Pearson Arab World Editions—Business & Economics

The Arab world's location between three continents ensures its place at the center of an increasingly integrated global economy, as distinctive as any business culture. We think learning should be as dynamic, relevant, and engaging as the business environment. Our new Arab World Editions for Business & Economics provides this uniquely Arab perspective, for students in and of the Arab world.

Each Arab World Edition integrates cases, companies, research, people, and discussions representing the diverse economic, political, and cultural situations across the nations that span the Arab world, whilst retaining the quality, research, and relevant global perspectives of the world's leading business thinkers.

We hope that you find this edition a valuable contribution to your teaching or business studies. We aim to set a new benchmark for contextualized learning with our adapted and new titles, and hope that they will prove a valuable contribution in the success of students and teachers along each step of their business program.

Supplementary support includes PowerPoint slides, instructor manuals, test bank generators, and MyLab online tutorials and homework systems.

Titles span a range of subjects and disciplines, including:

- Management—Robbins & Coulter
- Principles of Marketing—Kotler & Armstrong
- Economics—Hubbard & O'Brien
- Statistics for Business—Benghezal
- Principles of Managerial Finance—Gitman
- Marketing Management—Kotler & Keller
- Organizational Behavior—Robbins, Judge & Hasham
- Human Resource Management—Dessler
- Strategic Management—David
- Introductory Mathematical Analysis for Business, Economics, and Life and Social Sciences—Haeussler
- Marketing Research—Malhotra
- Operations Management—Heizer
- Auditing and Assurance Services—Arens

To find out more, go to www.pearson.com/middleeast/awe

PEARSON

OPERATIONS MANAGEMENT

ARAB WORLD EDITION

JAY HEIZER

Jesse H. Jones Professor of Business Administration
Texas Lutheran University

BARRY RENDER

Charles Harwood Professor of Operations Management
Crummer Graduate School of Business
Rollins College

ZU'BI AL-ZU'BI

Assistant Professor of Operations and Supply-Chain Management
Chairman of Business Management Department
University of Jordan

ALWAYS LEARNING   PEARSON

Acquisitions Editor: Rasheed Roussan
Development Editor: Kate Jamieson
Project Editor: Nicole Elliott
Editor: Lauren Dunn
Copy-editor: Jackie Mace
Proofreaders: Piers Maddox and Catherine Gaunt
Design Manager: Sarah Fach
Permissions Editor: Sarah Deakin
Picture Researchers: Zohir Naciri and Kevin Brown

Indexer: Indexing Specialists (UK) Ltd
Marketing Manager: Sue Mainey
Senior Manufacturing Controller: Christopher Crow
Cover Designer: Sarah Fach
Typesetter: Graphicraft Limited, Hong Kong
Typeface: Times LT Std 10/12 pt

Printed in Great Britain by Ashford Colour Press Ltd

Pearson Education Limited
Edinburgh Gate
Harlow
Essex CM20 2JE
England
and Associated Companies throughout the world

First published 2013

20 19 18
IMP 10 9 8 7 6 5 4 3 2

ISBN: 978-1-4479-0296-6

To: God almighty, whose world I have the privilege of studying,
and to my family, for continued inspiration

—Zu'bi Al Zu'bi

About the Authors

Jay Heizer Professor Emeritus, the Jesse H. Jones Chair of Business Administration, Texas Lutheran University, Seguin, Texas. He received his BBA and MBA from the University of North Texas and his Ph.D. in Management and Statistics from Arizona State University. He was previously a member of the faculty at the University of Memphis, the University of Oklahoma, Virginia Commonwealth University, and the University of Richmond. He has also held visiting positions at Boston University, George Mason University, the Czech Management Center, and the Otto-Von-Guericke University, Magdeburg.

Dr. Heizer's industrial experience is extensive. He learned the practical side of operations management as a machinist apprentice at Foringer and Company, as a production planner for Westinghouse Airbrake, and at General Dynamics, where he worked in engineering administration. In addition, he has been actively involved in consulting in the OM and MIS areas for a variety of organizations, including Philip Morris, Firestone, Dixie Container Corporation, Columbia Industries, and Tenneco. He holds the CPIM certification from APICS—the Association for Operations Management.

Professor Heizer has co-authored 5 books and has published more than 30 articles on a variety of management topics. His papers have appeared in the *Academy of Management Journal*, *Journal of Purchasing*, *Personnel Psychology*, *Production & Inventory Control Management*, *APICS—The Performance Advantage*, *Journal of Management History*, *IIE Solutions*, and *Engineering Management*, among others. He has taught operations management courses in undergraduate, graduate, and executive programs.

Barry Render Professor Emeritus, the Charles Harwood Professor of Operations Management, Crummer Graduate School of Business, Rollins College, Winter Park, Florida. He received his BS in Mathematics and Physics at Roosevelt University, and his MS in Operations Research and Ph.D. in Quantitative Analysis at the University of Cincinnati. He previously taught at George Washington University, University of New Orleans, Boston University, and George Mason University, where he held the Mason Foundation Professorship in Decision Sciences and was Chair of the Decision Science Department. Dr. Render has also worked in the aerospace industry, for General Electric, McDonnell Douglas, and NASA.

Professor Render has co-authored 10 textbooks for Prentice Hall, including *Managerial Decision Modeling with Spreadsheets*, *Quantitative Analysis for Management*, *Service Management*, *Introduction to Management Science*, and *Cases and Readings in Management Science*. *Quantitative Analysis for Management,* now in its 10th edition, is a leading text in that discipline in the United States and globally. Dr. Render's more than 100 articles on a variety of management topics have appeared in *Decision Sciences*; *Production and Operations Management*; *Interfaces*, *Information and Management*; *Journal of Management Information Systems*; *Socio-Economic Planning Sciences*; *IIE Solutions*; and *Operations Management Review*, among others.

Dr. Render has been honored as an AACSB Fellow and was twice named a Senior Fulbright Scholar. He was Vice President of the Decision Science Institute Southeast Region and served as Software Review Editor for *Decision Line* for six years and as Editor of the *New York Times* Operations Management special issues for five years. From 1984 to 1993, Dr. Render was President of Management Service Associates of Virginia, Inc., whose technology clients included the FBI; the U.S. Navy; Fairfax County, Virginia; and C&P Telephone.

Dr. Render has taught operations management courses in Rollins College's MBA and Executive MBA programs. He has received that school's Welsh Award as leading Professor and was selected by Roosevelt University as the 1996 recipient of the St. Claire Drake Award for Outstanding Scholarship. In 2005, Dr. Render received the Rollins College MBA Student Award for Best Overall Course, and in 2009 was named Professor of the Year by full-time MBA students.

Zu'bi Al-Zu'bi Assistant Professor of Operations and Supply-Chain Management at the Faculty of Business, University of Jordan. He received his BSc in Business Management from Mutah University, his MBA from the University of Jordan, and his Ph.D. in Operations and Supply-Chain Management from Durham Business School at Durham University, United Kingdom.

Dr. Zu'bi's experience in consultation and academia extends for more than a decade, working with many international, regional, governmental, and private organizations regarding their operations in the MENA region. During this time he has also taught operations and supply-chain management courses in undergraduate, graduate, and executive programs at universities in the United Kingdom and Jordan.

Dr. Zu'bi has authored a book about mass customization, and has published several articles on operations and supply-chain management in the *International Journal of Operations & Production Management*, *Journal of Product Innovation Management*, and *Production Planning & Control*, among others. He is a frequent correspondent for the Jordanian media and has organized and moderated many debating sessions for decision makers regarding economic and political issues.

Dr. Zu'bi has been elected to the Fellowship of the Higher Education Academy in the United Kingdom. For two years, he was President of the student body at Ustinov College at Durham University, for which he was voted the best college president in the Ernst & Young Durham Student Awards. He is currently the Chairman of the Business Management Department at the University of Jordan.

Brief Table of Contents

Table of Contents

Preface

Welcome to your Operations Management (OM) course. In this Arab World edition of *Operations Management*, we present a state-of-the-art view of the activities of the operations function. Operations are the core of business activity, and OM has a profound effect on the productivity of both manufacturing and services. Indeed, few other activities have so great an impact on the quality of our lives. The goal of this text is to present a broad introduction to the field of operations in a realistic, practical manner. OM includes a blend of topics from accounting, industrial engineering, management, management science, and statistics. Even if you are not planning on a career in the operations area, you will likely be working with people who are. Therefore, having a solid understanding of the role of operations in an organization will be of substantial benefit. This book will also help you understand how OM affects society and your life. Certainly, you will better understand what goes on behind the scenes when you purchase a bag of Frito-Lay potato chips, buy a meal at TcheTche, a falafel at Al Quds, or a product at Grand Stores, or when you enter New Mowasat Hospital for medical care.

Along with many of our readers who are OM graduates and undergraduates, we know that marketing, finance, accounting, and MIS students across the Arab world will also find the material both interesting and useful as we develop a fundamental working knowledge of the operations side of the firm. More than 600,000 readers of our earlier editions seem to have endorsed this premise.

NEW TO THE ARAB WORLD EDITION

A number of adaptations and new features have been added to the Arab World edition.

Arab World Case Studies: Each chapter contains case studies on operations management in an Arab world context, allowing students to see how the subject operates in their own region.

Regionalized Problems and Solved Problems: Hundreds of problems about the Arab world have been incorporated, allowing students to consolidate their learning at the end of each chapter. Some problems are solved so that students can appreciate the workings involved. The problems are given dots to indicate their level of difficulty.

English–Arabic Glossary: The Key Terms have translations to Arabic at the end of the book. Any instructor with experience in the Arab world knows how helpful this is for the students who studied Arabic in high school.

OTHER FEATURES AND PEDAGOGY

Ethical Dilemmas: The issue of ethics is integrated throughout the book, and the Ethical Dilemma at the end of each chapter can be used for classroom discussion or homework.

Examples: Each chapter includes several Arab world examples. In this way, students continuously see how operations management can be used in familiar situations, providing a real-world context.

Key Terms: New terminology is introduced in the text and then given a definition in the margin to make the navigation of the book that much easier for the student.

Author Comments: These notes indicate why a section, figure, or table is so important. The comments are meant to be motivational as well as educational.

Discussion Questions: These appear at the end of each chapter, supplement, and module, allowing students to explore the concepts they have just learned.

Rapid Review: At the end of each chapter, supplement, and module there is a review section that contains a summary of all the main points and equations in the chapter.

Self-Test: As part of the review section, there is a short test with questions linked to the learning objectives in that chapter.

Back-of-Book Answers: Answers to even-numbered problems appear in Appendix V.

STUDENT RESOURCES

To liven up the course and help students learn the content material, we have made available the following resources through www.pearsonmiddleeastawe.com/Heizer:

- **Twenty-seven exciting video cases**. These *Video Case Studies* feature real companies (Frito-Lay, Darden Restaurants, Regal Marine, Hard Rock Cafe, Red Lobster Restaurants, Ritz-Carlton, Wheeled Coach Ambulance, and Arnold Palmer Hospital) and allow students to watch short videos, read about the key topics, and answer questions. These case studies can also be assigned without using class time to show the videos. Each of them was developed and written by the text authors to specifically supplement the book's content.
- **DVD video clips**. We have provided 37 one- to two-minute video clips to illustrate chapter-related topics with videos at Frito-Lay, Ritz-Carlton, Hard Rock Cafe, Olive Garden, and other firms.
- **Virtual tours**. These company tours provide direct links to companies—ranging from a hospital to an auto manufacturer—that practice key concepts. After touring each website, students are asked questions directly related to the concepts discussed in the chapter.
- **Self-study quizzes**. These quizzes allow students to test their understanding of each topic. These extensive quizzes contain a broad assortment of questions, 20–25 per chapter, including multiple-choice, true/false, and internet essay questions. The quiz questions are graded and can be transmitted to the instructor for extra credit or serve as practice exams.
- **Excel OM data files** Examples in the text that can be solved with Excel OM appear on data files available throughout. They are identified at the end of each example.
- **POM for Windows software**. POM for Windows is a powerful tool for easily solving OM problems. Its 24 modules can be used to solve most of the homework problems in the text.
- **Excel OM problem-solving software**. Excel OM is our exclusive user-friendly Excel add-in. Excel OM automatically creates worksheets to model and solve problems. Users select a topic from the pull-down menu and fill in the data, and then Excel will display and graph (where appropriate) the results. This software is great for student homework, what-if analysis, and classroom demonstrations. This edition includes a new version of Excel OM that's compatible with Microsoft Excel 2007 as well as earlier versions of Excel.
- **Online Tutorial Chapters**. *Statistical Tools for Managers, Acceptance Sampling, The Simplex Method of Linear Programming, The MODI and VAM Methods of Solving Transportation Problems*, and *Vehicle Routing and Scheduling* are provided as additional material.
- **Virtual office hours**. Professors Heizer and Render appear on MyOMLab, walking students through 72 solved problems.
- **Additional practice problems**. These problems provide problem-solving experience. They supplement the examples and solved problems found in each chapter.
- **Additional case studies**. These additional case studies supplement the ones in the text. Detailed solutions appear in the Solutions Manual.

INSTRUCTOR RESOURCES

Register, Redeem, Log in At MyOMLab instructors can register and access a variety of print, media, and presentation resources that are available with this text in downloadable digital format. These can be accessed through www.pearsonmiddleeastawe.com/Heizer.

It Gets Better Once you register, you will not have additional forms to fill out or multiple usernames and passwords to remember to access new titles and/or editions. As a registered faculty member, you can log in directly to download resource files and receive immediate access and instructions for installing course management content to your campus server.

Need help? Our dedicated technical support team is ready to answer instructors' questions about the media supplements that accompany this text. Visit **http://247.pearsoned.co.uk** for answers to frequently asked questions and toll-free user support phone numbers. The supplements are available to adopting instructors. Detailed descriptions are provided at the Instructor's Resource Center.

Instructor's Resource Manual

The Instructor's Resource Manual contains many useful resources for instructors—course outlines, video notes, learning techniques, internet exercises and sample answers, case analysis ideas, additional teaching resources, and faculty notes. It also provides a snapshot of the PowerPoint lecture slides. Instructors can download the Instructor's Resource Manual from the Instructor's Resource Center, at MyOMLab.

Instructor's Solutions Manual The Instructor's Solutions Manual, written by the authors, contains the answers to all of the discussion questions, *Ethical Dilemmas* and cases in the text, as well as worked-out solutions to all the end-of-chapter problems, internet problems, and internet cases. Instructors can download the Instructor's Solutions Manual from the Instructor's Resource Center.

PowerPoint Presentations An extensive set of PowerPoint presentations is available for each chapter. Comprising well over 2,000 slides, this set has excellent color and clarity. These slides can also be downloaded from the Instructor's Resource Center.

Test Item File The test item file contains a variety of true/false, multiple-choice, fill-in-the-blank, short-answer, and problem- and topic-integrating questions for each chapter. Instructors can download the test item file from the Instructor's Resource Center.

TestGen The computerized TestGen package allows instructors to customize, save, and generate classroom tests. The test program permits instructors to edit, add, and delete questions from the test bank; edit existing graphics and create new graphics; analyze test results; and organize a database of test and student results. This software allows for extensive flexibility and ease of use. It provides many options for organizing and displaying tests, along with search and sort features. The software and the test banks can be downloaded from the Instructor's Resource Center.

MyOMLab This powerful tool, noted on the inside front cover, ties together all elements in this book into an innovative learning tool, an exam tool, a homework tool, and an assessment center. By using MyOMLab, instructors can assign thousands of problems from the text and/or problems/questions from the test item file for their students to take online at any time, as determined by the instructor. Visit MyOMLab at www.pearsonmiddleeastawe.com/Heizer for more information.

Video Package Designed and created by the authors specifically for their Heizer/Render texts, the video package contains the following 27 videos:

- Hard Rock Cafe: Operations Management in Services (Ch. 1)
- Frito-Lay: Operations Management in Manufacturing (Ch. 1)
- Strategy at Regal Marine (Ch. 2)
- Hard Rock Cafe's Global Strategy (Ch. 2)
- Project Management at Arnold Palmer Hospital (Ch. 3)
- Forecasting at Hard Rock Cafe (Ch. 4)
- Product Design at Regal Marine (Ch. 5)
- The Culture of Quality at Arnold Palmer Hospital (Ch. 6)
- Quality at the Ritz-Carlton Hotel Company (Ch. 6)
- Process Strategy at Wheeled Coach Ambulance (Ch. 7)
- Process Analysis at Arnold Palmer Hospital (Ch. 7)
- Green Manufacturing and Sustainability at Frito-Lay (Ch. 7)
- Capacity Planning at Arnold Palmer Hospital (Supp. 7)
- Where to Place the Hard Rock Cafe (Ch. 8)
- Locating the Next Red Lobster Restaurant (Ch. 8)
- Layout at Arnold Palmer Hospital's New Facility (Ch. 9)
- Facility Layout at Wheeled Coach Ambulance (Ch. 9)
- Hard Rock's Human Resource Strategy (Ch. 10)
- Darden's Global Supply Chain (Ch. 11)
- Arnold Palmer's Hospital Supply Chain (Ch. 11)
- Outsourcing Offshore at Darden (Supp. 11)
- Managing Inventory at Frito-Lay (Ch. 12)
- Inventory Control at Wheeled Coach Ambulance (Ch. 12)
- MRP at Wheeled Coach Ambulance (Ch. 14)
- Scheduling at Hard Rock Cafe (Ch. 15)
- JIT at Arnold Palmer Hospital (Ch. 16)
- Maintenance Drives Profits at Frito-Lay (Ch. 17)

ACKNOWLEDGMENTS

We express our appreciation to the following colleagues who contributed comments and suggestions that were valuable to us in the evolution of this text:

Dr. Amin Al-Algha, Department of Management and Marketing, University of Bahrain

Dr. Faisal N. M. Al-Madi, Faculty of Economic and Administrative Sciences, Hashemite University, Jordan

Abdel Latef Anouze, Olayan School of Business, American University of Beirut, Lebanon

Dr. Khaled Ahmed Bubshait, King Fahd University of Petroleum and Minerals (KFUPM), Saudi Arabia

Sheila Sison Biso, Kingdom University of Bahrain

Mohammed Nishat Faisal, Department of Management & Marketing, College of Business & Economics, Qatar University

Dr. Atef H Harb, Faculty of Business Administration and Economics, Notre Dame University, Lebanon

Willem Selen, Department of Business Administration, United Arab Emirates University

Many reviewers and contributors have provided valuable contributions and suggestions for previous editions of *Operations Management*. Many thanks to them for their insights, which have informed our work on this adaptation.

We wish you a pleasant and productive introduction to operations management.

1

Introduction to Operations Management

Chapter Outline

10

OM STRATEGY DECISIONS

▶ Design of Goods and Services
▶ Managing Quality
▶ Process Strategy
▶ Location Strategies
▶ Layout Strategies
▶ Human Resources
▶ Supply-Chain Management
▶ Inventory Management
▶ Scheduling
▶ Maintenance

OPERATIONS MANAGEMENT AT TCHETCHE CAFE

Operations managers are involved in the offering of products and services that meet the wants and needs of consumers. This is done in every organization, whether it is a manufacturer, a telecommunications company, a bank, or a café. The primary goal of operations management is to ensure the delivery of products—as the customer ordered them, when the customer wants them, and where the customer wants them. TcheTche Café is no exception. With close to 20 branches throughout the Middle East,

and over 600 employees, TcheTche is one of the leading chains of cafés in the region.

Amman-based TcheTche is a good story of operational success. It began in 1998 as a single coffee shop, but rapidly broadened its offerings to café-style food and sheesha. This was followed closely by expansion throughout Jordan and the Middle East. TcheTche made its name as the face of modern social dining, appealing particularly to Arabic youth due to the clever use of space and modern décor. However, TcheTche's biggest asset is the

The TcheTche Café logo has become one of the most well-known café brands in Jordan and the Middle East, particularly among young people, as it combines the old traditions of Arabia with the latest trends of the new millennium.

Customers are the main focus of TcheTche's strategy. Comments from customers are taken seriously by the staff; they act on feedback immediately where possible, often in front of the customer to demonstrate transparency.

value that it delivers to its visitors: by offering food, drinks, sheesha, and modern music at the same location, TcheTche combines the appeal of restaurants with traditional Arabic coffee houses, in a new and exciting package.

The operations managers at TcheTche work hard to ensure a broad variety of product offerings—there is always something new on the menu. In particular, there is an emphasis on the careful pricing of items to ensure that there is something for everyone. Menu items are priced to reflect the cost of the ingredients. However, what makes TcheTche special is its sheesha, which is the core product offering, with a fixed price across all menus.

Another important aspect of operations management at TcheTche is the standardization of service throughout the different branches. There is a set of standard operation guidelines by which the branches operate, and to which the employees must adhere. In this way, each branch has the same standards of operation and offers the same quality, menu, and ambience, to ensure the highest possible level of service in all locations. In order to achieve these high standards, TcheTche seeks to continuously train and develop the skills of its employees through a thorough set of on-the-job training programs.

Managers who successfully design and deliver goods and services throughout the world understand operations. In this text, we look at how this is achieved by operations managers across all sectors and industries. Operations Management is demanding, challenging, and exciting. It affects our lives every day. Ultimately, operations managers determine how well we live.

Source: **www.tchetchecafe.com**

Chapter 1 Learning Objectives

> **AUTHOR COMMENT**
> Let's begin by defining what this course is about.

LO1: Define operations management

> **VIDEO 1.1**
> Hard Rock Cafe: Operations Management in Services
>
> **VIDEO 1.2**
> Frito-Lay: Operations Management in Manufacturing

Production
The creation of goods and services.

Operations management (OM)
The set of activities that oversees the creation of goods and services.

WHAT IS OPERATIONS MANAGEMENT?

Operations Management (OM) applies to all companies, from cafés such as TcheTche, to manufacturing companies such as LG and EL Nasr Automotive Manufacturing Company. The techniques of OM are applied by managers in virtually all productive enterprises. It doesn't matter if the application is in an office, a hospital, a restaurant, a department store, or a factory—the production of goods and services requires operations management. And the *efficient* production of goods and services requires *effective* applications of the concepts, tools, and techniques of OM that we introduce in this book.

As we go through this textbook, we will discover how to manage operations in a changing global economy, with a particular focus on businesses in the Middle East. Our aim is to show how businesses create the goods and services that enrich our lives.

In this chapter, first we define operations management, explaining its evolution and exploring the exciting role that operations managers play in a huge variety of organizations. Then we discuss the concepts of production and productivity. This is followed by a discussion of operations in the service sector and the challenge of managing an effective and efficient production system.

Production is the creation of goods and services. **Operations management (OM)** is the set of activities that oversees the creation of goods and services. This is done by managing the conversion of inputs (such as raw materials or hours of labor) into valuable outputs (such as the finished goods or delivered services).

It is important to realize that we are not only dealing with tangible outputs, such as televisions or cars, which fall within the realm of production management. Operations management also deals with the creation of less visible outputs, such as services. These include treatment at a hospital, legal advice, and financial services such as car insurance or the transfer of funds from one bank account to another. Regardless of whether the end product is a good or service, the production activities that go on in the organization are often referred to as operations, or operations management.

> **AUTHOR COMMENT**
> Operations is one of the three functions that every organization performs.

ORGANIZING TO PRODUCE GOODS AND SERVICES

To create goods and services, all organizations perform three functions (see Figure 1.1). These functions are the necessary ingredients not only for production but also for an organization's survival. They are as follows.

1. *Marketing*, which generates the demand, or at least takes the order for a product or service (nothing happens until there is a sale).
2. *Production/operations*, which creates the product.
3. *Finance/accounting*, which tracks how well the organization is doing, pays the bills, and collects the money.

Factories, telecommunications companies, universities, and even charities all perform these functions. Figure 1.1 shows how a bank, an airline, and a manufacturing firm carry out these functions. The blue-shaded areas of Figure 1.1 show the operations functions in these firms.

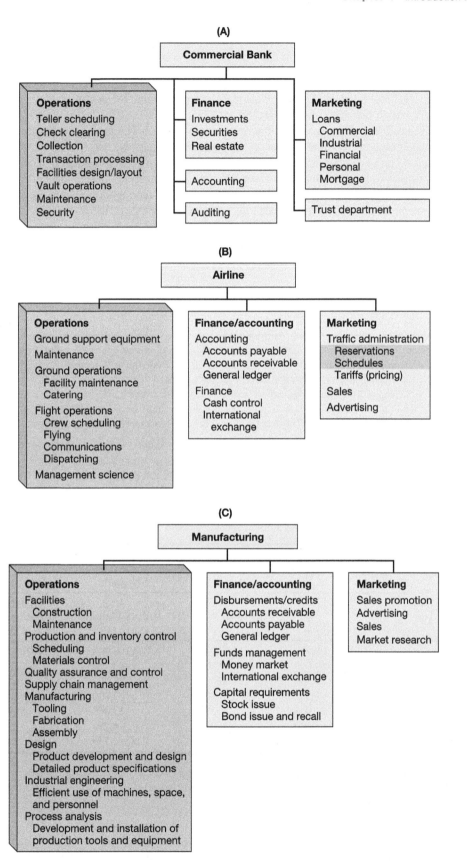

(A)

Commercial Bank

Operations
Teller scheduling
Check clearing
Collection
Transaction processing
Facilities design/layout
Vault operations
Maintenance
Security

Finance
Investments
Securities
Real estate

Accounting

Auditing

Marketing
Loans
   Commercial
   Industrial
   Financial
   Personal
   Mortgage

Trust department

(B)

Airline

Operations
Ground support equipment
Maintenance
Ground operations
   Facility maintenance
   Catering
Flight operations
   Crew scheduling
   Flying
   Communications
   Dispatching
Management science

Finance/accounting
Accounting
   Accounts payable
   Accounts receivable
   General ledger
Finance
   Cash control
   International
      exchange

Marketing
Traffic administration
   Reservations
   Schedules
   Tariffs (pricing)
Sales
Advertising

(C)

Manufacturing

Operations
Facilities
   Construction
   Maintenance
Production and inventory control
   Scheduling
   Materials control
Quality assurance and control
Supply chain management
Manufacturing
   Tooling
   Fabrication
   Assembly
Design
   Product development and design
   Detailed product specifications
Industrial engineering
   Efficient use of machines, space,
   and personnel
Process analysis
   Development and installation of
   production tools and equipment

Finance/accounting
Disbursements/credits
   Accounts receivable
   Accounts payable
   General ledger
Funds management
   Money market
   International exchange
Capital requirements
   Stock issue
   Bond issue and recall

Marketing
Sales promotion
Advertising
Sales
Market research

◀ **FIGURE 1.1**

Organization Charts for Two Service Organizations and One Manufacturing Organization

(A) A bank, (B) an airline, and (C) a manufacturing organization. The blue areas are OM activities.

AUTHOR COMMENT
The areas in blue indicate the significant role that OM plays in both manufacturing and service firms.

AUTHOR COMMENT
Good OM managers are scarce and, as a result, career opportunities and pay are excellent.

WHY STUDY OM?

We study OM for four reasons.

1. OM is one of the three major functions of any organization, and it is integrally related to all the other business functions. Since no business can run without OM, we study *how businesses organize their activities to be productive.*
2. We want to know *how goods and services are produced.* The production function is the segment of our society that creates the products and services we use.
3. To *understand what operations managers do.* Regardless of your job in an organization, you can perform better if you understand what operations managers do. In addition, understanding OM will help you explore the numerous and lucrative career opportunities in the field.
4. *It is such a costly part of an organization.* A large percentage of the revenue of most firms is spent on OM. Indeed, OM provides a major opportunity for an organization to improve its profitability by cutting costs and to enhance its service to society. Example 1 considers how a firm might increase its profitability via the production function.

EXAMPLE 1 ▶

Examining the options for increasing contribution

Beirut Solutions is a small consultation firm operating in Lebanon. It must double its dollar contribution to fixed costs and profit in order to be profitable enough to purchase the next generation of production equipment. Management has determined that if the firm fails to increase its contribution, its bank will not make the loan and the equipment cannot be purchased. If the firm cannot purchase the equipment, the limitations of the old equipment will force Beirut Solutions to go out of business and, in doing so, put its employees out of work and discontinue producing goods and services for its customers.

APPROACH ▶   Table 1.1 shows a simple profit-and-loss statement and three strategic options (marketing, finance/accounting, and operations) for the firm. The first option is a *marketing option*, where good marketing management may increase sales by 50 percent. By increasing sales by 50 percent, contribution in turn will increase 71 percent. But increasing sales by 50 percent may be difficult; it may even be impossible.

▶ **TABLE 1.1**

Options For Increasing Contribution

	Current	Marketing Option[a] Increase Sales Revenue 50%	Finance/Accounting Option[b] Reduce Finance Costs 50%	OM Option[c] Reduce Production Costs 20%
Sales	US$100,000	US$150,000	US$100,000	US$100,000
Costs of goods	−80,000	−120,000	−80,000	−64,000
Gross margin	20,000	30,000	20,000	36,000
Finance costs	−6,000	−6,000	−3,000	−6,000
Subtotal	14,000	24,000	17,000	30,000
Taxes at 25%	−3,500	−6,000	−4,250	−7,500
Contribution[d]	US$10,500	US$18,000	US$12,750	US$22,500

[a] Increasing sales by 50 percent increases contribution by US$7,500, or 71 percent (7,500 ÷ 10,500).
[b] Reducing finance costs by 50 percent increases contribution by US$2,250, or 21 percent (2,250 ÷ 10,500).
[c] Reducing production costs by 20 percent increases contribution by US$12,000, or 114 percent (12,000 ÷ 10,500).
[d] Contribution to fixed costs (excluding finance costs) and profit.

The second option is a *finance/accounting option*, where finance costs are cut in half through good financial management. But even a reduction of 50 percent is still inadequate for generating the necessary increase in contribution. Contribution is increased by only 21 percent.

The third option is an *OM option*, where management reduces production costs (costs of goods) by 20 percent and increases contribution by 114 percent.

SOLUTION ▶   Given the conditions of our brief example, Beirut Solutions has increased contribution from US$10,500 to US$22,500. It may now have a bank willing to lend it additional funds.

INSIGHT ▶ The OM option not only yields the greatest improvement in contribution but also may be the only feasible option. Both increasing sales by 50 percent and decreasing finance costs by 50 percent may be virtually impossible. Reducing operations costs by 20 percent may be difficult but feasible.

LEARNING EXERCISE ▶ What is the impact of only a 15 percent decrease in costs in the OM option? [Answer: A US$18,500 contribution; an 76 percent increase.]

Example 1 emphasizes the importance of an effective operations activity of a firm. Development of increasingly effective operations is the approach taken by many companies as they face growing global competition.

WHAT OPERATIONS MANAGERS DO

All good managers perform the basic functions of the **management process**, which are *planning*, *organizing*, *staffing*, *leading*, and *controlling*. Like all other managers, operations managers also perform these tasks in the ten major areas of decision-making in OM. These are shown in Table 1.2, and will be discussed in detail throughout this book. Typical issues relevant to these decisions and the chapter where each is discussed are also shown.

> **AUTHOR COMMENT**
> An operations manager must successfully address ten key decisions.

Management process
The application of planning, organizing, staffing, leading, and controlling to the achievement of objectives.

Where are the OM Jobs?

How does one get started on a career in operations? The ten OM decision areas identified in Table 1.2 are made by individuals who work in the disciplines shown in blue in Figure 1.1. Competent business students who have a good understanding of accounting, statistics, finance, and OM have a better chance of gaining entry-level positions in all of these areas. As you read

Ten Decision Areas	Issues	Chapter(s)
1. Design of goods and services	What good or service should we offer? How should we design these products?	5
2. Managing quality	How do we define quality? Who is responsible for quality?	6
3. Process and capacity design	What process and what capacity will these products require? What equipment and technology is necessary for these processes?	7, Supplement 7
4. Location strategy	Where should we put the facility? On what criteria should we base the location decision?	8
5. Layout strategy	How should we arrange the facility? How large must the facility be to meet our plan?	9
6. Human resources and job design	How do we provide a reasonable work environment? How much can we expect our employees to produce?	10
7. Supply-chain management	Should we make or buy this component? Who should be our suppliers and how can we integrate them into our strategy?	11, Supplement 11
8. Inventory, material requirements planning, and JIT (just-in-time)	How much inventory of each item should we have? When do we reorder?	12, 14, 16
9. Intermediate and short-term scheduling	Are we better off keeping people on the payroll during slowdowns? Which job do we perform next?	13, 15
10. Maintenance	How do we build reliability into our processes? Who is responsible for maintenance?	17

◀ TABLE 1.2
Ten Critical Decisions of Operations Management

> **AUTHOR COMMENT**
> Current OM emphasis on quality and the supply chain has increased job opportunities in these ten areas.

1/15   **Plant Manager**
Division of Fortune 1000 company seeks plant manager for plant located in the upper Hudson Valley area. This plant manufactures loading dock equipment for commercial markets. The candidate must be experienced in plant management including expertise in production planning, purchasing, and inventory management. Good written and oral communication skills are a must, along with excellent application of skills in managing people.

2/23   **Operations Analyst**
Expanding national coffee shop: top 10 'Best Places to Work' wants junior level systems analyst to join our excellent store improvement team. Business or I.E. degree, work methods, labor standards, ergonomics, cost accounting knowledge a plus. This is a hands-on job and excellent opportunity for a team player with good people skills. West coast US location. Some travel required.

3/18   **Quality Manager**
Several openings exist in our small package processing facilities in Northeast US, Florida, and Southern California for quality managers. These highly visible positions require extensive use of statistical tools to monitor all aspects of service, timeliness, and workload measurement. The work involves: (1) a combination of hands-on applications and detailed analysis using databases and spreadsheets; (2) process audits to identify areas for improvement; (3) management of implementation of changes. Positions involve night hours and weekends. Send resume.

4/6   **Supply Chain Manager and Planner**
Responsibilities entail negotiating contracts and establishing long-term relationships with suppliers. We will rely on the selected candidate to maintain accuracy in the purchasing system, invoices, and product returns. A bachelor's degree and up to 2 years related experience are required. Working knowledge of MRP, ability to use feedback to master scheduling and suppliers and consolidate orders for best price and delivery are necessary. Proficiency in all PC Windows applications, particularly Excel and Word, is essential. Knowledge of Oracle Business Systems I is a plus. Effective verbal and written communication skills are essential.

5/14   **Process Improvement Consultants**
An expanding consulting firm is seeking consultants to design and implement lean production and cycle time reduction plans in both service and manufacturing processes. Our firm is currently working with an international bank to improve its back office operations, as well as with several manufacturing firms. A business degree required; APICS certification a plus.

▲ **FIGURE 1.2** **Many Opportunities Exist for Operations Managers**

this text, identify the disciplines that can assist you in making these decisions, and take courses in those areas. The more background an OM student has in accounting, statistics, information systems, and mathematics, the more job opportunities will be available. About 40 percent of *all* jobs are in OM. In the Middle East, there is a shortage of graduates who have a well-rounded education in all aspects of management, particularly OM. This text aims to give you a firm foundation in the principles and practices of OM, which should put you on the right track for a good position in the corporate world.

THE EVOLUTION OF OPERATIONS MANAGEMENT

The field of OM is relatively young, but its history is rich and interesting. OM has its roots in the Industrial Revolution of the 1800s, when factories began to replace home-based manufacturing. As factories became larger, new technology was developed to meet the new demands. Over time, operations paradigms shifted from focusing on cost to quality, and finally to customers. With these changes came a necessary evolution of OM practices.

Operations management will continue to progress with contributions from other disciplines, including *industrial engineering* and *management science*. These disciplines, along with statistics, management, and economics, contribute to improved models and decision making. Innovations from the *physical sciences* (biology, anatomy, chemistry, and physics) have contributed also to advances in OM. These innovations include new adhesives, faster integrated circuits, gamma rays to sanitize food products, and higher-quality glass for LCD and plasma TVs. Especially important contributions to OM have come from *information technology*, which we define as the systematic processing of data to yield information. Information technology—with wireless links, internet, and eCommerce—is reducing costs and accelerating communication.

OPERATIONS IN THE SERVICE SECTOR

> **AUTHOR COMMENT**
> Services are especially important because almost 80 percent of all jobs are in service firms.

Manufacturers produce a tangible product, while service products are often intangible. It is important to remember, however, that many products are a combination of a good and a service. In this textbook, we define **services** as actions performed for the customer in a variety of sectors, such as professional expertise (legal advice, medical consultation, tax accounting), government, hospitality, transportation, and financial offerings.

Services
Economic activities that typically produce an intangible product (such as education, entertainment, hospitality, government, financial, and health services).

Differences Between Goods and Services

Let's examine some of the differences between goods and services.

- Services are usually *intangible* (for example, your purchase of a ride in an empty airline seat between two cities) as opposed to a tangible good, such as a cell phone or piece of furniture.
- Services are often *produced and consumed simultaneously*; there is no stored inventory. For instance, the beauty salon produces a haircut that is 'consumed' simultaneously, or the doctor produces an operation that is 'consumed' as it is produced.
- Services are often *unique*. Your mix of financial coverage, such as investments and insurance policies, may not be the same as anyone else's, just as the medical procedure or a haircut produced for you is not exactly like anyone else's.
- Services have *high customer interaction*. Services are often difficult to standardize, automate, and make as efficient as we would like because customer interaction demands uniqueness. In fact, in many cases this uniqueness is what the customer is paying for, therefore the operations manager must ensure that the product is designed (i.e. customized) so that it can be delivered in the required unique manner.
- Services have an *inconsistent product definition*. Product definition may be rigorous, as in the case of an automobile insurance policy, but inconsistent because policyholders change cars and mature.
- Services are often *knowledge-based*, as in the case of educational, medical, and legal services, and therefore hard to automate.
- Services are frequently *dispersed*. Dispersion occurs because services are frequently brought to the client or customer via a local office, a retail outlet, or even a house call.

LO2: Explain the distinction between goods and services

The activities of the operations function are often very similar for both goods and services. For instance, both goods and services must have quality standards established, and both must be designed and processed according to a schedule in a facility where human resources are employed.

Having made the distinction between goods and services, we should reiterate that in many cases the distinction is not clear-cut. In reality, almost all services and almost all goods are a mixture of a service and a tangible product. Even services such as consulting may require a tangible report. Similarly, the sale of most goods includes a service. For instance, many products have the service components of financing and delivery (e.g. car sales). Many also require after-sales training and maintenance (e.g. office copiers and machinery).

Growth of Services

Services constitute the largest economic sector in post-industrial societies. In the Middle East, where there are fewer manufacturing companies than elsewhere in the world, service companies comprise over 70 percent of all listed companies in the stock exchanges. In Jordan, the **service sector** comprises 67 percent of gross domestic product (GDP), while in Saudi Arabia, 71 percent of all labor is employed in service companies. In Lebanon, tourism alone contributes 20 percent of total GDP. Examples of firms in the service sector across the Middle East are shown in Table 1.3.

Service sector
The segment of the economy that includes trade, financial, hospitality, education, legal, medical, and other professional occupations.

▶ TABLE 1.3

Examples of Organizations in Each Sector

> **AUTHOR COMMENT**
> Service jobs with their operations component are growing as a percentage of all jobs.

Sector	Example
Service Sector	
Education, legal, medical, other	University of Cairo, Zu'bi Law, specialty hospital
Trade (retail, wholesale)	Carrefour stores, Mango clothing chain
Utilities, transportation	Qatargas, Emirates airlines
Professional and business services	Abu-Ghazaleh Consulting, United Insurers
Finance, information, real estate	Al Rajhi Bank, Batelco, Emaar Properties
Food, lodging, entertainment	Al Tazaj restaurants, Burj Al Arab Hotel, Ferrari City
Public administration	Bahrain, Greater Municipality of Amman
Manufacturing Sector	Almarai Foods, El Nasr Automotive Manufacturing Company
Construction Sector	Arabtec, Emaar
Agriculture	Kassatly Chtaura
Mining Sector	Aramco, Jordan Phosphates

> **AUTHOR COMMENT**
> Why is productivity important? Because it determines our standard of living.

THE PRODUCTIVITY CHALLENGE

Productivity
The ratio of outputs (goods and services) divided by one or more inputs (such as labor, capital, or management).

The creation of goods and services requires changing resources into goods and services. The more efficiently we make this change, the more productive we are and the more value is added to the good or service provided, thus making it more precious in the eyes of the consumer. **Productivity** is the ratio of outputs (goods and services) divided by the inputs (resources, such as labor and capital) (see Figure 1.3). The job of an operations manager is to enhance (improve) this ratio. Improving productivity means improving efficiency.

This improvement can be achieved in two ways: reducing inputs while keeping output constant or increasing output while keeping inputs constant. Both represent an improvement in productivity. In an economic sense, inputs are labor, capital, and management, which are integrated into a production system. Management creates this production system, which provides the conversion of inputs to outputs. Outputs are goods and services, including such diverse items as cars, milk, education, improved judicial systems, and swimming pools. *Production* is the making of goods and services. High production may imply only that more people are working and that employment levels are high (low unemployment), but it does not imply high *productivity*.

LO3: Explain the difference between production and productivity

Productivity is a significant issue for the world and one that the operations manager is uniquely qualified to address. Measurement of productivity is an excellent way to evaluate a country's ability to provide an improving standard of living for its people. *Only through increases in productivity can the standard of living improve*, because increases in productivity ensure that labor, capital, and management receive additional payments. If returns to labor, capital, or management are increased without increased productivity, prices rise, which causes inflation. In contrast, when productivity does increase, downward pressure is placed on prices, because more is being produced with the same resources.

The benefits of increased productivity are illustrated in the *OM in Action* box 'Improving Productivity at Starbucks.' In this text, we examine how to improve productivity through operations management.

▶ FIGURE 1.3

The Economic System Adds Value by Transforming Inputs to Outputs

An effective feedback loop evaluates performance against a strategy or standard. It also evaluates customer satisfaction and sends signals to managers controlling the inputs and transformation process.

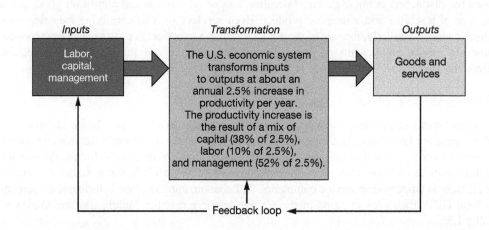

OM in Action ▶ Improving Productivity at Starbucks

"This is a game of seconds . . ." says Silva Peterson, whom Starbucks has put in charge of saving seconds. Her team of ten analysts are constantly asking themselves: "How can we shave time off this?"

Peterson's analysis suggested that there were some obvious opportunities. First, stop requiring signatures on credit-card purchases under US$25. This sliced 8 seconds off the transaction time at the cash register.

Second, analysts noticed that Starbucks' largest cold beverage, the Venti size, required two bending and digging motions to scoop up enough ice. The scoop was too small. Redesign of the scoop provided the proper amount in one motion and cut 14 seconds off the average time of 1 minute.

Third were new espresso machines: with the push of a button, the machines grind coffee beans and brew. This allowed the server, called a 'barista' in Starbucks'

vocabulary, to do other things. The savings: about 12 seconds per espresso shot.

As a result, operations improvements at Starbucks's outlets have increased the average yearly volume by nearly US$200,000 to about US$940,000 in the past 6 years. This is a 27 percent improvement in productivity—about 4.5 percent per year. In the service industry, a 4.5 percent per year increase is very tasty.

Sources: The Wall Street Journal (August 4, 2009): A1, A10 and (April 12, 2005): B2; B7; *Industrial Engineer* (January 2006): 66; and **www.finfacts.com**, October 6, 2005.

Productivity Measurement

LO4: Compute single-factor productivity

The measurement of productivity can be quite direct, for example when productivity is measured by labor-hours per ton of a specific type of steel. Although labor-hours is a common measure of input, other measures such as capital (money invested), materials (tons of ore), or energy (kilowatts of electricity) can be used.[1] An example of this can be summarized in the following equation:

$$\text{Productivity} = \frac{\text{Useful units produced}}{\text{Input used}} \qquad (1\text{-}1)$$

For example, if the units and labor-hours used is 250, then:

$$\text{Productivity} = \frac{\text{Useful units produced}}{\text{Input used}} = \frac{1{,}000}{250} = 4 \text{ units per labor-hour}$$

The use of just one resource input to measure productivity, as shown in Equation (1-1), is known as **single-factor productivity**. However, a broader view of productivity is **multi-factor productivity**, which includes some of the inputs (e.g. capital, labor, material, energy). Multi-factor productivity is also known as *total factor productivity* if all the inputs are included. Multi-factor productivity is calculated by combining the input units as shown here:

$$\text{Productivity} = \frac{\text{Output}}{\text{Labor} + \text{Material} + \text{Energy} + \text{Capital} + \text{Miscellaneous}} \qquad (1\text{-}2)$$

Single-factor productivity
Indicates the ratio of goods and services produced (outputs) to one resource (input).

Multi-factor productivity
Indicates the ratio of the goods and services produced (outputs) to some of the resources (inputs).

To aid in the computation of multi-factor productivity, the individual inputs (the denominator) can be expressed in terms of cost and summed as shown in Example 2.

Use of productivity measures aids managers in determining how well they are doing. However, results from the two measures can be expected to vary. If labor productivity growth is entirely the result of capital spending, then to solely measure labor will distort the results. Multi-factor productivity is usually better, but more complicated. Labor productivity is the more popular measure. Multi-factor productivity measures provide better information about the trade-offs among factors, but substantial measurement problems remain. Some of these measurement problems are as follows.

1. *Quality* may change while the quantity of inputs and outputs remains constant. Compare a high-definition TV of this decade with a black-and-white TV of the 1950s. Both are TVs, but few people would deny that the quality has improved. The unit of measure—a TV—is the same, but the quality has changed.

---

[1] The quality and time period are assumed to remain constant.

EXAMPLE 2 ▶

Computing single-factor and multi-factor gains in productivity

LO5: Compute multi-factor productivity

Kuwaiti Publishing Mill (KPM) wants to evaluate its labor and multi-factor productivity with a new computerized title-search system. The company has a staff of four, each working 8 hours per day (for a payroll cost of US$640/day) and overhead expenses of US$400 per day. KPM processes and closes on eight titles each day. The new computerized title-search system will allow the processing of 14 titles per day. Although the staff, their work hours, and pay are the same, the overhead expenses are now US$800 per day.

APPROACH ▶ KPM uses Equation (1-1) to compute labor productivity and Equation (1-2) to compute multi-factor productivity.

SOLUTION ▶

$$\text{Labor productivity with the old system: } \frac{8 \text{ titles per day}}{32 \text{ labor-hours}} = 0.25 \text{ titles per labor-hour}$$

$$\text{Labor productivity with the new system: } \frac{14 \text{ titles per day}}{32 \text{ labor-hours}} = 0.4375 \text{ titles per labor-hour}$$

$$\text{Multi-factor productivity with the old system: } \frac{8 \text{ titles per day}}{\text{US\$}640 + 400} = 0.0077 \text{ titles per dollar}$$

$$\text{Multi-factor productivity with the new system: } \frac{14 \text{ titles per day}}{\text{US\$}640 + 800} = 0.0097 \text{ titles per dollar}$$

Labor productivity has increased from 0.25 to 0.4375. The change is $(0.435 - 0.25) \div 0.25 = 0.74$ or a 74 percent increase in labor productivity. Multi-factor productivity has increased from 0.0077 to 0.0097. This change is $(0.0097 - 0.0077) \div 0.0077 = 0.26$ or a 26 percent increase in multi-factor productivity.

INSIGHT ▶ Both the labor (single-factor) and multi-factor productivity measures show an increase in productivity. However, the multi-factor measure provides a better picture of the increase because it includes all the costs connected with the increase in output.

LEARNING EXERCISE ▶ If the overhead expenses increases to US$960 (rather than US$800), what is the multi-factor productivity? [Answer: 0.00875.]

RELATED PROBLEMS ▶ 1.1, 1.2, 1.4, 1.5, 1.6, 1.8, 1.9, 1.12

2. *External elements* may cause an increase or a decrease in productivity for which the system under study may not be directly responsible. A more reliable electric power service may greatly improve production, thereby improving the firm's productivity because of this support system rather than because of managerial decisions made within the firm.
3. *Precise units of measure* may be lacking. Not all automobiles require the same inputs: the manufacture of a hybrid Prius differs greatly from that of a diesel-powered 4×4.

Productivity measurement is particularly difficult in the service sector, where the human element is highly involved and the end product can be hard to define. For example, economic statistics ignore the quality of your haircut, the outcome of a court case, or service at a retail store. In some cases, adjustments are made for the quality of the product sold but *not* for the quality of the sales presentation (e.g. the person selling the product) or the advantage of a broader product selection (e.g. in a large department store). Productivity measurements require specific inputs and outputs, but a free economy is producing worth—what people want—which includes convenience, speed, and safety, and these are difficult to measure in a quantitative way. Traditional measures of outputs may be a very poor indication of the worth of the products. For example, in a law office, where each case is different, the accuracy of the measure differs if defined by 'cases per labor-hour' or 'cases per employee.'

Productivity Variables

Productivity variables
The three factors critical to productivity improvement—labor, capital, and the art and science of management.

As we saw in Figure 1.3, productivity increases are dependent on three **productivity variables**.

1. *Labor*, which contributes about 10 percent of the annual increase in productivity.
2. *Capital*, which contributes about 38 percent of the annual increase in productivity.
3. *Management*, which contributes to the remaining 52 percent of the annual increase.

These three factors are critical to improved productivity. They represent the broad areas in which managers can take action to improve productivity.

Labor   The labor force is best able to contribute to increased productivity when it comprises healthy, well-educated individuals. Some increase also may be attributed to a shorter working week. Historically, about 10 percent of the annual improvement in productivity is attributed to improvement in the quality of labor. Three key variables for improved labor productivity are:

LO6: Identify the critical variables in enhancing productivity

1. basic education appropriate for an effective labor force
2. diet of the labor force
3. social overheads that makes labor available, such as transportation and sanitation.

Illiteracy and poor diet are a major impediment to productivity, costing countries up to 20 percent of their productivity. Infrastructure that yields clean drinking water and sanitation is also an opportunity for improved productivity, as well as an opportunity for better health, in much of the world. In addition to these factors is the challenge of *maintaining and enhancing the skills of labor* in the midst of rapidly expanding technology and knowledge.

Overcoming shortcomings in the quality of labor while other countries have a better labor force is a major challenge. Perhaps improvements can be found not only through increasing the competence of labor but also via *better utilized labor with a stronger commitment*. Training, motivation, team building, and the human resource strategies discussed in Chapter 10, as well as improved education, may be among the many techniques that contribute to increased labor productivity. Improvements in labor productivity are possible; however, they can be expected to be increasingly difficult and expensive.

Capital   All operations require the use of tools. Capital investment provides these tools. Capital investment has been increasing continuously in the Middle East over the past three decades, especially after the collapse of the Soviet Union and the entry of many Arab countries into the free market.

Inflation and taxes increase the cost of capital, making capital investment increasingly expensive. When the capital invested per employee drops, we can expect a drop in productivity. Using labor rather than capital may reduce unemployment in the short run, but it also makes economies less productive and therefore lowers wages in the long run. Capital investment is often a necessary but seldom sufficient ingredient in the battle for increased productivity.

The trade-off between capital and labor is continually in flux. A higher cost of capital means that more projects requiring capital are neglected: They are not pursued because the potential return on investment for a given risk has been reduced. Managers adjust their investment plans according to changes in capital cost.

Management   Management is a factor of production and an economic resource. Management is responsible for ensuring that labor and capital are used effectively to increase productivity. Management accounts for over half of the annual increase in productivity. This increase includes improvements made through the use of knowledge and the application of technology.

Using knowledge and technology is critical in post-industrial societies. Consequently, post-industrial societies are also known as knowledge societies. **Knowledge societies** are those in which much of the labor force has migrated from manual work to technical and information-processing tasks requiring ongoing education. The required education and training are important high-cost items that are the responsibility of operations managers, as they build organizations and workforces. The expanding knowledge base of contemporary society requires that managers use *technology and knowledge effectively.*

Knowledge society
A society in which much of the labor force has migrated from manual work to work based on knowledge.

More effective use of capital also contributes to productivity. It falls to the operations manager, as a productivity catalyst, to select the best new capital investments as well as to improve the productivity of existing investments.

The productivity challenge is difficult. A country cannot be a world-class competitor with second-class inputs. Poorly educated labor, inadequate capital, and outdated technology are second-class inputs. High productivity and high-quality outputs require high-quality inputs, including good operations managers.

Zain, a global telecommunications company based in Kuwait, has developed extensive training programs for its employees to ensure higher productivity. This is done through offering education opportunities to engineers and personnel from different managerial levels to guarantee a highly-skilled workforce.

Productivity and the Service Sector

The service sector provides a special challenge to the accurate measurement of productivity and productivity improvement. The traditional analytical framework of economic theory is based primarily on goods-producing activities; consequently, most published economic data relate to goods production. But the data do indicate that the contemporary service economy has increased in size, and there has been slower growth in productivity.

Productivity of the service sector has proven difficult to improve because service sector work is:

1. typically labor-intensive (for example, counseling, teaching)
2. frequently focused on unique individual attributes or desires (for example, investment advice)
3. often an intellectual task performed by professionals (for example, medical diagnosis)
4. often difficult to mechanize and automate (for example, a haircut)
5. often difficult to evaluate for quality (for example, the performance of a law firm).

The more intellectual and personal the task, the more difficult it is to achieve increases in productivity.

Low productivity improvement in the service sector is also due to the large number of activities in this sector that have lower productivity, such as child care, food preparation, house cleaning, and laundry service. These activities were previously performed in the home, and therefore were not included in the measured economy. Inclusion of these activities has probably resulted in lower measured productivity for the service sector, although, in fact, actual productivity has probably increased because these activities are now more efficiently produced than previously.

However, in spite of the difficulty of improving productivity in the service sector, improvements are being made. It is astonishing what can be achieved when management pays attention to how work actually gets done!

Because productivity is central to the operations manager's job and because the service sector is so large, we take special note in this text of how to improve productivity in the service sector. (See, for instance, the *OM in Action* box 'How Copenhagen County Hospital Can Save 8 Percent to 10 Percent of Its Costs.')

ETHICS AND SOCIAL RESPONSIBILITY

> **AUTHOR COMMENT**
> Ethics must drive all of a manager's decisions.

Operations managers are subjected to constant change and challenges. The systems they build to convert resources into goods and services are complex. The physical and social environment changes, as do laws and values. These changes present a variety of challenges that come from the conflicting perspectives of stakeholders such as customers, distributors, suppliers, owners, lenders, and employees. These stakeholders, as well as government agencies at various levels, require constant monitoring and thoughtful responses.

Identifying ethical and socially responsible responses while building productive systems is not always easy. Among the many ethical challenges facing operations managers are the following.

- Efficiently developing and producing safe, quality products.
- Sourcing ethically sound ingredients and materials.
- Paying fair prices to farmers in developing countries.
- Maintaining a sustainable environment.
- Providing a safe workplace.
- Honoring stakeholder commitments.

Managers must do all of this in an ethical and socially responsible way while meeting the demands of the marketplace. If operations managers have a *moral awareness and focus on increasing productivity* in a system where all stakeholders have a voice, then many of the ethical challenges will be successfully addressed. The organization will use fewer resources, the employees will be committed, the market will be satisfied, and the ethical climate will be enhanced. Throughout this text, we note the ways in which operations managers can take ethical and socially responsible action while successfully addressing these challenges of the market. We also conclude each chapter with an *Ethical Dilemma* exercise.

EXCITING NEW TRENDS IN OPERATIONS MANAGEMENT

> **AUTHOR COMMENT**
> One of the reasons OM is such an exciting discipline is that an operations manager is confronted with ever-changing issues, from technology to sustainability.

OM managers operate in an exciting and dynamic environment. This environment is the result of a variety of challenging forces, from globalization of world trade to the transfer of ideas, products, and money at electronic speeds. The direction now being taken by OM—where it has been and where it is going—is shown in Figure 1.4. Let's look at some of these challenges.

- *Ethics:* Operations managers' roles of buying from suppliers, transforming resources into finished goods, and delivering to customers place them at critical junctures where they must frequently make ethical decisions.
- *Global focus:* The rapid decline in communication and transportation costs has made markets global. Similarly, resources in the form of capital, materials, talent, and labor are now also

Traditional Approach	Reasons for Change	Current Challenges
Ethics and regulation not at the forefront	*Public concern over pollution, corruption, child labor, etc.*	High ethical and social responsibility; increased legal and professional standards (all chapters)
Local, regional, national focus	*Growth of reliable, low-cost communication and transportation*	Global focus; international collaboration (Chapters 2, 11)
Lengthy product development	*Shorter life cycles; growth of global communication; computer-aided design (CAD); Internet*	Rapid product development; design collaboration (Chapter 5)
Low-cost production, with little concern for environment; free resources (air, water) ignored	*Public sensitivity to environment; ISO 14000 standard; increasing disposal costs*	Environmentally sensitive production; green manufacturing; sustainability (Chapters 5, 7)
Low-cost standard products	*Rise of consumerism; increased affluence; individualism*	Mass customization (Chapters 5, 7)
Emphasis on specialized, often manual tasks	*Recognizing the importance of the employee's total contribution; knowledge society*	Empowered employees; enriched jobs (Chapter 10)
'In-house' production; low-bid purchasing	*Rapid technology change; increasing competitive forces*	Supply-chain partnering; joint ventures; alliances (Chapter 11, Supplement 11)
Large lot production	*Shorter product life; increasing need to reduce inventory*	Just-in-time performance; lean; continuous improvement (Chapter 16)

▲ FIGURE 1.4   **Changing Challenges for the Operations Manager**

global. As a result, countries throughout the world are contributing to globalization as they vie for economic growth. Operations managers are rapidly responding with creative designs, efficient production, and quality goods.

- *Rapid product development:* Rapid international communication of news, entertainment, and lifestyles is dramatically decreasing the life span of products. Operations managers are responding with management structures, technology, and alliances (partnerships) that are more responsive and effective.
- *Environmentally sensitive production:* Operations managers' continuing battle to improve productivity is increasingly concerned with designing products and processes that are ecologically sustainable. This means designing products and packaging that minimize resource use, are biodegradable, can be recycled, and are generally environmentally friendly.
- *Mass customization:* Once managers recognize the world as the marketplace, the cultural and individual differences become quite obvious. In a world where consumers are increasingly aware of innovation and options, substantial pressure is placed on firms to respond. Operations managers are responding with creative product designs and flexible production processes that cater to the individual whims of consumers. The goal is to produce customized products, whenever and wherever needed.
- *Empowered employees:* The knowledge explosion and more technical workplace have combined to require more competence in the workplace. Operations managers are responding by moving more decision making to individual workers.
- *Supply-chain partnering:* Shorter product life cycles, demanding customers, and fast changes in technology, material, and processes require supply-chain partners to be more in tune with the needs of end users. Because suppliers can contribute unique expertise, operations managers are outsourcing and building long-term partnerships with critical players in the supply chain.

- *Just-in-time performance:* Inventory requires financial resources and impedes response to rapid changes in the marketplace. These forces push operations managers to viciously cut inventories at every level, from raw materials to finished goods.

These trends are part of the exciting OM challenges that are discussed in this text.

CHAPTER SUMMARY

Operations, marketing, and finance/accounting are the three functions basic to all organizations. The operations function creates goods and services. Much of the progress of operations management has been made in the 20th century, but since the beginning of time, humankind has been attempting to improve its material well-being. Operations managers are key players in the battle to improve productivity.

As societies become increasingly affluent, more of their resources are devoted to services. In the Middle East, more than two-thirds of the workforce is employed in the service sector. Productivity improvements are difficult to achieve, but operations managers are the primary vehicle for making improvements.

Key Terms

Knowledge society (p. 13)
Management process (p. 7)
Multi-factor productivity (p. 11)
Operations management (OM) (p. 4)

Production (p. 4)
Productivity (p. 10)
Productivity variables (p. 12)
Service sector (p. 9)

Services (p. 9)
Single-factor productivity (p. 11)

Ethical Dilemma

Major corporations with overseas subcontractors (such as IKEA in Bangladesh, Unilever in India, and Nike in China) have been criticized, often with substantial negative publicity, when children as young as ten have been found working in the subcontractor's facilities. The standard response is to perform an audit and then enhance controls so that it does not happen again. In one such case, a 10-year-old was dismissed from the factory. Shortly thereafter, the family, without the 10-year-old's contribution to the family income, lost its modest home, and the 10-year-old was left to scrounge in the local dump for scraps of metal. Was the decision to hire the 10-year-old ethical? Was the decision to fire the 10-year-old ethical?

Discussion Questions

1. Why should one study operations management?
2. Figure 1.1 outlines the operations, finance/accounting, and marketing functions of three organizations. Prepare a chart similar to Figure 1.1 outlining the same functions for one of the following.
   a. a newspaper
   b. a drugstore
   c. a college library
   d. a summer camp
   e. a small costume-jewelry factory
3. Answer Question 2 for another organization, perhaps an organization where you have worked.
4. What are the three basic functions of a firm?
5. Name the ten decision areas of operations management.
6. Name four areas that are significant to improving labor productivity.
7. Society today has been described as a 'knowledge society.' How does this affect productivity measurement?
8. What are the measurement problems that occur when one attempts to measure productivity?
9. Mass customization and rapid product development were identified as current trends in modern manufacturing operations. What is the relationship, if any, between these trends? Can you cite any examples?
10. What are the five reasons why productivity is difficult to improve in the service sector?

Solved Problems   Virtual Office Hours help is available at MyOMLab

▼ SOLVED PROBLEM 1.1

Productivity can be measured in a variety of ways, such as by labor, capital, energy, material usage, and so on. At Modern Lumber, Inc., Art Binley, president and producer of apple crates sold to farmers, has been able with his current equipment to produce 240 crates per 100 logs. He currently purchases 100 logs per day, and each log requires 3 labor-hours to process. He believes that he can hire a professional buyer who can buy a better-quality log at the same cost. If this is the case, he can increase his production to 260 crates per 100 logs. His labor-hours will increase by 8 hours per day.

What will be the impact on productivity (measured in crates per labor-hour) if the buyer is hired?

▼ SOLUTION

(a) Current labor productivity $= \dfrac{240 \text{ crates}}{100 \text{ logs} \times 3 \text{ hours/log}}$

$= \dfrac{240}{300}$

$= 0.8$ crates per labor-hour

(b) Labor productivity with buyer

$= \dfrac{260 \text{ crates}}{(100 \text{ logs} \times 3 \text{ hours/log}) + 8 \text{ hours}}$

$= \dfrac{260}{308}$

$= 0.844$ crates per labor-hour

Using current productivity (0.80 from [a]) as a base, the increase will be 5.5 percent ($0.844 \div 0.8 = 1.055$, or a 5.5 percent increase).

▼ SOLVED PROBLEM 1.2

Art Binley has decided to look at his productivity from a multi-factor (total factor productivity) perspective (refer to Solved Problem 1.1). To do so, he has determined his labor, capital, energy, and material usage and decided to use US dollars as the common denominator. His total labor-hours are now 300 per day and will increase to 308 per day. His capital and energy costs will remain constant at US$350 and US$150 per day, respectively. Material costs for the 100 logs per day are US$1,000 and will remain the same. Because he pays an average of US$10 per hour (with fringes), Binley determines his productivity increase as follows:

▼ SOLUTION

Current System		
Labor:	300 hrs. @ 10 =	3,000
Material:	100 logs/day	1,000
Capital:		350
Energy:		150
Total Cost:		US$4,500

Multi-factor productivity of current system:
= 240 crates ÷ 4,500 = 0.0533 crates/dollar

System with Professional Buyer	
308 hrs. @ 10 =	US$3,080
	1,000
	350
	150
	US$4,580

Multi-factor productivity of proposed system:
= 260 crates ÷ 4,580 = 0.0568 crates/dollar

Using current productivity (0.0533) as a base, the increase will be 0.066. That is, $0.0568 \div 0.0533 = 1.066$, or a 6.6 percent increase.

Problems*

•   **1.1** Ali Shareef makes wooden boxes in which to ship motorcycles. Ali and his three employees invest a total of 40 hours per day making 120 boxes.
a) What is their productivity?
b) Ali and his employees have discussed redesigning the process to improve efficiency. If they can increase the rate to 125 per day, what will be their new productivity?
c) What will be their unit *increase* in productivity per hour?
d) What will be their percentage change in productivity? **Px**

•   **1.2** Sahara Metal Works produces cast bronze valves on a ten-person assembly line. On a recent day, 160 valves were produced during an 8-hour shift.
a) Calculate the labor productivity of the line.
b) The manager at Sahara changed the layout and was able to increase production to 180 units per 8-hour shift. What is the new labor productivity per labor-hour?
c) What is the percentage of productivity increase? **Px**

•   **1.3** This year, Ramtha, Inc. will produce 57,600 hot water heaters at its plant in Ramtha, Jordan, in order to meet expected

global demand. To accomplish this, each laborer at the Ramtha plant will work 160 hours per month. If the labor productivity at the plant is 0.15 hot water heaters per labor-hour, how many laborers are employed at the plant?

••   **1.4** Jamil Al-Omani makes footballs in his Muscat-based factory. With recent increases in his costs, he has a newfound interest in efficiency. Jamil is interested in determining the productivity of his organization. He would like to know if his organization is maintaining the manufacturing average of a 3 percent increase in productivity. He has the following data representing a month from last year and an equivalent month this year:

	Last Year	Now
Units produced	1,000	1,000
Labor (hours)	300	275
Leather (kg)	50	45
Capital invested (US$)	10,000	11,000
Energy (BTU)	3,000	2,850

Show the productivity percentage change for each category and then determine the improvement for labor-hours, the typical standard for comparison. **Px**

*Note: **Px** means the problem may be solved with POM for Windows and/or Excel OM.

•• **1.5** Jamil Al-Omani (using the data from Problem 1.4) determines his costs to be as follows:

- *Labor:* US$10 per hour
- *Leather:* US$5 per kg
- *Capital expense:* 1% per month of investment
- *Energy:* US$.50 per BTU.

Show the percentage change in productivity for one month last year versus one month this year, on a multi-factor basis with US dollars as the common denominator. **P**✕

• **1.6** Baghdadi Carpets cleaned 65 rugs in October, consuming the following resources:

Labor:	520 hours at US$13 per hour
Solvent:	100 liters at US$5 per liter
Machine rental:	20 days at US$50 per day

a) What is the labor productivity per dollar?
b) What is the multi-factor productivity? **P**✕

•• **1.7** Makhbaz Mazouzeh, a Lebanese bakery, is worried about increased costs—particularly energy. Last year's records can provide a fairly good estimate of the parameters for this year. Mazouzeh Azzeh, the owner, does not believe things have changed much, but she did invest an additional US$3,000 for modifications to the bakery's ovens to make them more energy-efficient. The modifications were supposed to make the ovens at least 15 percent more efficient. Mazouzeh has asked you to check the energy savings of the new ovens and also to look over other measures of the bakery's productivity to see if the modifications were beneficial. You have the following data to work with:

	Last Year	**Now**
Production (dozen)	1,500	1,500
Labor (hours)	350	325
Capital investment (US$)	15,000	18,000
Energy (BTU)	3,000	2,750

•• **1.8** Cairo Autos, Inc. modifies 375 cars per year. The manager, Amir Salah, is interested in obtaining a measure of overall performance. He has asked you to provide him with a multi-factor measure of last year's performance as a benchmark for future comparison. You have assembled the following data:

Labor:	10,000 hours at US$20 per hour
Kits:	500 kits at US$1,000 each
Energy:	100,000 kilowatt-hours at US$3 per kilowatt-hour

What do you tell Mr Salah? **P**✕

•• **1.9** Lake Latakia Seafood makes 500 wooden packing boxes for fresh seafood per day, working in two 10-hour shifts. Due to increased demand, plant managers have decided to operate three 8-hour shifts instead. The plant is now able to produce 650 boxes per day.

a) Calculate the company's productivity before the change in work rules and after the change.
b) What is the percentage increase in productivity?
c) If production is increased to 700 boxes per day, what is the new productivity? **P**✕

••• **1.10** Abdullah Al-Eini operates a kunafe shop in Damascus. Because of its excellent product and excellent location, demand has increased by 25 percent in the last year. On far too many occasions, customers have not been able to purchase the kunafe of their choice. Because of the size of the store, no new equipment can be added. At a staff meeting, one employee suggested ways to load the kunafe trays differently so that more kunafe can be made at one time. This new process will require that the trays be loaded by hand, requiring additional manpower. This is the only thing to be changed. If the shop makes 1,500 trays per month with a labor productivity of 2.344 trays per labor-hour, how many workers will Al-Eini need to add? (*Hint:* Each worker works 160 hours per month.)

•• **1.11** Refer to Problem 1.10. The pay will be US$8 per hour for employees. Abdullah Al-Eini can also improve the yield by purchasing a new oven. The new oven will mean an increase in his investment. This added investment has a cost of US$100 per month, but he will achieve the same output (an increase to 1,875) as the change in labor-hours. Which is the better decision?

a) Show the productivity change, in trays per dollar, with an increase in labor cost (from 640 to 800 hours).
b) Show the new productivity, in trays per dollar, with only an increase in investment (US$100 per month more).
c) Show the percentage change in productivity for labor and investment.

••• **1.12** Refer to Problems 1.10 and 1.11. If Abdullah's utility costs remain constant at US$500 per month, labor at US$8 per hour, and cost of ingredients at US$0.35 per tray, but Abdullah does not purchase the oven suggested in Problem 1.11, what will the productivity of the shop be? What will be the percentage increase or decrease?

•• **1.13** Layla Masri runs a small job shop where garments are made. The job shop employs eight workers. Each worker is paid US$10 per hour. During the first week of March, each worker worked 45 hours. Together, they produced a batch of 132 garments. Of these garments, 52 were 'seconds' (meaning that they were flawed). The seconds were sold for US$90 each at a market. The remaining 80 garments were sold to retail outlets at a price of US$198 per garment. What was the labor productivity, in dollars per labor-hour, at this job shop during the first week of March?

▶ **Refer to** MyOMLab **for additional homework problems.**

Case Studies

► Elhoudda Sardines Fishery, Casablanca

Elhoudda operates a sardine fishery where fish are purchased from local sources along the Atlantic Ocean, processed at the facility, and sold to customers for distribution. The plant manager is considering modernizing the fishery by introducing more modern technology at the plant. This will enable it to increase its capacity to meet the ever-increasing global demand for sardines. Currently, the plant operates five days a week, in two shifts of 30 workers per shift. The workers are paid US$10 per hour. Adding a third shift is not possible because the plant is cleaned during this period.

With the current equipment, the plant can process around 1,500 kilograms of sardines per hour, while the new equipment would be able to process 2,000 kilograms per hour. The updated equipment is made by the same manufacturer as the existing equipment, and the production personnel feel that they will be able to learn to use the new equipment quickly. For this reason, costs to train personnel are assumed to be negligible.

The production manager is skeptical about undergoing the plant modernization. The older equipment, he argues, is already

Adapted from Dr. Ian M. Langella, Shippensburg University, United States

paid for, and new equipment would cost US$10,000 per week. This cost comprises both principal and interest, and includes installation of the equipment. The control officer cautions that all costs should be included in the analysis, including energy consumption, which will be affected by the change. Energy costs are presently US$10 per unit, and the existing plant uses 1,000 units of energy per week. With the modernized plant, the consumption of energy would fall by 50 percent.

Discussion Questions

1. What is the productivity of the processing facility with the equipment currently in use?
2. What would the productivity of the plant become if the new system were purchased and implemented?
3. What would be the amount of additional expense on equipment that would make productivity of the two systems equal?
4. What might happen if energy costs increase in the future?

► Hard Rock Cafe: Operations Management in Services

Video Case

In its 42 years of existence, Hard Rock has grown from a modest London pub to a global power managing 129 cafés, 12 hotels/casinos, live music venues, and a huge annual Rockfest concert. This puts Hard Rock firmly in the service industry—a sector that employs over 75 percent of the people in the United States. Hard Rock moved its world headquarters to Orlando, Florida, in 1988 and has expanded to more than 40 locations throughout the United States, serving over 100,000 meals each day. Hard Rock chefs are modifying the menu from classic American—burgers and chicken wings—to include higher-end items such as stuffed veal chops and lobster tails. Just as taste in music changes over time, so does Hard Rock Cafe, with new menus, layouts, memorabilia, services, and strategies.

At Orlando's Universal Studios, a traditional tourist destination, Hard Rock Cafe serves over 3,500 meals each day. The café employs about 400 people. Most are employed in the restaurant, but some work in the retail shop. Retail is now a standard and increasingly prominent feature in Hard Rock Cafes (since close to 48 percent of revenue comes from this source). Café employees include kitchen and waiting staff, hosts and hostesses, and bartenders. Hard Rock employees are not only competent in their job skills but are also passionate about music and have engaging personalities. Café staff are scheduled down to 15-minute intervals to meet seasonal and daily demand changes in the tourist environment of Orlando. Surveys are done on a regular basis to evaluate the quality of food and service at the café. Scores are rated on a 1 to 7 scale, and if the score is not a 7, the food or service is a failure.

Hard Rock is adding a new emphasis on live music and is redesigning its restaurants to accommodate the changing tastes. Since Eric Clapton hung his guitar on the wall to mark his favorite bar stool, Hard Rock has become the world's leading collector and exhibitor of rock 'n' roll memorabilia, with changing exhibits at its cafés throughout the world. The collection includes thousands of pieces, valued at US$40 million. In keeping with the times, Hard Rock also maintains a website, (**www.hardrock.com**), which receives over 100,000 hits per week, and a weekly cable television program on VH1. Hard Rock's brand recognition, at 92 percent, is one of the highest in the world.

Discussion Questions*

1. From your knowledge of restaurants, from the video, and from the case itself, identify how each of the ten decisions of OM is applied at Hard Rock Cafe.
2. How would you determine the productivity of the kitchen staff and waiting staff at Hard Rock?
3. How are the ten decisions of OM different when applied to the operations manager of a service operation such as Hard Rock versus an automobile company such as Ford Motor Company?

*You may wish to view the video that accompanies this case before addressing these questions.

► Frito-Lay: Operations Management in Manufacturing

 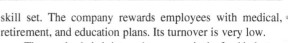

Frito-Lay, the massive subsidiary of PepsiCo, is an international organization with its own subsidiaries such as Lays Arabia (see the *Company Profile* in Chapter 13). Six of Frito-Lay's 41 brands exceed US$1 billion in sales: Fritos, Lay's Cheetos, Ruffles, Tostitos, Doritos, and Walker's Potato Chips. Operations is the focus of the firm—from designing products for new markets, to meeting changing consumer preferences, to adjusting to rising commodity costs, to subtle issues involving flavors and preservatives—OM is under constant cost, time, quality, and market pressure. Here is a look at how the ten decisions of OM are applied at this food processor.

In the food industry, product development kitchens experiment with new products, submit them to focus groups, and perform test marketing. Once the product specifications have been set, processes capable of meeting those specifications, and the necessary quality standards are created. At Frito-Lay, quality begins at the farm, with onsite inspection of the potatoes used in Ruffles and the corn used in Fritos. Quality continues throughout the manufacturing process, with visual inspections and with statistical process control of product variables such as oil, moisture, seasoning, salt, thickness, and weight. Additional quality evaluations are conducted throughout shipment, receipt, production, packaging, and delivery.

The production process at Frito-Lay is designed for large volumes and small variety, using expensive special-purpose equipment, and with swift movement of material through the facility. Product-focused facilities such as Frito-Lay's typically have high capital costs, tight schedules, and rapid processing. Frito-Lay's facilities are located regionally to aid in the rapid delivery of products because freshness is a critical issue. Sanitary issues and necessarily fast processing of products put a premium on an efficient layout. Production lines are designed for balanced throughput and high utilization. Cross-trained workers, who handle a variety of production lines, have promotion paths identified for their particular skill set. The company rewards employees with medical, retirement, and education plans. Its turnover is very low.

The supply chain is integral to success in the food industry; vendors must be chosen with great care. Moreover, the finished food product is highly dependent on perishable raw materials. Consequently, the supply chain brings raw materials (potatoes, corn, etc.) to the plant securely and rapidly to meet tight production schedules. For instance, from the time that potatoes are picked until they are unloaded at the plant, processed, packaged, and shipped from the plant is under 12 hours. The requirement for fresh product requires on-time, just-in-time deliveries combined with both low raw material and finished goods inventories. The continuous-flow nature of the specialized equipment in the production process permits little work-in-process inventory. The plants usually run 24/7. This means that there are four shifts of employees each day.

Tight scheduling to ensure the proper mix of fresh finished goods on automated equipment requires reliable systems and effective maintenance. Frito-Lay's workforce is trained to recognize problems early, and professional maintenance personnel are available on every shift. Downtime is very costly and can lead to late deliveries, making maintenance a high priority.

Discussion Questions

1. From your knowledge of production processes and from the case and the video, identify how each of the ten decisions of OM is applied at Frito-Lay.
2. How would you determine the productivity of the production process at Frito-Lay?
3. How are the ten decisions of OM different when applied by the operations manager of a production process such as Frito-Lay versus a service organization such as McDonald's?

Source: Professors Beverly Amer (Northern Arizona University), Barry Render (Rollins College), and Jay Heizer (Texas Lutheran University).

►**Additional Case Study:** Visit MyOMLab for this free case study:

Zychol Chemicals Corp.: The production manager must prepare a productivity report, which includes multi-factor analysis.

Chapter 1 *Rapid* Review

Main Heading	Review Material	MyOMLab
WHAT IS OPERATIONS MANAGEMENT? (p. 4)	**Production**—The creation of goods and services. **Operations management (OM)**—Activities that relate to the creation of goods and services through the transformation of inputs to outputs.	**OM AT TCHETCHE VIDEOS 1.1 and 1.2** Hard Rock Cafe: Operations Management in Services Frito-Lay: Operations Management in Manufacturing
ORGANIZING TO PRODUCE GOODS AND SERVICES (pp. 4–5)	All organizations perform three functions to create goods and services. 1. *Marketing*, which generates demand 2. *Production/operations*, which creates the product 3. *Finance/accounting*, which tracks how well the organization is doing, pays the bills, and collects the money.	
WHY STUDY OM? (pp. 6–7)	We study OM for four reasons. 1. To learn *how businesses organize their activities to be productive.* 2. To learn how goods and services are produced. 3. To understand what operations managers do. 4. Because OM is a costly part of an organization.	
WHAT OPERATIONS MANAGERS DO (pp. 7–8)	**Management process**—The application of planning, organizing, staffing, leading, and controlling to achieve objectives. Ten major OM decisions are required of operations managers. 1. Design of goods and services 2. Managing quality 3. Process and capacity design 4. Location strategy 5. Layout strategy 6. Human resources, job design, and work measurement 7. Supply-chain management 8. Inventory, material requirements planning, and JIT (just-in-time) 9. Intermediate and short-term scheduling 10. Maintenance About 40 percent of *all* jobs are in OM. Operations managers possess job titles such as plant manager, quality manager, process improvement consultant, and operations analyst.	
THE EVOLUTION OF OPERATIONS MANAGEMENT (pp. 8–9)	Operations Management has progressed with contributions from: ■ industrial engineering ■ management science ■ statistics ■ management ■ economics ■ innovations from the physical sciences.	
OPERATIONS IN THE SERVICE SECTOR (pp. 9–10)	**Services**—Economic activities that typically produce an intangible product (such as education, entertainment, lodging, government, financial, and health services). Almost all services and almost all goods are a mixture of a service and a tangible product. **Service sector**—The segment of the economy that includes trade, financial, lodging, education, legal, medical, and other professional occupations. Services now constitute the largest economic sector in post-industrial societies. The huge productivity increases in agriculture and manufacturing have allowed more of our economic resources to be devoted to services. Many service jobs pay very well.	

Main Heading	Review Material	
THE PRODUCTIVITY CHALLENGE (pp. 10–15)	**Productivity**—The ratio of outputs (goods and services) divided by one or more inputs (such as labor, capital, or management).	Problems: 1.1–1.13 Virtual Office Hours for Solved Problems: 1.1, 1.2
	High production means producing many units, while high productivity means producing units efficiently.	
	Only through increases in productivity can the standard of living of a country improve.	
	$$\text{Productivity} = \frac{\text{Useful units produced}}{\text{Input used}} \qquad (1\text{-}1)$$	
	Single-factor productivity—Indicates the ratio of one resource (input) to the goods and services produced (outputs).	
	Multi-factor productivity (total factor productivity)—Indicates the ratio of many or all resources (inputs) to the goods and services produced (outputs).	
	$$\text{Multi-factor Productivity} = \frac{\text{Output}}{\text{Labor} + \text{Material} + \text{Energy} + \text{Capital} + \text{Miscellaneous}} \qquad (1\text{-}2)$$	
	Measurement problems with productivity include the following: (1) the quality may change; (2) external elements may interfere; (3) precise units of measure may be lacking.	
	■ **Productivity variables**—The three factors critical to productivity improvement are labor (10 percent), capital (38 percent), and management (52 percent). ■ **Knowledge society**—A society in which much of the labor force has migrated from manual work to work based on knowledge.	
ETHICS AND SOCIAL RESPONSIBILITY (p. 15)	Among the many ethical challenges facing operations managers are: (1) efficiently developing and producing safe, quality products; (2) maintaining a clean environment; (3) providing a safe workplace; (4) honoring stakeholder commitments.	
EXCITING NEW TRENDS IN OPERATIONS MANAGEMENT (pp. 15–17)	Some of the current challenges for operations managers include: ■ high ethical and social responsibility; increased legal and professional standards ■ global focus; international collaboration ■ rapid product development; design collaboration ■ environmentally sensitive production; green manufacturing; sustainability ■ mass customization ■ empowered employees; enriched jobs ■ supply-chain partnering; joint ventures; alliances ■ just-in-time performance; lean; continuous improvement.	

Self-Test

■ **Before taking the self-test,** refer to the learning objectives listed at the beginning of the chapter and the key terms listed at the end of the chapter.

LO1. Productivity increases when:
  a) inputs increase while outputs remain the same
  b) inputs decrease while outputs remain the same
  c) outputs decrease while inputs remain the same
  d) inputs and outputs increase proportionately
  e) inputs increase at the same rate as outputs.

LO2. Services often:
  a) are tangible
  b) are standardized
  c) are knowledge-based
  d) are low in customer interaction
  e) have consistent product definition.

LO3. Productivity:
  a) can use many factors as the numerator
  b) is the same thing as production
  c) increases at about 2.5 percent per year
  d) is dependent upon labor, management, and capital
  e) is the same thing as effectiveness.

LO4. Single-factor productivity:
  a) remains constant
  b) is never constant
  c) usually uses labor as a factor
  d) seldom uses labor as a factor
  e) uses management as a factor.

LO5. Multi-factor productivity:
  a) remains constant
  b) is never constant
  c) usually uses substitutes as common variables for the factors of production
  d) seldom uses labor as a factor
  e) always uses management as a factor.

LO6. Productivity increases as a result of three factors:
  a) labor, capital, management
  b) engineering, labor, capital
  c) engineering, capital, quality control
  d) engineering, labor, data processing
  e) engineering, capital, data processing.

Answers: LO1. b; LO2. c; LO3. d; LO4. c; LO5. c; LO6. a.

2

The Global Environment and Operations Strategy

10

OM STRATEGY DECISIONS

- ▶ Design of Goods and Services
- ▶ Managing Quality
- ▶ Process Strategy
- ▶ Location Strategies
- ▶ Layout Strategies
- ▶ Human Resources
- ▶ Supply-Chain Management
- ▶ Inventory Management
- ▶ Scheduling
- ▶ Maintenance

EMAAR'S GLOBAL STRATEGY YIELDS THE TALLEST BUILDING IN THE WORLD

Emaar's strategy for its Burj Khalifa skyscraper has brought together the best of the world's engineering and technical skills to establish a structure that has broken several records. The skyscraper is considered the world's tallest freestanding structure and skyscraper (828 meters), with the most floors (160 floors), and with the world's highest and fastest elevator (64 km/h). In addition it has the world's highest place of worship (a mosque), highest outdoor observation deck, highest nightclub, and highest restaurant. Burj Khalifa incorporates the latest in a wide range of construction technologies and innovations, from concrete, steel, and aluminum to special silicon sealing for glass insulation, and the latest technology in cathodic protection systems to minimize corrosion.

Emaar has brought together the leading companies from all over the world to benefit from the best practitioners. The strategy was to select the best companies with a competitive edge in their domain and compose an integrated team that would excel in every aspect. The international contractors include: Skidmore, Owings & Merrill LLP from the United States (architecture), Besix from Belgium (construction), Samsung Engineering & Construction from South Korea (engineering), Arabtec from U.A.E. (construction), Turner from the United States (construction), Hyder from the United Kingdom (consulting), Grocon from Australia (construction), Otis from the United States (elevators and escalators), Lerch Bates from the United States (consulting), Far East Aluminum from Hong Kong (glazing fabricators), Arabian Aluminum from U.A.E. (aluminum), White Aluminum from U.A.E. (insulating), Bauer AG from Germany (foundations), Middle East Foundations from U.A.E. (geo-technical services), Cox Gomyl from Australia (window cleaning), and many others.

This state-of-the-art skyscraper is not only global in the sense that it was built and is maintained by

More than 7,500 skilled workers participated in constructing the Burj Khalifa.

Burj Khalifa is now the main tourist destination in Dubai, holding more than 35,000 people at any single point in time.

The water fountains surrounding Burj Khalifa resemble the desert flower, the hymenocallis.

Source: **www.emaar.com**

companies from all over the world, but also because it serves and hosts companies and people from different nationalities, ethnicities, and cultures. The first 40 floors are reserved for the Armani Hotel (Italy), the floors from 44 to 72 are residential, and floors 125 up to 135 are corporate suites.

The project cost AED 5.5 billion (US$1.5 billion), and now contains 900 apartments served by 57 elevators and eight escalators with the capacity of catering for almost 35,000 people at any one time. This skyscraper is functional, efficient, and built with the help of corporations from all around the world.

Chapter 2 Learning Objectives

> **AUTHOR COMMENT**
> As Professor Thomas Sewell
> observed, "No great civilization
> has developed in isolation."

A GLOBAL VIEW OF OPERATIONS

Today's operations manager must have a global view of operations strategy. The continuous removal of restrictions on international trade has provided companies with huge opportunities to extend their operations to other areas of the world, thus challenging them to find innovative strategies to expand into untraditional markets. Many companies in the Middle East have benefited from advances in technology, the spread of electronic trade, and cheap communication to launch operations in different parts of the world. For example:

Gulf Cooperation Council (GCC)

A political and economic union between Bahrain, Kuwait, Oman, Qatar, Saudi Arabia, and United Arab Emirates.

- Saudi Oger Ltd gained its competitive advantage from its global operations and expertise, carrying out complex and technologically advanced construction projects in Europe, the Middle East, and Africa.
- Almarai plc became one of the largest food companies in the Middle East by investing in storage and delivery systems, making it more flexible. Such state-of-the art design made it possible to serve fresh dairy products to Almarai customers throughout the **Gulf Cooperation Council (GCC)** daily.
- Patchi purchases cocoa from suppliers in Côte d'Ivoire, Brazil, Indonesia, and elsewhere around the world in addition to other ingredients from Switzerland and Belgium, to produce the finest chocolates in Lebanon to be sold in its 140 boutiques distributed around 35 countries worldwide.

Free Trade Zones

Zones that are free from customs interventions where businesses can manufacture goods from imported products and then export free of duties.

- **Free Trade Zones** encourage firms from around the world to relocate their operations to that area by offering a wide range of facilities provided by the local authorities. For example, Dubai Media City provides the facilities and infrastructure for global media organizations to set up their stations, news agencies, publishing houses, and so on, tax-free in Dubai—examples include CNN, BBC, Al Arabiya, the *Financial Times*, Reuters, and Sony.

Qualifying Industrial Zones (QIZs)

International factories located in Jordan that receive preferential tariff treatment.

This increase in economic integration and interdependence between countries signifies the importance of globalization for businesses. Domestic production and exporting no longer may be a viable business model, as there are new standards for global competitiveness that impact on quality, variety, and cost. As a result, companies should shift from dependence on domestic business to a more international approach. We will now discuss six ways in which companies can achieve this.

World Trade Organization (WTO)

An international organization that promotes world trade by lowering barriers to the free flow of goods across borders.

Reduce Costs   Many international operations seek to take advantage of tangible opportunities to reduce their costs. Foreign locations with lower wages can help lower both direct and indirect costs.

In Jordan, for example, the creation of **Qualifying Industrial Zones (QIZs)** encouraged many international manufacturers to relocate their operations to Jordan, as this guaranteed that their products would have quota-free entrance to the U.S. market without paying any duties or taxes. In addition, the less stringent government regulations on operations practices mean that the relocated companies can significantly cut costs. Other agreements around the world that aim to remove the tariff barriers between member nations include the **World Trade Organization (WTO)**, the **North American Free Trade Agreement (NAFTA)**, the **European Union (EU)**, and the Gulf Cooperation Council.

North American Free Trade Agreement (NAFTA)

A free trade agreement between Canada, Mexico, and the United States.

Such agreements guarantee access to lower-cost labor, which has the additional operational benefit of freeing higher-cost workers for more valuable tasks. This allows the savings to be invested in improved products/facilities and the retraining of existing workers at the home location. The impact of this approach is shown in the *OM in Action* box 'Going Global to Compete.'

European Union (EU)

A European political and trade group that has 27 members.

Improve the Supply Chain   The supply chain can often be improved by locating facilities in countries where unique resources are available. These resources may be expertise, labor, or raw materials. For example, most petrochemical industries want a presence in the Gulf region, where much of the world's oil reserves are available, thus providing significant savings in transportation logistics.

Provide Better Goods and Services   Although the characteristics of goods and services can be objective and measurable (e.g. number of on-time deliveries), they can also be subjective and less measurable (e.g. sensitivity to culture). Therefore, having operations abroad means that companies can better address the needs and wants of customers in different countries, and across different cultures. In addition, companies are more able to respond quickly to changes in customers' requirements.

Understand Markets   Because international operations require interaction with foreign customers, suppliers, and other competitive businesses, international firms inevitably learn about opportunities for new products and services. Knowledge of these markets not only helps firms understand where the market is going but also helps firms diversify their customer base, add production flexibility, expand existing product life cycles, and smooth the business cycle.

Learn to Improve Operations   Learning does not take place in isolation. Firms serve themselves and their customers well when they remain open to the free flow of ideas. For example, Yahoo! found that it could improve operations in the Arab world by acquiring Maktoob.com. This approach allowed Yahoo! to contribute its capital, resources, and technical know-how while the Arabic company contributed product ideas most suitable to the Arabic audience.

Attract and Retain Global Talent   Global organizations can attract and retain better employees by offering more employment opportunities. During economic downturns in one country or continent, a global firm has the means to relocate unneeded personnel to more prosperous locations.

So, to recap, successfully achieving a competitive advantage in our shrinking world means maximizing all of the possible opportunities, from tangible to intangible, that international operations can offer.

Cultural and Ethical Issues

While there are many forces driving firms toward globalization, many challenges remain. One of these challenges is reconciling differences in social and cultural behavior. With issues ranging from bribery, *wasta* (the use of personal connections to be favored in treatment over others), and child labor, to the environment, managers sometimes do not know how to respond when operating in a different culture. What one country's culture deems acceptable may be considered unacceptable or illegal in another. Therefore, it is important to have international laws and agreements to provide standard guidelines for managers to enable them to make ethical decisions. The WTO, for example, helps to make uniform the protection of both governments and industries from

---

OM in Action ▶ Going Global to Compete

Large companies such as IBM and Intel excel in developing new products and innovative solutions to the world of business, but they face very stiff competition from companies in the rapidly growing economies of China, India, and Brazil due to their lower cost structures.

One significant way of countering this competition is by cutting costs. IBM outsourced its African and Middle Eastern service delivery centers to Egypt, benefiting from the availability of high-skilled workers at a competitive wage structure. IBM also outsourced its back-office business processes, transaction processing operations, technical support operations, and call center operations. Intel acquired SySDSoft Ltd, a privately held Egyptian company based in Cairo, to benefit from its electrical engineers and computer scientists. Initially, Intel

outsourced some of its motherboard assembly to Egypt, from where more than 85 percent of its production was exported to African markets. SySDSoft Ltd became famous for designing Internet protocol-based solutions in the software stack and physical layer domain, and radio frequency/analog circuits embedded in mobile platforms. Its recent product portfolio covers technologies such as WiMAX, Wi-Fi, Bluetooth, wireless USB, and LTE.

Resourceful organizations such as IBM and Intel use a global perspective to become more efficient, which allows them to develop new products, retrain employees, and invest in new plant and equipment.

Sources: Newsroom-Intel (**newsroom.intel.com**) March 14, 2011 and **www.ameinfo.com**

firms that engage in unethical conduct. This is particularly important in the Arab world, as it opens up to the rest of the world. Managers must embrace this in their missions and strategies if they want their companies to succeed.

AUTHOR COMMENT
Getting an education and managing an organization both require a mission and strategy.

DEVELOPING MISSIONS AND STRATEGIES

An effective OM effort must have a *mission* so it knows where it is going, and a *strategy* so it knows how to get there. This is the case for a small domestic organization as well as a large international organization.

Mission

Mission
The purpose or rationale for an organization's existence.

LO1: Define mission and strategy

Economic success, indeed survival, is the result of identifying missions to satisfy a customer's needs and wants. We define the organization's **mission** as its purpose—what it will contribute to society. The mission states the rationale for the organization's existence. Developing a good strategy is difficult, but it is much easier if the mission has been well defined. Figure 2.1 provides examples of mission statements.

Once an organization's mission has been decided, each functional area within the firm determines its supporting mission. By *functional area* we mean the major disciplines required by the firm, such as marketing, finance/accounting, and production/operations. Missions for each function are developed to support the firm's overall mission. Then, within that function, lower-level supporting missions are established for the OM functions. Figure 2.2 provides such a hierarchy of sample missions.

Strategy

Strategy
How an organization expects to achieve its missions and goals.

With the mission established, strategy and its implementation can begin. **Strategy** is an organization's action plan to achieve the mission. Each functional area has a strategy for achieving its mission and for helping the organization reach the overall mission. These strategies exploit opportunities and strengths, neutralize threats, and avoid weaknesses. In the following sections, we will describe how strategies are developed and implemented.

Firms achieve missions in three conceptual ways: (1) differentiation; (2) cost leadership; (3) response. This means that operations managers are called on to deliver goods and services that are: (1) *better*, or at least different; (2) *cheaper*; (3) more *responsive*. Operations managers translate these *strategic concepts* into tangible tasks to be accomplished. Any one or combination of these three strategic concepts can generate a system that has a unique advantage over competitors. For example, Al Zamil, which operates in Saudi Arabia, Kuwait, Bahrain, Jordan,

▶ **FIGURE 2.1**
Mission Statements for Three Organizations

Sources: Annual reports: courtesy of Aramex, University of Jordan, and the Burj Al Arab.

Aramex
To be recognized as one of the top five global logistics and transportation companies by enabling and facilitating regional and global trade and commerce.
University of Jordan
The provision of quality education at both the undergraduate and graduate levels through the adoption of the principles of democracy in the education and decision-making processes, whilst encouraging interaction among students, with the local community, and at the international level to support goal-oriented research.
Burj Al Arab
To be a world class luxury international hotel and hospitality management company, committed to being the industry leader in all of our activities through dedication to our stakeholders; colleagues, customers, business partners and owners.

Sample Company Mission
To manufacture and service an innovative, growing, and profitable worldwide microwave communications business that exceeds our customers' expectations.

Sample Operations Management Mission
To produce products consistent with the company's mission as the worldwide low-cost manufacturer.

Sample OM Department Missions	
Product design	To design and produce products and services with outstanding quality and inherent customer value.
Quality management	To attain the exceptional value that is consistent with our company mission and marketing objectives by close attention to design, procurement, production, and field service opportunities.
Process design	To determine, design, and produce the production process and equipment that will be compatible with low-cost product, high quality, and a good quality of work life at economical cost.
Location	To locate, design, and build efficient and economical facilities that will yield high value to the company, its employees, and the community.
Layout design	To achieve, through skill, imagination, and resourcefulness in layout and work methods, production effectiveness and efficiency while supporting a high quality of work life.
Human resources	To provide a good quality of work life, with well-designed, safe, rewarding jobs, stable employment, and equitable pay, in exchange for outstanding individual contribution from employees at all levels.
Supply-chain management	To collaborate with suppliers to develop innovative products from stable, effective, and efficient sources of supply.
Inventory	To achieve low investment in inventory consistent with high customer service levels and high facility utilization.
Scheduling	To achieve high levels of throughput and timely customer delivery through effective scheduling.
Maintenance	To achieve high utilization of facilities and equipment by effective preventive maintenance and prompt repair of facilities and equipment.

◀ FIGURE 2.2
Sample Missions for a Company, the Operations Function, and Major OM Departments

Qatar, Oman, and U.A.E. has differentiated itself as a premier maker of quality air-conditioning units that are best suited to the extreme weather conditions in the Middle East; Nasr automobiles in Egypt has set itself apart by providing low-cost cars that are affordable for limited budget customers; and Aramex provides express delivery services that guarantee rapid transfer of parcels worldwide.

Clearly, strategies differ—and each strategy puts different demands on OM. Al Zamil's strategy is one of *differentiating* itself via quality from others in the industry. Nasr focuses on value at *low cost*, and Aramex's dominant strategy is a quick, reliable *response*.

ACHIEVING COMPETITIVE ADVANTAGE THROUGH OPERATIONS

Each of the three strategies provides an opportunity for operations managers to achieve competitive advantage. **Competitive advantage** implies the creation of a system that has a unique advantage over competitors. The idea is to create customer value in an efficient and

LO2: Identify and explain three strategic approaches to competitive advantage

VIDEO 2.1
Strategy at Regal Marine

AUTHOR COMMENT
For many organizations, the operations function provides competitive advantage.

Competitive advantage
The creation of a unique advantage over competitors.

sustainable way. Pure forms of these strategies may exist, but operations managers are more likely to be called on to implement some combination of them. Let us briefly look at how managers achieve competitive advantage via *differentiation*, *low cost*, and *response*.

Competing on Differentiation

Differentiation

Distinguishing the offerings of an organization in a way that the customer perceives as adding value.

Differentiation is concerned with providing *uniqueness*. A firm's opportunities for creating uniqueness are not located within a particular function or activity, but can arise in virtually everything the firm does. Moreover, because most products include some service, and most services include some product, the opportunities for creating this uniqueness are limitless. Therefore, effective operations managers assist in defining everything about a product or service that will influence the potential value to the customer. This may be the convenience of a broad product line, product features, or a service related to the product. Such services can manifest themselves through convenience (location of distribution centers, stores, or branches), training, product delivery and installation, or repair and maintenance services.

In the service sector, one option for extending product differentiation is through an *experience*. Differentiation by experience in services is a manifestation of the growing 'experience economy.' The idea of **experience differentiation** is to engage the customer—to use people's five senses so they become immersed, or even an active participant, in the product. Ferrari World in Abu Dhabi achieves this with 'Speed,' an attraction designed for children that uses 4D technology supported by humidity, lights, and movement, thus allowing children to experience the speed and power of a Ferrari as it chases after another driver through jungles, ice caves, and even through the ocean.

Experience differentiation

Engaging a customer with a product through imaginative use of the five senses, so the customer 'experiences' the product.

VIDEO 2.2
Hard Rock's Cafe's Global Strategy

Competing on Cost

Low-cost leadership

Achieving maximum value as perceived by the customer.

Low-cost leadership entails achieving maximum *value* as defined by the customer. It requires examining each of the ten OM decisions in a relentless effort to drive down costs while meeting customer expectations of value. A low-cost strategy does *not* imply low value or low quality. Lulu Hypermarkets in U.A.E. for example, thrives on providing high-quality fresh foods at the lowest price in the market. This strategy has enabled it to grow its market share in most of the Arab world countries such as Egypt, Qatar, Saudi Arabia, Oman, Bahrain, Kuwait, and Yemen. The key is in the operations strategy, by identifying the optimum size of investments, whether in inventory or storage space, in order to be able to spread overhead costs and have a cost advantage over competitors. This is done by continuous control of costs and the never-ending quest for more economically efficient alternatives for operations such as the transportation of goods, inventory pooling, and the optimal use of shelf space.

Competing on Response

Response

A set of values related to rapid, flexible, and reliable performance.

The third strategy option is **response**. Response is often thought of as *flexible* response, but it also refers to *reliable* and *quick* response. Indeed, we define response as including the entire range of values related to timely product development and delivery, as well as reliable scheduling and flexible performance.

These three critical aspects of response—the ability to match changes in a marketplace quickly while maintaining smooth operations—enable the company to have a competitive advantage over its competitors, which has greater perceived value by customers. Such a strategy has been pursued by Rubicon Group, which has demonstrated flexibility in responding to rapidly changing market needs in the digital content industry with reliable, high-quality solutions, such as its 3D technology in animation and its success with *Pink Panther and Pals*. The company's ability to reschedule quickly and innovate in its products has helped it to build a *sustainable competitive advantage*.

In practice, differentiation, low cost, and response can increase productivity and generate a sustainable competitive advantage (see Figure 2.3). Proper implementation of the following decisions by operations managers will allow these advantages to be achieved.

OM in Action ▶ Response Strategy at Petra

On the plant floor of Petra Engineering Industries, Co. in Amman, Jordan, you can see manufacturing personnel buzzing with energy and working hard to meet the next deadline. Established in 1987 to manufacture high-quality commercial and industrial HVAC (heating, ventilation, and air conditioning) equipment, Petra managed to expand from its small location near Amman to more than 20 facilities around the world. Its production lines include chillers, air handlers, dry cooler units, exhaust fans, fan coil units, split units, and bespoke customer solutions. The secret behind this rapid expansion and success is its response strategy.

Petra works very closely with customers and this enables it to pay close attention to what customers like and dislike. Whenever the manufacturing personnel are given a new task in coordination with the sales department, they quickly assemble a task team that aims to beat the deadlines. As one of the engineers puts it, "Deadlines are more of a personal challenge to us. We always aim to deliver one week earlier."

Of course, Petra wouldn't have achieved this without the support of the cutting-edge technology in which it heavily invests. Communications are of great importance as operations managers try to work effectively and efficiently with their global network of factories, R&D facilities, and design centers. Video conferencing is very important for the communication between the different managers, but a package of advanced electronic data interchange is used in addition to computer-aided design (CAD) and manufacturing.

Petra's main strength is its speed in product development, speed in production, and speed in delivering—hundreds of thousands of HVAC units are produced annually, mostly assembled in Jordan but delivered throughout the world, and this is done seamlessly.

Source: **www.petra-eng.com**

AUTHOR COMMENT
These ten decisions are used to implement a specific strategy and yield a competitive advantage.

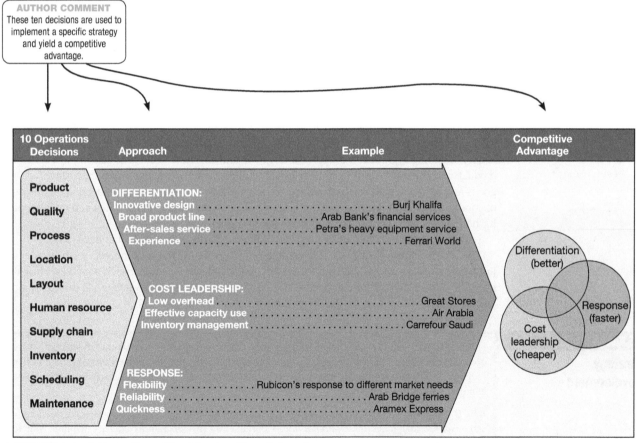

▲ **FIGURE 2.3** **Achieving Competitive Advantage Through Operations**

AUTHOR COMMENT
This book is structured around
these ten decisions.

Operations decisions
The strategic decisions of OM are
goods and service design, quality,
process design, location selection,
layout design, human resources
and job design, supply-chain
management, inventory,
scheduling, and maintenance.

TEN STRATEGIC OM DECISIONS

Differentiation, low cost, and response can be achieved when managers make effective decisions in ten areas of OM. These are collectively known as **operations decisions**. The ten decisions of OM that support missions and implement strategies are:

1. *Goods and service design:* Designing goods and services defines much of the transformation process. Costs, quality, and human resource decisions are often determined by design decisions. Designs usually determine the lower limits of cost and the upper limits of quality.
2. *Quality:* The customer's quality expectations must be determined, and policies and procedures established to identify and achieve that quality.
3. *Process and capacity design:* Process options are available for products and services. Process decisions commit management to specific technology, quality, human resource use, and maintenance. These expenses and capital commitments determine much of the firm's basic cost structure.
4. *Location selection:* Facility location decisions for both manufacturing and service organizations may determine the firm's ultimate success. Errors made at this juncture may overwhelm other efficiencies.
5. *Layout design:* Material flows, capacity needs, personnel levels, technology decisions, and inventory requirements influence layout.
6. *Human resources and job design:* People are an integral and expensive part of the total system design. Therefore, the quality of work life provided, the talent and skills required, and their costs must be determined.
7. *Supply-chain management:* These decisions determine what is to be made and what is to be purchased. Consideration is also given to quality, delivery, and innovation, all at a satisfactory price. Mutual trust between buyer and supplier is necessary for effective purchasing.
8. *Inventory:* Inventory decisions can be optimized only when customer satisfaction, suppliers, production schedules, and human resource planning are considered.
9. *Scheduling:* Feasible and efficient schedules of production must be developed; the demands on human resources and facilities must be determined and controlled.
10. *Maintenance:* Decisions must be made regarding the desired levels of reliability and stability, and systems must be established to maintain that reliability and stability.

LO3: Identify and define the ten decisions of operations management

Operations managers implement these ten decisions by identifying key tasks and the staffing needed to achieve them. However, the implementation of decisions is influenced by a variety of issues, including a product's proportion of goods and services (see Table 2.1 on page 36). Few products are either all goods or all services. Although the ten decisions remain the same for both goods and services, their relative importance and method of implementation depend on this ratio of goods and services. Throughout this text, we discuss how strategy is selected and implemented for both goods and services through these ten OM decisions.

Let's look at an example of strategy development through one of the ten decisions.

The ten decisions of OM are implemented in ways that provide competitive advantage, not just for fine-dining restaurants, but for all the goods and services that enrich our lives. How this might be done for two drug companies, one seeking a competitive advantage via differentiation, and the other via low cost, is shown in Table 2.2.

EXAMPLE 1 ►

Strategy development

Fadeel Al-Fadel has just completed culinary school and is ready to open his own restaurant. After examining both the external environment and his prospective strengths and weaknesses, he makes a decision on the mission for his restaurant, which he defines as "To provide outstanding Arabic fine dining for the people of Dubai."

APPROACH ►   Fadeel's supporting operations strategy is to ignore the options of *cost reduction* and *response* and focus on *differentiation*. Consequently, his operations strategy requires him to evaluate product designs (menus and meals) and selection of process, layout, and location. He must also evaluate the human resources, suppliers, inventory, scheduling, and maintenance that will support his mission and a differentiation strategy.

SOLUTION ►   Examining just one of these ten decisions, *process design*, requires that Fadeel consider the issues presented in the following figure.

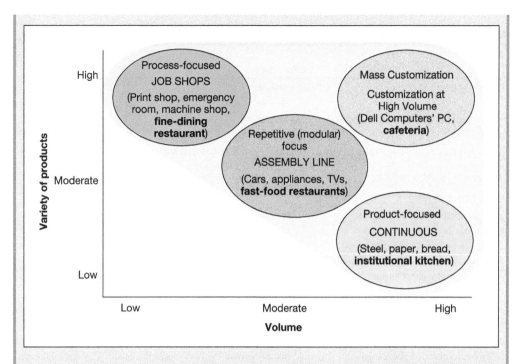

The first option is to operate in the lower-right corner of the above figure, where he could produce high volumes of food with a limited variety, much as in an institutional kitchen. Such a process could produce large volumes of standard items such as baked goods and mashed potatoes prepared with state-of-the-art automated equipment. Fadeel concludes that this is not an acceptable process option.

Alternatively, he can move to the middle of the figure, where he could produce more variety and lower volumes. Here he would have less automation and use prepared modular components for meals, much as a fast-food restaurant does. Again, he deems such process designs inappropriate for his mission.

Another option is to move to the upper-right corner and produce a high volume of customized meals, but neither Fadeel nor anyone else knows how to do this with Arabic gourmet meals.

Finally, Fadeel can design a process that operates in the upper-left corner of the figure, which requires little automation but lends itself to high variety. This process option suggests that he build an extremely flexible kitchen suitable for a wide variety of custom meals catering to the whims of each customer. With little automation, such a process would be suitable for a huge variety. This process strategy will support Fadeel's mission and desired product differentiation. Only with a process such as this can he provide the fine Arabic-style gourmet dining that he has in mind.

INSIGHT ▶   By considering the options inherent in each of the ten OM decisions, managers—Fadeel, in this case—can make decisions that support the mission.

LEARNING EXERCISE ▶   If Fadeel's mission were to offer less expensive meals and reduce the variety offered but still do so with an Arabic flair, what might his process strategy be? [Answer: Fadeel might try a repetitive (modular) strategy and mimic the Al Tazaj cafeteria-style restaurants.]

ISSUES IN OPERATIONS STRATEGY

AUTHOR COMMENT
An effective strategy finds the optimum fit for the firm's resources in the dynamic environment.

Whether the OM strategy is differentiation, cost, or response (as shown earlier in Figure 2.3), OM is a critical player. Therefore, prior to establishing and attempting to implement a strategy, some alternative perspectives may be helpful. One perspective is to take a **resources view**. This means thinking in terms of the financial, physical, human, and technological resources available and ensuring that the potential strategy is compatible with those resources. Another perspective is Porter's value-chain analysis.[1] **Value-chain analysis** is used to identify activities that represent strengths, or potential strengths, and may be opportunities for developing competitive advantage. These are areas where the firm adds its unique *value* through product research, design, human resources, supply-chain management, process innovation, or quality

Resources view

A method managers use to evaluate the resources at their disposal and manage or alter them to achieve competitive advantage.

Value-chain analysis

A way to identify those elements in the product/service chain that uniquely add value.

[1]M. E. Porter, *Competitive Advantage: Creating and Sustaining Superior Performance.* New York: The Free Press, 1985.

▼ TABLE 2.1

How the Differences between Goods and Services Influence How the Ten Operations Management Decisions Are Applied

Operations Decisions	Goods	Services
Goods and service design	Product is usually tangible (a computer).	Product is not tangible. A new range of product attributes (a smile).
Quality	Many objective quality standards (battery life).	Many subjective quality standards (nice color). Customer may be directly involved in the process (a haircut).
Process and capacity design	Customer is not involved in most of the process (auto assembly).	Capacity must match demand to avoid lost sales (customers often avoid waiting).
Location selection	May need to be near raw materials or labor force (steel plant near ore).	May need to be near customer (car rental).
Layout design	Layout can enhance production efficiency (assembly line).	Can enhance product as well as production (layout of a classroom or a fine-dining restaurant).
Human resources and job design	Workforce focused on technical skills (stone mason). Labor standards can be consistent (assembly line employee). Output-based wage system possible (garment sewing).	Direct workforce usually needs to be able to interact well with customer (bank teller); labor standards vary depending on customer requirements (legal cases).
Supply-chain management	Supply-chain relationships critical to final product.	Supply-chain relationships important but may not be critical.
Inventory	Raw materials, work-in-process, and finished goods may be inventoried (beverages).	Most services cannot be stored; so other ways must be found to accommodate fluctuations in demand (can't store haircuts, but even a barber shop has an inventory of supplies).
Scheduling	Goods are physically stored which helps in leveling production rates (lawnmowers and tree trimming).	Often concerned with meeting the customer's immediate schedule with human resources.
Maintenance	Maintenance is often preventive and takes place at the production site.	Maintenance is often 'repair' and takes place at the customer's site.

AUTHOR COMMENT
The production of both goods and services requires execution of the ten OM decisions.

AUTHOR COMMENT
Notice how the ten decisions are altered to build two distinct strategies in the same industry.

▼ TABLE 2.2

Operations Strategies of Two Drug Companies

	Brand Name Drugs, Inc.	Generic Drug Corp.
Competitive Advantage	**Product Differentiation**	**Low Cost**
Product Selection and Design	Heavy R&D investment; extensive labs; focus on development in a broad range of drug categories	Low R&D investment; focus on development of generic drugs
Quality	Quality is major priority, standards exceed regulatory requirements	Meets regulatory requirements on a country-by-country basis, as necessary
Process	Product and modular production process; tries to have long product runs in specialized facilities; builds capacity ahead of demand	Process-focused; general production processes; 'job shop' approach, short-run production; focus on high utilization
Location	Still located in city where it was founded	Recently moved to low-tax, low-labor cost environment
Layout	Layout supports automated product-focused production	Layout supports process-focused 'job shop' practices
Human Resources	Hire the best; nationwide searches	Very experienced top executives provide direction; other personnel paid below industry average
Supply Chain	Long-term supplier relationships	Tends to purchase competitively to find bargains
Inventory	Maintains high finished goods inventory primarily to ensure all demands are met	Process focus drives up work-in-process inventory; finished goods inventory tends to be low
Scheduling	Centralized production planning	Many short-run products complicate scheduling
Maintenance	Highly trained staff; extensive parts inventory	Highly trained staff to meet changing demands

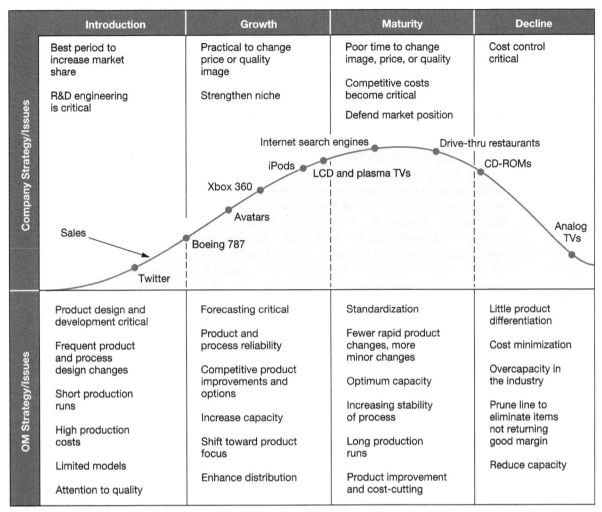

	Introduction	Growth	Maturity	Decline
Company Strategy/Issues	Best period to increase market share R&D engineering is critical	Practical to change price or quality image Strengthen niche	Poor time to change image, price, or quality Competitive costs become critical Defend market position	Cost control critical

Internet search engines

Drive-thru restaurants

iPods

CD-ROMs

LCD and plasma TVs

Xbox 360

Avatars

Analog TVs

Sales

Boeing 787

Twitter

	Introduction	Growth	Maturity	Decline
OM Strategy/Issues	Product design and development critical Frequent product and process design changes Short production runs High production costs Limited models Attention to quality	Forecasting critical Product and process reliability Competitive product improvements and options Increase capacity Shift toward product focus Enhance distribution	Standardization Fewer rapid product changes, more minor changes Optimum capacity Increasing stability of process Long production runs Product improvement and cost-cutting	Little product differentiation Cost minimization Overcapacity in the industry Prune line to eliminate items not returning good margin Reduce capacity

▲ **FIGURE 2.4** **Strategy and Issues During a Product's Life**

management. Porter also suggests analysis of competitors via what he calls his **five-forces model**.[2] These potential competing forces are immediate rivals, potential entrants, customers, suppliers, and substitute products.

In addition to the competitive environment, the operations manager needs to understand that the firm is operating in a system with many other external factors. These factors range from political and legal, to cultural. They influence strategy development and execution and require constant scanning of the environment.

The firm itself is also undergoing constant change. Everything from resources and technology, to product life cycles is in flux. Consider the significant changes required within the firm as its products move from introduction, to growth, to maturity, and to decline (see Figure 2.4). These internal changes, combined with external changes, require strategies that are dynamic.

In this chapter's *Company Profile*, Burj Khalifa provided an example of how strategy must change as technology and the environment change. Emaar Properties can now build even bigger structures using a global supply chain. Like many other OM strategies, Emaar's strategy has changed with technology and globalization. Microsoft has also had to adapt quickly to a changing environment. Microsoft Saudi Arabia is the best example of adaptation to the culture of customers in order to reach out to them. The translation of all the services and the products, and the process of offering solutions that are particular to the Arab world, has enabled the company to become closer to the hearts and minds of its Arab customers. In addition, changing customer preferences, faster processors, and the need for increased security issues have all driven changes at Microsoft.

Five-forces model

A method of analyzing the five forces in the competitive environment.

[2]Michael E. Porter, *Competitive Strategy: Techniques for Analyzing Industries and Competitors.* New York: The Free Press, 1980, 1998.

These forces have moved Microsoft's product strategy from operating systems to office products to internet service provider, and now to integrator of computers, cell phones, games, and television.

The more thorough the analysis and understanding of both the external and internal factors, the more likely a firm can find the optimum use of its resources. Once a firm understands itself and the environment, a SWOT analysis, which we discuss next, is in order.

STRATEGY DEVELOPMENT AND IMPLEMENTATION

SWOT analysis

A method of determining internal strengths and weaknesses and external opportunities and threats.

A **SWOT analysis** is a formal review of the internal Strengths and Weaknesses and the external Opportunities and Threats. Beginning with SWOT analyses, organizations position themselves, through their strategy, to have a competitive advantage. A firm may have excellent design skills or great talent at identifying outstanding locations. However, it may recognize the limitations of its manufacturing process or in finding good suppliers. The idea is to maximize opportunities and minimize threats in the environment while maximizing the advantages of the organization's strengths and minimizing the weaknesses. Any preconceived ideas about mission are then reevaluated to ensure that they are consistent with the SWOT analysis. Subsequently, a strategy for achieving the mission is developed. This strategy is continuously evaluated against the value provided to customers and competitive realities. The process is shown in Figure 2.5. From this process, key success factors are identified.

Key Success Factors and Core Competencies

Key success factors (KSFs)

Activities or factors that are key to achieving competitive advantage.

Core competencies

A set of skills, talents, and activities in which a firm is particularly strong.

Because no firm does everything exceptionally well, a successful strategy requires determining the firm's critical success factors and core competencies. **Key success factors (KSFs)** are those activities that are necessary for a firm to achieve its goals. KSFs can be so significant that a firm must get them right to survive in the industry. A KSF for McDonald's, for example, is layout. Without a play area, an effective drive-thru, and an efficient kitchen, McDonald's cannot be successful. KSFs are often necessary but not sufficient for competitive advantage. On the other hand, **core competencies** are the set of unique skills, talents, and capabilities that a firm has at a world-class standard. They allow a firm to set itself apart and develop a competitive advantage. Organizations that prosper identify their core competencies and nurture them. While McDonald's KSFs may include layout, its core competency may be consistency and quality. The idea is to build KSFs and core competencies that provide a competitive advantage and support a successful strategy and mission. A core competence may be a subset of KSFs or a combination of KSFs. The operations manager begins this inquiry by asking the following.

LO4: Understand the significance of key success factors and core competencies

- "What tasks must be done particularly well for a given strategy to succeed?"
- "Which activities will help the OM function provide a competitive advantage?"
- "Which elements contain the highest likelihood of failure, and which require additional commitment of managerial, monetary, technological, and human resources?"

Only by identifying and strengthening KSFs and core competencies can an organization achieve sustainable competitive advantage.

▶ **FIGURE 2.5**
Strategy Development Process

Analyze the Environment
Identify the strengths, weaknesses, opportunities, and threats.
Understand the environment, customers, industry, and competitors.

Determine the Corporate Mission
State the reason for the firm's existence and identify the value it wishes to create.

Form a Strategy
Build a competitive advantage, such as low price, design or volume flexibility, quality, quick delivery, dependability, after-sale services, or broad product lines.

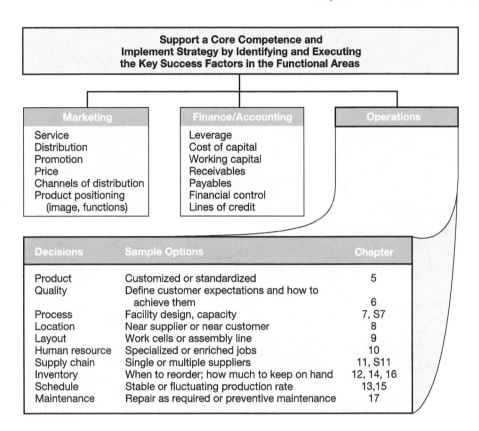

◀ **FIGURE 2.6**
**Implement Strategy by
Identifying and Executing Key
Success Factors that Support
Core Competencies**

In this text we focus on the ten OM decisions that typically include the KSFs. Potential KSFs for marketing, finance, and operations are shown in Figure 2.6. The ten OM decisions we develop in this text provide an excellent initial checklist for determining KSFs and identifying core competencies within the operations function.

Whatever the KSFs and core competencies, they must be supported by the related activities. One approach to identifying the activities is an **activity map**, which links competitive advantage, KSFs, and supporting activities. For example, Figure 2.7 shows how the U.S. company Southwest Airlines, whose core competence is operations, built a set of integrated activities to support its low-cost competitive advantage. Notice how the KSFs support operations and in turn are supported by other activities. The activities fit together and reinforce each other. The better they fit and reinforce each other, the more sustainable the competitive advantage. By focusing on enhancing its core competence and KSFs with a supporting set of activities, Southwest Airlines has become one of the great airline success stories.

Activity map
A graphical link of competitive advantage, KSFs, and supporting activities.

Build and Staff the Organization

The operations manager's job is a three-step process. Once a strategy and KSFs have been identified, the second step is to group the necessary activities into an organizational structure. The third step is to staff it with personnel who will get the job done. The manager works with subordinate managers to build plans, budgets, and programs that will successfully implement strategies that achieve missions. Firms tackle this organization of the operations function in a variety of ways. The organization charts shown in Chapter 1 (Figure 1.1) indicate the way that some firms have organized to perform the required activities.

Integrate OM with Other Activities

The organization of the operations function and its relationship to other parts of the organization vary with the OM mission. Moreover, the operations function is most likely to be successful when the operations strategy is integrated with other functional areas of the firm, such as marketing, finance, information technology, and human resources. In this way, all of the areas support the company's objectives. For example, short-term scheduling in the airline industry is dominated by volatile customer travel patterns. Day-of-week preference, holidays, seasonality, college schedules,

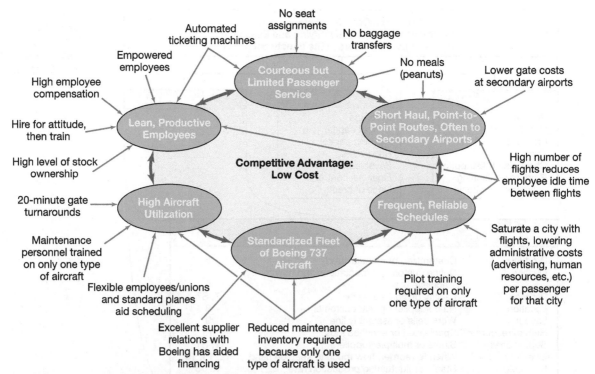

▲ **FIGURE 2.7** **Activity Mapping of Southwest Airlines's Low-Cost Competitive Advantage**
To achieve a low-cost competitive advantage, Southwest Airlines has identified a number of key success factors (connected by red arrows) and support activities (shown by blue arrows). As this figure indicates, a low-cost advantage is highly dependent on a very well-run operations function.

and so on, all play a role in changing flight schedules. Consequently, airline scheduling, although an OM activity, can be a part of marketing. Effective scheduling in the trucking industry is reflected in the amount of time that trucks travel loaded. However, scheduling of trucks requires information from delivery and pickup points, drivers, and other parts of the organization. When the OM function results in effective scheduling in the air passenger and commercial trucking industries, a competitive advantage can exist.

The operations manager transforms inputs into outputs. The transformations may be in terms of storage, transportation, manufacturing, dissemination of information, and utility of the product or service. *The operations manager's job is to implement an OM strategy, provide competitive advantage, and increase productivity.*

AUTHOR COMMENT
Firms that ignore the global economy will not survive.

GLOBAL OPERATIONS STRATEGY OPTIONS

As we suggested early in this chapter, many operations strategies now require an international dimension. We tend to call a firm with an international dimension an international business or a multinational corporation. An **international business** is any firm that engages in international trade or investment. This is a very broad category and is the opposite of a domestic, or local, firm.

A **multinational corporation (MNC)** is a firm with *extensive* international business involvement. MNCs buy resources, create goods or services, and sell goods or services in a variety of countries. The term *multinational corporation* applies to most of the world's large, well-known businesses. Petra Engineering Industries is a good example of an MNC. It imports heating, ventilation, and air conditioning (HVAC) components to Jordan from over 10 countries, exports HVAC equipment to over 50 countries, has facilities in 20 countries, and earns considerable sales and profits abroad.

Operations managers of international and multinational firms approach global opportunities with one of four operations strategies: *international, multidomestic, global,* or *transnational* (see Figure 2.8). The matrix of Figure 2.8 has a vertical axis of cost reduction and a horizontal axis of local responsiveness. Local responsiveness implies quick response and/or the differentiation necessary for the local market. The operations manager must know how to position the firm in this matrix. Let us briefly examine each of the four strategies.

International business
A firm that engages in cross-border transactions.

Multinational corporation (MNC)
A firm that has extensive involvement in international business, owning or controlling facilities in more than one country.

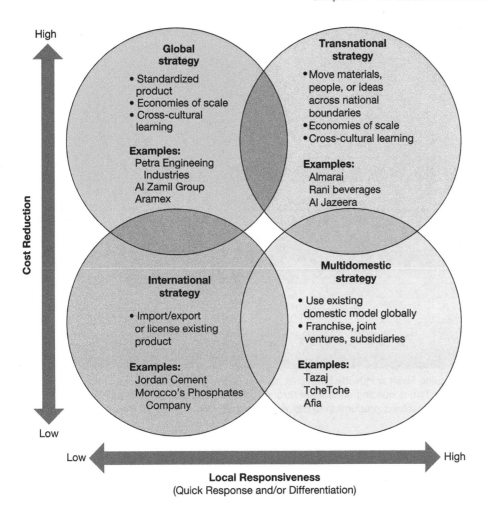

◀ **FIGURE 2.8**
Four International Operations Strategies

Source: Adapted from M. Hitt, R. D. Ireland, and R. E. Hoskisson, *Strategic Management, Competitiveness and Globalization*, 7th ed. Cincinnati: Southwestern College Publishing, 2009.

LO5: Identify and explain four global operations strategy options

International Strategy

An **international strategy** uses exports and licenses to penetrate the global arena. As Figure 2.8 suggests, the international strategy is the least advantageous, with little local responsiveness and little cost advantage. There is little responsiveness because we are exporting or licensing goods from the home country, and the cost advantages may be few because we are using the existing production process at some distance from the new market. However, an international strategy is often the easiest, as exports can require little change in existing operations, and licensing agreements often leave much of the risk to the licensee.

International strategy
A strategy in which global markets are penetrated using exports and licenses.

Multidomestic Strategy

The **multidomestic strategy** has decentralized authority with substantial autonomy at each business. Organizationally these are typically subsidiaries, franchises, or joint ventures with substantial independence. The advantage of this strategy is maximizing a competitive response for the local market; however, the strategy has little or no cost advantage. Many food producers, such as Tazaj in Saudi Arabia, use a multidomestic strategy to accommodate local tastes because global integration of the production process is not critical.

Multidomestic strategy
A strategy in which operating decisions are decentralized to each country to enhance local responsiveness.

Global Strategy

A **global strategy** has a high degree of centralization, with headquarters coordinating the organization to seek out standardization and learning between plants, thus generating economies of scale. This strategy is appropriate when the strategic focus is cost reduction, but has little to recommend it when the demand for local responsiveness is high. Al Zamil Group pursues global strategies which enable it to benefit from economies of scale and learning within each facility it has in the world.

Global strategy
A strategy in which operating decisions are centralized and headquarters coordinates the standardization and learning between facilities.

In a continuing fierce worldwide battle, Komatsu is seeking global advantage in the heavy equipment market. The firm is building equipment throughout the world as cost and logistics dictate. Their global strategy allows production to move as markets, risk, and exchange rates dictate.

Transnational Strategy

Transnational strategy

A strategy that combines the benefits of global-scale efficiencies with the benefits of local responsiveness.

A **transnational strategy** exploits economies of scale and learning, as well as pressure for responsiveness, by recognizing that core competence does not reside in just the 'home' country but can exist anywhere in the organization. *Transnational* describes a condition in which material, people, and ideas cross—or *transgress*—national boundaries. These firms have the potential to pursue all three operations strategies (i.e. differentiation, low cost, and response). Such firms can be thought of as 'world companies' whose country identity is not as important as its interdependent network of worldwide operations. Key activities in a transnational company are neither centralized in the parent company nor decentralized, so that each subsidiary can carry out its own tasks on a local basis. Instead, the resources and activities are dispersed but specialized, so as to be both efficient and flexible in an interdependent network. The Al Jazeera news network is a good example of transnational strategy because although it is mainly owned by Qatari shareholders and registered as a Qatari company, 99 percent of its news and programs are international and its employees are mainly non-Qatari citizens.

CHAPTER SUMMARY

Global operations provide an increase in both the challenges and opportunities for operations managers. Although the task is challenging, operations managers can and do improve productivity. They can build and manage OM functions that contribute in a significant way to competitiveness. Organizations identify their strengths and weaknesses. They then develop effective missions and strategies that account for these strengths and weaknesses and complement the opportunities and threats in the environment. If this procedure is performed well, the organization can have competitive advantage through some combination of product differentiation, low cost, and response. This competitive advantage is often achieved via a move to international, multidomestic, global, or transnational strategies.

Effective use of resources, whether domestic or international, is the responsibility of the professional manager, and professional managers are among the few in our society who *can* achieve this performance. The challenge is great, and the rewards to the manager and to society are substantial.

Key Terms

Activity map (p. 39)
Competitive advantage (p. 31)
Core competencies (p. 38)
Differentiation (p. 32)
European Union (EU) (p. 28)
Experience differentiation (p. 32)
Five-forces model (p. 37)
Free Trade Zones (p. 28)
Global strategy (p. 41)
Gulf Cooperation Council (GCC) (p. 28)

International business (p. 40)
International strategy (p. 41)
Key success factors (KSFs) (p. 38)
Low-cost leadership (p. 32)
Mission (p. 30)
Multidomestic strategy (p. 41)
Multinational corporation (MNC) (p. 40)
North American Free Trade Agreement
    (NAFTA) (p. 28)

Operations decisions (p. 34)
Qualifying Industrial Zones (QIZs) (p. 28)
Resources view (p. 35)
Response (p. 32)
Strategy (p. 30)
SWOT analysis (p. 38)
Transnational strategy (p. 42)
Value-chain analysis (p. 35)
World Trade Organization (WTO) (p. 28)

Ethical Dilemma

As a manufacturer of athletic shoes whose image, indeed performance, is widely regarded as socially responsible, you find your costs increasing. Traditionally, your athletic shoes have been made in Egypt and Algeria. Although the ease of doing business in those countries has been improving, wage rates have also been increasing. The labor–cost differential between your present suppliers and a contractor who will get the shoes made in China now exceeds US$1 per pair. Your sales next year are projected to be 10 million pairs, and your analysis suggests that this cost differential is not offset by any other tangible costs; you face only the political risk and potential damage to your commitment to social responsibility. Thus, this US$1 per pair saving should flow directly to your bottom line. There is no doubt that the Chinese government engages in censorship, remains repressive, and is a long way from a democracy. Moreover, you will have little or no control over working conditions, sexual harassment, and pollution. What do you do, and on what basis do you make your decision?

Discussion Questions

1. List six reasons to internationalize operations.
2. Define *mission*.
3. Define *strategy*.
4. Describe how an organization's *mission* and *strategy* have different purposes.
5. Identify the mission and strategy of an automobile repair garage. What are the manifestations of the ten OM decisions at the garage? That is, how is each of the ten decisions accomplished?
6. How does an OM strategy change during a product's life cycle?
7. There are three primary ways to achieve competitive advantage. Provide an example, not included in the text, of each. Support your choices.
8. How must an operations strategy integrate with marketing and accounting?

Solved Problem   Virtual Office Hours help is available at MyOMLab.

▼ SOLVED PROBLEM 2.1

The global tire industry continues to consolidate. Michelin buys Goodrich and Uniroyal and builds plants throughout the world. Bridgestone buys Firestone, expands its research budget, and focuses on world markets. Goodyear spends almost 4 percent of its sales revenue on research. These three aggressive firms have come to dominate the world tire market, with total market share approaching 60 percent. The German tire maker Continental AG has strengthened its position as fourth in the world, with a dominant presence in

Germany. Against this formidable array, the old-line Italian tire company Pirelli SpA found it difficult to respond effectively. Although Pirelli still had 5 percent of the market, it was losing millions a year while the competition was getting stronger. Tires are a tough, competitive business that rewards companies having strong market shares and long production runs. Pirelli has some strengths: an outstanding reputation for excellent high-performance tires and an innovative manufacturing function.

Use a SWOT analysis to establish a feasible strategy for Pirelli.

▼ SOLUTION

First, find an opportunity in the world tire market that avoids the threat of mass-market onslaught by the big three tire makers. Second, utilize the internal marketing strength represented by Pirelli's strong brand name and history of winning World Rally Championships. Third, maximize the internal innovative capabilities of the operations function.

To achieve these goals, Pirelli made a strategic shift out of low-margin standard tires and into higher-margin performance tires. Pirelli established deals with luxury brands Jaguar, BMW, Maserati, Ferrari, Bentley, and Lotus Elise and established itself as a provider of a large share of tires on new Porsches, S-class Mercedes, and Saabs. As a result, more than 70 percent of the company's tire production is now high-performance tires. People are willing to pay a premium for Pirellis.

The operations function continued to focus its design efforts on performance tires and developing a system of modular tire manufacture that allows much faster switching between models. This modular system, combined with investments in new manufacturing flexibility, has driven batch sizes down to as small as 150 to 200, making small-lot performance tires economically feasible. Manufacturing innovations at Pirelli have streamlined the production process, moving it from a 14-step process to a three-step process. A threat from the big three going after the performance market remains, but Pirelli has bypassed its weakness of having a small market share. The firm now has 24 plants in 12 countries and a presence in more than 160 countries, with sales exceeding US$4.5 billion.

Sources: Just Auto (February 2009): 14–15 and (December 2008): 14–15; *Hoover's Company Records* (October 15, 2005): 41369; and **www.pirelli.com/web/investors**.

Problems

• **2.1** The text provides three primary ways—strategic approaches (differentiation, cost, and response)—for achieving competitive advantage. Provide an example of each not given in the text. Support your choices. (*Hint:* Note the examples provided in the text.)

•• **2.2** Within the food service industry (restaurants that serve meals to customers, but not just fast food), find examples of firms that have sustained competitive advantage by competing on the basis of: (1) cost leadership; (2) response; (3) differentiation. Cite one example in each category; provide a sentence or two in support of each choice. Do not use fast-food chains for all categories. (*Hint:* A 'US$1 menu' is very easily copied and is not a good source of sustained advantage.)

•• **2.3** Identify how changes within an organization affect the OM strategy for a company. For instance, discuss what impact the following internal factors might have on OM strategy:

a) Maturing of a product.
b) Technology innovation in the manufacturing process.
c) Changes in laptop computer design that builds in wireless technology.

•• **2.4** Identify how changes in the external environment affect the OM strategy for a company. For instance, discuss what impact the following external factors might have on OM strategy:

a) Major increases in oil prices.
b) Water- and air-quality legislation.
c) Fewer young prospective employees entering the labor market.
d) Inflation versus stable prices.
e) Legislation moving health insurance from a pretax benefit to taxable income.

Case Studies

▶ ALDI

The grocery discounter ALDI was founded in 1913 as Albrecht Discount in Essen, Germany. Currently, ALDI operates stores in 18 countries in Europe, Australia, and the U.S.A. ALDI's strategy revolves around providing good-quality groceries for low prices. Quality is important to ALDI, which guarantees products sold with a no-questions-asked money-back guarantee.

ALDI achieves its low-cost strategy by using a variety of methods. First, it buys large quantities of items from vetted suppliers capable of delivering good-quality products, taking advantage of quantity discounts and economies of scale. ALDI stores are typically small, around 15,000 square feet, and are standardized with respect to appearance and layout while allowing for small differences between countries where they operate. A typical store sells around 700 products, compared with approximately 25,000 items stocked at a traditional supermarket. Usually there are only one or two brands of a certain item, and 95 percent of the items are store brands.

ALDI chooses inexpensive locations, usually outside town or on side streets, to minimize overheads. ALDI products are displayed on pallets rather than on shelving. Employees are cross-trained to be able to operate the checkout as well as restock items by replacing pallets. This results in flexibility, as more cash registers are opened when there are many customers, while when few customers are in the store, the employees replace empty pallets with full ones. Customers must pay for bags (or bring their own) and bring carts back to a standard location to recoup a coin deposit. ALDI stores typically operate with a 13 percent margin for overheads and labor, in contrast to other grocers, whose margin is around 30 percent.

Discussion Questions

1. How does ALDI's strategy lead to a competitive advantage? How does the company achieve this strategy?
2. Does ALDI's low-cost strategy imply that the company offers low quality? Why is quality important, regardless of competitive strategy?

Source: N. Kumar, "Strategies to Fight Low Cost Rivals." *Harvard Business Review* (December 2006): 104–112; ALDI website, **www.aldi.com**.
Case prepared by Dr. Ian M. Langella, Shippensburg University, United States.

▶ Strategy at Regal Marine

Regal Marine, one of the United States' ten largest power-boat manufacturers, achieves its mission—providing luxury performance boats to customers worldwide—by using the strategy of differentiation. It differentiates its products through constant innovation, unique features, and high quality. Increasing sales at the Orlando, Florida, family-owned firm suggest that the strategy is working.

As a quality boat manufacturer, Regal Marine starts with continuous innovation, as reflected in computer-aided design (CAD), high-quality molds, and close tolerances that are controlled through both defect charts and rigorous visual inspection. In-house quality is not enough, however. Because a product is only as good as the parts put into it, Regal has established close ties with a large number of its suppliers to ensure both flexibility and perfect parts. With the help of these suppliers, Regal can profitably produce a product line of 22 boats, ranging from a US$14,000 19-foot boat to the US$500,000 44-foot Commodore yacht.

"We build boats," says vice-president Tim Kuck, "but we're really in the 'fun' business. Our competition includes not only 300 other boat, canoe, and yacht manufacturers in our US$17 billion industry, but home theaters, the internet, and all kinds of alternative family entertainment." Fortunately Regal has been paying off debt and increasing market share.

Regal has also joined with scores of other independent boat makers in the American Boat Builders Association. Through economies of scale in procurement, Regal is able to navigate against billion-dollar competitor Brunswick (makers of the Sea Ray and Bayliner brands).

Discussion Questions*

1. State Regal Marine's mission in your own words.
2. Identify the strengths, weaknesses, opportunities, and threats that are relevant to the strategy of Regal Marine.
3. How would you define Regal's strategy?
4. How would each of the ten OM decisions apply to operations decision making at Regal Marine?

*You may wish to view the video that accompanies this case before addressing these questions.

▶ Hard Rock Cafe's Global Strategy

Hard Rock brings the concept of the 'experience economy' to its café operation. The strategy incorporates a unique 'experience' into its operations. This innovation is somewhat akin to mass customization in manufacturing. At Hard Rock, the experience concept is to provide not only a custom meal from the menu but also a dining event that includes a unique visual and sound experience not duplicated anywhere else in the world. This strategy is succeeding. Other themed restaurants have come and gone while Hard Rock continues to grow. As Professor C. Markides of the London Business School says, "The trick is not to play the game better than the competition, but to develop and play an altogether different game."[3] At Hard Rock, the different game is the experience game.

From the opening of its first café in London in 1971, during the British rock music explosion, Hard Rock has been serving food and rock music with equal enthusiasm. Hard Rock Cafe has 40 U.S. locations, about 12 in Europe, and the remainder scattered throughout the world, from Bangkok and Beijing to Beirut. New construction, leases, and investment in remodeling are long term, so a global strategy means special consideration of political risk, currency risk, and social norms in a context of a brand fit. Although Hard Rock is one of the most recognized brands in the world, this does not mean that its café is a natural fit everywhere. Special consideration must be given to the supply chain for the restaurant and its accompanying retail store. About 48 percent of a typical café's sales are from merchandise.

The Hard Rock Cafe business model is well defined, but because of various risk factors and differences in business practices and employment law, Hard Rock elects to franchise about half of its cafés. Social norms and preferences often suggest some tweaking of menus for local taste. For instance, Hard Rock focuses less on hamburgers and beef and more on fish and lobster in its British cafés.

Because 70 percent of Hard Rock's guests are tourists, recent years have found it expanding to 'destination' cities. While this has been a winning strategy for decades, allowing the firm to grow from one London café to 157 facilities in 57 countries, it has made Hard Rock susceptible to economic fluctuations that hit the tourist business hardest. So Hard Rock is signing a long-term lease for a new location in Nottingham, England, to join recently opened cafés in Manchester and Birmingham—cities that are not standard tourist destinations. At the same time, menus are being upgraded. Hopefully, repeat business from locals in these cities will smooth demand and make Hard Rock less dependent on tourists.

Discussion Questions[4]

1. Identify the strategy changes that have taken place at Hard Rock Cafe since its founding in 1971.
2. As Hard Rock Cafe has changed its strategy, how has its responses to some of the ten decisions of OM changed?
3. Where does Hard Rock fit in the four international operations strategies outlined in Figure 2.8? Explain your answer.

[3]Constantinos Markides, "Strategic Innovation." *MIT Sloan Management Review* 38, no. 3 (spring 1997): 9.

[4]You may wish to view the video that accompanies this case before addressing these questions.

▶ **Additional Case Study:** Visit MyOMLab for this free case study:
Motorola's Global Strategy: Focuses on Motorola's international strategy.

Main Heading	Review Material	
A GLOBAL VIEW OF OPERATIONS (pp. 28–30)	Domestic business operations decide to change to some form of international operations for six main reasons. 1. Reduce costs (labor, taxes, tariffs, etc.) 2. Improve supply chain. 3. Provide better goods and services. 4. Understand markets. 5. Learn to improve operations. 6. Attract and retain global talent. ■ **World Trade Organization (WTO)**—An international organization that promotes world trade by lowering barriers to the free flow of goods across borders. ■ **NAFTA**—A free trade agreement between Canada, Mexico, and the U.S.A. ■ **European Union (EU)**—A European trade group that has 27 member states. ■ **Gulf Cooperation Council (GCC)**—A political and economic union between the six Gulf nations. The WTO helps to make uniform the protection of both governments and industries from foreign firms that engage in unethical conduct.	
DEVELOPING MISSIONS AND STRATEGIES (pp. 30–31)	An effective operations management effort must have a *mission* so it knows where it is going, and a *strategy* so it knows how to get there. ■ **Mission**—The purpose or rationale for an organization's existence. ■ **Strategy**—How an organization expects to achieve its missions and goals. The three strategic approaches to competitive advantage are: 1. differentiation 2. cost leadership 3. response.	**VIDEO 2.1** Strategy at Regal Marine
ACHIEVING COMPETITIVE ADVANTAGE THROUGH OPERATIONS (pp. 31–33)	■ **Competitive advantage**—The creation of a unique advantage over competitors. ■ **Differentiation**—Distinguishing the offerings of an organization in a way that the customer perceives as adding value. ■ **Experience differentiation**—Engaging the customer with a product through imaginative use of the five senses, so the customer 'experiences' the product. ■ **Low-cost leadership**—Achieving maximum value, as perceived by the customer. ■ **Response**—A set of values related to rapid, flexible, and reliable performance. Differentiation can be attained, for example, through innovative design, by a broad product line, by offering excellent after-sales service, or through adding a sensory experience to the product or service offering. Cost leadership can be attained, for example, via low overheads, effective capacity use, or efficient inventory management. Response can be attained, for example, by offering a flexible product line, scheduling, or speedy delivery.	**VIDEO 2.2** Hard Rock Cafe's Global Strategy
TEN STRATEGIC OM DECISIONS (pp. 34–35)	■ **Operations decisions**—The strategic decisions of OM are goods and service design, quality, process and capacity design, location selection, layout design, human resources and job design, supply-chain management, inventory, scheduling, and maintenance.	
ISSUES IN OPERATIONS STRATEGY (pp. 35–38)	■ **Resources view**—A view in which managers evaluate the resources at their disposal and manage or alter them to achieve competitive advantage. ■ **Value-chain analysis**—A way to identify the elements in the product/service chain that uniquely add value. ■ **Five-forces model**—A way to analyze the five forces in the competitive environment. The potential competing forces in Porter's five-forces model are: (1) immediate rivals; (2) potential entrants; (3) customers; (4) suppliers; (5) substitute products. Different issues are emphasized during different stages of the product life cycle. • **Introduction**—Company strategy: Best period to increase market share, R&D engineering is critical. OM strategy: Product design and development critical, frequent product and process design changes, short production runs, high production costs, limited models, attention to quality. • **Growth**—Company strategy: Practical to change price or quality image, strengthen niche. OM strategy: Forecasting critical, product and process reliability, competitive product improvements and options, increase capacity, shift toward product focus, enhance distribution.	

Main Heading	Review Material	
	• **Maturity**—Company strategy: Poor time to change image or price or quality, competitive costs become critical, defend market position. OM strategy: Standardization, less rapid product changes (more minor changes), optimum capacity, increasing stability of process, long production runs, product improvement and cost-cutting. • **Decline**—Company strategy: Cost control critical. OM strategy: Little product differentiation, cost minimization, overcapacity in the industry, prune line to eliminate items not returning good margin, reduce capacity.	
STRATEGY DEVELOPMENT AND IMPLEMENTATION (pp. 38–40)	**SWOT analysis**—A method of determining internal strengths and weaknesses and external opportunities and threats. The strategy development process first involves performing environmental analysis, followed by determining the corporate mission, and finally forming a strategy. ■ **Key success factors (KSFs)**—Activities or factors that are key to achieving competitive advantage. ■ **Core competencies**—A set of skills, talents, and activities that a firm does particularly well. A core competence may be a subset or a combination, of KSFs. ■ **Activity map**—A graphical link of competitive advantage, KSFs, and supporting activities. An operations manager's job is to implement an OM strategy, provide competitive advantage, and increase productivity.	Virtual Office Hours for Solved Problem: 2.1
GLOBAL OPERATIONS STRATEGY OPTIONS (pp. 40–42)	■ **International business**—A firm that engages in cross-border transactions. ■ **Multinational corporation (MNC)**—A firm that has extensive involvement in international business, owning or controlling facilities in more than one country. ■ **International strategy**—A strategy in which global markets are penetrated using exports and licenses. ■ **Multidomestic strategy**—A strategy in which operating decisions are decentralized to each country to enhance local responsiveness. ■ **Global strategy**—A strategy in which operating decisions are centralized and headquarters coordinates the standardization and learning between facilities. ■ **Transnational strategy**—A strategy that combines the benefits of global-scale efficiencies with the benefits of local responsiveness. These firms transgress national boundaries. The four operations strategies for approaching global opportunities can be classified according to local responsiveness and cost reduction. 1. **International**—Little local responsiveness and little cost advantage 2. **Multidomestic**—Significant local responsiveness but little cost advantage 3. **Global**—Little local responsiveness but significant cost advantage 4. **Transnational**—Significant local responsiveness and significant cost advantage.	

Self-Test

■ **Before taking the self-test,** refer to the learning objectives listed at the beginning of the chapter and the key terms listed at the end of the chapter.

LO1. A mission statement is beneficial to an organization because it:
a) is a statement of the organization's purpose
b) provides a basis for the organization's culture
c) identifies important constituencies
d) details specific income goals
e) ensures profitability.

LO2. The three strategic approaches to competitive advantage are _____, _____, and _____.

LO3. The ten decisions of OM:
a) are functional areas of the firm
b) apply to both service and manufacturing organizations
c) are the goals that are to be achieved
d) form an action plan to achieve a mission
e) are key success factors.

LO4. The relatively few activities that make a difference between a firm having and not having a competitive advantage are known as:
a) activity maps
b) SWOT
c) key success factors
d) global profile
e) response strategy.

LO5. A company that is organized across international boundaries, with decentralized authority and substantial autonomy at each business via subsidiaries, franchises, or joint ventures, has:
a) a global strategy
b) a transnational strategy
c) an international strategy
d) a multidomestic strategy
e) a regional strategy.

Answers: LO1. a; LO2. differentiation, cost leadership, response; LO3. b; LO4. c; LO5. c.

3 Managing Projects

PROJECT MANAGEMENT: KEY TO SUCCESS FOR ARABTEC

Dubai-based Arabtec Construction LLC (**www.arabtecuae.com**) is one of the Middle East's largest contractors of construction and engineering projects.

The Arabtec beacon project is the Dubai Airport in partnership with Bechtel Inc.

Arabtec expanded its operation into the oil industry, which is still considered vital to the world with potential for growth.

Arabtec was established in 1975 amidst the construction hype that was sweeping the Middle East. The company started with small-sized projects that gained it market credibility and, in 1978, it was able to deliver three projects at three different locations in Abu Dhabi, Dubai, and Muscat. This greatly impressed potential clients and contracts began to flow in abundance. Soon after, Arabtec started to diversify its portfolio to include engineering projects to cover the market's needs. It became involved in the design and construction of oil facilities, residential compounds, hotels, commercial developments, and drainage works. But its great breakthrough came with an introduction to the international arena through partnership with Bechtel Corporation in the expansion of Dubai Airport. The high-quality work and excellent project management gained Arabtec an international reputation, and led to further expansion to new areas of work.

Arabtec's projects have included:

- *Burj Khalifa*. The tallest building in the world, with 160 floors, located in the heart of Dubai's downtown area, which aims to be the world's most prestigious square kilometer (US$1.5 billion).

- *Jumeirah Beach Residences 01 and 03*. A huge residential project that is part of the landmark Dubai Marine area. There are 13 towers providing 2,693 apartments, a shopping mall to house 350 retail outlets and 45 restaurants, and all the luxurious facilities that science can provide (US$500 million).

- *The Address*. Signature serviced apartments in downtown Dubai that won the 2008 World Hotel Award. It contains 64 floors, with 198 guest rooms, 628 serviced apartments, numerous restaurants, a banquet hall, a spa, a swimming pool, and gym (US$230 million).

- *Mubarraz Island*. This structural work in Abu Dhabi included gas installations and oil facilities, such as laboratories, control rooms, gas process plants, and pipelines. The project also included building offices, residences, mosques, roads, and supporting services for the island (US$200 million).

Arabtec is constructing the forthcoming Beverly Hills of Dubai—Emirates Hills—which will provide a unique community-living experience for the elite niche of Dubai residents, most specifically the expatriate community in Dubai.

- *Ocean Heights.* An architectural freehold residential masterpiece based in Dubai, with a twisting structure, making each floor unique in its design and plan. It will include 83 floors with 564 apartments, serviced by state-of-the-art amenities (US$175 million).

- *The Hanging Gardens.* This is a residential project in Egypt that reproduces Babylon's Hanging Gardens and is being developed by the Amer Group. The project will consist of 2.2 million square meters of cliff-face residences with a horizon view of the Red Sea, with access to the Telefric transportation and International Spa complex in Sokhna, Egypt (US$51.5 million).

- *Princess Nora Bint Abdulrahman University, Saudi Arabia.* In this educational project, Arabtec will construct housing for the married junior staff, comprising 46 buildings with a total area of 240,000 square meters (US$350 million).

- *Emirates Hills, Dubai.* This is an elite set of projects that aims at creating community-living with a unique style. The most notable project is the Villas, which is an exclusive freehold project from Emaar (a leading property developer in the Middle East), targeted at a specific luxurious niche in the market—ultra-luxury villas. The project prides itself on catering to the exact specifications of the owners, which means that every property will be different, giving a superior magnificence hard to find anywhere else with the aim of becoming the Beverly Hills of Dubai. Residents will also benefit from the other Emirates Living projects, the Lakes and the Meadows, which contain lifestyle facilities such as shops, schools, and cafés, and are centrally located near Dubai Marina and Dubai Media City.

The Infinity Tower constructed by Arabtec is the world's tallest tower to feature a 90-degree twist.

When companies or countries seek out firms to manage massive projects, they turn to companies like Arabtec, which, through excellent project management, has demonstrated its competitive advantage.

Source: **www.arabtecuae.com**

Chapter 3 Learning Objectives

THE IMPORTANCE OF PROJECT MANAGEMENT

When Arabtec Construction LLC, the subject of the Company Profile, won the contract for Burj Khalifa, it quickly had to mobilize an international force of manual workers, construction professionals, cooks, and even medical personnel. Its project management team had to access millions of tons of supplies and equipment to complete the project. When a supply of pipes can't reach the construction site on time due to an unexpected delay, Arabtec's project manager needs to be ready with a backup plan to ensure the availability of the supplies and the continuation of work.

This is the reality of growing project complexity and collapsing product/service life cycles. The strategic value of time-based competition is high, and continuous improvement is mandatory. Each new product/service introduction is seen as a unique event—a project. Projects are a common part of our everyday life. We may be planning a wedding or a surprise birthday party, remodeling a house, or preparing a semester-long class project. However, scheduling projects is a difficult challenge for operations managers and the stakes in project management are high. Cost overruns and unnecessary delays occur due to poor scheduling and poor controls.

Projects that take months or years to complete are usually developed outside the normal production system. Project organizations within the firm may be set up to handle such jobs and are often disbanded when the project is complete. On other occasions, managers find projects just a part of their job. The management of projects involves three phases (see Figure 3.1).

1. *Planning:* This phase includes goal setting, defining the project, and team organization.
2. *Scheduling:* This phase relates people, money, and supplies to specific activities, and relates activities to each other.
3. *Controlling:* Here the firm monitors resources, costs, quality, and budgets. It also revises or changes plans and shifts resources to meet time and cost demands.

We begin this chapter with a brief overview of these functions. Three popular techniques to allow managers to plan, schedule, and control—Gantt charts, Program Evaluation and Review Technique (PERT), and Critical Path Method (CPM)—are also described. The software package Microsoft® Project is discussed later in the chapter.

PROJECT PLANNING

Project organization
An organization formed to ensure that programs (projects) receive the proper management and attention.

Projects can be defined as a series of related tasks directed toward a major output. In some firms a **project organization** is developed to make sure that existing programs continue to run smoothly on a day-to-day basis while new projects are successfully completed.

For companies with multiple large projects, such as a construction firm, project organization is an effective way of assigning the people and physical resources needed. It is a temporary organization structure designed to achieve results by using specialists from throughout the firm.

The project organization works best when:

1. Work can be defined with a specific goal and deadline.
2. The job is unique or somewhat unfamiliar to the existing organization.
3. The work contains complex interrelated tasks requiring specialized skills.
4. The project is temporary but critical to the organization.
5. The project cuts across organizational lines.

The Project Manager

An example of a project organization is shown in Figure 3.2. Project team members are temporarily assigned to a project and report to the project manager. The manager heading the project

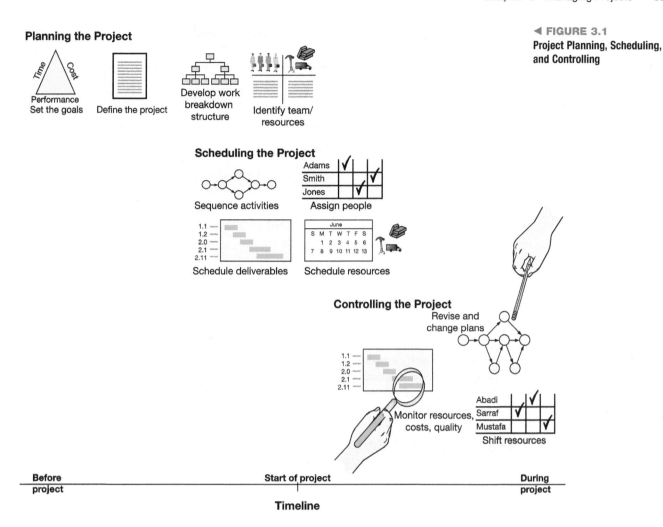

◀ FIGURE 3.1
Project Planning, Scheduling, and Controlling

Planning the Project

Time / Cost

Performance
Set the goals

Define the project

Develop work breakdown structure

Identify team/ resources

Scheduling the Project

Sequence activities

Assign people
Adams ✓
Smith ✓
Jones ✓

Schedule deliverables
1.1
1.2
2.0
2.1
2.11

Schedule resources
June
S M T W T F S
1 2 3 4 5 6
7 8 9 10 11 12 13

Controlling the Project

Revise and change plans

Monitor resources, costs, quality
1.1
1.2
2.0
2.1
2.11

Shift resources
Abadi ✓ ✓
Sarraf ✓
Mustafa ✓

Before project — Start of project — During project

Timeline

coordinates activities with other departments and reports directly to top management. Project managers receive high visibility in a firm and are responsible for making sure that: (1) all necessary activities are finished in proper sequence and on time; (2) the project comes in within budget; (3) the project meets its quality goals; (4) the people assigned to the project receive the motivation, direction, and information needed to do their jobs. This means that project managers should be good coaches and communicators, and be able to organize activities from a variety of disciplines.

Ethical Issues Faced in Project Management Project managers not only have high visibility but they also face ethical decisions on a daily basis. The way they act and respond to different situations establishes the code of conduct for the project. Project managers often deal with: (1) offers of gifts from contractors; (2) pressure to alter status reports to mask the reality of

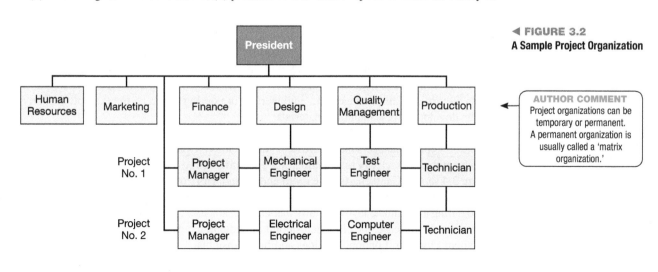

◀ FIGURE 3.2
A Sample Project Organization

President

Human Resources | Marketing | Finance | Design | Quality Management | Production

Project No. 1: Project Manager | Mechanical Engineer | Test Engineer | Technician

Project No. 2: Project Manager | Electrical Engineer | Computer Engineer | Technician

AUTHOR COMMENT
Project organizations can be temporary or permanent. A permanent organization is usually called a 'matrix organization.'

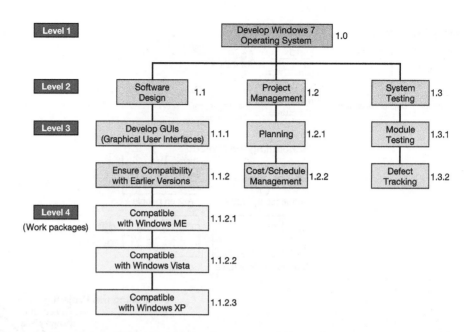

▶ **FIGURE 3.3**
Work Breakdown Structure

delays; (3) false reports for charges of time and expenses; (4) pressure to compromise quality to meet bonus or penalty schedules.

There are many institutes that provide guidelines and ethical codes to try to establish standards for project managers to follow. The Project Management Institute provides such codes (**www.pmi.org**).

Work Breakdown Structure

Work breakdown structure (WBS)

A hierarchical description of a project into more and more detailed components.

The project management team begins by carefully establishing the project's objectives, then breaking the project down into manageable parts. This **work breakdown structure (WBS)** defines the project by dividing it into its major subcomponents (or tasks), which are then subdivided into more detailed components, and finally into a set of activities and their related costs. Gross requirements for people, supplies, and equipment are also estimated in this planning phase.

The WBS typically decreases in size from top to bottom and is indented like this:

Level

1. Project
2.   Major tasks in the project
3.   Subtasks in major tasks
4.   Activities (or 'work packages') to be completed

This hierarchical framework can be illustrated with the development of Microsoft's operating system Windows 7, as we see in Figure 3.3.

AUTHOR COMMENT
Gantt charts are simple and visual, making them widely used.

PROJECT SCHEDULING

Project scheduling involves sequencing and allotting time to all project activities. At this stage, managers decide how long each activity will take and compute how many people and materials will be needed at each stage of production. Managers also chart separate schedules for personnel needs by type of skill (management, engineering, or pouring concrete, for example). Charts also can be developed for scheduling materials.

Gantt charts

Planning charts used to schedule resources and allocate time.

One popular project scheduling approach is the **Gantt chart**. Gantt charts are a low-cost means of helping managers make sure that: (1) activities are planned; (2) the order of performance is documented; (3) activity time estimates are recorded; (4) overall project time is developed. As Figure 3.4 shows, Gantt charts are easy to understand. Horizontal bars are drawn for each project activity along a time line. This illustration of a routine servicing of a Royal Jordanian Airbus A340 during a 40-minute layover shows that Gantt charts also can be used for scheduling repetitive operations. In this case, the chart helps point out potential delays. The *OM in Action* box 'Royal Jordanian Flights to London' provides additional insights.

Passengers	Deplaning					
	Baggage claim					
Baggage	Container offload					
Fueling	Pumping					
	Engine injection water					
Cargo and mail	Container offload					
Galley servicing	Main cabin door					
	Aft cabin door					
Lavatory servicing	Aft, center, forward					
Drinking water	Loading					
Cabin cleaning	First-class section					
	Economy section					
Cargo and mail	Container/bulk loading					
Flight service	Galley/cabin check					
	Receive passengers					
Operating crew	Aircraft check					
Baggage	Loading					
Passengers	Boarding					
		0	10	20	30	40

Time, minutes

◀ FIGURE 3.4
Gantt Chart of Service Activities for an Aircraft during a 40-Minute Layover

Air carriers such as Royal Jordanian hope to save millions a year with planned turnaround time; the shorter the turnaround time, the more the saving.

On simple projects, scheduling charts such as these allow managers to observe the progress of each activity and to spot and tackle problem areas. Gantt charts, though, do not adequately illustrate the interrelationships between the activities and the resources.

LO1: Use a Gantt chart for scheduling

PERT and CPM, the two widely used network techniques that we shall discuss here, *do* have the ability to consider precedence relationships and interdependency of activities. In complex projects, the scheduling of which is almost always computerized, PERT and CPM have an edge over the simpler Gantt charts. Even on huge projects, though, Gantt charts can be used to summarize project status and may complement the other network approaches.

To summarize, whatever the approach taken by a project manager, project scheduling serves several purposes.

1. It shows the relationship of each activity to others and to the whole project.
2. It identifies the precedence relationships among activities.
3. It encourages the setting of realistic time and cost estimates for each activity.
4. It helps make better use of people, money, and material resources by identifying critical bottlenecks in the project.

OM in Action ▶ Royal Jordanian Flights to London

Royal Jordanian flight 111 to London is one of the air carrier's busiest routes. The Airbus A340 has less than one hour to be ready to head back to Amman, and the ground crew have strict standards and limited time to get it ready for its five-hour flight.

The staff aim for a turnaround time of 40 minutes, and they have to ensure that passengers, luggage, and cargo are unloaded, fuel refilled, kitchen restocked, restroom tanks emptied and then cleaned, and that the plane undergoes an engineering and technical check-up. Only then can the next group of travelers and their belongings be loaded. A delay in any of these processes can mean a delayed departure, which will then affect travelers' plans and other flight connections.

Gantt charts, such as the one in Figure 3.4, aid Royal Jordanian and other airlines with the staffing and scheduling needed for this task.

Source: **www.rj.com/en/profile.html**

PROJECT CONTROLLING

The control of projects, like the control of any management system, involves the close monitoring of resources, costs, quality, and budgets. Control also means using a feedback loop to revise the project plan and having the ability to shift resources to where they are needed most. Computerized PERT/CPM reports and charts are widely available today on personal computers. Two of the most popular of these programs are Primavera (by Primavera Systems, Inc.) and Microsoft® Project (by Microsoft Corp.), which we illustrate in this chapter.

These programs produce a broad variety of reports, including: (1) detailed cost breakdowns for each task; (2) total program labor curves; (3) cost distribution tables; (4) functional cost and hour summaries; (5) raw material and expenditure forecasts; (6) variance reports; (7) time analysis reports; (8) work status reports.

PROJECT MANAGEMENT TECHNIQUES: PERT AND CPM

PERT and **CPM** were both developed in the 1950s to help managers schedule, monitor, and control large and complex projects.

The Framework of PERT and CPM

PERT and CPM both follow six basic steps.

1. Define the project and prepare the work breakdown structure.
2. Develop the relationships among the activities. Decide which activities must precede and which must follow others.
3. Draw the network connecting all the activities.
4. Assign time and/or cost estimates to each activity.
5. Compute the *longest* time path through the network. This is called the **critical path**.
6. Use the network to help plan, schedule, monitor, and control the project.

Program evaluation and review technique (PERT)

A project management technique that employs three time estimates for each activity.

Critical path method (CPM)

A project management technique that uses only one time factor per activity.

Critical path

The computed longest time path(s) through a network.

Step 5, finding the critical path, is a major part of controlling a project. The activities on the critical path represent tasks that will delay the entire project if they are not completed on time. Managers can gain the flexibility needed to complete critical tasks by identifying noncritical activities and replanning, rescheduling, and reallocating labor and financial resources.

Although PERT and CPM differ to some extent in terminology and in the construction of the network, their objectives are the same. Furthermore, the analysis used in both techniques is very similar. The major difference is that PERT employs three time estimates for each activity. These time estimates are used to compute expected values and standard deviations for the activity. CPM makes the assumption that activity times are known with certainty, and hence requires only one time factor for each activity.

For the purposes of illustration, the rest of this section concentrates on a discussion of PERT. Most of the comments and procedures described, however, apply just as well to CPM.

PERT and CPM are important because they can help us decide the project completion date, the critical and noncritical activities, and answers to queries regarding possible future scenarios. For example, if the project is to be finished in a shorter amount of time, what is the best way to accomplish this goal at the least cost?

Network Diagrams and Approaches

The first step in a PERT or CPM network is to divide the entire project into significant activities in accordance with the work breakdown structure. There are two approaches for drawing a project network: **activity-on-node (AON)** and **activity-on-arrow (AOA)**. Activities consume time and resources. The basic difference between AON and AOA is that the nodes in an AON diagram represent activities. In an AOA network, *arrows* represent activities and the nodes represent the starting and finishing times of an activity (also called *events*). So nodes in AOA consume neither time nor resources.

Figure 3.5 illustrates both conventions for a small portion of the airline turnaround Gantt chart (in Figure 3.4). The examples provide some background for understanding six common activity relationships in networks. In Figure 3.5(a), activity A must be finished before activity B

Activity-on-node (AON)

A network diagram in which nodes designate activities.

Activity-on-arrow (AOA)

A network diagram in which arrows designate activities.

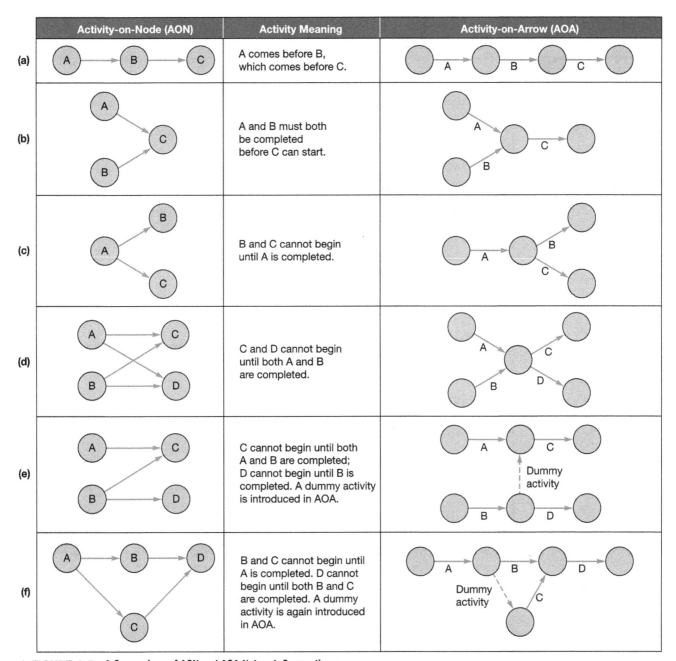

Activity-on-Node (AON)	Activity Meaning	Activity-on-Arrow (AOA)
(a)	A comes before B, which comes before C.	
(b)	A and B must both be completed before C can start.	
(c)	B and C cannot begin until A is completed.	
(d)	C and D cannot begin until both A and B are completed.	
(e)	C cannot begin until both A and B are completed; D cannot begin until B is completed. A dummy activity is introduced in AOA.	
(f)	B and C cannot begin until A is completed. D cannot begin until both B and C are completed. A dummy activity is again introduced in AOA.	

▲ **FIGURE 3.5** **A Comparison of AON and AOA Network Conventions**

is started, and B must, in turn, be completed before C begins. Activity A might represent 'deplaning passengers,' while B is 'cabin cleaning,' and C is 'boarding new passengers.'

Figures 3.5(e) and 3.5(f) illustrate that the AOA approach sometimes needs the addition of a **dummy activity** to clarify relationships. A dummy activity consumes no time or resources, but is required when a network has two activities with identical starting and ending events, or when two or more activities follow some, but not all, 'preceding' activities. The use of dummy activities is also important when computer software is employed to determine project completion time. A dummy activity has a completion time of zero and is shown graphically with a dashed line.

Although both AON and AOA are popular in practice, many of the project management software packages, including Microsoft® Project, use AON networks. For this reason, although we illustrate both types of networks in the next examples, we focus on AON networks in subsequent discussions in this chapter.

Dummy activity

An activity having no time that is inserted into a network to maintain the logic of the network.

Activity-on-Node Example

EXAMPLE 1 ▶

Activity-on-node for EEAA problem at Cairo Finest Paper Mills Ltd.

LO2: Draw AOA and AON networks

▶ **TABLE 3.1**

Cairo Finest Paper Mills' Activities and Predecessors

Cairo Finest Paper Mills Ltd. has long been delaying the expense of installing air pollution control equipment in its facility. The Egyptian Environmental Affairs Agency (EEAA) has recently given the manufacturer 16 weeks to install a complex air filter system. Cairo Finest Paper Mills has been warned that it may be forced to close the facility unless the device is installed in the allotted time. As a plant manager wanting to ensure that the installation of the filtering system progresses smoothly and on time, develop a table showing activity precedence relationships.

APPROACH ▶   Cairo Finest Paper Mills has identified the eight activities that need to be performed in order for the project to be completed. When the project begins, two activities can be simultaneously started: building the internal components for the device (activity A) and the modifications necessary for the floor and roof (activity B). The construction of the collection stack (activity C) can begin when the internal components are completed. Pouring the concrete floor and installation of the frame (activity D) can be started as soon as the internal components are completed and the roof and floor have been modified.

After the collection stack has been constructed, two activities can begin: building the high-temperature burner (activity E) and installing the pollution control system (activity F). The air pollution device can be installed (activity G) after the concrete floor has been poured, the frame has been installed, and the high-temperature burner has been built. Finally, after the control system and pollution device have been installed, the system can be inspected and tested (activity H).

Activity	Description	Immediate Predecessors
A	Build internal components	—
B	Modify roof and floor	—
C	Construct collection stack	A
D	Pour concrete and install frame	A, B
E	Build high-temperature burner	C
F	Install pollution control system	C
G	Install air pollution device	D, E
H	Inspect and test	F, G

SOLUTION ▶   Activities and precedence relationships may seem rather confusing when they are presented in this descriptive form. It is therefore convenient to list all the activity information in a table, as shown in Table 3.1. We see in the table that activity A is listed as an *immediate predecessor* of activity C. Likewise, both activities D and E must be performed prior to starting activity G.

INSIGHT ▶   To complete a network, all predecessors must be clearly defined.

LEARNING EXERCISE ▶   What is the impact on the sequence of activities if EEAA approval is required after *Inspect and Test*? [Answer: The immediate predecessor for the new activity would be H, *Inspect and Test*, with *EEAA Approval* as the last activity.]

Note that in Example 1, it is enough to list just the *immediate predecessors* for each activity. For instance, in Table 3.1, since activity A precedes activity C, and activity C precedes activity E, the fact that activity A precedes activity E is *implicit*. This relationship need not be explicitly shown in the activity precedence relationships.

When there are many activities in a project with fairly complicated precedence relationships, it is difficult for an individual to comprehend the complexity of the project from just the tabular information. In such cases, a visual representation of the project, using a *project network*, is convenient and useful. A project network is a diagram of all the activities and the precedence relationships that exist between these activities in a project. Example 2 illustrates how to construct a project network for Cairo Finest Paper Mills Ltd.

When we first draw a project network, it is not unusual that we place our nodes (activities) in the network in such a fashion that the arrows (precedence relationships) are not straight lines. That is, the lines could be intersecting each other, and even facing in opposite directions. For example, if we had switched the location of the nodes for activities E and F in Figure 3.8, the lines from F to H and E to G would have intersected. Although such a project network is perfectly valid, it is good practice to have a well-drawn network. One rule that we especially recommend

Draw the AON network for Cairo Finest Paper Mills Ltd., using the data in Example 1.

APPROACH ▶   In the AON approach, we denote each activity by a node. The lines, or arrows, represent the precedence relationships between the activities.

SOLUTION ▶   In this example, there are two activities (A and B) that do not have any predecessors. We draw separate nodes for each of these activities, as shown in Figure 3.6. Although not required, it is usually convenient to have a unique starting activity for a project. We have therefore included a *dummy activity* called *Start* in Figure 3.6. This dummy activity does not really exist and takes up zero time and resources. Activity *Start* is an immediate predecessor for both activities A and B, and serves as the unique starting activity for the entire project.

◀ EXAMPLE 2

AON graph for Cairo Finest Paper Mills Ltd.

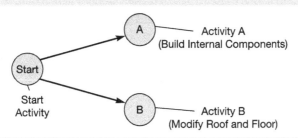

◀ FIGURE 3.6
Beginning AON Network for Cairo Finest Paper Mills

We now show the precedence relationships using lines with arrow symbols. For example, an arrow from activity *Start* to activity A indicates that *Start* is a predecessor for activity A. In a similar fashion, we draw an arrow from *Start* to B.

Next, we add a new node for activity C. Since activity A precedes activity C, we draw an arrow from node A to node C (see Figure 3.7). Likewise, we first draw a node to represent activity D. Then, since activities A and B both precede activity D, we draw arrows from A to D and from B to D (see Figure 3.7).

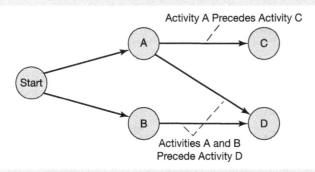

◀ FIGURE 3.7
Intermediate AON Network for Cairo Finest Paper Mills

We proceed in this fashion, adding a separate node for each activity and a separate line for each precedence relationship that exists. The complete AON project network for the Cairo Finest Paper Mills project is shown in Figure 3.8.

◀ FIGURE 3.8
Complete AON Network for Cairo Finest Paper Mills

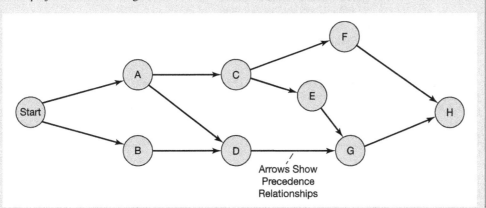

INSIGHT ▶   Drawing a project network properly takes some time and experience.

LEARNING EXERCISE ▶   If *EEAA Approval* occurs after *Inspect and Test*, what is the impact on the graph? [Answer: A straight line is extended to the right beyond H to reflect the additional activity.]

RELATED PROBLEMS ▶   3.3, 3.6, 3.7

is to place the nodes in such a fashion that all arrows point in the same direction. To achieve this, we suggest that you first draw a rough draft of the network, making sure all the relationships are shown. Then you can redraw the network to make appropriate changes in the location of the nodes.

As with the unique starting node, it is convenient to have the project network finish with a unique ending node. In the Cairo Finest Paper Mills example, it turns out that a unique activity, H, is the last activity in the project. We therefore automatically have a unique ending node. In situations in which a project has multiple ending activities, we include a 'dummy' ending activity.

Activity-on-Arrow Example

We saw earlier that in an AOA project network we can represent activities by arrows. A node represents an *event*, which marks the start or completion time of an activity. We usually identify an event (node) by a number.

EXAMPLE 3 ▶

Activity-on-arrow for Cairo Finest Paper Mills Ltd.

Draw the complete AOA project network for Cairo Finest Paper Mills problem.

APPROACH ▶ Using the data from Table 3.1 in Example 1, draw one activity at a time, starting with A.

SOLUTION ▶ We see that activity A starts at event 1 and ends at event 2. Likewise, activity B starts at event 1 and ends at event 3. Activity C, whose only immediate predecessor is activity A, starts at node 2 and ends at node 4. Activity D, however, has two predecessors (i.e. A and B). Hence, we need both activities A and B to end at event 3, so that activity D can start at that event. However, we cannot have multiple activities with common starting and ending nodes in an AOA network. To overcome this difficulty, in such cases, we may need to add a dummy line (activity) to enforce the precedence relationship. The dummy activity, shown in Figure 3.9 as a dashed line, is inserted between events 2 and 3 to make the diagram reflect the precedence between A and D. The remainder of the AOA project network for Cairo Finest Paper Mills example is also shown.

▶ FIGURE 3.9
Complete AOA Network (with Dummy Activity) for Cairo Finest Paper Mills

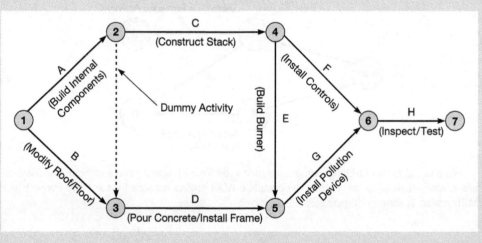

INSIGHT ▶ Dummy activities are common in AOA networks. They do not really exist in the project and take zero time.

LEARNING EXERCISE ▶ A new activity, *EEAA Approval*, follows activity H. Add it to Figure 3.9. [Answer: Insert an arrowed line from node 7, which ends at a new node 8, and is labeled I (EEAA Approval).]

RELATED PROBLEMS ▶ 3.4, 3.5

AUTHOR COMMENT
The dummy activity consumes no time, but note how it changes precedence. Now activity D cannot begin until *both* B and the dummy are complete.

AUTHOR COMMENT
We now add times to complete each activity. This lets us find the *critical path*.

DETERMINING THE PROJECT SCHEDULE

Look back at Figure 3.8 (in Example 2) for a moment to see Cairo Finest Paper Mills' completed AON project network. Once this project network has been drawn to show all the activities and their precedence relationships, the next step is to determine the project schedule. That is, we need to identify the planned starting and ending time for each activity.

Let us assume that Cairo Finest Paper Mills estimates the time required for each activity, in weeks, as shown in Table 3.2. The table indicates that the total time for all eight of the company's

Activity	Description	Time (weeks)
A	Build internal components	2
B	Modify roof and floor	3
C	Construct collection stack	2
D	Pour concrete and install frame	4
E	Build high-temperature burner	4
F	Install pollution control system	3
G	Install air pollution device	5
H	Inspect and test	2
	Total time (weeks)	25

◀ **TABLE 3.2**
Time Estimates for Cairo Finest Paper Mills

> **AUTHOR COMMENT**
> Does this mean the project will take 25 weeks to complete? No. Don't forget that several of the activities are being performed at the same time. It would take 25 weeks if they were done sequentially.

activities is 25 weeks. However, since several activities can take place simultaneously, it is clear that the total project completion time may be less than 25 weeks. To find out just how long the project will take, we perform the **critical path analysis** for the network.

As mentioned earlier, the critical path is the *longest* time path through the network. To find the critical path, we calculate two distinct starting and ending times for each activity. These are defined as follows.

Critical path analysis
A process that helps determine a project schedule.

> *Earliest start (ES)* = earliest time at which an activity can start, assuming all predecessors have been completed
> *Earliest finish (EF)* = earliest time at which an activity can be finished
> *Latest start (LS)* = latest time at which an activity can start so as to not delay the completion time of the entire project
> *Latest finish (LF)* = latest time by which an activity has to finish so as to not delay the completion time of the entire project

We use a two-pass process, consisting of a forward pass and a backward pass, to determine these time schedules for each activity. The early start and finish times (ES and EF) are determined during the **forward pass**. The late start and finish times (LS and LF) are determined during the backward pass.

Forward pass
A process that identifies all the early times.

Forward Pass

To clearly show the activity schedules on the project network, we use the notation shown in Figure 3.10. The ES of an activity is shown in the top left corner of the node denoting that activity. The EF is shown in the top right corner. The latest times, LS and LF, are shown in the bottom left and bottom right corners, respectively.

LO3: Complete forward and backward passes for a project

Earliest Start Time Rule Before an activity can start, *all* its immediate predecessors must be finished:

- If an activity has only a single immediate predecessor, its ES equals the EF of the predecessor.
- If an activity has multiple immediate predecessors, its ES is the maximum of all EF values of its predecessors. That is:

$$ES = Max \{EF \text{ of all immediate predecessors}\} \qquad (3\text{-}1)$$

> **AUTHOR COMMENT**
> *All* predecessor activities must be completed before an activity can begin.

◀ **FIGURE 3.10**
Notation Used in Nodes for Forward and Backward Pass

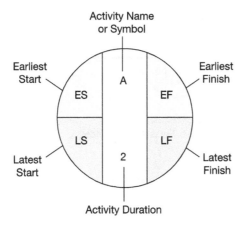

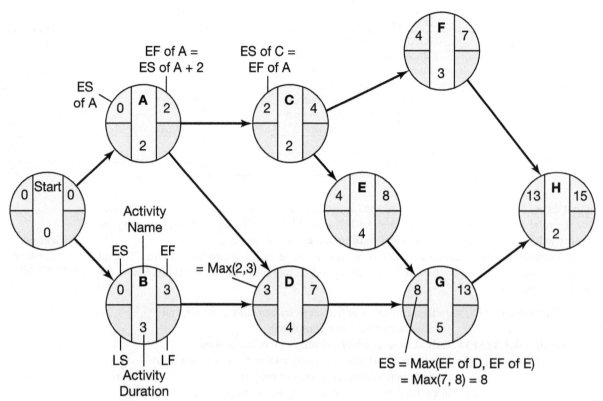

▲ FIGURE 3.11   Earliest Start and Earliest Finish Times for Cairo Finest Paper Mills

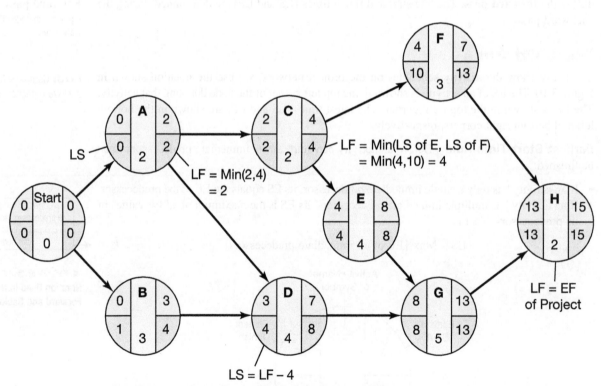

▲ FIGURE 3.12   Latest Start and Finish Times Are Now Added

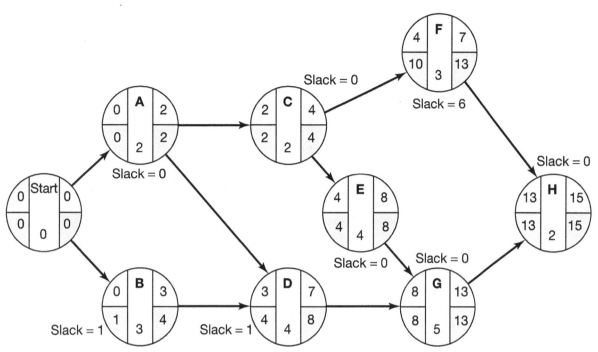

▲ FIGURE 3.13   **Slack Times Are Now Computed and Added**

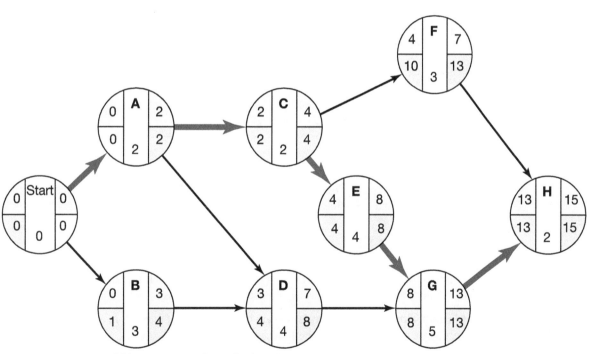

▲ FIGURE 3.14   **The Critical Path Is Now Shown in Five Thick Blue Lines**

Earliest Finish Rule   The earliest finish time (EF) of an activity is the sum of its earliest start time (ES) and its activity time. That is:

$$EF = ES + \text{Activity time}$$ (3-2)

EXAMPLE 4 ▶

Computing earliest start and finish times for Cairo Finest Paper Mills Ltd.

Calculate the earliest start and finish times for the activities in the Cairo Finest Paper Mills project.

APPROACH ▶   Use Table 3.2, which contains the activity times. Complete the project network for the company's project, along with the ES and EF values for all activities.

SOLUTION ▶   With the help of Figures 3.11–3.14, we describe how these values are calculated.

Since activity *Start* has no predecessors, we begin by setting its ES to 0. That is, activity *Start* can begin at time 0, which is the same as the beginning of week 1. If activity *Start* has an ES of 0, its EF is also 0, since its activity time is 0.

Next, we consider activities A and B, both of which have only *Start* as an immediate predecessor. Using the earliest start time rule, the ES for both activities A and B equals 0, which is the EF of activity *Start*. Now, using the earliest finish time rule, the EF for A is 2 (= 0 + 2), and the EF for B is 3 (= 0 + 3).

Since activity A precedes activity C, the ES of C equals the EF of A (= 2). The EF of C is therefore 4 (= 2 + 2).

We now come to activity D. Both activities A and B are immediate predecessors for B. Whereas A has an EF of 2, activity B has an EF of 3. Using the earliest start time rule, we compute the ES of activity D as follows:

$$\text{ES of D} = \text{Max(EF of A, EF of B)} = \text{Max}(2, 3) = 3$$

The EF of D equals 7 (= 3 + 4). Next, both activities E and F have activity C as their only immediate predecessor. Therefore, the ES for both E and F equals 4 (= EF of C). The EF of E is 8 (= 4 + 4), and the EF of F is 7 (= 4 + 3).

Activity G has both activities D and E as predecessors. Using the earliest start time rule, its ES is therefore the maximum of the EF of D and the EF of E. Hence, the ES of activity G equals 8 (= maximum of 7 and 8), and its EF equals 13 (= 8 + 5).

Finally, we come to activity H. Since it also has two predecessors, F and G, the ES of H is the maximum EF of these two activities. That is, the ES of H equals 13 (= maximum of 13 and 7). This implies that the EF of H is 15 (= 13 + 2). Since H is the last activity in the project, this also implies that the earliest time in which the entire project can be completed is 15 weeks.

INSIGHT ▶   The ES of an activity that has only one predecessor is simply the EF of that predecessor. For an activity with more than one predecessor, we must carefully examine the EFs of all immediate predecessors and choose the largest one.

LEARNING EXERCISE ▶   A new activity I, *EEAA Approval*, takes one week. Its predecessor is activity H. What are I's ES and EF? [Answer: 15, 16.]

RELATED PROBLEMS ▶   3.8, 3.9c

EXCEL OM Data File **Ch03Ex4.xls** can be found at MyOMLab.

Although the forward pass allows us to determine the earliest project completion time, it does not identify the critical path. To identify this path, we need to now conduct the backward pass to determine the LS and LF values for all activities.

Backward Pass

Backward pass
An activity that finds all the latest start and latest finish times.

Just as the forward pass began with the first activity in the project, the **backward pass** begins with the last activity in the project. For each activity, we first determine its LF value, followed by its LS value. The following two rules are used in this process.

Latest Finish Time Rule   This rule is again based on the fact that before an activity can start, all its immediate predecessors must be finished:

- If an activity is an immediate predecessor for just a single activity, its LF equals the LS of the activity that immediately follows it.
- If an activity is an immediate predecessor to more than one activity, its LF is the minimum of all LS values of all activities that immediately follow it. That is:

$$LF = \text{Min}\{LS \text{ of all immediate following activities}\} \qquad \text{(3-3)}$$

Latest Start Time Rule   The latest start time (LS) of an activity is the difference between its latest finish time (LF) and its activity time. That is:

$$LS = LF - \text{Activity time} \qquad \text{(3-4)}$$

Calculate the latest start and finish times for each activity in Cairo Finest Paper Mills' pollution project.

APPROACH ▶ Use Figure 3.11 as a beginning point. Figure 3.12 shows the complete project network for Cairo Finest Paper Mills, along with LS and LF values for all activities. In what follows, we see how these values were calculated.

SOLUTION ▶ We begin by assigning an LF value of 15 weeks for activity H. That is, we specify that the latest finish time for the entire project is the same as its earliest finish time. Using the latest start time rule, the LS of activity H is equal to 13 (= 15 − 2).

Since activity H is the lone succeeding activity for both activities F and G, the LF for both F and G equals 13. This implies that the LS of G is 8 (= 13 − 5), and the LS of F is 10 (= 13 − 3).

Proceeding in this fashion, we see that the LF of E is 8 (= LS of G), and its LS is 4 (= 8 − 4). Likewise, the LF of D is 8 (= LS of G), and its LS is 4 (= 8 − 4).

We now consider activity C, which is an immediate predecessor to two activities: E and F. Using the latest finish time rule, we compute the LF of activity C as follows:

$$\text{LF of C} = \text{Min(LS of E, LS of F)} = \text{Min}(4, 10) = 4$$

The LS of C is computed as 2 (= 4 − 2). Next, we compute the LF of B as 4 (= LS of D), and its LS as 1 (= 4 − 3).

We now consider activity A. We compute its LF as 2 (= minimum of LS of C and LS of D). Hence, the LS of activity A is 0 (= 2 − 2). Finally, both the LF and LS of activity *Start* are equal to 0.

INSIGHT ▶ The LF of an activity that is the predecessor of only one activity is just the LS of that following activity. If the activity is the predecessor to more than one activity, its LF is the smallest LS value of all activities that follow immediately.

LEARNING EXERCISE ▶ A new activity I, *EEAA Approval*, takes one week. Its predecessor is activity H. What are I's LS and LF? [Answer: 15, 16.]

RELATED PROBLEMS ▶ 3.8, 3.9c.

EXCEL OM Data File **Ch03Ex5.xls** can be found at MyOMLab.

◄ EXAMPLE 5

Computing latest start and finish times for Cairo Finest Paper Mills Ltd.

Calculating Slack Time and Identifying the Critical Path(s)

After we have computed the earliest and latest times for all activities, it is a simple matter to find the amount of **slack time** that each activity has. Slack is the length of time an activity can be delayed without delaying the entire project. Mathematically:

$$\text{Slack} = \text{LS} - \text{ES} \quad \text{or} \quad \text{Slack} = \text{LF} - \text{EF} \tag{3-5}$$

Slack time
Free time for an activity (Free Float, Free Time, or Free Slack).

Calculate the slack for the activities in the Cairo Finest Paper Mills project.

APPROACH ▶ Start with the data in Figure 3.12 and develop Table 3.3 one line at a time.

SOLUTION ▶ Table 3.3 summarizes the ES, EF, LS, LF, and slack time for all of the firm's activities. Activity B, for example, has 1 week of slack time since its LS is 1 and its ES is 0 (alternatively, its LF is 4 and its EF is 3). This means that activity B can be delayed by up to 1 week, and the whole project can still be finished in 15 weeks.

◄ EXAMPLE 6

Calculating slack times for Cairo Finest Paper Mills Ltd.

◄ TABLE 3.3

Cairo Finest Paper Mills' Schedule and Slack Times

Activity	Earliest Start ES	Earliest Finish EF	Latest Start LS	Latest Finish LF	Slack LS − ES	On Critical Path
A	0	2	0	2	0	Yes
B	0	3	1	4	1	No
C	2	4	2	4	0	Yes
D	3	7	4	8	1	No
E	4	8	4	8	0	Yes
F	4	7	10	13	6	No
G	8	13	8	13	0	Yes
H	13	15	13	15	0	Yes

On the other hand, activities A, C, E, G, and H have *no* slack time. This means that none of them can be delayed without delaying the entire project. Conversely, if the project manager at Cairo Finest Paper Mills wants to reduce the total project times, she will have to reduce the length of one of these activities.

Figure 3.13 shows the slack computed for each activity.

INSIGHT ▶ Slack may be computed from either early/late starts or early/late finishes. The key is to find which activities have zero slack.

LEARNING EXERCISE ▶ A new activity I, *EEAA Approval*, follows activity H and takes one week. Is it on the critical path? [Answer: Yes, LS − ES = 0.]

RELATED PROBLEMS ▶ 3.6, 3.8

EXCEL OM Data File **Ch03Ex6.xls** can be found at MyOMLab.

LO4: Determine a critical path

The activities with zero slack are called *critical activities* and are said to be on the critical path. The critical path is a continuous path through the project network that:

- Starts at the first activity in the project (*Start* in our example).
- Terminates at the last activity in the project (H in our example).
- Includes only critical activities (i.e. activities with no slack time).

EXAMPLE 7 ▶

Showing critical path with blue arrows

Show Cairo Finest Paper Mills' critical path and find the project completion time.

APPROACH ▶ We use Table 3.3 and Figure 3.14. Figure 3.14 indicates that the total project completion time of 15 weeks corresponds to the longest path in the network. That path is *Start*-A-C-E-G-H in network form. It is shown with thick blue arrows.

INSIGHT ▶ The critical path follows the activities with slack = 0. This is considered the longest path through the network.

LEARNING EXERCISE ▶ Why are activities B, D, and F not on the path with the thick blue line? [Answer: They are not critical and have slack values of 1, 1, and 6 weeks, respectively.]

RELATED PROBLEMS ▶ 3.3, 3.4, 3.5, 3.6, 3.9b, 3.10, 3.12a

Total Slack Time Look again at the project network in Figure 3.14. Consider activities B and D, which have slack of 1 week each. Does it mean that we can delay *each* activity by 1 week, and still complete the project in 15 weeks? The answer is no.

Let's assume that activity B is delayed by 1 week. It has used up its slack of 1 week and now has an EF of 4. This implies that activity D now has an ES of 4 and an EF of 8. Note that these are also its LS and LF values, respectively. That is, activity D also has no slack time now. Essentially, the slack of 1 week that activities B and D had is, for that path, *shared* between them. Delaying either activity by 1 week causes not only that activity, but also the other activity, to lose its slack. This type of slack time is referred to as **total slack**. Typically, when two or more noncritical activities appear successively in a path, they share total slack.

Total slack

Time shared among more than one activity.

AUTHOR COMMENT
PERT's ability to handle three time estimates for each activity enables us to compute the probability that we can complete the project by a target date.

VARIABILITY IN ACTIVITY TIMES

In identifying all earliest and latest times so far, and the associated critical path(s), we have adopted the CPM approach of assuming that all activity times are known and fixed constants. That is, there is no variability in activity times. However, in practice, it is likely that activity completion times vary depending on various factors.

For example, building internal components (activity A) for Cairo Finest Paper Mills Ltd. is estimated to finish in 2 weeks. Clearly, factors such as late arrival of raw materials, absence of key personnel, and so on, could delay this activity. Suppose activity A actually ends up taking

3 weeks. Since A is on the critical path, the entire project will now be delayed by 1 week to 16 weeks. If we had anticipated completion of this project in 15 weeks, we would obviously miss our deadline.

Although some activities may be relatively less prone to delays, others could be extremely susceptible to delays. For example, activity B (modify roof and floor) could be heavily dependent on weather conditions. A spell of bad weather could significantly affect its completion time.

This means that we cannot ignore the impact of variability in activity times when deciding the schedule for a project. PERT addresses this issue.

Three Time Estimates in PERT

In PERT, we employ a probability distribution based on three time estimates for each activity, as follows.

Optimistic time (a) = time an activity will take if everything goes as planned. In estimating this value, there should be only a small probability (say, 1/100) that the activity time will be < a.

Pessimistic time (b) = time an activity will take assuming very unfavorable conditions. In estimating this value, there should also be only a small probability (also, 1/100) that the activity time will be > b.

Most likely time (m) = most realistic estimate of the time required to complete an activity.

When using PERT, we often assume that activity time estimates follow the beta probability distribution (see Figure 3.15). This continuous distribution is often appropriate for determining the expected value and variance for activity completion times.

To find the *expected activity time*, t, the beta distribution weights the three time estimates as follows:

$$t = (a + 4m + b) \div 6 \qquad (3\text{-}6)$$

That is, the most likely time (m) is given four times the weight as the optimistic time (a) and pessimistic time (b). The time estimate t computed using Equation (3-6) for each activity is used in the project network to compute all earliest and latest times.

To compute the dispersion or variance of activity completion time, we use the formula:[1]

$$\text{Variance} = [(b - a) \div 6]^2 \qquad (3\text{-}7)$$

Optimistic time

The 'best' activity completion time that could be obtained in a PERT network.

Pessimistic time

The 'worst' activity time that could be expected in a PERT network.

Most likely time

The most probable time to complete an activity in a PERT network.

◄ **FIGURE 3.15**
Beta Probability Distribution with Three Time Estimates

[1]This formula is based on the statistical concept that from one end of the beta distribution to the other is 6 standard deviations (±3 standard deviations from the mean). Since ($b - a$) is 6 standard deviations, the variance is $[(b - a) \div 6]^2$.

EXAMPLE 8 ▶

Expected times and variances for Cairo Finest Paper Mills Ltd.

The project manager and the project management team at Cairo Finest Paper Mills want an expected time and variance for activity F (Installing the pollution control system) where:

$$a = 1 \text{ week}, m = 2 \text{ weeks}, b = 9 \text{ weeks}$$

APPROACH ▶   Use Equations 3-6 and 3-7 to compute the expected time and variance for F.

SOLUTION ▶   The expected time for activity F is:

$$t = \frac{a + 4m + b}{6} = \frac{1 + 4(2) + 9}{6} = \frac{18}{6} = 3 \text{ weeks}$$

The variance for activity F is:

$$\text{Variance} = \left[\frac{(b-a)}{6}\right]^2 = \left[\frac{(9-1)}{6}\right]^2 = \left(\frac{8}{6}\right)^2 = \frac{64}{36} = 1.78$$

LO5: Calculate the variance of activity times

INSIGHT ▶   The project manager now has information that allows her to understand and manage activity F. The expected time is, in fact, the activity time used in our earlier computation and identification of the critical path.

LEARNING EXERCISE ▶   Review the expected times and variances for all of the other activities in the project. These are shown in Table 3.4.

▶ TABLE 3.4

Time Estimates (in weeks) for Cairo Finest Paper Mills' Project

Activity	Optimistic a	Most Likely m	Pessimistic b	Expected Time $t = (a + 4m + b) \div 6$	Variance $[(b - a) \div 6]^2$
A	1	2	3	2	$[(3 - 1) \div 6]^2 = 4 \div 36 = 0.11$
B	2	3	4	3	$[(4 - 2) \div 6]^2 = 4 \div 36 = 0.11$
C	1	2	3	2	$[(3 - 1) \div 6]^2 = 4 \div 36 = 0.11$
D	2	4	6	4	$[(6 - 2) \div 6]^2 = 16 \div 36 = 0.44$
E	1	4	7	4	$[(7 - 1) \div 6]^2 = 36 \div 36 = 1.00$
F	1	2	9	3	$[(9 - 1) \div 6]^2 = 64 \div 36 = 1.78$
G	3	4	11	5	$[(11 - 3) \div 6]^2 = 64 \div 36 = 1.78$
H	1	2	3	2	$[(3 - 1) \div 6]^2 = 4 \div 36 = 0.11$

AUTHOR COMMENT
Can you see why the variance is higher in some activities than in others? Note the spread between the optimistic and pessimistic times.

RELATED PROBLEMS ▶   3.9a, 3.10a,b, 3.11a

EXCEL OM Data File **Ch03Ex8.xls** can be found at MyOMLab.

We see here a ship being repaired at a shipyard in Dubai, one of the Middle East's busiest ports. Managing this project uses the same techniques as managing the remodeling of a store or installing a new production line.

Probability of Project Completion

The critical path analysis helped us determine that Cairo Finest Paper Mills' expected project completion time is 15 weeks. The project manager at Cairo Finest Paper Mills knows, however, that there is significant variation in the time estimates for several activities. Variation in activities that are on the critical path can affect the overall project completion time—possibly delaying it. This is one occurrence that worries the plant manager considerably.

PERT uses the variance of critical path activities to help determine the variance of the overall project. Project variance is computed by summing variances of *critical* activities:

$$\sigma_p^2 = \text{Project variance} = \Sigma(\text{variances of activities on critical path}) \qquad \text{(3-8)}$$

Computing project variance and standard deviation for Cairo Finest Paper Mills Ltd.

Cairo Finest Paper Mills' managers now wish to know the project's variance and standard deviation.

APPROACH ▶ Because the activities are independent, we can add the variances of the activities on the critical path and then take the square root to determine the project's standard deviation.

SOLUTION ▶ From Example 8 (Table 3.4), we have the variances of all of the activities on the critical path. Specifically, we know that the variance of activity A is 0.11, the variance of activity C is 0.11, the variance of activity E is 1.00, the variance of activity G is 1.78, and the variance of activity H is 0.11.

Compute the total project variance and project standard deviation:

$$\text{Project variance } (\sigma_p^2) = 0.11 + 0.11 + 1.00 + 1.78 + 0.11 = 3.11$$

which implies:

$$\text{Project standard deviation } (\sigma_p) = \sqrt{\text{Project variance}} = \sqrt[2]{3.11} = 1.76 \text{ weeks}$$

INSIGHT ▶ Management now has an estimate not only of expected completion time for the project but also of the standard deviation of that estimate.

LEARNING EXERCISE ▶ If the variance for activity A is actually 0.30 (instead of 0.11), what is the new project standard deviation? [Answer: 1.817.]

RELATED PROBLEM ▶ 3.10e

EXCEL **OM** Data File **Ch03Ex9.xls** can be found at MyOMLab.

How can this information be used to help answer questions regarding the probability of finishing the project on time? PERT makes two more assumptions: (1) total project completion times follow a normal probability distribution; (2) activity times are statistically independent. With these assumptions, the bell-shaped normal curve shown in Figure 3.16 can be used to represent project completion dates. This normal curve implies that there is a 50 percent chance that the manufacturer's project completion time will be less than 15 weeks and a 50 percent chance that it will exceed 15 weeks.

Standard Deviation = 1.76 Weeks

15 Weeks

(Expected Completion Time)

◀ **FIGURE 3.16**
Probability Distribution for Project Completion Times at Cairo Finest Paper Mills Ltd.

Probability of completing a project on time

The project manager at Cairo Finest Paper Mills would like to find the probability that her project will be finished on or before the 16-week EEAA deadline.

APPROACH ▶   To do so, she needs to determine the appropriate area under the normal curve. This is the area to the left of the 16th week.

SOLUTION ▶   The standard normal equation can be applied as follows:

$$Z = (\text{Due date} - \text{Expected date of completion}) \div \sigma_p \tag{3-9}$$
$$= (16 \text{ weeks} - 15 \text{ weeks}) \div 1.76 \text{ weeks} = 0.57$$

> **AUTHOR COMMENT**
> Here is a chance to review your statistical skills and use of a normal distribution table (Appendix I).

where Z is the number of standard deviations the due date or target date lies from the mean or expected date.

Referring to the Normal Table in Appendix I, we find a Z value of 0.57 to the right of the mean indicates a probability of 0.7157. Thus, there is a 71.57 percent chance that the pollution control equipment can be put in place in 16 weeks or less. This is shown in Figure 3.17.

▶ **FIGURE 3.17**
Probability That Cairo Finest Paper Mills will Meet the 16-Week Deadline

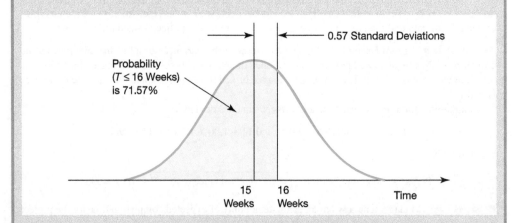

INSIGHT ▶   The shaded area to the left of the 16th week (71.57%) represents the probability that the project will be completed in less than 16 weeks.

LEARNING EXERCISE ▶   What is the probability that the project will be completed on or before the 17th week? [Answer: About 87.2 percent.]

RELATED PROBLEMS ▶   3.9d, 3.10f, 3.11d,e, 3.12b

Determining Project Completion Time for a Given Confidence Level   Let's say the project manager of Cairo Finest Paper Mills is worried that there is only a 71.57 percent chance that the pollution control equipment can be put in place in 16 weeks or less. She thinks that it may be possible to plead with the environmental group for more time. However, before she approaches the group, she wants to arm herself with sufficient information about the project. Specifically, she wants to find the deadline by which she has a 99 percent chance of completing the project. She hopes to use her analysis to convince the group to agree to this extended deadline.

Clearly, this due date would be greater than 16 weeks. However, what is the exact value of this new due date? To answer this question, we again use the assumption that Cairo Finest Paper Mills' project completion time follows a normal probability distribution with a mean of 15 weeks and a standard deviation of 1.76 weeks.

Computing probability for any completion date

The project manager at Cairo Finest Paper Mills wants to find the due date that gives her company's project a 99 percent chance of *on-time* completion.

APPROACH ▶   She first needs to compute the Z value corresponding to 99 percent, as shown in Figure 3.18. Mathematically, this is similar to Example 10, except the unknown is now Z rather than the due date.

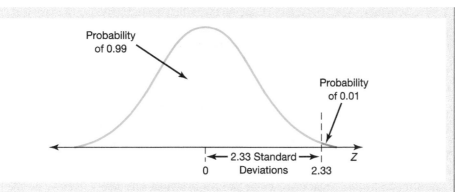

SOLUTION ▶   Referring again to the Normal Table in Appendix I, we identify a Z value of 2.33 as being closest to the probability of 0.99. That is, the project manager at Cairo Finest Paper Mills' due date should be 2.33 standard deviations above the mean project completion time. Starting with the standard normal equation (see Equation 3-9), we can solve for the due date and rewrite the equation as:

$$\text{Due date} = \text{Expected completion time} + (Z \times \sigma_p)$$
$$= 15 + (2.33 \times 1.76) = 19.1 \text{ weeks} \qquad (3\text{-}10)$$

INSIGHT ▶   If the project manager can get the environmental group to agree to give her a new deadline of 19.1 weeks (or more), she can be 99 percent sure of finishing the project on time.

LEARNING EXERCISE ▶   What due date gives the project a 95 percent chance of on-time completion? [Answer: About 17.9 weeks.]

RELATED PROBLEM ▶   3.12c

Variability in Completion Time of Noncritical Paths   In our discussion so far, we have focused exclusively on the variability in the completion times of activities on the critical path. This seems logical since these activities are, by definition, the more important activities in a project network. However, when there is variability in activity times, it is important that we also investigate the variability in the completion times of activities on *noncritical* paths.

Consider, for example, activity D in Cairo Finest Paper Mills' project. Recall from Figure 3.14 (in Example 7) that this is a noncritical activity, with a slack time of 1 week. We have therefore not considered the variability in activity D's time in computing the probabilities of project completion times. We observe, however, that D has a variance of 0.44 (see Table 3.4 in Example 8). In fact, the pessimistic completion time for D is 6 weeks. This means that if D ends up taking its pessimistic time to finish, the project will not finish in 15 weeks, even though D is not a critical activity.

For this reason, when we find probabilities of project completion times, it may be necessary for us to not focus only on the critical path(s). Indeed, some research has suggested that expending project resources to reduce the variability of activities not on the critical path can be an effective element in project management.[2] We may need also to compute these probabilities for noncritical paths, especially those that have relatively large variances. It is possible for a noncritical path to have a smaller probability of completion within a due date, when compared with the critical path. Determining the variance and probability of completion for a noncritical path is done in the same manner as Examples 9 and 10.

What Project Management Has Provided So Far   Project management techniques have thus far been able to provide the project manager at Cairo Finest Paper Mills with several valuable pieces of management information.

1. The project's expected completion date is 15 weeks.
2. There is a 71.57 percent chance that the equipment will be in place within the 16-week deadline. PERT analysis can easily find the probability of finishing by any date the project manager is interested in.

[2]F. M. Pokladnik, T. F. Anthony, R. R. Hill, G. Ulrich, "A Fresh Look at Estimated Project Duration: Noncritical Path Activity Contribution to Project Variance in PERT/CPM," *Proceedings of the 2003 Southwest Decision Science Conference*, Houston.

3. Five activities (A, C, E, G, and H) are on the critical path. If any one of these is delayed for any reason, the entire project will be delayed.
4. Three activities (B, D, and F) are not critical and have some slack time built in. This means that the project manager can borrow from their resources, and, if necessary, she may be able to speed up the whole project.
5. A detailed schedule of activity starting and ending dates, slack, and critical path activities has been made available (see Table 3.3 in Example 6).

AUTHOR COMMENT
When a project needs to be shortened, we want to find the most economical way of 'crashing' it.

COST–TIME TRADE-OFFS AND PROJECT CRASHING

While managing a project, it is not uncommon for a project manager to be faced with either (or both) of the following situations: (1) the project is behind schedule; (2) the scheduled project completion time has been moved forward. In either situation, some or all of the remaining activities need to be speeded up (usually by adding resources) to finish the project by the desired due date. The process by which we shorten the duration of a project in the cheapest manner possible is called project **crashing**.

Crashing
Shortening activity time in a network to reduce time on the critical path so total completion time is reduced.

CPM is a technique in which each activity has a *normal* or *standard time* that we use in our computations. Associated with this normal time is the *normal cost* of the activity. However, another time in project management is the *crash time*, which is defined as the shortest duration required to complete an activity. Associated with this crash time is the *crash cost* of the activity. Usually, we can shorten an activity by adding extra resources (e.g. equipment, people) to it. Hence, it is logical for the crash cost of an activity to be higher than its normal cost.

The amount by which an activity can be shortened (i.e. the difference between its normal time and crash time) depends on the activity in question. We may not be able to shorten some activities at all. For example, if a casting needs to be heat-treated in the furnace for 48 hours, adding more resources does not help shorten the time. In contrast, we may be able to shorten some activities significantly (e.g. frame a house in three days instead of ten days by using three times as many workers).

Likewise, the cost of crashing (or shortening) an activity depends on the nature of the activity. Managers are usually interested in speeding up a project at the least additional cost. Hence, when choosing which activities to crash, and by how much, we need to ensure the following:

- The amount by which an activity is crashed is, in fact, permissible.
- Taken together, the shortened activity durations will enable us to finish the project by the due date.
- The total cost of crashing is as small as possible.

LO6: Crash a project

Crashing a project involves four steps.

STEP 1: Compute the crash cost per week (or other time period) for each activity in the network. If crash costs are linear over time, the following formula can be used:

$$\text{Crash cost per period} = \frac{(\text{Crash cost} - \text{Normal cost})}{(\text{Normal time} - \text{Crash time})} \quad (3\text{-}11)$$

STEP 2: Using the current activity times, find the critical path(s) in the project network. Identify the critical activities.

STEP 3: If there is only one critical path, then select the activity on this critical path that (a) can still be crashed and (b) has the smallest crash cost per period. Crash this activity by one period.

If there is more than one critical path, then select one activity from each critical path such that (a) each selected activity can still be crashed and (b) the total crash cost per period of *all* selected activities is the smallest. Crash each activity by one period. Note that the same activity may be common to more than one critical path.

STEP 4: Update all activity times. If the desired due date has been reached, stop. If not, return to Step 2.

We illustrate project crashing in Example 12.

Suppose that Cairo Finest Paper Mills Ltd. has been given only 13 weeks (instead of 16 weeks) to install the new pollution control equipment or face a court-ordered shutdown. As you recall, the length of Cairo Finest Paper Mills' critical path was 15 weeks, but the project manager must now complete the project in 13 weeks.

APPROACH ▶   The project manager needs to determine which activities to crash, and by how much, to meet this 13-week due date. Naturally, she is interested in speeding up the project by 2 weeks, at the least additional cost.

SOLUTION ▶   The company's normal and crash times, and normal and crash costs, are shown in Table 3.5. Note, for example, that activity B's normal time is 3 weeks (the estimate used in computing the critical path), and its crash time is 1 week. This means that activity B can be shortened by up to 2 weeks if extra resources are provided. The cost of these additional resources is US$4,000 (= difference between the crash cost of US$34,000 and the normal cost of US$30,000). If we assume that the crashing cost is linear over time (i.e. the cost is the same each week), activity B's crash cost per week is US$2,000 (= US$4,000 ÷ 2).

◀ **EXAMPLE 12**

Project crashing to meet a deadline at Cairo Finest Paper Mills Ltd.

◀ **TABLE 3.5**

Normal and Crash Data for Cairo Finest Paper Mills Ltd.

Activity	Time (Weeks)		Cost (US$)		Crash Cost per Week (US$)	Critical Path?
	Normal	Crash	Normal	Crash		
A	2	1	22,000	22,750	750	Yes
B	3	1	30,000	34,000	2,000	No
C	2	1	26,000	27,000	1,000	Yes
D	4	3	48,000	49,000	1,000	No
E	4	2	56,000	58,000	1,000	Yes
F	3	2	30,000	30,500	500	No
G	5	2	80,000	84,500	1,500	Yes
H	2	1	16,000	19,000	3,000	Yes

This calculation for activity B is shown in Figure 3.19. Crash costs for all other activities can be computed in a similar fashion.

◀ **FIGURE 3.19**

Crash and Normal Times and Costs for Activity B

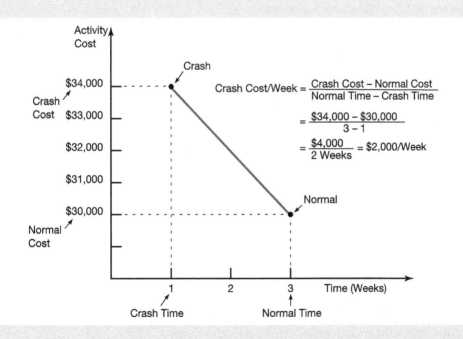

Steps 2, 3, and 4 can now be applied to reduce Cairo Finest Paper Mills' project completion time at a minimum cost. We show the project network for Cairo Finest Paper Mills again in Figure 3.20.

▶ **FIGURE 3.20**
Critical Path and Slack Times for Cairo Finest Paper Mills

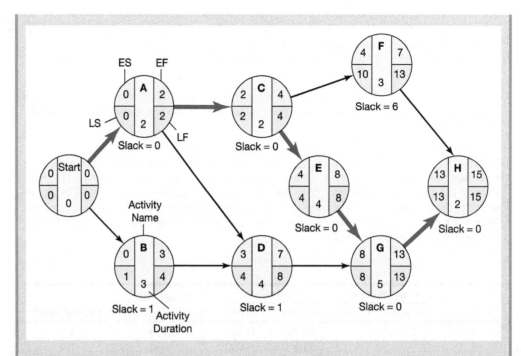

The current critical path (using normal times) is Start-A-C-E-G-H, in which Start is just a dummy starting activity. Of these critical activities, activity A has the lowest crash cost per week of US$750. The project manager at Cairo Finest Paper Mills should therefore crash activity A by 1 week to reduce the project completion time to 14 weeks. The cost is an additional US$750. Note that activity A cannot be crashed any further, since it has reached its crash limit of 1 week.

At this stage, the original path Start-A-C-E-G-H remains critical with a completion time of 14 weeks. However, a new path Start-B-D-G-H is also critical now, with a completion time of 14 weeks. Hence, any further crashing must be done to both critical paths.

On each of these critical paths, we need to identify one activity that can still be crashed. We also want the total cost of crashing an activity on each path to be the smallest. We might be tempted to simply pick the activities with the smallest crash cost per period in each path. If we did this, we would select activity C from the first path and activity D from the second path. The total crash cost would then be US$2,000 (= US$1,000 + US$1,000).

But we spot that activity G is common to both paths. That is, by crashing activity G, we will simultaneously reduce the completion time of both paths. Even though the US$1,500 crash cost for activity G is higher than that for activities C and D, we would still prefer crashing G, since the total crashing cost will now be only US$1,500 (compared with the US$2,000 if we crash C and D).

INSIGHT ▶ To crash the project down to 13 weeks, the project manager should crash activity A by 1 week, and activity G by 1 week. The total additional cost will be US$2,250 (= US$750 + US$1,500). This is important because many contracts for projects include bonuses or penalties for early or late finishes.

LEARNING EXERCISE ▶ Say the crash cost for activity B is US$31,000 instead of US$34,000. How does this change the answer? [Answer: No change.]

EXCEL OM Data File **Ch03Ex12.xls** can be found at MyOMLab.

AUTHOR COMMENT
Every technique has shortcomings as well as strengths. It is important to know both.

A CRITIQUE OF PERT AND CPM

As a critique of our discussions of PERT, here are some of its features about which operations managers need to be aware.

Advantages

1. Especially useful when scheduling and controlling large projects.
2. Straightforward concept and not mathematically complex.
3. Graphical networks help highlight relationships among project activities.
4. Critical path and slack time analyses help pinpoint activities that need to be closely watched.
5. Project documentation and graphs point out who is responsible for various activities.
6. Applicable to a wide variety of projects.
7. Useful in monitoring not only schedules but costs as well.

Limitations

1. Project activities have to be clearly defined, independent, and stable in their relationships.
2. Precedence relationships must be specified and networked together.
3. Time estimates tend to be subjective and are subject to fudging by managers who fear the dangers of being overly optimistic or not pessimistic enough.
4. There is the inherent danger of placing too much emphasis on the longest, or critical, path. Near-critical paths need to be monitored closely as well.

USING MICROSOFT® PROJECT TO MANAGE PROJECTS

> **AUTHOR COMMENT**
> Now that you understand the workings of PERT and CPM, you are ready to master this useful program. Knowing such software gives you an edge over others in the job market.

The approaches discussed so far are effective for managing small projects. However, for large or complex projects, specialized project management software is much preferred. In this section, we provide a brief introduction to the most popular example of such specialized software, Microsoft Project. Microsoft Project is extremely useful in drawing project networks, identifying the project schedule, and managing project costs and other resources.

Entering Data

Let us again consider the Cairo Finest Paper Mills Ltd. project. Recall that this project has eight activities (Table 3.6). The first step is to define the activities and their precedence relationships. To do so, we select File|New to open a blank project. We type the project start date (as July 1), then enter all activity information (see Program 3.1). For each activity (or task, as Microsoft Project calls it), we fill in the name and duration. The description of the activity is also placed in the *Task Name* column in Program 3.1. As we enter activities and durations, the software automatically inserts start and finish dates.

The next step is to define precedence relationships between these activities. To do so, we enter the relevant activity numbers (e.g. 1, 2) in the *Predecessors* column.

Viewing the Project Schedule

When all links have been defined, the complete project schedule can be viewed as a Gantt chart. We can also select View|Network Diagram to view the schedule as a project network (shown in Program 3.2). The critical path is shown in red on the screen in the network diagram. We can click on any of the activities in the project network to view details of the activities. Likewise, we can easily add or remove activities from the project network. Each time we do so, Microsoft Project automatically updates all start dates, finish dates, and the critical path(s). If desired, we can manually change the layout of the network (e.g. reposition activities) by changing the options in Format|Layout.

▼ **TABLE 3.6**

Time Estimates and Predecessors for Cairo Finest Paper Mills

Cairo Finest Paper Mills Ltd.		
Activities		
Activity	Time (wks)	Prede-cessors
A	2	—
B	3	—
C	2	A
D	4	A, B
E	4	C
F	3	C
G	5	D, E
H	2	F, G

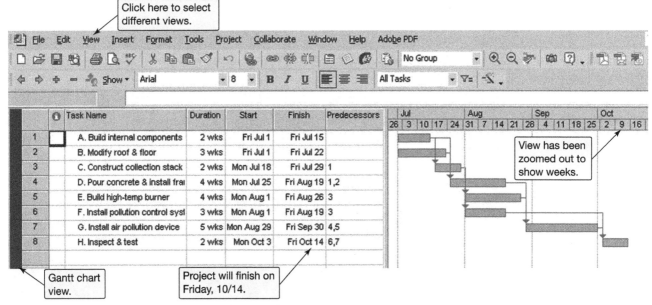

▲ **PROGRAM 3.1** **Gantt Chart in Microsoft Project for Cairo Finest Paper Mills Ltd.**

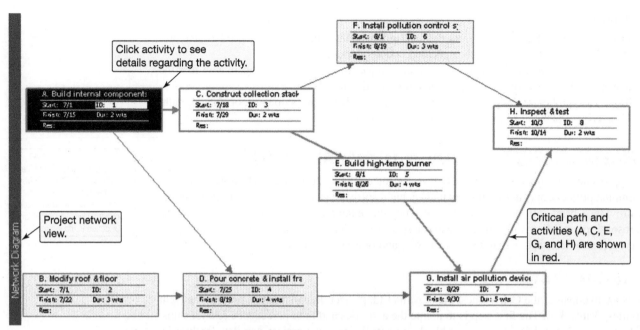

▲ **PROGRAM 3.2** **Project Network in Microsoft Project for Cairo Finest Paper Mills Ltd.**

Programs 3.1 and 3.2 show that if Cairo Finest Paper Mills' project starts on July 1, it can be finished on October 14. The start and finish dates for all activities are also clearly identified. Project management software, we see, can greatly simplify the scheduling procedures discussed earlier in this chapter.

PERT Analysis

Microsoft Project does not perform the PERT probability calculations discussed in Examples 10 and 11. However, by clicking View|Toolbars|PERT Analysis, we can get Microsoft Project to allow us to enter optimistic, most likely, and pessimistic times for each activity. We can then choose to view Gantt charts based on any of these three times for each activity.

Using PERT/CPM, Taco Bell built and opened this fast-food restaurant in Compton, California, in just 2 days! Typically, 2 months are needed to accomplish such a task. Good project management means a faster revenue stream instead of money tied up in construction.

Tracking the Time Status of a Project

Perhaps the biggest advantage of using software to manage projects is that it can track the progress of the project. In this regard, Microsoft Project has many features available to track individual activities in terms of time, cost, resource usage, and so on.

An easy way to track the time progress of tasks is to enter the percentage of work completed for each task. One way to do so is to double-click on any activity in the *Task Name* column in Program 3.1. A window is displayed that allows us to enter the percentage of work completed for each task.

Table 3.7 provides data regarding the percentage of each of Cairo Finest Paper Mills' activities as of today. (Assume that today is Friday, August 12, i.e. the end of the sixth week of the project schedule.)

As shown in Program 3.3, the Gantt chart immediately reflects this updated information by drawing a thick line within each activity's bar. The length of this line is proportional to the percentage of that activity's work that has been completed.

How do we know if we are on schedule? Notice that there is a vertical line shown on the Gantt chart corresponding to today's date. Microsoft Project will automatically move this line to correspond with the current date. If the project is on schedule, we should see all bars to the *left* of today's line indicate that they have been completed. For example, Program 3.3 shows that activities A, B, and C are on schedule. In contrast, activities D, E, and F appear to be behind schedule. These activities need to be investigated further to determine the reason for the delay. This type of easy *visual* information is what makes such software so useful in practice for project management.

▼ TABLE 3.7

Cairo Finest Paper Mills Status on August 12

Pollution Project Percentage Completed on Aug. 12	
Activity	**Completed**
A	100
B	100
C	100
D	10
E	20
F	20
G	0
H	0

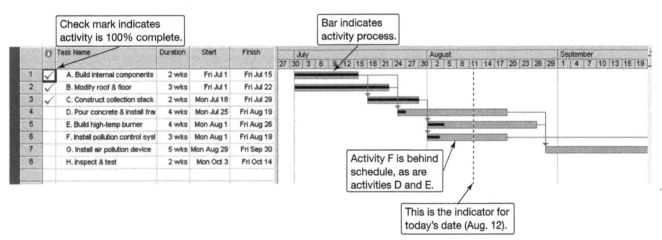

▲ PROGRAM 3.3   **Tracking Project Progress in Microsoft Project**

CHAPTER SUMMARY

PERT, CPM, and other scheduling techniques have proven to be valuable tools in controlling large and complex projects. With these tools, managers understand the status of each activity and know which activities are critical and which have slack; in addition, they know where crashing makes the most sense. Projects are segmented into discrete activities, and specific resources are identified. This allows project managers to respond aggressively to global competition. Effective project management also allows firms to create products and services for global markets. As with Microsoft Project illustrated in this chapter, a wide variety of software packages are available to help managers handle network modeling problems.

PERT and CPM do not, however, solve all the project scheduling and management problems. Good management practices, clear responsibilities for tasks, and straightforward and timely reporting systems are also needed. It is important to remember that the models we described in this chapter are only tools to help managers make better decisions.

Key Terms

Activity-on-arrow (AOA) (p. 56)
Activity-on-node (AON) (p. 56)
Backward pass (p. 64)
Crashing (p. 72)
Critical path (p. 56)
Critical path analysis (p. 61)
Critical path method (CPM) (p. 56)

Dummy activity (p. 57)
Forward pass (p. 61)
Gantt charts (p. 54)
Most likely time (p. 67)
Optimistic time (p. 67)
Pessimistic time (p. 67)

Program evaluation and review technique
    (PERT) (p. 56)
Project organization (p. 52)
Slack time (p. 65)
Total slack (p. 66)
Work breakdown structure (WBS) (p. 54)

Ethical Dilemma

One example of a mismanaged project is Amman's Bus Rapid Transit (BRT) system. BRT was considered to be a revolutionary project which would develop the transportation infrastructure in Amman and take it into the 21st century. The estimated project cost of US$1.2 billion made many skeptical about its feasibility, but the Greater Municipality of Amman estimated that the project would save Jordan's economy US$800 million a year, in the form of decreased congestion on the streets of the capital, and therefore fewer delays due to traffic. The project was started with great enthusiasm, but people were soon complaining about greater traffic congestion during the works' period, and financial analysts began to revisit the feasibility of the project. This led to the abandonment of the project in 2011 until further notice.

Read about this project (or another of your choice) and explain why it faced such problems. How and why do project managers allow such massive endeavors to fall into such a state? What do you think are the causes?

Discussion Questions

1. Explain the purpose of project organization.
2. What are the three phases involved in the management of a large project?
3. Define *work breakdown structure*. How is it used?
4. What is the use of Gantt charts in project management?
5. What is the difference between an activity-on-arrow (AOA) network and an activity-on-node (AON) network? Which is primarily used in this chapter?
6. What is the significance of the critical path?
7. What would a project manager have to do to crash an activity?
8. Describe how expected activity times and variances can be computed in a PERT network.
9. Define *early start*, *early finish*, *late start*, and *late finish* times.
10. Students are sometimes confused by the concept of critical path, and want to believe that it is the *shortest* path through a network. Convincingly explain why this is not so.
11. What are dummy activities? Why are they used in activity-on-arrow (AOA) project networks?
12. Would a project manager ever consider crashing a noncritical activity in a project network? Explain convincingly.
13. Describe the meaning of slack, and discuss how it can be determined.
14. How can we determine the probability that a project will be completed by a certain date? What assumptions are made in this computation?

Using Software to Solve Project Management Problems

In addition to the Microsoft Project software just illustrated, both Excel OM and POM for Windows are available to readers of this text as project management tools.

✗ Using Excel OM
Excel OM has a Project Scheduling module. Program 3.4 uses the data from the Cairo Finest Paper Mills Ltd. example in this chapter (see Examples 4 and 5). The PERT/CPM analysis also handles activities with three time estimates.

P Using POM for Windows
POM for Window's Project Scheduling module can also find the expected project completion time for a CPM and PERT network with either one or three time estimates. POM for Windows also performs project crashing. For further details refer to Appendix IV.

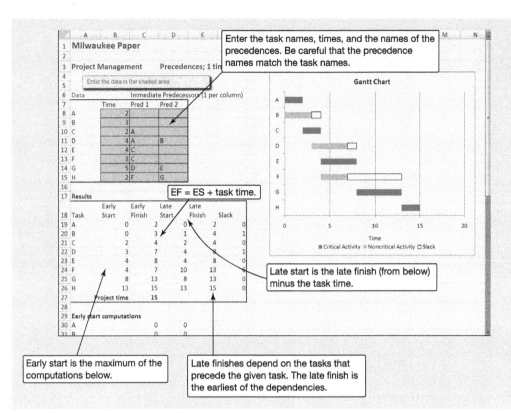

◀ **PROGRAM 3.4**
Excel OM's Use of Cairo Finest Paper Mills' Data from Examples 4 and 5

Solved Problems Virtual Office Hours help is available at MyOMLab.

▼ **SOLVED PROBLEM 3.1**

Construct an AON network based on the following:

Activity	Immediate Predecessor(s)
A	—
B	—
C	—
D	A, B
E	C

▼ **SOLUTION**

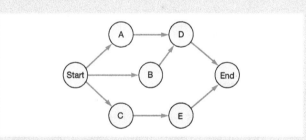

▼ **SOLVED PROBLEM 3.2**

Insert a dummy activity and event to correct the following AOA network:

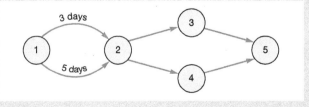

▼ **SOLUTION**

Since we cannot have two activities starting and ending at the same node, we add the following dummy activity and dummy event to obtain the correct AOA network:

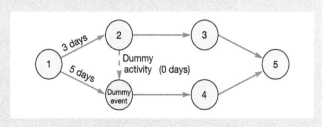

▼ SOLVED PROBLEM 3.3

Calculate the critical path, project completion time T, and project variance based on the following AON network information:

Activity	Time	Variance	ES	EF	LS	LF	Slack
A	2	$\frac{2}{6}$	0	2	0	2	0
B	3	$\frac{2}{6}$	0	3	1	4	1
C	2	$\frac{4}{6}$	2	4	2	4	0
D	4	$\frac{4}{6}$	3	7	4	8	1
E	4	$\frac{2}{6}$	4	8	4	8	0
F	3	$\frac{1}{6}$	4	7	10	13	6
G	5	$\frac{1}{6}$	8	13	8	13	0

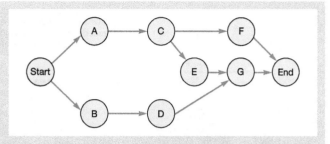

▼ SOLUTION

We conclude that the critical path is Start-A-C-E-G-End:

$$\text{Total project time} = T = 2 + 2 + 4 + 5 = 13$$

And

$$\sigma_p^2 = \Sigma \text{ variances on the critical path} = \frac{2}{6} + \frac{4}{6} + \frac{2}{6} + \frac{1}{6} = \frac{9}{6} = 1.5$$

▼ SOLVED PROBLEM 3.4

The following information has been computed from a project:

$$\text{Expected total project time} = T = 62 \text{ weeks}$$

$$\text{Project variance } (\sigma_p^2) = 81$$

What is the probability that the project will be completed 18 weeks *before* its expected completion date?

▼ SOLUTION

The desired completion date is 18 weeks before the expected completion date, 62 weeks. The desired completion date is 44 (or $62 - 18$) weeks:

$$\sigma_p = \sqrt{\text{Project variance}}$$

$$Z = \frac{\text{Due date} - \text{Expected completion date}}{\sigma_p}$$

$$= \frac{44 - 62}{9} = \frac{-18}{9} = -2.0$$

The normal curve appears as follows:

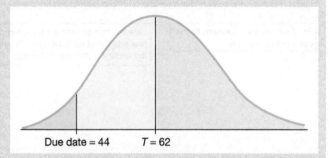

Due date = 44 $T = 62$

Because the normal curve is symmetrical and table values are calculated for positive values of Z, the area desired is equal to $1 - $ (table value). For $Z = +2.0$ the area from the table is 0.97725. Thus, the area corresponding to a Z value of -2.0 is 0.02275 (or $1 - 0.97725$). Hence, the probability of completing the project 18 weeks before the expected completion date is approximately 0.023, or 2.3%.

▼ SOLVED PROBLEM 3.5

Determine the least cost of reducing the project completion date by 3 months based on the following information:

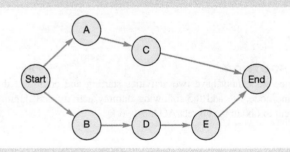

Activity	Normal Time (months)	Crash Time (months)	Normal Cost	Crash Cost
A	6	4	US$2,000	US$2,400
B	7	5	3,000	3,500
C	7	6	1,000	1,300
D	6	4	2,000	2,600
E	9	8	8,800	9,000

▼ SOLUTION

The first step in this problem is to compute ES, EF, LS, LF, and slack for each activity:

Activity	ES	EF	LS	LF	Slack
A	0	6	9	15	9
B	0	7	0	7	0
C	6	13	15	22	9
D	7	13	7	13	0
E	13	22	13	22	0

The critical path consists of activities B, D, and E.

Next, crash cost/month must be computed for each activity:

Activity	Normal Time – Crash Time	Crash Cost – Normal Cost	Crash Cost/Month	Critical Path?
A	2	US$400	US$200/month	No
B	2	500	250/month	Yes
C	1	300	300/month	No
D	2	600	300/month	Yes
E	1	200	200/month	Yes

Finally, we will select that activity on the critical path with the smallest crash cost/month. This is activity E. Thus, we can reduce

the total project completion date by 1 month for an additional cost of US$200. We still need to reduce the project completion date by 2 more months. This reduction can be achieved at least cost along the critical path by reducing activity B by 2 months for an additional cost of US$500. Neither reduction has an effect on noncritical activities. This solution is summarized in the following table:

Activity	Months Reduced	Cost
E	1	US$200
B	2	500
		Total: US$700

Problems*

• **3.1** The work breakdown structure (WBS) for building a house (levels 1 and 2) is shown below:

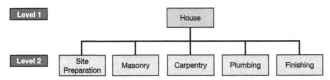

a) Add two level-3 activities to each of the level-2 activities to provide more detail to the WBS.
b) Select one of your level-3 activities and add two level-4 activities below it.

•• **3.2** Suhail Aljasser has decided to run for a seat in the National Assembly of Kuwait. He views his 8-month campaign for office as a major project and wishes to create a WBS to help control the detailed scheduling. So far, he has developed the following pieces of the WBS:

Level	Level ID No.	Activity
1	1.0	Develop political campaign
2	1.1	Fundraising plan
3	1.11	_____
3	1.12	_____
3	1.13	_____
2	1.2	Develop a position on major issues
3	1.21	_____
3	1.22	_____
3	1.23	_____
2	1.3	Staffing for campaign
3	1.31	_____
3	1.32	_____
3	1.33	_____
3	1.34	_____
2	1.4	Paperwork compliance for candidacy
3	1.41	_____
3	1.42	_____
2	1.5	Ethical plan/issues
3	1.51	_____

Help Mr. Aljasser by providing details where the blank lines appear. Are there any other major (level-2) activities to create? If so, add an ID no. 1.6 and insert them.

• **3.3** Draw the activity-on-node (AON) project network associated with the following activities for Firas Zain's consulting company project. How long should it take Firas and his team to complete this project? What are the critical path activities?

Activity	Immediate Predecessor(s)	Time (days)
A	—	3
B	A	4
C	A	6
D	B	6
E	B	4
F	C	4
G	D	6
H	E, F	8

Px

• **3.4** Given the activities whose sequence is described by the following table, draw the appropriate activity-on-arrow (AOA) network diagram.
a) Which activities are on the critical path?
b) What is the length of the critical path?

Activity	Immediate Predecessor(s)	Time (days)
A	—	5
B	A	2
C	A	4
D	B	5
E	B	5
F	C	5
G	E, F	2
H	D	3
I	G, H	5

Px

• **3.5** Using AOA, diagram the network described below for Tamer Omar's construction project. Calculate its critical path. How long is the minimum duration of this network?

*Note: **Px** means the problem may be solved with POM for Windows and/or Excel OM.

Activity	Nodes	Time (weeks)	Activity	Nodes	Time (weeks)
J	1–2	10	N	3–4	2
K	1–3	8	O	4–5	7
L	2–4	6	P	3–5	5
M	2–3	3			

•• **3.6** Murjana Al-Saleemi is developing a program in leadership training for middle-level managers. Murjana has listed a number of activities that must be completed before a training program of this nature could be conducted. The activities, immediate predecessors, and times appear in the accompanying table:

Activity	Immediate Predecessor(s)	Time (days)
A	—	2
B	—	5
C	—	1
D	B	10
E	A, D	3
F	C	6
G	E, F	8

a) Develop an AON network for this problem.
b) What is the critical path?
c) What is the total project completion time?
d) What is the slack time for each individual activity? **Px**

•• **3.7** The activities needed to build an experimental chemical contaminant tracking machine at Riyadh Industries are listed in the following table. Construct an AON network for these activities.

Activity	Immediate Predecessor(s)	Activity	Immediate Predecessor(s)
A	—	E	B
B	—	F	B
C	A	G	C, E
D	A	H	D, F

• **3.8** Riyadh Industries (see Problem 3.7) was able to determine the activity times for constructing a chemical contaminant tracking machine. Riyadh Industries would like to determine ES, EF, LS, LF, and slack for each activity. The total project completion time and the critical path should also be determined. Here are the activity times:

Activity	Time (weeks)	Activity	Time (weeks)
A	6	E	4
B	7	F	6
C	3	G	10
D	2	H	7

Px

•• **3.9** Mosul Carpet installs carpet in commercial offices. Muna has been very concerned with the amount of time it took to complete several recent jobs. Some of her workers are very unreliable. A list of activities and their optimistic completion time, the most likely completion time, and the pessimistic completion time (all in days) for a new contract are given in the following table:

Activity	Time (days) a	m	b	Immediate Predecessor(s)
A	3	6	8	—
B	2	4	4	—
C	1	2	3	—
D	6	7	8	C
E	2	4	6	B, D
F	6	10	14	A, E
G	1	2	4	A, E
H	3	6	9	F
I	10	11	12	G
J	14	16	20	C
K	2	8	10	H, I

a) Determine the expected completion time and variance for each activity.
b) Determine the total project completion time and the critical path for the project.
c) Determine ES, EF, LS, LF, and slack for each activity.
d) What is the probability that Mosul Carpet will finish the project in 40 days or less? **Px**

••• **3.10** Sameer Ghanama, president of Ghanama Construction, has developed the tasks, durations, and predecessor relationships in the following table for building new motels. Draw the AON network and answer the questions that follow.

Activity	Immediate Predecessor(s)	Time Estimates (in weeks) Optimistic	Most Likely	Pessimistic
A	—	4	8	10
B	A	2	8	24
C	A	8	12	16
D	A	4	6	10
E	B	1	2	3
F	E, C	6	8	20
G	E, C	2	3	4
H	F	2	2	2
I	F	6	6	6
J	D, G, H	4	6	12
K	I, J	2	2	3

a) What is the expected (estimated) time for activity C?
b) What is the variance for activity C?
c) Based on the calculation of estimated times, what is the critical path?
d) What is the estimated time of the critical path?
e) What is the activity variance along the critical path?
f) What is the probability of completion of the project before week 36? **Px**

••• **3.11** The estimated times and immediate predecessors for the activities in a project at Ahmad AlZoubi's retinal scanning company are given in the following table. Assume that the activity times are independent.

Activity	Immediate Predecessor	Time (weeks) a	m	b
A	—	9	10	11
B	—	4	10	16
C	A	9	10	11
D	B	5	8	11

a) Calculate the expected time and variance for each activity.
b) What is the expected completion time of the critical path? What is the expected completion time of the other path in the network?
c) What is the variance of the critical path? What is the variance of the other path in the network?
d) If the time to complete path A–C is normally distributed, what is the probability that this path will be finished in 22 weeks or less?
e) If the time to complete path B–D is normally distributed, what is the probability that this path will be finished in 22 weeks or less?
f) Explain why the probability that the *critical path* will be finished in 22 weeks or less is not necessarily the probability that the *project* will be finished in 22 weeks or less. **Px**

••• **3.12** Musa Oleeli Manufacturing produces custom-built pollution control devices for medium-size steel mills. The most recent project undertaken by Musa requires 14 different activities.
a) Musa's managers would like to determine the total project completion time (in days) and those activities that lie along the critical path. The appropriate data are shown in the following table.
b) What is the probability of being done in 53 days?
c) What date results in a 99 percent probability of completion?

Activity	Immediate Predecessor(s)	Optimistic Time	Most Likely Time	Pessimistic Time
A	—	4	6	7
B	—	1	2	3
C	A	6	6	6
D	A	5	8	11
E	B, C	1	9	18
F	D	2	3	6
G	D	1	7	8
H	E, F	4	4	6
I	G, H	1	6	8
J	I	2	5	7
K	I	8	9	11
L	J	2	4	6
M	K	1	2	3
N	L, M	6	8	10

Px

▶ **Refer to** MyOMLab **for additional homework problems.**

Case Studies

▶ Ojaman University: (A)*

Ojaman University is a large government university which enrolls close to 20,000 students. The university prides itself on having the best basketball team in the country, competing in the national premier league. To bolster the team's chances of reaching the elusive and long-desired number-one ranking, in 2003 the university hired the best coach in the country, Saleem Jamal.

One of Saleem's demands on joining Ojaman had been a new arena. With attendance increasing, Ojaman administrators began to face the issue head-on. After six months of research, much political arm wrestling, and some serious financial analysis, Dr. Mohammad Khaleel, president of Ojaman University, reached a decision to expand the capacity at its on-campus arena.

Adding thousands of seats, including dozens of luxury skyboxes, would not please everyone. The influential Saleem had expounded the need for a first-class arena, one with built-in dormitory rooms for his players and a palatial office appropriate for the coach of a future premier champion team. But the decision was made, and *everyone*, including the coach, would learn to live with it.

The job now was to get construction going immediately after the 2009 season ended. This would allow exactly 270 days until the 2010 season opening game. The contractor, Mustafa Arabi Contractors (Mustafa is an alumnus, of course), signed his contract. Mustafa looked at the tasks his engineers had outlined and looked President

Khaleel in the eye. "I guarantee the team will be able to take the field on schedule next year," he said with a sense of confidence. "I sure hope so," replied Khaleel. "The contract penalty of Dinar 10,000 per day for running late is nothing compared to what Coach Saleem will do to you if our opening game with the defending champions is delayed or canceled." Mustafa, sweating slightly, did not need to respond. In basketball crazy Ojaman, Mustafa Arabi Construction would be *mud* if the 270-day target was missed.

Back in his office, Mustafa again reviewed the data (see Table 3.8) and noted that optimistic time estimates can be used as crash times. He then gathered his foremen. "Folks, if we're not 75 percent sure we'll finish this arena in less than 270 days, I want this project crashed! Give me the cost figures for a target date of 250 days—also for 240 days. I want to be *early*, not just on time!"

Discussion Questions

1. Develop a network drawing for Mustafa Arabi Construction and determine the critical path. How long is the project expected to take?
2. What is the probability of finishing in 270 days?
3. If it is necessary to crash to 250 or 240 days, how would Mustafa do so, and at what costs? As noted in the case, assume that optimistic time estimates can be used as crash times.

*This integrated study runs throughout the text. Other issues facing Ojaman University's basketball expansion include (B) forecasting game attendance (Chapter 4); (C) quality of facilities (Chapter 6); (D) break-even analysis for food services (Supplement 7); (E) location of the new arena (Chapter 8); (F) inventory planning of basketball programs (Chapter 12); and (G) scheduling of campus security officers/staff for game days (Chapter 13).

▼ **TABLE 3.8**   **Ojaman University Project**

Activity	Description	Predecessor(s)	Optimistic	Most Likely	Pessimistic	Crash Cost/Day
			Time Estimates (days)			
A	Bonding, insurance, tax structuring	—	20	30	40	Dinar 1,500
B	Foundation, concrete footings for boxes	A	20	65	80	3,500
C	Upgrading skybox arena seating	A	50	60	100	4,000
D	Upgrading walkways, stairwells, elevators	C	30	50	100	1,900
E	Interior wiring, lathes	B	25	30	35	9,500
F	Inspection approvals	E	0.1	0.1	0.1	0
G	Plumbing	D, F	25	30	35	2,500
H	Painting	G	10	20	30	2,000
I	Hardware/AC/metal workings	H	20	25	60	2,000
J	Tile/carpet/windows	H	8	10	12	6,000
K	Inspection	J	0.1	0.1	0.1	0
L	Final detail work/cleanup	I, K	20	25	60	4,500

► **Project Management at Arnold Palmer Hospital**   **Video Case**

The equivalent of a new kindergarten class is born every day at Arnold Palmer Hospital in Orlando, Florida. With more than 12,300 births in 2005 in a hospital that was designed in 1989 for a capacity of 6,500 births a year, the newborn intensive care unit was stretched to the limit. Moreover, with continuing strong population growth in central Florida, the hospital was often full. It was clear that new facilities were needed. After much analysis, forecasting, and discussion, the management team decided to build a new 273-bed building across the street from the existing hospital. But the facility had to be built in accordance with the hospital's Guiding Principles and its uniqueness as a health center dedicated to the specialized needs of women and infants. Those Guiding Principles are: *family-centered focus; a healing environment where privacy and dignity are respected; sanctuary of caring that includes warm, serene surroundings with natural lighting; sincere and dedicated staff providing the highest quality care; and patient-centered flow and function.*

The vice president of business development, Karl Hodges, wanted a hospital that was designed from the inside out by the people who understood the Guiding Principles, who knew most about the current system, and who were going to use the new system, namely, the doctors and nurses. Hodges and his staff spent 13 months discussing expansion needs with this group, as well as with patients and the community before developing a proposal for the new facility on December 17, 2001. An administrative team created 35 user groups, which held over 1,000 planning meetings (lasting from 45 minutes to a whole day). They even created a 'Supreme Court' to deal with conflicting views on the multifaceted issues facing the new hospital.

Funding and regulatory issues added substantial complexity to this major expansion, and Hodges was very concerned that the project stayed on time and within budget. Tom Hyatt, director of facility development, was given the task of onsite manager of the

▼ **TABLE 3.9**   **Expansion Planning and Arnold Palmer Hospital Construction Activities and Times**[a]

Activity	Scheduled Time	Precedence Activity(ies)
1. Proposal and review	1 month	—
2. Establish master schedule	2 weeks	1
3. Architect selection process	5 weeks	1
4. Survey whole campus and its needs	1 month	1
5. Conceptual architect's plans	6 weeks	3
6. Cost estimating	2 months	2, 4, 5
7. Deliver plans to board for consideration/decision	1 month	6
8. Surveys/regulatory review	6 weeks	6
9. Construction manager selection	9 weeks	6
10. State review of need for more hospital beds ('Certificate of Need')	3.5 months	7, 8
11. Design drawings	4 months	10
12. Construction documents	5 months	9, 11
13. Site preparation/demolish existing building	9 weeks	11
14. Construction start/building pad	2 months	12, 13
15. Relocate utilities	6 weeks	12
16. Deep foundations	2 months	14
17. Building structure in place	9 months	16
18. Exterior skin/roofing	4 months	17
19. Interior buildout	12 months	17
20. Building inspections	5 weeks	15, 19
21. Occupancy	1 month	20

[a]This list of activities is abbreviated for purposes of this case study. For simplification, assume each week = 0.25 months (i.e. 2 weeks = 0.5 month, 6 weeks = 1.5 months, etc.).

US$100 million project, in addition to overseeing ongoing renovations, expansions, and other projects. The activities in the multiyear project for the new building at Arnold Palmer are shown in Table 3.7.

Discussion Questions*

1. Develop the network for planning and construction of the new hospital at Arnold Palmer.
2. What is the critical path and how long is the project expected to take?

3. Why is the construction of this 11-story building any more complex than construction of an equivalent office building?
4. What percentage of the whole project duration was spent in planning that occurred prior to the proposal and reviews? Prior to the actual building construction? Why?

*You may wish to view the video accompanying this case before addressing these questions.

▶ **Additional Case Study:** Visit MyOMLab for this free case study:

Shale Oil Company: This oil refinery must shut down for maintenance of a major piece of equipment.

Chapter 3 *Rapid* Review

Main Heading	Review Material	
THE IMPORTANCE OF PROJECT MANAGEMENT (p. 52)	The management of projects involves three phases: 1. **Planning**— This phase includes goal setting, defining the project, and team organization. 2. **Scheduling**— This phase relates people, money, and supplies to specific activities and relates activities to each other. 3. **Controlling**— Here the firm monitors resources, costs, quality, and budgets. It also revises or changes plans and shifts resources to meet time and cost demands.	
PROJECT PLANNING (pp. 52–54)	Projects can be defined as a series of related tasks directed toward a major output. ■ **Project organization**—An organization formed to ensure that programs (projects) receive the proper management and attention. ■ **Work breakdown structure (WBS)**—Defines a project by dividing it into more and more detailed components.	Problem 3.1
PROJECT SCHEDULING (pp. 54–55)	■ **Gantt charts**—Planning charts used to schedule resources and allocate time. Project scheduling serves several purposes: 1. It shows the relationship of each activity to others and to the whole project. 2. It identifies the precedence relationships among activities. 3. It encourages the setting of realistic time and cost estimates for each activity. 4. It helps make better use of people, money, and material resources by identifying critical bottlenecks in the project.	
PROJECT CONTROLLING (pp. 56)	Computerized programs produce a broad variety of PERT/CPM reports, including: (1) detailed cost breakdowns for each task; (2) total program labor curves; (3) cost distribution tables; (4) functional cost and hour summaries; (5) raw material and expenditure forecasts; (6) variance reports; (7) time analysis reports; (8) work status reports.	**VIDEO 3.1** Project Management at Arnold Palmer Hospital
PROJECT MANAGEMENT TECHNIQUES: PERT AND CPM (pp. 56–60)	■ **Program evaluation and review technique (PERT)**—A project management technique that employs three time estimates for each activity. ■ **Critical path method (CPM)**—A project management technique that uses only one estimate per activity. ■ **Critical path**—The computed *longest* time path(s) through a network. PERT and CPM both follow six basic steps. The activities on the critical path will delay the entire project if they are not completed on time. ■ **Activity-on-node (AON)**—A network diagram in which nodes designate activities. ■ **Activity-on-arrow (AOA)**—A network diagram in which arrows designate activities. In an AOA network, the nodes represent the starting and finishing times of an activity and are also called *events*. ■ **Dummy activity**—An activity having no time that is inserted into a network to maintain the logic of the network. A dummy ending activity can be added to the end of an AON diagram for a project that has multiple ending activities.	Problems: 3.3–3.7 Virtual Office Hours for Solved Problems: 3.1, 3.2
DETERMINING THE PROJECT SCHEDULE (pp. 60–66)	■ **Critical path analysis**—A process that helps determine a project schedule. To find the critical path, we calculate two distinct starting and ending times for each activity: • *Earliest start (ES)* = Earliest time at which an activity can start, assuming that all predecessors have been completed • *Earliest finish (EF)* = Earliest time at which an activity can be finished • *Latest start (LS)* = Latest time at which an activity can start, without delaying the completion time of the entire project • *Latest finish (LF)* = Latest time by which an activity has to finish so as to not delay the completion time of the entire project. ■ **Forward pass**—A process that identifies all the early start and early finish times. $$ES = \text{Max \{EF of all immediate predecessors\}} \qquad (3\text{-}1)$$ $$EF = ES + \text{Activity time} \qquad (3\text{-}2)$$ ■ **Backward pass**—A process that identifies all the late start and late finish times. $$LF = \text{Min \{LS of all immediate following activities\}} \qquad (3\text{-}3)$$ $$LS = LF - \text{Activity time} \qquad (3\text{-}4)$$	Problems: 3.8–10, 3.12 Virtual Office Hours for Solved Problem: 3.3

Main Heading	Review Material	MyOMLab
	■ **Slack time**—Free time for an activity. $$\text{Slack} = LS - ES \quad \text{or} \quad \text{Slack} = LF - EF \qquad (3\text{-}5)$$ The activities with zero slack are called *critical activities* and are said to be on the critical path. The critical path is a continuous path through the project network that starts at the first activity in the project, terminates at the last activity in the project, and includes only critical activities.	
VARIABILITY IN ACTIVITY TIMES (pp. 66–72)	■ **Optimistic time** (a)—The 'best' activity completion time that could be obtained in a PERT network. ■ **Pessimistic time** (b)—The 'worst' activity time that could be expected in a PERT network. ■ **Most likely time** (m)—The most probable time to complete an activity in a PERT network. When using PERT, we often assume that activity time estimates follow the beta distribution. $$\text{Expected activity time } t = (a + 4m + b) \div 6 \qquad (3\text{-}6)$$ $$\text{Variance of Activity Completion Time} = [(b - a) \div 6]^2 \qquad (3\text{-}7)$$ $$\sigma_p^2 = \text{Project variance} = \Sigma(\text{variances of activities on critical path}) \qquad (3\text{-}8)$$ $$Z = (\text{Due date} - \text{expected date of completion}) \div \sigma_p \qquad (3\text{-}9)$$ $$\text{Due date} = \text{Expected completion time} + (Z \times \sigma_p) \qquad (3\text{-}10)$$	Problems: 3.9, 3.11
COST–TIME TRADE-OFFS AND PROJECT CRASHING (pp. 72–74)	■ **Crashing**—Shortening activity time in a network to reduce time on the critical path so total completion time is reduced. $$\text{Crash cost per period} = \frac{(\text{Crash cost} - \text{Normal cost})}{(\text{Normal time} - \text{Crash time})} \qquad (3\text{-}11)$$	Virtual Office Hours for Solved Problem: 3.7
A CRITIQUE OF PERT AND CPM (pp. 74–75)	As with every technique for problem solving, PERT and CPM have a number of advantages as well as several limitations.	
USING MICROSOFT® PROJECT TO MANAGE PROJECTS (pp. 75–77)	Microsoft Project, the most popular example of specialized project management software, is extremely useful in drawing project networks, identifying the project schedule, and managing project costs and other resources.	

Self-Test

■ **Before taking the self-test,** refer to the learning objectives listed at the beginning of the chapter and the key terms listed at the end of the chapter.

LO1. Which of the following statements regarding Gantt charts is true?
   a) Gantt charts give a timeline and precedence relationships for each activity of a project.
   b) Gantt charts use the four standard spines: Methods, Materials, Manpower, and Machinery.
   c) Gantt charts are visual devices that show the duration of activities in a project.
   d) Gantt charts are expensive.
   e) All of the above are true.

LO2. Which of the following statements about AOA and AON networks is true?
   a) In AOA, arrows represent activities.
   b) In AON, nodes represent activities.
   c) Activities consume time and resources.
   d) Nodes are also called *events* in AOA.
   e) All of the above are true.

LO3. Slack time equals:
   a) $ES + t$
   b) $LS - ES$
   c) zero
   d) $EF - ES$.

LO4. The critical path of a network is the:
   a) shortest-time path through the network
   b) path with the fewest activities
   c) path with the most activities
   d) longest time path through the network.

LO5. PERT analysis computes the variance of the total project completion time as:
   a) the sum of the variances of all activities in the project
   b) the sum of the variances of all activities on the critical path
   c) the sum of the variances of all activities not on the critical path
   d) the variance of the final activity of the project.

LO6. The crash cost per period:
   a) is the difference in costs divided by the difference in times (crash and normal)
   b) is considered to be linear in the range between normal and crash
   c) needs to be determined so that the smallest cost values on the critical path can be considered for time reduction first
   d) is all of the above.

Answers: LO1. c; LO2. e; LO3. b; LO4. d; LO5. b; LO6. d.

4 Forecasting Demand

FORECASTING PROVIDES A COMPETITIVE ADVANTAGE FOR MARAH LAND

There are few amusement parks in the Arab world that provide entertainment for all family members to the extent that Marah Land parks do. The variety of games and theme parks spread all over the Middle East more than caters for every family member's taste.

Marah Land is owned by the Kuwait Commercial Markets Complex Company (KCMCC), which owns and operates more than 40 projects across the Middle East. Marah Land's portfolio is based in Kuwait, Bahrain, and Oman, and is expanding to other countries in the Arab world.

At Marah Land, revenues are all about people—how many visit the parks and how they spend money while there. The management looks closely at the daily number of visitors and their expenditure, and compares them to forecast reports made for the same time periods (whether daily or monthly). The *forecast* of every day's attendance at the different parks and games (such as the Ring of Fire, Beyond Time, Safari, Boating, and Marah Shot) and the *actual* attendance are compared and any deviations observed are scrutinized to find reasons and explanations.

The employees responsible for forecasting attendance not only provide daily predictions but also weekly, monthly, and annual forecasts to other departments in Marah Land and KCMCC. Such forecasts help the management, maintenance, operations, finance, and park scheduling and allow the company to be more efficient. Forecasters use a group of mathematical and judgmental models that aim to improve the accuracy of their estimates.

The forecasts go beyond mere calculation of attendance and expenditure, providing support statistics on the visitors' background, the size of their families, and the times spent queuing. The main

Marah Land became a popular destination for many Kuwaiti families due to its cheerful, safe environment and variety of activities for all members of the family.

Marah Land strives to have the latest games that will attract the younger generations.

method of data collection is direct observation and surveys. The data collected are analyzed for clear presentation to the decision makers. With the number of visiting families exceeding 800,000 annually in each of the Marah Land parks across the region, the task is not an easy one.

Such forecasts help Marah Land understand the expected demand for its services and products, and also help it design specific packages to people with different time pressures, travel destinations, family needs, and backgrounds.

A major use of the forecasting is capacity planning, which helps in calculating the number of working hours needed at different times, such as weekends or certain seasons. This helps to optimize the number of hours needed to operate and save unnecessary expenditure. It also helps in deciding the amount of food and beverages needed and also in deciding employees' working shifts.

At Marah Land, forecasting is a key driver in the company's success and competitive advantage.

Source: **http://www.kcmcc.com.kw**

Chapter 4 Learning Objectives

AUTHOR COMMENT
An increasingly complex world economy makes forecasting challenging.

WHAT IS FORECASTING?

In this chapter, we examine different types of forecasts and present a variety of forecasting models. Our purpose is to show that there are many ways for managers to forecast. We also provide an overview of business sales forecasting and describe how to prepare, monitor, and judge the accuracy of a forecast. Good forecasts are an *essential* part of efficient service and manufacturing operations.

Forecasting

The art and science of predicting future events.

Forecasting is the art and science of predicting future events. Forecasting may involve taking historical data and projecting them into the future with some sort of mathematical model. It may also be subjective or intuitive prediction. Or it may involve a combination of these—that is, a mathematical model adjusted by a manager's judgment based on previous experience and knowledge of the company, the industry, and the global trends.

As we introduce different forecasting techniques in this chapter, you will see that there is no one best method of forecasting and most of the time companies use a combination of forecasting methods. In addition, you will see that there are limits as to what can be expected from forecasts. They are rarely, if ever, perfect. They are also costly and time consuming to prepare and monitor. Yet the benefits of forecasting outweigh the drawbacks and make it worthwhile to invest in. Very few businesses can operate efficiently without some degree of forecasting.

Forecasting Time Horizons

LO1: Understand the three time horizons and which models apply for each

A forecast is usually classified by the *future time horizon* that it covers. Time horizons fall into three categories.

1. *Short-range forecast:* This forecast has a time span of up to 1 year but is generally less than 3 months. It is used for planning purchasing, job scheduling, workforce levels, job assignments, and production levels. The short-range forecast is characterized by being more accurate, dealing with more specific issues, and employing different methodologies than longer-term forecasting (such as moving averages, exponential smoothing, and trend extrapolation).
2. *Medium-range forecast:* A medium-range, or intermediate, forecast generally spans from 3 months to 3 years. It is useful in sales planning, production planning and budgeting, cash budgeting, and analysis of various operating plans. It is usually more accurate than long-term forecasting but less accurate than short-term forecasting.
3. *Long-range forecast:* Generally 3 years or more in time span, long-range forecasts are used in planning for new products, capital expenditures, facility location or expansion, and research and development. It is less accurate than the other two time horizons due to the more comprehensive issues it tries to forecast, and employs less quantitative methods in forecasting.

The Influence of Product Life Cycle

Another factor to consider when developing sales forecasts, especially longer ones, is product life cycle. Products, and even services, do not sell at a constant level throughout their lives. Most successful products pass through four stages: (1) introduction; (2) growth; (3) maturity; (4) decline.

Products in the first two stages of the life cycle (such as virtual reality) need longer forecasts than those in the maturity and decline stages (such as skateboards). Forecasts that reflect life cycle are useful in projecting different staffing levels, inventory levels, and factory capacity as the product passes from the first to the last stage. The challenge of introducing new products is treated in more detail in Chapter 5.

Types of Forecasts

Organizations use three major types of forecasts in planning future operations.

1. **Economic forecasts** address the business cycle by predicting inflation rates, money supplies, housing starts, and other planning indicators.
2. **Technological forecasts** are concerned with rates of technological progress, which can result in the birth of exciting new products, requiring new plants and equipment.
3. **Demand forecasts** are projections of demand for a company's products or services. These forecasts, also called *sales forecasts*, drive a company's production, capacity, and scheduling systems and serve as inputs to financial, marketing, and personnel planning.

Economic and technological forecasting are specialized techniques that may fall outside the role of the operations manager. The emphasis in this book will therefore be on demand forecasting.

THE STRATEGIC IMPORTANCE OF FORECASTING

Good forecasts are of critical importance in all aspects of a business: *The forecast is the only estimate of demand until actual demand becomes known.* Forecasts of demand therefore drive decisions in many areas. Let's look at the impact of product demand forecasting on three activities: (1) human resources; (2) capacity; (3) supply-chain management.

Human Resources

Hiring, training, and laying off workers all depend on anticipated demand. If the human resources department must hire additional workers without warning, the amount of training declines and the quality of the workforce suffers.

Capacity

When capacity is inadequate, the resulting shortages can lead to a loss of customers and market share. This is exactly what happened to Bloomsbury Qatar Foundation Publishing (BQFP) when it underestimated the huge demand for its new Arabic children's books. The books were sold out quickly, leaving some customers disappointed. On the other hand, when demand is overestimated, resulting in excess capacity, costs can skyrocket.

Economic forecasts
Planning indicators that are valuable in helping organizations prepare medium- to long-range forecasts.

Technological forecasts
Long-term forecasts concerned with the rates of technological progress.

Demand forecasts
Projections of a company's sales for each time period in the planning horizon.

VIDEO 4.1
Forecasting at Hard Rock Cafe

Hamda and Fisaikra, a Middle Eastern children's book with a story similar to *Cinderella*, sold out very quickly at Waterstones book store in Harrods, London. Bloomsbury Qatar Foundation Publishing didn't forecast such a huge demand within the first 2 weeks. The publishing house has since increased production of the Arabic children's book.

Supply-Chain Management

Good supplier relations and the ensuing price advantages for materials and parts depend on accurate forecasts. In the global marketplace, manufacturers seeking components for their products have a variety of resources to select from and to combine, in some cases by the hundreds; using forecasts to coordinate the different suppliers and the different price ranges is critical.

SEVEN STEPS IN THE FORECASTING SYSTEM

Forecasting follows seven basic steps. We use Marah Land, the focus of this chapter's *Company Profile*, as an example of each step.

1. *Determine the use of the forecast:* Marah Land uses park attendance forecasts to drive decisions about staffing, opening times, ride availability, and food supplies.
2. *Select the items to be forecasted:* For Marah Land, there are five locations across the Middle East. A forecast of daily attendance at each location is the main number that determines labor, maintenance, and scheduling.
3. *Determine the time horizon of the forecast:* Is it short, medium, or long term? Marah Land develops daily, weekly, monthly, annual, and 5-year forecasts.
4. *Select the forecasting model(s):* Marah Land uses a variety of statistical models that we shall discuss, including moving averages, econometrics, and regression analysis. It also employs judgmental, or non quantitative, models.
5. *Gather the data needed to make the forecast:* Marah Land has a forecasting team that works on collecting the necessary information to estimate future demand, the popularity of its games, the latest in the world of entertainment, and the new trends in the markets.
6. *Make the forecast.*
7. *Validate and implement the results:* At Marah Land, forecasts are reviewed daily to make sure they are valid. Error measures are applied; then the forecasts are used to schedule and plan daily shifts.

These seven steps present a systematic way of initiating, designing, and implementing a forecasting system. When the system is to be used to generate forecasts regularly over time, data must be routinely collected. Then actual computations are usually made by computer.

Regardless of the system that firms like Marah Land use, each company faces several realities:

Quantitative forecasts

Forecasts that employ mathematical modeling to forecast demand.

Qualitative forecasts

Forecasts that incorporate such factors as the decision maker's intuition, emotions, personal experiences, and value system.

- Forecasts are seldom perfect. This means that outside factors that we cannot predict or control often impact the forecast. Companies need to allow for this reality.
- Most forecasting techniques assume that there is some underlying stability in the system. Consequently, some firms automate their predictions using computerized forecasting software, then closely monitor only the product items whose demand is erratic.
- Both product family and aggregated forecasts are more accurate than individual product forecasts. Marah Land, for example, aggregates daily attendance forecasts of each park. This approach helps balance the over- and underpredictions of each of the five locations.

> **AUTHOR COMMENT**
> Forecasting is part science and part art.

FORECASTING APPROACHES

There are two general approaches to forecasting. One is quantitative analysis; the other is a qualitative approach. **Quantitative forecasts** use a variety of mathematical models that rely on historical data and/or associative variables to forecast demand. Subjective or **qualitative forecasts** incorporate such factors as the decision maker's intuition, emotions, personal experiences, and value system in reaching a forecast. Some firms use one approach and some use the other. In practice, a combination of the two is usually most effective.

Jury of executive opinion

A forecasting technique that uses the opinion of a small group of high-level managers to form a group estimate of demand.

Overview of Qualitative Methods

In this section, we consider four different *qualitative* forecasting techniques.

LO2: Explain when to use each of the four qualitative models

1. **Jury of executive opinion**: Under this method, the opinions of a group of high-level experts or managers, often in combination with statistical models, are pooled to arrive at a group estimate of demand.

2. **Delphi method**: There are three different types of participants in the Delphi method: decision makers, staff personnel, and respondents. Decision makers usually consist of a group of five to ten experts who will be making the actual forecast. Staff personnel assist decision makers by preparing, distributing, collecting, and summarizing a series of questionnaires and survey results. The respondents are a group of people, often located in different places, whose judgments are valued. This group provides inputs to the decision makers before the forecast is made.

3. **Sales force composite**: In this approach, each salesperson estimates what sales will be in his or her region. These forecasts are then reviewed to ensure that they are realistic. Then they are combined at the district and national levels to reach an overall forecast. A variation of this approach occurs at Lexus-Arab world, where, every quarter, Lexus dealers have a 'make meeting.' At this meeting, the dealers talk about what is selling, in what colors, and with what options, so the factory knows what to build.

4. **Consumer market survey**: This method solicits input from customers or potential customers regarding future purchasing plans. It can help not only in preparing a forecast but also in improving product design and planning for new products.

The consumer market survey and sales force composite methods can, however, suffer from overly optimistic forecasts that arise from customer input.

Delphi method
A forecasting technique using a group process that allows experts to make forecasts.

Sales force composite
A forecasting technique based on salespersons' estimates of expected sales.

Consumer market survey
A forecasting method that solicits input from customers or potential customers regarding future purchasing plans.

Overview of Quantitative Methods

Five quantitative forecasting methods, all of which use historical data, are described in this chapter. They fall into two categories:

1. Naive approach
2. Moving averages   } time-series models
3. Exponential smoothing
4. Trend projection
5. Linear regression   } associative model

Time-Series Models   **Time-series** models predict on the assumption that the future is derived from the past. In other words, they look at what has happened over a period of time and use a series of past data to make a forecast.

Associative Models   Associative models, such as linear regression, incorporate the variables or factors that might influence the quantity being forecast. For example, an associative model for baby diaper sales might use factors such as birth rate, advertising budget, and competitors' prices.

Time series
A forecasting technique that uses a series of past data points to make a forecast.

TIME-SERIES FORECASTING

A time series is based on a sequence of evenly spaced (weekly, monthly, quarterly, and so on) data points. Forecasting time-series data implies that future values are predicted *only* from past values and that other variables, no matter how potentially valuable, are ignored.

AUTHOR COMMENT
Here is the essence of this chapter. We now show you a wide variety of models that use time-series data.

Decomposition of a Time Series

Analyzing time series means breaking down past data into components and then projecting them forward. A time series has four components:

1. *Trend* is the gradual upward or downward movement of the data over time. Changes in income, population, age distribution, or cultural views may account for movement in trend.
2. *Seasonality* is a data pattern that repeats itself after a period of days, weeks, months, or quarters. There are six common seasonality patterns:

Period of Pattern	'Season' Length	Number of 'Seasons' in Pattern
Week	Day	7
Month	Week	4–$4\frac{1}{2}$
Month	Day	28–31
Year	Quarter	4
Year	Month	12
Year	Week	52

◄ **TABLE 4.1**
The six common seasonality patterns

AUTHOR COMMENT
The peak 'seasons' for coffee shops in the Arab world are the Champions League finals, the World Cup, and the weekends.

▶ **FIGURE 4.1**
Demand Charted over 4 Years with a Growth Trend and Seasonality Indicated

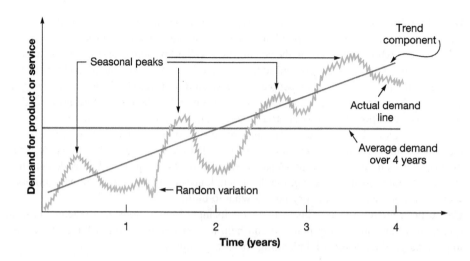

▶ **FIGURE 4.1**
Demand Charted over 4 Years with a Growth Trend and Seasonality Indicated

AUTHOR COMMENT
Forecasting is easy when demand is stable. But with trend, seasonality, and cycles considered, the job is a lot more interesting.

Restaurants and barber shops, for example, experience weekly seasons, with Friday being the peak of business. See the *OM in Action* box 'Forecasting at Zooka.' In addition, soda distributors forecast yearly patterns with monthly seasons, in particular the months of summer (June, July, August).

3. *Cycles* are patterns in the data that occur every several years. They are usually tied into the business cycle and are of major importance in short-term business analysis and planning. Predicting business cycles is difficult because they may be affected by political events or by international turmoil.

4. *Random variations* are irregularities in the data caused by chance and unusual situations. They follow no discernible pattern, so they cannot be predicted.

Figure 4.1 illustrates a demand over a 4-year period. It shows the average, trend, seasonal components, and random variations around the demand curve. The average demand is the sum of the demand for each period divided by the number of data periods.

Naive Approach

Naive approach
A forecasting technique which assumes that demand in the next period is equal to demand in the most recent period.

The simplest way to forecast is to assume that demand in the next period will be equal to demand in the most recent period. In other words, if sales of a product—say, Nasr automobiles—were 68 cars in January, we can forecast that February's sales will also be 68 cars. Does this make any sense? It turns out that for some product lines, this **naive approach** is the most cost-effective and efficient objective forecasting model. At least it provides a starting point against which more sophisticated models that follow can be compared.

Moving Averages

Moving average
A forecasting method that uses an average of the *n* most recent periods of data to forecast the next period.

A **moving-average** forecast uses a number of historical actual data values to generate a forecast. Moving averages are useful *if we can assume that market demands will stay fairly steady over time.* A 4-month moving average is found by simply summing the demand during the past 4 months and dividing by 4. With each passing month, the most recent month's data are added to the sum of the previous 3 months' data, and the earliest month is dropped. This practice tends to smooth out short-term irregularities in the data series.

Mathematically, the simple moving average (which serves as an estimate of the next period's demand) is expressed as

$$\text{Moving average} = \frac{\sum \text{demand in previous } n \text{ periods}}{n} \qquad (4\text{-}1)$$

where *n* is the number of periods in the moving average—for example, 4, 5, or 6 months, respectively, for a 4-, 5-, or 6-period moving average.

OM in Action ▶ Forecasting at Zoka

It's Friday night in Abdoun, the relaxed suburb of Amman, and the local Zoka restaurant and coffee shop is humming. Customers may wait an average of 30 minutes for a table, but they can admire scenic views of Amman while waiting. Then comes dinner, which makes people happy and feel the visit was worthwhile. The typical bill: under US$20 per person. Crowds flock to Zoka for value and consistency—and they get it.

Every night, Zoka's computer cranks out forecasts that tell the managers what demand to anticipate the next day. The forecasting software generates a total meal forecast and breaks that down into specific menu items. The system tells a manager, for example, that if 800 meals will be served the next day, "you need to get 10 kilos of steaks, 55 kilos of chicken, 42 portions of fish, and 75 portions of fries ready." Managers often fine tune the quantities based on local conditions, such as weather or an event taking place nearby, but they know what their customers are going to order.

By relying on demand history, the forecasting system has cut significant waste out of the system. The forecast also reduces labor costs by providing the necessary information for improved scheduling. Labor costs decreased almost a full percentage point in the first year, translating into additional thousands of US dollars in savings for Zoka. In the highly competitive restaurant business, every dollar counts.

Source: Interviews with Zoka Manager Mr. Rawashdeh.

Example 1 shows how moving averages are calculated.

◀ **EXAMPLE 1**

Determining the moving average

Salam Supply wants a 3-month moving-average forecast, including a forecast for next January, for shed sales.

APPROACH ▶ Storage shed sales are shown in the middle column of the table below. A 3-month moving average appears on the right.

Month	Actual Shed Sales	3-Month Moving Average
January	10	
February	12	
March	13	
April	16	$(10 + 12 + 13) \div 3 = 11\frac{2}{3}$
May	19	$(12 + 13 + 16) \div 3 = 13\frac{2}{3}$
June	23	$(13 + 16 + 19) \div 3 = 16$
July	26	$(16 + 19 + 23) \div 3 = 19\frac{1}{3}$
August	30	$(19 + 23 + 26) \div 3 = 22\frac{2}{3}$
September	28	$(23 + 26 + 30) \div 3 = 26\frac{1}{3}$
October	18	$(26 + 30 + 28) \div 3 = 28$
November	16	$(30 + 28 + 18) \div 3 = 25\frac{1}{3}$
December	14	$(28 + 18 + 16) \div 3 = 20\frac{2}{3}$

SOLUTION ▶ The forecast for December is $20\frac{2}{3}$. To project the demand for sheds in the coming January, we sum the October, November, and December sales and divide by 3: January forecast = $(18 + 16 + 14) \div 3 = 16$.

INSIGHT ▶ Management now has a forecast that averages sales for the last 3 months. It is easy to use and understand.

LEARNING EXERCISE ▶ If actual sales in December were 18 (rather than 14), what is the new January forecast? [Answer: $17\frac{1}{3}$]

RELATED PROBLEMS ▶ 4.1a, 4.2b, 4.7

EXCEL OM Data File **Ch04Ex1.xls** can be found at MyOMLab.

LO3: Apply the naive, moving-average, exponential smoothing, and trend methods

When a detectable trend or pattern is present, *weights* can be used to place more emphasis on recent values. This practice makes forecasting techniques more responsive to changes because more recent periods may be more heavily weighted. Choice of weights is somewhat arbitrary because there is no set formula to determine them. Therefore, deciding which weights to use requires some experience. For example, if the latest month or period is weighted too heavily, the forecast may reflect a large unusual change in the demand or sales pattern too quickly.

A weighted moving average may be expressed mathematically as:

$$\text{Weighted moving average} = \frac{\sum(\text{Weight for period } n)(\text{Demand in period } n)}{\sum \text{Weights}} \qquad (4\text{-}2)$$

Example 2 shows how to calculate a weighted moving average.

EXAMPLE 2 ▶

Determining the weighted moving average

Salam Supply (see Example 1) wants to forecast storage shed sales by weighting the past 3 months, with more weight given to recent data to make them more significant.

APPROACH ▶   Assign more weight to recent data, as follows:

Weights Applied	Period
3	Last month
2	Two months ago
1	Three months ago
6	Sum of weights

Forecast for this month =

$$\frac{3 \times \text{Sales last mo.} + 2 \times \text{Sales 2 mos. ago} + 1 \times \text{Sales 3 mos. ago}}{\text{Sum of the weights}}$$

SOLUTION ▶   The results of this weighted-average forecast are as follows:

Month	Actual Shed Sales	3-Month Weighted Moving Average
January	10	
February	12	
March	13	
April	16	$[(3 \times 13) + (2 \times 12) + (10)] \div 6 = 12\frac{1}{6}$
May	19	$[(3 \times 16) + (2 \times 13) + (12)] \div 6 = 14\frac{1}{3}$
June	23	$[(3 \times 19) + (2 \times 16) + (13)] \div 6 = 17$
July	26	$[(3 \times 23) + (2 \times 19) + (16)] \div 6 = 20\frac{1}{2}$
August	30	$[(3 \times 26) + (2 \times 23) + (19)] \div 6 = 23\frac{5}{6}$
September	28	$[(3 \times 30) + (2 \times 26) + (23)] \div 6 = 27\frac{1}{2}$
October	18	$[(3 \times 28) + (2 \times 30) + (26)] \div 6 = 28\frac{1}{3}$
November	16	$[(3 \times 18) + (2 \times 28) + (30)] \div 6 = 23\frac{1}{3}$
December	14	$[(3 \times 16) + (2 \times 18) + (28)] \div 6 = 18\frac{2}{3}$

INSIGHT ▶   In this particular forecasting situation, you can see that more heavily weighting the latest month provides a much more accurate projection.

LEARNING EXERCISE ▶   If the assigned weights were 0.50, 0.33, and 0.17 (instead of 3, 2, and 1) what is the forecast for January's weighted moving average? Why? [Answer: There is no change. These are the same *relative* weights. Note that $\sum$ weights = 1 now, so there is no need for a denominator. When the weights sum to 1, calculations tend to be simpler.]

RELATED PROBLEMS ▶   4.1b, 4.2c, 4.5

EXCEL OM Data File **Ch04Ex2.xls** can be found at MyOMLab.

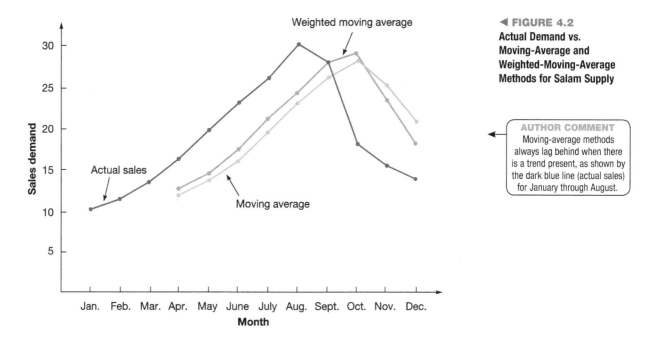

AUTHOR COMMENT
Moving-average methods
always lag behind when there
is a trend present, as shown by
the dark blue line (actual sales)
for January through August.

Both simple and weighted moving averages are effective in smoothing out sudden fluctuations in the demand pattern to provide stable estimates. Moving averages do, however, present three problems.

1. Increasing the size of n (the number of periods averaged) does smooth out fluctuations better, but it makes the method less sensitive to *real* changes in the data.
2. Moving averages cannot pick up trends very well. Because they are averages, they will always stay within past levels and will not predict changes to either higher or lower levels. That is, they *lag* the actual values.
3. Moving averages require extensive records of past data.

Figure 4.2, a plot of the data in Examples 1 and 2, illustrates the lag effect of the moving-average models. Note that both the moving-average and weighted-moving-average lines lag the actual demand. The weighted moving average, however, usually reacts more quickly to demand changes. Even in periods of downturn (see November and December) it more closely tracks the demand.

Exponential Smoothing

Exponential smoothing is a sophisticated weighted-moving-average forecasting method that is still fairly easy to use. It involves very *little* record keeping of past data. The basic exponential smoothing formula can be shown as follows:

New forecast = Last period's forecast
$$+ \alpha \text{ (Last period's actual demand} - \text{Last period's forecast)} \qquad \text{(4-3)}$$

where α is a weight, or **smoothing constant**, chosen by the forecaster, that has a value between 0 and 1. Equation (4-3) can also be written mathematically as:

$$F_t = F_{t-1} + \alpha(A_{t-1} - F_{t-1}) \qquad \text{(4-4)}$$

where F_t = new forecast
$\quad$ F_{t-1} = previous period's forecast
$\quad$ α = smoothing (or weighting) constant $(0 \le \alpha \le 1)$
$\quad$ A_{t-1} = previous period's actual demand

The concept is not complex. The latest estimate of demand is equal to the old estimate adjusted by a fraction of the difference between the last period's actual demand and the old estimate. Example 3 shows how to use exponential smoothing to derive a forecast.

Exponential smoothing
A weighted-moving-average forecasting technique in which data points are weighted by an exponential function.

Smoothing constant
The weighting factor used in an exponential smoothing forecast, a number between 0 and 1.

EXAMPLE 3 ▶

Determining a forecast via exponential smoothing

In January, a car dealer predicted February demand for 142 Ford Mustangs. Actual February demand was 153 cars. Using a smoothing constant chosen by management of $\alpha = 0.20$, the dealer wants to forecast March demand using the exponential smoothing model.

APPROACH ▶   The exponential smoothing model in Equations (4-3) and (4-4) can be applied.

SOLUTION ▶   Substituting the sample data into the formula, we obtain:

New forecast (for March demand) $= 142 + 0.2(153 - 142) = 142 + 2.2$
$$= 144.2$$

Thus, the March demand forecast for Ford Mustangs is rounded to 144.

INSIGHT ▶   Using just two pieces of data, the forecast and the actual demand, plus a smoothing constant, we developed a forecast of 144 Ford Mustangs for March.

LEARNING EXERCISE ▶   If the smoothing constant is changed to 0.30, what is the new forecast? [Answer: 145.3.]

RELATED PROBLEMS ▶   4.1c, 4.3, 4.4, 4.6, 4.9, 4.15, 4.17

The *smoothing constant*, α, is generally in the range from 0.05 to 0.50 for business applications. It can be changed to give more weight to recent data (when α is high) or more weight to past data (when α is low). When α reaches the extreme of 1.0, then in Equation (4-4), $F_t = 1.0A_{t-1}$. All the older values drop out, and the forecast becomes identical to the naive model mentioned earlier in this chapter. That is, the forecast for the next period is just the same as this period's demand.

Table 4.2 helps illustrate this concept. For example, when $\alpha = 0.5$, we can see that the new forecast is based almost entirely on demand in the last three or four periods. When $\alpha = 0.1$, the forecast places little weight on recent demand and takes many periods (about 19) of historical values into account.

▶ **TABLE 4.2**
The effect of changes in the smoothing constant

| | | *Weight Assigned to* | | | |
Smoothing Constant	Most Recent Period (α)	2nd Most Recent Period $\alpha(1 - \alpha)$	3rd Most Recent Period $\alpha(1 - \alpha)^2$	4th Most Recent Period $\alpha(1 - \alpha)^3$	5th Most Recent Period $\alpha(1 - \alpha)^4$
$\alpha = 0.1$	0.1	0.09	0.081	0.073	0.066
$\alpha = 0.5$	0.5	0.25	0.125	0.063	0.031

Selecting the Smoothing Constant   The exponential smoothing approach is easy to use, and it has been successfully applied in virtually every type of business. However, the appropriate value of the smoothing constant, α, can make the difference between an accurate forecast and an inaccurate forecast. High values of α are chosen when the underlying average is likely to change. Low values of α are used when the underlying average is fairly stable. In picking a value for the smoothing constant, the objective is to obtain the most accurate forecast.

Measuring Forecast Error

The overall accuracy of any forecasting model—moving average, exponential smoothing, or other—can be determined by comparing the forecasted values with the actual or observed values. If F_t denotes the forecast in period t, and A_t denotes the actual demand in period t, the *forecast error* (or deviation) is defined as:

Forecast error = Actual demand − Forecast value
$$= A_t - F_t$$

LO4: Compute three measures of forecast accuracy

Several measures are used in practice to calculate the overall forecast error. These measures can be used to compare different forecasting models, as well as to monitor forecasts to ensure they are performing well. Three of the most popular measures are mean absolute deviation (MAD), mean squared error (MSE), and mean absolute percent error (MAPE). We now describe and give an example of each.

Mean Absolute Deviation The first measure of the overall forecast error for a model is the **mean absolute deviation (MAD)**. This value is computed by taking the sum of the absolute values of the individual forecast errors (deviations) and dividing by the number of periods of data (n):

$$MAD = \frac{\sum |Actual - Forecast|}{n} \qquad (4\text{-}5)$$

Mean absolute deviation (MAD)
A measure of the overall forecast error for a model.

Example 4 applies MAD, as a measure of overall forecast error, by testing two values of α.

◄ **EXAMPLE 4**

Determining the MAD

During the past 8 quarters, the Port of Salalah in Oman has unloaded large quantities of grain from ships. The port's operations manager wants to test the use of exponential smoothing to see how well the technique works in predicting tonnage unloaded. He guesses that the forecast of grain unloaded in the first quarter was 175 tons. Two values of α are to be examined: $\alpha = 0.10$ and $\alpha = 0.50$.

APPROACH ▶ Compare the actual data with the data we forecast (using each of the two α values) and then find the absolute deviation and MADs.

SOLUTION ▶ The following table shows the *detailed* calculations for $\alpha = 0.10$ only.

Quarter	Actual Tonnage Unloaded	Forecast with $\alpha = 0.10$	Forecast with $\alpha = 0.50$
1	180	175	175
2	168	$175.50 = 175.00 + 0.10(180 - 175)$	177.50
3	159	$174.75 = 175.50 + 0.10(168 - 175.50)$	172.75
4	175	$173.18 = 174.75 + 0.10(159 - 174.75)$	165.88
5	190	$173.36 = 173.18 + 0.10(175 - 173.18)$	170.44
6	205	$175.02 = 173.36 + 0.10(190 - 173.36)$	180.22
7	180	$178.02 = 175.02 + 0.10(205 - 175.02)$	192.61
8	182	$178.22 = 178.02 + 0.10(180 - 178.02)$	186.30
9	?	$178.59 = 178.22 + 0.10(182 - 178.22)$	184.15

To evaluate the accuracy of each smoothing constant, we can compute forecast errors in terms of absolute deviations and MADs:

Quarter	Actual Tonnage Unloaded	Forecast with $\alpha = 0.10$	Absolute Deviation for $\alpha = 0.10$	Forecast with $\alpha = 0.50$	Absolute Deviation for $\alpha = 0.50$
1	180	175	5.00	175	5.00
2	168	175.50	7.50	177.50	9.50
3	159	174.75	15.75	172.75	13.75
4	175	173.18	1.82	165.88	9.12
5	190	173.36	16.64	170.44	19.56
6	205	175.02	29.98	180.22	24.78
7	180	178.02	1.98	192.61	12.61
8	182	178.22	3.78	186.30	4.30
	Sum of absolute deviations		82.45		98.62
	$MAD = \dfrac{\sum |Deviations|}{n}$		10.31		12.33

INSIGHT ▶ On the basis of this comparison of the two MADs, a smoothing constant of $\alpha = 0.10$ is preferred to $\alpha = 0.50$ because its MAD is smaller.

LEARNING EXERCISE ▶ If the smoothing constant is changed from $\alpha = 0.10$ to $\alpha = 0.20$, what is the new MAD? [Answer: 10.21.]

RELATED PROBLEMS ▶ 4.10, 4.15

EXCEL OM Data File **Ch04Ex4a.xls** and **Ch04Ex4b.xls** can be found at MyOMLab.

Most computerized forecasting software includes a feature that automatically finds the smoothing constant with the lowest forecast error. Some software modifies the α value if errors become larger than acceptable.

Mean squared error (MSE)

The average of the squared differences between the forecasted and observed values.

Mean Squared Error   The **mean squared error (MSE)** is a second way of measuring overall forecast error. MSE is the average of the squared differences between the forecasted and observed values. Its formula is:

$$MSE = \frac{\sum (\text{Forecast errors})^2}{n}$$ (4-6)

Example 5 finds the MSE for the Port of Salalah introduced in Example 4.

EXAMPLE 5 ▶

Determining the MSE

The operations manager for the Port of Salalah now wants to compute MSE for $\alpha = 0.10$.

APPROACH ▶   Use the same forecast data for $\alpha = 0.10$ from Example 4, then compute the MSE using Equation (4-6).

SOLUTION ▶

Quarter	Actual Tonnage Unloaded	Forecast for $\alpha = 0.10$	(Error)^2
1	180	175	$5^2 = 25$
2	168	175.50	$(-7.5)^2 = 56.25$
3	159	174.75	$(-15.75)^2 = 248.06$
4	175	173.18	$(1.82)^2 = 3.33$
5	190	173.36	$(16.64)^2 = 276.89$
6	205	175.02	$(29.98)^2 = 898.70$
7	180	178.02	$(1.98)^2 = 3.92$
8	182	178.22	$(3.78)^2 = 14.31$
			Sum of errors squared = 1,526.46

$$MSE = \frac{\sum (\text{Forecast errors})^2}{n} = 1,526.54 \div 8 = 190.8$$

INSIGHT ▶   Is this MSE = 190.8 good or bad? It all depends on the MSEs for other forecasting approaches. A low MSE is better because we want to minimize MSE. MSE exaggerates errors because it squares them.

LEARNING EXERCISE ▶   Find the MSE for $\alpha = 0.50$. [Answer: MSE = 195.24. The result indicates that $\alpha = 0.10$ is a better choice because we seek a lower MSE. Coincidentally, this is the same conclusion we reached using MAD in Example 4.]

A drawback of using the MSE is that it tends to accentuate large deviations due to the squared term. For example, if the forecast error for period 1 is twice as large as the error for period 2, the squared error in period 1 is four times as large as that for period 2. Hence, using MSE as the measure of forecast error typically indicates that we prefer to have several smaller deviations rather than even one large deviation.

Mean absolute percent error (MAPE)

The average of the absolute differences between the forecast and actual values, expressed as a percentage of actual values.

Mean Absolute Percent Error   A problem with both the MAD and MSE is that their values depend on the magnitude of the item being forecast. If the forecast item is measured in thousands, the MAD and MSE values can be very large. To avoid this problem, we can use the **mean absolute percent error (MAPE)**. This is computed as the average of the absolute difference between the forecasted and actual values, expressed as a percentage of the actual values. That is, if we have forecasted and actual values for n periods, the MAPE is calculated as:

$$MAPE = \frac{\sum_{i=1}^{n} 100|\text{Actual}_i - \text{Forecast}_i| \div \text{Actual}_i}{n}$$ (4-7)

Example 6 illustrates the calculations using the data from Examples 4 and 5.

The Port of Salalah wants to now calculate the MAPE when $\alpha = 0.10$.

APPROACH ▶ Equation (4-7) is applied to the forecast data computed in Example 4.

SOLUTION ▶

Quarter	Actual Tonnage Unloaded	Forecast for $\alpha = 0.10$	Absolute Percent Error 100 (|error| ÷ actual)
1	180	175.00	$100(5 \div 180) =$ 2.78%
2	168	175.50	$100(7.5 \div 168) =$ 4.46%
3	159	174.75	$100(15.75 \div 159) =$ 9.90%
4	175	173.18	$100(1.82 \div 175) =$ 1.05%
5	190	173.36	$100(16.64 \div 190) =$ 8.76%
6	205	175.02	$100(29.98 \div 205) =$ 14.62%
7	180	178.02	$100(1.98 \div 180) =$ 1.10%
8	182	178.22	$100(3.78 \div 182) =$ 2.08%
			Sum of % errors = 44.75%

$$\text{MAPE} = \frac{\Sigma \text{ absolute percent errors}}{n} = \frac{44.75\%}{8} = 5.59\%$$

INSIGHT ▶ MAPE expresses the error as a percentage of the actual values, undistorted by a single large value.

LEARNING EXERCISE ▶ What is MAPE when α is 0.50? [Answer: MAPE = 6.75%. As was the case with MAD and MSE, the $\alpha = 0.1$ was preferable for this series of data.]

The MAPE is perhaps the easiest measure to interpret. For example, a result that the MAPE is 6% is a clear statement that is not dependent on issues such as the magnitude of the input data.

Exponential Smoothing with Trend Adjustment

Simple exponential smoothing, the technique we just illustrated in Examples 3 to 6, is like any other moving-average technique: It fails to respond to trends. Other forecasting techniques that can deal with trends are certainly available. However, because exponential smoothing is such a popular modeling approach in business, let us look at it in more detail.

Here is why exponential smoothing must be modified when a trend is present. Assume that demand for our product or service has been increasing by 100 units per month and that we have been forecasting with $\alpha = 0.4$ in our exponential smoothing model. Table 4.3 shows a severe lag in the 2nd, 3rd, 4th, and 5th months, even when our initial estimate for month 1 is perfect.

Month	Actual Demand	Forecast for Month $T(F_t)$
1	100	$F_1 = 100$ (given)
2	200	$F_2 = F_1 + \alpha(A_1 - F_1) = 100 + 0.4(100 - 100) = 100$
3	300	$F_3 = F_2 + \alpha(A_2 - F_2) = 100 + 0.4(200 - 100) = 140$
4	400	$F_4 = F_3 + \alpha(A_3 - F_3) = 140 + 0.4(300 - 140) = 204$
5	500	$F_5 = F_4 + \alpha(A_4 - F_4) = 204 + 0.4(400 - 204) = 282$

◀ **TABLE 4.3**

The effect of using exponential smoothing when a trend is present

To improve our forecast, let us illustrate a more complex exponential smoothing model, one that adjusts for trend. The idea is to compute an exponentially smoothed average of the data and then adjust for positive or negative lag in trend. The new formula is:

Forecast including trend (FIT_t) = Exponentially smoothed forecast (F_t)
+ Exponentially smoothed trend (T_t) (4-8)

With trend-adjusted exponential smoothing, estimates for both the average and the trend are smoothed. This procedure requires two smoothing constants: α for the average and β for the trend. We then compute the average and trend each period:

$F_t = \alpha$(Actual demand last period) $+ (1 - \alpha)$(Forecast last period + Trend estimate last period) or:

$$F_t = \alpha(A_{t-1}) + (1 - \alpha)(F_{t-1} + T_{t-1}) \tag{4-9}$$

or:

$$T_t = \beta(F_t - F_{t-1}) + (1 - \beta)T_{t-1} \tag{4-10}$$

where F_t = exponentially smoothed forecast of the data series in period t
   T_t = exponentially smoothed trend in period t
   A_t = actual demand in period t
   α = smoothing constant for the average $(0 \le \alpha \le 1)$
   β = smoothing constant for the trend $(0 \le \beta \le 1)$

So the three steps to compute a trend-adjusted forecast are:

Step 1:   Compute F_t, the exponentially smoothed forecast for period t, using Equation (4-9).
Step 2:   Compute the smoothed trend, T_t, using Equation (4-10).
Step 3:   Calculate the forecast including trend, FIT_t, by the formula $FIT_t = F_t + T_t$ (from Equation 4-8).

Example 7 shows how to use trend-adjusted exponential smoothing.

EXAMPLE 7 ▶

Computing a trend-adjusted exponential smoothing forecast

A large Algerian manufacturer wants to forecast demand for a piece of pollution-control equipment. A review of past sales, as shown below, indicates that an increasing trend is present:

Month (t)	Actual Demand (A_t)	Month (t)	Actual Demand (A_t)
1	12	6	21
2	17	7	31
3	20	8	28
4	19	9	36
5	24	10	?

Smoothing constants are assigned the values of $\alpha = 0.2$ and $\beta = 0.4$. The firm assumes the initial forecast for month 1 (F_1) was 11 units and the trend over that period (T_1) was 2 units.

APPROACH ▶   A trend-adjusted exponential smoothing model, using Equations (4-8), (4-9), and (4-10) and the three steps above, is employed.

SOLUTION ▶

Step 1:   Forecast for month 2:

$$F_2 = \alpha A_1 + (1 - \alpha)(F_1 + T_1)$$
$$F_2 = (0.2)(12) + (1 - 0.2)(11 + 2)$$
$$= 2.4 + (0.8)(13) = 2.4 + 10.4 = 12.8 \text{ units}$$

Step 2:   Compute the trend in period 2:

$$T_2 = \beta(F_2 - F_1) + (1 - \beta)T_1$$
$$= 0.4(12.8 - 11) + (1 - 0.4)(2)$$
$$= (0.4)(1.8) + (0.6)(2) = 0.72 + 1.2 = 1.92$$

Step 3:   Compute the forecast including trend (FIT_t):

$$FIT_2 = F_2 + T_2$$
$$= 12.8 + 1.92$$
$$= 14.72 \text{ units}$$

We will also do the same calculations for the third month:

Step 1: $F_3 = \alpha A_2 + (1 - \alpha)(F_2 + T_2) = (0.2)(17) + (1 - 0.2)(12.8 + 1.92)$
$$= 3.4 + (0.8)(14.72) = 3.4 + 11.78 = 15.18$$

Step 2: $T_3 = \beta(F_3 - F_2) + (1 - \beta)T_2 = (0.4)(15.18 - 12.8) + (1 - 0.4)(1.92)$
$$= (0.4)(2.38) + (0.6)(1.92) = 0.952 + 1.152 = 2.10$$

Step 3: $FIT_3 = F_3 + T_3$
$$= 15.18 + 2.10 = 17.28$$

Table 4.4 completes the forecasts for the 10-month period.

Month	Actual Demand	Smoothed Forecast, F_t	Smoothed Trend, T_t	Forecast Including Trend, FIT_t
1	12	11	2	13.00
2	17	12.80	1.92	14.72
3	20	15.18	2.10	17.28
4	19	17.82	2.32	20.14
5	24	19.91	2.23	22.14
6	21	22.51	2.38	24.89
7	31	24.11	2.07	26.18
8	28	27.14	2.45	29.59
9	36	29.28	2.32	31.60
10	—	32.48	2.68	35.16

INSIGHT ▶   Figure 4.3 compares actual demand (A_t) to an exponential smoothing forecast that includes trend (FIT_t). *FIT* picks up the trend in actual demand. A simple exponential smoothing model (as we saw in Examples 3 and 4) trails far behind.

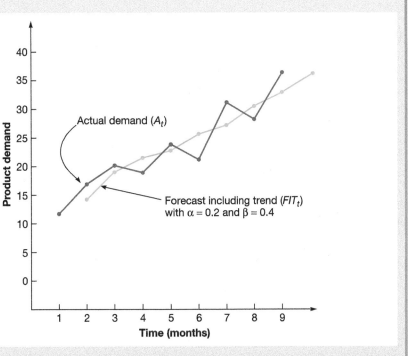

LEARNING EXERCISE ▶   Using the data for actual demand for the 9 months, compute the exponentially smoothed forecast *without* trend (using Equation (4-4) as we did earlier in Examples 3 and 4). Apply α = 0.2 and assume an initial forecast for month 1 of 11 units. Then plot the months 20–10 forecast values on Figure 4.3. What do you notice? [Answer: Month 10 forecast = 24.65. All the points are below and lag the trend-adjusted forecast.]

RELATED PROBLEM ▶   4.18

EXCEL OM Data File **Ch04Ex7.xls** can be found at MyOMLab.

The value of the trend-smoothing constant, β, resembles the α constant because a high β is more responsive to recent changes in trend. A low β gives less weight to the most recent trends and tends to smooth out the present trend. Values of β can be found by the trial-and-error approach or by using sophisticated commercial forecasting software, with the MAD used as a measure of comparison.

Simple exponential smoothing is often referred to as *first-order smoothing*, and trend-adjusted smoothing is called *second-order*, or *double smoothing*. Other advanced exponential-smoothing

▶ **FIGURE 4.4**

The Least-Squares Method for Finding the Best-Fitting Straight Line, Where the Asterisks Are the Locations of the Seven Actual Observations or Data Points

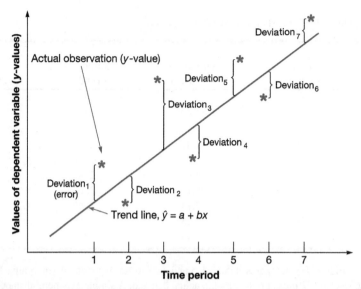

models are also used, including seasonal-adjusted and triple smoothing, but these are beyond the scope of this book.[1]

Trend Projections

Trend projection

A time-series forecasting method that fits a trend line to a series of historical data points and then projects the line into the future for forecasts.

The last time-series forecasting method we will discuss is **trend projection**. This technique fits a trend line to a series of historical data points and then projects the line into the future for medium- to long-range forecasts. Several mathematical trend equations can be developed (for example, exponential and quadratic), but in this section, we will look at *linear* (straight-line) trends only.

If we decide to develop a linear trend line by a precise statistical method, we can apply the *least-squares method*. This approach results in a straight line that minimizes the sum of the squares of the vertical differences or deviations from the line to each of the actual observations. Figure 4.4 illustrates the least-squares approach.

A least-squares line is described in terms of its y-intercept (the height at which it intercepts the y-axis) and its expected change (slope). If we can compute the y-intercept and slope, we can express the line with the following equation:

$$\hat{y} = a + bx \tag{4-11}$$

where $\hat{y}$ (called 'y hat') = computed value of the variable to be predicted (called the *dependent variable*)

a = y-axis intercept

b = slope of the regression line (or the rate of change in y for given changes in x)

x = the independent variable (which in this case is *time*)

Statisticians have developed equations that we can use to find the values of a and b for any regression line. The slope b is found by:

$$b = \frac{\sum xy - n\bar{x}\bar{y}}{\sum x^2 - n\bar{x}^2} \tag{4-12}$$

where b = slope of the regression line

Σ = summation sign

x = known values of the independent variable

y = known values of the dependent variable

$\bar{x}$ = average of the x-values

$\bar{y}$ = average of the y-values

n = number of data points or observations

We can compute the y-intercept a as follows:

$$a = \bar{y} - b\bar{x} \tag{4-13}$$

[1]For more details, see D. Groebner, P. Shannon, P. Fry, and K. Smith, *Business Statistics*, 8th ed. (Upper Saddle River, NJ: Prentice Hall, 2011).

Example 8 shows how to apply these concepts.

Forecasting with least squares

The demand for electric power at Cairo Team Ltd. over the period 2005 to 2011 is shown in the following table, in megawatts. The firm wants to forecast 2012 demand by fitting a straight-line trend to these data.

Year	Electrical Power Demand	Year	Electrical Power Demand
2005	74	2009	105
2006	79	2010	142
2007	80	2011	122
2008	90		

APPROACH ▶ With a series of data over time, we can minimize the computations by transforming the values of x (time) to simpler numbers. Thus, in this case, we can designate 2005 as year 1, 2006 as year 2, and so on. Then Equations (4-12) and (4-13) can be used to create the trend projection model.

SOLUTION ▶

Year	Time Period (x)	Electrical Power Demand (y)	x^2	xy
2005	1	74	1	74
2006	2	79	4	158
2007	3	80	9	240
2008	4	90	16	360
2009	5	105	25	525
2010	6	142	36	852
2011	7	122	49	854
	$\sum x = 28$	$\sum y = 692$	$\sum x^2 = 140$	$\sum xy = 3{,}063$

$$\bar{x} = \frac{\sum x}{n} = \frac{28}{7} = 4 \quad \bar{y} = \frac{\sum y}{n} = \frac{692}{7} = 98.86$$

$$b = \frac{\sum xy - n\bar{x}\bar{y}}{\sum x^2 - n\bar{x}^2} = \frac{3{,}063 - (7)(4)(98.86)}{140 - (7)(4^2)} = \frac{295}{28} = 10.54$$

$$a = \bar{y} - b\bar{x} = 98.86 - 10.54(4) = 56.70$$

Thus, the least-squares trend equation is $\hat{y} = 56.70 + 10.54x$. To project demand in 2012, we first denote the year 2011 in our new coding system as $x = 8$:

$$\text{Demand in 2012} = 56.70 + 10.54(8) = 141.02, \text{ or } 141 \text{ megawatts}$$

INSIGHT ▶ To evaluate the model, we plot both the historical demand and the trend line in Figure 4.5. In this case, we may wish to be cautious and try to understand the 2010 to 2011 swing in demand.

◀ **FIGURE 4.5**
Electrical Power and the Computed Trend Line

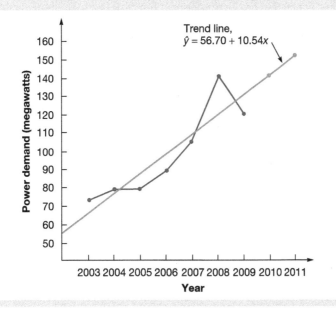

Notes on the Use of the Least-Squares Method   Using the least-squares method implies that we have met three requirements:

1. We always plot the data because least-squares data assume a linear relationship. If a curve appears to be present, curvilinear analysis is probably needed.
2. We do not predict time periods far beyond our given database. For example, if we have 20 months' worth of average prices of Microsoft stock, we can forecast only 3 or 4 months into the future. Forecasts beyond that have little statistical validity. Thus, you cannot take 5 years' worth of sales data and project 10 years into the future. The world is too uncertain.
3. Deviations around the least-squares line (see Figure 4.4) are assumed to be random. They are normally distributed, with most observations close to the line and only a smaller number farther out.

Seasonal Variations in Data

Seasonal variations

Regular upward or downward movements in a time series that tie to recurring events.

Demand for many products is seasonal. Yamaha, the manufacturer of these WaveRunners and snowmobiles, produces products with complementary demands to address seasonal fluctuations.

LO5: Develop seasonal indices

Seasonal variations in data are regular up-and-down movements in a time series that relate to recurring events such as weather or holidays. Demand for coal and fuel oil in the US, for example, peaks during cold winter months.

Seasonality may be applied to hourly, daily, weekly, monthly, or other recurring patterns. Fast-food restaurants experience *daily* surges at noon and again at 6 p.m. Movie theaters see higher demand on Friday and Saturday evenings.

Similarly, understanding seasonal variations is important for capacity planning in organizations that handle peak loads. These include electric power companies during extreme cold and warm periods, banks on Thursday afternoons, and buses during the morning and evening rush hours.

Time-series forecasts like those in Example 8 involve reviewing the trend of data over a series of time periods. The presence of seasonality makes adjustments in trend-line forecasts necessary. Seasonality is expressed in terms of the amount that actual values differ from average values in the time series. Analyzing data in monthly or quarterly terms usually makes it easy for a statistician to spot seasonal patterns. Seasonal indices can then be developed by several common methods.

In what is called a *multiplicative seasonal model*, seasonal factors are multiplied by an estimate of average demand to produce a seasonal forecast. Our assumption in this section is that trend has been removed from the data. Otherwise, the magnitude of the seasonal data will be distorted by the trend.

Here are the steps we will follow for a company that has 'seasons' of 1 month.

1. Find the *average historical demand each season* (or month in this case) by summing the demand for that month in each year and dividing by the number of years of data available. For example, if, in January, we have seen sales of 8, 6, and 10 units over the past 3 years, average January demand equals $(8 + 6 + 10) \div 3 = 8$ units.
2. Compute the *average demand over all months* by dividing the total average annual demand by the number of seasons. For example, if the total average demand for a year is 120 units and there are 12 seasons (each month), the average monthly demand is $120 \div 12 = 10$ units.
3. Compute a *seasonal index* for each season by dividing that month's actual historical demand (from step 1) by the average demand over all months (from step 2). For example, if the average historical January demand over the past 3 years is 8 units and the average demand

over all months is 10 units, the seasonal index for January is 8 ÷ 10 = 0.80 units. Likewise, a seasonal index of 1.20 for February would mean that February's demand is 20 percent larger than the average demand over all months.

4. Estimate next year's total annual demand.
5. Divide this estimate of total annual demand by the number of seasons, then multiply it by the seasonal index for that month. This provides the *seasonal forecast*.

Example 9 illustrates this procedure as it computes seasonal indices from historical data.

▶ **EXAMPLE 9**

Determining seasonal indices

A Manama distributor of Sony laptop computers wants to develop monthly indices for sales. Data from 2009–2011, by month, are available.

APPROACH ▶   Follow the five steps listed above.

SOLUTION ▶

Month	Demand 2009	2010	2011	Average 2009–2011 Demand	Average Monthly Demand[a]	Seasonal Index[b]
Jan.	80	85	105	90	94	0.957 (= 90 ÷ 94)
Feb.	70	85	85	80	94	0.851 (= 80 ÷ 94)
Mar.	80	93	82	85	94	0.904 (= 85 ÷ 94)
Apr.	90	95	115	100	94	1.064 (= 100 ÷ 94)
May	113	125	131	123	94	1.309 (= 123 ÷ 94)
June	110	115	120	115	94	1.223 (= 115 ÷ 94)
July	100	102	113	105	94	1.117 (= 105 ÷ 94)
Aug.	88	102	110	100	94	1.064 (= 100 ÷ 94)
Sept.	85	90	95	90	94	0.957 (= 90 ÷ 94)
Oct.	77	78	85	80	94	0.851 (= 80 ÷ 94)
Nov.	75	82	83	80	94	0.851 (= 80 ÷ 94)
Dec.	82	78	80	80	94	0.851 (= 80 ÷ 94)

Total average annual demand = 1,128

[a] Average monthly demand = $\frac{1,128}{12 \text{ months}}$ = 94   [b] Seasonal index = $\frac{\text{Average 2009–2011 monthly demand}}{\text{Average monthly demand}}$

If we expected the 2012 annual demand for computers to be 1,200 units, we would use these seasonal indices to forecast the monthly demand as follows:

Month	Demand	Month	Demand
Jan.	$\frac{1,200}{12} \times 0.957 = 96$	July	$\frac{1,200}{12} \times 1.117 = 112$
Feb.	$\frac{1,200}{12} \times 0.851 = 85$	Aug.	$\frac{1,200}{12} \times 1.064 = 106$
Mar.	$\frac{1,200}{12} \times 0.904 = 90$	Sept.	$\frac{1,200}{12} \times 0.957 = 96$
Apr.	$\frac{1,200}{12} \times 1.064 = 106$	Oct.	$\frac{1,200}{12} \times 0.851 = 85$
May	$\frac{1,200}{12} \times 1.309 = 131$	Nov.	$\frac{1,200}{12} \times 0.851 = 85$
June	$\frac{1,200}{12} \times 1.223 = 122$	Dec.	$\frac{1,200}{12} \times 0.851 = 85$

INSIGHT ▶   Think of these indices as percentages of average sales. The average sales (without seasonality) would be 94, but with seasonality, sales fluctuate from 85 percent to 131 percent of average.

LEARNING EXERCISE ▶   If 2012 annual demand is 1,150 laptops (instead of 1,200), what will the January, February, and March forecasts be? [Answer: 91.7, 81.5, and 86.6, which can be rounded to 92, 82, and 87.]

RELATED PROBLEM ▶   4.12

EXCEL OM Data File **Ch04Ex9.xls** can be found at MyOMLab.

For simplicity, only 3 periods are used for each monthly index in the preceding example. Example 10 illustrates how indices that have already been prepared can be applied to adjust trend-line forecasts for seasonality.

EXAMPLE 10 ▶

Applying both trend and seasonal indices

San Diego Hospital wants to improve its forecasting by applying both trend and seasonal indices to 66 months of data it has collected. It will then forecast 'patient-days' over the coming year.

APPROACH ▶   A trend line is created; then monthly seasonal indices are computed. Finally, a multiplicative seasonal model is used to forecast months 67 to 78.

SOLUTION ▶   Using 66 months of adult inpatient hospital days, the following equation was computed:

$$\hat{y} = 8,090 + 21.5x$$

where

$$\hat{y} = \text{patient days}$$
$$x = \text{time, in months}$$

Based on this model, which reflects only trend data, the hospital forecasts patient days for the next month (period 67) to be:

$$\text{Patient days} = 8,090 + (21.5)(67) = 9,530 \text{ (trend only)}$$

While this model, as plotted in Figure 4.6, recognized the upward trend line in the demand for inpatient services, it ignored the seasonality that the administration knew to be present.

▶ FIGURE 4.6

Trend Data for San Diego Hospital re-use

Source: From "Modern Methods Improve Hospital Forecasting" by W. E. Sterk and E. G. Shryock from *Healthcare Financial Management*, Vol. 41, no. 3, 97. Reprinted by permission of Healthcare Financial Management Association.

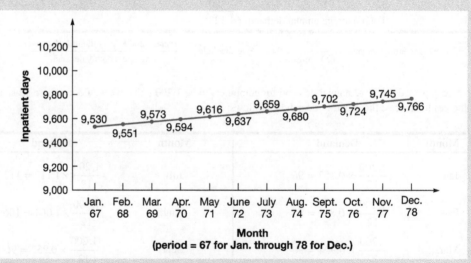

The following table provides seasonal indices based on the same 66 months. Such seasonal data, by the way, were found to be typical of hospitals nationwide.

Seasonality Indices for Adult Inpatient Days at San Diego Hospital			
Month	**Seasonality Index**	**Month**	**Seasonality Index**
January	1.04	July	1.03
February	0.97	August	1.04
March	1.02	September	0.97
April	1.01	October	1.00
May	0.99	November	0.96
June	0.99	December	0.98

These seasonal indices are graphed in Figure 4.7. Note that January, March, July, and August seem to exhibit significantly higher patient days on average, while February, September, November, and December experience lower patient days.

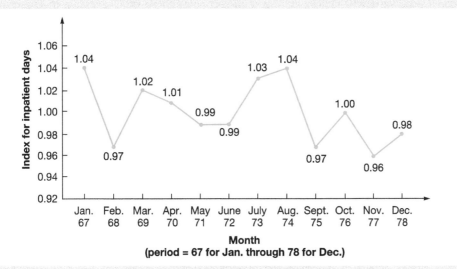

◄ **FIGURE 4.7**
Seasonal Index for San Diego Hospital

However, neither the trend data nor the seasonal data alone provide a reasonable forecast for the hospital. Only when the hospital multiplied the trend-adjusted data by the appropriate seasonal index did it obtain good forecasts. Thus, for period 67 (January):

Patient days = (Trend-adjusted forecast) (Monthly seasonal index) = (9,530)(1.04) = 9,911

The patient days for each month are:

Period	67	68	69	70	71	72	73	74	75	76	77	78
Month	Jan.	Feb.	Mar.	Apr.	May	June	July	Aug.	Sept.	Oct.	Nov.	Dec.
Forecast with Trend & Seasonality	9,911	9,265	9,764	9,691	9,520	9,542	9,949	10,068	9,411	9,724	9,355	9,572

A graph showing the forecast that combines both trend and seasonality appears in Figure 4.8.

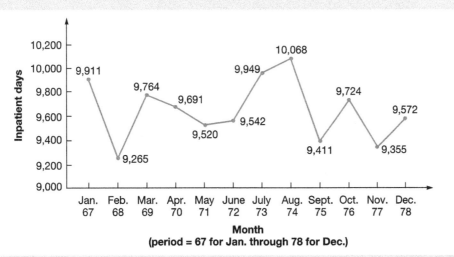

◄ **FIGURE 4.8**
Combined Trend and Seasonal Forecast

INSIGHT ▶ Notice that with trend only, the September forecast is 9,702, but with both trend and seasonal adjustments, the forecast is 9,411. By combining trend and seasonal data, the hospital was better able to forecast inpatient days and the related staffing and budgeting vital to effective operations.

LEARNING EXERCISE ▶ If the slope of the trend line for patient-days is 22.0 (rather than 21.5) and the index for December is 0.99 (instead of 0.98), what is the new forecast for December inpatient days? [Answer: 9,708.]

Cyclical Variations in Data

Cycles
Patterns in the data that occur every several years.

Cycles are like seasonal variations in data but occur every several *years*, not weeks, months, or quarters. Forecasting cyclical variations in a time series is difficult. This is because cycles include a wide variety of factors that cause the economy to go from recession to expansion to recession over a period of years. These factors include national or industry-wide overexpansion in times of euphoria and contraction in times of concern. Forecasting demand for individual products can also be driven by product life cycles—the stages products go through from introduction through decline. Life cycles exist for virtually all products; striking examples include floppy disks, video recorders, and the Atari VCS.

Developing associative techniques of variables that affect one another is our next topic.

AUTHOR COMMENT
We now deal with the same mathematical model that we saw earlier, the least-squares method. But we use any potential 'cause-and-effect' variable as *x*.

ASSOCIATIVE FORECASTING METHODS: REGRESSION AND CORRELATION ANALYSIS

Unlike time-series forecasting, *associative forecasting* models usually consider *several* variables that are related to the quantity being predicted. Once these related variables have been found, a statistical model is built and used to forecast the item of interest. This approach is more powerful than the time-series methods that use only the historical values for the forecasted variable.

Many factors can be considered in an associative analysis. For example, the sales of Pampers' diapers may be related to Pampers' advertising budget, the company's prices, competitors' prices and promotional strategies, and even the nation's birth rate, economy, and unemployment rates. In this case, diaper sales would be called the *dependent variable*, and the other variables would be called *independent variables*. The manager's job is to develop *the best statistical relationship between diaper sales and the independent variables*. The most common quantitative associative forecasting model is **linear-regression analysis**.

Linear-regression analysis
A straight-line mathematical model to describe the functional relationships between independent and dependent variables.

Using Regression Analysis for Forecasting

We can use the same mathematical model that we employed in the least-squares method of trend projection to perform a linear-regression analysis. The dependent variables that we want to forecast will still be $\hat{y}$. But now the independent variable, x, need no longer be time. We use the equation:

LO6: Conduct a regression and correlation analysis

$$\hat{y} = a + bx$$

where $\hat{y}$ = value of the dependent variable (in our example, sales)
   a = y-axis intercept
   b = slope of the regression line
   x = independent variable

Example 11 shows how to use linear regression.

EXAMPLE 11 ▶

Computing a linear regression equation

Shaer Construction Company renovates old homes in West Beirut, Lebanon. Over time, the company has found that its U.S. dollar volume of renovation work is dependent on the West Beirut area payroll. Management wants to establish a mathematical relationship to help predict sales.

APPROACH ▶   Shaer's vice president of operations has prepared the following table, which lists company revenues and the amount of money earned by wage earners in West Beirut during the past 6 years:

Shaer's Sales (in US$ millions), *y*	Area Payroll (in US$ billions), *x*	Shaer's Sales (in US$ millions), *y*	Area Payroll (in US$ billions), *x*
2.0	1	2.0	2
3.0	3	2.0	1
2.5	4	3.5	7

The vice president needs to determine whether there is a straight-line (linear) relationship between area payroll and sales. He plots the known data on a scatter diagram:

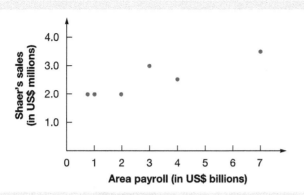

AUTHOR COMMENT
A scatter diagram is a powerful data analysis tool. It helps quickly size up the relationship between two variables.

From the six data points, there appears to be a slight positive relationship between the independent variable (payroll) and the dependent variable (sales). As payroll increases, Shaer's sales tend to be higher.

SOLUTION ▶ We can find a mathematical equation by using the least-squares regression approach:

Sales, y	Payroll, x	x^2	xy
2.0	1	1	2.0
3.0	3	9	9.0
2.5	4	16	10.0
2.0	2	4	4.0
2.0	1	1	2.0
3.5	7	49	24.5
$\Sigma y = 15.0$	$\Sigma x = 18$	$\Sigma x^2 = 80$	$\Sigma xy = 51.5$

$$\bar{x} = \frac{\Sigma x}{6} = \frac{18}{6} = 3$$

$$\bar{y} = \frac{\Sigma y}{6} = \frac{15}{6} = 2.5$$

$$b = \frac{\Sigma xy - n\bar{x}\bar{y}}{\Sigma x^2 - n\bar{x}^2} = \frac{51.5 - (6)(3)(2.5)}{80 - (6)(3^2)} = 0.25$$

$$a = \bar{y} - b\bar{x} = 2.5 - (0.25)(3) = 1.75$$

The estimated regression equation, therefore, is:

$$\hat{y} = 1.75 + 0.25x$$

or:

$$\text{Sales} = 1.75 + 0.25 \, (\text{payroll})$$

If the local chamber of commerce predicts that the West Beirut area payroll will be US$6 billion next year, we can estimate sales for Shaer with the regression equation:

$$\text{Sales (in US\$ millions)} = 1.75 + 0.25(6)$$
$$= 1.75 + 1.50 = 3.25$$

or:

$$\text{Sales} = \text{US\$3,250,000}$$

INSIGHT ▶ Given our assumptions of a straight-line relationship between payroll and sales, we now have an indication of the slope of that relationship: on average, sales increase at the rate of a million dollars for every quarter billion dollars in the local area payroll. This is because $b = 0.25$.

LEARNING EXERCISE ▶ What are Shaer's sales when the local payroll is US$8 billion? [Answer: US$3.75 million.]

RELATED PROBLEMS ▶ 4.13, 4.14, 4.16

► **FIGURE 4.9**
**Distribution about the
Point Estimate of
US$3.25 Million Sales**

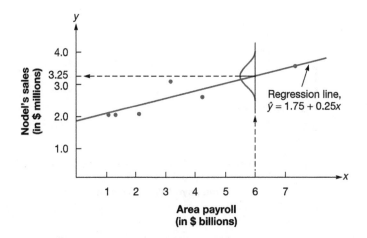

The final part of Example 11 shows a central weakness of associative forecasting methods like regression. Even when we have computed a regression equation, we must provide a forecast of the independent variable x—in this case, payroll—before estimating the dependent variable y for the next time period. Although this is not a problem for all forecasts, you can imagine the difficulty of determining future values of *some* common independent variables (such as unemployment rates, gross national product, price indices, and so on).

Standard Error of the Estimate

The forecast of US$3,250,000 for Shaer's sales in Example 11 is called a *point estimate* of y. The point estimate is really the *mean*, or *expected value*, of a distribution of possible values of sales. Figure 4.9 illustrates this concept.

**Standard error of the
estimate**

A measure of variability around
the regression line—its standard
deviation.

To measure the accuracy of the regression estimates, we must compute the **standard error of the estimate**, $S_{y,x}$. This computation is called the *standard deviation of the regression*. It measures the error from the dependent variable, y, to the regression line, rather than to the mean. Equation (4-14) is a similar expression to that found in most statistics books for computing the standard deviation of an arithmetic mean:

$$S_{y,x} = \sqrt{\frac{\Sigma(y - y_c)^2}{n - 2}}$$

(4-14)

where $y = y$-value of each data point
$y_c =$ computed value of the dependent variable, from the regression equation
$n =$ number of data points

Equation (4-15) may look more complex, but it is actually an easier-to-use version of Equation (4-14). Both formulae provide the same answer and can be used in setting up prediction intervals around the point estimate:[2]

$$S_{x,y} = \sqrt{\frac{\Sigma y^2 - a\Sigma y - b\Sigma xy}{n - 2}}$$

(4-15)

Example 12 shows how we would calculate the standard error of the estimate in Example 11.

EXAMPLE 12 ►

**Computing the
standard error of
the estimate**

Shaer's vice president of operations now wants to know the error associated with the regression line computed in Example 11.

APPROACH ►   Compute the standard error of the estimate, $S_{y,x}$, using Equation (4-15).

SOLUTION ►   The only number we need that is not available to solve for $S_{y,x}$ is Σy^2. Some quick addition reveals $\Sigma y^2 = 39.5$. Therefore:

[2]When the sample size is large ($n > 30$), the prediction value of y can be computed using normal tables. When the number of observations is small, the t-distribution is appropriate. See D. Groebner et al., *Business Statistics*, 8th ed. (Upper Saddle River, NJ: Prentice Hall, 2011).

$$S_{y,x} = \sqrt{\frac{\sum y^2 - a\sum y - b\sum xy}{n-2}}$$

$$= \sqrt{\frac{39.5 - 1.75(15.0) - 0.25(51.5)}{6-2}} = \sqrt{0.09375} = 0.306 \,(\text{in US\$ millions})$$

The standard error of the estimate is then US$306,000 in sales.

INSIGHT ▶ The interpretation of the standard error of the estimate is similar to the standard deviation; namely, ±1 standard deviation = 0.6827. So there is a 68.27 percent chance of sales being ±US$306,000 from the point estimate of US$3,250,000.

LEARNING EXERCISE ▶ What is the probability sales will exceed US$3,556,000? [Answer: About 16 percent.]

EXCEL OM Data File **Ch04Ex12.xls** can be found at MyOMLab.

Correlation Coefficients for Regression Lines

The regression equation is one way of expressing the nature of the relationship between two variables. Regression lines are not 'cause-and-effect' relationships. They merely describe the relationships among variables. The regression equation shows how one variable relates to the value and changes in another variable.

Another way to evaluate the relationship between two variables is to compute the **coefficient of correlation**. This measure expresses the degree or strength of the linear relationship. Usually identified as r, the coefficient of correlation can be any number between +1 and −1. Figure 4.10 illustrates what different values of r might look like.

To compute r, we use much of the same data needed earlier to calculate a and b for the regression line. The rather lengthy equation for r is:

$$r = \frac{n\sum xy - \sum x \sum y}{\sqrt{[n\sum x^2 - (\sum x)^2][n\sum y^2 - (\sum y)^2]}} \tag{4-16}$$

Example 13 shows how to calculate the coefficient of correlation for the data given in Examples 11 and 12.

Coefficient of correlation

A measure of the strength of the relationship between two variables.

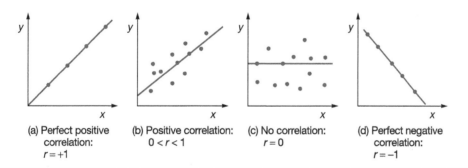

◀ FIGURE 4.10
Four Values of the Correlation Coefficient

(a) Perfect positive correlation: $r = +1$

(b) Positive correlation: $0 < r < 1$

(c) No correlation: $r = 0$

(d) Perfect negative correlation: $r = -1$

◀ EXAMPLE 13

Determining the coefficient of correlation

In Example 11, we looked at the relationship between Shaer Construction Company's renovation sales and payroll in its home town of West Beirut. The vice president now wants to know the strength of the association between area payroll and sales.

APPROACH ▶ We compute the r value using Equation (4-16). We need to first add one more column of calculations—for y^2.

SOLUTION ▶ The data, including the column for y^2 and the calculations, are shown here:

y	x	x^2	xy	y^2
2.0	1	1	2.0	4.0
3.0	3	9	9.0	9.0
2.5	4	16	10.0	6.25
2.0	2	4	4.0	4.0
2.0	1	1	2.0	4.0
3.5	7	49	24.5	12.25
$\sum y = 15.0$	$\sum x = 18$	$\sum x^2 = 80$	$\sum xy = 51.5$	$\sum y^2 = 39.5$

$$r = \frac{(6)(51.5) - (18)(15.0)}{\sqrt{[(6)(80) - (18)^2][(6)(39.5) - (15.0)^2]}}$$

$$= \frac{309 - 270}{\sqrt{(156)(12)}} = \frac{39}{\sqrt{1,872}}$$

$$= \frac{39}{43.3} = 0.901$$

INSIGHT ▶   This r of 0.901 appears to be a significant correlation and helps confirm the closeness of the relationship between the two variables.

LEARNING EXERCISE ▶   If the coefficient of correlation was −0.901 rather than +0.901, what would this tell you? [Answer: The negative correlation would tell you that as payroll went up, Shaer's sales went down—a rather unlikely occurrence that would suggest you recheck your math.]

RELATED PROBLEMS ▶   4.14d, 4.16c

Coefficient of determination

A measure of the amount of variation in the dependent variable about its mean that is explained by the regression equation.

Although the coefficient of correlation is the measure most commonly used to describe the relationship between two variables, another measure does exist. It is called the **coefficient of determination** and is simply the square of the coefficient of correlation—namely, r^2. The value of r^2 will always be a positive number in the range $0 \leq r^2 \leq 1$. The coefficient of determination is the percentage of variation in the dependent variable (y) that is explained by the regression equation. In Shaer's case, the value of r^2 is 0.81, indicating that 81 percent of the total variation is explained by the regression equation.

Multiple-Regression Analysis

Multiple regression

An associative forecasting method with more than one independent variable.

Multiple regression is a practical extension of the simple regression model we just explored. It allows us to build a model with several independent variables instead of just one variable. For example, if Shaer Construction wanted to include average annual interest rates in its model for forecasting renovation sales, the proper equation would be:

$$\hat{y} = a + b_1 x_1 + b_2 x_2 \tag{4-17}$$

where $\hat{y}$ = dependent variable, sales
            a = a constant, the y intercept
    x_1 and x_2 = values of the two independent variables, area payroll and
                interest rates, respectively
    b_1 and b_2 = coefficients for the two independent variables

The mathematics of multiple regression becomes quite complex (and is usually tackled by computer), so we leave the formulae for a, b_1, and b_2 to statistics textbooks. However, Example 14 shows how to interpret Equation (4-17) in forecasting Shaer's sales.

EXAMPLE 14 ▶

Using a multiple-regression equation

Shaer Construction wants to see the impact of a second independent variable, interest rates, on its sales.

APPROACH ▶   The new multiple-regression line for Shaer Construction, calculated by computer software, is:

$$\hat{y} = 1.80 + 0.30x_1 - 5.0x_2$$

We also find that the new coefficient of correlation is 0.96, implying the inclusion of the variable x_2, interest rates, adds even more strength to the linear relationship.

SOLUTION ▶   We can now estimate Shaer's sales if we substitute values for next year's payroll and interest rate. If West Beirut's payroll will be US\$6 billion and the interest rate will be 0.12 (12 percent), sales will be forecast as:

$$\text{Sales (US\$ millions)} = 1.80 + 0.30(6) - 5.0(0.12)$$
$$= 1.8 + 1.8 - 0.6$$
$$= 3.00$$

> or:
>
> Sales = US$3,000,000
>
> **INSIGHT ▶** By using both variables, payroll and interest rates, Shaer now has a sales forecast of US$3 million and a higher coefficient of correlation. This suggests a stronger relationship between the two variables and a more accurate estimate of sales.
>
> **LEARNING EXERCISE ▶** If interest rates were only 6 percent, what would be the sales forecast? [Answer: 1.8 + 1.8 −5.0(0.06) = 3.3, or US$3,300,000.]

MONITORING AND CONTROLLING FORECASTS

AUTHOR COMMENT
Using a tracking signal is a good way to make sure the forecasting system is continuing to do a good job.

Once a forecast has been completed, it should not be forgotten. No manager wants to be reminded that his or her forecast is horribly inaccurate, but a firm needs to determine why actual demand (or whatever variable is being examined) differed significantly from that projected. If the forecaster is accurate, that individual usually makes sure that everyone is aware of his or her talents.

One way to monitor forecasts to ensure that they are performing well is to use a tracking signal. A **tracking signal** is a measurement of how well a forecast is predicting actual values. As forecasts are updated every week, month, or quarter, the newly available demand data are compared to the forecast values.

Tracking signal
A measurement of how well a forecast is predicting actual values.

The tracking signal is computed as the cumulative error divided by the *mean absolute deviation (MAD)*:

$$\text{Tracking signal} = \frac{\text{Cumulative error}}{\text{MAD}}$$

(4-18)

$$= \frac{\sum(\text{Actual demand in period } i - \text{Forecast demand in period } i)}{\text{MAD}}$$

where

$$\text{MAD} = \frac{\sum |\text{Actual} - \text{Forecast}|}{n}$$

as seen earlier, in Equation (4-5).

Positive tracking signals indicate that demand is *greater* than forecast. *Negative* signals mean that demand is *less* than forecast. A good tracking signal—that is, one with a low cumulative error—has about as much positive error as it has negative error. In other words, small deviations are okay, but positive and negative errors should balance one another so that the tracking signal centers closely around zero. A consistent tendency for forecasts to be greater or less than the actual values (that is, for a high absolute cumulative error) is called a **bias** error. Bias can occur if, for example, the wrong variables or trend line are used or if a seasonal index is misapplied.

Bias
A forecast that is consistently higher or consistently lower than actual values of a time series.

Once tracking signals are calculated, they are compared with predetermined control limits. When a tracking signal exceeds an upper or lower limit, there is a problem with the forecasting method, and management may want to reevaluate the way it forecasts demand. Figure 4.11 shows the graph of a tracking signal that is exceeding the range of acceptable variation. If the model being used is exponential smoothing, perhaps the smoothing constant needs to be readjusted.

LO7: Use a tracking signal

How do firms decide what the upper and lower tracking limits should be? There is no single answer, but they try to find reasonable values—in other words, limits not so low as to be triggered with every small forecast error and not so high as to allow bad forecasts to be regularly overlooked. One MAD is equivalent to approximately 0.8 standard deviation, ±2 MADs = ±1.6 standard deviations, ±3 MADs = ±2.4 standard deviations, and ±4 MADs = ±3.2 standard deviations. This fact suggests that for a forecast to be 'in control,' 89 percent of the errors are expected to fall within ±2 MADs, 98 percent within ±3 MADs, or 99.9 percent within ±4 MADs.[3]

---

[3]To prove these three percentages to yourself, just set up a normal curve for ±1.6 standard deviations (*z*-values). Using the normal table in Appendix I, you find that the area under the curve is 0.89. This represents ±2 MADs. Likewise, ±3 MADs = ±2.4 standard deviations encompass 98 percent of the area, and so on for ±4 MADs.

▶ **FIGURE 4.11**
A Plot of Tracking Signals

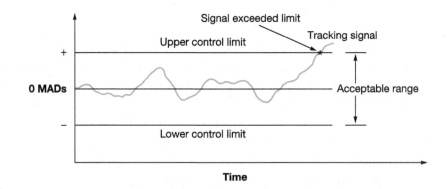

Example 15 shows how the tracking signal and cumulative error can be computed.

EXAMPLE 15 ▶

Computing the tracking signal at Jeddah Automatic Bakery

Jeddah Automatic Bakery wants to evaluate performance of its Arab bread forecast.

APPROACH ▶   Develop a tracking signal for the forecast and see if it stays within acceptable limits, which we define as ±4 MADs.

SOLUTION ▶   Using the forecast and demand data for the past 6 quarters for Arab bread sales, we develop a tracking signal in the table below:

Quarter	Actual Demand	Forecast Demand	Error	Cumulative Error	Absolute Forecast Error	Cumulative Absolute Forecast Error	MAD	Tracking Signal (Cumulative Quarter Error ÷ MAD)
1	90	100	−10	−10	10	10	10.0	−10 ÷ 10 = −1
2	95	100	−5	−15	5	15	7.5	−15 ÷ 7.5 = −2
3	115	100	+15	0	15	30	10.0	0 ÷ 10 = 0
4	100	110	−10	−10	10	40	10.0	−10 ÷ 10 = −1
5	125	110	+15	+5	15	55	11.0	+5 ÷ 11 = +0.5
6	140	110	+30	+35	30	85	14.2	+35 ÷ 14.2 = +2.5

$$\text{At the end of quarter 6, MAD} = \frac{\sum |\text{Forecast errors}|}{n} = \frac{85}{6} = 14.2$$

$$\text{and} \qquad \text{Tracking signal} = \frac{\text{Cumulative error}}{\text{MAD}} = \frac{35}{14.2} = 2.5 \text{ MADs}$$

INSIGHT ▶   Because the tracking signal drifted from −2 MADs to +2.5 MADs (between 1.6 and 2.0 standard deviations), we can conclude that it is within acceptable limits.

LEARNING EXERCISE ▶   If actual demand in quarter 6 was 130 (rather than 140), what would be the MAD and resulting tracking signal? [Answer: MAD for quarter 6 would be 12.5, and the tracking signal for period 6 would be 2 MADs.]

RELATED PROBLEMS ▶   4.15, 4.19

AUTHOR COMMENT
Forecasting at Kudu and Aramex is as important and complex as it is for manufacturers such as Lexus and Dell.

FORECASTING IN THE SERVICE SECTOR

Forecasting in the service sector presents some unusual challenges. A major technique in the retail sector is tracking demand by maintaining good short-term records. For instance, a barbershop catering to men expects peak flows on Fridays and is closed on Mondays. A downtown restaurant, on the other hand, may need to track conventions and holidays for effective short-term forecasting.

Specialty Retail Shops   Specialty retail facilities, such as flower shops, may have other unusual demand patterns, and those patterns will differ depending on the holiday; for example, whether it is Mother's Day, Eid, or a national day. The demand pattern differs according to the holiday; for a chocolate shop in the Middle East, if Mother's Day falls midweek, the demand for chocolate boxes differs than if it falls during weekends, when families tend to go out instead.

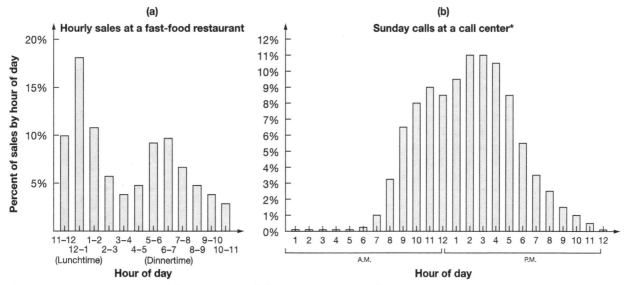

▲ FIGURE 4.12 **Forecasts Are Unique: Note the Variations between (a) Hourly Sales at a Fast-Food Restaurant and (b) Call Volume at the Call Center on a Sunday**

*Based on historical data: see *Journal of Business Forecasting* (Winter 1999–2000): 6–11.

Therefore, many service firms maintain records of sales, noting not only the day of the week but also unusual events, including the weather, so that patterns and correlations that influence demand can be developed.

Fast-Food Restaurants   Fast-food restaurants are well aware not only of weekly, daily, and hourly demand but even 15-minute variations in demand that influence sales. Therefore, detailed forecasts of demand are needed. Figure 4.12(a) shows the hourly forecast for a typical fast-food restaurant. Note the lunchtime and dinnertime peaks. This contrasts to the mid-morning and mid-afternoon peaks at a call center in Figure 4.12(b).

CHAPTER SUMMARY

Forecasts are a critical part of the operations manager's function. Demand forecasts drive a firm's production, capacity, and scheduling systems and affect the financial, marketing, and personnel planning functions.

There is a variety of qualitative and quantitative forecasting techniques. Qualitative approaches employ judgment, experience, intuition, and a host of other factors that are difficult to quantify. Quantitative forecasting uses historical data and causal, or associative, relations to project future demands. The Rapid Review for this chapter summarizes the formulae we introduced in quantitative forecasting. Forecast calculations are seldom performed by hand. Most operations managers turn to software packages such as Forecast PRO, SAP, AFS, SAS, SPSS, or Excel.

No forecasting method is perfect under all conditions. And even once management has found a satisfactory approach, it must still monitor and control forecasts to make sure errors do not get out of hand. Forecasting can often be a very challenging, but rewarding, part of managing.

Key Terms

Bias (p. 117)
Coefficient of correlation (p. 115)
Coefficient of determination (p. 116)
Consumer market survey (p. 95)
Cycles (p. 112)
Delphi method (p. 95)
Demand forecasts (p. 93)
Economic forecasts (p. 93)
Exponential smoothing (p. 99)
Forecasting (p. 92)

Jury of executive opinion (p. 94)
Linear-regression analysis (p. 112)
Mean absolute deviation (MAD) (p. 101)
Mean absolute percent error (MAPE) (p. 102)
Mean squared error (MSE) (p. 102)
Moving average (p. 96)
Multiple regression (p. 116)
Naive approach (p. 96)
Qualitative forecasts (p. 94)

Quantitative forecasts (p. 94)
Sales force composite (p. 95)
Seasonal variations (p. 108)
Smoothing constant (p. 99)
Standard error of the estimate (p. 114)
Technological forecasts (p. 93)
Time series (p. 95)
Tracking signal (p. 117)
Trend projection (p. 106)

Ethical Dilemma

In 2011, the board of trustees responsible for higher education funding in Saudi Arabia hired a consultant to develop a series of enrollment forecasting models, one for each university in Saudi. These models used historical data and exponential smoothing to forecast the following year's enrollments. Based on the model, which included a smoothing constant (α) for each school, each university's budget was set by the board. The head of the board personally selected each smoothing constant based on what he called his "gut reactions and political acumen."

What do you think the advantages and disadvantages of this system are? Answer from the perspective of (a) the board of trustees and (b) the president of each university. How can this model be abused and what can be done to remove any biases? How can a *regression model* be used to produce results that favor one forecast over another?

Discussion Questions

1. What is a qualitative forecasting model, and when is its use appropriate?
2. Identify and briefly describe the two general forecasting approaches.
3. Identify the three forecasting time horizons. State an approximate duration for each.
4. What three methods are used to determine the accuracy of any given forecasting method? How would you determine whether time-series regression or exponential smoothing is better in a specific application?
5. Explain the value of seasonal indices in forecasting. How are seasonal patterns different from cyclical patterns?
6. What is the purpose of a tracking signal?
7. What happens to the ability to forecast for periods farther into the future?

Using Software in Forecasting

This section presents three ways to solve forecasting problems with computer software. First, you can create your own Excel spreadsheets to develop forecasts. Second, you can use the Excel OM software that comes with the text. Third, POM for Windows is another program that is located at MyOMLab.

Creating Your Own Excel Spreadsheets

Excel spreadsheets (and spreadsheets in general) are frequently used in forecasting. Exponential smoothing, trend analysis, and regression analysis (simple and multiple) are supported by built-in Excel functions.

Program 4.1 illustrates how to build an Excel forecast for the data in Example 8. The goal for Cairo Team Ltd. is to create a trend analysis of the 2005–2011 data. Note that in cell D4 you can enter either = $B$16 + $B$17 * C4 *or* = TREND ($B$4: $B$10, $C$4: $C$10, C4).

▶ **PROGRAM 4.1**

Using Excel to Develop Your Own Forecast, with Data from Example 8

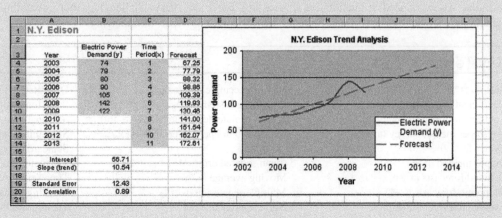

Computations			
Value	**Cell**	**Excel Formula**	**Action**
Trend line column	D4	=$B$16+$B$17*C4 (or =TREND($B$4:$B$10, $C$4:$C$10, C4))	Copy to D5:D14
Intercept	B16	=INTERCEPT(B4:B10, C4:C10)	
Slope (trend)	B17	=SLOPE(B4:B10, C4:C10)	
Standard error	B19	=STEYX(B4:B10, C4:C10)	
Correlation	B20	=CORREL(B4:B10, C4:C10)	

As an alternative, you may want to experiment with Excel's built-in regression analysis. To do so, under the *Data* menu bar selection choose *Data Analysis*, then *Regression*. Enter your *Y* and *X* data into two columns (say B and C). When the regression window appears, enter the *Y* and *X* ranges, then select *OK*. Excel offers several plots and tables to those interested in more rigorous analysis of regression problems.

✖ Using Excel OM

Excel OM's forecasting module has five components: (1) moving averages; (2) weighted moving averages; (3) exponential smoothing; (4) regression (with one variable only); (5) decomposition. Excel OM's error analysis is much more complete than that available with the Excel add-in.

Program 4.2 illustrates Excel OM's input and output, using Example 2's weighted-moving-average data.

ℙ Using POM for Windows

POM for Windows can project moving averages (both simple and weighted), handle exponential smoothing (both simple and trend adjusted), forecast with least-squares trend projection, and solve linear-regression (associative) models. A summary screen of error analysis and a graph of the data can also be generated. As a special example of exponential smoothing adaptive forecasting, when using an α of 0, POM for Windows will find the α value that yields the minimum MAD.

Appendix IV provides further details.

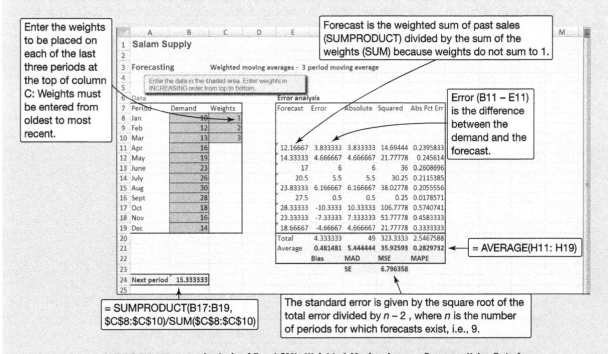

▲ **PROGRAM 4.2** **Analysis of Excel OM's Weighted-Moving-Average Program, Using Data from Example 2 as Input**

Solved Problems   Virtual Office Hours help is available at MyOMLab.

▼ SOLVED PROBLEM 4.1

Sales of Volkswagen's popular Beetle have grown steadily at auto dealerships in Nevada during the past 5 years (see table below). The sales manager had predicted in 2004 that 2005 sales would be 410 VWs. Using exponential smoothing with a weight of $\alpha = 0.30$, develop forecasts for 2006 through 2010.

Year	Sales	Forecast
2005	450	410
2006	495	
2007	518	
2008	563	
2009	584	
2010	?	

▼ SOLUTION

Year	Forecast
2005	410.0
2006	$422.0 = 410 + 0.3\,(450 - 410)$
2007	$443.9 = 422 + 0.3\,(495 - 422)$
2008	$466.1 = 443.9 + 0.3\,(518 - 443.9)$
2009	$495.2 = 466.1 + 0.3\,(563 - 466.1)$
2010	$521.8 = 495.2 + 0.3\,(584 - 495.2)$

▼ SOLVED PROBLEM 4.2

In Example 7, we applied trend-adjusted exponential smoothing to forecast demand for a piece of pollution-control equipment for months 2 and 3 (out of 9 months of data provided). Let us now continue this process for month 4. We want to confirm the forecast for month 4 shown in Table 4.4 and Figure 4.3 (p. 105).

For month 4, $A_4 = 19$, with $\alpha = 0.2$, and $\beta = 0.4$.

▼ SOLUTION

$$F_4 = \alpha A_3 + (1 - \alpha)(F_3 + T_3)$$
$$= (0.2)(20) + (1 - 0.2)(15.18 + 2.10)$$
$$= 4.0 + (0.8)(17.28)$$
$$= 4.0 + 13.82 = 17.82$$
$$T_4 = \beta(F_4 - F_3) + (1 - \beta)T_3$$
$$= (0.4)(17.82 - 15.18) + (1 - 0.4)(2.10)$$
$$= (0.4)(2.64) + (0.6)(2.10)$$
$$= 1.056 + 1.26 = 2.32$$
$$FIT_4 = 17.82 + 2.32$$
$$= 20.14$$

▼ SOLVED PROBLEM 4.3

Room registrations in the Toronto Towers Plaza Hotel have been recorded for the past 9 years. To project future occupancy, the management would like to determine the mathematical trend of guest registration. This estimate will help the hotel determine whether future expansion will be needed. Given the following time-series data, develop a regression equation relating registrations to time (e.g. a trend equation). Then forecast 2011 registrations. Room registrations are in the thousands:

2001: 17   2002: 16   2003: 16   2004: 21   2005: 20
2006: 20   2007: 23   2008: 25   2009: 24

▼ SOLUTION

Year	Transformed Year, x	Registrants, y (in thousands)	x^2	xy
2001	1	17	1	17
2002	2	16	4	32
2003	3	16	9	48
2004	4	21	16	84
2005	5	20	25	100
2006	6	20	36	120
2007	7	23	49	161
2008	8	25	64	200
2009	9	24	81	216
	$\sum x = 45$	$\sum y = 182$	$\sum x^2 = 285$	$\sum xy = 978$

$$b = \frac{\sum xy - n\bar{x}\bar{y}}{\sum x^2 - n\bar{x}^2} = \frac{978 - (9)(5)(20.22)}{285 - (9)(25)} = \frac{978 - 909.9}{285 - 225} = \frac{68.1}{60} = 1.135$$

$$a = \bar{y} - b\bar{x} = 20.22 - (1.135)(5) = 20.22 - 5.675 = 14.545$$

$$\hat{y}(\text{registrations}) = 14.545 + 1.135x$$

The projection of registrations in the year 2011 (which is $x = 11$ in the coding system used) is:

$$\hat{y} = 14.545 + (1.135)(11) = 27.03$$
or 27,030 guests in 2011

▼ SOLVED PROBLEM 4.4

Quarterly demand for Ford F150 pickups at a New York auto dealer is forecast with the equation:

$$\hat{y} = 10 + 3x$$

where x = quarters, and:

Quarter I of 2008 = 0
Quarter II of 2008 = 1
Quarter III of 2008 = 2
Quarter IV of 2008 = 3
Quarter I of 2009 = 4
and so on

and:

$$\hat{y} = \text{quarterly demand}$$

The demand for trucks is seasonal, and the indices for Quarters I, II, III, and IV are 0.80, 1.00, 1.30, and 0.90, respectively. Forecast demand for each quarter of 2010. Then, seasonalize each forecast to adjust for quarterly variations.

▼ SOLUTION

Quarter II of 2009 is coded $x = 5$; Quarter III of 2009, $x = 6$; and Quarter IV of 2009, $x = 7$. Hence, Quarter I of 2010 is coded $x = 8$; Quarter II, $x = 9$; and so on.

$$\hat{y} \text{ (2010 Quarter I)} = 10 + 3(8) = 34$$
$$\hat{y} \text{ (2010 Quarter II)} = 10 + 3(9) = 37$$
$$\hat{y} \text{ (2010 Quarter III)} = 10 + 3(10) = 40$$
$$\hat{y} \text{ (2010 Quarter IV)} = 10 + 3(11) = 43$$

Adjusted forecast = (0.80)(34) = 27.2
Adjusted forecast = (1.00)(37) = 37
Adjusted forecast = (1.30)(40) = 52
Adjusted forecast = (0.90)(43) = 38.7

Problems*

• **4.1** The following gives the number of pints of type A blood used at Damascus Hospital in the past 6 weeks:

Week Of	Pints Used
August 31	360
September 7	389
September 14	410
September 21	381
September 28	368
October 5	374

a) Forecast the demand for the week of October 12 using a 3-week moving average.
b) Use a 3-week weighted moving average, with weights of 0.1, 0.3, and 0.6, using 0.6 for the most recent week. Forecast demand for the week of October 12.
c) Compute the forecast for the week of October 12 using exponential smoothing with a forecast for August 31 of 360 and $\alpha = 0.2$. Px

•• **4.2**

Year	1	2	3	4	5	6	7	8	9	10	11
Demand	7	9	5	9	13	8	12	13	9	11	7

a) Plot the above data on a graph. Do you observe any trend, cycles, or random variations?
b) Starting in year 4 and going to year 12, forecast demand using a 3-year moving average. Plot your forecast on the same graph as the original data.
c) Starting in year 4 and going to year 12, forecast demand using a 3-year moving average with weights of 0.1, 0.3, and 0.6, using 0.6 for the most recent year. Plot this forecast on the same graph.
d) As you compare forecasts with the original data, which seems to give the better results? Px

• **4.3** Refer to Problem 4.2. Develop a forecast for years 2 through 12 using exponential smoothing with $\alpha = 0.4$ and a forecast for year 1 of 6. Plot your new forecast on a graph with the actual data and the naive forecast. Based on a visual inspection, which forecast is better? Px

*Note: Px means the problem may be solved with POM for Windows and/or Excel OM.

• **4.4** A check-processing center uses exponential smoothing to forecast the number of incoming checks each month. The number of checks received in June was 40 million, while the forecast was 42 million. A smoothing constant of 0.2 is used.
a) What is the forecast for July?
b) If the center received 45 million checks in July, what would be the forecast for August?
c) Why might this be an inappropriate forecasting method for this situation? Px

•• **4.5** The actual demand for the patients at Dhahran Emergency Medical Clinic for the first 6 weeks of this year follows:

Week	Actual No. of Patients
1	65
2	62
3	70
4	48
5	63
6	52

Clinic administrator Muhanna Hussein wants you to forecast patient demand at the clinic for week 7 by using this data. You decide to use a weighted moving average method to find this forecast. Your method uses four actual demand levels, with weights of 0.333 on the present period, 0.25 one period ago, 0.25 two periods ago, and 0.167 three periods ago.
a) What is the value of your forecast? Px
b) If instead the weights were 20, 15, 15, and 10, respectively, how would the forecast change? Explain why.
c) What if the weights were 0.40, 0.30, 0.20, and 0.10, respectively? Now what is the forecast for week 7?

•• **4.6** Consider the following actual and forecast demand levels for Kudu burgers at a local Kudu restaurant:

Day	Actual Demand	Forecast Demand
Monday	88	88
Tuesday	72	88
Wednesday	68	84
Thursday	48	80
Friday		

The forecast for Monday was derived by observing Monday's demand level and setting Monday's forecast level equal to this demand level. Subsequent forecasts were derived by using exponential smoothing with a smoothing constant of 0.25. Using this exponential smoothing method, what is the forecast for Kudu burger demand for Friday? **P✕**

•   4.7 Refer to Solved Problem 4.1 on page 122. Use a 3-year moving average to forecast the sales of Nasr automobiles in Cairo through 2013. What is the MAD? **P✕**

•   4.8 Refer to Solved Problem 4.1. Using the trend projection method, develop a forecast for the sales of Nasr automobiles in Cairo through 2013. What is the MAD? **P✕**

•   4.9 Refer to Solved Problem 4.1. Using smoothing constants of 0.6 and 0.9, develop forecasts for the sales of Nasr automobiles. What effect did the smoothing constant have on the forecast? Use MAD to determine which of the three smoothing constants (0.3, 0.6, or 0.9) gives the most accurate forecast. **P✕**

••   4.10 Sales of vegetable dehydrators at a discount department store in Doha over the past year are shown below. Management prepared a forecast using a combination of exponential smoothing and its collective judgment for the 4 months (March, April, May, and June of 2012):

Month	2011–2012 Unit Sales	Management's Forecast
July	100	
August	93	
September	96	
October	110	
November	124	
December	119	
January	92	
February	83	
March	101	120
April	96	114
May	89	110
June	108	108

a) Compute MAD and MAPE for management's technique.
b) Do management's results outperform (i.e. have smaller MAD and MAPE than) a naive forecast?
c) Which forecast do you recommend, based on lower forecast error?

•   4.11 The following gives the number of accidents that occurred on the Desert Highway in Saudi during the past 4 months:

Month	Number of Accidents
January	30
February	40
March	60
April	90

Forecast the number of accidents that will occur in May, using least-squares regression to derive a trend equation. **P✕**

••   4.12 Muna Sweilem owns a company that manufactures boats. Actual demand for Muna's boats during each season in 2009 through 2012 was as follows:

Season	Year			
	2009	2010	2011	2012
Winter	1,400	1,200	1,000	900
Spring	1,500	1,400	1,600	1,500
Summer	1,000	2,100	2,000	1,900
Fall	600	750	650	500

Muna has forecasted that annual demand for his sailboats in 2013 will equal 5,600 boats. Based on this data and the multiplicative seasonal model, what will the demand level be for Muna's boats in the spring of 2013?

••   4.13 Coffee Destination-Kuwait's manager, Saleem, suspects that demand for Arabic coffees depends on the price being charged. Based on historical observations, Saleem has gathered the following data, which show the numbers of these coffees sold over six different price values:

Price (US$)	Number Sold
US$2.70	760
US$3.50	510
US$2.00	980
US$4.20	250
US$3.10	320
US$4.05	480

Using these data, how many Arabic coffees would be forecast to be sold according to simple linear regression if the price per cup were US$2.80? **P✕**

••   4.14 Musa Juma, a real estate developer, has devised a regression model to help determine residential housing prices in Oman. The model was developed using recent sales in a particular neighborhood. The price (Y) of the house is based on the size (square footage = X) of the house. The model is:

$$Y = 13,473 + 37.65X$$

The coefficient of correlation for the model is 0.63.
a) Use the model to predict the selling price of a house that is 1,860 square feet.
b) A 1,860-square-foot house recently sold for US$95,000. Explain why this is not what the model predicted.
c) If you were going to use multiple regression to develop such a model, what other quantitative variables might you include?
d) What is the value of the coefficient of determination in this problem? **P✕**

••   4.15 Sales of music stands at Ali's music store in Alexandria, Egypt, over the past 10 weeks are shown in the table below.
a) Forecast demand for each week, including week 10, using exponential smoothing with α = 0.5 (initial forecast = 20).

Week	Demand	Week	Demand
1	20	6	29
2	21	7	36
3	28	8	22
4	37	9	25
5	25	10	28

b) Compute the MAD.
c) Compute the tracking signal. **P✕**

••   4.16 Damascus City Council has collected the following data on annual sales tax collections and new car registrations:

Annual Sales Tax Collections (in millions)	1.0	1.4	1.9	2.0	1.8	2.1	2.3
New Car Registrations (in thousands)	10	12	15	16	14	17	20

Determine the following:
a) The least-squares regression equation.
b) Using the results of part (a), find the estimated sales tax collections if new car registrations total 22,000.
c) The coefficients of correlation and determination. **P✕**

••• **4.17** Emergency calls in Baghdad, Iraq, for the past 24 weeks are shown in the following table:

Week	1	2	3	4	5	6	7	8	9	10	11	12
Calls	50	35	25	40	45	35	20	30	35	20	15	40
Week	13	14	15	16	17	18	19	20	21	22	23	24
Calls	55	35	25	55	55	40	35	60	75	50	40	65

a) Compute the exponentially smoothed forecast of calls for each week. Assume an initial forecast of 50 calls in the first week, and use $\alpha = 0.2$. What is the forecast for week 25?
b) Re-forecast each period using $\alpha = 0.6$.
c) Actual calls during week 25 were 85. Which smoothing constant provides a superior forecast? Explain and justify the measure of error you used. **Px**

••• **4.18** Using the emergency call data in Problem 4.17, forecast calls for weeks 2 through 25 with a trend-adjusted exponential smoothing model. Assume an initial forecast for 50 calls for week 1 and an initial trend of zero. Use smoothing constants of $\alpha = 0.3$ and $\beta = 0.2$. Is this model better than that of Problem 4.17? What adjustment might be useful for further improvement? (Again, assume that actual calls in week 25 were 85.) **Px**

••• **4.19** The following are monthly actual and forecast demand levels for May through December for units of a product manufactured by the N. Tamimi Pharmaceutical Company:

Month	Actual Demand	Forecast Demand
May	100	100
June	80	104
July	110	99
August	115	101
September	105	104
October	110	104
November	125	105
December	120	109

What is the value of the tracking signal as of the end of December?

Case Studies

▶ Ojaman University: (B)*

Ojaman University is a large government university which enrolls close to 20,000 students. The university prides itself on having the best basketball team in the country, competing in the national premier league. To bolster the team's chances of reaching the elusive and long-desired number-one ranking, in 2003 the university hired the best coach in the country, Saleem Jamal.

One of Saleem's demands on joining Ojaman had been a new arena. With attendance increasing, Ojaman administrators began to face the issue head-on. The following table indicates attendance at each game for the past 6 years.

Ojaman University's president, Dr. Mohammad Khaleel, decided it was time for his vice president of development to forecast when the existing arena would 'max out.' The expansion was, in his mind, a given. But Khaleel needed to know how long he could wait. He also sought a revenue projection, assuming an average ticket price of US$50 in 2012 and a 5 percent increase each year in future prices.

Discussion Questions

1. Develop a forecasting model, justifying its selection over other techniques, and project attendance through 2013.
2. What revenues are to be expected in 2012 and 2013?
3. Discuss the university's options.

Ojaman University Basketball Game Attendance, 2006–2011

	2006		2007		2008	
Game	Attendees	Opponent	Attendees	Opponent	Attendees	Opponent
1	34,200	TABEEKIA	36,100	RAMTHA	35,900	SHAJARA
2ª	39,800	DERAA	40,200	LUBEIDA	46,500	TORRA
3	38,200	AQABA	39,100	ZARQA	43,100	WEHDAT
4ᵇ	26,900	SALT	25,300	RMEITH	27,900	MAREEKH
5	35,100	MAAN	36,200	ORTHODOX	39,200	AHLI

	2009		2010		2011	
Game	Attendees	Opponent	Attendees	Opponent	Attendees	Opponent
1	41,900	DERRA	42,500	HAYNA	46,900	QUDS
2ª	46,100	RAMTHA	48,200	NAUR	50,100	SHOBAK
3	43,900	HOWARA	44,200	NASR	45,900	HILAL
4ᵇ	30,100	KARAK	33,900	MAREEKH	36,300	WEHDAT
5	40,500	TELA	47,800	AHLI	49,900	TORRA

ªHomecoming games.

ᵇDuring the 4th week of each season, Ojaman city hosted a hugely popular traditional crafts festival. This event brought tens of thousands of tourists to the town, especially on weekends, and had an obvious negative impact on game attendance.

*This integrated study runs throughout the text. Other issues facing Ojaman University's basketball expansion include (A) managing the arena project (Chapter 3); (C) quality of facilities (Chapter 6); (D) break-even analysis for food services (Supplement 7); (E) location of the new arena (Chapter 8); (F) inventory planning of basketball programs (Chapter 12); and (G) scheduling of campus security officers/staff for game days (Chapter 13).

▶ Forecasting at Hard Rock Cafe

With the growth of Hard Rock Cafe—from one pub in London in 1971 to more than 129 restaurants in more than 40 countries today—came a corporatewide demand for better forecasting. Hard Rock uses long-range forecasting in setting a capacity plan and intermediate-term forecasting for locking in contracts for leather goods (used in jackets) and for such food items as beef and chicken. Its short-term sales forecasts are conducted each month, by café, and then aggregated for a headquarters' view.

The heart of the sales forecasting system is the point-of-sale system (POS), which, in effect, captures transaction data on nearly every person who walks through a café's door. The sale of each entrée represents one customer; the entrée sales data are transmitted daily to the corporate headquarters' database in Orlando, Florida. There, the financial team, headed by Todd Lindsey, begins the forecast process. Lindsey forecasts monthly guest counts, retail sales, banquet sales, and concert sales (if applicable) at each café. The general managers of individual cafés tap into the same database to prepare a daily forecast for their sites. A café manager pulls up prior years' sales for that day, adding information from the local chamber of commerce or tourist board on upcoming events, such as a major convention, sporting event, or concert in the city where the café is located. The daily forecast is further broken down into hourly sales, which drives employee scheduling. An hourly forecast of US$5,500 in sales translates into 19 workstations, which are further broken down into a specific number of wait staff, hosts, bartenders, and kitchen staff. Computerized scheduling software plugs in people based on their availability. Variances between forecast and actual sales are then examined to see why errors occurred.

Hard Rock doesn't limit its use of forecasting tools to sales. To evaluate managers and set bonuses, a 3-year weighted moving average is applied to café sales. If café general managers exceed their targets, a bonus is computed. Todd Lindsey, at corporate headquarters, applies weights of 40 percent to the most recent year's sales, 40 percent to the year before, and 20 percent to sales 2 years ago in reaching his moving average.

An even more sophisticated application of statistics is found in Hard Rock's menu planning. Using multiple regression, managers can compute the impact on demand of other menu items if the price of one item is changed. For example, if the price of a cheeseburger increases from US$7.99 to US$8.99, Hard Rock can predict the effect this will have on sales of chicken sandwiches and salads. Managers do the same analysis on menu placement, with the center section driving higher sales volumes. When an item such as a hamburger is moved off the center to one of the side flaps, the corresponding effect on related items, say French fries, is determined.

Hard Rock's Moscow Cafe[a]

Month	1	2	3	4	5	6	7	8	9	10
Guest count (in thousands)	21	24	27	32	29	37	43	43	54	66
Advertising (in US$ thousand)	14	17	25	25	35	35	45	50	60	60

[a]These figures are only used for purposes of this case study.

Discussion Questions*

1. Describe three different forecasting applications at Hard Rock. Name three other areas in which you think Hard Rock could use forecasting models.
2. What is the role of the POS system in forecasting at Hard Rock?
3. Justify the use of the weighting system used for evaluating managers for annual bonuses.
4. Name several variables besides those mentioned in the case that could be used as good predictors of daily sales in each café.
5. At Hard Rock's Moscow restaurant, the manager is trying to evaluate how a new advertising campaign affects guest counts. Using data for the past 10 months (see the table) develop a least squares regression relationship and then forecast the expected guest count when advertising is US$65,000.

*You may wish to view the video that accompanies this case before answering these questions.

▶ Digital Cell Phone, Inc.

Jaleel Jasser has just been hired as a management analyst at Digital Cell Phone, Inc. Digital Cell manufactures a broad line of phones for the consumer market. Jaleel's boss, Osama Tareef, chief operations officer, has asked Jaleel to stop by his office this morning. After a brief exchange of pleasantries over a cup of coffee, he says he has a special assignment for Jaleel: "We've always just made an educated guess about how many phones we need to make each month. Usually we just look at how many we sold last month and plan to produce about the same number. This sometimes works fine. But most months we either have too many phones in inventory or we are out of stock. Neither situation is good."

Handing Jaleel the table shown here, Tareef continues, "Here are our actual orders entered for the past 36 months. There are 144 phones per case. I was hoping that since you graduated recently from the University of Jordan, you might have studied some techniques that would help us plan better. It's been awhile since I was in college—I think I forgot most of the details I learned then. I'd like you to analyze these data and give me an idea of what our business will look like over the next 6 to 12 months. Do you think you can handle this?"

"Of course," Jaleel replies, sounding more confident than he really is. "How much time do I have?"

"I need your report on Monday. I plan to take it home with me and read it over my holiday. Be sure that you explain things carefully so that I can understand your recommendation without having to ask you any more questions. Since you are new to the company, you should know that I like to see all the details and complete justification for recommendations from my staff."

With that, Jaleel was dismissed. Arriving back at his office, he began his analysis.

	Orders Received, by Month		
Month	**Cases 2010**	**Cases 2011**	**Cases 2012**
January	480	575	608
February	436	527	597
March	482	540	612
April	448	502	603
May	458	508	628
June	489	573	605
July	498	508	627
August	430	498	578
September	444	485	585
October	496	526	581
November	487	552	632
December	525	587	656

Discussion Questions

1. Prepare Jaleel's report to Osama Tareef using regression analysis. Provide a summary of the cell phone industry outlook as part of Jaleel's response.
2. Adding seasonality into your model, how does the analysis change?

Adapted from Source: Professor Victor E. Sower, Sam Houston State University.

▶ **Additional Case Study:** Visit MyOMLab for this free case study:

North-South Airlines: Reflects the merger of two airlines and addresses their maintenance costs.

Chapter 4 *Rapid* Review

Main Heading	Review Material	
WHAT IS FORECASTING? (pp. 92–93)	▪ **Forecasting**—The art and science of predicting future events. ▪ **Economic forecasts**—Planning indicators that are valuable in helping organizations prepare medium- to long-range forecasts. ▪ **Technological forecasts**—Long-term forecasts concerned with the rates of technological progress. ▪ **Demand forecasts**—Projections of a company's sales for each time period in the planning horizon.	
THE STRATEGIC IMPORTANCE OF FORECASTING (pp. 93–94)	*The forecast is the only estimate of demand until actual demand becomes known.* Forecasts of demand drive decisions in many areas, including: *Human Resources, Capacity, Supply-Chain Management.*	**VIDEO 4.1** Forecasting at Hard Rock Cafe
SEVEN STEPS IN THE FORECASTING SYSTEM (p. 94)	Forecasting follows seven basic steps: 1. Determine the use of the forecast; 2. Select the items to be forecasted; 3. Determine the time horizon of the forecast; 4. Select the forecasting model(s); 5. Gather the data needed to make the forecast; 6. Make the forecast; 7. Validate and implement the results.	
FORECASTING APPROACHES (pp. 94–95)	▪ **Quantitative forecasts**—Forecasts that employ mathematical modeling to forecast demand. ▪ **Qualitative forecasts**—Forecasts that incorporate such factors as the decision maker's intuition, emotions, personal experiences, and value system. ▪ **Jury of executive opinion**—Takes the opinion of a small group of high-level managers and results in a group estimate of demand. ▪ **Delphi method**—Uses an interactive group process that allows experts to make forecasts. ▪ **Sales force composite**—Based on salespersons' estimates of expected sales. ▪ **Consumer market survey**—Solicits input from customers or potential customers regarding future purchasing plans. ▪ **Time series**—Uses a series of past data points to make a forecast.	
TIME-SERIES FORECASTING (pp. 95–112)	▪ **Naive approach**—Assumes that demand in the next period is equal to demand in the most recent period. ▪ **Moving averages**—Uses an average of the *n* most recent periods of data to forecast the next period. $$\text{Moving average} = \frac{\sum \text{demand in previous } n \text{ periods}}{n} \quad (4\text{-}1)$$ $$\text{Weighted moving average} = \frac{\sum (\text{Weight for period } n)(\text{Demand in period } n)}{\sum \text{Weights}} \quad (4\text{-}2)$$ ▪ **Exponential smoothing**—A weighted-moving-average forecasting technique in which data points are weighted by an exponential function. ▪ **Smoothing constant**—The weighting factor, α, used in an exponential smoothing forecast, a number between 0 and 1. Exponential smoothing formula: $F_t = F_{t-1} + \alpha(A_{t-1} - F_{t-1})$ $\quad (4\text{-}4)$ ▪ **Mean absolute deviation (MAD)**—A measure of the overall forecast error for a model. $$\text{MAD} = \frac{\sum |\text{Actual} - \text{Forecast}|}{n} \quad (4\text{-}5)$$ ▪ **Mean squared error (MSE)**—The average of the squared differences between the forecast and observed values. $$\text{MSE} = \frac{\sum(\text{Forecast errors})^2}{n} \quad (4\text{-}6)$$ ▪ **Mean absolute percent error (MAPE)**—The average of the absolute differences between the forecast and actual values, expressed as a percentage of actual values. $$\text{MAPE} = \frac{\sum_{i=1}^{n} 100|\text{Actual}_i - \text{Forecast}_i| + \text{Actual}_i}{n} \quad (4\text{-}7)$$ ▪ **Exponential Smoothing with Trend Adjustment** $\text{Forecast including trend } (FIT_t) = \text{Exponentially smoothed forecast } (F_t)$ $\qquad\qquad\qquad\qquad\qquad + \text{Exponentially smoothed trend } (T_t) \quad (4\text{-}8)$	Problems: 4.1–4.9 Virtual Office Hours for Solved Problems: 4.1–4.4

Main Heading	Review Material	
	■ **Trend projection**—A time-series forecasting method that fits a trend line to a series of historical data points and then projects the line into the future for forecasts. Trend Projection and Regression Analysis $$\hat{y} = a + bx \text{ where } b = \frac{\sum xy - n\bar{x}\bar{y}}{\sum x^2 - n\bar{x}^2}, \text{ and } a = \bar{y} - b\bar{x} \qquad \text{(4-11), (4-12), (4-13)}$$ ■ **Seasonal variations**—Regular upward or downward movements in a time series that tie to recurring events. ■ **Cycles**—Patterns in the data that occur every several years.	
ASSOCIATIVE FORECASTING METHODS: REGRESSION AND CORRELATION ANALYSIS (pp. 112–117)	■ **Linear-regression analysis**—A straight-line mathematical model to describe the functional relationships between independent and dependent variables. ■ **Standard error of the estimate**—A measure of variability around the regression line. ■ **Coefficient of correlation**—A measure of the strength of the relationship between two variables. ■ **Coefficient of determination**—A measure of the amount of variation in the dependent variable about its mean that is explained by the regression equation. ■ **Multiple regression**—An associative forecasting method with > 1 independent variable. $$\text{Multiple regression forecast: } \hat{y} = a + b_1x_1 + b_2x_2 \qquad \text{(4-17)}$$	Problems: 4.13, 4.14, 4.16
MONITORING AND CONTROLLING FORECASTS (pp. 117–118)	■ **Tracking signal**—A measurement of how well the forecast is predicting actual values. $$\text{Tracking signal} = \frac{\sum(\text{Actual demand in period } i - \text{Forecast demand in period } i)}{\text{MAD}} \quad \text{(4-18)}$$ ■ **Bias**—A forecast that is consistently higher or lower than actual values of a time series.	Problems: 4.15, 4.19
FORECASTING IN THE SERVICE SECTOR (pp. 118–119)	Service-sector forecasting may require good short-term demand records, even per 15-minute intervals. Demand during holidays or specific weather events may also need to be tracked.	

*Self-*Test

■ **Before taking the self-test,** refer to the learning objectives listed at the beginning of the chapter and the key terms listed at the end of the chapter.

LO1. Forecasting time horizons include:
  a) long range
  b) medium range
  c) short range
  d) all of the above.

LO2. Qualitative methods of forecasting include:
  a) sales force composite
  b) jury of executive opinion
  c) consumer market survey
  d) exponential smoothing
  e) all except (d).

LO3. The difference between a *moving-average* model and an *exponential smoothing* model is that _____.

LO4. Three popular measures of forecast accuracy are:
  a) total error, average error, and mean error
  b) average error, median error, and maximum error
  c) median error, minimum error, and maximum absolute error
  d) mean absolute deviation, mean squared error, and mean absolute percent error.

LO5. Average demand for iPods in the Rome, Italy, Apple store is 800 units per month. The May monthly index is 1.25. What is the seasonally adjusted sales forecast for May?
  a) 640 units
  b) 798.75 units
  c) 800 units
  d) 1,000 units
  e) cannot be calculated with the information given.

LO6. The main difference between simple and multiple regression is _____.

LO7. The tracking signal is the:
  a) standard error of the estimate
  b) cumulative error
  c) mean absolute deviation (MAD)
  d) ratio of the cumulative error to MAD
  e) mean absolute percent error (MAPE).

5

Product Design

10

OM STRATEGY DECISIONS

- ► Design of Goods and Services
- ► Managing Quality
- ► Process Strategy
- ► Location Strategies
- ► Layout Strategies
- ► Human Resources
- ► Supply-Chain Management
- ► Inventory Management
- ► Scheduling
- ► Maintenance

PRODUCT STRATEGY PROVIDES COMPETITIVE ADVANTAGE AT GULF CRAFT, INC.

A long tradition of seafaring has made the Arabian Gulf one of the busiest marine regions in the world. Such history has equipped Gulf Craft, Inc. with the necessary experience needed to compete globally. Since its inception in 1982, Gulf Craft, Inc. has never stopped growing and expanding. It started as a local builder of 15-foot and 19-foot fishing boats and is now considered one of the most competitive international manufacturers of super yachts and luxury boats. Gulf Craft sells to clients in the Americas, Europe, Asia, and the Arab world. Its export capacity has reached all of the possible markets and the firm sells to more than 50 countries worldwide.

Gulf Craft's most important asset is its creativity department, where an international design team works on developing new designs to outmatch competitors in the market. The firm's continuous quest to satisfy the ever-changing tastes of its quite demanding customers, combined with its engineering excellence and its appetite to include the latest in technology in its boats, gives Gulf Craft an edge over its rivals. This continuous pressure to excel is important in a market that witnesses constant advancements in yacht and boat materials, and customers demanding higher value for their investments.

Gulf Craft uses computer-aided design (CAD) to help architects experiment with many different combinations of forms, technology, and shapes in the manufacture of new yachts to reach the perfect design for every new masterpiece they make. The rationale is that using such technology enables the firm to capitalize on its creativity while reducing the new product development time, cost, and difficulties.

One of Gulf Craft's most reputable brands is Majesty Yacht, which is considered to be at the cutting edge of fiberglass boats. The variety of technologies used in these boats reflects the complexity of their design and construction; from Gyro-Marine Stabilizers and composite construction, to vacuum infusion processes and water jet drives. Such sophistication and excellence in production extends also to Gulf Craft's other brands, such as Oryx and Silvercraft, thus helping it perform better in international markets. Currently, the company exports more than 70 percent of its production.

In addition to the manufacturing, Gulf Craft performs all the necessary servicing of its yachts. The engine installations and repairs are carried out by highly trained technicians who also administer the electrical repairs and trailer manufacturing. Also, the woodwork is fitted by the carpentry department, which employs highly skilled craftspeople from Europe, Asia, and the Arab world.

Today Gulf Craft has manufacturing units and marine service centers in the Maldives, Umm Al Quwain, and Ajman, where the firm's headquarters are located. Its competitive approach to manufacturing has enabled it to stay at the forefront of fiberglass yacht manufacturing, with an annual production capacity of 400 yachts.

Gulf Craft's excellence in yacht manufacturing is best seen in its 135-feet yachts, which incorporate the latest in marine technology and fiberglass designs.

Source: **www.gulfcraftinc.com.**

Gulf Craft is well known for its innovative designs and the special attention it gives to customer wants and specifications—resulting in the production of almost 400 distinctive yachts every year.

Gulf Craft focuses on excellent customer service: it operates specialized service centers with highly trained staff using the most advanced tools in order to cater for the different maintenance services needed by the yachts.

Chapter 5 **Learning Objectives**

AUTHOR COMMENT
Product strategy is critical to achieving competitive advantage.

GOODS AND SERVICES SELECTION

Gulf Craft, Inc. knows that the basis for its existence is the excellent boats it provides to society. To maximize the potential for success, top companies often concentrate on only a few products that are of the highest quality. For instance, Al Zamil in Dammam focuses on air conditioning and its products are all based on outstanding air conditioning technology. However, because most products have a limited and even predictable life cycle, companies must constantly be looking for new products to design, develop, and take to market. Good operations managers insist on strong communication among customers, product processes, and suppliers that results in a high success rate for their new products.

One product strategy is to build particular competence in customizing an established family of goods or services. This approach allows the customer to choose product variations while reinforcing the organization's strength. Computer manufacturer Dell, for example, has built a huge market by delivering computers with the exact hardware and software desired by end users. And Dell does it fast—it understands that speed to market is imperative to gain a competitive edge.

VIDEO 5.1
Product Design at Regal Marine

An effective product strategy links product decisions with investment, market share, and product life cycle, and defines the breadth of the product line. The *objective of the* **product decision** *is to develop and implement a product strategy that meets the demands of the marketplace with a competitive advantage.* As one of the ten decisions of OM, product strategy may focus on developing a competitive advantage via differentiation, low cost, rapid response, or a combination of these.

Product decision
The selection, definition, and design of products.

Product Strategy Options Support Competitive Advantage

A world of options exists in the selection, definition, and design of products. Product selection involves choosing the good or service to provide customers or clients. For instance, hospitals specialize in various types of patients and medical procedures. A hospital's management may decide to operate a general-purpose hospital or a maternity hospital or, as in the case of EyeHosp in Jordan, to specialize in eye care and surgery. Hospitals select their products when they decide what kind of hospital to be. Numerous other options exist for hospitals, just as they exist for Al Zamil.

Service organizations like EyeHosp *differentiate* themselves through their product. EyeHosp differentiates itself by offering a distinctly unique and high-quality product. Its renowned specialization in eye care and surgery is so effective that patients can return to normal living quickly and with very few complications.

Kudu, a chain of fast-food restaurants in Saudi Arabia, has developed and executed a *low-cost* strategy through product design. By designing a product (its menu) that can be produced with a minimum of labor in small kitchens, Kudu has developed a product line that is both low cost and high value.

Product decisions are fundamental to an organization's strategy and have major implications throughout the operations function. For instance, GM's steering columns are a good example of the strong role product design plays in both quality and efficiency. The redesigned steering column has a simpler design, with about 30 percent fewer parts than its predecessor. The result: assembly time is one-third that of the older column, and the new column's quality is about seven times higher. As an added bonus, machinery on the new line costs a third less than that on the old line.

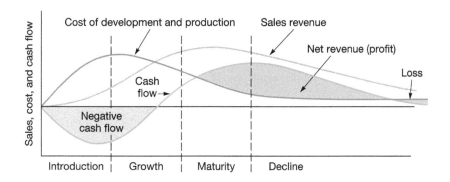

◀ FIGURE 5.1
Product Life Cycle, Sales, Cost, and Profit

Product Life Cycles

Products have a life cycle that starts with their introduction to the market and ends with the phasing out of demand. There are four phases in the life of a product. Those phases are introduction, growth, maturity, and decline.

Product life cycles may be a matter of a few hours (a newspaper), months (seasonal fashions), years (video cassette tapes and personal computers), or decades (Nasr cars in Egypt). Regardless of the length of the cycle, the task for the operations manager is the same: to design a system that helps introduce new products successfully.

Figure 5.1 shows the four life cycle stages and the relationship of product sales, cash flow, and profit over the life cycle of a product. Note that typically a firm has a negative cash flow while it develops a product. When the product is successful, those losses may be recovered. Eventually, the successful product may yield a profit prior to its decline. However, the profit is fleeting—hence, the constant demand for new products.

LO1: Define product life cycle

Life Cycle and Strategy

Just as operations managers must be prepared to develop new products, they must also be prepared to develop *strategies* for new and *existing* products. Periodic examination of products is appropriate because *strategies change as products move through their life cycle.* Successful product strategies require determining the best strategy for each product based on its position in its life cycle. A firm, therefore, identifies products or families of products and their position in the life cycle. Let us review some strategy options as products move through their life cycles.

Introductory phase   Because products in the introductory phase are still being 'fine-tuned' for the market, as are their production techniques, they may warrant unusual expenditures for: (1) research; (2) product development; (3) process modification and enhancement; (4) supplier development. For example, when cellular phones were first introduced, the features desired by the public were still being determined. At the same time, operations managers were still searching for the best manufacturing techniques.

Growth phase   In the growth phase, product design has begun to stabilize, and effective forecasting of capacity requirements is necessary. Adding capacity or enhancing existing capacity to accommodate the increase in product demand may be necessary.

Maturity phase   By the time a product is mature, competitors are established. So high-volume, innovative production may be appropriate. Improved cost control, reduction in options, and a paring down of the product line may be effective or necessary for profitability and market share.

Decline phase   Management may need to be ruthless with those products whose life cycle is at an end. Outdated products are typically poor products in which to invest resources and managerial talent. Unless they make some unique contribution to the firm's reputation or its product line, or can be sold with an unusually high contribution, their production should be terminated.[1]

---

[1]*Contribution* is defined as the difference between direct cost and selling price. Direct costs are labor and materials that go into the product.

Product-by-Value Analysis

Product-by-value analysis

A list of products, in descending order of their individual monetary contribution to the firm, as well as the total annual monetary contribution of the product.

The effective operations manager selects items that show the greatest promise. This is the Pareto principle (i.e. focus on the critical few, not the trivial many) applied to product mix: resources are to be invested in the critical few and not the trivial many. **Product-by-value analysis** lists products in descending order of their *individual monetary contribution* to the firm. It also lists the *total annual monetary contribution* of the product. Low contribution on a per-unit basis by a particular product may look substantially different if it represents a large portion of the company's sales.

A product-by-value report allows management to evaluate possible strategies for each product. These may include increasing cash flow (e.g. increasing contribution by raising selling price or lowering cost), increasing market penetration (improving quality and/or reducing cost or price), or reducing costs (improving the production process). The report may also tell management which product offerings should be eliminated and which fail to justify further investment in research and development or capital equipment. Product-by-value analysis focuses management's attention on the strategic direction for each product.

> **AUTHOR COMMENT**
> Societies reward those who supply new products that reflect their needs.

GENERATING NEW PRODUCTS

Product selection, definition, and design take place continuously due to their importance in replacing old products and generating higher revenues for the company. Consider recent product changes: TV to HDTV, radio to satellite radio, land lines to cell phones, Walkman to iPod, and so on. Knowing how to successfully find and develop new products is an important skill, not just for business but for social progress too.

New Product Opportunities

Aggressive new product development requires that organizations build structures internally that have open communication with customers, innovative organizational cultures, aggressive R&D, strong leadership, formal incentives, and training. Only then can a firm profitably and energetically focus on specific opportunities such as the following.

1. *Understanding the customer* is the main focus of new product development. Many commercially important products are initially thought of and even prototyped by users rather than producers. Such products tend to be developed by 'lead users'—companies, organizations, or individuals that are well ahead of market trends and have needs that go far beyond those of average users. The operations manager must be aware of the market and particularly these innovative lead users.
2. *Economic change* brings increasing levels of affluence in the long run but economic cycles and price changes in the short run. In the long run, for instance, more and more people can afford automobiles, but in the short run, a recession may weaken the demand for automobiles.
3. *Sociological and demographic change* may appear in such factors as decreasing family size. This trend alters the size preference for homes, apartments, and automobiles.
4. *Technological change* makes possible everything from cell phones to iPods to artificial hearts.
5. *Political/legal change* brings about new trade agreements, tariffs, and government requirements.
6. Other changes may be brought about through *market practice*, *professional standards*, *suppliers*, and *distributors*.

Operations managers must be aware of these dynamics and be able to anticipate changes in product opportunities, the products themselves, product volume, and product mix.

Importance of New Products

The importance of new products cannot be overestimated. Leading companies generate a substantial portion of their sales from products less than 5 years old. The need for new products is why Nokia developed its E72, in spite of continuing high sales of its successful E6.

Product selection, definition, and design occurs frequently—perhaps hundreds of times for each financially successful product. Operations managers and their organizations must be able to accept risk and tolerate failure. They must accommodate a high volume of new product ideas while maintaining the activities to which they are already committed.

PRODUCT DEVELOPMENT

Product Development System

The product development system determines not only product success but also the firm's future. An effective product strategy links product decisions with cash flow, market dynamics, product life cycle, and the organization's capabilities. Figure 5.2 shows the stages of product development. In this system, product options go through a series of steps, each having its own screening and evaluation criteria, but providing a continuing flow of information to prior steps.

The screening process extends to the operations function. Optimum product development depends not only on support from other parts of the firm but also on the successful integration of all ten of the OM decisions, from product design to maintenance. Identifying products that appear likely to capture market share, be cost effective, and profitable, but are in fact very difficult to produce, may lead to failure rather than success.

Quality Function Deployment (QFD)

Quality function deployment (QFD) refers to: (1) determining what will satisfy the customer; (2) translating those customer desires into the target design. The idea is to capture a rich understanding of customer wants and to identify alternative process solutions. This information is then integrated into the evolving product design. QFD is used early in the design process to help determine *what will satisfy the customer* and *where to deploy quality efforts*.

One of the tools of QFD is the house of quality. The **house of quality** is a graphic technique for defining the relationship between customer desires and product (or service). Only by defining this relationship in a rigorous way can operations managers design products and processes with features desired by customers. To build the house of quality, we perform seven basic steps:

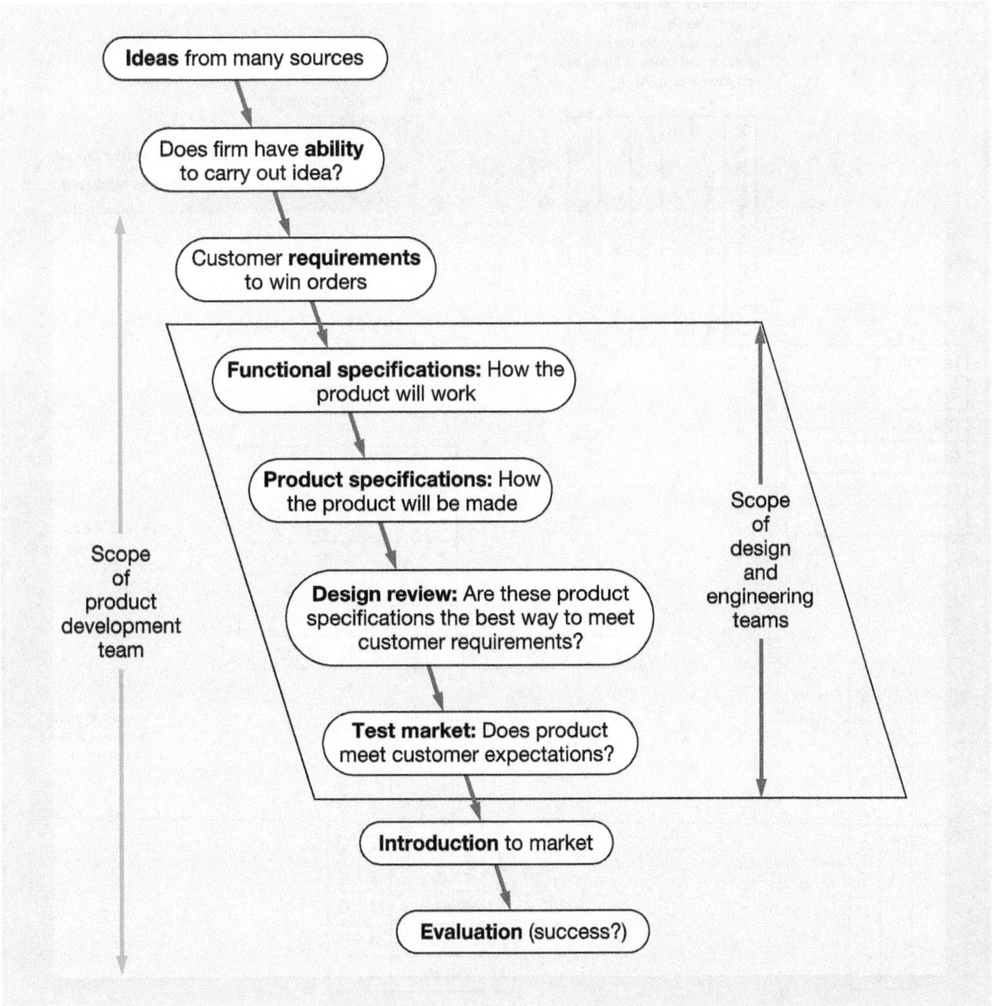

AUTHOR COMMENT
Motorola went through 3,000 working models before it developed its first pocket cell phone.

LO2: Describe a product development system

Quality function deployment (QFD)
A process for determining customer wants and translating them into the attributes that each functional area can understand and act on.

House of quality
A part of the quality function deployment process that utilizes a planning matrix to relate customer 'wants' to 'how' the firm is going to meet those 'wants.'

◀ **FIGURE 5.2**
Product Development Stages
Product concepts are developed from a variety of sources, both external and internal to the firm. Concepts that survive the product idea stage progress through various stages, with nearly constant review, feedback, and evaluation in a highly participative environment to minimize failure.

1. Identify customer *wants*. (What do prospective customers want in this product?)
2. Identify *how* the good/service will satisfy customer wants. (Identify specific product characteristics, features, or attributes and show how they will satisfy customer *wants*.)
3. Relate customer *wants* to product *hows*. (Build a matrix, as in Example 1, that shows this relationship.)
4. Identify relationships between the firm's *hows*. (How do our *hows* tie together? For instance, in the following example, there is a high relationship between low electricity requirements and auto focus, auto exposure, and a paint palette because they all require electricity. This relationship is shown in the 'roof' of the house in Example 1.)
5. Develop importance ratings. (Using the *customer's* importance ratings and weights for the relationships shown in the matrix, compute *our* importance ratings, as in Example 1.)
6. Evaluate competing products. (How well do competing products meet customer wants? Such an evaluation, as shown in the two columns on the right of the figure in Example 1, would be based on market research.)
7. Determine the desirable technical attributes, your performance, and the competitor's performance against these attributes. (This is done at the bottom of the figure in Example 1).

LO3: Build a house of quality

Example 1 shows how to construct a house of quality.

EXAMPLE 1 ▶

Constructing a house of quality

▶ **FIGURE 5.3** **Quality Function Deployment's (QFD) House of Quality**

First, through market research, Egypt Lenses and Cameras, Inc. determined what the customer wants. Those wants are shown on the left of the house of quality.

Second, the product development team determined how the organization is going to translate those customer wants into product design and process attribute targets. These hows are entered across the top portion of the house of quality.

Third, the team evaluated each of the customer wants against the hows. In the relationship matrix of the house, the team evaluated how well its design meets customer needs.

Fourth, the 'roof' of the house indicates the relationship between the attributes.

Fifth, the team developed importance ratings for its design attributes on the bottom row of the table. This was done by assigning values (5 for high, 3 for medium, and 1 for low) to each entry in the relationship matrix, and then multiplying each of these values by the customer's importance rating. The values in the 'Our importance ratings' row provide a ranking of how to proceed with product and process design, with the highest values being the most critical to a successful product.

Sixth, the house of quality is also used for the evaluation of competitors. The two columns on the right indicate how market research thinks competitors, A and B, satisfy customer wants (Good, Fair, or Poor). Products from other firms and even the proposed product can be added next to company B.

Seventh, the team identifies the technical attributes and evaluates how well Egypt Lenses and Cameras, Inc. and its competitors address these attributes. Here the team decided on the noted technical attributes.

Egypt Lenses and Cameras, Inc. wants a methodology that strengthens its ability to meet customer desires with its new digital camera.

APPROACH ▶   Use QFD's house of quality.

SOLUTION ▶   Build the house of quality for Egypt Lenses and Cameras, Inc. We do so in Figure 5.3, using steps 1–7 described.

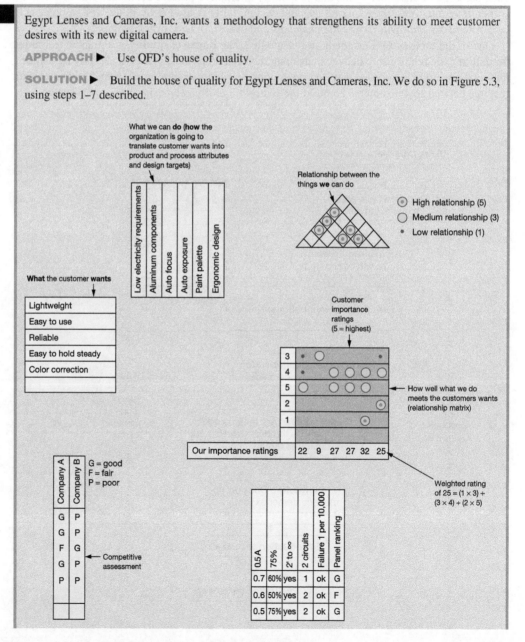

INSIGHT ▶   QFD provides an analytical tool that structures design features and technical issues, as well as providing importance rankings and competitor comparison.

LEARNING EXERCISE ▶   If the market research for another country indicates that 'lightweight' has the most important customer ranking (5), and reliability has a ranking of 3, what is the new total importance ranking for low electricity requirements, aluminum components, and ergonomic design? [Answer: 18, 15, 27, respectively.]

RELATED PROBLEMS ▶   5.1, 5.2, 5.3, 5.4

Another use of QFD is to show how the quality effort will be *deployed*. As Figure 5.4 shows, *design characteristics* of House 1 become the inputs to House 2, which are satisfied by *specific components* of the product. Similarly, the concept is carried to House 3, where the specific components are to be satisfied through particular *production processes*. Once those production processes are defined, they become requirements of House 4 to be satisfied by a *quality plan* that will ensure conformance of those processes. The quality plan is a set of specific tolerances, procedures, methods, and sampling techniques that will ensure that the production process meets the customer requirements.

Much of the QFD effort is devoted to meeting customer requirements with design characteristics (House 1 in Figure 5.4), and its importance is not to be underestimated. However, the *sequence* of houses is a very effective way of identifying, communicating, and allocating resources throughout the system. The series of houses helps operations managers determine where to *deploy* quality resources. In this way we meet customer requirements, produce quality products, and win orders.

Organizing for Product Development

There are four common approaches to organizing for product development. *First*, the traditional U.S. approach to product development is an organization with distinct departments: a research and development department to do the necessary research; an engineering department to design the product; a manufacturing engineering department to design a product that can be produced; and a production department that produces the product. The distinct advantage of this approach is that fixed duties and responsibilities exist. The distinct disadvantage is lack of forward thinking: How will downstream departments in the process deal with the concepts, ideas, and designs presented to them, and ultimately what will the customer think of the product?

A *second* and popular approach is to assign a product manager to 'champion' the product through the product development system and related organizations. However, a *third*, and perhaps the best, product development approach used seems to be the use of teams. Such teams are known variously as *product development teams, design for manufacturability teams*, and *value engineering teams*.

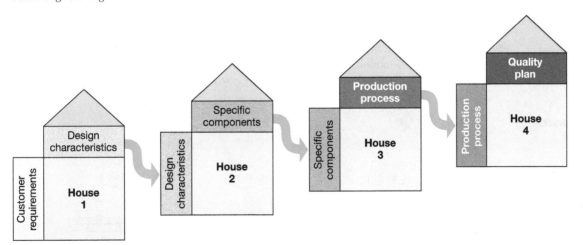

▲ **FIGURE 5.4   House of Quality Sequence Indicates How to Deploy Resources to Achieve Customer Requirements**
Product concepts are developed from a variety of sources, both external and internal to the firm. Concepts that survive the product idea stage progress through various stages, with nearly constant review, feedback, and evaluation in a highly participative environment to minimize failure.

The Japanese use a *fourth* approach. They bypass the team issue by not subdividing organizations into research and development, engineering, production, and so forth. Consistent with the Japanese style of group effort and teamwork, these activities are all in one organization. Japanese culture and management style are more collegial and the organization less structured than in most Western countries. Therefore, the Japanese find it unnecessary to have 'teams' to provide the necessary communication and coordination, contrary to the Western style.

Product development teams are charged with the responsibility of moving from market requirements for a product to achieving a product success (see Figure 5.2 on page 137). Regardless of the formal nature of the product development effort, research suggests that success is more likely in an open, highly participative environment where those with potential contributions are allowed to make them. The objective of a product development team is to make the good or service a success. This includes marketability, manufacturability, and serviceability.

Use of such teams is also called **concurrent engineering** and implies a team representing all affected areas (known as a *cross-functional* team). Concurrent engineering also implies speedier product development through simultaneous performance of various aspects of product development.[2] The team approach is the dominant structure for product development by leading organizations in the United States.

Product development teams

Teams charged with moving from market requirements for a product to achieving product success.

Concurrent engineering

Use of participating teams in design and engineering activities.

Manufacturability and Value Engineering

Manufacturability and value engineering

Activities that help improve a product's design, production, maintainability, and use.

Manufacturability and value engineering activities are concerned with improvement of design and specifications at the research, development, design, and production stages of product development. In addition to immediate, obvious cost reduction, design for manufacturability and value engineering may produce other benefits. These include:

1. Reduced complexity of the product.
2. Reduction of environmental impact.
3. Additional standardization of components, which would lower the costs significantly due to the uniformity of inputs and outputs.
4. Improvement of functional aspects of the product.
5. Improved job design and job safety.
6. Improved maintainability (serviceability) of the product.
7. Robust design.

Manufacturability and value engineering activities may be the best cost-avoidance techniques available to operations management. They yield value improvement by focusing on achieving the functional specifications necessary to meet customer requirements in an optimal way—as shown in Figure 5.5, which demonstrates the cost reduction achieved for a specific bracket via value engineering.

ISSUES FOR PRODUCT DESIGN

In addition to developing an effective system and organization structure for product development, several *techniques* are important to the design of a product. We will now review six of these: (1) robust design; (2) modular design; (3) computer-aided design (CAD); (4) computer-aided manufacturing (CAM); (5) virtual reality technology; (6) value analysis.

▶ **FIGURE 5.5**
Cost Reduction of a Bracket via Value Engineering

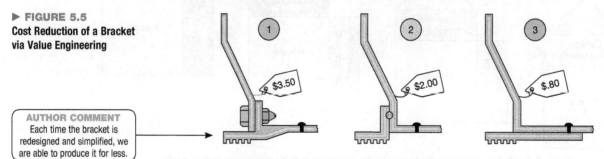

AUTHOR COMMENT
Each time the bracket is redesigned and simplified, we are able to produce it for less.

[2]Firms that have high technological or product change in their competitive environment tend to use more concurrent engineering practices. See X. Koufteros, M. Vonderembse, and W. Doll, "Concurrent Engineering and Its Consequences," *Journal of Operations Management* 19, no. 1 (January 2001): 97–115.

Robust Design

Robust design means that the product is designed so that small variations in production or assembly do not adversely affect the product. For instance, Nasr in Egypt tested different suspension systems to allow its cars to drive over a wide range of terrains, specifically in some parts of Egypt where streets are bumpy. The shock absorbers it developed were less sensitive to assembly variations because the cars were put together in fewer steps as a result of replacing the pressurized oil in the shock absorber with gas.

Robust design

A design that can be produced to requirements even with unfavorable conditions in the production process.

Modular Design

Modular designs offer flexibility to both production and marketing. Operations managers find modularity helpful because it makes product development, production, and subsequent changes easier. Moreover, marketing may like modularity because it adds flexibility to the ways customers can be satisfied. For instance, customers at Kudu restaurants can choose from a limited variety of 'modules' (cheese, lettuce, buns, sauces, pickles, fries, etc.) to make their favorite meal. This same concept of modularity is found in many industries, from airframe manufacturers to computer assembly. Airbus uses the same wing modules on several planes, just as Dell uses different hardware modules (processor, memory, video card type, hard drive storage, monitor size, etc.) to make a variety of personal computers.

Modular design

A design in which parts or components of a product are subdivided into modules that are easily interchanged or replaced.

Computer-Aided Design (CAD)

Computer-aided design (CAD) is the use of computers to interactively design products and prepare engineering documentation. Use and variety of CAD software is extensive and is rapidly expanding. CAD software allows designers to use three-dimensional drawings to save time and money by shortening development cycles for virtually all products (see the 3D design photos below). The speed and ease with which sophisticated designs can be manipulated, analyzed, and modified with CAD makes review of numerous options possible before final commitments are made. Faster development, better products, accurate flow of information to other departments—all contribute to a tremendous payoff for CAD. The payoff is particularly significant because most product costs are determined at the design stage.

Computer-aided design (CAD)

Interactive use of a computer to develop and document a product.

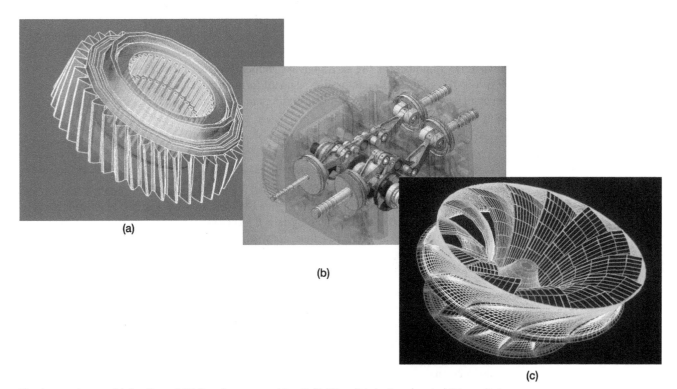

(a)

(b)

(c)

The increasing sophistication of CAD software provides (left) 3D solid design, (center) integrated assembly, and (right) analysis of stress, pressure, and thermal issues, which improves the design, speeds the design process, and provides computer code for CAM equipment while reducing costs.

Design for manufacture and assembly (DFMA)
Software that allows designers to look at the effect of design on manufacturing of the product.

3D object modeling
An extension of CAD that builds small prototypes.

This prototype wheel for a tire (at the left of the photo) is being built using 3D System's Stereolithography technology, a 3D object modeling system. This technology uses data from CAD and builds structures layer by layer in 0.001-inch increments. The technique reduces the time it takes to create a sample from weeks to hours while also reducing costs. The technique is also known as rapid prototyping.

One extension of CAD is **design for manufacture and assembly (DFMA)** software, which focuses on the effect of design on assembly. It allows designers to examine the integration of product designs before the product is manufactured. For instance, DFMA allows automobile designers to examine how a transmission will be placed in a car on the production line, even while both the transmission and the car are still in the design stage.

A second CAD extension is **3D object modeling**. The technology is particularly useful for small prototype development (as shown in the photo above). 3D object modeling rapidly builds up a model in very thin layers of synthetic materials for evaluation. This technology speeds development by avoiding a more lengthy and formal manufacturing process.

Some CAD systems have moved to the internet through e-commerce, where they link computerized design with purchasing, outsourcing, manufacturing, and long-term maintenance. This move supports rapid product change and the growing trend toward 'mass customization.' With CAD on the internet, customers can enter a supplier's design libraries and make design changes. The supplier's software can then automatically generate the drawings, update the bill of materials, and prepare instructions for the supplier's production process. The result is customized products produced faster and at less expense.

Standard for the exchange of product data (STEP)
A standard that provides a format allowing the electronic transmission of three-dimensional data.

As product life cycles shorten and design becomes more complex, collaboration among departments, facilities, and suppliers throughout the world becomes critical. The potential of such collaboration has proven so important that a standard for its exchange has been developed, known as the **standard for the exchange of product data (STEP)**. STEP allows manufacturers to express 3D product information in a standard format so it can be exchanged internationally, allowing geographically dispersed manufacturers to integrate design, manufacture, and support processes.[3]

Computer-Aided Manufacturing (CAM)

Computer-aided manufacturing (CAM)
The use of information technology to control machinery.

Computer-aided manufacturing (CAM) refers to the use of specialized computer programs to direct and control manufacturing equipment. When CAD information is translated into instructions for CAM, the result of these two technologies is CAD/CAM.

The benefits of CAD and CAM include:

1. *Product quality:* CAD allows the designer to investigate more alternatives, potential problems, and dangers.
2. *Shorter design time:* A shorter design phase lowers cost and allows a more rapid response to the market.
3. *Production cost reductions:* Reduced inventory, more efficient use of personnel through improved scheduling, and faster implementation of design changes results in lower costs.
4. *Database availability:* Provides information for other manufacturing software and accurate product data so everyone is operating from the same information, resulting in dramatic cost reductions.

[3]The STEP format is documented in the European Community's standard ISO 10303.

5. *New range of capabilities:* For instance, the abilities to rotate and depict objects in three-dimensional form, to check clearances, to relate parts and attachments, and to improve the use of numerically controlled machine tools—all provide new capability for manufacturing. CAD/CAM speeds up detail work, allowing designers to concentrate on the conceptual and imaginative aspects of their task. Al-Manar Engineering in Aleppo, Syria, has successfully deployed CAD/CAM technologies in creating innovative solutions for manufacturing industries, such as printing machines, rollers, centrifugal separators, steamers, and jets.

Virtual Reality Technology

Virtual reality is a visual form of communication in which images substitute for the real thing but still allow the user to respond interactively. The roots of virtual reality technology in operations are in CAD. Once design information is in a CAD system, it is also in electronic digital form for other uses, such as developing 3D layouts of everything from restaurants to amusement parks. Changes to mechanical design, restaurant layouts, or amusement park rides are much less expensive at the design stage than later.

Virtual reality
A visual form of communication in which images substitute for reality and typically allow the user to respond interactively.

Value Analysis

Although value engineering (discussed on page 140) focuses on *preproduction* design improvement, value analysis, a related technique, takes place *during* the production process, when it is clear that a new product is a success. **Value analysis** seeks improvements that lead to either a better product, or a product made more economically, or a product with less environmental impact. The techniques and advantages for value analysis are the same as for value engineering, although minor changes in implementation may be necessary because value analysis is taking place while the product is being produced.

Value analysis
A review of successful products that takes place during the production process.

ETHICS, ENVIRONMENTALLY FRIENDLY DESIGNS, AND SUSTAINABILITY

> **AUTHOR COMMENT**
> OM can do a lot to save our planet. Saving the planet is good practice and good ethics.

In an OM context, **sustainability** means ecological stability. This means operating a production system in a way that supports conservation and renewal of resources. The entire product life cycle—from design, to production, to final destruction or recycling—provides an opportunity to preserve resources. Operations managers have tools that can drive down costs or improve margins while preserving resources.

Sustainability
A production system that supports conservation and renewal of resources.

Many industries opt for more economical and environmentally friendly alternatives when it comes to selecting the materials to be included in the design of their new products, such as the replacement of chlorofluorocarbons (CFCs) in refrigeration by the less harmful hydrochlorofluorocarbons (HCFCs). At the production stage firms can encourage sustainability by using intranets or EDI (Electronic Data Interchange) instead of reams of paper. Sustainability can also be achieved by more recycling of the materials used in production. If enough consideration is given at the design phase, firms can recycle most of the materials used in their final products when the time comes for the products' destruction.

TIME-BASED COMPETITION

> **AUTHOR COMMENT**
> Fast communication, rapid technological change, and short product life cycles push product development.

As product life cycles shorten, the need for faster product development increases. Additionally, as technological sophistication of new products increases, so do the expense and risk. For instance, drug firms invest an average of 12 to 15 years and US$600 million in capital before receiving regulatory approval of each new drug. Even then, only 1 of 5 will actually be a success. Those operations managers who master this art of product development continuously gain on slower product developers. Swift development leads to competitive advantage. This concept is called **time-based competition**.

Often, the first company into production may have its product adopted for use in a variety of applications that will generate sales for years. It may become the 'standard.' Consequently, there is often more concern with getting the product to market than with optimum product design or process efficiency. Even so, rapid introduction to the market may be good management because until competition begins to introduce copies or improved versions, the product can sometimes

Time-based competition
Competition based on time; rapidly developing products and moving them to market.

▶ **FIGURE 5.6**
Product Development Continuum

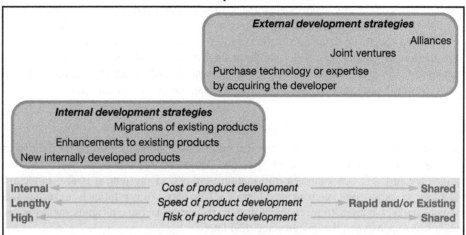

Product Development Continuum

**Product Development
Continuum**

LO4: Describe how time-based competition is implemented by OM

be priced high enough to justify somewhat inefficient production design and methods. For example, Fastlink in Jordan introduced wireless telecommunication solutions to the market at relatively high prices, knowing that competitors would need time to enter the market and provide cheaper alternatives.

Because time-based competition is so important, instead of developing new products from scratch (which has been the focus thus far in this chapter) a number of other strategies can be used. Figure 5.6 shows a continuum that goes from new, internally developed products (on the lower left) to 'alliances.' *Enhancements* and *migrations* use the organization's existing product strengths for innovation and therefore are typically faster while at the same time being less risky than developing entirely new products. Enhancements may be changes in color, size, weight, or features, such as are taking place in cellular phones (see *OM in Action* box 'Chasing Fads in the Cell Phone Industry').

The product development strategies on the lower left of Figure 5.6 are *internal* development strategies, while the three approaches we now introduce can be thought of as *external* development strategies. Firms use both. The external strategies are: (1) purchase the technology; (2) establish joint ventures; (3) develop alliances.

Purchasing Technology by Acquiring a Firm

Yahoo! is a good example of a company at the cutting edge of technology that speeds development by *acquiring entrepreneurial firms* that have already developed the technology that fits its mission. The acquisition of Maktoob (an Arab internet services company) in 2009 allowed Yahoo! to benefit from Maktoob's expertise and advancement in providing innovative solutions to its Arab audience in the MENA region. The issue became more one of fitting the purchased organization, its technology, its product lines, and its culture into the buying firm, rather than a product development issue.

Joint Ventures

Joint ventures
Firms establishing joint ownership to pursue new products or markets.

Joint ventures are combined ownership, usually between just two firms, to form a new entity. Ownership can be 50–50, or one owner can assume a larger portion to ensure tighter control. Joint ventures are often appropriate for exploiting specific product opportunities that may not be central to the firm's mission. Such ventures are more likely to work when the risks are known and can be equitably shared. For instance, Accenture and the Saudi Arabia-based Al Faisaliah Group entered into a joint venture to form Faisaliah Business and Technology Company (FBTC). Both companies saw a learning opportunity as well as a product they both needed in the Arabian market. FBTC focuses on providing enterprise resource planning solutions to companies in the region, benefiting from Accenture's knowledge and specialty in the field of technology, and Al Faisaliah's expertise in the Arabian market. The risks were well understood, as were the respective commitments.

OM in Action ▶ Chasing Fads in the Cell Phone Industry

In the shrinking world marketplace, innovations that appeal to customers in one region rapidly become global trends. The process shakes up the structure of one industry after another, from computers to automobiles to consumer electronics.

Nowhere has this impact been greater in recent years than in the cell phone industry. The industry sells about 1.3 billion phones each year, but product life cycle is short. Competition is intense. Higher margins go to the innovator—and manufacturers that jump on an emerging trend early can reap substantial rewards. The swiftest Chinese manufacturers, such as Ningbo Bird and TCL, now replace some phone models after just 6 months. In the past, Motorola, Nokia, and other industry veterans enjoyed what are now considered long life cycles—2 years. New styles and technological advances in cell phones constantly appear somewhere in the world. Wired, well-traveled consumers seek the latest innovation; local retailers rush to offer it; and telecommunication providers order it.

Contemporary cell phones may be a curvy, boxy, or a clamshell fashion item; have a tiny keyboard for quick and easy typing or a more limited number pad; have a built-in radio or a digital music player; have a camera, internet access, or TV clips; function on cellular or wireless (Wi-Fi) networks; or have games or personal organizers. Mattel and Nokia even have Barbie phones for preteen girls, complete with prepaid minutes, customized ringtones, and faceplates. The rapid changes in features and demand are forcing manufacturers into a frenzied race to keep up or simply to pull out.

"We got out of the handset business because we couldn't keep up with the cycle times," says Jeffrey Belk, Marketing Vice President for Qualcomm, Inc., the San Diego company that now focuses on making handset chips.

Developing new products is always a challenge, but in the dynamic global marketplace of cell phones, product development takes on new technology and new markets at breakneck speed.

Sources: Supply Chain Management Review (October, 2007): 28; *The Wall Street Journal* (October 30, 2003): A1 and (Sept. 8, 2004): D5; and *International Business Times* (March 3, 2009).

Alliances

Alliances are cooperative agreements that allow firms to remain independent but use complementing strengths to pursue strategies consistent with their individual missions. When new products are central to the mission, but substantial resources are required and sizable risk is present, then alliances may be a good strategy for product development. One example of an alliance is when Royal Jordanian joined British Airways in the Oneworld airline alliance, which enabled Royal Jordanian to order ten Boeing 787 Dreamliners—the latest in air travel technology. However, alliances are much more difficult to achieve and maintain than joint ventures because of the ambiguities associated with them. It may be helpful to think of an alliance as an incomplete contract between the firms. The firms remain separate.

Alliances
Cooperative agreements that allow firms to remain independent but pursue strategies consistent with their individual missions.

Networked Organizations

In the ever-changing market conditions of the 21st century, companies are seeking new ways to engage their workers with their surrounding environment to ensure that they are well prepared to meet any new challenges. The **networked organization** focuses on enabling its knowledge workers to continuously develop themselves to respond to the high uncertainty in the market with creative solutions. This is done by empowering and supporting the workers, and allowing them access to information. For example, Dell creates a free flow of information by connecting its workers and divisions through the use of advanced information and communication technologies.

Enhancements, migration, acquisitions, joint ventures, alliances, and networked organizations are all strategies for speeding product development. Moreover, they typically reduce the risk associated with product development while enhancing the human and capital resources available.

Networked organization
A group of autonomous units, divisions, or companies that become a single entity, using technology to coordinate and control the process.

DEFINING A PRODUCT

Once new goods or services are selected for introduction, they must be defined. First, a good or service is defined in terms of its *functions*—that is, what it is to *do*. The product is then designed, and the firm determines how the functions are to be achieved. Management typically has a variety of options as to how a product should achieve its functional purpose. For instance, when an alarm clock is produced, aspects of design such as the color, size, or location of buttons may make substantial differences in ease of manufacture, quality, and market acceptance.

AUTHOR COMMENT
Before anything can be produced, a product's functions and attributes must be defined.

► **FIGURE 5.7**
**Engineering Drawings
Such as This One Show
Dimensions, Tolerances,
Materials, and Finishes**

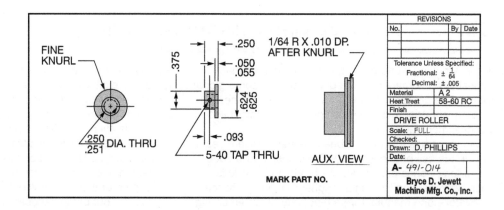

L05: Describe how products
and services are defined by OM

Engineering drawing

A drawing that shows the
dimensions, tolerances, materials,
and finishes of a component.

Bill of material (BOM)

A list of the components, their
description, and the quantity of
each required to make one unit of
a product.

Make-or-buy decision

A choice between producing a
component or service in-house
and purchasing it from an outside
source.

Group technology

A product and component coding
system that specifies the type of
processing and the parameters of
the processing; it allows similar
products to be grouped.

Rigorous specifications of a product are necessary to assure efficient production. Equipment, layout, and human resources cannot be determined until the product is defined, designed, and documented. Therefore, every organization needs documents to define its products. This is true of everything from meat patties, to cheese, to computers, to a medical procedure. In the case of cheese, a written specification is typical. On the other hand, most manufactured items as well as their components are defined by a drawing, usually referred to as an engineering drawing. An **engineering drawing** shows the dimensions, tolerances, materials, and finishes of a component. The engineering drawing will be an item on a bill of material. An engineering drawing is shown in Figure 5.7. The **bill of material (BOM)** lists the components, their description, and the quantity of each required to make one unit of a product.

Make-or-Buy Decisions

For many components of products, firms have the option of producing the components themselves or purchasing them from outside sources. Choosing between these options is known as the **make-or-buy decision**. Because of variations in quality, cost, and delivery schedules, the make-or-buy decision is critical to product definition. Many items can be purchased as a 'standard item' produced by someone else. We discuss the make-or-buy decision in more detail in Chapter 11.

Group Technology

Engineering drawings may also include codes to facilitate group technology. **Group technology** requires components to be identified by a coding scheme that specifies the type of processing (such as drilling) and the parameters of the processing (such as size). This facilitates standardization of materials, components, and processes as well as the identification of families of parts. As families of parts are identified, activities and machines can be grouped to minimize setups, routings, and material handling. An example of how families of parts may be grouped is shown in Figure 5.8.

► **FIGURE 5.8**
**A Variety of Group Technology
Coding Schemes Move
Manufactured Components
from (a) Ungrouped to
(b) Grouped (families of parts)**

(a) Ungrouped Parts	(b) Grouped Cylindrical Parts (families of parts)				
	Grooved	Slotted	Threaded	Drilled	Machined

Group technology provides a systematic way to review a family of components to see if an existing component might suffice on a new project. Using existing or standard components eliminates all the costs connected with the design and development of the new part, which is a major cost reduction. For these reasons, successful implementation of group technology leads to the following advantages.

1. Improved design (because more design time can be devoted to fewer components).
2. Reduced raw material and purchases.
3. Simplified production planning and control.
4. Improved layout, routing, and machine loading.
5. Reduced tooling setup time, and work-in-process and production time.

The application of group technology helps the entire organization, as many costs are reduced.

DOCUMENTS FOR PRODUCTION

Once a product is selected, designed, and ready for production, production is assisted by a variety of documents. We will briefly review some of these.

An **assembly drawing** simply shows an exploded view of the product. An assembly drawing is usually a three-dimensional drawing, known as an *isometric drawing*; the relative locations of components are drawn in relation to each other to show how to assemble the unit—see Figure 5.9(a).

The **assembly chart** shows in schematic form how a product is assembled. Manufactured components, purchased components, or a combination of both may be shown on an assembly chart. The assembly chart identifies the point of production at which components flow into subassemblies and ultimately into a final product. An example of an assembly chart is shown in Figure 5.9(b).

The **route sheet** lists the operations necessary to produce the component with the material specified in the bill of material. The route sheet for an item will have one entry for each operation to be performed on the item. When route sheets include specific methods of operation and labor standards, they are often known as *process sheets*.

The **work order** is an instruction to make a given quantity of a particular item, usually to a given schedule. The ticket that a waiter writes in your favorite restaurant is a work order. In a hospital or factory, the work order is a more formal document that provides authorization to draw various pharmaceuticals or items from inventory, to perform various functions, and to assign personnel to perform those functions.

Engineering change notices change some aspect of the product's definition or documentation, such as an engineering drawing or a bill of material. For a complex product that has a long manufacturing cycle, such as a Boeing 777, the changes may be so numerous that no two 777s

Assembly drawing
An exploded view of the product.

Assembly chart
A graphic means of identifying how components flow into subassemblies and final products.

Route sheet
A listing of the operations necessary to produce a component with the material specified in the bill of material.

Work order
An instruction to make a given quantity of a particular item.

Engineering change notice
A correction or modification of an engineering drawing or bill of material.

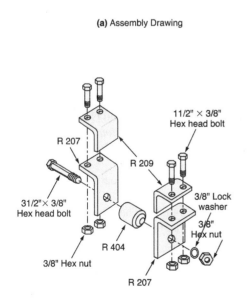

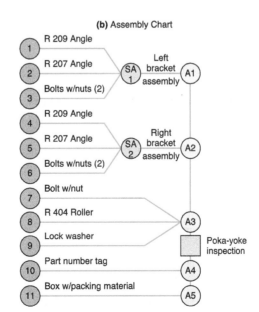

◄ FIGURE 5.9
Assembly Drawing and Assembly Chart

are built exactly alike—which is indeed the case. Such dynamic design change has fostered the development of a discipline known as configuration management, which is concerned with product identification, control, and documentation. **Configuration management** is the system by which a product's planned and changing configurations are accurately identified and for which control and accountability of change are maintained.

Product Life-Cycle Management (PLM)

Product life-cycle management (PLM) is an umbrella of software programs that attempts to bring together phases of product design and manufacture—including tying together many of the techniques discussed in the prior two sections, *Defining a Product* and *Documents for Production*. The idea behind PLM software is that product design and manufacture decisions can be performed more creatively, faster, and more economically when the data are integrated and consistent.

Although there is not one standard, PLM products often start with product design (CAD/CAM); move on to design for manufacture and assembly (DFMA); and then into product routing, materials, layout, assembly, maintenance, and even environmental issues.[4] Integration of these tasks makes sense because many of these decision areas require overlapping pieces of data.

Shorter life cycles, more technologically challenging products, more regulations about materials and manufacturing processes, and more environmental issues all make PLM an appealing tool for operations managers.

SERVICE DESIGN

Much of our discussion so far has focused on what we can call tangible products, that is, goods. On the other side of the product coin are, of course, services. Service industries include banking, finance, insurance, transportation, and communications.

Designing services is challenging because they often have unique characteristics. One reason productivity improvements in services are so low is because both the design and delivery of service products include customer interaction. When the customer participates in the design process, the service supplier may have a menu of services from which the customer selects options (see Figure 5.10a). At this point, the customer may even participate in the *design* of the service. Design specifications may take the form of a contract or a narrative description with photos (such as for cosmetic surgery or a hairstyle). Similarly, the customer may be involved in the *delivery* of a service (see Figure 5.10b) or in both *design and delivery*, a situation that maximizes the product design challenge (see Figure 5.10c).

However, as with goods, a large part of cost and quality of a service is defined at the design stage. Also as with goods, a number of techniques can both reduce costs and enhance the product. One technique is to design the product so that *customization is delayed* as late in the process as possible. This is the way a hair salon operates: Although shampooing and rinsing are done in a standard way with lower-cost labor, the tint and styling (customizing) are done last. It is also the way most restaurants operate: How would you like that cooked? Which dressing would you prefer with your salad?

The second approach is to *modularize* the product so that customization takes the form of changing modules. This strategy allows modules to be designed as 'fixed,' standard entities. For example, investment portfolios are put together on a modular basis, as are college curricula.

A third approach to the design of services is to divide the service into small parts and identify those parts that lend themselves to *automation* or *reduced customer interaction*. For instance, by isolating check-cashing activity via ATM machines, banks have been very effective at designing a product that both increases customer service and reduces costs.

Because of the high customer interaction in many service industries, a fourth technique is to focus design on the so-called moment of truth. The *moment of truth* is the moment that exemplifies, enhances, or detracts from the customer's expectations. That moment may be as simple as a smile or having the checkout clerk focus on you rather than talking over his shoulder

---

Configuration management
A system by which a product's planned and changing components are accurately identified.

Product life-cycle management (PLM)
Software programs that tie together many phases of product design and manufacture.

LO6: Describe the documents needed for production

AUTHOR COMMENT
Services also need to be defined and documented.

---

[4]Some PLM vendors include supply chain elements such as sourcing, material management, and vendor evaluation in their packages, but in most instances, these are considered part of the ERP systems discussed along with MRP in Chapter 14. See, for instance, SAP PLM (**www.mySAP.com**), Parametric Technology Corp. (**www.ptc.com**), Siemens PLM Software (**www.siemens.com/plm**), and Proplanner (**www.proplanner.com**).

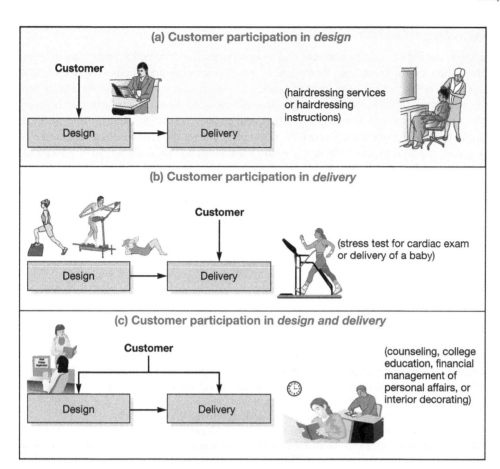

to the clerk at the next counter. Figure 5.11 shows a moment-of-truth analysis for a computer company's customer service hotline. The operations manager's task is to identify moments of truth and design operations that meet or exceed the customer's expectations.

Also worth mentioning is the current trend toward **servitization**, which seeks to understand customers' purchasing motivations and habits. Knowing how customers use the company's products and services helps the company provide a more specific service or product that will closely match what the customers want.

Servitization

The inclusion of a service component in each product to better meet the demands of the customers.

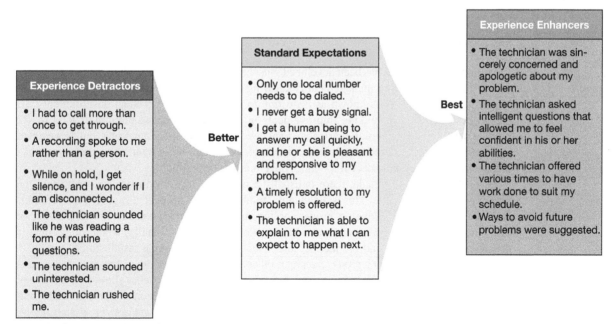

▲ **FIGURE 5.11**   **Moments of Truth: Customer Contacts at a Computer Company's Service Hotline Improve As We Move from Left to Right**

Documents for Services

LO7: Describe customer participation in the design and production of services

Because of the high customer interaction of most services, the documents for moving the product to production are different from those used in goods-producing operations. The documentation for a service will often take the form of explicit *job instructions* that specify what is to happen at the moment of truth. For instance, regardless of how good a bank's products may be in terms of checking, savings, trusts, loans, mortgages, and so forth, if the moment of truth is not done well, the product may be poorly received. Example 2 shows the kind of documentation a bank may use to move a product (drive-up window banking) to 'production.' In a telemarketing service, the product design is communicated to production personnel in the form of a *telephone script*, while a *storyboard* is used for movie and TV production.

EXAMPLE 2 ▶

Service documentation for production

First Bank Corp. wants to ensure effective delivery of service to its drive-up customers.

APPROACH ▶   Develop a 'production' document for the tellers at the drive-up window that provides the information necessary to do an effective job.

SOLUTION ▶

Documentation for Tellers at Drive-up Windows

Customers who use the drive-up teller windows rather than walk-in lobbies require a different customer relations technique. The distance and machinery between the teller and the customer raises communication barriers. Guidelines to ensure good customer relations at the drive-up window are:

- Be especially discreet when talking to the customer through the microphone.
- Provide written instructions for customers who must fill out forms you provide.
- Mark lines to be completed or attach a note with instructions.
- Always say "please" and "thank you" when speaking through the microphone.
- Establish eye contact with the customer if the distance allows it.
- If a transaction requires that the customer park the car and come into the lobby, apologize for the inconvenience.

Source: Adapted with permission from *Teller Operations* (Chicago, IL: The Institute of Financial Education, 1999): 32.

INSIGHT ▶   By providing documentation in the form of a script/guideline for tellers, the likelihood of effective communication and a good product/service is improved.

LEARNING EXERCISE ▶   Modify the guidelines above to show how they would be different for a drive-thru restaurant. [Answer: Written instructions, marking lines to be completed, or coming into the store are seldom necessary, but techniques for making change, and proper transfer of the order should be included.]

RELATED PROBLEM ▶   5.7

AUTHOR COMMENT
One of the arts of management is knowing when a product should move from development to production.

TRANSITION TO PRODUCTION

Eventually, a product that has been developed must move to the production phase or be terminated. One of the arts of modern management is knowing when to move a product from development to production; this move is known as *transition to production*. The product development staff are always interested in making improvements in a product. Because these staff tend to see product development as evolutionary, they may never have a completed product, but as we noted earlier, the cost of late product introduction is high. Although these conflicting pressures exist, management must make a decision—more development or production.

Once this decision is made, there is usually a period of trial production to ensure that the design is indeed producible. This is the manufacturability test. This trial also gives the operations staff the opportunity to develop proper tooling, quality control procedures, and training of personnel to ensure that production can be initiated successfully. Finally, when the product is deemed both marketable and producible, line management will assume responsibility.

Some companies appoint a *project manager*; others use *product development teams* to ensure that the transition from development to production is successful. Both approaches allow a wide range of resources and talents to be brought to bear to ensure satisfactory production of a product that is still in flux. A third approach is *integration of the product development and manufacturing organizations*. This approach allows for easy shifting of resources between the two organizations as needs change. The operations manager's job is to make the transition from R&D to production seamless.

CHAPTER SUMMARY

Effective product strategy requires selecting, designing, and defining a product and then transitioning that product to production. Only when this strategy is carried out effectively can the production function contribute its maximum to the organization. The operations manager must build a product development system that has the ability to conceive, design, and produce products that will yield a competitive advantage for the firm. As products move through their life cycle (introduction, growth, maturity, and decline), the options that the operations manager should pursue change. Both manufactured and service products have a variety of techniques available to aid in performing this activity efficiently.

Written specifications, bills of material, and engineering drawings help in defining products. Similarly, assembly drawings, assembly charts, route sheets, and work orders are often used to assist in the actual production of the product. Once a product is in production, value analysis is appropriate to ensure maximum product value. Engineering change notices and configuration management provide product documentation.

Key Terms

3D object modeling (p. 142)
Alliances (p. 145)
Assembly chart (p. 147)
Assembly drawing (p. 147)
Bill of material (BOM) (p. 146)
Computer-aided design (CAD) (p. 141)
Computer-aided manufacturing (CAM)
 (p. 142)
Concurrent engineering (p. 140)
Configuration management (p. 148)
Design for manufacture and assembly
 (DFMA) (p. 142)
Engineering change notice (p. 147)

Engineering drawing (p. 146)
Group technology (p. 146)
House of quality (p. 137)
Joint ventures (p. 144)
Make-or-buy decision (p. 146)
Manufacturability and value engineering
 (p. 140)
Modular design (p. 141)
Networked organization (p. 145)
Product decision (p. 134)
Product development teams (p. 140)
Product life-cycle management (PLM)
 (p. 148)

Product-by-value analysis (p. 136)
Quality function deployment (QFD)
 (p. 137)
Robust design (p. 141)
Route sheet (p. 147)
Servitization (p. 149)
Standard for the exchange of product data
 (STEP) (p. 142)
Sustainability (p. 143)
Time-based competition (p. 143)
Value analysis (p. 143)
Virtual reality (p. 143)
Work order (p. 147)

Ethical Dilemma

Hashem Hammoudeh, president of Hammoudeh Toy Company, Inc., in Doha, has just reviewed the design of a new toy train for 1- to 3-year-olds. Hashem's design and marketing staff are very enthusiastic about the market for the product and the potential of follow-on train cars. The sales manager is looking forward to a very good reception at the annual toy show in Tripoli next month. Hashem, too, is delighted, as he is faced with laying off staff if orders do not improve.

Hashem's production people have worked out the manufacturing issues and produced a successful pilot run. However, the quality testing staff suggest that under certain conditions, a hook to attach cars to the train and the crank for the bell can be broken off. This is an issue because children can choke on small parts such as these. In the quality test, 1- to 3-year-olds were unable to break off these parts; there were *no* failures. But when the test simulated the force of an adult tossing the train into a toy box or a 5-year-old throwing it on the floor, there were failures. The estimate is that one of the two parts can be broken off four times out of 100,000 throws. Neither the design nor the materials people know how to make the toy safer and still perform as designed. The failure rate is low and certainly normal

for this type of toy, but not at the level that Hashem's firm strives for. And, of course, someone, someday may sue. A child choking on the broken part is a serious matter. Also, Hashem was recently reminded in a discussion with legal counsel that the new Qatari laws suggest that new products may not be produced if there is 'actual or foreseeable knowledge of a problem' with the product.

The design of successful, ethically produced, new products, as suggested in this chapter, is a complex task. What should Hashem do?

Discussion Questions

1. Why is it necessary to document a product explicitly?
2. What techniques do we use to define a product?
3. In what ways is product strategy linked to product decisions?
4. Once a product is defined, what documents are used to assist production personnel in its manufacture?
5. What is time-based competition?
6. Describe the differences between joint ventures and alliances.
7. Describe four organizational approaches to product development. Which of these is generally thought to be best?
8. Explain what is meant by robust design.
9. What are three specific ways in which computer-aided design (CAD) benefits the design engineer?
10. What information is contained in a bill of material?
11. What information is contained in an engineering drawing?
12. What information is contained in an assembly chart? In a process sheet?
13. Explain what is meant in service design by the 'moment of truth.'
14. Explain how the house of quality translates customer desires into product/service attributes.
15. What is meant by *sustainability* in the context of operations management?
16. What strategic advantages does computer-aided design provide?

Problems

•• **5.1** Construct a house of quality matrix for a wristwatch. Be sure to indicate specific customer wants that you think the general public desires. Then complete the matrix to show how an operations manager might identify specific attributes that can be measured and controlled to meet those customer desires.

•• **5.2** Using the house of quality, pick a real product (a good or service) and analyze how an existing organization satisfies customer requirements.

•• **5.3** Prepare a house of quality for a mousetrap.

•• **5.4** Conduct an interview with a prospective purchaser of a new bicycle and translate the customer's *wants* into the specific *hows* of the firm.

•• **5.5** Prepare a bill of material for (a) a pair of eyeglasses and its case or (b) a fast-food sandwich (visit a local sandwich shop like Kudu; perhaps a manager will provide you with details on the quantity or weight of various ingredients—otherwise, estimate the quantities).

•• **5.6** Draw an assembly chart for a pair of eyeglasses and its case.

•• **5.7** Prepare a script for telephone callers at the university's annual 'phone-a-thon' fund raiser.

•• **5.8** Prepare an assembly chart for a table lamp.

••• **5.9** Prepare a product-by-value analysis for the following products, and given the position in its life cycle, identify the issues likely to confront the operations manager, and his or her possible actions. Product Aleph has annual sales of 1,000 units and a contribution of US$2,500; it is in the introductory stage. Product Ba' has annual sales of 1,500 units and a contribution of US$3,000; it is in the growth stage. Product Jeem has annual sales of 3,500 units and a contribution of US$1,750; it is in the decline stage.

•• **5.10** Given the contribution made on each of the three products in the following table and their position in the life cycle, identify a reasonable operations strategy for each:

Product	Product Contribution (% of selling price)	Company Contribution (%: total annual contribution divided by total annual sales)	Position in Life Cycle
Kindle	30	40	Growth
Netbook computer	30	50	Introduction
Hand calculator	50	10	Decline

•••• **5.11** Using the house of quality sequence, as described in Figure 5.4 on page 139, determine how you might deploy resources to achieve the desired quality for a product or service whose production process you understand.

▶ **Refer to** MyOMLab **for additional homework problems.**

Case Studies

▶ Temsa Global's Product Strategy

Temsa Global is an automotive company with factories in Adana, Adapazari, Egypt. It produces buses, minibuses, and light trucks in its factories in Turkey. The company started out its business as a licensor of Mitsubishi products in 1984, when it could manufacture only the licensed products. Since 2001, Temsa Global has gradually developed design capabilities to support the shift in its product strategy. In 2009, Temsa R&D and Technology, Inc., which was founded in 2003, had more than 200 employees.

In 2009, Temsa Global introduced its first city bus model, Avenue. Temsa Global has designed Avenue primarily for the European markets, in collaboration with its customer Arriva, a U.K.-based transport services company that has operations in 12 European countries. Temsa R&D and Technology, Inc. center cooperates with universities and research institutes on advanced technologies and breakthrough applications. Avenue was designed by Temsa Global's sister company Temsa R&D and Technology, Inc. and the new design has decreased the production costs considerably. The cost reduction is expected to allow Temsa Global to price its buses competitively with respect to its competitors' similar products. Currently the bus industry is moving toward hybrid power technologies, and green design continues to gain importance. Temsa Global has managed to catch this wave early; Avenue is over 1,700 pounds lighter than similar buses, thanks to the composite materials used in the body, and its hybrid version offers 25 percent savings on fuel consumption.

The next step is to market Avenue in other European countries, as well as in Turkey. Customers in different markets have specific requirements, and Avenue's modular design will play a pivotal role in offering customized products.

Through product design, Temsa has become a global brand in less than a decade. The next challenge Temsa faces is to support its customer-driven strategy with a service network that covers markets with seemingly different characteristics. This may require acquiring new skills.

Discussion Questions

1. What was the product strategy of Temsa Global in 2009? How was it different from the product strategy in 1984? What organizational changes are required to support this shift?
2. What are the possible advantages of investing in the R&D center for advanced technologies? Discuss the implications, considering the changing perceptions and demands of consumers.
3. What should be the focus of Temsa Global in supporting its market-driven product strategy and customized designs?

Sources: **www.temsaglobal.com.tr**; **www.busworld.org**; **www.hurriyet.com.tr**. Case prepared by Dr. Ervim Didem Gunes and Dr. Selcuk Karabati, College of Administrative Sciences and Economics, Koc University, Turkey.

▶ Product Design at Regal Marine

Video Case

With hundreds of competitors in the boat business, Regal Marine must work to differentiate itself from the flock. Regal continuously introduces innovative, high-quality new boats. Its differentiation strategy is reflected in a product line consisting of 22 models.

To maintain this stream of innovation, and with so many boats at varying stages of their life cycles, Regal constantly seeks design input from customers, dealers, and consultants. Design ideas rapidly find themselves in the styling studio, where they are placed onto CAD machines in order to speed the development process. Existing boat designs are always evolving as the company tries to stay stylish and competitive. Moreover, with life cycles as short as 3 years, a steady stream of new products is required. A few years ago, the new product was the three-passenger US$11,000 Rush, a small but powerful boat capable of pulling a water-skier. This was followed with a 20-foot inboard–outboard performance boat with so many innovations that it won prize after prize in the industry. Another new boat is a redesigned 44-foot Commodore that sleeps six in luxury staterooms. With all these models and innovations, Regal designers and production personnel are under pressure to respond quickly.

By getting key suppliers on board early and urging them to participate at the design stage, Regal improves both innovations and quality while speeding product development. Regal finds that the sooner it brings suppliers on board, the faster it can bring new boats to the market. After a development stage that constitutes concept and styling, CAD designs yield product specifications. The first stage in actual production is the creation of the 'plug,' a foam-based carving used to make the molds for fiberglass hulls and decks. Specifications from the CAD system drive the carving process. Once the plug is carved, the permanent molds for each new hull and deck design are formed. Molds take about 4 to 8 weeks to make and are all handmade. Similar molds are made for many of the other features in Regal boats—from galley and stateroom components to lavatories and steps. Finished molds can be joined and used to make thousands of boats.

Discussion Questions*

1. How does the concept of product life cycle apply to Regal Marine products?
2. What strategy does Regal use to stay competitive?
3. What kind of engineering savings is Regal achieving by using CAD technology rather than traditional drafting techniques?
4. What are the likely benefits of the CAD design technology?

*You may wish to view the video that accompanies this case before addressing these questions.

Chapter 5 *Rapid* Review

Main Heading	Review Material	
GOODS AND SERVICES SELECTION (pp. 134–136)	Although the term *products* may often refer to tangible goods, it also refers to offerings by service organizations. *The objective of the product decision is to develop and implement a product strategy that meets the demands of the marketplace with a competitive advantage.* ■ **Product decision**—The selection, definition, and design of products. The four phases of the product life cycle are introduction, growth, maturity, and decline. ■ **Product-by-value analysis**—A list of products, in descending order of their individual monetary contribution to the firm, as well as the *total annual monetary* contribution of the product.	**VIDEO 5.1** Product Design at Regal Marine Problem: 5.9
GENERATING NEW PRODUCTS (p. 136)	Product selection, definition, and design take place on a continuing basis. Changes in product opportunities, the products themselves, product volume, and product mix may arise due to understanding the customer, economic change, sociological and demographic change, technological change, political/legal change, market practice, professional standards, suppliers, or distributors.	
PRODUCT DEVELOPMENT (pp. 137–140)	■ **Quality function deployment (QFD)**—A process for determining customer requirements (customer 'wants') and translating them into attributes (the 'hows') that each functional area can understand and act on. ■ **House of quality**—A part of the quality function deployment process that utilizes a planning matrix to relate customer wants to how the firm is going to meet those wants. ■ **Product development teams**—Teams charged with moving from market requirements for a product to achieving product success. ■ **Concurrent engineering**—Use of participating teams in design and engineering activities. ■ **Manufacturability and value engineering**—Activities that help improve a product's design, production, maintainability, and use.	
ISSUES FOR PRODUCT DESIGN (pp. 140–143)	■ **Robust design**—A design that can be produced to requirements even with unfavorable conditions in the production process. ■ **Modular design**—A design in which parts or components of a product are subdivided into modules that are easily interchanged or replaced. ■ **Computer-aided design (CAD)**—Interactive use of a computer to develop and document a product. ■ **Design for manufacture and assembly (DFMA)**—Software that allows designers to look at the effect of design on the manufacturing of a product. ■ **3D object modeling**—An extension of CAD that builds small prototypes. ■ **Standard for the exchange of product data (STEP)**—A standard that provides a format allowing the electronic transmission of three-dimensional data. ■ **Computer-aided manufacturing (CAM)**—The use of information technology to control machinery. ■ **Virtual reality**—A visual form of communication in which images substitute for reality and typically allow the user to respond interactively. ■ **Value analysis**—A review of successful products that takes place during the production process.	
ETHICS, ENVIRONMENTALLY FRIENDLY DESIGNS, AND SUSTAINABILITY (p. 143)	■ **Sustainability**—A production system that supports conservation and renewal of resources.	
TIME-BASED COMPETITION (pp. 143–145)	■ **Time-based competition**—Competition based on time; rapidly developing products and moving them to market. *Internal development strategies* include: (1) new internally developed products; (2) enhancements to existing products; (3) migrations of existing products. *External development strategies* include: (1) purchase the technology or expertise by acquiring the developer; (2) establish joint ventures; (3) develop alliances. ■ **Joint ventures**—Firms establishing joint ownership to pursue new products or markets. ■ **Alliances**—Cooperative agreements that allow firms to remain independent but pursue strategies consistent with their individual missions. ■ **Networked organization**—A group of autonomous units, divisions, or companies that become a single entity through the use of social mechanisms for coordination and control, supported by information and communication technologies.	

Main Heading	Review Material
DEFINING A PRODUCT (pp. 145–147)	■ **Engineering drawing**—A drawing that shows the dimensions, tolerances, materials, and finishes of a component. ■ **Bill of material (BOM)**—A list of the components, their description, and the quantity of each required to make one unit of a product. ■ **Make-or-buy decision**—The choice between producing a component or a service and purchasing it from an outside source. ■ **Group technology**—A product and component coding system that specifies the type of processing and the parameters of the processing; it allows similar products to be grouped.
DOCUMENTS FOR PRODUCTION (pp. 147–148)	■ **Assembly drawing**—An exploded view of a product. ■ **Assembly chart**—A graphic means of identifying how components flow into subassemblies and final products. ■ **Route sheet**—A list of the operations necessary to produce a component with the material specified in the bill of material. ■ **Work order**—An instruction to make a given quantity of a particular item. ■ **Engineering change notice**—A correction or modification of an engineering drawing or bill of material. ■ **Configuration management**—A system by which a product's planned and changing components are accurately identified. ■ **Product life-cycle management (PLM)**—Software programs that tie together many phases of product design and manufacture.
SERVICE DESIGN (pp. 148–150)	Techniques to reduce costs and enhance the service offering include: (1) delaying customization; (2) modularizing; (3) automating; (4) designing for the 'moment of truth.' **Servitization** also aims to increase the service offerings in products, and is used in the manufacturing sector too.
TRANSITION TO PRODUCTION (p. 150)	One of the arts of modern management is knowing when to move a product from development to production; this move is known as *transition to production*.

Self-Test

■ **Before taking the self-test,** refer to the learning objectives listed at the beginning of the chapter and the key terms listed at the end of the chapter.

LO1. A product's life cycle is divided into four stages, including:
   a) introduction
   b) growth
   c) maturity
   d) all of the above.

LO2. Product development systems include:
   a) bills of material
   b) routing charts
   c) functional specifications
   d) product-by-values analysis
   e) configuration management.

LO3. A house of quality is:
   a) a matrix relating customer 'wants' to the firm's 'hows'
   b) a schematic showing how a product is put together
   c) a list of the operations necessary to produce a component
   d) an instruction to make a given quantity of a particular item
   e) a set of detailed instructions about how to perform a task.

LO4. Time-based competition focuses on:
   a) moving new products to market more quickly
   b) reducing the life cycle of a product
   c) linking QFD to PLM
   d) design database availability
   e) value engineering.

LO5. Products are defined by:
   a) value analysis
   b) value engineering
   c) routing sheets
   d) assembly charts
   e) engineering drawings.

LO6. A route sheet:
   a) lists the operations necessary to produce a component
   b) is an instruction to make a given quantity of a particular item
   c) is a schematic showing how a product is assembled
   d) is a document showing the flow of product components
   e) all of the above.

LO7. Four techniques available when a service is designed are:
   a) recognize political or legal change, technological change, sociological demographic change, and economic change
   b) understand product introduction, growth, maturity, and decline
   c) recognize functional specifications, product specifications, design review, and test markets
   d) ensure that customization is done as late in the process as possible, modularize the product, reduce customer interaction, and focus on the moment of truth.

Answers: LO1. d; **LO2.** c; **LO3.** a; **LO4.** a; **LO5.** e; **LO6.** a; **LO7.** d.

6 Quality Management and International Standards

10 OM STRATEGY DECISIONS

▶ Design of Goods and Services
▶ Managing Quality
▶ Process Strategy
▶ Location Strategies
▶ Layout Strategies
▶ Human Resources
▶ Supply-Chain Management
▶ Inventory Management
▶ Scheduling
▶ Maintenance

QUALITY-BASED COMPETITIVE ADVANTAGE

Established in 1965 as a private hospital, the New Mowasat Hospital (NMH) in Kuwait has been described as the highest quality health care provider in the country. The hospital's strategy has always focused on bringing the latest in health services and technology to Kuwait, to cater for the growing needs of the Kuwaiti population.

The hospital is divided into two main complexes: the inpatients' building and the outpatients' complex. The inpatients' building stretches over an area of 17,000 square meters and includes 96 fully serviced bed suites. It is equipped with various laboratories and a pharmacy, ultrasound scanning facilities, and a radiology department capable of CT scanning, bone densitometry, MRI, echo-cardiography, and mammography. The outpatients' complex is the medical plaza in Salmiya. It is considered one of the most prestigious medical specialty centers in Kuwait, incorporating state-of-the-art technology and the latest in modern medicine.

NMH thrives on excellence in quality; it continually introduces new technology, equipment, and programs in pursuit of a better service for its patients. The stress on quality is implemented through the continuous development approach by which NMH canvasses its patients, whether by questionnaires or follow-up procedures, on the quality of the services provided and what could have been done better. The feedback ranges from requesting new types of surgery to new hospital services.

Recently, due to increased awareness of the anxiety felt by children in hospital, NMH introduced a child-life program to make hospitalization friendlier for children and their parents. The program deals with every aspect of the hospitalization process, from preparing nurses, doctors, and care-givers, to dealing with children in a much more considered way, to health wards that are specifically designed for children. The children's wards have been painted in shiny, pleasant colors to match the smocks of the nurses and to create a happy atmosphere for the children that helps make them more emotionally prepared for treatment. Children are examined in a dedicated 'treatment room' rather than in their beds, to help them feel safer in their own beds. This emphasis on emotional aspects of treatment has guided the hospital to design a special area for therapeutic play in the pediatric department and if the children are not well enough to attend, then games and activities can be brought into their rooms. Of course, special attention has been given to the design of toys in order to ensure safety. For example, toys are selected that contain lead-free paint, no loose straps, or sharp ends.

NMH's focus on providing excellent child care has made it the number one destination for parents to take their sick children. The total quality approach pursued by NMH has given it a competitive advantage over the other hospitals in Kuwait. Many of the different aspects of quality management presented in this chapter are employed at NMH:

- *Continuous improvement:* This is clear in NMH's relentless quest for new ways to provide superior service.
- *Employee empowerment:* This is apparent in NMH's ongoing training programs and the systems that enable employees to provide direct feedback and take action in favor of a better service.

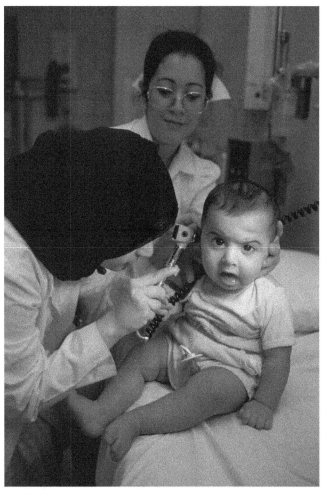

Specialized and well trained pediatricians monitor the operations in each clinic and ensure continuous care for the children.

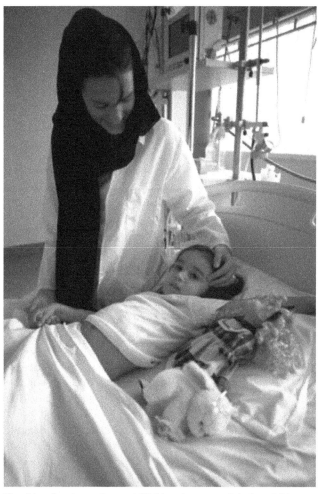

The friendly atmosphere at NMH reduces anxiety for children at the hospital.

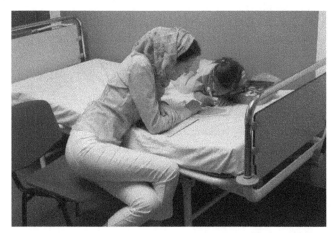

NMH strives to make the hospital a welcoming environment rather than a difficult time away from fun.

- *Benchmarking:* NMH is accredited by prestigious international health accreditation programs, such as the Canadian Council on Health Services Accreditation (CCHSA) and the Joint Commission International (JCI), which further indicates its commitment to the highest health standards.

- *Tools such as flowcharts:* These help NMH monitor processes and graphically identify problem areas, and suggest ways they can be improved.

This culture of quality and excellence drives the present and future of NMH, and ensures its superior position in Kuwait's health sector.

Source: **www.newmowasat.com**

Chapter 6 **Learning Objectives**

> **AUTHOR COMMENT**
> Quality is an issue that affects an entire organization.

QUALITY AND STRATEGY

As New Mowasat Hospital and many other organizations have found, quality is a great recipe for success. Managing quality helps build successful strategies of *differentiation*, *low cost*, and *response*. For instance, defining customer quality expectations has helped Qatar Airways successfully *differentiate* its flight services as among the best in the world. Jordan Cement has learned to produce quality cement at *low cost* by developing efficient processes that produce consistent quality. And Rubicon Studios rapidly *responds* to customer orders because quality systems have allowed it to rapidly respond to its customers' varying wants and specifications of digital content. Indeed, quality may be the critical success factor for these firms just as it is at New Mowasat Hospital.

> **VIDEO 6.1**
> The Culture of Quality at Arnold Palmer Hospital

As Figure 6.1 suggests, improvements in quality help firms increase sales and reduce costs, both of which can increase profitability. Increases in sales often occur as firms speed response, increase or lower selling prices, and improve their reputation for quality products. Similarly, improved quality allows costs to drop as firms increase productivity and lower rework, scrap, and warranty costs. One study found that companies with the highest quality were five times as productive (as measured by units produced per labor-hour) as companies with the poorest quality. Indeed, when the implications of an organization's long-term costs and the potential for increased sales are considered, total costs may well be at a minimum when 100 percent of the goods or services are perfect and defect free.

Quality, or the lack of quality, affects the entire organization from supplier to customer and from product design to maintenance. Perhaps more importantly, *building* an organization that can achieve quality is a demanding task. Figure 6.2 lays out the flow of activities for an organization to use to achieve total quality management (TQM). A successful quality strategy begins with an organizational culture that fosters quality, followed by an understanding of the principles of quality, and then engaging employees in the necessary activities to implement quality. When these things are done well, the organization typically satisfies its customers and obtains a competitive advantage. The ultimate goal is to win customers. Because quality causes so many other good things to happen, it is a great place to start.

> **AUTHOR COMMENT**
> To create a quality good or service, operations managers need to know what the customer expects.

DEFINING QUALITY

Quality
The ability of a product or service to meet customer needs.

An operations manager's objective is to build a total quality management system that identifies and satisfies customer needs. Total quality management takes care of the customer. Consequently, we define **quality** as *the ability of a product or service to meet customer wants and needs.*

▶ **FIGURE 6.1**

Ways Quality Improves Profitability

> **AUTHOR COMMENT**
> High-quality products and services are the most profitable.

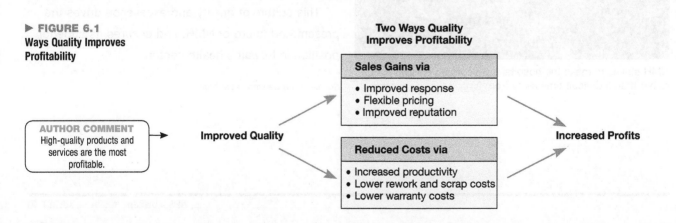

Two Ways Quality Improves Profitability

Sales Gains via
- Improved response
- Flexible pricing
- Improved reputation

Reduced Costs via
- Increased productivity
- Lower rework and scrap costs
- Lower warranty costs

Improved Quality

Increased Profits

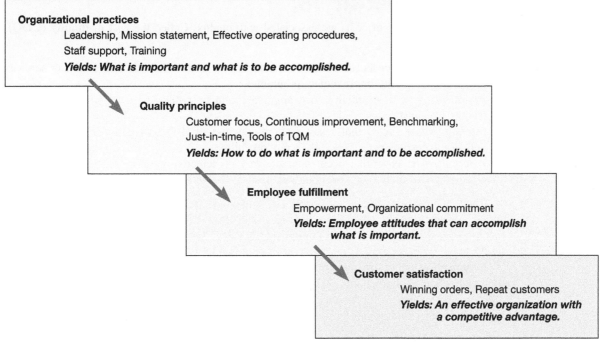

▲ FIGURE 6.2   **The Flow of Activities that are Necessary to Achieve Total Quality Management**

Definitions of quality fall into several categories. Some definitions are *user based*. They propose that quality 'lies in the eyes of the beholder.' Marketing people like this approach and so do customers. To them, higher quality means better performance, nicer features, and other (sometimes costly) improvements. To production managers, quality is *manufacturing based*. They believe that quality means conforming to standards and 'making it right the first time.' Yet a third approach is *product based*, which views quality as a precise and measurable variable. In this view, for example, really good ice cream has high butterfat levels.

LO1: Define quality and TQM

This text develops approaches and techniques to address all three categories of quality. The characteristics that suggest quality must first be identified through research (a user-based approach to quality). These characteristics are then translated into specific product attributes (a product-based approach to quality). Then, the manufacturing process is organized to ensure that products are made precisely to specifications (a manufacturing-based approach to quality). A process that ignores any one of these steps will not result in a quality product.

Implications of Quality

In addition to being a critical element in operations, quality has other implications. Here are three other reasons why quality is important.

1. *Company reputation:* An organization can expect its reputation for quality—be it good or bad—to follow it. Quality will show up in perceptions about the firm's new products, employment practices, and supplier relations. Self-promotion is not a substitute for quality products.
2. *Product liability:* The courts increasingly hold organizations that design, produce, or distribute faulty products or services liable for damages or injuries resulting from their use. Legislation such as the United States' Consumer Product Safety Act sets and enforces product standards by banning products that do not reach those standards. Impure foods that cause illness, nightgowns that burn, tires that fall apart, or auto fuel tanks that explode on impact can all lead to huge legal expenses, large settlements or losses, and terrible publicity.
3. *Global implications:* In this technological age, quality is an international, as well as an OM, concern. For both a company and a country to compete effectively in the global economy, products must meet global quality, design, and price expectations. Inferior products harm a firm's profitability and a nation's balance of payments.

Cost of Quality (COQ)

Cost of quality (COQ)
The cost of doing things wrong—that is, the price of nonconformance.

Four major categories of costs are associated with quality. Called the **cost of quality (COQ)**, they are:

- *Prevention costs:* costs associated with reducing the potential for defective parts or services (e.g. training, quality improvement programs).
- *Appraisal costs:* costs related to evaluating products, processes, parts, and services (e.g. testing, labs, inspectors).
- *Internal failure:* costs that result from production of defective parts or services before delivery to customers (e.g. rework, scrap, downtime).
- *External costs:* costs that occur after delivery of defective parts or services (e.g. rework, returned goods, liabilities, lost goodwill, costs to society).

The first three costs can be reasonably estimated, but external costs are very hard to quantify. When GE had to recall 3.1 million dishwashers in 1999 (because of a defective switch alleged to have started seven fires), the cost of repairs exceeded the value of all the machines. This leads to the belief by many experts that the cost of poor quality is consistently underestimated.

Observers of quality management believe that, on balance, the cost of quality products is only a fraction of the benefits. They think the real losers are organizations that fail to work aggressively at quality. For instance, Philip Crosby stated that quality is free. "What costs money are the unquality things—all the actions that involve not doing it right the first time."[1]

Leaders in Quality   Besides Crosby there are several other leaders in the field of quality management, including Deming, Feigenbaum, and Juran. Table 6.1 summarizes their philosophies and contributions.

Ethics and Quality Management

For operations managers, one of the most important jobs is to deliver healthy, safe, and quality products and services to customers. The development of poor-quality products, because of

▶ **TABLE 6.1**
Leaders in the Field of Quality Management

Leader	Philosophy/Contribution
W. Edwards Deming	Deming insisted management accept responsibility for building good systems. The employee cannot produce products that on average exceed the quality of what the process is capable of producing. His 14 points for implementing quality improvement are presented in this chapter.
Joseph M. Juran	A pioneer in teaching the Japanese how to improve quality, Juran believed strongly in top-management commitment, support, and involvement in the quality effort. He was also a believer in teams that continuously seek to raise quality standards. Juran differs from Deming somewhat in focusing on the customer and defining quality as fitness for use, not necessarily the written specifications.
Armand Feigenbaum	His 1961 book, *Total Quality Control*, laid out 40 steps to quality improvement processes. He viewed quality not as a set of tools but as a total field that integrated the processes of a company. His work in how people learn from each other's successes led to the field of cross-functional teamwork.
Philip B. Crosby	*Quality Is Free* was Crosby's attention-getting book published in 1979. Crosby believed that in the traditional trade-off between the cost of improving quality and the cost of poor quality, the cost of poor quality is understated. The cost of poor quality should include all of the things that are involved in not doing the job right the first time. Crosby coined the term *zero defects* and stated, "There is absolutely no reason for having errors or defects in any product or service."

[1]Philip B. Crosby, *Quality Is Free* (New York: McGraw-Hill, 1979). Further, J. M. Juran states, in his book *Juran on Quality by Design* (The Free Press 1992, 119), that costs of poor quality "are huge, but the amounts are not known with precision. In most companies the accounting system provides only a minority of the information needed to quantify this cost of poor quality. It takes a great deal of time and effort to extend the accounting system so as to provide full coverage."

inadequate design and production processes, results not only in higher production costs but also leads to injuries, lawsuits, and increased government regulation.

If a firm believes that it has introduced a questionable product, ethical conduct must dictate the responsible action. This may be a worldwide recall, as conducted by both Johnson & Johnson (for Tylenol) and Perrier (for sparkling water), when each of these products was found to be contaminated. A manufacturer must accept responsibility for any poor-quality product released to the public. In previous years, Ford (the Explorer SUV maker) and Firestone (the radial tire maker) have been accused of failing to issue product recalls, of withholding damaging information, and of handling complaints on an individual basis.[2]

There are many stakeholders involved in the production and marketing of poor-quality products, including stockholders, employees, customers, suppliers, distributors, and creditors. As a matter of ethics, management must ask if any of these stakeholders are being wronged. Every company needs to develop core values that become day-to-day guidelines for everyone from the CEO to production-line employees.

INTERNATIONAL QUALITY STANDARDS

ISO 9000

> **AUTHOR COMMENT**
> International quality standards grow in prominence every year. See **www.iso.ch** and **www.asq.org** to learn more about them.

ISO 9000
A set of quality standards developed by the International Organization for Standardization (ISO).

Quality is so important globally that the world is uniting around a single quality standard, **ISO 9000**. ISO 9000 is the only quality standard with international recognition. In 1987, 91 member nations published a series of quality assurance standards, known collectively as ISO 9000. The focus of the standards is to establish quality management procedures, through leadership, detailed documentation, work instructions, and recordkeeping. These procedures, we should note, say nothing about the actual quality of the product—they deal entirely with standards to be followed.

To become ISO 9000 certified, organizations go through a 9- to 18-month process that involves documenting quality procedures, an on-site assessment, and an ongoing series of audits of their products or services. To do business globally, being listed in the ISO directory is critical. As of 2011, there were over 1.7 million certifications awarded to firms in 175 countries.

LO2: Describe the ISO international quality standards

ISO upgraded its standards in 2008 into more of a quality management system, which is detailed in its ISO 9001: 2008 component. Leadership by top management and customer requirements and satisfaction play a much larger role, while documented procedures receive less emphasis under ISO 9001: 2008.

ISO 14000

ISO 14000
A series of environmental management standards established by the International Organization for Standardization (ISO).

The continuing internationalization of quality is evident with the development of **ISO 14000**. ISO 14000 is a series of environmental management standards that contain five core elements: (1) environmental management; (2) auditing; (3) performance evaluation; (4) labeling; (5) life cycle assessment. The new standard could have several advantages:

- Positive public image and reduced exposure to liability.
- Good systematic approach to pollution prevention through the minimization of ecological impact of products and activities.
- Compliance with regulatory requirements and opportunities for competitive advantage.
- Reduction in need for multiple audits.

This standard is being accepted worldwide, with ISO 14001, which addresses environmental impacts of activities systematically, receiving great attention. The *OM in Action* box 'Aramex: Becoming the World's First Carbon-Neutral Logistics Company' illustrates the growing application of the ISO 14000 series.

As a follow-on to ISO 14000, ISO 24700 reflects the business world's current approach to reusing recovered components from many products. These components must be 'qualified as good as new' and meet all safety and environmental criteria.

---

[2]For further reading, see O. Fisscher and A. Nijhof, "Implications of Business Ethics for Quality Management," *TQM Magazine* 17 (2005): 150–161; and M. R. Nayebpour and D. Koehn, "The Ethics of Quality: Problems and Preconditions," *Journal of Business Ethics* 44 (April 2003): 37–48.

OM in Action ▶ Aramex: Becoming the World's First Carbon-Neutral Logistics Company

Logistics companies have been notorious for their high carbon footprint; however, one company in the Arab world is trying to change this image, for good.

In 2006, Aramex published what it claimed to be the Arab world's first sustainability report and outlined its intention to become the world's first carbon-neutral logistics company. With the help of international standards for environmental management ISO 14000, Aramex set itself a series of goals to be achieved in the years ahead. Aramex committed to reduce its carbon emissions by 50 percent, to reduce its fuel use by 20 percent, and to generate 2 percent of its revenues from carbon-neutral services by 2009. The company promised to update its transportation fleet to include hybrid cars and upgraded trucks that met ISO 14000 and the latest European Union CO_2 emissions targets. In addition, Aramex set out its commitment to replace fuel with liquid gas to power the vans and trucks, which emits 25 percent less CO_2 than gasoline.

In response, the warehouse has been redesigned to meet ISO 14000 environmental management standards. Another act was the planting of 10,000 new trees to the south of the Jordanian port of Aqaba, calculating that each tree would compensate for 0.8 tonnes of CO_2, or 1,500 km of executive travel, in its 40-year lifetime. Fadi Ghandour, chief executive officer of Aramex, says this is

just one of several similar schemes it is backing in various countries, "It takes us to the heart of the way we manage our company."

Increasingly, companies, such as Aramex, that can prove their green credentials are likely to win more business from environmentally concerned manufacturers and shippers.

Source: **www.aramex.com/news**, September 4, 2009

AUTHOR COMMENT
The seven concepts that make up TQM are part of the lexicon of business.

Total quality management (TQM)

Management of an entire organization so that it excels in all aspects of products and services that are important to the customer.

TOTAL QUALITY MANAGEMENT

Total quality management (TQM) refers to a quality emphasis that encompasses the entire organization, from supplier to customer. TQM stresses a commitment by management to have a continuing companywide drive toward excellence in all aspects of products and services that are important to the customer. Each of the ten decisions made by operations managers deals with some aspect of identifying and meeting customer expectations. Meeting those expectations requires an emphasis on TQM if a firm is to compete as a leader in world markets.

Quality expert W. Edwards Deming used 14 points (see Table 6.2) to indicate how he implemented TQM. We develop these into seven concepts for an effective TQM program:

▶ **TABLE 6.2**

Deming's 14 Points for Implementing Quality Improvement

1. Create consistency of purpose.
2. Lead to promote change.
3. Build quality into the product; stop depending on inspections to catch problems.
4. Build long-term relationships based on performance instead of awarding business on the basis of price.
5. Continuously improve product, quality, and service.
6. Start training.
7. Emphasize leadership.
8. Drive out fear.
9. Break down barriers between departments.
10. Stop haranguing workers.
11. Support, help, and improve.
12. Remove barriers to pride in work.
13. Institute a vigorous program of education and self-improvement.
14. Put everybody in the company to work on the transformation.

Source: Deming, W. Edwards. *Out of the Crisis*, 23–24, © 2000 W. Edwards Deming Institute, published by The MIT Press. Reprinted by permission.

(1) continuous improvement; (2) Six Sigma; (3) employee empowerment; (4) benchmarking; (5) just-in-time (JIT); (6) Taguchi concepts; (7) knowledge of TQM tools.

Continuous Improvement

Total quality management requires a never-ending process of continuous improvement that covers people, equipment, suppliers, materials, and procedures. The basis of the philosophy is that every aspect of an operation can be improved. The end goal is perfection, which is never achieved but always sought.

Plan–Do–Check–Act   Walter Shewhart, another pioneer in quality management, developed a circular model known as **PDCA** (plan, do, check, act) as his version of continuous improvement. Deming later took this concept to Japan during his work there after World War II.[3] The PDCA cycle is shown in Figure 6.3 as a circle to stress the continuous nature of the improvement process.

PDCA

A continuous improvement model of plan, do, check, act

The Japanese use the word *kaizen* to describe this ongoing process of unending improvement—the setting and achieving of ever-higher goals. In the United States, *TQM* and *zero defects* are also used to describe continuous improvement efforts. But whether it's PDCA, kaizen, TQM, or zero defects, the operations manager is a key player in building a work culture that endorses continuous improvement.

◀ **FIGURE 6.3**
PDCA cycle

```
4. Act            1. Plan
Implement         Identify the
the plan,         problem and
document.         make a plan.

3. Check          2. Do
Is the plan       Test the
working?          plan.
```

Six Sigma

The term **Six Sigma**, popularized by Motorola, Honeywell, and General Electric, has two meanings in TQM. In a *statistical* sense, it describes a process, product, or service with an extremely high capability (99.9997 percent accuracy). For example, if 1 million passengers pass through Riyadh International Airport with checked baggage each month, a Six Sigma program for baggage handling will result in only 3.4 passengers with misplaced luggage. The more common *three-sigma* program would result in 2,700 passengers with misplaced bags every month. See Figure 6.4.

Six Sigma

A program to save time, improve quality, and lower costs.

The second TQM definition of Six Sigma is a program designed to reduce defects to help lower costs, save time, and improve customer satisfaction. Six Sigma is a comprehensive system—a strategy, a discipline, and a set of tools—for achieving and sustaining business success:

LO3: Explain what Six Sigma is

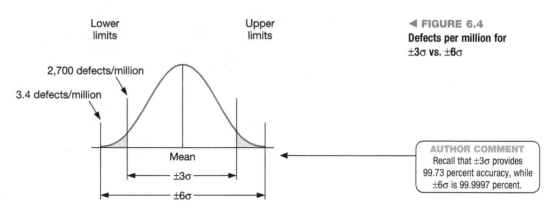

◀ **FIGURE 6.4**
Defects per million for ±3σ vs. ±6σ

AUTHOR COMMENT
Recall that ±3σ provides 99.73 percent accuracy, while ±6σ is 99.9997 percent.

[3] As a result, the Japanese refer to the PDCA cycle as a Deming circle, while others call it a Shewhart circle.

- It is a *strategy* because it focuses on total customer satisfaction.
- It is a *discipline* because it follows the formal Six Sigma Improvement Model known as DMAIC. This five-step process improvement model: (1) *Defines* the project's purpose, scope, and outputs and then identifies the required process information, keeping in mind the customer's definition of quality; (2) *Measures* the process and collects data; (3) *Analyzes* the data, ensuring repeatability (the results can be duplicated) and reproducibility (others get the same result); (4) *Improves*, by modifying or redesigning, existing processes and procedures; (5) *Controls* the new process to make sure performance levels are maintained.
- It is a *set of seven tools* that we introduce shortly in this chapter: check sheets, scatter diagrams, cause-and-effect diagrams, Pareto charts, flowcharts, histograms, and statistical process control.

It is easy to understand why a successful Six Sigma program requires a significant amount of time, because the components detailed above entail great commitment from top management and employees to devote their attention, resources, and efforts for the components' correct application.

Employee Empowerment

Employee empowerment means involving employees in every step of the production process. Consistently, business literature suggests that some 85 percent of quality problems have to do with materials and processes, not with employee performance. Therefore, the task is to design equipment and processes that produce the desired quality. This is best done with a high degree of involvement by those who understand the shortcomings of the system. Those dealing with the system on a daily basis understand it better than anyone else. One study indicated that TQM programs that delegate responsibility for quality to shop-floor employees tend to be twice as likely to succeed as those implemented with 'top-down' directives.[4]

When nonconformance occurs, the worker is seldom at fault. The product may have been badly designed, the system that makes the product may have been badly designed, or the employee may have been improperly trained. Although the employee may be able to help solve the problem, the employee rarely causes it.

Techniques for building employee empowerment include: (1) building communication networks that include employees; (2) developing open, supportive supervisors; (3) moving responsibility from both managers and staff to production employees; (4) building high-morale organizations; (5) creating such formal organization structures as teams and quality circles.

Teams can be built to address a variety of issues. One popular focus of teams is quality. Such teams are often known as quality circles. A **quality circle** is a group of employees who meet regularly to solve work-related problems. The members receive training in group planning, problem solving, and statistical quality control. They generally meet once a week (usually after work but sometimes during company time). Although the members are not rewarded financially, they do receive recognition from the firm. A specially trained team member, called the *facilitator*, usually helps train the members and keeps the meetings running smoothly. Teams with a quality focus have proven to be a cost-effective way to increase productivity as well as quality.

Employee empowerment

Enlarging employee jobs so that the added responsibility and authority is moved to the lowest level possible in the organization.

Quality circle

A group of employees meeting regularly with a facilitator to solve work-related problems in their work area.

Workers are their own inspectors. This woman is checking the quality of a suit she is working on.

---

[4]"The Straining of Quality," *The Economist* (January 14, 1995): 55. We also see that this is one of the strengths of Southwest Airlines, which offers bare-bones domestic service but whose friendly and humorous employees help it obtain number one ranking for quality. (See *Fortune* [March 6, 2006]: 65–69.)

Benchmarking

Benchmarking is another ingredient in an organization's TQM program. **Benchmarking** involves selecting a demonstrated standard of products, services, costs, or practices that represent the very best performance for processes or activities very similar to your own. The idea is to identify a target at which to shoot and then to develop a standard or benchmark against which to compare your performance. The steps for developing benchmarks are:

1. Determine what to benchmark.
2. Form a benchmark team.
3. Identify benchmarking partners.
4. Collect and analyze benchmarking information.
5. Take action to match or exceed the benchmark.

Typical performance measures used in benchmarking include percentage of defects, cost per unit or per order, processing time per unit, service response time, return on investment, customer satisfaction rates, and customer retention rates.

LO4: Explain how benchmarking is used in TQM

Benchmarks often take the form of 'best practices' found in other firms or in other divisions. Table 6.3 illustrates best practices for resolving customer complaints.

Internal Benchmarking When an organization is large enough to have many divisions or business units, a natural approach is the internal benchmark. Data are usually much more accessible than from outside firms. Typically, one internal unit has superior performance worth learning from.

Benchmarks can and should be established in a variety of areas. Total quality management requires no less.[5]

Best Practice	Justification
Make it easy for clients to complain.	It is free market research.
Respond quickly to complaints.	It adds customers and loyalty.
Resolve complaints on the first contact.	It reduces cost.
Use computers to manage complaints.	Discover trends, share them, and align your services.
Recruit the best for customer service jobs.	It should be part of formal training and career advancement.

◀ **TABLE 6.3**
Best Practices for Resolving Customer Complaints

Source: Canadian Government Guide on Complaint Mechanism.

Just-in-Time (JIT)

The philosophy behind just-in-time (JIT) is one of continuing improvement and enforced problem solving. JIT systems are designed to produce or deliver goods just as they are needed. JIT is related to quality in three ways:

- *JIT cuts the cost of quality:* This occurs because scrap, rework, inventory investment, and damage costs are directly related to inventory on hand. Because there is less inventory on hand with JIT, costs are lower. In addition, inventory hides bad quality, whereas JIT immediately *exposes* bad quality.
- *JIT improves quality:* As JIT shrinks lead time it keeps evidence of errors fresh and limits the number of potential sources of error. JIT creates, in effect, an early warning system for quality problems, both within the firm and with vendors.
- *Better quality means less inventory and a better, easier-to-employ JIT system:* Often the purpose of keeping inventory is to protect against poor production performance resulting from unreliable quality. If consistent quality exists, JIT allows firms to reduce all the costs associated with inventory.

[5]Note that benchmarking is good for evaluating how well you are doing the thing you are doing compared with the industry, but the more imaginative approach to process improvement is to ask, Should we be doing this at all? Comparing your warehousing operations to the marvelous job that L. L. Bean does is fine, but maybe you should be outsourcing the warehousing function (see Supplement 11).

▶ **FIGURE 6.5**

(a) Quality Loss Function and (b) Distribution of Products Produced

Taguchi aims for the target because products produced near the upper and lower acceptable specifications result in higher quality loss function.

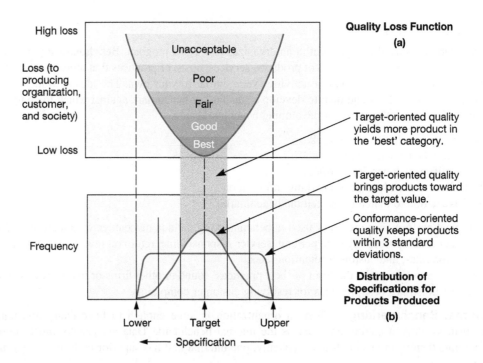

Quality Loss Function

(a)

Target-oriented quality yields more product in the 'best' category.

Target-oriented quality brings products toward the target value.

Conformance-oriented quality keeps products within 3 standard deviations.

Distribution of Specifications for Products Produced

(b)

Taguchi Concepts

Most quality problems are the result of poor product and process design. Genichi Taguchi has provided us with three concepts aimed at improving both product and process quality: *quality robustness*, *quality loss function*, and *target-oriented quality*.[6]

Quality robust

Products that are consistently built to meet customer needs in spite of adverse conditions in the production process.

Quality robust products are products that can be produced uniformly and consistently in adverse manufacturing and environmental conditions. Taguchi's idea is to remove the *effects* of adverse conditions instead of removing the causes. Taguchi suggests that removing the effects is often cheaper than removing the causes and more effective in producing a robust product. In this way, small variations in materials and process do not destroy product quality.

Quality loss function (QLF)

A mathematical function that identifies all costs connected with poor quality and shows how these costs increase as product quality moves from what the customer wants.

A **quality loss function (QLF)** identifies all costs connected with poor quality and shows how these costs increase as the product moves away from being exactly what the customer wants. These costs include not only customer dissatisfaction but also warranty and service costs; internal inspection, repair, and scrap costs; and costs that can best be described as costs to society. Notice that Figure 6.5(a) shows the quality loss function as a curve that increases at an increasing rate. It takes the general form of a simple quadratic formula:

$$L = D^2 C$$

where L = loss to society

D^2 = square of the distance from the target value

C = cost of the deviation at the specification limit

LO5: Explain quality robust products and Taguchi concepts

All the losses to society due to poor performance are included in the loss function. The smaller the loss, the more desirable the product. The farther the product is from the target value, the more severe the loss.

Taguchi observed that traditional conformance-oriented specifications (i.e. the product is good as long as it falls within the tolerance limits) are too simplistic. As shown in Figure 6.5(b), conformance-oriented quality accepts all products that fall within the tolerance limits, accepting more units farther from the target. Therefore, the loss (cost) is higher in terms of customer satisfaction and benefits to society. Target-oriented quality, on the other hand, strives to keep the product at the desired specification, resulting in more (and better) units near the target. **Target-oriented quality** is a philosophy of continuous improvement to bring the product exactly on target.

Target-oriented quality

A philosophy of continuous improvement to bring a product exactly on target.

[6]G. Taguchi, S. Chowdhury, and Y. Wu, *Taguchi's Quality Engineering Handbook* (New York: Wiley, 2004).

Knowledge of TQM Tools

To empower employees and implement TQM as a continuing effort, everyone in the organization must be trained in the techniques of TQM. In the following section, we focus on some of the diverse and expanding tools that are used in the TQM crusade.

TOOLS OF TQM

Seven tools that are particularly helpful in the TQM effort are shown in Figure 6.6. We will now introduce these tools.

AUTHOR COMMENT
These seven tools will prove useful in many of your courses and throughout your career.

Check Sheets

A check sheet is any kind of form that is designed for recording data. In many cases, the recording is done so the patterns are easily seen while the data are being taken, see Figure 6.6(a). Check sheets help analysts find the facts or patterns that may aid subsequent analysis. An example might be a drawing that shows a tally of the areas where defects are occurring or a check sheet showing the type of customer complaints.

LO6: Use the seven tools of TQM

Tools for Generating Ideas

(a) *Check Sheet:* An organized method of recording data

Defect	Hour							
	1	2	3	4	5	6	7	8
A	///	/		/	/	/	///	/
B	//	/	/	/			//	///
C	/	//					//	////

(b) *Scatter Diagram:* A graph of the value of one variable vs. another variable

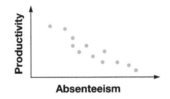

(c) *Cause-and-Effect Diagram:* A tool that identifies process elements (causes) that may affect an outcome

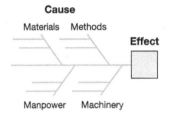

Tools for Organizing the Data

(d) *Pareto Chart:* A graph that identifies and plots problems or defects in descending order of frequency

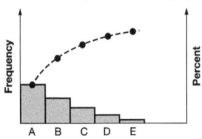

(e) *Flowchart (Process Diagram):* A chart that describes the steps in a process

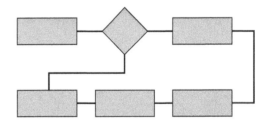

Tools for Identifying Problems

(f) *Histogram:* A distribution that shows the frequency of occurrences of a variable

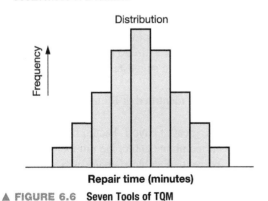

(g) *Statistical Process Control Chart:* A chart with time on the horizontal axis for plotting values of a statistic

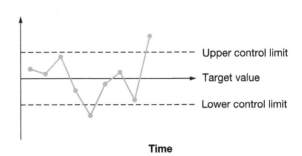

▲ **FIGURE 6.6**   **Seven Tools of TQM**

Scatter Diagrams

Scatter diagrams show the relationship between two measurements. An example is the positive relationship between length of a service call and the number of trips a repairperson makes back to the truck for parts. Another example might be a plot of productivity and absenteeism, as shown in Figure 6.6(b). If the two items are closely related, the data points will form a tight band. If a random pattern results, the items are unrelated.

Cause-and-Effect Diagrams

Cause-and-effect diagram

Also known as an *Ishikawa diagram* or a *fish-bone chart*. A schematic technique used to discover possible locations of quality problems.

Another tool for identifying quality issues and inspection points is the **cause-and-effect diagram**, also known as an *Ishikawa diagram* or a *fish-bone chart*. Figure 6.7 illustrates a chart (note the shape resembling the bones of a fish) for a basketball quality control problem—missed free-throws. Each 'bone' represents a possible source of error.

The operations manager starts with four categories: material, machinery/equipment, manpower, and methods. These four *M*s are the 'causes.' They provide a good checklist for initial analysis. Individual causes associated with each category are tied in as separate bones along that branch, often through a brainstorming process. For example, the method branch in Figure 6.7 has problems caused by hand position, follow-through, aiming point, bent knees, and balance. When a fish-bone chart is systematically developed, possible quality problems and inspection points are highlighted.

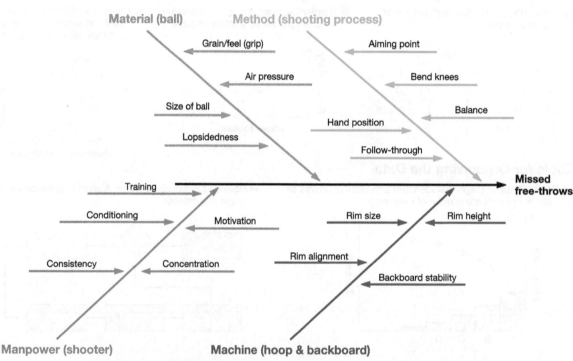

▲ FIGURE 6.7   Fish-Bone Chart (or Cause-and-Effect Diagram) for Problems with Missed Free-Throws
Source: Adapted from MoreSteam.com, 2007.

Pareto Charts

Pareto charts

Graphics that identify the few critical items as opposed to many less important ones.

Pareto charts (Figure 6.6(d)) are a method of organizing errors, problems, or defects to help focus on problem-solving efforts. They are based on the work of Vilfredo Pareto, a 19th-century economist. Joseph M. Juran popularized Pareto's work when he suggested that 80 percent of a firm's problems are a result of only 20 percent of the causes.

Example 1 indicates that of the five types of complaints identified at Ramtha Hotel, Jordan, the vast majority were of one type—poor room service.

Pareto analysis indicates which problems may yield the greatest payoff. Pacific Bell discovered this when it tried to find a way to reduce damage to buried phone cable, the number-one cause of phone outages. Pareto analysis showed that 41 percent of cable damage was caused by construction work. Armed with this information, Pacific Bell was able to devise a plan to reduce cable cuts by 24 percent in one year, saving US$6 million.

The Ramtha Hotel in Jordan has just collected the data from 75 complaint calls to the general manager during the month of October. The manager wants to prepare an analysis of the complaints. The data provided are room service, 54; check-in delays, 12; hours the pool is open, 4; minibar prices, 3; and miscellaneous, 2.

APPROACH ▶ A Pareto chart is an excellent choice for this analysis.

SOLUTION ▶ The Pareto chart shown below indicates that 72 percent of the calls were the result of one cause: room service. The majority of complaints will be eliminated when this one cause is corrected.

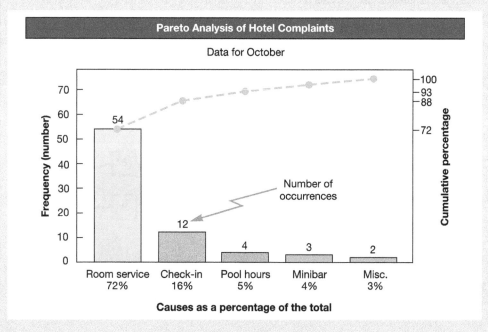

This visual means of summarizing data is very helpful—particularly with large amounts of data, as in the Ojaman University case study at the end of this chapter. We can immediately spot the top problems and prepare a plan to address them.

INSIGHT ▶ This visual means of summarizing data is very helpful—particularly with large amounts of data, as in the Ojaman University case study at the end of this chapter. We can immediately spot the top problems and prepare a plan to address them.

LEARNING EXERCISE ▶ Ramtha's restaurant manager decides to do a similar analysis on complaints she has collected over the past year: too expensive, 22; weak beverages, 15; slow service, 65; short hours, 8; unfriendly waiters, 12. Prepare a Pareto chart. [Answer: slow service, 53 percent; too expensive, 18 percent; weak beverages, 12 percent; unfriendly waiters, 10 percent; short hours, 7 percent.]

RELATED PROBLEMS ▶ 6.1, 6.3, 6.7b, 6.12

Flowcharts

Flowcharts graphically present a process or system using annotated boxes and interconnected lines, see Figure 6.6(e). They are a simple, but great tool for trying to make sense of a process or explain a process. Example 2 uses a flowchart to show the process of completing an MRI at a hospital.

Flowcharts
A drawing used to analyze movement of people or material.

Histograms

Histograms show the range of values of a measurement and the frequency with which each value occurs, see Figure 6.6(f). They show the most frequently occurring readings as well as the variations in the measurements. Descriptive statistics, such as the average and standard deviation, may be calculated to describe the distribution. However, the data should always be plotted so the shape of the distribution can be 'seen.' A visual presentation of the distribution may also provide insight into the cause of the variation.

EXAMPLE 2 ▶

A flowchart for hospital MRI service

New Mowasat Hospital has undertaken a series of process improvement initiatives. One of these is to make the MRI service efficient for patient, doctor, and hospital. The first step, the administrator believes, is to develop a flowchart for this process.

APPROACH ▶ A process improvement staffer observed a number of patients and followed them (and information flow) from start to end. Here are the 11 steps:

1. Physician schedules MRI after examining patient (START).
2. Patient taken to the MRI lab with test order and copy of medical records.
3. Patient signs in, completes required paperwork.
4. Patient is prepped by technician for scan.
5. Technician carries out the MRI scan.
6. Technician inspects film for clarity.
7. If MRI not satisfactory (20 percent of time), steps 5 and 6 are repeated.
8. Patient taken back to hospital room.
9. MRI is read by radiologist and report is prepared.
10. MRI and report are transferred electronically to physician.
11. Patient and physician discuss report (END).

SOLUTION ▶ Here is the flowchart:

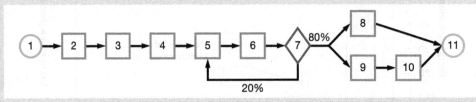

INSIGHT ▶ With the flowchart in hand, the hospital can analyze each step and identify value-added activities and activities that can be improved or eliminated.

LEARNING EXERCISE ▶ If the patient's blood pressure is over 200/120 when being prepped for the MRI, she is taken back to her room for 2 hours and the process returns to Step 2. How does the flowchart change? Answer:

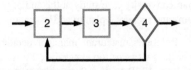

RELATED PROBLEMS ▶ 6.6, 6.13

AUTHOR COMMENT
Flowcharting any process is an excellent way to understand and then try to improve that process.

Statistical Process Control (SPC)

Statistical process control (SPC)

A process used to monitor standards, make measurements, and take corrective action as a product or service is being produced.

Statistical process control (SPC) monitors standards, makes measurements, and takes corrective action as a product or service is being produced. Samples of process outputs are examined; if they are within acceptable limits, the process is permitted to continue. If they fall outside certain specific ranges, the process is stopped and, typically, the assignable cause located and removed.

Control charts

Graphic presentations of process data over time, with predetermined control limits.

Control charts are graphic presentations of data over time that show upper and lower limits for the process we want to control, see Figure 6.6(g). Control charts are constructed in such a way that new data can be quickly compared with past performance data. We take samples of the process output and plot the average of each of these samples on a chart that has the limits on it. The upper and lower limits in a control chart can be in units of temperature, pressure, weight, length, and so on.

Figure 6.8 shows the plot of the average percentages of samples in a control chart. When the average of the samples falls within the upper and lower control limits and no discernible pattern is present, the process is said to be in control with only natural variation present. Otherwise, the process is out of control or out of adjustment.

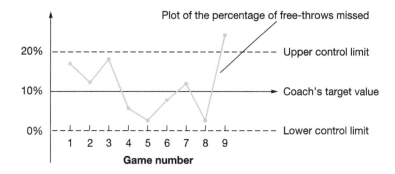

Control Chart for Percentage of Free-throws Missed by the Chicago Bulls in Their First Nine Games of the New Season

THE ROLE OF INSPECTION

> **AUTHOR COMMENT**
> One of the themes of quality is that 'quality cannot be inspected into a product.'

To make sure a system is producing at the expected quality level, control of the process is needed. The best processes have little variation from the standard expected. The operations manager's task is to build such systems and to verify, often by inspection, that they are performing to standard. This **inspection** can involve measurement, tasting, touching, weighing, or testing of the product (sometimes even destroying it when doing so). Its goal is to detect a bad process immediately. Inspection does not correct deficiencies in the system or defects in the products; nor does it change a product or increase its value. Inspection only finds deficiencies and defects. Moreover, inspections are expensive and do not add value to the product.

Inspection

A means of ensuring that an operation is producing at the quality level expected.

Inspection should be thought of as a vehicle for improving the system. Operations managers need to know critical points in the system: (1) *when to inspect*; (2) *where to inspect*.

When and Where to Inspect

Deciding when and where to inspect depends on the type of process and the value added at each stage. Inspections can take place at any of the following points.

1. At your supplier's plant while the supplier is producing.
2. At your facility upon receipt of goods from your supplier.
3. Before costly or irreversible processes.
4. During the step-by-step production process.
5. When production or service is complete.
6. Before delivery to your customer.
7. At the point of customer contact.

The seven tools of TQM discussed in the previous section aid in this 'when and where to inspect' decision. However, inspection is not a substitute for a robust product produced by well-trained employees in a good process. In one well-known experiment conducted by an independent research firm, 100 defective pieces were added to a 'perfect' lot of items and then subjected to 100 percent inspection.[7] The inspectors found only 68 of the defective pieces in their first inspection. It took another three passes by the inspectors to find the next 30 defects. The last two defects were never found. So the bottom line is that there is variability in the inspection process. Additionally, inspectors are only human: They become bored, they become tired, and the inspection equipment itself has variability. Even with 100 percent inspection, inspectors cannot guarantee perfection. Therefore, good processes, employee empowerment, and source control are a better solution than trying to find defects by inspection. You cannot inspect quality into the product.

For example, at Elzay Ready Wear Manufacturing Company, in Jordan, as in many organizations, quality was viewed by machine operators as the job of 'those quality people.' Inspections were based on random sampling, and if a part showed up bad, it was thrown out. The company decided to pay more attention to the system (operators, machine repair and design, measurement methods, communications, and responsibilities), and to invest more money in training. Over time as defects declined, Elzay was able to empower its own employees and make them responsible for the quality control.

---

[7]*Statistical Quality Control* (Springfield, MA: Monsanto Chemical Company, n.d.): 19.

Source Inspection

Source inspection

Controlling or monitoring at the point of production or purchase—at the source.

The best inspection can be thought of as no inspection at all; this 'inspection' is always done at the source—it is just doing the job properly with the operator ensuring that this is so. This may be called **source inspection** (or source control) and is consistent with the concept of employee empowerment, where individual employees self-check their own work. The idea is that each supplier, process, and employee *treats the next step in the process as the customer*, ensuring perfect product to the next 'customer.' This inspection may be assisted by the use of checklists and controls, such as a fail-safe device called a *poka-yoke*, a name borrowed from the Japanese.

Poka-yoke

Literally translated, 'foolproof'; it has come to mean a device or technique that ensures the production of a good unit every time.

A **poka-yoke** is a foolproof device or technique that ensures production of good units every time. These special devices avoid errors and provide quick feedback of problems. A simple example of a poka-yoke device is the diesel gas pump nozzle that will not fit into the unleaded gas tank opening on your car.

Service Industry Inspection

In *service*-oriented organizations, inspection points can be assigned at a wide range of locations, as illustrated in Table 6.4. Again, the operations manager must decide where inspections are justified and may find the seven tools of TQM useful when making these judgments.

▶ **TABLE 6.4**

Examples of Inspection in Services

Organization	What Is Inspected	Standard
Zubi Law Firm	Receptionist performance	Phone answered by the second ring
	Billing	Accurate, timely, and correct format
	Attorney	Promptness in returning calls
Manama Hotel	Reception desk	Use customer's name
	Doorman	Greet guest in less than 30 seconds
	Room	All lights working, spotless bathroom
	Minibar	Restocked and charges accurately posted to bill
New Mowasat Hospital	Billing	Accurate, timely, and correct format
	Pharmacy	Prescription accuracy, inventory accuracy
	Lab	Audit for lab-test accuracy
	Nurses	Charts immediately updated
	Admissions	Data entered correctly and completely
Zooka Restaurant	Busboy	Serves water and bread within 1 minute
	Busboy	Clears all entrée items and crumbs prior to dessert
	Waiter	Knows and suggests specials, desserts
Great Stores	Display areas	Attractive, well organized, stocked, good lighting
	Stockrooms	Rotation of goods, organized, clean
	Salesclerks	Neat, courteous, very knowledgeable

Inspection of Attributes versus Variables

Attribute inspection

An inspection that classifies items as being either good or defective.

When inspections take place, quality characteristics may be measured as either *attributes* or *variables*. **Attribute inspection** classifies items as being either good or defective. It does not address the *degree* of failure. For example, the lightbulb burns or it does not. **Variable inspection** measures such dimensions as weight, speed, size, or strength to see if an item falls within an acceptable range. If a piece of electrical wire is supposed to be 0.01 inch in diameter, a micrometer can be used to see if the product is close enough to pass inspection.

Variable inspection

Classifications of inspected items as falling on a continuum scale, such as dimension, or strength.

Knowing whether attributes or variables are being inspected helps us decide which statistical quality control approach to take.

AUTHOR COMMENT
The personal component of a service can make quality measurement difficult.

▶ TQM IN SERVICES

The personal component of services is more difficult to measure than the quality of the tangible component. Generally, the user of a service, like the user of a good, has features in mind that form a basis for comparison among alternatives. Lack of any one feature may eliminate the service from further consideration. Quality also may be perceived as a bundle of attributes in which many lesser characteristics are superior to those of competitors. This approach to product

UPS drivers are taught hundreds of methods of how to correctly deliver a package. Regimented? Absolutely. But UPS credits its uniformity and efficiency with laying the foundation for its high-quality service.

comparison differs little between goods and services. However, what is very different about the selection of services is the poor definition of the: (1) *intangible differences between products*; (2) *the intangible expectations customers have of those products*. Indeed, the intangible attributes may not be defined at all. They are often unspoken images in the purchaser's mind. This is why all of those marketing issues, such as advertising, image, and promotion, can make a difference (see the photo of the UPS driver).

The operations manager plays a significant role in addressing several major aspects of service quality. First, the *tangible component of many services is important*. How well the service is designed and produced does make a difference. This might be how accurate, clear, and complete your checkout bill at the hotel is, how warm the food is at Kudu restaurant, or how well your car runs after you pick it up at the repair shop.

Second, another aspect of service and service quality is the process. Notice in Table 6.5 that 9 out of 10 of the determinants of service quality are related to *the service process*. Such things as reliability and courtesy are part of the process. An operations manager can *design processes (service products) that have these attributes* and can ensure their quality through the TQM techniques discussed in this chapter.

Third, the operations manager should realize that the customer's expectations are the standard against which the service is judged. Customers' perceptions of service quality result from a comparison of their before-service expectations with their actual-service experience. In other words, service quality is judged on the basis of whether it meets expectations. The *manager may be able to influence both the quality of the service and the expectation*. Don't promise more than you can deliver.

Fourth, the manager must expect exceptions. There is a standard quality level at which the regular service is delivered, such as the bank teller's handling of a transaction. However, there are 'exceptions' or 'problems' initiated by the customer or by less-than-optimal operating

VIDEO 6.2
Quality at the Ritz-Carlton Hotel Company

▶ **TABLE 6.5**
Determinants of Service Quality

Reliability involves consistency of performance and dependability. It means that the firm performs the service right the first time and that the firm honors its promises.

Responsiveness concerns the willingness or readiness of employees to provide service. It involves timeliness of service.

Competence means possession of the required skills and knowledge to perform the service.

Access involves approachability and ease of contact.

Courtesy involves politeness, respect, consideration, and friendliness of contact personnel (including receptionists, telephone operators, etc.).

Communication means keeping customers informed in language they can understand and listening to them. It may mean that the company has to adjust its language for different consumers—increasing the level of sophistication with a well-educated customer and speaking simply and plainly with a novice.

Credibility involves trustworthiness, believability, and honesty. It involves having the customer's best interests at heart.

Security is the freedom from danger, risk, or doubt.

Understanding/knowing the customer involves making the effort to understand the customer's needs.

Tangibles include the physical evidence of the service.

Source: Adapted from A. Parasuranam, Valarie A. Zeithaml, and Leonard L. Berry, "A Conceptual Model of Service Quality and Its Implications for Future Research," *Journal of Marketing* (Fall 1985): 44; *Journal of Marketing*, 58, no. 1 (January 1994): 111–125; *Journal of Retailing* 70 (Fall 1994): 201–230.

conditions (e.g. the computer 'crashed'). This implies that the quality control system must recognize and *have a set of alternative plans for less-than-optimal operating conditions.*

Service recovery

Training and empowering frontline workers to solve a problem immediately.

Well-run companies have **service recovery** strategies. This means they train and empower frontline employees to immediately solve a problem. For instance, staff at Marriott Hotels are drilled in the LEARN routine—*Listen, Empathize, Apologize, React, Notify*—with the final step ensuring that the complaint is fed back into the system. And at the Ritz-Carlton, staff members are trained not to say merely "sorry" but "please accept my apology." The Ritz gives them a budget for reimbursing upset guests.

Designing the product, managing the service process, matching customer expectations to the product, and preparing for the exceptions are keys to quality services.

CHAPTER SUMMARY

Quality is a term that means different things to different people. We define quality as 'The ability of a product or service to meet customer needs.' Defining quality expectations are critical to effective and efficient operations.

Quality requires building a total quality management (TQM) environment because quality cannot be inspected into a product. The chapter also addresses seven TQM *concepts:* continuous improvement, Six Sigma, employee empowerment,

benchmarking, just-in-time, Taguchi concepts, and knowledge of TQM tools. The seven TQM *tools* introduced in this chapter are check sheets, scatter diagrams, cause and effect diagrams, Pareto charts, flowcharts, histograms, and statistical process control (SPC).

Key Terms

Attribute inspection (p. 174)
Benchmarking (p. 167)
Cause-and-effect diagram, Ishikawa
    diagram, or fish-bone chart
    (p. 170)
Control charts (p. 172)
Cost of quality (COQ) (p. 162)
Employee empowerment (p. 166)
Flowcharts (p. 171)

Inspection (p. 173)
ISO 9000 (p. 163)
ISO 14000 (p. 163)
Pareto charts (p. 170)
PDCA (p. 165)
Poka-yoke (p. 174)
Quality (p. 160)
Quality circle (p. 166)
Quality loss function (QLF) (p. 168)

Quality robust (p. 168)
Service recovery (p. 176)
Six Sigma (p. 165)
Source inspection (p. 174)
Statistical process control (SPC) (p. 172)
Target-oriented quality (p. 168)
Total quality management (TQM)
    (p. 164)
Variable inspection (p. 174)

Ethical Dilemma

A lawsuit a few years ago made headlines worldwide when a McDonald's drive-thru customer spilled a cup of scalding hot coffee on herself. Claiming the coffee was too hot to be safely consumed in a car, the badly burned 80-year-old woman won US$2.9 million in court. (The judge later reduced the award to US$640,000.) McDonald's claimed the product was served to the correct specifications and was of proper quality. Further, the cup read "Caution—Contents May Be Hot." McDonald's coffee, at 180°F, is substantially hotter (by

corporate rule) than typical restaurant coffee, despite hundreds of coffee-scalding complaints in the past 10 years. Similar court cases, incidentally, resulted in smaller verdicts, but again in favor of the plaintiffs. For example, Motor City Bagel Shop was sued for a spilled cup of coffee by a drive-thru patron, and Starbucks by a customer who spilled coffee on her own ankle.

Are McDonald's, Motor City, and Starbucks at fault in situations such as these? How do quality and ethics enter into these cases?

Discussion Questions

1. Explain how improving quality can lead to reduced costs.
2. Which 3 of Deming's 14 points do you think are most critical to the success of a TQM program? Why?
3. List the seven concepts that are necessary for an effective TQM program. How are these related to Deming's 14 points?
4. What are the seven tools of TQM?
5. How does fear in the workplace (and in the classroom) inhibit learning?
6. How can a university control the quality of its output (that is, its graduates)?
7. What is the purpose of using a Pareto chart for a given problem?
8. What are the four broad categories of 'causes' to help initially structure an Ishikawa diagram or cause-and-effect diagram?
9. What roles do operations managers play in addressing the major aspects of service quality?
10. Explain, in your own words, what is meant by *source inspection*.
11. What are the ten determinants of service quality?

Problems

• **6.1** An innovative clothing manufacturer in Lebanon runs a series of high-profile, risqué ads on a billboard on Highway 101 and regularly takes protest calls from people who are offended by them. The company has no idea how many people in total see the ads, but it has been collecting statistics on the number of phone calls from irate viewers:

Type	Description	Number of Complaints
R	Offensive racially/ethnically	10
M	Demeaning to men	4
W	Demeaning to women	14
I	Ad is incomprehensible	6
O	Other	2

a) Depict these data with a Pareto chart. Also depict the cumulative complaint line.
b) What percentage of the total complaints can be attributed to the most prevalent complaint?

• **6.2** Develop a scatter diagram for two variables of interest (say, pages in the newspaper by day of the week; see example in Figure 6.6b).

• **6.3** Develop a Pareto chart of the following causes of poor grades on an exam:

Reason for Poor Grade	Frequency
Insufficient time to complete	15
Late arrival to exam	7
Difficulty understanding material	25
Insufficient preparation time	2
Studied wrong material	2
Distractions in exam room	9
Calculator batteries died during exam	1
Forgot exam was scheduled	3
Felt ill during exam	4

• **6.4** Develop a histogram of the time it took for you or your friends to receive six recent orders at a fast-food restaurant.

•• **6.5** Suha's restaurant in Damascus, Syria, has recorded the following data for eight recent customers:

Customer Number, i	Minutes from Time Food Ordered Until Food Arrived (y_i)	No. of Trips to Kitchen by Waitress (x_i)
1	10.50	4
2	12.75	5
3	9.25	3
4	8.00	2
5	9.75	3
6	11.00	4
7	14.00	6
8	10.75	5

a) Suha wants you to graph the eight points (x_i, y_i), $i = 1, 2, \ldots, 8$. She has been concerned because customers have been waiting too long for their food, and this graph is intended to help her find possible causes of the problem.
b) This is an example of what type of graph?

•• **6.6** Develop a flowchart, as in Figure 6.6(e) and Example 2 showing all the steps involved in planning a party.

•• **6.7** Consider the types of poor driving habits that might occur at a traffic light. Make a list of the ten you consider most likely to happen. Add the category of 'other' to that list.
a) Compose a check sheet, like that in Figure 6.6(a) to collect the frequency of occurrence of these habits. Using your check sheet, visit a busy traffic light intersection at four different times of the day, with two of these times being during high-traffic periods (rush hour, lunch hour). For 15 to 20 minutes each visit, observe the frequency with which the habits you listed occurred.
b) Construct a Pareto chart showing the relative frequency of occurrence of each habit.

•• **6.8** Draw a fish-bone chart detailing reasons why an airline customer might be dissatisfied.

•• **6.9** Consider the everyday task of getting to work on time or arriving at your first class on time in the morning. Draw a fish-bone chart showing reasons why you might arrive late in the morning.

•• **6.10** Construct a cause-and-effect diagram to reflect 'student dissatisfied with university registration process.' Use the 'four Ms' or create your own organizing scheme. Include at least 12 causes.

•• **6.11** Draw a fish-bone chart depicting the reasons that might give rise to an incorrect fee statement at the time you go to pay for your registration at school.

• **6.12** Use Pareto analysis to investigate the following data collected on a printed-circuit-board assembly line:

Defect	Number of Defect Occurrences
Components not adhering	143
Excess adhesive	71
Misplaced transistors	601
Defective board dimension	146
Mounting holes improperly positioned	12
Circuitry problems on final test	90
Wrong component	212

a) Prepare a graph of the data.
b) What conclusions do you reach?

•• **6.13** Develop a flowchart for one of the following:
a) Filling up with gasoline at a self-serve station.
b) Determining your account balance and making a withdrawal at an ATM.
c) Getting a cone of yogurt or ice cream from an ice cream store.

▶ **Refer to** MyOMLab **for additional homework problems.**

Case Studies

Ojaman University: (C)*

The popularity of Ojaman University's basketball program under its new coach, Saleem Jamal, surged in each of the 6 years since his arrival. (See Ojaman University: (A) in Chapter 3 and (B) in Chapter 4.) With a basketball arena close to maximum capacity at 54,000 seats and a vocal coach pushing for a new arena, Ojaman president Dr. Mohammad Khaleel faced some difficult decisions. After a phenomenal upset victory over its archrival, the University

*This integrated case study runs throughout the text. Other issues facing Ojaman University's basketball arena include (A) managing the renovation project (Chapter 3); (B) forecasting game attendance (Chapter 4); (D) break-even analysis for food services (Supplement 7); (E) location of the new arena (Chapter 8); (F) inventory planning of basketball programs (Chapter 12); and (G) scheduling of campus security officers/staff for game days (Chapter 13).

of Tabeekia, at the homecoming game in the fall, Dr. Khaleel was not as happy as one would think. Instead of ecstatic alumni, students, and faculty, all Khaleel heard were complaints. "The lines at the concession stands were too long"; "Parking was harder to find and farther away than in the old days" (that is, before the team won regularly); "Seats weren't comfortable"; "Traffic was backed up halfway to Ojaman"; and on and on. "A college president just can't win," muttered Khaleel to himself.

At his staff meeting the following Monday, Khaleel turned to his vice president of administration, Laila Mahmoud. "I wish you would take care of these basketball complaints, Laila," he said. "See what the *real* problems are and let me know how you've resolved them." Laila wasn't surprised at the request. "I've already got a handle on it, Khaleel," she replied. "We've been randomly surveying 50 fans per game for the past year to see what's on their minds. It's

▼ TABLE 6.6
Fan Satisfaction Survey Results (N = 250)

		Overall Grade				
		A	**B**	**C**	**D**	**E**
Game Day	A. Parking	90	105	45	5	5
	B. Traffic	50	85	48	52	15
	C. Seating	45	30	115	35	25
	D. Entertainment	160	35	26	10	19
	E. Printed Program	66	34	98	22	30
Tickets	A. Pricing	105	104	16	15	10
	B. Season Ticket Plans	75	80	54	41	0
Concessions	A. Prices	16	116	58	58	2
	B. Selection of Foods	155	60	24	11	0
	C. Speed of Service	35	45	46	48	76

Respondents

Alumnus	113
Student	83
Faculty/Staff	16
None of the above	38

Open-Ended Comments on Survey Cards:

Parking a mess	More shawerma stands	Well done, OU	Cold coffee served at game
Add a skybox	Seats are all metal	Put in bigger seats	My company will buy a
Get better cheerleaders	Need skyboxes	Friendly ushers	skybox—build it!
Double the parking attendants	Seats smell	Need better seats	Programs overpriced
Everything is okay	Go OU!	Expand parking lots	Want softer seats
Too crowded	Lines are awful	Hate the bleacher seats	Beat those Tabeekia!
Seats too narrow	Seats are uncomfortable	Shawerma cold	I'll pay for a skybox
Great food	I will pay more for better view	3 dinars for a coffee? No way!	Seats too small
Abul Zooz for President!	Get a new arena	Get some skyboxes	Band was terrific
I smelled drugs being smoked	Student dress code needed	Love the new uniforms	Love Saleem
Arena is ancient	I want cushioned seats	Took an hour to park	Everything is great
Seats are like rocks	Not enough police	Coach is terrific	Build new arena
Not enough police for traffic	Students too rowdy	More water fountains	Move games to Amman
Game starts too late	Parking terrible	Better seats	No complaints
Hire more traffic police	Toilets weren't clean	Seats not comfy	Dirty bathroom
Need new band	Not enough disabled space in	Bigger parking lot	
Great!	parking lot	I'm too old for bench seats	

all part of my campuswide TQM effort. Let me tally things up and I'll get back to you in a week."

When she returned to her office, Laila pulled out the file her assistant had compiled (see Table 6.6). "There's a lot of information here," she thought.

Discussion Questions

1. Using at least two different quality tools, analyze the data and present your conclusions.
2. How could the survey have been more useful?
3. What is the next step?

▶ **The Culture of Quality at Arnold Palmer Hospital**

Video Case

Founded in 1989, Arnold Palmer Hospital is one of the largest hospitals for women and children in the United States, with 431 beds in two facilities totaling 676,000 square feet. Located in downtown Orlando, Florida, and named after its famed golf benefactor, the hospital, with more than 2,000 employees serves an 18-county area in central Florida and is the only Level 1 trauma center for children in that region. Arnold Palmer Hospital provides a broad range of medical services including neonatal and pediatric intensive care, pediatric oncology and cardiology, care for high-risk pregnancies, and maternal intensive care.

Quality health care is a goal all hospitals profess, but Arnold Palmer Hospital has actually developed comprehensive and scientific means of asking customers to judge the quality of care they receive. Participating in a national benchmark comparison against other hospitals, Arnold Palmer Hospital consistently scores in the top 10 percent in overall patient satisfaction. Executive Director Kathy Swanson states, "Hospitals in this area will be distinguished largely on the basis of their customer satisfaction. We must have accurate information about how our patients and their families judge the quality of our care, so I follow the questionnaire results daily. The in-depth survey helps me and others on my team to gain quick knowledge from patient feedback." Arnold Palmer Hospital employees are empowered to provide gifts in value up to US$200 to patients who find reason to complain about any hospital service such as food, courtesy, responsiveness, or cleanliness.

Swanson doesn't focus just on the customer surveys, which are mailed to patients 1 week after discharge, but also on a variety of internal measures. These measures usually start at the grassroots level, where the staff see a problem and develop ways to track performance. The hospital's longstanding philosophy supports the concept that each patient is important and respected as a person. That patient has the right to comprehensive, compassionate family-centered health care provided by a knowledgeable physician-directed team.

Some of the measures Swanson carefully monitors for continuous improvement are morbidity, infection rates, readmission rates, costs per case, and length of stays. The tools she uses daily include Pareto charts, flowcharts and process charts, in addition to benchmarking against hospitals both nationally and in the southeast region.

The result of all of these efforts has been a quality culture as manifested in Arnold Palmer's high ranking in patient satisfaction and one of the highest survival rates of critically ill babies.

Discussion Questions*

1. Why is it important for Arnold Palmer Hospital to get a patient's assessment of health care quality? Does the patient have the expertise to judge the health care she receives?
2. How would you build a culture of quality in an organization, such as Arnold Palmer Hospital?
3. What techniques does Arnold Palmer Hospital practice in its drive for quality and continuous improvement?
4. Develop a fish-bone diagram illustrating the quality variables for a patient who just gave birth at Arnold Palmer Hospital (or any other hospital).

*You may wish to view the video that accompanies this case before answering these questions.

▶ Quality at the Ritz-Carlton Hotel Company

Video Case

Ritz-Carlton. The name alone evokes images of luxury and quality. As the first hotel company to win the Malcolm Baldrige National Quality Award, the Ritz treats quality as if it is the heartbeat of the company. This means a daily commitment to meeting customer expectations and making sure that each hotel is free of any deficiency.

In the hotel industry, quality can be hard to quantify. Guests do not purchase a product when they stay at the Ritz: They buy an experience. Thus, creating the right combination of elements to make the experience stand out is the challenge and goal of every employee, from maintenance to management.

Before applying for the Baldrige Award, company management undertook a rigorous self-examination of its operations in an attempt to measure and quantify quality. Nineteen processes were studied, including room service delivery, guest reservation and registration, message delivery, and breakfast service. This period of self-study included statistical measurement of process work flows and cycle times for areas ranging from room service delivery times and reservations to valet parking and housekeeping efficiency. The results were used to develop performance benchmarks against which future activity could be measured.

With specific, quantifiable targets in place, Ritz-Carlton managers and employees now focus on continuous improvement. The goal is 100 percent customer satisfaction: If a guest's experience does not meet expectations, the Ritz-Carlton risks losing that guest to competition.

One way the company has put more meaning behind its quality efforts is to organize its employees into 'self-directed' work teams. Employee teams determine work scheduling, what work needs to be done, and what to do about quality problems in their own areas. In order that they can see the relationship of their specific area to the overall goals, employees are also given the opportunity to take additional training in hotel operations. Ritz-Carlton believes that a more educated and informed employee is in a better position to make decisions in the best interest of the organization.

Discussion Questions*

1. In what ways could the Ritz-Carlton monitor its success in achieving quality?
2. Many companies say that their goal is to provide quality products or services. What actions might you expect from a company that intends quality to be more than a slogan or buzzword?
3. Why might it cost the Ritz-Carlton less to 'do things right' the first time?
4. How could control charts, Pareto diagrams, and cause-and-effect diagrams be used to identify quality problems at a hotel?
5. What are some nonfinancial measures of customer satisfaction that might be used by the Ritz-Carlton?

*You may wish to view the video that accompanies this case before answering these questions.

Source: Adapted from C. T. Horngren, S. M. Datar, and G. Foster, *Cost Accounting*, 13th ed. (Upper Saddle River, NJ: Prentice Hall, 2009).

▶ **Additional Case Study:** Visit MyOMLab for this free case study:

Westover Electrical, Inc.: This electric motor manufacturer has a large log of defects in its wiring process.

Main Heading	Review Material	MyOMLab
QUALITY AND STRATEGY (p. 160)	Managing quality helps build successful strategies of *differentiation*, *low cost*, and *response*. Two ways that quality improves profitability are: ■ *Sales gains* via improved response, price flexibility, increased market share, and/or improved reputation ■ *Reduced costs* via increased productivity, lower rework and scrap costs, and/or lower warranty costs	**VIDEO 6.1** The Culture of Quality at Arnold Palmer Hospital
DEFINING QUALITY (pp. 160–163)	An operations manager's objective is to build a total quality management system that identifies and satisfies customer needs. ■ **Quality**—The ability of a product or service to meet customer needs. ■ **Cost of quality (COQ)**—The cost of doing things wrong; that is, the price of nonconformance. The four major categories of costs associated with quality are: *Prevention costs, Appraisal costs, Internal failure*, and *External costs*. Four leaders in the field of quality management are W. Edwards Deming, Joseph M. Juran, Armand Feigenbaum, and Philip B. Crosby.	
INTERNATIONAL QUALITY STANDARDS (pp. 163–164)	■ **ISO 9000**—A set of quality standards developed by the International Organization for Standardization (ISO). ISO 9000 is the only quality standard with international recognition. To do business globally, being listed in the ISO directory is critical. ■ **ISO 14000**—A series of environmental management standards established by the ISO. ISO 14000 contains five core elements: (1) environmental management; (2) auditing; (3) performance evaluation; (4) labeling; (5) life cycle assessment. As a follow-on to ISO 14000, ISO 24700 reflects the business world's current approach to reusing recovered components from many products.	
TOTAL QUALITY MANAGEMENT (pp. 164–169)	■ **Total quality management (TQM)**—Management of an entire organization so that it excels in all aspects of products and services that are important to the customer. Seven concepts for an effective TQM program are: (1) continuous improvement; (2) Six Sigma; (3) employee empowerment; (4) benchmarking; (5) just-in-time (JIT); (6) Taguchi concepts; (7) knowledge of TQM tools. ■ **PDCA**—A continuous improvement model that involves four stages: plan, do, check, and act. The Japanese use the word *kaizen* to describe the ongoing process of unending improvement—the setting and achieving of ever-higher goals. ■ **Six Sigma**—A program to save time, improve quality, and lower costs. In a statistical sense, Six Sigma describes a process, product, or service with an extremely high capability—99.9997 percent accuracy, or 3.4 defects per million. ■ **Employee empowerment**—Enlarging employees' jobs so that the added responsibility and authority is moved to the lowest level possible in the organization. Business literature suggests that some 85 percent of quality problems have to do with materials and processes, not with employee performance. ■ **Quality circle**—A group of employees meeting regularly with a facilitator to solve work-related problems in their work area. ■ **Benchmarking**—Selecting a demonstrated standard of performance that represents the very best performance for a process or an activity. The philosophy behind just-in-time (JIT) involves continuing improvement and enforced problem solving. JIT systems are designed to produce or deliver goods just as they are needed. ■ **Quality robust**—Products that are consistently built to meet customer needs, in spite of adverse conditions in the production process. ■ **Quality loss function (QLF)**—A mathematical function that identifies all costs connected with poor quality and shows how these costs increase as product quality moves from what the customer wants: $L = D^2C$. ■ **Target-oriented quality**—A philosophy of continuous improvement to bring the product exactly on target.	Problems: 6.1, 6.3, 6.5, 6.12

MyOMLab

Main Heading	Review Material	
TOOLS OF TQM (pp. 169–173)	TQM tools that generate ideas include the *check sheet* (organized method of recording data), *scatter diagram* (graph of the value of one variable vs. another variable), and *cause-and-effect diagram*. Tools for organizing the data are the *Pareto chart* and *flowchart*. Tools for identifying problems are the *histogram* (distribution showing the frequency of occurrences of a variable) and *statistical process control chart*. ■ **Cause-and-effect diagram**—A schematic technique used to discover possible locations of quality problems. (Also called an Ishikawa diagram or a fish-bone chart.) The 4 *Ms* (material, machinery/equipment, manpower, and methods) may be broad 'causes.' ■ **Pareto chart**—A graphic that identifies the few critical items as opposed to many less important ones. ■ **Flowchart**—A block diagram that graphically describes a process or system. ■ **Statistical process control (SPC)**—A process used to monitor standards, make measurements, and take corrective action as a product or service is being produced. ■ **Control chart**—A graphic presentation of process data over time, with predetermined control limits.	
THE ROLE OF INSPECTION (pp. 173–174)	■ **Inspection**—A means of ensuring that an operation is producing at the quality level expected. ■ **Source inspection**—Controlling or monitoring at the point of production or purchase: at the source. ■ **Poka-yoke**—Literally translated, 'foolproof'; it has come to mean a device or technique that ensures the production of a good unit every time. ■ **Attribute inspection**—An inspection that classifies items as being either good or defective. ■ **Variable inspection**—Classifications of inspected items as falling on a continuum scale, such as dimension, size, or strength.	
TQM IN SERVICES (pp. 174–176)	Determinants of service quality: reliability, responsiveness, competence, access, courtesy, communication, credibility, security, understanding/knowing the customer, and tangibles. ■ **Service recovery**—Training and empowering frontline workers to solve a problem immediately.	**VIDEO 6.2** Quality at the Ritz-Carlton Hotel Company

Self-Test

■ **Before taking the self-test,** refer to the learning objectives listed at the beginning of the chapter and the key terms listed at the end of the chapter.

LO1. In this chapter, *quality* is defined as:
  a) the degree of excellence at an acceptable price and the control of variability at an acceptable cost
  b) how well a product fits patterns of consumer preferences
  c) the ability of a product or service to meet customer needs
  d) being impossible to define, but you know what it is.

LO2. ISO 14000 is an international standard that addresses _____.

LO3. If 1 million passengers pass through the Riyadh International Airport with checked baggage each year, a successful Six Sigma program for baggage handling would result in how many passengers with misplaced luggage?
  a) 3.4
  b) 6.0
  c) 34
  d) 2,700
  e) 6 times the monthly standard deviation of passengers.

LO4. The process of identifying other organizations that are best at some facet of your operations and then modeling your organization after them is known as:
  a) continuous improvement
  b) employee empowerment
  c) benchmarking
  d) copycatting
  e) patent infringement.

LO5. The Taguchi method includes all except which of the following major concepts?
  a) employee involvement
  b) remove the effects of adverse conditions
  c) quality loss function
  d) target specifications.

LO6. The seven tools of total quality management are _____, _____, _____, _____, _____, _____, and _____.

7 Process Design

Chapter Outline

10

OM STRATEGY DECISIONS

- ▶ Design of Goods and Services
- ▶ Managing Quality
- ▶ Process Strategy
- ▶ Location Strategies
- ▶ Layout Strategies
- ▶ Human Resources
- ▶ Supply-Chain Management
- ▶ Inventory Management
- ▶ Scheduling
- ▶ Maintenance

REPETITIVE MANUFACTURING WORKS AT HARLEY-DAVIDSON

Since Harley-Davidson's founding in 1903, it has competed with hundreds of manufacturers, foreign and domestic. The competition has been tough. Recent competitive battles have been with the Japanese, and earlier battles were with the German, English, and Italian manufacturers. But after over 100 years. Harley is the only major U.S. motorcycle company. The company now has five U.S. facilities and an assembly plant in Brazil.

As a part of management's lean manufacturing effort, Harley groups production of parts that require similar processes together. The result is work cells. Using the latest technology, work cells perform in one location all the operations necessary for production of a specific module. Raw materials are moved to the work cells and then the modules proceed to the assembly line. As a double check on quality, Harley has also installed "light curtain" technology which uses an infrared sensor to verify the bin from which an operator is taking parts. Materials go to the assembly line on a just-in-time basis, or as Harley calls it, using a Materials as Needed (MAN) system.

The 12.5-million-square-foot facility in the U.S. includes manufacturing cells that perform tube bending, frame-building, machining, painting, and polishing. Innovative manufacturing techniques use robots to load machines and highly automated production to reduce machining time. Automation and precision sensors play a key role in maintaining tolerances and producing a quality product. Each day the facility produces up to 600 heavy-duty factory-custom motorcycles. Bikes are assembled

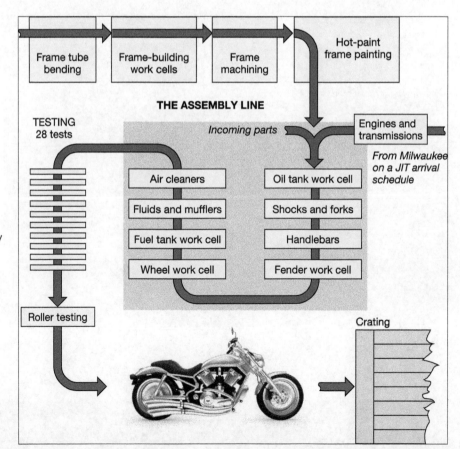

Flow Diagram Showing the Production Process at Harley-Davidson's Assembly Plant.

with different engine displacements, multiple wheel options, colors, and accessories. The result is a huge number of variations in the motorcycles available which allows customers to individualize their purchase. The Harley-Davidson production system works because high-quality modules are brought together on a tightly scheduled repetitive production line.

Engines, having arrived just-in-time from the Milwaukee engine plant in their own protective shipping containers, are placed on an overhead conveyor for movement to the assembly line.

Wheel assembly modules are prepared in a work cell for JIT delivery to the assembly line.

For manufacturers like Harley-Davidson, which produce a large number of end products from a relatively small number of options, modular bills of material provide an effective solution.

It all comes together on the line. Any employee who spots a problem has the authority to stop the line until the problem is corrected.

Chapter 7 **Learning Objectives**

> **AUTHOR COMMENT**
> The four process strategies are detrimental to production because they answer the basic question: How can we produce the new products we are questing?

FOUR PROCESS STRATEGIES

In Chapter 5, we examined the need for the selection, definition, and design of goods and services. Our purpose was to create environmentally friendly designs that could be delivered in an ethical, sustainable manner. We now turn to their production. A major decision for an operations manager is finding the best way to produce so as not to waste our planet's resources. Let's look at ways to help managers design a process for achieving this goal.

A **process** (or transformation) **strategy** is an organization's approach to transforming resources into goods and services. The objective of a process strategy is to build a production process that meets customer requirements and product specifications within cost and other managerial constraints. The process selected will have a long-term effect on efficiency and flexibility of production, as well as on cost and quality of the goods produced. Therefore, the limitations of a firm's operations strategy are determined at the time of the process decision.

Virtually every good or service is made by using some variation of one of four process strategies: (1) process focus; (2) repetitive focus; (3) product focus; (4) mass customization. The relationship of these four strategies to volume and variety is shown in Figure 7.1. We examine New Mowasat Hospital as an example of a process-focused firm, EGA as a repetitive producer, Cheetos from Frito-Lay as a product-focused operation, and Dell as a mass customizer.

Process strategy

An organization's approach to transforming resources into goods and services.

LO1: Describe four production processes

Process Focus

The vast majority of global production is devoted to making *low-volume, high-variety* products in places called 'job shops.' Such facilities are organized around specific activities or processes. In a factory, these processes might be departments devoted to welding, grinding, and painting. In an office, the processes might be accounts payable, sales, and payroll. In a restaurant, they might be grill and bakery. Such facilities are **process focused** in terms of equipment, layout, and supervision. They provide a high degree of product flexibility as products move between

Process focus

A production facility organized around processes to facilitate low-volume, high-variety production.

▶ **FIGURE 7.1**
Process Selected Must Fit with Volume and Variety

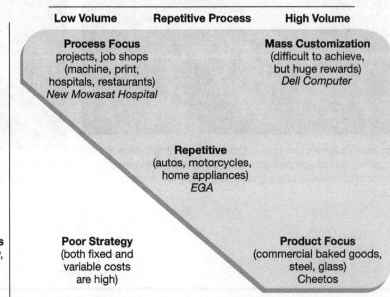

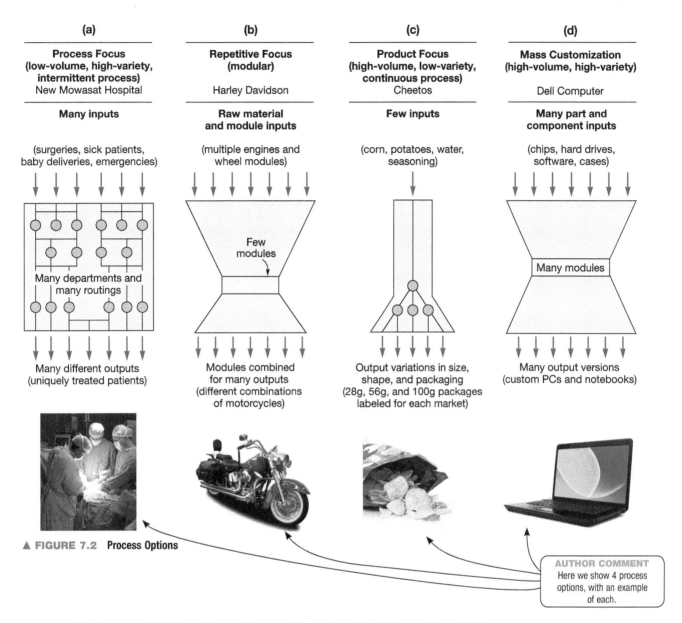

(a)	(b)	(c)	(d)
Process Focus **(low-volume, high-variety,** **intermittent process)** New Mowasat Hospital	**Repetitive Focus** **(modular)** Harley Davidson	**Product Focus** **(high-volume, low-variety,** **continuous process)** Cheetos	**Mass Customization** **(high-volume, high-variety)** Dell Computer
Many inputs	**Raw material** **and module inputs**	**Few inputs**	**Many part and** **component inputs**
(surgeries, sick patients, baby deliveries, emergencies)	(multiple engines and wheel modules)	(corn, potatoes, water, seasoning)	(chips, hard drives, software, cases)
Many departments and many routings	Few modules		Many modules
Many different outputs (uniquely treated patients)	Modules combined for many outputs (different combinations of motorcycles)	Output variations in size, shape, and packaging (28g, 56g, and 100g packages labeled for each market)	Many output versions (custom PCs and notebooks)

▲ **FIGURE 7.2** **Process Options**

> **AUTHOR COMMENT**
> Here we show 4 process options, with an example of each.

processes. Each process is designed to perform a wide variety of activities and handle frequent changes. Consequently, they are also called *intermittent processes*.

Process-focused facilities have high variable costs with extremely low utilization of facilities, as low as 5 percent. This is the case for many restaurants, hospitals, and machine shops. However, some facilities that lend themselves to electronic controls do somewhat better. With computer-controlled machines, it is possible to program machine tools, piece movement, tool changing, placement of the parts on the machine, and even the movement of materials between machines.

Repetitive Focus

A repetitive process falls between the product and process focuses seen in Figures 7.1 and 7.2(b). Repetitive processes, as we saw in the Company Profile on EGA, use modules. Modules are parts or components previously prepared, often in a continuous process.

The **repetitive process** is the classic assembly line. Widely used in the assembly of virtually all automobiles and household appliances, it has more structure and consequently less flexibility than a process-focused facility.

Fast-food firms are another example of a repetitive process using **modules**. This type of production allows more customizing than a product-focused facility; modules (for example, meat, cheese, sauce, tomatoes, onions) are assembled to get a quasi-custom product, a cheeseburger. In this manner, the firm obtains both the economic advantages of the continuous model (where many of the modules are prepared) and the custom advantage of the low-volume, high-variety model.

Repetitive process
A product-oriented production process that uses modules.

Modules
Parts or components of a product previously prepared, often in a continuous process.

Product Focus

Product focus

A facility organized around products; a product-oriented, high-volume, low-variety process.

High-volume, low-variety processes are **product focused**. The facilities are organized around *products*. They are also called *continuous processes*, because they have very long, continuous production runs. Products such as glass, paper, tin sheets, lightbulbs, and potato chips are made via a continuous process. Some products, such as lightbulbs, are discrete; others, such as rolls of paper, are nondiscrete. Still others, such as repaired hernias at specialized hospitals, are services. It is only with standardization and effective quality control that firms have established product-focused facilities. An organization producing the same lightbulb or hot dog bun day after day can organize around a product. Such an organization has an inherent ability to set standards and maintain a given quality, as opposed to an organization that is producing unique products every day, such as a print shop or general-purpose hospital. For example, Frito-Lay's family of products is also produced in a product-focused facility, see Figure 7.2(c). At Frito-Lay, corn, potatoes, water, and seasoning are the relatively few inputs, but outputs (like Cheetos, Doritos, and Lays) vary in seasoning and packaging within the product family.

A product-focused facility produces high volume and low variety. The specialized nature of the facility requires high fixed cost, but low variable costs reward high facility utilization.

Mass Customization Focus

Our increasingly wealthy and sophisticated world demands individualized goods and services. A peek at the rich variety of goods and services that operations managers are called on to supply is shown in Table 7.1. The explosion of variety has taken place in automobiles, movies, breakfast cereals, and thousands of other areas. In spite of this proliferation of products, operations managers have improved product quality while reducing costs. Consequently, the variety of products continues to grow. Operations managers use *mass customization* to produce this vast array of goods and services. **Mass customization** is the rapid, low-cost production of goods and services that fulfill increasingly unique customer desires. But mass customization (see the upper-right section of Figure 7.1) is not just about variety; it is about making precisely *what* the customer wants *when* the customer wants it, economically.

Mass customization

Rapid, low-cost production that caters to constantly changing unique customer desires.

Mass customization brings us the variety of products traditionally provided by low-volume manufacture (a process focus) at the cost of standardized high-volume (product-focused) production. However, achieving mass customization is a challenge that requires sophisticated operational capabilities. For example, Dell has a facility that allows customers to build their own computers. Building agile processes that rapidly and inexpensively produce custom products requires imaginative and aggressive use of organizational resources. And the link between sales, design, production, supply chain, and logistics must be tight.

Dell Computer, see Figure 7.2(d) has demonstrated that the payoff for mass customization can be substantial. More traditional manufacturers include Toyota, which recently announced delivery of custom-ordered cars in 5 days. Similarly, electronic controls allow designers in the

▶ **TABLE 7.1**

Mass Customization Provides More Choices than Ever

| | Number of Choices[a] | |
Item	1970s	21st Century
Vehicle models	140	286
Vehicle styles	18	1,212
Bicycle types	8	211,000[c]
Software titles	0	400,000
Websites	0	162,000,000[d]
Movie releases per year	267	765[e]
New book titles	40,530	300,000+
TV channels	5	185
Breakfast cereals	160	340
Items (SKUs) in supermarkets	14,000[b]	150,000[f]
LCD TVs	0	102

[a]Variety available in America; worldwide the variety increases even more. [b]1989.
[c]Possible combinations for one manufacturer. [d]Royal Pingdom Estimate (2008).
[e]www.movieweb.com (2009). [f]SKUs managed by H. E. Butts grocery chain.
Source: Various; however, many of the data are from the Federal Reserve Bank of Dallas.

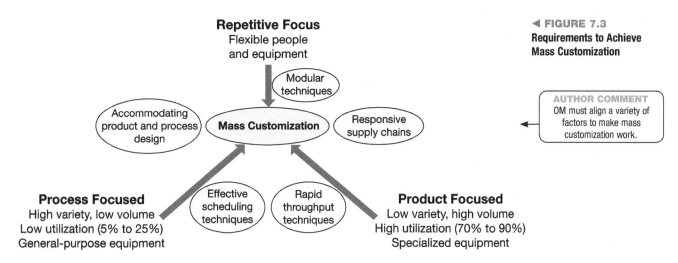

◄ **FIGURE 7.3**
Requirements to Achieve Mass Customization

AUTHOR COMMENT
OM must align a variety of factors to make mass customization work.

textile industry to rapidly revamp their lines and respond to changes. Nike, too, has introduced mass customization through its NIKEiD, which allows customers to design their own shoes through use of a specialized applet online.

The service industry is also moving toward mass customization. For instance, not very many years ago, most people had the same telephone service. Now, not only is the phone service full of options, from caller ID to voice mail, but contemporary phones are hardly phones. Smart phones are inclusive of all the functions a person might need while mobile; email, camera, computer, game player, GPS, and Web browsing are some of the services provided. Similarly, insurance companies are adding and tailoring new products with shortened development times to meet the unique needs of their customers. Mass customization places new demands on operations managers who must build the processes that provide this expanding variety of goods and services. Mass customization relies on modular design in addition to effective scheduling, personnel and facility flexibility, supportive supply chains, and rapid throughput to achieve its purpose, as shown in Figure 7.3. These items influence all ten of the OM decisions and therefore require excellent operations management.

Making Mass Customization Work Mass customization suggests a high-volume system in which products are built-to-order.[1] **Build-to-order (BTO)** means producing to customer orders, not forecasts. Build-to-order can be a successful order-winning strategy when executed well. But high-volume build-to-order is difficult. Some major challenges are:

- *Product design* must be imaginative and fast. Successful build-to-order designs often use modules. Dell uses different combinations of monitor size, memory, processor type, and hard drives to make thousands of variations of its desktop computers and laptops.
- *Process design* must be flexible and able to accommodate changes in both design and technology. For instance, **postponement** allows for customization late in the production process. Toyota installs unique interior modules very late in production for its popular Scion, a process also typical with customized vans. Postponement is further discussed in Chapter 11.
- *Inventory management* requires tight control. To be successful with build-to-order, a firm must avoid being stuck with unpopular or obsolete components. With virtually no raw material, Dell puts customized computers together in less than a day.
- *Tight schedules* that track orders and material from design through delivery are another requirement of mass customization.
- *Responsive partners* in the supply chain can yield effective collaboration. Forecasting, inventory management, and ordering for Jo Bedu shirts are all handled for the retailer by its supplier in Amman.

Mass customization/build-to-order is difficult, but is the new imperative for operations. There are advantages to mass customization and building to order: First, by meeting the demands of the marketplace, firms win orders and stay in business; in addition, they trim costs (from personnel

Build-to-order (BTO)
Produce to customer order rather than to a forecast.

Postponement
Delaying any modifications or customization to a product as long as possible in the production process.

---

[1]Build-to-order (BTO) may be referred to and refined as engineer-to-order (ETO) and design-to-order (DTO), depending on the extent of the customization.

▼ **TABLE 7.2**   **Comparison of the Characteristics of Four Types of Processes**

Process Focus (low volume, high variety) (e.g. New Mowasat Hospital)	Repetitive Focus (modular) (e.g. EGA)	Product Focus (high volume, low variety) (e.g. Cheetos from Frito-Lay)	Mass Customization (high volume, high variety) (e.g. Dell Computers)
1. Small quantity and large variety of products are produced.	1. Long runs, usually a standardized product with options, are produced from modules.	1. Large quantity and small variety of products are produced.	1. Large quantity and large variety of products are produced.
2. Equipment used is general purpose.	2. Special equipment aids in use of an assembly line.	2. Equipment used is special purpose.	2. Rapid changeover on flexible equipment.
3. Operators are broadly skilled.	3. Employees are modestly trained.	3. Operators are less broadly skilled.	3. Flexible operators are trained for the necessary customization.
4. There are many job instructions because each job changes.	4. Repetitive operations reduce training and changes in job instructions.	4. Work orders and job instructions are few because they are standardized.	4. Custom orders require many job instructions.
5. Raw material inventories are high relative to the value of the product.	5. Just-in-time procurement techniques are used.	5. Raw material inventories are low relative to the value of the product.	5. Raw material inventories are low relative to the value of the product.
6. Work-in-process is high compared to output.	6. Just-in-time inventory techniques are used.	6. Work-in-process inventory is low compared to output.	6. Work-in-process inventory is driven down by JIT, kanban, lean production.
7. Units move slowly through the facility.	7. Assembly is measured in hours and days.	7. Swift movement of units through the facility is typical.	7. Goods move swiftly through the facility.
8. Finished goods are usually made to order and not stored.	8. Finished goods are made to frequent forecasts.	8. Finished goods are usually made to a forecast and stored.	8. Finished goods are often build-to-order (BTO).
9. Scheduling is complex and concerned with the trade-off between inventory availability, capacity, and customer service.	9. Scheduling is based on building various models from a variety of modules to forecasts.	9. Scheduling is relatively simple and concerned with establishing a rate of output sufficient to meet sales forecasts.	9. Sophisticated scheduling is required to accommodate custom orders.
10. Fixed costs tend to be low and variable costs high.	10. Fixed costs are dependent on flexibility of the facility.	10. Fixed costs tend to be high and variable costs low.	10. Fixed costs tend to be high, but variable costs must be low.

to inventory to facilities) that exist because of inaccurate sales forecasting. Mass customization and build-to-order can be done—and operations managers in leading organizations are accepting the challenge.

Comparison of Process Choices

The characteristics of the four processes are shown in Table 7.2 and Figure 7.2. Advantages exist across the continuum of processes, and firms may find strategic advantage in any process. Each of the processes, when properly matched to volume and variety, can produce a low-cost advantage. For instance, unit costs will be less in the continuous-process case when high volume (and high utilization) exists. However, we do not always use the continuous process (that is, specialized equipment and facilities) because it is too expensive when volumes are low or flexibility is required. A low-volume, unique, highly differentiated good or service is more economical when produced under process focus; this is the way fine-dining restaurants and general-purpose hospitals are organized. Just as all four processes, when appropriately selected and well managed, can yield low cost, all four can also be responsive and produce differentiated products.

Figure 7.3 indicated that equipment utilization in a process-focused facility is often in the range of 5 percent to 25 percent. When utilization goes above 15 percent, moving toward a repetitive or product focus, or even mass customization, may be advantageous. A cost advantage usually exists by improving utilization, provided the necessary flexibility is maintained. McDonald's started an entirely new industry by moving its limited menu from process focus to repetitive focus. McDonald's is now trying to add more variety and move toward mass customization.

Much of what is produced in the world is still produced in very small lots—often as small as one. This is true for most legal services, medical services, dental services, and restaurants. An X-ray machine in a dentist's office and much of the equipment in a fine-dining restaurant have low utilization. Hospitals, too, have low utilization, which suggests why their costs are considered high. Why such low utilization? In part because excess capacity for peak loads is desirable. Hospital administrators, as well as managers of other service facilities and their patients and customers, expect equipment to be available as needed. Another reason is poor scheduling (although substantial efforts have been made to forecast demand in the service industry) and the resulting imbalance in the use of facilities.

Crossover charts The comparison of processes can be further enhanced by looking at the point where the total cost of the processes changes. For instance, Figure 7.4 shows three alternative processes compared on a single chart. Such a chart is sometimes called a **crossover chart**. Process A has the lowest cost for volumes below V_1, process B has the lowest cost between V_1 and V_2, and process C has the lowest cost at volumes above V_2.

Example 1 illustrates how to determine the exact volume at which one process becomes more expensive than another.

Crossover chart
A chart of costs at the possible volumes for more than one process.

Crossover Chart

Bahrain Island Enterprises would like to evaluate three accounting software products (A, B, and C) to support changes in its internal accounting processes. The resulting processes will have cost structures similar to those shown in Figure 7.4. The costs of the software for these processes are:

	Total Fixed Cost	Dollars Required per Accounting Report
Software A	US$200,000	US$60
Software B	US$300,000	US$25
Software C	US$400,000	US$10

APPROACH ► Solve for the crossover point for software A and B and then the crossover point for software B and C.

SOLUTION ► Software A yields a process that is most economical up to V_1 but to exactly what number of reports (volume)? To determine the volume at V_1 we set the cost of software A equal to the cost of software B. V_1 is the unknown volume:

$$200,000 + (60)V_1 = 30,000 + (25)V_1$$

$$35V_1 = 100,000$$

$$V_1 = 2,857$$

This means that software A is most economical from 0 reports to 2,857 reports (V_1).

Similarly, to determine the crossover point for V_2 we set the cost of software B equal to the cost of software C:

$$300,000 + (25)V_2 = 400,000 + (10)V_2$$

$$15V_2 = 100,000$$

$$V_2 = 6,666$$

This means that software B is most economical if the number of reports is between 2,857 (V_1) and 6,666 (V_2) and that software C is most economical if reports exceed 6,666 (V_2).

INSIGHT ► As you can see, the software and related process chosen is highly dependent on the forecasted volume.

LEARNING EXERCISE ► If the vendor of software A reduces the fixed cost to US$150,000, what is the new crossover point between A and B? [Answer: 4,286.]

RELATED PROBLEMS ► 7.5, 7.6, 7.7, 7.8, 7.9, 7.10

EXCEL **OM** Data File **Ch07Ex1.xls** can be found at MyOMLab.

▶ **FIGURE 7.4**
Crossover Charts

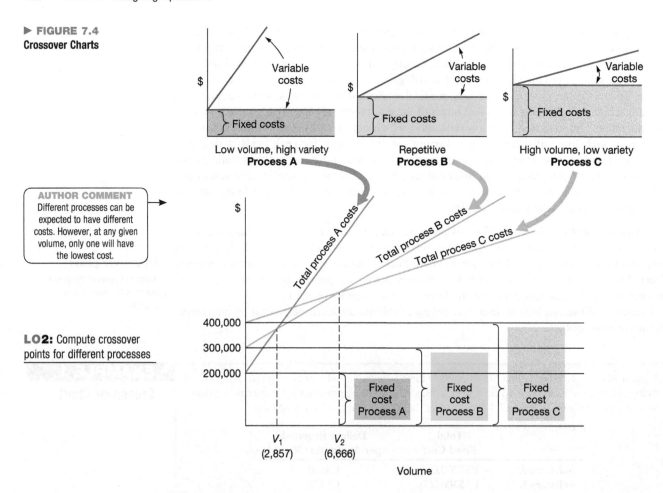

AUTHOR COMMENT
Different processes can be expected to have different costs. However, at any given volume, only one will have the lowest cost.

LO2: Compute crossover points for different processes

Focused processes   In an ongoing quest for efficiency, industrialized societies continue to move toward specialization. The focus that comes with specialization contributes to efficiency. Managers who focus on a limited number of activities, products, and technologies do better. As the variety of products in a facility increases, overhead costs increase even faster. Similarly, as the variety of products, customers, and technology increases, so does complexity. The resources necessary to cope with the complexity expand disproportionately. A focus on depth of product line as opposed to breadth is typical of outstanding firms, of which Intel, Nokia, and Almarai are world-class examples. Specialization, simplification, concentration, and *focus* yield efficiency. They also contribute to building a core competence that yields market and financial success. The focus can be:

VIDEO 7.1
Process Strategy at Wheeled Coach Ambulance

- *Customers* (such as Aramex, which focuses on customers who require quick delivery solutions)
- *Products* with similar attributes (such as the Arab Potash Company in Jordan, which processes only high-quality fertilizers to be exported to advanced industries around the world)
- *Service* (such as New Mowasat Hospital, with a focus on children and women)
- *Technology* (such as Advanced Electronics Company, in Saudi Arabia, with a focus on only certain specialized kinds of electronics manufacturing, system integration, and military systems).

The key for the operations manager is to move continuously toward specialization, focusing on the products, technology, customers, processes, and talents necessary to excel in that specialty.

Changing processes   Changing the production system from one process model to another is difficult and expensive. In some cases, the change may mean starting over. Consider what would be required of a seemingly simple change—Kudu fast-food restaurants in Saudi Arabia adding the flexibility necessary to serve you a charbroiled hamburger. What appears to be straightforward would require changes in many of our ten OM decisions. For instance, changes may be necessary in: (1) purchasing (a different quality of meat, perhaps with more fat content, and supplies such as charcoal); (2) quality standards (how long and at what temperature the patty will cook); (3) equipment (the charbroiler); (4) layout (space for the new process and for new exhaust vents); (5) training. So choosing where to operate on the process strategy continuum may determine the transformation strategy for an extended period. This critical decision must be done right the first time.

PROCESS ANALYSIS AND DESIGN

AUTHOR COMMENT
Here we look at five tools that help understand processes.

When analyzing and designing processes, we ask questions such as the following.

- Is the process designed to achieve competitive advantage in terms of differentiation, response, or low cost?
- Does the process eliminate steps that do not add value?
- Does the process maximize customer value as perceived by the customer?
- Will the process win orders?

A number of tools help us understand the complexities of process design and redesign. They are simply ways of making sense of what happens or must happen in a process. Let's look at five of them: flowcharts, time-function mapping, value-stream mapping, process charts, and service blueprinting.

LO3: Use the tools of process analysis

Flowchart

The first tool is the **flowchart**, which is a schematic or drawing of the movement of material, product, or people. Such charts can help understanding, analysis, and communication of a process.

Flowchart

A drawing used to analyze movement of people or material.

Time-Function Mapping

A second tool for process analysis and design is a flowchart, but with time added on the horizontal axis. Such charts are sometimes called **time-function mapping**, or *process mapping*. With time-function mapping, nodes indicate the activities and arrows indicate the flow direction, with time on the horizontal axis. This type of analysis allows users to identify and eliminate waste such as extra steps, duplication, and delay. Figure 7.5 shows the use of process mapping before and after process improvement at American National Can Company. In this example, substantial reduction in waiting time and process improvement in order processing contributed to a savings of 46 days.

Time-function mapping

Also known as *process mapping*, a flowchart with time added on the horizontal axis.

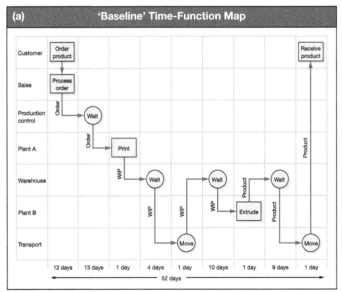

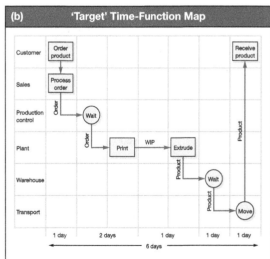

▲ **FIGURE 7.5** **Time-Function Mapping (Process Mapping) for a Product Requiring Printing and Extruding Operations at American National Can Company**

This technique clearly shows that waiting and order processing contributed substantially to the 46 days that can be eliminated in this operation.

Source: Excerpted from Elaine J. Labach, "Faster, Better, and Cheaper," *Target* no. 5: 43 with permission of the Association for Manufacturing Excellence, 380 West Palatine Road, Wheeling, IL 60090-5863, 847/520-3282. **www.ame.org**. Reprinted with permission of Target Magazine.

Value-stream mapping (VSM)

A process that helps managers understand how to add value in the flow of material and information through the entire production process.

Value-Stream Mapping

A variation of time-function mapping is **value-stream mapping (VSM)**; however, value-stream mapping takes an expanded look at where value is added (and not added) in the entire production process, including the supply chain. As with time-function mapping, the idea is to start with the customer and understand the production process, but value-stream mapping extends the analysis back to suppliers.

Value-stream mapping

EGA has received an order for 11,000 brake disks per month and wants to understand how the order will be processed through manufacturing.

APPROACH ▶   To fully understand the process from customer to supplier, EGA wants to prepare a value-stream map.

SOLUTION ▶   Although value-stream maps appear complex, their construction is easy. Here are the steps needed to complete the value-stream map shown in Figure 7.6.

1. Begin with symbols for customer, supplier, and production to ensure the big picture.
2. Enter customer order requirements.
3. Calculate the daily production requirements.
4. Enter the outbound shipping requirements and delivery frequency.
5. Determine inbound shipping method and delivery frequency.
6. Add the process steps (i.e. machine, assemble) in sequence, left to right.
7. Add communication methods, add their frequency, and show the direction with arrows.
8. Add inventory quantities (shown with ⚠) between every step of the entire flow.
9. Determine total working time (value-added time) and delay (non-value-added time).

▶ FIGURE 7.6
Value-Stream Mapping (VSM)

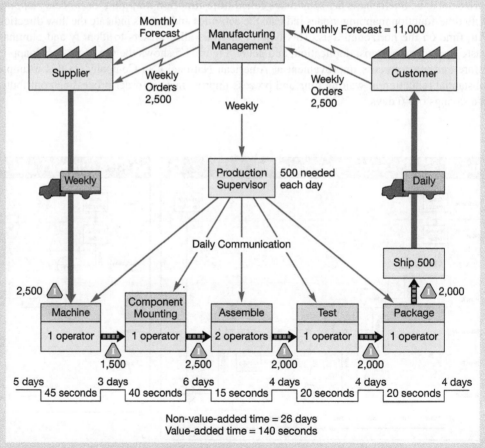

INSIGHT ▶   From Figure 7.6 we note that large inventories exist in incoming raw material and between processing steps, and that the value-added time is low as a proportion of the entire process.

LEARNING EXERCISE ▶   How might raw material inventory be reduced? [Answer: Have deliveries twice per week rather than once per week.]

Value-stream mapping takes into account not only the process but, as shown in Example 2, also the management decisions and information systems that support the process.

Process Charts

The fourth tool is the *process chart*. **Process charts** use symbols, time, and distance to provide an objective and structured way to analyze and record the activities that make up a process.[2] They allow us to focus on value-added activities. For instance, the process chart shown in Figure 7.7, which includes the present method of hamburger assembly at a fast-food restaurant, includes a value-added line to help us distinguish between value-added activities and waste. Identifying all value-added operations (as opposed to inspection, storage, delay, and transportation, which add no value) allows us to determine the percentage of value added to total activities.[3] We can see from the computation at the bottom of Figure 7.7 that the value added in this case is 85.7 percent. The operations manager's job is to reduce waste and increase the percentage of value added. The non-value-added items are a waste; they are resources lost to the firm and to society forever.

Process chart

A graphic representation that depicts a sequence of steps for a process.

Service Blueprinting

Products with a high service content may warrant use of yet a fifth process technique. **Service blueprinting** is a process analysis technique that focuses on the customer and the provider's interaction with the customer. For instance, the activities at level one of Figure 7.8 are under the control of the customer. In the second level are activities of the service provider interacting with the customer. The third level includes those activities that are performed away from, and not immediately visible to, the customer. Each level suggests different management issues. For instance, the top level may suggest educating the customer or modifying expectations, whereas the second level may require a focus on personnel selection and training. Finally, the third level lends itself to more typical process innovations. The service blueprint shown in Figure 7.8 also notes potential failure points and shows how poka-yoke techniques can be added to improve quality. The consequences of these failure points can be greatly reduced if identified at the design stage when modifications or appropriate poka-yokes can be included. A time dimension is included in Figure 7.8 to aid understanding, extend insight, and provide a focus on customer service.

Service blueprinting

A process analysis technique that lends itself to a focus on the customer and the provider's interaction with the customer.

[2] An additional example of a process chart is shown in Chapter 10.
[3] Waste includes *inspection* (if the task is done properly, then inspection is unnecessary); *transportation* (movement of material within a process may be a necessary evil, but it adds no value); *delay* (an asset sitting idle and taking up space is waste); *storage* (unless part of a 'curing' process, storage is waste).

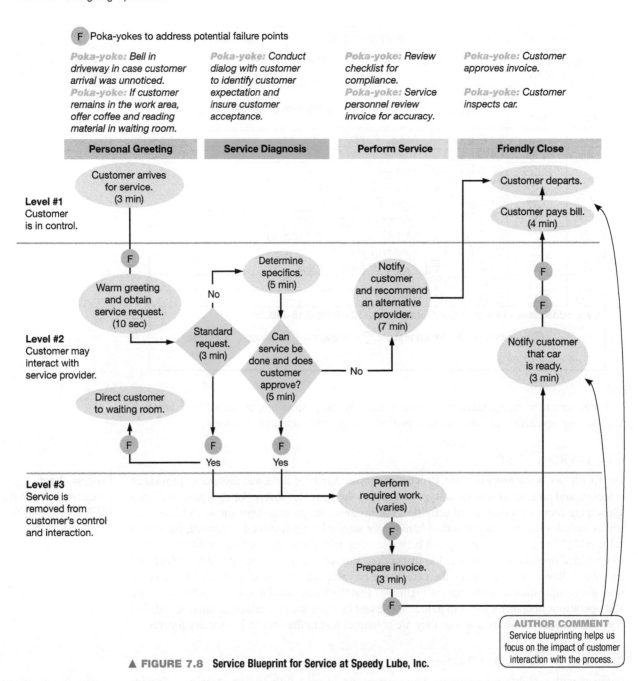

F   Poka-yokes to address potential failure points

Poka-yoke: Bell in driveway in case customer arrival was unnoticed.
Poka-yoke: If customer remains in the work area, offer coffee and reading material in waiting room.

Poka-yoke: Conduct dialog with customer to identify customer expectation and insure customer acceptance.

Poka-yoke: Review checklist for compliance.
Poka-yoke: Service personnel review invoice for accuracy.

Poka-yoke: Customer approves invoice.

Poka-yoke: Customer inspects car.

Personal Greeting | **Service Diagnosis** | **Perform Service** | **Friendly Close**

Level #1
Customer is in control.

Customer arrives for service. (3 min)

Customer departs.

Customer pays bill. (4 min)

Level #2
Customer may interact with service provider.

Warm greeting and obtain service request. (10 sec)

Determine specifics. (5 min)

No

Standard request. (3 min)

Can service be done and does customer approve? (5 min)

No

Notify customer and recommend an alternative provider. (7 min)

Notify customer that car is ready. (3 min)

Direct customer to waiting room.

F   Yes

F   Yes

Level #3
Service is removed from customer's control and interaction.

Perform required work. (varies)

F

Prepare invoice. (3 min)

F

AUTHOR COMMENT
Service blueprinting helps us focus on the impact of customer interaction with the process.

▲ FIGURE 7.8   **Service Blueprint for Service at Speedy Lube, Inc.**

Each of these five process analysis tools has its strengths and variations. Flowcharts are a quick way to view the big picture and try to make sense of the entire system. Time-function mapping adds some rigor and a time element to the macro analysis. Value-stream mapping extends beyond the immediate organization to customers and suppliers. Process charts are designed to provide a much more detailed view of the process, adding items such as value-added time, delay, distance, storage, and so forth. Service blueprinting, on the other hand, is designed to help us focus on the customer interaction part of the process. Because customer interaction is often an important variable in process design, we now examine some additional aspects of service process design.

AUTHOR COMMENT
Customer interaction with service processes increases the design challenge.

SPECIAL CONSIDERATIONS FOR SERVICE PROCESS DESIGN

Interaction with the customer often affects process performance adversely. But a service, by its very nature, implies that some interaction and customization is needed. Recognizing that the customer's unique desires tend to play havoc with a process, the more the manager designs the process to accommodate these special requirements, the more effective and efficient the process will be.

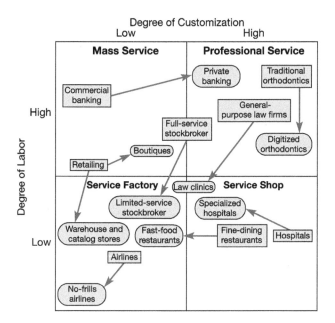

Degree of Customization

◀ **FIGURE 7.9**
Services Moving toward Specialization and Focus within the Service Process Matrix

Source: Adapted from work by Roger Schmenner, "Service Business and Productivity," *Decision Sciences* 35, no. 3 (Summer 2004): 333–347.

AUTHOR COMMENT
Notice how services find a competitive opportunity by moving from the rectangles to the ovals.

Customer Interaction and Process Design

The four quadrants of Figure 7.9 provide additional insight into how operations managers design service processes to find the best level of specialization and focus while maintaining the necessary customer interaction and customization. The ten operations decisions we introduced in Chapters 1 and 2 are used with a different emphasis in each quadrant. For instance:

LO4: Describe customer interaction in process design

- In the upper sections (quadrants) of *mass service* and *professional service*, where *labor content is high*, we expect the manager to focus extensively on human resources. This is often done with personalized services, requiring high labor involvement and therefore significant selection and training issues in the human resources area. This is particularly true in the professional service quadrant.

- The quadrants with *low customization* tend to: (1) standardize or restrict some offerings, as do fast-food restaurants; (2) automate, as have airlines with ticket-vending machines; (3) remove some services, such as seat assignments, as has Air Arabia. Offloading some aspect of the service through automation may require innovations in process design as well as capital investment. Such is the case with airline ticket vending and bank ATMs. This move to standardization and automation may require added capital expenditure, as well as putting operations managers under pressure to develop new skills for the purchase and maintenance of such equipment. A reduction in a customization capability will require added strength in other areas.

- Because customer feedback is lower in the quadrants with *low customization*, tight control may be required to maintain quality standards.

- Operations with *low labor intensity* may lend themselves particularly well to innovations in process technology and scheduling.

Table 7.3 shows some additional techniques for innovative process design in services. Managers focus on designing innovative processes that enhance the service.

More Opportunities to Improve Service Processes

Layout Layout design is an integral part of many service processes, particularly in retailing, dining, and banking. In retailing, layout can provide not only product exposure but also customer education and product enhancement. In restaurants, layout can enhance the dining experience as well as provide an effective flow between bar, kitchen, and dining area. In banks, layout provides security as well as work flow and personal comfort. Because layout is such an integral part of many services, it provides continuing opportunity for winning orders.

VIDEO 7.2
Process Analysis at Arnold Palmer Hospital

Human resources Because so many services involve direct interaction with the customer (as the upper quadrants of Figure 7.9 suggest), the human resource issues of recruiting and

► **TABLE 7.3**
**Techniques for Improving
Service Productivity**

Strategy	Technique	Example
Separation	*Structuring service* so customers must go where the service is offered	Bank customers go to a manager to open a new account, to loan officers for loans, and to tellers for deposits
Self-service	*Self-service* so customers examine, compare, and evaluate at their own pace	Supermarkets and department stores Internet ordering
Postponement	*Customizing at delivery*	Customizing vans at delivery rather than at production
Focus	*Restricting* the offerings	Limited-menu restaurant
Modules	*Modular* selection of service *Modular* production	Investment and insurance selection Pre-packaged food modules in restaurants
Automation	*Separating services* that may lend themselves to some type of automation	Automatic teller machines
Scheduling	Precise personnel *scheduling*	Scheduling ticket counter personnel at 15-minute intervals at airlines
Training	*Clarifying the service* options *Explaining how to avoid problems*	Investment counsellors, funeral directors After-sales maintenance personnel

training can be particularly important ingredients in service processes. Additionally, a committed workforce that exhibits flexibility when schedules are made and is cross-trained to fill in when the process requires less than a full-time person can have a tremendous impact on overall process performance.

SELECTION OF EQUIPMENT AND TECHNOLOGY

Ultimately, the decisions about a particular process require decisions about equipment and technology. Those decisions can be complex because alternative methods of production are present in virtually all operations functions, be they hospitals, restaurants, or manufacturing facilities. Picking the best equipment means understanding the specific industry and available processes and technology. That choice of equipment, be it an X-ray machine for a hospital, a computer-controlled lathe for a factory, or a new computer for an office, requires considering cost, quality, capacity, and flexibility. To make this decision, operations personnel develop documentation that indicates the capacity, size, and tolerances of each option, as well as its maintenance requirements. Any one of these attributes may be the deciding factor regarding selection.

The selection of equipment for a particular type of process can also provide competitive advantage. Many firms, for instance, develop unique machines or techniques within established processes that provide an advantage. This advantage may result in added flexibility in meeting customer requirements, lower cost, or higher quality. Innovations and equipment modification might also allow for a more stable production process requiring less adjustment, maintenance, and operator training. In any case, specialized equipment often provides a way to win orders.

Flexibility

The ability to respond with little penalty in time, cost, or customer value.

Modern technology also allows operations managers to enlarge the scope of their processes. As a result, an important attribute to look for in new equipment and process selection is flexible equipment. **Flexibility** is the ability to respond with little penalty in time, cost, or customer value. This may mean modular, movable, even cheap equipment. Flexibility may also mean the development of sophisticated electronic equipment, which increasingly provides the rapid changes that mass customization demands. The technological advances that influence OM process strategy are substantial and are discussed next.

LO5: Identify recent advances in production technology

PRODUCTION TECHNOLOGY

Advances in technology that enhance production and productivity have a wide range of applications in both manufacturing and services. In this section, we introduce nine areas of technology: (1) machine technology; (2) automatic identification systems; (3) process control; (4) vision systems; (5) robots; (6) automated storage and retrieval systems; (7) automated guided vehicles; (8) flexible manufacturing systems; (9) computer-integrated manufacturing.

Machine Technology

Machinery of the 21st century is often five times more productive than that of previous generations while being smaller and using less power. And continuing advances in lubricants now allow the use of water-based lubricants rather than oil-based. Using water-based lubricants eliminates hazardous waste and allows shavings to be easily recovered and recycled.

The intelligence now available for the control of new machinery via computer chips allows more complex and precise items to be made faster. Electronic controls increase speed by reducing changeover time, reducing waste (because of fewer mistakes), and enhancing flexibility. Machinery with its own computer and memory is called **computer numerical control (CNC)** machinery.

Automatic Identification Systems and Radio Frequency Identification

New equipment, from numerically controlled manufacturing machinery to ATM machines, is controlled by digital electronic signals. Electrons are a great vehicle for transmitting information, but they have a major limitation—most OM data do not start out in bits and bytes. Therefore, operations managers must get the data into an electronic form. Making data digital is done via computer keyboards, bar codes, radio frequencies, optical characters, and so forth. These **automatic identification systems (AISs)** help us move data into electronic form, where they are easily manipulated.

Because of its decreasing cost and increasing pervasiveness, **radio frequency identification (RFID)** warrants special note. RFID is integrated circuitry with its own tiny antennae that use radio waves to send signals a limited range—usually a matter of meters. These RFID tags (sometimes called RFID circuits) provide unique identification that enables the tracking and monitoring of parts, pallets, people, and pets—virtually everything that moves. RFID requires no line of sight between tag and reader.

Innovative OM examples of AISs and RFID include:

- Nurses reduce errors in hospitals by matching bar codes on medication to ID bracelets on patients.
- RFID tags in agriculture monitor the temperature at which fruit is kept. They can also track what chemicals and fertilizers have been used on the fruit.

Process Control

Process control is the use of information technology to monitor and control a physical process. For instance, process control is used to measure the moisture content and thickness of paper as it travels over a paper machine at thousands of meters per minute. Process control is also used to determine and control temperatures, pressures, and quantities in petroleum refineries, petrochemical processes, cement plants, steel mills, nuclear reactors, and other product-focused facilities.

Process-control systems operate in a number of ways, but the following is typical.

- Sensors collect data.
- Devices read data on some periodic basis, perhaps once a minute or once every second.
- Measurements are translated into digital signals, which are transmitted to a computer.
- Computer programs read the file (the digital data) and analyze the data.
- The resulting output may take numerous forms. These include messages on computer consoles or printers, signals to motors to change valve settings, warning lights or horns, or statistical process-control charts.

Vision Systems

Vision systems combine video cameras and computer technology and are often used in inspection roles. Visual inspection is an important task in most food-processing and manufacturing organizations. Moreover, in many applications, visual inspection performed by humans is tedious, mind-numbing, and error prone. Thus vision systems are widely used when the items being inspected are very similar. For instance, vision systems are used to inspect Frito-Lay's potato chips so that imperfections can be identified as the chips proceed down the production line. Vision systems are consistently accurate, do not become bored, and are of modest cost. These systems are vastly superior to individuals trying to perform these tasks.

Computer numerical control (CNC)
Machinery with its own computer and memory.

Automatic identification system (AIS)
A system for transforming data into electronic form, for example bar codes.

Radio frequency identification (RFID)
A wireless system in which integrated circuits with antennae send radio waves.

Process control
The use of information technology to control a physical process.

Vision systems
Systems that use video cameras and computer technology in inspection roles.

Security guards protect property using video surveillance and report any signs of crime or disorder to the emergency services.

Robots

Robot

A flexible machine with the ability to hold, move, or grab items. It functions through electronic impulses that activate motors and switches.

When a machine is flexible and has the ability to hold, move, and perhaps 'grab' items, we tend to use the word *robot*. **Robots** are mechanical devices that use electronic impulses to activate motors and switches. Robots may be used effectively to perform tasks that are especially monotonous or dangerous or those that can be improved by the substitution of mechanical for human effort. Such is the case when consistency, accuracy, speed, strength, or power can be enhanced by the substitution of machines for people. Ford, for example, uses robots to do 98 percent of the welding and most of the painting on some automobiles.

Automated Storage and Retrieval Systems

Automated storage and retrieval system (ASRS)

Computer-controlled warehouses that provide for the automatic placement of parts into and from designated places within a warehouse.

Because of the tremendous labor involved in error-prone warehousing, computer-controlled warehouses have been developed. These systems, known as **automated storage and retrieval systems (ASRSs)**, provide for the automatic placement and withdrawal of parts and products into and from designated places in a warehouse. Such systems are commonly used in distribution facilities of retailers such as Grand Stores. These systems are also found in inventory and test areas of manufacturing firms.

Automated Guided Vehicles

Automated guided vehicle (AGV)

Electronically guided and controlled cart used to move materials.

Automated material handling can take the form of monorails, conveyors, robots, or automated guided vehicles. **Automated guided vehicles (AGVs)** are electronically guided and controlled carts used in manufacturing to move parts and equipment. They are also used in offices to move mail and in hospitals and in jails to deliver meals.

Flexible Manufacturing Systems

Flexible manufacturing system (FMS)

A system that uses an automated work cell controlled by electronic signals from a common centralized computer facility.

When a central computer provides instructions to each workstation *and* to the material-handling equipment (which moves material to that station), the system is known as an automated work cell or, more commonly, a **flexible manufacturing system (FMS)**. An FMS is flexible because both the material-handling devices and the machines themselves are controlled by easily changed electronic signals (computer programs). Operators simply load new programs, as necessary, to produce different products. The result is a system that can economically produce low volume but high variety. For example, the Gulf Craft facility, near Umm Al Quwain, efficiently builds one-of-a-kind yachts for special clients. The costs associated with changeover and low utilization have been reduced substantially. FMSs bridge the gap between product-focused and process-focused facilities.

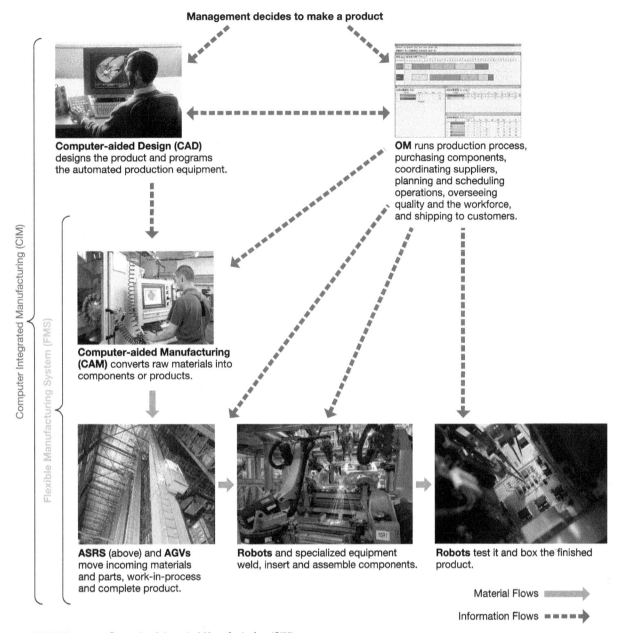

Management decides to make a product

Computer-aided Design (CAD) designs the product and programs the automated production equipment.

OM runs production process, purchasing components, coordinating suppliers, planning and scheduling operations, overseeing quality and the workforce, and shipping to customers.

Computer-aided Manufacturing (CAM) converts raw materials into components or products.

ASRS (above) and **AGVs** move incoming materials and parts, work-in-process and complete product.

Robots and specialized equipment weld, insert and assemble components.

Robots test it and box the finished product.

Computer Integrated Manufacturing (CIM)

Flexible Manufacturing System (FMS)

Material Flows

Information Flows

▲ **FIGURE 7.10** **Computer-Integrated Manufacturing (CIM)**

CIM includes computer-aided design (CAD), computer-aided manufacturing (CAM), flexible manufacturing systems (FMSs), automated storage and retrieval systems (ASRSs), automated guided vehicles (AGVs), and robots to provide an integrated and flexible manufacturing process.

Computer-Integrated Manufacturing

Flexible manufacturing systems can be extended backward electronically to the engineering and inventory control departments and forward to the warehousing and shipping departments. In this way, computer-aided design (CAD) generates the necessary electronic instructions to run a numerically controlled machine. In a computer-integrated manufacturing environment, a design change initiated at a CAD terminal can result in that change being made in the part produced on the shop floor in a matter of minutes. When this capability is integrated with inventory control, warehousing, and shipping as a part of a flexible manufacturing system, the entire system is called **computer-integrated manufacturing (CIM)** (Figure 7.10).

Flexible manufacturing systems and computer-integrated manufacturing are reducing the distinction between low-volume/high-variety and high-volume/low-variety production. Information technology is allowing FMS and CIM to handle increasing variety while expanding to include a growing range of volumes.

Computer-integrated manufacturing (CIM)

A manufacturing system in which CAD, FMS, inventory control, warehousing, and shipping are integrated.

AUTHOR COMMENT
Although less dramatic than manufacturing, technology also improves quality and productivity in services.

TECHNOLOGY IN SERVICES

Just as we have seen rapid advances in technology in the manufacturing sector, so we also find dramatic changes in the service sector. These range from electronic diagnostic equipment at auto repair shops, to blood- and urine-testing equipment in hospitals, to retinal security scanners at airports and high-security facilities. The hospitality industry provides other examples, as discussed in the *OM in Action* box 'Technology Changes the Hotel Industry.'

OM in Action ▶ Technology Changes the Hotel Industry

Technology is introducing 'intelligent rooms' to the hotel industry. Hotel management can now precisely track a maid's time through the use of a security system. When a maid enters a room, a card is inserted that notifies the front-desk computer of the maid's location. "We can show her a printout of how long she takes to do a room," says one manager.

Security systems also enable guests to use their own credit cards as keys to unlock their doors. There are also other uses for the system. The computer can bar a guest's access to the room after checkout time and automatically control the air conditioning or heat, turning it on at check-in and off at checkout.

Minibars are now equipped with sensors that alert the central computer system at the hotel when an item is removed. Such items are immediately billed to the room. And now, with a handheld infrared unit, housekeeping staff can check, from the hallway, to see if a room is physically occupied. This both eliminates the embarrassment of having a hotel staffer walk in on a guest *and* improves security for housekeepers.

At Loew's Portofino Bay Hotel at Universal Studios, Orlando, Florida, guest smart cards act as credit cards in both the theme park and the hotel, and staff smart cards (programmed for different levels of security access) create an audit trail of employee movement.

Sources: Hotel and MotelManagement (November 5, 2007): 16; *Hotels* (April 2004): 51–54; and *Newsweek* (international ed.) (September 27, 2004): 73.

In retail stores, point-of-sale (POS) terminals download prices quickly to reflect changing costs or market conditions, and sales are tracked in 15-minute segments to aid scheduling.

Table 7.4 provides a glimpse of the impact of technology on services. Operations managers in services, as in manufacturing, must be able to evaluate the impact of technology on their firm. This ability requires particular skill when evaluating reliability, investment analysis, human resource requirements, and maintenance/service.

▶ **TABLE 7.4**

Examples of Technology's Impact on Services

Service Industry	Example
Financial services	Debit cards, electronic funds transfer, ATMs, internet stock trading, QR (Quick Response) code scanning via smart phones.
Education	Online newspapers, online journals, e-books and Kindle, interactive assignments via Web CT or Blackboard Learning Systems, interactive whiteboards, and smart phones.
Utilities and government	Automated one-man garbage trucks, optical mail scanners, flood-warning systems, meters allowing homeowners to control energy usage and costs.
Restaurants and foods	Wireless orders from waiters to the kitchen, robot butchering.
Communications	Interactive TV, e-books via Kindle, networking technologies such as Skype.
Hotels	Electronic check-in/checkout, electronic key/lock systems, mobile Web bookings.
Wholesale/retail trade	Point-of-sale (POS) terminals, e-commerce, electronic communication between store and supplier, bar-coded data, RFID.
Transportation	Automatic toll booths, satellite-directed navigation systems, Wi-Fi in automobiles.
Health care	Online patient-monitoring systems, online medical information systems, robotic surgery.
Airlines	Ticketless travel, scheduling, internet purchases, boarding passes downloaded as two-dimensional bar codes on smart phones.

PROCESS REDESIGN

AUTHOR COMMENT
Most processes we design are existing processes, so the ability to redesign them is important.

Often a firm finds that the initial assumptions of its process are no longer valid. The world is a dynamic place, and customer desires, product technology, and product mix change. Consequently, processes are redesigned. **Process redesign** is the fundamental rethinking of business processes to bring about dramatic improvements in performance. Effective process redesign relies on reevaluating the purpose of the process and questioning both purpose and underlying assumptions. It works only if the basic process and its objectives are reexamined.

Process redesign also focuses on those activities that cross functional lines. Because managers are often in charge of specific 'functions' or specialized areas of responsibility, those activities (processes) that cross from one function or specialty to another may be neglected. Redesign casts aside all notions of how the process is currently being done and focuses on dramatic improvements in cost, time, and customer value. Any process is a candidate for radical redesign. The process can be a factory layout, a purchasing procedure, a new way of processing credit applications, or a new order-fulfillment process.

Process redesign
The fundamental rethinking of business processes to bring about dramatic improvements in performance.

SUSTAINABILITY

AUTHOR COMMENT
Process selection and management can support conservation and renewal of resources.

In Chapter 5 we discussed goods and services *design* and its potential impact on ethics, the environment, and sustainability. We now introduce the issue of sustainability in production *processes*.[4] Managers may find it helpful to think in terms of four R's as they address sustainability. These are: (1) the *resources* used by the production process; (2) the *recycling* of production materials and product components; (3) the *regulations* that apply; (4) the firm's *reputation*. All four areas provide impetus for managers to perform well as they develop and refine production processes.

Resources

Operations is often the primary user of the firm's resources. This puts special pressure on using human, financial, and material resources in a sustainable way. Most firms are good at reducing resource use as it is a win–win situation: Reducing resources lowers cost as well as being a positive force toward sustainability. Examples of sustainable use in production processes are:

- Aramex has reduced its dependency on fuel-operated vehicles to almost 30 percent and replaced them with hybrid trucks and cars.
- Pepsi has reduced the weight of its plastic bottles for Aquafina by 20 percent. This reduces resource use and saves weight with the added advantage of cutting delivery cost.
- Tesco plc and Frito-Lay have both driven down their water and energy use. (These firms' efforts in sustainability are discussed in the video cases at the end of this chapter.)

VIDEO 7.3
Green Manufacturing and Sustainability at Frito-Lay

Recycle

As managers seek sustainability, they should realize that there are only three things that can be done with waste: burn it, bury it, or reuse it. The first two have undesirable consequences. Burned waste pumps unwanted emissions into the atmosphere, and burying has the potential of releasing methane and ammonia, as well as creating fires, explosions, and water table issues. While recycling begins at design by specifying products and components that have recycle potential, managers must build processes that facilitate disassembly and reuse of those materials. Whether it is plastic, glass, or lead in an automobile or plastic bags and Styrofoam from the grocery store, recycling has a significant role in sustainability.

LO6: Discuss the four R's of sustainability

Regulations

Laws and regulations affecting transportation, waste, and noise are proliferating and can be as much of a challenge as reducing resource use. While the challenge can be difficult, firms must abide by the legal requirements of the host nation; society expects no less. The resources available from planet Earth are finite and many by-products are undesirable. So organizations are increasingly under pressure from regulatory agencies to reduce by-products that yield

---

[4]We define sustainable in an OM context as a production system that supports conservation and renewal of resources.

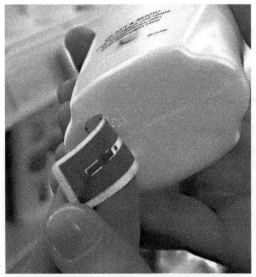 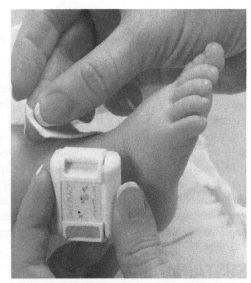

Pharmaceutical companies are counting on RFID to aid the tracking and tracing of drugs in the distribution system to reduce losses that total over US$30 billion a year.

Hospitals use RFID sensors to track patients, staff and equipment.

greenhouse gases and pollute the air and water. Greenhouse gases include carbon dioxide, methane, nitrous oxide, and fluorinated gases that are believed to contribute to global warming. To meet regulatory requirements, firms design, redesign, and invest substantial human and financial resources. For example, home builders are required not just to manage water runoff but to have a pollution prevention plan for each site.

Carbon footprint Another sustainability issue is evaluating and reducing the *carbon footprint*. This is a measurement of greenhouse gases for which international regulation is pending. A substantial portion of greenhouse gases are released naturally by farming, cattle, and decaying forests, but also by manufacturing and services. Operations personnel are being asked to contribute to their reduction.

Reputation

The marketplace may reward leadership in sustainability. The free enterprise system operates on a voluntary basis: If employees, suppliers, distributors, providers of capital, and, of course, customers, do not want to do business with a firm, they are not required to do so. Those organizations that do not meet society's expectations can expect these voluntary relationships to be difficult to build and maintain. A bad reputation does have negative consequences. Our society is increasingly transparent, and both good news and bad news travel rapidly. But green processes can yield good news, a good reputation, and good results. For example, the University of Jordan's decision to switch off electricity after 5 p.m. everyday (except for certain services) and its shift to energy-efficient lighting reduced its energy consumption by 35 percent and set a good example for its students in social responsibility.

Imaginative, well-led firms are finding opportunities to build sustainable production processes that conserve resources, recycle, meet regulatory requirements, and foster a positive reputation.

CHAPTER SUMMARY

Effective operations managers understand how to use process strategy as a competitive weapon. They select a production process with the necessary quality, flexibility, and cost structure to meet product and volume requirements. They also seek creative ways to combine the low unit cost of high-volume, low-variety manufacturing with the customization available through low-volume, high-variety facilities. Managers use the techniques of lean production and employee participation to encourage the development of efficient equipment and processes. They design their equipment and processes to have capabilities beyond the tolerance required by their customers, while ensuring the flexibility needed for adjustments in technology, features, and volumes.

Key Terms

Automated guided vehicle (AGV) (p. 200)
Automated storage and retrieval system (ASRS) (p. 200)
Automatic identification system (AIS) (p. 199)
Build-to-order (BTO) (p. 189)
Computer numerical control (CNC) (p. 199)
Computer-integrated manufacturing (CIM) (p. 201)
Crossover chart (p. 191)

Flexibility (p. 198)
Flexible manufacturing system (FMS) (p. 200)
Flowchart (p. 193)
Mass customization (p. 188)
Modules (p. 187)
Postponement (p. 189)
Process chart (p. 195)
Process control (p. 199)
Process focus (p. 186)
Process redesign (p. 203)

Process strategy (p. 186)
Product focus (p. 188)
Radio frequency identification (RFID) (p. 199)
Repetitive process (p. 187)
Robot (p. 200)
Service blueprinting (p. 195)
Time-function mapping (or process mapping) (p. 193)
Value-stream mapping (VSM) (p. 194)
Vision systems (p. 199)

Ethical Dilemma

For the sake of efficiency and lower costs, Sonokor Farms in Syria uses a standardized manufacturing process for its chicken farming. The process of raising hens in cages and confined spaces, such as inside a hangar, in such large numbers to acquire eggs for human consumption is controversial. In factory chicken farming chickens are fed in their cages without the freedom to move around. The food is mixed with vitamins and growth hormones to ensure the greatest weight gain and thus maximum profits. The free movement of chickens is controlled, which may cause osteoporosis in the birds. In addition, the chickens' beaks are trimmed to stop them from pecking their feathers or each other. This procedure is painful and causes severe distress to the chickens. The low light levels used in the farms, said to prevent vent-pecking and cannibalism, cause the chickens to become afraid of stronger lights, causing panic when normal lighting is on.

However, these procedures ensure high productivity of eggs at a low price, due to the reduced land, management, and feed costs.

Discuss the productivity and ethical implications of this industry and these two divergent opinions.

Discussion Questions

1. What is process strategy?
2. What type of process is used for making each of the following products?
   a) fizzy drinks
   b) wedding invitations
   c) automobiles
   d) paper
   e) Big Macs
   f) custom homes
   g) motorcycles.
3. What is service blueprinting?
4. What is process redesign?
5. What are the techniques for improving service productivity?
6. Name the four quadrants of the service process matrix. Discuss how the matrix is used to classify services into categories.
7. What is CIM?
8. What do we mean by a process-control system and what are the typical elements in such systems?
9. Identify *manufacturing* firms that compete on each of the four processes shown in Figure 7.1.
10. Identify the competitive advantage of each of the four firms identified in Discussion Question 9.
11. Identify *service* firms that compete on each of the four processes shown in Figure 7.1.
12. Identify the competitive advantage of each of the four firms identified in Discussion Question 11.
13. What are numerically controlled machines?
14. Describe briefly what an automatic identification system (AIS) is and how service organizations could use AIS to increase productivity and at the same time increase the variety of services offered.
15. Name some of the advances being made in technology that enhance production and productivity.
16. Explain what a flexible manufacturing system (FMS) is.
17. In what ways do CAD and FMS connect?
18. What are the four *R*'s of sustainability?

Solved Problem   Virtual Office Hours help is available at MyOMLab.

▼ SOLVED PROBLEM 7.1

Bagot Copy Shop has a volume of 125,000 black-and-white copies per month. Two salesmen have made presentations to Gordon Bagot for machines of equal quality and reliability. The first machine, Print Shop 5, has a cost of US$2,000 per month and a variable cost of US$0.03. The other machine (a Speed Copy 100) will cost only US$1,500 per month but the toner is more expensive, driving the cost per copy up to US$0.035. If cost and volume are the only considerations, which machine should Bagot Copy Shop purchase?

▼ SOLUTION

$$2,000 + 0.03X = 1,500 + 0.035X$$

$$2,000 - 1,500 = 0.035X - 0.03X$$

$$500 = 0.005X$$

$$100,000 = X$$

Because Bagot expects his volume to exceed 100,000 units, he should choose the Print Shop 5.

Problems*

• **7.1** Prepare a flowchart for one of the following:
a) the registration process at a school
b) the process at the local car wash
c) a shoe shine
d) some other process with the approval of the instructor.

• **7.2** Prepare a process chart for one of the activities in Problem 7.1.

•• **7.3** Prepare a time-function map for one of the activities in Problem 7.1.

•• **7.4** Prepare a service blueprint for one of the activities in Problem 7.1.

• **7.5** Doha Toy Shop, Inc. has a 1-year contract for the production of 200,000 parts for a new toy. Owner Jasem Al-Ali hopes the contract will be extended and the volume increased next year. Doha has developed costs for three alternatives. They are general-purpose equipment (GPE), flexible manufacturing system (FMS), and expensive, but efficient, dedicated machine (DM). The cost data follow:

	General-Purpose Equipment (GPE)	Flexible Manufacturing System (FMS)	Dedicated Machine (DM)
Annual contracted units	200,000	200,000	200,000
Annual fixed cost	US$100,000	US$200,000	US$500,000
Per unit variable cost	US$15.00	US$14.00	US$13.00

Which process is best for this contract? P✗

*Note: P✗ means the problem may be solved with POM for Windows and/or Excel OM.

• **7.6** Using the data in Problem 7.5, determine the economical volume for each process. P✗

• **7.7** Using the data in Problem 7.5, determine the best process for each of the following volumes: (1) 75,000; (2) 275,000; (3) 375,000.

• **7.8** Refer to Problem 7.5. If a contract for the second and third years is pending, what are the implications for process selection?

•• **7.9** Grand Riyadh Mechanical, Inc. is considering producing a gear assembly that it now purchases from Beit Najran Supply Ltd. Beit Najran Supply Ltd. charges US$4 per unit with a minimum order of 3,000 units. Grand Riyadh Mechanical, Inc. estimates that it will cost US$15,000 to set up the process and then US$1.82 per unit for labor and materials.
a) Draw a graph illustrating the crossover (or indifference) point.
b) Determine the number of units where either choice has the same cost. P✗

••• **7.10** Khazaneh Mumtazeh, Inc. needs to choose a production method for its new office shelf, the Taweela. To help accomplish this, the firm has gathered the following production cost data:

Process Type	Annualized Fixed Cost of Plant & Equip.	Variable Costs (per unit) (US$)		
		Labor	Material	Energy
Mass Customization	US$1,260,000	30	18	12
Intermittent	US$1,000,000	24	26	20
Repetitive	US$1,625,000	28	15	12
Continuous	US$1,960,000	25	15	10

Khazaneh Mumtazeh projects an annual demand of 24,000 units for the Taweela. The Taweela will sell for US$120 per unit.
a) Which process type will maximize the annual profit from producing the Taweela?
b) What is the value of this annual profit? P✗

Case Studies

► Environmental Sustainability at Tesco plc, UK

Tesco plc is the largest retailer in the United Kingdom and the third-largest grocery retailer in the world, with operations in 14 countries. The company manages its business using a model called Steering Wheel (SW), which is basically a balanced scorecard comprising the key elements of business: customers, operations, people, finance, and community. Environmental sustainability aspects are integrated into SW as part of the community element.

Tesco recognizes that tackling climate change is fundamental to its environmental strategies. It has set out three strategies as part of its climate change program: leading by example, reducing own direct carbon footprint; working with its supply chains and partners to reduce emissions more broadly; and leading a revolution in green consumption.

In addition to the climate change strategy, the company is actively involved in reducing waste, improving recycling, reducing unnecessary packaging, and promoting the use of sustainable products with minimal adverse impact on biodiversity. It regularly sets its own targets and aims to achieve the targets. In the past few years, the company has registered impressive performances in terms of setting and achieving targets: including being the first major retailer to carbon label 100 own-brand products in Ireland and the United Kingdom; new stores have been built using environmentally sustainable materials and principles; and the company halved its energy use per square meter in its UK stores (against a baseline of the year 2000).

Some targets the company set for itself, as per its Corporate Responsibility Report 2009, including halving emissions from existing buildings and new stores by 2020 and halving distribution emissions of each case of goods delivered by 2012, against a baseline of 2006.

Notable among the achievements of Tesco plc in terms of environmental sustainability are the following:

- The company committed around US$40 million to create the new Sustainable Consumption Institute (SCI) at the University of Manchester, United Kingdom.
- The company set for itself a target of halving the average energy use in its buildings compared to 2000 levels and achieved this target two years early—in 2008.
- It created the Sustainable Technology Fund to support environmentally sustainable technologies that are not yet commercially viable.
- The company reduced the amount of carbon emitted in its distribution network by 10 percent. It encourages the use of fully electric vans for its home delivery fleet.
- In 2008, the company reduced the amount of waste going into landfills by over one-third. It has set a target of diverting 95 percent of the waste away from landfills.

Through these initiatives, Tesco is aiming to be a leader in the global retailing market in terms of environmental sustainability.

Discussion Questions

1. How is Tesco doing in terms of environmental sustainability?
2. Based on library and internet research, report on other environmental sustainability practices used at Tesco.
3. Compare Tesco's environmental sustainability strategy to those of the other global retailers, such as Wal-Mart, Target, and Carrefour.
4. How much of Tesco's sustainability effort is (a) resource focused, (b) regulation focused, and (c) reputation focused?

Sources: Tesco plc Corporate Responsibility Report 2009 accessed at **www.tescoplc.com/plc/corporate_responsibility_09/**; and Tesco plc press releases accessed at **www.tescoplc.com/plc/media/pr/**. Case prepared by Dr. Ramakrishnan Ramanathan, Business School, Nottingham University, UK.

► Process Strategy at Wheeled Coach Ambulance

Video Case

Wheeled Coach, based in Winter Park, Florida, is the world's largest manufacturer of ambulances. Working four 10-hour days each week, 350 employees make only custom-made ambulances: Virtually every vehicle is unique. Wheeled Coach accommodates the marketplace by providing a wide variety of options and an engineering staff accustomed to innovation and custom design. Continuing growth, which now requires that more than 20 ambulances roll off the assembly line each week, makes process design a continuing challenge. Wheeled Coach's response has been to build a focused factory: Wheeled Coach builds nothing but ambulances. Within the focused factory, Wheeled Coach established work cells for every major module feeding an assembly line, including aluminum bodies, electrical wiring harnesses, interior cabinets, windows, painting, and upholstery.

Labor standards drive the schedule so that every work cell feeds the assembly line on schedule, just in time for installations. The chassis, usually that of a Ford truck, moves to a station at which the aluminum body is mounted. Then the vehicle is moved to painting. Following a custom paint job, it moves to the assembly line, where it will spend 7 days. During each of these 7 workdays, each work cell delivers its respective module to the appropriate

position on the assembly line. During the first day, electrical wiring is installed; on the second day, the unit moves forward to the station at which cabinetry is delivered and installed, then to a window and lighting station, on to upholstery, to fit and finish, to further customizing, and finally to inspection and road testing.

Discussion Questions*

1. Why do you think major auto manufacturers do not build ambulances?
2. What is an alternative process strategy to the assembly line that Wheeled Coach currently uses?
3. Why is it more efficient for the work cells to prepare 'modules' and deliver them to the assembly line than it would be to produce the component (e.g. interior upholstery) on the line?
4. How does Wheeled Coach manage the tasks to be performed at each work station?

*You may wish to view the video that accompanies this case before addressing these questions.

▶ Process Analysis at Arnold Palmer Hospital

 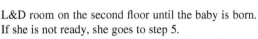

The Arnold Palmer Hospital (APH) in Orlando, Florida, is one of the busiest and most respected hospitals for the medical treatment of children and women in the United States. Since its opening on golfing legend Arnold Palmer's birthday, September 10, 1989, more than 1.6 million children and women have passed through its doors. It is the fourth busiest labor and delivery hospital in the United States and one of the largest neonatal intensive care units in the Southeast. APH ranks in the top 10 percent of hospitals nationwide in patient satisfaction.

"Part of the reason for APH's success," says Executive Director Kathy Swanson, "is our continuous improvement process. Our goal is 100 percent patient satisfaction. But getting there means constantly examining and reexamining everything we do, from patient flow, to cleanliness, to layout space, to a work-friendly environment, to speed of medication delivery from the pharmacy to a patient. Continuous improvement is a huge and never-ending task."

One of the tools the hospital uses consistently is the process flowchart (like that in Figure 7.8 in this chapter). Staffer Diane Bowles, who carries the title 'clinical practice improvement consultant,' charts scores of processes. Bowles's flowcharts help study ways to improve the turnaround of a vacated room (especially important in a hospital that has pushed capacity for years), speed up the admission process, and deliver warm meals warm.

Lately, APH has been examining the flow of maternity patients (and their paperwork) from the moment they enter the hospital until they are discharged, hopefully with their healthy baby a day or two later. The flow of maternity patients follows these steps:

1. Enter APH's Labor & Delivery (L&D) check-in desk entrance.
2. If the baby is born en route or if birth is imminent, the mother and baby are taken directly to L&D on the second floor and registered and admitted directly at the bedside. If there are no complications, the mother and baby go to step 6.
3. If the baby is *not* yet born, the front desk asks if the mother is pre-registered. (Most do pre-register at the 28- to 30-week pregnancy mark). If she is not registered, she goes to the registration office on the first floor.
4. The pregnant woman is then taken to L&D Triage on the eighth floor for assessment. If she is in active labor, she is taken to an

L&D room on the second floor until the baby is born. If she is not ready, she goes to step 5.
5. Pregnant women not ready to deliver (i.e. no contractions or false alarm) are either sent home to return on a later date and reenter the system at that time, or if contractions are not yet close enough, they are sent to walk around the hospital grounds (to encourage progress) and then return to L&D Triage at a prescribed time.
6. When the baby is born, if there are no complications, after 2 hours the mother and baby are transferred to a 'mother–baby care unit' room on floors 3, 4, or 5 for an average of 40–44 hours.
7. If there *are* complications with the mother, she goes to an operating room and/or intensive care unit. From there, she goes back to a mother–baby care room upon stabilization—or is discharged at another time if not stabilized. Complications for the baby may result in a stay in the neonatal intensive care unit (NICU) before transfer to the baby nursery near the mother's room. If the baby is not stable enough for discharge with the mother, the baby is discharged later.
8. Mother and/or baby, when ready, are discharged and taken by wheelchair to the discharge exit for pickup to travel home.

Discussion Questions*

1. As Diane's new assistant, you need to flowchart this process. Explain how the process might be improved once you have completed the chart.
2. If a mother is scheduled for a Caesarean-section birth (i.e. the baby is removed from the womb surgically), how would this flowchart change?
3. If *all* mothers were electronically (or manually) pre-registered, how would the flowchart change? Redraw the chart to show your changes.
4. Describe in detail a process that the hospital could analyze, besides the ones mentioned in this case.

*You may wish to view the video that accompanies this case before addressing these questions.

▶ Green Manufacturing and Sustainability at Frito-Lay

Frito-Lay, the multi-billion-US-dollar snack-food giant, requires vast amounts of water, electricity, natural gas, and fuel to produce its 41 well-known brands. In keeping with growing environmental concerns, Frito-Lay has initiated ambitious plans to produce environmentally friendly snacks. But even environmentally friendly snacks require resources. Recognizing the environmental impact, the firm is an aggressive 'green manufacturer,' with major initiatives in resource reduction and sustainability.

For instance, the company's energy management program includes a variety of elements designed to engage employees in reducing energy consumption. These elements include scorecards and customized action plans that empower employees and recognize their achievements.

At Frito-Lay's factory in Casa Grande, Arizona, more than 226,800 kg of potatoes arrive every day to be washed, sliced, fried, seasoned, and portioned into bags of Lay's and Ruffles chips. The process consumes enormous amounts of energy and creates vast amounts of wastewater, starch, and potato peelings. Frito-Lay plans

to take the plant off the power grid and run it almost entirely on renewable fuels and recycled water. The managers at the Casa Grande plant have also installed skylights in conference rooms, offices, and a finished goods warehouse to reduce the need for artificial light. More fuel-efficient ovens recapture heat from exhaust stacks. Vacuum hoses that pull moisture from potato slices to recapture the water and to reduce the amount of heat needed to cook the potato chips are also being used.

Frito-Lay has also built over 50 acres of solar concentrators behind its Modesto, California, plant to generate solar power. The solar power is being converted into heat and used to cook Sun Chips. A biomass boiler, which will burn agricultural waste, is also planned to provide additional renewable fuel.

Frito-Lay is installing high-tech filters that recycle most of the water used to rinse and wash potatoes. It also recycles corn by-products to make Doritos and other snacks; starch is reclaimed and sold, primarily as animal feed, and leftover sludge is burned to create methane gas to run the plant boiler.

There are benefits besides the potential energy savings. Like many other large corporations, Frito-Lay is striving to establish its green credentials as consumers become more focused on environmental issues. There are marketing opportunities, too. The company, for example, advertises that its popular Sun Chips snacks are made using solar energy.

At Frito-Lay's Florida plant, only 3.5 percent of the waste goes to landfills, but that is still nearly 7 million kilograms annually. The goal is zero waste to landfills. The snack-food maker earned its spot in the National Environmental Performance Track program by maintaining a sustained environmental compliance record and making new commitments to reduce, reuse, and recycle at this facility.

Substantial resource reductions have been made in the production process, with an energy reduction of 21 percent across Frito-Lay's 34 U.S. plants. But the continuing battle for resource reduction continues. The company is also moving toward biodegradable packaging and pursuing initiatives in areas such as office paper, packaging material, seasoning bags, and cans and bottles. While these multiyear initiatives are expensive, they have backing at the highest levels of Frito-Lay as well as from corporate executives at PepsiCo, the parent company.

Discussion Questions*

1. Using resources, regulation, and reputation as a basis, what are the sources of pressure on firms such as Frito-Lay to reduce their environmental footprint?
2. Identify the specific techniques that Frito-Lay is using to become a 'green manufacturer.'
3. Select another company and compare its green policies to those of Frito-Lay.

*You may wish to view the video that accompanies this case before addressing these questions.

Source: Professors Beverly Amer, Northern Arizona University; Barry Render, Rollins College; and Jay Heizer, Texas Lutheran University.

▶ **Additional Case Study:** Visit MyOMLab *for this free case study:*
Matthew Yachts, Inc.: Examines a possible process change as the market for yachts changes.

Chapter 7 *Rapid* Review

Main Heading	Review Material	
FOUR PROCESS STRATEGIES (pp. 186–193)	■ **Process strategy**—An organization's approach to transforming resources into goods and services. *The objective of a process strategy is to build a production process that meets customer requirements and product specifications within cost and other managerial constraints.* Virtually every good or service is made by using some variation of one of four process strategies. ■ **Process focus**—A facility organized around processes to facilitate low-volume, high-variety production. The vast majority of global production is devoted to making low-volume, high-variety products in process-focused facilities, also known as job shops or *intermittent process* facilities. Process-focused facilities have high variable costs with extremely low utilization (5 percent to 25 percent) of facilities. ■ **Repetitive process**—A product-oriented production process that uses modules. ■ **Modules**—Parts or components of a product previously prepared, often in a continuous process. The repetitive process is the classic assembly line. It allows the firm to use modules and combine the economic advantages of the product-focused model with the customization advantages of the process-focused model. ■ **Product focus**—A facility organized around products; a product-oriented, high-volume, low-variety process. Product-focused facilities are also called *continuous processes,* because they have very long, continuous production runs. The specialized nature of a product-focused facility requires high fixed cost; however, low variable costs reward high facility utilization. ■ **Mass customization**—Rapid, low-cost production that caters to constantly changing unique customer desires. ■ **Build-to-order (BTO)**—Produce to customer order rather than to a forecast. Major challenges of a build-to-order system include: *Product design, Process design, Inventory management, Tight schedules* and *Responsive partners.* ■ **Postponement**—The delay of any modifications or customization to a product as long as possible in the production process. ■ **Crossover chart**—A chart of costs at the possible volumes for more than one process.	Problems: 7.5–7.10 **VIDEO 7.1** Process Strategy at Wheeled Coach Ambulance Virtual Office Hours for Solved Problem: 7.1
PROCESS ANALYSIS AND DESIGN (pp. 193–196)	Five tools of process analysis are: ■ **Flowchart**—A drawing used to analyze movement of people or materials. ■ **Time-function mapping** (or **process mapping**)—A flowchart with time added on the horizontal axis. ■ **Value-stream mapping (VSM)**—A tool that helps managers understand how to add value in the flow of material and information through the entire production process. ■ **Process charts**—Charts that use symbols to analyze the movement of people or material. Process charts allow managers to focus on value-added activities and to compute the percentage of value-added time (= operation time/total time). ■ **Service blueprinting**—A process analysis technique that lends itself to a focus on the customer and the provider's interaction with the customer.	Problems: 7.2, 7.3

Main Heading	Review Material	MyOMLab
SPECIAL CONSIDERATIONS FOR SERVICE PROCESS DESIGN (pp. 196–198)	Services can be classified into one of four quadrants, based on relative degrees of labor and customization: 1. *Service factory* 2. *Service shop* 3. *Mass service* 4. *Professional service* Techniques for improving service productivity include: ■ *Separation*—Structuring service so customers must go where the service is offered ■ *Self-service*—Customers examining, comparing, and evaluating at their own pace ■ *Postponement*—Customizing at delivery ■ *Focus*—Restricting the offerings ■ *Modules*—Modular selection of service; modular production ■ *Automation*—Separating services that may lend themselves to a type of automation ■ *Scheduling*—Precise personnel scheduling ■ *Training*—Clarifying the service options; explaining how to avoid problems	**VIDEO** 7.2 Process Analysis at Arnold Palmer Hospital
SELECTION OF EQUIPMENT AND TECHNOLOGY (p. 198)	Picking the best equipment involves understanding the specific industry and available processes and technology. The choice requires considering cost, quality, capacity, and flexibility. ■ **Flexibility**—The ability to respond with little penalty in time, cost, or customer value.	
PRODUCTION TECHNOLOGY (pp. 198–201)	■ **Computer numerical control (CNC)**—Machinery with its own computer and memory. ■ **Automatic identification system (AIS)**—A system for transforming data into electronic form (e.g. bar codes). ■ **Radio frequency identification (RFID)**—A wireless system in which integrated circuits with antennae send radio waves. ■ **Process control**—The use of information technology to control a physical process. ■ **Vision systems**—Systems that use video cameras and computer technology in inspection roles. ■ **Robot**—A flexible machine with the ability to hold, move, or grab items. ■ **Automated storage and retrieval systems (ASRS)**—Computer-controlled warehouses that provide for the automatic placement of parts into and from designated places within a warehouse. ■ **Automated guided vehicle (AGV)**—Electronically guided and controlled cart used to move materials. ■ **Flexible manufacturing system (FMS)**—Automated work cell controlled by electronic signals from a common centralized computer facility. ■ **Computer-integrated manufacturing (CIM)**—A manufacturing system in which CAD, FMS, inventory control, warehousing, and shipping are integrated.	
TECHNOLOGY IN SERVICES (p. 202)	Many rapid technological developments have occurred in the service sector. These range from POS terminals and RFID to online newspapers and e-books.	
PROCESS REDESIGN (p. 203)	■ Process redesign—The fundamental rethinking of business processes to bring about dramatic improvements in performance. Process redesign often focuses on activities that cross functional lines.	
SUSTAINABILITY (pp. 203–204)	There are four *Rs* to consider when addressing sustainability: (1) the *resources* used by the production process; (2) the *recycling* of production materials and product components; (3) the *regulations* that apply; (4) the firm's *reputation*.	**VIDEO** 7.3 Green Manufacturing and Sustainability at Frito-Lay

*Self-*Test

■ **Before taking the self-test,** refer to the learning objectives listed at the beginning of the chapter and the key terms listed at the end of the chapter.

LO1. Low-volume, high-variety processes are also known as:
   a) continuous processes
   b) process focused
   c) repetitive processes
   d) product focused.

LO2. A crossover chart for process selection focuses on:
   a) labor costs
   b) material cost
   c) both labor and material costs
   d) fixed and variable costs
   e) fixed costs.

LO3. Tools for process analysis include all of the following except:
   a) flowchart
   b) vision systems
   c) service blueprinting
   d) time-function mapping
   e) value-stream mapping.

LO4. Customer feedback in process design is lower as:
   a) the degree of customization is increased
   b) the degree of labor is increased
   c) the degree of customization is lowered
   d) both a and b
   e) both b and c.

LO5. Computer-integrated manufacturing (CIM) includes manufacturing systems that have:
   a) computer-aided design, direct numerical control machines, and material handling equipment controlled by automation
   b) transaction processing, a management information system, and decision support systems
   c) automated guided vehicles, robots, and process control
   d) robots, automated guided vehicles, and transfer equipment.

LO6. The four *R*'s of sustainability are:

_____, _____, _____, _____.

When designing a stadium, management hopes that the forecasted capacity (the product mix—football teams, carnivals and special events—and the technology needed for these events) is accurate and adequate for operation above the break-even point. However, in many stadiums, even when operating at full capacity, break-even is not achieved and supplemental funding must be obtained.

Supplement 7 Learning Objectives

> **AUTHOR COMMENT**
> Too little capacity loses customers and too much capacity is expensive.

CAPACITY

What should be the seating capacity of a football stadium? How many customers per day should Kudu fast-food restaurants be able to serve daily? In this supplement we look at some tools that help a manager make these decisions.

After selection of a production process (Chapter 7), managers need to determine capacity. **Capacity** is the 'throughput,' or the number of units a facility can hold, receive, store, or produce in a given time. Capacity decisions often determine capital requirements and therefore a large portion of fixed cost. Capacity also determines whether demand will be satisfied or whether facilities will be idle. If a facility is too large, portions of it will sit unused and add cost to existing production. If a facility is too small, customers—and perhaps entire markets—will be lost. Determining facility size, with an objective of achieving high levels of utilization and a high return on investment, is critical.

Capacity planning can be viewed in three time horizons. In Figure S7.1 we note that long-range capacity (greater than 1 year) is a function of adding facilities and equipment that have a long lead time. In the intermediate range (3 to 18 months), we can add equipment, personnel, and shifts; we can subcontract; and we can build or use inventory. This is the 'aggregate planning' task. In the short run (usually up to 3 months), we are primarily concerned with scheduling jobs and people, as well as allocating machinery. Modifying capacity in the short run is difficult, as we are usually constrained by existing capacity.

Capacity

The 'throughput' or number of units a facility can hold, receive, store, or produce in a period of time.

LO1: Define capacity

Design and Effective Capacity

Design capacity is the maximum theoretical output of a system in a given period under ideal conditions. It is normally expressed as a rate, such as the number of tons of steel that can be produced per week, per month, or per year. For many companies, measuring capacity can be

Design capacity

The theoretical maximum output of a system in a given period under ideal conditions.

Options for Adjusting Capacity

Time Horizon

Long-range planning
- Add facilities.
- Add long lead time equipment. ★

Intermediate-range planning
(aggregate planning)
- Subcontract.
- Add equipment.
- Add shifts.
- Add personnel.
- Build or use inventory.

Short-range planning
(scheduling)
★
- Schedule jobs.
- Schedule personnel.
- Allocate machinery.

Modify capacity   Use capacity

★ Difficult to adjust capacity as limited options exist

straightforward: It is the maximum number of units the company is capable of producing in a specific time. However, for some organizations, determining capacity can be more difficult. Capacity can be measured in terms of beds (a hospital), active members (a church), or classroom size (a school). Other organizations use total work time available as a measure of overall capacity.

Most organizations operate their facilities at a rate less than the design capacity. They do so because they have found that they can operate more efficiently when their resources are not stretched to the limit. For example, Zoka café in Amman, Jordan, has tables set with 2 or 4 chairs, seating a total of 210 guests. But the tables are never filled that way. Some tables will have 1 or 3 guests; tables can be pulled together for parties of 6 or 8. There are always unused chairs. Design capacity is 210, but *effective capacity* is often closer to 160, which is 76.2 percent of design capacity.

Effective capacity is the capacity a firm *expects* to achieve given the current operating constraints. Effective capacity is often lower than design capacity because the facility may have been designed for an earlier version of the product or a different product mix than is currently being produced.

Two measures of system performance are particularly useful: utilization and efficiency. **Utilization** is simply the percentage of *design capacity* actually achieved. **Efficiency** is the percentage of *effective capacity* actually achieved. Depending on how facilities are used and managed, it may be difficult or impossible to reach 100 percent efficiency. Operations managers tend to be evaluated on efficiency. The key to improving efficiency is often found in correcting quality problems and in effective scheduling, training, and maintenance. Utilization and efficiency are computed below.

Effective capacity
The capacity a firm can expect to achieve, given its product mix, methods of scheduling, maintenance, and standards of quality.

Utilization
Actual output as a percentage of design capacity.

Efficiency
Actual output as a percentage of effective capacity.

$$\text{Utilization} = \text{Actual output} \div \text{Design capacity} \quad \text{(S7-1)}$$

$$\text{Efficiency} = \text{Actual output} \div \text{Effective capacity} \quad \text{(S7-2)}$$

In Example S1 we determine these values.

◀ **EXAMPLE S1**

Determining capacity utilization and efficiency

Sara James Bakery has a plant for processing *Deluxe* breakfast rolls and wants to better understand its capability. Determine the design capacity, utilization, and efficiency for this plant when producing this *Deluxe* roll.

APPROACH ▶ Last week the facility produced 148,000 rolls. The effective capacity is 175,000 rolls. The production line operates 7 days per week, with three 8-hour shifts per day. The line was designed to process the nut-filled, cinnamon-flavored *Deluxe* roll at a rate of 1,200 per hour. The firm first computes the design capacity and then uses Equation (S7-1) to determine utilization and Equation (S7-2) to determine efficiency.

SOLUTION ▶

Design capacity = (7 days × 3 shifts × 8 hours) × (1,200 rolls per hour) = 201,600 rolls

Utilization = Actual output ÷ Design capacity = 148,000 ÷ 201,600 = 73.4%

Efficiency = Actual output ÷ Effective capacity = 148,000 ÷ 175,000 = 84.6%

> **INSIGHT** ▶   The bakery now has the information necessary to evaluate efficiency.
>
> **LEARNING EXERCISE** ▶   If the actual output is 150,000 rolls, what is the efficiency? [Answer: 85.7%.]
>
> **RELATED PROBLEMS** ▶   S7.1, S7.2, S7.4, S7.5

LO2: Determine design capacity, effective capacity, and utilization

Design capacity, utilization, and efficiency are all important measures for an operations manager. But managers often need to know the expected output of a facility or process. To do this, we solve for actual (or in this case, future or expected) output as shown in Equation (S7-3):

$$\text{Actual (or Expected) output} = (\text{Effective capacity})(\text{Efficiency}) \tag{S7-3}$$

Expected output is sometimes referred to as *rated capacity*. With a knowledge of effective capacity and efficiency, a manager can find the expected output of a facility. We do so in Example S2.

EXAMPLE S2 ▶

Determining expected output

The manager of Sara James Bakery (see Example S1) now needs to increase production of the increasingly popular *Deluxe* roll. To meet this demand, she will be adding a second production line.

APPROACH ▶   The manager must determine the expected output of this second line for the sales department. Effective capacity on the second line is the same as on the first line, which is 175,000 *Deluxe* rolls. The first line is operating at an efficiency of 84.6 percent, as computed in Example S1. But output on the second line will be less than the first line because the crew will be primarily new hires; so the efficiency can be expected to be no more than 75 percent. What is the expected output?

SOLUTION ▶   Use Equation (S7-3) to determine the expected output:

$$\text{Expected output} = (\text{Effective capacity})(\text{Efficiency}) = (175,000)(0.75) = 131,250 \text{ rolls}$$

INSIGHT ▶   The sales department can now be told the expected output is 131,250 *Deluxe* rolls.

LEARNING EXERCISE ▶   After 1 month of training, the crew on the second production line is expected to perform at 80 percent efficiency. What is the revised expected output of *Deluxe* rolls? [Answer: 140,000.]

RELATED PROBLEM ▶   S7.3

If the expected output is inadequate, additional capacity may be needed. Much of the remainder of this supplement addresses how to effectively and efficiently add that capacity.

Capacity and Strategy

Sustained profits come from building competitive advantage, not just from a good financial return on a specific process. Capacity decisions must be integrated into the organization's mission and strategy. Investments are not to be made as isolated expenditures, but as part of a coordinated plan that will place the firm in an advantageous position. The questions to be asked are, "Will these investments eventually win profitable customers?" and "What competitive advantage (such as process flexibility, speed of delivery, improved quality, and so on) do we obtain?"

All ten decisions of operations management that we discuss in this text, as well as other organizational elements such as marketing and finance, are affected by changes in capacity. Changes in capacity will have sales and cash flow implications, just as capacity changes have quality, supply-chain, human resource, and maintenance implications. All must be considered.

Capacity Considerations

In addition to tight integration of strategy and investments, there are four special considerations for a good capacity decision:

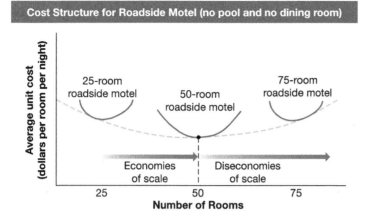

> **AUTHOR COMMENT**
> Each industry and technology
> has an optimum size.

1. *Forecast demand accurately:* An accurate forecast is paramount to the capacity decision. The new product may be a new dish at Zooka's that places added demands on the restaurant's food service, or it may be a new maternity capability at New Mowasat Hospital, or the new hybrid Lexus. Whatever the new product, its prospects and the life cycle of existing products must be determined. Management must know which products are being added and which are being dropped, as well as their expected volumes.

2. *Understand the technology and capacity increments:* The number of initial alternatives may be large, but once the volume is determined, technology decisions may be aided by analysis of cost, human resources required, quality, and reliability. Such a review often reduces the number of alternatives to a few. The technology may dictate the capacity increment. Meeting added demand with a few extra tables in Zooka may not be difficult, but meeting increased demand for a new automobile by adding a new assembly line at EGA may be very difficult—and expensive. The operations manager is held responsible for the technology and the correct capacity increment.

3. *Find the optimum operating size (volume):* Technology and capacity increments often dictate an optimal size for a facility. A roadside motel may require 50 rooms to be viable. If smaller, the fixed cost is too burdensome; if larger, the facility becomes more than one manager can supervise. A hypothetical optimum for the motel is shown in Figure S7.2. This issue is known as *economies and diseconomies of scale*.

4. *Build for change:* In our fast-paced world, change is inevitable. So operations managers build flexibility into the facility and equipment. They evaluate the sensitivity of the decision by testing several revenue projections on both the upside and downside for potential risks. Buildings can often be built in phases; and buildings and equipment can be designed with modifications in mind to accommodate future changes in product, product mix, and processes.

Rather than strategically manage capacity, managers may tactically manage demand.

Managing Demand

Even with good forecasting and facilities built to that forecast, there may be a poor match between the actual demand that occurs and available capacity. A poor match may mean demand exceeds capacity or capacity exceeds demand. However, in both cases, firms have options.

Demand Exceeds Capacity   When *demand exceeds capacity*, the firm may be able to curtail demand simply by raising prices, scheduling long lead times (which may be inevitable), and discouraging marginally profitable business. However, because inadequate facilities reduce revenue below what is possible, the long-term solution is usually to increase capacity.

Capacity Exceeds Demand   When *capacity exceeds demand*, the firm may want to stimulate demand through price reductions or aggressive marketing, or it may accommodate the market through product changes. When decreasing customer demand is combined with old and inflexible processes, layoffs and plant closures may be necessary to bring capacity in line with demand.

Adjusting to Seasonal Demands   A seasonal or cyclical pattern of demand is another capacity challenge. In such cases, management may find it helpful to offer products with

▶ **FIGURE S7.3**
By Combining Products That Have Complementary Seasonal Patterns, Capacity Can Be Better Utilized

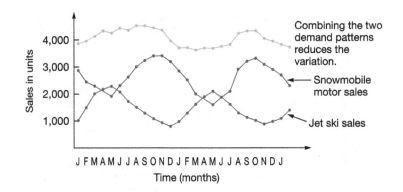

Combining the two demand patterns reduces the variation.

Snowmobile motor sales

Jet ski sales

Sales in units

J F M A M J J A S O N D J F M A M J J A S O N D J
Time (months)

AUTHOR COMMENT
A smoother sales demand contributes to improved scheduling and better human resource strategies.

complementary demand patterns—that is, products for which the demand is high for one when low for the other. For example, in Figure S7.3 the firm is adding a line of snowmobile motors to its line of jet skis to smooth demand. With appropriate complementing of products, perhaps the utilization of facility, equipment, and personnel can be smoothed.

Tactics for Matching Capacity to Demand   Various tactics for matching capacity to demand exist. Options for adjusting capacity include:

1. Making staffing changes (increasing or decreasing the number of employees or shifts)
2. Adjusting equipment (purchasing additional machinery or selling or leasing out existing equipment)
3. Improving processes to increase throughput
4. Redesigning products to facilitate more throughput
5. Adding process flexibility to better meet changing product preferences
6. Closing facilities

The foregoing tactics can be used to adjust demand to existing facilities. The strategic issue is, of course, how to have a facility of the correct size.

Demand and Capacity Management in the Service Sector

In the service sector, scheduling customers is *demand management*, and scheduling the workforce is *capacity management*.

Demand Management   When demand and capacity are fairly well matched, demand management can often be handled with appointments, reservations, or a first-come, first-served

Matching capacity and demand can be a challenge. When market share is declining, the mismatch between demand and capacity means empty plants and laying off employees (left photo). On the other hand, when demand exceeds capacity, as at this opening of the Dubai Aquarium, U.A.E. the mismatch may force customers to leave the queue which would cause a loss in revenue (right photo).

rule. In some businesses, such as doctors' and lawyers' offices, an *appointment system* is the schedule and is adequate. *Reservations systems* work well in rental car agencies, hotels, and some restaurants as a means of minimizing customer waiting time and avoiding disappointment over unfilled service. In retail shops, a post office, or a fast-food restaurant, a *first-come, first-served* rule for serving customers may suffice. Each industry develops its own approaches to matching demand and capacity. Other more aggressive approaches to demand management include many variations of discounts: 'early bird' specials in restaurants, discounts for matinee performances or for seats at odd hours on an airline, and cheap weekend phone calls.

Capacity Management When managing demand is not feasible, then managing capacity through changes in full-time, temporary, or part-time staff may be an option. This is the approach in many services. For instance, hospitals may find capacity limited by a shortage of board-certified radiologists willing to cover the graveyard shifts.

BOTTLENECK ANALYSIS AND THE THEORY OF CONSTRAINTS

AUTHOR COMMENT
There are always bottlenecks; a manager must identify and manage them.

As managers seek to match capacity to demand, decisions must be made about the size of specific operations or work areas in the larger system. Each of the interdependent work areas can be expected to have its own unique capacity. **Capacity analysis** involves determining the throughput capacity of workstations in a system and ultimately the capacity of the entire system.

A key concept in capacity analysis is the role of a constraint or bottleneck. A **bottleneck** is an operation that is the limiting factor or constraint. The term *bottleneck* refers to the neck of a bottle that constrains flow or, in the case of a production system, constrains throughput. A bottleneck has the lowest effective capacity of any operation in the system and thus limits the system's output. Bottlenecks occur in all facets of life—from job shops where a machine is constraining the work flow to highway traffic where two lanes converge into one inadequate lane, resulting in traffic congestion.

Capacity analysis
A means of determining throughput capacity of workstations or an entire production system.

Bottleneck
The limiting factor or constraint in a system.

LO3: Perform bottleneck analysis

Process Times for Stations, Systems, and Cycles

Three metrics are important to help us analyze production system capacity. First, we define the **process time of a station** as the time to produce a given number of units (or a batch of units) at that workstation. For example, if 60 windshields on a Ford assembly line can be installed in 30 minutes, then the process time is 0.5 minutes per windshield. (Process time is simply the inverse of capacity, which in this case is 60 minutes per hour ÷ 0.5 minutes per windshield = 120 windshields installed per hour.) The **process time of a system** is the time of the longest process (the slowest workstation) in the system, which is defined as the process time of the bottleneck. **Process cycle time**, on the other hand, is the time it takes for a unit of product, such as a car, to go through the entire empty system, from start to finish.[1]

Process time of a system and *process cycle time* may be quite different. For example, a Ford assembly line may roll out a new car every minute (process time of the system, because this is the longest workstation), but it may take 30 hours to actually make a car from start to finish (process cycle time). This is because the assembly line has many workstations, with each station contributing to the completed car. Thus, the system's process time determines its capacity (one car per minute), while its process cycle time determines potential ability to build a product (30 hours).

Figure S7.4 displays a simple assembly line using a flowchart, with the individual *process station times* shown as 2, 4, and 3 minutes. The *process time for the system* is 4 minutes because station B is the slowest station, the bottleneck, with a 4-minute process time. Station A could work faster than that, but the result would be a pile of inventory continuously building in front of station B. Station C could also potentially work faster than 4 minutes per unit, but there is no way to tap into its excess capacity because station B will not be able to feed products to station C to work on any faster than one every 4 minutes. Thus, we see that the excess capacity at non-bottleneck stations cannot be used to somehow 'make up for the bottleneck.' Finally, the time to produce a new unit, *the process cycle time*, is 2 + 4 + 3 = 9 minutes.

Process time of a station
The time to produce units at a single workstation.

Process time of a system
The time of the longest (slowest) process; the bottleneck.

Process cycle time
The time it takes for a product to go through the production process with no waiting.

---

[1]The more general term is *manufacturing cycle time*, but we use *process cycle time* here to note that we are defining the time in an empty system. Cycle time varies, depending on the status of the system, which ranges from empty to substantial work-in-process.

▶ **FIGURE S7.4**

Three-Station Assembly Line

A box represents an operation, a triangle represents inventory, and arrows represent precedence relationships.

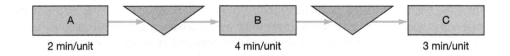

The following two examples illustrate capacity analysis for slightly more complex systems. Example S3 introduces the concept of parallel processes, and Example S4 introduces the concept of simultaneous processing.

EXAMPLE S3 ▶

Capacity analysis with parallel processes

Yazeed's sandwich shop provides healthy sandwiches for customers. Yazeed has two identical sandwich assembly lines. A customer first places and pays for an order, which takes approximately 30 seconds. The order is then sent to one of the two lines. Each assembly line has two workers and three major operations: (1) worker 1 retrieves and cuts the bread (15 seconds/sandwich); (2) worker 2 adds ingredients and places the sandwich onto the toaster conveyor belt (20 seconds/sandwich); (3) the toaster heats the sandwich (40 seconds/sandwich). A wrapper then wraps heated sandwiches coming from both lines and provides final packaging for the customer (37.5 seconds/sandwich). A flowchart of the customer order is shown below.

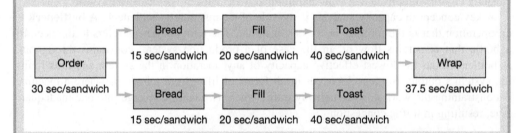

APPROACH ▶   Clearly the toaster is the single slowest resource in the five-step process, but is it the bottleneck? Yazeed should first determine the process time of each assembly line, then the process time of the combined assembly lines, and finally the process time of the entire operation.

SOLUTION ▶   Because each of the three assembly-line operations uses a separate resource (worker or machine), separate partially completed sandwiches can be worked on simultaneously at each station. Thus, the process time of each assembly line is the longest process time of each of the three operations. In this case, the 40-second toasting time represents the longest process time of each assembly line. Next, the process time of the combined assembly-line operations is 40 seconds per two sandwiches, or 20 seconds per sandwich. Therefore, the wrapping and delivering operation becomes the bottleneck for the entire customer order operation, and the system process time is 37.5 seconds—the maximum of 30, 20, and 37.5. The capacity per hour equals 3,600 seconds per hour ÷ 37.5 seconds per sandwich = 96 sandwiches per hour. Finally, the process cycle time equals 30 + 15 + 20 + 40 + 37.5 = 142.5 seconds (or 2 minutes and 22.5 seconds), assuming no waiting in line to begin with.

INSIGHT ▶   If *n* parallel (redundant) operations are added, the process time of the combined operation will equal 1 ÷ *n* times the process time of the original.

LEARNING EXERCISE ▶   If Yazeed hires an additional wrapper, what will be the new hourly capacity? [Answer: The new bottleneck is now the order-taking station: Capacity = 3,600 seconds per hour ÷ 30 seconds per sandwich = 120 sandwiches per hour.]

RELATED PROBLEM ▶   S7.6

In Example S3, how could we claim that the process time of the toaster was 20 seconds per sandwich when it takes 40 seconds to toast a sandwich? Because we had two toasters, two sandwiches could be toasted every 40 seconds, for an average of 1 sandwich every 20 seconds. And that time for a toaster can actually be achieved if the start times for the two are *staggered* (i.e. a new sandwich is placed in a toaster every 20 seconds). In that case, even though each sandwich will sit in the toaster for 40 seconds, a sandwich could emerge from one of the two toasters every 20 seconds. As we see, doubling the number of resources effectively cuts the process time in half, resulting in a doubling of the capacity of those resources.

Dr. Omar's dentistry practice has been cleaning customers' teeth for decades. The process for a basic dental cleaning is relatively straightforward: (1) the customer checks in (2 minutes); (2) a lab technician takes and develops four X-rays (2 and 4 minutes, respectively); (3) the dentist processes and examines the X-rays (5 minutes) *while* the hygienist cleans the teeth (24 minutes); (4) the dentist meets with the patient to poke at a few teeth, explain the X-ray results, and tell the patient to floss more often (8 minutes); (5) the customer pays and books her next appointment (6 minutes). A flowchart of the customer visit is shown below.

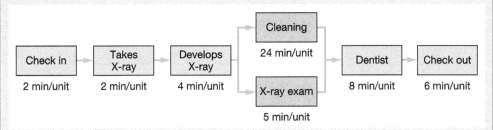

APPROACH ▶ With simultaneous processes, an order or a product is essentially *split* into different paths to be rejoined later on. To find the process time, each operation is treated separately, just as though all operations were on a sequential path. To find the process cycle time, the time over *all* paths must be computed, and it is the *longest* path.

SOLUTION ▶ The bottleneck in this system is the hygienist, at 24 minutes per patient, resulting in an hourly system capacity of 60 minutes ÷ 24 minutes per patient = 2.5 patients. The process cycle time is the maximum of the two paths through the system. The path through the X-ray exam is 2 + 2 + 4 + 5 + 8 + 6 = 27 minutes, while the path through the hygienist is 2 + 2 + 4 + 24 + 8 + 6 = 46 minutes. Thus a patient should be out the door after 46 minutes (i.e. the maximum of 27 and 46).

INSIGHT ▶ With simultaneous processing, all process times in the entire system are not simply added together to compute process cycle time, because some operations are occurring at the same time. Instead, the longest path through the system is deemed the process cycle time.

LEARNING EXERCISE ▶ Suppose that the same technician now has the hygienist start immediately after the X-rays are taken (allowing the hygienist to start 4 minutes sooner). The technician then processes the X-rays while the hygienist is cleaning teeth. The dentist still analyzes the X-rays while the teeth cleaning is occurring. What would be the new system capacity and process cycle time? [Answer: The X-ray development/processing operation is no longer on the initial path, reducing the total patient visit duration by 4 minutes, for a process cycle time of 42 minutes (the maximum of 27 and 42). However, the hygienist is still the bottleneck, so the capacity remains at 2.5 patients per hour.]

RELATED PROBLEM ▶ S7.7

To summarize: (1) the *system process time* is the process time of the bottleneck, which is the operation with the longest (slowest) process time, after dividing by the number of parallel (redundant) operations; (2) the *system capacity* is the inverse of the system process time; (3) the *process cycle time* is the total time through the longest path in the system, assuming no waiting.

Theory of Constraints

The **theory of constraints (TOC)** has been popularized by the book *The Goal: A Process of Ongoing Improvement,* by Goldratt and Cox.[2] TOC is a body of knowledge that deals with anything that limits or constrains an organization's ability to achieve its goals. Constraints can be physical (e.g. process or personnel availability, raw materials, or supplies) or nonphysical (e.g. procedures, morale, and training). The TOC process is comprised of five main steps to recognize and manage the limitations that constrain an organization's ability.

Theory of constraints (TOC)

A body of knowledge that deals with anything that limits an organization's ability to achieve its goals.

Step 1: Identify the constraints.
Step 2: Develop a plan for overcoming the identified constraints.
Step 3: Focus resources on accomplishing Step 2.
Step 4: Reduce the effects of the constraints by offloading work or by expanding capability. Make sure that the constraints are recognized by all those who can have an impact on them.
Step 5: When one set of constraints is overcome, go back to Step 1 and identify new constraints.

[2]See E. M. Goldratt and J. Cox, *The Goal: A Process of Ongoing Improvement*, 3rd rev. ed., Great Barrington, MA: North River Press, 2004.

Bottleneck Management

A crucial constraint in any system is the bottleneck, and managers must focus significant attention on it. We present four principles of bottleneck management:

1. *Release work orders to the system at the pace set by the bottleneck's capacity:* The theory of constraints utilizes the concept of *drum, buffer, rope* to aid in the implementation of bottleneck and non-bottleneck scheduling. In brief, the *drum* is the beat of the system. It provides the schedule—the pace of production. The *buffer* is the resource, usually inventory, which may be helpful to keep the bottleneck operating at the pace of the drum. Finally, the *rope* provides the synchronization or communication necessary to pull units through the system. The rope can be thought of as signals between workstations.

2. *Lost time at the bottleneck represents lost capacity for the whole system:* This principle implies that the bottleneck should always be kept busy with work. Well-trained and cross-trained employees and inspections prior to the bottleneck can reduce lost capacity at a bottleneck.

3. *Increasing the capacity of a non-bottleneck station is a mirage:* Increasing the capacity of *non-bottleneck* stations has no impact on the system's overall capacity. Working faster on a non-bottleneck station may just create extra inventory, with all of its adverse effects. This implies that non-bottlenecks should have planned idle time. Extra work or setups at non-bottleneck stations will not cause delay, which allows for smaller batch sizes and more frequent product changeovers at non-bottleneck stations.

4. *Increasing the capacity of the bottleneck increases capacity for the whole system:* Managers should focus improvement efforts on the bottleneck. Bottleneck capacity may be improved by various means, including offloading some of the bottleneck operations to another workstation (e.g. let the milk froth settle next to the nozzle at the bar, not under it, so the next cappuccino can be served), increasing capacity of the bottleneck (adding resources, working longer or working faster), subcontracting, developing alternative routings, and reducing setup times.

Even when managers have process and quality variability under control, changing technology, personnel, products, product mixes, and volumes can create multiple and shifting bottlenecks. Identifying and managing bottlenecks is a required operations task, but by definition, bottlenecks cannot be 'eliminated.' A system will always have at least one.

Break-even analysis
A means of finding the point, in dollars and units, at which costs equal revenues.

BREAK-EVEN ANALYSIS

Break-even analysis is the critical tool for determining the capacity a facility must have to achieve profitability. The objective of **break-even analysis** is to find the point, in monetary terms and units, at which costs equal revenue. This point is the break-even point. Firms must operate above this level to achieve profitability. As shown in Figure S7.5, break-even analysis requires an estimation of fixed costs, variable costs, and revenue.

Fixed costs are costs that continue even if no units are produced. Examples include depreciation, taxes, debt, and mortgage payments. *Variable costs* are those that vary with the volume of units produced. The major components of variable costs are labor and materials. However, other costs, such as the portion of the utilities that varies with volume, are also variable costs. The difference between selling price and variable cost is *contribution*. Only when total contribution exceeds total fixed cost will there be profit.

Another element in break-even analysis is the *revenue function*. In Figure S7.5, revenue begins at the origin and proceeds upward to the right, increasing by the selling price of each unit. Where the revenue function crosses the total cost line (the sum of fixed and variable costs), is the break-even point, with a profit corridor to the right and a loss corridor to the left.

Assumptions

A number of assumptions underlie the basic break-even model. Notably, costs and revenue are shown as straight lines. They are shown to increase linearly—that is, in direct proportion to the volume of units being produced. However, neither fixed costs nor variable costs (nor, for that matter, the revenue function) need be a straight line. For example, fixed costs change as more capital equipment or warehouse space is used; labor costs change with overtime or as marginally skilled workers are employed; the revenue function may change due to such factors as volume discounts.

Graphic Approach

The first step in the graphic approach to break-even analysis is to define those costs that are fixed and sum them. The fixed costs are drawn as a horizontal line beginning at that dollar amount on the vertical axis. The variable costs are then estimated by an analysis of labor, materials, and other costs connected with the production of each unit. The variable costs are shown as an incrementally increasing cost, originating at the intersection of the fixed cost on the vertical axis and increasing with each change in volume as we move to the right on the volume (or horizontal) axis.

LO4: Compute break-even

Algebraic Approach

The formulas for the break-even point in units produced and monetary terms are shown below. Let:

BEP_x = break-even point in units

$BEP_\$$ = break-even point in monetary terms

P = price per unit (after all discounts)

x = number of units produced

TR = total revenue = Px

F = fixed costs

V = variable costs per unit

TC = total costs = $F + Vx$

The break-even point occurs where total revenue equals total costs. Therefore:

$$TR = TC \quad \text{or} \quad Px = F + Vx$$

Solving for x, we get

$$\text{Break-even point in units } (BEP_x) = \frac{F}{P - V}$$

and:

$$\text{Break-even point in monetary terms } (BEP_\$) = BEP_x P = \frac{F}{P - V} P = \frac{F}{(P - V) \div P} = \frac{F}{1 - V \div P}$$

$$\text{Profit} = TR - TC = Px - (F + Vx) = Px - F - Vx = (P - V)x - F$$

Using these equations, we can solve directly for break-even point and profitability. The two break-even formulas of particular interest are:

$$\text{Break-even in units} = \frac{\text{Total fixed cost}}{\text{Price} - \text{Variable cost}} \tag{S7-4}$$

$$\text{Break-even in monetary terms} = \frac{\text{Total fixed cost}}{1 - \dfrac{\text{Variable cost}}{\text{Selling price}}} \tag{S7-5}$$

Single-Product Case

In Example S5, we determine the break-even point in dollars and units for one product.

EXAMPLE S5 ▶

Single product break-even analysis

Fadeel, Inc., in Oman, wants to determine the minimum monetary value and unit volume needed at its new facility to break even.

APPROACH ▶ The firm first determines that it has fixed costs of US$10,000 this period. Direct labor is US$1.50 per unit, and material is US$0.75 per unit. The selling price is US$4.00 per unit.

SOLUTION ▶ The break-even point in U.S. dollars is computed as follows:

$$BEP_\$ = \frac{F}{1 - (V/P)} = \frac{US\$10,000}{1 - [(1.50 + 0.75)/(4.00)]} = \frac{US\$10,000}{0.4375} = US\$22,857.14$$

The break-even point in units is:

$$BEP_x = \frac{F}{P - V} = \frac{US\$10,000}{4.00 - (1.50 + 0.75)} = 5,714$$

Note that we use total variable costs (that is, both labor and material).

INSIGHT ▶ The management of Fadeel, Inc. now has an estimate in both units and dollars of the volume necessary for the new facility.

LEARNING EXERCISE ▶ If Fadeel finds that fixed costs will increase to US$12,000, what happens to the break-even in units and dollars? [Answer: The break-even in units increases to 6,857, and break-even in dollars increases to US$27,428.57.]

RELATED PROBLEMS ▶ S7.8, S7.9, S7.10

EXCEL OM Data File **sup07SExS3.xls** can be found at MyOMLab.

Multiproduct Case

Most firms, from manufacturers to restaurants (even fast-food restaurants), have a variety of offerings. Each offering may have a different selling price and variable cost. Utilizing break-even analysis, we modify Equation (S7-5) to reflect the proportion of sales for each product.

Recessions (e.g. 2008–2010) and terrorist attacks (e.g. September 11, 2001) can make even the best capacity decision for an airline look bad. Excess capacity for an airline can be very expensive, with storage costs running as high as US$60,000 per month per aircraft. Here, as a testimonial to excess capacity, aircrafts sit idle in the Mojave Desert.

Paper machines such as the one shown here require a high capital investment. This investment results in a high fixed cost but allows production of paper at a very low variable cost. The production manager's job is to maintain utilization above the break-even point to achieve profitability.

We do this by 'weighting' each product's contribution by its proportion of sales. The formula is then:

$$\text{Break-even point in dollars } (BEP_\$) = \frac{F}{\sum\left[\left(1 - \frac{V_i}{P_i}\right) \times (W_i)\right]}$$

(S7-6)

where V = variable cost per unit W = percentage each product is of total sales
P = price per unit i = each product
F = fixed cost

Example S6 shows how to determine the break-even point for the multiproduct case at the Eman Bistro restaurant.

► **EXAMPLE S6**

Multiproduct break-even analysis

Eman Bistro in Tunisia, like most other resturants, makes more than one product and would like to know its break-even point in U.S. dollars.

APPROACH ► Information for Eman Bistro follows. Fixed costs are US$3,000 per month.

Item	Price	Cost	Annual Forecasted Sales Units
Sandwich	US$5.00	US$3.00	9,000
Drinks	1.50	0.50	9,000
Baked potato	2.00	1.00	7,000

With a variety of offerings, we proceed with break-even analysis just as in a single-product case, except that we weight each of the products by its proportion of total sales using Equation (S7-6).

SOLUTION ► Multiproduct Break-even: Determining Contribution

1	2	3	4	5	6	7	8
Item (i)	Selling Price (P)	Variable Cost (V)	($V \div P$)	$1 - (V \div P)$	Annual Forecasted Sales US$	% of Sales	Weighted Contribution (col. 5 × col. 7)
Sandwich	US$5.00	US$3.00	0.60	0.40	US$45,000	0.621	0.248
Drinks	1.50	0.50	0.33	0.67	13,500	0.186	0.125
Baked potato	2.00	1.00	0.50	0.50	14,000	0.193	0.096
					US$72,500	1.000	0.469

Note: Revenue for sandwiches is US$45,000 (5.00 × 9,000), which is 62.1 percent of the total revenue of US$72,500. Therefore, the contribution for sandwiches is 'weighted' by 0.621. The weighted contribution is 0.621 × 0.40 = 0.248. In this manner, its *relative* contribution is properly reflected.

Using this approach for each product, we find that the total weighted contribution is 0.469 for each dollar of sales, and the break-even point in dollars is US$76,759:

$$BEP_\$ = \frac{F}{\sum\left[\left(1 - \frac{V_i}{P_i}\right) \times (W_i)\right]} = \frac{US\$3,000 \times 12}{0.469} = \frac{US\$36,000}{0.469} = US\$76,759$$

The information given in this example implies total daily sales (52 weeks at 6 days each) of:

$$\frac{US\$76,759}{312 \text{ days}} = US\$246.02$$

INSIGHT ▶ The management of Eman Bistro now knows that it must generate average sales of US$246.02 each day to break even. Management also knows that if the forecasted sales of US$72,500 are correct, Eman Bistro will lose money, as break-even is US$76,759.

LEARNING EXERCISE ▶ If the manager of Eman Bistro wants to make an additional US$1,000 per month in salary, and considers this a fixed cost, what is the new break-even point in average sales per day? [Answer: US$328.03.]

Break-even figures by product provide the manager with added insight as to the realism of his or her sales forecast. They indicate exactly what must be sold each day, as we illustrate in Example S7.

EXAMPLE S7 ▶

Unit sales at break-even

Eman Bistro also wants to know the break-even for the number of sandwiches that must be sold every day.

APPROACH ▶ Using the data in Example S6, we take the forecast sandwich sales of 62.1 percent times the daily break-even of US$246.02 divided by the selling price of each sandwich (US$5.00).

SOLUTION ▶ At break-even, sandwich sales must then be:

$$\frac{0.621 \times US\$246.02}{5.00} = \text{Number of sandwiches} = 30.6 \approx 31 \text{ sandwiches each day}$$

INSIGHT ▶ With knowledge of individual product sales, the manager has a basis for determining material and labor requirements.

LEARNING EXERCISE ▶ At a dollar break-even of US$328.03 per day, how many sandwiches must Eman Bistro sell each day? [Answer: 40.]

Once break-even analysis has been prepared, analyzed, and judged to be reasonable, decisions can be made about the type and capacity of equipment needed. Indeed, a better judgment of the likelihood of success of the enterprise can now be made.

AUTHOR COMMENT
Capacity decisions require matching capacity to forecasts, which is always difficult.

VIDEO S7.1
Capacity Planning at Arnold Palmer Hospital

REDUCING RISK WITH INCREMENTAL CHANGES

When demand for goods and services can be forecast with a reasonable degree of precision, determining a break-even point and capacity requirements can be rather straightforward. But, more likely, determining the capacity and how to achieve it will be complicated, as many factors are difficult to measure and quantify. Factors such as technology, competitors, building restrictions, cost of capital, human resource options, and regulations make the decision interesting. To complicate matters further, demand growth is usually in small units, while capacity additions are likely to be both instantaneous and in large units. This contradiction adds to the capacity decision risk. To reduce risk, incremental changes that hedge demand forecasts may be a good option. Figure S7.6 illustrates three approaches to new capacity.

(a) Leading Strategy
Management leads capacity in periodic increments. Management could also add enough capacity in one period to handle expected demand for multiple periods.

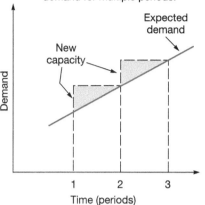

(b) Lag Strategy
Here management lags (chases) demand.

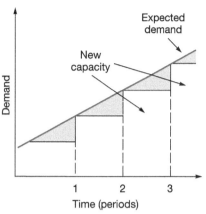

(c) Straddle Strategy
Here management uses average capacity increments to straddle demand.

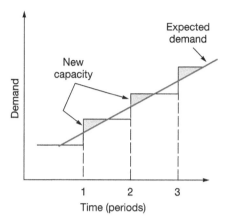

▲ FIGURE S7.6   **Approaches to Capacity Expansion**

Alternative Figure S7.6(a) *leads* capacity—that is, acquires capacity to stay ahead of demand, with new capacity being acquired at the beginning of period 1. This capacity handles increased demand, until the beginning of period 2. At the beginning of period 2, new capacity is again acquired, which will allow the organization to stay ahead of demand until the beginning of period 3. This process can be continued indefinitely into the future. Here capacity is acquired *incrementally*—at the beginning of period 1 *and* at the beginning of period 2. But managers can also elect to make a larger increase at the beginning of period 1—an increase that may satisfy expected demand until the beginning of period 3.

Excess capacity gives operations managers flexibility. For instance, in the hotel industry, added (extra) capacity in the form of rooms can allow a wider variety of room options and perhaps flexibility in room cleanup schedules. In manufacturing, excess capacity can be used to do more setups, shorten production runs, and drive down inventory costs.

But Figure S7.6(b) shows an option that *lags* capacity, perhaps using overtime or subcontracting to accommodate excess demand. Figure S7.6(c) *straddles* demand by building capacity that is 'average,' sometimes lagging demand and sometimes leading it. Both the lag and straddle option have the advantage of delaying capital expenditure.

In cases where the business climate is stable, deciding between alternatives can be relatively easy. The total cost of each alternative can be computed, and the alternative with the least total cost can be selected. However, when capacity requirements are subject to significant unknowns, 'probabilistic' models may be appropriate.

SUPPLEMENT SUMMARY

Managers tie equipment selection and capacity decisions to the organization's missions and strategy. Four additional considerations are critical: (1) accurately forecasting demand; (2) understanding the equipment, processes, and capacity increments; (3) finding the optimum operating size; (4) ensuring the flexibility needed for adjustments in technology, product features and mix, and volumes.

Some of the techniques that are particularly useful to operations managers when making capacity decisions include good forecasting, bottleneck analysis, and break-even analysis.

Key Terms

Bottleneck (p. 219)
Break-even analysis (p. 222)
Capacity (p. 214)
Capacity analysis (p. 219)

Design capacity (p. 214)
Effective capacity (p. 215)
Efficiency (p. 215)
Process cycle time (p. 219)

Process time of a station (p. 219)
Process time of a system (p. 219)
Theory of constraints (TOC) (p. 221)
Utilization (p. 215)

Discussion Questions

1. Distinguish between design capacity and effective capacity.
2. What is effective capacity?
3. What is efficiency?
4. How is actual, or expected, output computed?
5. Explain why doubling the capacity of a bottleneck may not double the system capacity.
6. Distinguish between process time of a system and process cycle time.
7. What is the theory of constraints?
8. What are the assumptions of break-even analysis?
9. What keeps plotted revenue data from falling on a straight line in a break-even analysis?
10. Under what conditions would a firm want its capacity to lag demand? to lead demand?
11. Describe the five-step process that serves as the basis of the theory of constraints.
12. What are the techniques available to operations managers to deal with a bottleneck operation? Which of these does not decrease process cycle time?

Using Software for Break-Even Analysis

Excel, Excel OM, and POM for Windows all handle break-even and cost–volume analysis problems.

Using Excel

It is a straightforward task to develop the formulas to do a break-even analysis in Excel. You can see similar spreadsheet analysis in the Excel OM preprogrammed software that accompanies this text.

✗ Using Excel OM

Excel OM's Break-Even Analysis module provides the Excel formulas needed to compute the break-even points, and the solution and graphical output.

P Using POM for Windows

Similar to Excel OM, POM for Windows also contains a break-even/cost–volume analysis module.

Solved Problems   Virtual Office Hours help is available at MyOMLab.

▼ SOLVED PROBLEM S7.1

Sara James Bakery, described in Examples S1 and S2, has decided to increase its facilities by adding one additional process line. The firm will have two process lines, each working 7 days a week, 3 shifts per day, 8 hours per shift, with effective capacity of 300,000 rolls. This addition, however, will reduce overall system efficiency to 85 percent. Compute the expected production with this new effective capacity.

▼ SOLUTION

Expected production = (Effective capactiy)(Efficiency)
$$= 300,000(0.85)$$
$$= 255,000 \text{ rolls per week}$$

▼ SOLVED PROBLEM S7.2

John has been asked to determine whether the US$22.50 cost of tickets for the community dinner theater will allow the group to achieve break-even and whether the 175 seating capacity is adequate. The cost for each performance of a 10-performance run is US$2,500. The facility rental cost for the entire 10 performances is US$10,000. Drinks and parking are extra charges and have their own price and variable costs, as shown below:

1	2	3	4	5	6	7	8	9
	Selling Price (P)	Variable Cost (V)	Percentage Variable Cost $(V \div P)$	Contribution $1 - (V \div P)$	Estimated Quantity of Sales Units (sales)	Dollar Sales (Sales $\times$ P)	Percentage of Sales	Contribution Weighted by Percentage of Sales (col. 5 $\times$ col. 8)
Tickets with Dinner	US$22.50	US$10.50	0.467	0.533	175	US$3,938	0.741	0.395
Drinks	US$5.00	US$1.75	0.350	0.650	175	US$875	0.165	0.107
Parking	US$5.00	US$2.00	0.400	0.600	100	US$500	0.094	0.056
					450	US$5,313	1.000	0.558

▼ SOLUTION

$$BEP_s = \frac{F}{\sum\left[\left(1 - \frac{V_i}{P_i}\right) \times (W_i)\right]} = \frac{US\$(10 \times 2,500) + US\$10,000}{0.558} = \frac{US\$35,000}{0.558} = US\$62,724$$

Revenue for each performance (from column 7) = US$5,313

Total forecasted revenue for the 10 performances = (10 × US$5,313) = US$53,130

Forecasted revenue with this mix of sales shows a break-even of US$62,724

Thus, given this mix of costs, sales, and capacity John determines that the theater will not break even.

▼ SOLVED PROBLEM S7.3

T. Smunt Manufacturing Corp. has the process displayed below. The drilling operation occurs separately from and simultaneously with the sawing and grinding operations. The product only needs to go through one of the three assembly operations (the assembly operations are 'parallel').

a. Which operation is the bottleneck?
b. What is the system's process time?
c. What is the process cycle time for the overall system?

d. If the firm operates 8 hours per day, 22 days per month, what is the monthly capacity of the manufacturing process?
e. Suppose that a second drilling machine is added, and it has the same process time as the original drilling machine. What is the new process time of the system?
f. Suppose that a second drilling machine is added, and it has the same process time as the original drilling machine. What is the new process cycle time?

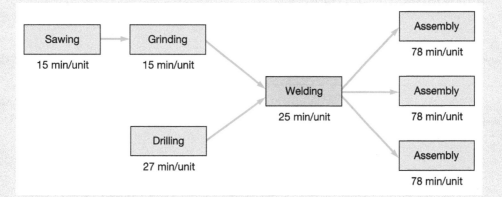

▼ SOLUTION

a. The process time of Assembly is 78 minutes ÷ 3 operators = 26 minutes per unit, so the station with the longest process time, hence the bottleneck, is Drilling, at 27 minutes.
b. The system's process time is 27 minutes per unit (the longest process, Drilling).
c. System process cycle time is the maximum of (15 + 15 + 25 + 78), (27 + 25 + 78) = maximum of (133, 130) = 133 minutes.

d. Monthly capacity = (60 minutes)(8 hours) ÷ 22 days) ÷ 27 minutes per unit = 10,560 minutes per month ÷ 27 minutes per unit = 391.11 units/month.
e. The bottleneck shifts to Assembly, with a process time of 26 minutes per unit.
f. Redundancy does not affect process cycle time. It is still 133 minutes.

Problems*

• **S7.1** If a plant was designed to produce 7,000 hammers per day but is limited to making 6,000 hammers per day because of the time needed to change equipment between styles of hammers, what is the utilization?

• **S7.2** For the past month, the plant in Problem S7.1, which has an effective capacity of 6,500, has made only 4,500 hammers

per day because of material delay, employee absences, and other problems. What is its efficiency?

• **S7.3** If a plant has an effective capacity of 6,500 and an efficiency of 88 percent, what is the actual (planned) output?

• **S7.4** A plant has an effective capacity of 900 units per day and produces 800 units per day with its product mix; what is its efficiency?

*Note: Px means the problem may be solved with POM for Windows and/or Excel OM.

• **S7.5** Material delays have routinely limited production of household sinks to 400 units per day. If the plant efficiency is 80 percent, what is the effective capacity?

•• **S7.6** The three-station work cell illustrated in Figure S7.7 has a product that must go through one of the two machines at station 1 (they are parallel) before proceeding to station 2.
a) What is the process time of the system?
b) What is the bottleneck time of this work cell?
c) What is the process cycle time?
d) If the firm operates 10 hours per day, 5 days per week, what is the weekly capacity of this work cell?

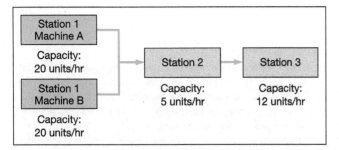

▲ **FIGURE S7.7**   **Three-Station Work Cell**

•• **S7.7** A production process at Rmaith Manufacturing is shown in Figure S7.8. The drilling operation occurs separately from, and simultaneously with, the sawing and sanding operations. A product needs to go through only one of the three assembly operations (the operations are in parallel).

a) Which operation is the bottleneck?
b) What is the process time of the overall system?
c) What is the process cycle time of the overall system?
d) If the firm operates 8 hours per day, 20 days per month, what is the monthly capacity of the manufacturing process?

•• **S7.8** You are considering opening a copy service in the student union. You estimate your fixed cost at US$15,000 and the variable cost of each copy sold at US$.01. You expect the selling price to average US$0.05.
a) What is the break-even point in dollars?
b) What is the break-even point in units? **Px**

•• **S7.9** An electronics firm in Morocco is currently manufacturing an item that has a variable cost of US$.50 per unit and a selling price of US$1.00 per unit. Fixed costs are US$14,000. Current volume is 30,000 units. The firm can substantially improve the product quality by adding a new piece of equipment at an additional fixed cost of US$6,000. Variable cost would increase to US$.60, but volume should jump to 50,000 units due to a higher-quality product. Should the company buy the new equipment? **Px**

•• **S7.10** The electronics firm in Problem S7.9 is now considering the new equipment and increasing the selling price to US$1.10 per unit. With the higher-quality product, the new volume is expected to be 45,000 units. Under these circumstances, should the company purchase the new equipment and increase the selling price? **Px**

▶ Refer to MyOMLab **for additional homework problems.**

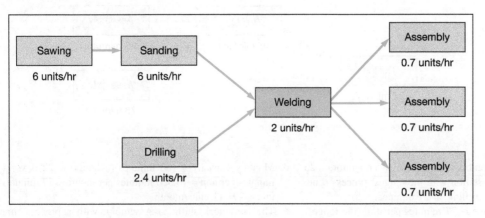

◀ **FIGURE S7.8**
Work Cell with Parallel Operations

Case Study

▶ **Capacity Planning at Arnold Palmer Hospital**

Since opening day, Arnold Palmer Hospital has experienced an explosive growth in demand for its services. One of only six hospitals in the United States to specialize in health care for women and children, Arnold Palmer Hospital has cared for over 1,500,000 patients who came to the Orlando, Florida facility from all 50 states and more than 100 countries. With patient satisfaction scores in the top 10 percent of U.S. hospitals surveyed (over 95 percent of patients would recommend the hospital to others), one of Arnold Palmer Hospital's main focuses is delivery of babies. Originally built with 281 beds and a capacity for 6,500 births per year, the hospital

steadily approached and then passed 10,000 births. Looking at Table S7.1, Executive Director Kathy Swanson knew an expansion was necessary.

With continuing population growth in its market area serving 18 central Florida counties, Arnold Palmer Hospital was delivering the equivalent of a kindergarten class of babies every day and still not meeting demand. Supported with substantial additional demographic analysis, the hospital was ready to move ahead with a capacity expansion plan and a new 11-story hospital building across the street from the existing facility.

▼ TABLE S7.1   Births at Arnold Palmer Hospital

Year	Births
1995	6,144
1996	6,230
1997	6,432
1998	6,950
1999	7,377
2000	8,655
2001	9,536
2002	9,825
2003	10,253
2004	10,555
2005	12,316
2006	13,070
2007	14,028
2008	14,634

Thirty-five planning teams were established to study such issues as: (1) specific forecasts; (2) services that would transfer to the new facility; (3) services that would remain in the existing facility; (4) staffing needs; (5) capital equipment; (6) pro forma accounting data; (7) regulatory requirements. Ultimately, Arnold Palmer Hospital was ready to move ahead with a budget of US$100 million and a commitment to an additional 150 beds. But given the growth of the central Florida region, Swanson decided to expand the hospital in stages: the top two floors would be empty interiors ('shells') to be completed at a later date, and the fourth-floor operating room could be doubled in size when needed. "With the new facility in place, we are now able to handle up to 16,000 births per year," says Swanson.

Discussion Questions*

1. Given the capacity planning discussion in the text (see Figure S7.6), what approach is being taken by Arnold Palmer Hospital toward matching capacity to demand?
2. What kind of major changes could take place in Arnold Palmer Hospital's demand forecast that would leave the hospital with an underutilized facility (namely, what are the risks connected with this capacity decision)?
3. Use regression analysis to forecast the point at which Swanson needs to expand into the top two floors of the new building, namely, when demand will exceed 16,000 births.

* You may wish to view the video accompanying this case before addressing these questions.

▶ **Additional Case Study:** Visit MyOMLab *for this free case study:*
Ojaman University D: Requires the development of a multiproduct break-even solution.

Main Heading	Review Material	
CAPACITY (PP. 214–219)	▪ **Capacity**—The 'throughput,' or number of units a facility can hold, receive, store, or produce in a period of time.	Problems: S7.1–S7.5
	Capacity decisions often determine capital requirements and therefore a large portion of fixed cost. Capacity also determines whether demand will be satisfied or whether facilities will be idle.	
	Determining facility size, with an objective of achieving high levels of utilization and a high return on investment, is critical.	
	Capacity planning can be viewed in three time horizons:	Virtual Office Hours for Solved Problems: S7.1
	1. *Long range* (>1 year)—Adding facilities and long lead-time equipment 2. *Intermediate range* (3–18 months)—'Aggregate planning' tasks, including adding equipment, personnel, and shifts; subcontracting; and building or using inventory 3. *Short* range (<3 months)—Scheduling jobs and people, and allocating machinery	
	▪ **Design capacity**—The theoretical maximum output of a system in a given period, under ideal conditions. Most organizations operate their facilities at a rate less than the design capacity.	
	▪ **Effective capacity**—The capacity a firm can expect to achieve, given its product mix, methods of scheduling, maintenance, and standards of quality. ▪ **Utilization**—Actual output as a percentage of design capacity. ▪ **Efficiency**—Actual output as a percentage of effective capacity.	
	$$\text{Utilization} = \text{Actual output} \div \text{Design capacity} \qquad \text{(S7-1)}$$ $$\text{Efficiency} = \text{Actual output} \div \text{Effective capacity} \qquad \text{(S7-2)}$$ $$\text{Actual (or Expected) output} = (\text{Effective capacity}) (\text{Efficiency}) \qquad \text{(S7-3)}$$	
	Expected output is sometimes referred to as *rated capacity.*	
	When demand exceeds capacity, a firm may be able to curtail demand simply by raising prices, increasing lead times (which may be inevitable), and discouraging marginally profitable business.	
	When capacity exceeds demand, a firm may want to stimulate demand through price reductions or aggressive marketing, or it may accommodate the market via product changes.	
	In the service sector, scheduling customers is *demand management,* and scheduling the workforce is *capacity management.*	
	When demand and capacity are fairly well matched, demand management in services can often be handled with appointments, reservations, or a first-come, first-served rule. Otherwise, discounts based on time of day may be used (e.g. 'early bird' specials, matinee pricing).	
	When managing demand in services is not feasible, managing capacity through changes in full-time, temporary, or part-time staff may be an option.	
BOTTLENECK ANALYSIS AND THEORY OF CONSTRAINTS (PP. 219–222)	▪ **Capacity analysis**—Determining throughput capacity of workstations or an entire production system. ▪ **Bottleneck**—The limiting factor or constraint in a system. ▪ **Process time of a station**—The time to produce a given number of units at that single workstation. ▪ **Process time of a system**—The time of the longest (slowest) process, the bottleneck. ▪ **Process cycle time**—The time it takes for a product to go through the production process with no waiting: the longest path through the system.	Problems: S7.6–S7.7
	A system's process time determines its capacity (e.g. one car per minute), while its process cycle time determines potential ability to build product (e.g. 30 hours). If *n* parallel (redundant) operations are added, the process time of the combined operations will equal $1 \div n$ times the process time of the original. With simultaneous processing, an order or product is essentially *split* into different paths to be rejoined later on. The longest path through the system is deemed the process cycle time.	
	▪ **Theory of constraints (TOC)**—A body of knowledge that deals with anything limiting an organization's ability to achieve its goals.	

Main Heading	Review Material	MyOMLab
BREAK-EVEN ANALYSIS (PP. 222–226)	■ **Break-even analysis**—A means of finding the point, in monetary terms and units, at which costs equal revenues. *Fixed costs* are costs that exist even if no units are produced. Variable costs are those that vary with the volume of units produced. In the break-even model, costs and revenue are assumed to increase linearly. $$\text{Break-even in units} = \frac{\text{Total fixed cost}}{\text{Price} - \text{Variable cost}} \quad (S7\text{-}4)$$ $$\text{Break-even in monetary terms} = \frac{\text{Total fixed cost}}{1 - \dfrac{\text{Variable cost}}{\text{Selling price}}} \quad (S7\text{-}5)$$ $$\text{Break-even point in monetary terms } (BEP_\$) = \frac{F}{\sum\left[\left(1 - \dfrac{V_i}{P_i}\right) \times (W_i)\right]} \quad (S7\text{-}6)$$	Problems: S7.8–S7.10 Virtual Office Hours for Solved Problem: S7.2
REDUCING RISK WITH INCREMENTAL CHANGES (PP. 226–227)	Demand growth is usually in small units, while capacity additions are likely to be both instantaneous and in large units. To reduce risk, incremental changes that hedge demand forecasts may be a good option. Three approaches to capacity expansion are: (1) *leading* strategy; (2) *lag* strategy; (3) *straddle* strategy. Both lag strategy and straddle strategy delay capital expenditure.	**VIDEO S7.1** Capacity Planning at Arnold Palmer Hospital

*Self-*Test

■ **Before taking the self-test,** refer to the learning objectives listed at the beginning of the supplement and the key terms listed at the end of the supplement.

LO**1.** Capacity decisions should be made on the basis of:
   a) building sustained competitive advantage
   b) good financial returns
   c) a coordinated plan
   d) integration into the company's strategy
   e) all of the above.

LO**2.** Effective capacity is:
   a) the capacity a firm expects to achieve, given the current operating constraints
   b) the percentage of design capacity actually achieved
   c) the percentage of capacity actually achieved
   d) actual output
   e) efficiency.

LO**3.** System capacity is based on:
   a) process time of the bottleneck
   b) throughput time
   c) process time of the fastest station
   d) throughput time plus waiting time
   e) none of the above.

LO**4.** The break-even point is:
   a) adding processes to meet the point of changing product demands
   b) improving processes to increase throughput
   c) the point in monetary terms or units at which cost equals revenue
   d) adding or removing capacity to meet demand
   e) the total cost of a process alternative.

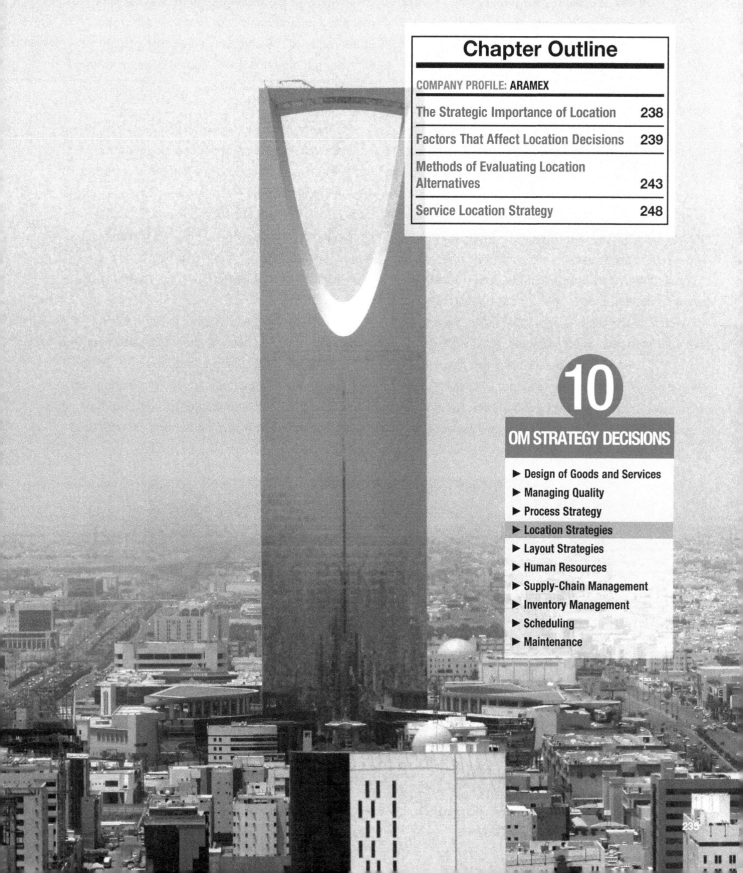

8 Location Decisions

10

OM STRATEGY DECISIONS

► Design of Goods and Services
► Managing Quality
► Process Strategy
► Location Strategies
► Layout Strategies
► Human Resources
► Supply-Chain Management
► Inventory Management
► Scheduling
► Maintenance

LOCATION PROVIDES COMPETITIVE ADVANTAGE FOR ARAMEX

Aramex started its operations as an express company in Amman, Jordan, in 1982. The central location of Jordan, linking the three continents of Africa, Asia, and Europe, allowed Aramex to provide express solutions to neighboring countries, specifically in the Arabian Gulf region.

In 1997, Aramex became the first Arabic company to be listed in NASDAQ. But in 2002 the shareholders decided to delist it from NASDAQ and listed it as a public company in Dubai, where the firm established its biggest regional hub. Aramex's expansion strategy aimed primarily at gaining entry into key locations such as the United States, Europe, and China that would enable it to provide a superior quality of service at a competitive price. The firm's global network stretches to 60 countries.

In 2009, Hong Kong became a major hub for express and freight movements out of China. Country Manager, Samer Marei, commented that Hong Kong's superior logistics infrastructure, highly developed economy, and advanced transportation network made it a natural choice for Aramex as it grows in the region. "The company views Hong Kong as a key regional hub and a critical gateway to the Chinese mainland, which holds endless possibilities," he continued.

Aramex's international expansion into Hong Kong adds significant value and services to its network of 353 offices in 60 countries around the world. Its 12,800 employees work around the clock to ensure speedy delivery and superior logistics to customers, generating a turnover of over US$700 million for Aramex as a company, and US$8 billion for the Global Distribution Alliance (GDI), which Aramex leads.

Mr Marei also noted: "A base in Hong Kong provides businesses such as ours access to mainland China, which is a global manufacturing hub. On the other hand, the Middle East, which is one of our core markets, is primarily a consumer market that depends on imports from China and other parts of Asia. So a

Aramex's choice of Hong Kong as their main hub in the Far East provides them with important access to China.

Well planned rotating schedules are prepared at Aramex headquarters to ensure that each container arrives in time with the contained packages.

The highly automated and state-of-the-art sorting center ensures Aramex's competitive advantage in maintaining almost error-free shipment.

presence in Hong Kong is valuable to us in serving our clients on this major trade route."

Aramex's location decisions are a direct example of the immense opportunities a well-considered location provides. Its presence in Hong Kong, for example, provides the firm with a cost-effective routing solution that is much more appealing to agents and customers in that region.

Source: "On the Move," from *Hong Kong Trader* [online] at **http://www.hktdc.com/info/mi/a/hkthk/en/1X06SDDK/1/ Hong-Kong-Trader-Hong-Kong-Edition/On-The-Move.htm**, May 19, 2010, accessed June 13, 2012.

Chapter 8 **Learning Objectives**

> **AUTHOR COMMENT**
> The location decision can make or break a major business; this chapter will explain the sophisticated techniques companies use to ensure they made the right one!

VIDEO 8.1
Where to Place the Hard Rock Cafe

THE STRATEGIC IMPORTANCE OF LOCATION

When Aramex opened its Asian hub in Hong Kong in 2009, it facilitated the movement of its packages around the globe in a seamless manner. The strategic impact, cost, and international aspect of this decision, as demonstrated in the *Company Profile*, indicate how significant location decisions are.

Firms throughout the world are using the concepts and techniques of this chapter to address the location decision because location greatly affects both fixed and variable costs. Location has a major impact on the overall risk and profit of the company. For instance, depending on the product and type of production or service taking place, transportation costs alone can total as much as 25 percent of the product's selling price. That is, one-fourth of a firm's total revenue may be needed just to cover freight expenses of the raw materials coming in and finished products going out. Other costs that may be influenced by location include taxes, wages, raw material costs, and rents. When all costs are considered, location may alter total operating expenses as much as 50 percent.

Companies make location decisions relatively infrequently, usually because demand has outgrown the current plant's capacity or because of changes in labor productivity, exchange rates, costs, or local attitudes. Companies may also relocate their manufacturing or service facilities because of shifts in demographics and customer demand.

Location options include: (1) expanding an existing facility instead of moving; (2) maintaining current sites while adding another facility elsewhere; (3) closing the existing facility and moving to another location.

The location decision often depends on the type of business. For industrial location decisions, the strategy is usually minimizing costs, although innovation and creativity may also be critical. For retail and professional service organizations, the strategy focuses on maximizing revenue. Warehouse location strategy, however, may be driven by a combination of cost and speed of delivery. *The objective of location strategy is to maximize the benefit of location to the firm.*

Location and Costs

Because location is such a significant cost and revenue driver, location often has the power to make (or break) a company's business strategy. Key multinationals in every major industry, from automobiles to cellular phones, now have or are planning a presence in each of their major markets. Location decisions to support a low-cost strategy require particularly careful consideration.

Once management is committed to a specific location, many costs are firmly in place and difficult to reduce. For instance, if a new factory location is in a region with high energy costs, even good management with an outstanding energy strategy is starting at a disadvantage. Management is in a similar bind with its human resource strategy if labor in the selected location is expensive, ill-trained, or has a poor work ethic. Consequently, hard work to determine an optimal facility location is a good investment.

Location and Innovation

When creativity, innovation, and research and development investments are critical to the operations strategy, the location criteria may change from a focus on costs. When innovation is the focus, four attributes seem to affect overall competitiveness as well as innovation:[1]

---

[1] See Michael E. Porter and Scott Stern, "Innovation: Location Matters," *MIT Sloan Management Review* 42, no. 4 (Summer 2001): 28–36.

- The presence of high-quality and specialized inputs such as scientific and technical talent
- An environment that encourages investment and intense local rivalry
- Pressure and insight gained from a sophisticated local market
- Local presence of related and supporting industries

Almarai is a good example of a firm that has rejected low-cost locations when those locations could not support other important aspects of the strategy. When analysis indicated that the infrastructure and skill levels could not support specific production qualities and technologies, the locations were removed from consideration, even if they were low cost.

FACTORS THAT AFFECT LOCATION DECISIONS

Selecting a facility location is becoming much more complex with the globalization of the workplace. As we saw in Chapter 2, globalization has taken place because of the development of: (1) market economics; (2) better international communications; (3) more rapid, reliable travel and shipping; (4) ease of capital flow between countries; (5) high differences in labor costs. Many firms now consider opening new offices, factories, retail stores, or banks outside their home country. Location decisions transcend national borders. In fact, as Figure 8.1 shows, the sequence of location decisions often begins with choosing a country in which to operate.

One approach to selecting a country is to identify what the parent organization believes are key success factors (KSFs) needed to achieve competitive advantage. Six possible country KSFs are listed at the top of Figure 8.1. Using such factors (including some negative ones, such as crime), the World Economic Forum biannually ranks the global competitiveness of 142 countries (see Table 8.1). In 2011–2012, Switzerland was top of the 142 countries, and Qatar ranked fourteenth (highest in the Arab world) because of its high rates of savings and investments, openness to trade, quality education, and efficient government.

Once a firm decides which country is best for its location, it focuses on a region of the chosen country and a community. The final step in the location decision process is choosing a specific site within a community. The company must pick the one location that is best suited for shipping and receiving, zoning, utilities, size, and cost. Again, Figure 8.1 summarizes this series of decisions and the factors that affect them.

▼ **TABLE 8.1**

Competitiveness of 142 selected countries, based on annual surveys of 14,000 business executives

Country	2011–2012 Ranking
Switzerland	1
⋮	
United States	5
⋮	
United Kingdom	10
⋮	
Qatar	14
⋮	
Saudi Arabia	17
⋮	
China	26
⋮	
U.A.E.	27
⋮	
Oman	32
⋮	
Kuwait	34
⋮	
Bahrain	37
⋮	
Tunisia	40
⋮	
India	56
⋮	
Russian Federation	66
⋮	
Jordan	71
⋮	
Lebanon	89
⋮	
Egypt	94
⋮	
Chad	142

Source: **www.weforum.org**, 2011. Used with permission of World Economic Forum.

Country Decision

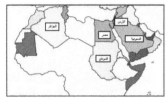

Key Success Factors

1. Political risks, government rules, attitudes, incentives
2. Cultural and economic issues
3. Location of markets
4. Labor talent, attitudes, productivity, costs
5. Availability of supplies, communications, energy
6. Exchange rates and currency risk

Region/Community Decision

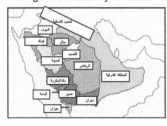

1. Corporate desires
2. Attractiveness of region (culture, taxes, climate, etc.)
3. Labor availability, costs, attitudes toward unions
4. Cost and availability of utilities
5. Environmental regulations of state and town
6. Government incentives and fiscal policies
7. Proximity to raw materials and customers
8. Land/construction costs

Site Decision

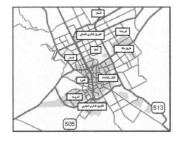

1. Site size and cost
2. Air, rail, highway, and waterway systems
3. Zoning restrictions
4. Proximity of services/supplies needed
5. Environmental impact issues

◀ **FIGURE 8.1**

Some Considerations and Factors That Affect Location Decisions

Besides globalization, a number of other factors affect the location decision. Among these are labor productivity, foreign exchange, culture, changing attitudes toward the industry, and proximity to markets, suppliers, and competitors.

Labor Productivity

When deciding on a location, management may be tempted by an area's low wage rates. However, wage rates cannot be considered by themselves; management must also consider productivity.

As discussed in Chapter 1, differences exist in productivity in various countries. What management is really interested in is the combination of production and the wage rate. For example, if a company pays US\$70 per day with 60 units produced per day in Beirut, it will spend less on labor than at a different location that pays US\$25 per day with production of 20 units per day:

$$\frac{\text{Labor cost per day}}{\text{Production (that is, units per day)}} = \text{Labor cost per unit}$$

Case 1: Beirut plant:

$$\frac{\text{US\$70 Wages per day}}{60 \text{ Units produced per day}} = \frac{\text{US\$70}}{60} = \text{US\$1.17 per unit}$$

Case 2: Different location plant:

$$\frac{\text{US\$25 Wages per day}}{20 \text{ Units produced per day}} = \frac{\text{US\$25}}{20} = \text{US\$1.25 per unit}$$

Employees with poor training, poor education, or poor work habits may not be a good buy even at low wages. By the same token, employees who cannot or will not always reach their places of work are not much good to the organization, even at low wages. (Labor cost per unit is sometimes called the *labor content* of the product.)

Exchange Rates and Currency Risk

Although wage rates and productivity may make a country seem economical, unfavorable exchange rates may negate any savings. Sometimes, though, firms can take advantage of a particularly favorable exchange rate by relocating or exporting to a foreign country. However, the values of foreign currencies continually rise and fall in most countries. Such changes could well make what was a good location in 2010 a disastrous one in 2015.

Costs

Tangible costs

Readily identifiable costs that can be measured with some precision.

We can divide location costs into two categories, tangible and intangible. **Tangible costs** are those costs that are readily identifiable and precisely measured. They include utilities, labor, material, taxes, depreciation, and other costs that the accounting department and management can identify. In addition, such costs as transportation of raw materials, transportation of finished goods, and site construction are all factored into the overall cost of a location. Government incentives, as we see in the *OM in Action* box 'How Egypt Won the Auto Industry,' certainly affect a location's cost.

Intangible costs

A category of location costs that cannot be easily quantified, such as quality of life and government.

Intangible costs are less easily quantified. They include quality of education, public transportation facilities, community attitudes toward the industry and the company, and quality and attitude of prospective employees. They also include quality-of-life variables, such as climate and sports teams, that may influence personnel recruiting.

Ethical Issues   Location decisions based on costs alone may create ethical situations, such as the European Company case in Arabia (see the *Ethical Dilemma* at the end of this chapter). The European Company accepted multiple millions of dollars in incentives to open a facility in that location, only to renege a decade later, leaving residents and government in the lurch.[2]

---

[2]So what's a city, county, or state to do? According to *Forbes* (June 19, 2006): 42, "Keep taxes low. Don't grant favors. Pursue non-discriminatory reforms like reining in debt and public spending. Remove barriers rather than trying to steer economic growth to this favored corporation or that one." While many inner cities have languished, Chicago has prospered by focusing on infrastructure and quality-of-life issues. Also see "Is There a Better Way to Court a Company?" *Business Week* (July 23, 2007): 55.

OM in Action ▶ How Egypt Won the Auto Industry

Egypt has provided incentives for investment in the auto industry. This has enabled local manufacturers to expand their capacities and has encouraged international manufacturers to invest in and launch car production and assembly plants in the country.

Fiat was the first company to enter the Egyptian market with the establishment of El Nasr Automotive Manufacturing Company in 1960. The production of the different Fiat series, such as Fiat 1100, 1300, 2300, 128, 125, 133, 126, and 127, marked the firm's early production throughout the 1960s and the 1970s, until it started its agreement with the Turkish manufacturer Tofaş in the 1990s and later with the Serbian auto manufacturer, Zastava. Nasr's presence provided huge job opportunities in the Egyptian market and provided a good source of revenue for the government.

The successful production of these cars in Egypt encouraged American car manufacturers such as Buick, Cadillac, and Chevrolet to start production in Egypt through the Ghabbour Group. Their success also led to the signing of contracts with Bajaj Auto, Volvo, Mitsubishi, and Hyundai. With a production of 150,000 units a year, Ghabbour is the largest auto manufacturer in the Arab world, with over 3,000 jobs created from its inception.

In 1978, Arab American Vehicles managed to attract companies such as Daimler AG, KIA, Peugeot, Chrysler LLC, Suzuki, and Citroën to manufacture their cars in Egypt. Such a move encouraged most manufacturers to start taking Egypt seriously as a major manufacturing hub of the Middle East, especially with the special investment laws that Egypt introduced to attract major manufacturers (such as tax holidays for foreign investors in industry).

To further cement Egypt's reputation as a leading auto-making center in the Arab world, Mercedes Benz made one of the biggest investments in the Arab world's history by starting a joint venture to produce Mercedes cars in Egypt, thus creating more jobs for the Egyptian population. Such a move was countered by an effort by BMW in 2003 to start an enterprise to produce its cars for the Middle East and the Common Market for Eastern and Southern Africa regions.

By supporting these investments in the auto industry, Egypt has gained much more than it has spent. Profitability and employability in the industry depend on more than the original equipment manufacturers (OEMs) and their assembly plants. General Motors, Daimler, BMW, Volkswagen, and Nissan have created their own supply base in Egypt, which has much higher employment capacity than an OEM. This successful policy, supported by investment promotion laws and financial incentive packages, has brought international car manufacturers and suppliers to Egypt and created thousands of additional jobs.

Source: **www.mfti.gov.eg/english/index.htm**

To what extent do companies owe long-term allegiance to a particular country or state or town if they are losing money—or if the firm can make greater profits elsewhere? Is it ethical for developed countries to locate plants in undeveloped countries where sweatshops and child labor are commonly used? Where low wages and poor working conditions are the norm? It has been said that the factory of the future will be a large ship, capable of moving from port to port as costs in one port become noncompetitive.

Political Risk, Values, and Culture

The political risk associated with national, state, and local governments' attitudes toward private and intellectual property, zoning, pollution, and employment stability may be in flux. Governmental positions at the time a location decision is made may not be lasting ones. However, management may find that these attitudes can be influenced by their own leadership.

Worker values may also differ from country to country, region to region, and small town to city. Worker views regarding turnover, unions, and absenteeism are all relevant factors. In turn, these values can affect a company's decision about whether to make offers to current workers if the firm relocates to a new location.

One of the greatest challenges in a global operations decision is dealing with another country's culture. Cultural variations in punctuality by employees and suppliers make a marked difference in production and delivery schedules. Bribery, likewise, creates substantial economic inefficiency, as well as ethical and legal problems in the global arena. As a result, operations managers face significant challenges when building effective supply chains across cultures. Table 8.2 provides a ranking of corruption in countries around the world.

Proximity to Markets

For many firms, locating near customers is extremely important. Particularly, service organizations, like drugstores, restaurants, post offices, or barbers, find that proximity to market

▶ **TABLE 8.2**

Ranking corruption in selected countries (score of 10 represents a corruption-free country)

Rank	Score
1 New Zealand	9.5
⋮	
16 United Kingdom, Barbados, Austria	7.8 (tie)
⋮	
22 Qatar, Chile	7.2 (tie)
⋮	
24 United States	7.1
⋮	
28 U.A.E.	6.8
⋮	
46 Bahrain, Macao, Mauritius	5.1 (tie)
⋮	
50 Oman	4.8
⋮	
56 Jordan	4.5
⋮	
57 Saudi Arabia, Czech Republic, Namibia	4.4 (tie)
⋮	
69 Italy, Ghana, FYR Macedonia, Samoa	3.9 (tie)
⋮	
112 Egypt, Algeria, Vietnam	2.9 (tie)
⋮	
134 Lebanon	2.5
⋮	
143 Russia	2.4
⋮	
182 Somalia, North Korea	1.0 (tie)

Source: Transparency International's 2011 survey, at **www.transparency.org**. Used with permission of Transparency International.

is *the* primary location factor. Manufacturing firms find it useful to be close to customers when transporting finished goods is expensive or difficult (perhaps because they are bulky, heavy, or fragile). Foreign-owned manufacturers such as Mercedes, LG, and Carrier are building millions of units each year in the Arab world.

In addition, with just-in-time production, suppliers want to locate near users. For a firm like Coca-Cola, whose product's primary ingredient is water, it makes sense to have bottling plants in many cities rather than shipping heavy (and sometimes fragile glass) containers cross-country.

Proximity to Suppliers

Firms locate near their raw materials and suppliers because of: (1) perishability; (2) transportation costs; (3) bulk. Bakeries, dairy plants, and frozen seafood processors deal with *perishable* raw materials, so they often locate close to suppliers. Companies dependent on inputs of heavy or bulky raw materials (such as steel producers using coal and iron ore) face expensive inbound *transportation costs*, so transportation costs become a major factor. And goods for which there is a *reduction in bulk* during production (such as cement mills located near limestone resources) typically need to be near the raw material.

Proximity to Competitors (Clustering)

Clustering

The location of competing companies near each other, often because of a critical mass of information, talent, venture capital, or natural resources.

Both manufacturing and service organizations also like to locate, somewhat surprisingly, near competitors. This tendency, called **clustering**, often occurs when a major resource is found in that region. Such resources include natural resources, information resources, venture capital resources, and talent resources. Table 8.3 presents nine examples of industries that exhibit clustering, and the reasons why.

▼ **TABLE 8.3** Clustering of Companies

Industry	Locations	Reason for Clustering
Petrochemical industries	Gulf region (Saudi Arabia)	Natural resource of land
Software firms	Silicon Valley, Boston, Bangalore (India)	Talent resources of bright graduates in scientific/technical areas, venture capitalists nearby
Race car building	Huntingdon/Northampton region (England)	Critical mass of talent and information
Theme parks (including Disney World, Universal Studios, and Sea World)	Orlando, Florida	A hot spot for entertainment, warm weather, tourists, and inexpensive labor
Electronics firms (such as Sony, IBM, HP, Motorola, and Panasonic)	Northern Mexico	NAFTA, duty-free export to United States (24 percent of all televisions are built here)
Computer hardware manufacturing	Singapore, Taiwan	High technological penetration rates and per capita GDP, skilled/educated workforce with large pool of engineers
Fast-food chains (such as Kudu, McDonald's, Burger King, and Pizza Hut)	Sites within 1 mile of one another	Stimulate food sales, high traffic flows
General aviation aircraft (including Cessna, Learjet, Boeing, and Raytheon)	Wichita, Kansas	Mass of aviation skills (60–70 percent of the world's small planes/jets are built here)
Orthopedic device manufacturing	Warsaw, Indiana	Ready supply of skilled workers, strong U.S. market

METHODS OF EVALUATING LOCATION ALTERNATIVES

AUTHOR COMMENT
Here are four techniques that help in making good location decisions.

Four major methods are used for solving location problems: the factor-rating method, locational break-even analysis, the center-of-gravity method, and the transportation model. This section describes these approaches.

The Factor-Rating Method

There are many factors, both qualitative and quantitative, to consider in choosing a location. Some of these factors are more important than others, so managers can use weightings to make the decision process more objective. The **factor-rating method** is popular because a wide variety of factors, from education to recreation to labor skills, can be objectively included. Figure 8.1 listed a few of the many factors that affect location decisions.

Factor-rating method
A location method that instills objectivity into the process of identifying hard-to-evaluate costs.

The factor-rating method has six steps:

1. Develop a list of relevant factors called *key success factors* (such as those in Figure 8.1).
2. Assign a weight to each factor to reflect its relative importance in the company's objectives.
3. Develop a scale for each factor (for example, 1 to 10 or 1 to 100 points).
4. Have management score each location for each factor, using the scale in step 3.
5. Multiply the score by the weights for each factor and total the score for each location.
6. Make a recommendation based on the maximum point score, considering the results of other quantitative approaches as well.

Marah Land, a Kuwaiti chain of family-oriented theme parks, wishes to expand overseas by opening its first park in Europe. It wishes to select between France and Denmark.

APPROACH ▶ The ratings sheet in Table 8.4 lists key success factors that management has decided are important; their weightings and their rating for two possible sites—Dijon, France, and Copenhagen, Denmark—are shown.

◀ **EXAMPLE 1**

Factor-rating method for an expanding theme park

▶ **TABLE 8.4**

Weights, Scores, and Solution

AUTHOR COMMENT
These weights do not need to be on a 0–1 scale or total to 1. We can use a 1–10 scale, 1–100 scale, or any other scale we prefer.

Key Success Factor	Weight	Scores (out of 100) France	Scores (out of 100) Denmark	Weighted Scores France	Weighted Scores Denmark
Labor availability and attitude	0.25	70	60	(0.25)(70) = 17.5	(0.25)(60) = 15.0
People-to-car ratio	0.05	50	60	(0.05)(50) = 2.5	(0.05)(60) = 3.0
Per capita income	0.10	85	80	(0.10)(85) = 8.5	(0.10)(80) = 8.0
Tax structure	0.39	75	70	(0.39)(75) = 29.3	(0.39)(70) = 27.3
Education and health	0.21	60	70	(0.21)(60) = 12.6	(0.21)(70) = 14.7
Totals	1.00			70.4	68.0

LO3: Apply the factor-rating method

SOLUTION ▶ Table 8.4 uses weights and scores to evaluate alternative site locations. Given the option of 100 points assigned to each factor, the French location is preferable.

INSIGHT ▶ By changing the points or weights slightly for those factors about which there is some doubt, we can analyze the sensitivity of the decision. For instance, we can see that changing the scores for 'labor availability and attitude' by 10 points can change the decision. The numbers used in factor weighting can be subjective and the model's results are not 'exact' even though this is a quantitative approach.

LEARNING EXERCISE ▶ If the weight for 'tax structure' drops to 0.20 and the weight for 'education and health' increases to 0.40, what is the new result? [Answer: Denmark is now preferable, with a 68.0 vs. a 67.5 score for France.]

RELATED PROBLEMS ▶ 8.3, 8.4, 8.5, 8.6, 8.7

EXCEL OM Data File **Ch08Ex1.xls** can be found at MyOMLab.

When a decision is sensitive to minor changes, further analysis of the weighting and the points assigned may be appropriate. Alternatively, management may conclude that these intangible factors are not the proper criteria on which to base a location decision. Managers therefore place primary weight on the more quantitative aspects of the decision.

Locational Break-Even Analysis

Locational break-even analysis

A cost–volume analysis to make an economic comparison of location alternatives.

Locational break-even analysis is the use of cost–volume analysis to make an economic comparison of location alternatives. By identifying fixed and variable costs and graphing them for each location, we can determine which one provides the lowest cost. Locational break-even analysis can be done mathematically or graphically. The graphic approach has the advantage of providing the range of volume over which each location is preferable.

The three steps to locational break-even analysis are as follows.

1. Determine the fixed and variable cost for each location.
2. Plot the costs for each location, with costs on the vertical axis of the graph and annual volume on the horizontal axis.
3. Select the location that has the lowest total cost for the expected production volume.

EXAMPLE 2 ▶

Locational break-even for a parts manufacturer

Musa Alzam, owner of Alzam Manufacturing, needs to expand his capacity. He is considering three locations—Ramtha, Allan, and Nahle—for a new plant. The company wishes to find the most economical location for an expected volume of 2,000 units per year.

APPROACH ▶ Musa conducts locational break-even analysis. To do so, he determines that fixed costs per year at the sites are US$30,000, US$60,000, and US$110,000, respectively; and variable costs are US$75 per unit, US$45 per unit, and US$25 per unit, respectively. The expected selling price of each ignition system produced is US$120.

SOLUTION ▶ For each of the three locations, Musa can plot the fixed costs (those at a volume of zero units) and the total cost (fixed costs + variables costs) at the expected volume of output. These lines have been plotted in Figure 8.2.

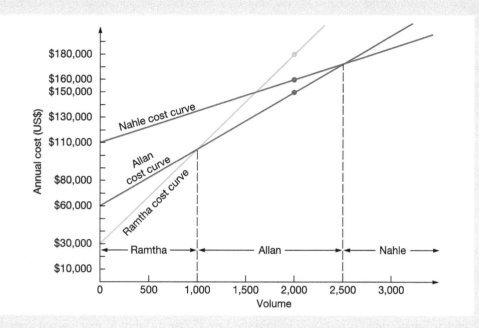

◀ **FIGURE 8.2**
Crossover Chart for Locational Break-Even Analysis

For Ramtha:

$$\text{Total cost} = \text{US\$}30{,}000 + \text{US\$}75(2{,}000) = \text{US\$}180{,}000$$

For Allan:

$$\text{Total cost} = \text{US\$}60{,}000 + \text{US\$}45(2{,}000) = \text{US\$}150{,}000$$

For Nahle:

$$\text{Total cost} = \text{US\$}110{,}000 + \text{US\$}25(2{,}000) = \text{US\$}160{,}000$$

LO4: Complete a locational break-even analysis graphically and mathematically

With an expected volume of 2,000 units per year, Allan provides the lowest cost location. The expected profit is:

$$\text{Total revenue} - \text{Total cost} = \text{US\$}120(2{,}000) - \text{US\$}150{,}000 = \text{US\$}90{,}000 \text{ per year}$$

The crossover point for Ramtha and Allan is:

$$30{,}000 + 75(x) = 60{,}000 + 45(x)$$
$$30(x) = 30{,}000$$
$$x = 1{,}000$$

and the crossover point for Allan and Nahle is:

$$60{,}000 + 45(x) = 110{,}000 + 25(x)$$
$$20(x) = 50{,}000$$
$$x = 2{,}500$$

INSIGHT ▶ As with every other OM model, locational break-even results can be sensitive to input data. For example, for a volume of less than 1,000, Ramtha would be preferred. For a volume greater than 2,500, Nahle would yield the greatest profit.

LEARNING EXERCISE ▶ The variable cost for Nahle is now expected to be US$22 per unit. What is the new crossover point between Allan and Nahle? [Answer: 2,174 units.]

RELATED PROBLEMS ▶ 8.8, 8.9

EXCEL OM Data File **Ch08Ex2.xls** can be found at MyOMLab.

Center-of-Gravity Method

Center-of-gravity method

A mathematical technique used for finding the best location for a single distribution point that services several stores or areas.

The **center-of-gravity method** is a mathematical technique used for finding the location of a distribution center that will minimize distribution costs. The method takes into account the location of markets, the volume of goods shipped to those markets, and shipping costs in finding the best location for a distribution center.

The first step in the center-of-gravity method is to place the locations on a coordinate system. This will be illustrated in Example 3. The origin of the coordinate system and the scale used are arbitrary, just as long as the relative distances are correctly represented. This can be done easily by placing a grid over an ordinary map. The center of gravity is determined using Equations (8-1) and (8-2):

$$x\text{-coordinate of the center of gravity} = \frac{\sum_i d_{ix} Q_i}{\sum_i Q_i} \tag{8-1}$$

$$y\text{-coordinate of the center of gravity} = \frac{\sum_i d_{iy} Q_i}{\sum_i Q_i} \tag{8-2}$$

LO5: Use the center-of-gravity method

where d_{ix} = x-coordinate of location i
d_{iy} = y-coordinate of location i
Q_i = Quantity of goods moved to or from location i

Note that Equations (8-1) and (8-2) include the term Q_i, the quantity of supplies transferred to or from location i.

Since the number of containers shipped each month affects cost, distance alone should not be the principal criterion. The center-of-gravity method assumes that cost is directly proportional to both distance and volume shipped. The ideal location is that which minimizes the weighted distance between the warehouse and its retail outlets, where the distance is weighted by the number of containers shipped.[3]

EXAMPLE 3 ▶

Center of gravity

Salma's Discount Department Stores, a chain of four large Target-type outlets in Jordan, has store locations in Amman, Ramtha, Zarqa, and Aqaba; they are currently being supplied out of an old and inadequate warehouse in Ramtha, the site of the chain's first store. The firm wants to find some 'central' location in which to build a new warehouse.

APPROACH ▶   Salma will apply the center-of-gravity method. It gathers data on demand rates at each outlet (see Table 8.5).

▶ TABLE 8.5

Demand for Salma's Discount Department Stores

Store Location	Number of Containers Shipped per Month
Amman	2,000
Ramtha	1,000
Zarqa	1,000
Aqaba	2,000

[3]Equations (8-1) and (8-2) compute a center of gravity (COG) under 'squared Euclidean' distances and may actually result in transportation costs slightly (less than 2 percent) higher than an *optimal* COG computed using 'Euclidean' (straight-line) distances. The latter, however, is a more complex and involved procedure mathematically, so the formulas we present are generally used as an attractive substitute. See C. Kuo and R. E. White, "A Note on the Treatment of the Center-of-Gravity Method in Operations Management Textbooks," *Decision Sciences Journal of Innovative Education* 2 (Fall 2004): 219–227.

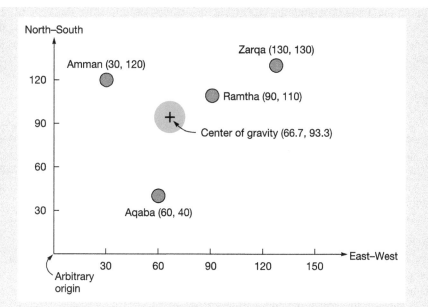

Its current store locations are shown in Figure 8.3. For example, location 1 is Amman, and from Table 8.5 and Figure 8.3, we have:

$$d_{1x} = 30$$
$$d_{1y} = 120$$
$$Q_1 = 2,000$$

SOLUTION ▶ Using the data in Table 8.5 and Figure 8.3 for each of the other cities, and Equations (8-1) and (8-2) we find:

x-coordinate of the center of gravity:

$$= \frac{(30)(2,000) + (90)(1,000) + (130)(1,000) + (60)(2,000)}{2,000 + 1,000 + 1,000 + 2,000} = \frac{400,000}{6,000}$$
$$= 66.7$$

y-coordinate of the center of gravity:

$$= \frac{(120)(2,000) + (110)(1,000) + (130)(1,000) + (40)(2,000)}{2,000 + 1,000 + 1,000 + 2,000} = \frac{560,000}{6,000}$$
$$= 93.3$$

This location (66.7, 93.3) is shown by the crosshairs in Figure 8.3.

INSIGHT ▶ By overlaying a map of Jordan on this exhibit, we find this location is near Madaba. The firm may well wish to consider Madaba, Maeen, or a nearby city as an appropriate location. But it is important to have the highways near the city selected to make delivery times quicker.

LEARNING EXERCISE ▶ The number of containers shipped per month to Aqaba is expected to grow quickly to 3,000. How does this change the center of gravity, and where should the new warehouse be located? [Answer: (65.7, 85.7), which is closer to Karak.]

RELATED PROBLEMS ▶ 8.10, 8.11

EXCEL OM Data File **Ch08Ex3.xls** can be found at MyOMLab

Transportation Model

The objective of the **transportation model** is to determine the best pattern of shipments from several points of supply (sources) to several points of demand (destinations) so as to minimize total production and transportation costs. Every firm with a network of supply-and-demand points faces such a problem.

Transportation model
A technique for solving a class of linear programming problems.

Although the linear programming (LP) technique can be used to solve this type of problem, more efficient, special-purpose algorithms have been developed for the transportation application. The transportation model finds an initial feasible solution and then makes step-by-step improvements until an optimal solution is reached.

AUTHOR COMMENT
Retail stores often attract more shoppers when competitors are close.

SERVICE LOCATION STRATEGY

While the focus in industrial-sector location analysis is on minimizing cost, the focus in the service sector is on maximizing revenue. This is because manufacturing firms find that costs tend to vary substantially among locations, while service firms find that location often has more impact on revenue than cost. Therefore, for the service firm, a specific location often influences revenue more than it does cost. This means that the location focus for service firms should be on determining the volume of business and revenue.

There are eight major determinants of volume and revenue for a service firm:

1. Purchasing power of the customer-drawing area
2. Service and image compatibility with demographics of the customer-drawing area
3. Competition in the area
4. Quality of the competition
5. Uniqueness of the firm's and competitors' locations
6. Physical qualities of facilities and neighboring businesses
7. Operating policies of the firm
8. Quality of management

Realistic analysis of these factors can provide a reasonable picture of the revenue expected. The techniques used in the service sector include correlation analysis, traffic counts, demographic analysis, purchasing power analysis, the factor-rating method, the center-of-gravity method, and geographic information systems. Table 8.6 provides a summary of location strategies for both service and goods-producing organizations.

▶ **TABLE 8.6**
Location Strategies—Service vs. Goods-Producing Organizations

SERVICE/RETAIL/PROFESSIONAL	GOODS-PRODUCING
Revenue Focus	**Cost Focus**

Volume/revenue
   Drawing area; purchasing power
   Competition; advertising/pricing
 Physical quality
   Parking/access; security/lighting;
     appearance/image
	Tangible costs
	   Transportation cost of raw material
	   Shipment cost of finished goods
	   Energy and utility cost; labor; raw
	     material; taxes, and so on

Cost determinants
   Rent
   Management caliber
   Operation policies (hours, wage rates)
	Intangible and future costs
	   Attitude toward union
	   Quality of life
	   Education expenditures by state
	   Quality of state and local government

Techniques	**Techniques**
Regression models to determine importance of various factors Factor-rating method Traffic counts Demographic analysis of drawing area Purchasing power analysis of area Center-of-gravity method Geographic information systems	Transportation method Factor-rating method Locational break-even analysis Crossover charts
Assumptions	**Assumptions**

Location is a major determinant of revenue
 High customer-contact issues are critical
 Costs are relatively constant for a given area;
   therefore, the revenue function is critical
	Location is a major determinant of cost
	 Most major costs can be identified explicitly
	   for each site
	 Low customer contact allows focus on the
	   identifiable costs
	 Intangible costs can be evaluated

AUTHOR COMMENT
This table helps differentiate between service- and manufacturing-sector decisions. Almost every aspect of the decision is different.

LO6: Understand the differences between service- and industrial-sector location analysis

How Hotel Chains Select Sites

One of the most important decisions in the hospitality industry is location. Hotel chains that pick good sites more accurately and quickly than competitors have a distinct strategic advantage. Hotel chains usually use statistical regression analysis to locate their next site. They start by testing all the different independent variables that would have an effect on profitability, the dependent variable. The aim is to find the variables with the highest correlation with profitability to build a regression model to provide a cutoff that will give the best results for predicting the success or failure of a site. A spreadsheet is then used to implement the model, which applies the decision rule and suggests 'build' or 'don't build.'

The Call Center Industry

Industries and office activities that require neither face-to-face contact with the customer nor movement of materials broaden location options substantially. A case in point is the call center industry, in which the traditional variables are no longer relevant. Where inexpensive fiber-optic phone lines are available, the cost and availability of labor may drive the location decision.

With the prevalence of globalization, international companies started hiring call center staff in low-wage countries like India and Egypt to deal with customer contact jobs, such as product support, hotel reservations, and bill collection. Egypt's highly educated, English-speaking workforce still attracts a large call center business in the Arab world due to its proximity to the culture of these organizations. On the global scale, India and Mexico are the main destinations of choice for European and American businesses due to the employees' similar education and in-depth knowledge of European and American popular culture. How to use quantitative techniques to locate call centers is discussed in detail in Supplement 11.

Geographic Information Systems

Geographic information systems are an important tool to help firms make successful, analytical decisions with regard to location. A **geographic information system (GIS)** stores and displays information that can be linked to a geographical location. For instance, retailers, banks, food chains, gas stations, and print shop franchises can all use geographically coded files from a GIS to conduct demographic analyses. By combining population, age, income, traffic flow, and density figures with geography, a retailer can pinpoint the best location for a new store or restaurant.

Here are some of the geographic databases available in many GISs.

- Census data by block, tract, city, county, congressional district, metropolitan area, state, zip code
- Maps of every street, highway, bridge, and tunnel in the United States.
- Utilities such as electrical, water, and gas lines
- All rivers, mountains, lakes, forests
- All major airports, colleges, hospitals

For example, airlines use GISs to identify airports where ground services are the most effective. This information is then used to help schedule and to decide where to purchase fuel, meals, and other services.

Commercial office building developers use GISs in the selection of cities for future construction. Building new office space takes several years so developers value the database approach that a GIS can offer. GIS is used to analyze factors that influence the location decisions by addressing five elements for each city: (1) residential areas; (2) retail shops; (3) cultural and entertainment centers; (4) crime incidence; (5) transportation options.

The *Video Case Study* 'Locating the Next Red Lobster Restaurant' that appears at the end of this chapter describes how that chain uses its GIS to define trade areas based on market size and population density.

Geographic information system (GIS)
A system that stores and displays information that can be linked to a geographic location.

VIDEO 8.2
Locating the Next Red Lobster Restaurant

Geographic information systems (GISs) are used by a variety of firms to identify target markets by income, ethnicity, product use, age, etc. Here, data from StreatPro helps with competitive analysis.

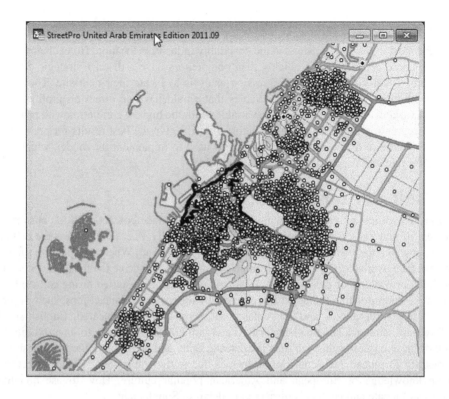

CHAPTER SUMMARY

Location may determine up to 50 percent of operating expense. Location is also a critical element in determining revenue for the service, retail, or professional firm. Industrial firms need to consider both tangible and intangible costs. Industrial location problems are typically addressed via a factor-rating method, locational break-even analysis, the center-of-gravity method, and the transportation method of linear programming.

For service, retail, and professional organizations, analysis is typically made of a variety of variables including purchasing power of a drawing area, competition, advertising and promotion, physical qualities of the location, and operating policies of the organization.

Key Terms

Center-of-gravity method (p. 246)
Clustering (p. 242)
Factor-rating method (p. 243)

Geographic information
system (GIS) (p. 249)
Intangible costs (p. 240)

Locational break-even analysis (p. 244)
Tangible costs (p. 240)
Transportation model (p. 247)

Ethical Dilemma

In this chapter, we have discussed a number of location decisions. Consider another: A European company announced its competition to select an Arab world location for a new multibillion-Euro aircraft-repair base. The bidding for the prize of 7,500 jobs paying at least €25 per hour was fast, with Egypt offering 100 percent tax-free earnings for the first 5 years as an incentive and Sudan offering the same percentage for 10 years. Syria also offered 100 percent for 10 years and zero import duties on the components, while Marrakech, in Morocco, made a similar offer with free land for the project.

When the European company finally selected from among the countries bidding on the base, the winner was Marrakech. But in 2008, with the company near bankruptcy due to the global financial crisis, and having fulfilled its legal obligation, it walked away from the massive project. This left Marrakech and its government out of pocket, with no new tenant in sight. The city now even owns the tools, neatly arranged in each of the 20 elaborately equipped construction sites. The company outsourced its maintenance to mechanics at a European city (which pays one-third of what the company gave out in salary and benefits in Marrakech).

What are the ethical, legal, and economic implications of such location bidding wars? Who pays for such giveaways? Are local citizens allowed to vote on offers made by their cities, counties, or states? Should there be limits on these incentives?

Discussion Questions

1. How is Aramex's location a competitive advantage? Discuss.
2. Why do so many international firms build facilities in other countries?
3. Why do so many foreign companies build facilities in the Arab world?
4. What is clustering?
5. How does factor weighting incorporate personal preference in location choices?
6. What are the advantages and disadvantages of a qualitative (as opposed to a quantitative) approach to location decision making?
7. Provide two examples of clustering in the service sector.
8. What are the major factors that firms consider when choosing a country in which to locate?
9. What factors affect region/community location decisions?
10. Although most organizations may make the location decision infrequently, there are some organizations that make the decision quite regularly and often. Provide one or two examples. How might their approach to the location decision differ from the norm?
11. List factors, other than globalization, that affect the location decision.
12. Explain the assumptions behind the center-of-gravity method. How can the model be used in a service facility location?
13. What are the three steps to locational break-even analysis?
14. "Manufacturers locate near their resources, retailers locate near their customers." Discuss this statement, with reference to the proximity-to-markets arguments covered in the text. Can you think of a counterexample in each case? Support your choices.
15. Why shouldn't low wage rates alone be sufficient to select a location?
16. List the techniques used by service organizations to select locations.
17. Contrast the location of a food distributor and a supermarket. (The distributor sends truckloads of food, meat, produce, etc., to the supermarket.) Show the relevant considerations (factors) they share; show those where they differ.

Using Software to Solve Location Problems

This section presents three ways to solve location problems with computer software. First, you can create your own spreadsheets to compute factor ratings, the center of gravity, and break-even analysis. Second, Excel OM (free with your text) is programmed to solve all three models. Third, POM for Windows is also found at MyOMLab and can solve all problems labelled with a P.

Creating Your Own Excel Spreadsheets

Excel (and other spreadsheets) are easily developed to solve most of the problems in this chapter. We do not provide an example here, but you can see from Program 8.1 how the formulas are created.

✗ Using Excel OM

Excel OM may be used to solve Example 1 (with the Factor Rating module), Example 2 (with the Break-Even Analysis module), and Example 3 (with the Center-of-Gravity module), as well as other location problems. To illustrate the factor-rating method, consider the case of Marah Land (Example 1), which wishes to expand its corporate presence to Europe. Program 8.1 provides the data inputs for five important factors, including their weights, and ratings on a 1–100 scale (where 100 is the highest rating) for each country. As we see, France is more highly rated, with a 70.4 score versus 68.0 for Denmark.

▶ **PROGRAM 8.1**

Excel OM's Factor Rating
Module, Including Inputs,
Selected Formulas, and
Outputs Using Marah Land
Data in Example 1

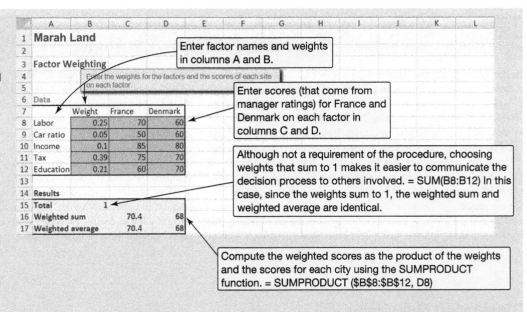

Using POM for Windows

POM for Windows also includes three different facility location models: the factor-rating method, the center-of-gravity model, and locational break-even analysis. For details, refer to Appendix IV.

Solved Problems   Virtual Office Hours help is available at MyOMLab

▼ SOLVED PROBLEM 8.1

Just as cities and communities can be compared for location selection by the weighted approach model, as we saw earlier in this chapter, so can actual site decisions within those cities. Table 8.7 illustrates four factors of importance to Washington, DC, and the health officials charged with opening that city's first public drug treatment clinic. Of primary concern (and given a weight of 5) was location of the clinic so it would be as accessible as possible to the largest number of patients. Due to a tight budget, the annual lease cost was also of some concern. A suite in the city hall, at 14th and U Streets, was highly rated because its rent would be free. An old office building near the downtown bus station received a much lower rating because of its cost. Equally important as lease

cost was the need for confidentiality of patients and, therefore, for a relatively inconspicuous clinic. Finally, because so many of the staff at the clinic would be donating their time, the safety, parking, and accessibility of each site were of concern as well.

Using the factor-rating method, which site is preferred?

▼ SOLUTION

In the three rightmost columns in Table 8.7, the weighted scores are summed. The bus terminal area has a low score and can be excluded from further consideration. The other two sites are virtually identical in total score. The city may now want to consider other factors, including political ones, in selecting between the two remaining sites.

▼ TABLE 8.7

Potential Clinic Sites in Damascus

		Potential Locations[a]			*Weighted Scores*		
Factor	**Importance Weight**	**Homeless Shelter (2nd and D, SE)**	**City Hall (14th and U, NW)**	**Bus Terminal Area (7th and H, NW)**	**Homeless Shelter**	**City Hall**	**Bus Terminal Area**
Accessibility for addicts	5	9	7	7	45	35	35
Annual lease cost	3	6	10	3	18	30	9
Inconspicuous	3	5	2	7	15	6	21
Accessibility for health staff	2	3	6	2	6	12	4
				Total scores:	84	83	69

[a]All sites are rated on a 1 to 10 basis, with 10 as the highest score and 1 as the lowest.

▼ SOLVED PROBLEM 8.2

Ching-Chang Kau is considering opening a new foundry in Denton, Texas; Edwardsville, Illinois; or Fayetteville, Arkansas, to produce high-quality rifle sights. He has assembled the following fixed-cost and variable-cost data:

		Per-Unit Costs		
Location	**Fixed Cost per Year**	**Material**	**Variable Labor**	**Overhead**
Denton	US$200,000	US$0.20	US$0.40	US$0.40
Edwardsville	US$180,000	US$0.25	US$0.75	US$0.75
Fayetteville	US$170,000	US$1.00	US$1.00	US$1.00

a) Graph the total cost lines.
b) Over what range of annual volume is each facility going to have a competitive advantage?
c) What is the volume at the intersection of the Edwardsville and Fayetteville cost lines?

▼ SOLUTION

(a) A graph of the total cost lines is shown in Figure 8.4.
(b) Below 8,000 units, the Fayetteville facility will have a competitive advantage (lowest cost); between 8,000 units and 26,666 units, Edwardsville has an advantage; and above 26,666, Denton has the advantage. (We have made the assumption in this problem that other costs—that is, delivery and intangible factors—are constant regardless of the decision.)
(c) From Figure 8.4, we see that the cost line for Edwardsville and the cost line for Fayetteville cross at about 8,000. We can also determine this point with a little algebra:

$$US\$180,000 + 1.75Q = US\$170,000 + 3.00Q$$
$$US\$10,000 = 1.25Q$$
$$8,000 = Q$$

▶ **FIGURE 8.4**
Graph of Total Cost Lines for Ching-Chang Kau

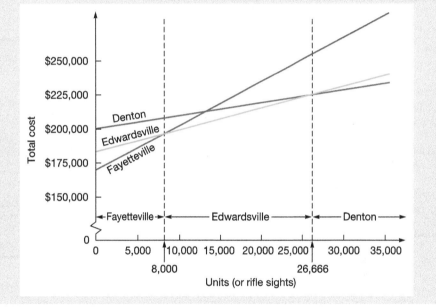

Problems*

•• **8.1** You have been asked to analyze the bids for 200 polished disks used in solar panels. These bids have been submitted by three suppliers: Egypt Polishing, Syria Shine, and American Glow. Egypt Polishing has submitted a bid of EGP 2,000. Syria Shine has submitted a bid of SYP 2,000. American Glow has submitted a bid of US$200. You check with your local bank and find that US$1 = EGP 10 and US$1 = SYP 8. Which company should you choose?

• **8.2** Refer to Problem 8.1. If the final destination is Damascus, Syria, and there is a 30 percent import tax, which firm should you choose?

•• **8.3** Subway is planning for a new restaurant in Muscat, Oman. Three locations are being considered. The following table gives the factors for each site.

*Note: ▶✕ means the problem may be solved with POM for Windows and/or Excel OM.

Factor	Weight	Downtown	Dahiya	Muala
Space	0.30	60	70	80
Costs	0.25	40	80	30
Traffic density	0.20	50	80	60
Neighborhood income	0.15	50	70	40
Zoning laws	0.10	80	20	90

a) At which site should Subway open the new restaurant?
b) If the weights for Space and Traffic density are reversed, how would this affect the decision? ▶✕

•• **8.4** Insurance Company of Arabia (ICA) is considering opening an office in U.A.E. The two cities under consideration are Dubai and Abu Dhabi. The factor ratings (higher scores are better) for the two cities are given in the following table. In which city should ICA locate?

Factor	Weight	Dubai	Abu Dhabi
Customer convenience	0.25	70	80
Bank accessibility	0.20	40	90
Computer support	0.20	85	75
Rental costs	0.15	90	55
Labor costs	0.10	80	50
Taxes	0.10	90	50 **Px**

•• **8.5** A location analysis for Taj Controls, a small manufacturer of parts for high-technology cable systems in Egypt, has been narrowed down to four locations. Taj will need to train assemblers, testers, and robotics maintainers in local training centers. Alia Taj, the president, has asked each potential site to offer training programs, tax breaks, and other industrial incentives. The critical factors, their weights, and the ratings for each location are shown in the following table. High scores represent favorable values.

Factor	Weight	Location Alexandria	Location Cairo	Location Mansoura	Location Sharm
Labor availability	0.15	90	80	90	80
Technical school quality	0.10	95	75	65	85
Operating cost	0.30	80	85	95	85
Land and construction cost	0.15	60	80	90	70
Industrial incentives	0.20	90	75	85	60
Labor cost	0.10	75	80	85	75

a) Compute the composite (weighted average) rating for each location.
b) Which site would you choose?
c) Would you reach the same conclusion if the weights for operating cost and labor cost were reversed? Recompute as necessary and explain. **Px**

•• **8.6** A company is planning on expanding and building a new plant in one of three Middle Eastern countries. Jamal Sulaim, the manager charged with making the decision, has determined that five key success factors can be used to evaluate the prospective countries. Sulaim used a rating system of 1 (least desirable country) to 5 (most desirable) to evaluate each factor.

Key Success Factors	Weight	Candidate Country Ratings Lebanon	Candidate Country Ratings Egypt	Candidate Country Ratings Jordan
Technology	0.2	4	5	1
Level of education	0.1	4	1	5
Political and legal aspects	0.4	1	3	3
Social and cultural aspects	0.1	4	2	3
Economic factors	0.2	3	3	2

a) Which country should be selected for the new plant?
b) Political unrest in Lebanon results in a lower score, 2, for Political and legal aspects. Does your conclusion change?
c) What if Lebanon's score drops even further, to a 1, for Political and legal aspects? **Px**

•• **8.7** Salam Fadeel, owner of Fadeel Manufacturing, must expand by building a new factory. The search for a location for this factory has been narrowed to four sites: A, B, C, or D. The following table shows the results thus far obtained by Salam by using the factor-rating method to analyze the problem. The scale used for each factor scoring is 1 through 5.

Factor	Weight	Site Scores A	Site Scores B	Site Scores C	Site Scores D
Quality of labor	10	5	4	4	5
Construction cost	8	2	3	4	1
Transportation costs	8	3	4	3	2
Proximity to markets	7	5	3	4	4
Taxes	6	2	3	3	4
Weather	6	2	5	5	4
Energy costs	5	5	4	3	3

a) Which site should Salam choose?
b) If site D's score for Energy costs increases from a 3 to a 5, do results change?
c) If site A's Weather score is adjusted to a 4, what is the impact? What should Salam do at this point? **Px**

•• **8.8** The fixed and variable costs for three potential manufacturing plant sites for a rattan chair weaver are shown:

Site	Fixed Cost per Year	Variable Cost per Unit
1	US$500	US$11
2	1,000	7
3	1,700	4

a) Over what range of production is each location optimal?
b) For a production of 200 units, which site is best? **Px**

••• **8.9** Audi Motors is considering three sites—A, B, and C—at which to locate a factory to build its new-model automobile, the Audi SUV XL500. The goal is to locate at a minimum-cost site, where cost is measured by the annual fixed plus variable costs of production. Audi Motors has gathered the following data:

Site	Annualized Fixed Cost	Variable Cost per Auto Produced
A	US$10,000,000	US$2,500
B	US$20,000,000	US$2,000
C	US$25,000,000	US$1,000

The firm knows it will produce between 0 and 60,000 SUV XL500s at the new plant each year, but, thus far, that is the extent of its knowledge about production plans.

a) For what values of volume, V, of production, if any, is site C a recommended site?
b) What volume indicates site A is optimal?
c) Over what range of volume is site B optimal? Why? **Px**

•• **8.10** The following table gives the map coordinates and the shipping loads for a set of cities that we wish to connect through a central hub.

City	Map Coordinate (x, y)	Shipping Load
A	(5, 10)	5
B	(6, 8)	10
C	(4, 9)	15
D	(9, 5)	5
E	(7, 9)	15
F	(3, 2)	10
G	(2, 6)	5

a) Near which map coordinates should the hub be located?
b) If the shipments from city A triple, how does this change the coordinates? **P✗**

•• **8.11** Omar's Video, a major video rental and TV sales chain headquartered in Kuwait, is about to open its first outlet in Amman, Jordan, and wants to select a site that will place the new outlet in the center of Amman's population base. Omar examines the seven administrative areas in Amman, plots the coordinates of the center of each from a map, and looks up the population base in each to use as a weighting. The information gathered appears in the following table.

Administrative Areas	Population in Census Tract	X, Y Map Coordinates
101	2,000	(25, 45)
102	5,000	(25, 25)
103	10,000	(55, 45)
104	7,000	(50, 20)
105	10,000	(80, 50)
106	20,000	(70, 20)
107	14,000	(90, 25)

a) At what center-of-gravity coordinates should the new store be located?
b) Administrative areas 103 and 105 are each projected to grow by 20 percent in the next year. How will this influence the new store's coordinates? **P✗**

▶ **Refer to** MyOMLab **for additional homework problems.**

Case Studies

▶ Finding a Location for Electronics Component Manufacturing in Asia

ACM is an electronics component manufacturer that has been located in Singapore since 1991, supplying original equipment manufacturers (OEMs) with quality components. In the past several years, ACM has experienced increasing pressure from other manufacturers located in other countries. In Singapore, while labor remains quite inexpensive, there has been a relatively steady increase in labor costs. In addition, utility costs—most notably water and energy costs—have led the firm to contemplate moving operations elsewhere in Asia in an attempt to make the firm more competitive. ACM remains profitable, but margins have shrunk, and management is interested in ensuring that the firm remains competitive in the medium term to long term against other component manufacturers.

A team of senior management has formed a committee to reach a decision regarding possible relocation. The committee has identified two additional locations as possible candidates for relocation: Hong Kong (People's Republic of China, PRC) and Kuching (Malaysia). Hong Kong's main attractions stem from the fact that since 1997, when its sovereignty was transferred back to the PRC, labor costs have decreased as access to labor has increased. Hong Kong enjoys a large seaport and very good transportation infrastructure, and this is important in moving in raw materials and moving out finished components to customers. Presently, the customers are geographically dispersed, making access to a seaport very important in delivering products to customers. Senior management believes that an increasing number of OEMs will move to the PRC in the next several years, as has been the case in the past decade. This will only increase the attractiveness of locating the manufacturing facility in Hong Kong.

Kuching is located in the Malaysian province of Sarawak, on the island of Borneo. It is the fourth-largest city in Malaysia and home to a population of around 650,000. Several points make Kuching attractive to the relocation committee. First, locating here

would give access to natural resources and other production inputs. Second, the transportation infrastructure is good, and the city hosts a deep seaport for moving raw materials in and finished goods out. That said, the port is not as large or accessible as those of Hong Kong or Singapore, and several committee members have expressed concern about the frequency of ship visits to Kuching. If the port does not receive regular service from container ships, transportation costs to ship components to OEMs will undoubtedly increase. Finally, another selling point is that labor is relatively stable and inexpensive in Malaysia.

The committee has contacted the government of Singapore to elicit possible incentives to not relocate to another country. Singapore is offering a 5-year exemption on taxes for ACM if the plant remains in Singapore. The government will also assist by partially subsidizing labor, water, and energy costs for 5 years. Committee members realize that the Singapore plant, which has been operating for years, has already been amortized, and opening a new plant would require additional capital costs. That said, opening a new factory would also provide an opportunity to upgrade production equipment to more productive and energy-efficient alternatives.

Discussion Questions

1. What advantages and disadvantages does each potential location offer?
2. What other relevant factors that are not mentioned in this case study might play a role in this decision?
3. Why is transportation infrastructure so important in this decision?
4. This is a long-term, strategic decision; what factors might change in the next 10 to 20 years? How will this influence the decision?
5. Which alternative would you recommend, under which circumstances?

Source: Dr. Ian M. Langella, Shippensburg University, United States.

▶ Where to Place the Hard Rock Cafe

Some people would say that Oliver Munday, Hard Rock's vice president for café development, has the best job in the world. Travel the world to pick a country for Hard Rock's next café, select a city, and find the ideal site. It's true that selecting a site involves lots of incognito walking around, visiting nice restaurants, and drinking in bars. But that is not where Mr. Munday's work begins, nor where it ends. At the front end, selecting the country and city first involves a great deal of research. At the back end, Munday not only picks the final site and negotiates the deal but then works with architects and planners and stays with the project through the opening and first year's sales.

Munday is currently looking heavily into global expansion in Europe, Latin America, and Asia. "We've got to look at political risk, currency, and social norms—how our brand fits into the country," he says. Once the country is selected, Munday focuses on the region and city. His research checklist is extensive:

Site location now tends to focus on the tremendous resurgence of city centers, where nightlife tends to concentrate. That's what Munday selected in Moscow and Bogota, although in both locations

Hard Rock's Standard Market Report (for offshore sites)
A. Demographics (local, city, region, SMSA), with trend analysis
  1. Population of area
  2. Economic indicators
B. Visitor market, with trend analysis
  1. Tourists/business visitors
  2. Hotels
  3. Convention center
  4. Entertainment
  5. Sports
  6. Retail
C. Transportation
  1. Airport
  2. Rail
  3. Road
  4. Sea/river
D. Restaurants and nightclubs (a selection in key target market areas)
E. Political risk
F. Real estate market
G. Hard Rock Cafe comparable market analysis

subcategories include:
(a) age of airport
(b) no. of passengers
(c) airlines
(d) direct flights
(e) hubs

he chose to find a local partner and franchise the operation. In these two political environments, "Hard Rock wouldn't dream of operating by ourselves," says Munday. The location decision also is at least a 10- to 15-year commitment by Hard Rock, which employs tools such as break-even analysis to help decide whether to purchase land and build, or to remodel an existing facility.

Currently, Munday is considering four European cities for Hard Rock's next expansion. Although he could not provide the names, for competitive reasons, the following is known:

Factor	European City under Consideration				Importance of This Factor at This Time
	A	B	C	D	
A. Demographics	70	70	60	90	20
B. Visitor market	80	60	90	75	20
C. Transportation	100	50	75	90	20
D. Restaurants/ nightclubs	80	90	65	65	10
E. Low political risk	90	60	50	70	10
F. Real estate market	65	75	85	70	10
G. Comparable market analysis	70	60	65	80	10

Discussion Questions*

1. From Munday's Standard Market Report checklist, select any other four categories, such as population (A1), hotels (B2), or restaurants/nightclubs (D), and provide three subcategories that should be evaluated. (See item C1 (airport) for a guide.)
2. Which is the highest rated of the four European cities under consideration, using the table above?
3. Why does Hard Rock put such serious effort into its location analysis?
4. Under what conditions do you think Hard Rock prefers to franchise a café?

*You may wish to view the video that accompanies this case before answering the questions.

▶ Locating the Next Red Lobster Restaurant

From its first Red Lobster in 1968, Darden Restaurants has grown the chain to 690 locations, with over US$2.6 billion in U.S. sales annually. The casual dining market may be crowded, with competitors such as Chili's, Ruby Tuesday, Applebee's, TGI Friday's, and Outback, but Darden's continuing success means the chain thinks there is still plenty of room to grow. Robert Reiner, director of market development, is charged with identifying the sites that will maximize new store sales without cannibalizing sales at the existing Red Lobster locations.

Characteristics for identifying a good site have not changed in 40 years; they still include real estate prices, customer age, competition, ethnicity, income, family size, population density, nearby hotels, and buying behavior, to name just a few. What *has* changed is the powerful software that allows Reiner to analyze a new site in

5 minutes, as opposed to the 8 hours he spent just a few years ago.

Darden has partnered with MapInfo Corp., whose geographic information system (GIS) contains a powerful module for analyzing a trade area (see the discussion of GIS in the chapter). With the United States geo-coded down to the individual block, MapInfo allows Reiner to create a psychographic profile of existing and potential Red Lobster trade areas. "We can now target areas with greatest sales potential," says Reiner.

The United States is segmented into 72 'clusters' of customer profiles by MapInfo. If, for example, cluster #7, Equestrian Heights (see MapInfo description below), represents 1.7 percent of a household base within a Red Lobster trade area, but this segment also accounts for 2.4 percent of sales, Reiner computes that this

Cluster	PSYTE 2003	Snap Shot Description
7	Equestrian Heights	They may not have a stallion in the barn, but they likely pass a corral on the way home. These families with teens live in older, larger homes adjacent to, or between, suburbs but not usually tract housing. Most are married with teenagers, but 40 percent are empty nesters. They use their graduate and professional school education—56 percent are dual earners. Over 90 percent are white, non-Hispanic. Their mean family income is US$99,000, and they live within commuting distance of central cities. They have white-collar jobs during the week but require a riding lawn mower to maintain their gardens on weekends.

segment is effectively spending 1.39 times more than average (Index = 2.4 ÷ 1.7) and adjusts his analysis of a new site to reflect this added weight.

When Reiner maps the United States, a state, or a region for a new site, he wants one that is at least 3 miles from the nearest Red Lobster and won't negatively impact its sales by more than 8 percent; MapInfo pinpoints the best spot. The software also recognizes the nearness of non-Darden competition and assigns a probability of success (as measured by reaching sales potential).

The specific spot selected depends on Darden's seven real estate brokers, whose list of considerations include proximity to a vibrant retail area, proximity to a freeway, road visibility, nearby hotels, and a corner location at a primary intersection.

"Picking a new Red Lobster location is one of the most critical functions we can do at Darden," says Reiner. "And the software we use serves as an independent voice in assessing the quality of an existing or proposed location."

Discussion Questions*

1. Visit the website for MapInfo (**www.mapinfo.com**). Describe the psychological profiling (PSYTE) clustering system. Select an industry, other than restaurants, and explain how the software can be used for that industry.
2. What are the major differences in site location for a restaurant vs. a retail store vs. a manufacturing plant?
3. Red Lobster also defines its trade areas based on market size and population density. Here are its seven density classes:

Density Class	Description	Households per Sq. Mile
1	Super Urban	8,000+
2	Urban	4,000–7,999
3	Light Urban	2,000–3,999
4	First Tier Suburban	1,000–1,999
5	Second Tier Suburban	600–999
6	Exurban/Small	100–599
7	Rural	0–99

Note: Density classes are based on the households and land area within 3 miles of the geography (e.g. census tract) using population-weighted centroids.

Ninety-two percent of the Red Lobster restaurants fall into three of these classes. Which three classes do you think the chain has the most restaurants in? Why?

*You may wish to view the video that accompanies this case before answering the questions.

▶**Additional Case Study:** Visit MyOMLab *for this free case study:* **Ojaman University (E)**:
The university faces three choices where to locate its basketball arena.

Chapter 8 *Rapid* Review

MyOMLab

Main Heading	Review Material	
THE STRATEGIC IMPORTANCE OF LOCATION (pp. 238–239)	Location has a major impact on the overall risk and profit of the company. Transportation costs alone can total as much as 25 percent of the product's selling price. When all costs are considered, location may alter total operating expenses as much as 50 percent. Companies make location decisions relatively infrequently, usually because demand has outgrown the current plant's capacity or because of changes in labor productivity, exchange rates, costs, or local attitudes. Companies may also relocate their manufacturing or service facilities because of shifts in demographics and customer demand. Location options include: (1) expanding an existing facility instead of moving; (2) maintaining current sites while adding another facility elsewhere; (3) closing the existing facility and moving to another location. For industrial location decisions, the location strategy is usually minimizing costs. For retail and professional service organizations, the strategy focuses on maximizing revenue. Warehouse location strategy may be driven by a combination of cost and speed of delivery. *The objective of location strategy is to maximize the benefit of location to the firm.* When innovation is the focus, overall competitiveness and innovation are affected by: (1) the presence of high-quality and specialized inputs such as scientific and technical talent; (2) an environment that encourages investment and intense local rivalry; (3) pressure and insight gained from a sophisticated local market; (4) local presence of related and supporting industries.	**VIDEO 8.1** Where to Place the Hard Rock Cafe
FACTORS THAT AFFECT LOCATION DECISIONS (pp. 239–243)	Globalization has taken place because of the development of: (1) market economics; (2) better international communications; (3) more rapid, reliable travel and shipping; (4) ease of capital flow between countries; (5) large differences in labor costs. Labor cost per unit is sometimes called the *labor content* of the product: Labor cost per unit = Labor cost per day ÷ Production (that is, units per day) Sometimes firms can take advantage of a particularly favorable exchange rate by relocating or exporting to (or importing from) a foreign country. ■ **Tangible costs**—Readily identifiable costs that can be measured with some precision. ■ **Intangible costs**—A category of location costs that cannot be easily quantified, such as quality of life and government. Many service organizations find that proximity to market is *the* primary location factor. Firms locate near their raw materials and suppliers because of: (1) perishability; (2) transportation costs; (3) bulk. ■ **Clustering**—Location of competing companies near each other, often because of a critical mass of information, talent, venture capital, or natural resources.	Problems: 8.1–8.2
METHODS OF EVALUATING LOCATION ALTERNATIVES (pp. 243–248)	■ **Factor-rating method**—A location method that instills objectivity into the process of identifying hard-to-evaluate costs. The six steps of the factor-rating method are: 1. Develop a list of relevant factors called *key success factors*. 2. Assign a weight to each factor to reflect its relative importance in the company's objectives. 3. Develop a scale for each factor (for example, 1 to 10 or 1 to 100 points). 4. Have management score each location for each factor, using the scale in step 3. 5. Multiply the score by the weight for each factor and total the score for each location. 6. Make a recommendation based on the maximum point score, considering the results of other quantitative approaches as well. ■ **Locational break-even analysis**—A cost–volume analysis used to make an economic comparison of location alternatives. The three steps to locational break-even analysis are: 1. Determine the fixed and variable cost for each location. 2. Plot the costs for each location, with costs on the vertical axis of the graph and annual volume on the horizontal axis. 3. Select the location that has the lowest total cost for the expected production volume. ■ **Center-of-gravity method**—A mathematical technique used for finding the best location for a single distribution point that services several stores or areas.	Problems: 8.3–8.11 Virtual Office Hours for Solved Problems: 8.1, 8.2

Main Heading	Review Material	MyOMLab

The center-of-gravity method chooses the ideal location that minimizes the *weighted* distance between itself and the locations it serves, where the distance is weighted by the number of containers shipped, Q_i:

$$x\text{-coordinate of the center of gravity} = \frac{\sum_i d_{ix} Q_i}{\sum_i Q_i} \qquad (8\text{-}1)$$

$$y\text{-coordinate of the center of gravity} = \frac{\sum_i d_{iy} Q_i}{\sum_i Q_i} \qquad (8\text{-}2)$$

■ **Transportation model**—A technique for solving a class of linear programming problems.

The transportation model determines the best pattern of shipments from several points of supply to several points of demand in order to minimize total production and transportation costs.

SERVICE LOCATION STRATEGY
(pp. 248–250)

The eight major determinants of volume and revenue for the service firm are:

1. Purchasing power of the customer-drawing area
2. Service and image compatibility with demographics of the customer-drawing area
3. Competition in the area
4. Quality of the competition
5. Uniqueness of the firm's and competitors' locations
6. Physical qualities of facilities and neighboring businesses
7. Operating policies of the firm
8. Quality of management

■ **Geographic information system (GIS)**—A system that stores and displays information that can be linked to a geographic location.

Some of the geographic databases available in many GISs include: (1) census data by block, tract, city, county, congressional district, metropolitan area, state, and zip code; (2) maps of every street, highway, bridge, and tunnel in the United States; (3) utilities such as electrical, water, and gas lines; (4) all rivers, mountains, lakes, and forests; (5) all major airports, colleges, and hospitals.

VIDEO 8.2
Locating the Next Red Lobster Restaurant

Self-Test

■ **Before taking the self-test,** refer to the learning objectives listed at the beginning of the chapter and the key terms listed at the end of the chapter.

LO1. The factors involved in location decisions include:
 a) foreign exchange
 b) attitudes
 c) labor productivity
 d) all of the above.

LO2. If Ali Tech pays US$30 per day to a worker in its Mansoura, Egypt, plant, and the employee completes four instruments per 8-hour day, the labor cost/unit is:
 a) US$30.00
 b) US$3.75
 c) US$7.50
 d) US$4.00
 e) US$8.00.

LO3. Evaluating location alternatives by comparing their composite (weighted-average) scores involves:
 a) factor-rating analysis
 b) cost–volume analysis
 c) transportation model analysis
 d) linear regression analysis
 e) crossover analysis.

LO4. On the crossover chart where the costs of two or more location alternatives have been plotted, the quantity at which two cost curves cross is the quantity at which:

 a) fixed costs are equal for two alternative locations
 b) variable costs are equal for two alternative locations
 c) total costs are equal for all alternative locations
 d) fixed costs equal variable costs for one location
 e) total costs are equal for two alternative locations.

LO5. A regional bookstore chain is about to build a distribution center that is centrally located for its eight retail outlets. It will most likely employ which of the following tools of analysis?
 a) Assembly-line balancing
 b) Load–distance analysis
 c) Center-of-gravity model
 d) Linear programming
 e) All of the above.

LO6. What is the major difference in focus between location decisions in the service sector and in the manufacturing sector?
 a) There is no difference in focus
 b) The focus in manufacturing is revenue maximization, while the focus in service is cost minimization
 c) The focus in service is revenue maximization, while the focus in manufacturing is cost minimization
 d) The focus in manufacturing is on raw materials, while the focus in service is on labor.

Answers: LO1. d; LO2. c; LO3. a; LO4. e; LO5. c; LO6. c.

9

Layout Decisions

10

OM STRATEGY DECISIONS

- ► Design of Goods and Services
- ► Managing Quality
- ► Process Strategy
- ► Location Strategies
- ► Layout Strategies
- ► Human Resources
- ► Supply-Chain Management
- ► Inventory Management
- ► Scheduling
- ► Maintenance

McDONALD'S LOOKS FOR COMPETITIVE ADVANTAGE THROUGH LAYOUT

In its half-century of existence, McDonald's revolutionized the restaurant industry by inventing the limited-menu fast-food restaurant. It has also made seven major innovations. The first, the introduction of *indoor seating* (1950s), was a layout issue, as was the second, *drive-thru windows* (1970s). The third, adding *breakfasts* to the menu (1980s), was a product strategy. The fourth, *adding play areas* (late 1980s), was again a layout decision.

In the 1990s, McDonald's completed its fifth innovation, a radically new *redesign of the kitchens* in its outlets to facilitate a mass customization process. Dubbed the 'Made by You' kitchen system, sandwiches were assembled to order with the revamped layout.

In 2004, the chain began the rollout of its sixth innovation, a new food ordering layout: the *self-service kiosk*. Kiosks take up less space than an employee and reduce waiting line time. Now, McDonald's is working on its seventh innovation, and not surprisingly, it also deals with restaurant layout. The company, on an unprecedented scale, is redesigning all 30,000 eateries around the globe to take on a *21st century look*. The dining area will be separated into three sections with distinct personalities: (1) the 'linger' zone focuses on young adults and offers comfortable furniture and Wi-Fi connections; (2) the 'grab and go' zone features tall counters, bar stools, and plasma TVs; (3) the 'flexible' zone has colorful family booths, flexible seating, and child-oriented music. The cost per outlet: a whopping US$300,000–US$400,000 renovation fee.

As McDonald's has discovered, facility layout is indeed a source of competitive advantage.

Due to the global approach of McDonald's, their brand should be familiar to the customer in local terms; here the brand name is written in Arabic in one of their branches in Dubai.

McDonald's understand the different needs of their customers and this dictates the design of their service areas, such as this playground for children accompanying their parents to the restaurant.

This attractive seating area at one of the McDonald's branches makes it welcoming for people wanting to hang out and socialize.

Chapter 9 Learning Objectives

THE STRATEGIC IMPORTANCE OF LAYOUT DECISIONS

Layout has numerous strategic implications because it establishes an organization's competitive priorities in regard to capacity, processes, flexibility, and cost, as well as quality of work life, customer contact, and image. An effective layout can help an organization achieve a strategy that supports differentiation, low cost, or response. This can be done through a layout design that aims at achieving:

- higher utilization of space, equipment, and people
- improved flow of information, materials, or people
- improved employee morale and safer working conditions
- improved customer/client interaction
- flexibility (whatever the layout is now, it will need to change).

In our increasingly short-life-cycle, mass-customized world, layout designs need to be viewed as dynamic. This means considering small, movable, and flexible equipment. Store displays need to be movable, office desks and partitions modular, and warehouse racks prefabricated. To make quick and easy changes in product models and in production rates, operations managers must design flexibility into layouts. To obtain flexibility in layout, managers cross-train their workers, maintain equipment, keep investments low, place workstations close together, and use small, movable equipment. In some cases, equipment on wheels is appropriate, in anticipation of the next change in product, process, or volume.

TYPES OF LAYOUT

Layout decisions include the best placement of machines (in production settings), offices and desks (in office settings), or service centers (in settings such as hospitals or department stores). An effective layout facilitates the flow of materials, people, and information within and between areas. To achieve these objectives, a variety of approaches have been developed. We will discuss seven of them in this chapter.

1. *Office layout:* Positions workers, their equipment, and spaces/offices to provide for movement of information.
2. *Retail layout:* Allocates shelf space and responds to customer behavior.
3. *Warehouse layout:* Addresses trade-offs between space and material handling.
4. *Fixed-position layout:* Addresses the layout requirements of large, bulky projects such as ships and buildings.
5. *Process-oriented layout:* Deals with low-volume, high-variety production (also called 'job shop' or intermittent production).
6. *Work-cell layout:* Arranges machinery and equipment to focus on production of a single product or group of related products.
7. *Product-oriented layout:* Seeks the best personnel and machine utilization in repetitive or continuous production.

Examples for each of these classes of layouts are noted in Table 9.1.

Because only a few of these seven classes can be modeled mathematically, the layout and design of physical facilities is still something of an art. However, we do know that a good layout requires determining the following:

▼ TABLE 9.1 Layout Strategies

	Objectives	Examples
Office	Locate workers requiring frequent contact close to one another	Middle East Insurance (Jordan)
Retail	Expose customer to high-margin items	Grand Stores (Saudi Arabia)
Warehouse (storage)	Balance low-cost storage with low-cost material handling	City Mall (Jordan)
Project (fixed position)	Move material to the limited storage areas around the site	El Zay distribution center (Jordan)
Job Shop (process oriented)	Manage varied material flow for each product	Dubai International Airport (U.A.E.)
Work Cell (product families)	Identify a product family, build teams, cross train team members	TcheTche (Jordan, Egypt, U.A.E, Saudi Arabia, and Lebanon)
Repetitive/Continuous (product oriented)	Equalize the task time at each workstation	Nasr (Egypt)

- *Material handling equipment:* Managers must decide about equipment to be used, including conveyors, cranes, automated storage and retrieval systems, and automatic carts to deliver and store material.
- *Capacity and space requirements:* Only when personnel, machines, and equipment requirements are known can managers proceed with layout and provide space for each component. In the case of office work, operations managers must make judgments about the space requirements for each employee. It may be a 2 × 2-meter cubicle plus allowance for hallways, aisles, rest rooms, cafeterias, stairwells, elevators, and so forth, or it may be spacious executive offices and conference rooms. Management must also consider allowances for requirements that address safety, noise, dust, fumes, temperature, and space around equipment and machines.
- *Environment and aesthetics:* Layout concerns often require decisions about windows, planters, and height of partitions to facilitate air flow, reduce noise, provide privacy, and so forth.
- *Flows of information:* Communication is important to any organization and must be facilitated by the layout. This issue may require decisions about proximity as well as decisions about open spaces versus half-height dividers versus private offices.
- *Cost of moving between various work areas:* There may be unique considerations related to moving materials or to the importance of having certain areas next to each other. For example, moving molten steel is more difficult than moving cold steel.

This open office offers a large shared space that encourages employees to interact. Before Steelcase, the office furniture maker, adopted an open office system, 80 percent of its office space was private; now it is just 20 percent private. The CEO even went from a private 700-square-meter office to a 48-square-meter enclosure in an open area. This dramatically increases unplanned and spontaneous communication between employees.

► **FIGURE 9.1**
Office Relationship Chart

Source: Adapted from Richard Muther, *Simplified Systematic Layout Planning,* 3rd ed. (Kansas City, Mgt. & Ind'l Research Publications). Used by permission of the publisher.

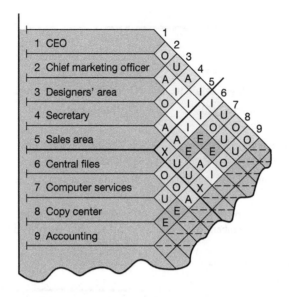

Value	CLOSENESS
A	Absolutely necessary
E	Especially important
I	Important
O	Ordinary OK
U	Unimportant
X	Not desirable

OFFICE LAYOUT

Office layout

The grouping of workers, their equipment, and spaces/offices to provide for comfort, safety, and movement of information.

Office layouts require the grouping of workers, their equipment, and spaces to provide for comfort, safety, and movement of information. The main distinction of office layouts is the importance placed on the flow of information. Office layouts are in constant flux as the technological change sweeping society alters the way offices function.

Even though the movement of information is increasingly electronic, analysis of office layouts still requires a task-based approach. Paper correspondence, contracts, legal documents, confidential patient records, and hard-copy scripts, artwork, and designs still play a major role in many offices. Managers therefore examine both electronic and conventional communication patterns, separation needs, and other conditions affecting employee effectiveness. A useful tool for such an analysis is the *relationship chart* shown in Figure 9.1. This chart, prepared for an office of product designers, indicates that the chief marketing officer must be: (1) near the designers' area; (2) less near the secretary and central files; (3) not at all near the copy center or accounting department.

LO1: Discuss important issues in office layout

General office-area guidelines allot an average of about 10 square meters per person (including corridors). A major executive is allotted about 40 square meters, and a conference room area is based on 2.5 square meters per person.

On the other hand, some layout considerations are universal (many of which apply to factories as well as to offices). They have to do with working conditions, teamwork, authority, and status. Should offices be private or open cubicles, have low file cabinets to foster informal communication or high cabinets to reduce noise and contribute to privacy? (See the Steelcase photo on the previous page.) Should all employees use the same entrance, rest rooms, lockers, and cafeteria? As mentioned earlier, layout decisions are part art and part science.

As a final comment on office layout, we note two major trends. First, technology, such as cell phones, iPads, the internet, laptop computers, and PDAs, allows increasing layout flexibility by moving information electronically and allowing employees to work offsite. Second, modern firms create dynamic needs for space and services.

AUTHOR COMMENT
The goal in a retail layout is to maximize profit per square meter of store space.

RETAIL LAYOUT

Retail layout

An approach that addresses flow, allocates space, and responds to customer behavior.

Retail layouts are based on the idea that sales and profitability vary directly with customer exposure to products. Thus, most retail operations managers try to expose customers to as many products as possible. Studies show that the greater the rate of exposure, the greater the sales and the higher the return on investment. The operations manager can change exposure with store arrangement and the allocation of space to various products within that arrangement.

Five ideas are helpful for determining the overall arrangement of many stores:

1. Locate the high-draw items around the periphery of the store. Thus, we tend to find dairy products on one side of a supermarket and bread and bakery products on another. An example of this tactic is shown in Figure 9.2.

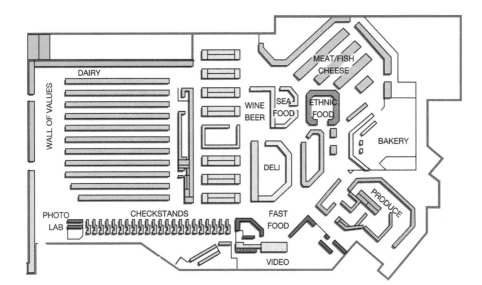

2. Use prominent locations for high-impulse and high-margin items. Smart Buy puts fast-growing, high-margin digital goods—such as cameras and DVDs—in the front and center of its stores.

3. Distribute what are known in the trade as 'power items'—items that may dominate a purchasing trip—to both sides of an aisle, and disperse them to increase the viewing of other items. For example, items such as eggs, milk, and margarine are dispersed and located throughout the entire shopping area to increase the exposure of the other items and encourage customers to look at them for possible purchase.

4. Use end-aisle locations because they have a very high exposure rate.

5. Convey the mission of the store by carefully selecting the position of the lead-off department. For instance, if prepared foods are part of a supermarket's mission, position the bakery and deli at the front to appeal to convenience-oriented customers.

LO2: Define the objectives of retail layout

Once the overall layout of a retail store has been decided, products need to be arranged for sale. Many considerations go into this arrangement. However, the main *objective of retail layout is to maximize profitability per square meter of floor space* (or, in some stores, on linear meter of shelf space). Big-ticket, or expensive, items may yield greater sales, but the profit per square meter may be lower. Computerized programs are available to assist managers in evaluating the profitability of various merchandising plans for hundreds of categories: this technique is known as category management.

An additional, and somewhat controversial, issue in retail layout is called slotting. **Slotting fees** are fees manufacturers pay to get their goods on the shelf in a retail store or supermarket chain. The result of massive new-product introductions, retailers can now demand up to US$25,000 to place an item in their chain. During the last decade, marketplace economics, consolidations, and technology have provided retailers with this leverage. The competition for shelf space is advanced by POS systems and scanner technology, which improve supply-chain management and inventory control. Many small firms question the legality and ethics of slotting fees, claiming the fees stifle new products, limit their ability to expand, and cost consumers money. Grand Stores is one of the few major retailers in the Arab world that does not demand slotting fees. This removes the barrier to entry that small companies usually face. (See the *Ethical Dilemma* at the end of this chapter.)

Slotting fees
Fees manufacturers pay to get shelf space for their products.

Servicescapes

Although the main objective of retail layout is to maximize profit through product exposure, there are other aspects of the service that managers consider. The term **servicescape** describes the physical surroundings in which the service is delivered and how the surroundings have a humanistic effect on customers and employees. To provide a good service layout, a firm considers three elements:

Servicescape
The physical surroundings in which a service takes place, and how they affect customers and employees.

A critical component of the Hard Rock brand is merchandise, and each Hard Rock Café location has a dedicated retail space known as a Rock Shop. These retail spaces are laid out in conjunction with the restaurant area to create the maximum traffic flow before and after eating.

1. *Ambient conditions*, which are background characteristics such as lighting, sound, smell, and temperature. All these affect workers *and* customers and can affect how much is spent and how long a person stays in the building—For example, fine-dining restaurants with linen tablecloths and candlelit atmosphere; Fakhreddine restaurant in Amman with its oriental décor; leather chairs at Starbucks.
2. *Spatial layout and functionality*, which involve customer circulation path planning, aisle characteristics (such as width, direction, angle, and shelf spacing), and product grouping. An example would be Carrefour's long aisles and high shelves; Smart Buy's wide center aisle.
3. *Signs, symbols, and artefacts*, which are characteristics of building design that carry social significance (such as carpeted areas of a department store that encourage shoppers to slow down and browse)—For example, Blue Fig's wall of paintings in Jordan and TcheTche's uniform red décor.

> **AUTHOR COMMENT**
> In warehouse layout, we want to maximize use of the whole building—from floor to ceiling.

Warehouse layout
A design that attempts to minimize total cost by addressing trade-offs between space and material handling.

WAREHOUSING AND STORAGE LAYOUTS

The objective of **warehouse layout** *is to find the optimum trade-off between handling cost and costs associated with warehouse space.* Consequently, management's task is to maximize the utilization of the total 'cube' of the warehouse—that is, utilize its full volume while maintaining low material handling costs. We define *material handling costs* as all the costs related to the transaction. This consists of incoming transport, storage, and outgoing transport of the materials to be warehoused. These costs include equipment, people, material, supervision, insurance, and depreciation. Effective warehouse layouts do, of course, also minimize the damage and spoilage of material within the warehouse.

Management minimizes the sum of the resources spent on finding and moving material plus the deterioration and damage to the material itself. The variety of items stored and the number of items 'picked' has direct bearing on the optimum layout. A warehouse storing a few different items lends itself to higher density than a warehouse storing a large variety of items. Modern warehouse management is, in many instances, an automated procedure using *automated storage and retrieval systems* (ASRSs).

The Wolfsburg, Germany, parking garage photo indicates that an ASRS can take many forms.

An important component of warehouse layout is the relationship between the receiving/unloading area and the shipping/loading area. Facility design depends on the type of supplies unloaded, what they are unloaded from (trucks, rail cars, barges, and so on), and where they are unloaded. In some companies, the receiving and shipping facilities, or *docks*, as they are called, are even in the same area; sometimes they are receiving docks in the morning and shipping docks in the afternoon.

LO3: Discuss modern warehouse management and terms such as ASRS, cross-docking, and random stocking

Automated storage and retrieval systems are not only found in traditional warehouses. This parking garage in Wolfsburg, Germany, occupies only 20 percent of the space of a traditionally designed garage. The ASRS 'retrieves' autos in less time, without the potential of the cars being damaged by an attendant.

Cross-docking

Cross-docking means to avoid placing materials or supplies in storage by processing them as they are received. In a manufacturing facility, product is received directly at the assembly line. In a distribution center, labeled and presorted loads arrive at the shipping dock for immediate rerouting, thereby avoiding formal receiving, stocking/storing, and order-selection activities. Because these activities add no value to the product, their elimination is 100 percent cost savings. Although cross-docking reduces product handling, inventory, and facility costs, it requires both: (1) tight scheduling; (2) accurate inbound product identification. Wal-Mart provides us with an excellent example of successful cross-docking in action; when Wal-Mart adopted the strategy in the late 1980s it quickly became one of the firm's core competencies. Wal-Mart used a satellite system that linked its points of sale, trucks, and distribution centers to the headquarters to ensure strict real-time scheduling, which reduced the firm's handling and inventory costs significantly and led to high savings, better performance, and strong competitive position.

Cross-docking
Avoiding the placement of materials or supplies in storage by processing them as they are received from shipment.

AISs, such as bar codes, are used for item identification.

Random Stocking

Random stocking

Used in warehousing to locate stock wherever there is an open location.

Automatic identification systems (AISs), usually in the form of bar codes and radio frequency identification (RFID), allow accurate and rapid item identification. When automatic identification systems are combined with effective management information systems, operations managers know the quantity and location of every unit. This information can be used with human operators or with automatic storage and retrieval systems to load units anywhere in the warehouse—randomly. Accurate inventory quantities and locations mean the potential utilization of the whole facility because space does not need to be reserved for certain stock-keeping units (SKUs) or part families. Computerized **random stocking** systems often include the following tasks.

1. Maintaining a list of 'open' locations
2. Maintaining accurate records of existing inventory and its locations
3. Sequencing items to minimize the travel time required to 'pick' orders
4. Combining orders to reduce picking time
5. Assigning certain items or classes of items, such as high-usage items, to particular warehouse areas so that the total distance traveled within the warehouse is minimized

Random stocking systems can increase facility utilization and decrease labor cost, but they require accurate records.

Customizing

Customizing

Using warehousing to add value to a product through component modification, repair, labeling, and packaging through the use of postponement.

Although we expect warehouses to store as little product as possible and hold it for as short a time as possible, we are now asking warehouses to customize products. Warehouses can be places where value is added through **customizing**. Warehouse customization is a particularly useful way to generate competitive advantage in markets where products have multiple configurations through the use of postponement. For instance, a warehouse can be a place where computer components are put together, software loaded, and repairs made at the last stages before being delivered to the customers as per their details. Warehouses may also provide customized labeling and packaging for retailers so items arrive ready for display.

Increasingly, this type of work goes on adjacent to major airports, in facilities such as Dubai Cargo Village terminal in Dubai International Airport, which hosts major logistics and service providers such as Aramex. Adding value at warehouses adjacent to major airports also facilitates overnight delivery. For example, if your computer has failed, the replacement may be sent to you from such a warehouse for delivery the next morning. When your old machine arrives back at the warehouse, it is repaired and sent to someone else. These value-added activities at 'quasi-warehouses' contribute to strategies of differentiation, low cost, and rapid response.

AUTHOR COMMENT
Fixed-position layout brings all the workers and materials to the project's site.

FIXED-POSITION LAYOUT

Fixed-position layout

A system that addresses the layout requirements of stationary projects.

In a **fixed-position layout**, the project remains in one place and workers and equipment come to that one work area. Examples of this type of project are a ship, a highway, a bridge, a house, and an operating table in a hospital operating room.

The techniques for addressing the fixed-position layout are complicated by three factors. First, there is limited space at virtually all sites. Second, at different stages of a project, different

A house built via traditional fixed-position layout would be constructed onsite, with equipment, materials, and workers brought to the site. Then a 'meeting of the trades' would assign space for various time periods. However, the home pictured here can be built at a much lower cost. The house is built in two transportable modules in a factory. Scaffolding and hoists make the job easier, quicker, and cheaper, and the indoor work environment aids labor productivity.

materials are needed; therefore, different items become critical as the project develops. Third, the volume of materials needed is dynamic.

Because problems with fixed-position layouts are so difficult to solve well onsite, an alternative strategy is to complete as much of the project as possible offsite. This approach is used in the home-building industry. As the photo shows, many home builders are moving from a fixed-position layout strategy to one that is more product oriented. In addition, many houses that are built onsite (fixed position) have the majority of components, such as doors, windows, fixtures, trusses, stairs, and wallboard, built as modules with more efficient offsite processes.

LO4: Identify when fixed-position layouts are appropriate

PROCESS-ORIENTED LAYOUT

A **process-oriented layout** can simultaneously handle a wide variety of products or services. This is the traditional way to support a product differentiation strategy. It is most efficient when making products with different requirements or when handling customers, patients, or clients with different needs. A process-oriented layout is typically the low-volume, high-variety strategy discussed in Chapter 7. In this job-shop environment, each product or each small group of products undergoes a different sequence of operations. A product or small order is produced by moving it from one department to another in the sequence required for that product. A good example of the process-oriented layout is a hospital or clinic. Figure 9.3 illustrates the process for two patients, A and B, at an emergency clinic in Beirut. An inflow of patients, each with his or her own needs, requires routing through admissions, laboratories, operating rooms, radiology, pharmacies, nursing beds, and so on. Equipment, skills, and supervision are organized around these processes.

Process-oriented layout
A layout that deals with low-volume, high-variety production in which like machines and equipment are grouped together.

VIDEO 9.1
Layout at Arnold Palmer Hospital's New Facility

A big advantage of process-oriented layout is its flexibility in equipment and labor assignments. The breakdown of one machine, for example, need not halt an entire process; work can be transferred to other machines in the department. Process-oriented layout is also especially good for handling the manufacture of parts in small batches, or **job lots**, and for the production of a wide variety of parts in different sizes or forms.

Job lots
Groups or batches of parts processed together.

The disadvantages of process-oriented layout come from the general-purpose use of the equipment. Orders take more time to move through the system because of difficult scheduling, changing setups, and unique material handling. In addition, general-purpose equipment requires high labor skills, and work-in-process inventories are higher because of imbalances in the production process. High labor-skill needs also increase the required level of training and experience, and high work-in-process levels increase capital investment.

When designing a process layout, the most common tactic is to arrange departments or work centers so as to minimize the costs of material handling. In other words, departments with large flows of parts or people between them should be placed next to one another. Material handling costs in this approach depend on: (1) the number of loads (or people) to be moved between two departments during some period of time; (2) the distance-related costs of moving loads (or people) between departments. Cost is assumed to be a function of distance between departments. The objective can be expressed as follows:

LO5: Explain how to achieve a good process-oriented facility layout

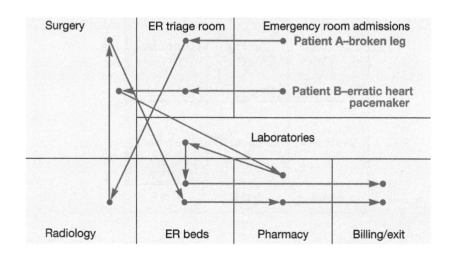

◀ FIGURE 9.3
An Emergency Room Process Layout Showing the Routing of Two Patients

AUTHOR COMMENT
Patient A (broken leg) proceeds (blue arrow) to ER triage, to radiology, to surgery, to a bed, to pharmacy, to billing. Patient B (pacemaker problem) moves (red arrow) to ER triage, to surgery, to pharmacy, to lab, to a bed, to billing.

$$\text{Minimize cost} = \sum_{i=1}^{n} \sum_{j=1}^{n} X_{ij}C_{ij} \qquad (9\text{-}1)$$

where n = total number of work centers or departments
   i, j = individual departments
   X_{ij} = number of loads moved from department i to department j
   C_{ij} = cost to move a load between department i and department j

Process-oriented facilities (and fixed-position layouts as well) try to minimize loads, or trips, times distance-related costs. The term combines distance and other costs into one factor. We thereby assume not only that the difficulty of movement is equal but also that the pickup and setdown costs are constant. Although they are not always constant, for simplicity's sake we summarize these data (that is, distance, difficulty, and pickup and setdown costs) in this one variable, cost. The best way to understand the steps involved in designing a process layout is to look at an example.

EXAMPLE 1 ▶

Designing a process layout

Salma's Company management wants to arrange the six departments of its factory in a way that will minimize interdepartmental material handling costs. Management makes an initial assumption (to simplify the problem) that each department is 20×20 meters and that the building is 60 meters long and 40 meters wide.

APPROACH AND SOLUTION ▶   The process layout procedure that the management follows involves six steps:

STEP 1: *Construct a 'from–to matrix'* showing the flow of parts or materials from department to department (see Figure 9.4).

▶ **FIGURE 9.4**
Interdepartmental Flow of Parts

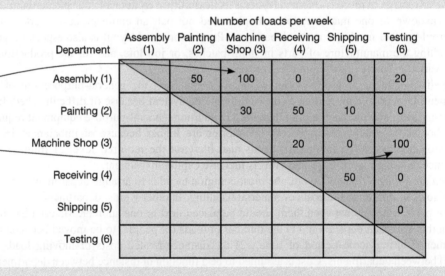

Department	Assembly (1)	Painting (2)	Machine Shop (3)	Receiving (4)	Shipping (5)	Testing (6)
Assembly (1)		50	100	0	0	20
Painting (2)			30	50	10	0
Machine Shop (3)				20	0	100
Receiving (4)					50	0
Shipping (5)						0
Testing (6)						

Number of loads per week

AUTHOR COMMENT
The high flows between 1 and 3 and between 3 and 6 are immediately apparent. Departments 1, 3, and 6, therefore, should be close together.

STEP 2: *Determine the space requirements* for each department. (Figure 9.5 shows available plant space.)

▶ **FIGURE 9.5**
Building Dimensions and One Possible Department Layout

AUTHOR COMMENT
Think of this as a starting, initial, layout. Our goal is to improve it, if possible.

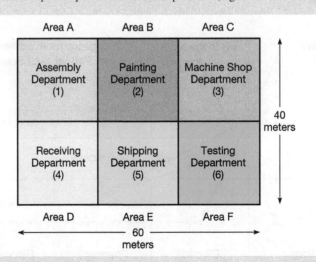

Area A   Area B   Area C

Assembly Department (1)	Painting Department (2)	Machine Shop Department (3)
Receiving Department (4)	Shipping Department (5)	Testing Department (6)

40 meters

Area D   Area E   Area F

◀—— 60 meters ——▶

STEP 3: *Develop an initial schematic diagram* showing the sequence of departments through which parts must move. Try to place departments with a heavy flow of materials or parts next to one another. (See Figure 9.6.)

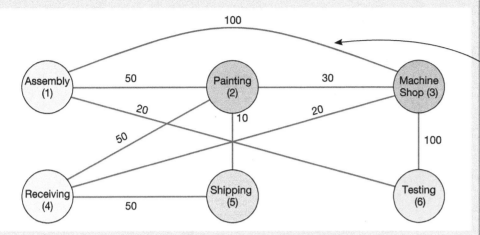

◄ **FIGURE 9.6**
Interdepartmental Flow Graph Showing Number of Weekly Loads

AUTHOR COMMENT
This shows that 100 loads also move weekly between Assembly and the Machine Shop. We will probably want to move these two departments closer to one another to minimize the flow of parts through the factory.

STEP 4: *Determine the cost of this layout* by using the material-handling cost equation:

$$\text{Cost} = \sum_{i=1}^{n}\sum_{j=1}^{n} X_{ij} C_{ij}$$

For this problem, Salma's Company assumes that a forklift carries all interdepartmental loads. The cost of moving one load between adjacent departments is estimated to be US$1. Moving a load between non-adjacent departments costs US$2. Looking at Figures 9.4 and 9.5, we thus see that the handling cost between departments 1 and 2 is US$50 (US$1 × 50 loads), US$200 between departments 1 and 3 (US$2 × 100 loads), US$40 between departments 1 and 6 (US$2 × 20 loads), and so on. Work areas that are diagonal to one another, such as 2 and 4, are treated as adjacent. The total cost for the layout shown in Figure 9.6 is:

$$
\begin{aligned}
\text{Cost} = \quad &\underset{(1\text{ and }2)}{\text{US}\$50} + \underset{(1\text{ and }3)}{\text{US}\$200} + \underset{(1\text{ and }6)}{\text{US}\$40} + \underset{(2\text{ and }3)}{\text{US}\$30} + \underset{(2\text{ and }4)}{\text{US}\$50} \\
&+ \underset{(2\text{ and }5)}{\text{US}\$10} + \underset{(3\text{ and }4)}{\text{US}\$40} + \underset{(3\text{ and }6)}{\text{US}\$100} + \underset{(4\text{ and }5)}{\text{US}\$50} \\
&= \text{US}\$570
\end{aligned}
$$

STEP 5: By trial and error (or by a more sophisticated computer program approach that we discuss shortly), *try to improve the layout* pictured in Figure 9.5 to establish a better arrangement of departments.

By looking at both the flow graph (Figure 9.6) and the cost calculations, we see that placing departments 1 and 3 closer together appears desirable. They currently are nonadjacent, and the high volume of flow between them causes a large handling expense. Looking the situation over, we need to check the effect of shifting departments and possibly raising, instead of lowering, overall costs.

One possibility is to switch departments 1 and 2. This exchange produces a second departmental flow graph (Figure 9.7), which shows a reduction in cost to US$480, a saving in material handling of US$90:

$$
\begin{aligned}
\text{Cost} = \quad &\underset{(1\text{ and }2)}{\text{US}\$50} + \underset{(1\text{ and }3)}{\text{US}\$100} + \underset{(1\text{ and }6)}{\text{US}\$20} + \underset{(2\text{ and }3)}{\text{US}\$60} + \underset{(2\text{ and }4)}{\text{US}\$50} \\
&+ \underset{(2\text{ and }5)}{\text{US}\$10} + \underset{(3\text{ and }4)}{\text{US}\$40} + \underset{(3\text{ and }6)}{\text{US}\$100} + \underset{(4\text{ and }5)}{\text{US}\$50} \\
&= \text{US}\$480
\end{aligned}
$$

Suppose Salma's Company is satisfied with the cost figure of US$480 and the flow graph of Figure 9.7. The problem may not be solved yet. Often, a sixth step is necessary:

STEP 6: *Prepare a detailed plan* arranging the departments to fit the shape of the building and its nonmovable areas (such as the loading dock, washrooms, and stairways). Often this step involves ensuring that the final plan can be accommodated by the electrical system, floor loads, aesthetics, and other factors.

In the case of Salma's Company, space requirements are a simple matter (see Figure 9.8).

► **FIGURE 9.7**
**Second Interdepartmental
Flow Graph**

AUTHOR COMMENT
Notice how Assembly and
Machine Shop are now
adjacent. Testing stayed close
to the Machine Shop also.

► **FIGURE 9.8**
**A Feasible Layout for
Salma's Company**

AUTHOR COMMENT
Here we see the departments
moved to areas A–F to try to
improve the flow.

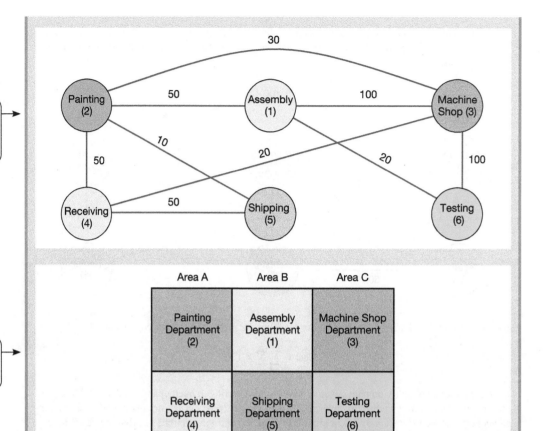

INSIGHT ► This switch of departments is only one of a large number of possible changes. For a six-department problem, there are actually 720 (or 6! = 6 × 5 × 4 × 3 × 2 × 1) potential arrangements! In layout problems, we may not find the optimal solution and may have to be satisfied with a 'reasonable' one.

LEARNING EXERCISE ► Can you improve on the layout in Figures 9.7 and 9.8? [Answer: Yes, it can be lowered to US$430 by placing Shipping in area A, Painting in area B, Assembly in area C, Receiving in area D (no change), Machine Shop in area E, and Testing in area F (no change).]

RELATED PROBLEMS ► 9.1, 9.2, 9.3, 9.4

EXCEL OM Data File **Ch09Ex1.xls** can be found at MyOMLab.

Computer Software for Process-Oriented Layouts

The graphic approach in Example 1 is fine for small problems. It does not, however, suffice for larger problems. When 20 departments are involved in a layout problem, more than 600 *trillion* different department configurations are possible. Fortunately, computer programs have been written to handle large layouts. These programs often add sophistication with flowcharts, multiple-story capability, storage and container placement, material volumes, time analysis, and cost comparisons. Such programs include CRAFT (Computerized Relative Allocation of Facilities Technique) (see Figure 9.9), Automated Layout Design Program (ALDEP), Computerized Relationship Layout Planning (CORELAP), and Factory Flow. These programs tend to be interactive—that is, require participation by the user. And most only claim to provide 'good,' not 'optimal,' solutions.

Work cell

An arrangement of machines and personnel that focuses on making a single product or family of related products.

AUTHOR COMMENT
Using work cells is a big step
toward manufacturing
efficiency. They can make jobs
more interesting, save space,
and cut inventory.

WORK CELLS

A **work cell** reorganizes people and machines that would ordinarily be dispersed in various departments into a group so that they can focus on making a single product or a group of related products (Figure 9.10). Cellular work arrangements are used when volume warrants a special

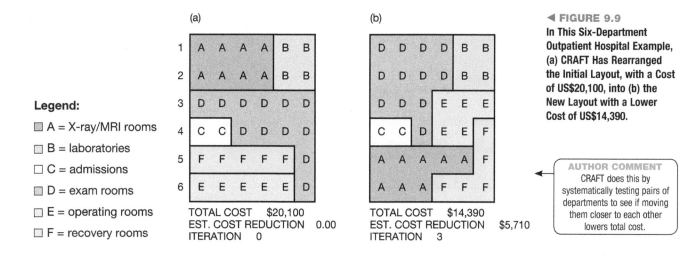

Legend:

■ A = X-ray/MRI rooms

□ B = laboratories

□ C = admissions

■ D = exam rooms

□ E = operating rooms

□ F = recovery rooms

◀ **FIGURE 9.9**
In This Six-Department Outpatient Hospital Example, (a) CRAFT Has Rearranged the Initial Layout, with a Cost of US$20,100, into (b) the New Layout with a Lower Cost of US$14,390.

AUTHOR COMMENT
CRAFT does this by systematically testing pairs of departments to see if moving them closer to each other lowers total cost.

arrangement of machinery and equipment. In a manufacturing environment, *group technology* (Chapter 5) identifies products that have similar characteristics and lend themselves to being processed in a particular work cell. These work cells are reconfigured as product designs change or volume fluctuates. Although the idea of work cells was first presented by R. E. Flanders in 1925, only with the increasing use of group technology has the technique reasserted itself. The advantages of work cells are:

1. *Reduced work-in-process inventory* because the work cell is set up to provide one-piece flow from machine to machine.
2. *Less floor space* required because less space is needed between machines to accommodate work-in-process inventory.
3. *Reduced raw material and finished goods inventories* because less work-in-process allows more rapid movement of materials through the work cell.
4. *Reduced direct labor cost* because of improved communication among employees, better material flow, and improved scheduling.
5. *Heightened sense of employee participation* in the organization and the product: Employees accept the added responsibility of product quality because it is directly associated with them and their work cell.
6. *Increased equipment and machinery utilization* because of better scheduling and faster material flow.
7. *Reduced investment in machinery and equipment* because good utilization reduces the number of machines and the amount of equipment and tooling.

LO6: Define work cell and the requirements of a work cell

Requirements of Work Cells

The requirements of cellular production include:

- Identification of families of products, often through the use of group technology codes or equivalents
- A high level of training, flexibility, and empowerment of employees
- Being self-contained, with its own equipment and resources
- Test (poka-yoke) at each station in the cell

Work cells have at least five advantages over assembly lines and process facilities: (1) because tasks are grouped, inspection is often immediate; (2) fewer workers are needed; (3) workers can reach more of the work area; (4) the work area can be more efficiently balanced; (5) communication is enhanced. Work cells are sometimes organized in a U shape, as shown in the right-hand side of Figure 9.10.

Staffing and Balancing Work Cells

Once the work cell has the appropriate equipment located in the proper sequence, the next task is to staff and balance the cell. Efficient production in a work cell requires appropriate staffing.

▶ FIGURE 9.10

Improving Layouts by Moving to the Work Cell Concept

Note in both (a) and (b) that U-shaped work cells can reduce material and employee movement. The U shape may also reduce space requirements, enhance communication, cut the number of workers, and make inspection easier.

(a)

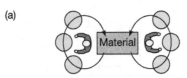

Current layout—workers in small closed areas.

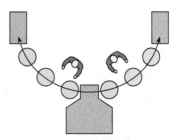

Improved layout—cross-trained workers can assist each other. May be able to add a third worker as added output is needed.

(b)

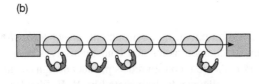

Current layout—straight lines make it hard to balance tasks because work may not be divided evenly.

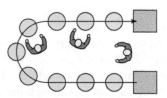

Improved layout—in U shape, workers have better access. Four cross-trained workers were reduced to three.

Takt time

Pace of production to meet customer demands.

This involves two steps. First, determine the **takt time**,[1] which is the pace (frequency) of production units necessary to meet customer orders:

$$\text{Takt time} = \text{Total work time available/Units required} \qquad (9\text{-}2)$$

Second, determine the number of operators required. This requires dividing the total operation time in the work cell by the takt time:

$$\text{Workers required} = \text{Total operation time required/Takt time} \qquad (9\text{-}3)$$

Example 2 considers these two steps when staffing work cells.

Contemporary software such as this from e-factory (UGS Corp.) allows operations managers to quickly place and connect symbols for factory equipment for a full three-dimensional view of the layout. Such presentations provide added insight into the issues of facility layout in terms of process, material handling, efficiency and safety.

[1]*Takt* is German for 'time,' 'measure,' or 'beat' and is used in this context as the rate at which completed units must be produced to satisfy customer demand.

OM in Action ► Work Cells Increase Productivity at Canon

Look quickly at Canon's factory near Tokyo, and you might think you stepped back a few decades. Instead of the swiftly moving assembly lines you might expect to see in a high-cost, sophisticated digital camera and photo copier giant, you see workers gathered in small groups called *work cells*. Each cell is responsible for one product or a small family of products. The product focus encourages employees to exchange ideas about how to improve the assembly process. They also accept more responsibility for their work.

Canon's work cells have increased productivity by 30 percent. But how?

First, conveyor belts and their spare parts take up space, an expensive commodity in Japan. The shift to the cell system has freed 12 miles of conveyor-belt space at 54 plants and allowed Canon to close 29 parts warehouses, saving US$280 million in real estate costs.

Employees are encouraged to work in ever-tighter cells, with prizes given to those who free up the most space.

Second, the cells enable Canon to change the product mix more quickly to meet market demands for innovative products—a big advantage as product life cycles become shorter and shorter.

Third, staff morale has increased because instead of performing a single task over and over, employees are trained to put together whole machines. Some of Canon's fastest workers are so admired that they have become TV celebrities.

A layout change that improves morale while increasing productivity is a win–win for Canon.

Sources: The Wall Street Journal (September 27, 2004): R11; and *Financial Times* (September 23, 2003): 14.

Jumelan company in Cairo makes auto mirrors. The major customer is the Nasr plant nearby. Nasr expects 600 mirrors delivered daily, and the work cell producing the mirrors is scheduled for 8 hours. Jumelan wants to determine the takt time and the number of workers required.

APPROACH ► Jumelan uses Equations (9-2) and (9-3) and develops a work balance chart to help determine the time for each operation in the work cell, as well as total time.

SOLUTION ►

Takt time = (8 hours × 60 minutes) ÷ 600 units = 480 ÷ 600 = 0.8 minute = 48 seconds

Therefore, the customer requirement is one mirror every 48 seconds.

The *work balance chart* in Figure 9.11 shows that five operations are necessary, for a total operation time of 140 seconds:

$$\text{Workers required} = \text{Total operation time required} \div \text{Takt time}$$
$$= (50 + 45 + 10 + 20 + 15) \div 48$$
$$= 140 \div 48 = 2.92$$

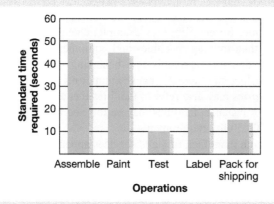

◄ **FIGURE 9.11**
Work Balance Chart for Mirror Production

INSIGHT ► To produce one unit every 48 seconds will require 2.92 people. With three operators this work cell will be producing one unit each 46.67 seconds (140 seconds ÷ 3 employees = 46.67) and 617 units per day (480 minutes available × 60 seconds) ÷ 46.67 seconds for each unit = 617).

LEARNING EXERCISE ► If testing time is expanded to 20 seconds, what is the staffing requirement? [Answer: 3.125 employees.]

The Boeing 737, the world's most popular commercial airplane, is produced on a moving production line, traveling at 5 cm a minute through the final assembly process. The moving line, one of several lean manufacturing innovations at the Washington facility, has enhanced quality, reduced flow time, slashed inventory levels, and cut space requirements. Final assembly is only 11 days—a time saving of 50 percent—and inventory is down more than 55 percent. Boeing has expanded the moving line concept to its 747 jumbo jet.

A *work balance chart* (like the one in Example 2) is also valuable for evaluating the operation times in work cells. Some consideration must be given to determining the bottleneck operation. Bottleneck operations can constrain the flow through the cell. Imbalance in a work cell is seldom an issue if the operation is manual, as cell members by definition are part of a cross-trained team. Consequently, the inherent flexibility of work cells typically overcomes modest imbalance issues within a cell. However, if the imbalance is a machine constraint, then an adjustment in machinery, process, or operations may be necessary. In such situations the use of traditional assembly-line-balancing analysis, the topic of our next section, may be helpful.

In many arrangements, without cells and without cross-training, if one operation is halted for whatever reason (reading a drawing, getting a tool, machine maintenance, etc.), the entire flow stops. Multiple-operator cells are therefore preferred. However, we should note that the increasing capability of multitasking machines can complicate work cell design and staffing.

The success of work cells is not limited to manufacturing. Rahwanji Cards designs high-quality wedding and greetings cards in the Arab world market and produces millions of cards annually using cellular design. Its work cells, consisting of artists, writers, designers, and administration staff, produce a significant variety of cards in a speedy manner.

Commercial software, such as ProPlanner and Factory Flow, is available to aid managers in their move to work cells. These programs typically require information that includes AutoCAD layout drawings; part routing data; and cost, times, and speeds of material handling systems.

The Focused Work Center and the Focused Factory

Focused work center

A permanent or semi-permanent product-oriented arrangement of machines and personnel.

Focused factory

A facility designed to produce similar products or components.

When a firm has *identified a family of similar products that have a large and stable demand*, it may organize a focused work center. A **focused work center** moves production from a general-purpose, process-oriented facility to a large work cell that remains part of the present plant. If the focused work center is in a separate facility, it is often called a **focused factory**. A fast-food restaurant is a focused factory—most are easily reconfigured for adjustments to product mix and volume. Burger King, for example, changes the number of personnel and task assignments rather than moving machines and equipment. In this manner, Burger King 'balances' the assembly line (see assembly-line balancing on page 279) to meet changing production demands. In effect, the 'layout' changes numerous times each day.

The term *focused factories* may also refer to facilities that are focused in ways other than by product line or layout. For instance, facilities may be focused in regard to meeting quality, new product introduction, or flexibility requirements.

Focused facilities in both manufacturing and services appear to be better able to stay in tune with their customers, to produce quality products, and to operate at higher margins. This is true whether they are steel mills like Hadeed (Saudi Arabia), restaurants like McDonald's and Jasmi's (Bahrain), or a hospital like the New Mowasat Hospital (Kuwait).

Table 9.2 summarizes our discussion of work cells, focused work centers, and focused factories.

AUTHOR COMMENT
The traditional assembly line handles repetitive production.

REPETITIVE AND PRODUCT-ORIENTED LAYOUT

Product-oriented layouts are organized around products or families of similar high-volume, low-variety products. Repetitive production and continuous production, which are discussed in Chapter 7, use product layouts. The assumptions are that:

◀ **TABLE 9.2**

Work Cells, Focused Work Centers, and the Focused Factory

	Work Cell	Focused Work Center	Focused Factory
Description	A work cell is a temporary product-oriented arrangement of machines and personnel in what is ordinarily a process-oriented facility	A focused work center is a permanent product-oriented arrangement of machines and personnel in what is ordinarily a process-oriented facility	A focused factory is a permanent facility to produce a product or component in a product-oriented facility. Many of the focused factories currently being built were originally part of a process-oriented facility
Example	A job shop with machinery and personnel rearranged to produce 300 unique control panels	Pipe bracket manufacturing at a shipyard	A plant to produce window mechanisms or seat belts for automobiles

1. Volume is adequate for high equipment utilization
2. Product demand is stable enough to justify high investment in specialized equipment
3. Product is standardized or approaching a phase of its life cycle that justifies investment in specialized equipment
4. Supplies of raw materials and components are adequate and of uniform quality (adequately standardized) to ensure that they will work with the specialized equipment

LO7: Define product-oriented layout

Two types of a product-oriented layout are fabrication and assembly lines. The **fabrication line** builds components, such as automobile tires or metal parts for a refrigerator, on a series of machines, while an **assembly line** puts the fabricated parts together at a series of workstations. However, both are repetitive processes, and in both cases, the line must be 'balanced': That is, the time spent to perform work on one machine must equal or 'balance' the time spent to perform work on the next machine in the fabrication line, just as the time spent at one workstation by one assembly-line employee must 'balance' the time spent at the next workstation by the next employee.

Fabrication line

A machine-paced, product-oriented facility for building components.

Fabrication lines tend to be machine-paced and require mechanical and engineering changes to facilitate balancing. Assembly lines, on the other hand, tend to be paced by work tasks assigned to individuals or to workstations. Assembly lines, therefore, can be balanced by moving tasks from one individual to another. The central problem, then, in product-oriented layout planning is to balance the tasks at each workstation on the production line so that it is nearly the same while obtaining the desired amount of output.

Assembly line

An approach that puts fabricated parts together at a series of workstations; used in repetitive processes.

Management's goal is to create a smooth, continuing flow along the assembly line with a minimum of idle time at each workstation. A well-balanced assembly line has the advantage of high personnel and facility utilization and equity among employees' work loads. Some union contracts require that work loads be nearly equal among those on the same assembly line. The term most often used to describe this process is **assembly-line balancing**. Indeed, the *objective of the product-oriented layout is to minimize imbalance in the fabrication or assembly line.*

Assembly-line balancing

Obtaining output at each workstation on a production line so delay is minimized.

The main advantages of product-oriented layout are:

1. The low variable cost per unit usually associated with high-volume, standardized products
2. Low material handling costs
3. Reduced work-in-process inventories
4. Easier training and supervision
5. Rapid throughput

The disadvantages of product layout are:

1. The high volume required because of the large investment needed to establish the process
2. Work stoppage at any one point ties up the whole operation
3. A lack of flexibility when handling a variety of products or production rates

Because the problems of fabrication lines and assembly lines are similar, we focus our discussion on assembly lines. On an assembly line, the product typically moves via automated means, such

VIDEO 9.2
Facility Layout at Wheeled Coach Ambulance

Elapsed time	0:00	0:11	0:31	0:45		1:30
Task time (seconds)		11	20	14	0	45
Task	1. Order	2. Bun toasting	3. Assembly with condiments	4. Wrapping of patty with bun	5. Order picked up immediately to keep it fresh	6. Customer service (order and payment)

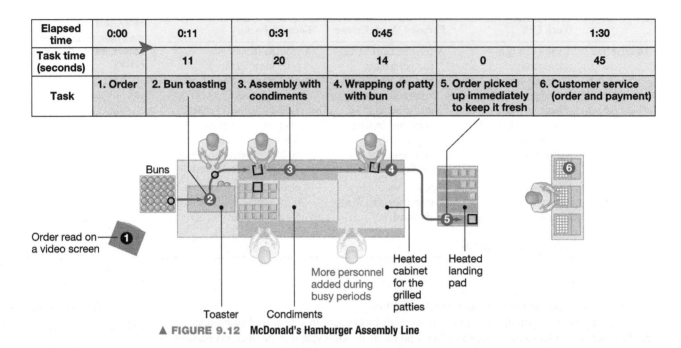

▲ **FIGURE 9.12   McDonald's Hamburger Assembly Line**

as a conveyor, through a series of workstations until completed. This is the way fast-food hamburgers are made (see Figure 9.12), automobiles are assembled, and television sets and ovens are produced. Product-oriented layouts use more automated and specially designed equipment than do process layouts.

Assembly-Line Balancing

LO8: Explain how to balance production flow in a repetitive or product-oriented facility

Line balancing is usually undertaken to minimize imbalance between machines or personnel while meeting a required output from the line. To produce at a specified rate, management must know the tools, equipment, and work methods used. Then the time requirements for each assembly task (e.g. drilling a hole, tightening a nut, or spray-painting a part) must be determined. Management also needs to know the *precedence relationship* among the activities—that is, the sequence in which various tasks must be performed. Example 3 shows how to turn these task data into a precedence diagram.

◄ **EXAMPLE 3** ►

Developing a precedence diagram for an assembly line

▶ **FIGURE 9.13**
Precedence Diagram

Gulf Air wants to develop a precedence diagram for an electrostatic wing component that requires a total assembly time of 66 minutes.

APPROACH ▶   Staff gather tasks, assembly times, and sequence requirements for the component in Table 9.3.

SOLUTION ▶   Figure 9.13 shows the precedence diagram.

Task	Assembly Time (minutes)	Task Must Follow This Task	
A	10	—	This means that tasks B and E
B	11	A	cannot be done until task A
C	5	B	has been completed.
D	4	B	
E	12	A	
F	3	C, D	
G	7	F	
H	11	E	
I	3	G, H	
	Total time 66		

◀ **TABLE 9.3** **Precedence Data For Wing Component**

INSIGHT ▶ The diagram helps structure an assembly line and workstations, and it makes it easier to visualize the sequence of tasks.

LEARNING EXERCISE ▶ If task D had a second preceding task (C), how would Figure 9.13 change? [Answer: There would also be an arrow pointing from C to D.]

RELATED PROBLEMS ▶ 9.6a, 9.7a, 9.8a

Once we have constructed a precedence chart summarizing the sequences and performance times, we turn to the job of grouping tasks into job stations so that we can meet the specified production rate. This process involves three steps.

1. Take the number of units required (demand or production rate) per day and divide it into the productive time available per day (in minutes or seconds). This operation gives us what is called the **cycle time**[2]—namely, the maximum time allowed at each workstation if the production rate is to be achieved:

$$\text{Cycle time} = \frac{\text{Production time available per day}}{\text{Units required per day}} \quad \text{(9-4)}$$

Cycle time

The time it takes a product to be made.

2. Calculate the theoretical minimum number of workstations. This is the total task-duration time (the time it takes to make the product) divided by the cycle time. Fractions are rounded to the next higher whole number:

$$\text{Minimum number of workstations} = \frac{\sum_{i=1}^{n} \text{Time for task } i}{\text{Cycle time}} \quad \text{(9-5)}$$

where n is the number of assembly tasks.

3. Balance the line by assigning specific assembly tasks to each workstation. An efficient balance is one that will complete the required assembly, follow the specified sequence, and keep the idle time at each workstation to a minimum. A formal procedure for doing this is the following.
   a. Identify a master list of tasks.
   b. Eliminate those tasks that have been assigned.
   c. Eliminate those tasks whose precedence relationship has not been satisfied.
   d. Eliminate those tasks for which inadequate time is available at the workstation.
   e. Use one of the line-balancing 'heuristics' described in Table 9.4. The five choices are: (1) longest task time; (2) most following tasks; (3) ranked positional weight; (4) shortest task time; (5) least number of following tasks. You may wish to test several of these

[2]*Cycle time* is the actual time to accomplish a task or process step. Several process steps may be necessary to complete the product. *Takt time*, discussed earlier, is determined by the customer and is the speed at which completed units must be produced to satisfy customer demand.

▶ **TABLE 9.4**
Layout Heuristics That May Be Used To Assign Tasks To Workstations In Assembly-Line Balancing

1. *Longest task (operation) time*	From the available tasks, choose the task with the longest task time.
2. *Most following tasks*	From the available tasks, choose the task with the largest number of following tasks.
3. *Ranked positional weight*	From the available tasks, choose the task for which the sum of the times for each following task is longest. (In Example 4 we see that the ranked positional weight of task C = 5(C) + 3(F) + 7(G) + 3(I) = 18, whereas the ranked positional weight of task D = 4(D) + 3(F) + 7(G) + 3(I) = 17; therefore, C would be chosen first, using this heuristic.)
4. *Shortest task (operations) time*	From the available tasks, choose the task with the shortest task time.
5. *Least number of following tasks*	From the available tasks, choose the task with the least number of subsequent tasks.

Heuristic

Problem solving using procedures and rules rather than mathematical optimization.

heuristics to see which generates the 'best' solution—that is, the smallest number of workstations and highest efficiency. Remember, however, that although heuristics provide solutions, they do not guarantee an optimal solution.

Example 4 illustrates a simple line-balancing procedure.

EXAMPLE 4 ▶

Balancing the assembly line

On the basis of the precedence diagram and activity times given in Example 3, Gulf Air determines that there are 480 productive minutes of work available per day. Furthermore, the production schedule requires that 40 units of the wing component be completed as output from the assembly line each day. It now wants to group the tasks into workstations.

APPROACH ▶   Following the three steps above, we compute the cycle time using Equation (9-4) and minimum number of workstations using Equation (9-5), and we assign tasks to workstations—in this case using the *most following tasks* heuristic.

SOLUTION ▶

$$\text{Cycle time (in minutes)} = \frac{480 \text{ minutes}}{40 \text{ units}}$$

$$= 12 \text{ minutes/unit}$$

$$\text{Minimum number of workstations} = \frac{\text{Total task time}}{\text{Cycle time}} = \frac{66}{12}$$

$$= 5.5 \text{ or } 6 \text{ stations}$$

Figure 9.14 shows one solution that does not violate the sequence requirements and that groups tasks into six one-person stations. To obtain this solution, activities with the most following tasks were moved into workstations to use as much of the available cycle time of 12 minutes as possible. The first workstation consumes 10 minutes and has an idle time of 2 minutes.

▶ **FIGURE 9.14**
A Six-Station Solution to the Line-Balancing Problem

AUTHOR COMMENT
Tasks C, D, and F can be grouped together in one workstation, provided that the physical facilities and skill levels meet the work requirements.

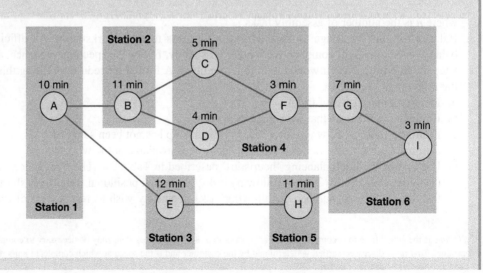

We can compute the efficiency of a line balance by dividing the total task time by the product of the number of workstations required times the assigned (actual) cycle time of the longest workstation:

$$\text{Efficiency} = \frac{\Sigma \text{ Task times}}{(\text{Actual number of workstations}) \times (\text{Largest assigned cycle time})} \tag{9-6}$$

Operations managers compare different levels of efficiency for various numbers of workstations. In this way, a firm can determine the sensitivity of the line to changes in the production rate and workstation assignments.

Gulf Air needs to calculate the balance efficiency for Example 4.

APPROACH ▶ Equation (9-6) is applied.

SOLUTION ▶

$$\text{Efficiency} = \frac{66 \text{ minutes}}{(6 \text{ stations}) \times (12 \text{ minutes})} = \frac{66}{72} = 91.7\%$$

Note that opening a seventh workstation, for whatever reason, would decrease the efficiency of the balance to 78.6 percent (assuming that at least one of the workstations still required 12 minutes):

$$\text{Efficiency} = \frac{66 \text{ minutes}}{(7 \text{ stations}) \times (12 \text{ minutes})} = 78.6\%$$

INSIGHT ▶ Increasing efficiency may require that some tasks be divided into smaller elements and reassigned to other tasks. This facilitates a better balance between workstations and means higher efficiency.

LEARNING EXERCISE ▶ What is the efficiency if an eighth workstation is opened? [Answer: Efficiency = 68.75%.]

RELATED PROBLEMS ▶ 9.6f, 9.7c, 9.8e, g

Large-scale line-balancing problems, like large process-layout problems, are often solved by computers. Several computer programs are available to handle the assignment of workstations on assembly lines with 100 (or more) individual work activities. Two computer routines, COMSOAL (Computer Method for Sequencing Operations for Assembly Lines) and ASYBL (General Electric's Assembly Line Configuration program), are widely used in larger problems to evaluate the thousands, or even millions, of possible workstation combinations much more efficiently than could ever be done by hand.

CHAPTER SUMMARY

Layouts make a substantial difference in operating efficiency. The seven layout situations discussed in this chapter are: (1) office; (2) retail; (3) warehouse; (4) fixed position; (5) process oriented; (6) work cells; (7) product oriented. A variety of techniques has been developed to solve these layout problems. Office layouts often seek to maximize information flows, retail firms focus on product exposure, and warehouses attempt to optimize the trade-off between storage space and material handling cost.

The fixed-position layout problem attempts to minimize material handling costs within the constraint of limited space at the site. Process layouts minimize travel distances times the number of trips. Product layouts focus on reducing waste and the imbalance in an assembly line. Work cells are the result of identifying a family of products that justify a special configuration of machinery and equipment that reduces

material travel and adjusts imbalances with cross-trained personnel.

Often, the issues in a layout problem are so wide-ranging that finding an optimal solution is not possible. For this reason, layout decisions, although the subject of substantial research effort, remain something of an art.

Key Terms

Assembly line (p. 279)
Assembly-line balancing (p. 279)
Cross-docking (p. 269)
Customizing (p. 270)
Cycle time (p. 281)
Fabrication line (p. 279)
Fixed-position layout (p. 270)

Focused factory (p. 278)
Focused work center (p. 278)
Heuristic (p. 282)
Job lots (p. 271)
Office layout (p. 266)
Process-oriented layout (p. 271)
Random stocking (p. 270)

Retail layout (p. 266)
Servicescape (p. 267)
Slotting fees (p. 267)
Takt time (p. 276)
Warehouse layout (p. 268)
Work cell (p. 274)

Ethical Dilemma

Although buried by mass customization and a proliferation of new products of numerous sizes and variations, grocery chains continue to seek to maximize payoff from their layout. Their layout includes a marketable commodity—shelf space—and they charge for it. This charge is known as a *slotting fee*.* Recent estimates are that food manufacturers now spend some 13 percent of sales on trade promotions, which is paid to grocers to get them to promote and discount the manufacturer's products. A portion of these fees is for slotting; but slotting fees drive up the manufacturer's cost. They also put the small company with a new product at a disadvantage, because small companies with limited resources are squeezed out of the marketplace. Slotting fees may also mean that customers may no longer be able to find the special local brand. How ethical are slotting fees?

*For an interesting discussion of slotting fees, see J. G. Kaikati and A. M. Kaikati, "Slotting and Promotional Allowances," *Supply Chain Management* 11, no. 2 (2006): 140–147; or J. L. Stanton and K. C. Herbst, "Slotting Allowances," *International Journal of Retail & Distribution Management* 34, no. 2/3 (2006): 187–197.

Discussion Questions

1. What are the seven layout strategies presented in this chapter?
2. What are the three factors that complicate a fixed-position layout?
3. What are the advantages and disadvantages of process layout?
4. How would an analyst obtain data and determine the number of trips in:
   (a) a hospital?
   (b) a machine shop?
   (c) an auto-repair shop?
5. What are the advantages and disadvantages of product layout?
6. What are the four assumptions (or preconditions) of establishing layout for high-volume, low-variety products?
7. What are the three forms of work cells discussed in the textbook?
8. What are the advantages and disadvantages of work cells?
9. What are the requirements for a focused work center or focused factory to be appropriate?
10. What are the two major trends influencing office layout?
11. What layout variables would you consider particularly important in an office layout where computer programs are written?
12. What layout innovations have you noticed recently in retail establishments?
13. What are the variables that a manager can manipulate in a retail layout?
14. Visit a local supermarket and sketch its layout. What are your observations regarding departments and their locations?
15. What is random stocking?
16. What information is necessary for random stocking to work?
17. Explain the concept of cross-docking.
18. What is a heuristic? Name several that can be used in assembly-line balancing.

Using Software to Solve Layout Problems

In addition to the many commercial software packages available for addressing layout problems, Excel OM and POM for Windows, both of which accompany this text, contain modules for the process problem and the assembly-line-balancing problem.

Using Excel OM

Excel OM can assist in evaluating a series of department work assignments like the one we saw for the Salma's Company in Example 1. The layout module can generate an optimal solution by enumeration or by computing the 'total movement' cost for each layout you wish to examine. As such, it provides a speedy calculator for each flow–distance pairing.

Program 9.1 illustrates our inputs in the top two tables. We first enter department flows, then provide distances between work areas. Entering area assignments on a trial-and-error basis in the upper

▼ **PROGRAM 9.1**   **Using Excel OM's Process Layout Module to Solve the Salma's Company Problem in Example 1**

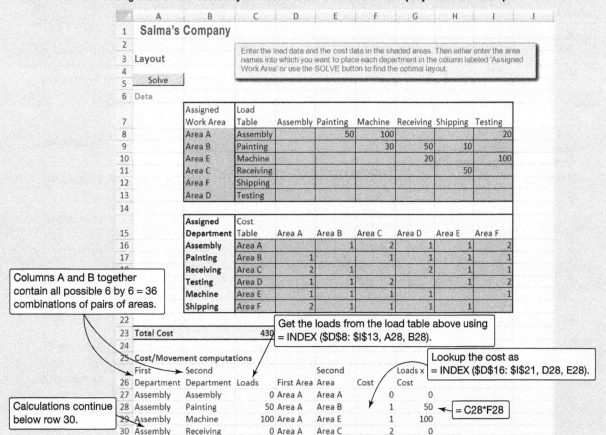

left of the top table generates movement computations at the bottom of the screen. Total movement is recalculated each time we try a new area assignment. It turns out that the assignment shown is optimal at 430 meters of movement.

P Using POM for Windows

The POM for Windows facility layout module can be used to place up to 10 departments in 10 rooms to minimize the total distance traveled as a function of the distances between the rooms and the flow between departments. The program exchanges departments until no exchange will reduce the total amount of movement, meaning an optimal solution has been reached.

The POM for Windows and Excel OM modules for line balancing can handle a line with up to 99 tasks, each with up to 6 immediate predecessors. In this program, cycle time can be entered either: (1) *given*, if known; (2) the *demand* rate can be entered with time available as shown. All five 'heuristic rules' are used: (1) longest operation (task) time; (2) most following tasks; (3) ranked positional weight; (4) shortest operation (task) time; (5) least number of following tasks. No one rule can guarantee an optimal solution, but POM for Windows displays the number of stations needed for each rule.

Appendix IV discusses further details regarding POM for Windows.

Solved Problems Virtual Office Hours help is available at MyOMLab.

▼ SOLVED PROBLEM 9.1

Aero Maintenance is a small aircraft engine maintenance facility located in Wichita, Kansas. Its new administrator, Ann Daniel, decides to improve material flow in the facility, using the process-layout method she studied at the Wichita State University. The current layout of Aero Maintenance's eight departments is shown in Figure 9.15.

Current Aero Maintenance Layout

Area A	Area B	Area C	Area D	
Entrance (1)	Receiving (2)	Parts (3)	Metallurgy (4)	10m
Breakdown (5)	Assembly (6)	Inspection (7)	Test (8)	10m
Area E	Area F	Area G	Area H	

40m

▲ FIGURE 9.15   Aero Maintenance Layout

The only physical restriction perceived by Daniel is the need to keep the entrance in its current location. All other departments can be moved to a different work area (each 10 meters square) if layout analysis indicates a move would be beneficial.

First, Daniel analyzes records to determine the number of material movements among departments in an average month. These data are shown in Figure 9.16. Her objective, Daniel decides, is to lay out the departments so as to minimize the total movement (distance traveled) of material in the facility. She writes her objective as:

$$\text{Minimize material movement} = \sum_{i=1}^{n} \sum_{j=1}^{n} X_{ij} C_{ij}$$

where X_{ij} = number of material movements per month (loads or trips) moving from department i to department j

C_{ij} = distance in meters between departments i and j (which, in this case, is the equivalent of cost per load to move between departments)

Note that this is only a slight modification of the cost-objective equation shown earlier in the chapter.

▶ FIGURE 9.16
Number of Material Movements (Loads) between Departments in One Month

	Entrance (1)	Receiving (2)	Parts (3)	Metallurgy (4)	Breakdown (5)	Assembly (6)	Inspection (7)	Test (8)	Department
		100	100	0	0	0	0	0	Entrance (1)
			0	50	20	0	0	0	Receiving (2)
				30	30	0	0	0	Parts (3)
					20	0	0	20	Metallurgy (4)
						20	0	10	Breakdown (5)
							30	0	Assembly (6)
								0	Inspection (7)
									Test (8)

Daniel assumes that adjacent departments, such as the Entrance (now in work area A) and Receiving (now in work area B), have a walking distance of 10 meters. Diagonal departments are also considered adjacent and assigned a distance of 10 meters. Nonadjacent departments, such as the Entrance and Parts (now in area C) or the Entrance and Inspection (area G) are 20 meters apart, and nonadjacent rooms, such as the Entrance and Metallurgy (area D), are 30 meters apart. (Hence, 10 meters is considered 10 units of cost, 20 meters is 20 units of cost, and 30 meters is 30 units of cost.)

Given the above information, redesign Aero Maintenance's layout to improve its material flow efficiency.

▼ SOLUTION

First, establish Aero Maintenance's current layout, as shown in Figure 9.17. Then, by analyzing the current layout, compute material movement:

$$
\begin{aligned}
\text{Total movement} = &\ \underset{\text{1 to 2}}{(100 \times 10 \text{ m})} + \underset{\text{1 to 3}}{(100 \times 20 \text{ m})} + \underset{\text{2 to 4}}{(50 \times 20 \text{ m})} + \underset{\text{2 to 5}}{(20 \times 10 \text{ m})} \\
& + \underset{\text{3 to 4}}{(30 \times 10 \text{ m})} + \underset{\text{3 to 5}}{(30 \times 20 \text{ m})} + \underset{\text{4 to 5}}{(20 \times 30 \text{ m})} + \underset{\text{4 to 8}}{(20 \times 10 \text{ m})} \\
& + \underset{\text{5 to 6}}{(20 \times 10 \text{ m})} + \underset{\text{5 to 8}}{(10 \times 30 \text{ m})} + \underset{\text{6 to 7}}{(30 \times 10 \text{ m})} \\
= &\ 1{,}000 + 2{,}000 + 1{,}000 + 200 + 300 + 600 + 600 + 200 + 200 \\
& + 300 + 300 \\
= &\ 6{,}700 \text{ meters}
\end{aligned}
$$

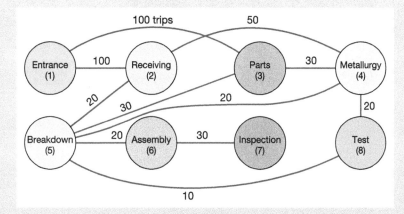

◀ FIGURE 9.17
Current Material Flow

Propose a new layout that will reduce the current figure of 6,700 meters. Two useful changes, for example, are to switch departments 3 and 5 and to interchange departments 4 and 6. This change would result in the schematic shown in Figure 9.18:

$$
\begin{aligned}
\text{Total movement} = &\ \underset{\text{1 to 2}}{(100 \times 10 \text{ m})} + \underset{\text{1 to 3}}{(100 \times 10 \text{ m})} + \underset{\text{2 to 4}}{(50 \times 10 \text{ m})} + \underset{\text{2 to 5}}{(20 \times 10 \text{ m})} \\
& + \underset{\text{3 to 4}}{(30 \times 10 \text{ m})} + \underset{\text{3 to 5}}{(30 \times 20 \text{ m})} + \underset{\text{4 to 5}}{(20 \times 10 \text{ m})} + \underset{\text{4 to 8}}{(20 \times 20 \text{ m})} \\
& + \underset{\text{5 to 6}}{(20 \times 10 \text{ m})} + \underset{\text{5 to 8}}{(10 \times 10 \text{ m})} + \underset{\text{6 to 7}}{(30 \times 10 \text{ m})} \\
= &\ 1{,}000 + 1{,}000 + 500 + 200 + 300 + 600 + 200 + 400 + 200 \\
& + 100 + 300 \\
= &\ 4{,}800 \text{ meters}
\end{aligned}
$$

Do you see any room for further improvement?

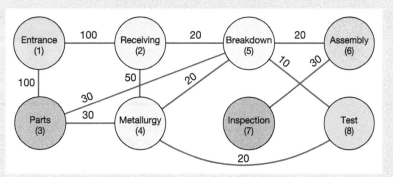

◀ FIGURE 9.18
Improved Layout

▼ SOLVED PROBLEM 9.2

The assembly line whose activities are shown in Figure 9.19 has an 8-minute cycle time. Draw the precedence graph and find the minimum possible number of one-person workstations. Then arrange the work activities into workstations so as to balance the line. What is the efficiency of your line balance?

Task	Performance Time (minutes)	Task Must Follow This Task
A	5	—
B	3	A
C	4	B
D	3	B
E	6	C
F	1	C
G	4	D, E, F
H	$\underline{2}$	G
	28	

▶ **FIGURE 9.19**
Four-Station Solution to the Line-Balancing Problem

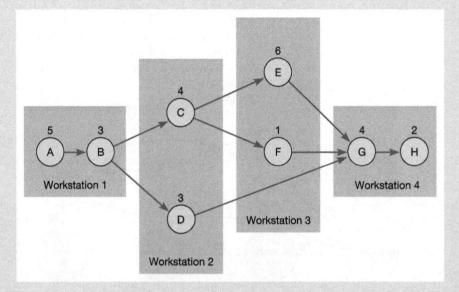

▼ SOLUTION

The theoretical minimum number of workstations is:

$$\frac{\sum t_i}{\text{Cycle time}} = \frac{28 \text{ minutes}}{8 \text{ minutes}} = 3.5, \text{ or 4 stations}$$

The precedence graph and one good layout are shown in Figure 9.19.

$$\text{Efficiency} = \frac{\text{Total task time}}{(\text{Number of workstations}) \times (\text{Largest cycle time})} = \frac{28}{(4)(8)} = 87.5\%$$

Problems*

•• **9.1** Jumana's job shop has four work areas, A, B, C, and D. Distances in meters between centers of the work areas are:

	A	**B**	**C**	**D**
A	—	4	9	7
B	—	—	6	8
C	—	—	—	10
D	—	—	—	—

Work pieces moved, in 100s of work pieces per week, between pairs of work areas, are:

	A	**B**	**C**	**D**
A	—	8	7	4
B	—	—	3	2
C	—	—	—	6
D	—	—	—	—

It costs Jumana US$1 to move one work piece 1 meter. What is the weekly total material handling cost of the layout? ⫽

•• **9.2** Three departments—milling (M), drilling (D), and sawing (S)—are assigned to three work areas in Laila's machine

*Note: ⫽ means the problem may be solved with POM for Windows and/or Excel OM.

shop in Manama. The number of work pieces moved per day and the distances between the centers of the work areas, in meters, are as follows:

Pieces Moved Between Work Areas Each Day

	M	D	S
M	—	23	32
D	—	—	20
S	—	—	—

Distances Between Centers of Work Areas (Departments) in Meters

	M	D	S
M	—	10	5
D	—	—	8
S	—	—	—

It costs US$2 to move one work piece 1 meter.
What is the cost? **P✗**

•• **9.3** Registration at Baghdad University has always been a time of emotion, commotion, and lines. Students must move among four stations to complete the trying semiannual process. Last semester's registration, held in the Registration Hall, is described in Figure 9.20. You can see, for example, that 450 students moved from the Paperwork station (A) to Advising (B), and 550 went directly from A to picking up their class cards (C). Graduate students, who for the most part had preregistered, proceeded directly from A to the station where registration is verified and payment collected (D). The layout used last semester is also shown in Figure 9.20. The registrar is preparing to set up this semester's stations and is anticipating similar numbers.

Interstation Activity Mix

	Pick up paperwork and forms (A)	Advising station (B)	Pick up class cards (C)	Verification of status and payment (D)
Paperwork/forms (A)	—	450	550	50
Advising (B)	350	—	200	0
Class cards (C)	0	0	—	750
Verification/payment (D)	0	0	0	—

Existing Layout

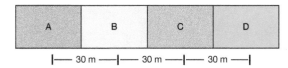

|— 30 m —|— 30 m —|— 30 m —|

▲ **FIGURE 9.20** **Registration Flow of Students**

a) What is the 'load × distance,' or 'movement cost,' of the layout shown?
b) Provide an improved layout and compute its movement cost. **P✗**

•• **9.4** Six processes are to be laid out in six areas along a long corridor at Hasheem Accounting Services. The distance between adjacent work centers is 40 meters. The number of trips between work centers is given in the following table:

				To		
From	**A**	**B**	**C**	**D**	**E**	**F**
A		18	25	73	12	54
B			96	23	31	45
C				41	22	20
D					19	57
E						48
F						

a) Assign the processes to the work areas in a way that minimizes the total flow, using a method that places processes with highest flow adjacent to each other.
b) What assignment minimizes the total traffic flow? **P✗**

•• **9.5** Tripoli Electronics wants to establish an assembly line for producing a new product, the Personal Little Assistant (PLA). The tasks, task times, and immediate predecessors for the tasks are as follows:

Task	Time (sec)	Immediate Predecessors
A	12	—
B	15	A
C	8	A
D	5	B, C
E	20	D

Tripoli's goal is to produce 180 PLAs per hour.

a) What is the cycle time?
b) What is the theoretical minimum for the number of workstations that Tripoli can achieve in this assembly line?
c) Can the theoretical minimum actually be reached when workstations are assigned? **P✗**

•• **9.6** Fallah Toy Company has decided to manufacture a new toy tractor, the production of which is broken down into six steps. The demand for the tractor is 4,800 units per 40-hour working week:

Task	Performance Time (sec)	Predecessors
A	20	None
B	30	A
C	15	A
D	15	A
E	10	B, C
F	30	D, E

a) Draw a precedence diagram of this operation.
b) Given the demand, what is the cycle time for this operation?
c) What is the *theoretical* minimum number of workstations?
d) Assign tasks to workstations.
e) How much total idle time is present each cycle?
f) What is the overall efficiency of the assembly line with five stations; and with six stations? **P✗**

•• **9.7** Tailwind, Inc. produces high-quality but expensive training shoes for runners. The Tailwind shoe, which sells for US$210, contains both gas- and liquid-filled compartments to provide more stability and better protection against knee, foot, and back injuries.

Manufacturing the shoes requires 10 separate tasks. There are 400 minutes available for manufacturing the shoes in the plant each day. Daily demand is 60. The information for the tasks is as follows:

Task	Performance Time (min)	Task Must Follow This Task
A	1	—
B	3	A
C	2	B
D	4	B
E	1	C, D
F	3	A
G	2	F
H	5	G
I	1	E, H
J	3	I

a) Draw the precedence diagram.
b) Assign tasks to the minimum feasible number of workstations according to the 'ranked positioned weight' decision rule.
c) What is the efficiency of the process?
d) What is the idle time per cycle? **Px**

••• **9.8** Dr. Mohammad Baker, operations manager at Nesa Electronics, prides himself on excellent assembly-line balancing. He has been told that the firm needs to complete 96 instruments per 24-hour day. The assembly-line activities are:

Task	Time (min)	Predecessors
A	3	—
B	6	—
C	7	A
D	5	A, B
E	2	B
F	4	C
G	5	F
H	7	D, E
I	1	H
J	6	E
K	4	G, I, J
	50	

a) Draw the precedence diagram.
b) If the daily (24-hour) production rate is 96 units, what is the highest allowable cycle time?

c) If the cycle time after allowances is given as 10 minutes, what is the daily (24-hour) production rate?
d) With a 10-minute cycle time, what is the theoretical minimum number of workstations with which the line can be balanced?
e) With a 10-minute cycle time and six workstations, what is the efficiency?
f) What is the total idle time per cycle with a 10-minute cycle time and six workstations?
g) What is the best workstation assignment you can make without exceeding a 10-minute cycle time and what is its efficiency? **Px**

•• **9.9** Suppose production requirements in Solved Problem 9.2 (see page 288) increase and require a reduction in cycle time from 8 minutes to 7 minutes. Balance the line once again, using the new cycle time. Note that it is not possible to combine task times so as to group tasks into the minimum number of workstations. This condition occurs in actual balancing problems fairly often. **Px**

•• **9.10** The pre-induction physical examination given by the army involves the following seven activities:

Activity	Average Time (min)
Medical history	10
Blood tests	8
Eye examination	5
Measurements (i.e. weight, height, blood pressure)	7
Medical examination	16
Psychological interview	12
Exit medical evaluation	10

These activities can be performed in any order, with two exceptions: Medical history must be taken first, and Exit medical evaluation is last. At present, there are three paramedics and two physicians on duty during each shift. Only physicians can perform exit evaluations and conduct psychological interviews. Other activities can be carried out by either physicians or paramedics.
a) Develop a layout and balance the line.
b) How many people can be processed per hour?
c) Which activity accounts for the current bottleneck?
d) What is the total idle time per cycle?
e) If one more physician can be placed on duty, how would you redraw the layout? What is the new throughput?

▶ Refer to MyOMLab for additional homework problems.

Case Studies

Layout of Saudi Aramco's Refineries Optimizes Operations

Saudi Aramco is the world's biggest oil company in terms of its production and reserves. It has more than 112 oil and gas fields in Saudi Arabia and a refining capacity of 4.16 million barrels per day (bpd) across the world, including its international refineries (joint ventures). A rapid supply of crude oil to refineries around the world is necessary to ensure adequate amounts reach the market.

In 2011 Aramco started putting in place the plans for its new Jazan Refinery. One of the first critical decisions the firm had to make

was the layout design. First, Aramco had to decide on the capacity required to meet the demand of the market in that region—a massive 400,000 bpd. The different engineering work needed for the front-end engineering and design (FEED) also needed to be considered. The huge task of developing the process design, layout, integration, and optimization of the facility was awarded to KBR, Inc.

The refinery layout is complex: There are many different processes involved, including the logistics of oil supply to the refinery through tanks or ships, and the eventual distribution of the oil. However, it is the refinery's internal operations that basically determine how the processes are arranged. The desalting stage comes first, where the crude oil is washed from salt, followed by continuous distillation (separating the crude oil into fractions), followed by vacuum distillation, naphtha hydro-treatment (to desulfurize it), distillate hydro-treatment, fluid catalytic cracking, hydro-cracking, visbreaking, coking, and many other chemical processes that lead to different end products with unique characteristics.

The Jazan Refinery will provide the needed foundation for economic development in the region, which is increasing demand on petroleum products. It will allow Aramco to meet its corporate objectives, particularly increasing market share, but only if its layout allows the proper flow of work with minimal costs, time, and effort.

Discussion Questions

1. What are the possible layout designs available to Aramco's oil refineries?
2. What suggestions would you make to Aramco on the layout of its oil refineries?
3. How would you measure the 'efficiency' of this layout?

Sources: **www.arabianoilandgas.com/article-8480-saudi-aramco-awards-kbr-jazan-refinery-feed-study/**; **www.epcengineer.com/projects/details/1512/jazan-refinery**; and **www.saudiaramco.com**

▶ Layout at Arnold Palmer Hospital's New Facility

Video Case

When the Arnold Palmer Hospital in Orlando, Florida began plans to create a new 273-bed, 11-story hospital across the street from its existing facility, which was bursting at the seams in terms of capacity, a massive planning process began. The US$100 million building, opened in 2006, was long overdue, according to Executive Director Kathy Swanson: "We started Arnold Palmer Hospital in 1989, with a mission to provide quality services for children and women in a comforting, family-friendly environment. Since then we have served well over 1.5 million women and children and now deliver more than 12,000 babies a year. By 2001, we simply ran out of room, and it was time for us to grow."

The new facility's unique, circular pod design provides an efficient layout in all areas of the hospital, creating a patient-centered environment. *Servicescape* design features include a serene environment created through the use of warm colors, private rooms with pull-down beds for family members, over 4 m high ceilings, and natural lighting with oversized windows in patient rooms. But these radical new features did not come easily. "This pod concept with a central nursing area and pie-shaped rooms resulted from over 1,000 planning meetings of 35 user groups, extensive motion and time studies, and computer simulations of the daily movements of nurses," says Swanson.

In a traditional linear hospital layout, called the *racetrack* design, patient rooms line long hallways, and a nurse might walk 4.3 km per day serving patient needs at Arnold Palmer. "Some nurses spent 30 percent of their time simply walking. With the nursing shortage and the high cost of health care professionals, efficiency is a major concern," added Swanson. With the nursing station in the center of 10- or 12-bed circular pods, no patient room is more than 4 m from a station. The time savings are in the 20 percent range. Swanson pointed to Figures 9.21 and 9.22 as examples of the old and new walking and trip distances.*

"We have also totally redesigned our neonatal rooms," says Swanson. "In the old system, there were 16 neonatal beds in a large and often noisy rectangular room. The new building features semiprivate rooms for these tiny babies. The rooms are much improved, with added privacy and a quiet, simulated night atmosphere, in addition to pull-down beds for parents to use. Our research shows that babies improve and develop much more quickly with this layout design. Layout and environment indeed impact patient care!"

*Layout and walking distances, including some of the numbers in Figures 9.21 and 9.22, have been simplified for purposes of this case.

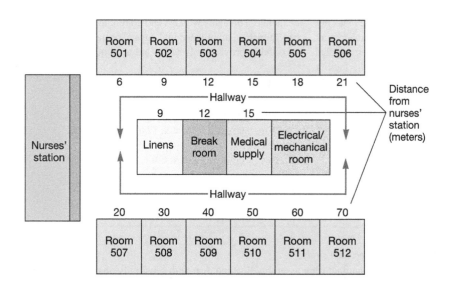

◀ **FIGURE 9.21**

Traditional Hospital Layout

Patient rooms are on two linear hallways with exterior windows. Supply rooms are on interior corridors. This layout is called a 'race track' design.

▶ **FIGURE 9.22**
New Pod Design for Hospital Layout

Note that each room is 4 m from the pod's *local* nursing station. The *break rooms* and the *central medical station* are each about 18 m from the local nursing pod. Pod *linen supply* rooms are also 4 m from the local nursing station.

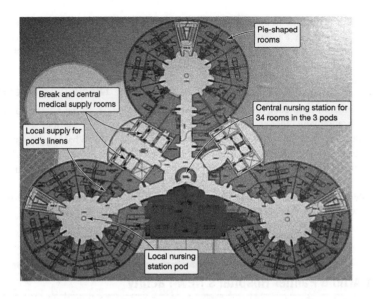

- Pie-shaped rooms
- Break and central medical supply rooms
- Central nursing station for 34 rooms in the 3 pods
- Local supply for pod's linens
- Local nursing station pod

Discussion Questions*

1. Identify the many variables that a hospital needs to consider in layout design.
2. What are the advantages of the circular pod design over the traditional linear hallway layout found in most hospitals?
3. Figure 9.21 illustrates a sample linear hallway layout. During a period of random observation, nurse Thomas Smith's day includes 6 trips from the nursing station to each of the 12 patient rooms (back and forth), 20 trips to the medical supply room, 5 trips to the break room, and 12 trips to the linen supply room. What is his total distance traveled in meters?

4. Figure 9.22 illustrates an architect's drawing of Arnold Palmer Hospital's new circular pod system. If nurse Susan Jones's day includes 7 trips from the nursing pod to each of the 12 rooms (back and forth), 20 trips to central medical supply, 6 trips to the break room, and 12 trips to the pod linen supply, how many meters does she walk during her shift? What are the differences in the travel times between the two nurses for this random day?
5. The concept of *servicescapes* is discussed in this chapter. Describe why this is so important at Arnold Palmer Hospital and give examples of its use in layout design.

*You may wish to view the video that accompanies this case before addressing these questions.

▶ Facility Layout at Wheeled Coach Ambulance

Video Case

When President Bob Collins began his career at Wheeled Coach, the world's largest manufacturer of ambulances, there were only a handful of employees. Now the firm's Florida plant has a workforce of 350. The physical plant has also expanded, with offices, R&D, final assembly, and wiring, cabinetry, and upholstery work cells in one large building. Growth has forced the painting work cell into a separate building, aluminum fabrication and body installation into another, inspection and shipping into a fourth, and warehousing into yet another.

Like many other growing companies, Wheeled Coach was not able to design its facility from scratch. And although management realizes that material handling costs are a little higher than an ideal layout would provide, Collins is pleased with the way the facility has evolved and employees have adapted. The aluminum cutting work cell lies adjacent to body fabrication, which, in turn, is located next to the body-installation work cell. And while the vehicle must be driven across a street to one building for painting and then to another for final assembly, at least the ambulance is on wheels. Collins is also satisfied with the flexibility shown in design of the work cells. Cell construction is flexible and can accommodate changes in product mix and volume. In addition, work cells are typically small and movable, with many work benches and staging racks borne on wheels so that

they can be easily rearranged and products transported to the assembly line.

Assembly-line balancing is one key problem facing Wheeled Coach and every other repetitive manufacturer. Produced on a schedule calling for four 10-hour work days per week, once an ambulance is on one of the six final assembly lines, it *must* move forward each day to the next workstation. Balancing just enough workers and tasks at each of the seven workstations is a never-ending challenge. Too many workers end up running into each other, too few can't finish an ambulance in 7 days. Constant shifting of design and mix and improved analysis has led to frequent changes.

Discussion Questions*

1. What analytical techniques are available to help a company like Wheeled Coach deal with layout problems?
2. What suggestions would you make to Bob Collins about his layout?
3. How would you measure the 'efficiency' of this layout?

*You may wish to view the video that accompanies this case before addressing these questions.

▶ **Additional Case Study:** Visit MyOMLab *for this free case study:*

Microfix, Inc.: This company needs to balance its PC manufacturing assembly line and deal with sensitivity analysis of time estimates.

Main Heading	Review Material	MyOMLab
THE STRATEGIC IMPORTANCE OF LAYOUT DECISIONS (p. 264)	Layout has numerous strategic implications because it establishes an organization's competitive priorities in regard to capacity, processes, flexibility, and cost, as well as quality of work life, customer contact, and image. *The objective of layout strategy is to develop an effective and efficient layout that will meet the firm's competitive requirements.*	
TYPES OF LAYOUT (pp. 264–266)	Types of layout and examples of their typical objectives include: 1. *Office layout:* Locate workers requiring frequent contact close to one another. 2. *Retail layout:* Expose customers to high-margin items. 3. *Warehouse layout:* Balance low-cost storage with low-cost material handling. 4. *Fixed-position layout:* Move material to the limited storage areas around the site. 5. *Process-oriented layout:* Manage varied material flow for each product. 6. *Work-cell layout:* Identify a product family, build teams, and cross-train team members. 7. *Product-oriented layout:* Equalize the task time at each workstation.	
OFFICE LAYOUT (p. 266)	■ **Office layout**—The grouping of workers, their equipment, and spaces/offices to provide for comfort, safety, and movement of information. A *relationship chart* displays a 'closeness value' between each pair of people and/or departments that need to be placed in the office layout.	
RETAIL LAYOUT (pp. 266–268)	■ **Retail layout**—An approach that addresses flow, allocates space, and responds to customer behavior. Retail layouts are based on the idea that sales and profitability vary directly with customer exposure to products. The main *objective of retail layout is to maximize profitability per square meter of floor space* (or, in some stores, per linear meter of shelf space). ■ **Slotting fees**—Fees manufacturers pay to get shelf space for their products. ■ **Servicescape**—The physical surroundings in which a service takes place and how they affect customers and employees.	
WAREHOUSING AND STORAGE LAYOUTS (pp. 268–270)	■ **Warehouse layout**—A design that attempts to minimize total cost by addressing trade-offs between space and material handling. The variety of items stored and the number of items 'picked' has direct bearing on the optimal layout. Modern warehouse management is often an automated procedure using *automated storage and retrieval systems* (ASRSs). ■ **Cross-docking**—Avoiding the placement of materials or supplies in storage by processing them as they are received for shipment. Cross-docking requires both tight scheduling and accurate inbound product identification. ■ **Random stocking**—Used in warehousing to locate stock wherever there is an open location. ■ **Customizing**—Using warehousing to add value to a product through component modification, repair, labeling, and packaging.	
FIXED-POSITION LAYOUT (pp. 270–271)	■ **Fixed-position layout**—A system that addresses the layout requirements of stationary projects. Fixed-position layouts involve three complications: (1) there is limited space at virtually all sites; (2) different materials are needed at different stages of a project; (3) the volume of materials needed is dynamic.	
PROCESS-ORIENTED LAYOUT (pp. 271–274)	■ **Process-oriented layout**—A layout that deals with low-volume, high-variety production in which like machines and equipment are grouped together. ■ **Job lots**—Groups or batches of parts processed together. $$\text{Material handling cost minimization} = \sum_{i=1}^{n}\sum_{j=1}^{n} X_{ij}C_{ij} \qquad (9\text{-}1)$$	Problems: 9.1–9.4 Virtual Office Hours for Solved Problem: 9.1 **VIDEO 9.1** Layout at Arnold Palmer Hospital's New Facility

Rapid Review

9

Main Heading	Review Material	
WORK CELLS (pp. 274–278)	■ **Work cell**—An arrangement of machines and personnel that focuses on making a single product or family of related products. ■ **Takt time**—Pace of production to meet customer demands. $$\text{Takt time} = \text{Total work time available/Units required} \quad (9\text{-}2)$$ $$\text{Workers required} = \text{Total operation time required/Takt time} \quad (9\text{-}3)$$ ■ **Focused work center**—A permanent or semi-permanent product-oriented arrangement of machines and personnel. ■ **Focused factory**—A facility designed to produce similar products or components.	
REPETITIVE AND PRODUCT-ORIENTED LAYOUT (pp. 278–283)	■ **Fabrication line**—A machine-paced, product-oriented facility for building components. ■ **Assembly line**—An approach that puts fabricated parts together at a series of workstations; a repetitive process. ■ **Assembly-line balancing**—Obtaining output at each workstation on a production line in order to minimize delay. $$\text{Cycle time} = \text{Production time available per day} \div \text{Units required per day} \quad (9\text{-}4)$$ $$\text{Minimum number of workstations} = \sum_{i=1}^{n} \text{Time for task } i \div \text{Cycle time} \quad (9\text{-}5)$$ ■ **Heuristic**—Problem solving using procedures and rules rather than mathematical optimization. Line balancing heuristics include longest task (operation) time, most following tasks, ranked positional weight, shortest task (operation) time, and least number of following tasks. $$\text{Efficiency} = \frac{\sum \text{Task times}}{(\text{Actual number of workstations}) \times (\text{Largest assigned cycle time})} \quad (9\text{-}6)$$	Problems: 9.5–9.10 **VIDEO 9.2** Facility Layout at Wheeled Coach Ambulance Virtual Office Hours for Solved Problem: 9.2

Self-Test

■ **Before taking the self-test,** refer to the learning objectives listed at the beginning of the chapter and the key terms listed at the end of the chapter.

LO1. Which of the statements below best describes *office layout*?
 a) groups workers, their equipment, and spaces/offices to provide for movement of information
 b) addresses the layout requirements of large, bulky projects, such as ships and buildings
 c) seeks the best personnel and machine utilization in repetitive or continuous production
 d) allocates shelf space and responds to customer behavior
 e) deals with low-volume, high-variety production.

LO2. Which of the following does *not* support the retail layout objective of maximizing customer exposure to products?
 a) locate high-draw items around the periphery of the store
 b) use prominent locations for high-impulse and high-margin items
 c) maximize exposure to expensive items
 d) use end-aisle locations
 e) convey the store's mission with the careful positioning of the lead-off department.

LO3. The major problem addressed by the warehouse layout strategy is:
 a) minimizing difficulties caused by material flow varying with each product
 b) requiring frequent contact close to one another
 c) addressing trade-offs between space and material handling
 d) balancing product flow from one workstation to the next
 e) none of the above.

LO4. A fixed-position layout:
 a) groups workers to provide for movement of information
 b) addresses the layout requirements of large, bulky projects, such as ships and buildings
 c) seeks the best machine utilization in continuous production

 d) allocates shelf space based on customer behavior
 e) deals with low-volume, high-variety production.

LO5. A process-oriented layout:
 a) groups workers to provide for movement of information
 b) addresses the layout requirements of large, bulky projects, such as ships and buildings
 c) seeks the best machine utilization in continuous production
 d) allocates shelf space based on customer behavior
 e) deals with low-volume, high-variety production.

LO6. For a focused work center or focused factory to be appropriate, the following three factors are required:
 a) _____
 b) _____
 c) _____

LO7. Before considering a product-oriented layout, it is important to be certain that:
 a) _____
 b) _____
 c) _____
 d) _____

LO8. An assembly line is to be designed for a product whose completion requires 21 minutes of work. The factory works 400 minutes per day. Can a production line with five workstations make 100 units per day?
 a) Yes, with exactly 100 minutes to spare.
 b) No, but four workstations would be sufficient.
 c) No, it will fall short even with a perfectly balanced line.
 d) Yes, but the line's efficiency is very low.
 e) Cannot be determined from the information given.

Answers: LO1. a; **LO2.** c; **LO3.** c; **LO4.** b; **LO5.** e; **LO6.** family of products, stable forecast (demand), volume; **LO7.** adequate volume, stable demand, standardized product, adequate/quality supplies; **LO8.** c.

10

Job Design and Work Measurement

Chapter Outline

COMPANY PROFILE: FALAFEL AL QUDS

10

OM STRATEGY DECISIONS

- ► Design of Goods and Services
- ► Managing Quality
- ► Process Strategy
- ► Location Strategies
- ► Layout Strategies
- ► Human Resources
- ► Supply-Chain Management
- ► Inventory Management
- ► Scheduling
- ► Maintenance

295

SPEEDY TEAMWORK MAKES THE DIFFERENCE

Since 1966, Falafel Al Quds has been serving its tasty falafels to locals and tourists in the Jordanian capital, Amman. However, the success of Al Quds led to an enormous increase in demand and challenged the firm with the task of serving hundreds of customers from its 12-square-meter branch.

The manager, Adib Hani Rasas, indicated that the business's biggest asset is its workers. The falafel industry is very competitive due to the fact that falafel is one of the most popular delicacies in the Arab world. Many companies enter and exit the market every year due to the small initial capital needed to start up a falafel joint. But Al Quds' secret is not only in the ingredients but also in the corporate culture of the company. "Many tried to copy our recipe, and a few did succeed, but their attempts to clone us failed, because they can't clone the spirit of work that we have," Adib explains.

Falafel Al Quds operates with six personnel who serve hundreds, and sometimes thousands, of falafel lovers each day, especially when there are municipal and tourist events in the area. The six workers function with complete synchronization and can serve a falafel sandwich in less than 15 seconds. More remarkably, they perform all work manually, with no specialized machinery.

Falafels are primarily made from chickpeas that are ground and then pressed into balls and deep fried. The falafels are then placed in a variety of different breads with different combinations of pickles, tomatoes, onions, and creamy sauces. "We studied carefully the way we like to make our falafel sandwiches and this enabled us to come up with a clear job design for the group and the workers," Adib states. "The workers are aligned according to specialization, following the order of the processes to ensure seamless flow of work and maximum speed."

Al-Quds' falafel sandwich has a prescribed list of ingredients that are closely monitored by the staff to ensure they deliver the intended taste.

Although the shop space is very limited, workers are well trained to maximize its utility.

Every work movement is well studied and then taught to workers to ensure the minimum failure rate—if not zero mistakes.

The employees are specialized in the different processes of the production, but Al Quds' job expansion strategies include training them to do different tasks, which ensures a high level of enthusiasm while working. For example, the recipe is handled by a chef, but all the other workers are trained to replace him whenever he is absent or on a break. The sauce specialist also trains others to step in for him at any moment, and the same goes for the sandwich maker. It is a total production method that allows for specialization, job rotation, enrichment, and enlargement all at the same time. This is evident in the staff's attitude—they are always cheerful and very approachable, which creates a great rapport with their customers. They are trained to deal with all manner of complaints with a positive attitude and a welcoming mentality.

The workers fulfill many customized orders for take outs or home delivery for parties and feasts, so they have to be ready for the challenge of unique orders. "Once we were asked to make a thousand sandwiches in less than half a day, with a strange sauce that was detailed to our chef over the phone," one employee explains. He continues, "We accepted the challenge and completed the order on time."

The careful design of the jobs at Al Quds, in addition to thorough management of its human resource, provides it with a competitive advantage that keeps it ahead of its rivals and retains its customer base.

Source: **Adib Hani Rasas at Al Quds**

Chapter 10 Learning Objectives

AUTHOR COMMENT
Mutual trust and commitment are key to a successful human resource strategy.

HUMAN RESOURCE STRATEGY FOR COMPETITIVE ADVANTAGE

Building and sustaining good human resource strategies are daily challenges. Falafel Al Quds, like many other organizations, including Aramex and Qatar Gas, have demonstrated that sustainable competitive advantage can be built through a human resource strategy. The payoff can be significant and difficult for others to duplicate. In this chapter, we will examine some of the tools available to operations managers for achieving competitive advantage via human resource management.

The objective of a human resource strategy is to manage labor and design jobs so people are effectively and efficiently utilized. As we focus on a human resource strategy, we want to ensure that people:

VIDEO 10.1
Hard Rock's Human Resource Strategy

1. Are efficiently utilized within the constraints of other operations management decisions
2. Have a reasonable quality of work life in an atmosphere of mutual commitment and trust

By reasonable *quality of work life* we mean a job is not only reasonably safe, with equitable pay, but also that both physical and psychological requirements are met. *Mutual commitment* means that both management and employee strive to meet common objectives. *Mutual trust* is reflected in reasonable, documented employment policies that are honestly and equitably implemented to the satisfaction of both management and employee.[1] When management has a genuine respect for its employees and their contributions to the firm, establishing a reasonable quality of work life and mutual trust is relatively simple.

This chapter is devoted to showing how operations managers can contribute to an effective human resource strategy (working with human resource managers), which may provide a competitive advantage, as in the case of Falafel Al Quds.

Constraints on Human Resource Strategy

As Figure 10.1 suggests, many decisions made about people are constrained by other decisions. First, the product mix may determine seasonality and stability of employment. Second, technology, equipment, and processes may have implications for safety and job content. Third, the location decision may have an impact on the ambient environment in which the employees work. Finally, layout decisions, such as assembly line versus work cell, influence job content.

So, the trade-offs necessary to reach a tolerable quality of work life are difficult. Effective managers consider such decisions simultaneously. The result: an effective, efficient system in which both individual and team performance are enhanced through optimum job design.

Acknowledging the constraints imposed on human resource strategy, we now look at three distinct decision areas of human resource strategy: *labor planning, job design,* and *labor standards.*

---

[1]We find many companies calling their employees *associates, individual contributors,* or members of a particular team.

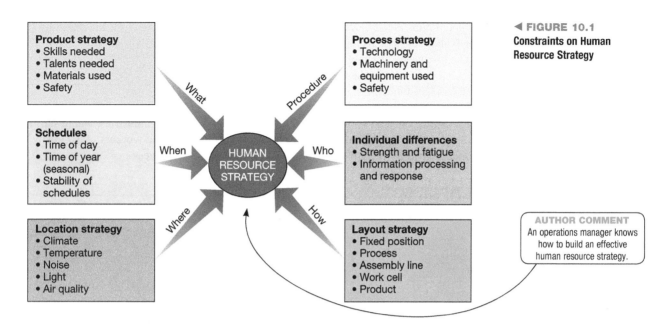

◀ **FIGURE 10.1**
Constraints on Human Resource Strategy

> **AUTHOR COMMENT**
> An operations manager knows how to build an effective human resource strategy.

LABOR PLANNING

> **AUTHOR COMMENT**
> Achieving employment stability, favorable work schedules, and acceptable work rules can be challenging.

Labor planning is determining staffing policies that deal with: (1) employment stability; (2) work schedules.

Employment-Stability Policies

Labor planning
A means of determining staffing policies dealing with employment stability, work schedules, and work rules.

Employment stability deals with the number of employees maintained by an organization at any given time. There are two very basic policies for dealing with stability.

1. *Follow demand exactly:* Following demand exactly keeps direct labor costs tied to production but incurs other costs. These other costs include (a) hiring and layoff costs, (b) unemployment insurance, and (c) premium wages to entice personnel to accept unstable employment. This policy tends to treat labor as a variable cost.
2. *Hold employment constant:* Holding employment levels constant maintains a trained workforce and keeps hiring, layoff, and unemployment costs to a minimum. However, with employment held constant, employees may not be utilized fully when demand is low, and the firm may not have the human resources it needs when demand is high. This policy tends to treat labor as a fixed cost.

The above policies are only two of many that can be efficient *and* provide a reasonable quality of work life. Firms must determine policies about employment stability.

LO1: Describe labor planning policies

Work Schedules

Although the standard work schedule in many countries around the world is five 8-hour days, many variations exist. A currently popular variation is a work schedule called **flextime**. A flextime policy might allow an employee (with proper notification) to be at work at 8 a.m. plus or minus 2 hours. This policy allows more autonomy and independence on the part of the employee. Some firms have found flextime a low-cost fringe benefit that enhances job satisfaction. The problem from the OM perspective is that much production work requires full staffing for efficient operations. A machine that requires three people cannot run at all if only two show up. Having a waiter show up to serve lunch at 1.30 p.m. rather than 11.30 a.m. is not much help either.

Flextime
A work schedule policy that allows employees, within limits, to determine their own work schedules.

Similarly, some industries find that their process strategies severely constrain their human resource scheduling options. For instance, paper manufacturing, petroleum refining, and power stations require around-the-clock staffing except for maintenance and repair shutdown. A good example of companies using flextime would be companies that are based on creativity, such as research institutions, software, and advertising companies: i.e. University of Qatar, Microsoft in the United States, and Think Arabia.

Another option is the *flexible workweek*. This plan often calls for fewer but longer days, such as four 10-hour days or, as in the case of light-assembly plants, 12-hour shifts. Working 12-hour shifts usually means working 3 days one week and 4 the next. Such shifts are sometimes called *compressed workweeks*. These schedules are viable for many operations functions—as long as suppliers and customers can be accommodated.

A further option is shorter days rather than longer days. This plan often moves employees to *part-time status*. Such an option is particularly attractive in service industries, where staffing for peak loads is necessary. Banks and restaurants often hire part-time workers. Also, many firms reduce labor costs by reducing fringe benefits for part-time employees.

JOB DESIGN

Job design specifies the tasks that constitute a job for an individual or a group. We examine five components of job design: (1) labor specialization; (2) job expansion; (3) psychological components; (4) self-directed teams; (5) motivation and incentive systems.

Job design
An approach that specifies the tasks that constitute a job for an individual or a group.

Labor Specialization

The importance of job design as a management variable is credited to the 18th-century economist Adam Smith. Smith suggested that **division of labor**, also known as *labor specialization* (or *job specialization*), would assist in reducing labor costs of multi-skilled artisans. This is accomplished in several ways:

Division of labor
Also known as labor specialization or job specialization; the division of labor into unique ('special') tasks.

1. *Development of dexterity* (specialized skills) and faster learning by the employee because of repetition
2. *Less loss of time* because the employee would not be changing jobs or tools
3. *Development of specialized tools* and the reduction of investment because each employee has only a few tools needed for a particular task.

The 19th-century British mathematician Charles Babbage determined that a fourth consideration was also important for labor efficiency. Because pay tends to follow skill with a rather high correlation, Babbage suggested *paying exactly the wage needed for the particular skill required*. If the entire job consists of only one skill, then we would pay for only that skill. Otherwise, we would tend to pay for the highest skill contributed by the employee. These four advantages of labor specialization are still valid today.

LO2: Identify the major issues in job design

A classic example of labor specialization is the assembly line. Such a system is often very efficient, although it may require employees to do short, repetitive, mind-numbing jobs. The wage rate for many of these jobs, however, is very good. Given the relatively high wage rate for the modest skills required in many of these jobs, there is often a large pool of employees from which to choose.

From the manager's point of view, a major limitation of specialized jobs is their failure to fully utilize each worker's skills. Job specialization tends to bring only the employee's manual skills to work. In an increasingly sophisticated knowledge-based society, managers may want employees to bring their mind to work as well.

Job Expansion

Moving from labor specialization toward more varied job design may improve the quality of work life. The theory is that variety makes the job 'better' and that the employee therefore enjoys a higher quality of work life. This flexibility thus benefits the employee and the organization.

Job enlargement
The grouping of a variety of tasks about the same skill level; horizontal enlargement.

We modify jobs in a variety of ways. The first approach is **job enlargement**, which occurs when we add tasks requiring similar skill to an existing job, such as adding shelf-arrangement, labeling, and price tagging tasks to the job of a shop floor assistant. **Job rotation** is a version of job enlargement that occurs when the employee is allowed to move from one specialized job to another, such as sending a secretary to work as a field data collector. Variety has been added to the employee's perspective of the job. In the context of restaurants, rotating the employees between the different food-processing stages would also be considered rotation, as the employees would have a greater variety of tasks to perform. Another approach is **job enrichment**, which adds planning and control to the job. For example, department store salespeople could be responsible for ordering, as well as selling, their goods. Job enrichment can be thought of as *vertical expansion*, as opposed to job enlargement, which is *horizontal*. These ideas are shown in Figure 10.2.

Job rotation
A system in which an employee is moved from one specialized job to another.

Job enrichment
A method of giving an employee more responsibility that includes some of the planning and control necessary for job accomplishment; vertical expansion.

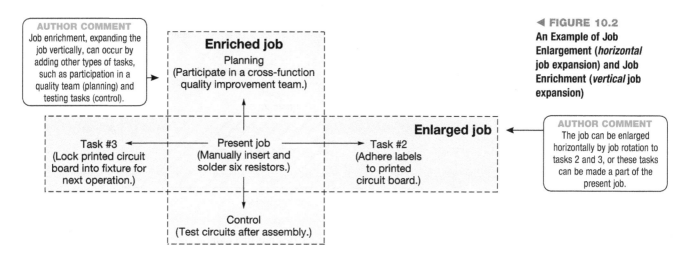

A popular extension of job enrichment, **employee empowerment** is the practice of enriching jobs so employees accept responsibility for a variety of decisions normally associated with staff specialists. Empowering employees helps them take 'ownership' of their jobs so they have a personal interest in improving performance.

Employee empowerment
Enlarging employee jobs so that the added responsibility and authority is moved to the lowest level possible in the organization.

Psychological Components of Job Design

An effective human resource strategy also requires consideration of the psychological components of job design. These components focus on how to design jobs that meet some minimum psychological requirements.

Hawthorne Studies   The Hawthorne studies introduced psychology to the workplace. They were conducted in the late 1920s at Western Electric's Hawthorne plant near Chicago. These studies were initiated to determine the impact of lighting on productivity. Instead, they found the dynamic social system and distinct roles played by employees to be more important. They also found that individual differences may be a critical factor in shaping the expectations of both the employee and the employer.

Core Job Characteristics   In the decades since the Hawthorne studies, substantial research regarding the psychological components of job design has taken place. Hackman and Oldham have incorporated much of that work into five desirable characteristics of job design.[2] They suggest that jobs should include the following characteristics:

1. *Skill variety*, requiring the worker to use a variety of skills and talents
2. *Job identity*, allowing the worker to perceive the job as a whole and recognize a start and a finish
3. *Job significance*, providing a sense that the job has an impact on the organization and society
4. *Autonomy*, offering freedom, independence, and discretion
5. *Feedback*, providing clear, timely information about performance.

Including these five ingredients in job design is consistent with job enlargement, job enrichment, and employee empowerment. We now want to look at some of the ways in which teams can be used to expand jobs and achieve these five job characteristics.

Self-directed Teams

Many world-class organizations have adopted teams to foster mutual trust and commitment, and provide the core job characteristics. One team concept of particular note is the **self-directed team**: a group of empowered individuals working together to reach a common goal. These teams may be organized for long- or short-term objectives. Teams are effective primarily because they can easily provide employee empowerment, ensure core job characteristics, and satisfy many of the psychological needs of individual team members. A job design continuum is shown in Figure 10.3.

Self-directed team
A group of empowered individuals working together to reach a common goal.

[2]See "Motivation Through the Design of Work," in Jay Richard Hackman and Greg R. Oldham, eds., *Work Redesign* (Reading, MA: Addison-Wesley, 1980), and A. Thomas, W. C. Buboltz, and C. Winkelspecht, "Job Characteristics and Personality as Predictors of Job Satisfaction," *Organizational Analysis*, 12, no. 2 (2004): 205–219.

▶ **FIGURE 10.3**
Job Design Continuum

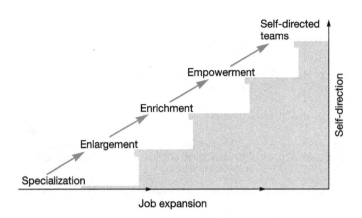

Limitations of Job Expansion   If job designs that enlarge, enrich, empower, and use teams are so good, why are they not universally used? Mostly it is because of costs. Here are a few limitations of expanded job designs.

- *Higher capital cost:* Job expansion may require additional equipment and facilities.
- *Individual differences:* Some employees opt for the less complex jobs.
- *Higher wage rates:* Expanded jobs may well require a higher average wage.
- *Smaller labor pool:* Because expanded jobs require more skill and acceptance of more responsibility, job requirements have increased.
- *Higher training costs:* Job expansion requires training and cross-training. Therefore, training budgets need to increase.

Despite these limitations, firms can find a substantial payoff in job expansion.

Motivation and Incentive Systems

Our discussion of the psychological components of job design provides insight into the factors that contribute to job satisfaction and motivation. In addition to these psychological factors, there are monetary factors. Money often serves as a psychological as well as a financial motivator. Monetary rewards take the form of bonuses, profit and gain sharing, and incentive systems.

Bonuses, typically in cash or stock options, are often used at executive level to reward management. Profit-sharing systems provide some part of the profit for distribution to employees. A variation of profit sharing is gain sharing, which rewards employees for improvements made in an organization's performance. One type of these is the Scanlon plan, in which any reduction in the cost of labor is shared between management and labor.

Incentive systems based on individual or group productivity are used throughout the world in a wide variety of applications. Production incentives often require employees or crews to produce at or above a predetermined standard. The standard can be based on a 'standard time' per task or number of pieces made. Both systems typically guarantee the employee at least a base rate. Incentives, of course, need not be monetary. Awards, recognition, and other kinds of preferences, such as a preferred work schedule, can be effective.

With the increasing use of teams, various forms of team-based pay are also being developed. Many are based on traditional pay systems supplemented with some form of bonus or incentive system. However, because many team environments require cross-training of enlarged jobs, *knowledge-based* pay systems have also been developed. Under knowledge-based (or skill-based) pay systems, a portion of the employee's pay depends on demonstrated knowledge or skills possessed. At Al Rajhi Banking Group, employees receive pay rises *when* they have mastered new skills, such as scheduling, budgeting, and risk analysis.

▶ ERGONOMICS AND THE WORK ENVIRONMENT

With the foundation provided by Frederick W. Taylor, the father of the era of scientific management, we have developed a body of knowledge about people's capabilities and limitations. This knowledge is necessary because humans are hand/eye animals possessing exceptional capabilities and some limitations. Because managers must design jobs that can be done, we now introduce a few of the issues related to people's capabilities and limitations.

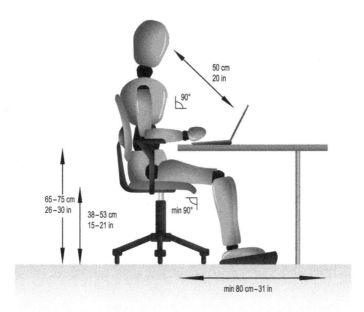

Ergonomic issues occur in the office as well as in the factory. Posture, which is related to desk height, chair height and position, keyboard placement and computer screen, is an important factor in reducing back and neck pain that can be caused by extended hours at a computer.

Ergonomics

The operations manager is interested in building a good interface between humans, the environment, and machines. Studies of this interface are known as **ergonomics**. Ergonomics means 'the study of work'—*Ergon* is the Greek word for 'work.' The term *human factors* is often substituted for the word *ergonomics*. Understanding ergonomic issues helps to improve human performance. The design of the workplace can make the job easier or impossible. Additionally, we now have the ability, through the use of computer modeling, to analyze human motions and efforts.

Ergonomics
The study of the human interface with the environment and machines.

LO3: Identify major ergonomic and work environment issues

Operator Input to Machines

Operator response to machines, be they hand tools, pedals, levers, or buttons, needs to be evaluated. Operations managers need to be sure that operators have the strength, reflexes, perception, and mental capacity to provide necessary control. Such problems as *carpal tunnel syndrome* may result when a tool as simple as a keyboard is poorly designed.

Feedback to Operators

Feedback to operators is provided by sight, sound, and feel; it should not be left to chance. Relatively simple issues make a difference in operator response and, therefore, performance.

The Work Environment

The physical environment in which employees work affects their performance, safety, and quality of work life. Illumination, noise and vibration, temperature, humidity, and air quality are work environment factors under the control of the organization and the operations manager. The manager must approach them as controllable.

Drivers of race cars have no time to grasp for controls or to look for small hidden gauges. Controls and instrumentation for modern race cars have migrated to the steering wheel itself—the critical interface between man and machine.

An important human factor/ergonomic issue in the aircraft industry is cockpit design. Newer 'glass cockpits' (on the right) display information in more concise form than the traditional rows of round analog dials and gauges (on the left). New displays reduce the chance of human error, which is a factor in about two-thirds of commercial air accidents. Fractions of a second can mean the difference between life and death.

Illumination is necessary, but the proper level depends on the work being performed. Figure 10.4 provides some guidelines. However, other lighting factors are important. These include reflective ability, contrast of the work surface with surroundings, glare, and shadows.

Noise of some form is usually present in the work area, and most employees seem to adjust well. However, high levels of sound will damage hearing. Figure 10.5 provides indications of the sound generated by various activities. Extended periods of exposure to decibel levels above 85 dB are permanently damaging. Government organizations, such as the Ministries of Labor around the Middle East, impose certain requirements to protect the health of workers, such as requiring ear protection above 85 dB if exposure equals or exceeds 8 hours. Even at low levels, noise and vibration can be distracting and can raise a person's blood pressure, so managers make substantial effort to reduce noise and vibration through good machine design, enclosures, or insulation.

Temperature and humidity parameters have also been well established. Managers with activities operating outside the established comfort zone should expect adverse effect on performance.

AUTHOR COMMENT
Methods analysis provides the tools for understanding systems.

Methods analysis
A system that involves developing work procedures that are safe and produce quality products efficiently.

LO4: Use the tools of methods analysis

METHODS ANALYSIS

Methods analysis focuses on *how* a task is accomplished. Whether controlling a machine or making or assembling components, how a task is done makes a difference in performance, safety, and quality. Using knowledge from ergonomics and methods analysis, methods engineers are charged with ensuring that quality and quantity standards are achieved efficiently and safely. Methods analysis and related techniques are useful in office environments as well as in the factory. Methods techniques are used to analyze:

1. *Movement of individuals or material.* The analysis is performed using *flow diagrams* and *process charts* with varying amounts of detail.
2. *Activity of human and machine and crew activity.* This analysis is performed using *activity charts* (also known as man–machine charts and crew charts).

500 and up
Exacting Tasks
(electronic and watch assembly, dentistry)

100–200
Small Details
(engraving, detail drafting)

75–100
Normal Visual
(office, classroom, machining)

50–75
Assembly Tasks
(parts assembly)

25–50
General Interiors
(conference, rest rooms, restaurants)

10–25
Large Objects
(warehouses, hallways)

▲ **FIGURE 10.4** **Recommended Levels of Illumination (using foot-candles (ft-c) as the measure of illumination)**

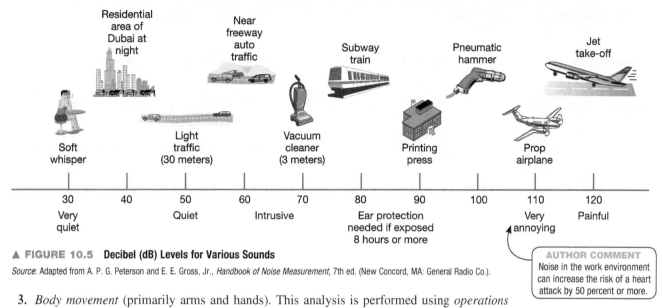

▲ **FIGURE 10.5** **Decibel (dB) Levels for Various Sounds**

Source: Adapted from A. P. G. Peterson and E. E. Gross, Jr., *Handbook of Noise Measurement*, 7th ed. (New Concord, MA: General Radio Co.).

> **AUTHOR COMMENT**
> Noise in the work environment can increase the risk of a heart attack by 50 percent or more.

3. *Body movement* (primarily arms and hands). This analysis is performed using *operations charts*.

Flow diagrams are schematics (drawings) used to investigate movement of people or materials. The factory in Figure 10.6 shows one style of flow diagram. The factory's old method is shown

Flow diagram

A drawing used to analyze the movement of people or materials.

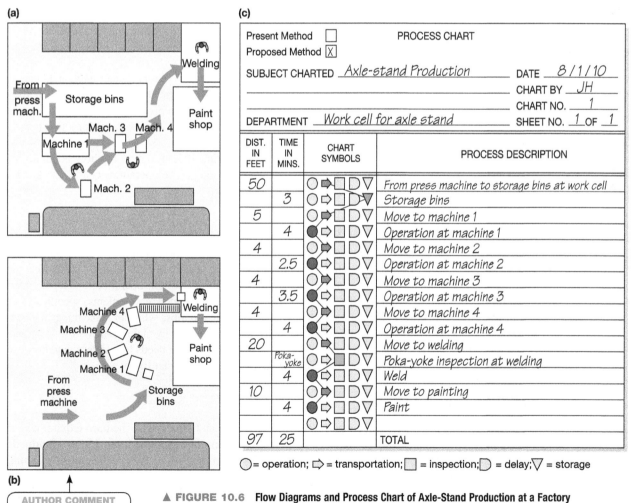

▲ **FIGURE 10.6** **Flow Diagrams and Process Chart of Axle-Stand Production at a Factory**

(a) Old method; (b) new method; (c) process chart of axle-stand production using the factory's new method (shown in (b)).

> **AUTHOR COMMENT**
> Flow diagrams provide an excellent way of understanding layout issues.

▼ **FIGURE 10.7** **Activity Chart for Two-Person Crew Doing an Oil Change in 12 Minutes at Quick Car Lube**

ACTIVITY CHART

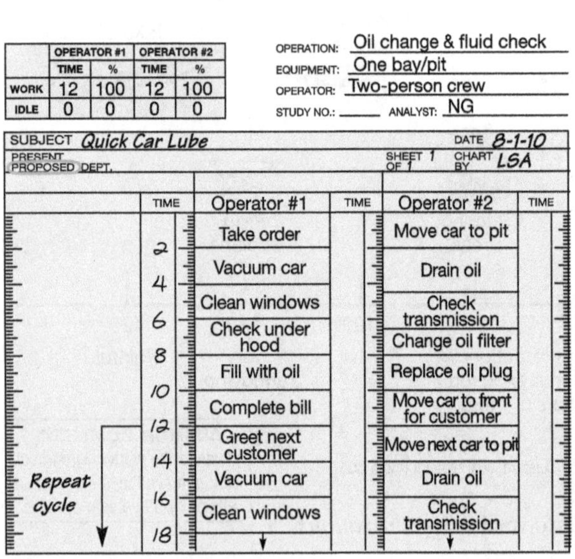

	OPERATOR #1		OPERATOR #2	
	TIME	%	TIME	%
WORK	12	100	12	100
IDLE	0	0	0	0

OPERATION: Oil change & fluid check
EQUIPMENT: One bay/pit
OPERATOR: Two-person crew
STUDY NO.: _____   ANALYST: NG

SUBJECT *Quick Car Lube*					DATE *8-1-10*	
PRESENT PROPOSED DEPT.					SHEET 1 OF 1 CHART BY *LSA*	

	TIME	Operator #1	TIME	Operator #2	TIME
	2	Take order		Move car to pit	
	4	Vacuum car		Drain oil	
	6	Clean windows		Check transmission	
	8	Check under hood		Change oil filter	
	10	Fill with oil		Replace oil plug	
	12	Complete bill		Move car to front for customer	
	14	Greet next customer		Move next car to pit	
Repeat cycle	16	Vacuum car		Drain oil	
	18	Clean windows		Check transmission	

Process chart

A graphic representation that depicts a sequence of steps for a process.

Activity chart

A way of improving utilization of an operator and a machine or some combination of operators (a crew) and machines.

Operations chart

A chart depicting right- and left-hand motions.

Visual workplace

Uses a variety of visual communication techniques to rapidly communicate information to stakeholders.

Labor standards

The amount of time required to perform a job or part of a job.

▼ **FIGURE 10.8** **Operations Chart for Bolt–Washer Assembly**

OPERATIONS CHART

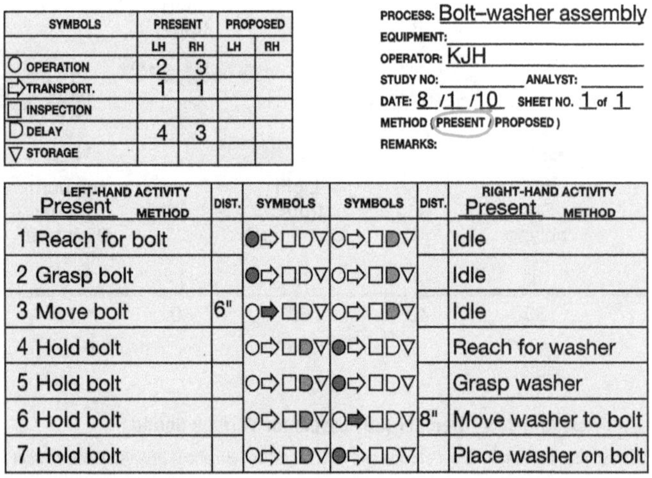

SYMBOLS	PRESENT		PROPOSED	
	LH	RH	LH	RH
○ OPERATION	2	3		
⇨ TRANSPORT.	1	1		
☐ INSPECTION				
D DELAY	4	3		
▽ STORAGE				

PROCESS: Bolt–washer assembly
EQUIPMENT: _____
OPERATOR: KJH
STUDY NO.: _____   ANALYST: _____
DATE: 8 /1 /10   SHEET NO. 1 of 1
METHOD (PRESENT / PROPOSED)
REMARKS:

LEFT-HAND ACTIVITY Present METHOD	DIST.	SYMBOLS	SYMBOLS	DIST.	RIGHT-HAND ACTIVITY Present METHOD
1 Reach for bolt		●⇨☐DV	O⇨☐DV		Idle
2 Grasp bolt		●⇨☐DV	O⇨☐DV		Idle
3 Move bolt	6"	O⇨☐DV	O⇨☐DV		Idle
4 Hold bolt		O⇨☐DV	●⇨☐DV		Reach for washer
5 Hold bolt		O⇨☐DV	●⇨☐DV		Grasp washer
6 Hold bolt		O⇨☐DV	O⇨☐DV	8"	Move washer to bolt
7 Hold bolt		O⇨☐DV	●⇨☐DV		Place washer on bolt

in Figure 10.6(a), and a new method, with improved work flow and requiring less storage and space, is shown in Figure 10.6(b). **Process charts** use symbols, as in Figure 10.6(c), to help us understand the movement of people or material. In this way non value-added activities can be recognized and operations made more efficient. Figure 10.6(c) is a process chart used to supplement the flow diagrams shown in Figure 10.6(b).

Activity charts are used to study and improve the utilization of an operator and a machine or some combination of operators (a 'crew') and machines. The typical approach is for the analyst to record the present method through direct observation and then propose the improvement on a second chart. Figure 10.7 is an activity chart to show a proposed improvement for a two-person crew at Quick Car Lube in Dubai.

Body movement is analyzed by an **operations chart**. It is designed to show economy of motion by pointing out wasted motion and idle time (delay). The operations chart (also known as a *right-hand/left-hand chart*) is shown in Figure 10.8.

THE VISUAL WORKPLACE

A **visual workplace** uses low-cost visual devices to share information quickly and accurately. Well-designed displays and graphs eliminate confusion and replace difficult-to-understand printouts and paperwork. Because workplace data change quickly and often, operations managers need to share accurate and up-to-date information. Changing customer requirements, specifications, schedules, and other details must be rapidly communicated to those who can make things happen.

The visual workplace can eliminate non value-added activities by making standards, problems, and abnormalities visual (see Figure 10.9). The visual workplace needs less supervision because employees understand the standard, see the results, and know what to do.

LABOR STANDARDS

So far in this chapter, we have discussed labor planning and job design. The third requirement of an effective human resource strategy is the establishment of labor standards. **Labor standards** are the amount of time required to perform a job or part of a job. Effective manpower planning is dependent on knowledge of the labor required.

Modern labor standards originated with the works of Frederick W. Taylor and Frank and Lillian Gilbreth at the beginning of the 20th century. At that time, a large proportion of work was manual, and the resulting labor content of products was high. Little was known about what constituted a fair day's work, so managers initiated studies to improve work methods and

Visual utensil holder encourages housekeeping.

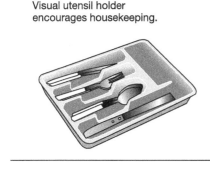

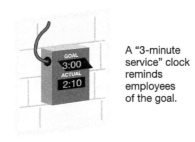

A "3-minute service" clock reminds employees of the goal.

Visual signals at the machine notify support personnel.

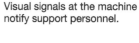
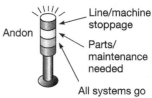

Andon

Line/machine stoppage

Parts/ maintenance needed

All systems go

Visual kanbans reduce inventory and foster JIT.

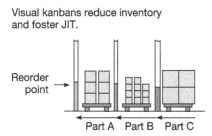

Reorder point

Part A   Part B   Part C

Quantities in bins indicate ongoing daily requirements and clipboards provide information on schedule changes.

Process specifications and operating procedures are posted in each work area.

▲ **FIGURE 10.9** **The Visual Workplace**

understand human effort. These efforts continue to this day. Although labor costs are often less than 10 percent of sales, labor standards remain important and continue to play a major role in both service and manufacturing organizations. They are often a beginning point for determining staffing requirements.

Effective operations management requires meaningful standards that help a firm determine:

1. Labor content of items produced (the labor cost)
2. Staffing needs (how many people it will take to meet required production)
3. Cost and time estimates prior to production (to assist in a variety of decisions, from cost estimates to make-or-buy decisions)
4. Crew size and work balance (who does what in a group activity or on an assembly line)
5. Expected production (so that both manager and worker know what constitutes a fair day's work)
6. Basis of wage-incentive plans (what provides a reasonable incentive)
7. Efficiency of employees and supervision (a standard is necessary against which to determine efficiency)

Properly set labor standards represent the amount of time that it should take an average employee to perform specific job activities under normal working conditions. Labor standards are set in four ways:

LO5: Identify four ways of establishing labor standards

1. Historical experience
2. Time studies
3. Predetermined time standards
4. Work sampling

Historical Experience

Labor standards can be estimated based on *historical experience*—that is, how many labor-hours were required to do a task the last time it was performed. Historical standards have the advantage of being relatively easy and inexpensive to obtain. They are usually available from employee time cards or production records. However, they are not objective, and we do not know their accuracy, whether they represent a reasonable or a poor work pace, and whether unusual occurrences are included. Because these variables are unknown, their use is not recommended. Instead, time studies, predetermined time standards, and work sampling are preferred.

Time Studies

The classical stopwatch study, or **time study**, originally proposed by Frederick W. Taylor in 1881, involves timing a sample of a worker's performance and using it to set a standard. A trained and experienced person can establish a standard by following these eight steps.

Time study

Timing a sample of a worker's performance and using it as a basis for setting a standard time.

1. Define the task to be studied (after methods analysis has been conducted).
2. Divide the task into precise elements (parts of a task that often take no more than a few seconds).
3. Decide how many times to measure the task (the number of job cycles or samples needed).
4. Time and record elemental times and ratings of performance.

Average observed time

The arithmetic mean of the times for each element measured, adjusted for unusual influence for each element.

5. Compute the average observed (actual) time. The **average observed time** is the arithmetic mean of the times for *each* element measured, adjusted for unusual influence for each element:

$$\text{Average observed time} = \frac{(\text{Sum of the times recorded to perform each element})}{\text{Number of observations}} \quad (10\text{-}1)$$

Normal time

The average observed time, adjusted for pace.

6. Determine performance rating (work pace) and then compute the **normal time** for each element.

$$\text{Normal time} = (\text{Average observed time}) \times (\text{Performance rating factor}) \quad (10\text{-}2)$$

The performance rating adjusts the average observed time to what a trained worker could expect to accomplish working at a normal pace. For example, a worker should be able to walk 3 miles per hour. He or she should also be able to deal a deck of 52 cards into 4 equal piles in 30 seconds. A performance rating of 1.05 would indicate that the observed worker performs the task slightly *faster* than average. Numerous videos specify work pace on which professionals agree, and benchmarks have been established by the Society for the Advancement of Management in the U.S. Performance rating, however, is still something of an art.

7. Add the normal times for each element to develop a total normal time for the task.

Standard time

An adjustment to the total normal time; the adjustment provides allowances for personal needs, unavoidable work delays, and fatigue.

8. Compute the **standard time**. This adjustment to the total normal time provides for allowances such as *personal* needs, unavoidable work *delays*, and worker *fatigue*:

$$\text{Standard time} = \frac{\text{Total normal time}}{1 - \text{Allowance factor}} \quad (10\text{-}3)$$

Personal time allowances are often established in the range of 4 percent to 7 percent of total time, depending on nearness to rest rooms, water fountains, and other facilities. *Delay allowances* are often set as a result of the actual studies of the delay that occurs. *Fatigue allowances* are based on our growing knowledge of human energy expenditure under various physical and environmental conditions. A sample set of personal and fatigue allowances is shown in Table 10.1. Example 1 illustrates the computation of standard time.

▼ **TABLE 10.1** Allowance Factors (in percent) for Various Classes of Work

1. Constant allowances:			(D) Bad light:	
(A) Personal allowance	5		(i) Well below recommended	2
(B) Basic fatigue allowance	4		(ii) Quite inadequate	5
2. Variable allowances:			(E) Atmospheric conditions (heat and humidity): Variable	0–10
(A) Standing allowance	2		(F) Close attention:	
(B) Abnormal position allowance:			(i) Fine or exacting	2
(i) Awkward (bending)	2		(ii) Very fine or very exacting	5
(ii) Very awkward (lying, stretching)	7		(G) Noise level:	
(C) Use of force or muscular energy in lifting, pulling, pushing Weight lifted (kilograms):			(i) Intermittent—loud	2
			(ii) Intermittent—very loud or high pitched	5
10	3		(H) Mental strain:	
20	9		(i) Complex or wide span of attention	4
30	17		(ii) Very complex	8
			(I) Tediousness:	
			(i) Tedious	2
			(ii) Very tedious	5

◄ EXAMPLE 1

Determining normal and standard time

The time study of a work operation at a falafel restaurant yielded an average observed time of 4.0 minutes. The analyst rated the observed worker at 85 percent. This means the worker performed at 85 percent of normal when the study was made. The firm uses a 13 percent allowance factor. The falafel restaurant wants to compute the normal time and the standard time for this operation.

APPROACH ▶ The firm needs to apply Equations (10-2) and (10-3).

SOLUTION ▶

Average observed time = 4.0 min

Total normal time = (Average observed time) × (Performance rating factor)
= (4.0)(0.85)
= 3.4 min

$$\text{Standard time} = \frac{\text{Total normal time}}{1 - \text{Allowance factor}} = \frac{3.4}{1 - 0.13} = \frac{3.4}{0.87}$$
= 3.9 min

INSIGHT ▶ Because the observed worker was rated at 85 percent (slower than average), the normal time is less than the worker's 4.0-minute average time.

LEARNING EXERCISE ▶ If the observed worker is rated at 115 percent (faster than average), what are the new normal and standard times? [Answer: 4.6 min, 5.287 min.]

RELATED PROBLEMS ▶ 10.8, 10.9, 10.10, 10.11, 10.12

EXCEL OM Data File **Ch10Ex1.xls** can be found at MyOMLab.

LO6: Compute the normal and standard times in a time study

Example 2 uses a series of actual stopwatch times for each element.

◄ EXAMPLE 2

Using time studies to compute standard time

Management Science Associates promotes its management development seminars by mailing thousands of individually composed and typed letters to various firms. A time study has been conducted on the task of preparing letters for mailing. On the basis of the following observations, Management Science Associates wants to develop a time standard for this task. The firm's personal, delay, and fatigue allowance factor is 15 percent.

Job Element	Observations (minutes)					Performance Rating
	1	2	3	4	5	
(A) Compose and type letter	8	10	9	21*	11	120%
(B) Type envelope address	2	3	2	1	3	105%
(C) Stuff, stamp, seal, and sort envelopes	2	1	5*	2	1	110%

APPROACH ▶ Once the data have been collected, the procedure is to:

1. Delete unusual or nonrecurring observations.
2. Compute the *average time* for each element, using Equation (10-1).
3. Compute the *normal time* for each element, using Equation (10-2).
4. Find the total normal time.
5. Compute the *standard time*, using Equation (10-3).

SOLUTION ▶

1. Delete observations such as those marked with an asterisk (*). (These may be due to business interruptions, conferences with the boss, or mistakes of an unusual nature; they are not part of the job element, but may be personal or delay time.)
2. Average time for each job element:

$$\text{Average time for A} = \frac{8 + 10 + 9 + 11}{4}$$
= 9.5 min

$$\text{Average time for B} = \frac{2 + 3 + 2 + 1 + 3}{5}$$
= 2.2 min

$$\text{Average time for C} = \frac{2 + 1 + 2 + 1}{4}$$
= 1.5 min

3. Normal time for each job element:

$$\text{Normal time for A} = (\text{Average observed time}) \times (\text{Performance rating})$$
$$= (9.5)(1.2)$$
$$= 11.4 \text{ min}$$
$$\text{Normal time for B} = (2.2)(1.05)$$
$$= 2.31 \text{ min}$$
$$\text{Normal time for C} = (1.5)(1.10)$$
$$= 1.65 \text{ min}$$

Note: Normal times are computed for each element because the performance rating factor (work pace) may vary for each element, as it did in this case.

4. Add the normal times for each element to find the total normal time (the normal time for the whole job):

$$\text{Total normal time} = 11.40 + 2.31 + 1.65$$
$$= 15.36 \text{ min}$$

5. Standard time for the job:

$$\text{Standard time} = \frac{\text{Total normal time}}{1 - \text{Allowance factor}} = \frac{15.36}{1 - 0.15}$$
$$= 18.07 \text{ min}$$

Thus, 18.07 minutes is the time standard for this job.

INSIGHT ▶   When observed times are not consistent they need to be reviewed. Abnormally short times may be the result of an observational error and are usually discarded. Abnormally long times need to be analyzed to determine if they, too, are an error. However, they may *include* a seldom occurring but legitimate activity for the element (such as a machine adjustment) or may be personal, delay, or fatigue time.

LEARNING EXERCISE ▶   If the two observations marked with an asterisk were *not* deleted, what would be the total normal time and the standard time? [Answer: 18.89 min, 22.22 min.]

RELATED PROBLEMS ▶   10.13, 10.14, 10.16a,b

Time study requires a sampling process; so the question of sampling error in the average observed time naturally arises. In statistics, error varies inversely with sample size. Thus, to determine just how many cycles we should time, we must consider the variability of each element in the study.

To determine an adequate sample size, three items must be considered:

1. How accurate we want to be (e.g. is ±5 percent of observed time close enough?).
2. The desired level of confidence (e.g. the *z*-value; is 95 percent adequate or is 99 percent required?).
3. How much variation exists within the job elements (e.g. if the variation is large, a larger sample will be required).

The formula for finding the appropriate sample size, given these three variables, is:

$$\text{Required sample size} = n = \left(\frac{zs}{h\bar{x}}\right)^2 \tag{10-4}$$

where h = accuracy level (acceptable error) desired in percentage of the job element, expressed as a decimal (5% = 0.5)

z = number of standard deviations required for desired level of confidence (90% confidence = 1.65; see Table 10.2 or Appendix I for more *z*-values)

s = standard deviation of the initial sample

$\bar{x}$ = mean of the initial sample

n = required sample size

▼ TABLE 10.2

Common *z*-Values

Desired Confidence (%)	*z*-Value (standard deviation required for desired level of confidence)
90.0	1.65
95.0	1.96
95.45	2.00
99.0	2.58
99.73	3.00

We demonstrate with Example 3.

Rana Co. has asked you to check a labor standard prepared by a recently terminated analyst. Your first task is to determine the correct sample size. Your accuracy is to be within 5 percent and your confidence level at 95 percent. The standard deviation of the sample is 1.0 and the mean 3.00.

APPROACH ▶ You apply Equation (10-4).

SOLUTION ▶
$$h = 0.05 \qquad \bar{x} = 3.00 \qquad s = 1.0$$
$$z = 1.96 \text{ (from Table 10.2 or Appendix I)}$$

$$n = \left(\frac{zs}{h\bar{x}}\right)^2$$

$$n = \left(\frac{1.96 \times 1.0}{0.05 \times 3}\right)^2 = 170.74 \approx 171$$

Therefore, you recommend a sample size of 171.

INSIGHT ▶ Notice that as the confidence level required increases, the sample size also increases. Similarly, as the desired accuracy level increases (say, from 5 percent to 1 percent), the sample size increases.

LEARNING EXERCISE ▶ The confidence level for Rana Co. can be set lower, at 90 percent, while retaining the same ±5 percent accuracy levels. What sample size is needed now? [Answer: $n = 121$.]

RELATED PROBLEMS ▶ 10.15, 10.16c

EXCEL OM Data File **Ch10Ex3.xls** can be found at MyOMLab.

Now let's look at two variations of Example 3.

First, if h, the desired accuracy, is expressed as an absolute amount of error (say, 1 minute of error is acceptable), then substitute e for $h\bar{x}$, and the appropriate formula is:

$$n = \left(\frac{zs}{e}\right)^2 \tag{10-5}$$

where e is the absolute time amount of acceptable error.

Second, for those cases when s, the standard deviation of the sample, is not provided (which is typically the case outside the classroom), it must be computed. The formula for doing so is:

$$s = \sqrt{\frac{\sum(x_i - \bar{x})^2}{n-1}} = \sqrt{\frac{\sum(\text{Each sample observation} - \bar{x})^2}{\text{Number in sample} - 1}} \tag{10-6}$$

where x_i = value of each observation
$\bar{x}$ = mean of the observations
n = number of observations in the sample

An example of this computation is provided in Solved Problem 10.3 on page 318.

Although time studies provide accuracy in setting labor standards (see the *OM in Action* box 'Aramex: Competing Through Accuracy'), they have two disadvantages. First, they require a trained staff of analysts. Second, these standards cannot be set before tasks are actually performed. This leads us to two alternative work-measurement techniques that we discuss next.

LO7: Find the proper sample size for a time study

Predetermined time standards
A division of manual work into small basic elements that have established and widely accepted times.

AUTHOR COMMENT
Families of predetermined time standards have been developed for many occupations.

Predetermined Time Standards

In addition to historical experience and time studies, we can set production standards by using predetermined time standards. **Predetermined time standards** divide manual work into small basic elements that already have established times (based on very large samples of workers). To estimate the time for a particular task, the time factors for each basic element of that task are added together. Developing a comprehensive system of predetermined time standards would be prohibitively expensive for any given firm. Consequently, a number of systems are commercially available. The most common predetermined time standard is *methods time measurement* (MTM), which is a product of the MTM Association.[3]

OM in Action ▶ Aramex: Competing Through Accuracy

Aramex employs 6,000 people and delivers thousands of parcels a day to locations throughout the world, particularly the Arab world. To achieve its promise of delivering an express service, Aramex invests a significant sum of capital, time, and energy in training its employees to respond quickly, using the latest technology in the most effective and efficient manner.

Specialists and planners at Aramex use the latest GPS and tracking systems to help drivers take the shortest route to their pickup and delivery destinations. The aim is to avoid any unpredicted traffic jams and road maintenance to ensure the smooth flow of the delivery process. The GPS technology also helps Aramex to set time standards for each delivery to ensure that drivers are maximizing the use of their time, thus minimizing the cost. Most importantly, these standards serve as controlling criteria against which drivers are measured for performance.

Aramex also focuses on training its drivers to better use their time and energy through motion guidance. They are trained on the most specific details of driving procedures and handling techniques and then provided with these instructions in a written format. The company issues a manual for its drivers to refer to at every step. Such detailed instructions are needed to increase productivity and to ensure that the drivers are on time, every time.

Source: **www.aramex.com**

Therbligs

Basic physical elements of motion.

Time measurement units (TMUs)

Units for very basic micromotions in which 1 TMU = 0.0006 minute or 100,000 TMUs = 1 hour.

Predetermined time standards are an outgrowth of basic motions called **therbligs**. The term *therblig* was coined by Frank Gilbreth and is *Gilbreth* spelled backwards, with the *t* and *h* reversed. Therbligs include such activities as select, grasp, position, assemble, reach, hold, rest, and inspect. These activities are stated in terms of **time measurement units (TMUs)**, which are equal to only 0.00001 hour, or 0.0006 minute each. MTM values for various therbligs are specified in very detailed tables. Figure 10.10, for example, provides the set of time standards for the motion GET and PLACE. To use GET and PLACE, one must know what is being moved, its approximate weight, and where and how far it is supposed to be placed.

Example 4 shows the use of predetermined time standards in setting service labor standards.

▶ **FIGURE 10.10**

Sample MTM Table for GET and PLACE Motion

Time values are in TMUs.

Source: Copyrighted by the MTM Association for Standards and Research. No reprint permission without consent from the MTM Association, 16–01 Broadway, Fair Lawn, NJ 07410. Used with permission of the MTM Association for Standards and Research.

GET and PLACE				DISTANCE RANGE IN IN.	<8	>8 <20	>20 <32
WEIGHT	CONDITIONS OF GET	PLACE ACCURACY	MTM CODE	1	2	3	
<2 LB	EASY	APPROXIMATE	AA	20	35	50	
		LOOSE	AB	30	45	60	
		TIGHT	AC	40	55	70	
	DIFFICULT	APPROXIMATE	AD	20	45	60	
		LOOSE	AE	30	55	70	
		TIGHT	AF	40	65	80	
	HANDFUL	APPROXIMATE	AG	40	65	80	
>2 LB <18 LB		APPROXIMATE	AH	25	45	55	
		LOOSE	AJ	40	65	75	
		TIGHT	AK	50	75	85	
>18 LB <45 LB		APPROXIMATE	AL	90	106	115	
		LOOSE	AM	95	120	130	
		TIGHT	AN	120	145	160	

---

[3]MTM is really a family of products available from the Methods Time Measurement Association. For example, MTM-HC deals with the health care industry, MTM-C handles clerical activities, MTM-M involves microscope activities, MTM-V deals with machine shop tasks, and so on.

General Hospital wants to set the standard time for lab technicians to pour a tube specimen using MTM.[4]

APPROACH ▶ This is a repetitive task for which the MTM data in Table 10.3 may be used to develop standard times. The sample tube is in a rack and the centrifuge tubes in a nearby box. A technician removes the sample tube from the rack, uncaps it, gets the centrifuge tube, pours, and places both tubes in the rack.

Element Description	Element	Time
Get tube from rack	AA2	35
Uncap, place on counter	AA2	35
Get centrifuge tube, place at sample tube	AD2	45
Pour (3 sec)	PT	83
Place tubes in rack	PC2	40
	Total TMU	238

$0.0006 \times 238 =$ Total standard minutes $= 0.143$ or about 8.6 seconds

SOLUTION ▶ The first work element involves getting the tube from the rack. The conditions for GETTING the tube and PLACING it in front of the technician are:

- *Weight:* (less than 1 kilogram)
- *Conditions of GET:* (easy)
- *Place accuracy:* (approximate)
- *Distance range:* (20 to 50 centimeters)

Then the MTM element for this activity is AA2 (as seen in Figure 10.10). The rest of Table 10.3 is developed from similar MTM tables.

INSIGHT ▶ Most MTM calculations are computerized, so the user need only key in the appropriate MTM codes, such as AA2 in this example.

LEARNING EXERCISE ▶ General Hospital decides that the first step in this process really involves a distance range of 10 cm (getting the tube from the rack). The other work elements are unchanged. What is the new standard time? [Answer: 0.134 min. or just over 8 seconds]

RELATED PROBLEM ▶ 10.19

Predetermined time standards have several advantages over direct time studies. First, they may be established in a laboratory environment, where the procedure will not upset actual production activities (which time studies tend to do). Second, because the standard can be set *before* a task is actually performed, it can be used for planning. Third, no performance ratings are necessary. Fourth, unions tend to accept this method as a fair means of setting standards. Finally, predetermined time standards are particularly effective in firms that do substantial numbers of studies of similar tasks. To ensure accurate labor standards, some firms use both time studies and predetermined time standards.

Work Sampling

The fourth method of developing labor or production standards, work sampling, was developed in England by L. Tippet in the 1930s. **Work sampling** estimates the percentage of the time that a worker spends on various tasks. Random observations are used to record the activity that a worker is performing. The results are primarily used to determine how employees allocate their time among various activities. Knowledge of this allocation may lead to staffing changes, reassignment of duties, estimates of activity cost, and the setting of delay allowances for labor standards. When work sampling is done to establish delay allowances, it is sometimes called a *ratio delay study.*

The work-sampling procedure can be summarized in five steps:

Work sampling

An estimate, via sampling, of the percentage of the time that a worker spends on various tasks.

[4]A. S. Helms, B. W. Shaw, and C. A. Lindner, "The Development of Laboratory Workload Standards through Computer-Based Work Measurement Technique, Part I," *Journal of Methods-Time Measurement* 12: 43. Used with permission of MTM Association for Standards and Research.

Using the techniques of this chapter to develop labor standards, operations managers at Orlando's Arnold Palmer Hospital determined that nurses walked an average of 4.35 km per day. This constitutes up to 30 percent of the nurse's time, a terrible waste of critical talent. Analysis resulted in a new layout design that has reduced walking distances by 20 percent.

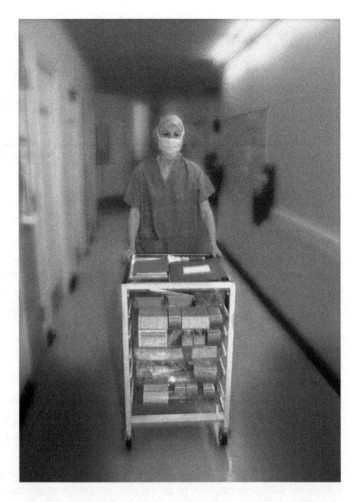

1. Take a preliminary sample to obtain an estimate of the parameter value (e.g. percentage of time a worker is busy).
2. Compute the sample size required.
3. Prepare a schedule for observing the worker at appropriate times. The concept of random numbers is used to provide for random observation. For example, let's say we draw the following five random numbers from a table: 7, 12, 22, 25, and 49. These can then be used to create an observation schedule of 9.07 a.m., 9.12, 9.22, 9.25, and 9.49.
4. Observe and record worker activities.
5. Determine how workers spend their time (usually as a percentage).

To determine the number of observations required, management must decide on the desired confidence level and accuracy. First, however, the analyst must select a preliminary value for the parameter under study (Step 1 above). The choice is usually based on a small sample of perhaps 50 observations. The following formula then gives the sample size for a desired confidence and accuracy:

$$n = \frac{z^2 p(1-p)}{h^2}$$

(10-7)

where n = required sample size
   z = number of standard deviations for the desired confidence level ($z = 1$ for 68 percent confidence, $z = 2$ for 95.45 percent confidence, and $z = 3$ for 99.73 percent confidence—these values are obtained from Table 10.2 or the normal table in Appendix I)
   p = estimated value of sample proportion (of time worker is observed busy or idle)
   h = acceptable error level, in percent

Example 5 shows how to apply this formula.

The manager of Jeddah Public Library, Dana Samir, estimates that her employees are idle 25 percent of the time. She would like to take a work sample that is accurate within 3 percent and wants to have 95.45 percent confidence in the results.

APPROACH ▶ Dana applies Equation (10-7) to determine how many observations should be taken.

SOLUTION ▶ Dana computes n:

$$n = \frac{z^2 p(1-p)}{h^2}$$

where n = required sample size
   z = 2 for 95.45 percent confidence level
   p = estimate of idle proportion = 25 percent = 0.25
   h = acceptable error of 3 percent = 0.03

She finds that

$$n = \frac{(2)^2(0.25)(0.75)}{(0.03)^2} = 833 \text{ observations}$$

INSIGHT ▶ Thus, 833 observations should be taken. If the percentage of idle time observed is not close to 25 percent as the study progresses, then the number of observations may have to be recalculated and increased or decreased as appropriate.

LEARNING EXERCISE ▶ If the confidence level increases to 99.73 percent, how does the sample size change? [Answer: n = 1,875.]

RELATED PROBLEM ▶ 10.18

◀ EXAMPLE 5
Determining the number of work sample observations needed

The focus of work sampling is to determine how workers allocate their time among various activities. This is accomplished by establishing the percentage of time individuals spend on these activities rather than the exact amount of time spent on specific tasks. The analyst simply records in a random, nonbiased way the occurrence of each activity. Example 6 shows the procedure for evaluating employees at the public library introduced in Example 5.

Dana Samir, the manager of Jeddah Public Library, wants to be sure her employees have adequate time to provide prompt, helpful service. She believes that service to library clients who phone or walk in with a question deteriorates rapidly when employees are busy more than 75 percent of the time. Consequently, she does not want her employees to be occupied with client service activities more than 75 percent of the time.

APPROACH ▶ The study requires several things: First, based on the calculations in Example 5, 833 observations are needed. Second, observations are to be made in a random, nonbiased way over a period of 2 weeks to ensure a true sample. Third, the analyst must define the activities that are 'work.' In this case, work is defined as all the activities necessary to take care of the client (inquiry handling, filing, meetings, data entry, discussions with the supervisor, etc.). Fourth, personal time is to be included in the 25 percent of nonwork time. Fifth, the observations are made in a nonintrusive way so as not to distort the normal work patterns. At the end of the 2 weeks, the 833 observations yield the following results:

◀ EXAMPLE 6
Determining employee time allocation with work sampling

No. of Observations	Activity
485	On the phone or meeting with a library client
126	Idle
62	Personal time
23	Discussions with supervisor
137	Filing, meeting, and computer data entry
833	

SOLUTION ▶ The analyst concludes that all but 188 observations (126 idle and 62 personal) are work related. Since 22.6 percent (= 188 ÷ 833) is less idle time than Dana believes necessary to ensure a high client service level, she needs to find a way to reduce current workloads. This could be done through a reassignment of duties or the hiring of additional personnel.

INSIGHT ▶ Work sampling is particularly helpful when determining staffing needs or the reallocation of duties (see Figure 10.11).

LEARNING EXERCISE ▶ The analyst working for Dana recategorizes several observations. There are now 450 'on the phone or meeting with a library client' observations, 156 'idle,' and 67 'personal time' observations. The last two categories saw no changes. Do the conclusions change? [Answer: Yes; now about 27 percent of employee time is not work related—over the 25 percent Dana desires.]

RELATED PROBLEM ▶ 10.17

The results of similar studies of salespeople and assembly-line employees are shown in Figure 10.11.

Work sampling offers several advantages over time-study methods. First, because a single observer can observe several workers simultaneously, it is less expensive. Second, observers usually do not require much training, and no timing devices are needed. Third, the study can be temporarily delayed at any time with little impact on the results. Fourth, because work sampling uses instantaneous observations over a long period, the worker has little chance of affecting the study's outcome. Fifth, the procedure is less intrusive and therefore less likely to generate objections.

The disadvantages of work sampling are: (1) it does not divide work elements as completely as time studies; (2) it can yield biased or incorrect results if the observer does not follow random routes of travel and observation; (3) because it is less intrusive, it tends to be less accurate; this is particularly true when job content times are short.

> **AUTHOR COMMENT**
> Mutual trust and commitment cannot be achieved without ethical behavior.

ETHICS

Ethics in the workplace presents some interesting challenges. As we have suggested in this chapter, many constraints influence job design. The issues of fairness, equity, and ethics are pervasive. Whether the issue is equal opportunity or safe working conditions, an operations manager is often the one responsible. Managers do have some guidelines. By knowing the law, working with government agencies, unions, trade associations, insurers, and employees, managers can often determine the parameters of their decisions. Human resource and legal departments are also available for help and guidance through the labyrinth of laws and regulations.

Management's role is to educate employees; specify the necessary equipment, work rules, and work environment; and then enforce those requirements, even when, for example, employees think it is not necessary to wear safety equipment. We began this chapter with a discussion of mutual trust and commitment, and that is the environment that managers should foster. Ethical management requires no less.

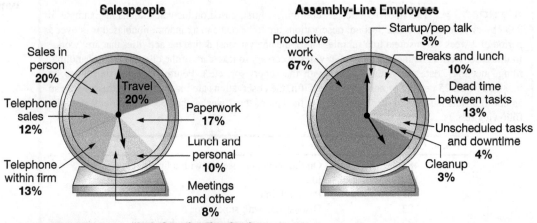

▲ FIGURE 10.11 Work-Sampling Time Studies

These two work-sampling time studies were done to determine the activities of salespeople at a wholesale electronics distributor (left) and a composite of several auto assembly-line employees (right).

CHAPTER SUMMARY

Outstanding firms know that their human resource strategy can yield a competitive advantage. Often a large percentage of employees and a large part of labor costs are under the direction of OM. Consequently, an operations manager usually has a major role to play in achieving human resource objectives. A requirement is to build an environment with mutual respect and commitment and a reasonable quality of work life. Successful organizations have designed jobs that use both the mental and physical capabilities of their employees. Regardless of the strategy chosen, the skill with which a firm manages its human resources ultimately determines its success.

Labor standards are required for an efficient operations system. They are needed for production planning, labor planning, costing, and evaluating performance. They are used throughout industry—from the factory to finance, sales, and the office. They can also be used as a basis for incentive systems. Standards may be established via historical data, time studies, predetermined time standards, and work sampling.

Key Terms

Activity chart (p. 306)
Average observed time (p. 308)
Division of labor (p. 300)
Employee empowerment (p. 301)
Ergonomics (p. 303)
Flextime (p. 299)
Flow diagram (p. 305)
Job design (p. 300)
Job enlargement (p. 300)

Job enrichment (p. 300)
Job rotation (p. 300)
Labor planning (p. 299)
Labor standards (p. 306)
Methods analysis (p. 304)
Normal time (p. 308)
Operations chart (p. 306)
Predetermined time standards (p. 311)
Process chart (p. 306)

Self-directed team (p. 301)
Standard time (p. 308)
Therbligs (p. 312)
Time measurement units (TMUs) (p. 312)
Time study (p. 308)
Visual workplace (p. 306)
Work sampling (p. 313)

Ethical Dilemma

Arabicana Steel, Inc. is a maker of cast-iron water and sewer pipes. In a very dangerous industry, Arabicana is perhaps the most unsafe company, with four times the injury rate of its six competitors combined. Its worker death rate is six times that of its industry's average. Arabicana plants were also found to be in violation of pollution and emission limits.

Workers who protest dangerous work conditions claim they are targeted for termination. Supervisors have bullied injured workers and intimidated union leaders. Line workers who fail to make daily quotas get disciplinary actions. Managers have put up safety signs *after* a worker was injured to make it appear the worker ignored posted policies. They alter safety records and doctor machines to cover up hazards.

Arabicana plants have also been repeatedly fined for failing to stop production to repair broken pollution controls. Five plants have been designated 'high priority' violators by the environment protection agency. Inside the plants, workers have repeatedly complained of blurred vision, severe headaches, and respiratory problems after being exposed, without training or protection, to chemicals used to make pipes. It is 'standard procedure' to illegally dump industrial contaminants into local rivers and creeks.

Given the following fictional scenario, what is your position, and what action should you take?

(a) On your spouse's recent move, you accepted a job, perhaps somewhat naively, as a company nurse in one of the Arabicana plants. After 2 weeks on the job you became aware of the work environment noted above.

(b) You are a contractor who has traditionally used Arabicana's products, which meet specifications. Arabicana is consistently the lowest bidder. Your customers are happy with the product.

(c) You are Arabicana's banker.

(d) You are a supplier to Arabicana.

Discussion Questions

1. How would you define a good quality of work life?
2. What are some of the worst jobs you know about? Why are they bad jobs? Why do people want these jobs?
3. If you were redesigning the jobs described in Question 2, what changes would you make? Are your changes realistic? Would they improve productivity (not just *production* but *productivity*)?
4. Can you think of any jobs that push the man–machine interface to the limits of human capabilities?
5. What are the five core characteristics of a good job design?
6. What are the differences among job enrichment, job enlargement, job rotation, job specialization, and employee empowerment?
7. Define ergonomics. Discuss the role of ergonomics in job design.
8. List the techniques available for carrying out methods analysis.
9. Identify four ways in which labor standards are set.
10. What are some of the uses to which labor standards are put?

11. How would you classify the following job elements? Are they personal, fatigue, or delay?
    (a) The operator stops to talk to you.
    (b) The operator lights up a cigarette.
    (c) The operator opens his lunch (it is not lunch time), removes an apple, and takes an occasional bite.
12. How do you classify the time for a drill press operator who is idle for a few minutes at the beginning of every job waiting for the setup person to complete the setup? Some of the setup time is used in going for stock, but the operator typically returns with stock before the setup person is finished with the setup.
13. How do you classify the time for a machine operator who, between every job and sometimes in the middle of jobs, turns off the machine and goes for stock?
14. The operator drops a part, which you pick up and hand to him. Does this make any difference in a time study? If so, how?

Solved Problems   Virtual Office Hours help is available at MyOMLab

▼ SOLVED PROBLEM 10.1

A work operation consisting of three elements has been subjected to a stopwatch time study. The recorded observations are shown in the following table. By union contract, the allowance time for the operation is personal time 5 percent, delay 5 percent, and fatigue 10 percent. Determine the standard time for the work operation.

Job	Observations (minutes)						Performance
Element	1	2	3	4	5	6	Rating (%)
A	0.1	0.3	0.2	0.9	0.2	0.1	90
B	0.8	0.6	0.8	0.5	3.2	0.7	110
C	0.5	0.5	0.4	0.5	0.6	0.5	80

▼ SOLUTION

First, delete the two observations that appear to be very unusual (0.9 minute for job element A and 3.2 minutes for job element B). Then:

$$\text{A's average observed time} = \frac{0.1 + 0.3 + 0.2 + 0.2 + 0.1}{5} = 0.18 \text{ min}$$

$$\text{B's average observed time} = \frac{0.8 + 0.6 + 0.8 + 0.5 + 0.7}{5} = 0.68 \text{ min}$$

$$\text{C's average observed time} = \frac{0.5 + 0.5 + 0.4 + 0.5 + 0.6 + 0.5}{6} = 0.50 \text{ min}$$

$$\text{A's normal time} = (0.18)(0.90) = 0.16 \text{ min}$$

$$\text{B's normal time} = (0.68)(1.10) = 0.75 \text{ min}$$

$$\text{C's normal time} = (0.50)(0.80) = 0.40 \text{ min}$$

$$\text{Normal time for job} = 0.16 + 0.75 + 0.40 - 1.31 \text{ min}$$

Note, the total allowance factor = 0.05 + 0.05 + 0.10 = 0.20

$$\text{Then: Standard time} = \frac{1.31}{1 - 0.20} = 1.64 \text{ min}$$

▼ SOLVED PROBLEM 10.2

The preliminary work sample of an operation indicates the following:

Number of times operator working	60
Number of times operator idle	40
Total number of preliminary observations	100

What is the required sample size for a 99.73 percent confidence level with ±4 percent precision?

▼ SOLUTION

$$z = 3 \text{ for 99.73 percent confidence}; \quad p = \frac{60}{100} = 0.6; \quad h = 0.04$$

So:

$$n = \frac{z^2 p(1-p)}{h^2} = \frac{(3)^2(0.6)(0.4)}{(0.04)^2} = 1,350 \text{ sample size}$$

▼ SOLVED PROBLEM 10.3

Amor Manufacturing Co. of Geneva, Switzerland has just observed a job in its laboratory in anticipation of releasing the job to the factory for production. The firm wants rather good accuracy for costing and labor forecasting. Specifically, it wants to provide a 99 percent confidence level and a cycle time that is within 3 percent of the true value. How many observations should it make? The data collected so far are as follows:

Observation	Time
1	1.7
2	1.6
3	1.4
4	1.4
5	1.4

▼ SOLUTION

First, solve for the mean, $\bar{x}$, and the sample standard deviation, s:

$$s = \sqrt{\frac{\sum(\text{Each sample observation} - \bar{x})^2}{\text{Number in sample} - 1}}$$

Observation	x_i	$\bar{x}$	$x_i - \bar{x}$	$(x_i - \bar{x})^2$
1	1.7	1.5	0.2	0.04
2	1.6	1.5	0.1	0.01
3	1.4	1.5	−0.1	0.01
4	1.4	1.5	−0.1	0.01
5	1.4	1.5	−0.1	0.01
	$\bar{x} = 1.5$			$0.08 = \sum(x_i - \bar{x})^2$

$$s = \sqrt{\frac{0.08}{n-1}} = \sqrt{\frac{0.08}{4}} = 0.141$$

Then, solve for

$$n = \left(\frac{zs}{h\bar{x}}\right)^2 = \left[\frac{(2.58)(0.141)}{(0.03)(1.5)}\right]^2 = 65.3$$

where $\bar{x} = 1.5$
$s = 0.141$
$z = 2.58$ (from Table 10.2)
$h = 0.03$

Therefore, you round up to 66 observations.

Problems*

• **10.1** Make a process chart for changing the right rear tire on an automobile.

• **10.2** Draw an activity chart for a machine operator with the following operation. The relevant times are as follows:

Prepare mill for loading (cleaning, oiling, and so on)	0.50 min
Load mill	1.75 min
Mill operating (cutting material)	2.25 min
Unload mill	0.75 min

•• **10.3** Make an operations chart of one of the following:
a) Putting a new eraser in (or on) a pencil
b) Putting a paper clip on two pieces of paper
c) Putting paper in a printer

• **10.4** Develop a process chart for installing a new memory board in your personal computer.

• **10.5** Rate a job you have had using Hackman and Oldham's core job characteristics (see page 301) on a scale from 1 to 10. What is your total score? What about the job could have been changed to make you give it a higher score?

••• **10.6** Draw an activity chart for washing the dishes in a double-sided sink. Two people participate, one washing, the other rinsing and drying. The rinser dries a batch of dishes from the drip rack as the washer fills the right sink with clean but unrinsed dishes. Then the rinser rinses the clean batch and places them on the drip rack. All dishes are stacked before being placed in the cabinets.

•••• **10.7** Design a process chart for printing a short document on a laser printer at an office. Unknown to you, the printer in the hallway is out of paper. The paper is located in a supply room at the other end of the hall. You wish to make five stapled copies of the document once it is printed. The copier, located next to the printer, has a sorter but no stapler. How could you make the task more efficient with the existing equipment?

*Note: **P✕** means the problem may be solved with POM for Windows and/or Excel.

• **10.8** If Saleha has times of 8.4, 8.6, 8.3, 8.5, 8.7, and 8.5 and a performance rating of 110 percent, what is the normal time for this operation? Is she faster or slower than normal? **P✕**

• **10.9** If Saleha, the worker in Problem 10.8, has a performance rating of 90 percent, what is the normal time for the operation? Is she faster or slower than normal? **P✕**

•• **10.10** Refer to Problem 10.8.
a) If the allowance factor is 15 percent, what is the standard time for this operation?
b) If the allowance factor is 18 percent and the performance rating is now 90 percent, what is the standard time for this operation? **P✕**

• **10.11** After being observed many times, Jamileh, a hospital lab analyst, had an average observed time for blood tests of 12 minutes. Jamileh's performance rating is 105 percent. The hospital has a personal, fatigue, and delay allowance of 16 percent.
a) Find the normal time for this process.
b) Find the standard time for this blood test. **P✕**

• **10.12** After training, Mariam, a computer technician, had an average observed time for memory-chip tests of 12 seconds. Mariam's performance rating is 100 percent. The firm has a personal fatigue and delay allowance of 15 percent.
a) Find the normal time for this process.
b) Find the standard time for this process. **P✕**

• **10.13** The results of a time study to perform a quality control test are shown in the following table. On the basis of these observations, determine the normal and standard time for the test, assuming a 23 percent allowance factor. **P✕**

Task Element	Performance Rating (%)	Observations (minutes)				
		1	2	3	4	5
1	97	1.5	1.8	2.0	1.7	1.5
2	105	0.6	0.4	0.7	3.7[a]	0.5
3	86	0.5	0.4	0.6	0.4	0.4
4	90	0.6	0.8	0.7	0.6	0.7

[a]Disregard—employee is smoking a cigarette (included in personal time).

•• **10.14** Botros Jalil, a loan processor at the National Bank, has been timed performing four work elements, with the results shown in the following table. The allowances for tasks such as this are personal, 7 percent; fatigue, 10 percent; and delay, 3 percent.

Task Element	Performance Rating (%)	Observations (minutes)				
		1	2	3	4	5
1	110	0.5	0.4	0.6	0.4	0.4
2	95	0.6	0.8	0.7	0.6	0.7
3	90	0.6	0.4	0.7	0.5	0.5
4	85	1.5	1.8	2.0	1.7	1.5

a) What is the normal time?
b) What is the standard time? **Px**

•• **10.15** A time study of a factory worker has revealed an average observed time of 3.20 minutes, with a standard deviation of 1.28 minutes. These figures were based on a sample of 45 observations. Is this sample adequate in size for the firm to be 99 percent confident that the standard time is within 5 percent of the true value? If not, what should be the proper number of observations? **Px**

•• **10.16** Based on a careful work study in the Rushdi Corp., the results shown in the following table have been observed:

Element	Observations (minutes)					Performance Rating (%)
	1	2	3	4	5	
Prepare daily reports	35	40	33	42	39	120
Photocopy results	12	10	36[a]	15	13	110
Label and package reports	3	3	5	5	4	90
Distribute reports	15	18	21	17	45[b]	85

[a]Photocopying machine broken; included as delay in the allowance factor.
[b]Power outage; included as delay in the allowance factor.

a) Compute the normal time for each work element.
b) If the allowance for this type of work is 15 percent, what is the standard time?

c) How many observations are needed for a 95 percent confidence level within 5 percent accuracy? (*Hint*: Calculate the sample size of each element.)

••• **10.17** A random work sample of operators taken over a 160-hour working month at Tele-Marketing, Inc., Jordan, has produced the following results. What is the percentage of time spent working?

On phone with customer	858
Idle time	220
Personal time	85

•• **10.18** A total of 300 observations of Luay, an assembly-line worker, were made over a 40-hour working week. The sample also showed that Luay was busy working (assembling the parts) during 250 observations.
a) Find the percentage of time Luay was working.
b) If you want a confidence level of 95 percent, and if 3 percent is an acceptable error, what size should the sample be?
c) Was the sample size adequate? **Px**

• **10.19** Sharpening your pencil is an operation that may be divided into eight small elemental motions. In MTM terms, each element may be assigned a certain number of TMUs:

Reach 14 centimeters for the pencil	6 TMU
Grasp the pencil	2 TMU
Move the pencil 16 centimeters	10 TMU
Position the pencil	20 TMU
Insert the pencil into the sharpener	4 TMU
Sharpen the pencil	120 TMU
Disengage the pencil	10 TMU
Move the pencil 16 centimeters	10 TMU

What is the total normal time for sharpening one pencil? Convert your answer into minutes and seconds.

▶ **Refer to** MyOMLab **for additional homework problems.**

Case Studies

Jameelah Manufacturing Company

Kamila, vice president of operations at Jameelah Manufacturing Company, has just received a request for quote (RFQ) from Odai Electric Supply for 400 units per week of a motor armature. The components are standard and either easy to work into the existing production schedule or readily available from established suppliers on a JIT basis. But there is some difference in assembly. Kamila has identified eight tasks that Jameelah must perform to assemble the armature. Seven of these tasks are very similar to ones performed by Jameelah in the past; therefore, the average time and resulting labor standard of those tasks is known.

The eighth task, an *overload* test, requires performing a task that is very different from any performed previously, however. Kamila has asked you to conduct a time study on the task to determine the standard time. Then an estimate can be made of the cost to assemble the armature. This information, combined with other cost data, will allow the firm to put together the information needed for the RFQ.

To determine a standard time for the task, an employee from an existing assembly station was trained in the new assembly process. Once proficient, the employee was then asked to perform the task 17 times so a standard could be determined. The actual times observed (in minutes) were as follows:

1	2	3	4	5	6	7	8	9	10	11	12	13	14	15	16	17
2.05	1.92	2.01	1.89	1.77	1.80	1.86	1.83	1.93	1.96	1.95	2.05	1.79	1.82	1.85	1.85	1.99

The worker had a 115 percent performance rating. The task can be performed in a sitting position at a well-designed ergonomic workstation in an air-conditioned facility. Although the armature itself weighs 10.5 kilograms, there is a carrier that holds it so that the operator need only rotate the armature. But the detailed work remains high; therefore, the fatigue allowance should be 8 percent. The company has an established personal allowance of 6 percent. Delay should be very low. Previous studies of delay in this department average 2 percent. This standard is to use the same figure.

The working day is 7.5 hours, but operators are paid for 8 hours at an average of US$12.50 per hour.

Adapted from Source: Professor Hank Maddux, Sam Houston State University, United States.

Discussion Questions

In your report to Kamila, you realize you will want to address several factors:

1. How big should the sample be for a statistically accurate standard (at, say, the 99.73 percent confidence level and accuracy of 5 percent)?
2. Is the sample size adequate?
3. How many units should be produced at this workstation per day?
4. What is the cost per unit for this task in direct labor cost?

Hard Rock's Human Resource Strategy

Video Case

Everyone—managers and hourly employees alike—who goes to work for Hard Rock Cafe takes Rock 101, an initial 2-day training class. There they receive their wallet-sized 'Hard Rock Values' card which they carry at all times. The Hard Rock value system is to bring a fun, healthy, nurturing environment into the Hard Rock Cafe culture.* This initial course and many other courses help employees develop both personally and professionally. The human resource department plays a critical role in any service organization, but at Hard Rock, with its 'experience strategy,' the human resource department takes on added importance.

Long before Jim Knight, manager of corporate training, begins the class, the human resource strategy of Hard Rock has had an impact. Hard Rock's strategic plan includes building a culture that allows for acceptance of substantial diversity and individuality. From a human resource perspective, this has the benefit of enlarging the pool of applicants as well as contributing to the Hard Rock culture.

Creating a work environment above and beyond a paycheck is a unique challenge. Outstanding pay and benefits are a start, but the key is to provide an environment that works for the employees. This includes benefits that start for part-timers who work at least 19 hours per week (while others in the industry start at 35 hours per week); a unique respect for individuality; continuing training; and a high level of internal promotions—some 60 percent of the managers are promoted from hourly employee ranks. The company's training is very specific, with job-oriented interactive CDs covering kitchen, retail, and front-of-house service. Outside volunteer work is especially encouraged to foster a bond between the workers, their community, and issues of importance to them.

Applicants also are screened on their interest in music and their ability to tell a story. Hard Rock builds on a hiring criterion of bright, positive-attitude, self-motivated individuals with an employee bill of rights and substantial employee empowerment. The result is a unique culture and work environment which, no doubt, contributes to the low turnover of hourly people—one-half the industry average.

The layout, memorabilia, music, and videos are important elements in the Hard Rock 'experience,' but it falls on the waiters and waitresses to make the experience come alive. They are particularly focused on providing an authentic and memorable dining experience. Like Southwest Airlines, Hard Rock is looking for people with a cause—people who like to serve. By succeeding with its human resource strategy, Hard Rock obtains a competitive advantage.

Hard Rock Values

1. Innovate and create at every opportunity.
2. Encourage our employees to maximize their potential.
3. Love All–Serve All... treat every individual with respect.
4. Deliver exceptional quality... exceed expectations.
5. Ensure the long-term growth and success of our organization.
6. Save the Planet... actively participate in the well-being of our planet and its people.
7. Practice honesty, integrity and professionalism.

Discussion Questions[†]

1. What has Hard Rock done to lower employee turnover to half the industry average?
2. How does Hard Rock's human resource department support the company's overall strategy?
3. How would Hard Rock's value system work for automobile assembly-line workers? (*Hint*: Consider Hackman and Oldham's core job characteristics.)
4. How might you adjust a traditional assembly line to address more 'core job characteristics'?

*Hard Rock Cafe's mission, mottos, and operating values are available at **www.hardrock.com/corporate/careers.**

[†]Before answering these questions, you may wish to view the video that accompanies this case.

▶ **Additional Case Studies:** Visit MyOMLab for these free case studies:

Chicago Southern Hospital: Examines the requirements for a work-sampling plan for nurses.
Karstadt versus JCPenney: Compares the work culture in retailing in the United States and Germany.
The Fleet That Wanders: Requires a look at ergonomic issues for truck drivers.

Main Heading	Review Material	MyOMLab
HUMAN RESOURCE STRATEGY FOR COMPETITIVE ADVANTAGE (pp. 298–299)	*The objective of a human resource strategy is to manage labor and design jobs so people are effectively and efficiently utilized.* *Quality of work life* refers to a job that is not only reasonably safe with equitable pay but that also achieves an appropriate level of both physical and psychological requirements. *Mutual commitment* means that both management and employees strive to meet common objectives. *Mutual trust* is reflected in reasonable, documented employment policies that are honestly and equitably implemented to the satisfaction of both management and employees.	**VIDEO 10.1** Hard Rock's Human Resource Strategy
LABOR PLANNING (pp. 299–300)	▪ **Labor planning**—A means of determining staffing policies dealing with employment stability, work schedules, and work rules. ▪ **Flextime**—Allows employees, within limits, to determine their own schedules. *Flexible* (or *compressed*) *working weeks* often call for fewer but longer working days. *Part-time status* is particularly attractive in service industries with fluctuating demand loads.	
JOB DESIGN (pp. 300–302)	▪ **Job design**—Specifies the tasks that constitute a job for an individual or group. ▪ **Division of labor** (also **labor specialization** (or **job specialization**)—The division of labor into unique ('special') tasks. ▪ **Job enlargement**—The grouping of a variety of tasks about the same skill level; horizontal enlargement. ▪ **Job rotation**—A system in which an employee is moved from one specialized job to another. ▪ **Job enrichment**—A method of giving an employee more responsibility that includes some of the planning and control necessary for job accomplishment; vertical expansion. ▪ **Employee empowerment**—Enlarging employee jobs so that the added responsibility and authority is moved to the lowest level possible. ▪ **Self-directed team**—A group of empowered individuals working together to reach a common goal.	
ERGONOMICS AND THE WORK ENVIRONMENT (pp. 302–304)	▪ **Ergonomics**—The study of the human interface with the environment and machines. The physical environment affects performance, safety, and quality of work life. Illumination, noise and vibration, temperature, humidity, and air quality are controllable by management.	
METHODS ANALYSIS (pp. 304–306)	▪ **Methods analysis**—A system that involves developing work procedures that are safe and produce quality products efficiently. ▪ **Flow diagram**—A drawing used to analyze movement of people or materials. ▪ **Process chart**—A graphic representation that depicts a sequence of steps for a process. ▪ **Activity chart**—A way of improving utilization of an operator and a machine or some combination of operators (a crew) and machines. ▪ **Operations chart**—A chart depicting right- and left-hand motions.	
THE VISUAL WORKPLACE (p. 306)	▪ **Visual workplace**—Uses a variety of visual communication techniques to rapidly communicate information to stakeholders.	Virtual Office Hours for Solved Problems: 10.1–10.4

MyOMLab

Main Heading	Review Material	
LABOR STANDARDS (pp. 306–316)	■ **Labor standards**—The amount of time required to perform a job or part of a job. Labor standards are set in four ways: (1) historical experience; (2) time studies; (3) predetermined time standards; (4) work sampling. ■ **Time study**—Timing a sample of a worker's performance and using it as a basis for setting a standard time. ■ **Average observed time**—The arithmetic mean of the times for each element measured, adjusted for unusual influence for each element: $$\text{Average observed time} = \frac{\text{(Sum of the times recorded to perform each element)}}{\text{Number of observations}} \quad (10\text{-}1)$$ ■ **Normal time**—The average observed time, adjusted for pace: $$\text{Normal time} = \text{(Average observed time)} \times \text{(Performance rating factor)} \quad (10\text{-}2)$$ ■ **Standard time**—An adjustment to the total normal time; the adjustment provides allowances for personal needs, unavoidable work delays, and fatigue: $$\text{Standard time} = \frac{\text{Total normal time}}{1 - \text{Allowance factor}} \quad (10\text{-}3)$$ *Personal time allowances* are often established in the range of 4 percent to 7 percent of total time. $$\text{Required sample size} = n = \left(\frac{zs}{h\bar{x}}\right)^2 \quad (10\text{-}4)$$ $$n = \left(\frac{zs}{e}\right)^2 \quad (10\text{-}5)$$ $$s = \sqrt{\frac{\sum (x_i - \bar{x})^2}{n-1}} = \sqrt{\frac{\sum (\text{Each sample observation} - \bar{x})^2}{\text{Number in sample} - 1}} \quad (10\text{-}6)$$ ■ **Predetermined time standards**—A division of manual work into small basic elements that have established and widely accepted times. The most common predetermined time standard is *methods time measurement* (MTM). ■ **Therbligs**—Basic physical elements of motion. ■ **Time measurement units (TMUs)**—Units for very basic micromotions in which 1 TMU = 0.0006 minute or 100,000 TMUs = 1 hour. ■ **Work sampling**—An estimate, via sampling, of the percentage of the time that a worker spends on various tasks. Work sampling sample size for a desired confidence and accuracy: $$n = \frac{z^2 p(1-p)}{h^2} \quad (10\text{-}7)$$	Problems 10.8–10.19
ETHICS (p. 316)	Management's role is to educate the employee; specify the necessary equipment, work rules, and work environment; and then enforce those requirements.	

*Self-*Test

■ **Before taking the self-test,** refer to the learning objectives listed at the beginning of the chapter and the key terms listed at the end of the chapter.

LO1. When product demand fluctuates and yet you maintain a constant level of employment, some of your cost savings might include:
 a) reduction in hiring costs
 b) reduction in layoff costs and unemployment insurance costs
 c) lack of need to pay a premium wage to get workers to accept unstable employment
 d) having a trained workforce rather than having to retrain new employees each time you hire for an upswing in demand
 e) all of the above.

LO2. The difference between *job enrichment* and *job enlargement* is that:
 a) enlarged jobs contain a larger number of similar tasks, while enriched jobs include some of the planning and control necessary for job accomplishment
 b) enriched jobs contain a larger number of similar tasks, while enlarged jobs include some of the planning and control necessary for job accomplishment
 c) enriched jobs enable an employee to do a number of boring jobs instead of just one
 d) all of the above.

LO3. The work environment includes these factors:
 a) Lighting, noise, temperature, and air quality
 b) Illumination, carpeting, and high ceilings
 c) Enough space for meetings and videoconferencing
 d) Noise, humidity, and number of coworkers
 e) Job enlargement and space analysis.

LO4. *Methods analysis* focuses on:
 a) the design of the machines used to perform a task
 b) how a task is accomplished
 c) the raw materials that are consumed in performing a task
 d) reducing the number of steps required to perform a task.

LO5. The least preferred method of establishing labor standards is:
 a) time studies
 b) work sampling
 c) historical experience
 d) predetermined time standards.

LO6. The allowance factor in a time study:
 a) adjusts normal time for errors and rework
 b) adjusts standard time for lunch breaks
 c) adjusts normal time for personal needs, unavoidable delays, and fatigue
 d) allows workers to rest every 20 minutes.

LO7. To set the required sample size in a time study, you must know:
 a) the number of employees
 b) the number of parts produced per day
 c) the desired accuracy and confidence levels
 d) management's philosophy toward sampling.

11 Managing the Supply Chain

10 OM STRATEGY DECISIONS

- ► Design of Goods and Services
- ► Managing Quality
- ► Process Strategy
- ► Location Strategies
- ► Layout Strategies
- ► Human Resources
- ► **Supply-Chain Management**
- ► Inventory Management
- ► Scheduling
- ► Maintenance

LANDMARK'S SUPPLY CHAIN YIELDS A COMPETITIVE EDGE

As one of the most successful retailers in the Middle East, the Landmark Group has developed a supply chain that is the envy of rivals throughout the region.

Founded back in the 1970s with a single store in Bahrain, the Landmark Group has emerged as one of the Middle East's most successful retailers, with over 900 stores across the region, in addition to countries such as India, Pakistan, Turkey and Egypt.

"We provide a value-driven product range for the entire family," explains Vipin Sethi, CEO of Landmark Group. "Quality is not a question of price for our company. Across our retail concepts, we strive to provide value at every price point."

Diversity has obviously played a fundamental role in developing the Landmark Group's market-leading position, with a portfolio that covers footwear and accessories (Shoe Mart), fashion (Splash), children's clothing (Baby Shop), furniture (Home Center and Q Home Décor) and home décor (Lifestyle). Even outside of retail, the group has interests in everything from indoor entertainment centers for children to specialty good offerings and even budget hotels. "Our various offerings have evolved into the preferred choice for consumers and have become category killers," continues Sethi.

While a number of chief executives have made similar claims about their brands in the Middle East, the fact that Landmark Group has achieved a consistent annual growth rate of 25 percent is perfect support to Sethi's assertion about the company, which currently employs around 31,000 personnel in total.

Further evidence is provided by the numerous trophies that decorate his office, including Retailer of the Year from the Retail City Awards, to the Business Excellence Award in the re-export category at the Mohammed Bin Rashid Al Maktoum Business Awards.

"With so much activity within the Landmark Group, our supply chain operations must be efficient. The products are sent to the Middle East from across the world, with a particular focus on India, China, Hong Kong, and Indonesia," states Sethi, who has a refreshing knowledge of supply chain issues.

"We use a combination of different transportation modes. The majority arrives by sea freight, although airfreight is used for high-priority movements, based on criticality of the shipments. The use of roads is based on the feasibility and nature of cargo being moved. For instance, road transport is avoided for fragile cargo movement to ensure no in-transit damages are caused to our merchandise."

Once the products arrive in the region, they are transported to one of the Landmark Group's growing number of logistics facilities, including a regional distribution center (RDC), central distribution center (CDC) in Jebel Ali Free Zone, and origin-consolidated freight stations (CFS).

"Our facilities are located across the Middle East and each warehouse is equipped with modern storage equipment and material handling solutions, which have been acquired from market leaders such as Famco," continues Sethi. "This includes everything from multi-level racking, VNA racking and selective racking to electric forklifts, reach trucks and hand pallet trolleys. Our operations are also supported by Oracle WMS for real-time visibility of inventory, assisting us to make the required decisions."

Landmark Group has opted for a combined in-house and 3PL model to manage its supply chain operations. "This helps us in serving our customers better. Transportation is outsourced at all our locations as it gives us the flexibility to manage our business volumes. Our inter-GCC movement contracts are door-to-door, which means our service providers handle transportation and border clearances efficiently," explains Sethi. "Our warehousing operation is done in-house as the necessary infrastructure and skills have been developed by us to specifically cater to the group's growing needs."

The executive admits that, like any growing organization, Landmark Group has grappled with various supply chain challenges at various times. Much of this has centered on developing the right infrastructure at the right time to handle the growth in business and volumes. In addition, his logistics team has worked tirelessly to meet country-specific regulations and requirements on product standards and documentation.

"This is critical as it impacts the lead times of product delivery from the point-of-origin to the point-of-consumption," he maintains. "We also have challenges such as port congestion and border congestion impacting transit lead times, in addition to inflationary pressures which drive up the supply chain cost."

Landmark's supply chain comprises a complex and highly sophisticated network of hundreds of suppliers from all over the globe.

Sethi is evidently proud that Landmark Group's supply chain has proved a success is battling these challenges. And with high ambitions to develop the group even further in the coming years, there are various initiatives in place to continue strengthening its logistics processes.

"There are three key stages to our supply chain development plan. Firstly, we will continually evaluate and modify the network design to ensure minimum lead times and cost," he explains. "Secondly, we will invest in state-of-the-art IT systems for efficiency and effectiveness in operations. And finally, we have a dedicated supply chain process improvement cell, which is responsible for benchmarking the best supply chain practices around the world and implementing it in Landmark. With these three factors, I am confident our supply chain will continue to support all growth predictions for the coming years."

Landmark expanded at an incredible pace, to include several outlets in the Gulf region, due to its highly efficient supply chain management.

Source: ITP Business Publishing Ltd., Arabia Supply Chain.com, Landmark Group, Dubai (2010), from **www.arabiansupplychain.com/ article-4003-logistics-case-study-landmark-group-dubai/**.

Chapter 11 Learning Objectives

AUTHOR COMMENT
Competition today is not between companies; it is between supply chains.

THE SUPPLY CHAIN'S STRATEGIC IMPORTANCE

Most firms, like Landmark, spend a huge portion of their revenues on purchases. Because an increasing percentage of an organization's costs are determined by purchasing, relationships with suppliers are increasingly integrated and long term. Joint efforts that improve innovation, speed design, and reduce costs are common. Such efforts, when part of a corporate-wide strategy, can dramatically improve both partners' competitiveness. This integrated focus places added emphasis on managing supplier relationships.

Supply-chain management is the integration of the activities that procure materials and services, transform them into intermediate goods and final products, and deliver them to customers. These activities include purchasing and outsourcing activities, plus many other functions that are important to the relationship with suppliers and distributors. Supply-chain management includes determining: (1) transportation vendors; (2) credit and cash transfers; (3) suppliers; (4) distributors; (5) accounts payable and receivable; (6) warehousing and inventory; (7) order fulfillment; (8) sharing customer, forecasting, and production information. The *objective is to build a chain of suppliers that focuses on maximizing value to the ultimate customer.*

Supply-chain management

Management of activities that procure materials and services, transform them into intermediate goods and final products, and deliver them through a distribution system.

As firms strive to increase their competitiveness via product customization, high quality, cost reductions, and speed to market, added emphasis is placed on the supply chain. Effective supply-chain management makes suppliers 'partners' in the firm's strategy to satisfy an ever-changing marketplace. A competitive advantage may depend on a close long-term strategic relationship with a few suppliers.

LO1: Explain the strategic importance of the supply chain

To ensure that the supply chain supports the firm's strategy, managers need to consider the supply-chain issues shown in Table 11.1[1]. Activities of supply-chain managers cut across accounting, finance, marketing, and the operations discipline. Just as the OM function supports the firm's overall strategy, the supply chain must support the OM strategy. Strategies of low cost or rapid response demand different things from a supply chain than a strategy of differentiation. For instance, a low-cost strategy, as Table 11.1 indicates, requires suppliers be selected primarily on cost. Such suppliers should have the ability to design low-cost products that meet the functional requirements, minimize inventory, and drive down lead times.

▼ **TABLE 11.1**   How Supply-Chain Decisions Affect Strategy*

	Low-Cost Strategy	**Response Strategy**	**Differentiation Strategy**
Supplier's goal	Supply demand at lowest possible cost (e.g. Emerson Electric, Al Tazaj in Saudi Arabia)	Respond quickly to changing requirements and demand to minimize stockouts (e.g. Dell Computer)	Share market research; jointly develop products and options (e.g. Elzay in Jordan)
Primary selection criteria	Select primarily for cost	Select primarily for capacity, speed, and flexibility	Select primarily for product development skills
Process characteristics	Maintain high average utilization	Invest in excess capacity and flexible processes	Use modular processes that lend themselves to mass customization
Inventory characteristics	Minimize inventory throughout the chain to hold down costs	Develop responsive system, with buffer stocks positioned to ensure supply	Minimize inventory in the chain to avoid obsolescence
Lead-time characteristics	Shorten lead time as long as it does not increase costs	Invest aggressively to reduce production lead time	Invest aggressively to reduce development lead time
Product-design characteristics	Maximize performance and minimize cost	Use product designs that lead to low setup time and rapid production ramp-up	Use modular design to postpone product differentiation for as long as possible

[1]See related table and discussion in Marshall L. Fisher, "What Is the Right Supply Chain for Your Product?" *Harvard Business Review* (March–April 1997): 105.

Firms must achieve integration of strategy up and down the supply chain, and must expect that strategy to be different for different products and to change as products move through their life cycle. Landmark Group, as noted in the opening *Company Profile*, competes in a huge, worldwide retailing industry through following the best-in-class techniques and processes in its supply chain.

Supply-Chain Risk

VIDEO 11.1
Darden's Global Supply Chain

> **AUTHOR COMMENT**
> The environment, controls, and process performance all affect supply-chain risk.

In this age of increasing specialization, low communication cost, and fast transportation, companies are making less and buying more. This means more reliance on supply chains and more risk. Managing the new integrated supply chain is a strategic challenge. Having fewer suppliers makes the supplier and customer more dependent on each other, increasing risk for both. This risk is compounded by globalization and logistical complexity. In any supply chain, vendor reliability and quality may be challenging, but the new paradigm of a tight, fast, low-inventory supply chain, operating across political and cultural boundaries, adds a new dimension to risk. As organizations go global, shipping time may increase, logistics may be less reliable, and tariffs and quotas may block companies from doing business. In addition, international supply chains complicate information flows and increase political and currency risks.

Thus, the development of a successful strategic plan for supply-chain management requires careful research, an understanding of the risk involved, and innovative planning. Reducing risk in this increasingly global environment suggests that management must be able to mitigate and react to disruptions in:

1. *Processes* (raw material and component availability, quality, and logistics)
2. *Controls* (management metrics and reliable secure communication for financial transactions, product designs, and logistics scheduling)
3. *Environment* (customs duties, tariffs, security screening, natural disaster, currency fluctuations, terrorist attacks, and political issues)

Let's look at how several organizations address these risks in their supply chains.

- To reduce *process risk*, McDonald's planned its supply chain 6 years in advance of its opening in Russia. Creating a US$60 million 'food town,' it developed independently owned supply plants in Moscow to keep its transportation costs and handling times low and its quality and customer-service levels high.
- Ford's *process risk* reduction strategy is to develop a global network of *few but exceptional* suppliers who will provide the lowest cost and highest quality. This has driven one division's supplier base down to only 227 suppliers worldwide, compared with 700 previously.
- Landmark Group has placed extensive *controls*, including third-party audits, on supplier processes and logistics to ensure constant monitoring and reduction of risk.

Tight integration of the supply chain can have significant benefits, but the risks can and must be managed.

ETHICS AND SUSTAINABILITY

> **AUTHOR COMMENT**
> Because so much money passes through the supply chain, the opportunity for ethical lapses is significant.

Let's look at three aspects of ethics in the supply chain: personal ethics, ethics within the supply chain, and ethical behavior regarding the environment.

Personal Ethics

Ethical decisions are critical to the long-term success of any organization. However, the supply chain is particularly susceptible to ethical lapses, as the opportunities for unethical behavior are enormous. With sales personnel anxious to sell and purchasing agents spending huge sums, temptations abound. Many salespeople become friends with customers, do favors for them, take them to lunch, or present small (or large) gifts. Determining when tokens of friendship become bribes can be challenging. Many companies have strict rules and codes of conduct that limit what is acceptable. Recognizing these issues, in the U.S. the Institute for Supply Management has developed principles and standards to be used as guidelines for ethical behavior (as shown in Table 11.2). As the supply chain becomes international, operations managers need to expect an additional set of ethical issues to manifest themselves as they deal with new cultural values.

▼ **TABLE 11.2**

Principles and Standards of Ethical Supply Management Conduct

INTEGRITY IN YOUR DECISIONS AND ACTIONS; VALUE FOR YOUR EMPLOYER; LOYALTY TO YOUR PROFESSION

1   **PERCEIVED IMPROPRIETY** Prevent the intent and appearance of unethical or compromising conduct in relationships, actions, and communications.

2   **CONFLICTS OF INTEREST** Ensure that any personal, business, or other activity does not conflict with the lawful interests of your employer.

3   **ISSUES OF INFLUENCE** Avoid behaviors or actions that may negatively influence, or appear to influence, supply management decisions.

4   **RESPONSIBILITIES TO YOUR EMPLOYER** Uphold fiduciary and other responsibilities using reasonable care and granted authority to deliver value to your employer.

5   **SUPPLIER AND CUSTOMER RELATIONSHIPS** Promote positive supplier and customer relationships.

6   **SUSTAINABILITY AND SOCIAL RESPONSIBILITY** Champion social responsibility and sustainability practices in supply management.

7   **CONFIDENTIAL AND PROPRIETARY INFORMATION** Protect confidential and proprietary information.

8   **RECIPROCITY** Avoid improper reciprocal agreements.

9   **APPLICABLE LAWS, REGULATIONS, AND TRADE AGREEMENTS** Know and obey the letter and spirit of laws, regulations, and trade agreements applicable to supply management.

10 **PROFESSIONAL COMPETENCE** Develop skills, expand knowledge, and conduct business that demonstrates competence and promotes the supply management profession.

Source: **www.ism.ws**

Ethics within the Supply Chain

In this age of hyper-specialization, much of any organization's resources are purchased, putting great stress on ethics in the supply chain. Managers may be tempted to ignore ethical lapses by suppliers or offload pollution to suppliers. But firms must establish standards for their suppliers, just as they have established standards for themselves. Society expects ethical performance throughout the supply chain. For instance, Gap, Inc. reported that of its 3,000-plus factories worldwide, about 90 percent failed their initial evaluation.[2] The report indicated that 10 percent to 25 percent of Gap's Chinese factories engaged in psychological or verbal abuse, and more than 50 percent of the factories visited in sub-Saharan Africa operated without proper safety devices. The challenge of enforcing ethical standards is significant, but responsible firms, such as Gap, are finding ways to deal with this difficult issue.

Ethical Behavior Regarding the Environment

While ethics on both a personal basis and in the supply chain are important, so is ethical behavior in regard to the environment. Good ethics extends to doing business in a way that supports conservation and renewal of resources. This requires evaluation of the entire environmental impact, from raw material, to manufacture, through use, and final disposal. For instance, Al Fulk National Co. Ltd., which owns one of the biggest shrimp farms in the Arab world, abides by the standards of the Global Aquaculture Alliance in order to satisfy the conditions of many of its customers. These standards must be met if suppliers want to maintain the business relationship. Operations managers also ensure that sustainability is reflected in the performance of second- and third-tier suppliers. Enforcement can be done by in-house inspectors, third-party auditors, governmental agencies, or nongovernmental watchdog organizations. All four approaches are used.

The incoming supply chain garners most of the attention, but it is only part of the ethical challenge of sustainability. The 'return' supply chain is also significant. Returned products can only be burned, buried, or reused. And the first two options have adverse consequences. Once viewed in this manner, the need for operations managers to evaluate the entire product life cycle is apparent.

[2]Amy Merrick, "Gap Offers Unusual Look at Factory Conditions," *The Wall Street Journal* (May 12, 2004): A1, A12.

While 84 percent of an automobile and 90 percent of an airplane is recycled, these levels are not easily achieved. Recycling efforts began at product and process design. Then special end-of-product-life processes were developed. Oil, lead, gasoline, explosives in air bags, acid in batteries, and the many components (axles, differentials, jet engines, hydraulic valves) that still have many years of service all demand their own unique recovery, remanufacturing, or recycling process. This complexity places significant demands on the producer as well as return and reuse supply chains in the quest for sustainability. But pursuing this quest is the ethical thing to do. Saving the Earth is a challenging task.

> **AUTHOR COMMENT**
> A huge part of a firm's revenue is typically spent on purchases, so this is a good place to look for savings.

SUPPLY-CHAIN ECONOMICS

The supply chain receives such attention because it is an integral part of a firm's strategy and the most costly activity in most firms. For both goods and services, supply-chain costs as a percentage of sales are often substantial (see Table 11.3). Because such a huge portion of revenue is devoted to the supply chain, an effective strategy is vital. The supply chain provides a major opportunity to reduce costs and increase contribution margins.

Table 11.4 and Example 1 illustrate the amount of leverage available to the operations manager through the supply chain.

These numbers indicate the strong role that supply chains play in profitability.

▼ **TABLE 11.3**

Supply-Chain Costs as a Percentage of Sales

Industry	% Purchased
Automobile	67
Beverages	52
Chemical	62
Food	60
Lumber	61
Metals	65
Paper	55
Petroleum	79
Transportation	62

◀ **EXAMPLE 1**

Profit potential in the supply chain

Suha Furniture, Inc. of Lebanon spends 50 percent of its sales dollars in the supply chain and has a net profit of 4 percent. The company wants to know how many dollars of sales is equivalent to supply-chain savings of US$1.[a]

APPROACH ▶ Table 11.4 (given Suha's assumptions) can be used to make the analysis.

SOLUTION ▶ Table 11.4 indicates that every US$1 Suha can save in the supply chain results in the same profit that would be generated by US$3.70 in sales.

◀ **TABLE 11.4**

Dollars of Additional Sales Needed to Equal US$1 Saved through the Supply Chain

Percentage Net Profit of Firm	Percentage of Sales Spent in the Supply Chain						
	30%	40%	50%	60%	70%	80%	90%
2	US$2.78	US$3.23	US$3.85	US$4.76	US$6.25	US$9.09	US$16.67
4	US$2.70	US$3.13	US$3.70	US$4.55	US$5.88	US$8.33	US$14.29
6	US$2.63	US$3.03	US$3.57	US$4.35	US$5.56	US$7.69	US$12.50
8	US$2.56	US$2.94	US$3.45	US$4.17	US$5.26	US$7.14	US$11.11
10	US$2.50	US$2.86	US$3.33	US$4.00	US$5.00	US$6.67	US$10.00

[a]The required increase in sales assumes that 50 percent of the costs other than purchases are variable and that half the remaining costs (less profit) are fixed. Therefore, at sales of US$100 (50 percent purchases and 2 percent margin), US$50 are purchases, US$24 are other variable costs, US$24 are fixed costs, and US$2 profit. Increasing sales by US$3.85 yields the following:

Purchases at 50%	US$51.93 (50% of US$103.85)
Other Variable Costs	24.92 (24% of US$103.85)
Fixed Cost	24.00 (fixed)
Profit	3.00 (from US$2 to US$3 profit)
	US$103.85

Through US$3.85 of additional sales, we have increased profit by US$1, from US$2 to US$3. The same increase in margin could have been obtained by reducing supply-chain costs by US$1.

INSIGHT ▶ Effective management of the supply chain can generate substantial benefits.

LEARNING EXERCISE ▶ If Suha increases its profit to 6 percent, how much of an increase in sales is necessary to equal US$1 savings? [Answer: US$3.57.]

RELATED PROBLEMS ▶ 11.4, 11.5

Make-or-Buy Decisions

Make-or-buy decision

A choice between producing a component or service in-house and purchasing it from an outside source.

A wholesaler or retailer buys everything that it sells; a manufacturing operation hardly ever does. Manufacturers, restaurants, and assemblers of products buy components and subassemblies that go into final products. Choosing whether products and services can be advantageously obtained *externally* or produced *internally* is known as the **make-or-buy decision**. Supply-chain personnel evaluate alternative suppliers and provide current, accurate, and complete data relevant to the buy alternative. Increasingly, firms focus not on an analytical make-or-buy decision but on identifying their core competencies.

Outsourcing

Outsourcing

Transferring a firm's activities that have traditionally been internal to external suppliers.

Outsourcing transfers some of what are traditional internal activities and resources of a firm to outside vendors, making it slightly different from the traditional make-or-buy decision. Outsourcing is part of the continuing trend toward utilizing the efficiency that comes with specialization. The vendor performing the outsourced service is an expert in that particular specialty. This leaves the outsourcing firm to focus on its critical success factors, that is, its core competencies that yield a competitive advantage. Outsourcing is the focus of the supplement to this chapter.

AUTHOR COMMENT
Supply-chain strategies come in many varieties; choosing the correct one is key.

SUPPLY-CHAIN STRATEGIES

LO2: Identify six supply-chain strategies

For goods and services to be obtained from outside sources, the firm must decide on a supply-chain strategy. One such strategy is the approach of *negotiating with many suppliers* and playing one supplier against another. A second strategy is to develop *long-term 'partnering'* relationships with a few suppliers to satisfy the end customer. A third strategy is *vertical integration*, in which a firm actually buys the supplier. A fourth approach is some type of collaboration that allows two or more firms to combine resources—typically in what is called a *joint venture*—to produce a component. A fifth variation is a combination of few suppliers and vertical integration, known as a *keiretsu*. In a *keiretsu*, *suppliers become part of a company coalition*. Finally, a sixth strategy is to develop *virtual companies that use suppliers on an as-needed basis*. We will now discuss each of these strategies.

Many Suppliers

With the many-suppliers strategy, a supplier responds to the demands and specifications of a 'request for quotation,' with the order usually going to the low bidder. This is a common strategy when products are commodities. This strategy plays one supplier against another and places the burden of meeting the buyer's demands on the supplier. Suppliers aggressively compete with one another. This approach holds the supplier responsible for maintaining the necessary technology, expertise, and forecasting abilities, as well as cost, quality, and delivery competencies.

Few Suppliers

A strategy of few suppliers implies that rather than looking for short-term attributes, such as low cost, a buyer is better off forming a long-term relationship with a few dedicated suppliers. Long-term suppliers are more likely to understand the broad objectives of the procuring firm and the end customer. Using few suppliers can create value by allowing suppliers to have economies of scale and a learning curve that yields both lower transaction costs and lower production costs.

Few suppliers, each with a large commitment to the buyer, may also be more willing to participate in JIT systems as well as provide design innovations and technological expertise. Many firms have moved aggressively to incorporate suppliers into their supply systems. On occasion these relationships yield contracts that extend through the product's life cycle. The expectation is that both the purchaser and supplier collaborate, becoming more efficient and reducing prices over time. The natural outcome of such relationships is fewer suppliers, but those that remain have long-term relationships.

Service companies, like Grand Stores, have also demonstrated that cooperation with suppliers can yield cost savings for customers and suppliers alike. This strategy has resulted in suppliers that develop new products, winning customers for Grand Stores and the supplier. The move toward tight integration of the suppliers and purchasers is occurring in both manufacturing and services.

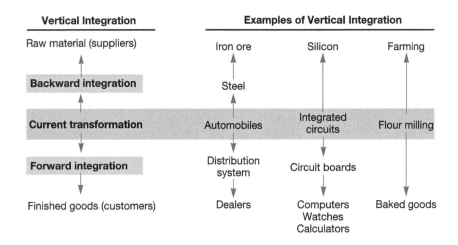

Like all strategies, a downside exists. With few suppliers, the cost of changing partners is huge, so both buyer and supplier run the risk of becoming captives of the other. Poor supplier performance is only one risk the purchaser faces. The purchaser must also be concerned about trade secrets and suppliers that make other alliances or venture out on their own. This happened when the Jordan-based company One World Software Solutions was partially acquired by its suppliers, Cisco and Microsoft, which recognized its potential in understanding the Arab world market, thus forming Estarta.

Vertical Integration

Purchasing can be extended to take the form of vertical integration. By **vertical integration**, we mean developing the ability to produce goods or services previously purchased or to actually buy a supplier or a distributor. As shown in Figure 11.1, vertical integration can take the form of *forward* or *backward integration.*

Backward integration suggests a firm purchases its suppliers, as in the case of Grand Stores deciding to have its own bakery. Forward integration, on the other hand, suggests that a manufacturer of components makes the finished product. An example is Jordan Cement Factories, a manufacturer of cement, using its existing technology to make express dry cement and white cement for its other customers who would otherwise get it from other intermediaries. Jordan Cement acquired some of these companies and started providing this product and service directly to its customers.

Vertical integration can offer a strategic opportunity for the operations manager. For firms with the capital, managerial talent, and required demand, vertical integration may provide substantial opportunities for cost reduction, quality adherence, and timely delivery. Other advantages, such as inventory reduction and scheduling, can accrue to the company that effectively manages vertical integration or close, mutually beneficial relationships with suppliers.

Because purchased items represent such a large part of the costs of sales, it is obvious why so many organizations find interest in vertical integration. Vertical integration appears to work best when the organization has a large market share and the management talent to operate an acquired vendor successfully.

The relentless march of specialization continues, meaning that a model of vertical integration or 'doing everything' is increasingly difficult. Backward integration may be particularly dangerous for firms in industries undergoing technological change if management cannot keep abreast of those changes or invest the financial resources necessary for the next wave of technology. Most organizations are better served concentrating on their specialty and leveraging the partners' contributions. Exceptions do exist. Where capital, management talent, and technology are available and the components are also highly integrated, vertical integration may make sense.

Joint Ventures

Because vertical integration is so dangerous, firms may opt for some form of formal collaboration. As we noted in Chapter 5, firms may engage in collaboration to enhance their new product prowess or technological skills. But firms also engage in collaboration to secure supply or reduce

Vertical integration

Developing the ability to produce goods or services previously purchased or actually buying a supplier or a distributor.

costs. One version of a joint venture is the current Daimler–BMW effort to develop and produce standard automobile components. Given the global consolidation of the auto industry, these two rivals in the luxury segment of the automobile market are at a disadvantage in volume. Their relatively low volume means fewer units over which to spread fixed costs, hence the interest in consolidating to cut development and production costs. As in all other such collaborations, the trick is to cooperate without diluting the brand or conceding a competitive advantage.

Keiretsu Networks

Keiretsu

A Japanese term that describes suppliers who become part of a company coalition.

Many large Japanese manufacturers have found another strategy; it is part collaboration, part purchasing from few suppliers, and part vertical integration. These manufacturers are often financial supporters of suppliers through ownership or loans. The supplier becomes part of a company coalition known as a **keiretsu**. Members of the keiretsu are assured long-term relationships and are therefore expected to collaborate as partners, providing technical expertise and stable quality production to the manufacturer. Members of the keiretsu can also have suppliers further down the chain, making second- and even third-tier suppliers part of the coalition.

Virtual Companies

Virtual companies

Companies that rely on a variety of supplier relationships to provide services on demand. Also known as hollow corporations or network companies.

Virtual companies rely on a variety of supplier relationships to provide services on demand. Virtual companies have fluid, moving organizational boundaries that allow them to create a unique enterprise to meet changing market demands. Suppliers may provide a variety of services that include doing the payroll, hiring personnel, designing products, providing consulting services, manufacturing components, conducting tests, or distributing products. The relationships may be short or long term and may include true partners, collaborators, or simply able suppliers and subcontractors. Whatever the formal relationship, the result can be exceptionally lean performance. The advantages of virtual companies include specialized management expertise, low capital investment, flexibility, and speed. The result is efficiency.

The apparel business provides a *traditional* example of virtual organizations. For example, Ashekman, in Lebanon, links designers, manufacturers, and sewers together in a seamless manner. In fact, the designers of clothes seldom manufacture their designs; rather, they license the manufacture. The manufacturer may then rent space, lease sewing machines, and contract for labor. The result is an organization that has low overheads, remains flexible, and can respond rapidly to the market.

AUTHOR COMMENT
Trust, agreed-upon goals, and compatible cultures make supply-chain management easier.

VIDEO 11.2
Arnold Palmer's Hospital Supply Chain

MANAGING THE SUPPLY CHAIN

As managers move toward integration of the supply chain, substantial efficiencies are possible. The cycle of materials—as they flow from suppliers, to production, to warehousing, to distribution, to the customer—takes place among separate and often very independent organizations. Therefore, there are significant management issues that may result in serious inefficiencies. Success begins with mutual agreement on goals, followed by mutual trust, and continues with compatible organizational cultures.

Mutual Agreement on Goals

An integrated supply chain requires more than just agreement on the contractual terms of a buy/sell relationship. Partners in the chain must appreciate that the only entity that puts money into a supply chain is the end customer. Therefore, establishing a mutual understanding of the mission, strategy, and goals of participating organizations is essential. The integrated supply chain is about adding economic value and maximizing the total content of the product.

Trust

Trust is critical to an effective and efficient supply chain. Members of the chain must enter into a relationship that shares information. Visibility throughout the supply chain is a requirement. Supplier relationships are more likely to be successful if risk and cost savings are shared—and activities such as end-customer research, sales analysis, forecasting, and production planning are joint activities. Such relationships are built on mutual trust.

Compatible Organizational Cultures

A positive relationship between the purchasing and supplying organizations that comes with compatible organizational cultures can be a real advantage when making a supply chain a success. A champion within one of the two firms promotes both formal and informal contacts, and those contacts contribute to the alignment of the organizational cultures, further strengthening the relationship, and thus ensuring higher market penetration, greater customer loyalty, product availability, and market growth. Such a notion has been researched by John Gattorna, who examined the concept of *strategic supply-chain alignment* to provide an in-depth analysis of the culture role on the long term—thus ensuring higher market penetration, greater customer loyalty, product availability, and market growth.

The operations manager is dealing with a supply chain that is made up of independent specialists, each trying to satisfy its own customers at a profit. This leads to actions that may not optimize the entire chain. On the other hand, the supply chain is replete with opportunities to reduce waste and enhance value. We now look at some of the significant issues and opportunities.

Issues in an Integrated Supply Chain

Three issues complicate development of an efficient, integrated supply chain: **local optimization**, incentives, and large lots.

Local Optimization   Members of the chain are inclined to focus on maximizing local profit or minimizing immediate cost based on their limited knowledge. Slight upturns in demand are overcompensated for because no one wants to be caught short. Similarly, slight downturns are overcompensated for because no one wants to be caught holding excess inventory. So fluctuations are magnified. For instance, a pasta distributor does not want to run out of pasta for its retail customers; the natural response to an extra large order from the retailer is to compensate with an even larger order to the manufacturer on the assumption that retail sales are picking up. Neither the distributor nor the manufacturer knows that the retailer had a major one-time promotion that moved a lot of pasta.

Incentives (Sales Incentives, Quantity Discounts, Quotas, and Promotions)
Incentives push merchandise into the chain for sales that have not occurred. This generates fluctuations that are ultimately expensive to all members of the chain.

Large Lots   There is often a bias toward large lots because large lots tend to reduce unit costs. A logistics manager wants to ship large lots, preferably in full trucks, and a production manager wants long production runs. Both actions drive down unit shipping and production costs, but fail to reflect actual sales and increased holding costs.

These three common occurrences—local optimization, incentives, and large lots—contribute to distortions of information about what is really occurring in the supply chain. A well-running supply system needs to be based on accurate information about how many products are truly being pulled through the chain. The inaccurate information is unintentional, but it results in distortions and fluctuations in the supply chain and causes what is known as the bullwhip effect.

The **bullwhip effect** occurs as orders are relayed from retailers, to distributors, to wholesalers, to manufacturers, with fluctuations increasing at each step in the sequence. The 'bullwhip' fluctuations in the supply chain increase the costs associated with inventory, transportation, shipping, and receiving, while decreasing customer service and profitability. Egypt Phosphate Company found that although the demand for its fertilizers was steady and the store orders had little fluctuation, as orders moved through the supply chain, fluctuations increased. By the time orders were initiated for raw material, the variability was substantial.

The bullwhip effect can occur when orders decrease as well as when they increase. A number of opportunities exist for reducing the bullwhip effect and improving opportunities in the supply chain. These are discussed in the following section.

Opportunities in an Integrated Supply Chain

Opportunities for effective management in the supply chain include the following 11 items.

Accurate 'Pull' Data   Accurate **pull data** are generated by sharing: (1) point-of-sales (POS) information so that each member of the chain can schedule effectively; (2) computer-assisted

LO3: Explain issues and opportunities in the supply chain

Local optimization
When sub-units of a system or members of a group focus on maximizing their immediate interest rather than on the system or the group's overall interest.

Bullwhip effect
The increasing fluctuation in orders that often occurs as orders move through the supply chain.

Pull data
Accurate sales data that initiate transactions to 'pull' a product through the supply chain.

ordering (CAO). This implies using POS systems that collect sales data and then adjusting that data for market factors, inventory on hand, and outstanding orders. Then a net order is sent directly to the supplier who is responsible for maintaining the finished-goods inventory.

Lot Size Reduction   Lot sizes are reduced through aggressive management. This may include (1) developing economical shipments of less than truckload lots, (2) providing discounts based on total annual volume rather than size of individual shipments, and (3) reducing the cost of ordering through techniques such as standing orders and various forms of electronic purchasing.

Single-stage control of replenishment

Fixing responsibility for monitoring and managing inventory for the retailer.

Single-Stage Control of Replenishment   **Single-stage control of replenishment** means designating a member in the chain as responsible for monitoring and managing inventory in the supply chain based on the 'pull' from the end user. This approach removes distorted information and multiple forecasts that create the bullwhip effect. Control may be in the hands of:

- A sophisticated *retailer* who understands demand patterns. Wal-Mart does this for some of its inventory with radio frequency ID (RFID) tags as shown in the *OM in Action* box 'Radio Frequency Tags: Keeping the Shelves Stocked.'
- A *distributor* who manages the inventory for a particular distribution area. Distributors who handle grocery items and soft drinks may do this. Pepsi Arabia manages the cola inventory and delivery for many of its customers.
- A *manufacturer* who has a well-managed forecasting, manufacturing, and distribution system.

Vendor-managed inventory (VMI)

A system in which a supplier maintains material for the buyer, often delivering directly to the buyer's using department.

Vendor-managed inventory   **Vendor-managed inventory (VMI)** means the use of a local supplier (usually a distributor) to maintain inventory for the manufacturer or retailer. The supplier delivers directly to the purchaser's using department rather than to a receiving dock or stockroom. If the supplier can maintain the stock of inventory for a variety of customers who use the same product or whose differences are very minor (say, at the packaging stage), then there should be net savings. These systems work without the immediate direction of the purchaser.

Collaborative planning, forecasting, and replenishment (CPFR)

A joint effort of members of a supply chain to share information in order to reduce supply-chain costs.

Collaborative Planning, Forecasting, and Replenishment (CPFR)   Like single-stage control and vendor-managed inventory, **collaborative planning, forecasting, and replenishment (CPFR)**

OM in Action ▶ Radio Frequency Tags: Keeping the Shelves Stocked

Supply chains work smoothly when sales are steady, but often break down when confronted by a sudden surge or rapid drop in demand. Radio frequency ID (or RFID) tags can change that by providing real-time information about what's happening on store shelves. Here's how the system works for Procter & Gamble's (P&G's) Pampers.

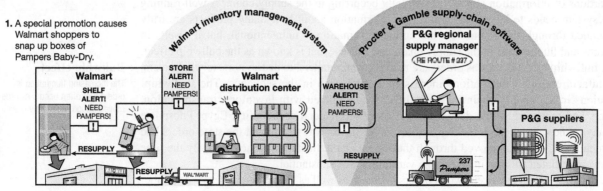

1. A special promotion causes Walmart shoppers to snap up boxes of Pampers Baby-Dry.

2. Each box of Pampers has an RFID tag. Shelf-mounted scanners alert the stockroom of urgent need for restock.

3. Walmart's inventory management system tracks and links its in-store stock and its warehouse stock, prompting quicker replenishment and providing accurate real-time data.

4. Walmart's systems are linked to the P&G supply-chain management system. Demand spikes reported by RFID tags are immediately visible throughout the supply chain.

5. P&G's logistics software tracks its trucks with GPS locators, and tracks their contents with RFID tag readers. Regional managers can reroute trucks to fill urgent needs.

6. P&G suppliers also use RFID tags and readers on their raw materials, giving P&G visibility several tiers down the supply chain, and giving suppliers the ability to accurately forecast demand and production.

Sources: Financial Times (August 22, 2008): 12; Business 2.0 (May 2002): 86; and Knight Ridder Tribune Business News (August 6, 2006): 1.

is another effort to manage inventory in the supply chain. With CPFR, members of the supply chain share planning, forecasting, and inventory information. Partners in a CPFR effort begin with collaboration on product definition and a joint marketing plan. Promotion, advertising, forecasts, and timing of shipments are all included in the plan in a concerted effort to drive down inventory and related costs.

Blanket Orders Blanket orders are unfilled orders with a vendor.[3] A **blanket order** is a contract to purchase certain items from a vendor. It is not an authorization to ship anything. Shipment is made only on receipt of an agreed-on document, perhaps a shipping requisition or shipment release.

Blanket order

A long-term purchase commitment to a supplier for items that are to be delivered against short-term releases to ship.

Standardization The purchasing department should make special efforts to increase levels of standardization. That is, rather than obtaining a variety of similar components with labeling, coloring, packaging, or perhaps even slightly different engineering specifications, the purchasing agent should try to have those components standardized.

Postponement **Postponement** withholds any modification or customization to the product (keeping it generic) for as long as possible. The concept is to minimize internal variety while maximizing external variety. For instance, after analyzing the supply chain for its printers, Hewlett-Packard (HP) determined that if the printer's power supply was moved out of the printer itself and into a power cord, HP could ship the basic printer anywhere in the world. HP modified the printer, its power cord, its packaging, and its documentation so that only the power cord and documentation needed to be added at the final distribution point. This modification allowed the firm to manufacture and hold centralized inventories of the generic printer for shipment as demand changed. Only the unique power system and documentation had to be held in each country. This understanding of the entire supply chain reduced both risk and investment in inventory.

Postponement

Delaying any modifications or customization to a product as long as possible in the production process.

Drop Shipping and Special Packaging **Drop shipping** means the supplier will ship directly to the end consumer, rather than to the seller, saving both time and reshipping costs. Other cost-saving measures include the use of special packaging, labels, and optimal placement of labels and bar codes on containers. The final location down to the department and number of units in each shipping container can also be indicated. Substantial savings can be obtained through management techniques such as these. Some of these techniques can be of particular benefit to wholesalers and retailers by reducing shrinkage (lost, damaged, or stolen merchandise) and handling cost.

Drop shipping

Shipping directly from the supplier to the end consumer rather than from the seller, saving both time and reshipping costs.

Pass-through Facility A **pass-through facility** is a distribution center where merchandise is held, but it functions less as a holding area and more as a shipping hub. These facilities, often run by logistics vendors, use the latest technology and automated systems to expedite orders.

Pass-through facility

Expedites shipment by holding merchandise and delivering from shipping hubs.

Channel Assembly Channel assembly is an extension of the pass-through facility. **Channel assembly** sends individual components and modules, rather than finished products, to the distributor. The distributor then assembles, tests, and ships. Channel assembly treats distributors more as manufacturing partners than as distributors. This technique has proven successful in industries where products are undergoing rapid change, such as personal computers. With this strategy, finished-goods inventory is reduced because units are built to a shorter, more accurate forecast. Consequently, market response is better, with lower investment—a nice combination.

Channel assembly

Postpones final assembly of a product so the distribution channel can assemble it.

E-PROCUREMENT

E-procurement uses the internet to facilitate purchasing. E-procurement speeds purchasing, reduces costs, and integrates the supply chain, enhancing an organization's competitive advantage. The traditional supply chain is full of paper transactions, such as requisitions, requests for bids, bid evaluations, purchase orders, order releases, receiving documents, invoices, and the issuance of checks. E-procurement reduces this barrage of paperwork and at the same time provides purchasing personnel with an extensive database of vendor, delivery, and quality data. With this history, vendor selection has improved.

AUTHOR COMMENT
The internet has revolutionized procurement.

E-procurement

Purchasing facilitated through the internet.

In this section, we discuss traditional techniques of electronic ordering and funds transfer and then move on to online catalogs, auctions, RFQs, and real-time inventory tracking.

---

[3]Unfilled orders are also referred to as 'open' orders, or 'incomplete' orders.

Electronic Ordering and Funds Transfer

Electronic data interchange (EDI)

A standardized data-transmission format for computerized communications between organizations.

Advanced shipping notice (ASN)

A shipping notice delivered directly from vendor to purchaser.

Electronic ordering and bank transfers are traditional approaches to speeding transactions and reducing paperwork. Transactions between firms often use **electronic data interchange (EDI)**, which is a standardized data-transmission format for computerized communications between organizations. EDI provides data transfer for virtually any business application, including purchasing. Under EDI, data for a purchase order, such as order date, due date, quantity, part number, purchase order number, address, and so forth, are fitted into the standard EDI format. EDI also provides for the use of **advanced shipping notice (ASN)**, which notifies the purchaser that the vendor is ready to ship. Although some firms are still moving to EDI and ASN, the internet's ease of use and lower cost is proving more popular.

Online Catalogs

Purchase of standard items is often accomplished via online catalogs. Such catalogs provide current information about products in electronic form. Online catalogs support cost comparisons and incorporate voice and video clips, making the process efficient for both buyers and sellers. Online catalogs are available in three versions:

1. *Catalogs provided by vendors.*
2. *Catalogs provided by intermediaries*—internet sites where business buyers and sellers can meet. These intermediaries typically create industry-specific catalogs with content from many suppliers.
3. Online *exchanges provided by buyers.* Burj Al Arab Hotel, in Dubai, has a website for suppliers to ensure the most economic purchase.

Such exchanges—and there are many—move companies from a multitude of individual phone calls, faxes, and e-mails to a centralized online system, and drive billions of dollars of waste out of the supply chain.

Auctions

Online auction sites can be maintained by sellers, buyers, or intermediaries. Operations managers find online auctions a fertile area for disposing of excess raw material and discontinued or excess inventory. Online auctions lower entry barriers, encouraging sellers to join, and simultaneously increase the potential number of buyers.

The key for auction firms is to find and build a huge base of potential bidders, improve client buying procedures, and qualify new suppliers.

RFQs

When purchasing requirements are nonstandard, time spent preparing requests for quotes (RFQs) and the related bid package can be substantial. Consequently, e-procurement has now moved these often expensive parts of the purchasing process online, allowing purchasing agents to inexpensively attach electronic copies of the necessary drawings to RFQs.

Real-Time Inventory Tracking

Aramex provides a real-time tracking service for packages from pickup to delivery, and many companies have followed suit. As operations managers move to an era of mass customization, with customers ordering exactly the cars they want, customers will expect to know where their cars are and exactly when they can be picked up. E-procurement, supported by bar codes and RFID, can provide economical inventory tracking on the shop floor, in warehouses, and in logistics.

VENDOR SELECTION

For those goods and services a firm buys, vendors must be selected. Vendor selection considers numerous factors, such as strategic fit, vendor competence, delivery, and quality performance. Because a firm may have some competence in all areas and may have exceptional competence in only a few, selection can be challenging. Procurement policies also need to be established. Those might address issues such as percentage of business done with any one supplier or with minority businesses. We now examine vendor selection as a three-stage process: (1) vendor evaluation; (2) vendor development; (3) negotiations.

LO4: Describe the steps in vendor selection

Vendor Evaluation

The first stage of vendor selection, *vendor evaluation*, involves finding potential vendors and determining the likelihood of their becoming good suppliers. This phase requires the development of evaluation criteria, such as the criteria shown in Example 2. However, both the criteria and the weights selected vary depending on the supply-chain strategy being implemented. (Refer to Table 11.1, on page 330.)

◄ **EXAMPLE 2**

Weighted approach to vendor evaluation

Majed Amin, president of Arabic Fun Toys, is interested in evaluating suppliers who will work with him to make nontoxic, environmentally friendly paints and dyes for his line of children's toys. This is a critical strategic element of his supply chain, and he desires a firm that will contribute to his product.

APPROACH ▶ Majed begins his analysis of one potential supplier, Jaser Paint and Dye, by using the weighted approach to vendor evaluation.

SOLUTION ▶ Majed first reviews the supplier differentiation attributes in Table 11.1 and develops the following list of selection criteria. He then assigns the weights shown to help him perform an objective review of potential vendors. His staff assign the scores shown and compute the total weighted score.

Criteria	Weights	Scores (1–5) (5 highest)	Weight × Score
Engineering/research/innovation skills	0.20	5	1.0
Production process capability (flexibility/technical assistance)	0.15	4	0.6
Distribution/delivery capability	0.05	4	0.2
Quality systems and performance	0.10	2	0.2
Facilities/location	0.05	2	0.1
Financial and managerial strength (stability and cost structure)	0.15	4	0.6
Information systems capability (e-procurement, ERP)	0.10	2	0.2
Integrity (environmental compliance/ethics)	0.20	5	1.0
	1.00		3.9 Total

Jaser Paint and Dye receives an overall score of 3.9.

INSIGHT ▶ Majed now has a basis for comparison with other potential vendors, selecting the one with the highest overall rating.

LEARNING EXERCISE ▶ If Majed believes that the weight for 'engineering/research/innovation skills' should be increased to 0.25 and the weight for 'financial and managerial strength' reduced to 0.10, what is the new score? [Answer: Jaser Paint and Dye now goes to 3.95.]

RELATED PROBLEMS ▶ 11.2, 11.3

EXCEL OM Data File **Ch11Ex2.xls** can be found at MyOMLab.

The selection of competent suppliers is critical. If good suppliers are not selected, then all other supply-chain efforts are wasted. As firms move toward using fewer longer-term suppliers, the issues of financial strength, quality, management, research, technical ability, and potential for a close long-term relationship play an increasingly important role. These attributes should be noted in the evaluation process.

Vendor Development

The second stage of vendor selection is *vendor development*. Assuming that a firm wants to proceed with a particular vendor, how does it integrate this supplier into its system? The buyer makes sure the vendor has an appreciation of quality requirements, product specifications, schedules and delivery, the purchaser's payment system, and procurement policies. *Vendor development* may include everything from training, to engineering and production help, to procedures for information transfer.

Negotiations

Regardless of the supply-chain strategy adopted, negotiations regarding the critical elements of the contractual relationship must take place. These negotiations often focus on quality, delivery, payment, and cost. We will look at three classic types of **negotiation strategies**: the cost-based price model, the market-based price model, and competitive bidding.

Negotiation strategies
Approaches taken by supply-chain personnel to develop contractual relationships with suppliers.

Cost-Based Price Model   The *cost-based price model* requires that the supplier open its books to the purchaser. The contract price is then based on time and materials or on a fixed cost with an escalation clause to accommodate changes in the vendor's labor and materials cost.

Market-Based Price Model   In the market-based price model, price is based on a published, auction, or index price. Many commodities (agricultural products, paper, metal, etc.) are priced this way. Paperboard prices, for instance, are available via the *Official Board Markets'* weekly publication (**www.advanstar.com**). Nonferrous metal prices are quoted in *Platt's Metals Week* (**www.platts.com**), and prices of other metals are quoted at **www.metalworld.com**.

Competitive Bidding   When suppliers are not willing to discuss costs or where near-perfect markets do not exist, competitive bidding is often appropriate. Infrequent work (such as construction, tooling, and dies) is usually purchased based on a bid. Bidding may take place via mail, fax, or an internet auction. Competitive bidding is the typical policy in many firms for the majority of their purchases. Bidding policies usually require that the purchasing agent have several potential suppliers of the product (or its equivalent) and quotations from each. The major disadvantage of this method, as mentioned earlier, is that the development of long-term relations between buyer and seller is hindered. Competitive bidding may effectively determine initial cost. However, it may also make difficult the communication and performance that are vital for engineering changes, quality, and delivery.

Yet a fourth approach is *to combine one or more* of the preceding negotiation techniques. The supplier and purchaser may agree on review of certain cost data, accept some form of market data for raw material costs, or agree that the supplier will 'remain competitive.' In any case, a good supplier relationship is one in which both partners have established a degree of mutual trust and a belief in each other's competence, honesty, and fair dealing.

AUTHOR COMMENT
Time, cost, and reliability variables make logistic decisions demanding.

LOGISTICS MANAGEMENT

Procurement activities may be combined with various shipping, warehousing, and inventory activities to form a logistics system. The purpose of **logistics management** is to obtain efficiency of operations through the integration of all material acquisition, movement, and storage activities. When transportation and inventory costs are substantial on both the input and output sides of the production process, an emphasis on logistics may be appropriate. When logistics issues are significant or expensive, many firms opt for outsourcing the logistics function. Logistics specialists can often bring expertise not available in-house. For instance, logistics companies often have tracking technology that reduces transportation losses and supports delivery schedules that adhere to precise delivery windows. The potential for competitive advantage is found via both reduced costs and improved customer service.

Logistics management
An approach that seeks efficiency of operations through the integration of all material acquisition, movement, and storage activities.

Firms recognize that the distribution of goods to and from their facilities can represent as much as 25 percent of the cost of products. In addition, the total distribution cost in the Arab world is over 18 percent of the gross national product (GNP). Because of this high cost, firms constantly evaluate their means of distribution. Five major means of distribution are trucking, railroads, airfreight, waterways, and pipelines.

Distribution Systems

Trucking   The vast majority of manufactured goods are moved by truck. The flexibility of shipping by truck is only one of its many advantages. Companies that have adopted JIT programs in recent years have put increased pressure on truckers to pick up and deliver on time, with no damage to the goods, with paperwork in order, and at low cost. Trucking firms are using computers to monitor weather, find the most effective route, reduce fuel cost, and analyze the most efficient way to unload. In spite of these advances, the motor carrier industry averages a capacity utilization of only 50 percent. That underutilized space wastes millions of US dollars per year. To improve logistics efficiency, the industry is establishing websites that let shippers and truckers find each other to use some of this idle capacity. Shippers may pick from thousands of approved carriers that have registered with the website.

Railroads   Railroads in the Middle East are not the favorite method of shipping due to the poor infrastructure, but containerization has made intermodal shipping of truck trailers on railroad flat cars a new means of distribution in the Arab world. However, due to the growth of JIT, rail transport has lost out yet more in the MENA region because small-batch manufacture requires frequent, smaller shipments that are likely to move via truck or air.

LO5: Explain major issues in logistics management

Airfreight   Airfreight represents only about 5 percent of tonnage shipped in the Arab world. However, the recent proliferation of airfreight carriers such as Aramex, UPS, and DHL makes it the fastest-growing mode of shipping. Clearly, for national and international movement of lightweight items, such as medical and emergency supplies, flowers, fruits, and electronic components, airfreight offers speed and reliability.

Waterways   Waterways are one of the Arab world's oldest means of freight transportation, dating back to construction of the Suez Canal in 1869. The usual cargo on waterways is bulky, low-value cargo such as iron ore, grains, cement, coal, chemicals, limestone, and petroleum products. Internationally, millions of containers are shipped at very low cost via huge oceangoing ships each year. Water transportation is important when shipping cost is more important than speed.

Pipelines   Pipelines are an important form of transporting crude oil, natural gas, and other petroleum and chemical products. For example, pipelines are the preferred method for the transportation of crude oil in the Arab world.

Third-Party Logistics

Supply-chain managers may find that outsourcing logistics is advantageous in driving down inventory investment and costs while improving delivery reliability and speed. Specialized logistics firms support this goal by coordinating the supplier's inventory system with the service capabilities of the delivery firm. Aramex, for example, uses the internet for online tracking. At **www.aramex.com**, a customer can compute shipping costs, print labels, adjust invoices, and track package status all on the same website. Aramex, FedEx, DHL, and UPS play a core role in other firms' logistics processes. In some cases, they even run the server for retailer websites. In other cases, such as for Majid Al Futtaim Fashion, Aramex operates warehouses that pick, pack, test, and assemble products, then it handles delivery and customs clearance when necessary. The *OM in Action* box 'Aramex's Role in the Supply Chain' shows how outsourcing logistics can reduce costs while shrinking inventory and delivery times.

As this photo of the port of Jebel Ali shows, with millions of containers entering U.A.E. annually, tracking location, content, and condition of trucks and containers is a challenge. But new technology may improve both security and JIT shipments.

OM in Action ▶ Aramex's Role in the Supply Chain

Delivering fashion to customers is an art. It is an art that Majid Al Futtaim Fashion (MAFF) has mastered pretty well, with over 90 retail outlets across the Arab world—a number that is expected to grow further within the next few years.

In early 2010, with the Dubai Shopping Festival in the background, MAFF needed the support of Aramex in managing huge and yet very time-constrained orders. Time was of the essence; the group wanted to be able to focus on the creative part of its work, without worrying about the logistics of delivering thousands of pieces with different designs to different customers with maximum speed and minimum costs. "Due to the forecasted growth in sales, it was important for us to find a logistics partner that would help us in bringing various fashion products to our clients in the most cost-effective manner," observed Mr. Mohammed Shoaib Hai, Head of Supply Chain at MAFF.

Whereas on the retail side the process might seem self-explanatory, behind the curtain is a complex logistics network that ensures inventories are kept, clothing items are shipped, and last-minute demands are catered to. One of those back-end solutions is warehousing. "Specifically, a positively evolving warehouse process from Aramex has enabled MAFF to adapt to the challenges in the business," Mohammed commented. Aramex's experience in warehouse management gave it a competitive advantage in performing the functions of warehousing and shipping.

Aramex aims at reducing inventory costs, increasing transaction speed, and improving sales by implementing customer requirements more efficiently. Aramex also provides record management and e-commerce services for its customers, which further supports the supply-chain functions at competitive clients such as MAFF.

Source: The Navigator, "Delivering in Style with Majid Al Futtaim Fashion," (June, 2010), from **http://navigator.aramex.com/Issues/2010/June/ CaseStudyMajidAlFuttaimFashion.aspx**, accessed June 12, 2012; **www.aramex.com**

Cost of Shipping Alternatives

The longer a product is in transit, the longer the firm has its money invested. But faster shipping is usually more expensive than slow shipping. A simple way to obtain some insight into this trade-off is to evaluate holding cost against shipping options. We do this in Example 3.

EXAMPLE 3 ▶

Determining daily cost of holding

A shipment of new connectors for semiconductors needs to go from Aleppo to Dubai for assembly. The value of the connectors is US$1,750 and the holding cost is 40 percent per year. One airfreight carrier can ship the connectors 1 day faster than its competitor, at an extra cost of US$20.00. Which carrier should be selected?

APPROACH ▶   First we determine the daily holding cost and then compare the daily holding cost with the cost of faster shipment.

SOLUTION ▶

$$\text{Daily cost of holding the product} = (\text{Annual holding cost} \times \text{Product value}) \div 365$$
$$= (0.40 \times \text{US\$1,750}) \div 365$$
$$= \text{US\$1.92}$$

Since the cost of saving 1 day is US$20.00, which is much more than the daily holding cost of US$1.92, we decide on the less costly of the carriers and take the extra day to make the shipment. This saves US$18.08 (US$20.00 – US$1.92).

INSIGHT ▶   The solution becomes radically different if the 1-day delay in getting the connectors to Dubai delays delivery (making a customer angry) or delays payment of a US$150,000 final bill. (Even 1 day's interest on US$150,000 or an angry customer makes a saving of US$18.08 insignificant.)

LEARNING EXERCISE ▶   If the holding cost is 100 percent per year, what is the decision? [Answer: Even with a holding cost of US$4.79 per day, the less costly carrier is selected.]

RELATED PROBLEMS ▶   11.6, 11.7

Example 3 looks only at holding costs versus shipping cost. For the operations or logistics manager there are many other considerations, including coordinating shipments to maintain a schedule, getting a new product to market, and keeping a customer happy. Estimates of these other costs can be added to the estimate of daily holding cost. Determining the impact and cost of these many other considerations makes the evaluation of shipping alternatives interesting.

Speed and accuracy in the supply chain are supported by bar-code tracking of shipments. At each step of a journey, from initial pickup to final destination, bar codes are read and stored. Within seconds, this tracking information is available online to customers worldwide (left).

Security and JIT

Globalization has affected societies in many different ways, most notably free trade. In the Middle East millions of containers enter the ports each year, along with thousands of airplanes, cars, and trucks each day. Even under the best of conditions, some 5 percent of the container movements are misrouted, stolen, damaged, or excessively delayed.

Since the September 11, 2001 terrorist attacks in the United States, supply chains have become more complex. Technological innovations, though, in the supply chain are improving security and JIT, making logistics more reliable. Technology is now capable of knowing truck and container location, content, and condition. New devices can detect whether someone has broken into a sealed container and can communicate that information to the shipper or receiver via satellite or radio. Motion detectors can also be installed inside containers. Other sensors can record interior data, including temperature, shock, radioactivity, and whether a container is moving. Tracking lost containers, identifying delays, or just reminding individuals in the supply chain that a shipment is on its way will help expedite shipments. Improvements in security may aid JIT, and improvements in JIT may aid security—both of which can improve supply-chain logistics.

MEASURING SUPPLY-CHAIN PERFORMANCE

> **AUTHOR COMMENT**
> If you can't measure it, you can't control it.

Like all other managers, supply-chain managers require standards (or *metrics*, as they are often called) to evaluate performance. Evaluation of the supply chain is particularly critical for these managers because they spend most of the organization's money. In addition, they make scheduling and quantity decisions that determine the assets committed to inventory. Only with effective metrics can managers determine: (1) how well the *supply chain is performing*; (2) *the assets committed to inventory*. We will now discuss these two metrics.

LO6: Compute the percentage of assets committed to inventory and inventory turnover

Supply-Chain Performance The benchmark metrics shown in Table 11.5 focus on procurement and vendor performance issues. World-class benchmarks are the result of well-managed supply chains that drive down costs, lead times, late deliveries, and shortages while improving quality.

Assets Committed to Inventory Three specific measures can be helpful here. The first is the amount of money invested in inventory, usually expressed as a percentage of assets, as shown in Equation (11-1) and Example 4:

Percentage invested in inventory = (Total inventory investment ÷ Total assets) × 100   (11-1)

**Tracking Mahallat's
inventory investment**

Mahallat's management wishes to track its investment in inventory as one of its performance measures. Mahallat had US$11.4 billion invested in inventory and total assets of US$44.4 billion in 2011.

APPROACH ▶ Determine the investment in inventory and total assets and then use Equation (11-1).

SOLUTION ▶ Percentage invested in inventory = (11.4 ÷ 44.4) × 100 = 25.7%

INSIGHT ▶ Over one-fourth of Mahallat's assets are committed to inventory.

LEARNING EXERCISE ▶ If Mahallat can drive its investment down to 20 percent of assets, how much money will it free up for other uses? [Answer: 11.4 − (44.4 × 0.2) = US$2.52 billion.]

Specific comparisons with competitors may assist evaluation. Total assets committed to inventory in manufacturing approach 15 percent, in wholesale 34 percent, and in retail 27 percent—with wide variations, depending on the specific business model, the business cycle, and management (see Table 11.6).

The second common measure of supply-chain performance is *inventory turnover* (see Table 11.7). Its reciprocal, *weeks of supply*, is the third. **Inventory turnover** is computed on an annual basis, using Equation (11-2):

Inventory turnover
Cost of goods sold divided by average inventory.

$$\text{Inventory turnover} = \text{Cost of goods sold} \div \text{Inventory investment} \qquad \text{(11-2)}$$

Cost of goods sold is the cost to produce the goods or services sold for a given period. Inventory investment is the average inventory value for the same period. This may be the average of several periods of inventory or beginning and ending inventory added together and divided by 2. Often, average inventory investment is based on nothing more than the inventory investment at the end of the period—typically at year-end.[4]

In Example 5, we look at inventory turnover applied to PepsiCo, Inc.

▼ **TABLE 11.5** Metrics for Supply-Chain Performance

	Typical Firms	Benchmark Firms
Lead time (weeks)	15	8
Time spent placing an order	42 minutes	15 minutes
Percentage of late deliveries	33%	2%
Percentage of rejected material	1.5%	0.0001%
Number of shortages per year	400	4

Source: Adapted from a McKinsey & Company report.

▼ **TABLE 11.6**

Inventory as Percentage of Total Assets (with Examples of Exceptional Performance)

Manufacturer	15%
(Toyota 5%)	
Wholesale	34%
(Coca-Cola 2.9%)	
Restaurants	2.9%
(McDonald's 0.05%)	
Retail	27%
(Home Depot 25.7%)	

▼ **TABLE 11.7**

Examples of Annual Inventory Turnover

Food, Beverage, Retail	
Anheuser Busch	15
Coca-Cola	14
Home Depot	5
McDonald's	112
Manufacturing	
Dell Computer	90
Johnson Controls	22
Toyota (overall)	13
Nissan (assembly)	150

[4]Inventory quantities often fluctuate wildly, and various types of inventory exist (e.g. raw material, work-in-process, finished goods, and maintenance, repair, and operating supplies, (MRO). Therefore, care must be taken when using inventory values; they may reflect more than just supply-chain performance.

PepsiCo, Inc., manufacturer and distributor of drinks, Frito-Lay, and Quaker Foods, provides the following in its 2010 annual report (shown here in US$ billions). Determine PepsiCo's turnover.

Net revenue		US$32.5
Cost of goods sold		US$14.2
Inventory:		
Raw material inventory	US$0.74	
Work-in-process inventory	US$0.11	
Finished goods inventory	US$0.84	
Total inventory investment		US$1.69

APPROACH ▶ Use the inventory turnover computation in Equation (11-2) to measure inventory performance. Cost of goods sold is US$14.2 billion. Total inventory is the sum of raw materials at US$0.74 billion, work-in-process at US$0.11 billion, and finished goods at US$0.84 billion, for total inventory investment of US$1.69 billion.

SOLUTION ▶

$$\text{Inventory Turnover} = \text{Cost of goods sold} \div \text{Inventory investment}$$
$$= 14.2 \div 1.69$$
$$= 8.4$$

INSIGHT ▶ We now have a standard, popular measure by which to evaluate performance.

LEARNING EXERCISE ▶ If PepsiCo's cost of goods sold is US$10.8 billion and inventory investment is US$0.76 billion, what is its inventory turnover? [Answer: 14.2.]

RELATED PROBLEM ▶ 11.8a

Weeks of supply, as shown in Example 6, may have more meaning in the wholesale and retail portions of the service sector than in manufacturing. It is computed below as the reciprocal of inventory turnover:

$$\text{Weeks of supply} = \text{Inventory investment} \div (\text{Annual cost of goods sold} \div 52 \text{ weeks}) \quad \text{(11-3)}$$

Using the PepsiCo data in Example 5, management wants to know the weeks of supply.

APPROACH ▶ We know that inventory investment is US$1.69 billion and that weekly sales equal annual cost of goods sold (US$14.2 billion) divided by 52 = US$14.2 ÷ 52 = US$0.273 billion

SOLUTION ▶ Using Equation (11-3), we compute weeks of supply as:

$$\text{Weeks of supply} = (\text{Inventory investment} \div \text{Average weekly cost of goods sold})$$
$$= 1.69 \div 0.273 = 6.19 \text{ weeks}$$

INSIGHT ▶ We now have a standard measurement by which to evaluate a company's continuing performance or by which to compare companies.

LEARNING EXERCISE ▶ If PepsiCo's average inventory investment is US$0.76 billion and its average weekly cost of goods sold is US$0.207 billion, what is the firm's weeks of supply? [Answer: 3.67 weeks.]

Supply-chain management provides a competitive advantage when firms effectively respond to the demands of global markets and global sources.

The SCOR Model

In addition to the metrics presented above, the Supply-Chain Council (SCC) has developed 200 process elements, 550 metrics, and 500 best practices. The SCC (**www.supply-chain.org**) is a 900-member not-for-profit association for the improvement of supply-chain effectiveness.

▶ **FIGURE 11.2**
**The Supply-Chain Operations
Reference (SCOR) Model**

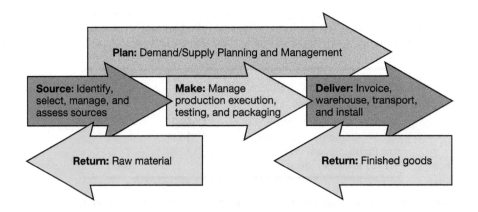

Plan: Demand/Supply Planning and Management

Source: Identify, select, manage, and assess sources

Make: Manage production execution, testing, and packaging

Deliver: Invoice, warehouse, transport, and install

Return: Raw material

Return: Finished goods

Supply-Chain Operations Reference (SCOR) model

A set of processes, metrics, and best practices developed by the Supply-Chain Council (**www.supply-chain.org**).

The council has developed the five-part **Supply-Chain Operations Reference (SCOR) model**. The five parts are Plan, Source, Make, Deliver, and Return, as shown in Figure 11.2.

The council believes the model provides a structure for its processes, metrics, and best practices to be: (1) implemented for competitive advantage; (2) defined and communicated precisely; (3) measured, managed, and controlled; (4) fine-tuned as necessary to a specific application.

CHAPTER SUMMARY

Competition is no longer between companies but between supply chains. For many firms, the supply chain determines a substantial portion of product cost and quality, as well as opportunities for responsiveness and differentiation. Six supply-chain strategies have been identified: (1) many suppliers; (2) few suppliers; (3) vertical integration; (4) joint ventures; (5) *keiretsu* networks; (6) virtual companies. Skillful supply-chain management provides a great strategic opportunity for competitive advantage.

Key Terms

Advanced shipping notice (ASN) (p. 340)
Blanket order (p. 339)
Bullwhip effect (p. 337)
Channel assembly (p. 339)
Collaborative planning, forecasting, and
  replenishment (CPFR) (p. 338)
Drop shipping (p. 339)
Electronic data interchange (EDI) (p. 340)
E-procurement (p. 339)

Inventory turnover (p. 346)
Keiretsu (p. 336)
Local optimization (p. 337)
Logistics management (p. 342)
Make-or-buy decision (p. 334)
Negotiation strategies (p. 342)
Outsourcing (p. 334)
Pass-through facility (p. 339)
Postponement (p. 339)

Pull data (p. 337)
Single-stage control of replenishment
  (p. 338)
Supply-chain management (p. 330)
Supply-Chain Operations Reference
  (SCOR) model (p. 348)
Vendor-managed inventory (VMI) (p. 338)
Vertical integration (p. 335)
Virtual companies (p. 336)

Ethical Dilemma

Al-Waha Ceramics operates extensively in the Middle East region, providing ceramics to industrial customers, construction companies, retailers, and end users. Their supply-chain strategy has always been to diversify their raw materials' sources with a commitment of no more than 40 percent to one major supplier to ensure the agility of their processes and not to affect the supplier's market position.

Conversely, Gold Pyramid Ceramics Ltd. depends heavily on one supplier, and over time they have become this supplier's only customer. This has lead to the supplier making employees redundant to reduce costs, since no sales force is needed.

Al-Waha is has had to downsize its operations in the Middle East due to lower demand rates and is in negotiations to be sold to another main ceramics producer. On the other hand, Gold Pyramids has hired more people and is expanding at an accelerating rate in the region.

What are the ethical issues involved, and which firm has a more ethical position?

Discussion Questions

1. Define *supply-chain management.*
2. What are the objectives of supply-chain management?
3. What is the objective of logistics management?
4. How do we distinguish between the types of risk in the supply chain?
5. What is vertical integration? Give examples of backward and forward integration.
6. What are three basic approaches to negotiations?
7. How does a traditional adversarial relationship with suppliers change when a firm makes a decision to move to a few suppliers?
8. What is the difference between postponement and channel assembly?
9. What is CPFR?
10. What is the value of online auctions in e-commerce?
11. What are blanket orders? How do they differ from invoiceless purchasing?
12. What can purchasing do to implement just-in-time deliveries?
13. What is e-procurement?
14. What is SCOR, and what purpose does it serve?

Solved Problem   Virtual Office Hours help is available at MyOMLab

▼ SOLVED PROBLEM 11.1

Jack's Pottery Outlet has total end-of-year assets of US$5 million. The first-of-the-year inventory was US$375,000, with a year-end inventory of US$325,000. The annual cost of goods sold was US$7 million. The owner, Eric Jack, wants to evaluate his supply-chain performance by measuring his percentage of assets in inventory, his inventory turnover, and his weeks of supply. We use Equations (11-1), (11-2), and (11-3) to provide these measures.

▼ SOLUTION

First, determine *average inventory*:

$$(US\$375,000 + US\$325,000) \div 2 = US\$350,000$$

Then, use Equation (11-1) to determine percentage invested in inventory:

Percentage invested in inventory = (Total inventory investment ÷ Total assets) × 100

$$= (350,000 \div 5,000,000) \times 100$$

$$= 7\%$$

Third, determine inventory turnover, using Equation (11-2):

Inventory turnover = Cost of goods sold ÷ Inventory investment

$$= 7,000,000 \div 350,000$$

$$= 20$$

Finally, to determine weeks of inventory, use Equation (11-3), adjusted to weeks:

Weeks of inventory = Inventory investment ÷ Weekly cost of goods sold

$$= 350,000 \div (7,000,000 \div 52)$$

$$= 350,000 \div 134,615$$

$$= 2.6$$

We conclude that Jack's Pottery Outlet has 7 percent of its assets invested in inventory, that the inventory turnover is 20, and that weeks of supply is 2.6.

Problems

•• **11.1** Choose a local establishment that is a member of a relatively large chain. From interviews with workers and information from the internet, identify the elements of the supply chain. Determine whether the supply chain represents a low-cost, rapid response, or differentiation strategy (refer to Chapter 2). Are the supply-chain characteristics significantly different from one product to another?

•• **11.2** As purchasing agent for Géant, in Tunisia, you ask your buyer to provide you with a ranking of 'excellent,' 'good,' 'fair,' or 'poor' for a variety of characteristics for two potential vendors. You suggest that 'Products' total be weighted 40 percent and the other three categories' totals be weighted 20 percent each. The buyer has returned the following ranking:

VENDOR RATING

Company	Excellent (4)	Good (3)	Fair (2)	Poor (1)
Financial Strength			K	D
Manufacturing Range			KD	
Research Facilities	K		D	
Geographical Locations		K	D	
Management		K	D	
Labor Relations			K	D
Trade Relations			KD	

Service	Excellent (4)	Good (3)	Fair (2)	Poor (1)
Deliveries on Time		KD		
Handling of Problems		KD		
Technical Assistance		K	D	

Products	Excellent (4)	Good (3)	Fair (2)	Poor (1)
Quality	KD			
Price			KD	
Packaging			KD	

Sales	Excellent (4)	Good (3)	Fair (2)	Poor (1)
Product Knowledge			D	K
Sales Calls			K	D
Sales Service			K	D

DONNA INC. = D
KAY CORP. = K

Which of the two vendors would you select?

•• **11.3** Using the data in Problem 11.2, assume that both Donna, Inc. and Kay Corp. are able to move all their 'poor' ratings to 'fair.' How would you then rank the two firms?

• **11.4** Using Table 11.4, determine the sales necessary to equal a dollar of savings on purchases for a company that has:
a) A net profit of 4 percent and spends 40 percent of its revenue on purchases.
b) A net profit of 6 percent and spends 80 percent of its revenue on purchases.

• **11.5** Using Table 11.4, determine the sales necessary to equal a dollar of savings on purchases for a company that has:
a) A net profit of 6 percent and spends 60 percent of its revenue on purchases.
b) A net profit of 8 percent and spends 80 percent of its revenue on purchases.

•• **11.6** Your options for shipping US$100,000 of machine parts from Jedda, Saudi Arabia, to Doha, Qatar, are: (1) use a ship that will take 15 days at a cost of US$3,800; (2) truck the parts to Adan in Yemen and then ship at a total cost of US$4,800. The second option will take only 10 days. You are paid via a letter of credit the day the parts arrive. Your holding cost is estimated at 30 percent of the value per year.
a) Which option is more economical?
b) What customer issues are not included in the data presented?

•• **11.7** If you have a third option for the data in Problem 11.6, and it costs US$4,000 and also takes 10 days, what is your most economical plan?

•• **11.8** Baker Mfg, Inc. (see Table 11.8) wishes to compare its inventory turnover to those of the industry leader, Arrow Distributing Corp., which has turnover of about 13 times per year and 8 percent of its assets invested in inventory.
a) What is Baker's inventory turnover?
b) What is Baker's percentage of assets committed to inventory?
c) How does Baker's performance compare with the industry leaders?

▼ **TABLE 11.8** For Problem 11.8

Arrow Distributing Corp.	
Net revenue	US$16,500
Cost of sales	US$13,500
Inventory	US$1,000
Total assets	US$8,600

Baker Mfg Inc.	
Net revenue	US$27,500
Cost of sales	US$21,500
Inventory	US$1,250
Total assets	US$16,600

▶ **Refer to** MyOMLab **for additional homework problems.**

Case Studies

▶ Supply-Chain Management at Gulf Craft

Like most other manufacturers, Gulf Craft (GC) finds that it must spend a huge portion of its revenue on purchases. GC has also found that the better its suppliers understand its end users, the better are both the supplier's product and GC's final product. GC is trying to differentiate its products from the vast number of boats supplied by other companies. Thus, the firm works closely with suppliers to ensure innovation, quality, and timely delivery.

GC has done a number of things to drive down costs while driving up quality, responsiveness, and innovation. First, working on partnering relationships with suppliers ranging from providers of windshields to providers of instrument panel controls, GC has brought timely innovation at reasonable cost to its product. Key vendors are so tightly linked with the company that they meet with designers to discuss material changes to be incorporated into new product designs.

Second, the company has joined other boat manufacturers in a purchasing group, to work with suppliers on reducing the costs of large purchases. Third, GC is working with a number of local vendors to supply hardware and fasteners directly to the assembly line on a just-in-time basis. In some of these cases, GC has worked out an arrangement with the vendor so that title does not transfer until parts are used by GC. In other cases, title transfers when items are delivered to the property. This practice drives down total inventory and the costs associated with large-lot delivery.

Finally, GC works with a personnel agency to outsource part of the recruiting and screening process for employees. In all these cases, GC is demonstrating innovative approaches to supply-chain management that help the firm and, ultimately, the end user.

Discussion Questions

1. What other techniques might GC use to improve supply-chain management?
2. What kind of response might members of the supply chain expect from GC in response to their 'partnering' in the supply chain?
3. Why is supply-chain management important to GC?

▶ Darden's Global Supply Chain

Video Case

Darden Restaurants, owner of popular brands such as Olive Garden and Red Lobster, requires unique supply chains to serve more than 300 million meals annually. Darden's strategy is operations excellence, and Senior Vice President Jim Lawrence's task is to ensure competitive advantage via Darden's supply chains. For a firm with purchases exceeding US$1.5 billion, managing the supply chains is a complex and challenging task.

Darden, like other casual dining restaurants, has unique supply chains that reflect its menu options. Darden's supply chains are rather shallow, often having just one tier of suppliers. But it has four distinct supply chains.

First, 'smallware' is a restaurant-industry term for items such as linens, dishes, tableware and kitchenware, and silverware. These are purchased, with Darden taking title as they are received at the Darden Direct Distribution (DDD) warehouse in Orlando, Florida. From this single warehouse, smallware items are shipped via common carrier (trucking companies) to Olive Garden, Red Lobster, Bahama Breeze, and Seasons 52 restaurants.

Second, frozen, dry, and canned food products are handled economically by Darden's 11 distribution centers in North America, which are managed by major U.S. food distributors, such as MBM, Maines, and Sygma. This is Darden's second supply line.

Third, the fresh food supply chain (not frozen and not canned), where life is measured in days, includes dairy products, produce, and meat. This supply chain is B2B, where restaurant managers directly place orders with a preselected group of independent suppliers.

Fourth, Darden's worldwide seafood supply chain is the final link. Here Darden has developed independent suppliers of salmon, shrimp, tilapia, scallops, and other fresh fish that are source inspected by Darden's overseas representatives to ensure quality. These fresh products are flown to the United States and shipped to 16 distributors, with 22 locations, for quick delivery to the restaurants. With suppliers in 35 countries, Darden must be on the cutting edge when it comes to collaboration, partnering, communication, and food safety. It does this with heavy travel schedules for purchasing and quality control personnel, native-speaking employees onsite, and aggressive communication. Communication is a critical element; Darden tries to develop as much forecasting transparency as possible. "Point of sale (POS) terminals," says Lawrence, "feed actual sales every night to suppliers."

Discussion Questions*

1. What are the advantages of each of Darden's four supply chains?
2. What are the complications of having four supply chains?
3. Where would you expect ownership/title to change in each of Darden's four supply chains?
4. How do Darden's four supply chains compare with those of other firms, such as Dell or an automobile manufacturer? Why do the differences exist, and how are they addressed?

*You may wish to view the video that accompanies this case before answering these questions.

► **Arnold Palmer's Hospital Supply Chain**

Arnold Palmer Hospital, one of the nation's top hospitals dedicated to serving women and children, is a large business with over 2,000 employees working in a 431-bed facility in Orlando, Florida. Like many other hospitals, and other companies, Arnold Palmer Hospital had been a long-time member of a large buying group, one servicing 900 members. But the group did have a few limitations. For example, it might change suppliers for a particular product every year (based on a new lower-cost bidder) or stock only a product that was not familiar to the physicians at Arnold Palmer Hospital. The buying group was also not able to negotiate contracts with local manufacturers to secure the best pricing.

So, in 2003, Arnold Palmer Hospital, together with seven other partner hospitals in central Florida, formed its own much smaller, but still powerful (with US$200 million in annual purchases) Healthcare Purchasing Alliance (HPA) corporation. The new alliance saved the HPA members US$7 million in its first year with two main changes. First, it was structured and staffed to assure that the bulk of the savings associated with its contracting efforts went to its eight members. Second, it struck even better deals with vendors by guaranteeing a *committed* volume and signing not 1-year deals but 3- to 5-year contracts. "Even with a new internal cost of US$400,000 to run HPA, the savings and ability to contract for what our member hospitals really want makes the deal a winner," says George DeLong, head of HPA.

Effective supply-chain management in manufacturing often focuses on development of new product innovations and efficiency through buyer–vendor collaboration. However, the approach in a service industry has a slightly different emphasis. At Arnold Palmer Hospital, supply-chain opportunities often manifest themselves through the Medical Economic Outcomes Committee. This committee (and its subcommittees) consists of users (including the medical and nursing staff) who evaluate purchase options with a goal of better

medicine while achieving economic targets. For instance, the heart pacemaker negotiation by the cardiology subcommittee allowed for the standardization to two manufacturers, with annual savings of US$2 million for just this one product.

Arnold Palmer Hospital is also able to develop custom products that require collaboration down to the third tier of the supply chain. This is the case with custom packs that are used in the operating room. The custom packs are delivered by a distributor, McKesson General Medical, but assembled by a pack company that uses materials the hospital wanted purchased from specific manufacturers. The HPA allows Arnold Palmer Hospital to be creative in this way. With major cost savings, standardization, blanket purchase orders, long-term contracts, and more control of product development, the benefits to the hospital are substantial.

Discussion Questions*

1. How does this supply chain differ from that in a manufacturing firm?
2. What are the constraints on making decisions based on economics alone at Arnold Palmer Hospital?
3. What role do doctors and nurses play in supply-chain decisions in a hospital? How is this participation handled at Arnold Palmer Hospital?
4. Dr. Smith just returned from the Annual Physician's Orthopedic Conference, where she saw a new hip joint replacement demonstrated. She decides she wants to start using the replacement joint at Arnold Palmer Hospital. What process will Dr. Smith have to go through at the hospital to introduce this new product into the supply chain for future surgical use?

*You may wish to view the video that accompanies this case before answering the questions.

► **Additional Case Study:** Visit MyOMLab for this free case study:

Amazon.com: Discusses opportunities and issues in an innovative business model for the internet.

Main Heading	Review Material	
THE SUPPLY CHAIN'S STRATEGIC IMPORTANCE (pp. 330–331)	Most firms spend a huge portion of their sales money on purchases. ■ **Supply-chain management**—Management of activities related to procuring materials and services, transforming them into intermediate goods and final products, and delivering them through a distribution system. The *objective is to build a chain of suppliers that focuses on maximizing value to the ultimate customer.* Competition is no longer between companies; it is between supply chains.	**VIDEO 11.1** Darden's Global Supply Chain **VIDEO 11.2** Arnold Palmer's Hospital Supply Chain
ETHICS AND SUSTAINABILITY (pp. 331–333)	Ethics includes personal ethics, ethics within the supply chain, and ethical behavior regarding the environment. The Institute for Supply Management has developed a set of Principles and Standards for ethical conduct.	
SUPPLY-CHAIN ECONOMICS (pp. 333–334)	■ **Make-or-buy decision**—A choice between producing a component or service in-house or purchasing it from an outside source. ■ **Outsourcing**—Transferring to external suppliers a firm's activities that have traditionally been internal.	Problems: 11.6, 11.7
SUPPLY-CHAIN STRATEGIES (pp. 334–336)	Six supply-chain strategies for goods and services to be obtained from outside sources are: 1. Negotiating with many suppliers and playing one supplier against another 2. Developing long-term partnering relationships with a few suppliers 3. Vertical integration 4. Joint ventures 5. Developing *keiretsu* networks 6. Developing virtual companies that use suppliers on an as-needed basis ■ **Vertical integration**—Developing the ability to produce goods or services previously purchased or actually buying a supplier or a distributor. ■ ***Keiretsu***—A Japanese term that describes suppliers who become part of a company coalition. ■ **Virtual companies**—Companies that rely on a variety of supplier relationships to provide services on demand. Also known as hollow corporations or network companies.	
MANAGING THE SUPPLY CHAIN (pp. 336–339)	Supply-chain integration success begins with mutual agreement on goals, followed by mutual trust, and continues with compatible organizational cultures. Three issues complicate the development of an efficient, integrated supply chain: local optimization, incentives, and large lots. ■ **Bullwhip effect**—Increasing fluctuation in orders or cancellations that often occurs as orders move through the supply chain. ■ **Pull data**—Accurate sales data that initiate transactions to 'pull' a product through the supply chain. ■ **Single-stage control of replenishment**—Fixing responsibility for monitoring and managing inventory for the retailer. ■ **Vendor-managed inventory (VMI)**—A system in which a supplier maintains material for the buyer, often delivering directly to the buyer's using department. ■ **Collaborative planning, forecasting, and replenishment (CPFR)**—A system in which members of a supply chain share information in a joint effort to reduce supply-chain costs. ■ **Blanket order**—A long-term purchase commitment to a supplier for items that are to be delivered against short-term releases to ship. The purchasing department should make special efforts to increase levels of standardization. ■ **Postponement**—Delaying any modifications or customization to a product for as long as possible in the production process. Postponement strives to minimize internal variety while maximizing external variety. ■ **Drop shipping**—Shipping directly from the supplier to the end consumer rather than from the seller, saving both time and reshipping costs. ■ **Pass-through facility**—A facility that expedites shipment by holding merchandise and delivering from shipping hubs. ■ **Channel assembly**—A system that postpones final assembly of a product so the distribution channel can assemble it.	

Main Heading	Review Material	
E-PROCUREMENT (pp. 339–340)	■ **E-procurement**—Purchasing facilitated through the internet. ■ **Electronic data interchange (EDI)**—A standardized data-transmission format for computerized communications between organizations. ■ **Advanced shipping notice (ASN)**—A shipping notice delivered directly from vendor to purchaser. Online catalogs move companies from a multitude of individual phone calls, faxes, and emails to a centralized online system and drive billions of dollars of waste out of the supply chain.	
VENDOR SELECTION (pp. 340–342)	Vendor selection is a three-stage process: (1) vendor evaluation; (2) vendor development; (3) negotiations. *Vendor evaluation* involves finding potential vendors and determining the likelihood of their becoming good suppliers. *Vendor development* may include everything from training, to engineering and production help, to procedures for information transfer. ■ **Negotiation strategies**—Approaches taken by supply-chain personnel to develop contractual relationships with suppliers. Three classic types of negotiation strategies are: (1) the cost-based price model; (2) the market-based price model; (3) competitive bidding.	Problems: 11.2, 11.3
LOGISTICS MANAGEMENT (pp. 342–345)	■ **Logistics management**—An approach that seeks efficiency of operations through the integration of all material acquisition, movement, and storage activities. The total distribution cost in the Arab world is over 18 percent of the gross national product (GNP). Five major means of distribution are trucking, railroads, airfreight, waterways, and pipelines. The vast majority of manufactured goods move by truck.	Problem: 11.8
MEASURING SUPPLY-CHAIN PERFORMANCE (pp. 345–348)	Typical supply-chain benchmark metrics include lead time, time spent placing an order, percentage of late deliveries, percentage of rejected material, and number of shortages per year: Percentage invested in inventory = (Total inventory investment/Total assets) × 100 (11-1) ■ **Inventory turnover**—Cost of goods sold divided by average inventory: Inventory turnover = Cost of goods sold/Inventory investment (11-2) Weeks of supply = (Inventory investment/Average weekly cost of goods sold) (11-3) ■ **Supply-Chain Operations Reference (SCOR) Model**—A set of processes, metrics, and best practices developed by the Supply Chain Council. The five parts of the SCOR model are Plan, Source, Make, Deliver, and Return.	Virtual Office Hours for Solved Problem: 11.1

Self-Test

■ **Before taking the self test,** refer to the learning objectives listed at the beginning of the chapter and the key terms listed at the end of the chapter.

LO1. The objective of supply-chain management is to _____.

LO2. The term *vertical integration* means to:
 a) develop the ability to produce products that complement or supplement the original product
 b) produce goods or services previously purchased
 c) develop the ability to produce the specified good more efficiently
 d) all of the above.

LO3. The bullwhip effect can be aggravated by:
 a) local optimization d) promotions
 b) sales incentives e) all of the above.
 c) quantity discounts

LO4. Vendor selection requires:
 a) vendor evaluation and effective third-party logistics
 b) vendor development and logistics
 c) negotiations, vendor evaluation, and vendor development
 d) an integrated supply chain
 e) inventory and supply-chain management.

LO5. A major issue in logistics is:
 a) cost of purchases
 b) vendor evaluation
 c) product customization
 d) cost of shipping alternatives
 e) excellent suppliers.

LO6. Inventory turnover =
 a) Cost of goods sold ÷ Weeks of supply
 b) Weeks of supply ÷ Annual cost of goods sold
 c) Annual cost of goods sold ÷ 52 weeks
 d) Inventory investment ÷ Cost of goods sold
 e) Cost of goods sold ÷ Inventory investment.

Answers: LO1. build a chain of suppliers that focuses on maximizing value to the ultimate customer; **LO2.** b; **LO3.** e; **LO4.** c; **LO5.** d; **LO6.** e.

SUPPLEMENT 11

Outsourcing as a Supply-Chain Strategy

Supplement Outline

Supplement 11 Learning Objectives

LO1: Explain how core competencies relate to outsourcing   357

LO2: Describe the risks of outsourcing   358

LO3: Use factor rating to evaluate both country and provider outsourcers   360

LO4: List the advantages and disadvantages of outsourcing   361

> **AUTHOR COMMENT**
> Outsourcing is a supply-chain strategy that can deliver tremendous value to an organization.

WHAT IS OUTSOURCING?

Outsourcing is a creative management strategy. Indeed, some organizations use outsourcing to replace entire purchasing, IT support, marketing, finance, and operations departments. Outsourcing is applicable to firms throughout the world. And because outsourcing decisions are risky and many are not successful, making the right decision may mean the difference between success and failure.[1]

Because outsourcing grows by double digits every year, students and managers need to understand the issues, concepts, models, philosophies, procedures, and practices of outsourcing. This supplement describes current concepts, methodologies, and outsourcing strategies.

Outsourcing

Transferring a firm's activities that have traditionally been internal to external suppliers.

Outsourcing means procuring from external suppliers services or products that are normally a part of an organization. In other words, a firm takes functions it was performing in-house (such as accounting, janitorial, or call center functions) and has another company do the same job. If a company owns two plants and reallocates production from the first to the second, this is not considered outsourcing. If a company moves some of its business processes to a foreign country but retains control, we define this move as **offshoring**, not outsourcing. For example, Jordan's Zalloum Group offshored a US$30 million confectionery factory to Egypt (with huge savings in transportation costs).

Offshoring

Moving a business process to a foreign country but retaining control of it.

Early in their lives, many businesses handle their activities internally. As businesses mature and grow, however, they often find competitive advantage in the specialization provided by outside firms. They may also find limitations on locally available labor, services, materials, or other resources. So organizations balance the potential benefits of outsourcing with its potential risks. Outsourcing the wrong activities can cause major problems.

Outsourcing is not a new concept; it is simply an extension of the long-standing practice of *subcontracting* production activities. Indeed, the classic make-or-buy decision concerning products (which we discussed in Chapter 11) is an example of outsourcing.

So why has outsourcing expanded to become a major strategy in business the world over? From an economic perspective, it is due to the continuing move toward specialization in an increasingly technological society. More specifically, outsourcing's continuing growth is due to: (1) increasing expertise; (2) reduced costs of more reliable transportation; (3) the rapid development and deployment of advancements in telecommunications and computers. Low-cost communication, including the internet, permits firms anywhere in the world to provide previously limited information services.

Examples of outsourcing include.

- Call centers for the United States and England in Egypt and India
- Aljazeera's legal services routed to Jordan
- Arab Bank handing travel services and payroll to Aramex
- Production of the Mercedes E Class by EGA in Cairo, Egypt
- Libya's Ministry of Health sending sophisticated-surgery patients to Jordan

VIDEO S11.1
Outsourcing Offshore at Darden

Outsourced manufacturing, also known as *contract manufacturing*, is becoming standard practice in many industries, from computers to automobiles.

Paralleling the growth of outsourcing is the growth of international trade. With the passage of landmark trade agreements like the Gulf Cooperation Council, the work of the World

---

[1]The authors wish to thank Professor Marc J. Schneiderjans, of the University of Nebraska–Lincoln, for help with the development of this supplement. His book *Outsourcing and Insourcing in an International Context*, with Ashlyn Schniederjans and Dara Schniederjans (Armonk, NY: M.E. Sharpe, 2005), provided insight, content, and references that shaped our approach to the topic.

Trade Organization and the European Union, and other international trade zones established throughout the world, we are witnessing the greatest expansion of international commerce in history.

Table S11.1 provides a ranking of the outsourcing locations (out of 50 countries) in the annual A.T. Kearney Global Location Index. Scores are based on financial attractiveness, workforce availability, employee skill set, and business environment.

Types of Outsourcing

Nearly any business activity can be outsourced. A general contractor in the building industry, who subcontracts various construction activities needed to build a home, is a perfect example of an outsourcer. Every component of the building process, including the architect's design, a consultant's site location analysis, a lawyer's work to obtain the building permits, plumbing, electrical work, dry walling, painting, furnace installation, landscaping, and sales, is usually outsourced. Outsourcing implies an agreement (typically a legally binding contract) with an external organization.

Among the business processes outsourced are: (1) purchasing; (2) logistics; (3) R&D; (4) operation of facilities; (5) management of services; (6) human resources; (7) finance/accounting; (8) customer relations; (9) sales/marketing; (10) training; (11) legal processes. Note that the first six of these are OM functions that we discuss in this text.

STRATEGIC PLANNING AND CORE COMPETENCIES

As we saw in Chapter 2, organizations develop missions, long-term goals, and strategies as general guides for operating their businesses. The strategic planning process begins with a basic mission statement and the establishing of goals. Given the mission and goals, strategic planners next undertake an internal analysis of the organization to identify how much or little each business activity contributes to the achievement of the mission.

During such an analysis, firms identify their strengths—what they do well or better than their competitors. These unique skills, talents, and capabilities are called **core competencies**. Core competencies may include specialized knowledge, proprietary technology or information, and unique production methods. The trick is to identify what the organization does better than anyone else. Common sense dictates that core competencies are the activities that a firm should perform. By contrast, *non-core activities*, which can be a sizable portion of an organization's total business, are good candidates for outsourcing.

Sony's core competency, for example, is electromechanical design of chips. This is its core, and Sony is one of the best in the world when it comes to rapid response and specialized production of these chips. But, as Figure S11.1 suggests, outsourcing could offer Sony continuous innovation and flexibility. Leading specialized outsource providers are likely to come up with major innovations in such areas as software, human resources, and distribution. That is their business, not Sony's.

Managers evaluate their strategies and core competencies and ask themselves how to use the assets entrusted to them. Do they want to be the offshore company that does low-margin work at 3 or 4 percent or the innovative firm that makes a 30 to 40 percent margin? PC or iPod assemblers in China and Taiwan earn 3 to 4 percent, but Apple, which innovates, designs, and sells, has a margin ten times as large.

Management must be cautious in outsourcing those elements of the product or service that provide a competitive advantage. For example, when considering Knowledge Process Outsourcing (KPO), which depends on outsourcing the activities relating to knowledge and information, a company would need to seek an outsourcing agent with competence and credible expertise in the processes in order to manage such high-value work. A good example would be Rubicon Group Holding, which outsources some of its knowledge processes to digital companies in the Philippines.

The Theory of Comparative Advantage

The motivation for international outsourcing comes from the **theory of comparative advantage**. This theory focuses on the basic economics of outsourcing internationally. According to the theory, if an external provider, regardless of its geographic location, can perform activities more

▼ **TABLE S11.1**
Desirable Outsourcing Destinations

Rank	Country	Score
1	India	7.01
2	China	6.49
3	Malaysia	5.99
4	Egypt	5.81
15	U.A.E.	5.41
16	United Kingdom	5.41
18	United States	5.35
22	Jordan	5.23
23	Tunisia	5.23
37	Morocco	4.96
50	Portugal	4.15

Source: Based on A. T. Kearney, 2011.

Core competencies
A set of skills, talents, and activities in which a firm is particularly strong.

LO1: Explain how core competencies relate to outsourcing

Theory of comparative advantage
A theory which states that countries benefit from specializing in (and exporting) products and services in which they have relative advantage, and importing goods in which they have a relative disadvantage.

▶ **FIGURE S11.1**
Sony, an Outsourcing Company
Based on J. B. Quinn. "Outsourcing Innovation." *Sloan Management Review* (Summer 2000): 20.

Outsourcers *could* provide Sony with:

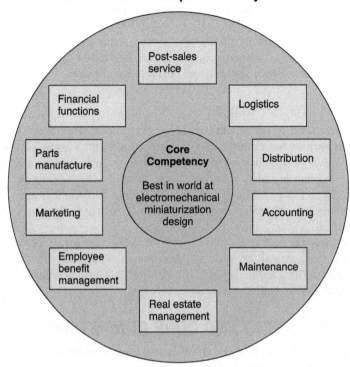

productively than the purchasing firm, then the external provider should do the work. This allows the purchasing firm to focus on what it does best, its core competencies.

However, comparative advantage is not static. Companies, and indeed countries, strive to find comparative advantage. Countries such as U.A.E, India, China, and Russia have made it a government priority and set up agencies to support the easy transition of foreign firms into their outsourcing markets. Work and jobs go to countries that reduce risk through the necessary legal structures, effective infrastructure, and an educated workforce.

Backsourcing
The return of business activity to the original firm.

Consistent with the theory of comparative advantage, the trend toward outsourcing continues to grow. This does not mean all existing outsourcing decisions are perfect. The term **backsourcing** has been used to describe the return of business activity to the original firm. This happened to Zain, which returned its call centers to the headquarters in Jordan after they were outsourced to a Lebanese third-party company that yielded low customer satisfaction.

We will now discuss the risks associated with outsourcing.

AUTHOR COMMENT
The substantial risk in outsourcing requires managers to invest the effort to make sure they do it right.

RISKS OF OUTSOURCING

Risk management starts with a realistic analysis of risks and results in a strategy that minimizes the impact of these uncertainties. Indeed, outsourcing can look very risky. And it is. Perhaps half of all outsourcing agreements fail because of inappropriate planning and analysis. For one thing, few promoters of international outsourcing mention the erratic power grids in some foreign countries or the difficulties with local government officials, inexperienced managers, and unmotivated employees. On the other hand, when managers set an outsourcing goal of 75 percent cost reduction and receive only a 30 to 40 percent cost reduction, they view the outsourcing as a failure, when, in fact, it may be a success.

LO2: Describe the risks of outsourcing

Quality can also be at risk. A recent survey found that companies that outsourced customer service saw a drop in their score on the Consumer Satisfaction Index. This was true regardless of whether the companies outsourced domestically or overseas.[2]

[2]J. Whitaker, M. S. Krishnan, and C. Fornell. "How Offshore Outsourcing Affects Customer Satisfaction." *The Wall Street Journal* (July 7, 2008): R4.

Outsourcing Process	Examples of Possible Risks
Identify non-core competencies	Can be incorrectly identified as a non-core competency.
Identify non-core activities that should be outsourced	Just because the activity is not a core competency for your firm does not mean an outsource provider is more competent and efficient.
Identify impact on existing facilities, capacity, and logistics	Failing to understand the change in resources and talents needed internally.
Establish goals and draft outsourcing agreement specifications	Setting goals so high that failure is certain.
Identify and select outsource provider	Selecting the wrong outsource provider.
Negotiate goals and measures of outsourcing performance	Misinterpreting measures and goals, how they are measured, and what they mean.
Monitor and control current outsourcing program	Being unable to control product development, schedules, and quality.
Evaluate and give feedback to outsource provider	Having a non-responsive provider (i.e. one that ignores feedback).
Evaluate international political and currency risks	Country's currency may be unstable, a country may be politically unstable, or cultural and language differences may inhibit successful operations.
Evaluate coordination needed for shipping and distribution	Understanding of the timing necessary to manage flows to different facilities and markets.

◄ **TABLE S11.2**

The Outsourcing Process and Related Risks

> **AUTHOR COMMENT**
> Cultural differences may indeed be why companies are less frequently outsourcing their call centers.

Another risk is the political backlash that results from outsourcing to foreign countries. The perceived loss of jobs could be used by the general public to cause political actions against the government.

Table S11.2 lists some of the risks inherent in outsourcing.

In addition to the external risks, operations managers must deal with other issues that outsourcing brings. These include: (1) changes in employment levels; (2) changes in facilities and processes needed to receive components in a different state of assembly; (3) vastly expanded logistics issues, including insurance, customs, and timing.

What can be done to mitigate the risks of outsourcing? Research indicates that of all the reasons given for outsourcing failure, the most common is that the decision was made without sufficient understanding and analysis. The next section provides a methodology that helps analyze the outsourcing decision process.

EVALUATING OUTSOURCING RISK WITH FACTOR RATING

> **AUTHOR COMMENT**
> The factor-rating model adds objectivity to decision making.

The factor-rating method, first introduced in Chapter 8, is an excellent tool for dealing with both country risk assessment and provider selection problems.

Rating International Risk Factors

Suppose a company has identified for outsourcing an area of production that is a non-core competency. Example S1 shows how to rate several international risk factors using an *unweighted* factor-rating approach.

◄ **EXAMPLE S1**

Establishing risk factors for four countries

EGA Airbags produces auto and truck airbags for Nissan, Chrysler, Mercedes, and BMW. It wants to conduct a risk assessment of outsourcing manufacturing. Four countries—England, Mexico, Spain, and Egypt (the current home nation)—are being considered. Only English- or Spanish-speaking countries are included because they 'fit' with organizational capabilities.

APPROACH ▶ EGA's management identifies nine factors, listed in Table S11.3, and rates each country on a 0–3 scale, where 0 is no risk and 3 is high risk. Risk ratings are added to find the lowest-risk location.

► **TABLE S11.3**
EGA Airbag's International Risk Factors, by Country (an unweighted approach)*

Risk Factor	England	Mexico	Spain	Egypt (home country)
Economic: Labor cost/laws	1	0	2	1
Economic: Capital availability	0	2	1	0
Economic: Infrastructure	0	2	2	0
Culture: Language	0	0	0	0
Culture: Social norms	2	0	1	2
Migration: Uncontrolled	0	2	0	0
Politics: Ideology	2	0	1	2
Politics: Instability	0	1	2	2
Politics: Legalities	3	0	2	3
Total risk rating scores	8	7	11	10

*Risk rating scale: 0 = no risk, 1 = minor risk, 2 = average risk, 3 = high risk

SOLUTION ►   Based on these ratings, Mexico is the least risky of the four locations being considered.

INSIGHT ►   As with many other quantitative methods, assessing risk factors is not easy and may require considerable research, but the technique adds objectivity to a decision.

LEARNING EXERCISE ►   Social norms in England have just been rescored by an economist, and the new rating is 'no risk.' How does this affect EGA's decision? [Answer: England now has the lowest rating, at 6, for risk.]

RELATED PROBLEM ►   S11.1

EXCEL OM Data File **ChS11ExS1.xls** can be found at MyOMLab.

LO3: Use factor rating to evaluate both country and provider outsourcers

In Example S1, EGA Airbags considered only English- and Spanish-speaking countries. But it is worth mentioning that countries like China, India, and Russia have millions of English-speaking personnel. This may have an impact on the final decision.

Example S1 considered the home country of the outsourcing firm. This inclusion helps document the risks that a domestic outsourcing provider poses compared with the risks posed by international providers. Including the home country in the analysis also helps justify final strategy selection to stakeholders who might question it.

Nearshoring

Choosing an outsource provider in the home country or in a nearby country.

Indeed, **nearshoring** (i.e. choosing an outsource provider located in the home country or in a nearby country) can be a good strategy for businesses and governments seeking both control and cost advantages. Gulf State firms are interested in nearshoring to Yemen or Oman because of their cultural similarity and geographic proximity to the Arabian Gulf. This allows the company wanting to outsource to exert more control than would be possible when outsourcing to most other countries. Nearshoring represents a compromise in which some cost savings are sacrificed for greater control because Yemen or Oman have a smaller wage differential, which limits the labor cost reduction advantage.

Rating Outsource Providers

In Chapter 8, Example 1, we illustrated the factor-rating method's computations when each factor has its own importance weight. We now apply that concept in Example S2 to compare outsourcing providers being considered by a firm.

EXAMPLE S2 ►

Rating provider selection criteria

Arabic Architects, Inc., a designer of high-rise buildings, has decided to outsource its information technology (IT) function. Three outsourcing providers are being actively considered: one in the United States, one in India, and one in Lebanon.

APPROACH ►   Arabic's VP–Operations, Susan Abdulghani, has made a list of seven criteria she considers critical. After putting together a committee of four other VPs, she has rated each firm (on a 1–5 scale, with 5 being highest) and has also placed an importance weight on each of the factors, as shown in Table S11.4.

Factor (criterion)*	Importance Weight	Outsource Providers		
		BIM (U.S.A.)	S.P.C. (India)	IT5 (Lebanon)
1. Can reduce operating costs	0.2	3	3	5
2. Can reduce capital investment	0.2	4	3	3
3. Skilled personnel	0.2	5	4	3
4. Can improve quality	0.1	4	5	2
5. Can gain access to technology not in company	0.1	5	3	5
6. Can create additional capacity	0.1	4	2	4
7. Aligns with policy/philosophy/culture	0.1	2	3	5
Totals	1.0	3.9	3.3	3.8

*These seven major criteria are based on a survey of 165 procurement executives, as reported in J. Schildhouse, "Outsourcing Ins and Outs," *Inside Supply Management* (December 2005): 22–29.

SOLUTION ▶ Susan multiplies each rating by the weight and sums the products in each column to generate a total score for each outsourcing provider. She selects BIM, which has the highest overall rating.

INSIGHT ▶ When the total scores are as close (3.9 vs. 3.8) as they are in this case, it is important to examine the sensitivity of the results to inputs. For example, if one of the importance weights or factor scores changes even marginally, the final selection may change. Management preference may also play a role here.

LEARNING EXERCISE ▶ Susan decides that 'Skilled personnel' should instead get a weight of 0.1 and 'Aligns with policy/philosophy/culture' should increase to 0.2. How do the total scores change? [Answer: BIM = 3.6, S.P.C. = 3.2, and IT5 = 4, so IT5 is selected.]

RELATED PROBLEMS ▶ S11.2, S11.3, S11.4

EXCEL OM Data File **ChS11ExS2.xls** can be found at MyOMLab.

ADVANTAGES AND DISADVANTAGES OF OUTSOURCING

Advantages of Outsourcing

As mentioned earlier, companies outsource for five main reasons. They are, in order of importance: (1) cost savings; (2) gaining outside expertise; (3) improving operations and service; (4) focusing on core competencies; (5) gaining outside technology.

LO4: List the advantages and disadvantages of outsourcing

Cost Savings The number-one reason driving outsourcing for many firms is the possibility of significant cost savings, particularly for labor.

Gaining Outside Expertise In addition to gaining access to a broad base of skills that are unavailable in-house, an outsourcing provider may be a source of innovation for improving products, processes, and services.

Improving Operations and Service An outsourcing provider may have production flexibility. This may allow the firm outsourcing its work to win orders by more quickly introducing new products and services.

Focusing on Core Competencies An outsourcing provider brings *its* core competencies to the supply chain. This frees up a firm's human, physical, and financial resources to reallocate to core competencies.

Gaining Outside Technology Firms can outsource to state-of-the-art providers instead of retaining old (legacy) systems. This means they do not have to invest in new technology, thereby cutting risks.

Other Advantages There are additional advantages in outsourcing. For example, a firm may improve its performance and image by associating with an outstanding supplier. Outsourcing can also be used as a strategy for downsizing, or 'reengineering,' a firm.

Disadvantages of Outsourcing

There are a number of potential disadvantages in outsourcing. Here are just a few.

Increased Transportation Costs Delivery costs may rise substantially if distance increases from an outsourcing provider to a firm using that provider.

Loss of Control This disadvantage can permeate and link to all other problems with outsourcing. When managers lose control of some operations, costs may increase because it's harder to assess and control them. For example, production of most of the world's laptops is now outsourced. This means that companies like Dell and HP find themselves using the same contractor (Quanta) to make their machines in China. This can leave them struggling to maintain control over the supplier.

Creating Future Competition Intel, for example, outsourced a core competency, chip production, to AMD when it could not keep up with early demands. Within a few years, AMD became a leading competitor, manufacturing its own chips.

Negative Impact on Employees Employee morale may drop when functions are outsourced, particularly when friends lose their jobs. Employees believe they may be next, and indeed they may be. Productivity, loyalty, and trust—all of which are needed for a healthy, growing business—may suffer.

Longer-Term Impact Some disadvantages of outsourcing tend to be longer term than the advantages of outsourcing. In other words, many of the risks firms run by outsourcing may not show up on the bottom line until some time in the future. This permits CEOs who prefer short-term planning and are interested only in bottom-line improvements to use the outsourcing strategy to make quick gains at the expense of longer-term objectives.

The advantages and disadvantages of outsourcing may or may not occur but should be thought of as possibilities to be managed effectively.

AUDITS AND METRICS TO EVALUATE PERFORMANCE

Regardless of the techniques and success in the selection of outsourcing providers, agreements must specify results and outcomes. Whatever the outsourced component or service, management needs an evaluation process to ensure satisfactory continuing performance. At a minimum, the product or service must be defined in terms of quality, customer satisfaction, delivery, cost, and improvement. The mix and detail of the performance measures will depend on the nature of the product.

In situations where the outsourced product or service plays a major role in strategy and winning orders, the relationship needs to be more than after-the-fact audits and reports. It needs to be based on continuing communication, understanding, trust, and performance. The relationship should manifest itself in the mutual belief that 'we are in this together' and go well beyond the written agreement.

However, when outsourcing is for less critical components, agreements that include the traditional mix of audits and metrics (such as cost, logistics, quality, and delivery) may be reported weekly or monthly. When a *service* has been outsourced, more imaginative metrics may be necessary. For instance, in an outsourced call center, these metrics may deal with personnel evaluation and training, call volume, call type, and response time, as well as tracking complaints. In this dynamic environment, reporting of such metrics may be required daily.

> **AUTHOR COMMENT**
> Because outsourcing is rife with potential abuse, companies have to be careful not to harm individuals, societies, or nature.

ETHICAL ISSUES IN OUTSOURCING

Laws, trade agreements, and business practices are contributing to a growing set of international, ethical practices for the outsourcing industry. Table S11.5 presents several tenets of conduct that have fairly universal acceptance.

In the electronics industry, HP, Dell, IBM, Intel, and 12 other companies have created the Electronics Industry Code of Conduct (EICC). The EICC sets environmental standards, bans child labor and excessive overtime, and audits outsourcing producers to ensure compliance.

Ethics Principle	Outsourcing Linkage
Do no harm to indigenous cultures	Avoid outsourcing in a way that violates religious holidays (e.g. making employees work during religious holidays).
Do no harm to the ecological systems	Don't use outsourcing to move pollution from one country to another.
Uphold universal labor standards	Don't use outsourcing to take advantage of cheap labor that leads to employee abuse.
Uphold basic human rights	Don't accept outsourcing that violates basic human rights.
Pursue long-term involvement	Don't use outsourcing as a short-term arrangement to reduce costs; view it as a long-term partnership.
Share knowledge and technology	Don't think outsourcing agreements will prevent loss of technology, but use the inevitable sharing to build good relationships.

◀ **TABLE S11.5**

Ethical Principles and Related Outsourcing Linkages

SUPPLEMENT SUMMARY

Companies can give many different reasons why they outsource, but the reality is that outsourcing's most attractive feature is that it helps firms cut costs. Workers in low-cost countries simply work much more cheaply, with fewer fringe benefits, work rules, and legal restrictions, than their counterparts in the outsourcing countries. For example, a comparable hourly wage of US$20 in the United States and US$30 in Europe is well above the US$2.5 per hour in Egypt, yet Egypt often achieves quality levels equivalent to (or even higher than) plants in the outsourcing countries.

There is a growing economic pressure to outsource. But there is also a need for planning outsourcing to make it acceptable to all participants. When outsourcing is done in the right way, it creates a win–win situation.

Key Terms

Backsourcing (p. 358)
Core competencies (p. 357)

Nearshoring (p. 360)
Offshoring (p. 356)

Outsourcing (p. 356)
Theory of comparative advantage (p. 357)

Discussion Questions

1. How would you summarize outsourcing trends?
2. What potential cost saving advantages might firms experience by using outsourcing?
3. What internal issues must managers address when outsourcing?
4. How should a company select an outsourcing provider?
5. What are international risk factors in the outsourcing decision?
6. How can ethics be beneficial in an outsourcing organization?
7. What are some of the possible consequences of poor outsourcing?

Using Software to Solve Outsourcing Problems

Excel, Excel OM, and POM for Windows may be used to solve most of the problems in this supplement.

Excel OM and POM for Windows both contain Factor Rating modules that can address issues such as the ones we saw in Examples S1 and S2. The Factor Rating module was illustrated earlier in Program 8.1 in Chapter 8.

Problems*

• **S11.1** Salima Prama Technologies, Inc., in Iraq, has narrowed its choice of outsourcing provider to two firms located in different countries. Prama wants to decide which one of the two countries is the better choice, based on risk-avoidance criteria. She has polled her executives and established four criteria. The resulting ratings for the two countries are presented in the table below, where 1 is a lower risk and 3 is a higher risk.

a) Using the unweighted factor-rating method, which country would you select?

b) If the first two factors (price and nearness) are given a weight of 2, and the last two factors (technology and history) are given a weight of 1, how does your answer change? **PX**

Selection Criterion	Lebanon	Qatar
Price of service from outsourcer	2	3
Nearness of facilities to client	3	1
Level of technology	1	3
History of successful outsourcing	1	2

• **S11.2** Using the same ratings given in Problem S11.1, assume that the executives have determined four criteria weightings: Price, with a weight of 0.1; Nearness, with 0.6; Technology, with 0.2; and History, with 0.1.

a) Using the weighted factor-rating method, which country would you select?

b) Double each of the weights used in part (a) (to 0.2, 1.2, 0.4, and 0.2, respectively). What effect does this have on your answer? Why? **PX**

S11.3 Mashi Accounting Software in Yemen is marketed to small accounting firms throughout the Arab world. Owner Muhaseb Mashi has decided to outsource the company's help desk and is considering three providers: Manila Call Center (Philippines), Delhi Services (India), and Beirut Call (Lebanon). The following table

*Note: **PX** means the problem may be solved with POM for Windows and/or Excel OM.

summarizes the data Mashi has assembled. Which outsourcing firm has the best rating? (Higher weights imply higher importance and higher ratings imply more desirable providers.) **PX**

Criterion	Importance Weight	Manila	Delhi	Beirut
		Provider Ratings		
Flexibility	0.5	5	1	9
Trustworthiness	0.1	5	5	2
Price	0.2	4	3	6
Delivery	0.2	5	6	6

•••• **S11.4** Samara Technologies, a high-tech manufacturer, is considering outsourcing some of its electronics production. Four firms have responded to its request for bids, and CEO Samara has started to perform an analysis on the scores his OM team has entered in the table below.

Factor	Weight	A	B	C	D
		Ratings of Outsource Providers			
Labor	w	5	4	3	5
Quality procedures	30	2	3	5	1
Logistics system	5	3	4	3	5
Price	25	5	3	4	4
Trustworthiness	5	3	2	3	5
Technology in place	15	2	5	4	4
Management team	15	5	4	2	1

Weights are on a scale from 1 through 30, and the outsourcing provider scores are on a scale of 1 through 5. The weight for the labor factor is shown as a w because Samara's OM team cannot agree on a value for this weight. For what range of values of w, if any, is company C a recommended outsourcing provider, according to the factor-rating method?

Case Studies

▶ Outsourcing to Tata

While some states in the United States, such as Tennessee, have been quick to ban or limit international outsourcing of government activities, other state governments have sought to take advantage of low-cost opportunities that international outsourcing can offer.

The state of New Mexico's Labor Department hired Tata Consultancy Services, an Indian outsourcing firm, to reprogram New Mexico's unemployment compensation computer system. While Tata had completed work for other states, including Pennsylvania and New York, it had never worked on an unemployment compensation system. Also, New Mexico agreed to allow Tata to do all computer software work in India, apparently with insufficient monitoring of progress by New Mexico officials responsible for the outsourcing project.

The new system should have been completed in 6 months, which put the due date in December 2001. Unfortunately, things did not work out well. The initial system was delivered 1 year later. But in late 2004 it was still not working. Also, the outsourcing project

went way over the budget of US$3.6 million, up to US$13 million. The warranty for the system ended in 2003, leaving New Mexico with a situation of either suing Tata to complete the project (it was estimated at 80 percent complete) or hiring someone to fix it. Tata's position was that it had complied with the outsourcing agreement and was willing to continue fixing the system if it could receive additional compensation to justify additional work.

Discussion Questions

1. Use the process in Table S11.2 to analyze what New Mexico could have done to achieve a more successful outcome.
2. Is this a case of cultural misunderstanding, or could the same result have occurred if a U.S. firm, such as IBM, had been selected?
3. Conduct your own research to assess the risks of outsourcing any information technology project. (*Computerworld* is one good source.)

▶ **Outsourcing Offshore at Darden**

Video Case

Darden Restaurants, owner of popular brands such as Olive Garden and Red Lobster, serves more than 300 million meals annually in over 1,700 restaurants across the United States and Canada. To achieve competitive advantage via its supply chain, Darden must achieve excellence at each step. With purchases from 35 countries, and seafood products with a shelf life as short as 4 days, this is a complex and challenging task.

Those 300 million meals annually mean 18 million kg of shrimp and huge quantities of tilapia, swordfish, and other fresh purchases. Fresh seafood is typically flown to the United States and monitored each step of the way to ensure that 1°C is maintained.

Darden's purchasing agents travel the world to find competitive advantage in the supply chain. Darden personnel from supply chain and development, quality assurance, and environmental relations contribute to developing, evaluating, and checking suppliers. Darden also has seven native-speaking representatives living on other continents to provide continuing support and evaluation of suppliers. All suppliers must abide by Darden's food standards, which typically exceed Food and Drug Administration (FDA) and other industry standards. Darden expects continuous improvement in durable relationships that increase quality and reduce cost.

Darden's aggressiveness and development of a sophisticated supply chain provides an opportunity for outsourcing. Much food preparation is labor intensive and is often more efficient when handled in bulk. This is particularly true where large volumes may justify capital investment. For instance, Tyson and Iowa Beef prepare meats to Darden's specifications much more economically than can individual restaurants. Similarly, Darden has found that it can outsource both the cutting of salmon to the proper portion size and the cracking/peeling of shrimp more cost-effectively offshore than in U.S. distribution centers or individual restaurants.

Discussion Questions*

1. What are some outsourcing opportunities in a restaurant?
2. What supply-chain issues are unique to a firm sourcing from 35 countries?
3. Examine how other firms or industries develop international supply chains as compared to Darden.
4. Why does Darden outsource harvesting and preparation of much of its seafood?

*You may wish to view the video that accompanies this case study before answering these questions.

Main Heading	Review Material	
WHAT IS OUTSOURCING? (pp. 356–357)	■ **Outsourcing**—Procuring from external sources services or products that are normally part of an organization. Some organizations use outsourcing to replace entire purchasing, information systems, marketing, finance, and operations departments. ■ **Offshoring**—Moving a business process to a foreign country but retaining control of it. Outsourcing is not a new concept; it is simply an extension of the long-standing practice of *subcontracting* production activities. Outsourced manufacturing, also known as contract manufacturing, is becoming standard practice in many industries. Outsourcing implies an agreement (typically a legally binding contract) with an external organization.	**VIDEO S11.1** Outsourcing Offshore at Darden
STRATEGIC PLANNING AND CORE COMPETENCIES (pp. 357–358)	■ **Core competencies**—An organization's unique skills, talents, and capabilities. Core competencies may include specialized knowledge, proprietary technology or information, and unique production methods. *Non-core activities*, which can be a sizable portion of an organization's total business, are good candidates for outsourcing. ■ **Theory of comparative advantage**—A theory which states that countries benefit from specializing in (and exporting) products and services in which they have relative advantage and importing goods in which they have a relative disadvantage. ■ **Backsourcing**—The return of business activity to the original firm.	
RISKS OF OUTSOURCING (pp. 358–359)	Perhaps half of all outsourcing agreements fail because of inappropriate planning and analysis. Potential risks of outsourcing include: ■ In some countries, erratic power grids, difficult local government officials, inexperienced managers, or unmotivated employees ■ A drop in quality or customer service ■ Political backlash that results from outsourcing to foreign countries ■ Changes in employment levels ■ Changes in facilities and processes needed to receive components in a different state of assembly ■ Vastly expanded logistics issues, including insurance, customs, and timing The most common reason given for outsourcing failure is that the decision was made without sufficient understanding and analysis.	
EVALUATING OUTSOURCING RISK WITH FACTOR RATING (pp. 359–361)	The factor-rating method is an excellent tool for dealing with both country risk assessment and provider selection problems. Including the home country of the outsourcing firm in a factor-rating analysis helps document the risks that a domestic outsourcing provider poses compared with the risks posed by international providers. Including the home country in the analysis also helps justify final strategy selection to stakeholders who might question it. ■ **Nearshoring**—Choosing an outsource provider in the home country or in a nearby country. Nearshoring can be a good strategy for businesses and governments seeking both control and cost advantages.	Problems: S11.1–S11.4
ADVANTAGES AND DISADVANTAGES OF OUTSOURCING (pp. 361–362)	Advantages of outsourcing include: ■ *Cost savings*: The number-one reason driving outsourcing for many firms is the possibility of significant cost savings, particularly for labor. ■ *Gaining outside expertise*: In addition to gaining access to a broad base of skills that are unavailable in-house, an outsourcing provider may be a source of innovation for improving products, processes, and services. ■ *Improving operations and service*: An outsourcing provider may have production flexibility. This may allow the client firm to win orders by more quickly introducing new products and services. ■ *Focusing on core competencies*: An outsourcing provider brings *its* core competencies to the supply chain. This frees up the firm's human, physical, and financial resources to reallocate to the firm's own core competencies. ■ *Gaining outside technology*: Firms can outsource to state-of-the-art providers instead of retaining old (legacy) systems. These firms do not have to invest in new technology, thereby cutting risks. ■ *Other advantages*: The client firm may improve its performance and image by associating with an outstanding supplier. Outsourcing can also be used as a strategy for downsizing, or 'reengineering,' a firm.	

Main Heading	Review Material	
	Potential disadvantages of outsourcing include: ■ *Increased transportation costs*: Delivery costs may rise substantially if distance increases from an outsourcing provider to a client firm. ■ *Loss of control*: This disadvantage can permeate and link to all other problems with outsourcing. When managers lose control of some operations, costs may increase because it's harder to assess and control them. ■ *Creating future competitors* ■ *Negative impact on employees*: Employee morale may drop when functions are outsourced, particularly when friends lose their jobs. ■ *Longer-term impact*: Some disadvantages of outsourcing tend to be longer term than the advantages of outsourcing. In other words, many of the risks firms run by outsourcing may not show up on the bottom line until some time in the future.	
AUDITS AND METRICS TO EVALUATE PERFORMANCE (p. 362)	Outsourcing agreements must specify results and outcomes. Management needs an evaluation process to ensure satisfactory continuing performance. At a minimum, the product or service must be defined in terms of quality, customer satisfaction, delivery, cost, and improvement. When the outsourced product or service plays a major role in strategy and winning orders, the relationship needs to be based on continuing communication, understanding, trust, and performance.	
ETHICAL ISSUES IN OUTSOURCING (pp. 362–363)	Some outsourcing policies linked to ethical principles include: avoid outsourcing in a way that violates religious holidays; don't use outsourcing to move pollution from one country to another; don't use outsourcing to take advantage of cheap labor that leads to employee abuse; don't accept outsourcing that violates basic human rights; don't use outsourcing as a short-term arrangement to reduce costs—view it as a long-term partnership; and don't think an outsourcing agreement will prevent loss of technology, but use the inevitable sharing to build a good relationship with outsourcing firms.	

Self-Test

■ **Before taking the self-test,** refer to the learning objectives listed at the beginning of the supplement and the key terms listed at the end of the supplement.

LO1. Core competencies are those strengths in a firm that include:
  a) specialized skills
  b) unique production methods
  c) proprietary information/knowledge
  d) things a company does better than others
  e) all of the above.

LO2. Outsourcing can be a risky proposition because:
  a) about half of all outsourcing agreements fail
  b) it saves only about 30 percent in labor costs
  c) labor costs are increasing throughout the world
  d) a non-core competency is outsourced
  e) shipping costs are increasing.

LO3. Evaluating outsourcing providers by comparing their weighted average scores involves:
  a) factor-rating analysis
  b) cost-volume analysis
  c) transportation model analysis
  d) linear regression analysis
  e) crossover analysis.

LO4. Advantages of outsourcing include:
  a) focusing on core competencies and cost savings
  b) gaining outside technology and creating new markets in India for U.S. products
  c) improving operations by closing plants in Malaysia
  d) employees wanting to leave the firm
  e) reduced problems with logistics.

12

Managing Inventory

10

OM STRATEGY DECISIONS

- ► Design of Goods and Services
- ► Managing Quality
- ► Process Strategy
- ► Location Strategies
- ► Layout Strategies
- ► Human Resources
- ► Supply-Chain Management
  - ■ Independent Demand
  - ■ Dependent Demand
  - ■ JIT & Lean Operations
- ► Inventory Management
- ► Scheduling
- ► Maintenance

INVENTORY MANAGEMENT PROVIDES COMPETITIVE ADVANTAGE AT ALMARAI FOODS

Almarai Foods is the biggest foods company in the Arab world. Established in 1976 as a partnership to produce fresh dairy products for the Saudi population, Almarai invested heavily in its inventory management system from the start. It had to meet the challenge of producing thousands of tonnes of perishable items, such as milk, cheese, yogurt, and bakery products, storing them and then distributing them to many countries across the region in a way that guaranteed freshness upon delivery.

Managing this massive inventory has made Almarai a pioneer in using technologically advanced warehouses, temperature-controlled vessels, and computer-controlled logistics and distribution trucks.

Almarai uses a variety of inventory management techniques to ensure speed and responsiveness in dealing with any market changes or demands. These computer-based inventory systems are used for tracking stock levels, clients' orders, sales figures, and deliveries. In addition, they create work orders and bills of materials, thus speeding up the manufacturing process. At Almarai, computerized inventory management ensures an optimal level of stock that will reduce costs, spoilage, and waste.

So, next time you buy some yogurt, remember, you are actually at the end of a very sophisticated and technologically advanced process that makes sure that there are enough yogurts in the shop and that those yogurts are fresh.

Almarai has one of the biggest warehouses in the Middle East region to cater for its expanding market share.

The availability of a dependable and reliable road haulage fleet guarantees the delivery of Almarai products fresh to the market.

The variety of foodstaffs available means that an accurate record of all products needs to be kept.

Source: **www.almarai.com**

Almarai products	Stock Control					
Product	Date	Opening stock	Deliveries	Order No.	Closing stock	Name
Skimmed Milk	24.08.2012	4325	12	3264/AL HAK	3658	A Hassan
Milk	24.08.2012	848	8	84216	602	A Hassan
Yoghurt	24.08.2012	1503	5	65100	1249	A Hassan
Dessert	29.07.2012	4362	9	1652	3850	A Hassan
Single cream	29.07.2012	5297	4	65165	3658	A Hassan
Double cream	29.07.2012	378	3	65169	3658	A Hassan
Milk-Condensed	18.07.2012	158	8	2651	3658	A Hassan
Milk-Long Life	15.07.2012	4025	10	2659	3658	A Hassan
New Stock						

The use of information technology systems in managing inventory minimizes the waste and the loss of units, and increases the accuracy of forecasting future storage.

Chapter 12 Learning Objectives

THE IMPORTANCE OF INVENTORY

Inventory is one of the most expensive assets of many companies, representing as much as 50 percent of total invested capital. Operations managers around the globe have long recognized that good inventory management is crucial. On the one hand, a firm can reduce costs by reducing inventory. On the other hand, production may stop and customers become dissatisfied when an item is out of stock. *The objective of inventory management is to strike a balance between inventory investment and customer service.* You can never achieve a low-cost strategy without good inventory management.

All organizations have some type of inventory planning and control system. A bank has methods to control its inventory of cash. A hospital has methods to control blood supplies and pharmaceuticals. Government agencies, schools, and, of course, virtually every manufacturing and production organization are concerned with inventory planning and control.

In cases of physical products, the organization must determine whether to produce goods or to purchase them. Once this decision has been made, the next step is to forecast demand, as discussed in Chapter 4. Then operations managers determine the inventory necessary to service that demand. In this chapter, we discuss the functions, types, and management of inventory. We then address two basic inventory issues: how much to order and when to order.

VIDEO 12.1
Managing Inventory at Frito-Lay

Functions of Inventory

Inventory can serve several functions that add flexibility to a firm's operations. The four functions of inventory are:

1. To '*decouple' or separate various parts of the production process.* For example, if a firm's supplies fluctuate, extra inventory may be necessary to decouple the production process from suppliers.

Hedging inventories of oil is complicated when onshore storage units are full. This supertanker is the world's newest kind of inventory warehouse. When oil traders are betting that prices will rise and want to store oil, a supertanker may be used as a warehouse. These huge floating warehouses can stay at sea for months, waiting for a price that makes the hedge successful.

2. To *decouple the firm from fluctuations in demand* and *provide a stock of goods that will provide a selection for customers*. Such inventories are typical in retail establishments.
3. To *take advantage of quantity discounts*, because purchases in larger quantities may reduce the cost of goods or their delivery.
4. To *hedge against inflation* and upward price changes (as shown in the supertanker photo).

Types of Inventory

To accommodate the functions of inventory, firms maintain four types of inventories: (1) raw material inventory; (2) work-in-process inventory; (3) maintenance/repair/operating supply (MRO) inventory; (4) finished-goods inventory.

Raw material inventory has been purchased but not processed. This inventory can be used to decouple (i.e. separate) suppliers from the production process. However, the preferred approach is to eliminate supplier variability in quality, quantity, or delivery time so that separation is not needed. **Work-in-process (WIP) inventory** is components or raw materials that have undergone some change but are not completed. WIP exists because of the time it takes for a product to be made—called **cycle time**. Reducing cycle time reduces inventory. Often this task is not difficult: During most of the time a product is 'being made,' it is in fact sitting idle. As Figure 12.1 shows, actual work time, or 'run' time, is a small portion of the material flow time, perhaps as low as 5 percent.

Maintenance/repair/operating (MRO) inventories are devoted to supplies necessary to keep machinery and processes productive. They exist because the need and timing for maintenance and repair of some equipment are unknown. Although the demand for MRO inventory is often a function of maintenance schedules, other unscheduled MRO demands must be anticipated. **Finished-goods inventory** is completed product awaiting shipment. Finished goods may be inventoried because future customer demands are unknown.

Raw material inventory
Materials that are usually purchased but have yet to enter the manufacturing process.

Work-in-process (WIP) inventory
Products or components that are no longer raw materials but have yet to become finished products.

Cycle time
The time it takes a product to be made.

Maintenance/repair/operating (MRO)
Maintenance, repair, and operating materials.

Finished-goods inventory
An end item ready to be sold, but still an asset on the company's books.

MANAGING INVENTORY

Operations managers establish systems for managing inventory. In this section, we briefly examine two ingredients of such systems: (1) how inventory items can be classified (called *ABC analysis*); (2) how accurate inventory records can be maintained. We will then look at inventory control in the service sector.

> **AUTHOR COMMENT**
> Firms must carefully control critical items, keep accurate records, count inventory regularly, and avoid theft and damage.

ABC Analysis

ABC analysis divides on-hand inventory into three classifications on the basis of monetary volume. ABC analysis is an inventory application of what is known as the *Pareto principle* (named after Vilfredo Pareto, a 19th-century Italian economist). The Pareto principle states that there are a 'critical few and trivial many.' The idea is to establish inventory policies that focus resources on the *few critical* inventory parts and not the many trivial ones. It is not realistic to monitor inexpensive items with the same intensity as very expensive items.

To determine annual monetary volume for ABC analysis, we measure the *annual demand* of each inventory item times the *cost per unit*. *Class A* items are those on which the annual monetary volume is high. Although such items may represent only about 15 percent of the total inventory

ABC analysis
A method for dividing on-hand inventory into three classifications based on annual dollar volume.

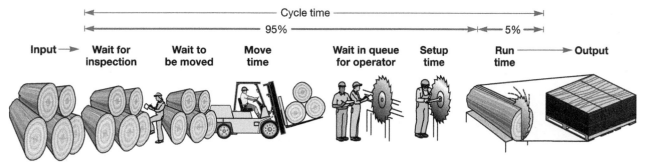

▲ **FIGURE 12.1** **The Material Flow Cycle**
Most of the time that work is in-process (95 percent of the cycle time) is not productive time.

► **FIGURE 12.2**
Graphic Representation of ABC Analysis

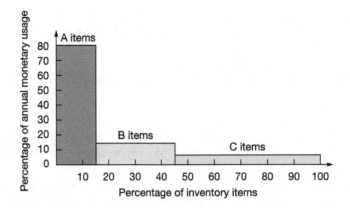

AUTHOR COMMENT
A, B, and C categories need not be exact. The idea is to recognize that levels of control should match the risk.

items, they represent 70 percent to 80 percent of the total financial usage. *Class B* items are those inventory items of medium annual monetary volume. These items may represent about 30 percent of inventory items and 15 percent to 25 percent of the total value. Those with low annual monetary volume are *Class C*, which may represent only 5 percent of the annual monetary volume but about 55 percent of the total inventory items.

Graphically, the inventory of many organizations would appear as presented in Figure 12.2. An example of the use of ABC analysis is shown in Example 1.

EXAMPLE 1 ►

ABC analysis for a chip manufacturer

Qatar Chips, Inc., maker of customized chips, wants to categorize its 10 major inventory items using ABC analysis.

APPROACH ► ABC analysis organizes the items on an annual money-volume basis (using US dollars as their standard currency). Shown below (in columns 1–4) are the 10 items (identified by stock numbers), their annual demands, and unit costs.

SOLUTION ► Annual dollar volume is computed in column 5, along with the percentage of the total represented by each item in column 6. Column 7 groups the 10 items into A, B, and C categories.

					ABC Calculation				
(1)	(2)	(3)		(4)		(5)	(6)		(7)
Item Stock Number	Percentage of Number of Items Stocked	Annual Volume (units)	×	Unit Cost US$	=	Annual Dollar Volume US$	Percentage of Annual Dollar Volume		Class
#10286	20%	1,000		90.00		90,000	38.8%	72%	A
#11526		500		154.00		77,000	33.2%		A
#12760	30%	1,550		17.00		26,350	11.3%	23%	B
#10867		350		42.86		15,001	6.4%		B
#10500		1,000		12.50		12,500	5.4%		B
#12572	50%	600		14.17		8,502	3.7%	5%	C
#14075		2,000		0.60		1,200	0.5%		C
#01036		100		8.50		850	0.4%		C
#01307		1,200		0.42		504	0.2%		C
#10572		250		0.60		150	0.1%		C
		8,550				232,057	100.0%		

LO1: Conduct an ABC analysis

INSIGHT ► The breakdown into A, B, and C categories is not hard and fast. The objective is to try to separate the 'important' from the 'unimportant.'

LEARNING EXERCISE ► The unit cost for Item #10286 has increased from US$90.00 to US$120.00. How does this impact the ABC analysis? [Answer: The total annual dollar volume increases by US$30,000, to US$262,057, and the two A items now comprise 75% of that amount.]

RELATED PROBLEM ► 12.1

EXCEL OM Data File **Ch12Ex1.xls** can be found at MyOMLab.

Criteria other than annual monetary volume can determine item classification. For instance, anticipated engineering changes, delivery problems, quality problems, or high unit cost may dictate upgrading items to a higher classification. The advantage of dividing inventory items into classes allows policies and controls to be established for each class.

Policies that may be based on ABC analysis include the following.

1. Purchasing resources expended on supplier development should be much higher for individual A items than for C items.
2. A items, as opposed to B and C items, should have tighter physical inventory control; perhaps they belong in a more secure area, and perhaps the accuracy of inventory records for A items should be verified more frequently.
3. Forecasting A items may warrant more care than forecasting other items.

Better forecasting, physical control, supplier reliability, and an ultimate reduction in safety stock can all result from appropriate inventory management policies. ABC analysis guides the development of those policies.

Record Accuracy

Good inventory policies are meaningless if management does not know what inventory is on hand. Accuracy of records is a critical ingredient in production and inventory systems. Record accuracy allows organizations to focus on those items that are needed, rather than settling for being sure that 'some of everything' is in inventory. Only when an organization can determine accurately what it has on hand can it make precise decisions about ordering, scheduling, and shipping.

To ensure accuracy, incoming and outgoing record keeping must be good, as must be stockroom security. A well-organized stockroom will have limited access, good housekeeping, and storage areas that hold fixed amounts of inventory. Bins, shelf space, and parts will be labeled accurately.

Cycle Counting

Even though an organization may have made substantial efforts to record inventory accurately, these records must be verified through a continuing audit. Such audits are known as **cycle counting**. Historically, many firms performed annual physical inventories. This practice often meant shutting down the facility and having inexperienced people count parts and material. Inventory records should instead be verified via cycle counting. Cycle counting uses inventory classifications developed through ABC analysis. With cycle counting procedures, items are counted, records are verified, and inaccuracies are periodically documented. The cause of inaccuracies is then traced and appropriate remedial action taken to ensure integrity of the inventory system.

Cycle counting
A continuing reconciliation of inventory with inventory records.

A items will be counted frequently, perhaps once a month; **B** items will be counted less frequently, perhaps once a quarter; and **C** items will be counted perhaps once every 6 months. Example 2 illustrates how to compute the number of items of each classification to be counted each day.

◄ **EXAMPLE 2**

Cycle counting at a truck manufacturer

Alexandria Trucks, Inc., a builder of high-quality refuse trucks, has about 5,000 items in its inventory. It wants to determine how many items to cycle count each day.

APPROACH ▶ After hiring Mohammad Fadel, a bright young OM student, for the summer, the firm determined that it has 500 A items, 1,750 B items, and 2,750 C items. Company policy is to count all A items every month (every 20 working days), all B items every quarter (every 60 working days), and all C items every 6 months (every 120 working days). The firm then allocates some items to be counted each day.

SOLUTION ▶

Item Class	Quantity	Cycle Counting Policy	Number of Items Counted per Day
A	500	Each month (20 working days)	500 ÷ 20 = 25/day
B	1,750	Each quarter (60 working days)	1,750 ÷ 60 = 29/day
C	2,750	Every 6 months (120 working days)	2,750 ÷ 120 = 23/day
			77/day

Seventy-seven items are counted each day.

> **INSIGHT ▶** This daily audit of 77 items is much more efficient and accurate than conducting a massive inventory count once a year.
>
> **LEARNING EXERCISE ▶** Alexandria Trucks reclassifies some B and C items so there are now 1,500 B items and 3,000 C items. How does this change the cycle count? [Answer: B and C both change to 25 items each per day, for a total of 75 items per day.]

LO2: Explain and use cycle counting

In Example 2, the particular items to be cycle counted can be sequentially or randomly selected each day. Another option is to cycle count items when they are reordered.

Cycle counting also has the following advantages:

1. Eliminates the shutdown and interruption of production necessary for annual physical inventories.
2. Eliminates annual inventory adjustments.
3. Trained personnel audit the accuracy of inventory.
4. Allows the cause of the errors to be identified and remedial action to be taken.
5. Maintains accurate inventory records.

Control of Service Inventories

Management of service inventories deserves special consideration. Extensive inventory is held in wholesale and retail businesses, making inventory management crucial and often a factor in a manager's advancement. In the food-service business, for example, control of inventory can make the difference between success and failure. Moreover, inventory that is in transit or idle in a warehouse is lost value. Similarly, inventory damaged or stolen prior to sale is a loss. In retailing, inventory that is unaccounted for between receipt and time of sale is known as **shrinkage**. Shrinkage occurs from damage and theft as well as from sloppy paperwork. Inventory theft is also known as **pilferage**. Retail inventory loss of 1 percent of sales is considered good, but many stores exceed 3 percent. Because the impact on profitability is substantial, inventory accuracy and control are critical. Applicable techniques include the following:

Shrinkage

Retail inventory that is unaccounted for between receipt and sale.

Pilferage

A small amount of theft.

1. *Good personnel selection, training, and discipline:* These are never easy but very necessary in food-service, wholesale, and retail operations, where employees have access to directly consumable merchandise.
2. *Tight control of incoming shipments:* This task is being addressed by many firms through the use of bar code and radio frequency ID (RFID) systems that read every incoming shipment and automatically check tallies against purchase orders. When properly designed, these systems are very hard to defeat. Each item has its own unique stock-keeping unit (SKU; pronounced 'skew').
3. *Effective control of all goods leaving the facility.* This job is accomplished with bar codes on items being shipped, magnetic strips on merchandise, or via direct observation. Direct observation can be personnel stationed at exits (as at Giant Stores and Carrefour) and in potentially high-loss areas or can take the form of one-way mirrors and video surveillance.

Successful retail operations require very good store-level control with accurate inventory in its proper location. One recent study found that consumers and clerks could not find 16 percent of the items at one of the United States' largest retailers—not because the items were out of stock but because they were misplaced (in a backroom, a storage area, or on the wrong aisle). By the researcher's estimates, major retailers lose 10 percent to 25 percent of overall profits due to poor or inaccurate inventory records.[1]

---

[1] See E. Malykhina, "Retailers Take Stock," *Information Week* (February 7, 2005): 20–22 and A. Raman, N. DeHoratius, and Z. Ton, "Execution: The Missing Link in Retail Operations," *California Management Review* 43, no. 3 (Spring 2001): 136–141.

INVENTORY MODELS

We now examine a variety of inventory models and the costs associated with them.

Independent vs. Dependent Demand

Inventory control models assume that demand for an item is either independent of or dependent on the demand for other items. For example, the demand for refrigerators is *independent* of the demand for ovens. However, the demand for oven components is *dependent* on the demand for ovens.

This chapter focuses on managing inventory where demand is *independent*. Chapter 14 presents *dependent* demand management.

Holding, Ordering, and Setup Costs

Before elaborating on the three types of costs it is important to differentiate between *average costs*, which are the result of dividing total costs by total input (such as labor-hours, inventory units) in a given period of time, and *marginal costs*, which are the costs that will be realized because of slight changes in units of activity (usually expressed as the increase of one unit). Experts and scholars have found that using marginal cost estimates is much more accurate than using average costs estimates. This is because the average costs can be overstated as they do not take into account fixed costs that might change afterwards; whereas, marginal cost estimates change as the inputs change. Therefore, it is more accurate to use marginal costs when estimating the holding, ordering, and setup costs.

Holding costs are the costs associated with holding or 'carrying' inventory over time. Therefore, holding costs also include obsolescence and costs related to storage, such as insurance, extra staffing, and interest payments. Many firms fail to include all the inventory holding costs. Consequently, inventory holding costs are often understated. Table 12.1 shows the kinds of costs that need to be evaluated to determine holding costs.

Ordering cost includes costs of supplies, forms, order processing, purchasing, clerical support, and so forth. When orders are being manufactured, ordering costs also exist, but they are a part of what is called setup costs. **Setup cost** is the cost to prepare a machine or process for manufacturing an order. This includes time and labor to clean and change tools or holders. Operations managers can lower ordering costs by reducing setup costs and by using such efficient procedures as electronic ordering and payment.

In manufacturing environments, setup cost is highly correlated with **setup time**. Setups usually require a substantial amount of work even before a setup is actually performed at the work center. With proper planning much of the preparation required by a setup can be done prior to shutting down the machine or process. Setup times can thus be reduced substantially. Machines and processes that traditionally have taken hours to set up are now being set up in less than a minute by the more imaginative world-class manufacturers. As we shall see later in this chapter, reducing setup times is an excellent way to reduce inventory investment and to improve productivity.

Holding cost
The cost to keep or carry inventory in stock.

Ordering cost
The cost of the ordering process.

Setup cost
The cost to prepare a machine or process for production.

Setup time
The time required to prepare a machine or process for production.

INVENTORY MODELS FOR INDEPENDENT DEMAND

In this section, we introduce three inventory models that address two important questions: *when to order* and *how much to order*. These *independent* demand models are:

1. Basic economic order quantity (EOQ) model
2. Production order quantity model
3. Quantity discount model

The Basic Economic Order Quantity Model

The **economic order quantity model** is one of the most commonly used inventory-control techniques. This technique is relatively easy to use but is based on several assumptions:

1. Demand for an item is known, reasonably constant, and independent of decisions for other items.
2. Lead time—that is, the time between placement and receipt of the order—is known and consistent.

Economic order quantity model

An inventory-control technique that minimizes the total of ordering and holding costs.

▼ TABLE 12.1
Determining Inventory Holding Costs

Category	Cost (and range) as a Percentage of Inventory Value
Housing costs (building rent or depreciation, operating cost, taxes, insurance)	6% (3–10%)
Material handling costs (equipment lease or depreciation, power, operating cost)	3% (1–3.5%)
Labor cost (receiving, warehousing, security)	3% (3–5%)
Investment costs (borrowing costs, taxes, and insurance on inventory)	11% (6–24%)
Pilferage, scrap, and obsolescence (much higher in industries undergoing rapid change like PCs and cell phones)	3% (2–5%)
Overall carrying cost	26%

Note: All numbers are approximate, as they vary substantially depending on the nature of the business, location, and current interest rates.

> **AUTHOR COMMENT**
> An overall inventory carrying cost of less than 15 percent is very unlikely, but this cost can exceed 40 percent, especially in high-tech and fashion industries.

3. Receipt of inventory is instantaneous and complete. In other words, the inventory from an order arrives in one batch at one time.
4. Quantity discounts are not possible.
5. The only variable costs are the cost of setting up or placing an order (setup or ordering cost) and the cost of holding or storing inventory over time (holding or carrying cost). These costs were discussed in the previous section.
6. Stockouts (shortages) can be completely avoided if orders are placed at the right time.

LO3: Explain and use the EOQ model for independent inventory demand

With these assumptions, the graph of inventory usage over time has a saw tooth shape, as in Figure 12.3. In Figure 12.3, Q represents the amount that is ordered. If this amount is 500 dresses, all 500 dresses arrive at one time (when an order is received). Thus, the inventory level jumps from 0 to 500 dresses. In general, an inventory level increases from 0 to Q units when an order arrives.

Because demand is constant over time, inventory drops at a uniform rate over time. (Refer to the sloped lines in Figure 12.3.) Each time the inventory level reaches 0, the new order is placed and received, and the inventory level again jumps to Q units (represented by the vertical lines). This process continues indefinitely over time.

Minimizing Costs

The objective of most inventory models is to minimize total costs. With the assumptions just given, significant costs are setup (or ordering) cost and holding (or carrying) cost. All other costs, such as the cost of the inventory itself, are constant. Thus, if we minimize the sum of setup and holding costs, we will also be minimizing total costs. To help you visualize this, in Figure 12.4 we graph total costs as a function of the order quantity, Q. The optimal order size, Q^*, will be the quantity that minimizes the total costs. As the quantity ordered increases, the total number of orders placed per year will decrease. Thus, as the quantity ordered increases, the annual setup or ordering cost will decrease (Figure 12.4[a]). But as the order quantity increases, the holding cost will increase due to the larger average inventories that are maintained (Figure 12.4[b]).

As we can see in Figure 12.4(c), a reduction in either holding or setup cost will reduce the total cost curve. A reduction in the setup cost curve also reduces the optimal order quantity

▶ **FIGURE 12.3**
Inventory Usage over Time

> **AUTHOR COMMENT**
> If the maximum we can ever have is Q (say, 500 units) and the minimum is zero, then if inventory is used (or sold) at a fairly steady rate, the average = $(Q + 0) \div 2 = Q/2$.

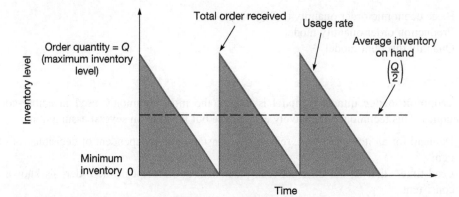

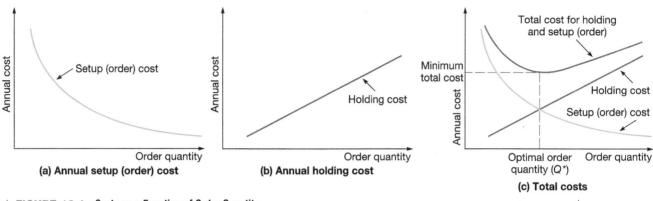

▲ FIGURE 12.4   Costs as a Function of Order Quantity

AUTHOR COMMENT
This graph is the heart of EOQ inventory modeling. We want to find the smallest total cost (top curve), which is the sum of the two curves below it.

(lot size). In addition, smaller lot sizes have a positive impact on quality and production flexibility.

You should note that in Figure 12.4(c), the optimal order quantity occurs at the point where the ordering-cost curve and the carrying-cost curve intersect. This was not by chance. With the EOQ model, the optimal order quantity will occur at a point where the total setup cost is equal to the total holding cost.[2] We use this fact to develop equations that solve directly for Q^*. The necessary steps are:

1. Develop an expression for setup or ordering cost.
2. Develop an expression for holding cost.
3. Set setup (order) cost equal to holding cost.
4. Solve the equation for the optimal order quantity.

Using the following variables, we can determine setup and holding costs and solve for Q^*:

$$Q = \text{Number of units per order}$$
$$Q^* = \text{Optimum number of units per order (EOQ)}$$
$$D = \text{Annual demand in units for the inventory item}$$
$$S = \text{Setup or ordering cost for each order}$$
$$H = \text{Holding or carrying cost per unit per year}$$

1. Annual setup cost = (Number of orders placed per year) × (Setup or order cost per order)

$$= \left(\frac{\text{Annual demand}}{\text{Number of units in each order}} \right) (\text{Setup or order cost per order})$$

$$= \left(\frac{D}{Q} \right)(S) = \frac{D}{Q} S$$

2. Annual holding cost = (Average inventory level) × (Holding cost per unit per year)

$$= \left(\frac{\text{Order quantity}}{2} \right)(\text{Holding cost per unit per year})$$

$$= \left(\frac{Q}{2} \right)(H) = \frac{Q}{2} H$$

3. Optimal order quantity is found when annual setup (order) cost equals annual holding cost, namely:

$$\frac{D}{Q} S = \frac{Q}{2} H$$

---

[2]This is the case when holding costs are linear and begin at the origin—that is, when inventory costs do not decline (or they increase) as inventory volume increases and all holding costs are in small increments. In addition, there is probably some learning each time a setup (or order) is executed—a fact that lowers subsequent setup costs. Consequently, the EOQ model is probably a special case. However, we abide by the conventional wisdom that this model is a reasonable approximation.

4. To solve for Q^*, simply cross-multiply terms and isolate Q on the left of the equal sign:

$$2DS = Q^2H$$

$$Q^2 = \frac{2DS}{H}$$

$$Q^* = \sqrt{\frac{2DS}{H}} \tag{12-1}$$

Now that we have derived the equation for the optimal order quantity, Q^*, it is possible to solve inventory problems directly, as in Example 3.

EXAMPLE 3 ▶

Finding the optimal order size at Syriana, Inc.

Syriana, Inc., a company that markets painless hypodermic needles to hospitals, would like to reduce its inventory cost by determining the optimal number of hypodermic needles to obtain per order.

APPROACH ▶ The annual demand is 1,000 units; the setup or ordering cost is US$10 per order; and the holding cost per unit per year is US$0.50.

SOLUTION ▶ Using these figures, we can calculate the optimal number of units per order:

$$Q^* = \sqrt{\frac{2DS}{H}}$$

$$Q^* = \sqrt{\frac{2(1,000)(10)}{0.50}} = \sqrt{40,000} = 200 \text{ units}$$

INSIGHT ▶ Syriana, Inc. now knows how many needles to order per order. The firm also has a basis for determining ordering and holding costs for this item, as well as the number of orders to be processed by the receiving and inventory departments.

LEARNING EXERCISE ▶ If D increases to 1,200 units, what is the new Q^*? [Answer: $Q^* = 219$ units.]

RELATED PROBLEMS ▶ 12.2, 12.3, 12.6, 12.7

EXCEL **OM** Data File **Ch12Ex3.xls** can be found at MyOMLab.

We can also determine the expected number of orders placed during the year (N) and the expected time between orders (T), as follows:

$$\text{Expected number of orders} = N = \frac{\text{Demand}}{\text{Order quantity}} = \frac{D}{Q^*} \tag{12-2}$$

$$\text{Expected time between orders} = T = \frac{\text{Number of working days per year}}{N} \tag{12-3}$$

Example 4 illustrates this concept.

EXAMPLE 4 ▶

Computing number of orders and time between orders at Syriana, Inc.

Syriana, Inc. (in Example 3) has a 250-day working year and wants to find the number of orders (N) and the expected time between orders (T).

APPROACH ▶ Using Equations (12-2) and (12-3), Syriana enters the data given in Example 3.

SOLUTION ▶

$$N = \frac{\text{Demand}}{\text{Order quantity}} = \frac{1,000}{200} = 5 \text{ orders per year}$$

$$T = \frac{\text{Number of working days per year}}{\text{Expected number of orders}}$$

$$= \frac{250 \text{ working days per year}}{5 \text{ orders}} = 50 \text{ days between orders}$$

As mentioned earlier in this section, the total annual variable inventory cost is the sum of setup and holding costs:

$$\text{Total annual cost} = \text{Setup (order) cost} + \text{Holding cost} \tag{12-4}$$

In terms of the variables in the model, we can express the total cost, TC, as:

$$TC = \frac{D}{Q}S + \frac{Q}{2}H \tag{12-5}$$

Example 5 shows how to use this formula.

◀ **EXAMPLE 5**

Computing combined cost of ordering and holding

Syriana, Inc. (from Examples 3 and 4) wants to determine the combined annual ordering and holding costs.

APPROACH ▶ Apply Equation (12-5), using the data in Example 3.

SOLUTION ▶

$$TC = \frac{D}{Q}S + \frac{Q}{2}H$$

$$= \frac{1,000}{200}(US\$10) + \frac{200}{2}(US\$.50)$$

$$= (5)(US\$10) + (100)(US\$.50)$$

$$= US\$50 + US\$50 = US\$100$$

INSIGHT ▶ These are the annual setup and holding costs. The US$100 total does not include the actual cost of goods. Notice that in the EOQ model, holding costs always equal setup (order) costs.

LEARNING EXERCISE ▶ Find the total annual cost if $D = 1,200$ units in Example 3. [Answer: US$109.54.]

RELATED PROBLEMS ▶ 12.6, 12.7

Inventory costs may also be expressed to include the actual cost of the material purchased. If we assume that the annual demand and the price per hypodermic needle are known values (e.g. 1,000 hypodermics per year at $P = US\$10$) and total annual cost should include purchase cost, then Equation (12-5) becomes:

$$TC = \frac{D}{Q}S + \frac{Q}{2}H + PD$$

Because material cost does not depend on the particular order policy, we still incur an annual material cost of $D \times P = (1,000)(US\$10) = US\$10,000$. (Later in this chapter we will discuss the case in which this may not be true—namely, when a quantity discount is available.)[3]

---

[3]The formula for the economic order quantity (Q^*) can also be determined by finding where the total cost curve is at a minimum (i.e. where the slope of the total cost curve is zero). Using calculus, we set the derivative of the total cost with respect to Q^* equal to 0.

The calculations for finding the minimum of $TC = \frac{D}{Q}S + \frac{Q}{2}H + PD$ are $\frac{d(TC)}{dQ} = \left(\frac{-DS}{Q^2}\right) + \frac{H}{2} + 0 = 0$

Thus, $Q^* = \sqrt{\frac{2DS}{H}}$.

This store takes 4 weeks to get an order for Levi's 501 jeans filled by the manufacturer. If the store sells 10 pairs of size 30–32 Levi's a week, the store manager could set up two containers, keep 40 pairs of jeans in the second container, and place an order whenever the first container is empty. This would be a fixed-quantity reordering system. It is also called a 'two-bin' system and is an example of a very elementary, but effective, approach to inventory management.

Robust

Giving satisfactory answers even with substantial variation in the parameters.

Robust Model   A benefit of the EOQ model is that it is robust. By **robust** we mean that it gives satisfactory answers even with substantial variation in its parameters. As we have observed, determining accurate ordering costs and holding costs for inventory is often difficult. Consequently, a robust model is advantageous. Total cost of the EOQ changes little in the neighborhood of the minimum. The curve is very shallow. This means that variations in setup costs, holding costs, demand, or even EOQ make relatively modest differences in total cost. Example 6 shows the robustness of EOQ.

EXAMPLE 6 ▶

EOQ is a robust model

Management in the Syriana, Inc. examples underestimates total annual demand by 50 percent (say demand is actually 1,500 needles rather than 1,000 needles) while using the same Q. How will the annual inventory cost be impacted?

APPROACH ▶   We will solve for annual costs twice. First, we will apply the wrong EOQ; then we will recompute costs with the correct EOQ.

SOLUTION ▶   If demand in Example 5 is actually 1,500 needles rather than 1,000, but management uses an order quantity of $Q = 200$ (when it should be $Q = 244.9$ based on $D = 1,500$), the sum of holding and ordering cost increases to US\$125:

$$\text{Annual cost} = \frac{D}{Q}S + \frac{Q}{2}H$$

$$= \frac{1,500}{200}(\text{US\$10}) + \frac{200}{2}(\text{US\$.50})$$

$$= \text{US\$75} + \text{US\$50} = \text{US\$125}$$

However, had we known that the demand was for 1,500 with an EOQ of 244.9 units, we would have spent US\$122.47, as shown:

$$\text{Annual cost} = \frac{1,500}{244.9}(\text{US\$10}) + \frac{244.9}{2}(\text{US\$.50})$$

$$= 6.125(\text{US\$10}) + 122.45(\text{US\$.50})$$

$$= \text{US\$61.25} + \text{US\$61.22} = \text{US\$122.47}$$

INSIGHT ▶   Note that the expenditure of US\$125.00, made with an estimate of demand that was substantially wrong, is only 2 percent (US\$2.52 ÷ US\$122.47) higher than we would have paid had we known the actual demand and ordered accordingly. Note also that were it not due to rounding, the annual holding costs and ordering costs would be exactly equal.

LEARNING EXERCISE ▶   Demand at Syriana remains at 1,000, H is still US\$0.50, and we order 200 needles at a time (as in Example 5). But if the true order cost = S = US\$15 (rather than US\$10), what is the annual cost? [Answer: Annual order cost increases to US\$75, and annual holding cost stays at US\$50. So the total cost = US\$125.]

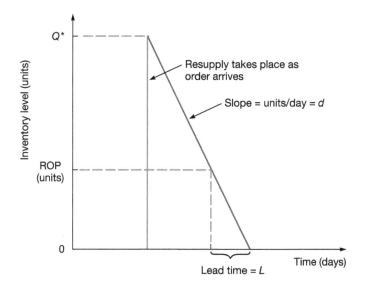

◄ **FIGURE 12.5**
The Reorder Point (ROP)
$Q*$ is the optimum order quantity, and lead time represents the time between placing and receiving an order.

We may conclude that the EOQ is indeed robust and that significant errors do not cost us very much. This attribute of the EOQ model is most convenient because our ability to accurately determine demand, holding cost, and ordering cost is limited.

Reorder Points

Now that we have decided *how much* to order, we will look at the second inventory question, *when* to order. Simple inventory models assume that receipt of an order is instantaneous. In other words, they assume: (1) that a firm will place an order when the inventory level for that particular item reaches zero; (2) that it will receive the ordered items immediately. However, the time between placement and receipt of an order, called **lead time**, or delivery time, can be as short as a few hours or as long as months. Thus, the when-to-order decision is usually expressed in terms of a **reorder point (ROP)**—the inventory level at which an order should be placed (see Figure 12.5).

The ROP is given as:

$$\text{ROP} = (\text{Demand per day}) \times (\text{Lead time for a new order in days})$$
$$= d \times L \tag{12-6}$$

This equation for ROP *assumes that demand during lead time and lead time itself are constant.* When this is not the case, extra stock, often called **safety stock**, should be added.

The demand per day, d, is found by dividing the annual demand, D, by the number of working days in a year:

$$d = \frac{D}{\text{Number of working days in a year}}$$

Computing the ROP is demonstrated in Example 7.

Lead time
In purchasing systems, the time between placing an order and receiving it; in production systems, the wait, move, queue, setup, and run times for each component produced.

Reorder point (ROP)
The inventory level (point) at which action is taken to replenish the stocked item.

Safety stock
Extra stock to allow for uneven demand; a buffer.

An Apple distributor in Dubai has a demand for 8,000 iPods per year. The firm operates a 250-day working year. On average, delivery of an order takes 3 working days. It wants to calculate the reorder point.

APPROACH ▶   Compute the daily demand and then apply Equation (12-6).

SOLUTION ▶

$$d = \frac{D}{\text{Number of working days in a year}} = \frac{8,000}{250}$$

$$= 32 \text{ units}$$

$$\text{ROP} = d \times L = 32 \text{ units per day} \times 3 \text{ days}$$

$$= 96 \text{ units}$$

◄ **EXAMPLE 7**

Computing reorder points (ROP) for iPods

LO4: Compute a reorder point and explain safety stock

INSIGHT ▶ Thus, when iPod inventory stock drops to 96 units, an order should be placed. The order will arrive 3 days later, just as the distributor's stock is depleted.

LEARNING EXERCISE ▶ If there are only 200 working days per year, what is the correct ROP? [Answer: 120 iPods.]

RELATED PROBLEMS ▶ 12.4, 12.5, 12.7f

Safety stock is especially important in firms whose raw material deliveries may be uniquely unreliable. For example, Zoka's restaurants in Amman use Aberdeen Angus beef imported from the United Kingdom. Because the normal mode of delivery is highly variable, safety stock may be substantial.

Production Order Quantity Model

In the previous inventory model, we assumed that the entire inventory order was received at one time. There are times, however, when the firm may receive its inventory over a period of time. Such cases require a different model, one that does not require the instantaneous-receipt assumption. This model is applicable under two situations: (1) when inventory continuously flows or builds up over a period of time after an order has been placed; (2) when units are produced and sold simultaneously. Under these circumstances, we take into account daily production (or inventory-flow) rate and daily demand rate. Figure 12.6 shows inventory levels as a function of time (and inventory dropping to zero between orders).

Production order quantity model

An economic order quantity technique applied to production orders.

Because this model is especially suitable for the production environment, it is commonly called the **production order quantity model**. It is useful when inventory continuously builds up over time, and traditional economic order quantity assumptions are valid. We derive this model by setting ordering or setup costs equal to holding costs and solving for optimal order size, Q^*. Using the following symbols, we can determine the expression for annual inventory holding cost for the production order quantity model:

Q = Number of units per order
H = Holding cost per unit per year
p = Daily production rate
d = Daily demand rate, or usage rate
t = Length of the production run in days

LO5: Apply the production order quantity model

1. $\left(\begin{array}{c}\text{Annual inventory}\\ \text{holding cost}\end{array}\right) = (\text{Average inventory level}) \times \left(\begin{array}{c}\text{Holding cost}\\ \text{per unit per year}\end{array}\right)$

2. $(\text{Average inventory level}) = (\text{Maximum inventory level}) \div 2$

3. $\left(\begin{array}{c}\text{Maximum}\\ \text{inventory level}\end{array}\right) = \left(\begin{array}{c}\text{Total production during}\\ \text{the production run}\end{array}\right) - \left(\begin{array}{c}\text{Total used during}\\ \text{the production run}\end{array}\right)$

$= pt - dt$

However, Q = total produced = pt, and thus $t = Q \div P$. Therefore:

$$\text{Maximum inventory level} = p\left(\frac{Q}{p}\right) - d\left(\frac{Q}{p}\right)$$

$$= Q - \frac{d}{p}Q = Q\left(1 - \frac{d}{p}\right)$$

▶ **FIGURE 12.6**
Change in Inventory Levels over Time for the Production Model

AUTHOR COMMENT
Note that inventory buildup is not instantaneous but gradual. So the formula reduces the average inventory and thus the holding cost by the ratio of that buildup.

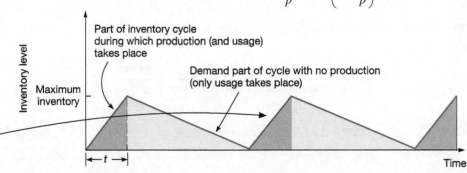

Part of inventory cycle during which production (and usage) takes place

Demand part of cycle with no production (only usage takes place)

Maximum inventory

Inventory level

$\leftarrow t \rightarrow$

Time

Each order may require a change in the way a machine or process is set up. Reducing setup time usually means a reduction in setup cost; and reductions in setup costs make smaller batches (lots) more economical to produce. Increasingly, set up (and operation) is performed by computer-controlled machines, such as this one, operating from previously written programs.

4. Annual inventory holding cost (or simply holding cost) =

$$\frac{\text{Maximum inventory level}}{2}(H) = \frac{Q}{2}\left[1 - \left(\frac{d}{p}\right)\right]H$$

Using this expression for holding cost and the expression for setup cost developed in the basic EOQ model, we solve for the optimal number of pieces per order by equating setup cost and holding cost:

$$\text{Setup cost} = (D \div Q)S$$

$$\text{Holding cost} = \tfrac{1}{2}HQ[1 - (d \div p)]$$

Set ordering cost equal to holding cost to obtain Q_p^*:

$$\frac{D}{Q}S = \tfrac{1}{2}HQ[1 - (d \div p)]$$

$$Q^2 = \frac{2DS}{H[1 - (d \div p)]}$$

$$Q_p^* = \sqrt{\frac{2DS}{H[1 - (d \div p)]}} \tag{12-7}$$

In Example 8, we use the above equation (12-7), to solve for the optimum order or production quantity when inventory is consumed as it is produced.

◄ EXAMPLE 8

A production order quantity model

Alshula Manufacturing, Inc., in Baghdad, makes and sells specialty hubcaps for the retail automobile aftermarket. Alshula's forecast for its wire-wheel hubcap is 1,000 units next year, with an average daily demand of 4 units. However, the production process is most efficient at 8 units per day. So the company produces 8 per day but uses only 4 per day. The company wants to solve for the optimum number of units per order. (*Note*: This plant schedules production of this hubcap only as needed, during the 250 days per year the shop operates.)

APPROACH ▶ Gather the cost data and apply Equation (12-7):

$$\text{Annual demand} = D = 1,000 \text{ units}$$

$$\text{Setup costs} = S = \text{US\$10}$$

$$\text{Holding cost} = H = \text{US\$0.50 per unit per year}$$

$$\text{Daily production rate} = p = 8 \text{ units daily}$$

$$\text{Daily demand rate} = d = 4 \text{ units daily}$$

You may want to compare this solution with the answer in Example 3, which had identical D, S, and H values. Eliminating the instantaneous-receipt assumption, where $p = 8$ and $d = 4$, resulted in an increase in Q^* from 200 in Example 3 to 283 in Example 8. This increase in Q^* occurred because holding cost dropped from US\$0.50 to [US\$0.50 $\times (1 - d \div p)$], making a larger order quantity optimal. Also note that:

$$d = 4 = \frac{D}{\text{Number of days the plant is in operation}}$$

$$= \frac{1,000}{250}$$

We can also calculate Q_p^* when *annual* data are available. When annual data are used, we can express Q_p^* as:

$$Q_p^* = \sqrt{\frac{2DS}{H\left(1 - \dfrac{\text{Annual demand rate}}{\text{Annual production rate}}\right)}} \tag{12-8}$$

AUTHOR COMMENT
Think of the discount model as the EOQ model run once for *each* of the discount price levels offered.

Quantity Discount Models

Quantity discount
A reduced price for items purchased in large quantities.

To increase sales, many companies offer quantity discounts to their customers. A **quantity discount** is simply a reduced price (P) for an item when it is purchased in larger quantities. Discount schedules with several discounts for large orders are common. A typical quantity discount schedule appears in Table 12.2. As can be seen in the table, the normal price of the item is US\$5. When 1,000 to 1,999 units are ordered at one time, the price per unit drops to US\$4.80; when the quantity ordered at one time is 2,000 units or more, the price is US\$4.75 per unit. As always, management must decide when and how much to order. However, with an opportunity to save money on quantity discounts, how does the operations manager make these decisions?

▼ **TABLE 12.2**
A Quantity Discount Schedule

Discount Number	Discount Quantity	Discount (%)	Discount Price (P) in US\$
1	0 to 999	no discount	5.00
2	1,000 to 1,999	4	4.80
3	2,000 and over	5	4.75

As with other inventory models discussed so far, the overall objective is to minimize total cost. Because the unit cost for the third discount in Table 12.2 is the lowest, you may be tempted to order 2,000 units or more merely to take advantage of the lower product cost. Placing an order for that quantity, however, even with the greatest discount price, may not minimize total inventory cost. Granted, as discount quantity goes up, the product cost goes down. However, holding cost increases because orders are larger. Thus the major trade-off when considering quantity discounts is between *reduced product cost* and *increased holding cost*. When we include the cost of the product, the equation for the total annual inventory cost can be calculated as follows:

Total cost = Ordering (setup) cost + Holding cost + Product cost

LO6: Explain and use the quantity discount model

or

$$TC = \frac{D}{Q}S + \frac{Q}{2}H + PD \qquad (12\text{-}9)$$

where Q = Quantity ordered
D = Annual demand in units
S = Ordering or setup cost per order
P = Price per unit
H = Holding cost per unit per year

Now, we have to determine the quantity that will minimize the total annual inventory cost. Because there are several discounts, this process involves four steps:

STEP 1: For each discount, calculate a value for optimal order size Q^*, using the following equation:

$$Q^* = \sqrt{\frac{2DS}{IP}} \qquad (12\text{-}10)$$

Note that the holding cost is IP instead of H. Because the price of the item is a factor in annual holding cost, we cannot assume that the holding cost is a constant when the price per unit changes for each quantity discount. Thus, it is common to express the holding cost as a percentage (I) of unit price (P) instead of as a constant cost per unit per year, H.

STEP 2: For any discount, if the order quantity is too low to qualify for the discount, adjust the order quantity upward to the *lowest* quantity that will qualify for the discount. For example, if Q^* for discount 2 in Table 12.2 were 500 units, you would adjust this value up to 1,000 units. (Look at the second discount in Table 12.2. Order quantities between 1,000 and 1,999 will qualify for the 4 percent discount. Thus, if Q^* is below 1,000 units, we will adjust the order quantity up to 1,000 units.)

The reasoning for Step 2 may not be obvious. If the order quantity, Q^*, is below the range that will qualify for a discount, a quantity within this range may still result in the lowest total cost.

As shown in Figure 12.7, the total cost curve is broken into three different total cost curves. There is a total cost curve for the first ($0 \leq Q \leq 999$), second ($1,000 \leq Q \leq 1,999$), and third ($Q \geq 2,000$) discount. Look at the total cost (TC) curve for discount 2. Q^* for discount 2 is less than the allowable discount range, which is from 1,000 to 1,999 units. As the figure shows, the lowest allowable quantity in this range, which is 1,000 units, is the quantity that minimizes total cost. Thus, the second step is needed to ensure that we do not discard an order quantity that may indeed produce the minimum cost. Note that an order quantity computed in step 1 that is *greater* than the range that would qualify it for a discount may be discarded.

STEP 3: Using the preceding total cost equation, compute a total cost for every Q^* determined in Steps 1 and 2. If you had to adjust Q^* upward because it was below the allowable quantity range, be sure to use the adjusted value for Q^*.

STEP 4: Select the Q^* that has the lowest total cost, as computed in Step 3. It will be the quantity that will minimize the total inventory cost.

Let us see how this procedure can be applied with an example.

▶ **FIGURE 12.7**
Total Cost Curve for the Quantity Discount Model

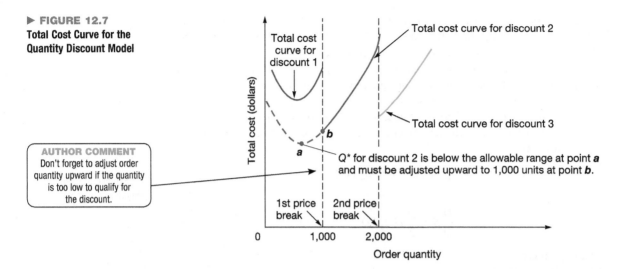

AUTHOR COMMENT
Don't forget to adjust order quantity upward if the quantity is too low to qualify for the discount.

EXAMPLE 9 ▶

Quantity discount model

Giant Discount Store in Muscat stocks toy race cars. Recently, the store has been given a quantity discount schedule for these cars. This quantity schedule was shown in Table 12.2. Thus, the normal cost for the toy race cars is US$5.00. For orders between 1,000 and 1,999 units, the unit cost drops to US$4.80; for orders of 2,000 or more units, the unit cost is only US$4.75. Furthermore, ordering cost is US$49.00 per order, annual demand is 5,000 race cars, and inventory carrying charge, as a percentage of cost, I, is 20 percent, or 0.2. What order quantity will minimize the total inventory cost?

APPROACH ▶   We will follow the four steps just outlined for a quantity discount model.

SOLUTION ▶   The first step is to compute Q^* for every discount in Table 12.2. This is done as follows:

$$Q_1^* = \sqrt{\frac{2(5,000)(49)}{(0.2)(5.00)}} = 700 \text{ cars per order}$$

$$Q_2^* = \sqrt{\frac{2(5,000)(49)}{(0.2)(4.80)}} = 714 \text{ cars per order}$$

$$Q_3^* = \sqrt{\frac{2(5,000)(49)}{(0.2)(4.75)}} = 718 \text{ cars per order}$$

The second step is to adjust upward those values of Q^* that are below the allowable discount range. Since Q_1^* is between 0 and 999, it need not be adjusted. Because Q_2^* is below the allowable range of 1,000 to 1,999, it must be adjusted to 1,000 units. The same is true for Q_3^*. It must be adjusted to 2,000 units. After this step, the following order quantities must be tested in the total cost equation:

$$Q_1^* = 700$$
$$Q_2^* = 1,000 - \text{adjusted}$$
$$Q_3^* = 2,000 - \text{adjusted}$$

The third step is to use Equation (12-9) and compute a total cost for each order quantity. This step is taken with the aid of Table 12.3, which presents the computations for each level of discount introduced in Table 12.2.

▼ **TABLE 12.3**
Total Cost Computations for Giant Discount Store

Discount Number	Unit Price (US$)	Order Quantity (US$)	Annual Product Cost (US$)	Annual Ordering Cost (US$)	Annual Holding Cost (US$)	Total (US$)
1	5.00	700	25,000	350	350	25,700
2	4.80	1,000	24,000	245	480	24,725
3	4.75	2,000	23,750	122.50	950	24,822.50

The fourth step is to select that order quantity with the lowest total cost. Looking at Table 12.3, you can see that an order quantity of 1,000 toy race cars will minimize the total cost. You should see, however, that the total cost for ordering 2,000 cars is only slightly greater than the total cost for ordering

1,000 cars. Thus, if the third discount cost is lowered to US$4.65, for example, then this quantity might be the one that minimizes total inventory cost.

INSIGHT ▶ The quantity discount model's third cost factor, annual product cost, is now a major variable with impact on the final cost and decision. It takes substantial increases in order and holding costs to compensate for a large quantity price break.

LEARNING EXERCISE ▶ Giant Discount Store has just been offered a third price break. If it orders 2,500 or more cars at a time, the unit cost drops to US$4.60. What is the optimal order quantity now? [Answer: Q_4^*, for a total cost of US$24,248.]

RELATED PROBLEMS ▶ 12.11, 12.12, 12.13, 12.14

EXCEL OM Data File **CH12EX9.xls** can be found at MyOMLab.

AUTHOR COMMENT
Probabilistic models are a real-world adjustment because demand and lead time won't always be known and constant.

PROBABILISTIC MODELS AND SAFETY STOCK

All the inventory models we have discussed so far make the assumption that demand for a product is constant and certain. We now relax this assumption. The following inventory models apply when product demand is not known but can be specified by means of a probability distribution. These types of models are called **probabilistic models**.

An important concern of management is maintaining an adequate service level in the face of uncertain demand. The **service level** is the *complement* of the probability of a stockout. For instance, if the probability of a stockout is 0.05, then the service level is 0.95. Uncertain demand raises the possibility of a stockout. One method of reducing stockouts is to hold extra units in inventory. As we noted, such inventory is usually referred to as safety stock. It involves adding a number of units as a buffer to the reorder point (ROP). As you recall from our previous discussion:

$$ROP = d \times L$$

where d = Daily demand
L = Order lead time, or number of working days it takes to deliver an order

The inclusion of safety stock (ss) changes the expression to:

$$ROP = d \times L + ss \tag{12-11}$$

The amount of safety stock maintained depends on the cost of incurring a stockout and the cost of holding the extra inventory. Annual stockout cost is computed as follows:

Annual stockout costs = The sum of the units short for each demand level
× The probability of that demand level × The stockout cost/unit
× The number of orders per year (12-12)

Example 10 illustrates this concept.

Probabilistic model
A statistical model applicable when product demand or any other variable is not known but can be specified by means of a probability distribution.

Service level
The complement of the probability of a stockout.

◀ EXAMPLE 10

Determining safety stock with probabilistic demand and constant lead time

Shami Optical in Kuwait has determined that its reorder point for eyeglass frames is 50 units. Its carrying cost per frame per year is US$5, and stockout (or lost sale) cost is US$40 per frame. The store has experienced the following probability distribution for inventory demand during the lead time (reorder period). The optimum number of orders per year is six.

	Number of Units	Probability
	30	0.2
	40	0.2
ROP →	50	0.3
	60	0.2
	70	0.1
		1.0

How much safety stock should Shami keep on hand?

APPROACH ▶   The objective is to find the amount of safety stock that minimizes the sum of the additional inventory holding costs and stockout costs. The annual holding cost is simply the holding cost per unit multiplied by the units added to the ROP. For example, a safety stock of 20 frames, which implies that the new ROP, with safety stock, is 70(= 50 + 20) raises the annual carrying cost by US$5(20) = US$100.

However, computing annual stockout cost is more interesting. For any level of safety stock, stockout cost is the expected cost of stocking out. We can compute it, as in Equation (12-12), by multiplying the number of frames short (Demand—ROP) by the probability of demand at that level, by the stockout cost, by the number of times per year the stockout can occur (which in our case is the number of orders per year). Then we add stockout costs for each possible stockout level for a given ROP.

SOLUTION ▶   We begin by looking at zero safety stock. For this safety stock, a shortage of 10 frames will occur if demand is 60, and a shortage of 20 frames will occur if the demand is 70. Thus the stockout costs for zero safety stock are:

$$(10 \text{ frames short})(0.2)(\text{US\$40 per stockout})(6 \text{ possible stockouts per year})$$

$$+ (20 \text{ frames short})(0.1)(\text{US\$40})(6) = \text{US\$960}$$

The following table summarizes the total costs for each of the three alternatives:

Safety Stock	Additional Holding Cost (US$)	Stockout Cost (US$)	Total Cost (US$)
20	(20)(5) = 100	0	100
10	(10)(5) = 50	(10)(0.1)(40)(6) = 240	290
0	0	(10)(0.2)(40)(6) + (20)(0.1)(40)(6) = 960	960

The safety stock with the lowest total cost is 20 frames. Therefore, this safety stock changes the reorder point to 50 + 20 = 70 frames.

INSIGHT ▶   The optical company now knows that a safety stock of 20 frames will be the most economical decision.

LEARNING EXERCISE ▶   Shami Optical's holding cost per frame is now estimated to be US$20, while the stockout cost is US$30 per frame. Does the reorder point change? [Answer: Safety stock = 10 now, with a total cost of US$380, which is the lowest of the three. ROP = 60 frames.]

RELATED PROBLEMS ▶   12.18, 12.19

When it is difficult or impossible to determine the cost of being out of stock, a manager may decide to follow a policy of keeping enough safety stock on hand to meet a prescribed customer service level. For instance, Figure 12.8 shows the use of safety stock when demand (for hospital resuscitation kits) is probabilistic. We see that the safety stock in Figure 12.8 is 16.5 units, and the reorder point is also increased by 16.5.

The manager may want to define the service level as meeting 95 percent of the demand (or, conversely, having stockouts only 5 percent of the time). Assuming that demand during lead time (the reorder period) follows a normal curve, only the mean and standard deviation are needed to define the inventory requirements for any given service level. Sales data are usually adequate for computing the mean and standard deviation. In the following example we use a normal curve with a known mean (μ) and standard deviation (σ) to determine the reorder point and safety stock necessary for a 95 percent service level. We use the following formula:

$$\text{ROP} = \text{Expected demand during lead time} + Z\sigma_{dLT} \qquad \text{(12-13)}$$

where Z = Number of standard deviations

    σ_{dLT} = Standard deviation of demand during lead time

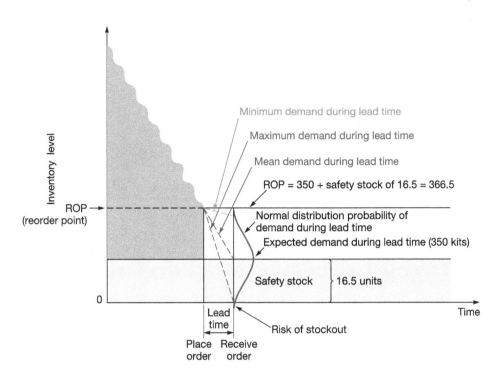

◄ **FIGURE 12.8**
Probabilistic Demand for a Hospital Item
Expected number of kits needed during lead time is 350, but for a 95 percent service level, the reorder point should be raised to 366.5.

◄ **EXAMPLE 11**

Safety stock with probabilistic demand

Red Crescent Hospital stocks a 'code blue' resuscitation kit that has a normally distributed demand during the reorder period. The mean (average) demand during the reorder period is 350 kits, and the standard deviation is 10 kits. The hospital administrator wants to follow a policy that results in stockouts only 5 percent of the time.

(a) What is the appropriate value of Z? (b) How much safety stock should the hospital maintain? (c) What reorder point should be used?

APPROACH ▶ The hospital determines how much inventory is needed to meet the demand 95 percent of the time. The figure in this example may help you visualize the approach. The data are as follows:

$$\mu = \text{Mean demand} = 350 \text{ kits}$$
$$\sigma_{dLT} = \text{Standard deviation of demand during lead time} = 10 \text{ kits}$$
$$Z = \text{Number of standard normal deviations}$$

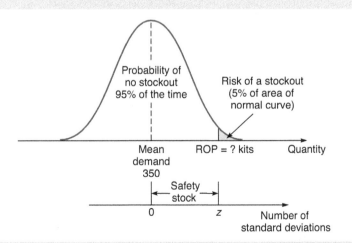

AUTHOR COMMENT
Recall that the service level is 1 minus the risk of a stockout.

SOLUTION ▶

a. We use the properties of a standardized normal curve to get a Z-value for an area under the normal curve of 0.95 (or 1 − 0.05). Using a normal table (see Appendix I), we find a Z-value of 1.65 standard deviations from the mean.

b. Because: Safety stock $= x - \mu$

and: $Z = \dfrac{x - \mu}{\sigma_{dLT}}$

then: Safety stock $= Z\sigma_{dLT}$ (12-14)

Solving for safety stock, as in Equation (12-14), gives:

$$\text{Safety stock} = 1.65(10)$$
$$= 16.5 \text{ kits}$$

This is the situation illustrated in Figure 12.8.

c. The reorder point is:

$$\text{ROP} = \text{Expected demand during lead time} + \text{Safety stock}$$
$$= 350 \text{ kits} + 16.5 \text{ kits of safety stock}$$
$$= 366.5, \text{ or } 367 \text{ kits}$$

INSIGHT ▶ The cost of the inventory policy increases dramatically (exponentially) with an increase in service levels.

LEARNING EXERCISE ▶ What policy results in stockouts 10 percent of the time? [Answer: $Z = 1.28$; safety stock $= 12.8$; ROP $= 363$ kits.]

RELATED PROBLEMS ▶ 12.16, 12.17

Other Probabilistic Models

Equations (12-13) and (12-14) assume that both an estimate of expected demand during lead times and its standard deviation are available. When data on lead time demand are *not* at hand, these formulas cannot be applied. However, three other models are available. We need to determine which model to use for three situations:

1. Demand is variable and lead time is constant
2. Lead time is variable, and demand is constant
3. Both demand and lead time are variable

LO7: Understand service levels and probabilistic inventory models

All three models assume that demand and lead time are independent variables. Note that our examples use days, but weeks can also be used. Let us examine these three situations separately, because a different formula for the ROP is needed for each.

Demand Is Variable and Lead Time Is Constant When *only the demand is variable*, then:

$$\text{ROP} = (Average \text{ daily demand} \times \text{Lead time in days}) + z\sigma_{dLT} \qquad (12\text{-}15)$$

where σ_{dLT} = Standard deviation of demand during lead time $- \sigma_d \sqrt{\text{Lead time}}$

and σ_d = Standard deviation of demand per day

EXAMPLE 12 ▶

ROP for variable demand and constant lead time

The *average* daily demand for Apple iPods at a Doha store is 15, with a standard deviation of 5 units. The lead time is constant at 2 days. Find the reorder point if management wants a 90 percent service level (i.e. risk stockouts only 10 percent of the time). How much of this is safety stock?

APPROACH ▶ Apply Equation (12-15) to the following data:

$$\text{Average daily demand (normally distributed)} = 15$$
$$\text{Lead time in days (constant)} = 2$$
$$\text{Standard deviation of daily demand} = \sigma_d = 5$$
$$\text{Service level} = 90\%$$

SOLUTION ▶ From the normal table (Appendix I), we derive a Z-value for 90 percent of 1.28. Then:

$$ROP = (15 \text{ units} \times 2 \text{ days}) + Z\sigma_d\sqrt{\text{Lead time}}$$

$$= 30 + 1.28(5)(\sqrt{2})$$

$$= 30 + 1.28(5)(1.41) = 30 + 9.02 = 39.02 \cong 39$$

Thus, safety stock is about 9 iPods.

INSIGHT ▶ The value of Z depends on the manager's stockout risk level. The smaller the risk, the higher the Z.

LEARNING EXERCISE ▶ If the Doha manager wants a 95 percent service level, what is the new ROP? [Answer: ROP = 41.63, or 42.]

RELATED PROBLEM ▶ 12.20

Lead Time Is Variable and Demand Is Constant When the demand is constant and *only the lead time is variable*, then:

$$ROP = (\text{Daily demand} \times Average \text{ lead time in days}) + Z(\text{Daily demand}) \times \sigma_{LT} \quad \text{(12-16)}$$

where σ_{LT} = Standard deviation of lead time in days

◀ **EXAMPLE 13**

ROP for constant demand and variable lead time

The Doha store in Example 12 sells about 10 digital cameras a day (almost a constant quantity). Lead time for camera delivery is normally distributed with a mean time of 6 days and a standard deviation of 3 days. A 98 percent service level is set. Find the ROP.

APPROACH ▶ Apply Equation (12-16) to the following data:

$$\text{Daily demand} = 10$$

$$\text{Average lead time} = 6 \text{ days}$$

$$\text{Standard deviation of lead time} = \sigma_{LT} = 3 \text{ days}$$

$$\text{Service level} = 98\%, \text{ so } Z \text{ (from Appendix I)} = 2.055$$

SOLUTION ▶ From the equation we get:

$$ROP = (10 \text{ units} \times 6 \text{ days}) + 2.055(10 \text{ units})(3)$$

$$= 60 + 61.65 = 121.65$$

The reorder point is about 122 cameras.

INSIGHT ▶ Note how the very high service level of 98 percent drives the ROP up.

LEARNING EXERCISE ▶ If a 90 percent service level is applied, what does the ROP drop to? [Answer: ROP = 60 + (1.28)(10)(3) = 60 + 38.4 = 98.4; since the Z-value is only 1.28.]

RELATED PROBLEM ▶ 12.21

Both Demand and Lead Time Are Variable When both the demand and lead time are variable, the formula for reorder point becomes more complex:[4]

$$ROP = (\text{Average daily demand} \times \text{Average lead time}) + Z\sigma_{dLT} \quad \text{(12-17)}$$

where σ_d = Standard deviation of demand per day

σ_{LT} = Standard deviation of lead time in days

and $\sigma_{dLT} = \sqrt{(\text{Average lead time} \times \sigma_d^2) + (\text{Average daily demand})^2 \sigma_{LT}^2}$

---

[4]Refer to S. Narasimhan, D. W. McLeavey, and P. Billington, *Production Planning and Inventory Control*, 2nd ed. (Upper Saddle River, NJ: Prentice Hall, 1995), Chap. 6, for details. Note that Equation (12-17) can also be expressed as

$ROP = \text{Average daily demand} \times \text{Average lead time} + z\sqrt{(\text{Average lead time} \times \sigma_d^2) + d^{-2}\sigma_{LT}^2}$.

EXAMPLE 14 ▶

ROP for variable demand and variable lead time

The Doha store's most popular item is a six-pack of 9-volt batteries. About 150 packs are sold per day, following a normal distribution with a standard deviation of 16 packs. Batteries are ordered from an overseas distributor; lead time is normally distributed with an average of 5 days and a standard deviation of 1 day. To maintain a 95 percent service level, what ROP is appropriate?

APPROACH ▶   Determine a quantity at which to reorder by applying Equation (12-17) to the following data:

Average daily demand = 150 packs

Standard deviation of demand = σ_d = 16 packs

Average lead time = 3 days

Standard deviation of lead time = σ_{LT} = 1 day

Service level = 95%, so Z = 1.65 (from Appendix I)

SOLUTION ▶   From the equation we compute:

$$ROP = (150 \text{ packs} \times 5 \text{ days}) + 1.65\sigma_{dLT}$$

where

$$\sigma_{dLT} = \sqrt{(5 \text{ days} \times 16^2) + (150^2 \times 1^2)}$$
$$= \sqrt{(5 \times 256) + (22,500 \times 1)}$$
$$= \sqrt{1,280 + 22,500} = \sqrt{23,780} \cong 154$$

So ROP = $(150 \times 5) + 1.65(154) \cong 750 + 254 = 1,004$ packs

INSIGHT ▶   When both demand and lead time are variable, the formula looks quite complex. But it is just the result of squaring the standard deviations in Equations (12-15) and (12-16) to get their variances, then summing them, and finally taking the square root.

LEARNING EXERCISE ▶   For an 80 percent service level, what is the ROP? [Answer: Z = 0.84 and ROP = 879 packs.]

RELATED PROBLEM ▶   12.22

SINGLE-PERIOD MODEL

Single-period inventory model

A system for ordering items that have little or no value at the end of a sales period.

A **single-period inventory model** describes a situation in which *one* order is placed for a product. At the end of the sales period, any remaining product has little or no value. This is a typical problem for seasonal goods, bakery goods, newspapers, and magazines. (Indeed, this inventory issue is often called the 'newsstand problem'.) In other words, even though items at a newsstand are ordered weekly or daily, they cannot be held over and used as inventory in the next sales period. So our decision is how much to order at the beginning of the period.

Because the exact demand for such seasonal products is never known, we consider a probability distribution related to demand. If the normal distribution is assumed, and we stocked and sold an average (mean) of 100 Ramadan lanterns each season, then there is a 50 percent chance we would stock out and a 50 percent chance we would have lanterns left over. To determine the optimal stocking policy for lanterns before the season begins, we also need to know the standard deviation and consider these two marginal costs:

C_s = Cost of shortage (we underestimated) = Sales price/unit − Cost/unit

C_o = Cost of overage (we overestimated) = Cost/unit − Salvage value/unit (if there is any)

The service level, that is, the probability of *not* stocking out, is set at:

$$\text{Service level} = \frac{C_s}{C_s + C_o} \qquad (12\text{-}18)$$

Therefore, we should consider increasing our order quantity until the service level is less than or equal to the ratio of $[C_s \div (C_s + C_o)]$.

This model, illustrated in Example 15, is used in many service industries, from hotels to airlines to bakeries to clothing retailers.

Ali's newsstand, just outside the National Museum in Khartoum, usually sells 120 copies of the *Alrai* newspaper each day. Ali believes the sale of *Alrai* is normally distributed, with a standard deviation of 15 papers. He pays 70 cents for each paper, which sells for US$1.25. *Alrai* gives him a 30-cent credit for each unsold paper. He wants to determine how many papers he should order each day and the stockout risk for that quantity.

APPROACH ▶   Ali's data are as follows:

$$C_s = \text{cost of shortage} = \text{US\$1.25} - \text{US\$0.70} = \text{US\$0.55}$$

$$C_o = \text{cost of overage} = \text{US\$0.70} - \text{US\$0.30 (salvage value)} = \text{US\$0.40}$$

Ali will apply Equation (12-18) and the normal table, using $\mu = 120$ and $\sigma = 15$.

SOLUTION ▶

(a) Service level $= \dfrac{C_s}{C_s + C_o} = \dfrac{0.55}{0.55 + 0.40} = \dfrac{0.55}{0.95} = 0.578$

(b) Ali needs to find the Z score for his normal distribution that yields a probability of 0.578.

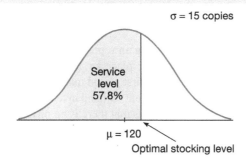

So 57.8% of the area under the normal curve must be to the left of the optimal stocking level.

(c) Using Appendix I,[5] for an area of 0.578, the Z value $\cong 0.20$.

Then, the optimal stocking level $= 120$ copies $+ (0.20)(\sigma)$

$$= 120 + (0.20)(15) = 120 + 3 = 123 \text{ papers}$$

The stockout risk if Ali orders 123 copies of *Alrai* each day is $1 - \text{service level} = 1 - 0.578 = 0.422 = 42.2\%$.

INSIGHT ▶   If the service level is ever under 0.50, Ali should order fewer than 120 copies per day.

LEARNING EXERCISE ▶   How does Ali's decision change if *Alrai* changes its policy and offers *no credit* for unsold papers, a policy many publishers are adopting?
[Answer: Service level $= 0.44$, $Z = -0.15$. Therefore, stock $120 + (-0.15)(15) = 117.75$ or 118 papers.]

FIXED-PERIOD (P) SYSTEMS

AUTHOR COMMENT
A fixed-period model orders a different quantity each time.

The inventory models that we have considered so far are **fixed-quantity systems** (or *Q systems*). That is, the same fixed amount is added to inventory every time an order for an item is placed. We saw that orders are event triggered. When inventory decreases to the reorder point (ROP), a new order for Q units is placed.

To use the fixed-quantity model, inventory must be continuously monitored.[6] This requires a **perpetual inventory system**. Every time an item is added to or withdrawn from inventory, records must be updated to determine whether the ROP has been reached.

In a **fixed-period system** (also called a *periodic review*, or *P system*), on the other hand, inventory is ordered at the end of a given period. Then, and only then, is on-hand inventory counted. Only the amount necessary to bring total inventory up to a pre-specified target level (*T*) is ordered. Figure 12.9 illustrates this concept.

Fixed-quantity system
Also known as a *Q system*; an ordering system with the same order amount each time.

Perpetual inventory system
A system that keeps track of each withdrawal or addition to inventory continuously, so records are always current.

Fixed-period system
Also known as a *periodic review*, or *P system*; a system in which inventory orders are made at regular time intervals.

[5]Alternatively, Microsoft Excel's NORMSINV (probability) function can be applied.
[6]Some in OM call these continuous review systems.

▶ **FIGURE 12.9**

Inventory Level in a Fixed-Period (P) System

Various amounts (Q_1, Q_2, Q_3, etc.) are ordered at regular time intervals (P) based on the quantity necessary to bring inventory up to the target quantity (T).

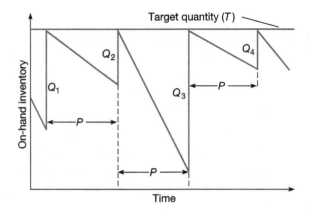

Fixed-period systems have several of the same assumptions as the basic EOQ fixed-quantity system:

- The only relevant costs are the ordering and holding costs.
- Lead times are known and constant.
- Items are independent of one another.

The downward-sloped lines in Figure 12.9 again represent on-hand inventory levels. But now, when the time between orders (P) passes, we place an order to raise inventory up to the target quantity (T). The amount ordered during the first period may be Q_1, the second period Q_2, and so on. The Q_i value is the difference between current on-hand inventory and the target inventory level.

The advantage of the fixed-period system is that there is no physical count of inventory items after an item is withdrawn—this occurs only when the time for the next review comes up. This procedure is also convenient administratively.

A fixed-period system is appropriate when vendors make routine (i.e. at fixed-time interval) visits to customers to take fresh orders or when purchasers want to combine orders to save ordering and transportation costs (therefore, they will have the same review period for similar inventory items). For example, a vending machine company may come to refill its machines every Tuesday. This is also the case at Teeba Dairies, whose reps visit their stores every Thursday, as discussed in *OM in Action* box 'Teeba's Weekly Visit'.

The disadvantage of the P system is that because there is no tally of inventory during the review period, there is the possibility of a stockout during this time. This scenario is possible if a large sale draws the inventory level down to zero right after an order is placed. Therefore, a higher level of safety stock (as compared to a fixed-quantity system) needs to be maintained to provide protection against stockout during both the time between reviews and the lead time.

OM in Action ▶ Teeba's weekly visit

When Mohammad Othman, sales rep for Teeba Dairies, visits his customers' stores each Thursday—whether they are large retailers such as Carrefour, Safeway, and Cozmo or one of dozens of small marts he covers in the Jordanian capital—managers and officers eagerly await his arrival and welcome his suggestions and recommendations. "His visit is so important that we find a way to spend as much time as we can with him," says one of the customers.

What makes Mohammad and other sales reps for Teeba Dairies so precious? It's their wide and extensive network of information. Sellers, drivers, sales reps, and marketers collect information on the sales of the dairies in the Jordanian market in a sophisticated manner. Whether they collect information on the inventory, displays, or even customers' preferred tastes, they feed it back to their headquarters for processing and dissemination.

Matching these data with information published by the Department of Statistics regarding the demographics, population figures, growth rates, and the economy's indices, provides a great source for data mining for the team at the research and development unit. This helps the company not only to predict market trends but also to satisfy the specific needs of each neighborhood. This is the reason why Teeba's popularity in Jordan and its market share continue to grow, as well as its annual profits.

www.teeba.jo/

CHAPTER SUMMARY

Inventory represents a major investment for many firms. This investment is often larger than it should be because firms find it easier to have 'just-in-case' inventory rather than 'just-in-time' inventory. Inventories are of four types:

1. Raw material and purchased components
2. Work-in-process
3. Maintenance, repair, and operating (MRO)
4. Finished goods

In this chapter, we discussed independent inventory, ABC analysis, record accuracy, cycle counting, and inventory models used to control independent demands. The EOQ model, production order quantity model, and quantity discount model can all be solved using Excel, Excel OM, or POM for Windows software.

Key Terms

ABC analysis (p. 373)
Cycle counting (p. 375)
Cycle time (p. 373)
Economic order quantity (EOQ) model (p. 377)
Finished-goods inventory (p. 373)
Fixed-period system (p. 395)
Fixed-quantity system (p. 395)
Holding cost (p. 377)
Lead time (p. 383)

Maintenance/repair/operating (MRO) (p. 373)
Ordering cost (p. 377)
Perpetual inventory system (p. 395)
Pilferage (p. 376)
Probabilistic model (p. 389)
Production order quantity model (p. 384)
Quantity discount (p. 386)
Raw material inventory (p. 373)

Reorder point (ROP) (p. 383)
Robust (p. 382)
Safety stock (p. 383)
Service level (p. 389)
Setup cost (p. 377)
Setup time (p. 377)
Shrinkage (p. 376)
Single-period inventory model (p. 394)
Work-in-process (WIP) inventory (p. 373)

Ethical Dilemma

Akilah Hospital in Tripoli, Libya, faces a problem common to large hospitals as well as small, remote ones like itself. That problem is deciding how much of each type of blood to keep in stock. Because blood is expensive and has a limited shelf life (up to 5 weeks under 1–6°C refrigeration), Akilah naturally wants to keep its stock as low as possible. Unfortunately, past disasters such as a major transportation accident or natural disasters have demonstrated that lives would be lost when not enough blood was available to handle massive needs. The hospital administrator wants to set an 85 percent service level based on demand over the past decade. Discuss the implications of this decision. What is the hospital's responsibility with regard to stocking lifesaving medicines with short shelf lives? How would you set the inventory level for a commodity such as blood?

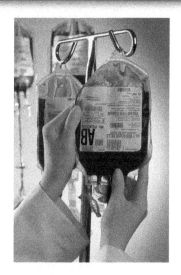

Discussion Questions

1. Describe the four types of inventory.
2. With the advent of low-cost computing, do you see alternatives to the popular ABC classifications?
3. What is the purpose of the ABC classification system?
4. Identify and explain the types of costs that are involved in an inventory system.
5. Explain the major assumptions of the basic EOQ model.
6. What is the relationship of the economic order quantity to demand? To the holding cost? To the setup cost?
7. Explain why it is not necessary to include product cost (price or price times quantity) in the EOQ model, but the quantity discount model requires this information.
8. What are the advantages of cycle counting?
9. What impact does a decrease in setup time have on EOQ?
10. Explain what is meant by the expression 'robust model.' Specifically, what would you tell a manager who exclaimed, "Uh-oh, we're in trouble! The calculated EOQ is wrong; actual demand is 10 percent greater than estimated."

Using Software to Solve Inventory Problems

This section presents three ways to solve inventory problems with computer software. First, you can create your own Excel spreadsheets. Second, you can use the Excel OM software that comes with this text. Third, POM for Windows, also on our MyOMLab, can solve all problems marked with a **P**.

Creating Your Own Excel Spreadsheets

Program 12.1 illustrates how you can make an Excel model to solve Example 8 (p. 385). This is a production order quantity model. A listing of the formulas needed to create the spreadsheet is shown.

▶ **PROGRAM 12.1**

Using Excel for a Production Model, with Data from Example 8

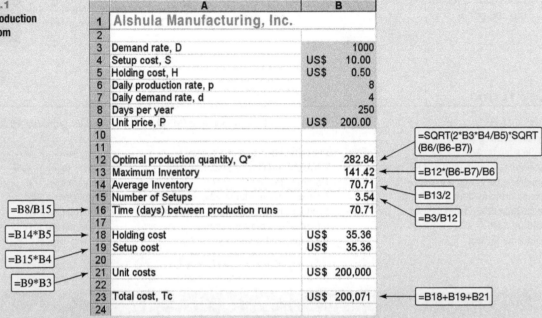

	A	B
1	**Alshula Manufacturing, Inc.**	
2		
3	Demand rate, D	1000
4	Setup cost, S	US$ 10.00
5	Holding cost, H	US$ 0.50
6	Daily production rate, p	8
7	Daily demand rate, d	4
8	Days per year	250
9	Unit price, P	US$ 200.00
10		
11		
12	Optimal production quantity, Q*	282.84
13	Maximum Inventory	141.42
14	Average Inventory	70.71
15	Number of Setups	3.54
16	Time (days) between production runs	70.71
17		
18	Holding cost	US$ 35.36
19	Setup cost	US$ 35.36
20		
21	Unit costs	US$ 200,000
22		
23	Total cost, Tc	US$ 200,071
24		

Formula annotations:
- B12: =SQRT(2*B3*B4/B5)*SQRT(B6/(B6-B7))
- B13: =B12*(B6-B7)/B6
- B14: =B13/2
- B16: =B3/B12
- B16 (days): =B8/B15
- B18: =B14*B5
- B19: =B15*B4
- B21: =B9*B3
- B23: =B18+B19+B21

✗ Using Excel OM

Excel OM allows us to easily model inventory problems ranging from ABC analysis, to the basic EOQ model, to the production model, to quantity discount situations.

Program 12.2 shows the input data, selected formulas, and results for an ABC analysis, using data from Example 1 (on p. 374). After the data are entered, we use the *Data* and *Sort* Excel commands to rank the items from largest to smallest dollar volumes.

▶ **PROGRAM 12.2**

Using Excel OM for an ABC Analysis, with Data from Example 1

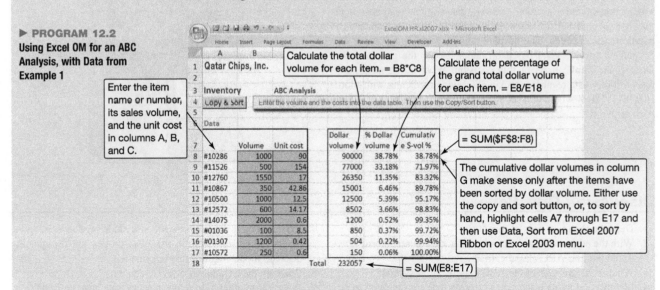

Enter the item name or number, its sales volume, and the unit cost in columns A, B, and C.

Calculate the total dollar volume for each item. = B8*C8

Calculate the percentage of the grand total dollar volume for each item. = E8/E18

	A	B			Dollar volume	% Dollar volume	Cumulative S-vol %
1	Qatar Chips, Inc.						
3	Inventory		ABC Analysis				
4	Copy & Sort						
6	Data						
7		Volume	Unit cost				
8	#10286	1000	90		90000	38.78%	38.78%
9	#11526	500	154		77000	33.18%	71.97%
10	#12760	1550	17		26350	11.35%	83.32%
11	#10867	350	42.86		15001	6.46%	89.78%
12	#10500	1000	12.5		12500	5.39%	95.17%
13	#12572	600	14.17		8502	3.66%	98.83%
14	#14075	2000	0.6		1200	0.52%	99.35%
15	#01036	100	8.5		850	0.37%	99.72%
16	#01307	1200	0.42		504	0.22%	99.94%
17	#10572	250	0.6		150	0.06%	100.00%
18				Total	232057		

= SUM($F$8:F8)

= SUM(E8:E17)

The cumulative dollar volumes in column G make sense only after the items have been sorted by dollar volume. Either use the copy and sort button, or, to sort by hand, highlight cells A7 through E17 and then use Data, Sort from Excel 2007 Ribbon or Excel 2003 menu.

P Using POM for Windows

The POM for Windows Inventory module can also solve the entire EOQ family of problems. Please refer to Appendix IV for further details.

Solved Problems Virtual Office help is available at MyOMLab

▼ SOLVED PROBLEM 12.1

David Alexander has compiled the following table of six items in inventory at Angelo Products, along with the unit cost and the annual demand in units:

Identification Code	Unit Cost (US$)	Annual Demand (units)
XX1	5.84	1,200
B66	5.40	1,110
3CPO	1.12	896
33CP	74.54	1,104
R2D2	2.00	1,110
RMS	2.08	961

Use ABC analysis to determine which item(s) should be carefully controlled using a quantitative inventory technique and which item(s) should not be closely controlled.

▼ SOLUTION

The item that needs strict control is 33CP, so it is an A item. Items that do not need to be strictly controlled are 3CPO, R2D2, and RMS; these are C items. The B items will be XX1 and B66.

Code	Annual US Dollar Volume = Unit Cost × Demand (US$)
XX1	7,008.00
B66	5,994.00
3CPO	1,003.52
33CP	82,292.16
R2D2	2,220.00
RMS	1,998.88

Total cost = US$100,516.56
70 percent of total cost = US$70,347.92

▼ SOLVED PROBLEM 12.2

The Warren W. Fisher Computer Corporation purchases 8,000 transistors each year as components in minicomputers. The unit cost of each transistor is US$10, and the cost of carrying one transistor in inventory for a year is US$3. Ordering cost is US$30 per order.

What are (a) the optimal order quantity, (b) the expected number of orders placed each year, and (c) the expected time between orders? Assume that Fisher operates on a 200-day working year.

▼ SOLUTION

a) $Q^* = \sqrt{\dfrac{2DS}{H}} = \sqrt{\dfrac{2(8,000)(30)}{3}} = 400$ units

b) $N = \dfrac{D}{Q^*} = \dfrac{8,000}{400} = 20$ orders

c) Time between orders $= T = \dfrac{\text{Number of working days}}{N} = \dfrac{200}{20} = 10$ working days

With 20 orders placed each year, an order for 400 transistors is placed every 10 working days.

▼ SOLVED PROBLEM 12.3

Annual demand for notebook binders at Meyer's Stationery Shop is 10,000 units. Brad Meyer operates his business 300 days per year and finds that deliveries from his supplier generally take 5 working days. Calculate the reorder point for the notebook binders.

▼ SOLUTION

$$L = 5 \text{ days}$$

$$d = \frac{10,000}{300} = 33.3 \text{ units per day}$$

$$\text{ROP} = d \times L = (33.3 \text{ units per day})(5 \text{ days})$$
$$= 166.7 \text{ units}$$

Thus, Brad should reorder when his stock reaches 167 units.

▼ SOLVED PROBLEM 12.4

Leonard Presby, Inc. has an annual demand rate of 1,000 units but can produce at an average production rate of 2,000 units. Setup cost is US$10; carrying cost is US$1. What is the optimal number of units to be produced each time?

▼ SOLUTION

$$Q_p^* = \sqrt{\frac{2DS}{H\left(1 - \dfrac{\text{Annual demand rate}}{\text{Annual production rate}}\right)}} = \sqrt{\frac{2(1,000)(10)}{1[1 - (1,000 \div 2,000)]}}$$

$$= \sqrt{\frac{20,000}{1 \div 2}} = \sqrt{40,000} = 200 \text{ units}$$

Problems*

•• **12.1** Baghdad Super Plastics is a large manufacturer of injection-molded plastics in Iraq. An investigation of the company's manufacturing facility in Baghdad yields the information presented in the table below. How would the plant classify these items according to an ABC classification system? **P✗**

Item Code #	Average Inventory (units)	Value (US$/unit)
1289	400	3.75
2347	300	4.00
2349	120	2.50
2363	75	1.50
2394	60	1.75
2395	30	2.00
6782	20	1.15
7844	12	2.05
8210	8	1.80
8310	7	2.00
9111	6	3.00

• **12.2** Mai's computer training school, in Doha, stocks workbooks with the following characteristics:

Demand D = 19,500 units/year

Ordering cost S = US$25/order

Holding cost H = US$4/unit/year

a) Calculate the EOQ for the workbooks.
b) What are the annual holding costs for the workbooks?
c) What are the annual ordering costs? **P✗**

• **12.3** If D = 8,000 per month, S = US$45 per order, and H = US$2 per unit per month:
a) What is the economic order quantity?
b) How does your answer change if the holding cost doubles?
c) What if the holding cost drops in half? **P✗**

• **12.4** Lead time for one of your fastest-moving products is 21 days. Demand during this period averages 100 units per day.
a) What would be an appropriate reorder point?
b) How does your answer change if demand during lead time doubles?
c) How does your answer change if demand during lead time drops in half?

• **12.5** Annual demand for the notebook binders at Dana's Stationery Shop is 10,000 units. Dana operates her business 300 days per year and finds that deliveries from her supplier generally take 5 working days.
a) Calculate the reorder point for the notebook binders that she stocks.
b) Why is this number important to Dana?

•• **12.6** Taher is the purchasing manager for the headquarters of a large insurance company chain with a central inventory operation. Taher's fastest-moving inventory item has a demand of 6,000 units per year. The cost of each unit is US$100, and the inventory carrying cost is US$10 per unit per year. The average ordering cost is US$30 per order. It takes about 5 days for an order to arrive, and the demand for 1 week is 120 units. (This is a corporate operation, and there are 250 working days per year.)
a) What is the EOQ?
b) What is the average inventory if the EOQ is used?

*P✗ means the problem may be solved with POM for Windows and/or Excel OM.

c) What is the optimal number of orders per year?
d) What is the optimal number of days in between any two orders?
e) What is the annual cost of ordering and holding inventory?
f) What is the total annual inventory cost, including cost of the 6,000 units? **P✗**

•• **12.7** Jameel's machine shop uses 2,500 brackets during the course of a year. These brackets are purchased from a supplier 90 miles away. The following information is known about the brackets:

Annual demand:	2,500
Holding cost per bracket per year:	US$1.50
Order cost per order:	US$18.75
Lead time:	2 days
Working days per year:	250

a) Given the above information, what would be the economic order quantity (EOQ)?
b) Given the EOQ, what would be the average inventory? What would be the annual inventory holding cost?
c) Given the EOQ, how many orders would be made each year? What would be the annual order cost?
d) Given the EOQ, what is the total annual cost of managing the inventory?
e) What is the time between orders?
f) What is the reorder point (ROP)? **P✗**

•• **12.8** EGA Motors is an Egyptian car manufacturer. At its largest manufacturing facility, near Cairo, the company produces subcomponents at a rate of 300 per day, and it uses these subcomponents at a rate of 12,500 per year (of 250 working days). Holding costs are US$2 per item per year, and ordering costs are US$30 per order.
a) What is the economic production quantity?
b) How many production runs per year will be made?
c) What will be the maximum inventory level?
d) What percentage of time will the facility be producing components?
e) What is the annual cost of ordering and holding inventory? **P✗**

•• **12.9** Khaleel Manufacturing Company, in Kuwait, makes flashing lights for toys. The company operates its production facility 300 days per year. It has orders for about 12,000 flashing lights per year and has the capability of producing 100 per day. Setting up the light production costs US$50. The cost of each light is US$1. The holding cost is US$0.10 per light per year.
a) What is the optimal size of the production run?
b) What is the average holding cost per year?
c) What is the average setup cost per year?
d) What is the total cost per year, including the cost of the lights? **P✗**

•• **12.10** Jehan is the production manager of Dawaleeb, a small producer of metal parts in Jordan. Dawaleeb supplies Sayyarat, a larger assembly company, with 10,000 wheel bearings each year. This order has been stable for some time. Setup cost for Dawaleeb is US$40, and holding cost is US$0.60 per wheel bearing per year. Dawaleeb can produce 500 wheel bearings per day. Seyyarat is a just-in-time manufacturer and requires that 50 bearings be shipped to it each business day.
a) What is the optimum production quantity?
b) What is the maximum number of wheel bearings that will be in inventory at Dawaleeb?

c) How many production runs of wheel bearings will Dawaleeb have in a year?
d) What is the total setup + holding cost for Dawaleeb? **P**✗

•• **12.11** Jeddah New Computers purchases integrated chips at US$350 per chip. The holding cost is US$35 per unit per year, the ordering cost is US$120 per order, and sales are steady, at 400 per month. The company's supplier, Manama Chip Manufacturing, Inc., decides to offer price concessions in order to attract larger orders. The price structure is shown below.

Manama Chip's Price Structure

Quantity Purchased	Price (US$)/Unit
1–99 units	350
100–199 units	325
200 or more units	300

a) What is the optimal order quantity and the minimum cost for Jeddah New Computers to order, purchase, and hold these integrated chips?
b) Jeddah New Computers wishes to use a 10 percent holding cost rather than the fixed US$35 holding cost in part (a). What is the optimal order quantity, and what is the optimal cost? **P**✗

•• **12.12** Dawood Distributors, in Qatar, has an annual demand for an airport metal detector of 1,400 units. The cost of a typical detector to Dawood is US$400. Carrying cost is estimated to be 20 percent of the unit cost, and the ordering cost is US$25 per order. If Dawood orders in quantities of 300 or more, the company can get a 5 percent discount on the cost of the detectors. Should Dawood take the quantity discount? **P**✗

•• **12.13** Naser Tire Center, in U.A.E. sells 20,000 go-cart tires per year. The ordering cost for each order is US$40, and the holding cost is 20 percent of the purchase price of the tires per year. The purchase price is US$20 per tire if fewer than 500 tires are ordered, US$18 per tire if 500 or more—but fewer than 1,000—tires are ordered, and US$17 per tire if 1,000 or more tires are ordered.
a) How many tires should Naser order each time it places an order?
b) What is the total cost of this policy? **P**✗

•• **12.14** Muna Manufacturing, in Bahrain, has gone out on bid for a regulator component. Expected demand is 700 units per month. The item can be purchased from either Suad Manufacturing or Baker Manufacturing. Their price lists are shown in the table. Ordering cost is US$50, and annual holding cost per unit is US$5.

Suad Mfg.		Baker Mfg.	
Quantity	Unit Price (US$)	Quantity	Unit Price (US$)
1–499	16.00	1–399	16.10
500–999	15.50	400–799	15.60
1,000+	15.00	800+	15.10

a) What is the economic order quantity?
b) Which supplier should be used? Why?
c) What is the optimal order quantity and total annual cost of ordering, purchasing, and holding the component? **P**✗

••• **12.15** Hikma Pharmaceutical uses an unstable chemical compound that must be kept in an environment where both temperature and humidity can be controlled. Hikma uses 800 kilograms per month of the chemical, estimates the holding cost to be 50 percent of the purchase price (because of spoilage), and estimates order costs to be US$50 per order. The cost schedules of two suppliers are as follows:

Vendor 1		Vendor 2	
Quantity	Price (US$)/kg	Quantity	Price (US$)/kg
1–499	17.00	1–399	17.10
500–999	16.75	400–799	16.85
1,000+	16.50	800–1,199	16.60
		1,200+	16.25

a) What is the economic order quantity for each supplier?
b) What quantity should be ordered, and which supplier should be used?
c) What is the total cost for the most economic order size?
d) What factor(s) should be considered besides total cost? **P**✗

•• **12.16** Sameera is in charge of maintaining hospital supplies at Ajman Hospital. During the past year, the mean lead time demand for bandage BX-5 was 60 (and was normally distributed). Furthermore, the standard deviation for BX-5 was 7. Sameera would like to maintain a 90 percent service level.
a) What safety stock level do you recommend for BX-5?
b) What is the appropriate reorder point? **P**✗

•• **12.17** Based on available information, lead time demand for PC jump drives averages 50 units (normally distributed), with a standard deviation of 5 drives. Management wants a 97 percent service level.
a) What value of Z should be applied?
b) How many drives should be carried as safety stock?
c) What is the appropriate reorder point? **P**✗

•• **12.18** Tobacco is shipped from Yemen to a cigarette manufacturer in Jordan once a year. The reorder point, without safety stock, is 200 kilograms. The carrying cost is US$15 per kilo per year, and the cost of a stockout is US$70 per kilo per year. Given the following demand probabilities during the lead time, how much safety stock should be carried?

Demand During Lead Time (kilos)	Probability
0	0.1
100	0.1
200	0.2
300	0.4
400	0.2 **P**✗

••• **12.19** Rashaka, a Bahraini organization that sells weight training sets, has an ordering cost of US$40 for the BB-1 set. (BB-1 stands for Body Beautiful Number 1.) The carrying cost for BB-1 is US$5 per set per year. To meet demand, Rashaka orders large quantities of BB-1 seven times a year. The stockout cost for BB-1 is estimated to be US$50 per set. Over the past several years, Rashaka has observed the following demand during the lead time for BB-1:

Demand During Lead Time	Probability
40	0.1
50	0.2
60	0.2
70	0.2
80	0.2
90	0.1
	1.0

The reorder point for BB-1 is 60 sets. What level of safety stock should be maintained for BB-1? **P**✗

•• **12.20** Petra Grand Hotel distributes a mean of 1,000 bath towels per day to guests at the pool and in their rooms. This demand is normally distributed with a standard deviation of 100 towels per day, based on occupancy. The laundry firm that has the linen contract requires a 2-day lead time. The hotel expects a 98 percent service level to satisfy high guest expectations.
a) What is the ROP?
b) What is the safety stock? **Px**

•• **12.21** Rabwa Printing has contracts with legal firms in Riyadh to copy their court documents. Daily demand is almost constant at 12,500 pages of documents. The lead time for paper delivery is normally distributed with a mean of 4 days and a standard deviation of 1 day. A 97 percent service level is expected. Compute Rabwa's ROP. **Px**

••• **12.22** Homs Cigars, in Syria, stocks Cuban cigars that have variable lead times because of the difficulty in importing the product:

Lead time is normally distributed with an average of 6 weeks and a standard deviation of 2 weeks. Demand is also a variable and normally distributed with a mean of 200 cigars per week and a standard deviation of 25 cigars.
a) For a 90 percent service level, what is the ROP?
b) What is the ROP for a 95 percent service level?
c) Explain what these two service levels mean. Which is preferable? **Px**

•• **12.23** Bahrain Oyster Restaurant buys fresh oysters for US$5 per kg and sells them for US$9 per kg. Any oysters not sold that day are sold to a nearby grocery store, for US$2 per kg. Bahrain Oyster Restaurant believes that demand follows the normal distribution, with a mean of 100 kilos and a standard deviation of 15 kg. How many kilos should the restaurant order each day?

▶ **Refer to MyOMLab for additional homework problems.**

Case Studies

▶ Herrer's Bicycle Shop, Tilburg, the Netherlands

Jo Herrer started Herrer's Bicycle Shop in Tilburg at the end of the 1980s, and the business has thrived in this very green university town in the Netherlands. Jo imports bikes from renowned global suppliers as kits, assembles them, and sells directly to consumers.

The Flying Dutchman bicycle has been a great seller, easily the best-selling bike in the past years, and Jo is looking for some help in making ordering decisions on this important product. Jo obtains the bike kits from a supplier in Asia, with a lead time of one month from the time the order is placed until the time it is received in Jo's shop. There are significant ordering costs associated with placing an order; Jo estimates US$100 for each order. Jo purchases each bike for US$200 and sells each one, assembled, for US$350. Jo estimates holding cost to be 18 percent of the purchase (not selling) price per year.

Jo would like to maintain a high service level of 95 percent. Because the bike sells so well, Jo is also considering a higher service level, which will result in more holding costs but perhaps additional sales and revenue. Monthly sales data for the bike in years 2008, 2009, and a forecast for 2010 are given in the adjacent table.

Monthly Sales of Flying Dutchman Bicycle

Month	2008	2009	2010 Forecast
January	12	14	16
February	23	26	30
March	43	51	59
April	83	97	113
May	162	193	225
June	83	97	113
July	62	73	85
August	33	39	45
September	21	25	29
October	22	25	29
November	42	51	59
December	61	73	85

Discussion Questions

1. Given the data, can you provide advice to Jo on the order quantity and reorder point?
2. If Jo wanted to increase service to 99 percent, what would the new reorder point be? How much additional holding costs would result?
3. What critical assumption is not met in the analysis above? What improvements on the policy can you imagine?

Source: Dr. Ian M. Langella, Shippensburg University, United States.

▶ Managing Inventory at Frito-Lay

Video Case

Frito-Lay has flourished since its origin—the 1931 purchase of a small San Antonio firm for US$100 that included a recipe, 19 retail accounts, and a hand-operated potato ricer. The multi-billion-US dollar company, headquartered in Dallas, now has 41 products—15 with sales of over US$100 million per year and 7 at over US$1 billion in sales. Production takes place in 36 product-focused plants in the United States and Canada, with 48,000 employees.

Inventory is a major investment and an expensive asset in most firms. Holding costs often exceed 25 percent of product value, but in Frito-Lay's prepared food industry, holding cost can be much higher because the raw materials are perishable. In the food industry, inventory spoils. So poor inventory management is not only expensive but can also yield an unsatisfactory product that in the extreme can also ruin market acceptance.

Major ingredients at Frito-Lay are corn meal, corn, potatoes, oil, and seasoning. Using potato chips to illustrate rapid inventory flow: potatoes are moved via truck from farm, to regional plants for processing, to warehouse, to the retail store. This happens in a matter of hours—not days or weeks. This keeps freshness high and holding costs low.

Frequent deliveries of main ingredients at the Florida plant, for example, take several forms:

- Potatoes are delivered in 10 truckloads per day, with 150,000 lb consumed in one shift: The entire potato storage area will only hold $7\frac{1}{2}$ hours' worth of potatoes.
- Oil inventory arrives by rail car, which lasts only $4\frac{1}{2}$ days.
- Corn meal arrives from various farms in the Midwest, and inventory typically averages 4 days' production.
- Seasoning inventory averages 7 days.
- Packaging inventory averages 8 to 10 days.

Frito-Lay's product-focused facility is expensive. It represents a major capital investment that must achieve high utilization to be efficient. The capital cost must be spread over a substantial volume to drive down total cost of the snack foods produced. This demand for high utilization requires reliable equipment and tight schedules. Reliable machinery requires an inventory of critical components: This is known as MRO, or maintenance, repair, and operating supplies.

MRO inventory of motors, switches, gears, bearings, and other critical specialized components can be costly but is necessary.

Frito-Lay's non-MRO inventory moves rapidly. Raw material quickly becomes work-in-process, moving through the system and out the door as a bag of chips in about $1\frac{1}{2}$ shifts. Packaged finished products move from production to the distribution chain in less than 1.4 days.

Discussion Questions*

1. How does the mix of Frito-Lay's inventory differ from those at a machine or cabinet shop (a process-focused facility)?
2. What are the major inventory items at Frito-Lay, and how rapidly do they move through the process?
3. What are the four types of inventory? Give an example of each at Frito-Lay.
4. How would you rank the dollar investment in each of the four types (from the most investment to the least investment)?
5. Why does inventory flow so quickly through a Frito-Lay plant?
6. Why does the company keep so many plants open?
7. Why doesn't Frito-Lay make all its 41 products at each of its plants?

*You may wish to view the video that accompanies this case before answering these questions.

Source: Professors Jay Heizer, Texas Lutheran University; Barry Render, Rollins College; and Bev Amer, Northern Arizona University.

▶ Inventory Control at Wheeled Coach Ambulance

Video Case

Controlling inventory is one of Wheeled Coach's toughest problems. Operating according to a strategy of mass customization and responsiveness, management knows that success is dependent on tight inventory control. Anything else results in an inability to deliver promptly, chaos on the assembly line, and a huge inventory investment. Wheeled Coach finds that almost 50 percent of the US$40,000 to US$100,000 cost of every ambulance it manufactures is purchased materials. A large proportion of that 50 percent is in chassis (purchased from Ford), aluminum (from Reynolds Metal), and plywood used for flooring and cabinetry construction (from local suppliers). Wheeled Coach tracks these A inventory items quite carefully, maintaining tight security/control and ordering carefully so as to maximize quantity discounts while minimizing on-hand stock. Because of long lead times and scheduling needs at Reynolds, aluminum must actually be ordered as much as 8 months in advance.

In a crowded ambulance industry in which it is the only giant, its 45 competitors don't have the purchasing power to draw the same discounts as Wheeled Coach. But this competitive cost advantage cannot be taken lightly, according to President Bob

Collins. "Cycle counting in our stockrooms is critical. No part can leave the locked stockrooms without appearing on a bill of materials."

Accurate bills of material (BOM) are a requirement if products are going to be built on time. Additionally, because of the custom nature of each vehicle, most orders are won only after a bidding process. Accurate BOMs are critical to cost estimation and the resulting bid. For these reasons, Collins was emphatic that Wheeled Coach maintain outstanding inventory control.

Discussion Questions*

1. Explain how Wheeled Coach implements ABC analysis.
2. If you were to take over as inventory control manager at Wheeled Coach, what additional policies and techniques would you initiate to ensure accurate inventory records?
3. How would you go about implementing these suggestions?

*You may wish to view the video that accompanies this case before answering these questions.

▶**Additional Case Studies:** Visit MyOMLab *for these free case studies:*

Ojaman University (F): The university must decide how many basketball day programs to order, and from whom.

LaPlace Power and Light: This utility company is evaluating its current inventory policies.

Main Heading	Review Material	MyOMLab
THE IMPORTANCE OF INVENTORY (pp. 372–373)	Inventory is one of the most expensive assets of many companies. *The objective of inventory management is to strike a balance between inventory investment and customer service.* The two basic inventory issues are how much to order and when to order. ■ **Raw material inventory**—Materials that are usually purchased but have yet to enter the manufacturing process. ■ **Work-in-process (WIP) inventory**—Products or components that are no longer raw materials but have yet to become finished products. ■ **Cycle time**—The time it takes for a product to be made. ■ **MRO**—Maintenance, repair, and operating materials. ■ **Finished-goods inventory**—An end item ready to be sold but still an asset on the company's books.	**VIDEO 12.1** Managing Inventory at Frito-Lay
MANAGING INVENTORY (pp. 373–376)	■ **ABC analysis**—A method for dividing on-hand inventory into three classifications based on annual monetary volume. ■ **Cycle counting**—A continuing reconciliation of inventory with inventory records. ■ **Shrinkage**—Retail inventory that is unaccounted for between receipt and sale. ■ **Pilferage**—A small amount of theft.	Problem: 12.1 Virtual Office Hours for Solved Problem: 12.1
INVENTORY MODELS (p. 377)	■ **Holding cost**—The cost to keep or carry inventory in stock. ■ **Ordering cost**—The cost of the ordering process. ■ **Setup cost**—The cost to prepare a machine or process for production. ■ **Setup time**—The time required to prepare a machine or process for production.	
INVENTORY MODELS FOR INDEPENDENT DEMAND (pp. 377–389)	**Economic order quantity (EOQ) model**—An inventory-control technique that minimizes the total of ordering and holding costs: $$Q^* = \sqrt{\frac{2DS}{H}} \qquad (12\text{-}1)$$ $$\text{Expected number of orders} = N = \frac{\text{Demand}}{\text{Order quantity}} = \frac{D}{Q^*} \qquad (12\text{-}2)$$ $$\text{Expected time between orders} = T = \frac{\text{Number of working days per year}}{N} \qquad (12\text{-}3)$$ $$\text{Total annual cost} = \text{Setup (order) cost} + \text{Holding cost} \qquad (12\text{-}4)$$ $$TC = \frac{D}{Q}S + \frac{Q}{2}H \qquad (12\text{-}5)$$ ■ **Robust**—Giving satisfactory answers even with substantial variation in the parameters. ■ **Lead time**—In purchasing systems, the time between placing an order and receiving it; in production systems, the wait, move, queue, setup, and run times for each component produced. ■ **Reorder point (ROP)**—The inventory level (point) at which action is taken to replenish the stocked item. *ROP for known demand:* $$\text{ROP} = (\text{Demand per day}) \times (\text{Lead time for a new order in days})$$ $$= d \times L \qquad (12\text{-}6)$$ ■ **Safety stock**—Extra stock to allow for uneven demand; a buffer. ■ **Production order quantity model**—An economic order quantity technique applied to production orders: $$Q_p^* = \sqrt{\frac{2DS}{H[1 - (d \div p)]}} \qquad (12\text{-}7)$$ $$Q_p^* = \sqrt{\frac{2DS}{H\left(1 - \dfrac{\text{Annual demand rate}}{\text{Annual production rate}}\right)}} \qquad (12\text{-}8)$$ ■ **Quantity discount**—A reduced price for items purchased in large quantities: $$TC = \frac{D}{Q}S + \frac{Q}{2}H + PD \qquad (12\text{-}9)$$ $$Q^* = \sqrt{\frac{2DS}{IP}} \qquad (12\text{-}10)$$	Problems: 12.2–12.15 Virtual Office Hours for Solved Problems: 12.2–12.4 **VIDEO 12.2** Inventory Control at Wheeled Coach Ambulance

Main Heading	Review Material	
PROBABILISTIC MODELS AND SAFETY STOCK (pp. 389–394)	▪ **Probabilistic model**—A statistical model applicable when product demand or any other variable is not known but can be specified by means of a probability distribution. ▪ **Service level**—The complement of the probability of a stockout. *ROP for unknown demand:* $$\text{ROP} = d \times L + ss \qquad (12\text{-}11)$$ Annual stockout costs = The sum of the units short for each demand level × The probability of that demand level × The stockout cost/unit × The number of orders per year $\qquad (12\text{-}12)$ *ROP for unknown demand and given service level:* $$\text{ROP} = \text{Expected demand during lead time} + Z\sigma_{dLT} \qquad (12\text{-}13)$$ $$\text{Safety stock} = Z\sigma_{dLT} \qquad (12\text{-}14)$$ *ROP for variable demand and constant lead time:* $$\text{ROP} = (\text{Average daily demand} \times \text{Lead time in days}) + Z\sigma_{dLT} \qquad (12\text{-}15)$$ *ROP for constant demand and variable lead time:* $$\text{ROP} = (\text{Daily demand} \times \textit{Average lead time in days}) + Z(\text{Daily demand}) \times \sigma_{LT} \qquad (12\text{-}16)$$ *ROP for variable demand and variable lead time:* $$\text{ROP} = (\text{Average daily demand} \times \text{Average lead time}) + Z\sigma_{dLT} \qquad (12\text{-}17)$$ In each case, $\sigma_{dLT} = \sqrt{(\text{Average lead time} \times \sigma_d^2) + d^{-2}\sigma_{LT}^2}$ but under constant demand: $\sigma_d^2 = 0$, while under constant lead time: $\sigma_{LT}^2 = 0$.	Problems: 12.16–12.22
SINGLE-PERIOD MODEL (pp. 394–395)	▪ **Single-period inventory model**—A system for ordering items that have little or no value at the end of the sales period: $$\text{Service level} = \frac{C_s}{C_s + C_o} \qquad (12\text{-}18)$$	
FIXED-PERIOD (P) SYSTEMS (pp. 395–396)	▪ **Fixed-quantity (Q) system**—An ordering system with the same order amount each time. ▪ **Perpetual inventory system**—A system that keeps track of each withdrawal or addition to inventory continuously, so records are always current. ▪ **Fixed-period (P) system**—A system in which inventory orders are made at regular time intervals.	

*Self-*Test

Before taking the self-test, refer to the learning objectives listed at the beginning of the chapter and the key terms listed at the end of the chapter.

LO1. ABC analysis divides on-hand inventory into three classes, based on:
   a) unit price   **c)** annual demand
   b) the number of units on hand   **d)** annual monetary values.

LO2. Cycle counting:
   a) provides a measure of inventory turnover
   b) assumes that all inventory records must be verified with the same frequency
   c) is a process by which inventory records are periodically verified
   d) is all of the above.

LO3. The two most important inventory-based questions answered by the typical inventory model are:
   a) when to place an order and the cost of the order
   b) when to place an order and how much of an item to order
   c) how much of an item to order and the cost of the order
   d) how much of an item to order and with whom the order should be placed.

LO4. Extra units in inventory to help reduce stockouts are called:
   a) reorder point   **c)** just-in-time inventory
   b) safety stock   **d)** all of the above.

LO5. The difference(s) between the basic EOQ model and the production order quantity model is(are) that:
   a) the production order quantity model does not require the assumption of known, constant demand
   b) the EOQ model does not require the assumption of negligible lead time
   c) the production order quantity model does not require the assumption of instantaneous delivery
   d) all of the above.

LO6. The EOQ model with quantity discounts attempts to determine:
   a) the lowest amount of inventory necessary to satisfy a certain service level
   b) the lowest purchase price
   c) whether to use a fixed-quantity or fixed-period order policy
   d) how many units should be ordered
   e) the shortest lead time.

LO7. The appropriate level of safety stock is typically determined by:
   a) minimizing an expected stockout cost
   b) choosing the level of safety stock that assures a given service level
   c) carrying sufficient safety stock so as to eliminate all stockouts
   d) annual demand.

Answers: LO1. d; LO2. c; LO3. b; LO4. b; LO5. d; LO6. c; LO7. b.

13 Aggregate Scheduling

10

OM STRATEGY DECISIONS

▶ Design of Goods and Services
▶ Managing Quality
▶ Process Strategy
▶ Location Strategies
▶ Layout Strategies
▶ Human Resources
▶ Supply-Chain Management
▶ Inventory Management
▶ Scheduling
  ■ Aggregate
  ■ Short-Term
▶ Maintenance

AGGREGATE PLANNING PROVIDES A COMPETITIVE ADVANTAGE AT LAY'S ARABIA

Like other organizations throughout the world, Saudi Snack Foods (Lay's Arabia)— a subsidiary of Frito-Lay *PepsiCo Asia, Middle East & Africa* division—relies on effective aggregate planning to match fluctuating multi-million-US dollar demand to capacity in its Asian, Middle Eastern, and African plants. Planning for the intermediate term (3 to 18 months) is the heart of aggregate planning. Effective aggregate planning, combined with tight scheduling, effective maintenance, and efficient employee and facility scheduling, are the keys to high plant utilization. High utilization is a critical factor in facilities such as Lay's Arabia where capital investment is substantial.

Saudi Snack Foods has more than a dozen brands of snacks and chips, such as the well-known names of Lay's, Doritos, Cheetos, and Tostitos. Unique processes using specially designed equipment are required to produce each of these products. Because these specialized processes generate high fixed cost, they must operate at very high volume. But such product-focused facilities benefit by having low variable costs. High utilization and performance above the break-even point require a good match between demand and capacity. Idle equipment is disastrous.

At Lay's Arabia, Saudi Snack Foods' headquarters in Riyadh, planners create a total demand profile in line with Frito-Lay's central headquarters in Dallas. They use historical product sales, forecasts of new products, product innovations, product promotions, and dynamic local demand data from account managers to forecast demand. Planners then match the total demand profile to existing capacity, capacity expansion plans, and cost. This becomes the aggregate plan. The aggregate plan of Frito-Lay is communicated to each of the firm's regions, including Asia, the Middle East, and Africa, and to their plants. Every quarter, headquarters and each plant modify the respective plans to incorporate changing market conditions and plant performance.

Each plant uses its quarterly plan to develop a 4-week plan, which in turn assigns specific products to specific product lines for production runs. Finally, each week raw materials and labor are assigned to each process. Effective aggregate planning is a major factor in high utilization and low cost. As the company's 60 percent market share indicates, excellent aggregate planning yields a competitive advantage at Frito-Lay.

The aggregate plan adjusts for farm location, yield and quantities for timely delivery of Lay's unique varieties of potatoes. During harvest times, potatoes go directly to the plant. During non-harvest months, potatoes are stored in climate-controlled environments to maintain quality, texture, and taste.

As potatoes arrive at the plant, they are promptly washed and peeled to ensure freshness and taste. After peeling, potatoes are cut into thin slices, rinsed of excess starch, and cooked in sunflower and/or corn oil.

After cooking is complete, inspection, bagging, weighing and packing operations prepare Lay's potato chips for shipment to customers—all in a matter of hours.

Lay's Arabia became one of the most well-known brands in the Arab world for its quality and Arabic-tastes approach.

Chapter 13 **Learning Objectives**

> **AUTHOR COMMENT**
> Idle capacity is expensive, and inadequate capacity loses customers.

Aggregate planning

Also known as *aggregate scheduling*; an approach to determine the quantity and timing of production for the intermediate future (usually 3 to 18 months ahead).

THE PLANNING PROCESS

Manufacturers such as Frito-Lay face tough decisions when trying to schedule products such as snack foods, the demand for which is heavily dependent on seasonal variation or certain events, for example, sport tournaments. Developing plans that minimize costs connected with such forecasts is *aggregate planning*, one of the main functions of an operations manager. **Aggregate planning** (also known as *aggregate scheduling*) is concerned with determining the quantity and timing of production for the intermediate future, often from 3 to 18 months ahead. Operations managers try to determine the best way to meet forecasted demand by adjusting production rates, labor levels, inventory levels, overtime work, subcontracting rates, and other controllable variables. Usually, *the objective of aggregate planning is to meet forecasted demand while minimizing cost over the planning period.* However, other strategic issues may be more important than low cost. These strategies may be to smooth employment levels, to drive down inventory levels, or to meet a high level of service.

For manufacturers, the aggregate schedule ties the firm's strategic goals to production plans, but for service organizations, the aggregate schedule ties strategic goals to workforce schedules.

Four things are needed for aggregate planning:

LO1: Define aggregate planning

1. A logical overall unit for measuring sales and output, such as kilograms of Doritos at Frito-Lay.
2. A forecast of demand for a reasonable intermediate planning period in these aggregate terms.
3. A method for determining the relevant costs.
4. A model that combines forecasts and costs so that scheduling decisions can be made for the planning period.

In this chapter we describe the aggregate planning decision, show how the aggregate plan fits into the overall planning process, and describe several techniques that managers use when developing an aggregate plan. We stress both manufacturing and service-sector firms.

Planning Horizons

In Chapter 4, we saw that demand forecasting can address short-, medium-, and long-range problems. Long-range forecasts help managers deal with capacity and strategic issues and are the responsibility of top management (see Figure 13.1). Top management formulates policy-related questions, such as facility location and expansion, new product development, research funding, and investment over a period of several years.

Scheduling decisions

Plans that match production to changes in demand.

Medium-range planning begins once long-term capacity decisions are made. This is the job of the operations manager. **Scheduling decisions** address the problem of matching productivity to fluctuating demands. These plans need to be consistent with top management's long-range strategy and work within the resources allocated by earlier strategic decisions. Medium- (or 'intermediate-') range planning is accomplished by building an aggregate production plan.

Short-range planning may extend up to a year but is usually less than 3 months. This plan is also the responsibility of operations personnel, who work with supervisors to 'disaggregate' the intermediate plan into weekly, daily, and hourly schedules. Tactics for dealing with short-term planning involve loading, sequencing, expediting, and dispatching, which are discussed in Chapter 15.

Figure 13.1 illustrates the time horizons and features for short-, intermediate-, and long-range planning.

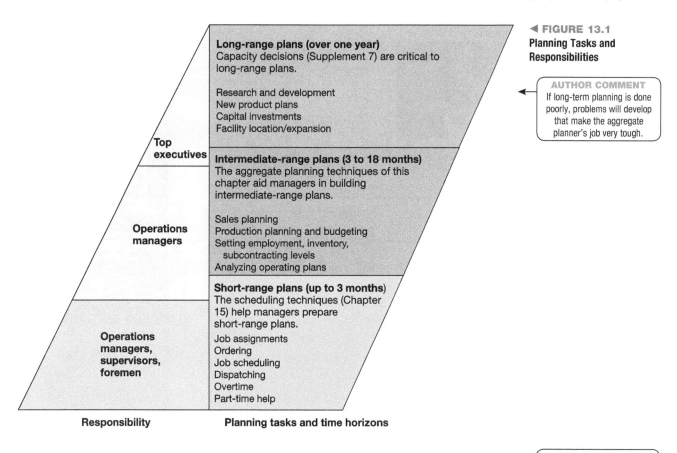

> **AUTHOR COMMENT**
> If long-term planning is done poorly, problems will develop that make the aggregate planner's job very tough.

Top executives

Long-range plans (over one year)
Capacity decisions (Supplement 7) are critical to long-range plans.

Research and development
New product plans
Capital investments
Facility location/expansion

Operations managers

Intermediate-range plans (3 to 18 months)
The aggregate planning techniques of this chapter aid managers in building intermediate-range plans.

Sales planning
Production planning and budgeting
Setting employment, inventory, subcontracting levels
Analyzing operating plans

Operations managers, supervisors, foremen

Short-range plans (up to 3 months)
The scheduling techniques (Chapter 15) help managers prepare short-range plans.
Job assignments
Ordering
Job scheduling
Dispatching
Overtime
Part-time help

Responsibility   **Planning tasks and time horizons**

THE NATURE OF AGGREGATE PLANNING

> **AUTHOR COMMENT**
> Aggregate plans are formulated in a variety of units, such as kilograms of Fritos, tons of steel, or number of students.

As the term *aggregate* implies, an aggregate plan means combining appropriate resources into general, or overall, terms. Given demand forecast, facility capacity, inventory levels, workforce size, and related inputs, the planner has to select the rate of output for a facility over the next 3 to 18 months. The plan can be for firms such as Frito-Lay and Whirlpool, hospitals, colleges, or Pearson, the company that published this textbook.

Aggregate planning is part of a larger production planning system. Therefore, understanding the interfaces between the plan and several internal and external factors is useful. Figure 13.2 shows that the operations manager not only receives input from the marketing department's demand forecast, but must also deal with financial data, personnel, capacity, and availability of raw materials. In a manufacturing environment, the process of breaking the aggregate plan down into greater detail is called **disaggregation**. Disaggregation results in a **master production schedule**, which provides input to material requirements planning (MRP) systems. The master production schedule addresses the purchasing or production of parts or components needed to make final products (see Chapter 14). Detailed work schedules for people and priority scheduling for products result as the final step of the production planning system (and are discussed in Chapter 15).

Disaggregation
The process of breaking an aggregate plan into greater detail.

Master production schedule (MPS)
A timetable that specifies what is to be made and when.

AGGREGATE PLANNING STRATEGIES

> **AUTHOR COMMENT**
> Managers can meet aggregate plans by adjusting either capacity or demand.

When generating an aggregate plan, the operations manager must answer several questions:

1. Should inventories be used to absorb changes in demand during the planning period?
2. Should changes be accommodated by varying the size of the workforce?
3. Should part-timers be used, or should overtime and idle time absorb fluctuations?
4. Should subcontractors be used on fluctuating orders so a stable workforce can be maintained?
5. Should prices or other factors be changed to influence demand?

All of these are legitimate planning strategies. They involve the manipulation of inventory, production rates, labor levels, capacity, and other controllable variables. We will now examine eight options in more detail. The first five are called *capacity options* because they do not try to change demand but attempt to absorb demand fluctuations. The last three are *demand options* through which firms try to smooth out changes in the demand pattern over the planning period.

LO2: Identify optional strategies for developing an aggregate plan

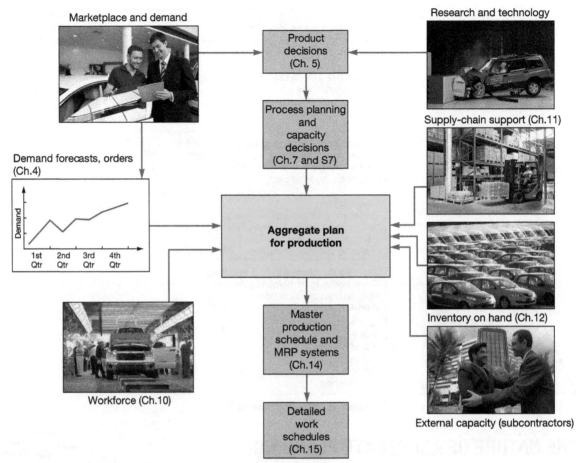

▲ **FIGURE 13.2   Relationships of an Aggregate Plan**

Capacity Options

A firm can choose from the following basic capacity (production) options:

1. *Changing inventory levels:* Managers can increase inventory during periods of low demand to meet high demand in future periods. If this strategy is selected, costs associated with storage, insurance, handling, obsolescence, pilferage, and capital invested will increase. On the other hand, with low inventory on hand and increasing demand, shortages can occur, resulting in longer lead times and poor customer service.

2. *Varying workforce size by hiring or layoffs:* One way to meet demand is to hire or lay off production workers to match production rates. However, new employees need to be trained, and productivity drops temporarily as they are absorbed into the workforce. Layoffs or terminations, of course, lower the morale of all workers and also lead to lower productivity.

3. *Varying production rates through overtime or idle time:* Keeping a constant workforce while varying working hours may be possible. Yet when demand is on a large upswing, there is a limit on how much overtime is realistic. Overtime pay increases costs and too much overtime can result in worker fatigue and a drop in productivity. Overtime also implies added overhead costs to keep a facility open. On the other hand, when there is a period of decreased demand, the company must somehow absorb workers' idle time—often a difficult and expensive process.

4. *Subcontracting:* A firm can acquire temporary capacity by subcontracting work during peak demand periods. Subcontracting, however, has several pitfalls. First, it may be costly; second, it risks opening the door to a competitor. Third, developing the perfect subcontract supplier can be a challenge.

5. *Using part-time workers:* Especially in the service sector, part-time workers can fill labor needs. This practice is common in restaurants, retail stores, and supermarkets.

Arab Bank incentivizes using cash machines by charging customers for carrying out certain services over the counter that do not require human input.

Demand Options

The basic demand options are:

1. *Influencing demand:* When demand is low, a company can try to increase demand through advertising, promotion, personal selling, and price cuts. Airlines and hotels offer weekend discounts and off-season rates; telephone companies charge less at night; some colleges give discounts to senior citizens; and air conditioners are least expensive in winter. However, even special advertising, promotions, selling, and pricing are not always able to balance demand with production capacity.

2. *Back ordering during high-demand periods:* Back orders are orders for goods or services that a firm accepts but is unable (either on purpose or by chance) to fill at the moment. If customers are willing to wait without loss of their goodwill or order, back ordering is a possible strategy. Many firms back order, but the approach often results in lost sales.

3. *Counterseasonal product and service mixing:* A widely used active smoothing technique among manufacturers is to develop a product mix of counterseasonal items. Examples include companies that make both furnaces and air conditioners. However, companies that follow this approach may find themselves involved in products or services beyond their area of expertise or beyond their target market.

These eight options, along with their advantages and disadvantages, are summarized in Table 13.1.

Mixing Options to Develop a Plan

Although each of the five capacity options and three demand options discussed above may produce an effective aggregate schedule, some combination of capacity options and demand options may be better.

Many manufacturers assume that the use of the demand options has been fully explored by the marketing department and those reasonable options incorporated into the demand forecast. The operations manager then builds the aggregate plan based on that forecast. However, using the five capacity options at his or her command, the operations manager still has a multitude of possible plans. These plans can embody, at one extreme, a *chase strategy* and, at the other, a *level-scheduling strategy*. They may, of course, fall somewhere in between.

Chase Strategy   A **chase strategy** typically attempts to achieve output rates for each period that match the demand forecast for that period. This strategy can be accomplished in a variety

Chase strategy

A planning strategy that sets production equal to forecasted demand.

▼ **TABLE 13.1** Aggregate Planning Options: Advantages And Disadvantages

Option	Advantages	Disadvantages	Comments
Changing inventory levels	Changes in human resources are gradual or none; no abrupt production changes.	Inventory holding costs may increase. Shortages may result in lost sales.	Applies mainly to production, not service, operations.
Varying workforce size by hiring or layoffs	Avoids the costs of other alternatives.	Hiring, layoff, and training costs may be significant.	Used where size of labor pool is large.
Varying production rates through overtime or idle time	Matches seasonal fluctuations without hiring/training costs.	Overtime premiums; tired workers; may not meet demand.	Allows flexibility within the aggregate plan.
Subcontracting	Permits flexibility and smoothing of the firm's output.	Loss of quality control; reduced profits; loss of future business.	Applies mainly in production settings.
Using part-time workers	Is less costly and more flexible than full-time workers.	High turnover/training costs; quality suffers; scheduling difficult.	Good for unskilled jobs in areas with large temporary labor pools.
Influencing demand	Tries to use excess capacity. Discounts draw new customers.	Uncertainty in demand. Hard to match demand to supply exactly.	Creates marketing ideas. Overbooking used in some businesses.
Back ordering during high-demand periods	May avoid overtime. Keeps capacity constant.	Customer must be willing to wait, but goodwill is lost.	Many companies back order.
Counterseasonal product and service mixing	Fully utilizes resources; allows stable workforce.	May require skills or equipment outside firm's areas of expertise.	Risky finding products or services with opposite demand patterns.

of ways. For example, the operations manager can vary workforce levels by hiring or laying off or can vary production by means of overtime, idle time, part-time employees, or subcontracting. Many service organizations favor the chase strategy because the changing inventory levels option is difficult or impossible to adopt. Industries that have moved toward a chase strategy include education, hospitality, and construction.

Level scheduling

Maintaining a constant output rate, production rate, or workforce level over the planning horizon.

Level Strategy A level strategy (or **level scheduling**) is an aggregate plan in which production is uniform from period to period. Firms like Toyota and Nissan attempt to keep production at uniform levels and may: (1) let the finished-goods inventory vary to buffer the difference between demand and production; (2) find alternative work for employees. Their philosophy is that a stable workforce leads to a better-quality product, less turnover and absenteeism, and more employee commitment to corporate goals. Other hidden savings include employees who are more experienced, easier scheduling and supervision, and fewer dramatic startups and shutdowns. Level scheduling works well when demand is reasonably stable.

Mixed strategy

A planning strategy that uses two or more controllable variables to set a feasible production plan.

For most firms, neither a chase strategy nor a level strategy is likely to prove ideal, so a combination of the eight options (called a **mixed strategy**) must be investigated to achieve minimum cost. However, because there are a huge number of possible mixed strategies, managers find that aggregate planning can be a challenging task. Finding the one 'optimal' plan is not always possible, but as we will see in the next section, a number of techniques have been developed to aid the aggregate planning process.

AUTHOR COMMENT
Managers must commit to employment levels, material purchases, and inventory levels; aggregate plans help managers do that.

METHODS FOR AGGREGATE PLANNING

In this section, we introduce several techniques that operations managers use to develop aggregate plans. They range from the widely used graphical method to a series of more formal mathematical approaches, including the transportation method of linear programming.

Graphical techniques

Aggregate planning techniques that work with a few variables at a time to allow planners to compare projected demand with existing capacity.

Graphical Methods

Graphical techniques are popular because they are easy to understand and use. These plans work with a few variables at a time to allow planners to compare projected demand with existing capacity. They are trial-and-error approaches that do not guarantee an optimal production plan, but they require only limited computations and can be performed by clerical staff. Following are the five steps in the graphical method:

1. Determine the demand in each period.
2. Determine capacity for regular time, overtime, and subcontracting each period.
3. Find labor costs, hiring and layoff costs, and inventory holding costs.
4. Consider company policy that may apply to the workers or to stock levels.
5. Develop alternative plans and examine their total costs.

These steps are illustrated in Examples 1 through 4.

◀ **EXAMPLE 1**

Graphical approach to aggregate planning for a roofing supplier

A Juarez, Mexico, manufacturer of roofing supplies has developed monthly forecasts for a family of products. Data for the 6-month period January to June are presented in Table 13.2. The firm would like to begin development of an aggregate plan.

Month	Expected Demand	Production Days	Demand per Day (computed)
Jan.	900	22	41
Feb.	700	18	39
Mar.	800	21	38
Apr.	1,200	21	57
May	1,500	22	68
June	1,100	20	55
	6,200	124	

◀ **TABLE 13.2**
Monthly Forecasts

APPROACH ▶ Plot daily and average demand to illustrate the nature of the aggregate planning problem.

SOLUTION ▶ First, compute demand per day by dividing the expected monthly demand by the number of production days (working days) each month and drawing a graph of those forecasted demands (Figure 13.3). Second, draw a dotted line across the chart that represents the production rate required to meet average demand over the 6-month period. The chart is computed as follows:

$$\text{Average requirement} = \frac{\text{Total expected demand}}{\text{Number of production days}} = \frac{6{,}200}{124} = 50 \text{ units per day}$$

◀ **FIGURE 13.3**
Graph of Forecast and Average Forecast Demand

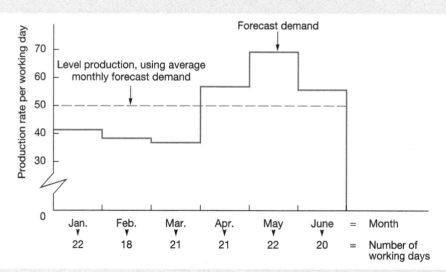

INSIGHT ▶ Changes in the production rate become obvious when the data are graphed. Note that in the first 3 months, expected demand is lower than average, while expected demand in April, May, and June is above average.

LEARNING EXERCISE ▶ If demand for June increases to 1,200 (from 1,100), what is the impact on Figure 13.3? [Answer: The daily rate for June will go up to 60, and average production will increase to 50.8 (6,300 ÷ 124).]

RELATED PROBLEM ▶ 13.1

The graph in Figure 13.3 illustrates how the forecast differs from the average demand. Some strategies for meeting the forecast were listed earlier. The firm, for example, might staff in order to yield a production rate that meets *average* demand (as indicated by the dashed line). Or it might produce a steady rate of, say, 30 units and then subcontract excess demand to other roofing suppliers. Other plans might combine overtime work with subcontracting to absorb demand. Examples 2 to 4 illustrate three possible strategies.

EXAMPLE 2 ▶

Plan 1 for the roofing supplier—a constant workforce

One possible strategy (call it plan 1) for the manufacturer described in Example 1 is to maintain a constant workforce throughout the 6-month period. A second (plan 2) is to maintain a constant workforce at a level necessary to meet the lowest demand month (March) and to meet all demand above this level by subcontracting. Both plan 1 and plan 2 have level production and are, therefore, called *level strategies*. Plan 3 is to hire and lay off workers as needed to produce exact monthly requirements—*a chase strategy*. Table 13.3 provides cost information necessary for analyzing these three alternatives:

▶ TABLE 13.3
Cost Information

Inventory carrying cost	US$5 per unit per month
Subcontracting cost per unit	US$20 per unit
Average pay rate	US$10 per hour (US$80 per day)
Overtime pay rate	US$17 per hour (above 8 hours per day)
Labor-hours to produce a unit	1.6 hours per unit
Cost of increasing daily production rate (hiring and training)	US$300 per unit
Cost of decreasing daily production rate (layoffs)	US$600 per unit

ANALYSIS OF PLAN 1. APPROACH ▶ Here we assume that 50 units are produced per day and that we have a constant workforce, no overtime or idle time, no safety stock, and no subcontractors. The firm accumulates inventory during the slack period of demand, January through March, and depletes it during the higher-demand warm season, April through June. We assume beginning inventory = 0 and planned ending inventory = 0.

SOLUTION ▶

Month	Production Days	Production at 50 Units per Day	Demand Forecast	Monthly Inventory Change	Ending Inventory
Jan.	22	1,100	900	+200	200
Feb.	18	900	700	+200	400
Mar.	21	1,050	800	+250	650
Apr.	21	1,050	1,200	−150	500
May	22	1,100	1,500	−400	100
June	20	1,000	1,100	−100	0
					1,850

Total units of inventory carried over from one month to the next month = 1,850 units

Workforce required to produce 50 units per day = 10 workers

Because each unit requires 1.6 labor-hours to produce, each worker can make 5 units in an 8-hour day. Therefore, to produce 50 units, 10 workers are needed.

Finally, the costs of plan 1 are computed as follows:

Cost		Calculations
Inventory carrying	US$9,250	(= 1,850 units carried × US$5 per unit)
Regular-time labor	99,200	(= 10 workers × US$80/day × 124 days)
Other costs (overtime, hiring, layoffs, subcontracting)	0	
Total cost	US$108,450	

The graph for Example 2 was shown in Figure 13.3. Some planners prefer a *cumulative* graph to display visually how the forecast deviates from the average requirements. Such a graph is provided in Figure 13.4. Note that both the level production line and the forecast line produce the same total production.

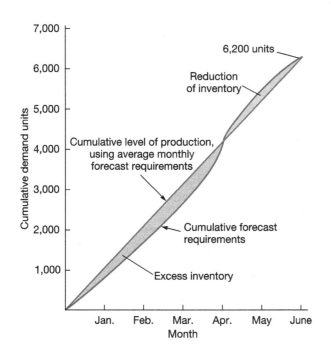

◀ **FIGURE 13.4**
Cumulative Graph for Plan 1

AUTHOR COMMENT
We saw another way to graph this data in Figure 13.3.

◀ **EXAMPLE 3**

Plan 2 for the roofing supplier—use of subcontractors within a constant workforce

ANALYSIS OF PLAN 2. APPROACH ▶   Although a constant workforce is also maintained in plan 2, it is set low enough to meet demand only in March, the lowest demand-per-day month. To produce 38 units per day (800 ÷ 21) in-house, 7.6 workers are needed. (You can think of this as 7 full-time workers and 1 part-timer.) *All* other demand is met by subcontracting. Subcontracting is thus required in every other month. No inventory holding costs are incurred in plan 2.

SOLUTION ▶   Because 6,200 units are required during the aggregate plan period, we must compute how many can be made by the firm and how many must be subcontracted:

$$\text{In-house production} = 38 \text{ units per day} \times 124 \text{ production days}$$
$$= 4{,}712 \text{ units}$$

$$\text{Subcontract units} = 6{,}200 - 4{,}712 = 1{,}488 \text{ units}$$

The costs of plan 2 are computed as follows:

Cost		Calculations
Regular-time labor	US$75,392	(= 7.6 workers × US$80/day × 124 days)
Subcontracting	29,760	(= 1,488 units × US$20 per unit)
Total cost	US$105,152	

INSIGHT ▶ Note the lower cost of regular labor but the added subcontracting cost.

LEARNING EXERCISE ▶ If demand for June increases to 1,200 (from 1,100), what is the change in cost? [Answer: Subcontracting requirements increase to 1,588 at US$20 per unit, for a subcontracting cost of US$31,760 and a total cost of US$107,152.]

RELATED PROBLEMS ▶ 13.2, 13.3, 13.4, 13.5, 13.8

EXAMPLE 4 ▶

Plan 3 for the roofing supplier—hiring and layoffs

ANALYSIS OF PLAN 3. APPROACH ▶ The final strategy, plan 3, involves varying the workforce size by hiring and laying off staff as necessary. The production rate will equal the demand, and there is no change in production from the previous month, December.

SOLUTION ▶ Table 13.4 shows the calculations and the total cost of plan 3. Recall that it costs US$600 per unit produced to reduce production from the previous month's daily level and US$300 per unit change to increase the daily rate of production through hirings.

▶ TABLE 13.4

Cost Computations for Plan 3

Month	Forecast (units)	Daily Production Rate	Basic Production Cost (demand × 1.6 hr per unit × US$10 per hr)	Extra Cost of Increasing Production (hiring cost (US$))	Extra Cost of Decreasing Production (layoff cost (US$))	Total Cost (US$)
Jan.	900	41	14,400	—	—	14,400
Feb.	700	39	11,200	—	1,200 (= 2 × 600)	12,400
Mar.	800	38	12,800	—	600 (= 1 × 600)	13,400
Apr.	1,200	57	19,200	5,700 (= 19 × 300)	—	24,900
May	1,500	68	24,000	3,300 (= 11 × 300)	—	27,300
June	1,100	55	17,600	—	7,800 (= 13 × 600)	25,400
			99,200	9,000	9,600	117,800

Thus, the total cost, including production, hiring, and layoff, for plan 3 is US$117,800.

INSIGHT ▶ Note the substantial cost associated with changing (both increasing and decreasing) the production levels.

LEARNING EXERCISE ▶ If demand for June increases to 1,200 (from 1,100), what is the change in cost? [Answer: Daily production for June is 60 units, which is a decrease of 8 units in the daily production rate from May's 68 units, so the new June layoff cost is US$4,800(= 8 × US$600), with a total plan 3 cost of US$114,800.]

RELATED PROBLEMS ▶ 13.2, 13.3, 13.4, 13.5, 13.8

The final step in the graphical method is to compare the costs of each proposed plan and to select the approach with the least total cost. A summary analysis is provided in Table 13.5. We see that because plan 2 has the lowest cost, it is the best of the three options.

▶ TABLE 13.5

Comparison of the Three Plans

Cost	Plan 1 (constant workforce of 10 workers) (US$)	Plan 2 (workforce of 7.6 workers plus subcontract) (US$)	Plan 3 (hiring and layoffs to meet demand) (US$)
Inventory carrying	9,250	0	0
Regular labor	99,200	75,392	99,200
Overtime labor	0	0	0
Hiring	0	0	9,000
Layoffs	0	0	9,600
Subcontracting	0	29,760	0
Total cost	108,450	105,152	117,800

Of course, many other feasible strategies can be considered in a problem like this, including combinations that use some overtime. Although graphing is a popular management tool, its help is in evaluating strategies, not generating them. To generate strategies, a systematic approach that considers all costs and produces an effective solution is needed.

Mathematical Approaches

This section briefly describes some of the mathematical approaches to aggregate planning.

The Transportation Method of Linear Programming When an aggregate planning problem is viewed as one of allocating operating capacity to meet forecasted demand, it can be formulated in a linear programming format. The **transportation method of linear programming** is not a trial-and-error approach like graphing but rather produces an optimal plan for minimizing costs. It is also flexible in that it can specify regular and overtime production in each time period, the number of units to be subcontracted, extra shifts, and the inventory carryover from period to period.

Transportation method of linear programming

A way of solving for the optimal solution to an aggregate planning problem.

In Example 5, the supply consists of on-hand inventory and units produced by regular time, overtime, and subcontracting. Costs per unit, in the upper-right corner of each cell of the matrix in Table 13.7, relate to units produced in a given period or units carried in inventory from an earlier period.

◄ **EXAMPLE 5**

Aggregate planning with the transportation method

Tunis Tire Company would like to develop an aggregate plan via the transportation method. Data that relate to production, demand, capacity, and cost at its Tunisian plant are shown in Table 13.6.

	Sales Period		
	Mar.	**Apr.**	**May**
Demand	800	1,000	750
Capacity:			
Regular	700	700	700
Overtime	50	50	50
Subcontracting	150	150	130
Beginning inventory	100 tires		

Costs (US$)	
Regular time	40 per tire
Overtime	50 per tire
Subcontract	70 per tire
Carrying cost	2 per tire per month

◄ **TABLE 13.6**

Tunis's Production, Demand, Capacity, And Cost Data

APPROACH ► Solve the aggregate planning problem by minimizing the costs of matching production in various periods to future demands.

SOLUTION ► Table 13.7 illustrates the structure of the transportation table and an initial feasible solution.

When setting up and analyzing this table, you should note the following:

1. Carrying costs are US$2/tire per month. Tires produced in 1 period and held for 1 month will have a US$2 higher cost. Because holding cost is linear, 2 months' holdover costs US$4. So when you move across a row from left to right, regular time, overtime, and subcontracting costs are lowest when output is used the same period it is produced. If goods are made in one period and carried over to the next, holding costs are incurred. Beginning inventory, however, is generally given a unit cost of 0 if it is used to satisfy demand in period 1.

2. Transportation problems require that supply equals demand; so, a dummy column called 'unused capacity' has been added. Costs of not using capacity are zero.

3. Because back ordering is not a viable alternative for this particular company, no production is possible in those cells that represent production in a period to satisfy demand in a past period (i.e. those periods with an 'X'). If back ordering is allowed, costs of expediting, loss of goodwill, and loss of sales revenues are summed to estimate backorder cost.

► TABLE 13.7
Tunis's Transportation Table[a]

| SUPPLY FROM | DEMAND FOR | | | | TOTAL CAPACITY AVAILABLE (supply) |
	Period 1 (Mar.)	Period 2 (Apr.)	Period 3 (May)	Unused Capacity (dummy)	
Beginning inventory	0 / 100	2	4	0	100
Period 1 — Regular time	40 / 700	42	44	0	700
Period 1 — Overtime	50	52 / 50	54	0	50
Period 1 — Subcontract	70	72 / 150	74	0	150
Period 2 — Regular time	×	40 / 700	42	0	700
Period 2 — Overtime	×	50 / 50	52	0	50
Period 2 — Subcontract	×	70 / 50	72	0 / 100	150
Period 3 — Regular time	×	×	40 / 700	0	700
Period 3 — Overtime	×	×	50 / 50	0	50
Period 3 — Subcontract	×	×	70	0 / 130	130
TOTAL DEMAND	800	1,000	750	230	2,780

[a]Cells with an x indicate that back orders are not used at Tunis. When using Excel OM or POM for Windows to solve, you must insert a *very* high cost (e.g. 9,999) in each cell that is not used for production.

LO4: Solve an aggregate plan via the transportation method of linear programming

4. Quantities in red in each column of Table 13.7 designate the levels of inventory needed to meet demand requirements (shown in the bottom row of the table). Demand of 800 tires in March is met by using 100 tires from beginning inventory and 700 tires from regular time.

5. In general, to complete the table, allocate as much production as you can to a cell with the smallest cost without exceeding the unused capacity in that row or demand in that column. If there is still some demand left in that column, allocate as much as you can to the next-lowest-cost cell. You then repeat this process for periods 2 and 3 (and beyond, if necessary). When you are finished, the sum of all your entries in a row must equal the total row capacity, and the sum of all entries in a column must equal the demand for that period. (This step can be accomplished by the transportation method or by using POM for Windows or Excel OM software.)

Try to confirm that the cost of this initial solution is US$105,900. The initial solution is not optimal, however. See if you can find the production schedule that yields the least cost (which turns out to be US$105,700) using software or by hand.

INSIGHT ► The transportation method is flexible when costs are linear but does not work when costs are nonlinear.

LEARNING EXERCISE ► What is the impact on this problem if there is no beginning inventory? [Answer: Total capacity (units) available is reduced by 100 units and the need to subcontract increases by 100 units.]

RELATED PROBLEMS ► 13.6, 13.7

EXCEL OM Data File Ch13Ex5.xls can be found at MyOMLab.

The transportation method of linear programming described in the above example was originally formulated by E. H. Bowman in 1956. Although it works well in analyzing the effects of holding inventories, using overtime, and subcontracting, it does not work when nonlinear or negative factors are introduced. Thus, when other factors such as hiring and layoffs are introduced, the more general method of linear programming must be used.

Management Coefficients Model   Bowman's **management coefficients model**[1] builds a formal decision model around a manager's experience and performance. The assumption is that the manager's past performance is pretty good; therefore, it can be used as a basis for future decisions. The technique uses a regression analysis of past production decisions made by managers. The regression line provides the relationship between variables (such as demand and labor) for future decisions. According to Bowman, managers' deficiencies are mostly inconsistencies in decision making.

Management coefficients model
A formal planning model built around a manager's experience and performance.

Other Models   Two additional aggregate planning models are the linear decision rule and simulation. The *linear decision rule (LDR)* attempts to specify an optimum production rate and workforce level over a specific period. It minimizes the total costs of payroll, hiring, layoffs, overtime, and inventory through a series of quadratic cost curves.[2]

A computer model called *scheduling by simulation* uses a search procedure to look for the minimum-cost combination of values for workforce size and production rate.

Comparison of Aggregate Planning Methods

Although these mathematical models have been found by researchers to work well under certain conditions, and linear programming has found some acceptance in industry, the fact is that most sophisticated planning models are not widely used. Why? Perhaps it reflects the average manager's attitude about what he or she views as overly complex models. Like all of us, planners like to understand how and why the models on which they are basing important decisions work. Additionally, operations managers need to make decisions quickly based on the changing dynamics of the competitive environment—and building good models is time-consuming. This may explain why the simpler graphical approach is more generally accepted.

Table 13.8 highlights some of the main features of graphing, transportation, management coefficients, and simulation planning models.

Technique	Solution Approaches	Important Aspects
Graphical methods	Trial and error	Simple to understand and easy to use. Many solutions; one chosen may not be optimal.
Transportation method of linear programming	Optimization	LP software available; permits sensitivity analysis and new constraints; linear functions may not be realistic.
Management coefficients model	Heuristic	Simple, easy to implement; tries to mimic manager's decision process; uses regression.
Simulation	Change parameters	Complex; model may be difficult to build and for managers to understand.

◀ **TABLE 13.8**
Summary Of Four Major Aggregate Planning Methods

AGGREGATE PLANNING IN SERVICES

AUTHOR COMMENT
The major variable in capacity management for services is labor.

Some service organizations conduct aggregate planning in exactly the same way as we did in Examples 1 through 5 in this chapter, but with demand management taking a more active role. Because most services pursue *combinations* of the eight capacity and demand options discussed

[1]E. H. Bowman, "Consistency and Optimality in Managerial Decision Making," *Management Science* 9, no. 2 (January 1963): 310–321.

[2]Because LDR was developed by Charles C. Holt, Franco Modigliani, John F. Muth, and Herbert Simon, it is popularly known as the HMMS rule. For details, see Martin K. Starr, *Production and Operations Management* (Cincinnati, OH: Atomic Dog Publishing, 2004): 490–493.

Aramex runs one of the most complex transportation networks in the Middle East, Africa and Asia through sophisticated planning and scheduling programs to ensure optimal assignment.

earlier, they usually formulate mixed aggregate planning strategies. In industries such as banking, trucking, and fast foods, aggregate planning may be easier than in manufacturing.

Controlling the cost of labor in service firms is critical. Successful techniques include:

1. Accurate scheduling of labor-hours to insure quick response to customer demand.
2. An on-call labor resource that can be added or deleted to meet unexpected demand.
3. Flexibility of individual worker skills that permits reallocation of available labor.
4. Flexibility in rate of output or hours of work to meet changing demand.

These options may seem demanding, but they are not unusual in service industries, in which labor is the primary aggregate planning vehicle. For instance:

• Excess capacity is used to provide study and planning time by real estate and auto salespersons.
• Police and fire departments have provisions for calling in off-duty personnel for major emergencies. Where the emergency is extended, police or fire personnel may work longer hours and extra shifts.
• When business is unexpectedly light, restaurants and retail stores send personnel home early.
• Supermarket stock clerks work cash registers when checkout lines become too lengthy.
• Experienced waitresses increase their pace and efficiency of service as crowds of customers arrive.

Approaches to aggregate planning differ by the type of service provided. Here we discuss five service scenarios.

Restaurants

In a business with a highly variable demand, such as a restaurant, aggregate scheduling is directed toward: (1) smoothing the production rate; (2) finding the optimal size of the workforce. The general approach usually requires building very modest levels of inventory during slack periods and depleting inventory during peak periods, but using labor to accommodate most of the changes in demand. Because this situation is very similar to those found in manufacturing, traditional aggregate planning methods may be applied to services as well. One difference that should be noted is that even modest amounts of inventory may be perishable. In addition, the relevant units of time may be much smaller than in manufacturing. For example, in fast-food restaurants, peak and slack periods may be measured in fractions of an hour and the 'product' may be inventoried for as little as 10 minutes.

Hospitals

Hospitals face aggregate planning problems in allocating money, staff, and supplies to meet the demands of patients. Amman's Surgical Hospital, for example, plans for bed capacity and personnel needs in light of a patient-load forecast developed by moving averages. The necessary labor focus of its aggregate plan has led to the creation of a new floating staff pool serving each nursing pod.

National Chains of Small Service Firms

With the advent of national chains of small service businesses, such as funeral homes, oil change outlets, and photocopy/printing centers, the question of aggregate planning versus independent planning at each business establishment becomes an issue. Both purchases and production capacity may be centrally planned when demand can be influenced through special promotions. This approach to aggregate scheduling is often advantageous because it reduces costs and helps manage cash flow at independent sites.

Miscellaneous Services

Most 'miscellaneous' services—financial, transportation, and many communication and recreation services—provide intangible output. Aggregate planning for these services deals mainly with planning for human resource requirements and managing demand. The twofold goal is to level demand peaks and to design methods for fully utilizing labor resources during low-demand periods. Example 6 illustrates such a plan for a legal firm.

Johara, a medium-sized law firm of 32 legal professionals in Doha, wants to develop an aggregate plan for the next quarter. The firm has developed three forecasts of billable hours for the next quarter for each of five categories of legal business it performs (column 1, Table 13.9). The three forecasts (best, likely, and worst) are shown in columns 2, 3, and 4 of Table 13.9.

◄ EXAMPLE 6

Aggregate planning in a law firm

◄ TABLE 13.9

Labor Allocation at Johara, Forecasts For Coming Quarter (1 Lawyer = 500 Hours Of Labor)

(1)	Labor-Hours Required			Capacity Constraints	
	(2)	(3)	(4)	(5)	(6)
		Forecasts		Maximum	Number of
Category of Legal Business	Best (hours)	Likely (hours)	Worst (hours)	Demand in People	Qualified Personnel
Trial work	1,800	1,500	1,200	3.6	4
Legal research	4,500	4,000	3,500	9.0	32
Corporate law	8,000	7,000	6,500	16.0	15
Real estate law	1,700	1,500	1,300	3.4	6
Criminal law	3,500	3,000	2,500	7.0	12
Total hours	19,500	17,000	15,000		
Lawyers needed	39	34	30		

APPROACH ▶ If we make some assumptions about the working week and skills, we can provide an aggregate plan for the firm. Assuming a 40-hour working week and that 100 percent of each lawyer's hours are billed, about 500 billable hours are available from each lawyer this fiscal quarter.

SOLUTION ▶ We divide hours of billable time (which is the demand) by 500 to provide a count of lawyers needed (lawyers represent the capacity) to cover the estimated demand. Capacity then is shown to be 39, 34, and 30 for the three forecasts, best, likely, and worst, respectively. For example, the best-case scenario of 19,500 total hours, divided by 500 hours per lawyer, equals 39 lawyers needed. Because all 32 lawyers at Johara are qualified to perform basic legal research, this skill has maximum scheduling flexibility (column 6). The most highly skilled (and capacity-constrained) categories are trial work and corporate law. The firm's best-case forecast just barely covers trial work, with 3.6 lawyers needed (see column 5) and 4 qualified (column 6). And corporate law is short by one full person.

Overtime may be used to cover the excess this quarter, but as business expands, it may be necessary to hire or develop talent in both of these areas. Available staff adequately covers real estate and criminal practice, as long as other needs do not use their excess capacity. With its current legal staff of 32, Johara's best-case forecast will increase the workload by $[(39 - 32) \div 32 =]21.8$ percent (assuming no new hires). This represents one extra day of work per lawyer per week. The worst-case scenario will result in about a 6 percent underutilization of talent. For both of these scenarios, the firm has determined that available staff will provide adequate service.

INSIGHT ▶ While our definitions of demand and capacity are different than for a manufacturing firm, aggregate planning is as appropriate, useful, and necessary in a service environment as in manufacturing.

LEARNING EXERCISE ▶ If the criminal law best-case forecast increases to 4,500 hours, what happens to the number of lawyers needed? [Answer: The demand for lawyers increases to 41.]

RELATED PROBLEMS ▶ 13.9, 13.10

Source: Adapted from Glenn Bassett, *Operations Management for Service Industries* (Westport, CT: Quorum Books, 1992): 110.

Airline Industry

Airlines and auto-rental firms also have unique aggregate scheduling problems. Consider an airline that has its headquarters in Dubai, two hub sites in cities such as Amman and Casablanca, and 150 offices in airports throughout the Arab world. This planning is considerably more complex than aggregate planning for a single site or even for a number of independent sites.

Aggregate planning consists of tables or schedules for: (1) number of flights in and out of each hub; (2) number of flights on all routes; (3) number of passengers to be serviced on all flights; (4) number of air personnel and ground personnel required at each hub and airport; (5) determining the seats to be allocated to various fare classes. Techniques for determining seat allocation are called yield, or revenue, management, our next topic.

AUTHOR COMMENT
Yield management changes the focus of aggregate planning from capacity management to demand management.

YIELD MANAGEMENT

Most operations models, like most business models, assume that firms charge all customers the same price for a product. In fact, many firms work hard at charging different prices. The idea is to match the demand curve by charging based on differences in the customer's willingness to pay. The management challenge is to identify those differences and price accordingly. The technique for multiple price points is called yield management.

**Yield (or revenue)
management**

Capacity decisions that determine the allocation of resources to maximize profit or yield.

LO5: Understand and solve a yield management problem

Yield (or revenue) management is the aggregate planning process of allocating the company's scarce resources to customers at prices that will maximize yield or revenue. The *OM in Action* box 'Yield Management at Hertz' describes this practice in the rental car industry.

Organizations that have *perishable inventory*, such as airlines, hotels, car rental agencies, cruise lines, and even electrical utilities, have the following shared characteristics that make yield management of interest:[3]

1. Service or product can be sold in advance of consumption.
2. Demand fluctuates.
3. The resource (capacity) is relatively fixed.
4. Demand can be segmented.
5. Variable costs are low and fixed costs are high.

Example 7 illustrates how yield management works in a hotel.

[3] R. Oberwetter, "Revenue Management," *OR/MS Today* (June 2001): 41–44.

OM in Action ► Yield Management at Hertz

For over 90 years, Hertz has been renting standard cars for a fixed amount per day. During the past two decades, however, a significant increase in demand has derived from airline travelers flying for business purposes. As the auto-rental market has changed and matured, Hertz has offered more options, including allowing customers to pick up and drop off in different locations. This option has resulted in excess capacity in some cities and shortages in others.

These shortages and overages alerted Hertz to the need for a yield management system similar to those used in the airline industry. The system is used to set prices, regulate the movement, and ultimately determine the availability of cars at each location. Through research, Hertz found that different city locations peak on different days of the week. So cars are moved to peak-demand locations from locations where the demand is low. By

altering both the price and quantity of cars at various locations, Hertz has been able to increase 'yield' and boost revenue.

The yield management system is primarily used by regional and local managers to better deal with changes in demand in the market. Hertz's plan to go global with the system, however, faces major challenges in the Arab world, where restrictions against moving empty cars across national borders are common.

Sources: The Wall Street Journal (December 30, 2003): D1 and (March 3, 2000): W-4; and *Cornell Hotel and Restaurant Quarterly* (December 2001): 33–46.

Jeezan Hotel in Sharm El Shiekh, Egypt, is a 100-room hotel that charges one set price for its rooms, US$150 per night. The variable cost of a room being occupied is low. Management believes the cleaning, air-conditioning, and incidental costs of soap, shampoo, and so forth, are US$15 per room per night. Sales average 50 rooms per night. Figure 13.5 illustrates the current pricing scheme. Net sales are US$6,750 per night with a single price point.

APPROACH ► Analyze pricing from the perspective of yield management. We note in Figure 13.5 that some guests would have been willing to spend more than US$150 per room—'money left on the table.' Others would be willing to pay more than the variable cost of US$15 but less than US$150—'passed-up contribution.'

◄ **EXAMPLE 7**

Yield management

◄ **FIGURE 13.5**
Hotel Sets Only One Price Level

```
Room Sales
           Demand curve
    100 ──┐↗
         │╲   Potential customers exist who
         │ ╲  are willing to pay more than the
         │  ╲ US$15 variable cost of the room,
         │   ╲ but not US$150.
         │Passed-up
         │contribution
     50 ─┤      ╲
         │       ╲  Some customers who paid
         │        ╲ US$150 were actually willing
Total US$ contribution =  ╲ to pay more for the room.
(Price) × (50 rooms) =     ╲
(US$150 – US$15)(50) =      ╲ Money left
US$6,750                     ╲ on the table
         └────┬────────┬──────╲──────► Price
           US$15    US$150
         Variable cost  Price charged
         of room        for room
         (e.g. cleaning, A/C)
```

SOLUTION ► In Figure 13.6, the hotel decides to set *two* price levels. It estimates that 30 rooms per night can be sold at US$100 and another 30 rooms at US$200, using yield management software that is widely available.

Source: Adapted from S. Kimes and K. McGuire, "Function Space Revenue Management," *Cornell Hotel and Restaurant Administration Quarterly* 42, no. 6 (December 2001): 33–46.

▶ **FIGURE 13.6**
Hotel with Two Price Levels

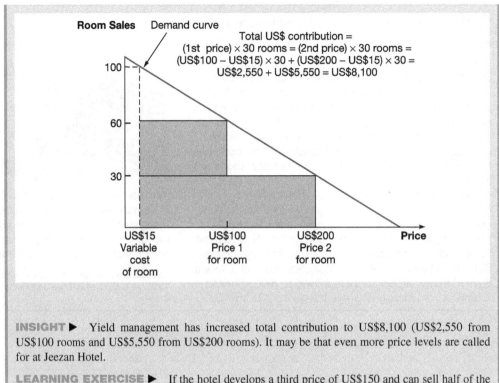

INSIGHT ▶ Yield management has increased total contribution to US$8,100 (US$2,550 from US$100 rooms and US$5,550 from US$200 rooms). It may be that even more price levels are called for at Jeezan Hotel.

LEARNING EXERCISE ▶ If the hotel develops a third price of US$150 and can sell half of the US$100 rooms at the increased rate, what is the contribution?

[Answer: US$8,850 = (15 × US$85) + (15 × US$135) + 30 × US$185.]

Industries traditionally associated with revenue management operate in quadrant 2 of Figure 13.7. They are able to apply variable pricing for their product and control product use or availability (number of airline seats or hotel rooms sold at economy rate). On the other hand, movie theaters, arenas, or performing arts centers (quadrant 1) have less pricing flexibility but still use time (evening or matinee) and location (orchestra, side, or balcony) to manage revenue. In both cases, management has control over the amount of the resource used—both the quantity and the duration of the resource.

▶ **FIGURE 13.7**
Yield Management Matrix

Industries in quadrant 2 are traditionally associated with revenue management.

		Price	
		Tend to be fixed	**Tend to be variable**
Use	**Tend to be predictable**	Quadrant 1: Movies Stadiums/arenas Convention centers Hotel meeting space	Quadrant 2: Hotels Airlines Rental cars Cruise lines
	Tend to be uncertain	Quadrant 3: Restaurants Golf courses Internet service providers	Quadrant 4: Hospitals Continuing care

In the lower half of Figure 13.7, the manager's job is more difficult because the duration of the use of the resource is less controllable. However, with imagination, managers are using excess capacity even for these industries. For instance, the golf course may sell less desirable tee times at a reduced rate, and the restaurant may have an 'early bird' special to generate business before the usual dinner hour.

To make yield management work, the company needs to manage three issues:

1. *Multiple pricing structures:* These structures must be feasible and appear logical (and preferably fair) to the customer. Such justification may take various forms, for example, first-class seats on an airline or the preferred starting time at a golf course. (See the Ethical Dilemma at the end of this chapter.)
2. *Forecasts of the use and duration of the use:* How many economy seats should be available? How much will customers pay for a room with an ocean view?
3. *Changes in demand:* This means managing the increased use as more capacity is sold. It also means dealing with issues that occur because the pricing structure may not seem logical and fair to all customers. Finally, it means managing new issues, such as overbooking because the forecast was not perfect.

Precise pricing through yield management has substantial potential. Therefore, several firms now have software available to address the issue. These include NCR's Teradata, SPS, DemandTec, and Oracle with Profit Logic.

CHAPTER SUMMARY

Aggregate planning provides companies with a necessary weapon to help capture market shares in the global economy. The aggregate plan gives both manufacturing and service firms the ability to respond to changing customer demands while still producing at low-cost and high-quality levels.

Aggregate schedules set levels of inventory, production, subcontracting, and employment over an intermediate time range, usually 3 to 18 months. This chapter describes several aggregate planning techniques, ranging from the popular graphical approach to a variety of mathematical models, such as linear programming.

The aggregate plan is an important responsibility of an operations manager and a key to efficient use of existing capital investment. Output from the aggregate schedule leads to a more detailed master production schedule, which is the basis for disaggregation, job scheduling, and MRP systems.

Aggregate plans for manufacturing firms and service systems are similar. Restaurants, airlines, and hotels are all service systems that employ aggregate plans, and have an opportunity to implement yield management. But regardless of the industry or planning method, the most important issue is the implementation of the plan. In this respect, managers appear to be more comfortable with faster, less complex, and less mathematical approaches to planning.

Key Terms

Ethical Dilemma

Airline passengers today stand in numerous lines, are crowded into small seats on mostly full airplanes, and often spend time on taxiways because of air-traffic problems or lack of open gates. But what gripes travelers almost as much as these annoyances is finding out that the person sitting next to them paid a much lower fare than they did for their seat. This concept of 'yield management' or 'revenue management' results in ticket pricing that can range from free to thousands of dollars on the same plane. Figure 13.8

illustrates what passengers recently paid for various seats on an 11.35 a.m. flight from Beirut to Muscat, Oman, on an Airbus A320.

Make the case for, and then against, this pricing system. Does the general public seem to accept yield management? What would happen if you overheard the person in front of you in line getting a better room rate at a Jumeirah Hotel? How do customers manipulate the airline systems to get better fares?

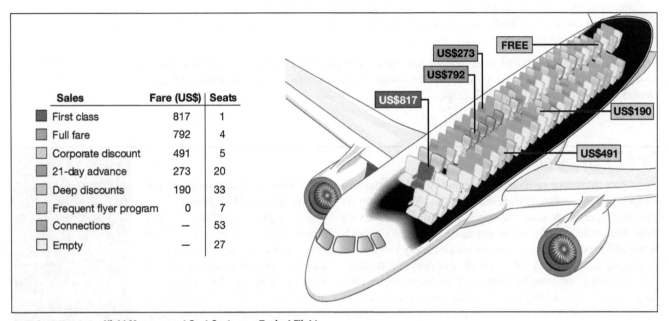

Sales	Fare (US$)	Seats
First class	817	1
Full fare	792	4
Corporate discount	491	5
21-day advance	273	20
Deep discounts	190	33
Frequent flyer program	0	7
Connections	–	53
Empty	–	27

▲ **FIGURE 13.8** **Yield Management Seat Costs on a Typical Flight**

Discussion Questions

1. Define *aggregate planning*.
2. Explain what the term *aggregate* in 'aggregate planning' means.
3. List the strategic objectives of aggregate planning. Which one of these is most often addressed by the quantitative techniques of aggregate planning? Which one of these is generally the most important?
4. Define *chase strategy*.
5. What is a pure strategy? Provide a few examples.
6. What is level scheduling? What is the basic philosophy underlying it?
7. Define *mixed strategy*. Why would a firm use a mixed strategy instead of a simple pure strategy?

8. What are the advantages and disadvantages of varying the size of the workforce to meet demand requirements each period?
9. Why are mathematical models not more widely used in aggregate planning?
10. How does aggregate planning in service differ from aggregate planning in manufacturing?
11. What is the relationship between the aggregate plan and the master production schedule?
12. Why are graphical aggregate planning methods useful?
13. What are major limitations of using the transportation method for aggregate planning?
14. How does yield management impact an aggregate plan?

Using Software for Aggregate Planning

This section illustrates the use of Excel OM and POM for Windows in aggregate planning.

USING EXCEL OM

Excel OM's Aggregate Planning module is demonstrated in Program 13.1. Again using data from Example 2, Program 13.1 provides input and some of the formulas used to compute the costs of regular time, overtime, subcontracting, holding, shortage, and increase or decrease in production. The user must provide the production plan for Excel OM to analyze.

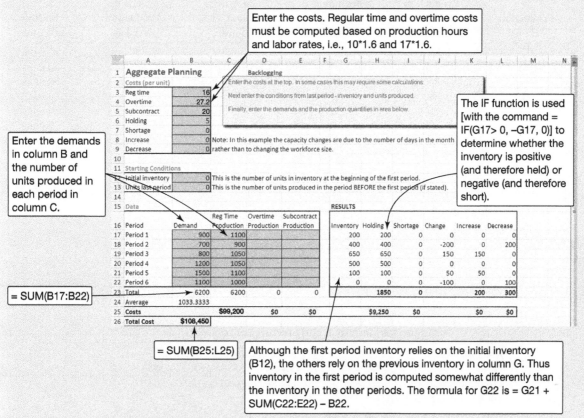

Enter the costs. Regular time and overtime costs must be computed based on production hours and labor rates, i.e., 10*1.6 and 17*1.6.

Enter the demands in column B and the number of units produced in each period in column C.

The IF function is used [with the command = IF(G17> 0, –G17, 0)] to determine whether the inventory is positive (and therefore held) or negative (and therefore short).

= SUM(B17:B22)

= SUM(B25:L25)

Although the first period inventory relies on the initial inventory (B12), the others rely on the previous inventory in column G. Thus inventory in the first period is computed somewhat differently than the inventory in the other periods. The formula for G22 is = G21 + SUM(C22:E22) – B22.

▲ **PROGRAM 13.1**   **Using Excel OM for Aggregate Planning, with Example 2 Data**

USING POM FOR WINDOWS

The POM for Windows Aggregate Planning module performs aggregate or production planning for up to 90 time periods. Given a set of demands for future periods, you can try various plans to determine the lowest-cost plan based on holding, shortage, production, and changeover costs. Four methods are available for planning. More help is available on each after you choose the method. See Appendix IV for further details.

Solved Problems   Virtual Office Hours help is available at MyOMLab

▼ SOLVED PROBLEM 13.1

The roofing manufacturer described in Examples 1 to 4 of this chapter wishes to consider yet a fourth planning strategy (plan 4). This one maintains a constant workforce of eight people and uses overtime whenever necessary to meet demand. Use the information found in Table 13.3 on page 416. Again, assume beginning and ending inventories are equal to zero.

▼ SOLUTION

Employ eight workers and use overtime when necessary. Note that carrying costs will be encountered in this plan.

Month	Production Days	Production at 40 Units per Day	Beginning-of-Month Inventory	Forecast Demand This Month	Overtime Production Needed	Ending Inventory
Jan.	22	880	—	900	20 units	0 units
Feb.	18	720	0	700	0 units	20 units
Mar.	21	840	20	800	0 units	60 units
Apr.	21	840	60	1,200	300 units	0 units
May	22	880	0	1,500	620 units	0 units
June	20	800	0	1,100	300 units	0 units
					1,240 units	80 units

Carrying cost totals = 80 units × US$5/unit/month = US$400

Regular pay:

8 workers × US$80/day × 124 days = US$79,360

Overtime pay:
To produce 1,240 units at overtime rate requires 1,240 × 1.6 hours/unit = 1,984 hours:

Overtime cost = US$17/hour × 1,984 hours = US$33,728

PLAN 4

Costs (workforce of 8 plus overtime) in US$

Carrying cost	400	(80 units carried × US$5/unit)
Regular labor	79,360	(8 workers × US$80/day × 124 days)
Overtime	33,728	(1,984 hours × US$17/hour)
Hiring or firing	0	
Subcontracting	0	
Total costs	113,488	

Plan 2 is still preferable at US$105,152.

▼ SOLVED PROBLEM 13.2

A Dover, Delaware, plant has developed the accompanying supply, demand, cost, and inventory data. The firm has a constant workforce and meets all its demand. Allocate production capacity to satisfy demand at a minimum cost. What is the cost of this plan?

Demand Forecast

Period	Demand (units)
1	450
2	550
3	750

Supply Capacity Available (units)

Period	Regular Time	Overtime	Subcontract
1	300	50	200
2	400	50	200
3	450	50	200

Other Data

Initial inventory	50 units
Regular-time cost per unit	US$50
Overtime cost per unit	US$65
Subcontract cost per unit	US$80
Carrying cost per unit per period	US$1
Back order cost per unit per period	US$4

▼ **SOLUTION**

		DEMAND FOR				TOTAL CAPACITY AVAILABLE (supply)
SUPPLY FROM		*Period 1*	*Period 2*	*Period 3*	*Unused Capacity (dummy)*	
Beginning inventory		0 50	1	2	0	50
P e r i o d 1	*Regular time*	50 300	51	52	0	300
	Overtime	65 50	66	67	0	50
	Subcontract	80 50	81	82	0 150	200
P e r i o d 2	*Regular time*	54	50 400	51	0	400
	Overtime	69	65 50	66	0	50
	Subcontract	84	80 100	81 50	0 50	200
P e r i o d 3	*Regular time*	58	54	50 450	0	450
	Overtime	73	69	65 50	0	50
	Subcontract	88	84	80 200	0	200
TOTAL DEMAND		450	550	750	200	1,950

Cost of plan:

Period 1: 50(US$0) + 300(US$50) + 50(US$65) + 50(US$80) = US$22,250
Period 2:   400(US$50) + 50(US$65) + 100(US$80) = US$31,250
Period 3: 50(US$81) + 450(US$50) + 50(US$65) + 200(US$80) = US$45,800*
Total cost   US$99,300

*Includes 50 units of subcontract and carrying cost.

Problems*

• **13.1** Prepare a graph of the monthly forecasts and average forecasted demand for Industrial Air Corp., a manufacturer of a variety of large air conditioners for commercial applications.

Month	Production Days	Demand Forecast
January	22	1,000
February	18	1,100
March	22	1,200
April	21	1,300
May	22	1,350
June	21	1,350
July	21	1,300
August	22	1,200
September	21	1,100
October	22	1,100
November	20	1,050
December	20	900

•• **13.2** a) Develop another plan for the roofing manufacturer described in Examples 1 to 4 (pages 415–418) and Solved Problem 13.1 (page 430). For this plan, plan 5, the firm wants to maintain a constant workforce of six, using subcontracting to meet remaining demand. Is this plan preferable?

b) The same roofing manufacturer in Examples 1 to 4 and Solved Problems 13.1 has yet a sixth plan. A constant workforce of seven is selected, with the remainder of demand filled by subcontracting. What is the cost of this plan?

c) Is this better than plans 1–5? **Px**

••• **13.3** Salam Fadeel, Inc., U.A.E. is a disk manufacturer in need of an aggregate plan for July through December. The company has gathered the following data:

Note: **Px** means the problem may be solved with POM for Windows and/or Excel OM.

	Costs (US$)
Holding cost	8/disk/month
Subcontracting	80/disk
Regular-time labor	12/hour
Overtime labor	18/hour for hours above 8 hours/worker/day
Hiring cost	40/worker
Layoff cost	80/worker

Demand*	
July	400
Aug.	500
Sept.	550
Oct.	700
Nov.	800
Dec.	700

*No costs are incurred for unmet demand.

Other Data	
Current workforce (June)	8 people
Labor-hours/disk	4 hours
Workdays/month	20 days
Beginning inventory	150 disks**
Ending inventory	0 disks

**Note that there is no holding cost for June.

What will each of the two following strategies cost?

a) Vary the workforce so that production meets demand. Salam had eight workers on board in June.

b) Vary overtime only and use a constant workforce of eight. **Px**

•• **13.4** You manage a consulting firm down the street from Salam Fadeel, Inc., and to get your foot in the door, you have told Mr. Fadeel (see Problem 13.3) that you can do a better job at

aggregate planning than his current staff. He said, "Fine. You do that, and you have a 1-year contract." You now have to make good on your boast using the data in Problem 13.3. You decide to hire five workers in August and five more in October.

••• **13.5** Juhaina Beauty Products, in Egypt, has developed a new shampoo and you need to develop its aggregate schedule. The cost accounting department has supplied you the cost relevant to the aggregate plan and the marketing department has provided a four-quarter forecast. All are shown as follows:

Quarter	Forecast
1	1,400
2	1,200
3	1,500
4	1,300

	Costs (US$)
Previous quarter's output	1,500 units
Beginning inventory	0 units
Stockout cost for backorders	50 per unit
Inventory holding cost	10 per unit for every unit held at the end of the quarter
Hiring workers	40 per unit
Laying off workers	80 per unit
Unit cost	30 per unit
Overtime	15 extra per unit
Subcontracting	Not available

Your job is to develop an aggregate plan for the next four quarters.

a) First, try a chase plan by hiring and layoffs (to meet the forecast) as necessary.

b) Then try a plan that holds employment steady.

c) Which is the more economical plan for Juhaina Beauty Products? **Px**

•• **13.6** Sameera's Saudi firm has developed the following supply, demand, cost, and inventory data. Allocate production capacity to meet demand at a minimum cost using the transportation method. What is the cost? Assume that the initial inventory has no holding cost in the first period and backorders are not permitted.

Supply Available

Period	Regular Time	Overtime	Subcontract	Demand Forecast
1	30	10	5	40
2	35	12	5	50
3	30	10	5	40

Initial inventory	20 units
Regular-time cost per unit	US$100
Overtime cost per unit	US$150
Subcontract cost per unit	US$200
Carrying cost per unit per month	US$4

Px

••• **13.7** A large Jeddah feed mill prepares its 6-month aggregate plan by forecasting demand for 50-kilogram bags of cattle feed as follows: January, 1,000 bags; February, 1,200; March, 1,250; April, 1,450; May, 1,400; and June, 1,400. The feed mill plans to begin the new year with no inventory left over from the previous year and backorders are not permitted. It projects that capacity (during regular hours) for producing bags of feed will remain constant at 800 until the end of April, and then increase to 1,100 bags per month when a planned expansion is completed on May 1. Overtime capacity is set at 300 bags per month until the expansion, at which time it will increase to 400 bags per month. A friendly competitor in Riyadh is also available as a backup source to meet demand—but can provide only 500 bags total during the 6-month period. Develop a 6-month production plan for the feed mill using the transportation method.

Cost data are as follows:

Regular-time cost per bag (until April 30)	US$12.00
Regular-time cost per bag (after May 1)	US$11.00
Overtime cost per bag (during entire period)	US$16.00
Cost of outside purchase per bag	US$18.50
Carrying cost per bag per month	US$1.00

••• **13.8** Shaher, owner of a Kuwaiti firm that manufactures display cabinets, develops an 8-month aggregate plan. Demand and capacity (in units) are forecast as follows:

Capacity Source (units)	Jan.	Feb.	Mar.	Apr.	May	June	July	Aug.
Regular time	235	255	290	300	300	290	300	290
Overtime	20	24	26	24	30	28	30	30
Subcontract	12	16	15	17	17	19	19	20
Demand	255	294	321	301	330	320	345	340

The cost of producing each unit is US$1,000 on regular time, US$1,300 on overtime, and US$1,800 on a subcontract. Inventory carrying cost is US$200 per unit per month. There is no beginning or ending inventory in stock, and no backorders are permitted from period to period.
a) Set up a production plan that minimizes cost by producing exactly what the demand is each month. Let the workforce vary by using regular time first, then overtime, and then subcontracting. This plan allows no backorders or inventory. What is this plan's cost?
b) Through better planning, regular-time production can be set at exactly the same amount, 275 units, per month. Does this alter the solution?

c) If overtime costs rise from US$1,300 to US$1,400, will your answer to part (a) change? What if overtime costs then fall to US$1,200?

••• **13.9** Jameel and Salama is a small accounting firm in Qatar, managed by Shahin Salama since the retirement in December of his partner Jameel Srour. Shahin and his three CPAs can together bill 640 hours per month. When Shahin or another accountant bills more than 160 hours per month, he or she gets an additional 'overtime' pay of US$62.50 for each of the extra hours: This is above and beyond the US$5,000 salary each draws during the month. (Shahin draws the same base pay as his employees.) Shahin strongly discourages any CPA from working (billing) more than 240 hours in any given month. The demand for billable hours for the firm over the next 6 months is estimated below:

Month	Estimate of Billable Hours
Jan.	600
Feb.	500
Mar.	1,000
Apr.	1,200
May	650
June	590

Shahin has an agreement with Jameel, his former partner, to help out during the busy tax season, if needed, for an hourly fee of US$125. Shahin will not even consider laying off one of his colleagues in the case of a slow economy. He could, however, hire another CPA at the same salary, as business dictates.
a) Develop an aggregate plan for the 6-month period.
b) Compute the cost of Shahin's plan of using overtime and Jameel.
c) Should the firm remain as is, with a total of four CPAs?

•• **13.10** Refer to the CPA firm in Problem 13.9. In planning for next year, Shahin estimates that billable hours will increase by 10 percent in each of the 6 months. He therefore proceeds to hire a fifth CPA. The same regular time, overtime, and outside consultant (i.e. Jameel) costs still apply.
a) Develop the new aggregate plan and compute its costs.
b) Comment on the staffing level with five accountants. Was it a good decision to hire the additional accountant?

▶ **Refer to** MyOMLab **for additional homework problems.**

Case Study

Ojaman University: (G)*

With the rising demands of a successful basketball program, the campus police chief at Ojaman University, Salih Taki, wants to develop a 2-year plan that involves a request for additional resources.

The OU department currently has 26 sworn officers. The size of the force has not changed over the past 15 years, but the following changes have prompted the chief to seek more resources:

- The size of the athletic program, especially basketball, has increased.
- The college has expanded geographically, with some new research facilities and laboratories now miles away from the main campus.
- Traffic and parking problems have increased.

- More portable, expensive computers with high theft potential are dispersed across the campus.
- Addiction problems have increased.
- The size of the surrounding community has doubled.
- The police need to spend more time on education and prevention programs.

The college is located in Ojaman, a small town. During the summer months, the student population is around 5,000. This number swells to 20,000 during fall and spring semesters. Thus, demand for police and other services is significantly lower during the summer months. Demand for police services also varies by:

- Time of day (peak time is between 10 p.m. and 2 a.m.).
- Day of the week (weekends are the busiest).
- Weekend of the year (on basketball weekends, 50,000 extra people come to campus).
- Special events (check-in, checkout, commencement).

Basketball weekends are especially difficult to staff. Extra police services are typically needed from 8 a.m. to 5 p.m. on five basketball Saturdays. All 26 officers are called in to work double shifts. More than 40 law enforcement officers from surrounding locations are paid to come in on their own time, and a dozen state police lend a hand free of charge (when available). Twenty-five students and local residents are paid to handle traffic and parking. During the last academic year (a 9-month period), overtime payments to campus police officers totaled over US$120,000.

Other relevant data include the following:

- The average starting salary for a police officer is US$28,000.
- Work-study and part-time students and local residents who help with traffic and parking are paid US$9.00 an hour.
- Overtime is paid to police officers who work over 40 hours a week at the rate of US$18.00 an hour. Extra officers who are hired part time from outside agencies also earn US$18.00 an hour.
- There seems to be an unlimited supply of officers who will work for the college when needed for special events.
- With days off, vacations, and average sick leave considered, it takes five persons to cover one 24-hour, 7-day-a-week position.

The schedule of officers during fall and spring semesters is:

	Weekdays	Weekend
First shift (7 a.m.–3 p.m.)	5	4
Second shift (3 p.m.–11 p.m.)	5	6
Third shift (11 p.m.–7 a.m.)	6	8

Source: Adapted from C. Haksever, B. Render, and R. Russell, *Service Management and Operations*, 2nd ed. (Upper Saddle River, NJ: Prentice Hall, 2000), 308–309. Reprinted by permission of Prentice Hall, Inc.

Staffing for basketball weekends and special events is *in addition to* the preceding schedule. Summer staffing is, on average, half that shown.

Taki thinks that his present staff are stretched to the limit. Fatigued officers are potential problems for the department and the community. In addition, neither time nor personnel has been set aside for crime prevention, safety, or health programs. Interactions of police officers with students, faculty, and staff are minimal and usually negative in nature. In light of these problems, the chief would like to request funding for four additional officers, two assigned to new programs and two to alleviate the overload of his current staff. He would also like to begin limiting overtime to 10 hours per week for each officer.

Discussion Questions

1. Which variations in demand for police services should be considered in an aggregate plan for resources? Which variations can be accomplished with short-term scheduling adjustments?
2. Evaluate the current staffing plan. What does it cost? Are 26 officers sufficient to handle the normal workload?
3. What would be the additional cost of the chief's proposal? How would you suggest that he justify his request?
4. How much does it currently cost the college to provide police services for basketball games? What would be the pros and cons of completely subcontracting this work to outside law enforcement agencies?
5. Propose other alternatives.

*This integrated case study runs throughout the text. Other issues facing Ojaman's basketball expansion include: (A) managing the arena project (Chapter 3); (B) forecasting game attendance (Chapter 4); (C) quality of facilities (Chapter 6); (D) break-even analysis for food services (Supplement 7); (E) where to locate the new arena (Chapter 8); (F) inventory planning of basketball programs (Chapter 12).

▶ **Additional Case Study:** Visit MyOMLab for this free case study:

Cornwell Glass: Involves setting a production schedule for an auto glass producer.

Main Heading	Review Material	MyOMLab
THE PLANNING PROCESS (pp. 410–411)	■ **Aggregate planning** (or **aggregate scheduling**)—An approach to determine the quantity and timing of production for the intermediate future (usually 3 to 18 months ahead). Usually, *the objective of aggregate planning is to meet forecasted demand while minimizing cost over the planning period.* Four things are needed for aggregate planning: 1. A logical overall unit for measuring sales and output. 2. A forecast of demand for a reasonable intermediate planning period in these aggregate terms. 3. A method for determining the relevant costs. 4. A model that combines forecasts and costs so that scheduling decisions can be made for the planning period. ■ **Scheduling decisions**—Plans that match production to changes in demand.	
THE NATURE OF AGGREGATE PLANNING (p. 411)	An aggregate plan looks at production *in the aggregate* (a family of products), not as a product-by-product breakdown. ■ **Disaggregation**—The process of breaking an aggregate plan into greater detail. ■ **Master production schedule**—A timetable that specifies what is to be made and when.	
AGGREGATE PLANNING STRATEGIES (pp. 411–414)	The basic aggregate planning capacity (production) options are: • Changing inventory levels • Varying workforce size by hiring or layoffs • Varying production rates through overtime or idle time • Subcontracting • Using part-time workers The basic aggregate planning demand options are: • Influencing demand • Back ordering during high-demand periods • Counterseasonal product and service mixing ■ **Chase strategy**—A planning strategy that sets production equal to forecasted demand. Many service organizations favor the chase strategy because the inventory option is difficult or impossible to adopt. ■ **Level scheduling**—Maintaining a constant output rate, production rate, or workforce level over the planning horizon. Level scheduling works well when demand is reasonably stable. ■ **Mixed strategy**—A planning strategy that uses two or more controllable variables to set a feasible production plan.	
METHODS FOR AGGREGATE PLANNING (pp. 414–421)	■ **Graphical techniques**—Aggregate planning techniques that work with a few variables at a time to allow planners to compare projected demand with existing capacity. Graphical techniques are trial-and-error approaches that do not guarantee an optimal production plan, but they require only limited computations. The five steps of the graphical method are: 1. Determine the demand in each period. 2. Determine capacity for regular time, overtime, and subcontracting each period. 3. Find labor costs, hiring and layoff costs, and inventory-holding costs. 4. Consider company policy that may apply to the workers or to stock levels. 5. Develop alternative plans and examine their total costs. A *cumulative* graph displays visually how the forecast deviates from the average requirements. ■ **Transportation method of linear programming**—A way of solving for the optimal solution to an aggregate planning problem. The transportation method of linear programming is flexible in that it can specify regular and overtime production in each time period, the number of units to be subcontracted, extra shifts, and the inventory carryover from period to period. Transportation problems require that supply equals demand, so when it does not, a dummy column called 'unused capacity' may be added. Costs of not using capacity are zero.	Problems: 13.2–13.8 Virtual Office Hours for Solved Problems: 13.1, 13.2

MyOMLab

Main Heading	Review Material
	Demand requirements are shown in the bottom row of a transportation table. Total capacity available (supply) is shown in the far right column.
	In general, to complete a transportation table, allocate as much production as you can to a cell with the smallest cost, without exceeding the unused capacity in that row or demand in that column. If there is still some demand left in that column, allocate as much as you can to the next lowest-cost cell. You then repeat this process for periods 2 and 3 (and beyond, if necessary). When you are finished, the sum of all your entries in a row must equal total row capacity, and the sum of all entries in a column must equal the demand for that period.
	The transportation method was originally formulated by E. H. Bowman in 1956.
	The transportation method does not work when nonlinear or negative factors are introduced.
	■ **Management coefficients model**—A formal planning model built around a manager's experience and performance.
AGGREGATE PLANNING IN SERVICES (pp. 421–424)	Successful techniques for controlling the cost of labor in service firms include: 1. Accurate scheduling of labor-hours to ensure quick response to customer demand. 2. An on-call labor resource that can be added or deleted to meet unexpected demand. 3. Flexibility of individual worker skills that permits reallocation of available labor. 4. Flexibility in rate of output or hours of work to meet changing demand.
YIELD MANAGEMENT (pp. 424–427)	■ **Yield** (or **revenue**) **management**—Capacity decisions that determine the allocation of resources to maximize profit or yield. Organizations that have *perishable inventory*, such as airlines, hotels, car rental agencies, and cruise lines, have the following shared characteristics that make yield management of interest: 1. Service or product can be sold in advance of consumption. 2. Demand fluctuates. 3. The resource (capacity) is relatively fixed. 4. Demand can be segmented. 5. Variable costs are low, and fixed costs are high. To make yield management work, the company needs to manage three issues: 1. *Multiple pricing structures* 2. *Forecasts of the use and duration of the use* 3. *Changes in demand.*

Self-Test

■ **Before taking the self-test,** refer to the learning objectives listed at the beginning of the chapter and the key terms listed at the end of the chapter.

LO1. Aggregate planning is concerned with determining the quantity and timing of production in the:
a) short term
b) intermediate term
c) long term
d) all of the above.

LO2. Aggregate planning deals with a number of constraints. These typically are:
a) job assignments, job ordering, dispatching, and overtime help
b) part-time help, weekly scheduling, and SKU production scheduling
c) subcontracting, employment levels, inventory levels, and capacity
d) capital investment, expansion or contracting capacity, and R&D
e) facility location, production budgeting, overtime, and R&D.

LO3. Which of the following is not one of the graphical method steps?
a) Determine the demand in each period
b) Determine capacity for regular time, overtime, and subcontracting each period

c) Find labor costs, hiring and layoff costs, and inventory holding costs
d) Construct the transportation table
e) Consider company policy that may apply to the workers or stock levels
f) Develop alternative plans and examine their total costs.

LO4. When might a dummy column be added to a transportation table?
a) When supply does not equal demand
b) When overtime is greater than regular time
c) When subcontracting is greater than regular time
d) When subcontracting is greater than regular time plus overtime
e) When production needs to spill over into a new period.

LO5. Yield management requires management to deal with:
a) multiple pricing structures
b) changes in demand
c) forecasts of use
d) forecasts of duration of use
e) all of the above.

Answers: LO1. b; **LO2.** c; **LO3.** d; **LO4.** a; **LO5.** e.

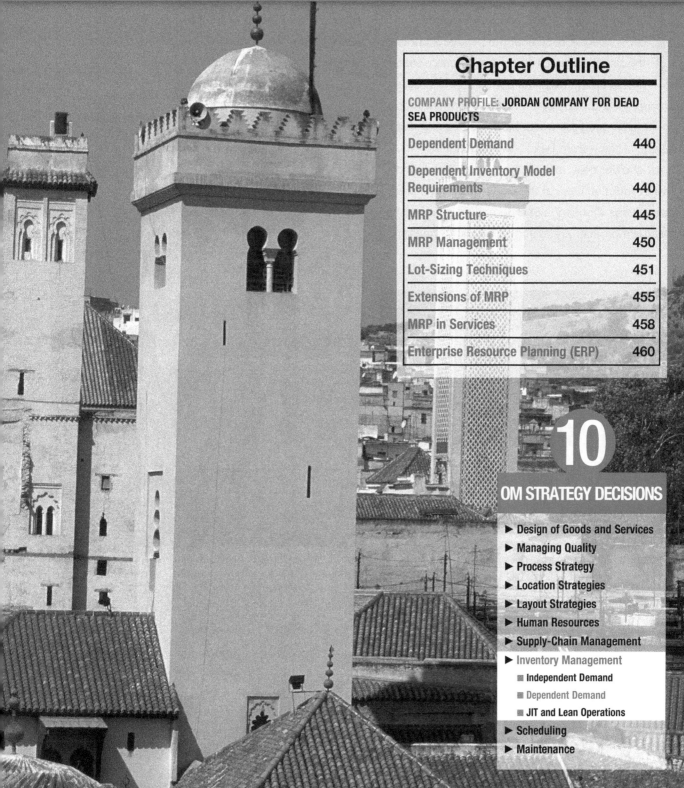

10

OM STRATEGY DECISIONS

► Design of Goods and Services
► Managing Quality
► Process Strategy
► Location Strategies
► Layout Strategies
► Human Resources
► Supply-Chain Management
► Inventory Management
  ■ Independent Demand
  ■ Dependent Demand
  ■ JIT and Lean Operations
► Scheduling
► Maintenance

MRP PROVIDES A COMPETITIVE ADVANTAGE FOR JORDAN COMPANY FOR DEAD SEA PRODUCTS

Jordan Company for Dead Sea Products produces Dead Sea natural products under the brand name La Cure. The Amman-based firm is an international competitor that sells its cosmetics and body care products to more than 53 countries around the world. More than 52 signature products, ranging from Dead Sea mud, soaps, oil, creams, shower gels, and shampoos, are produced on five production lines at the Dead Sea plant. The company uses thousands of different inventory items, of which almost half are manufactured and the rest are purchased. Most of the product line is custom designed and assembled to meet the specific and unique requirements of the customers.

La Cure has a wide range of products that are extracted from Dead Sea salts, mud and water. The production of such a huge variety needs careful requirement planning to ensure effective production without interruptions.

Workers at La Cure are trained to use the highly sophisticated machinery, but are also given a special course in manual processes to ensure the continuous flow of products.

This variety of products and the nature of the process demand good material requirements planning (MRP). Effective use of an MRP system requires accurate bills of material and inventory records. Jordan Company for Dead Sea Products, which uses custom-made MRP software, provides daily updates and has reduced inventory by more than 50 percent in just 12 months.

Jordan Company for Dead Sea Products insists that four key tasks be performed properly. First, the material plan must meet both the requirements of the master schedule and the capabilities of the production facility at the Dead Sea. Second, the plan must be executed as designed by the operations department. Third, inventory investment must be minimized through effective 'time-phased' material deliveries, consignment inventories, and a constant review of purchase methods. Finally, excellent record integrity must be maintained. Record accuracy is recognized as a fundamental ingredient of Jordan Company for Dead Sea Products' successful MRP program. The company uses MRP as the catalyst for low inventory, high quality, tight schedules, and accurate records. It has found competitive advantage via MRP.

Source: **www.special-lacure.com**

VIDEO 14.1
MRP at Wheeled Coach Ambulance

Chapter 14 Learning Objectives

Material requirements planning (MRP)
A dependent demand technique that uses a bill of material, inventory, expected receipts, and a master production schedule to determine material requirements.

DEPENDENT DEMAND

Jordan Company for Dead Sea Products and many other firms have found important benefits in **material requirements planning (MRP)**. These benefits include: (1) better response to customer orders as the result of improved adherence to schedules; (2) faster response to market changes; (3) improved utilization of facilities and labor; (4) reduced inventory levels. Better response to customer orders and to the market wins orders and market share. Better utilization of facilities and labor yields higher productivity and return on investment. Less inventory frees up capital and floor space for other uses. These benefits are the result of a strategic decision to use a *dependent* inventory scheduling system.

Demand for items is dependent when the relationship between the items can be determined. Therefore, once management receives an order or makes a forecast for the final product, quantities for all components can be computed. All components are dependent items. The Egyptian German Automotive operations manager who schedules the company's production of cars, for example, knows the requirements down to the last rivet. For any product, all components of that product are dependent demand items. *More generally, for any product for which a schedule can be established, dependent techniques should be used.*

When the requirements of MRP are met, dependent models are preferable to the EOQ models described in Chapter 12.[1] Dependent models are better not only for manufacturers and distributors but also for a wide variety of firms, from restaurants to hospitals. The dependent technique used in a production environment is called material requirements planning (MRP).

Because MRP provides such a clean structure for dependent demand, it has evolved as the basis for enterprise resource planning (ERP). ERP is an information system for identifying and planning the enterprise-wide resources needed to take, make, ship, and account for customer orders. We will discuss ERP in the latter part of this chapter.

DEPENDENT INVENTORY MODEL REQUIREMENTS

Effective use of dependent inventory models requires the operations manager to know the following:

1. Master production schedule (what is to be made and when).
2. Specifications or bill of material (materials and parts required to make the product).
3. Inventory availability (what is in stock).
4. Purchase orders outstanding (what is on order, also called expected receipts).
5. Lead times (how long it takes to get various components).

We now discuss each of these requirements in the context of material requirements planning.

Master Production Schedule

Master production schedule (MPS)
A timetable that specifies what is to be made and when.

A **master production schedule (MPS)** specifies what is to be made (i.e. the number of finished products or items) and when. The schedule must be in accordance with a production plan. The production plan sets the overall level of output in broad terms (e.g. product families, standard hours, or monetary volume). The plan also includes a variety of inputs, including financial plans, customer demand, engineering capabilities, labor availability, inventory fluctuations, supplier

---

[1]The inventory models (EOQ) discussed in Chapter 12 assumed that the demand for one item was independent of the demand for another item. For example, EOQ assumes the demand for refrigerator parts is *independent* of the demand for refrigerators and that demand for parts is constant.

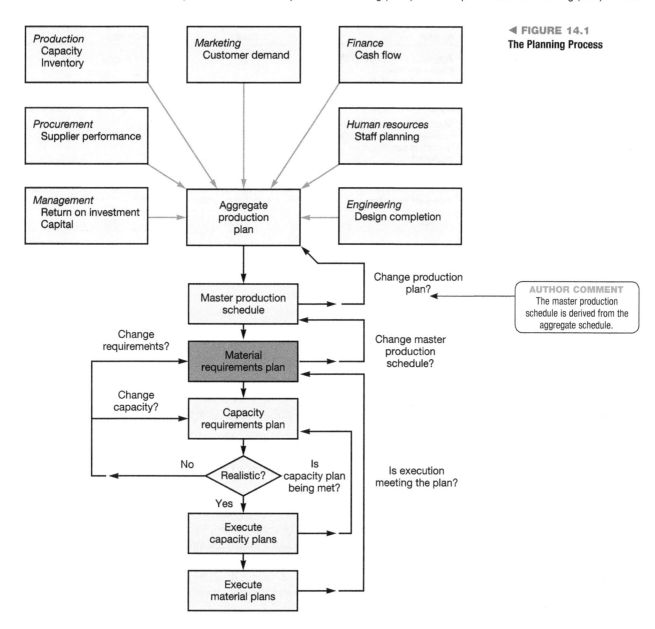

AUTHOR COMMENT
The master production schedule is derived from the aggregate schedule.

performance, and other considerations. Each of these inputs contributes in its own way to the production plan, as shown in Figure 14.1.

As the planning process moves from the production plan to execution, each of the lower-level plans must be feasible. When one is not, feedback to the next higher level is used to make the necessary adjustment. One of the major strengths of MRP is its ability to determine precisely the feasibility of a schedule within aggregate capacity constraints. This planning process can yield excellent results. The production plan sets the upper and lower bounds on the master production schedule. The result of this production planning process is the master production schedule.

The master production schedule tells us what is required to satisfy demand and meet the production plan. This schedule establishes what items to make and when: It *disaggregates* the aggregate production plan. While the *aggregate production plan* (as discussed in Chapter 13) is established in gross terms such as families of products or tons of steel, the *master production schedule* is established in terms of specific products. Figure 14.2 shows the master production schedules for three stereo models that flow from the aggregate production plan for a family of stereo amplifiers.

Managers must adhere to the schedule for a reasonable length of time (usually a major portion of the production cycle—the time it takes to produce a product). Many organizations establish a master production schedule and establish a policy of not changing ('fixing') the near-term portion of the plan. This near-term portion of the plan is then referred to as the 'fixed,' 'firm,' or

► **FIGURE 14.2**
The Aggregate Production Plan Is the Basis for Development of the Detailed Master Production Schedule

Months	January				February				
Aggregate Production Plan (Shows the total quantity of amplifiers)	1,500				1,200				
Weeks	1	2	3	4	5	6	7	8	
Master Production Schedule (Shows the specific type and quantity of amplifier to be produced)									
240-watt amplifier	100		100		100		100		
150-watt amplifier		500		500		450		450	
75-watt amplifier				300				100	

'frozen' schedule. Jordan Company for Dead Sea Products, the subject of the *Company Profile* for this chapter, fixes the first 21 days of its schedule. Only changes farther out, beyond the fixed schedule, are permitted. The master production schedule is a 'rolling' production schedule. For example, a fixed 5-week plan has an additional week added to it as each week is completed, so a 5-week fixed schedule is maintained. Note that the master production schedule is a statement of *what is to be produced*, not a forecast of demand. The master production schedule can be expressed in any of the following terms:

1. A *customer order in a job shop* (make-to-order) company.
2. *Modules in a repetitive* (assemble-to-order or forecast) company.
3. An *end item in a continuous* (stock-to-forecast) company.

This relationship of the master production schedule to the processes is shown in Figure 14.3.

A master production schedule for two of Ali's Restaurant products, lamb meat shawerma and chicken meat shawerma, might look like Table 14.1.

Bills of Material

Bill of material (BOM)

A list of the components, their description, and the quantity of each required to make one unit of a product.

Defining what goes into a product may seem simple, but it can be difficult in practice. As we noted in Chapter 5, to aid this process, manufactured items are defined via a bill of material. A **bill of material (BOM)** is a list of quantities of components, ingredients, and materials required to make a product. Individual drawings describe not only physical dimensions but also any special processing, as well as the raw materials from which each part is made. Ali's Restaurant

AUTHOR COMMENT
The type of process determines the units in the master production schedule.

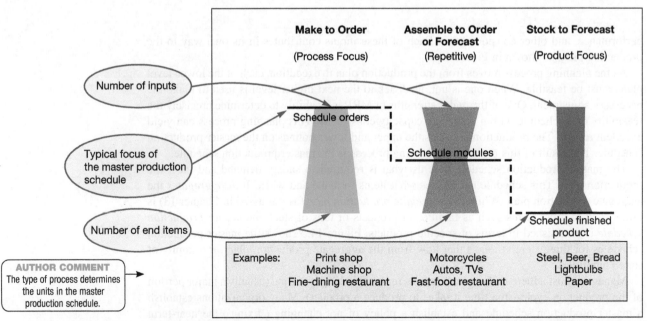

▲ **FIGURE 14.3** **Typical Focus of the Master Production Schedule in Three Process Strategies**

Gross Requirements for Lamb Meat Shawerma									
Day	6	7	8	9	10	11	12	13	14	and so on
Amount	50		100	47	60		110	75		

Gross Requirements for Chicken Meat Shawerma									
Day	7	8	9	10	11	12	13	14	15	16	and so on
Amount	100	200	150			60	75		100		

◀ **TABLE 14.1**

Master Production Schedule for Lamb Meat Shawerma and Chicken Meat Shawerma at Ali's Restaurant

has a recipe for shawerma, specifying ingredients and quantities, just as Jordan Company for Dead Sea Products has a full set of ingredients for its products. Both are bills of material (although we call the first a recipe, and they do vary somewhat in scope).

Because there is often a rush to get a new product to market, however, drawings and bills of material may be incomplete or even nonexistent. Moreover, complete drawings and bills of material (as well as other forms of specifications) often contain errors in dimensions, quantities, or countless other areas. When errors are identified, engineering change notices (ECNs) are created, further complicating the process. An *engineering change notice* is a change or correction to an engineering drawing or bill of material.

One way a bill of material defines a product is by providing a product structure. Example 1 shows how to develop the product structure and 'explode' it to reveal the requirements for each component. A bill of materials for item A in Example 1 consists of items B and C. Items above any level are called *parents*; items below any level are called *components* or *children*. By convention, the top level in a bill of materials is the 0 level.

Medina Speakers Ltd. packages high-fidelity components for mail order. Components for the high-end speaker kit, 'Awesome' (A), include two standard 30 cm speaker kits (Bs) and three speaker kits with amp-boosters (Cs).

Each B consists of two speakers (Ds) and two shipping boxes each with an installation kit (E). Each of the three 300-watt speaker kits (Cs) has two speaker boosters (Fs) and two installation kits (Es). Each speaker booster (F) includes two speakers (Ds) and one amp-booster (G). The total for each Awesome is four standard 30 cm speakers and twelve 30 cm speakers with the amp-booster. (Most purchasers require hearing aids within 3 years, and at least one court case is pending because of structural damage to a men's dormitory.) As we can see, the demand for B, C, D, E, F, and G is completely dependent on the master production schedule for A—the Awesome speaker kits.

APPROACH ▶ Given the above information, we construct a product structure and 'explode' the requirements.

SOLUTION ▶ This structure has four levels: 0, 1, 2, and 3. There are four parents: A, B, C, and F. Each parent item has at least one level below it. Items B, C, D, E, F, and G are components because each item has at least one level above it. In this structure, B, C, and F are both parents and components. Numbers in parentheses indicate how many units of that particular item are needed to make the item immediately above it. Thus, $B_{(2)}$ means that it takes two units of B for every unit of A, and $F_{(2)}$ means that it takes two units of F for every unit of C.

◀ **EXAMPLE 1**

Developing a product structure and gross requirements

LO1: Develop a product structure

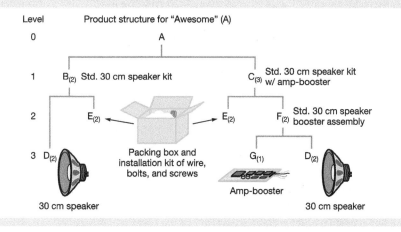

Once we have developed the product structure, we can determine the number of units of each item required to satisfy demand for a new order of 50 Awesome speaker kits. We 'explode' the requirements as shown:

Part B:	$2 \times$ number of As =	(2)(50) =	100
Part C:	$3 \times$ number of As =	(3)(50) =	150
Part D:	$2 \times$ number of Bs + $2 \times$ number of Fs =	(2)(100) + (2)(300) =	800
Part E:	$2 \times$ number of Bs + $2 \times$ number of Cs =	(2)(100) + (2)(150) =	500
Part F:	$2 \times$ number of Cs =	(2)(150) =	300
Part G:	$1 \times$ number of Fs =	(1)(300) =	300

INSIGHT ▶   We now have a visual picture of the Awesome speaker kit requirements and knowledge of the quantities required. Thus, for 50 units of A, we will need 100 units of B, 150 units of C, 800 units of D, 500 units of E, 300 units of F, and 300 units of G.

LEARNING EXERCISE ▶   If there are 100 Fs in stock, how many Ds do you need? [Answer: 600.]

RELATED PROBLEMS ▶   14.1, 14.3a

EXCEL OM Data File **Ch14Ex1.xls** can be found at MyOMLab.

Bills of material not only specify requirements but also are useful for costing, and they can serve as a list of items to be issued to production or assembly personnel. When bills of material are used in this way, they are usually called *pick lists*.

Modular bills

Bills of material organized by major subassemblies or by product options.

Modular Bills   Bills of material may be organized around product modules (see Chapter 5). *Modules* are not final products to be sold but are components that can be produced and assembled into units. They are often major components of the final product or product options. Bills of material for modules are called **modular bills**. Bills of material are sometimes organized as modules (rather than as part of a final product) because production scheduling and production are often facilitated by organizing around relatively few modules rather than a multitude of final assemblies. For instance, a firm may make 138,000 different final products but may have only 40 modules that are mixed and matched to produce those 138,000 final products. The firm builds an aggregate production plan and prepares its master production schedule for the 40 modules, not the 138,000 configurations of the final product. This approach allows the MPS to be prepared for a reasonable number of items (the narrow portion of the middle graphic in Figure 14.3) and to postpone assembly. The 40 modules can then be configured for specific orders at final assembly.

Planning bills

Also known as *'pseudo' bills*, *kitted material*, or *kit*; a material grouping created in order to assign an artificial parent to a bill of material.

Phantom bills of material

Bills of material for components, usually assemblies, that exist only temporarily; they are never inventoried.

Planning Bills and Phantom Bills   Two other special kinds of bills of material are planning bills and phantom bills. **Planning bills** (sometimes called 'pseudo' bills or super bills) are created in order to assign an artificial parent to the bill of material. Such bills are used: (1) when we want to group subassemblies so the number of items to be scheduled is reduced; (2) when we want to issue 'kits' to the production department. For instance, it may not be efficient to issue inexpensive items such as washers and cotter pins with each of numerous subassemblies, so we call this a *kit* and generate a planning bill. The planning bill specifies the *kit* to be issued. Consequently, a planning bill may also be known as *kitted material*, or *kit*. **Phantom bills of material** are bills of material for components, usually subassemblies, that exist only temporarily. These components go directly into another assembly and are never inventoried. Therefore, components of phantom bills of material are coded to receive special treatment; lead times are zero, and they are handled as an integral part of their parent item. An example is a transmission shaft with gears and bearings assembly that is placed directly into a transmission.

Low-level coding

A number that identifies items at the lowest level at which they occur.

Low-Level Coding   Low-level coding of an item in a bill of material is necessary when identical items exist at various levels in the bill of material. **Low-level coding** means that the item is coded at the lowest level at which it occurs. For example, item D in Example 1 is coded at the lowest level at which it is used. Item D could be coded as part of B and occur at level 2. However, because D is also part of F, and F is level 2, item D becomes a level-3 item. Low-level coding is a convention to allow easy computing of the requirements of an item. When the bill of material has thousands of items or when requirements are frequently recomputed, the ease and speed of computation become a major concern.

Accurate Inventory Records

As we saw in Chapter 12, knowledge of what is in stock is the result of good inventory management. Good inventory management is an absolute necessity for an MRP system to work. If the firm does not exceed 99 percent record accuracy, then material requirements planning will not work.[2]

Purchase Orders Outstanding

Knowledge of outstanding orders exists as a by-product of well-managed purchasing and inventory-control departments. When purchase orders are executed, records of those orders and their scheduled delivery dates must be available to production personnel. Only with good purchasing data can managers prepare meaningful production plans and effectively execute an MRP system.

Lead Times for Components

Once managers determine when products are needed, they determine when to acquire them. The time required to acquire (that is, purchase, produce, or assemble) an item is known as **lead time**. Lead time for a manufactured item consists of *move*, *setup*, and *assembly* or *run times* for each component. For a purchased item, the lead time includes the time between recognition of need for an order and when it is available for production.

When the bill of material for Awesome speaker kits, in Example 1, is turned on its side and modified by adding lead times for each component (see Table 14.2), we then have a *time-phased product structure*. Time in this structure is shown on the horizontal axis of Figure 14.4 with item A due for completion in week 8. Each component is then offset to accommodate lead times.

MRP STRUCTURE

Although most MRP systems are computerized, the MRP procedure is straightforward and we can illustrate a small one by hand. A master production schedule, a bill of material, inventory and purchase records, and lead times for each item are the ingredients of an MRP system (see Figure 14.5).

▼ TABLE 14.2

Lead Times for Awesome Speaker Kits

Component	Lead Time
A	1 week
B	2 weeks
C	1 week
D	1 week
E	2 weeks
F	3 weeks
G	2 weeks

Lead time

In purchasing systems, the time between placing an order and receiving it; in production systems, the wait, move, queue, setup, and run times for each component produced.

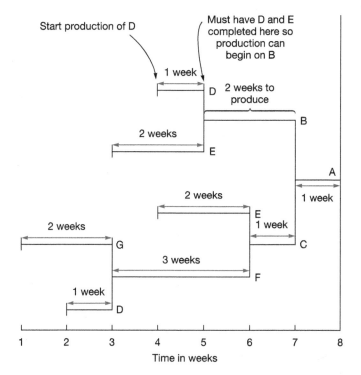

Start production of D

Must have D and E completed here so production can begin on B

1 week

D 2 weeks to produce

B

2 weeks

E

A

2 weeks

1 week

E 1 week

2 weeks

G

C

3 weeks

F

1 week

D

| 1 | 2 | 3 | 4 | 5 | 6 | 7 | 8 |

Time in weeks

◄ FIGURE 14.4

Time-Phased Product Structure

AUTHOR COMMENT
This is a product structure on its side, with lead times.

[2]Record accuracy of 99 percent may sound good, but note that even when each component has an availability of 99 percent and a product has only seven components, the likelihood of a product being completed is only 0.932 (because $0.99^7 = 0.932$).

▶ FIGURE 14.5
Structure of the MRP System

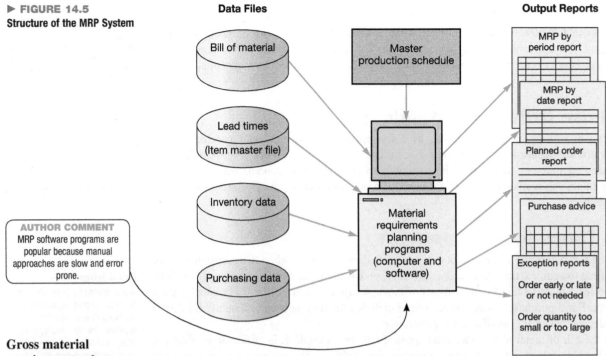

Data Files

Bill of material

Lead times
(Item master file)

Inventory data

Purchasing data

Master
production schedule

Material
requirements
planning
programs
(computer and
software)

Output Reports

MRP by
period report

MRP by
date report

Planned order
report

Purchase advice

Exception reports

Order early or late
or not needed

Order quantity too
small or too large

> **AUTHOR COMMENT**
> MRP software programs are
> popular because manual
> approaches are slow and error
> prone.

**Gross material
requirements plan**

A schedule that shows the total
demand for an item (prior to
subtraction of on-hand inventory
and scheduled receipts) and:
(1) when it must be ordered from
suppliers; (2) when production
must be started to meet its
demand by a particular date.

Once these ingredients are available and accurate, the next step is to construct a gross material requirements plan. The **gross material requirements plan** is a schedule, as shown in Example 2. It combines a master production schedule (that requires one unit of A in week 8) and the time-phased structure (Figure 14.4). It shows when an item must be ordered from suppliers if there is no inventory on hand or when the production of an item must be started to satisfy demand for the finished product by a particular date.

EXAMPLE 2 ▶

**Building a gross
requirements plan**

Each Awesome speaker kit (item A of Example 1) requires all the items in the product structure for A. Lead times are shown in Table 14.2.

APPROACH ▶   Using the information in Example 1 and Table 14.2, we construct the gross material requirements plan with a production schedule that will satisfy the demand of 50 units of A by week 8.

SOLUTION ▶   We prepare a schedule as shown in Table 14.3.

▶ TABLE 14.3

Gross Material Requirements
Plan for 50 Awesome Speaker
Kits

					Week					
		1	2	3	4	5	6	7	8	**Lead Time**
A.	Required date								50	
	Order release date							50		1 week
B.	Required date						100			
	Order release date				100					2 weeks
C.	Required date						150			
	Order release date					150				1 week
E.	Required date					200	300			
	Order release date			200	300					2 weeks
F.	Required date						300			
	Order release date			300						3 weeks
D.	Required date			600		200				
	Order release date		600		200					1 week
G.	Required date			300						
	Order release date	300								2 weeks

LO2: Build a gross
requirements plan

You can interpret the gross material requirements shown in Table 14.3 as follows: If you want 50 units of A at week 8, you must start assembling A in week 7. Thus, in week 7, you will need 100 units of B and 150 units of C. These two items take 2 weeks and 1 week, respectively, to produce. Production of B, therefore, should start in week 5, and production of C should start in week 6 (lead time subtracted from the required date for these items). Working backward, we can perform the same computations for all of the other items. Because D and E are used in two different places in Awesome speaker kits, there are two entries in each data record.

INSIGHT ▶ The gross material requirements plan shows when production of each item should begin and end in order to have 50 units of A at week 8. Management now has an initial plan.

LEARNING EXERCISE ▶ If the lead time for G decreases from 2 weeks to 1 week, what is the new order release date for G? [Answer: 300 in week 2.]

RELATED PROBLEMS ▶ 14.2, 14.4, 14.6, 14.8a

EXCEL OM Data File **Ch14Ex2.xls** can be found at MyOMLab.

So far, we have considered *gross material requirements*, which assumes that there is no inventory on hand. When there is inventory on hand, we prepare a **net material requirements plan**. When considering on-hand inventory, we must realize that many items in inventory contain subassemblies or parts. If the gross requirement for Awesome speaker kits is 100 and there are 20 of those speakers on hand, the net requirement for Awesome speaker kits is 80 (that is, 100 – 20). However, each Awesome speaker kit on hand contains 2 Bs. As a result, the requirement for Bs drops by 40 Bs. Therefore, if inventory is on hand for a parent item, the requirements for the parent item and all its components decrease because each Awesome speaker kit contains the components for lower-level items. Example 3 shows how to create a net material requirements plan.

Net material requirements plan
The result of adjusting gross requirements for inventory on hand and scheduled receipts.

◀ EXAMPLE 3
Determining net requirements

Medina Speakers Ltd. developed a product structure from a bill of material in Example 1. Example 2 developed a gross requirements plan. Given the following on-hand inventory, Medina Speakers Ltd. now wants to construct a net requirements plan.

Item	On Hand	Item	On Hand
A	10	E	10
B	15	F	5
C	20	G	0
D	10		

APPROACH ▶ A net material requirements plan includes gross requirements, on-hand inventory, net requirements, planned order receipt, and planned order release for each item. We begin with A and work backward through the components.

SOLUTION ▶ Shown in the chart below is the net material requirements plan for product A.

Constructing a net requirements plan is similar to constructing a gross requirements plan. Starting with item A, we work backward to determine net requirements for all items. To do these computations, we refer to the product structure, on-hand inventory, and lead times. The gross requirement for A is 50 units in week 8. Ten items are on hand; therefore, the net requirements and the scheduled **planned order receipt** are both 40 items in week 8. Because of the 1-week lead time, the **planned order release** is 40 items in week 7 (see the arrow connecting the order receipt and order release). Referring to week 7 and the product structure in Example 1, we can see that 80 (2 × 40) items of B and 120 (3 × 40) items of C are required in week 7 to have a total for 50 items of A in week 8. The letter superscripted A to the right of the gross figure for items B and C was generated as a result of the demand for the parent, A. Performing the same type of analysis for B and C yields the net requirements for D, E, F, and G. Note the on-hand inventory in row E in week 6 is zero. It is zero because the on-hand inventory (10 units) was used to make B in week 5. By the same token, the inventory for D was used to make F in week 3.

Planned order receipt
The quantity planned to be received at a future date.

Planned order release
The scheduled date for an order to be released.

INSIGHT ▶ Once a net requirement plan has been completed, management knows the quantities needed, and can draw up an ordering schedule, and a production schedule for each component.

Lot Size	Lead Time (weeks)	On Hand	Safety Stock	Allocated	Low-Level Code	Item Identification			Week 1	Week 2	Week 3	Week 4	Week 5	Week 6	Week 7	Week 8
Lot-for-Lot	1	10	—	—	0	A	Gross Requirements									50
							Scheduled Receipts									
							Projected On Hand	10	10	10	10	10	10	10	10	10
							Net Requirements									40
							Planned Order Receipts									40
							Planned Order Releases								40	
Lot-for-Lot	2	15	—	—	1	B	Gross Requirements								80^A	
							Scheduled Receipts									
							Projected On Hand	15	15	15	15	15	15	15	15	
							Net Requirements								65	
							Planned Order Receipts								65	
							Planned Order Releases						65			
Lot-for-Lot	1	20	—	—	1	C	Gross Requirements								120^A	
							Scheduled Receipts									
							Projected On Hand	20	20	20	20	20	20	20	20	
							Net Requirements								100	
							Planned Order Receipts								100	
							Planned Order Releases							100		
Lot-for-Lot	2	10	—	—	2	E	Gross Requirements							130^B	200^C	
							Scheduled Receipts									
							Projected On Hand	10	10	10	10	10	10			
							Net Requirements							120	200	
							Planned Order Receipts							120	200	
							Planned Order Releases					120	200			
Lot-for-Lot	3	5	—	—	2	F	Gross Requirements								200^C	
							Scheduled Receipts									
							Projected On Hand	5	5	5	5	5	5	5		
							Net Requirements								195	
							Planned Order Receipts								195	
							Planned Order Releases					195				
Lot-for-Lot	1	10	—	—	3	D	Gross Requirements						390^F		130^B	
							Scheduled Receipts									
							Projected On Hand	10	10	10	10					
							Net Requirements						380		130	
							Planned Order Receipts						380		130	
							Planned Order Releases					380		130		
Lot-for-Lot	2	0	—	—	3	G	Gross Requirements						195^F			
							Scheduled Receipts									
							Projected On Hand						0			
							Net Requirements						195			
							Planned Order Receipts						195			
							Planned Order Releases				195					

▲ FIGURE 14.6   Net Material Requirements Plan for Product A
The superscript is the source of the demand.

LEARNING EXERCISE ▶   If the on-hand inventory quantity of component F is 95 rather than 5, how many units of G will need to be ordered in week 1? [Answer: 105 units.]

RELATED PROBLEMS ▶   14.5, 14.7, 14.8b, 14.9

EXCEL OM Data File Ch14Ex3.xls can be found at MyOMLab.

Examples 2 and 3 considered only product A, the Awesome speaker kit, and its completion only in week 8. Fifty units of A were required in week 8. Normally, however, there is a demand for many products over time. For each product, management must prepare a master production schedule (as we saw earlier in Table 14.1). Scheduled production of each product is added to the

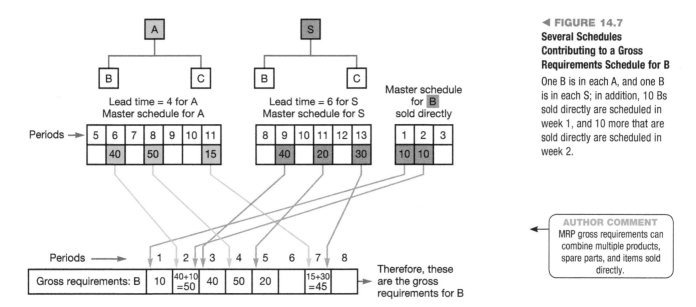

◀ **FIGURE 14.7**
Several Schedules Contributing to a Gross Requirements Schedule for B

One B is in each A, and one B is in each S; in addition, 10 Bs sold directly are scheduled in week 1, and 10 more that are sold directly are scheduled in week 2.

AUTHOR COMMENT
MRP gross requirements can combine multiple products, spare parts, and items sold directly.

master schedule and ultimately to the net material requirements plan. Figure 14.7 shows how several product schedules, including requirements for components sold directly, can contribute to one gross material requirements plan.

Most inventory systems also note the number of units in inventory that have been assigned to specific future production but not yet used or issued from the stockroom. Such items are often referred to as *allocated* items. Allocated items increase requirements and may then be included in an MRP planning sheet, as shown in Figure 14.8.

The allocated quantity has the effect of increasing the requirements (or, alternatively, reducing the quantity on hand). The logic, then, of a net requirements MRP is:

$$\underbrace{[(\text{Gross requirements}) + (\text{Allocations})]}_{\text{Total requirements}} - \underbrace{[(\text{On hand}) + (\text{Scheduled receipts})]}_{\text{Available inventory}} = \frac{\text{Net}}{\text{requirements}}$$

LO3: Build a net requirements plan

Safety Stock

The continuing task of operations managers is to remove variability. This is the case in MRP systems as in other operations systems. Realistically, however, managers need to realize that bills of material and inventory records, like purchase and production quantities, as well as lead times, may not be perfect. This means that some consideration of safety stock may be prudent. Because of the significant domino effect of any change in requirements, safety stock should be minimized, with a goal of ultimate elimination. When safety stock is deemed absolutely necessary, the usual policy is to build it into the projected on-hand inventory of the MRP logic. Distortion can be minimized when safety stock is held at the finished goods level and at the purchased component or raw material level.

Lot Size	Lead Time	On Hand	Safety Stock	Allocated	Low-Level Code	Item ID		Period							
								1	2	3	4	5	6	7	8
Lot For Lot	1	0	0	10	0	Z	Gross Requirements								80 90
							Scheduled Receipts								0
							Projected On Hand 0	0	0	0	0	0	0	0	0
							Net Requirements								90
							Planned Order Receipts								90
							Planned Order Releases							90	

▲ **FIGURE 14.8** **Sample MRP Planning Sheet for Item Z**

MRP MANAGEMENT

The material requirements plan is not static. And since MRP systems increasingly are integrated with just-in-time (JIT) techniques, we now discuss these two issues.

MRP Dynamics

Bills of material and material requirements plans are altered as changes in design, schedules, and production processes occur. In addition, changes occur in material requirements whenever the master production schedule is modified. Regardless of the cause of any changes, the MRP model can be manipulated to reflect them. In this manner, an up-to-date requirements schedule is possible.

The inputs to MRP (the master schedule, bill of material, lead times, purchasing, and inventory) frequently change. Conveniently, a central strength of MRP systems is timely and accurate replanning. This occurs in one of two ways: by recomputing (also known as 'regenerating') the requirement and schedule periodically, often weekly, or via a 'net change' calculation. Net change in an MRP system means that the MRP system creates new requirements in response to transactions. However, many firms do not want to respond to minor scheduling or quantity changes even if they are aware of them. These frequent changes generate what is called **system nervousness** and can create havoc in purchasing and production departments if implemented. Consequently, OM personnel reduce such nervousness by evaluating the need and impact of changes prior to disseminating requests to other departments. Two tools are particularly helpful when trying to reduce MRP system nervousness.

The first is time fences. **Time fences** allow a segment of the master schedule to be designated as 'not to be rescheduled.' This segment of the master schedule is therefore not changed during the periodic regeneration of schedules. The second tool is pegging. **Pegging** means tracing upward in the bill of material from the component to the parent item. By pegging upward, the production planner can determine the cause for the requirement and make a judgment about the necessity for a change in the schedule.

With MRP, the operations manager *can* react to the dynamics of the real world. How frequently the manager wishes to impose those changes on the firm requires professional judgment. Moreover, if the nervousness is caused by legitimate changes, then the proper response may be to investigate the production environment—not adjust via MRP.

System nervousness
Frequent changes in an MRP system.

Time fences
A means for allowing a segment of the master schedule to be designated as 'not to be rescheduled.'

Pegging
In material requirements planning systems, tracing upward in the bill of material from the component to the parent item.

MRP and JIT

MRP does not do detailed scheduling—it plans. MRP will tell you that a job needs to be completed on a certain week or day but does not tell you that Job X needs to run on Machine A at 10.30 a.m. and be completed by 11.30 a.m. so that Job X can then run on Machine B. MRP is also a planning technique with *fixed* lead times. Fixed lead times can be a limitation. For instance, the lead time to produce 50 units may vary substantially from the lead time to produce 5 units. These limitations complicate the marriage of MRP and just-in-time (JIT). What is needed is a way to make MRP more responsive to moving material rapidly in small batches. An MRP system combined with JIT can provide the best of both worlds. MRP provides the plan and an accurate picture of requirements; then JIT rapidly moves material in small batches, reducing work-in-process inventory. Let's look at four approaches for integrating MRP and JIT: finite capacity scheduling, small buckets, balanced flow, and supermarkets.

Finite Capacity Scheduling (FCS) Most MRP software loads work into infinite size 'buckets.' The **buckets** are time units, usually one week. Traditionally, when work is to be done in a given week, MRP puts the work there without regard to capacity. Consequently, MRP is considered an *infinite* scheduling technique. Frequently, as you might suspect, this is not realistic. Finite capacity scheduling (FCS), which we discuss in Chapter 15, considers department and machine capacity, which is *finite*, hence the name. FCS provides the precise scheduling needed for rapid material movement. We are now witnessing a convergence of FCS and MRP. Sophisticated FCS systems modify the output from MRP systems to provide a finite schedule.

Buckets
Time units in a material requirements planning system.

Small Bucket Approach MRP is an excellent tool for resource and scheduling management in process-focused facilities, that is, in job shops. Such facilities include machine shops, hospitals, and restaurants, where lead times are relatively stable and poor balance between work centers is expected. Schedules are often driven by work orders, and lot sizes are the exploded bill-of-material size. In these enterprises, MRP can be integrated with JIT through the following steps.

STEP 1: Reduce MRP 'buckets' from weekly to daily to perhaps hourly. Buckets are time units in an MRP system. Although the examples in this chapter have used weekly *time buckets,* many firms now use daily or even fraction-of-a-day time buckets. Some systems use a **bucketless system** in which all time-phased data have dates attached rather than defined time periods or buckets.

STEP 2: The planned receipts that are part of a firm's planned orders in an MRP system are communicated to the work areas for production purposes and used to sequence production.

STEP 3: Inventory is moved through the plant on a JIT basis.

STEP 4: As products are completed, they are moved into inventory (typically finished-goods inventory) in the normal way. Receipt of these products into inventory reduces the quantities required for subsequent planned orders in the MRP system.

STEP 5: A system known as *back flush* is used to reduce inventory balances. **Back flushing** uses the bill of material to deduct component quantities from inventory as each unit is completed.

Bucketless system
Time-phased data are referenced using dated records rather than defined time periods, or buckets.

Back flush
A system to reduce inventory balances by deducting everything in the bill of material on completion of the unit.

The focus in these facilities becomes one of maintaining schedules. Nissan achieves success with this approach by computer communication links to suppliers. These schedules are confirmed, updated, or changed every 15 to 20 minutes. Suppliers provide deliveries 4 to 16 times per day. Master schedule performance is 99 percent on time, as measured every hour. On-time delivery from suppliers is 99.9 percent and for manufactured piece parts, 99.5 percent.

Balanced Flow Approach MRP supports the planning and scheduling necessary for repetitive operations, such as the assembly lines at Egyptian German Automotive and a thousand other places. In these environments, the planning portion of MRP is combined with JIT execution. The JIT portion uses kanbans, visual signals, and reliable suppliers to pull the material through the facility. In these systems, execution is achieved by maintaining a carefully balanced flow of material to assembly areas with small lot sizes.

Supermarket Another technique that joins MRP and JIT is the use of a 'supermarket.' In many firms, subassemblies, their components, and hardware items are common to a variety of products. In such cases, releasing orders for these common items with traditional lead-time offset, as is done in an MRP system, is not necessary. The subassemblies, components, and hardware items can be maintained in a common area, sometimes called a **supermarket**, adjacent to the production areas where they are used.

Supermarket
An inventory area that holds common items that are replenished by a kanban system.

LOT-SIZING TECHNIQUES

An MRP system is an excellent way to determine production schedules and net requirements. However, whenever we have a net requirement, a decision must be made about *how much* to order. This decision is called a **lot-sizing decision**. There are a variety of ways to determine lot sizes in an MRP system; commercial MRP software usually includes the choice of several lot-sizing techniques. We now review a few of them.

AUTHOR COMMENT
Managers need to know how to group/order the 'planned order releases.'

Lot-sizing decision
The process of, or techniques used in, determining lot size.

Lot-for-Lot

In Example 3, we used a lot-sizing technique known as **lot-for-lot**, which produced exactly what was required. This decision is consistent with the objective of an MRP system, which is to meet the requirements of *dependent* demand. Thus, an MRP system should produce units only as needed, with no safety stock and no anticipation of further orders. When frequent orders are economical and JIT inventory techniques implemented, lot-for-lot can be very efficient. However, when setup costs are significant or management has been unable to implement JIT, lot-for-lot can be expensive. Example 4 uses the lot-for-lot criteria and determines cost for 10 weeks of demand.

Lot-for-lot
A lot-sizing technique that generates exactly what is required to meet the plan.

Lot sizing with lot-for-lot

Medina Speakers Ltd. wants to compute its ordering and carrying cost of inventory on lot-for-lot criteria.

APPROACH ▶ With lot-for-lot, we order material only as it is needed. Once we have the cost of ordering (setting up), the cost of holding each unit for a given time period, and the production schedule, we can assign orders to our net requirements plan.

SOLUTION ▶ Medina Speakers Ltd. has determined that, for the 30 cm speaker unit, setup cost is US$100 and holding cost is US$1 per period. The production schedule, as reflected in net requirements for assemblies, is as follows:

MRP Lot Sizing: Lot-for-Lot Technique*

		1	2	3	4	5	6	7	8	9	10
Gross requirements		35	30	40	0	10	40	30	0	30	55
Scheduled receipts											
Projected on hand	35	35	0	0	0	0	0	0	0	0	0
Net requirements		0	30	40	0	10	40	30	0	30	55
Planned order receipts			30	40		10	40	30		30	55
Planned order releases		30	40		10	40	30		30	55	

*Holding costs = US$1/unit/week; setup cost = US$100; gross requirements average per week = 27; lead time = 1 week.

The lot-sizing solution using the lot-for-lot technique is shown in the table. The holding cost is zero as there is never any inventory. (Inventory in the first period is used immediately and therefore has no holding cost.) But seven separate setups (one associated with each order) yield a total cost of US$700. (Holding cost = $0 \times 1 = 0$; ordering cost = $7 \times 100 = $US$700.)

INSIGHT ▶ When supply is reliable and frequent orders are inexpensive, but holding cost or obsolescence is high, lot-for-lot ordering can be very efficient.

LEARNING EXERCISE ▶ What is the impact on total cost if holding cost is US$2 per period rather than US$1? [Answer: Total holding cost remains zero, as no units are held from one period to the next with lot-for-lot.]

RELATED PROBLEMS ▶ 14.10

Economic Order Quantity

As discussed in Chapter 12, EOQ can be used as a lot-sizing technique. But as we indicated there, EOQ is preferable when *relatively constant* independent demand exists, not when we *know* the demand. EOQ is a statistical technique using averages (such as average demand for a year), whereas the MRP procedure assumes *known* (dependent) demand reflected in a master production schedule. Operations managers should take advantage of demand information when it is known, rather than assuming a constant demand. EOQ is examined in Example 5.

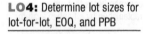

LO4: Determine lot sizes for lot-for-lot, EOQ, and PPB

This Nissan line in Tennessee, has little inventory because Nissan schedules to a razor's edge. At Nissan, MRP helps reduce inventory to world-class standards. World-class automobile assembly requires that purchased parts have a turnover of slightly more than once a day and that overall turnover approaches 150 times per year.

With a setup cost of US$100 and a holding cost per week of US$1, Medina Speakers Ltd. wants to examine its cost with lot sizes based on an EOQ criteria.

APPROACH ▶   Using the same cost and production schedule as in Example 4, we determine net requirements and EOQ lot sizes.

SOLUTION ▶   Ten-week usage equals a gross requirement of 270 units; therefore, weekly usage equals 27, and 52 weeks (annual usage) equals 1,404 units. From Chapter 12, the EOQ model is:

$$Q^* = \sqrt{\frac{2DS}{H}}$$

where

D = annual usage = 1,404
S = setup cost = US$100
H = holding (carrying) cost, on an annual basis per unit
  = US$1 × 52 weeks = US$52

$$Q^* = 73 \text{ units}$$

MRP Lot Sizing: EOQ Technique*

		1	2	3	4	5	6	7	8	9	10
Gross requirements		35	30	40	0	10	40	30	0	30	55
Scheduled receipts											
Projected on hand	35	35	0	43	3	3	66	26	69	69	39
Net requirements		0	30	0	0	7	0	4	0	0	16
Planned order receipts			73			73		73			73
Planned order releases		73			73		73		73		

*Holding costs = US$1/unit/week; setup cost = US$100; gross requirements average per week = 27; lead time = 1 week.

$$\text{Setups} = 1,404 \div 73 = 19 \text{ per year}$$

$$\text{Annual Setup cost} = 19 \times \text{US}\$100 = \text{US}\$1,900$$

$$\text{Annual Holding cost} = \frac{73}{2} \times (\text{US}\$1 \times 52 \text{ weeks}) = \text{US}\$1,898$$

$$\text{Annual Setup cost} + \text{Holding cost} = \text{US}\$1,900 + \text{US}\$1,898 = \text{US}\$3,798$$

The EOQ solution yields a computed 10-week cost of US$730 [US$3,798 × (10 weeks ÷ 52 weeks) = US$730].

INSIGHT ▶   EOQ can be an effective lot-sizing technique when demand is relatively constant. However, notice that actual holding cost will vary from the computed US$730, depending on the rate of actual usage. From the preceding table, we can see that in our 10-week example, costs really are US$400 for four setups, plus a holding cost of 375 units (includes 57 remaining at the end of the period) at US$1 per week for a total of US$775. Because usage was not constant, the actual computed cost was in fact more than the theoretical EOQ (US$730) and the lot-for-lot rule (US$700). If any stockouts had occurred, these costs too would need to be added to our actual EOQ cost of US$775.

LEARNING EXERCISE ▶   What is the impact on total cost if holding cost is US$2 per period rather than US$1? [Answer: The EOQ quantity becomes 52, the theoretical annual total cost becomes US$5,404, and the 10-week cost is US$1,039 (US$5,404 × (10 ÷ 52)).]

RELATED PROBLEMS ▶   14.11

Part Period Balancing

Part period balancing (PPB) is a more dynamic approach to balance setup and holding cost.[3] PPB uses additional information by changing the lot size to reflect requirements of the next lot size in the future. PPB attempts to balance setup and holding cost for known demands. Part

Part period balancing (PPB)

An inventory ordering technique that balances setup and holding costs by changing the lot size to reflect requirements of the next lot size in the future.

[3]J. J. DeMatteis, "An Economic Lot-Sizing Technique: The Part-Period Algorithms," *IBM Systems Journal* 7 (1968): 30–38.

Economic part period (EPP)

A period of time when the ratio of setup cost to holding cost is equal.

period balancing develops an **economic part period (EPP)**, which is the ratio of setup cost to holding cost. For our Medina Speakers Ltd. example, EPP = US\$100 ÷ US\$1 = 100 units. Therefore, holding 100 units for one period would cost US\$100, exactly the cost of one setup. Similarly, holding 50 units for two periods also costs US\$100 (2 periods × US\$1 × 50 units). PPB merely adds requirements until the number of part periods approximates the EPP—in this case, 100. Example 6 shows the application of part period balancing.

EXAMPLE 6 ▶

Lot sizing with part period balancing

Medina Speakers Ltd. wants to compute the costs associated with lot sizing using part period balancing. It will use a setup cost of US\$100 and a US\$1 holding cost.

APPROACH ▶ Using the same costs and production schedule as Examples 3 and 4, we develop a format that helps us compute the PPB quantity and apply that to our net requirements plan.

SOLUTION ▶ The procedure for computing the order releases of 80, 100, and 55 is shown in the following PPB calculation. In the second table, we apply the PPB order quantities to the net requirements plan.

PPB Calculations

Periods Combined	Trial Lot Size (cumulative net requirements)	Part Periods	Costs (US\$) Setup	Costs (US\$) Holding	Costs (US\$) Total
2	30	0		40 units held for 1 period = 40	
2, 3	70	$40 = 40 \times 1$		10 units held for 3 periods = 30	
2, 3, 4	70	40			
2, 3, 4, 5	80	$70 = 40 \times 1 + 10 \times 3$	100 +	70	= 170
2, 3, 4, 5, 6	120	$230 = 40 \times 1 + 10 \times 3 + 40 \times 4$			

(Therefore, combine periods 2 through 5; 70 is as close to our EPP of 100 as we are going to get.)

6	40	0			
6, 7	70	$30 = 30 \times 1$			
6, 7, 8	70	$30 = 30 \times 1 + 0 \times 2$			
6, 7, 8, 9	100	$120 = 30 \times 1 + 30 \times 3$	100 +	120	= 220

(Therefore, combine periods 6 through 9; 120 is as close to our EPP of 100 as we are going to get.)

10	55	0	100 +	0	= 100
			300 +	190	= 490

MRP Lot Sizing: PPB Technique*

		1	2	3	4	5	6	7	8	9	10
Gross requirements		35	30	40	0	10	40	30	0	30	55
Scheduled receipts											
Projected on hand	35	35	0	50	10	10	0	60	30	30	0
Net requirements		0	30	0	0	0	40	0	0	0	55
Planned order receipts			80				100				55
Planned order releases		80				100				55	

*Holding costs = US\$1/unit/week; setup cost = US\$100; gross requirements average per week = 27; lead time = 1 week.

EPP is 100 (setup cost divided by holding cost = US\$100 ÷ US\$1). The first lot is to cover periods 2, 3, 4, and 5 and is 80.

The total costs are US\$490, with setup costs totaling US\$300 and holding costs totaling US\$190.

INSIGHT ▶ Both the EOQ and PPB approaches to lot sizing balance holding cost and ordering cost. But PPB places an order each time holding cost equals ordering cost, while EOQ takes a longer averaging approach.

LEARNING EXERCISE ▶ What is the impact on total cost if holding cost is US\$2 per period rather than US\$1? [Answer: With higher holding costs [PPB becomes 100 ÷ 2 = 50], reorder points become more frequent, with orders now being placed for 70 units in period 1, 50 in period 4, 60 in period 6, and 55 in period 9.]

RELATED PROBLEMS ▶ 14.12

Wagner–Whitin Procedure

The **Wagner–Whitin procedure** is a dynamic programming model that adds some complexity to the lot-size computation. It assumes a finite time horizon beyond which there are no additional net requirements. It does, however, provide good results.[4]

Lot-Sizing Summary

In the three Medina Speakers lot-sizing examples, we found the following costs:

Lot-for-lot	US$700
EOQ	US$730
Part period balancing	US$490

These examples should not, however, lead operations personnel to hasty conclusions about the preferred lot-sizing technique. In theory, new lot sizes should be computed whenever there is a schedule or lot-size change anywhere in the MRP hierarchy, because cost optimization only happens at the top level and negative cost implications of the lot-sizing decision at lower levels is ignored. However, in practice, such changes cause the instability and system nervousness referred to earlier in this chapter. Consequently, such frequent changes are not made. This means that all lot sizes are wrong because the production system cannot respond to frequent changes.

In general, lot-sizing in MRP is avoided; the lot-for-lot approach should be used whenever low-cost deliveries can be achieved. Lot-for-lot is the goal. Lots can be modified as necessary for scrap allowances, process constraints (for example, a heat-treating process may require a lot of a given size), or raw material purchase lots (for example, a truckload of chemicals may be available in only one lot size). However, caution should be exercised prior to any modification of lot size because the modification can cause substantial distortion of actual requirements at lower levels in the MRP hierarchy. When setup costs are significant and demand is reasonably smooth, PPB, Wagner–Whitin, or even EOQ should provide satisfactory results. Too much concern with lot sizing yields false accuracy because of MRP dynamics. A correct lot size can be determined only after the fact, based on what actually happened in terms of requirements. And that is the reason why in current operations management practice to avoid lot-sizing, if possible, in MRP.

EXTENSIONS OF MRP

In this section, we review three extensions of MRP.

Material Requirements Planning II (MRP II)

Material requirements planning II (MRP II) is an extremely powerful technique. Once a firm has MRP in place, requirements data can be enriched by resources other than just components. When MRP is used this way, *resource* is usually substituted for *requirements*, and MRP becomes MRP II. It then stands for material *resource* planning.

So far in our discussion of MRP, we have scheduled products and their components. However, products require many resources, such as energy and money, beyond the product's tangible components. In addition to these resource inputs, *outputs* can be generated as well. Outputs can include such things as scrap, packaging waste, effluent, and carbon emissions. As OM becomes increasingly sensitive to the environmental and sustainability issues, identifying and managing by-products becomes increasingly important. MRP II provides a vehicle for doing so. Table 14.5 provides an example of labor-hours, machine-hours, weight of scrap, and cash, in the format of a gross requirements plan. With MRP II, management can identify the inputs and outputs, as well as the relevant schedule. MRP II provides another tool in OM's battle for sustainable operations.

Wagner–Whitin procedure

A technique for lot-size computation that assumes a finite time horizon beyond which there are no additional net requirements to arrive at an ordering strategy.

◄ **TABLE 14.4**

Costs of ordering and carrying stock for Medina Speakers Ltd. using different lot-sizing techniques.

Material requirements planning II (MRP II)

A system that allows, with MRP in place, inventory data to be augmented by other resource variables; in this case, MRP becomes material resource planning.

LO5: Describe MRP II

---

[4]We leave discussion of the algorithm to mathematical programming texts. The Wagner–Whitin algorithm yields a cost of US$455 for the data in Examples 4, 5, and 6.

Many MRP programs, such as *Resource Manager for Excel* and *DB*, are commercially available. *Resource Manager's* initial menu screen is shown here. A demo program is available for student use at **www.usersolutions.com**.

▶ **TABLE 14.5**

Material Resource Planning (MRP II)

By utilizing the logic of MRP, resources such as labor, machine-hours, scrap, and cost can be accurately determined and scheduled. Weekly demand for labor, machine-hours, scrap, and payables for 100 computers are shown.

	Lead Time	Weeks			
		5	6	7	8
Computer	1				100
Labor-hours: 0.2 each					20
Machine-hours: 0.2 each					20
Scrap: 28 g fiberglass each					2.8 kg
Payables: US$0					US$0
PC board (1 each)	2			100	
Labor-hours: 0.15 each				15	
Machine-hours: 0.1 each				10	
Scrap: 14 g copper each				1.5 kg	
Payables: raw material at US$5 each				US$500	
Processors (5 each)	4	500			
Labor-hours: 0.2 each		100			
Machine-hours: 0.2 each		100			
Scrap: 0.28 g of acid waste each		0.1418 kg			
Payables: processors at US$10 each		US$5,000			

Closed-loop MRP system

A system that provides feedback to the capacity plan, master production schedule, and production plan so planning can be kept valid at all times.

LO6: Describe closed-loop MRP

Load report

A report showing the resource requirements in a work center for all work currently assigned there as well as all planned and expected orders.

MRP II systems are seldom stand-alone programs. Most are tied into other computer software that provides data to the MRP system or receives data from the MRP system. Purchasing, production scheduling, capacity planning, inventory, and warehouse management are a few examples of this data integration.

Closed-Loop MRP

Closed-loop material requirements planning implies an MRP system that provides feedback to scheduling from the inventory control system. Specifically, a **closed-loop MRP system** provides information to the capacity plan, master production schedule, and ultimately to the production plan (as shown in Figure 14.9). Virtually all commercial MRP systems are closed-loop.

Capacity Planning

In keeping with the definition of closed-loop MRP, feedback about workload is obtained from each work center. **Load reports** show the resource requirements in a work center for all work

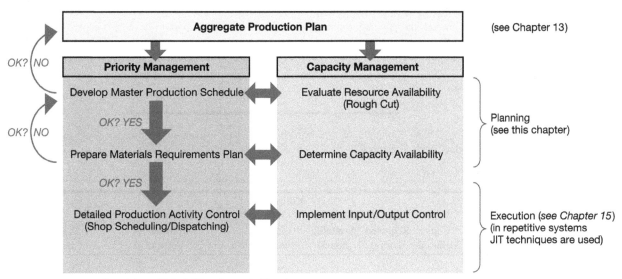

▲ **FIGURE 14.9**   **Closed-Loop Material Requirements Planning**

currently assigned to the work center, all work planned, and expected orders. Figure 14.10(a) shows that the initial load in the milling center exceeds capacity on days 2, 3, and 5. Closed-loop MRP systems allow production planners to move the work between time periods to smooth the load or at least bring it within capacity. (This is the 'capacity planning' part of Figure 14.9.) The closed-loop MRP system can then reschedule all items in the net requirements plan (see Figure 14.10[b]).

Tactics for smoothing the load and minimizing the impact of changed lead time include the following:

1. *Overlapping*, which reduces the lead time, sends pieces to the second operation before the entire lot is completed on the first operation.
2. *Operations splitting* sends the lot to two different machines for the same operation. This involves an additional setup, but results in shorter throughput times, because only part of the lot is processed on each machine.
3. *Order* or, *lot splitting*, involves breaking up the order and running part of it earlier (or later) in the schedule.

Example 7 shows a brief detailed capacity scheduling example using order splitting to improve utilization.

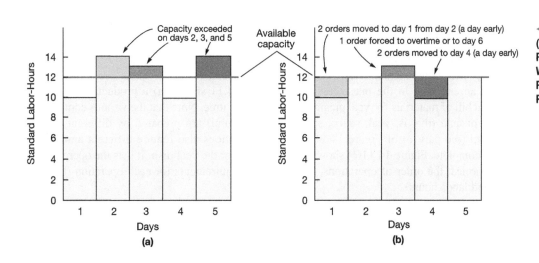

◀ **FIGURE 14.10**
(a) Initial Resource Requirements Profile for a Work Center (b) Smoothed Resource Requirements Profile for a Work Center

EXAMPLE 7 ▶
Order splitting

Omar Dawood, the production planner at Manama Products, needs to develop a capacity plan for a work center. He has the production orders shown below for the next 5 days. There are 12 hours available in the work cell each day. The parts being produced require 1 hour each.

Day	1	2	3	4	5
Orders	10	14	13	10	14

APPROACH ▶ Compute the time available in the work center and the time necessary to complete the production requirements.

SOLUTION ▶

Day	Units Ordered	Capacity Required (hours)	Capacity Available (hours)	Utilization: Over/ (Under) (hours)	Production Planner's Action	New Production Schedule
1	10	10	12	(2)		12
2	14	14	12	2	Split order: move 2 units to day 1	12
3	13	13	12	1	Split order: move 1 unit to day 6 or request overtime	13
4	10	10	12	(2)		12
5	14	14	12	2	Split order: move 2 units to day 4	12
	61					

INSIGHT ▶ By moving orders, the production planner is able to utilize capacity more effectively and still meet the order requirements, with only one order produced on overtime in day 3.

LEARNING EXERCISE ▶ If the units ordered for day 5 increase to 16, what are the production planner's options? [Answer: In addition to moving two units to day 4, move two units of production to day 6, or request overtime.]

RELATED PROBLEMS ▶ 14.15, 14.16, 14.17 in MyOMLab.

When the workload consistently exceeds work-center capacity, the tactics just discussed are not adequate. This may mean adding capacity. Options include adding capacity via personnel, machinery, overtime, or subcontracting.

MRP IN SERVICES

The demand for many services or service items is classified as dependent demand when it is directly related to or derived from the demand for other services. Such services often require product-structure trees, bills of material and labor, and scheduling. MRP can make a major contribution to operational performance in such services. Examples from restaurants, hospitals, and hotels follow.

Restaurants   In restaurants, ingredients and side dishes (bread, vegetables, and condiments) are typically meal components. These components are dependent on the demand for meals. The meal is an end item in the master schedule. Figure 14.11 shows (a) a product-structure tree and (b) a bill of materials for veal picante, a top-selling entrée. Note that the various components of veal picante (that is, veal, sauce, spinach, and linguini) are prepared by different kitchen personnel (see part [a] of Figure 14.11). These preparations also require different amounts of time to complete. Figure 14.11(c) shows a bill of labor for the veal dish. It lists the operations to be performed, the order of operations, and the labor requirements for each operation (types of labor and labor-hours).

Hospitals   MRP is also applied in hospitals, especially when dealing with surgeries that require known equipment, materials, and supplies. Baghdad Surgical Hospital and many hospital suppliers, for example, use the technique to improve the scheduling and management of expensive surgical inventory.

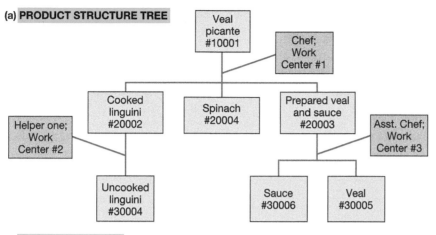

(a) PRODUCT STRUCTURE TREE

◄ **FIGURE 14.11**

Product Structure Tree, Bill of Material, and Bill of Labor for Veal Picante

Source: Adapted from John G. Wacker, "Effective Planning and Cost Control for Restaurants," *Production and Inventory Management* (Vol. 26, no. 1): 60. Reprinted by permission of American Production and Inventory Control Society.

(b) BILL OF MATERIALS

Part Number	Description	Quantity	Unit of Measure	Unit Cost
10001	Veal picante	1	Serving	—
20002	Cooked linguini	1	Serving	—
20003	Prepared veal and sauce	1	Serving	—
20004	Spinach	0.1	Bag	0.94
30004	Uncooked linguini	0.5	Pound	—
30005	Veal	1	Serving	2.15
30006	Sauce	1	Serving	0.80

(c) BILL OF LABOR FOR VEAL PICANTE

Work Center	Operation	Labor Type	Labor-Hours Setup Time	Labor-Hours Run Time
1	Assemble dish	Chef	0.0069	0.0041
2	Cook linguini	Helper one	0.0005	0.0022
3	Cook veal and sauce	Assistant chef	0.0125	0.0500

Hotels   Jumeira Hotels develops a bill of materials and a bill of labor when it renovates each of its hotel rooms. Jumeira managers explode the bill of materials to compute requirements for materials, furniture, and decorations. MRP then provides net requirements and a schedule for use by purchasing and contractors.

Distribution Resource Planning

When dependent techniques are used in the supply chain, they are called distribution resource planning (DRP). **Distribution resource planning (DRP)** is a time-phased stock-replenishment plan for all levels of the supply chain.

DRP procedures and logic are analogous to MRP. With DRP, expected demand becomes gross requirements. Net requirements are determined by allocating available inventory to gross requirements. The DRP procedure starts with the forecast at the retail level (or the most distant point of the distribution network being supplied). All other levels are computed. As is the case with MRP, inventory is then reviewed with an aim to satisfy demand. So that stock will arrive when it is needed, net requirements are offset by the necessary lead time. A planned order release quantity becomes the gross requirement at the next level down the distribution chain.

DRP *pulls* inventory through the system. Pulls are initiated when the retail level orders more stock. Allocations are made to the retail level from available inventory and production after being adjusted to obtain shipping economies. Effective use of DRP requires an integrated information system to rapidly convey planned order releases from one level to the next. The goal of the DRP system is small and frequent replenishment within the bounds of economical ordering and shipping.[5]

Distribution resource planning (DRP)

A time-phased stock-replenishment plan for all levels of a distribution network.

[5]For an expanded discussion of time-phased stock-replenishment plans, see the section 'Opportunities in an Integrated Supply Chain' (page 337).

**Enterprise resource
planning (ERP)**

An information system for
identifying and planning the
enterprise-wide resources needed
to take, make, ship, and account
for customer orders.

ENTERPRISE RESOURCE PLANNING

Advances in MRP II systems that tie customers and suppliers to MRP II have led to the development of enterprise resource planning (ERP) systems. **Enterprise resource planning (ERP)** is software that allows companies to: (1) automate and integrate many of their business processes; (2) share a common database and business practices throughout the enterprise; (3) produce information in real time. A schematic showing some of these relationships for a manufacturing firm appears in Figure 14.12.

The objective of an ERP system is to coordinate a firm's whole business, from supplier evaluation to customer invoicing. This objective is seldom achieved, but ERP systems are evolving as umbrella systems that tie together a variety of specialized systems. This is accomplished by using a centralized database to assist the flow of information among business functions. Exactly what is tied together, and how, varies on a case-by-case basis. In addition to the traditional components of MRP, ERP systems usually provide financial and human resource (HR) management information. ERP systems also include:

LO7: Describe ERP

- *Supply-chain management (SCM)* software to support sophisticated vendor communication, e-commerce, and those activities necessary for efficient warehousing and logistics. The idea is to tie operations (MRP) to procurement, to materials management, and to suppliers, providing the tools necessary for effective management of all four areas.
- *Customer relationship management (CRM)* software for the incoming side of the business. CRM is designed to aid analysis of sales, target the most profitable customers, and manage the sales force.

▶ **FIGURE 14.12**
**MRP and ERP Information
Flows, Showing Customer
Relationship Management
(CRM), Supply-Chain
Management (SCM), and
Finance/Accounting**

Other functions such as
human resources are often also
included in ERP systems.

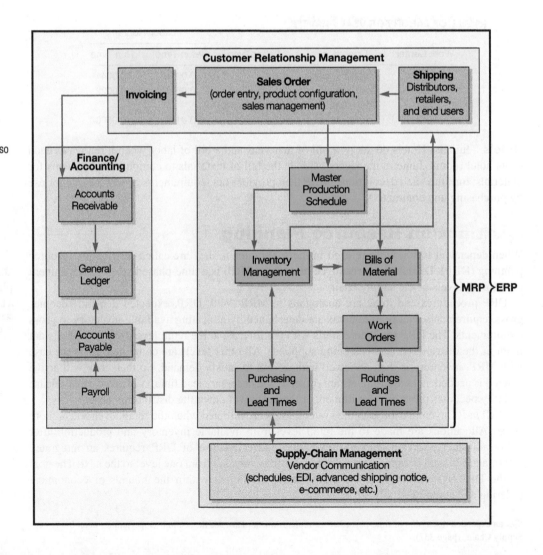

In addition to data integration, ERP software promises reduced transaction costs and fast, accurate information. A strategic emphasis on just-in-time systems and supply-chain integration drives the desire for enterprise-wide software. The *OM in Action* box 'Managing Benetton with ERP Software' provides an example of how ERP software helps integrate company operations.

OM in Action ▶ Managing Benetton with ERP Software

Thanks to ERP, the Italian clothing company Benetton can probably claim to have the world's fastest factory and the most efficient distribution in the garment industry. Located in Ponzano, Italy, Benetton makes and ships 50 million pieces of clothing each year. That is 30,000 boxes every day—boxes that must be filled with exactly the items ordered going to the correct store of the 5,000 Benetton outlets in 60 countries. This highly automated distribution center uses only 19 people. Without ERP, hundreds of people would be needed.

Here is how ERP software works:

1. *Ordering:* A salesperson in the south Boston, MA store finds that she is running out of a best-selling blue sweater. Using a laptop PC, her local Benetton sales agent taps into the ERP sales module.
2. *Availability:* ERP's inventory software simultaneously forwards the order to the mainframe in Italy and finds that half the order can be filled immediately from the Italian warehouse. The rest will be manufactured and shipped in 4 weeks.
3. *Production:* Because the blue sweater was originally created by computer-aided design (CAD), ERP

manufacturing software passes the specifications to a knitting machine. The knitting machine makes the sweaters.

4. *Warehousing:* The blue sweaters are boxed with a radio frequency ID (RFID) tag addressed to the Boston store and placed in one of the 300,000 slots in the Italian warehouse. A robot flies by, reading RFID tags, picks out any and all boxes ready for the Boston store, and loads them for shipment.
5. *Order tracking:* The Boston salesperson logs onto the ERP system through the internet and sees that the sweaters (and other items) are completed and being shipped.
6. *Planning:* Based on data from ERP's forecasting and financial modules, Benetton's chief buyer decides that blue sweaters are in high demand and quite profitable. She decides to add three new hues.

Sources: The Wall Street Journal (April 10, 2007): B1; *Frontline Solutions* (April 2003): 54; and *MIT Sloan Management Review* (Fall 2001): 46–53.

In an ERP system, data are entered only once into a common, complete, and consistent database shared by all applications. Each ERP vendor produces unique products. The major vendors, ASWAQ6 by Ajyal (a Kuwaiti firm), SAP AG (a German firm), BEA (Canada), and SSAGlobal, American Software, PeopleSoft/Oracle, and CMS Software (all of the United States), sell software or modules designed for specific industries (a set of SAP's modules is shown in Figure 14.13). However, companies must determine if their way of doing business will fit the standard ERP module. If they determine that the product will not fit the standard ERP product, they can change the way they do business to accommodate the software. But such a change can have an adverse impact on their business process, reducing competitive advantage. Alternatively, ERP software can be customized to meet companies' specific process requirements. Although the vendors build the software to keep the customization process simple, many companies spend up to five times the cost of the software to customize it. In addition to the expense, the major downside of customization is that when ERP vendors provide an upgrade or enhancement to the software, the customized part of the code must be rewritten to fit into the new version.

ERP programs cost from a minimum of US$300,000 for a small company to hundreds of millions of US dollars for global giants like Almarai, Ford, and Coca-Cola. It is easy to see, then, that ERP systems are expensive, full of hidden issues, and time-consuming to install. However, plug-and-play modules are now providing a solution to these issues as they allow ERP implementation to move away from the earlier SAP approach. Plug-and-play modules save time and are considered simpler to use, with the added benefit of being cheaper due to the lower cost of purchasing. Additionally, they don't require significant IT intervention, which makes them very suitable for small-to-medium enterprises (SMEs) who need to apply them in order to respond to globalization, but don't have the necessary IT support departments.

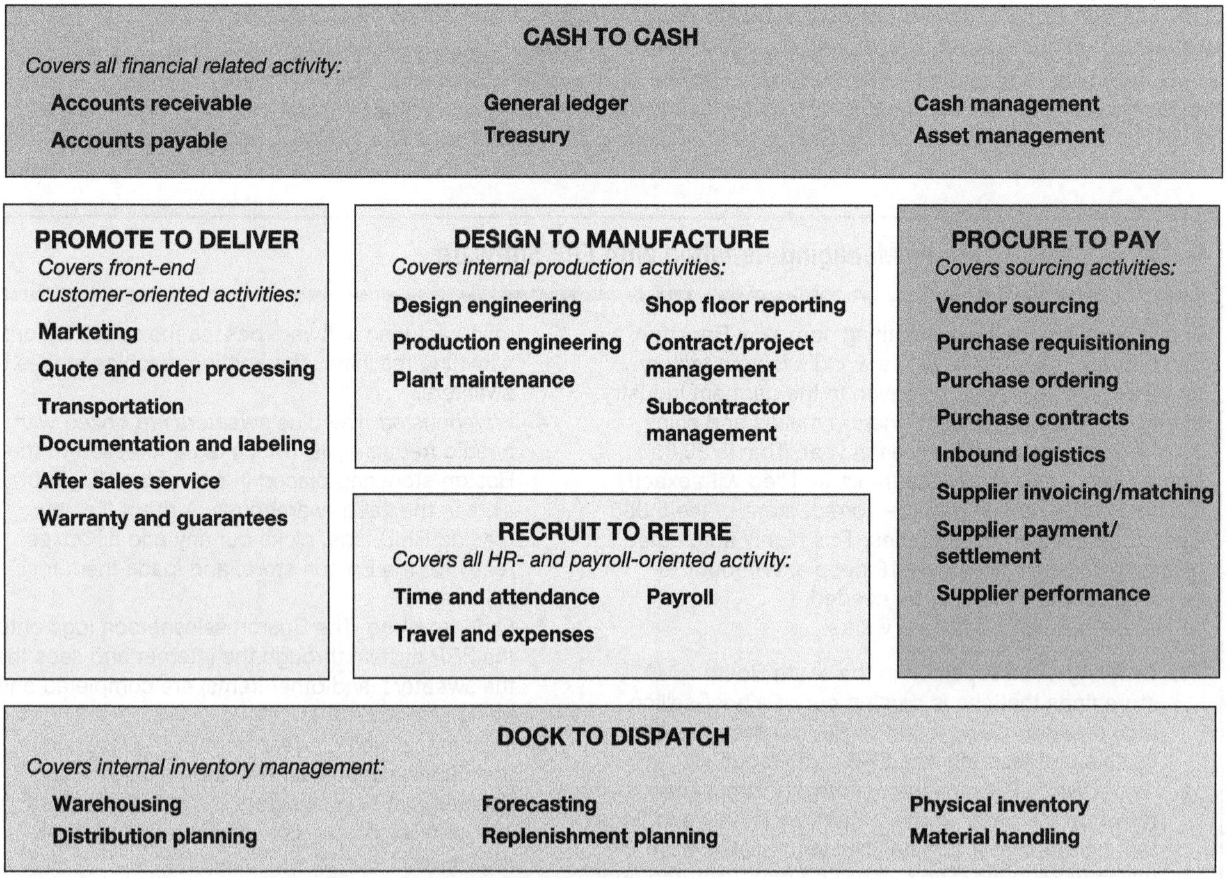

CASH TO CASH

Covers all financial related activity:

Accounts receivable	General ledger	Cash management
Accounts payable	Treasury	Asset management

PROMOTE TO DELIVER
Covers front-end customer-oriented activities:

Marketing

Quote and order processing

Transportation

Documentation and labeling

After sales service

Warranty and guarantees

DESIGN TO MANUFACTURE
Covers internal production activities:

Design engineering	Shop floor reporting
Production engineering	Contract/project management
Plant maintenance	Subcontractor management

RECRUIT TO RETIRE
Covers all HR- and payroll-oriented activity:

Time and attendance	Payroll
Travel and expenses	

PROCURE TO PAY
Covers sourcing activities:

Vendor sourcing

Purchase requisitioning

Purchase ordering

Purchase contracts

Inbound logistics

Supplier invoicing/matching

Supplier payment/settlement

Supplier performance

DOCK TO DISPATCH

Covers internal inventory management:

Warehousing	Forecasting	Physical inventory
Distribution planning	Replenishment planning	Material handling

▲ **FIGURE 14.13**   **SAP's Modules for ERP**

Advantages and Disadvantages of ERP Systems

We have alluded to some of the pluses and minuses of ERP. Here is a more complete list of both.

Advantages:
1. Provides integration of the supply chain, production, and administrative process.
2. Creates commonality of databases.
3. Can incorporate improved, reengineered, 'best processes.'
4. Increases communication and collaboration among business units and sites.
5. Has a software database that is off-the-shelf coding.
6. May provide a strategic advantage over competitors.

Disadvantages:
1. Is very expensive to purchase, and even more costly to customize.
2. Implementation may require major changes in the company and its processes.
3. Is so complex that many companies cannot adjust to it.
4. Involves an ongoing process for implementation, which may never be completed.
5. Expertise in ERP is limited, with staffing an ongoing problem.

ERP in the Service Sector

Efficient consumer response (ECR)

Supply-chain management systems in the grocery industry that tie sales to buying, to inventory, to logistics, and to production.

ERP vendors have developed a series of service modules for such markets as health care, government, retail stores, and financial services. At Le Royal Hotels and Resorts in Amman, there are ERP packages with software that handles all front- and back-office functions. This system integrates tasks such as maintaining guest histories, booking room and dinner reservations, scheduling golf tee times, and managing multiple properties in a chain. In the grocery industry, these supply-chain systems are known as **efficient consumer response (ECR)** systems. As is the case in manufacturing, efficient consumer response (ECR) systems tie sales to buying, to inventory, to logistics, and to production.

CHAPTER SUMMARY

Material requirements planning (MRP) schedules production and inventory when demand is dependent. For MRP to work, management must have a master schedule, precise requirements for all components, accurate inventory and purchasing records, and accurate lead times.

Production should often be lot-for-lot in an MRP system. When properly implemented, MRP can contribute in a major way to reduction in inventory while improving customer service levels. MRP techniques allow the operations manager to schedule and replenish stock on a 'need-to-order' basis rather than simply a 'time-to-order' basis.

The continuing development of MRP systems has led to MRP's use with lean manufacturing techniques. In addition, MRP can integrate production data with a variety of other activities, including the supply chain and sales. As a result, we now have integrated database-oriented enterprise resource planning (ERP) systems. These expensive and difficult-to-install ERP systems, when successful, support strategies of differentiation, response, and cost leadership.

Key Terms

Back flush (p. 451)
Bill of material (BOM) (p. 442)
Bucketless system (p. 451)
Buckets (p. 450)
Closed-loop MRP system (p. 456)
Distribution resource planning (DRP) (p. 459)
Economic part period (EPP) (p. 454)
Efficient consumer response (ECR) (p. 462)
Enterprise resource planning (ERP) (p. 460)
Gross material requirements plan (p. 446)

Lead time (p. 445)
Load report (p. 456)
Lot-for-lot (p. 451)
Lot-sizing decision (p. 451)
Low-level coding (p. 444)
Master production schedule (MPS) (p. 440)
Material requirements planning (MRP) (p. 440)
Material requirements planning II (MRP II) (p. 455)
Modular bills (p. 444)

Net material requirements plan (p. 447)
Part period balancing (PPB) (p. 453)
Pegging (p. 450)
Phantom bills of material (p. 444)
Planned order receipt (p. 447)
Planned order release (p. 447)
Planning bills (p. 444)
Supermarket (p. 451)
System nervousness (p. 450)
Time fences (p. 450)
Wagner–Whitin procedure (p. 455)

Ethical Dilemma

For many months your prospective ERP customer has been analyzing the hundreds of assumptions built into the US$90,000 ERP software you are selling. You have been working extremely hard to make this sale; if it goes through, you will reach your yearly quota and get a nice bonus, but loss of this sale may mean you start looking for other employment.

The accounting, human resource, supply chain, and marketing teams put together by the client have reviewed the specifications and finally recommended purchase of the software. However, as you

looked over their shoulders and helped them through the evaluation process, you began to realize that their purchasing procedures—with much of the purchasing being done at hundreds of regional stores—were not a good fit for the software. At the very least, the customizing will add US$250,000 to the implementation and training cost. The team is not aware of the issue, and you know that the necessary US$250,000 is not in the budget.

What do you do?

Discussion Questions

1. What is the difference between a *gross* requirements plan and a *net* requirements plan?
2. Once a material requirements plan (MRP) has been established, what other managerial applications might be found for the technique?
3. What are the similarities between MRP and distribution resource planning (DRP)?
4. How does MRP II differ from MRP?
5. Which is the best lot-sizing policy for manufacturing organizations?

6. What impact does ignoring carrying cost in the allocation of stock in a DRP system have on lot sizes?
7. MRP is more than an inventory system; what additional capabilities does MRP possess?
8. What are the options for the production planner who has: (a) scheduled more than capacity in a work center next week? (b) a consistent lack of capacity in that work center?
9. Master schedules are expressed in three different ways depending on whether the process is continuous, a job shop, or repetitive. What are these three ways?

Using Software to Solve MRP Problems

There are many commercial MRP software packages, for companies of all sizes. MRP software for small and medium-sized companies includes User Solutions, Inc., a demo of which is available at **www.usersolutions.com,** and MAX, from Exact Software North America, Inc. Software for larger systems is available from SAP, CMS, BEA, Oracle, i2 Technologies, and many others. The Excel OM software that accompanies this text includes an MRP module, as does POM for Windows. The use of both is explained in the following sections.

X Using Excel OM

Using Excel OM's MRP module requires the careful entry of several pieces of data. The initial MRP screen is where we enter: (1) the total number of occurrences of items in the bill of material (including the top item); (2) what we want the bill of material items to be called (i.e. Item no., Part); (3) total number of periods to be scheduled; (4) what we want the periods to be called (i.e. days, weeks).

Excel OM's second MRP screen provides the data entry for an indented bill of material. Here we enter: (1) the name of each item in the bill of material; (2) the quantity of that item in the assembly; (3) the correct indent (i.e. parent/child relationship) for each item. The indentations are critical as they provide the logic for the bill of material explosion. The indentations should follow the logic of the product structure tree, with indents for each assembly item in that assembly.

Excel OM's third MRP screen repeats the indented bill of material and provides the standard MRP tableau for entries. This is shown in Program 14.1 using the data from Examples 1, 2 and 3.

▶ **PROGRAM 14.1**
Using Excel OM's MRP Module to Solve Examples 1, 2, and 3

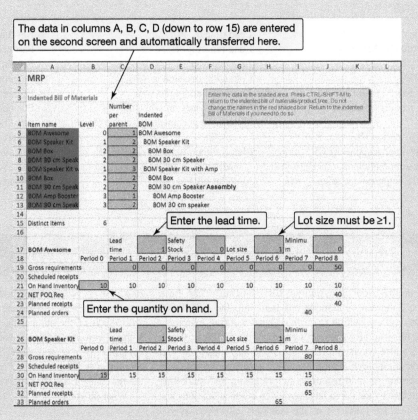

P Using POM for Windows

The POM for Windows MRP module can also solve Examples 1 to 3. Up to 18 periods can be analyzed. Here are the inputs required:

1. *Item names:* The item names are entered in the left column. The same item name will appear in more than one row if the item is used by two parent items. Each item must follow its parents.
2. *Item level:* The level in the indented bill of material must be given here. The item *cannot* be placed at a level more than one below the item immediately above.
3. *Lead-time:* The lead time for an item is entered here. The default is 1 week.
4. *Number per parent:* The number of units of this subassembly needed for its parent is entered here. The default is 1.
5. *On hand:* List current inventory on hand once, even if the subassembly is listed twice.
6. *Lot size:* The lot size can be specified here. A 0 or 1 will perform lot-for-lot ordering. If another number is placed here, then all orders for that item will be in integer multiples of that number.
7. *Demands:* The demands are entered in the end item row in the period in which the items are demanded.
8. *Scheduled receipts:* If units are scheduled to be received in the future, they should be listed in the appropriate time period (column) and item (row). (An entry here in level 1 is a demand; all other levels are receipts.)

Further details regarding POM for Windows are seen in Appendix IV.

Solved Problems Virtual Office Hours help is available at MyOMLab

▼ SOLVED PROBLEM 14.1

Determine the low-level coding and the quantity of each component necessary to produce 10 units of an assembly we will call Alpha. The product structure and quantities of each component needed for each assembly are noted in parentheses.

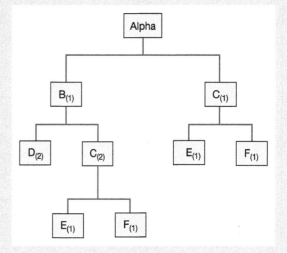

▼ SOLUTION

Redraw the product structure with low-level coding. Then multiply down the structure until the requirements of each branch are determined. Then add across the structure until the total for each is determined.

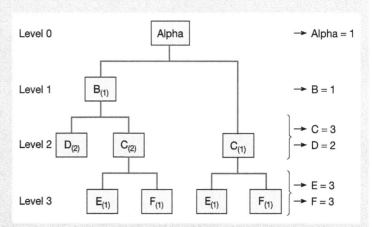

Es required for left branch:

$$(1_{alpha} \times 1_B \times 2_C \times 1_E) = 2 \text{ E}$$

and Es required for right branch:

$$(1_{alpha} \times 1_B \times 2_C \times 1_E) = \underline{1 \text{ E}}$$
$$\qquad\qquad\qquad\qquad 3 \text{ E required in total}$$

Then 'explode' the requirement by multiplying each by 10, as shown in the table.

Level	Item	Quantity per Unit	Total Requirements for 10 Alpha
0	Alpha	1	10
1	B	1	10
2	C	3	30
2	D	2	20
3	E	3	30
3	F	3	30

▼ SOLVED PROBLEM 14.2

Using the product structure for Alpha in Solved Problem 14.1, and the following lead times, quantity on hand, and master production schedule, prepare a net MRP table for Alphas.

Item	Lead Time	Quantity on Hand
Alpha	1	10
B	2	20
C	3	0
D	1	100
E	1	10
F	1	50

Master Production Schedule for Alpha

Period	6	7	8	9	10	11	12	13
Gross requirements			50			50		100

▼ SOLUTION

See Figure 14.14.

Net Material Requirements Planning Sheet for Alpha

Item attributes (Lot Size / Lead Time (# of Periods) / On Hand / Safety Stock / Allocated / Low-Level Code / Item ID):

Item ID	Lot Size	Lead Time	On Hand	Safety Stock	Allocated	Low-Level Code
Alpha (A)	Lot-for-Lot	1	10	—	—	0
B	Lot-for-Lot	2	20	—	—	1
C	Lot-for-Lot	3	0	—	—	2
D	Lot-for-Lot	1	100	—	—	2
E	Lot-for-Lot	1	10	—	—	3
F	Lot-for-Lot	1	50	—	—	3

Period (week, day):

Alpha (A) — On Hand 10

Row	1	2	3	4	5	6	7	8	9	10	11	12	13
Gross Requirements								50			50		100
Scheduled Receipts													
Projected On Hand (10)								10					
Net Requirements								40			50		100
Planned Order Receipts								40			50		100
Planned Order Releases							40			50		100	

B — On Hand 20

Row	1	2	3	4	5	6	7	8	9	10	11	12	13
Gross Requirements							40(A)			50(A)		100(A)	
Scheduled Receipts													
Projected On Hand (20)							20						
Net Requirements							20			50		100	
Planned Order Receipts							20			50		100	
Planned Order Releases					20			50		100			

C — On Hand 0

Row	1	2	3	4	5	6	7	8	9	10	11	12	13
Gross Requirements					40(B)		40(A)	100(B)		200(B) + 50(A)		100(A)	
Scheduled Receipts													
Projected On Hand (0)					0								
Net Requirements					40		40	100		250		100	
Planned Order Receipts					40		40	100		250		100	
Planned Order Releases		40		40	100		250		100				

D — On Hand 100

Row	1	2	3	4	5	6	7	8	9	10	11	12	13
Gross Requirements					40(B)			100(B)		200(B)			
Scheduled Receipts													
Projected On Hand (100)				0				60					
Net Requirements								40		200			
Planned Order Receipts								40		200			
Planned Order Releases							40		200				

E — On Hand 10

Row	1	2	3	4	5	6	7	8	9	10	11	12	13
Gross Requirements		40(C)		40(C)	100(C)		250(C)		100(C)				
Scheduled Receipts													
Projected On Hand (10)		10											
Net Requirements		30		40	100		250		100				
Planned Order Receipts		30		40	100		250		100				
Planned Order Releases	30		40	100		250		100					

F — On Hand 50

Row	1	2	3	4	5	6	7	8	9	10	11	12	13
Gross Requirements		40(C)		40(C)	100(C)		250(C)		100(C)				
Scheduled Receipts													
Projected On Hand (50)		50		10					—				
Net Requirements		0		30	100		250		100				
Planned Order Receipts			30		100		250		100				
Planned Order Releases			30	100		250		100					

▲ FIGURE 14.14 **Net Material Requirements Planning Sheet for Alpha**
The letter in parentheses indicates the source of the demand.

Problems*

• **14.1** You have developed the following simple product structure of items needed for your gift bag for a rush party for prospective pledges in your organization. You forecast 200 attendees. Assume that there is no inventory on hand of any of the items. Explode the bill of material. (Subscripts indicate the number of units required.)

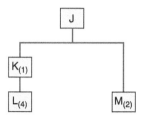

*P_X means the problem may be solved with POM for Windows and/or Excel OM. The exercises in this chapter (14.1 through 14.12) can be done on *Resource Manager for Excel*, a commercial system made available by User Solutions, Inc. Access to a trial version of the software and a set of notes for the user is available at **www.usersolutions.com**.

•• **14.2** You are expected to have the gift bags in Problem 14.1 ready at 5 p.m. sharp. However, you need to personalize the items (monogrammed pens, note pads, literature from the printer, etc.). The lead time is 1 hour to assemble 200 Js once the other items are prepared. The other items will take a while as well. Given the volunteers you have, the other time estimates are item K (2 hours), item L (1 hour), and item M (4 hours). Develop a time-phased assembly plan to prepare the gift bags.

•• **14.3** The demand for subassembly S is 100 units in week 7. Each unit of S requires 1 unit of T and 2 units of U. Each unit of T requires 1 unit of V, 2 units of W, and 1 unit of X. Finally, each unit of U requires 2 units of Y and 3 units of Z. One firm manufactures all items. It takes 2 weeks to make S, 1 week to make T, 2 weeks to make U, 2 weeks to make V, 3 weeks to make W, 1 week to make X, 2 weeks to make Y, and 1 week to make Z.
a) Construct a product structure. Identify all levels, parents, and components.
b) Prepare a time-phased product structure.

•• **14.4** Using the information in Problem 14.3, construct a gross material requirements plan. P_X

•• **14.5** Using the information in Problem 14.3, construct a net material requirements plan using the following on-hand inventory.

Lot Size	Lead Time (# of periods)	On Hand	Safety Stock	Allo-cated	Low-Level Code	Item ID		Period (week, day)							
								1	2	3	4	5	6	7	8
							Gross Requirements								
							Scheduled Receipts								
							Projected On Hand								
							Net Requirements								
							Planned Order Receipts								
							Planned Order Releases								
							Gross Requirements								
							Scheduled Receipts								
							Projected On Hand								
							Net Requirements								
							Planned Order Receipts								
							Planned Order Releases								
							Gross Requirements								
							Scheduled Receipts								
							Projected On Hand								
							Net Requirements								
							Planned Order Receipts								
							Planned Order Releases								
							Gross Requirements								
							Scheduled Receipts								
							Projected On Hand								
							Net Requirements								
							Planned Order Receipts								
							Planned Order Releases								
							Gross Requirements								
							Scheduled Receipts								
							Projected On Hand								
							Net Requirements								
							Planned Order Receipts								
							Planned Order Releases								

▲ **FIGURE 14.15** **MRP Form for Homework Problems in Chapter 14**
For several problems in this chapter, a copy of this form may be helpful.

Item	On-Hand Inventory	Item	On-Hand Inventory
S	20	W	30
T	20	X	25
U	40	Y	240
V	30	Z	40 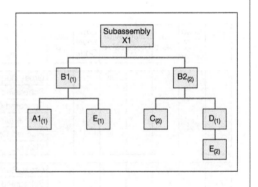

•• **14.6** Refer again to Problems 14.3 and 14.4. In addition to 100 units of S, there is also a demand for 20 units of U, which is a component of S. The 20 units of U are needed for maintenance purposes. These units are needed in week 6. Modify the *gross material requirements plan* to reflect this change. **Px**

•• **14.7** Refer again to Problems 14.3 and 14.5. In addition to 100 units of S, there is also a demand for 20 units of U, which is a component of S. The 20 units of U are needed for maintenance purposes. These units are needed in week 6. Modify the *net material requirements plan* to reflect this change. **Px**

••• **14.8** Given the following product structure, master production schedule, and inventory status (Figure 14.16) and assuming the requirements for each bill of material item is 1: (a) develop a gross requirements plan for Item C; (b) develop a net requirements plan for Item C. **Px**

•••• **14.9** Based on the data in Figure 14.16, complete a net material requirements schedule for:
a) All items (10 schedules in all), assuming the requirement for each bill of material item is 1.
b) All 10 items, assuming the requirement for all items is 1, except B, C, and F, which require *2 each*. **Px**

Data Table for Problems 14.10 through 14.12*

Period	1	2	3	4	5	6	7	8	9	10	11	12
Gross requirements	30		40		30	70	20		10	80		50

* Holding cost = US$2.50/unit/week; setup cost = US$150; lead time = 1 week; beginning inventory = 40.

••• **14.10** Develop a lot-for-lot solution and calculate total relevant costs for the data in the preceding table. **Px**

••• **14.11** Develop an EOQ solution and calculate total relevant costs for the data in the preceding table. Stockout costs equal US$10 per unit. **Px**

••• **14.12** Develop a PPB solution and calculate total relevant costs for the data in the preceding table. **Px**

Master Production Schedule for X1

PERIOD	7	8	9	10	11	12
Gross requirements		50		20		100

ITEM	LEAD TIME	ON HAND		ITEM	LEAD TIME	ON HAND
X1	1	50		C	1	0
B1	2	20		D	1	0
B2	2	20		E	3	10
A1	1	5				

▲ **FIGURE 14.16** Information for Problems 14.8 and 14.9

Case Studies

▶ Homs Automotive, Inc.

Homs Automotive, Inc. is an aftermarket producer and distributor of automotive replacement parts. Homs has slowly expanded the business, which began as a supplier of hard-to-get auto air-conditioning units for classic cars and hot rods. The firm has limited manufacturing capability, but a state-of-the-art MRP system and extensive inventory and assembly facilities. Components are purchased, assembled, and repackaged. Among its products are private-label air-conditioning, carburetors, and ignition kits. The downturn in the economy, particularly the company's discretionary segment, has put downward pressure on volume and margins. Profits have fallen considerably. In addition, customer service levels have declined, with late deliveries now exceeding 25 percent of orders. And to make matters worse, customer returns have been rising at a rate of 3 percent per month.

Ammar Zu'bi, vice president of sales, claims that most of the problem lies with the assembly department. He says that although the firm has accurate bills of materials, indicating what goes into each product, it is not producing the proper mix of the product. He also believes the firm has poor quality control and low productivity, and as a result its costs are too high.

Shahd Letanee, treasurer, believes that problems are due to investing in the wrong inventories. She thinks that marketing has too many options and products. Shahd also thinks that purchasing department buyers have been hedging their inventories and requirements with excess purchasing commitments.

The assembly manager, Mohammad Suleiman, says, "The symptom is that we have a lot of parts in inventory, but no place to assemble them in the production schedule. When we have the right part, it is not very good, but we use it anyway to meet the schedule."

Eman Al-Azzeh, manager of purchasing, has taken the stance that purchasing has not let Homs Automotive down. He has stuck by his old suppliers, used historical data to determine requirements, maintained what he views as excellent prices from suppliers, and evaluated new sources of supply with a view toward lowering cost. Where possible, Eman reacted to the increased pressure for profitability by emphasizing low cost and early delivery.

Discussion Questions

1. Prepare a plan for Homs Automotive, Inc. that gets the firm back on a course toward improved profitability. Be sure to identify the symptoms, the problems, and the specific changes you would implement.
2. Explain how MRP plays a role in this plan.

▶ MRP at Wheeled Coach Ambulance

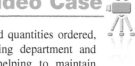
Video Case

Wheeled Coach, the world's largest manufacturer of ambulances, builds thousands of different and constantly changing configurations of its products. The custom nature of its business means lots of options and special designs—and a potential scheduling and inventory nightmare. Wheeled Coach addressed such problems, and succeeded in solving a lot of them, with an MRP system. As with most MRP installations, however, solving one set of problems uncovers a new set.

One of the new issues that had to be addressed by plant manager Lynn Whalen was newly discovered excess inventory. Managers discovered a substantial amount of inventory that was not called for in any finished products. Excess inventory was evident because of the new level of inventory accuracy required by the MRP system. The other reason was a new series of inventory reports generated by the IBM MAPICS MRP system purchased by Wheeled Coach. One of those reports indicates where items are used and is known as the 'Where Used' report. Interestingly, many inventory items were not called out on bills of material (BOMs) for any current products. In some cases, the reason some parts were in the stockroom remained a mystery.

The discovery of this excess inventory led to renewed efforts to ensure that the BOMs were accurate. With substantial work, BOM accuracy increased and the number of engineering change notices (ECNs) decreased. Similarly, purchase-order accuracy,

with regard to both part numbers and quantities ordered, was improved. Additionally, receiving department and stockroom accuracy went up, all helping to maintain schedule, costs, and ultimately, shipping dates and quality.

Eventually, Lynn Whalen concluded that the residual amounts of excess inventory were the result, at least in part, of rapid changes in ambulance design and technology. Another source was customer changes made after specifications had been determined and materials ordered. This latter excess occurs because, even though Wheeled Coach's own throughput time is only 17 days, many of the items that it purchases require much longer lead times.

Discussion Questions*

1. Why is accurate inventory such an important issue at Wheeled Coach?
2. Why does Wheeled Coach have excess inventory, and what kind of a plan would you suggest for dealing with it?
3. Be specific in your suggestions for reducing inventory and how to implement them.

*You may wish to view the video that accompanies this case before answering the questions.

▶ Additional Case Study: Visit MyOMLab for this free case study:

Ikon's attempt at ERP: The giant office technology firm faces hurdles with ERP implementation.

Main Heading	Review Material	MyOMLab
DEPENDENT DEMAND (p. 440)	Demand for items is *dependent* when the relationship between the items can be determined. For any product, all components of that product are dependent demand items. ■ **Material requirements planning (MRP)**—A dependent demand technique that uses a bill of material, inventory, expected receipts, and a master production schedule to determine material requirements.	**VIDEO 14.1** MRP at Wheeled Coach Ambulance
DEPENDENT INVENTORY MODEL REQUIREMENTS (pp. 440–445)	Dependent inventory models require operations managers to know the: (1) master production schedule; (2) specifications or bill of material; (3) inventory availability; (4) purchase orders outstanding; (5) lead times. ■ **Master production schedule (MPS)**—A timetable that specifies what is to be made and when. The MPS is a statement of *what is to be produced*, not a forecast of demand. ■ **Bill of material (BOM)**—A listing of the components, their description, and the quantity of each required to make one unit of a product. Items above any level in a BOM are called *parents*; items below any level are called *components*, or *children*. The top level in a BOM is the 0 level. ■ **Modular bills**—Bills of material organized by major subassemblies or by product options. ■ **Planning bills (or kits)**—A material grouping created in order to assign an artificial parent to a bill of material; also called 'pseudo' bills. ■ **Phantom bills of material**—Bills of material for components, usually subassemblies, that exist only temporarily; they are never inventoried. ■ **Low-level coding**—A number that identifies items at the lowest level at which they occur. ■ **Lead time**—In purchasing systems, the time between recognition of the need for an order and receiving it; in production systems, it is the order, wait, move, queue, setup, and run times for each component. When a bill of materials is turned on its side and modified by adding lead times for each component, it is called a *time-phased product structure*.	Problems: 14.1, 14.3 Virtual Office Hours for Solved Problem: 14.1
MRP STRUCTURE (pp. 445–449)	■ **Gross material requirements plan**—A schedule that shows the total demand for an item (prior to subtraction of on-hand inventory and scheduled receipts) and: (1) when it must be ordered from suppliers; (2) when production must be started to meet its demand by a particular date. ■ **Net material requirements plan**—The result of adjusting gross requirements for inventory on hand and scheduled receipts. ■ **Planned order receipt**—The quantity planned to be received at a future date. ■ **Planned order release**—The scheduled date for an order to be released. Net requirements = Gross requirements + Allocations – (On hand + Scheduled receipts)	Problems: 14.2, 14.4–14.8 Virtual Office Hours for Solved Problem: 14.2
MRP MANAGEMENT (pp. 450–451)	■ **System nervousness**—Frequent changes in an MRP system. ■ **Time fences**—A means for allowing a segment of the master schedule to be designated as 'not to be rescheduled.' ■ **Pegging**—In material requirements planning systems, tracing upward the bill of material from the component to the parent item. Four approaches for integrating MRP and JIT are: (1) finite capacity scheduling; (2) small buckets; (3) balanced flow; (4) supermarkets. ■ **Buckets**—Time units in a material requirements planning system. Finite capacity scheduling (FCS) considers department and machine capacity. FCS provides the precise scheduling needed for rapid material movement. ■ **Bucketless system**—Time-phased data are referenced using dated records rather than defined time periods, or buckets. ■ **Back flush**—A system to reduce inventory balances by deducting everything in the bill of materials on completion of the unit. ■ **Supermarket**—An inventory area that holds common items that are replenished by a kanban system.	
LOT-SIZING TECHNIQUES (pp. 451–455)	■ **Lot-sizing decision**—The process of, or techniques used in, determining lot size. ■ **Lot-for-lot**—A lot-sizing technique that generates exactly what is required to meet the plan. ■ **Part period balancing (PPB)**—An inventory ordering technique that balances setup and holding costs by changing the lot size to reflect requirements of the next lot size in the future.	Problems: 14.10–14.12

Main Heading	Review Material
	■ **Economic part period (EPP)**—A period of time when the ratio of setup cost to holding cost is equal. ■ **Wagner–Whitin procedure**—A technique for lot-size computation that assumes a finite time horizon beyond which there are no additional net requirements to arrive at an ordering strategy. In general, the lot-for-lot approach should be used whenever low-cost deliveries can be achieved.
EXTENSIONS OF MRP (pp. 455–458)	■ **Material requirements planning II (MRP II)**—A system that allows, with MRP in place, inventory data to be augmented by other resource variables; in this case, MRP becomes *material resource planning.* ■ **Closed-loop MRP system**—A system that provides feedback to the capacity plan, master production schedule, and production plan so planning can be kept valid at all times. ■ **Load report**—A report for showing the resource requirements in a work center for all work currently assigned there as well as all planned and expected orders. Tactics for smoothing the load and minimizing the impact of changed lead time include: *Overlapping, Operations splitting,* and *Order,* or *lot, splitting.*
MRP IN SERVICES (pp. 458–459)	■ **Distribution resource planning (DRP)**—A time-phased stock-replenishment plan for all levels of a distribution network.
ENTERPRISE RESOURCE PLANNING (ERP) (pp. 460–462)	■ **Enterprise resource planning (ERP)**—An information system for identifying and planning the enterprise-wide resources needed to take, make, ship, and account for customer orders. In an ERP system, data are entered only once into a common, complete, and consistent database shared by all applications. ■ **Efficient consumer response (ECR)**—Supply-chain management systems in the grocery industry that tie sales to buying, to inventory, to logistics, and to production.

Self-Test

■ **Before taking the self-test,** refer to the learning objectives listed at the beginning of the chapter and the key terms listed at the end of the chapter.

LO1. In a product structure diagram:
  a) parents are found only at the top level of the diagram
  b) parents are found at every level in the diagram
  c) children are found at every level of the diagram except the top level
  d) all items in the diagrams are both parents and children
  e) all of the above.

LO2. The difference between a gross material requirements plan (gross MRP) and a net material requirements plan (net MRP) is:
  a) the gross MRP may not be computerized, but the net MRP must be computerized
  b) the gross MRP includes consideration of the inventory on hand, whereas the net MRP doesn't include the inventory consideration
  c) the net MRP includes consideration of the inventory on hand, whereas the gross MRP doesn't include the inventory consideration
  d) the gross MRP doesn't take taxes into account, whereas the net MRP includes the tax considerations
  e) the net MRP is only an estimate, whereas the gross MRP is used for actual production scheduling.

LO3. Net requirements =
  a) Gross requirements + Allocations − On-hand inventory + Scheduled receipts
  b) Gross requirements − Allocations − On-hand inventory − Scheduled receipts
  c) Gross requirements − Allocations − On-hand inventory + Scheduled receipts
  d) Gross requirements + Allocations − On-hand inventory − Scheduled receipts.

LO4. A lot-sizing procedure that assumes a finite time horizon beyond which there are no additional net requirements is:
  a) Wagner–Whitin procedure
  b) part period balancing
  c) economic order quantity
  d) all of the above.

LO5. MRP II stands for:
  a) material resource planning
  b) management requirements planning
  c) management resource planning
  d) material revenue planning
  e) material risk planning.

LO6. A(n) _____ MRP system provides information to the capacity plan, to the master production schedule, and ultimately to the production plan.
  a) dynamic
  b) closed-loop
  c) continuous
  d) retrospective
  e) introspective.

LO7. Which system extends MRP II to tie in customers and suppliers?
  a) MRP III
  b) JIT
  c) IRP
  d) ERP
  e) Enhanced MRP II.

Answers: LO1. c; **LO2.** c; **LO3.** d; **LO4.** a; **LO5.** a; **LO6.** b; **LO7.** d.

15 Scheduling for the Short Term

10

OM STRATEGY DECISIONS

- ► Design of Goods and Services
- ► Managing Quality
- ► Process Strategy
- ► Location Strategies
- ► Layout Strategies
- ► Human Resources
- ► Supply-Chain Management
- ► Inventory Management
- ► Scheduling
  - ■ Aggregate
  - ■ Short-Term
- ► Maintenance

SCHEDULING AIRPLANES WHEN WEATHER IS THE ENEMY

Operations managers at airlines learn to expect the unexpected. Events that require rapid rescheduling are a regular part of life. Throughout the ordeals of thunderstorms, snowstorms, and fog, airlines across the globe struggle to cope with delays, cancellations, and furious passengers. The inevitable changes to the schedule often create a ripple effect that impacts on passengers at dozens of airports in the network. Almost 8 percent of Emirates' flights are disrupted because of bad weather: The cost is hundreds of millions of US dollars in lost revenue, overtime pay, and food and lodging vouchers. It is estimated that Emirates loses US$150 for each minute of delay.

Emirates realized the importance of responding quickly to such disruptions and embarked on an operational strategy for disruption management. The purpose was to ensure that all flight operations were integrated in such a way that would allow Emirates' control personnel to plan, observe, and respond to disruptions quickly. Most importantly, the data collected from each disruption could be analyzed to

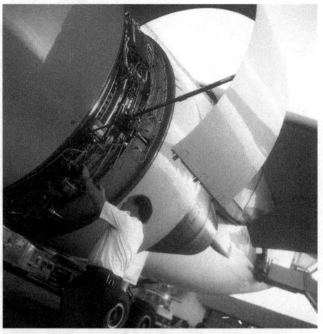

The intense working schedule for the planes necessitates periodic maintenance to ensure zero margin for mistakes.

improve Emirates' performance and create more satisfied travelers.

To this end, Emirates created a high-tech Network Control Center (NCC). This center monitors Emirates' worldwide aircraft flow 24/7. It plans Emirates' flights

Emirates is one of the world's largest airlines with more than 120 destinations worldwide.

Emirates' disruption management approach aims to minimize the effects of flight disruptions on the passengers as a first priority.

3 months in advance, but can help the crew in any critical situation that would require a change in route or hub in seconds, such as disruptions caused by bad weather.

Emirates' disruption management approach minimizes the effects of flight disruptions on the passengers, the company, and the different stakeholders. Using computers and telecommunications systems, the NCC advises personnel and notifies customers of schedule changes, reroutes flights, and gets jets into the air. Keeping flights flowing as smoothly as possible in spite of weather (or other types of disruption) is a competitive edge that Emirates would like to maintain.

Chapter 15 Learning Objectives

> **AUTHOR COMMENT**
> Good scheduling means lower costs and faster and more dependable delivery.

THE IMPORTANCE OF SHORT-TERM SCHEDULING

In the course of scheduling its flights, Emirates schedules thousands of pilots and flight attendants to accommodate passengers who wish to reach their destinations. This schedule, based on huge computer programs, plays a major role in satisfying customers. Emirates finds competitive advantage with its flexibility for last-minute adjustments to demand and weather disruptions.

Manufacturing firms also make schedules that match production to customer demands. Gulf Craft, Inc, based in U.A.E, schedules machines, tools, and people to make boat parts. Gulf Craft's mainframe computer downloads schedules for parts production into a flexible machining system (FMS), in which a manager makes the final scheduling decision. The FMS allows parts of many sizes or shapes to be made, in any order. This scheduling versatility results in parts produced on a just-in-time basis, with low setup times, little work-in-process, and high machine utilization. Efficient scheduling is how companies meet due dates promised to customers and face time-based competition.

The strategic importance of scheduling is clear:

- Effective scheduling means faster movement of goods and services through a facility. This means greater use of assets and hence greater capacity per dollar invested, which, in turn, *lowers cost*.
- Added capacity, faster throughput, and the related flexibility mean better customer service through *faster delivery*.
- Good scheduling also contributes to realistic commitments and hence *dependable delivery*.

> **AUTHOR COMMENT**
> Scheduling decisions range from years, for capacity planning, to minutes/hours/days, called short-term scheduling. This chapter focuses on the latter.

SCHEDULING ISSUES

Scheduling deals with the timing of operations. The types of scheduling decisions made in five organizations—a hospital, a college, a manufacturer, a restaurant, and an airline—are shown in Table 15.1. As you can see from Figure 15.1, a sequence of decisions affects scheduling. Schedule decisions begin with *capacity* planning, which involves total facility and equipment

> ▶ **TABLE 15.1**
> **Scheduling Decisions**

> **VIDEO 15.1**
> Scheduling at Hard Rock Cafe

Organization	Managers Schedule the Following:
New Mowasat Hospital, Kuwait	Operating room use Patient admissions Nursing, security, maintenance staff Outpatient treatments
Kingdom University of Bahrain	Classrooms and audiovisual equipment Student and instructor schedules Graduate and undergraduate courses
Gulf Craft, Inc., U.A.E.	Production of goods Purchases of materials Workers
TcheTche Cafe, Jordan	Chef, waiters, Delivery of fresh foods Opening of dining areas
Emirates	Maintenance of aircraft Departure timetables Flight crews, catering, gate, and ticketing personnel

Capacity Planning
(Long term; years)
Changes in Facilities
Changes in Equipment
See Chapter 7 and Supplement 7

Capacity Plan for New Facilities
Adjust capacity to the demand suggested by strategic plan

Aggregate Planning
(Intermediate term; quarterly or monthly)
Facility utilization
Personnel changes
Subcontracting
See Chapter 13

Aggregate Production Plan for All Bikes
(Determine personnel or subcontracting necessary to
match aggregate demand to existing facilities/capacity)

Month	1	2
Bike Production	800	850

Master Production Schedule for Bike Models
(Determine weekly capacity schedule)

	Month 1				Month 2			
Week	1	2	3	4	5	6	7	8
Model 22		200		200		200		200
Model 24	100		100		150		100	
Model 26	100		100		100		100	

Master Schedule
(Intermediate term; weekly)
Material requirements planning
Disaggregate the aggregate plan
See Chapters 13 and 14

Work Assigned to Specific Personnel and Work Centers
Make finite capacity schedule by matching specific
tasks to specific people and machines

Short-Term Scheduling
(Short term; days, hours, minutes)
Work center loading
Job sequencing/dispatching
See this chapter

Assemble
Model 22 in
work center 6

▲ FIGURE 15.1 The Relationship between Capacity Planning, Aggregate Planning, Master Schedule, and Short-Term Scheduling for a Bike Co.

resources available (discussed in Chapter 7 and Supplement 7). *Capacity plans* are usually annual or quarterly as new equipment and facilities are purchased or discarded. *Aggregate planning* (Chapter 13) makes decisions regarding the use of facilities, inventory, people, and outside contractors. Aggregate plans are typically monthly, and resources are allocated in terms of an aggregate measure such as total units, tons, or shop hours. However, the *master schedule* breaks down the aggregate plan and develops a schedule for specific products or product lines for each week. *Short-term schedules* then translate capacity decisions, aggregate (intermediate) planning, and master schedules into job sequences and specific assignments of personnel, materials, and machinery. In this chapter, we describe the narrow issue of scheduling goods and services in the *short run* (that is, matching daily or hourly requirements to specific personnel and equipment).

The objective of scheduling is to allocate and prioritize demand (generated by either forecasts or customer orders) to available facilities. Two significant factors in achieving this allocation and prioritizing are: (1) the type of scheduling, forward or backward; (2) the criteria for priorities. We discuss these two topics next.

LO1: Explain the relationship between short-term scheduling, capacity planning, aggregate planning, and a master schedule

Forward and Backward Scheduling

Scheduling involves assigning due dates to specific jobs, but many jobs compete simultaneously for the same resources. To help address the difficulties inherent in scheduling, we can categorize scheduling techniques as: (1) forward scheduling; (2) backward scheduling.

Forward scheduling
Scheduling that begins the schedule as soon as the requirements are known.

Forward scheduling starts the schedule as soon as the job requirements are known. Forward scheduling is used in a variety of organizations such as hospitals, clinics, fine-dining restaurants, and machine tool manufacturers. In these facilities, jobs are performed to customer order, and delivery is often requested as soon as possible. Forward scheduling is usually designed to produce a schedule that can be accomplished even if it means not meeting the due date. In many instances, forward scheduling causes a buildup of work-in-process inventory.

Backward scheduling
Scheduling that begins with the due date and schedules the final operation first and the other job steps in reverse order.

Backward scheduling begins with the due date, scheduling the *final* operation first. Steps in the job are then scheduled, one at a time, in reverse order. By subtracting the lead time for each item, the start time is obtained. However, the resources necessary to accomplish the schedule may not exist. Backward scheduling is used in many manufacturing environments, as well as service environments such as catering a banquet or scheduling surgery. In practice, a combination of forward and backward scheduling is often used to find a reasonable trade-off between what can be achieved and customer due dates.

Machine breakdowns, absenteeism, quality problems, shortages, and other factors further complicate scheduling. (See the *OM in Action* box 'Scheduling Workers Who Fall Asleep Is a Killer—Literally.') Consequently, assignment of a date does not ensure that the work will be performed according to the schedule. Many specialized techniques have been developed to aid in preparing reliable schedules.

Scheduling Criteria

The correct scheduling technique depends on the volume of orders, the nature of operations, and the overall complexity of jobs, as well as the importance placed on each of four criteria. These four criteria are:

1. *Minimize completion time:* This criterion is evaluated by determining the average completion time per job.
2. *Maximize utilization:* This is evaluated by determining the percentage of the time the facility is utilized.
3. *Minimize work-in-process (WIP) inventory:* This is evaluated by determining the average number of jobs in the system. The relationship between the number of jobs in the system and WIP inventory will be high. Therefore, the fewer the number of jobs that are in the system, the lower the inventory.
4. *Minimize customer waiting time:* This is evaluated by determining the average number of late days.

At Qatar Gas, the scheduling and control processes are run centrally in the headquarters in Doha; the central control room ensures that the processes are performing as intended and that any deviation is dealt with immediately.

OM in Action ▶ Scheduling Workers Who Fall Asleep Is a Killer—Literally

The accidents at the nuclear plants at Three Mile Island, Pennsylvania, and Chernobyl, Russia, and the disaster at Bhopal, India, all had one thing in common: they occurred between midnight and 4.00 a.m. These facilities had other problems, but the main issue was that the need for sleep results in unreliable workplace performance. In some cases, unable to cope with a constantly changing work schedule, workers simply fall asleep.

The same is true for pilots. Their inconsistent schedules and long flights often force them to snooze in the cockpit to get enough sleep. (Emirates' flight from Dubai to San Francisco takes about 16 hours, non-stop.) The Bombardier regional jet flying from Honolulu to Hilo, Hawaii, encountered a serious problem in 2008 as it flew over Maui: Both pilots were so fast asleep that they failed to respond to frantic calls from air-traffic controllers for 18 minutes. The plane, with 40 passengers, overshot its destination as it flew 26 miles over the Pacific.

Millions of people work in industries that maintain round-the-clock schedules. Employees from graveyard shifts report tales of seeing sleeping assembly-line workers fall off their stools, batches of defective parts sliding past dozing inspectors, and exhausted forklift operators crashing into walls. Virtually all shift workers are sleep-deprived. The National Highway Traffic Safety Administration of the United States indicates that drowsiness may be a factor in as many as 100,000 crashes annually.

Scheduling is a major problem in firms with 24/7 shifts, but some managers are taking steps to deal with schedule-related sleep problems among workers. Motorola, Dow Chemical, Detroit Edison, Pennzoil, and Exxon, for instance, all give workers several days off between shift changes.

Operations managers can make shift work less dangerous with shifts that do not exceed 12 hours, encourage 8 hours of sleep each day, and have extended time off between shift changes. As more is learned about the economic toll of non-daytime schedules and changing schedules, companies are learning to improve scheduling.

Sources: The Wall Street Journal (September 12, 2008): A1, A14 and (October 25, 2009): A:1; and *Air Safety and Health* (January 2004): 14.

◀ **TABLE 15.2**
Different Processes Suggest Different Approaches to Scheduling

Process-focused facilities (job shops)
- Focus is on generating a forward-looking schedule.
- MRP generates due dates that are refined with finite capacity scheduling techniques.
- *Examples:* foundries, machine shops, cabinet shops, print shops, many restaurants, and the fashion industry.

Work cells (focused facilities that process families of similar components)
- Focus is on generating a forward-looking schedule.
- MRP generates due dates, and subsequent detailed scheduling/dispatching is done at the work cell with kanbans and priority rules.
- *Examples:* boat engine rebuilder Gulf Craft, Inc., greeting-card maker Rahwanji Cards (Syria).

Repetitive facilities (assembly lines)
- Focus is on generating a forward-looking schedule that is achieved by balancing the line with traditional assembly-line techniques.
- Pull techniques, such as JIT and kanban, signal component scheduling to support the assembly line.
- Challenging scheduling problems typically occur only when the process is new or when products or models change.
- *Examples:* assembly lines for a wide variety of products from autos to home appliances and computers.

Product-focused facilities (continuous)
- Focus is on generating a forward-looking schedule that can meet a reasonably stable demand with the existing fixed capacity.
- Capacity in such facilities is usually limited by long-term capital investment.
- Capacity is usually known, as is the setup and run time for the limited range of products.
- *Examples:* facilities with very high-volume production and limited-variety products such as paper on huge machines at International Paper (Jordan) or rolled steel in a Saudi steel plant.

These four criteria are used in this chapter, as they are in industry, to evaluate scheduling performance. In addition, good scheduling approaches should be simple, clear, easily understood, easy to carry out, flexible, and realistic.

Table 15.2 provides an overview of different processes and approaches to scheduling. We now examine scheduling in process-focused facilities, in repetitive facilities, and in the service sector.

AUTHOR COMMENT
The facilities discussed here
are built around processes.

SCHEDULING PROCESS-FOCUSED FACILITIES

Process-focused facilities (also known as *intermittent* or *job-shop facilities*),[1] as we see in Table 15.2, are high-variety, low-volume systems commonly found in manufacturing and service organizations. These are production systems in which products are made to order. Items made under this system usually differ considerably in terms of materials used, order of processing, processing requirements, time of processing, and setup requirements. Because of these differences, scheduling can be complex. To run a facility in a balanced and efficient manner, the manager needs a production planning and control system. This system should:

- Schedule incoming orders without violating capacity constraints of individual work centers.
- Check the availability of tools and materials before releasing an order to a department.
- Establish due dates for each job and check progress against need dates and order lead times.
- Check work-in-progress as jobs move through the shop.
- Provide feedback on plant and production activities.
- Provide work efficiency statistics and monitor operator times for payroll and labor distribution analyses.

Whether the scheduling system is manual or automated, it must be accurate and relevant. This means it requires a production database with both planning and control files. Three types of *planning files* are:

1. An *item master file*, which contains information about each component the firm produces or purchases.
2. A *routing file*, which indicates each component's flow through the shop.
3. A *work-center master file*, which contains information about the work center, such as capacity and efficiency.

Control files track the actual progress made against the plan for each work order.

LOADING JOBS

Loading
The assigning of jobs to work or processing centers.

Loading means the assignment of jobs to work or processing centers. Operations managers assign jobs to work centers so that costs, idle time, or completion times are kept to a minimum. Loading work centers takes two forms.[2] One is oriented to capacity; the second is related to assigning specific jobs to work centers.

First, we examine loading from the perspective of capacity via a technique known as *input–output* control. Then, we present two approaches used for loading: *Gantt charts* and the *assignment method* of linear programming.

Input–Output Control

Many firms have difficulty scheduling (that is, achieving effective throughput) because they overload the production processes. This often occurs because they do not know actual performance in the work centers. Effective scheduling depends on matching the schedule to performance. Lack of knowledge about capacity and performance causes reduced throughput.

Input–output control
A system that allows operations personnel to manage facility work flows by tracking work added to a work center and its work completed.

Input–output control is a technique that allows operations personnel to manage facility work flows. If the work is arriving faster than it is being processed, the facility is overloaded, and a backlog develops. Overloading causes crowding in the facility, leading to inefficiencies and quality problems. If the work is arriving at a slower rate than jobs are being performed, the facility is underloaded, and the work center may run out of work. Underloading the facility results in idle capacity and wasted resources. Example 1 shows the use of input–output controls.

---

[1]Much of the literature on scheduling is about manufacturing; there, the traditional term *job-shop scheduling* is often used.

[2]Note that this discussion can apply to facilities that might be called a 'shop' in a manufacturing firm, a 'unit' in a hospital, or a 'department' in an office or a large kitchen.

Tripoli Machining Ltd. manufactures driveway security fences and gates. It wants to develop an input–output control report for the aluminum machining work center for 5 weeks (weeks 6/6 through 7/4). The planned input is 280 standard hours per week. The actual input is close to this figure, varying between 250 and 285. Output is scheduled at 320 standard hours, which is the assumed capacity. A backlog exists in the work center.

APPROACH ▶ Tripoli Machining Ltd. uses schedule information to create Figure 15.2, which monitors the workload-capacity relationship at the work center.

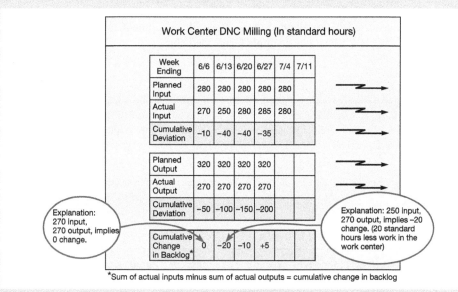

◀ FIGURE 15.2
Input–Output Control

SOLUTION ▶ The deviations between scheduled input and actual output are shown in Figure 15.2. Actual output (270 hours) is substantially less than planned. Therefore, neither the input plan nor the output plan is being achieved.

INSIGHT ▶ The backlog of work in this work center has actually increased by 5 hours by week 6/27. This increases work-in-process inventory, complicating the scheduling task and indicating the need for manager action.

LEARNING EXERCISE ▶ If actual output for the week of 6/27 was 275 (instead of 270), what changes? [Answer: Output cumulative deviation now is –195, and cumulative change in backlog is 0.]

RELATED PROBLEM ▶ 15.12

Input–output control can be maintained by a system of **ConWIP cards**, which control the amount of work in a work center. ConWIP is an acronym for *constant work-in-process*. The ConWIP card travels with a job (or batch) through the work center. When the job is finished, the card is released and returned to the initial workstation, authorizing the entry of a new batch into the work center. The ConWIP card effectively limits the amount of work in the work center, controls lead time, and monitors the backlog.

The options available to operations personnel to manage facility work flow include the following:

1. Correcting performances.
2. Increasing capacity.
3. Increasing or reducing input to the work center by (a) routing work to or from other work centers, (b) increasing or decreasing subcontracting, (c) producing less (or producing more).

Producing less is not a popular solution, but the advantages can be substantial. First, customer-service levels may improve because units may be produced on time. Second, efficiency may actually improve because there is less work in process cluttering the work center and adding to overhead costs. Third, quality may improve because less work in process hides fewer problems.

ConWIP cards
Cards that control the amount of work in a work center, aiding input–output control.

Gantt Charts

Gantt charts

Planning charts used to schedule resources and allocate time.

Gantt charts are visual aids that are useful in loading and scheduling. The name is derived from Henry Gantt, who developed the charts in the late 1800s. The charts show the use of resources, such as work centers and labor.

When used in *loading*, Gantt charts show the loading and idle times of several departments, machines, or facilities. They display the relative workloads in the system so that the manager knows what adjustments are appropriate. For example, when one work center becomes overloaded, employees from a low-load center can be transferred temporarily to increase the workforce. Or if waiting jobs can be processed at different work centers, some jobs at high-load centers can be transferred to low-load centers. Versatile equipment may also be transferred among centers. Example 2 illustrates a simple Gantt load chart.

EXAMPLE 2 ►

Gantt Load Chart

An Abu Dhabi washing machine manufacturer accepts special orders for machines to be used in such unique facilities as hospitals and large industrial laundries. The production of each machine requires varying tasks and durations. The company wants to build a load chart for the week of March 8.

APPROACH ►   The Gantt chart is selected as the appropriate graphical tool.

SOLUTION ►   Figure 15.3 shows the completed Gantt chart.

► **FIGURE 15.3**
Gantt Load Chart for the Week of March 8.

Work Center \ Day	Monday	Tuesday	Wednesday	Thursday	Friday
Metalworks	Job 349	✕	←————— Job 350 —————→		
Mechanical		←——— Job 349 ———→		Job 408	
Electronics	Job 408			Job 349	
Painting	←——— Job 295 ———→		Job 408	✕	Job 349

Processing	Unscheduled	✕ Center not available (e.g. maintenance time, repairs, shortages)

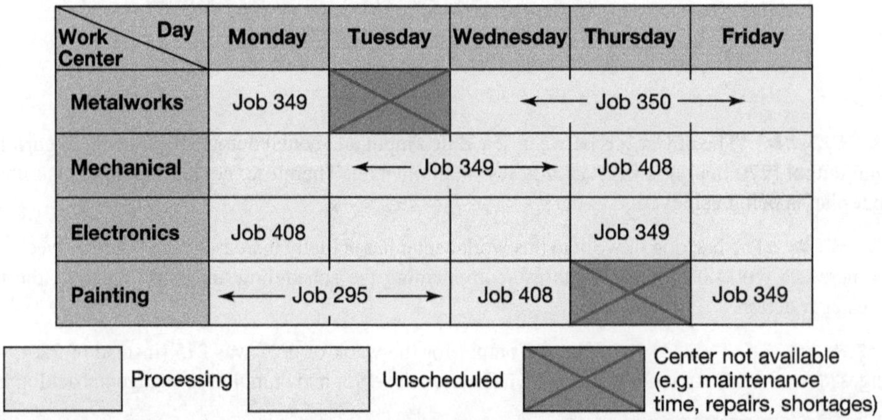

INSIGHT ►   The four work centers process several jobs during the week. This particular chart indicates that the metalworks and painting centers are completely loaded for the entire week. The mechanical and electronics centers have some idle time scattered during the week. We also note that the metalworks center is unavailable on Tuesday, and the painting center is unavailable on Thursday, perhaps for preventive maintenance.

LEARNING EXERCISE ►   What impact results from the electronics work center closing on Tuesday for preventive maintenance? [Answer: None.]

RELATED PROBLEM ►   15.1b

LO2: Draw Gantt loading and scheduling charts

The Gantt *load chart* has a major limitation: It does not account for production variability such as unexpected breakdowns or human errors that require reworking a job. Consequently, the chart must also be updated regularly to account for new jobs and revised time estimates.

A Gantt *schedule chart* is used to monitor jobs in progress (and is also used for project scheduling). It indicates which jobs are on schedule and which are ahead of or behind schedule. In practice, many versions of the chart are found. The schedule chart in Example 3 places jobs in progress on the vertical axis and time on the horizontal axis.

Printing House Ltd. wants to use a Gantt chart to show the scheduling of three orders, jobs A, B, and C.

APPROACH ▶ In Figure 15.4, each pair of brackets on the time axis denotes the estimated starting and finishing of a job enclosed within it. The solid bars reflect the actual status or progress of the job. We are just finishing day 5.

SOLUTION ▶

◀ **EXAMPLE 3**

Gantt scheduling chart

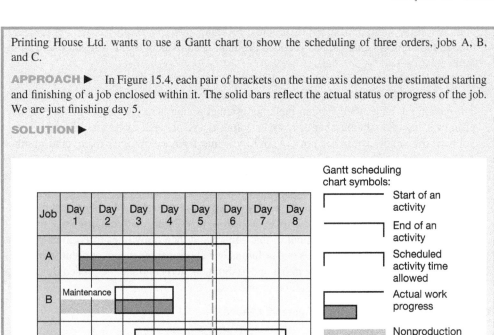

◀ **FIGURE 15.4**
Gantt Scheduling Chart for Jobs A, B, and C at a Printing Firm

INSIGHT ▶ Figure 15.4 illustrates that job A is about a half-day behind schedule at the end of day 5. Job B was completed after equipment maintenance. We also see that job C is ahead of schedule.

LEARNING EXERCISE ▶ Redraw the Gantt chart to show that job A is a half-day *ahead* of schedule. [Answer: The orangish bar now extends all the way to the end of the activity.]

RELATED PROBLEMS ▶ 15.1a, 15.2

Assignment Method

The **assignment method** involves assigning tasks or jobs to resources. Examples include assigning jobs to machines, contracts to bidders, people to projects, and salespeople to territories. The objective is most often to minimize total costs or time required to perform the tasks at hand. One important characteristic of assignment problems is that only one job (or worker) is assigned to one machine (or project).

Each assignment problem uses a table. The numbers in the table will be the costs or times associated with each particular assignment. For example, if Printing House Ltd. has three available typesetters (A, B, and C) and three new jobs to be completed, its table might look like Table 15.3. The dollar entries represent the firm's estimate of what it will cost for each job to be completed by each typesetter.

Assignment method
A special class of linear programming models that involves assigning tasks or jobs to resources.

LO3: Apply the assignment method for loading jobs

◀ **TABLE 15.3**
Cost estimates for three new jobs at Printing House Ltd.

Job	Typesetter		
	A	**B**	**C**
R-34	US$11	US$14	US$6
S-66	US$8	US$10	US$11
T-50	US$9	US$12	US$7

The assignment method involves adding and subtracting appropriate numbers in the table to find the lowest *opportunity cost*[3] for each assignment. There are four steps to follow:

1. Subtract the smallest number in each row from every number in that row, for columns that do not contain zero, and then, from the resulting matrix, subtract the smallest number in each column from every number in that column. This step has the effect of reducing the

[3]Opportunity costs are those profits forgone or not obtained.

numbers in the table until a series of zeros, meaning *zero opportunity costs*, appear. Even though the numbers change, this reduced problem is equivalent to the original one, and the same solution will be optimal.

2. Draw the minimum number of vertical and horizontal straight lines necessary to cover all zeros in the table. If the number of lines equals either the number of rows or the number of columns in the table, then we can make an optimal assignment (see step 4). If the number of lines is less than the number of rows or columns, we proceed to step 3.

3. Subtract the smallest number not covered by a line from every other uncovered number. Add the same number to any number(s) lying at the intersection of any two lines. Do not change the value of the numbers that are covered by only one line. Return to step 2 and continue until an optimal assignment is possible.

4. Optimal assignments will always be at zero locations in the table. One systematic way of making a valid assignment is first to select a row or column that contains only one zero square. We can make an assignment to that square and then draw lines through its row and column. From the uncovered rows and columns, we choose another row or column in which there is only one zero square. We make that assignment and continue the procedure until we have assigned each person or machine to one task.

Example 4 shows how to use the assignment method.

EXAMPLE 4 ▶

Assignment method

AUTHOR COMMENT
You can also tackle assignment problems with our Excel OM or POM software or with Excel's Solver add-in.

Printing House Ltd. wants to find the minimum total cost assignment of three jobs to three typesetters.

APPROACH ▶ The cost table shown earlier in this section is repeated here, and steps 1 through 4 are applied.

JOB \ TYPESETTER	A	B	C
R-34	$11	$14	$6
S-66	$8	$10	$11
T-50	$9	$12	$7

SOLUTION ▶

STEP 1A: Using the previous table, subtract the smallest number in each row from every number in the row. The result is shown in the table on the left.

JOB \ TYPESETTER	A	B	C
R-34	5	8	0
S-66	0	2	3
T-50	2	5	0

JOB \ TYPESETTER	A	B	C
R-34	5	6	0
S-66	0	0	3
T-50	2	3	0

STEP 1B: Using the above left table, for columns that do not contain zero, subtract the smallest number in each column from every number in the column. The result is shown in the table on the right.

STEP 2: Draw the minimum number of vertical and horizontal straight lines needed to cover all zeros. Because two lines suffice, the solution is not optimal.

JOB \ TYPESETTER	A	B	C
R-34	5	6	0
S-66	0	0	3
T-50	②	3	0

Smallest uncovered number

STEP 3: Subtract the smallest uncovered number (2 in this table) from every other uncovered number and add it to numbers at the intersection of two lines.

JOB \ TYPESETTER	A	B	C
R-34	3	4	0
S-66	0	0	5
T-50	0	1	0

Return to step 2. Cover the zeros with straight lines again.

JOB \ TYPESETTER	A	B	C
R-34	3	4	0
S-66	0	0	5
T-50	0	1	0

Because three lines are necessary, an optimal assignment can be made (see step 4 in the text for an explanation). Assign R-34 to person C, S-66 to person B, and T-50 to person A. Referring to the original cost table, we see that:

$$\text{Minimum cost} = \text{US\$6} + \text{US\$10} + \text{US\$9} = \text{US\$25}$$

INSIGHT ▶ If we had assigned S-66 to typesetter A, we could not assign T-50 to a zero location.

LEARNING EXERCISE ▶ If it costs US$10 for Typesetter C to complete R-34 (instead of US$6), how does the solution change? [Answer: R-34 to A, S-66 to B, T-50 to C: cost = US$28.]

RELATED PROBLEMS ▶ 15.3, 15.4, 15.5

EXCEL **OM** Data File **Ch15Ex4.xls** can be found at MyOMLab.

Some assignment problems entail *maximizing* profit, effectiveness, or payoff of an assignment of people to tasks or of jobs to machines. An equivalent minimization problem can be obtained by converting every number in the table to an *opportunity loss*. To convert a maximizing problem to an equivalent minimization problem, we create a minimizing table by subtracting every number in the original payoff table from the largest single number in that table. We then proceed to step 1 of the four-step assignment method. Minimizing the opportunity loss produces the same assignment solution as the original maximization problem.

SEQUENCING JOBS

Scheduling provides a basis for assigning jobs to work centers. Loading is a capacity-control technique that highlights overloads and underloads. **Sequencing** (also referred to as dispatching) specifies the order in which jobs should be done at each center. For example, suppose that ten patients are assigned to a medical clinic for treatment. In what order should they be treated? Should the first patient to be served be the one who arrived first or the one who needs emergency treatment? Sequencing methods provide such guidelines. These methods are referred to as priority rules for sequencing or dispatching jobs to work centers.

Priority Rules for Dispatching Jobs

Priority rules provide guidelines for the sequence in which jobs should be worked. The rules are especially applicable for process-focused facilities such as clinics, print shops, and manufacturing job shops. We will examine a few of the most popular priority rules. Priority rules try to minimize completion time, number of jobs in the system, and job lateness while maximizing facility utilization.

> **AUTHOR COMMENT**
> Once jobs are loaded, managers must decide the sequence in which they are to be completed.

Sequencing
Determining the order in which jobs should be done at each work center.

Priority rules
Rules used to determine the sequence of jobs in process-oriented facilities.

The most popular priority rules are:

- **First come, first served (FCFS):** the first job to arrive at a work center is processed first.
- **Shortest processing time (SPT):** the shortest jobs are handled first and completed.
- **Earliest due date (EDD):** the job with the earliest due date is selected first.
- **Longest processing time (LPT):** the longer, bigger jobs are often very important and are selected first.

Example 5 compares these rules.

EXAMPLE 5 ▶

Priority Rules For Dispatching

Five architectural rendering jobs are waiting to be assigned at Fujeira Architects. Their work (processing) times and due dates are given in the following table. The firm wants to determine the sequence of processing according to: (1) FCFS; (2) SPT; (3) EDD; (4) LPT rules. Jobs were assigned a letter in the order they arrived.

JOB	JOB WORK (PROCESSING) TIME (DAYS)	JOB DUE DATE (DAYS)
A	6	8
B	2	6
C	8	18
D	3	15
E	9	23

APPROACH ▶   Each of the four priority rules is examined in turn. Four measures of effectiveness can be computed for each rule and then compared to see which rule is best for the company.

SOLUTION ▶

1. The *FCFS* sequence shown in the next table is simply A–B–C–D–E. The 'flow time' in the system for this sequence measures the time each job spends waiting plus time being processed. Job B, for example, waits 6 days while job A is being processed, then takes 2 more days of operation time itself; so it will be completed in 8 days—which is 2 days later than its due date.

JOB SEQUENCE	JOB WORK (PROCESSING) TIME	FLOW TIME	JOB DUE DATE	JOB LATENESS
A	6	6	8	0
B	2	8	6	2
C	8	16	18	0
D	3	19	15	4
E	9	28	23	5
	28	77		11

The first-come, first-served rule results in the following measures of effectiveness:

a. Average completion time $= \dfrac{\text{Sum of total flow time}}{\text{Number of jobs}}$

$= \dfrac{77 \text{ days}}{5} = 15.4 \text{ days}$

b. Utilization metric $= \dfrac{\text{Total job work (processing) time}}{\text{Sum of total flow time}}$

$= \dfrac{28}{77} = 36.4\%$

c. Average number of jobs in the system $= \dfrac{\text{Sum of total flow time}}{\text{Total job work (processing) time}}$

$= \dfrac{77 \text{ days}}{28 \text{ days}} = 2.75 \text{ jobs}$

d. Average job lateness $= \dfrac{\text{Total late days}}{\text{Number of jobs}} = \dfrac{11}{5} = 2.2 \text{ days}$

2. The *SPT* rule shown in the next table results in the sequence B–D–A–C–E. Orders are sequenced according to processing time, with the highest priority given to the shortest job.

JOB SEQUENCE	JOB WORK (PROCESSING) TIME	FLOW TIME	JOB DUE DATE	JOB LATENESS
B	2	2	6	0
D	3	5	15	0
A	6	11	8	3
C	8	19	18	1
E	9	28	23	5
	28	65		9

Measurements of effectiveness for SPT are:

a. Average completion time $= \dfrac{65}{3} = 13$ days

b. Utilization metric $= \dfrac{28}{65} = 43.1\%$

c. Average number of jobs in the system $= \dfrac{65}{28} = 2.32$ jobs

d. Average job lateness $= \dfrac{9}{5} = 1.8$ days

3. The *EDD* rule shown in the next table gives the sequence B–A–D–C–E. Note that jobs are ordered by earliest due date first.

JOB SEQUENCE	JOB WORK (PROCESSING) TIME	FLOW TIME	JOB DUE DATE	JOB LATENESS
B	2	2	6	0
A	6	8	8	0
D	3	11	15	0
C	8	19	18	1
E	9	28	23	5
	28	68		6

Measurements of effectiveness for EDD are:

a. Average completion time $= \dfrac{68}{5} = 13.6$ days

b. Utilization metric $= \dfrac{28}{68} = 41.2\%$

c. Average number of jobs in the system $= \dfrac{68}{28} = 2.43$ jobs

d. Average job lateness $= \dfrac{6}{5} = 1.2$ days

4. The *LPT* rule shown in the next table results in the order E–C–A–D–B.

JOB SEQUENCE	JOB WORK (PROCESSING) TIME	FLOW TIME	JOB DUE DATE	JOB LATENESS
E	9	9	23	0
C	8	17	18	0
A	6	23	8	15
D	3	26	15	11
B	2	28	6	22
	28	103		48

LO4: Name and describe each of the priority sequencing rules

Measures of effectiveness for LPT are:

a. Average completion time $= \dfrac{103}{5} = 20.6$ days

b. Utilization metric $= \dfrac{28}{103} = 27.2\%$

c. Average number of jobs in the system $= \dfrac{103}{28} = 3.68$ jobs

d. Average job lateness $= \dfrac{48}{5} = 9.6$ days

The results of these four rules are summarized in the following table:

RULE	AVERAGE COMPLETION TIME (DAYS)	UTILIZATION METRIC (%)	AVERAGE NUMBER OF JOBS IN SYSTEM	AVERAGE LATENESS (DAYS)
FCFS	15.4	36.4	2.75	2.2
SPT	13.0	43.1	2.32	1.8
EDD	13.6	41.2	2.43	1.2
LPT	20.6	27.2	3.68	9.6

INSIGHT ▶ LPT is the least effective measurement for sequencing for the Fujeira Architects firm. SPT is superior in three measures, and EDD is superior in the fourth (average lateness).

LEARNING EXERCISE ▶ If job A takes 7 days (instead of 6), how do the four measures of effectiveness change under the FCFS rule? [Answer: 16.4 days, 35.4%, 2.83 jobs, 2.8 days late.]

RELATED PROBLEMS ▶ 15.6, 15.7

EXCEL OM Data File **Ch15Ex5.xls** can be found at MyOMLab.

The results in Example 5 are typically true in the real world also. No one sequencing rule always excels on all criteria. Experience indicates the following:

1. *Shortest processing time* is generally the best technique for minimizing job flow and minimizing the average number of jobs in the system. Its chief disadvantage is that long-duration jobs may be continuously pushed back in priority in favor of short-duration jobs. Customers may view this dimly, and a periodic adjustment for longer jobs must be made.
2. *First come, first served* does not score well on most criteria (but neither does it score particularly poorly). It has the advantage, however, of appearing fair to customers, which is important in service systems.
3. *Earliest due date* minimizes maximum tardiness, which may be necessary for jobs that have a very heavy penalty after a certain date. In general, EDD works well when lateness is an issue.

Critical Ratio

Critical ratio (CR)

A sequencing rule that is an index number computed by dividing the time remaining until due date by the work time remaining.

Another type of sequencing rule is the critical ratio. The **critical ratio (CR)** is an index number computed by dividing the time remaining until due date by the work time remaining. As opposed to the priority rules, critical ratio is dynamic and easily updated. It tends to perform better than FCFS, SPT, EDD, or LPT on the average job-lateness criterion.

The critical ratio gives priority to jobs that must be done to keep shipping on schedule. A job with a low critical ratio (less than 1.0) is one that is falling behind schedule. If CR is exactly 1.0, the job is on schedule. A CR greater than 1.0 means the job is ahead of schedule and has some slack.

The formula for critical ratio is:

$$CR = \frac{\text{Time remaining}}{\text{Workdays remaining}} = \frac{\text{Due date} - \text{Today's date}}{\text{Work (lead) time remaining}}$$

Your doctor may use a first-come, first-served priority satisfactorily. However, such a rule may be less than optimal for this emergency room. What priority rule might be best, and why? What priority rule is often used on TV hospital dramas?

Example 6 shows how to use the critical ratio.

◄ **EXAMPLE 6**

Critical ratio

Today is day 25 on Zyco Medical Testing Laboratories' production schedule. Three jobs are on order, as indicated here:

Job	Due Date	Workdays Remaining
A	30	4
B	28	5
C	27	2

APPROACH ► Zyco wants to compute the critical ratios, using the formula for CR.

SOLUTION ►

Job	Critical Ratio	Priority Order
A	$(30 - 25) \div 4 = 1.25$	3
B	$(28 - 25) \div 5 = 0.60$	1
C	$(27 - 25) \div 2 = 1.00$	2

INSIGHT ► Job B has a critical ratio of less than 1, meaning it will be late unless expedited. Thus, it has the highest priority. Job C is on time and job A has some slack. Once job B has been completed, we would recompute the critical ratios for jobs A and C to determine whether their priorities have changed.

LEARNING EXERCISE ► Today is day 24 (a day earlier) on Zyco's schedule. Recompute the CRs and determine the priorities. [Answer: 1.5, 0.8, 1.5; B is still number 1, but now jobs A and C are tied for second.]

In most production scheduling systems, the critical-ratio rule can help do the following:

1. Determine the status of a specific job.
2. Establish relative priority among jobs on a common basis.
3. Relate both make-to-stock and make-to-order jobs on a common basis.
4. Adjust priorities (and revise schedules) automatically for changes in both demand and job progress.
5. Dynamically track job progress.

Sequencing *N* Jobs on Two Machines: Johnson's Rule

The next step in complexity is the case in which *N* jobs (where *N* is 2 or more) must go through two different machines or work centers in the same order. This is called the *N*/2 problem.

Johnson's rule can be used to minimize the processing time for sequencing a group of jobs through two work centers. It also minimizes total idle time on the machines. *Johnson's rule* involves four steps:

Johnson's rule

An approach that minimizes processing time for sequencing a group of jobs through two work centers while minimizing total idle time in the work centers.

1. All jobs are to be listed, and the time that each requires on a machine is to be shown.
2. Select the job with the shortest activity time. If the shortest time lies with the first machine, the job is scheduled first. If the shortest time lies with the second machine, schedule the job last. Ties in activity times can be broken arbitrarily.
3. Once a job is scheduled, eliminate it.
4. Apply Steps 2 and 3 to the remaining jobs, working toward the center of the sequence.

Example 7 shows how to apply Johnson's rule.

EXAMPLE 7 ▶

Johnson's rule

Five specialty jobs at a Marrakech Tool and Die Shop must be processed through two work centers (drill press and lathe). The time for processing each job follows:

Work (processing) Time for Jobs (hours)

Job	Work Center 1 (drill press)	Work Center 2 (lathe)
A	5	2
B	3	6
C	8	4
D	10	7
E	7	12

The owner, Laith, wants to set the sequence to minimize his total processing time for the five jobs.

APPROACH ▶   Laith applies the four steps of Johnson's rule.

SOLUTION ▶

1. The job with the shortest processing time is A, in work center 2 (with a time of 2 hours). Because it is at the second center, schedule A last. Eliminate it from consideration.

				A

2. Job B has the next shortest time (3 hours). Because that time is at the first work center, we schedule it first and eliminate it from consideration.

B				A

LO5: Use Johnson's rule

3. The next shortest time is job C (4 hours) on the second machine. Therefore, it is placed as late as possible.

B			C	A

4. There is a tie (at 7 hours) for the shortest remaining job. We can place E, which was on the first work center, first. Then D is placed in the last sequencing position.

B	E	D	C	A

The sequential times are:

Work center 1	3	7	10	8	5
Work center 2	6	12	7	4	2

The time-phased flow of this job sequence is best illustrated graphically:

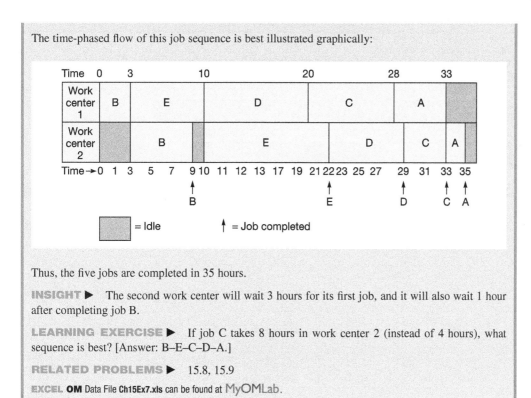

Thus, the five jobs are completed in 35 hours.

INSIGHT ▶ The second work center will wait 3 hours for its first job, and it will also wait 1 hour after completing job B.

LEARNING EXERCISE ▶ If job C takes 8 hours in work center 2 (instead of 4 hours), what sequence is best? [Answer: B–E–C–D–A.]

RELATED PROBLEMS ▶ 15.8, 15.9

EXCEL OM Data File **Ch15Ex7.xls** can be found at MyOMLab.

Limitations of Rule-Based Dispatching Systems

The scheduling techniques just discussed are rule-based techniques, but rule-based systems have a number of limitations. Among these are the following:

1. Scheduling is dynamic; therefore, rules need to be revised to adjust to changes in orders, process, equipment, product mix, and so forth.
2. Rules do not look upstream or downstream; idle resources and bottleneck resources in other departments may not be recognized.
3. Rules do not look beyond due dates. For instance, two orders may have the same due date. One order involves restocking a distributor and the other is a custom order that will shut down the customer's factory if not completed. Both may have the same due date, but clearly the custom order is more important.

Despite these limitations, schedulers often use sequencing rules such as SPT, EDD, or critical ratio. They apply these methods at each work center and then modify the sequence to deal with a multitude of real-world variables. They may do this manually or with finite capacity scheduling software.

FINITE CAPACITY SCHEDULING

Short-term scheduling is also called finite capacity scheduling.[4] **Finite capacity scheduling (FCS)** overcomes the disadvantages of systems based exclusively on rules by providing the scheduler with interactive computing and graphic output. In dynamic scheduling environments such as job shops (with a high variety, low volume, and shared resources) we expect changes— but changes disrupt schedules. Therefore, operations managers are moving toward FCS systems that allow virtually instantaneous change by the operator. Improvements in communication on the shop floor are also enhancing the accuracy and speed of information necessary for effective control in job shops. Computer-controlled machines can monitor events and collect information in near real-time. This means the scheduler can make schedule changes based on up-to-the-minute

Finite capacity scheduling

Computerized short-term scheduling that overcomes the disadvantage of rule-based systems by providing the user with graphical interactive computing.

---

[4]Finite capacity scheduling (FCS) systems go by a number of names, including finite scheduling and advance planning systems (APS). The name manufacturing execution systems (MES) may also be used, but MES tends to suggest an emphasis on the reporting system from shop operations back to the scheduling activity.

▶ **FIGURE 15.5**

This Lekin® finite capacity scheduling software presents a schedule of the five jobs and the two work centers shown in Example 7 (pages 490–491) in Gantt chart form. The software is capable of using a variety of priority rules, several shop types, up to 50 jobs, 20 work centers, and 100 machines to generate a schedule. The Lekin software is available for free at **www.stern.nyc.edu/om/ software/lekin/download/html** and can solve many of the problems at the end of this chapter.

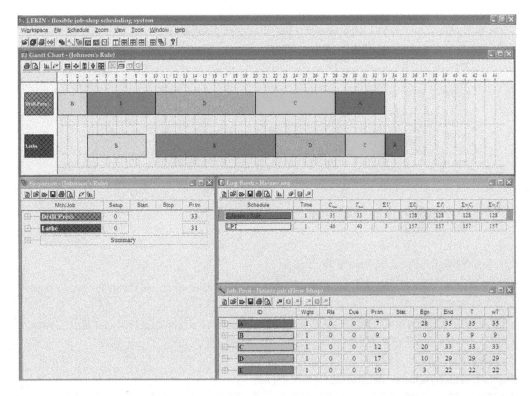

LO6: Define finite capacity scheduling

information. These schedules are often displayed in Gantt chart form. In addition to including priority rule options, many of the current FCS systems also combine an 'expert system' or simulation techniques and allow the scheduler to assign costs to various options. The scheduler has the flexibility to handle any situation, including order, labor, or machine changes.

The initial data for finite scheduling systems is often the output from an MRP system. The output from MRP systems is traditionally in weekly 'buckets' that have no capacity constraint. These systems just tell the planner when the material is needed, ignoring the capacity issue. Because *infinite*-size buckets are unrealistic and inadequate for detailed scheduling, MRP data require refinement. MRP output is combined with routing files, due dates, capacity of work centers, tooling, and other resource availability to provide the data needed for effective FCS. These are the same data needed in any manual system, but FCS software formalizes them, speeds analysis, and makes changes easier. The combining of MRP and FCS data, priority rules, models to assist analysis, and Gantt chart output is shown in Figure 15.6.

▶ **FIGURE 15.6**

Finite Capacity Scheduling Systems Combine MRP and Shop Floor Production Data to Generate a Gantt Chart That Can Be Manipulated by the User on a Computer Screen

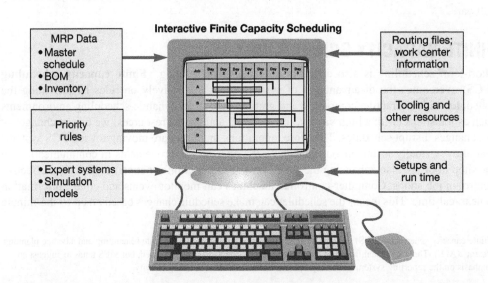

Finite capacity scheduling allows delivery requirements to be based on today's conditions and today's orders, not according to some predefined rule. The scheduler determines what constitutes a 'good' schedule. FCS software packages such as Lekin, ProPlanner, Preactor, Asprova, Tactic, and Jobplan are the most commonly used around the world.

SCHEDULING REPETITIVE FACILITIES

AUTHOR COMMENT
Repetitive producers create forward-looking schedules with level material use.

The scheduling goals defined at the beginning of this chapter are also appropriate for repetitive production. You may recall from Chapter 7 that repetitive producers make standard products from modules. The usual approach is to develop a forward-looking schedule on a balanced assembly line. (Refer to Table 15.2 on page 479.)

Repetitive producers want to satisfy customer demands, lower inventory investment, and reduce the batch (or lot) size, with existing equipment and processes. A technique to move toward these goals is to use a level-material-use schedule. **Level material use** means frequent, high-quality, small lot sizes that contribute to just-in-time production. This is exactly what world-class producers such as Harley-Davidson, Almarai, and Johnson Controls do. The advantages of level material use are:

Level material use
The use of frequent, high-quality, small lot sizes that contribute to just-in-time production.

1. Lower inventory levels, which releases capital for other uses.
2. Faster product throughput (that is, shorter lead times).
3. Improved component quality and hence improved product quality.
4. Reduced floor-space requirements.
5. Improved communication among employees because they are closer together (which can result in improved teamwork and *esprit de corps*).
6. Smoother production process because large lots have not 'hidden' the problems.

Suppose a repetitive producer runs large monthly batches: With a level-material-use schedule, management would move toward shortening this monthly cycle to a weekly, daily, or even hourly cycle.

One way to develop a level-material-use schedule is to first determine the minimum lot size that will keep the production process moving. This is illustrated in the next chapter, 'JIT and Lean Operations.'

SCHEDULING SERVICES

AUTHOR COMMENT
Scheduling people to perform services can be even more complex than scheduling machines.

Scheduling service systems differs from scheduling manufacturing systems in several ways:

- In manufacturing, the scheduling emphasis is on machines and materials; in services, it is on staffing levels.
- Inventories can help smooth demand for manufacturers, but many service systems do not maintain inventories.
- Services are labor intensive, and the demand for this labor can be highly variable.
- Legal considerations, such as wage and hour laws and union contracts that limit hours worked per shift, week, or month, constrain scheduling decisions.
- Because services usually schedule people rather than material, behavioral, social, seniority, and status issues complicate scheduling.

The following examples note the complexity of scheduling services.

Hospitals   A hospital is an example of a service facility that may use a scheduling system every bit as complex as one found in a job shop. Hospitals seldom use a machine shop priority system such as first come, first served (FCFS) for treating emergency patients. However, they do schedule products (such as surgeries) just like a factory, and capacities must meet wide variations in demand.

Banks   Cross-training of the workforce in a bank allows loan officers and other managers to provide short-term help for tellers if there is a surge in demand. Banks also employ part-time personnel to provide a variable capacity.

Retail Stores   Scheduling optimization systems, such as Workbrain, Cybershift, and Kronos, are used at retailers including Grand Stores, Cozmo, Payless Shoes, Target, and Radio Shack.

These systems track individual store sales, transactions, units sold, and customer traffic in 15-minute increments to create work schedules. For these large national firms, scheduling employees used to take thousands of managers' hours; now staffing is drawn up nationwide in a few hours, and customer checkout experience has improved dramatically.

Airlines   Airlines face two constraints when scheduling flight crews: (1) a complex set of Federal Aviation Administration (FAA) work-time limitations; (2) union contracts that guarantee crew are paid for some number of hours each day or each trip. Airline planners must build crew schedules that meet or exceed crews' pay guarantees. Planners must also make efficient use of their other expensive resource: aircraft. These schedules are typically built using linear programming models.

24/7 Operations   Emergency hotlines, police/fire departments, mail-order businesses, telephone operations, and call centers (such as Kuwaiti firm Zain) schedule employees 24 hours a day, 7 days a week. To allow management flexibility in staffing, sometimes part-time workers can be employed. This provides both benefits (in using odd shift lengths or matching anticipated workloads) and difficulties (from the large number of possible alternatives in terms of days off, lunch-hour times, rest periods, starting times). Most companies use computerized scheduling systems to cope with these complexities.

Scheduling Service Employees with Cyclical Scheduling

A number of techniques and algorithms exist for scheduling service-sector employees such as police officers, nurses, restaurant staff, tellers, and retail sales clerks. Managers, trying to set a timely and efficient schedule that keeps personnel happy, can spend substantial time each month developing employee schedules. Such schedules often consider a fairly long planning period (say, 6 weeks). One approach that is workable yet simple is *cyclical scheduling*.

LO7: Use the cyclical scheduling technique

Cyclical Scheduling   Cyclical scheduling with inconsistent staffing needs is often the case in services such as restaurants and police work. Here the objective focuses on developing a schedule with the minimum number of workers. In these cases, each employee is assigned to a shift and has time off. Let's look at Example 8.

EXAMPLE 8 ▶

Cyclical scheduling

Hospital administrator Mazouzeh Al-Azzeh wants to staff the oncology ward using a standard 5-day working week with two consecutive days off, but also wants to minimize the staff. However, as in most hospitals, she faces an inconsistent demand. Weekends have low usage. Doctors tend to work early in the week, and patients peak on Wednesday then taper off.

APPROACH ▶   Mazouzeh must first establish staffing requirements. Then the following five-step process is applied.

SOLUTION ▶

1. Determine the necessary daily staffing requirements. Mazouzeh has done this:

Day	Monday	Tuesday	Wednesday	Thursday	Friday	Saturday	Sunday
Staff required	5	5	6	5	4	3	3

2. Identify the two consecutive days that have the *lowest total requirement* and circle these. Assign these two days off to the first employee. In this case, the first employee has Saturday and Sunday off because 3 plus 3 is the *lowest sum* of any 2 days. In the case of a tie, choose the days with the lowest adjacent requirement, or by first assigning Saturday and Sunday as an 'off' day. If there are more than one, make an arbitrary decision.
3. We now have an employee working each of the uncircled days; therefore, make a new row for the next employee by subtracting 1 from the first row (because one day has been worked)—except for the circled days (which represent the days not worked) and any day that has a zero. That is, do not subtract from a circled day or a day that has a value of zero.
4. In the new row, identify the two consecutive days that have the lowest total requirement and circle them. Assign the next employee to the remaining days.

5. Repeat the process (steps 3 and 4) until all staffing requirements are met.

	Monday	Tuesday	Wednesday	Thursday	Friday	Saturday	Sunday
Employee 1	5	5	6	5	4	③	③
Employee 2	4	4	5	4	3	③	③
Employee 3	3	3	4	3	②	③	3
Employee 4	2	2	3	②	②	3	2
Employee 5	①	①	2	2	2	2	1
Employee 6	1	1	1	1	1	①	⓪
Employee 7						1	
Capacity (measured in number of employees)	5	5	6	5	4	3	3
Excess capacity	0	0	0	0	0	1	0

Mazouzeh needs six full-time employees to meet the staffing needs and one employee to work Saturday.

Notice that capacity (number of employees) equals requirements, provided an employee works overtime on Saturday, or a part-time employee is hired for Saturday.

INSIGHT ▶ Mazouzeh has implemented an efficient scheduling system that accommodates 2 consecutive days off for every employee.

LEARNING EXERCISE ▶ If Mazouzeh meets the staffing requirement for Saturday with a full-time employee, how does she schedule that employee? [Answer: That employee can have any 2 days off, except Saturday, and capacity will exceed requirements by one person each day the employee works (except Saturday).]

RELATED PROBLEMS ▶ 15.10, 15.11

Other cyclical scheduling techniques have been developed to aid service scheduling. Some approaches use linear programming. This is how Hard Rock Cafe schedules its services (see the Video Case Study at the end of this chapter). There is a natural bias in scheduling to use tools that are understood and yield solutions that are accepted.

CHAPTER SUMMARY

Scheduling involves the timing of operations to achieve the efficient movement of units through a system. This chapter addressed the issues of short-term scheduling in process-focused, repetitive, and service environments. We saw that process-focused facilities are production systems in which products are made to order and that scheduling tasks in them can become complex. Several aspects and approaches to scheduling, loading, and sequencing of jobs were introduced. These ranged from Gantt charts and the assignment method of scheduling to a series of priority rules, the critical-ratio rule, Johnson's rule for sequencing, and finite capacity scheduling.

Service systems generally differ from manufacturing systems. This leads to the use of first-come, first-served rules and appointment and reservation systems, as well as to heuristics and linear programming approaches for matching capacity to demand in service environments.

Key Terms

Assignment method (p. 483)
Backward scheduling (p. 478)
ConWIP cards (p. 481)
Critical ratio (CR) (p. 488)
Earliest due date (EDD) (p. 486)
Finite capacity scheduling (FCS) (p. 491)

First come, first served (FCFS) (p. 486)
Forward scheduling (p. 478)
Gantt charts (p. 482)
Input–output control (p. 480)
Johnson's rule (p. 490)
Level material use (p. 493)

Loading (p. 480)
Longest processing time (LPT) (p. 486)
Priority rules (p. 485)
Sequencing (p. 485)
Shortest processing time (SPT) (p. 486)

Ethical Dilemma

Scheduling people to work second and third shifts (evening and 'graveyard') is a problem in almost every 24-hour company. The *OM in Action* box 'Scheduling Workers Who Fall Asleep Is a Killer—Literally,' on page 479, describes potentially dangerous issues on working the night shifts. Perhaps even more significantly, ergonomic data indicate the body does not respond well to significant shifts in its natural circadian rhythm of sleep. There are also significant long-term health issues with frequent changes in work and sleep cycles.

Consider yourself the manager of a nonunion steel mill that must operate 24-hour days, and where the physical demands are such that 8-hour days are preferable to 10- or 12-hour days. Your empowered employees have decided that they want to work weekly rotating shifts. That is, they want a repeating work cycle of 1 week, 7 a.m. to 3 p.m., followed by a second week from 3 p.m. to 11 p.m., and the third week from 11 p.m. to 7 a.m. You are sure this is not a good idea in terms of both productivity and the long-term health of the employees. If you do not accept their decision, you undermine the work empowerment program, generate a morale issue, and perhaps,

more significantly, generate few more votes for a union. What is the ethical position and what do you do?

Discussion Questions

1. What is the overall objective of scheduling?
2. List the four criteria for determining the effectiveness of a *scheduling* decision. How do these criteria relate to the four criteria for *sequencing* decisions?
3. Describe what is meant by 'loading' work centers. What are the two ways work centers can be loaded? What are two techniques used in loading?
4. Name five priority sequencing rules. Explain how each works to assign jobs.
5. What are the advantages and disadvantages of the shortest processing time (SPT) rule?
6. What is a due date?
7. Explain the terms *flow time* and *lateness*.
8. Which shop-floor scheduling rule would you prefer to apply if you were the leader of the only team of experts charged with defusing several time bombs scattered throughout your building? You can see the bombs; they are of different types. You can tell how long each one will take to defuse. Discuss.
9. When is Johnson's rule best applied in job-shop scheduling?
10. State the four effectiveness measures for dispatching rules.
11. What are the steps of the assignment method of linear programming?
12. What are the advantages of level material flow?
13. What is input–output control?

Using Software for Short-Term Scheduling

In addition to the commercial software we noted in this chapter, short-term scheduling problems can be solved with the Excel OM software that comes free at MyOMLab. POM for Windows also includes a scheduling module. The use of each of these programs is explained next.

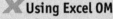 Using Excel OM

Excel OM has two modules that help solve short-term scheduling problems: Assignment and Job Shop Scheduling. The Assignment module is illustrated in Programs 15.1 and 15.2. The input screen, using the Example 4 data, appears first, as Program 15.1. Once the data are all entered, we choose the 'Tools' command, followed by the 'Solver' command. Excel's Solver uses linear programming to optimize assignment problems. The constraints are also shown in Program 15.1. We then select the 'Solve' command and the solution appears in Program 15.2.

Excel OM's Job Shop Scheduling module is illustrated in Program 15.3. Program 15.3 uses Example 5's data. Because jobs are listed in the sequence in which they arrived (see column A), the results are for the FCFS rule. Program 15.3 also shows some of the formulas (columns F, G, H, I, J) used in the calculations.

To solve with the SPT rule, we need four intermediate steps: (1) Select (that is, highlight) the data in columns A, B, and C for all jobs; (2) invoke the 'Data' command; (3) invoke the 'Sort' command; (4) sort by 'Time' (column C) in *ascending* order. To solve for EDD, step 4 changes to sort by 'Due Date' (column D) in *ascending* order. Finally, for an LPT solution, step 4 becomes sort by 'Due Date' (column D) in *descending* order.

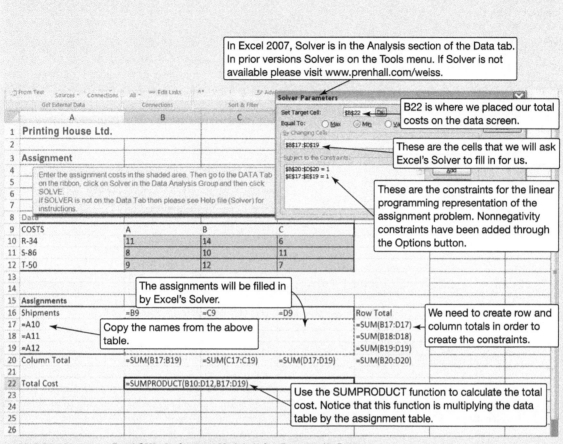

▲ **PROGRAM 15.1** **Excel OM's Assignment Module Using Example 4's Data**

After entering the problem data in the yellow area, select Tools, then Solver.

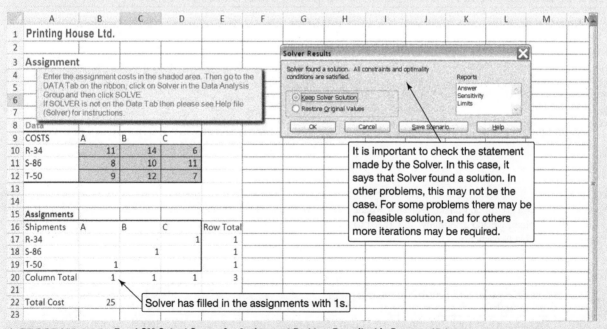

▲ **PROGRAM 15.2** **Excel OM Output Screen for Assignment Problem Described in Program 15.1**

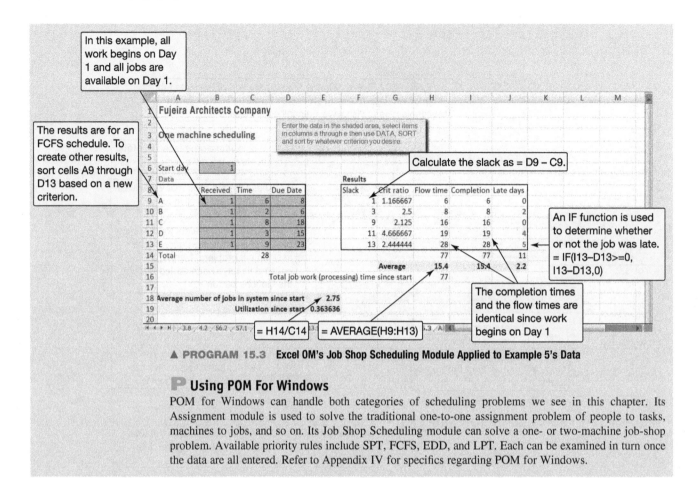

▲ PROGRAM 15.3   Excel OM's Job Shop Scheduling Module Applied to Example 5's Data

P Using POM For Windows

POM for Windows can handle both categories of scheduling problems we see in this chapter. Its Assignment module is used to solve the traditional one-to-one assignment problem of people to tasks, machines to jobs, and so on. Its Job Shop Scheduling module can solve a one- or two-machine job-shop problem. Available priority rules include SPT, FCFS, EDD, and LPT. Each can be examined in turn once the data are all entered. Refer to Appendix IV for specifics regarding POM for Windows.

Solved Problems   Solved Problems Virtual Office Hours help is available at MyOMLab

▼ SOLVED PROBLEM 15.1

King Finance Corporation, headquartered in New York, wants to assign three recently hired college graduates, Julie Jones, Al Smith and Pat Wilson, to regional offices. However, the firm also has an opening in New York and would send one of the three there if it were more economical than a move to Omaha, Dallas or Miami. It will cost US$1,000 to relocate Jones to New York, US$800 to relocate Smith there, and US$1,500 to move Wilson. What is the optimal assignment of personnel to offices?

OFFICE HIREE	OMAHA	MIAMI	DALLAS
Jones	US$800	US$1,100	US$1,200
Smith	US$500	US$1,600	US$1,300
Wilson	US$500	US$1,000	US$2,300

▼ SOLUTION

(a) The cost table has a fourth column to represent Riyadh. To 'balance' the problem, we add a 'dummy' row (person) with a zero relocation cost to each city.

(b) Subtract the smallest number in each row and cover all zeros (column subtraction of each column's zero will give the same numbers and therefore is not necessary):

OFFICE HIREE	OMAHA	MIAMI	DALLAS	NEW YORK
Jones	US$800	US$1,100	US$1,200	US$1,000
Smith	US$500	US$1,600	US$1,300	US$800
Wilson	US$500	US$1,000	US$2,300	US$1,500
Dummy	0	0	0	0

OFFICE HIREE	OMAHA	MIAMI	DALLAS	NEW YORK
Jones	0	300	400	200
Smith	0	1,100	800	300
Wilson	0	500	1,800	1,000
Dummy	0	0	0	0

(c) Only two lines cover, so subtract the smallest uncovered number (200) from all uncovered numbers, and add it to each square where two lines intersect. Then cover all zeros:

OFFICE / HIREE	OMAHA	MIAMI	DALLAS	NEW YORK
Jones	0	100	200	0
Smith	0	900	600	100
Wilson	0	300	1,600	800
Dummy	200	0	0	0

(d) Only three lines cover, so subtract the smallest uncovered number (100) from all uncovered numbers, and add it to each square where two lines intersect. Then cover all zeros:

OFFICE / HIREE	OMAHA	MIAMI	DALLAS	NEW YORK
Jones	100	0	100	0
Smith	0	700	400	0
Wilson	0	100	1,400	700
Dummy	400	0	0	100

(e) Still only three lines cover, so subtract the smallest uncovered number (100) from all uncovered numbers, add it to squares where two lines intersect, and cover all zeros:

OFFICE / HIREE	OMAHA	MIAMI	DALLAS	NEW YORK
Jones	0	0	100	0
Smith	0	800	500	100
Wilson	0	200	1,500	800
Dummy	300	0	0	100

(f) Because it takes four lines to cover all zeros, an optimal assignment can be made at zero squares. We assign:

Wilson to Omaha
Jones to Miami
Dummy (no one) to Dallas
Smith to New York

$$\text{Cost} = \text{US\$500} + \text{US\$1,100} + \text{US\$0} + \text{US\$800}$$
$$= \text{US\$2,400}$$

▼ SOLVED PROBLEM 15.2

A defense contractor in Dallas has six jobs awaiting processing. Processing time and due dates are given in the table. Assume that jobs arrive in the order shown. Set the processing sequence according to FCFS and evaluate.

JOB	JOB PROCESSING TIME (DAYS)	JOB DUE DATE (DAYS)
A	6	22
B	12	14
C	14	30
D	2	18
E	10	25
F	4	34

▼ SOLUTION

FCFS has the sequence A–B–C–D–E–F.

JOB SEQUENCE	JOB PROCESSING TIME	FLOW TIME	DUE DATE	JOB LATENESS
A	6	6	22	0
B	12	18	14	4
C	14	32	30	2
D	2	34	18	16
E	10	44	25	19
F	4	48	34	14
	48	182		55

1. Average completion time = 182 ÷ 6 = 30.33 days
2. Average number of jobs in system = 182 ÷ 48 = 3.79 jobs
3. Average job lateness = 55 ÷ 6 = 9.16 days
4. Utilization = 48 ÷ 182 = 26.4%

▼ SOLVED PROBLEM 15.3

The Dallas firm in Solved Problem 15.2 also wants to consider job sequencing by the SPT priority rule. Apply SPT to the same data and provide a recommendation.

▼ SOLUTION

SPT has the sequence D–F–A–E–B–C.

JOB SEQUENCE	JOB PROCESSING TIME	FLOW TIME	DUE DATE	JOB LATENESS
D	2	2	18	0
F	4	6	34	0
A	6	12	22	0
E	10	22	25	0
B	12	34	14	20
C	14	48	30	18
	48	124		38

1. Average completion time = 124 ÷ 6 = 20.67 days
2. Average number of jobs in system = 124 ÷ 48 = 2.58 jobs
3. Average job lateness = 38 ÷ 6 = 6.33 days
4. Utilization = 48 ÷ 124 = 38.7%

SPT is superior to FCFS in this case on all four measures. If we were to also analyze EDD, we would, however, find its average job lateness to be lowest at 5.5 days. SPT is a good recommendation. SPT's major disadvantage is that it makes long jobs wait, sometimes for a long time.

▼ **SOLVED PROBLEM 15.4**

Use Johnson's rule to find the optimum sequence for processing the jobs shown through two work centers. Times at each center are in hours.

JOB	WORK CENTER 1	WORK CENTER 2
A	6	12
B	3	7
C	18	9
D	15	14
E	16	8
F	10	15

▼ SOLUTION

B	A	F	D	C	E

The sequential times are:

Work center 1	3	6	10	15	18	16
Work center 2	7	12	15	14	9	8

▼ **SOLVED PROBLEM 15.5**

Illustrate the throughput time and idle time at the two work centers in Solved Problem 15.4 by constructing a time-phased chart.

▼ SOLUTION

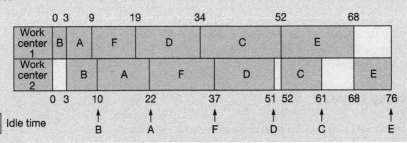

Problems*

15.1 Mousa's excavation company uses both Gantt scheduling charts and Gantt load charts.

a) Today, which is the end of day 7, Mousa is reviewing the Gantt chart depicting these schedules:

- Job #151 was scheduled to begin on day 3 and to take 6 days. As of now, it is 1 day ahead of schedule.
- Job #177 was scheduled to begin on day 1 and take 4 days. It is currently on time.
- Job #179 was scheduled to start on day 7 and take 2 days. It actually got started on day 6 and is progressing according to plan.
- Job #211 was scheduled to begin on day 5, but missing equipment delayed it until day 6. It is progressing as expected and should take 3 days.
- Job #215 was scheduled to begin on day 4 and take 5 days. It got started on time but has since fallen behind 2 days.

Draw the Gantt scheduling chart for the activities above.

b) Mousa now wants to use a Gantt load chart to see how much work is scheduled in each of his three work teams: Jalal, Bakkar, and Kamal. Five jobs constitute the current workload for these three work teams: Job #250, requiring 48 hours and #275 requiring 32 hours for Work Team Jamal; Jobs #210, and #280 requiring 16 and 24 hours, respectively, for Team Bakkar; and Job #225, requiring 40 hours, for Team Kamal.

Prepare the Gantt load chart for these activities.

15.2 Printing House Ltd. has four more jobs to be scheduled, in addition to those shown in Example 3 in the chapter. Production scheduling personnel are reviewing the Gantt chart at the end of day 4.

- Job D was scheduled to begin early on day 2 and to end on the middle of day 9. As of now (the review point after day 4), it is 2 days ahead of schedule.
- Job E should begin on day 1 and end on day 3. It was on time.
- Job F was to begin on day 3, but maintenance forced a delay of $1\frac{1}{2}$ days. The job should now take 5 full days. It is now on schedule.
- Job G is a day behind schedule. It started at the beginning of day 2 and should require 6 days to complete.

Develop a Gantt schedule chart for Printing House Ltd.

15.3 The Aleppo Cab Company has a taxi waiting at each of four cabstands in Castle. Four customers have called and requested service. The distances, in kilometers, from the waiting taxis to the customers are given in the following table. Find the optimal assignment of taxis to customers so as to minimize total driving distances to the customers.

	Customer			
Cab Site	A	B	C	D
Stand 1	7	3	4	8
Stand 2	5	4	6	5
Stand 3	6	7	9	6
Stand 4	8	6	7	4

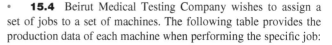

15.4 Beirut Medical Testing Company wishes to assign a set of jobs to a set of machines. The following table provides the production data of each machine when performing the specific job:

	Machine			
Job	A	B	C	D
1	7	9	8	10
2	10	9	7	6
3	11	5	9	6
4	9	11	5	8

a) Determine the assignment of jobs to machines that will *maximize* total production.
b) What is the total production of your assignments?

15.5 Alexandria Manufacturing Company is putting out four new electronic components. Each of the four plants has the capacity to add one more product to its current line of electronic parts. The unit-manufacturing costs for producing the different parts at the four plants are shown in the accompanying table. How should the company assign the new products to the plants to minimize manufacturing costs?

Electronic	Plant			
Component	1	2	3	4
C53	US$0.10	US$0.12	US$0.13	US$0.11
C81	0.05	0.06	0.04	0.08
D5	0.32	0.40	0.31	0.30
D44	0.17	0.14	0.19	0.15

15.6 The following jobs are waiting to be processed at Mustafa's machine center. Mustafa's machine center has a relatively long backlog and sets fresh schedules every 2 weeks, which do not disturb earlier schedules. Below are the jobs received during the previous 2 weeks. They are ready to be scheduled today, which is day 241 (day 241 is a work day). Job names refer to names of clients and contract numbers.

Job	Date Job Received	Production Days Needed	Date Job Due
BR-02	228	15	300
CX-01	225	25	270
DE-06	230	35	320
RG-05	235	40	360
SY-11	231	30	310

a) Complete the table below. (Show your supporting calculations.)
b) Which dispatching rule has the best score for flow time?
c) Which dispatching rule has the best score for utilization metric?
d) Which dispatching rule has the best score for lateness?
e) Which dispatching rule would you select? Support your decision.

Dispatching Rule	Job Sequence	Flow Time	Utilization Metric	Average Number of Jobs	Average Lateness
EDD					
SPT					
LPT					
FCFS					

*Note: means the problem may be solved with POM for Windows and/or Excel OM.

•• **15.7** The following jobs are waiting to be processed at Oman's Machine Center:

Job	Date Order Received	Production Days Needed	Date Order Due
A	110	20	180
B	120	30	200
C	122	10	175
D	125	16	230
E	130	18	210

In what sequence would the jobs be ranked according to the following rules: (a) FCFS, (b) EDD, (c) SPT, and (d) LPT? All dates are according to shop calendar days. Today on the planning calendar is day 130, and none of the jobs have been started or scheduled. Which rule is best? **Px**

•• **15.8** Baraka Tailors has been asked to make three different types of wedding suits for separate customers. The table below highlights the time taken in hours for: (1) cutting and sewing; (2) delivery of each of the suits. Which schedule finishes sooner: First-come, first-served (123) or a schedule using Johnson's rule?

Times Taken for Different Activities (hours)

Suit	Cut and Sew	Deliver
1	4	2
2	7	7
3	6	5

Px

••• **15.9** Six jobs are to be processed through a two-step operation. The first operation involves sanding, and the second involves painting. Processing times are as follows:

Job	Operation 1 (hours)	Operation 2 (hours)
A	10	5
B	7	4
C	5	7
D	3	8
E	2	6
F	4	3

Determine a sequence that will minimize the total completion time for these jobs. Illustrate graphically. **Px**

•• **15.10** Juma's Barber Shop at Abdali in Amman is open 7 days a week but has fluctuating demand. Juma is interested in treating his barbers as well as he can with steady work and preferably 5 days of work with two consecutive days off. His analysis of his staffing needs resulted in the following plan. Schedule Juma's staff with the minimum number of barbers.

	Day						
	Mon.	Tue.	Wed.	Thu.	Fri.	Sat.	Sun.
Barbers needed	6	5	5	5	6	4	3

•• **15.11** Given the following demand for waiters and waitresses at Shorta Grill, determine the minimum wait staff needed with a policy of two consecutive days off.

	Day						
	Mon.	Tue.	Wed.	Thu.	Fri.	Sat.	Sun.
Wait staff needed	3	4	4	5	6	7	4

•• **15.12** Dawood owns an automated machine shop that makes precision auto parts. He has just compiled an input–output report for the grinding work center. Complete this report and analyze the results.

Input–Output Report

Period	1	2	3	4	Total
Planned input	80	80	100	100	
Actual input	85	85	85	85	
Deviation					
Planned output	90	90	90	90	
Actual output	85	85	80	80	
Deviation					
Initial backlog: 30					

▶ Refer to MyOMLab for additional homework problems.

Case Studies

▶ Quds Wood Store

In 2011, Mahmoud started the Quds Wood Store to manufacture Quds tables. Each table is carefully constructed by hand using the highest-quality olive trees. Quds tables can support more than 250 kilograms, and since the start of the Quds Wood Store, not one table has been returned because of faulty workmanship or structural problems. In addition to being rugged, each table is beautifully finished using a urethane varnish that Mahmoud developed over 20 years of working with wood-finishing materials.

The manufacturing process consists of four steps: preparation, assembly, finishing, and packaging. Each step is performed by one person. In addition to overseeing the entire operation, Mahmoud

does all of the finishing. Khaleel performs the preparation step, which involves cutting and forming the basic components of the tables. Haroun is in charge of the assembly, and Rana performs the packaging.

Although each person is responsible for only one step in the manufacturing process, everyone can perform any one of the steps. It is Mahmoud's policy that occasionally everyone should complete several tables on his or her own without any help or assistance. A small competition is used to see who can complete an entire table in the least amount of time. Mahmoud maintains average total and intermediate completion times. The data are shown in Figure 15.7.

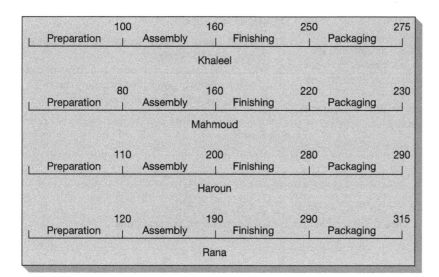

◀ **FIGURE 15.7**
Manufacturing Time in Minutes

◀ **FIGURE 15.8**
Samer's Completion Times in Minutes

It takes Rana longer than the other employees to construct a table. In addition to being slower than the other employees, Rana is also unhappy about her current responsibility of packaging, which leaves her idle most of the day. Her first preference is finishing, and her second preference is preparation.

In addition to quality, Mahmoud is concerned with costs and efficiency. When one of the employees misses a day, it causes major scheduling problems. In some cases, Mahmoud assigns another employee overtime to complete the necessary work. At other times, Mahmoud simply waits until the employee returns to work to complete his or her step in the manufacturing process. Both solutions cause problems. Overtime is expensive, and waiting causes delays and sometimes stops the entire manufacturing process.

To overcome some of these problems, Samer was hired. Samer's major duties are to perform miscellaneous jobs and to help out if one of the employees is absent. Mahmoud has given Samer training in all phases of the manufacturing process, and he is pleased with the speed at which Samer has been able to learn how to completely assemble Quds tables. Samer's average total and intermediate completion times are given in Figure 15.8.

Discussion Questions

1. What is the fastest way to manufacture Quds tables using the original crew? How many could be made per day?
2. Would production rates and quantities change significantly if Mahmoud would allow Samer to perform one of the four functions and make one of the original crew the backup person?
3. What is the fastest time to manufacture a table with the original crew if Rana is moved to either preparation or finishing?
4. Whoever performs the packaging function is severely underutilized. Can you find a better way of utilizing the four- or five-person crew than either giving each a single job or allowing each to manufacture an entire table? How many tables could be manufactured per day with this scheme?

► **Scheduling at Hard Rock Cafe**

Video Case

Whether it's scheduling nurses at Mayo Clinic, pilots at Southwest Airlines, classrooms at UCLA (the University of California, Los Angeles), or servers at a Hard Rock Cafe, it's clear that good scheduling is important. Proper schedules use an organization's assets: (1) more effectively, by serving customers promptly; (2) more efficiently, by lowering costs.

Hard Rock Cafe at Universal Studios, Orlando, Florida is the world's largest restaurant, with 1,100 seats on two main levels. With typical turnover of employees in the restaurant industry at 80 percent to 100 percent per year, Hard Rock General Manager Ken Hoffman takes scheduling very seriously. Hoffman wants his 160 servers to be effective, but he also wants to treat them fairly. He has done so well with scheduling software and flexibility that has increased productivity while contributing to turnover that is half the industry average. His goal is to find the fine balance that gives employees financially

productive daily work shifts while setting the schedule tight enough so as to not overstaff between lunch and dinner.

The weekly schedule begins with a sales forecast. "First, we examine last year's sales at the café for the same day of the week," says Hoffman. "Then we adjust our forecast for this year based on a variety of closely watched factors. For example, we call the Orlando Convention Bureau every week to see what major groups will be in town. Then we send two researchers out to check on the occupancy of nearby hotels. We watch closely to see what concerts are scheduled at Hard Rock Live—the 3,000-seat concert stage next door. From the forecast, we calculate how many people we need to have on duty each day for the kitchen, the bar, as hosts, and for table service."

Once Hard Rock determines the number of staff needed, servers submit request forms, which are fed into the software's linear programming mathematical model. Individuals are given priority rankings from 1 to 9, based on their seniority and how important they are to fill each day's schedule. Schedules are then posted by day and by workstation. Trades are handled between employees, who understand the value of each specific shift and station.

Hard Rock employees like the system, as does the general manager, since sales per labor-hour are rising and turnover is dropping.

Discussion Questions*

1. Name and justify several factors that Hoffman could use in forecasting weekly sales.
2. What can be done to lower turnover in large restaurants?
3. Why is seniority important in scheduling servers?
4. How does the schedule impact on productivity?

*You may wish to view the video accompanying this case before addressing these questions.

▶**Additional Case Study:** Visit MyOMLab for this free case study:

Payroll Planning, Inc.: Describes setting a schedule for handling the accounting for dozens of client firms.

Main Heading	Review Material	
THE IMPORTANCE OF SHORT-TERM SCHEDULING (p. 476)	The strategic importance of scheduling is clear: ■ Effective scheduling means *faster movement* of goods and services through a facility. This means greater use of assets and hence greater capacity per dollar invested, which, in turn, *lowers cost*. ■ Added capacity, faster throughput, and the related flexibility mean better customer service through *faster delivery*. ■ Good scheduling contributes to realistic commitments, hence *dependable delivery*.	
SCHEDULING ISSUES (pp. 476–479)	*The objective of scheduling is to allocate and prioritize demand (generated by either forecasts or customer orders) to available facilities.* ■ **Forward scheduling**—Begins the schedule as soon as the requirements are known. ■ **Backward scheduling**—Begins with the due date by scheduling the final operation first and the other job steps in reverse order. The four scheduling criteria are: (1) *minimize completion time*; (2) *maximize utilization*; (3) *minimize work-in-process (WIP) inventory*; (4) *minimize customer waiting time*.	**VIDEO 15.1** Scheduling at Hard Rock Cafe
SCHEDULING PROCESS-FOCUSED FACILITIES (p. 480)	A process-focused facility is a high-variety, low-volume system commonly found in manufacturing and services. It is also called an intermittent, or job shop, facility. Control files track the actual progress made against the plan for each work order.	
LOADING JOBS (pp. 480–485)	■ **Loading**—The assigning of jobs to work or processing centers. ■ **Input–output control**—Allows operations personnel to manage facility work flows by tracking work added to a work center and its work completed. ■ **ConWIP cards**—Cards that control the amount of work in a work center, aiding input–output control. ConWIP is an acronym for *constant work-in-process*. A ConWIP card travels with a job (or batch) through the work center. When the job is finished, the card is released and returned to the initial workstation, authorizing the entry of a new batch into the work center. ■ **Gantt charts**—Planning charts used to schedule resources and allocate time. The Gantt *load chart* shows the loading and idle times of several departments, machines, or facilities. It displays the relative workloads in the system so that the manager knows what adjustments are appropriate. The Gantt *schedule chart* is used to monitor jobs in progress (and is also used for project scheduling). It indicates which jobs are on schedule and which are ahead of or behind schedule. ■ **Assignment method**—A special class of linear programming models that involves assigning tasks or jobs to resources. In assignment problems, only one job (or worker) is assigned to one machine (or project). The assignment method involves adding and subtracting appropriate numbers in the table to find the lowest *opportunity cost* for each assignment.	Problems: 15.1–15.5, 15.12 Virtual Office Hours for Solved Problems: 15.1
SEQUENCING JOBS (pp. 485–491)	■ **Sequencing**—Determining the order in which jobs should be done at each work center. ■ **Priority rules**—Rules used to determine the sequence of jobs in process-oriented facilities. ■ **First come, first served (FCFS)**—Jobs are completed in the order in which they arrived. ■ **Shortest processing time (SPT)**—Jobs with the shortest processing times are assigned first. ■ **Earliest due date (EDD)**—Earliest due date jobs are performed first. ■ **Longest processing time (LPT)**—Jobs with the longest processing time are completed first: $$\text{Average completion time} = \frac{\text{Sum of total flow time}}{\text{Number of jobs}}$$ $$\text{Utilization metric} = \frac{\text{Total job work (processing) time}}{\text{Sum of total flow time}}$$ $$\text{Average number of jobs in the system} = \frac{\text{Sum of total flow time}}{\text{Total job work (processing) time}}$$ $$\text{Average job lateless} = \frac{\text{Total late days}}{\text{Number of jobs}}$$	Problems: 15.6–15.9 Virtual Office Hours for Solved Problems: 15.2–15.5

Main Heading	Review Material	
	SPT is the best technique for minimizing job flow and average number of jobs in the system.	
	FCFS performs about average on most criteria, and it appears fair to customers.	
	EDD minimizes maximum tardiness.	
	■ **Critical ratio (CR)**—A sequencing rule that is an index number computed by dividing the time remaining until due date by the work time remaining: $$CR = \frac{\text{Time remaining}}{\text{Workdays remaining}} = \frac{\text{Due date} - \text{Today's date}}{\text{Work (lead) time remaining}}$$ As opposed to the priority rules, the critical ratio is dynamic and easily updated. It tends to perform better than FCFS, SPT, EDD, or LPT on the average job-lateness criterion.	
	■ **Johnson's rule**—An approach that minimizes processing time for sequencing a group of jobs through two work centers while minimizing total idle time in the work centers.	
	Rule-based scheduling systems have the following limitations: (1) scheduling is dynamic; (2) rules do not look upstream or downstream; (3) rules do not look beyond due dates.	
FINITE CAPACITY SCHEDULING (FCS) (pp. 491–493)	**Finite capacity scheduling (FCS)**—Computerized short-term scheduling that overcomes the disadvantage of rule-based systems by providing the user with graphical interactive computing.	
SCHEDULING REPETITIVE FACILITIES (p. 493)	**Level material use**—The use of frequent, high-quality, small lot sizes that contribute to just-in-time production.	
	Advantages of level material use are: (1) lower inventory levels; (2) faster product throughput; (3) improved component and product quality; (4) reduced floor-space requirements; (5) improved communication among employees; (6) a smoother production process.	
SCHEDULING SERVICES (pp. 493–495)	Cyclical scheduling with inconsistent staffing needs is often the case in services. The objective focuses on developing a schedule with the minimum number of workers. In these cases, each employee is assigned to a shift and has time off.	Problems: 15.10–15.11

Self-Test

■ **Before taking the self-test**, refer to the learning objectives listed at the beginning of the chapter and the key terms listed at the end of the chapter.

LO1. Which of the following decisions covers the longest time period?
   a) short-term scheduling
   b) capacity planning
   c) aggregate planning
   d) a master schedule.

LO2. A visual aid used in loading and scheduling jobs is a:
   a) Gantt chart
   b) planning file
   c) bottleneck
   d) load-schedule matrix
   e) level material chart.

LO3. The assignment method involves adding and subtracting appropriate numbers in the table to find the lowest _____ for each assignment.
   a) profit
   b) number of steps
   c) number of allocations
   d) range per row
   e) opportunity cost.

LO4. The most popular priority rules include:
   a) FCFS
   b) EDD
   c) SPT
   d) all of the above.

LO5. The job that should be scheduled last when using Johnson's rule is the job with the:
   a) largest total processing time on both machines
   b) smallest total processing time on both machines
   c) longest activity time if it lies with the first machine
   d) longest activity time if it lies with the second machine
   e) shortest activity time if it lies with the second machine.

LO6. Computerized short-term scheduling that overcomes the disadvantage of rule-based systems by providing the user with graphical interactive computing is called:
   a) LPT
   b) FCS
   c) CSS
   d) FCFS
   e) GIC.

LO7. Cyclical scheduling is used to schedule:
   a) jobs
   b) machines
   c) shipments
   d) employees.

16 JIT, Lean Operations, and the Toyota Production System

10

OM STRATEGY DECISIONS

▶ Design of Goods and Services
▶ Managing Quality
▶ Process Strategy
▶ Location Strategies
▶ Layout Strategies
▶ Human Resources
▶ Supply-Chain Management
▶ Inventory Management
  ▪ Independent Demand
  ▪ Dependent Demand
  ▪ JIT and Lean Operations
▶ Scheduling
▶ Maintenance

ACHIEVING COMPETITIVE ADVANTAGE WITH LEAN OPERATIONS AT TOYOTA MOTOR CORPORATION

Toyota Motor Corporation, with annual sales of over 9 million cars and trucks, is the largest vehicle manufacturer in the world. Two techniques, just-in-time (JIT) and the Toyota Production System (TPS), have been instrumental in this post-WWII growth. Toyota, with a wide range of vehicles, competes head-to-head with successful long-established companies in Europe and the United States. Taiichi Ohno, a former executive vice president of Toyota, created the basic framework for the world's most discussed systems for improving productivity: JIT and TPS. These two concepts provide much of the foundation for lean operations:

- Central to JIT is a philosophy of continued problem solving. In practice, JIT means making only what is

needed, when it is needed. JIT provides an excellent vehicle for finding and eliminating problems because problems are easy to find in a system that has no slack. When excess inventory is eliminated, quality, layout, scheduling, and supplier issues become immediately evident—as does excess production.

- Central to TPS is employee learning and a continuing effort to create and produce products under ideal conditions. Ideal conditions exist only when facilities, machines, and people are brought together, adding value without waste. Waste undermines productivity by diverting resources to excess inventory, unnecessary processing, and poor quality. Respect for people, extensive training, cross-training, and standard work practices of empowered employees focusing on driving out waste are fundamental to TPS.

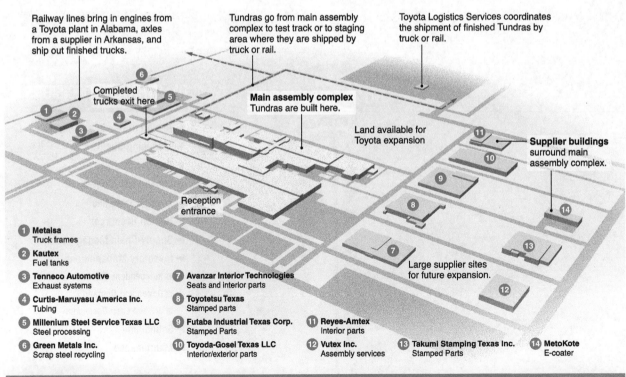

Railway lines bring in engines from a Toyota plant in Alabama, axles from a supplier in Arkansas, and ship out finished trucks.

Tundras go from main assembly complex to test track or to staging area where they are shipped by truck or rail.

Toyota Logistics Services coordinates the shipment of finished Tundras by truck or rail.

Completed trucks exit here

Main assembly complex
Tundras are built here.

Land available for Toyota expansion

Supplier buildings surround main assembly complex.

Reception entrance

Large supplier sites for future expansion.

1 **Metalsa**
Truck frames

2 **Kautex**
Fuel tanks

3 **Tenneco Automotive**
Exhaust systems

4 **Curtis-Maruyasu America Inc.**
Tubing

5 **Millenium Steel Service Texas LLC**
Steel processing

6 **Green Metals Inc.**
Scrap steel recycling

7 **Avanzar Interior Technologies**
Seats and interior parts

8 **Toyotetsu Texas**
Stamped parts

9 **Futaba Industrial Texas Corp.**
Stamped Parts

10 **Toyoda-Gosei Texas LLC**
Interior/exterior parts

11 **Reyes-Amtex**
Interior parts

12 **Vutex Inc.**
Assembly services

13 **Takumi Stamping Texas Inc.**
Stamped Parts

14 **MetoKote**
E-coater

14 Suppliers outside the main plant

Outside, Toyota has an 8 km² site with 14 of the 21 onsite suppliers, adjacent rail lines and a nearby interstate highway. The site provides expansion space for both Toyota and for its suppliers, and provides an environment for JIT.

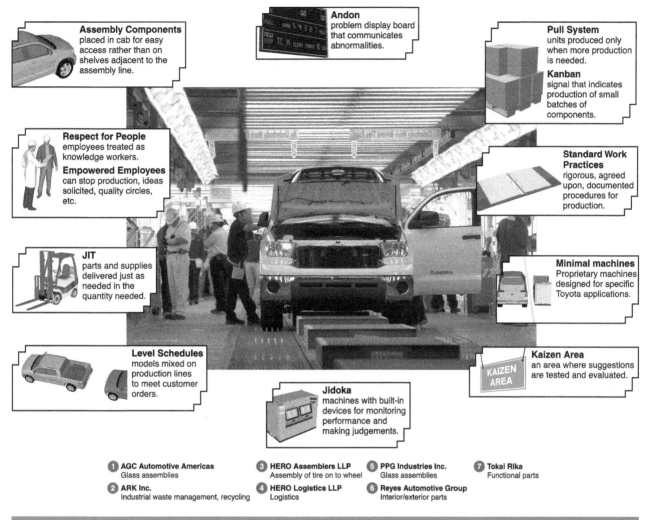

Assembly Components placed in cab for easy access rather than on shelves adjacent to the assembly line.

Andon problem display board that communicates abnormalities.

Pull System units produced only when more production is needed.

Kanban signal that indicates production of small batches of components.

Respect for People employees treated as knowledge workers.

Empowered Employees can stop production, ideas solicited, quality circles, etc.

Standard Work Practices rigorous, agreed upon, documented procedures for production.

JIT parts and supplies delivered just as needed in the quantity needed.

Minimal machines Proprietary machines designed for specific Toyota applications.

Level Schedules models mixed on production lines to meet customer orders.

Jidoka machines with built-in devices for monitoring performance and making judgements.

Kaizen Area an area where suggestions are tested and evaluated.

KAIZEN AREA

① **AGC Automotive Americas** Glass assemblies

② **ARK Inc.** Industrial waste management, recycling

③ **HERO Assemblers LLP** Assembly of tire on to wheel

④ **HERO Logistics LLP** Logistics

⑤ **PPG Industries Inc.** Glass assemblies

⑥ **Reyes Automotive Group** Interior/exterior parts

⑦ **Tokai Rika** Functional parts

7 Suppliers inside the main plant

Toyota's San Antonio plant has interior space of about 610 km², providing the facilities within the final assembly building for 7 of the 21 onsite suppliers, and capacity to build 200,000 pick-up trucks annually. But most importantly, Toyota practices the world-class Toyota Production System and expects its suppliers to do the same thing wherever they are.

Toyota's latest implementation of TPS and JIT is present at its new plant in San Antonio, Texas, the largest Toyota land site for an automobile assembly plant in the United States. Interestingly, despite its annual production capability of 200,000 Tundra pick-up trucks, the building itself is one of the smallest in the industry. Modern automobiles have 30,000 parts, but at Toyota, independent suppliers combine many of these parts into subassemblies. Twenty-one of these suppliers are on site and transfer components to the assembly line on a JIT basis.

Operations such as these taking place in the new San Antonio plant are why Toyota continues to perform near the top in quality and maintain the lowest labor-hour assembly time in the industry. JIT, TPS, and lean operations work—and they provide a competitive advantage at Toyota Motor Corporation.

Chapter 16 Learning Objectives

AUTHOR COMMENT
World-class firms everywhere are using these three techniques.

LO1: Define just-in-time, TPS, and lean operations

Just-in-time (JIT)
Continuous and forced problem solving via a focus on throughput and reduced inventory.

Toyota Production System (TPS)
Focus on continuous improvement, respect for people, and standard work practices.

Lean operations
Eliminates waste through a focus on exactly what the customer wants.

JUST-IN-TIME, THE TOYOTA PRODUCTION SYSTEM, AND LEAN OPERATIONS

As shown in the *Company Profile*, the Toyota Production System (TPS) contributes to a world-class operation at Toyota Motor Corporation. In this chapter, we discuss JIT, TPS, and lean operations as approaches to continuing improvement that drive out waste and lead to world-class organizations.

Just-in-time (JIT) is an approach of continuous and forced problem solving via a focus on throughput and reduced inventory. The **Toyota Production System (TPS)**, with its emphasis on continuous improvement, respect for people, and standard work practices, is particularly suited for assembly lines. **Lean operations** supplies the customer with exactly what the customer wants when the customer wants it, without waste, through continuous improvement. Lean operations are driven by workflow initiated by the 'pull' of the customer's order. When implemented as a comprehensive manufacturing strategy, JIT, TPS, and lean systems sustain competitive advantage and result in increased overall returns.

If there is any distinction between JIT, TPS, and lean operations, it is that:

- JIT emphasizes forced problem solving.
- TPS emphasizes employee learning and empowerment in an assembly-line environment.
- Lean operations emphasize understanding the customer.

However, in practice, there is little difference, and the terms are often used interchangeably. Leading organizations use the approaches and techniques that make sense for them. In this chapter, we use the term *lean operations* to encompass all of the related approaches and techniques.

Regardless of the label put on operations improvement, good production systems require that managers address three issues that are pervasive and fundamental to operations management: eliminate waste, remove variability, and improve throughput. We first introduce these three issues and then discuss the major attributes of JIT, TPS, and lean operations. Finally, we look at lean operations applied to services.

Eliminate Waste

LO2: Define the seven wastes and the 5Ss

Traditional producers have limited goals—accepting, for instance, the production of some defective parts and some inventory. Lean producers set their sights on perfection: no bad parts, no inventory, only value-added activities, and no waste. Any activity that does not add value in the eyes of the customer is a waste. The customer defines product value. If the customer does not want to pay for it, it is a waste. Taiichi Ohno, noted for his work on the Toyota Production System, identified seven categories of waste. These categories have become popular in lean organizations and cover many of the ways organizations waste or lose money. Ohno's **seven wastes** are:

Seven wastes
Overproduction
Queues
Transportation
Inventory
Motion
Overprocessing
Defective product

- *Overproduction:* Producing more than the customer orders or producing early (before it is demanded) is waste. Inventory of any kind is usually a waste.
- *Queues:* Idle time, storage, and waiting are wastes (they add no value).
- *Transportation:* Moving material between plants or between work centers and handling more than once is waste.
- *Inventory:* Unnecessary raw material, work-in-process (WIP), finished goods, and excess operating supplies add no value and are wastes.
- *Motion:* Movement of equipment or people that adds no value is waste.

- *Overprocessing:* Work performed on the product that adds no value is waste.
- *Defective product:* Returns, warranty claims, rework, and scrap are a waste.

A broader perspective—one that goes beyond immediate production—suggests that other resources, such as energy, water, and air, are often wasted but should not be. Efficient, sustainable production minimizes inputs and maximizes outputs, wasting nothing.

For over a century, managers have pursued 'housekeeping' for a neat, orderly, and efficient workplace and as a means of reducing waste. Operations managers have embellished 'housekeeping' to include a checklist—now known as the **5Ss**.[1] The Japanese developed the initial 5Ss. Not only are the 5Ss a good checklist for lean operations, they also provide an easy vehicle with which to assist the culture change that is often necessary to bring about lean operations. The 5Ss follow:

5Ss

A lean production checklist:
Sort
Simplify
Shine
Standardize
Sustain

- *Sort/segregate:* Keep what is needed and remove everything else from the work area; when in doubt, throw it out. Identify non-value items and remove them. Getting rid of these items makes space available and usually improves work flow.
- *Simplify/straighten:* Arrange and use methods analysis tools (see Chapter 7 and Chapter 10) to improve work flow and reduce wasted motion. Consider long-run and short-run ergonomic issues. Label and display for easy use only what is needed in the immediate work area. For examples of visual displays see Figure 10.9, page 307.
- *Shine/sweep:* Clean daily; eliminate all forms of dirt, contamination, and clutter from the work area.
- *Standardize:* Remove variations from the process by developing standard operating procedures and checklists; good standards make the abnormal obvious. Standardize equipment and tooling so that cross-training time and cost are reduced. Train and retrain the work team so that when deviations occur, they are readily apparent to all.
- *Sustain/self-discipline:* Review periodically to recognize efforts and to motivate to sustain progress. Use visuals wherever possible to communicate and sustain progress.

International managers such as those in Europe and the United States often add two additional Ss that contribute to establishing and maintaining a lean workplace:

- *Safety:* Build good safety practices into the above five activities.
- *Support/maintenance:* Reduce variability, unplanned downtime, and costs. Integrate daily shine tasks with preventive maintenance.

Remove Variability

Managers seek to remove variability caused by both internal and external factors. **Variability** is any deviation from the optimum process that delivers perfect product on time, every time. Variability is a polite word for problems. The less variability in a system, the less waste in the system. Most variability is caused by tolerating waste or by poor management. Among the many sources of variability are:

Variability

Any deviation from the optimum process that delivers perfect product on time, every time.

- Poor production processes that allow employees and suppliers to produce improper quantities or late or non-conforming units.
- Unknown customer demands.
- Incomplete or inaccurate drawings, specifications, and bills of material.

Both JIT and inventory reduction are effective tools for identifying causes of variability. The precise timing of JIT makes variability evident, just as reducing inventory exposes variability. The removal of variability allows managers to move good materials on schedule, add value at each step of the production process, drive down costs, and win orders.

Improve Throughput

Throughput time

The time required to move orders through the production process, from receipt to delivery.

Throughput time is the time that it takes to move an order from receipt to delivery. Each minute products remain on the books, costs accumulate and competitive advantage is lost. The time that

---

[1]The term 5S comes from the Japanese words seiri (*sort* and clear out), seiton (*straighten* and configure), seiso (*scrub* and cleanup), seiketsu (maintain *sanitation* and cleanliness of self and workplace), and shitsuke (*self-discipline and standardization* of these practices).

Manufacturing cycle time

The time between the arrival of raw materials and the shipping of finished products.

an order is in the shop is called **manufacturing cycle time**. This is the time between the arrival of raw materials and the shipping of finished product. For example, phone-system manufacturer Hatef now has materials pulled directly from qualified suppliers to the assembly line. This effort has reduced a segment of Hatef's manufacturing cycle time from one month to just one day, the incoming inspection staff from 89 to 35, and problems on the shop floor caused by defective materials by 90 percent. Driving down manufacturing cycle time can make a major improvement in throughput.

Pull system

A concept that results in material being produced only when requested and moved to where it is needed just as it is needed.

A technique for increasing throughput is a pull system. A **pull system** *pulls* a unit to where it is needed just as it is needed. Pull systems are a standard tool of JIT systems. Pull systems use signals to request production and delivery from supplying stations to stations that have production capacity available. The pull concept is used both within the immediate production process and with suppliers. By *pulling* material through the system in very small lots—just as it is needed—waste and inventory are removed. As inventory is removed, clutter is reduced, problems become evident, and continuous improvement is emphasized. Removing the cushion of inventory also reduces both investment in inventory and manufacturing cycle time. A push system dumps orders on the next downstream workstation, regardless of timelines and resource availability. Push systems are the antithesis of JIT. Pulling material through a production process as it is needed rather than in a 'push' mode typically lowers cost and improves schedule performance, enhancing customer satisfaction.

AUTHOR COMMENT
JIT places added demands on performance, but that is why it pays off.

JUST-IN-TIME (JIT)

With its forced problem solving via a focus on rapid throughput and reduced inventory, JIT provides a powerful strategy for improving operations. With JIT, materials arrive *where* they are needed only *when* they are needed. When good units do not arrive just as needed, a 'problem' has been identified. By driving out waste and delay in this manner, JIT reduces costs associated with excess inventory, cuts variability and waste, and improves throughput. JIT is a key ingredient of lean operations and is particularly helpful in supporting strategies of rapid response and low cost. Every moment material is held, an activity that adds value should be occurring. Consequently, as Figure 16.1 suggests, JIT often yields a competitive advantage.

Effective JIT requires a meaningful buyer–supplier partnership.

JIT Partnerships

Just-in-time (JIT) partnerships

Partnerships of suppliers and purchasers that remove waste and drive down costs for mutual benefits.

A **just-in-time (JIT) partnership** exists when a supplier and a purchaser work together with open communication and a goal of removing waste and driving down costs. Close relationships

Many services have adopted JIT techniques as a normal part of their business. Restaurants like Al Tazaj expect and receive JIT deliveries. Both buyer and supplier expect fresh, high-quality produce delivered without fail just when it is needed. The system doesn't work any other way.

JIT TECHNIQUES:

Suppliers:	Few vendors; Supportive supplier relationships; Quality deliveries on time, directly to work areas.
Layout:	Work-cells; Group technology; Flexible machinery; Organized workplace; Reduced space for inventory.
Inventory:	Small lot sizes; Low setup time; Specialized parts bins
Scheduling:	Zero deviation from schedules; Level schedules; Suppliers informed of schedules; Kanban techniques
Preventive maintenance:	Scheduled; Daily routine; Operator involvement
Quality production:	Statistical process control; Quality suppliers; Quality within the firm
Employee empowerment:	Empowered and cross-trained employees; Training support; Few job classifications to ensure flexibility of employees
Commitment:	Support of management, employees, and suppliers

WHICH RESULTS IN:

Rapid throughput frees assets

Quality improvement reduces waste

Cost reduction adds pricing flexibility

Variability reduction

Rework reduction

WHICH WINS ORDERS BY:

Faster response to the customer at lower cost and higher quality—

A Competitive Advantage

and trust are critical to the success of JIT. Figure 16.2 shows the characteristics of JIT partnerships. Some specific goals of JIT partnerships are:

- *Removal of unnecessary activities*, such as receiving, incoming inspection, and paperwork related to bidding, invoicing, and payment.
- *Removal of in-plant inventory* by delivery in small lots directly to the using department as needed.
- *Removal of in-transit inventory* by encouraging suppliers to locate nearby and provide frequent small shipments. The shorter the flow of material in the resource pipeline, the less inventory. Inventory can also be reduced through a technique known as *consignment*. **Consignment inventory** a variation of vendor-managed inventory (Chapter 11), means the supplier maintains the title to the inventory until it is used. For instance, an assembly plant may find a hardware supplier that is willing to locate its warehouse where the user currently has its stockroom. In this manner, when hardware is needed, it is no farther than the stockroom. Schedule and production information must be shared with the consignment supplier, or inventory holding costs will just be transferred from the buyer to the supplier, with no net cost reduction. Another option is to have the supplier ship to other, perhaps smaller, purchasers from the 'stockroom.'
- *Obtain improved quality and reliability* through long-term commitments, communication, and cooperation.

Consignment inventory

An arrangement in which the supplier maintains title to the inventory until it is used.

Leading organizations view suppliers as extensions of their own organizations and expect suppliers to be fully committed to improvement. Such relationships require a high degree of respect by both supplier and purchaser. Supplier concerns can be significant; Harley-Davidson, for example, initially had difficulty implementing JIT because supplier issues outweighed the perceived benefits.

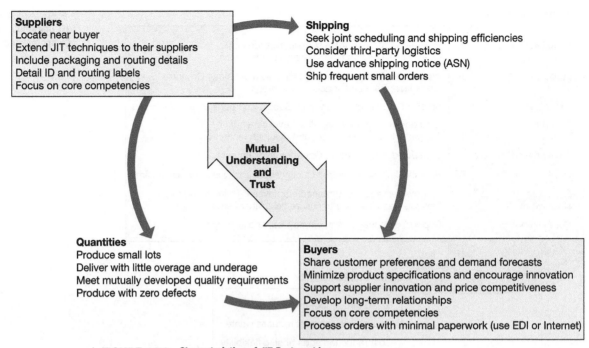

Suppliers
Locate near buyer
Extend JIT techniques to their suppliers
Include packaging and routing details
Detail ID and routing labels
Focus on core competencies

Shipping
Seek joint scheduling and shipping efficiencies
Consider third-party logistics
Use advance shipping notice (ASN)
Ship frequent small orders

Mutual Understanding and Trust

Quantities
Produce small lots
Deliver with little overage and underage
Meet mutually developed quality requirements
Produce with zero defects

Buyers
Share customer preferences and demand forecasts
Minimize product specifications and encourage innovation
Support supplier innovation and price competitiveness
Develop long-term relationships
Focus on core competencies
Process orders with minimal paperwork (use EDI or Internet)

▲ **FIGURE 16.2   Characteristics of JIT Partnerships**

Concerns of Suppliers

LO3: Explain JIT partnerships

Successful JIT partnerships require that supplier concerns be addressed. These concerns include:

1. *Diversification:* Suppliers may not want to tie themselves to long-term contracts with one customer. The suppliers' perception is that they reduce their risk if they have a variety of customers.
2. *Scheduling:* Many suppliers have little faith in the purchaser's ability to produce orders to a smooth, coordinated schedule.
3. *Lead time:* Engineering or specification changes can play havoc with JIT because of inadequate lead time for suppliers to implement the necessary changes.
4. *Quality:* Suppliers' capital budgets, processes, or technology may limit ability to respond to changes in product and quality.
5. *Lot sizes:* Suppliers may see frequent delivery in small lots as a way to transfer buyers' holding costs to suppliers.

JIT LAYOUT

▼ **TABLE 16.1**

JIT Layout Tactics

Build work cells for families of products

Include a large number of operations in a small area

Minimize distance

Design little space for inventory

Improve employee communication

Use poka-yoke devices

Build flexible or movable equipment

Cross-train workers to add flexibility

JIT layouts reduce another kind of waste—movement. The movement of material on a factory floor (or paper in an office) does not add value. Consequently, managers want flexible layouts that reduce the movement of both people and material. JIT layouts place material directly in the location where needed. For instance, an assembly line should be designed with delivery points next to the line so material need not be delivered first to a receiving department and then moved again. This is what Toyota did when they placed hardware and components in the chassis of each vehicle moving down the assembly line. This is not only convenient, but it allows Toyota to save space and opens areas adjacent to the assembly line previously occupied by shelves. When a layout reduces distance, firms often save labor and space and may have the added bonus of eliminating potential areas for accumulation of unwanted inventory. Table 16.1 provides a list of JIT layout tactics.

Distance Reduction

Reducing distance is a major contribution of work cells, work centers, and focused factories (see Chapter 9). The days of long production lines and huge economic lots, with goods passing through monumental, single-operation machines, are gone. Now firms use work cells, often arranged in a U shape, containing several machines performing different operations. These work cells are often based on group technology codes (as discussed in Chapter 5). Group technology codes help identify components with similar characteristics so we can group them into families. Once families are identified, work cells are built for them. The result can be thought of as a small product-oriented facility where the 'product' is actually a group of similar products—a family of products. The cells produce one good unit at a time, and ideally they produce the units *only* after a customer orders them.

Increased Flexibility

Modern work cells are designed so they can be easily rearranged to adapt to changes in volume, product improvements, or even new designs. Almost nothing in these new departments is bolted down. This same concept of layout flexibility applies to office environments. Not only is most office furniture and equipment movable, but so are office walls, computer connections, and telecommunications. Equipment is modular. Layout flexibility aids the changes that result from product *and* process improvements that are inevitable with a philosophy of continuous improvement.

Impact on Employees

JIT layouts allow cross-trained employees to bring flexibility and efficiency to the work cell. Employees working together can tell each other about problems and opportunities for improvement. When layouts provide for sequential operations, feedback can be immediate. Defects are waste. When workers produce units one at a time, they test each product or component at each subsequent production stage. Machines in work cells with self-testing poka-yoke functions detect defects and stop automatically when they occur. Before JIT, defective products were replaced from inventory. Because surplus inventory is not kept in JIT facilities, there are no such buffers. Getting it right the first time is critical.

Reduced Space and Inventory

Because JIT layouts reduce travel distance, they also reduce inventory by removing space for inventory. When there is little space, inventory must be moved in very small lots or even single units. Units are always moving because there is no storage.

JIT INVENTORY

Inventories in production and distribution systems often exist 'just in case' something goes wrong. That is, they are used just in case some variation from the production plan occurs. The 'extra' inventory is then used to cover variations or problems. Effective inventory tactics require 'just in time,' not 'just in case.' **Just-in-time (JIT) inventory** is the minimum inventory necessary to keep a perfect system running. With just-in-time inventory, the exact amount of goods arrives at the moment it is needed, not a minute before or a minute after. Some useful JIT inventory tactics are shown in Table 16.2 and discussed in more detail in the following sections.

> **AUTHOR COMMENT**
> Accountants book inventory as an asset, but operations managers know it is costly.

Just-in-time (JIT) inventory
The minimum inventory necessary to keep a perfect system running.

Reduce Inventory and Variability

Operations managers move toward JIT by first removing inventory. The idea is to eliminate variability in the production system hidden by inventory. Reducing inventory uncovers the 'rocks' in Figure 16.3(a) that represent the variability and problems currently being tolerated. With reduced inventory, management chips away at the exposed problems. After the lake (inventory) is lowered, managers make additional cuts in inventory and continue to chip away at the next level of exposed problems (see Figure 16.3[b,c]). Ultimately, there will be virtually no inventory and no problems (variability).

Reduce Lot Sizes

Just-in-time has also come to mean elimination of waste by reducing investment in inventory. The key to JIT is producing good product in small lot sizes. Reducing the size of batches can be a major help in reducing inventory and inventory costs. As we saw in Chapter 12, when

▼ **TABLE 16.2**
JIT Inventory Tactics

Use a pull system to move inventory
Reduce lot size
Develop just-in-time delivery systems with suppliers
Deliver directly to the point of use
Perform to schedule
Reduce setup time
Use group technology

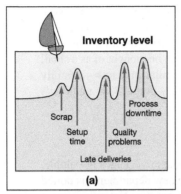 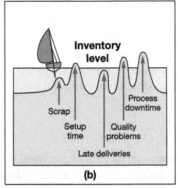 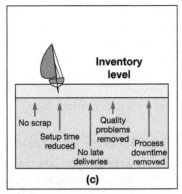

▲ FIGURE 16.3 High levels of inventory hide problems (a), but as we reduce inventory, problems are exposed (b), and finally after reducing inventory and removing problems we have lower inventory, lower costs, and smooth sailing (c).

► **FIGURE 16.4**
Frequent Orders Reduce Average Inventory

A lower order size increases the number of orders and total ordering cost but reduces average inventory and total holding cost.

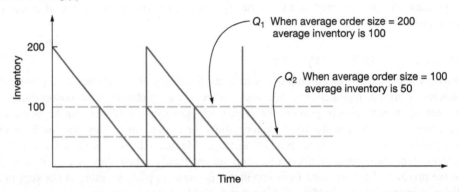

inventory usage is constant, the average inventory level is the sum of the maximum inventory plus the minimum inventory divided by 2. Figure 16.4 shows that lowering the order size increases the number of orders but drops inventory levels.

Ideally, in a JIT environment, order size is one, and single units are being pulled from one adjacent process to another. More realistically, analysis of the process, transportation time, and containers used for transport are considered when determining lot size. Such analysis typically results in a small lot size but a lot size larger than one. Once a lot size has been determined, the EOQ production order quantity model can be modified to determine the desired setup time. We saw in Chapter 12 that the production order quantity model takes the form:

$$Q^* = \sqrt{\frac{2DS}{H[1 - (d \div p)]}}$$ (16-1)

where D = Annual demand d = Daily demand
        S = Setup cost p = Daily production
        H = Holding cost

Example 1 shows how to determine the desired setup time.

EXAMPLE 1 ▶	
Determining optimal setup time	Aqsa Furniture, Inc., a Kuwaiti firm that produces rustic furniture, desires to move toward a reduced lot size. Aqsa Furniture's production analyst, Ala' Ribhi, determined that a 2-hour production cycle would be acceptable between two departments. Further, she concluded that a setup time that would accommodate the 2-hour cycle time should be achieved.

APPROACH ▶   Ala' developed the following data and procedure to determine optimum setup time analytically:

D = Annual demand = 400,000 units

d = Daily demand = 400,000 per 250 days = 1,600 units per day

p = Daily production rate = 4,000 units per day

Q = EOQ desired = 400 (which is the 2-hour demand; that is, 1,600 per day per four 2-hour periods)

H = Holding cost = US\$20 per unit per year

S = Setup cost (to be determined)

SOLUTION ▶ Ala' determines that the cost, on an hourly basis, of setting up equipment is US$30. Further, she computes that the setup cost per setup should be:

$$Q = \sqrt{\frac{2DS}{H(1 - d \div p)}}$$

$$Q^2 = \frac{2DS}{H(1 - d \div p)}$$

$$S = \frac{(Q^2)(H)(1 - d \div p)}{2D} \tag{16-2}$$

$$= \frac{(400)^2(20)(1 - 1{,}600 \div 4{,}000)}{2(400{,}000)}$$

$$= \frac{(3{,}200{,}000)(0.6)}{800{,}000}$$

$$= \text{US\$20.40}$$

$$\text{Setup time} = \text{US\$2.40/(hourly labor rate)}$$

$$= \text{US\$2.40/(US\$30 per hour)}$$

$$= 0.08 \text{ hour, or } 4.8 \text{ minutes}$$

INSIGHT ▶ Now, rather than produce components in large lots, Aqsa Furniture can produce in a 2-hour cycle with the advantage of an inventory turnover of four *per day*.

LEARNING EXERCISE ▶ If labor cost goes to US$40 per hour, what should be the setup time? [Answer: 0.06 hour, or 3.6 minutes.]

LO4: Determine optimal setup time

Only two changes need to be made for small lot material flow to work. First, material handling and work flow need to be improved. With short production cycles, there can be very little wait time. Improving material handling is usually easy and straightforward. The second change is more challenging, and that is a radical reduction in setup times. We discuss setup reduction next.

Reduce Setup Costs

Both inventory and the cost of holding it go down as the inventory-reorder quantity and the maximum inventory level drop. However, because inventory requires incurring an ordering or setup cost that must be applied to the units produced, managers tend to purchase (or produce) large orders. With large orders, each unit purchased or ordered absorbs only a small part of the setup cost. Consequently, the way to drive down lot sizes *and* reduce average inventory is to reduce setup cost, which in turn lowers the optimum order size.

The effect of reduced setup costs on total cost and lot size is shown in Figure 16.5. Moreover, smaller lot sizes hide fewer problems. In many environments, setup cost is highly correlated with

AUTHOR COMMENT
Reduced lot sizes must be accompanied by reduced setup times.

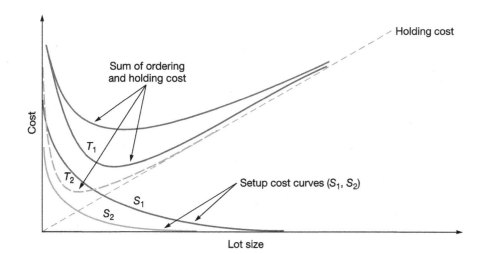

◀ FIGURE 16.5
Lower Setup Costs Will Lower Total Cost

More frequent orders require reducing setup costs; otherwise, inventory costs will rise. As the setup costs are lowered (from S_1 to S_2), total inventory costs also fall (from T_1 to T_2).

▶ **FIGURE 16.6**
Steps for Reducing Setup Times

Reduced setup times are a major JIT component.

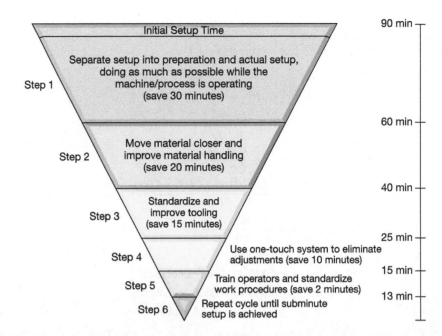

		90 min
	Initial Setup Time	
Step 1	Separate setup into preparation and actual setup, doing as much as possible while the machine/process is operating (save 30 minutes)	60 min
Step 2	Move material closer and improve material handling (save 20 minutes)	40 min
Step 3	Standardize and improve tooling (save 15 minutes)	25 min
Step 4	Use one-touch system to eliminate adjustments (save 10 minutes)	15 min
Step 5	Train operators and standardize work procedures (save 2 minutes)	13 min
Step 6	Repeat cycle until subminute setup is achieved	

▼ **TABLE 16.3**
JIT Scheduling Tactics

Communicate schedules to suppliers
Make level schedules
Freeze part of the schedule
Perform to schedule
Seek one-piece-make and one-piece-move
Eliminate waste
Produce in small lots
Use kanbans
Make each operation produce a perfect part

AUTHOR COMMENT
Effective scheduling is required for effective use of capital and personnel.

setup time. In a manufacturing facility, setups usually require a substantial amount of preparation. Much of the preparation required by a setup can be done prior to shutting down the machine or process. Setup times can be reduced substantially, as shown in Figure 16.6.

Just as setup costs can be reduced at a machine in a factory, setup time can also be reduced during the process of getting the order ready. It does little good to drive down factory setup time from hours to minutes if orders are going to take 2 weeks to process or 'set up' in the office. This is exactly what happens in organizations that forget that JIT concepts have applications in offices as well as in the factory. Reducing setup time (and cost) is an excellent way to reduce inventory investment and to improve productivity.

JIT SCHEDULING

Effective schedules, communicated both within the organization and to outside suppliers, support JIT. Better scheduling also improves the ability to meet customer orders, drives down inventory by allowing smaller lot sizes, and reduces work-in-process. For instance, as we saw in our opening *Company Profile*, Toyota has moved its seat supplier inside the new Tundra plant; this has driven down delivery time significantly.

Table 16.3 suggests several items that can contribute to achieving these goals, but two techniques (in addition to communicating schedules) are paramount. They are *level schedules* and *kanban*.

Level Schedules

Level schedules

Scheduling products so that each day's production meets the demand for that day.

Level schedules process frequent small batches rather than a few large batches. Figure 16.7 contrasts a traditional large-lot approach using large batches with a JIT level schedule using many small batches. The operations manager's task is to make and move small lots so the level schedule is economical. This requires success with the issues discussed in this chapter that allow small lots. As lots get smaller, the constraints may change and become increasingly challenging. At some point, processing a unit or two may not be feasible. The constraint may be the way units are sold and shipped (four to a carton), or an expensive paint changeover (on an automobile assembly line), or the proper number of units in a sterilizer (for a food-canning line).

The scheduler may find that *freezing* the portion of the schedule closest to due dates allows the production system to function and the schedule to be met. Freezing means not allowing changes to be part of the schedule. Operations managers expect the schedule to be achieved with no deviations from the schedule.

JIT Level Material-Use Approach

AA BBB C AA BBB C AA BBB C AA BBB C AA BBB C AA BBB C AA BBB C AA BBB C AA BBB C

Large-Lot Approach

AAAAAA BBBBBBBBB CCC AAAAAA BBBBBBBBB CCC AAAAAA BBBBBBBBB CCC

Time

▲ **FIGURE 16.7**   **Scheduling Small Lots of Parts A, B, and C Increases Flexibility to Meet Customer Demand and Reduces Inventory**

The JIT approach to scheduling produces just as many of each model per time period as the large-lot approach, provided that setup times are lowered.

Kanban

One way to achieve small lot sizes is to move inventory through the shop only as needed rather than *pushing* it on to the next workstation whether or not the personnel there are ready for it. As noted earlier, when inventory is moved only as needed, it is referred to as a *pull* system, and the ideal lot size is one. The Japanese call this system *kanban*. Kanbans allow arrivals at a work center to match (or nearly match) the processing time.

Kanban is a Japanese word for *card*. In their effort to reduce inventory, the Japanese use systems that 'pull' inventory through work centers. They often use a 'card' to signal the need for another container of material—hence the name *kanban*. *The card is the authorization for the next container of material to be produced.* Typically, a kanban signal exists for each container of items to be obtained. An order for the container is then initiated by each kanban and 'pulled' from the producing department or supplier. A sequence of kanbans 'pulls' the material through the plant.

The system has been modified in many facilities so that even though it is called a *kanban*, the card itself does not exist. In some cases, an empty position on the floor is sufficient indication that the next container is needed. In other cases, some sort of signal, such as a flag or rag (Figure 16.8) alerts that it is time for the next container.

When there is visual contact between producer and user, the process works like this:

1. The user removes a standard-size container of parts from a small storage area, as shown in Figure 16.8.
2. The signal at the storage area is seen by the producing department as authorization to replenish the using department or storage area. Because there is an optimum lot size, the producing department may make several containers at a time.

Figure 16.9 shows how a kanban works, pulling units as needed from production. This system is similar to the resupply that occurs in your neighborhood supermarket: The customer buys; the stock clerk observes the shelf or receives notice from the end-of-day sales list and

Kanban

The Japanese word for card, which has come to mean 'signal'; a kanban system moves parts through production via a 'pull' from a signal.

LO5: Define kanban

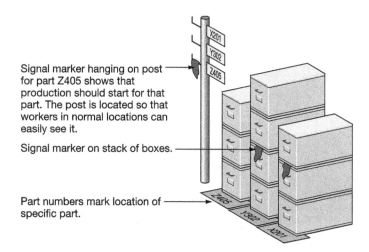

◀ **FIGURE 16.8**
Diagram of Outbound Stockpoint with Warning-Signal Marker

Signal marker hanging on post for part Z405 shows that production should start for that part. The post is located so that workers in normal locations can easily see it.

Signal marker on stack of boxes.

Part numbers mark location of specific part.

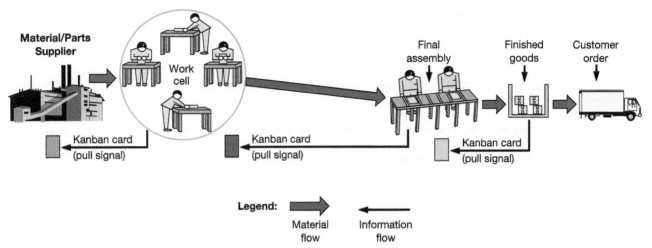

Legend:

Material flow   Information flow

▲ **FIGURE 16.9** **Kanban Signals 'Pull' Material Through the Production Process**

As a customer 'pulls' an order from finished goods, a signal (kanban card) is sent to the final assembly area. Final assembly produces and resupplies finished goods. When final assembly needs components, it sends a signal to *its* supplier, a work cell. The work cell, in turn, sends a signal to the material/parts supplier.

restocks. When the limited supply, if any, in the store's storage is depleted, a 'pull' signal is sent to the warehouse, distributor, or manufacturer for resupply, usually that night. The complicating factor in a manufacturing firm is the time needed for actual manufacturing (production) to take place.

Several additional points regarding kanbans may be helpful:

- When the producer and user are not in visual contact, a card can be used; otherwise, a light or flag or empty spot on the floor may be adequate.
- Because a pull station may require several resupply components, several kanban pull techniques can be used for different products at the same pull station.
- Usually, each card controls a specific quantity of parts, although multiple card systems are used if the producing work cell produces several components or if the lot size is different from the move size.
- In an MRP system (see Chapter 14), the schedule can be thought of as a 'build' authorization and the kanban as a type of 'pull' system that initiates the actual production.
- The kanban cards provide a direct control (limit) on the amount of work-in-process between cells.
- If there is an immediate storage area, a two-card system may be used—one card circulates between user and storage area, and the other circulates between the storage area and the producing area.

A kanban need not be as formal as signal lights or empty carts. The cook in a fast-food restaurant knows that when six cars are in line, eight meat patties and six orders of French fries should be cooking.

Determining the Number of Kanban Cards or Containers   The number of kanban cards, or containers, in a JIT system sets the amount of authorized inventory. To determine the number of containers moving back and forth between the using area and the producing areas, management first sets the size of each container. This is done by computing the lot size, using a model such as the production order quantity model (discussed in Chapter 12 and shown again on page 516 in Equation [16–1]). Setting the number of containers involves knowing: (1) lead time needed to produce a container of parts; (2) the amount of safety stock needed to account for variability or uncertainty in the system. The number of kanban cards is computed as follows:

$$\text{Number of kanbans (containers)} = \frac{\text{Demand during lead time} + \text{Safety stock}}{\text{Size of container}} \qquad \text{(16-3)}$$

Example 2 illustrates how to calculate the number of kanbans needed.

◄ **EXAMPLE 2**

Determining the number of kanban containers

Saj Bakery produces short runs of cakes that are shipped to grocery stores. The owner, Ayman Homsi, wants to try to reduce inventory by changing to a kanban system. He has developed the following data and asked you to finish the project.

$$\text{Daily demand} = 500 \text{ cakes}$$

$$\text{Production lead time} = \text{Wait time} + \text{Material handling time} + \text{Processing time} = 2 \text{ days}$$

$$\text{Safety stock} = \tfrac{1}{2} \text{ day}$$

$$\text{Container size (determined on a production order size EOQ basis)} = 250 \text{ cakes}$$

APPROACH ▶   Having determined that the EOQ size is 250, we then determine the number of kanbans (containers) needed.

SOLUTION ▶   Demand during lead time = Lead time × daily demand
$$= 2 \text{ days} \times 500 \text{ cakes} = 1{,}000$$
Safety stock = 250

$$\text{Number of kanbans (containers) needed} = \frac{\text{Demand during lead time} + \text{Safety stock}}{\text{Container size}}$$
$$= \frac{1{,}000 + 250}{250} = 5$$

INSIGHT ▶   Once the reorder point is hit, five containers should be released.

LEARNING EXERCISE ▶   If lead time drops to 1 day, how many containers are needed? [Answer: 3.]

RELATED PROBLEMS ▶   16.1, 16.2, 16.3, 16.4, 16.5

LO6: Compute the required number of kanbans

Advantages of Kanban   Containers are typically very small, usually a matter of a few hours' worth of production. Such a system requires tight schedules. Small quantities must be produced several times a day. The process must run smoothly with little variability in quality of lead time because any shortage has an almost immediate impact on the entire system. Kanban places added emphasis on meeting schedules, reducing the time and cost required by setups, and economical material handling.

Whether it is called kanban or something else, the advantages of small inventory and *pulling* material through the plant only when needed are significant. For instance, small batches allow only a very limited amount of faulty or delayed material. Problems are immediately evident. Numerous aspects of inventory are bad; only one aspect—availability—is good. Among the bad aspects are poor quality, obsolescence, damage, occupied space, committed assets, increased insurance, increased material handling, and increased accidents. Kanban systems put downward pressure on all these negative aspects of inventory.

In-plant kanban systems often use standardized, reusable containers that protect the specific quantities to be moved. Such containers are also desirable in the supply chain. Standardized containers reduce weight and disposal costs, generate less wasted space in trailers, and require less labor to pack, unpack, and prepare items.

This auto plant, like most JIT facilities, empowers employees so that they can stop the entire production line by pulling the overhead cord if any quality problems are spotted.

▼ TABLE 16.4
JIT Quality Tactics

Use statistical process
  control
Empower employees
Build fail-safe methods
  (poka-yoke,
  checklists, etc.)
Expose poor quality with
  small lot JIT
Provide immediate
  feedback

JIT QUALITY

The relationship between JIT and quality is a strong one. They are related in three ways. First, JIT cuts the cost of obtaining good quality. This saving occurs because scrap, rework, inventory investment, and damage costs are buried in inventory. JIT forces down inventory; therefore, fewer bad units are produced and fewer units must be reworked. In short, whereas inventory *hides* bad quality, JIT immediately *exposes* it.

Second, JIT improves quality. As JIT shrinks queues and lead time, it keeps evidence of errors fresh and limits the number of potential sources of error. In effect, JIT creates an early warning system for quality problems so that fewer bad units are produced and feedback is immediate. This advantage can accrue both within the firm and with goods received from outside vendors.

Finally, better quality means fewer buffers are needed and, therefore, a better, easier-to-employ JIT system can exist. Often the purpose of keeping inventory is to protect against unreliable quality. If consistent quality exists, JIT allows firms to reduce all costs associated with inventory. Table 16.4 suggests some requirements for quality in a JIT environment.

TOYOTA PRODUCTION SYSTEM

Toyota Motor's Eiji Toyoda and Taiichi Ohno are given credit for the Toyota Production System (TPS) (see the *Company Profile* that opens this chapter). Three core components of TPS are continuous improvement, respect for people, and standard work practice.

Continuous Improvement

Kaizen
A focus on continuous improvement.

Continuous improvement under TPS means building an organizational culture and instilling in its people a value system stressing that processes can be improved—indeed, that improvement is an integral part of every employee's job. This process is formalized in TPS by **kaizen**, the Japanese word for change for the good, or what is more generally known as *continuous improvement*. In application, it means making a multitude of small or incremental changes as one seeks elusive perfection. Instilling the mantra of continuous improvement begins at recruiting and continues through extensive and continuing training. One of the reasons continuous improvement works at Toyota, we should note, is because of another core value at Toyota, Toyota's respect for people.

Respect for People

At Toyota, people are recruited, trained, and treated as knowledge workers. Aided by aggressive cross-training and few job classifications, TPS engages the mental as well as physical capacities of employees in the challenging task of improving operations. Employees are empowered. They are empowered to make improvements. They are empowered to stop machines and processes when quality problems exist. Indeed, empowered employees are a necessary part of TPS. This means that those tasks that have traditionally been assigned to management are moved to employees. Toyota recognizes that employees know more about their jobs than anyone else. TPS respects employees by giving them the opportunity to enrich both their jobs and their lives.

Standard Work Practice

Standard work practice at Toyota includes these underlying principles:

- Work is completely specified as to content, sequence, timing, and outcome.
- Internal and external customer–supplier connections are direct, specifying personnel, methods, timing, and quantity.
- Product and service flows are to be simple and direct. Goods and services are directed to a specific person or machine.
- Improvements in the system must be made in accordance with the 'scientific method,' at the lowest possible level in the organization.[2]

> **LO7:** Explain the principles of the Toyota Production System

TPS requires that activities, connections, and flows include built-in tests to automatically signal problems. Any gap between what is expected and what occurs becomes immediately evident. The education and training of Toyota's employees and the responsiveness of the system to problems make the seemingly rigid system flexible and adaptable to changing circumstances. The result is ongoing improvements in reliability, flexibility, safety, and efficiency.

LEAN OPERATIONS

> **AUTHOR COMMENT**
> Lean drives out non-value-added activities.

Lean production can be thought of as the end result of a well-run OM function. While JIT and TPS tend to have an *internal* focus, lean production begins *externally* with a focus on the customer. Understanding what the customer wants and ensuring customer input and feedback are starting points for lean production. Lean operations means identifying customer value by analyzing all the activities required to produce the product and then optimizing the entire process from the customer's perspective.

Building a Lean Organization

The transition to lean production is difficult. Building an organizational culture where learning, empowerment, and continuous improvement are the norm is a challenge. However, organizations that focus on JIT, quality, and employee empowerment are often lean producers. Such firms drive out activities that do not add value in the eyes of the customer: they include leaders like Aramex, Emaar, and of course Toyota. Lean operations adopt a philosophy of minimizing waste by striving for perfection through continuous learning, creativity, and teamwork. They tend to share the following attributes:

- *Use JIT techniques* to eliminate virtually all inventory.
- *Build systems that help employees* produce a perfect part every time.
- *Reduce space requirements* by minimizing travel distance.
- *Develop partnerships with suppliers*, helping them to understand the needs of the ultimate customer.
- *Educate suppliers* to accept responsibility for satisfying end customer needs.
- *Eliminate all but value-added activities*. Material handling, inspection, inventory, and rework are the likely targets because these do not add value to the product.
- *Develop employees* by constantly improving job design, training, employee commitment, teamwork, and empowerment.

[2]Adopted from Steven J. Spear, "Learning to Lead at Toyota," *Harvard Business Review* 82, no. 5 (May 2004): 78–86; and Steven Spear and H. Kent Bowen, "Decoding the DNA of the Toyota Production System," *Harvard Business Review* 77, no. 5 (September–October 1999): 97–106.

- *Make jobs challenging*, pushing responsibility to the lowest level possible.
- *Build worker flexibility* through cross-training and reducing job classifications.

Success requires the full commitment and involvement of managers, employees, and suppliers. The rewards that lean producers reap are spectacular. Lean producers often become benchmark performers.

AUTHOR COMMENT
JIT, TPS, and lean began in factories but are now also used in services throughout the world.

LEAN OPERATIONS IN SERVICES

The features of lean operations apply to services just as they do in other sectors. (See the *OM in Action* box 'Toyota University Teaches Lean Thinking.') Here are some examples applied to suppliers, layout, inventory, and scheduling in the service sector.

Suppliers

As we have noted, virtually every restaurant deals with its suppliers on a JIT basis. Those that do not are usually unsuccessful. The waste is too evident—food spoils, and customers complain or get sick.

Layouts

Lean layouts are required in restaurant kitchens, where cold food must be served cold and hot food hot. McDonald's, for example, has reconfigured its kitchen layout at great expense to drive

Lean operations take on an unusual form in an operating room. Hospital suppliers provide surgical supplies for hospitals on a JIT basis: (1) They deliver prepackaged surgical supplies based on hospital operating schedules; (2) the surgical packages themselves are prepared so supplies are available in the sequence in which they will be used during surgery.

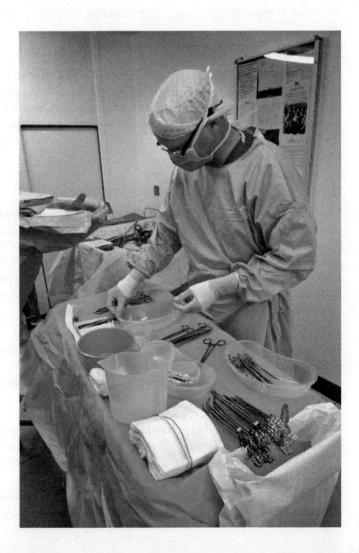

seconds out of the production process, thereby speeding delivery to customers. With the new process, McDonald's can produce made-to-order hamburgers in 45 seconds. Layouts also make a difference in airline baggage claim, where customers expect their bags just-in-time.

Inventory

Stockbrokers drive inventory down to nearly zero every day. Most sell and buy orders occur on an immediate basis because an unexecuted sell or buy order is not acceptable to the client. A broker may be in serious trouble if left holding an unexecuted trade. Similarly, McDonald's reduces inventory waste by maintaining a finished-goods inventory of only 10 minutes; after that, it is thrown away. Hospitals, such as New Mowasat and Arnold Palmer (described in this chapter's *Video Case Study*), manage JIT inventory and low safety stocks for many items. Even critical supplies such as pharmaceuticals may be held to low levels by developing community networks as backup systems. In this manner, if one pharmacy runs out of a needed drug, another member of the network can supply it until the next day's shipment arrives.

VIDEO 16.1
JIT at Arnold Palmer Hospital

Scheduling

At airline ticket counters, the focus of the system is on adjusting to customer demand. But rather than being accommodated by inventory availability, demand is satisfied by personnel. Through elaborate scheduling, ticket counter personnel show up just-in-time to cover peaks in customer demand. In other words, rather than 'things' inventoried, personnel are scheduled. At a salon, the focus is only slightly different: the *customer* and the staff are scheduled to assure prompt service. At McDonald's, scheduling of personnel is down to 15-minute increments, based on precise forecasting of demand. Additionally, at McDonald's, production is done in small lots to ensure that fresh, hot hamburgers are delivered just-in-time. In short, both personnel and production are scheduled to meet specific demand. Notice that in all three of these lean organizations—the airline ticket counter, the salon, and McDonald's—scheduling is a key ingredient. Excellent forecasts drive those schedules. Those forecasts may be very elaborate, with seasonal, daily, and even hourly components in the case of the airline ticket counter (holiday sales, flight time, etc.), seasonal and weekly components at the salon (holidays and Fridays create special problems), and down to a few minutes (to respond to the daily meal cycle) at McDonald's.

To deliver goods and services to customers under continuously changing demand, suppliers need to be reliable, inventories lean, cycle times short, and schedules nimble. A lean focus engages and empowers employees to create and deliver the customer's perception of value, eliminating whatever does not contribute to this goal. Lean operations are currently being developed with great success in many firms, regardless of their products. Lean techniques are widely used in both goods-producing and service-producing firms; they just look different.

OM in Action ▶ Toyota University Teaches Lean Thinking

Based in Gardena, California, Toyota University teaches its employees the Toyota Production System. But Toyota has also opened its door to others. As a public service, Toyota has been teaching lean thinking classes to the Los Angeles Police Department and the U.S. military. Classes begin, as one might expect, with a car-building exercise. Using model cars and desks as workstations and delivery areas, students begin with a focus on fast throughput and high production goals. This results in a 'push' system, with lots of work-in-process piling up, lots of defects to be reworked, and too many of the wrong kind of cars on the 'dealer's' lot.

The exercise is then revised, and students are taught to respond to orders and to form *kaizen* (continuous improvement) teams. The revised exercise then uses a 'pull' system that responds to orders and fixes even the most minor problems immediately. With a focus only on filling orders and 'pulling' demand through the production process with no defects, a faster, more efficient production line is formed.

Instructor Matthew May's observation about adapting lean methods beyond the factory: "If you can do it with LAPD, you can do it anywhere."

Sources: The Wall Street Journal (March 5, 2007): B1, B4; and **www.isosupport.com**.

CHAPTER SUMMARY

JIT, TPS, and lean operations are philosophies of continuous improvement. Lean operations focus on customer desires, TPS focuses on respect for people and standard work practices, and JIT focuses on driving out waste by reducing inventory. But all three approaches reduce waste in the production process. And because waste is found in anything that does not add value, organizations that implement these techniques are adding value more efficiently than other firms. The expectation of these systems is that empowered employees work with committed management to build systems that respond to customers with ever-lower cost and higher quality.

Key Terms

5Ss (p. 511)
Consignment inventory (p. 513)
Just-in-time (JIT) (p. 510)
Just-in-time (JIT) inventory (p. 515)
Just-in-time (JIT) partnerships (p. 512)

Kaizen (p. 522)
Kanban (p. 519)
Lean operations (p. 510)
Level schedules (p. 518)
Manufacturing cycle time (p. 512)

Pull system (p. 512)
Seven wastes (p. 510)
Throughput time (p. 511)
Toyota Production System (TPS) (p. 510)
Variability (p. 511)

Ethical Dilemma

In this lean operations world, in an effort to lower handling costs, speed delivery, and reduce inventory, retailers are forcing their suppliers to do more and more in the way of preparing their merchandise for their cross-docking warehouses, shipment to specific stores, and shelf presentation. Your company, a small manufacturer of aquarium decorations, is in a tough position. First, Mega-Mart wanted you to develop bar-code technology, then special packaging, then small individual shipments bar coded for each store (this way when the merchandise hits the warehouse it is cross-docked immediately to the correct truck and store and is ready for shelf placement). And now Mega-Mart wants you to develop RFID (Radio Frequency Identification) immediately: using radio frequency to transfer coded data from a small tag or device for automatic identification and tracking by the recipient monitor or control systems. Mega-Mart has made it clear that suppliers that cannot keep up with the technology will be dropped.

Earlier, when you didn't have the expertise for bar codes, you had to borrow money and hire an outside firm to do the development, purchase the technology, and train your shipping clerk. Then, meeting the special packaging requirement drove you into a loss for several months, resulting in a loss for last year. Now it appears that the RFID request is impossible. Your business, under the best of conditions, is marginally profitable, and the bank may not be willing to bail you out again. Over the years, Mega-Mart has slowly become your major customer and without them, you are probably out of business. What are the ethical issues and what do you do?

Discussion Questions

1. What is JIT?
2. What is a lean producer?
3. What is TPS?
4. What is level scheduling?
5. JIT attempts to remove delays, which do not add value. How then does JIT cope with weather and its impact on crop harvest and transportation times?
6. What are three ways in which JIT and quality are related?
7. How does TPS contribute to competitive advantage?
8. What are the characteristics of just-in-time partnerships with respect to suppliers?
9. Discuss how the Japanese word for *card* has application in the study of JIT.
10. Standardized, reusable containers have fairly obvious benefits for shipping. What is the purpose of these devices within the plant?
11. Does lean production work in the service sector? Provide an illustration.
12. Which lean techniques work in both the manufacturing *and* service sectors?

Solved Problems Virtual Office Hours help is available at MyOMLab.

▼ SOLVED PROBLEM 16.1

Krupp Refrigeration, Inc. is trying to reduce inventory and wants you to install a kanban system for compressors on one of its assembly lines. Determine the size of the kanban and the number of kanbans (containers) needed.

Setup cost = US$10

Annual holding cost per compressor = US$100

Daily production = 25,000 (50 weeks × 5 days each)
　　　　　　　　　　　　× daily usage of 100 compressors)

Lead time = 3 days

Safety stock = $\frac{1}{2}$ day's production of compressors

▼ SOLUTION

First, we must determine kanban container size. To do this, we determine the production order quantity (see discussion in Chapter 12 or Equation [16-1]), which determines the kanban size:

$$Q_p^* = \sqrt{\frac{2DS}{H\left(1 - \dfrac{d}{p}\right)}} = \sqrt{\frac{2(25,000)(10)}{H\left(1 - \dfrac{d}{p}\right)}} = \sqrt{\frac{500,000}{100\left(1 - \dfrac{100}{200}\right)}} = \sqrt{\frac{500,000}{50}}$$

$$= \sqrt{10,000} = 100 \text{ compressors. So the production order size and the size of the kanban container} = 100.$$

Then we determine the number of kanbans:

Demand during lead time = 300 (= 3 days × daily usage of 100)

Safety stock = 100 (= $\frac{1}{2}$ × daily productin of 200)

$$\text{Number of kanbans} = \frac{\text{Demand during lead time} + \text{Safety stock}}{\text{Size of container}}$$

$$= \frac{300 + 100}{100} = \frac{400}{100} = 4 \text{ containers}$$

Problems*

•　**16.1** Shabab Electronics, Inc. produces short runs of custom airwave scanners for the defense industry. You have been asked by the owner, Naser, to reduce inventory by introducing a kanban system. After several hours of analysis, you develop the following data for scanner connectors used in one work cell. How many kanbans do you need for this connector?

Daily demand	1,000 connectors
Lead time	2 days
Safety stock	$\frac{1}{2}$ day
Kanban size	500 connectors

•　**16.2** Samer's company wants to establish kanbans to feed a newly established work cell. The following data have been provided. How many kanbans are needed?

Daily demand	250 units
Production lead time	$\frac{1}{2}$ day
Safety stock	$\frac{1}{4}$ day
Kanban size	50 units

•　**16.3** Geeza Manufacturing, Inc., is moving to kanbans to support its telephone switching-board assembly lines. Determine the size of the kanban for subassemblies and the number of kanbans needed.

Setup cost = US$30

Annual holding　　　cost = US$120 per subassembly

Daily production = 20 subassemblies

Annual usage = 2,500 (50 weeks × 5 days each)
　　　　　　　　　× daily usage of 10 subassemblies

　Lead time = 16 days

　Safety stock = 4 days' production of subassemblies. **Px**

•　**16.4** Jezan-Mart, a major retailer, wants to determine the economic order quantity (see Chapter 12 for EOQ formulas) for its halogen lamps. It currently buys all halogen lamps from Noor Manufacturing in Marka. Annual demand is 2,000 lamps, ordering cost per order is US$30, annual carrying cost per lamp is US$12.

a) What is the EOQ?

b) What are the total annual costs of holding and ordering (managing) this inventory?

c) How many orders should Jezan-Mart place with Noor per year? **Px**

•••　**16.5** Jezan-Mart (see Problem 16.4), as part of its new JIT program, has signed a long-term contract with Noor and will place orders electronically for its halogen lamps. Ordering costs will drop to US$0.50 per order, but Jezan-Mart also reassessed its carrying costs and raised them to US$20 per lamp.

a) What is the new economic order quantity?

b) How many orders will now be placed?

c) What is the total annual cost of managing the inventory with this policy? **Px**

••　**16.6** How do your answers to Problems 16.4 and 16.5 provide insight into a JIT purchasing strategy?

*Note: **Px** means the problem may be solved with POM for Windows and/or Excel OM.

▶ **Refer to** MyOMLab **for additional homework problems.**

Case Studies

▶ JIT after a Catastrophe

You name the catastrophe, and JIT has been through it and survived. Toyota Motor Corporation has had its world-renowned JIT system tested by fire. The massive fire incinerated the main source of crucial brake valves that Toyota buys from the Aisin Seiki plant in Kariya, Japan, and uses in most of its cars. The impact was the loss of 70,000 cars not produced while Toyota got the supply chain repaired. Then an earthquake destroyed Toyota's transmission supplier, Riken, shutting down production in a dozen factories. Chrysler and many others had their JIT systems tested on September 11, 2001, when the terrorist attacks shut down their state-of-the-art air delivery systems. And on February 5, 2008, during the second shift at Caterpillar's high-pressure couplings plant in Oxford, Mississippi, a tornado all but destroyed the facility. Despite these catastrophes, managers at these firms, like other executives all over the world, are still cutting costs by consolidating production, reducing inventory, and implementing JIT.

Consistent with JIT practice, these firms maintain minimal inventory of components and tight supply chains. There are very few components in these closely knit networks that constitute their respective supply chains. Without critical components, production comes to a rapid halt. And in Caterpillar's case, the Oxford plant is the only plant in the world that makes this unique coupling. The

couplings link hydraulic hoses on *every* piece of machinery Caterpillar makes. Depending on a single source and holding little inventory is a risk, but it also keeps firms lean and costs low.

The morning after the tornado tore apart the Oxford plant, Greg Folley, who runs Caterpillar's parts division, toured the plant. Much of the roof, including 10-ton heating and air-conditioning units, had fallen onto three critical metal stamping machines. The first piece of equipment was up and running in 2 weeks; getting production back to normal would take 6 months. But the Oxford plant had been making over 1 million of the critical couplings each month; this left a huge hole in Caterpillar's supply line.

Discussion Questions

1. If you are Mr. Folley, looking over the devastation at the Oxford plant, what do you do to keep Caterpillar's worldwide production running?
2. Given the inherent risk in JIT and the trauma that the companies have experienced, why has JIT survived?
3. What do these experiences, and the continuing popularity of JIT, tell you about just-in-time?
4. What actions or changes in policy do you suggest for Caterpillar?

Sources: Case is based on material in: *The Wall Street Journal* (May 19, 2008): B1, B2; (July 20, 2007): B1; **www.USAToday.com/money/world/ 2007-07-18-toyota-quake**; and *Harvard Business Review* (September–October 1999): 97–106.

▶ JIT at Arnold Palmer Hospital

Video Case

Orlando's Arnold Palmer Hospital, founded in 1989, specializes in treatment of women and children and is renowned for its high-quality rankings (top 10 percent of 2,000 benchmarked hospitals), its labor and delivery volume (more than 16,000 births per year, and growing), and its neonatal intensive care unit (one of the highest survival rates in the nation). But quality medical practices and high patient satisfaction require costly inventory—some US$30 million per year and thousands of SKUs.* With pressure on medical care to manage and reduce costs, Arnold Palmer Hospital has turned toward controlling its inventory with just-in-time (JIT) techniques.

Within the hospital, for example, drugs are now distributed at nursing workstations via dispensing machines (almost like vending machines) that electronically track patient usage and post the related charge to each patient. The dispensing stations are refilled each night, based on patient demand and prescriptions written by doctors.

To address JIT issues externally, Arnold Palmer Hospital turned toward a major distribution partner, McKesson General Medical, which as a first-tier supplier provides the hospital with about one quarter of all its medical/surgical inventory. McKesson supplies sponges, basins, towels, mayo stand covers, syringes, and hundreds of other medical/surgical items. To ensure coordinated daily delivery of inventory purchased from McKesson, an account executive has been assigned to the hospital on a full-time basis, as well as two other individuals who address customer service and product issues. The result has been a drop in Central Supply average

daily inventory from US$400,000 to US$114,000 since JIT was introduced.

JIT success has also been achieved in the area of *custom surgical packs*. Custom surgical packs are the sterile coverings, disposable plastic trays, gauze, and the like, specialized to each type of surgical procedure. Arnold Palmer Hospital uses ten different custom packs for various surgical procedures. "Over 50,000 packs are used each year, for a total cost of about US$1.5 million," says George DeLong, head of Supply-Chain Management.

The packs are not only delivered in a JIT manner but packed that way as well. That is, they are packed in the reverse order they are used so each item comes out of the pack in the sequence it is needed. The packs are bulky, expensive, and must remain sterile. Reducing the inventory and handling while maintaining an assured sterile supply for scheduled surgeries presents a challenge to hospitals.

Here is how the supply chain works: Custom packs are *assembled* by a packing company with *components supplied* primarily from manufacturers selected by the hospital, and *delivered* by McKesson from its local warehouse. Arnold Palmer Hospital works with its own surgical staff (through the Medical Economics Outcome Committee) to identify and standardize the custom packs to reduce the number of custom pack SKUs. With this integrated system, pack safety stock inventory has been cut to one day.

The procedure to drive the custom surgical pack JIT system begins with a 'pull' from the doctors' daily surgical schedule. Then, Arnold Palmer Hospital initiates an electronic order to McKesson between 1.00 and 2.00 p.m. daily. At 4.00 a.m. the next day, McKesson delivers the packs. Hospital personnel arrive at 7.00 a.m. and stock the shelves for scheduled surgeries. McKesson then reorders from the packing company, which in turn 'pulls' necessary inventory for the quantity of packs needed from the manufacturers.

Arnold Palmer Hospital's JIT system reduces inventory investment, expensive traditional ordering, and bulky storage, and supports quality with a sterile delivery.

Discussion Questions**

1. What do you recommend be done when an error is found in a pack as it is opened for an operation?

2. How might the procedure for custom surgical packs described here be improved?

3. When discussing JIT in services, the text notes that suppliers, layout, inventory, and scheduling are all used. Provide an example of each of these at Arnold Palmer Hospital.

4. When a doctor proposes a new surgical procedure, how do you recommend the SKU for a new custom pack be entered into the hospital's supply-chain system?

*SKU = stock keeping unit

**You may wish to view the video that accompanies this case before answering these questions.

Chapter 16 *Rapid* Review

Main Heading	Review Material	
JUST-IN-TIME, THE TOYOTA PRODUCTION SYSTEM, AND LEAN OPERATIONS (pp. 510–512)	▪ **Just-in-time (JIT)**—Continuous and forced problem solving via a focus on throughput and reduced inventory. ▪ **Toyota Production System (TPS)**—Focus on continuous improvement, respect for people, and standard work practices. ▪ **Lean operations**—Eliminates waste through a focus on exactly what the customer wants. *When implemented as a comprehensive manufacturing strategy, JIT, TPS, and lean systems sustain competitive advantage and result in increased overall returns.* ▪ **Seven wastes**—Overproduction, queues, transportation, inventory, motion, overprocessing, and defective product. ▪ **5Ss**—A lean production checklist: sort, simplify, shine, standardize, and sustain. U.S. managers often add two additional *S*s to the 5 original ones: *safety* and *support/maintenance.* ▪ **Variability**—Any deviation from the optimum process that delivers perfect product on time, every time. Both JIT and inventory reduction are effective tools for identifying causes of variability. ▪ **Throughput**—The time required to move orders through the production process, from receipt to delivery. ▪ **Manufacturing cycle time**—The time between the arrival of raw materials and the shipping of finished products. ▪ **Pull system**—A concept that results in material being produced only when requested and moved to where it is needed just as it is needed. Pull systems use signals to request production and delivery from supplying stations to stations that have production capacity available.	
JUST-IN-TIME (JIT) (pp. 512–514)	▪ **JIT partnerships**—Partnerships of suppliers and purchasers that remove waste and drive down costs for mutual benefits. Some specific goals of JIT partnerships are: *removal of unnecessary activities*, *removal of in-plant inventory*; *removal of in-transit inventory*; and *obtain improved quality and reliability.* ▪ **Consignment inventory**—An arrangement in which the supplier maintains title to the inventory until it is used. Concerns of suppliers in JIT partnerships include: (1) diversification; (2) scheduling; (3) lead time; (4) quality; (5) lot sizes.	
JIT LAYOUT (pp. 514–515)	JIT layout tactics include building work cells for families of products, include a large number of operations in a small area, minimizing distance, designing little space for inventory, improving employee communication, using poka-yoke devices, building flexible or movable equipment, and cross-training workers to add flexibility.	
JIT INVENTORY (pp. 515–518)	▪ **Just-in-time inventory**—The minimum inventory necessary to keep a perfect system running. The idea behind JIT is to eliminate inventory that hides variability in the production system. JIT inventory tactics include using a pull system to move inventory, reducing lot size, developing just-in-time delivery systems with suppliers, delivering directly to the point of use, performing to schedule, reducing setup time, and using group technology. $$Q^* = \sqrt{\frac{2DS}{H[1 - (d \div p)]}} \qquad (16\text{-}1)$$ Using (16–1), for a given desired lot size, Q, we can solve for the optimal setup cost, S: $$S = \frac{(Q^2)(H)(1 - d \div p)}{2D} \qquad (16\text{-}2)$$	Problems: 16.8–16.10

Main Heading	Review Material	MyOMLab
JIT SCHEDULING (pp. 518–522)	JIT scheduling tactics include: communicate schedules to suppliers, make level schedules, freeze part of the schedule, perform to schedule, seek one-piece-make and one-piece-move, eliminate waste, produce in small lots, use kanbans, and make each operation produce a perfect part. ■ **Level schedules**—Scheduling products so that each day's production meets the demand for that day. ■ **Kanban**—The Japanese word for *card*, which has come to mean 'signal'; a kanban system moves parts through production via a 'pull' from a signal: $$\text{Number of Kanbans (containers)} = \frac{\text{Demand during lead time} + \text{Safety stock}}{\text{Size of container}} \quad (16\text{-}3)$$	Problems: 16.1–16.5 Virtual Office Hours for Solved Problem: 16.1
JIT QUALITY (p. 522)	Whereas inventory *hides* bad quality, JIT immediately *exposes* it. JIT quality tactics include using statistical process control, empowering employees, building fail-safe methods (poka-yoke, checklists, etc.), exposing poor quality with small lot JIT, and providing immediate feedback.	
TOYOTA PRODUCTION SYSTEM (pp. 522–523)	■ **Kaizen**—A focus on continuous improvement. At Toyota, people are recruited, trained, and treated as knowledge workers. They are empowered. TPS employs aggressive cross-training and few job classifications.	
LEAN OPERATIONS (pp. 523–524)	Lean operations tend to share the following attributes: *use JIT techniques* to eliminate virtually all inventory; *build systems that help employees* produce a perfect part every time; *reduce space requirements* by minimizing travel distance; *develop partnerships with suppliers*, helping them to understand the needs of the ultimate customer; *educate suppliers* to accept responsibility for satisfying end customer needs; *eliminate all but value-added activities*; *develop employees* by constantly improving job design, training, employee commitment, teamwork, and empowerment; *make jobs challenging*, pushing responsibility to the lowest level possible; and *build worker flexibility* through cross-training and reducing job classifications.	
LEAN OPERATIONS IN SERVICES (pp. 524–526)	The features of lean operations apply to services just as they do in other sectors. Forecasts in services may be very elaborate, with seasonal, daily, hourly, or even shorter components.	**VIDEO 16.1** JIT at Arnold Palmer Hospital

Self-Test

■ **Before taking the self-test,** refer to the learning objectives listed at the beginning of the chapter and the key terms listed at the end of the chapter.

LO1. Continuous improvement and forced problem solving via a focus on throughput and reduced inventory is a reasonable definition of:
 a) lean operations
 b) expedited management
 c) the 5Ss of housekeeping
 d) just-in-time
 e) Toyota Production System.

LO2. The 5Ss for lean production are _____, _____, _____, _____, and _____.

LO3. Concerns of suppliers when moving to JIT include:
 a) small lots sometimes seeming economically prohibitive
 b) realistic quality demands
 c) changes without adequate lead time
 d) erratic schedules
 e) all of the above.

LO4. What is the formula for optimal setup time?
 a) $\sqrt{2DQ \div [H(1 - d \div p)]}$
 b) $\sqrt{Q^2 H \div (1 - d \div p) \div (2D)}$
 c) $QH(1 - d \div p) \div (2D)$
 d) $Q^2 H(1 - d \div p) \div (2D)$
 e) $H(1 - d \div p)$.

LO5. Kanban is the Japanese word for:
 a) car
 b) pull
 c) card
 d) continuous improvement
 e) level schedule.

LO6. The required number of kanbans equals:
 a) 1
 b) Demand during lead time/Q
 c) Size of container
 d) Demand during lead time
 e) (Demand during lead time + safety stock)/Size of container.

LO7. TPS's standard work practices include:
 a) completely specified work
 b) 'pull' systems
 c) level scheduling
 d) kanbans
 e) JIT techniques.

Answers: LO1. d; LO2. sort, simplify, shine, standardize, sustain; LO3. e; LO4. e; LO5. d; LO6. e; LO7. a.

17

Maintenance and Reliability Decisions

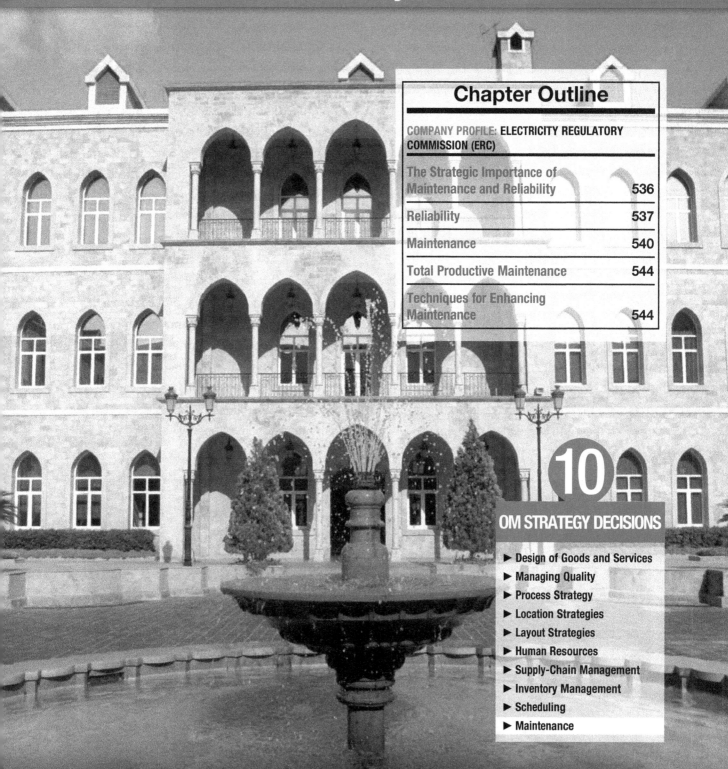

Chapter Outline

10

OM STRATEGY DECISIONS

- ► Design of Goods and Services
- ► Managing Quality
- ► Process Strategy
- ► Location Strategies
- ► Layout Strategies
- ► Human Resources
- ► Supply-Chain Management
- ► Inventory Management
- ► Scheduling
- ► Maintenance

MAINTENANCE PROVIDES A COMPETITIVE ADVANTAGE FOR ERC

The Electricity Regulatory Commission (ERC) fully owns, partially owns, and operates six power generating companies that supply power to Jordan. These are National Electric Power Co. (NEPCO), Central Electrical Generation Co. (CEGCO), Samra Electric Power Generation Co. (SEPGCO), Jordan Electric Power Co. (JEPCO), Irbid Electrical Power Co. (IDECO), and Electricity Distribution Co. (EDCO). Every year, ERC takes each one of its power-generating units off-line for 1 week to perform maintenance work.

Additionally, each unit is also taken off-line every 2 years for a complete overhaul and turbine generator inspection. Overhauls are scheduled for fall, just before the strong winter reaches Jordan, when the weather is mild and demand for power is relatively low. These overhauls last 1 month.

Units at ERC's Jordan Electric Power Co. (JEPCO) require that maintenance personnel perform thousands of repair and preventive maintenance tasks a year. To accomplish these tasks efficiently, many of these jobs are scheduled daily via a computerized maintenance management program. The computer generates preventive maintenance work orders and lists of required materials.

Every day that a plant is down for maintenance costs ERC about US$15,000 extra for the replacement cost of power that must be generated elsewhere. However, these costs pale beside the costs associated with a forced outage. An unexpected outage could cost ERC an additional US$70,000 to US$140,000 each day!

Scheduled overhauls are not easy; each one has distinct tasks and requires significant labor-hours. But the maintenance has huge preventive value; a cracked blade in a turbine generator, for example, could destroy other equipment totaling millions in value. At ERC, preventive maintenance is worth its weight in gold. As a result, ERC was awarded the Global Energy Award in 2007 for its effective and efficient management of energy.

Source: **www.erc.gov.jo**

The Electricity Regulatory Commission (ERC) in Jordan owns huge power plants such as this one in Samra.

Scheduled overhauls have huge preventive value; a cracked blade in a turbine generator, for example, could destroy other equipment—resulting in millions of US dollars' damage.

ERC's Jordan Electricity Company manages the biggest portion of Jordan's electrical grid which requires that maintenance personnel perform thousands of reparative and preventive maintenance tasks each year.

Chapter 17 **Learning Objectives**

AUTHOR COMMENT
If the system is not reliable, everything else is more difficult.

VIDEO 17.1
Maintenance Drives Profits at Frito-Lay

Maintenance

The activities involved in keeping a system's equipment in working order.

Reliability

The probability that a machine part or product will function properly for a specified time under stated conditions.

THE STRATEGIC IMPORTANCE OF MAINTENANCE AND RELIABILITY

Managers at Jordan's Electricity Regulatory Commission (ERC), fight for reliability to avoid the undesirable results of equipment failure. At ERC, a generator failure is very expensive for both the company and its customers. Power outages are instantaneous, with potentially devastating consequences. Similarly, managers at Aramex are intolerant of failures or breakdowns. Aramex's reliable maintenance strategy keeps its delivery vehicles operating and looking as good as new.

These companies, like most others, know that poor maintenance can be disruptive, inconvenient, wasteful, and expensive in financial terms and even in lives. As Figure 17.1 illustrates, the interdependency of operator, machine, and mechanic is a hallmark of successful maintenance and reliability. Good maintenance and reliability management enhances a firm's performance and protects its investment.

The objective of maintenance and reliability is to maintain the capability of the system. Good maintenance removes variability. Systems must be designed and maintained to reach expected performance and quality standards. **Maintenance** includes all activities involved in keeping a system's equipment in working order. **Reliability** is the probability that a machine part or product will function properly for a specified time under stated conditions.

In this chapter, we examine four important tactics for improving the reliability and maintenance not only of products and equipment but also of the systems that produce them. The four tactics are organized around reliability and maintenance.

The reliability tactics are:

1. Improving individual components.
2. Providing redundancy.

The maintenance tactics are:

1. Implementing or improving preventive maintenance.
2. Increasing repair capabilities or speed.

Variability corrupts processes and creates waste. The operations manager must drive out variability: Designing for reliability and managing for maintenance are crucial ingredients for doing so.

AUTHOR COMMENT
Employee commitment makes a big difference.

▶ **FIGURE 17.1**
Good Maintenance and Reliability Management Requires Employee Involvement and Good Procedures

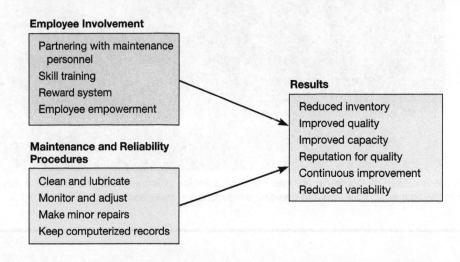

Employee Involvement
- Partnering with maintenance personnel
- Skill training
- Reward system
- Employee empowerment

Maintenance and Reliability Procedures
- Clean and lubricate
- Monitor and adjust
- Make minor repairs
- Keep computerized records

Results
- Reduced inventory
- Improved quality
- Improved capacity
- Reputation for quality
- Continuous improvement
- Reduced variability

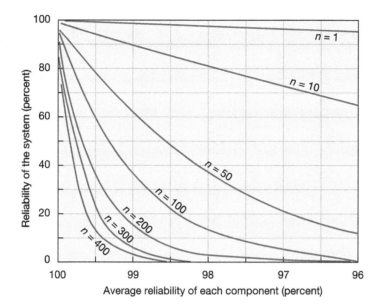

◀ **FIGURE 17.2**
Overall System Reliability as a Function of Number of *n* Components (Each with the Same Reliability) and Component Reliability with Components in a Series

RELIABILITY

Systems are composed of a series of individual interrelated components, each performing a specific job. If any *one* component fails to perform, for whatever reason, the overall system (for example, an airplane or machine) can fail. First, we discuss improving individual components, and then we discuss providing redundancy.

◀ **AUTHOR COMMENT**
Designing for reliability is an excellent place to start reducing variability.

LO1: Describe how to improve system reliability

Improving Individual Components

Because failures do occur in the real world, understanding their occurrence is an important reliability concept. We now examine the impact of failure in a series. Figure 17.2 shows that as the number of components in a *series* increases, the reliability of the whole system declines very quickly. A system of $n = 50$ interacting parts, each of which has a 99.5 percent reliability, has an overall reliability of 78 percent. If the system or machine has 100 interacting parts, each with an individual reliability of 99.5 percent, the overall reliability will be only about 60 percent!

To measure reliability in a system in which each individual part or component may have its own unique rate of reliability, we cannot use the reliability curve in Figure 17.2. However, the method of computing system reliability (R_s) is simple. It consists of finding the product of individual reliabilities as follows:

$$R_s = R_1 \times R_2 \times R_3 \times \cdots \times R_n \qquad \text{(17-1)}$$

where R_1 = reliability of component 1
         R_2 = reliability of component 2

and so on.

Equation (17-1) assumes that the reliability of an individual component does not depend on the reliability of other components (that is, each component is independent). Additionally, in this equation as in most reliability discussions, reliabilities are presented as *probabilities*. Thus, a 0.90 reliability means that the unit will perform as intended 90 percent of the time. It also means that it will fail $1 - 0.90 = 0.10 = 10$ percent of the time. We can use this method to evaluate the reliability of a service or a product, such as the one we examine in Example 1.

Component reliability is often a design or specification issue for which engineering design personnel may be responsible. However, supply-chain personnel may be able to improve components of systems by staying abreast of suppliers' products and research efforts. Supply-chain personnel can also contribute directly to the evaluation of supplier performance.

The basic unit of measure for reliability is the *product failure rate* (FR). Firms producing high-technology equipment often provide failure-rate data on their products. As shown in Equations (17-2) and (17-3), the failure rate measures the percentage of failures among the total number of products tested, FR(%), or a number of failures during a period of time, FR(*N*):

Reliability in a series

The Jordan Kuwait Bank processes loan applications through three clerks set up in series, with reliabilities of 0.90, 0.80, and 0.99. It wants to find the system reliability.

APPROACH ▶   Apply Equation (17-1) to solve for R_s.

SOLUTION ▶   The reliability of the loan process is:

$$R_s = R_1 \times R_2 \times R_3 = (0.90)(0.80)(0.99) = 0.713, \text{ or } 71.3\%$$

LO2: Determine system reliability

INSIGHT ▶   Because each clerk in the series is less than perfect, the error probabilities are cumulative and the resulting reliability for this series is 0.713, which is less than any one clerk.

LEARNING EXERCISE ▶   If the lowest-performing clerk (0.80) is replaced by a clerk performing at 0.95 reliability, what is the new expected reliability? [Answer: 0.846.]

RELATED PROBLEMS ▶   17.1, 17.2, 17.5

EXCEL OM Data File **Ch17Ex1.xls** can be found at MyOMLab.

$$FR(\%) = \frac{\text{Number of failures}}{\text{Number of units tested}} \times 100\% \qquad (17\text{-}2)$$

$$FR(N) = \frac{\text{Number of failures}}{\text{Number of unit-hours of operation time}} \qquad (17\text{-}3)$$

Mean time between failures (MTBF)

The expected time between a repair and the next failure of a component, machine, process, or product.

Perhaps the most common term in reliability analysis is the **mean time between failures (MTBF)**, which is the reciprocal of $FR(N)$:

$$MTBF = \frac{1}{FR(N)} \qquad (17\text{-}4)$$

In Example 2, we compute the percentage of failure $FR(\%)$, number of failures $FR(N)$, and mean time between failures.

Determining mean time between failures

Twenty air-conditioning systems designed for use by Emaar in Offices Complex One, Dubai, were operated for 1,000 hours at the subcontractor's test facility. Two of the systems failed during the test—one after 200 hours and the other after 600 hours.

APPROACH ▶   To determine the percentage of failures [$FR(\%)$], the number of failures per unit of time [$FR(N)$], and the mean time between failures (MTBF), we use Equations (17-2), (17-3), and (17-4), respectively.

SOLUTION ▶   Percentage of failures:

$$FR(\%) = \frac{\text{Number of failures}}{\text{Number of units tested}} = \frac{2}{20}(100\%) = 10\%$$

Number of failures per operating hour:

$$FR(N) = \frac{\text{Number of failures}}{\text{Operating time}}$$

where   Total time $= (1,000 \text{ hr})(20 \text{ units}) = 20,000$ unit-hour

Non-operating time $= 800$ hr for 1st failure $+ 400$ hr for 2nd failure
$= 1,200$ unit-hour

Operating time $=$ Total time $-$ Non-operating time

$$FR(N) = \frac{2}{20,000 - 1,200} = \frac{2}{18,800}$$

$$= 0.000106 \text{ failure/unit-hour}$$

Because $\text{MTBF} = \dfrac{1}{\text{FR}(N)}$

$$\text{MTBF} = \frac{1}{0.000106} = 9{,}434 \text{ hr}$$

LO3: Determine mean time between failures (MTBF)

If the typical working week for the building is 6 days, Emaar may be interested in the failure rate per week:

$$\text{Failure rate} = (\text{Failures/unit-hr})(24 \text{ hr/day})(6 \text{ days/week})$$

$$= (0.000106)(24)(6) = 0.0153 \text{ failure/week}$$

INSIGHT ▶ Mean time between failures (MTBF) is the standard means of stating reliability.

LEARNING EXERCISE ▶ If non-operating time drops to 800, what is the new MTBF? [Answer: 9,606 hr.]

RELATED PROBLEM ▶ 17.6

If the failure rate recorded in Example 2 is too high, Emaar will have to either increase the reliability of individual components, and thus of the system, or install several backup air-conditioning units. Backup units provide redundancy.

Providing Redundancy

To increase the reliability of systems, **redundancy** is added. The technique here is to 'back up' components with additional components. This is known as putting units in parallel and is a standard operations management tactic. Redundancy is provided to ensure that if one component fails, the system has recourse to another. For instance, say that reliability of a component is 0.80 and we back it up with another component with reliability of 0.80. The resulting reliability is the probability of the first component working plus the probability of the backup (or parallel) component working multiplied by the probability of needing the backup component ($1 - 0.8 = 0.2$). Therefore:

Redundancy
The use of components in parallel to raise reliability.

$$\begin{pmatrix} \text{Probability} \\ \text{of first} \\ \text{component} \\ \text{working} \end{pmatrix} + \left[\begin{pmatrix} \text{Probability} \\ \text{of second} \\ \text{component} \\ \text{working} \end{pmatrix} \times \begin{pmatrix} \text{Probability} \\ \text{of needing} \\ \text{second} \\ \text{component} \\ \text{working} \end{pmatrix} \right] =$$

$$(0.8) \quad + \ [(0.8) \quad \times (1 - 0.8)] \quad = 0.8 + 0.16 = 0.96$$

Example 3 shows how redundancy can improve the reliability of the loan process presented in Example 1.

◀ EXAMPLE 3

Reliability with a parallel process

The Jordan Kuwait Bank is disturbed that its loan-application process has a reliability of only 0.713 (see Example 1) and would like to improve this situation.

APPROACH ▶ The bank decides to provide redundancy for the two least reliable clerks.

SOLUTION ▶ This procedure results in the following system:

$$\begin{array}{ccc} R_1 & R_2 & R_3 \\ 0.90 & 0.80 & \\ \downarrow & \downarrow & \end{array}$$

$$\boxed{0.90} : \boxed{0.80} : \boxed{0.99} = [0.9 + 0.9(1 - 0.9)] \times [0.8 + 0.8(1 - 0.8)] \times 0.99$$
$$= [0.9 + (0.9)(0.1)] \times [0.8 + (0.8)(0.2)] \times 0.99$$
$$= 0.99 \times 0.96 \times 0.99 = 0.94$$

INSIGHT ▶ By providing redundancy for two clerks, Jordan Kuwait Bank has increased reliability of the loan process from 0.713 to 0.94.

LEARNING EXERCISE ▶ What happens when the bank replaces both clerks with one new clerk who has a reliability of 0.90? [Answer: $R_s = 0.88$.]

RELATED PROBLEMS ▶ 17.7, 17.8, 17.11

EXCEL OM Data File **Ch17Ex3.xls** can be found at MyOMLab.

AUTHOR COMMENT
Even the most reliable systems require maintenance.

Preventive maintenance

A plan that involves routine inspections, servicing, and keeping facilities in good repair to prevent failure.

Breakdown maintenance

Remedial maintenance that occurs when equipment fails and must be repaired on an emergency or priority basis.

Infant mortality

The failure rate early in the life of a product or process.

LO4: Distinguish between preventive and breakdown maintenance

LO5: Describe how to improve maintenance

MAINTENANCE

There are two types of maintenance: preventive maintenance and breakdown maintenance. **Preventive maintenance** involves performing routine inspections and servicing and keeping facilities in good repair. These activities are intended to build a system that will find potential failures and make changes or repairs that will prevent failure. Preventive maintenance is much more than just keeping machinery and equipment running. It also involves designing technical and human systems that will keep the productive process working within tolerance; it allows the system to perform. The emphasis of preventive maintenance is on understanding the process and keeping it working without interruption. **Breakdown maintenance** occurs when equipment fails and must be repaired on an emergency or priority basis.

Implementing Preventive Maintenance

Preventive maintenance implies that we can determine when a system needs service or will need repair. Therefore, to perform preventive maintenance, we must know when a system requires service or when it is likely to fail. Failures occur at different rates during the life of a product. A high initial failure rate, known as **infant mortality**, may exist for many products.[1] This is why many electronic firms 'burn in' their products prior to shipment: That is to say, they execute a variety of tests (such as a full wash cycle at Whirlpool washing machines) to detect 'startup' problems prior to shipment. Firms may also provide 90-day warranties. We should note that many infant mortality failures are not product failures per se, but rather failure due to improper use. This fact points up the importance in many industries of operations management's building an after-sales service system that includes installing and training.

Once the product, machine, or process 'settles in,' a study can be made of the mean time between failures (MTBF) distribution. Such distributions often follow a normal curve. When these distributions exhibit small standard deviations, then we know we have a candidate for preventive maintenance, even if the maintenance is expensive.

Once our firm has a candidate for preventive maintenance, we want to determine *when* preventive maintenance is economical. Typically, the more expensive the maintenance, the narrower must be the MTBF distribution (that is, have a small standard deviation). In addition, if the process is no more expensive to repair when it breaks down than the cost of preventive maintenance, perhaps we should let the process break down and then do the repair. However, the consequence of the breakdown must be fully considered. Even some relatively minor breakdowns have catastrophic consequences. (See the *OM in Action* box 'Preventive Maintenance Saves Lives' on the next page). At the other extreme, preventive maintenance costs may be so incidental that preventive maintenance is appropriate even if the MTBF distribution is rather flat (that is, it has a large standard deviation). In any event, consistent with job enrichment practices, machine operators must be held responsible for preventive maintenance of their own equipment and tools.

With good reporting techniques, firms can maintain records of individual processes, machines, or equipment. Such records can provide a profile of both the kinds of maintenance required and the timing of maintenance needed. Maintaining equipment history is an important part of a preventive maintenance system, as is a record of the time and cost to make the repair. Such records can also provide information about the family of equipment and suppliers.

Reliability and maintenance are of such importance that most systems are now computerized. Figure 17.3 shows the major components of such a system with files to be maintained on the left and reports generated on the right.

Figure 17.4(a) shows a traditional view of the relationship between preventive maintenance and breakdown maintenance. In this view, operations managers consider a *balance* between the two costs. Allocating more resources to preventive maintenance will reduce the number of breakdowns. At some point, however, the decrease in breakdown maintenance costs may be less than the increase in preventive maintenance costs. At this point, the total cost curve begins to rise. Beyond this optimal point, the firm will be better off waiting for breakdowns to occur and repairing them when they do.

---

[1]Infant mortality failures often follow a negative exponential distribution.

Data Files

Output Reports

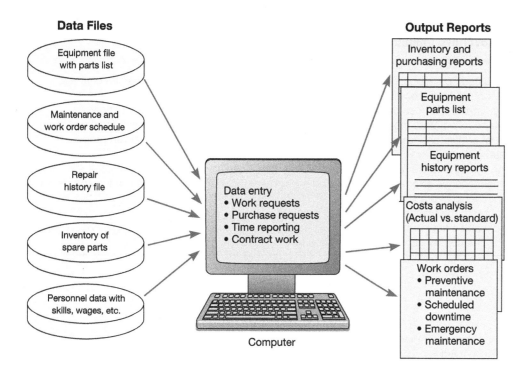

Computer

Unfortunately, cost curves such as in Figure 17.4(a) seldom consider the *full costs of a breakdown*. Many costs are ignored because they are not *directly* related to the immediate breakdown. For instance, the cost of inventory maintained to compensate for downtime is not typically considered. Moreover, downtime can have a devastating effect on safety and morale. Employees may also begin to believe that performance to standard and maintaining equipment are not important. Finally, downtime adversely affects delivery schedules, destroying customer relations and future sales. When the full impact of breakdowns is considered, Figure 17.4(b) may be a better representation of maintenance costs. In Figure 17.4(b), total costs are at a minimum when the system does not break down.

Assuming that all potential costs associated with downtime have been identified, the operations staff can compute the optimal level of maintenance activity on a theoretical basis. Such analysis, of course, also requires accurate historical data on maintenance costs, breakdown probabilities, and repair times. Example 4 shows how to compare preventive and breakdown maintenance costs to select the least expensive maintenance policy.

> **AUTHOR COMMENT**
> When all breakdown costs are considered, much more maintenance may be advantageous.

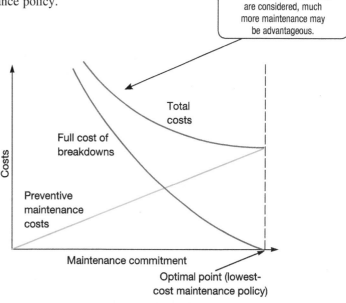

(a) Traditional View of Maintenance

(b) Full Cost View of Maintenance

▲ FIGURE 17.4 **Maintenance Costs**

OM in Action ▶ Preventive Maintenance Saves Lives

Flight 5481's trip was short. It lasted 70 seconds. The flight left the Charlotte Airport, bound for Greenville/Spartanburg, but seconds after lift-off, the nose of the aircraft pitched upward, the plane rolled, and, moments later, slammed into the corner of a maintenance facility at the airport, killing 21 people.

The National Transportation Safety Board's focus in this situation is a preventive maintenance error made two days prior to the crash. The mechanic and a supervisor skipped at least 12 steps required in the maintenance of the tension of the pitch-control cables during the *Detail 6* check that includes the pitch of the control cable tension.

Data show that the control column position changed during the maintenance and the plane lost about two-thirds down-elevator capability. Investigators believe that the aircraft would have been flyable with fully functioning controls had it been given proper preventive maintenance.

Maintenance can improve quality, reduce costs, and win orders. It can also be a matter of life and death.

Sources: Aviation Week and Space Technology (May 26, 2003): 52; *USA Today* (May 21, 2003): 8A; and *The Wall Street Journal* (May 21, 2003): D3 and (May 20, 2003): D1, D3.

EXAMPLE 4 ▶

Comparing preventive and breakdown maintenance costs

TAG is a firm specializing in payroll preparation. The firm has been successful in automating much of its work, using high-speed printers for check processing and report preparation. The computerized approach, however, has problems. Over the past 20 months, the printers have broken down at the rate indicated in the following table:

Number of Breakdowns	Number of Months That Breakdowns Occurred
0	2
1	8
2	6
3	4
	Total: 20

Each time the printers break down, TAG estimates that it loses an average of US$300 in production time and service expenses. One alternative is to purchase a service contract for preventive maintenance. Even if TAG contracts for preventive maintenance, there will still be breakdowns, *averaging* one breakdown per month. The price for this service is US$150 per month.

APPROACH ▶   To determine if TAG should follow a 'run until breakdown' policy or contract for preventive maintenance, we follow a 4-step process:

STEP 1. Compute the *expected number* of breakdowns (based on past history) if the firm continues as is, without the service contract.

STEP 2. Compute the expected breakdown cost per month with no preventive maintenance contract.

STEP 3. Compute the cost of preventive maintenance.

STEP 4. Compare the two options and select the one that will cost less.

SOLUTION ▶   STEP 1.

LO6: Compare preventive and breakdown maintenance costs

Number of Breakdowns	Frequency	Number of Breakdowns	Frequency
0	2 ÷ 20 = 0.1	2	6 ÷ 20 = 0.3
1	8 ÷ 20 = 0.4	3	4 ÷ 20 = 0.2

$$\begin{pmatrix} \text{Expected number} \\ \text{of breakdowns} \end{pmatrix} = \sum \left[\begin{pmatrix} \text{Number of} \\ \text{breakdowns} \end{pmatrix} \times \begin{pmatrix} \text{Corresponding} \\ \text{frequency} \end{pmatrix} \right]$$

$$= (0)(0.1) + (1)(0.4) + (2)(0.3) + (3)(0.2)$$

$$= 0 + 0.4 + 0.6 + 0.6$$

$$= 1.6 \text{ breakdowns/month}$$

STEP 2.

$$\text{Expected breakdown cost} = \left(\begin{array}{c}\text{Expected number}\\\text{of breakdowns}\end{array}\right) \times \left(\begin{array}{c}\text{Cost per}\\\text{breakdown}\end{array}\right)$$

$$= (1.6)(\text{US}\$300)$$

$$= \text{US}\$480/\text{month}$$

STEP 3.

$$\left(\begin{array}{c}\text{Preventive}\\\text{maintenance cost}\end{array}\right) = \left(\begin{array}{c}\text{Cost of expected}\\\text{breakdowns if service}\\\text{contract signed}\end{array}\right) + (\text{Cost of service contract})$$

$$= (1 \text{ breakdown/month})(\text{US}\$300) + \text{US}\$150/\text{month}$$

$$= \text{US}\$450/\text{month}$$

STEP 4. Because it is less expensive overall to hire a maintenance service firm (US$450) than to not do so (US$480), TAG should hire the service firm.

INSIGHT ▶ Determining the expected number of breakdowns for each option is crucial to making a good decision. This typically requires good maintenance records.

LEARNING EXERCISE ▶ What is the best decision if the preventive maintenance contract cost increases to US$195 per month? [Answer: At US$495 (=US$300 + US$195) per month, 'run until breakdown' becomes less expensive (assuming that all costs are included in the US$300 per breakdown cost).]

RELATED PROBLEMS ▶ 17.3, 17.4, 17.10

Using variations of the technique shown in Example 4, operations managers can examine maintenance policies.

Increasing Repair Capabilities

Because reliability and preventive maintenance are seldom perfect, most firms opt for some level of repair capability. Enlarging or improving repair facilities can get the system back in operation faster. A good maintenance facility should have these six features:

1. Well-trained personnel.
2. Adequate resources.
3. Ability to establish a repair plan and priorities[2].
4. Ability and authority to do material planning.
5. Ability to identify the cause of breakdowns.
6. Ability to design ways to extend MTBF.

However, not all repairs can be done in the firm's facility. Managers must, therefore, decide where repairs are to be performed. Figure 17.5 provides a continuum of options and how they rate in terms of speed, cost, and competence. Moving to the right in Figure 17.5 may improve the competence of the repair work, but at the same time it increases costs and replacement time.

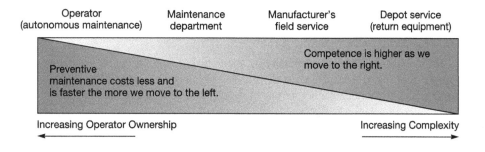

◀ **FIGURE 17.5**
The Operations Manager Determines How Maintenance Will Be Performed

[2]You may recall from our discussion of network planning in Chapter 3 that DuPont developed the critical path method (CPM) to improve the scheduling of maintenance projects.

LO7: Define autonomous maintenance

Autonomous maintenance

Operators partner with maintenance personnel to observe, check, adjust, clean, and notify.

Autonomous Maintenance

Preventive maintenance policies and techniques must include an emphasis on employees accepting responsibility for the 'observe, check, adjust, clean, and notify' type of equipment maintenance. Such policies are consistent with the advantages of employee empowerment. This approach is known as **autonomous maintenance**. Employees can predict failures, prevent breakdowns, and prolong equipment life. With autonomous maintenance, the manager is making a step toward both employee empowerment and maintaining system performance.

> **AUTHOR COMMENT**
> Maintenance improves productivity.

Total productive maintenance (TPM)

Combines total quality management with a strategic view of maintenance from process and equipment design to preventive maintenance.

TOTAL PRODUCTIVE MAINTENANCE

Many firms have moved to bring total quality management concepts to the practice of preventive maintenance with an approach known as **total productive maintenance (TPM)**. It involves the concept of reducing variability through autonomous maintenance and excellent maintenance practices. Total productive maintenance includes:

- Designing machines that are reliable, easy to operate, and easy to maintain.
- Emphasizing total cost of ownership when purchasing machines, so that service and maintenance are included in the cost.
- Developing preventive maintenance plans that utilize the best practices of operators, maintenance departments, and depot service.
- Training for autonomous maintenance so operators maintain their own machines and partner with maintenance personnel.

High utilization of facilities, tight scheduling, low inventory, and consistent quality demand reliability. Total productive maintenance is the key to reducing variability and improving reliability.

> **AUTHOR COMMENT**
> Both OM techniques and the physical sciences can improve maintenance.

TECHNIQUES FOR ENHANCING MAINTENANCE

Three techniques have proven beneficial to effective maintenance: simulation, expert systems, and sensors.

Simulation

Because of the complexity of some maintenance decisions, computer simulation is a good tool for evaluating the impact of various policies. For instance, operations personnel can decide whether to add more staff by determining the trade-offs between machine reliability and the costs of additional labor. Management can also simulate the replacement of parts that have not yet failed as a way of preventing future breakdowns. Simulation via physical models can also be useful. For example, a physical model can vibrate an airplane to simulate thousands of hours of flight time to evaluate maintenance needs.

Expert Systems

OM managers use expert systems (that is, computer programs that mimic human logic) to assist staff in isolating and repairing various faults in machinery and equipment. For instance, Almarai's DSS system asks a series of detailed questions that aid the user in identifying a problem. Royal Jordanian uses expert systems to monitor equipment and to train repair personnel.

Automated Sensors

Sensors warn when production machinery is about to fail or is becoming damaged by heat, vibration, or fluid leaks. The goal of such procedures is not only to avoid failures but also to perform preventive maintenance before machines are damaged.

CHAPTER SUMMARY

Operations managers focus on design improvements and backup components to improve reliability. Reliability improvements also can be obtained through the use of preventive maintenance and excellent repair facilities.

Firms give employees 'ownership' of their equipment. When workers repair or do preventive maintenance on their own machines, breakdowns are less common. Well-trained and empowered employees ensure reliable systems through preventive

maintenance. In turn, reliable, well-maintained equipment not only provides higher utilization but also improves quality and performance to schedule. Top firms build and maintain systems that drive out variability so that customers can rely on products and services to be produced to specifications and on time.

Key Terms

Autonomous maintenance (p. 544)
Breakdown maintenance (p. 540)
Infant mortality (p. 540)
Maintenance (p. 536)

Mean time between failures (MTBF)
  (p. 538)
Preventive maintenance (p. 540)
Redundancy (p. 539)

Reliability (p. 536)
Total productive maintenance (TPM)
  (p. 544)

Ethical Dilemma

The Space Shuttle *Columbia* disintegrated on its 2003 return to Earth. The *Challenger* exploded shortly after launch in 1986. An *Apollo 1* spacecraft imploded in fire on the launch pad in 1967. In each case, the lives of all crew members were lost. The hugely complex shuttle may look a bit like an airplane, but it is very different. In reality, its overall statistical reliability was such that about 1 out of every 50 flights had a major malfunction. In fact, there were 135 shuttle flights in total.

NASA cut safety inspections by more than 50 percent after 1989. Employees often faced a cumbersome process for bringing safety

issues to management. And the agency continued to face pressure to launch the shuttle on missions to the space station and elsewhere. Of course, as one aerospace manager has stated "you can be perfectly safe and never get off the ground."

Given the huge reliability and maintenance issues NASA faced (e.g. seals cracking in cold weather, heat shielding tiles falling off), should astronauts have been allowed to fly? (In earlier *Atlas* rockets, men were inserted not out of necessity but because test pilots and politicians thought they should be there.) What are the pros and cons of manned space exploration from an ethical perspective?

Discussion Questions

1. What is the objective of maintenance and reliability?
2. How does one identify a candidate for preventive maintenance?
3. Explain the notion of 'infant mortality' in the context of product reliability.
4. Why is simulation often an appropriate technique for maintenance problems?
5. What is the trade-off between operator-performed maintenance versus supplier-performed maintenance?
6. How can a manager evaluate the effectiveness of the maintenance function?

7. How does machine design contribute to either increasing or alleviating the maintenance problem?
8. What roles can information technology play in the maintenance function?
9. During an argument as to the merits of preventive maintenance at Windsor Printers, the company owner asked, "Why fix it before it breaks?" How would you, as the director of maintenance, respond?
10. Will preventive maintenance eliminate *all* breakdowns?

Using Software to Solve Reliability Problems

Px Excel OM and POM for Windows may be used to solve reliability problems. The reliability module allow us to enter: (1) number of systems (components) in the series (1 through 10); (2) number of backup, or parallel, components (1 through 12); (3) component reliability for both series and parallel data.

Solved Problems   Virtual Office Hours help is available at MyOMLab

▼ SOLVED PROBLEM 17.1

The semiconductor used in the Sullivan Wrist Calculator has five circuits, each of which has its own reliability rate. Component 1 has a reliability of 0.90; component 2, 0.95; component 3, 0.98; component 4, 0.90; and component 5, 0.99. What is the reliability of one semiconductor?

▼ SOLUTION

Semiconductor reliability, $R_s = R_1 \times R_2 \times R_3 \times R_4 \times R_5$

$$= (0.90)(0.95)(0.98)(0.90)(0.99)$$

$$= 0.7466$$

▼ SOLVED PROBLEM 17.2

A recent engineering change at Sullivan Wrist Calculator places a backup component in each of the two least reliable transistor circuits. The new circuits will look like the following:

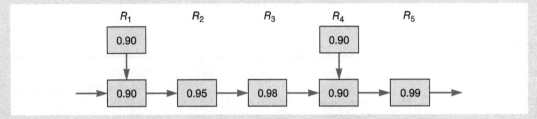

What is the reliability of the new system?

▼ SOLUTION

$$\text{Reliability} = [0.9 + (1 - 0.9) \times 0.9] \times 0.95 \times 0.98 \times [0.9 + (1 - 0.9) \times 0.9] \times 0.99$$

$$= [0.9 + 0.09] \times 0.95 \times 0.98 \times [0.9 + 0.09] \times 0.99$$

$$= 0.99 \times 0.95 \times 0.98 \times 0.99 \times 0.99$$

$$= 0.903$$

Problems*

•   **17.1**   The Beta II computer's electronic processing unit contains 50 components in series. The average reliability of each component is 99.0 percent. Using Figure 17.2, determine the overall reliability of the processing unit.

•   **17.2**   A testing process at Gulf Craft has 400 components in series. The average reliability of each component is 99.5 percent. Use Figure 17.2 to find the overall reliability of the whole testing process.

•   **17.3**   What are the *expected* number of yearly breakdowns for the power generator at ERC that has exhibited the following data over the past 20 years? **Px**

Number of breakdowns	0	1	2	3	4	5	6
Number of years in which breakdown occurred	2	2	5	4	5	2	0

•   **17.4**   Each breakdown of a graphic plotter table at EGA Industries costs US$50. Find the expected daily breakdown cost, given the following data: **Px**

Number of breakdowns	0	1	2	3	4
Daily breakdown probability	0.1	0.2	0.4	0.2	0.1

••   **17.5**   A new aircraft control system is being designed that must be 98 percent reliable. This system consists of three components in series. If all three of the components are to have the same level of reliability, what level of reliability is required? **Px**

*Note: **Px** means the problem may be solved with POM for Windows and/or Excel OM.

••   **17.6**   A manufacturer of disk drives for notebook computers wants a MTBF of at least 50,000 hours. Recent test results for 10 units were one failure at 10,000 hrs, another at 25,000 hrs, and two more at 45,000 hrs. The remaining units were still running at 60,000 hours. Determine the following:
a) Percentage of failures.
b) Number of failures per unit-hour
c) MTBF at this point in the testing

••   **17.7**   What is the reliability of the following production process? $R_1 = 0.95$, $R_2 = 0.90$, $R_3 = 0.98$.

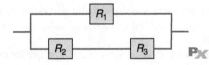

••   **17.8**   What is the reliability that bank loans will be processed accurately if each of the 5 clerks shown in the chart has the reliability shown?

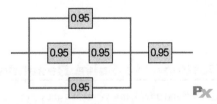

••   **17.9**   The maintenance department at Mechanical Dynamics has presented you with the following failure curve. What does it suggest?

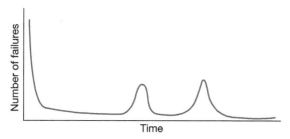

• • • 17.10 The fire department has a number of failures with its oxygen masks and is evaluating the possibility of outsourcing preventive maintenance to the manufacturer. Because of the risk associated with a failure, the cost of each failure is estimated at US$2,000. The current maintenance policy (with station employees performing maintenance) has yielded the following history:

Number of breakdowns	0	1	2	3	4	5
Number of years in which breakdowns occurred	4	3	1	5	5	0

This manufacturer will guarantee repairs on any and all failures as part of a service contract. The cost of this service is US$5,000 per year.
a) What is the expected number of breakdowns per year with station employees performing maintenance?
b) What is the cost of the current maintenance policy?
c) What is the more economical policy?

• • • 17.11 As VP for operations at Bairaq Engineering, you must decide which product design, A or B, has the higher reliability. B is designed with backup units for components R_3 and R_4. What is the reliability of each design?

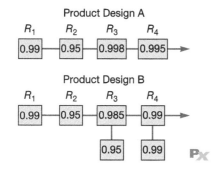

Product Design A

R_1 R_2 R_3 R_4
0.99 — 0.95 — 0.998 — 0.995

Product Design B

R_1 R_2 R_3 R_4
0.99 — 0.95 — 0.985 — 0.99
                0.95   0.99

• • • • 17.12 A typical retail transaction consists of several smaller steps, which can be considered components subject to failure. A list of such components might include:

Component	Description	Definition of Failure
1	Find product in proper size, color, etc.	Can't find product
2	Enter cashier line	No lines open; lines too long; line experiencing difficulty
3	Scan product UPC for name, price, etc.	Won't scan; item not on file; scans incorrect name or price
4	Calculate purchase total	Wrong weight; wrong extension; wrong data entry; wrong tax
5	Make payment	Customer lacks cash; check not acceptable; credit card refused
6	Make change	Makes change incorrectly
7	Bag merchandise	Damages merchandise while bagging; bag splits
8	Conclude transaction and exit	No receipt; unfriendly, rude, or aloof clerk

Let the eight probabilities of success be 0.92, 0.94, 0.99, 0.99, 0.98, 0.97, 0.95, and 0.96. What is the reliability of the system, that is, the probability that there will be a satisfied customer? If you were the store manager, what do you think should be an acceptable value for this probability? Which components would be good candidates for backup, which for redesign?

▶ **Refer to** MyOMLab **for additional homework problems.**

Case Study

▶ **Maintenance Drives Profits at Frito-Lay**

Video Case

Frito-Lay, the multi-billion-dollar subsidiary of food and beverage giant PepsiCo, produces dozens of snacks, including the well-known Lay's, Fritos, Cheetos, Doritos, Ruffles, and Tostitos brands, each of which sells over US$1 billion per year.

Frito-Lay plants produce in the high-volume, low-variety process model common to commercial baked goods, steel, glass, and beer industries. In this environment, preventive maintenance of equipment takes a major role by avoiding costly downtime. Tom Rao, Vice President for Florida operations, estimates that each 1 percent of downtime has a negative annual profit impact of US$200,000. He is proud of the 1.5 percent unscheduled downtime his plant is able

to reach—well below the 2 percent that is considered the 'world-class' benchmark. This excellent performance is possible because the maintenance department takes an active role in setting the parameters for preventive maintenance. This is done with weekly input to the production schedule.

Maintenance policy impacts energy use as well. The Florida plant's technical manager, Jim Wentzel, states, "By reducing production interruptions, we create an opportunity to bring energy and utility use under control. Equipment maintenance and a solid production schedule are keys to utility efficiency. With every production interruption, there is substantial waste."

As a part of its total productive maintenance (TPM) program,* Frito-Lay empowers employees with what it calls the 'Run Right' system. Run Right teaches employees to 'identify and do.' This means each shift is responsible for identifying problems and making the necessary corrections, when possible. This is accomplished through: (1) a 'power walk' at the beginning of the shift to ensure that equipment and process settings are performing to standard; (2) mid-shift and post-shift reviews of standards and performance; (3) posting of any issues on a large whiteboard in the shift office. Items remain on the whiteboard until corrected, which is seldom more than a shift or two.

With good manpower scheduling and tight labor control to hold down variable costs, making time for training is challenging. But supervisors, including the plant manager, are available to fill in on the production line when that is necessary to free an employee for training.

*At Frito-Lay preventive maintenance, autonomous maintenance, and total productive maintenance are part of a Frito-Lay program known as total productive manufacturing.

Source: Professors Barry Render (Rollins College), Jay Heizer (Texas Lutheran University), and Beverly Amer (Northern Arizona University).

The 30 maintenance personnel hired to cover operations at the Florida plant all come with multi-craft skills (e.g. welding, electrical, plumbing). "Multi-craft maintenance personnel are harder to find and cost more," says Wentzel, "but they more than pay for themselves."

Discussion Questions**

1. What might be done to help take Frito-Lay to the next level of outstanding maintenance? Consider factors such as sophisticated software.
2. What are the advantages and disadvantages of giving more responsibility for machine maintenance to the operator?
3. Discuss the pros and cons of hiring multi-craft maintenance personnel.

**You may wish to view the video that accompanies this case before answering these questions.

▶ **Additional Case Studies**: Visit MyOMLab for these free case studies:

Cartak's Department Store: Requires the evaluation of the impact of an additional invoice verifier.

Worldwide Chemical Company: The maintenance department in this company is in turmoil.

Main Heading	Review Material	MyOMLab
THE STRATEGIC IMPORTANCE OF MAINTENANCE AND RELIABILITY (pp. 536–537)	Poor maintenance can be disruptive, inconvenient, wasteful, and expensive in financial terms, and even in lives. The interdependency of operator, machine, and mechanic is a hallmark of successful maintenance and reliability.	**VIDEO 17.1** Maintenance Drives Profits at Frito-Lay
	Good maintenance and reliability management requires employee involvement and good procedures; it enhances a firm's performance and protects its investment.	
	The objective of maintenance and reliability is to maintain the capability of the system.	
	▪ **Maintenance**—All activities involved in keeping a system's equipment in working order. ▪ **Reliability**—The probability that a machine part or product will function properly for a specified time under stated conditions.	
	The two main tactics for improving reliability are:	
	1. Improving individual components 2. Providing redundancy	
	The two main tactics for improving maintenance are:	
	1. Implementing or improving preventive maintenance 2. Increasing repair capabilities or speed	
RELIABILITY (pp. 537–539)	A system is composed of a series of individual interrelated components, each performing a specific job. If any *one* component fails to perform, the overall system can fail.	Problems: 17.1–17.2, 17.5–17.8, 17.11, 17.12
	As the number of components in a *series* increases, the reliability of the whole system declines very quickly:	Virtual Office Hours for Solved Problems: 17.1, 17.2
	$$R_s = R_1 \times R_2 \times R_3 \times \cdots \times R_n \qquad (17\text{-}1)$$	
	where R_1 = reliability of component 1, R_2 = reliability of component 2, and so on.	
	Equation (17-1) assumes that the reliability of an individual component does not depend on the reliability of other components.	
	A 0.90 reliability means that the unit will perform as intended 90 percent of the time, and it will fail 10 percent of the time.	
	The basic unit of measure for reliability is the *product failure rate* (FR).	
	FR(N) is the number of failures during a period of time:	
	$$FR(\%) = \frac{\text{Number of failures}}{\text{Number of units tested}} \times 100\% \qquad (17\text{-}2)$$	
	$$FR(N) = \frac{\text{Number of failures}}{\text{Number of unit-hours of operation time}} \qquad (17\text{-}3)$$	
	▪ **Mean time between failures (MTBF)**—The expected time between a repair and the next failure of a component, machine, process, or product.	
	$$MTBF = \frac{1}{FR(N)} \qquad (17\text{-}4)$$	
	▪ **Redundancy**—The use of components in parallel to raise reliability.	
	The reliability of a component along with its backup equals:	
	(Probability that 1st component works) + [(Prob. that backup works) × (Prob. that 1st fails)]	
MAINTENANCE (pp. 540–544)	▪ **Preventive maintenance**—Involves routine inspections, servicing, and keeping facilities in good repair to prevent failure. ▪ **Breakdown maintenance**—Remedial maintenance that occurs when equipment fails and must be repaired on an emergency or priority basis. ▪ **Infant mortality**—The failure rate early in the life of a product or process.	Problems: 17.3, 17.4, 17.9, 17.10
	Consistent with job enrichment practices, machine operators must be held responsible for preventive maintenance of their own equipment and tools.	
	Reliability and maintenance are of such importance that most maintenance systems are now computerized.	
	Costs of a breakdown that may get ignored include:	
	• The cost of inventory maintained to compensate for downtime • Downtime, which can have a devastating effect on safety and morale and which adversely affects delivery schedules, destroying customer relations and future sales	
	▪ **Autonomous maintenance**—Partners operators with maintenance personnel to observe, check, adjust, clean, and notify.	

MyOMLab

Main Heading	Review Material
	Employees can predict failures, prevent breakdowns, and prolong equipment life. With autonomous maintenance, the manager is making a step toward both employee empowerment and maintaining system performance.
TOTAL PRODUCTIVE MAINTENANCE (p. 544)	■ **Total productive maintenance (TPM)**—Combines total quality management with a strategic view of maintenance from process and equipment design to preventive maintenance. Total productive maintenance includes: • Designing machines that are reliable, easy to operate, and easy to maintain • Emphasizing total cost of ownership when purchasing machines, so that service and maintenance are included in the cost • Developing preventive maintenance plans that utilize the best practices of operators, maintenance departments, and depot service • Training for autonomous maintenance so operators maintain their own machines and partner with maintenance personnel
TECHNIQUES FOR ENHANCING MAINTENANCE (p. 544)	Three techniques that have proven beneficial to effective maintenance are simulation, expert systems, and sensors: • Computer simulation is a good tool for evaluating the impact of various policies • Expert systems are computer programs that mimic human logic • Automatic sensors warn when production machinery is about to fail or is becoming damaged by heat, vibration, or fluid leaks

Self-Test

■ **Before taking the self-test,** refer to the learning objectives listed at the beginning of the chapter and the key terms listed at the end of the chapter.

LO1. The two main tactics for improving reliability are _____ and _____.

LO2. The reliability of a system with *n* independent components equals:
a) the sum of the individual reliabilities
b) the minimum reliability among all components
c) the maximum reliability among all components
d) the product of the individual reliabilities
e) the average of the individual reliabilities.

LO3. What is the formula for the mean time between failures?
a) Number of failures ÷ Number of unit-hours of operation time
b) Number of unit-hours of operation time ÷ Number of failures
c) (Number of failures ÷ Number of units tested) × 100%
d) (Number of units tested ÷ Number of failures) × 100%
e) 1 ÷ FR(%).

LO4. The process that is intended to find potential failures and make changes or repairs is known as:
a) breakdown maintenance
b) failure maintenance
c) preventive maintenance
d) all of the above.

LO5. The two main tactics for improving maintenance are _____ and _____.

LO6. The appropriate maintenance policy is developed by balancing preventive maintenance costs with breakdown maintenance costs. The problem is that:
a) preventive maintenance costs are very difficult to identify
b) full breakdown costs are seldom considered
c) preventive maintenance should be performed, regardless of the cost
d) breakdown maintenance must be performed, regardless of the cost.

LO7. _____ maintenance partners operators with maintenance personnel to observe, check, adjust, clean, and notify.
a) Partnering
b) Operator
c) Breakdown
d) Six Sigma
e) Autonomous.

A

QUANTITATIVE MODULE
Decision Modeling

Module A **Learning Objectives**

THE DECISION PROCESS IN OPERATIONS

Operations managers are decision makers. To achieve the goals of their organizations, managers must understand how decisions are made and know which decision-making tools to use. To a great extent, the success or failure of both people and companies depends on the quality of their decisions. Overcoming uncertainty is a manager's challenge.

What makes the difference between a good decision and a bad decision? A 'good' decision—one that uses analytic decision making—is based on logic and considers all available data and possible alternatives. It also follows these seven steps:

1. Clearly define the problem and the factors that influence it.
2. Develop specific and measurable objectives.
3. Develop a model—that is, a relationship between objectives and variables (which are measurable quantities).
4. Select the proper evaluation tool/method.
5. Evaluate each alternative solution based on its merits and drawbacks.
6. Select the best alternative.
7. Implement the decision and set a timetable for completion.

Throughout this book, we have introduced a broad range of mathematical models and tools that help operations managers make better decisions. Effective operations depend on careful decision making. Fortunately, there are a whole variety of analytic tools to help make these decisions. This module introduces two of them—decision tables and decision trees. They are used in a wide number of OM situations, ranging from new-product analysis (Chapter 5), to capacity planning (Supplement 7), to location planning (Chapter 8), to scheduling (Chapter 15), and to maintenance planning (Chapter 17).

AUTHOR COMMENT
This section uses a decision tree to introduce the terminology of decision theory.

FUNDAMENTALS OF DECISION MAKING

Regardless of the complexity of a decision or the sophistication of the technique used to analyze it, all decision makers are faced with alternatives and 'states of nature.' The following notation will be used in this module:

1. Terms:
    a. *Alternative*—A course of action or strategy that may be chosen by a decision maker (e.g. not carrying an umbrella tomorrow).
    b. *State of nature*—An occurrence or a situation over which the decision maker has little or no control (e.g. tomorrow's weather).

2. Symbols used in a decision tree:
    a. □—decision node from which one of several alternatives may be selected.
    b. ○—a state-of-nature node out of which one state of nature will occur.

To present a manager's decision alternatives, we can develop *decision trees* using the above symbols. When constructing a decision tree, we must be sure that all alternatives and states of nature are in their correct and logical places and that we include *all* possible alternatives and states of nature.

◄ **EXAMPLE A1**

**A simple
decision tree**

Geeza Products in Egypt is investigating the possibility of producing and marketing backyard storage sheds. Undertaking this project would require the construction of either a large or a small manufacturing plant. The market for the product produced—storage sheds—could be either favorable or unfavorable. Geeza, of course, has the option of not developing the new product line at all.

APPROACH ▶ Geeza decides to build a decision tree.

SOLUTION ▶ Figure A.1 illustrates Geeza's decision tree.

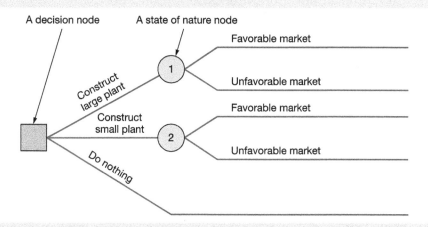

◄ **FIGURE A.1**
Geeza Products Decision Tree

INSIGHT ▶ We never want to overlook the option of 'doing nothing' as that is usually a possible decision.

LO1: Create a simple decision tree

LEARNING EXERCISE ▶ Geeza now considers constructing a medium-sized plant as a fourth option. Redraw the tree in Figure A.1 to accommodate this. [Answer: Your tree will have a new node and branches between 'Construct large plant' and 'Construct small plant.']

RELATED PROBLEMS ▶ A.2e, A.8a, A.9

DECISION TABLES

AUTHOR COMMENT
Decision tables force logic into decision making.

We may also develop a decision or payoff table to help Geeza Products define its alternatives. For any alternative and a particular state of nature, there is a *consequence* or *outcome*, which is usually expressed as a monetary value. This is called a *conditional value*. Note that all of the alternatives in Example A2 are listed down the left side of the table, that states of nature (outcomes) are listed across the top, and that conditional values (payoffs) are in the body of the **decision table**.

Decision table
A tabular means of analyzing decision alternatives and states of nature.

◄ **EXAMPLE A2**

A decision table

Geeza Products now wishes to organize the following information into a table. With a favorable market, a large facility will give Geeza Products a net profit of US$200,000. If the market is unfavorable, a US$180,000 net loss will occur. A small plant will result in a net profit of US$100,000 in a favorable market, but a net loss of US$20,000 will be encountered if the market is unfavorable.

APPROACH ▶ These numbers become conditional values in the decision table. We list alternatives in the left column and states of nature across the top of the table.

SOLUTION ▶ The completed table is shown in Table A.1.

LO2: Build a decision table

◄ **TABLE A.1**
Decision Table with Conditional Values for Geeza Products

	States of Nature	
Alternatives	**Favorable Market**	**Unfavorable Market**
Construct large plant	US$200,000	−US$180,000
Construct small plant	US$100,000	−US$20,000
Do nothing	US$0	US$0

INSIGHT ▶ The toughest part of decision tables is obtaining the data to analyze.

LEARNING EXERCISE ▶ In Examples A3 and A4, we see how to use decision tables to make decisions.

AUTHOR COMMENT
Depending on the certainty of information, there are three approaches in decision theory.

LO3: Explain when to use each of the three types of decision-making environments

TYPES OF DECISION-MAKING ENVIRONMENTS

The types of decisions people make depend on how much knowledge or information they have about the situation. There are three decision-making environments:

- Decision making under uncertainty.
- Decision making under risk.
- Decision making under certainty.

Decision Making under Uncertainty

When there is complete *uncertainty* as to which state of nature in a decision environment may occur (i.e. when we cannot even assess probabilities for each possible outcome), we rely on three decision methods:

Maximax

A criterion that finds an alternative that maximizes the maximum outcome.

Maximin

A criterion that finds an alternative that maximizes the minimum outcome.

Equally likely

A criterion that assigns equal probability to each state of nature.

1. The **maximax** method finds an alternative that *maximizes* the *maximum* outcome for every alternative. First, we find the maximum outcome within every alternative, and then we pick the alternative with the maximum number. Because this decision criterion locates the alternative with the *highest* possible *gain*, it has been called an 'optimistic' decision criterion.
2. The **maximin** method finds the alternative that *maximizes* the *minimum* outcome for every alternative. First, we find the minimum outcome within every alternative, and then we pick the alternative with the maximum number. Because this decision criterion locates the alternative that has the *least* possible *loss*, it has been called a 'pessimistic' decision criterion.
3. The **equally likely** method finds the alternative with the highest average outcome. First, we calculate the average outcome for every alternative, which is the sum of all outcomes divided by the number of outcomes. We then pick the alternative with the maximum number. The equally likely approach assumes that each state of nature is equally likely to occur.

EXAMPLE A3 ▶

A decision table analysis under uncertainty

▶ TABLE A.2

Decision Table for Decision Making under Uncertainty

Geeza Products would like to apply each of these three approaches now.

APPROACH ▶   Given Geeza's decision table of Example A2, he determines the maximax, maximin, and equally likely decision criteria.

SOLUTION ▶   Table A.2 provides the solution.

Alternatives	States of Nature		Maximum in Row	Minimum in Row	Row Average
	Favorable Market	Unfavorable Market			
Construct large plant	US$200,000	−US$180,000	US$200,000 ◀	−US$180,000	US$10,000
Construct small plant	US$100,000	−US$20,000	US$100,000	−US$420,000	US$40,000 ◀
Do nothing	US$0	US$0	US$0	US$0 ◀	US$0
			Maximax ⌐	Maximin ⌐	Equally likely ⌐

1. The maximax choice is to construct a large plant. This is the *maximum* of the *maximum* number within each row, or alternative.
2. The maximin choice is to do nothing. This is the *maximum* of the *minimum* number within each row, or alternative.
3. The equally likely choice is to construct a small plant. This is the maximum of the average outcome of each alternative. This approach assumes that all outcomes for any alternative are *equally likely*.

INSIGHT ▶   There are optimistic decision makers ('maximax') and pessimistic ones ('maximin'). Maximax and maximin present best case–worst case planning scenarios.

LEARNING EXERCISE ▶   Geeza reestimates the outcome for constructing a large plant when the market is favorable and raises it to US$250,000. What numbers change in Table A.2? Do the decisions change? [Answer: The maximax is now US$250,000, and the row average is US$35,000 for a large plant. No decision changes.]

RELATED PROBLEMS ▶   A.1, A.2b–d, A.4

Decision Making under Risk

Decision making under risk, a more common occurrence, relies on probabilities. Several possible states of nature may occur, each with an assumed probability. The states of nature must be mutually exclusive and collectively exhaustive and their probabilities must sum to 1.[1] Given a decision table with conditional values and probability assessments for all states of nature, we can determine the **expected monetary value (EMV)** for each alternative. This figure represents the expected value or *mean* return for each alternative *if we could repeat this decision (or similar types of decisions) a large number of times.*

The EMV for an alternative is the sum of all possible payoffs from the alternative, each weighted by the probability of that payoff occurring:

EMV (Alternative i) = (Payoff of 1st state of nature) × (Probability of 1st state of nature)

$\qquad$ + (Payoff of 2nd state of nature) × (Probability of 2nd state of nature)

$\qquad$ + ⋯ + (Payoff of last state of nature) × (Probability of last state of nature)

Example A4 illustrates how to compute the maximum EMV.

Expected monetary value (EMV)

The expected payout or value of a variable that has different possible states of nature, each with an associated probability.

LO4: Calculate an expected monetary value (EMV)

◀ **EXAMPLE A4**

Expected monetary value

◀ TABLE A.3   Decision Table for Geeza Products

Geeza would like to find the EMV for each alternative.

APPROACH ▶   Geeza Products' operations manager believes that the probability of a favorable market is exactly the same as that of an unfavorable market; that is, each state of nature has a 0.50 chance of occurring. He can now determine the EMV for each alternative (see Table A.3):

Alternatives	States of Nature	
	Favorable Market	**Unfavorable market**
Construct large plant (A_1)	US$200,000	−US$180,000
Construct small plant (A_2)	US$100,000	−US$20,000
Do nothing (A_3)	US$0	US$0
Probabilities	0.50	0.50

SOLUTION ▶

1. EMV(A_1) = (0.5)(US$200,000) + (0.5)(−US$180,000) = US$10,000
2. EMV(A_2) = (0.5)(US$100,000) + (0.5)(−US$20,000) = US$40,000
3. EMV(A_3) = (0.5)(US$0) + (0.5)(US$0) = US$0

INSIGHT ▶   The maximum EMV is seen in alternative A_2. Thus, according to the EMV decision criterion, Geeza would build the small facility.

LEARNING EXERCISE ▶   What happens to the three EMVs if Geeza increases the conditional value on the 'large plant/favorable market' result to US$250,000? [Answer: EMV($A_1$) = US$35,000. No change in decision.]

RELATED PROBLEMS ▶   A.2e, A.3a, A.5a, A.6, A.7, A.8a,b, A.10

EXCEL OM Data File **ModAExA4.xls** can be found at MyOMLab.

Decision Making under Certainty

Now suppose that the Geeza operations manager has been approached by a marketing research firm that proposes to help him make the decision about whether to build the plant to produce storage sheds. The marketing researchers claim that their technical analysis will tell Geeza with certainty whether the market is favorable for the proposed product. In other words, it will change Geeza's environment from one of decision making *under risk* to one of decision making *under certainty*. This information could prevent Geeza from making a very expensive mistake. The marketing research firm would charge Geeza US$65,000 for the information. What would

---

[1]To review these other statistical terms, refer to Tutorial 1, "Statistical Review for Managers" at MyOMLab.

you recommend? Should the operations manager hire the firm to make the study? Even if the information from the study is perfectly accurate, is it worth US\$65,000? What might it be worth? Although some of these questions are difficult to answer, determining the value of such *perfect information* can be very useful. It places an upper bound on what you would be willing to spend on information, such as that being sold by a marketing consultant. This is the concept of the expected value of perfect information, which we now introduce.

Expected Value of Perfect Information

If a manager were able to determine which state of nature would occur, then he or she would know which decision to make. Once a manager knows which decision to make, the payoff increases because the payoff is now a certainty, not a probability. Because the payoff will increase with knowledge of which state of nature will occur, this knowledge has value. Therefore, we now look at how to determine the value of this information. We call this difference between the payoff under perfect information and the payoff under risk the **expected value of perfect information (EVPI)**.

Expected value of perfect information (EVPI)

The difference between the payoff under perfect information and the payoff under risk.

Expected value with perfect information (EVwPI)

The expected (average) return if perfect information is available.

LO5: Compute the expected value of perfect information (EVPI)

$$\text{EVPI} = \text{Expected value with perfect information} - \text{Maximum EMV}$$

To find the EVPI, we must first compute the **expected value with perfect information (EVwPI)**, which is the expected (average) return if we have perfect information before a decision has to be made. To calculate this value, we choose the best alternative for each state of nature and multiply its payoff times the probability of occurrence of that state of nature:

Expected value *with* perfect information (EVwPI)

= (Best outcome or consequence for 1st state of nature) × (Probability of 1st state of nature)

+ (Best outcome for 2nd state of nature) × (Probability of 2nd state of nature)

+ · · · + (Best outcome for last state of nature) × (Probability of last state of nature)

In Example A5 we use the data and decision table from Example A4 to examine the expected value of perfect information.

EXAMPLE A5 ▶

Expected value of perfect information

Geeza Products' operations manager would like to calculate the maximum that he would pay for information—that is, the expected value of perfect information, or EVPI.

APPROACH ▶　Referring to Table A.3 in Example A4, he follows a two-stage process. First, the expected value *with* perfect information (EVwPI) is computed. Then, using this information, EVPI is calculated.

SOLUTION ▶

1. The best outcome for the state of nature 'favorable market' is 'build a large facility' with a payoff of US\$200,000. The best outcome for the state of nature 'unfavorable market' is 'do nothing' with a payoff of US\$0. Expected value *with* perfect information = (US\$200,000)(0.50) + (US\$0)(0.50) = US\$100,000. Thus, if we had perfect information, we would expect (on average) US\$100,000 if the decision could be repeated many times.

2. The maximum EMV is US\$40,000 for A_2, which is the expected outcome without perfect information. Thus:

$$\text{EVPI} = \text{EVwPI} - \text{Maximum EMV} = \text{US\$100,000} - \text{US\$40,000} = \text{US\$60,000}$$

INSIGHT ▶　The *most* Geeza should be willing to pay for perfect information is US\$60,000. This conclusion, of course, is again based on the assumption that the probability of each state of nature is 0.50.

LEARNING EXERCISE ▶　How does the EVPI change if the 'large plant/favorable market' conditional value is US\$250,000? [Answer: EVPI = US\$85,000.]

RELATED PROBLEMS ▶　A.3b, A.5, A.8

EXCEL OM Data File **ModAExA5.xls** can be found at MyOMLab.

The decision regarding drilling to excavate oil is one of the most risky and requires a rational decision making process to minimize uncertainty and decrease risk.

DECISION TREES

Decisions that lend themselves to display in a decision table also lend themselves to display in a decision tree. We will therefore analyze some decisions using decision trees. Although the use of a decision table is convenient in problems having one set of decisions and one set of states of nature, many problems include *sequential* decisions and states of nature.

When there are two or more sequential decisions, and later decisions are based on the outcome of prior ones, the decision tree approach becomes appropriate. A **decision tree** is a graphic display of the decision process that indicates decision alternatives, states of nature and their respective probabilities, and payoffs for each combination of decision alternative and state of nature.

Expected monetary value (EMV) is the most commonly used criterion for decision tree analysis. One of the first steps in such analysis is to graph the decision tree and to specify the monetary consequences of all outcomes for a particular problem.

Analyzing problems with *decision trees* involves five steps:

1. Define the problem.
2. Structure or draw the decision tree.
3. Assign probabilities to the states of nature.
4. Estimate payoffs for each possible combination of decision alternatives and states of nature.
5. Solve the problem by computing the expected monetary values (EMV) for each state-of-nature node. This is done by working *backward*—that is, by starting at the right of the tree and working back to decision nodes on the left.

> **AUTHOR COMMENT**
> Decision trees can become complex, so we illustrate three of them in this section.

Decision tree

A graphical means of analyzing decision alternatives and states of nature.

Geeza wants to develop a completed and solved decision tree.

APPROACH ▶ The payoffs are placed at the right-hand side of each of the tree's branches (see Figure A.2). The probabilities (first used by Geeza in Example A4) are placed in parentheses next to each state of nature. The expected monetary values for each state-of-nature node are then calculated and placed by their respective nodes. The EMV of the first node is US$10,000. This represents the branch from the decision node to 'construct a large plant.' The EMV for node 2, to 'construct a small plant,' is US$40,000. The option of 'doing nothing' has, of course, a payoff of US$0.

SOLUTION ▶ The branch leaving the decision node leading to the state-of-nature node with the highest EMV will be chosen. In Geeza's case, a small plant should be built.

> **◀ EXAMPLE A6**
>
> **Solving a tree for EMV**

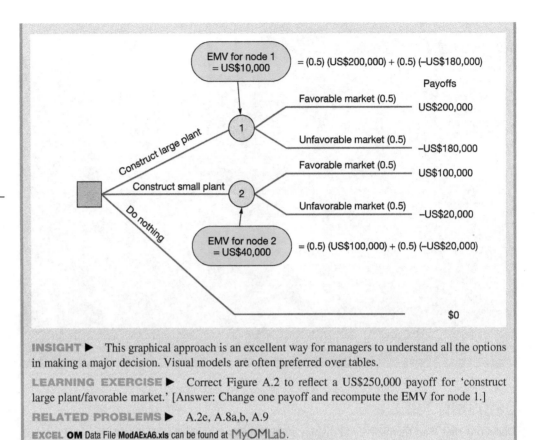

INSIGHT ▶ This graphical approach is an excellent way for managers to understand all the options in making a major decision. Visual models are often preferred over tables.

LEARNING EXERCISE ▶ Correct Figure A.2 to reflect a US$250,000 payoff for 'construct large plant/favorable market.' [Answer: Change one payoff and recompute the EMV for node 1.]

RELATED PROBLEMS ▶ A.2e, A.8a,b, A.9

EXCEL OM Data File **ModAExA6.xls** can be found at MyOMLab.

A More Complex Decision Tree

When a *sequence* of decisions must be made, decision trees are much more powerful tools than are decision tables. Let's say that Geeza Products has two decisions to make, with the second decision dependent on the outcome of the first. Before deciding about building a new plant, Geeza has the option of conducting its own marketing research survey, at a cost of US$10,000. The information from this survey could help it decide whether to build a large plant, to build a small plant, or not to build at all. Geeza recognizes that although such a survey will not provide it with *perfect* information, it may be extremely helpful.

Geeza's new decision tree is represented in Figure A.3 of Example A7. Take a careful look at this more complex tree. Note that *all possible outcomes and alternatives* are included in their logical sequence. This procedure is one of the strengths of using decision trees. The manager is forced to examine all possible outcomes, including unfavorable ones. He or she is also forced to make decisions in a logical, sequential manner.

◀ EXAMPLE A7

A decision tree with sequential decisions

Geeza Products wishes to develop the new tree for this sequential decision.

APPROACH ▶ Examining the tree in Figure A.3, we see that Geeza's first decision point is whether to conduct the US$10,000 market survey. If it chooses not to do the study (the lower part of the tree), it can either build a large plant, a small plant, or no plant. This is Geeza's second decision point. If the decision is to build, the market will be either favorable (0.50 probability) or unfavorable (also 0.50 probability). The payoffs for each of the possible consequences are listed along the right-hand side. As a matter of fact, this lower portion of Geeza's tree is *identical* to the simpler decision tree shown in Figure A.2.

SOLUTION ▶ The upper part of Figure A.3 reflects the decision to conduct the market survey. State-of-nature node number 1 has 2 branches coming out of it. Let us say there is a 45 percent chance that the survey results will indicate a favorable market for the storage sheds. We also note that the probability is 0.55 that the survey results will be negative.

The rest of the probabilities shown in parentheses in Figure A.3 are all *conditional* probabilities. For example, 0.78 is the probability of a favorable market for the sheds given a favorable result from the market survey. Of course, you would expect to find a high probability of a favorable market given that the research indicated that the market was good. Don't forget, though: There is a chance that

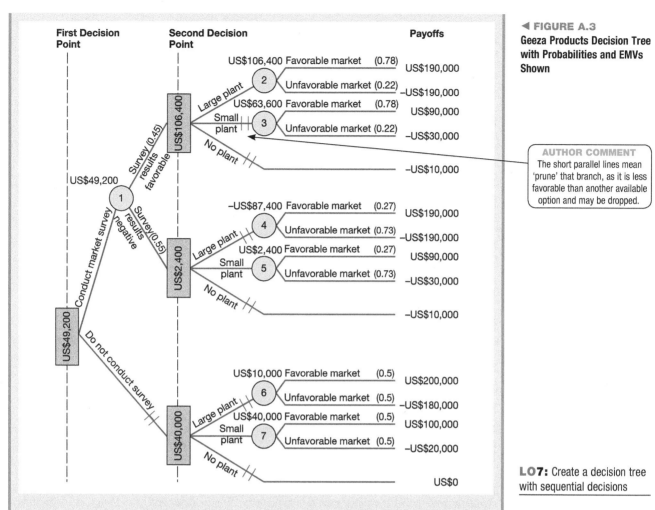

◀ **FIGURE A.3**
Geeza Products Decision Tree with Probabilities and EMVs Shown

> **AUTHOR COMMENT**
> The short parallel lines mean 'prune' that branch, as it is less favorable than another available option and may be dropped.

LO7: Create a decision tree with sequential decisions

Geeza's US$10,000 market survey did not result in perfect or even reliable information. Any market research study is subject to error. In this case, there remains a 22 percent chance that the market for sheds will be unfavorable given positive survey results.

Likewise, we note that there is a 27 percent chance that the market for sheds will be favorable given negative survey results. The probability is much higher, 0.73, that the market will actually be unfavorable given a negative survey.

Finally, when we look to the payoff column in Figure A.3, we see that US$10,000—the cost of the marketing study—has been subtracted from each of the top 10 tree branches. Thus, a large plant constructed in a favorable market would normally net a US$200,000 profit. Yet because the market study was conducted, this figure is reduced by US$10,000. In the unfavorable case, the loss of US$180,000 would increase to US$190,000. Similarly, conducting the survey and building *no plant* now results in a −US$10,000 payoff.

With all probabilities and payoffs specified, we can start calculating the expected monetary value of each branch. We begin at the end or right-hand side of the decision tree and work back toward the origin. When we finish, the best decision will be known.

1. Given favorable survey results:

     EMV (node 2) = (0.78)(US$190,000) + (0.22)(−US$190,000) = US$106,400
     EMV (node 3) = (0.78)(US$90,000) + (0.22)(−US$30,000) = US$63,600

   The EMV of no plant in this case is −US$10,000. Thus, if the survey results are favorable, a large plant should be built.

2. Given negative survey results:

     EMV (node 4) = (0.27)(US$190,000) + (0.73)(−US$190,000) = −US$87,400
     EMV (node 5) = (0.27)(US$90,000) + (0.73)(−US$30,000) = US$2,400

   The EMV of no plant is again −US$10,000 for this branch. Thus, given a negative survey result, Geeza should build a small plant with an expected value of US$2,400.

3. Continuing on the upper part of the tree and moving backward, we compute the expected value of conducting the market survey:

     EMV (node 1) = (0.45)(US$106,400) + (0.55)(US$2,400) = US$49,200

4. If the market survey is *not* conducted:

$$\text{EMV (node 6)} = (0.50)(\text{US}\$200,000) + (0.50)(-\text{US}\$180,000) = \text{US}\$10,000$$

$$\text{EMV (node 7)} = (0.50)(\text{US}\$100,000) + (0.50)(-\text{US}\$20,000) = \text{US}\$40,000$$

The EMV of no plant is US$0. Thus, building a small plant is the best choice, given the marketing research is not performed.

5. Because the expected monetary value of conducting the survey is US$49,200—versus an EMV of US$40,000 for not conducting the study—the best choice is to *seek marketing information*. If the survey results are favorable, Geeza Products should build the large plant; if they are unfavorable, it should build the small plant.

INSIGHT ▶ You can reduce complexity in a large decision tree by viewing and solving a number of smaller trees—start at the end branches of a large one. Take one decision at a time.

LEARNING EXERCISE ▶ Geeza estimates that if he conducts a market survey, there is really only a 35 percent chance the results will indicate a favorable market for the sheds. How does the tree change? [Answer: The EMV of conducting the survey = US$38,800, so Geeza should not do it now.]

RELATED PROBLEM ▶ A.9

Using Decision Trees in Ethical Decision Making

Decision trees can also be a useful tool to aid ethical corporate decision making. The decision tree illustrated in Example A8, developed by Harvard Professor Constance Bagley, provides guidance as to how managers can both maximize shareholder value and behave ethically. The tree can be applied to any action a company contemplates, whether it is expanding operations in a developing country or reducing a workforce at home.

EXAMPLE A8 ▶

Ethical decision making

Dubai Jeelani Corp. is opening a plant in Iraq, a country with much less stringent environmental laws than U.A.E, its home nation. Dubai Jeelani Corp. can save US$18 million in building the manufacturing facility—and boost its profits—if it does not install pollution-control equipment that is mandated in the U.A.E, but not in Iraq. But Dubai Jeelani Corp. also calculates that pollutants emitted from the plant, if unscrubbed, could damage the local fishing industry. This could cause a loss of millions of Dirhams in income as well as create health problems for local inhabitants.

APPROACH ▶ Dubai Jeelani Corp. decides to build a decision tree to model the problem.

SOLUTION ▶ Figure A.4 outlines the choices management can consider. For example, if in management's best judgment the harm to the Iraqi community by building the plant will be greater than the loss in company returns, the response to the question "Is it ethical?" will be "no".

Now, say Dubai Jeelani Corp. proposes building a somewhat different plant, one *with* pollution controls, despite a negative impact on company returns. That decision takes us to the branch "Is it ethical *not* to take action?" If the answer (for whatever reason) is "no", the decision tree suggests proceeding with the plant but notifying the Dubai Jeelani Board, shareholders, and others about its impact.

INSIGHT ▶ This tree allows managers to view the options graphically. This is a good way to start the process.

◀ FIGURE A.4
Dubai Jeelani's Decision Tree for Ethical Dilemma

Source: Modified from Constance E. Bagley, "The Ethical Leader's Decision Tree," *Harvard Business Review* (January–February 2003): 18–19.

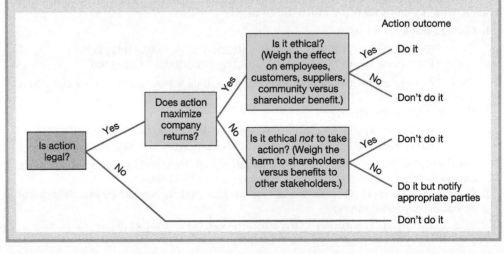

Ethical decisions can be quite complex: What happens, for example, if a company builds a polluting plant overseas, but this allows the company to sell a life-saving drug at a lower cost around the world? Does a decision tree deal with all possible ethical dilemmas? No—but it does provide managers with a framework for examining those choices.

MODULE SUMMARY

This module examines two of the most widely used decision techniques—decision tables and decision trees. These techniques are especially useful for making decisions under risk. Many decisions in research and development, plant and equipment, and even new buildings and structures can be analyzed with these decision models. Problems in inventory control, aggregate planning, maintenance, scheduling, and production control also lend themselves to decision table and decision tree applications.

Key Terms

Decision table (p. 553)
Decision tree (p. 557)
Equally likely (p. 554)
Expected monetary value (EMV) (p. 555)

Expected value of perfect information
  (EVPI) (p. 556)
Expected value with perfect information
  (EVwPI) (p. 556)

Maximax (p. 554)
Maximin (p. 554)

Discussion Questions

1. Identify the seven steps in the decision process.
2. Give an example of a good decision you made that resulted in a bad outcome. Also give an example of a bad decision you made that had a good outcome. Why was each decision good or bad?
3. What is the *equally likely* decision model?
4. Discuss the differences between decision making under certainty, under risk, and under uncertainty.
5. What is a decision tree?
6. Explain how decision trees might be used in several of the 10 OM decisions.
7. What is the expected value of perfect information?
8. What is the expected value *with* perfect information?
9. Identify the five steps in analyzing a problem using a decision tree.
10. Why are the maximax and maximin strategies considered to be optimistic and pessimistic, respectively?
11. The expected value criterion is considered to be the rational criterion on which to base a decision. Is this true? Is it rational to consider risk?
12. When are decision trees most useful?

Using Software for Decision Models

Analyzing decision tables is straightforward with Excel, Excel OM, and POM for Windows. When decision trees are involved, Excel OM or commercial packages such as DPL, Tree Plan, and Supertree provide flexibility, power, and ease. POM for Windows will also analyze trees but does not have graphic capabilities.

Using Excel OM

Excel OM allows decision makers to evaluate decisions quickly and to perform sensitivity analysis on the results. Program A.1 uses the Geeza data to illustrate input, output, and selected formulas needed to compute the EMV and EVPI values.

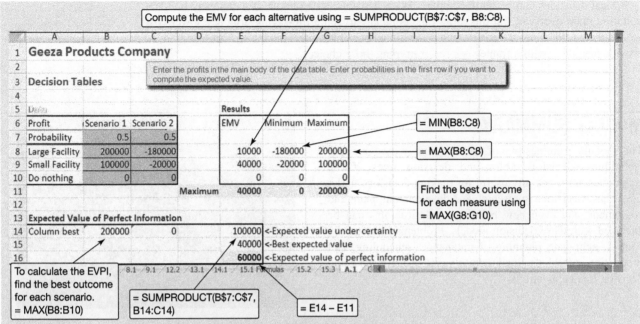

▲ **PROGRAM A.1** Using Excel OM to Compute EMV and Other Measures for Geeza

Program A.2 uses Excel OM to create the decision tree for Geeza Products shown earlier in Example A6. The tool to create the tree is seen in the window on the right.

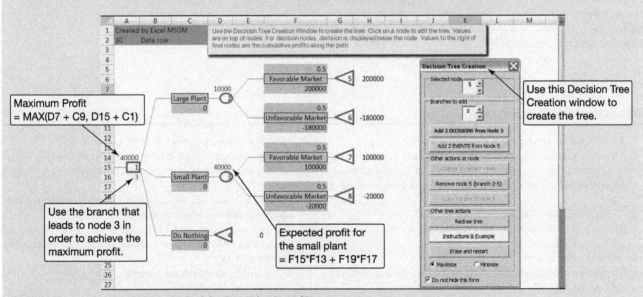

▲ **PROGRAM A.2** Geeza Products' Decision Tree Using Excel OM

P Using POM for Windows

POM for Windows can be used to calculate all of the information described in the decision tables and decision trees in this module. For details on how to use this software, please refer to Appendix IV.

Solved Problems   Virtual Office Hours help is available at MyOMLab

▼ SOLVED PROBLEM A.1

Stella Yan Hua is considering the possibility of opening a small dress shop on Fairbanks Avenue, a few blocks from the university. She has located a good mall that attracts students. Her options are to open a small shop, a medium-sized shop, or no shop at all. The market for a dress shop can be good, average, or bad. The probabilities for these three possibilities are 0.2 for a good market, 0.5 for an average market, and 0.3 for a bad market. The net profit or loss for the medium-sized or small shops for the various market conditions are given in the following table. Building no shop at all yields no loss and no gain. What do you recommend?

	States of Nature		
Alternatives	**Good Market (US$)**	**Average Market (US$)**	**Bad Market (US$)**
Small shop	75,000	25,000	−40,000
Medium-sized shop	100,000	35,000	−60,000
No shop	0	0	0
Probabilities	0.20	0.50	0.30

▼ SOLUTION

The problem can be solved by computing the expected monetary value (EMV) for each alternative:

EMV (Small shop) = (0.2)(US$75,000) + (0.5)(US$25,000) + (0.3)(−US$40,000) = US$15,500
EMV (Medium-sized shop) = (0.2)(US$100,000) + (0.5)(US$35,000) + (0.3)(−US$60,000) = US$19,500
EMV (No shop) = (0.2)(US$0) + (0.5)(US$0) + (0.3)(US$0) = US$0

As you can see, the best decision is to build the medium-sized shop. The EMV for this alternative is US$19,500.

▼ SOLVED PROBLEM A.2

T.S. Amer's Ski Shop in Nevada has a 100-day season. T.S. has established the probability of various store traffic, based on historical records of skiing conditions, as indicated in the table to the right. T.S. has four merchandising plans, each focusing on a popular name brand. Each plan yields a daily net profit as noted in the table. Using the weather forecast for the following day, T.S. can implement one of his four merchandising plans.

a) What is the expected monetary value (EMV) under risk?
b) What is the expected value *with* perfect information (EVwPI)?
c) What is the expected value of perfect information (EVPI)?

Decision Alternatives (merchandising plan focusing on:)	**Traffic in Store Because of Ski Conditions (states of nature) (US$)**			
	1	**2**	**3**	**4**
Patagonia	40	92	20	48
North Face	50	84	10	52
Cloud Veil	35	80	40	64
Columbia	45	72	10	60
Probabilities	0.20	0.25	0.30	0.25

▼ SOLUTION

a) The highest expected monetary value under risk is:

EMV (Patagonia) = 0.20(40) + 0.25(92) + 0.30(20) + 0.25(48) = US$49
EMV (North Face) = 0.20(50) + 0.25(84) + 0.30(10) + 0.25(52) = US$47
EMV (Cloud Veil) = 0.20(35) + 0.25(80) + 0.30(40) + 0.25(64) = US$55
EMV (Columbia) = 0.20(45) + 0.25(72) + 0.30(10) + 0.25(60) = US$45

So the maximum EMV = US$55

b) The expected value *with* perfect information is:

EVwPI = 0.20(50) + 0.25(92) + 0.30(40) + 0.25(64) = 10 + 23 + 12 + 16 = US$61

c) The expected value of perfect information is:

EVPI = EVwPI − Maximum EMV = 61 − 55 = US$6

▼ SOLVED PROBLEM A.3

Daily demand for cases of Tidy Bowl cleaner at Ravinder Nath's Supermarket has always been 5, 6, or 7 cases. Develop a decision tree that illustrates her decision alternatives as to whether to stock 5, 6, or 7 cases.

▼ SOLUTION

The decision tree is shown in Figure A.5.

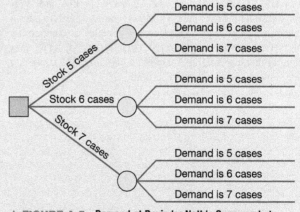

▲ **FIGURE A.5   Demand at Ravinder Nath's Supermarket**

Problems*

·   A.1 Given the following conditional value table, determine the appropriate decision under uncertainty using:
a) Maximax
b) Maximin
c) Equally likely **Px**

| | States of Nature | | |
Alternatives	Very Favorable Market	Average Market	Unfavorable Market
Build new plant	US$350,000	US$240,000	–US$300,000
Subcontract	US$180,000	US$90,000	–US$20,000
Overtime	US$110,000	US$60,000	–US$10,000
Do nothing	US$0	US$0	US$0

··   A.2 Even though independent gasoline stations have been having a difficult time, Suad has been thinking about starting her own independent gasoline station. Suad's problem is to decide how large her station should be. The annual returns will depend on both the size of her station and a number of marketing factors related to the oil industry and demand for gasoline. After a careful analysis, Suad developed the following table:

Size of First Station	Good Market (US$)	Fair Market (US$)	Poor Market (US$)
Small	50,000	20,000	–10,000
Medium	80,000	30,000	–20,000
Large	100,000	30,000	–40,000
Very large	300,000	25,000	–160,000

For example, if Suad constructs a small station and the market is good, she will realize a profit of US$50,000.
a) Develop a decision table for this decision, like the one illustrated in Table A.2 earlier.
b) What is the maximax decision?
c) What is the maximin decision?
d) What is the equally likely decision?
e) Develop a decision tree. Assume each outcome is equally likely, then find the highest EMV. **Px**

·   A.3 Hatem, Inc. is considering building a sensitive new airport scanning device. Hatem's managers believe that there is a probability of 0.4 that the ATR Co. will come out with a competitive product. If Hatem adds an assembly line for the product and ATR Co. does not follow with a competitive product, Hatem's expected profit is US$40,000; if Hatem adds an assembly line and ATR follows suit, Hatem still expects US$10,000 profit. If Hatem adds a new plant addition and ATR does not produce a competitive product, Hatem expects a profit of US$600,000; if ATR does compete for this market, Hatem expects a loss of US$100,000.
a) Determine the EMV of each decision.
b) Compute the expected value of perfect information. **Px**

··   A.4 Dua's factory is considering three approaches for meeting an expected increase in demand. These three approaches are increasing capacity, using overtime, and buying more equipment. Demand will increase either slightly (S), moderately (M), or greatly (G). The profits for each approach under each possible scenario are as follows:

| | Demand Scenario | | |
Approach	S (US$)	M (US$)	G (US$)
Increasing Capacity	700,000	700,000	700,000
Using Overtime	500,000	600,000	1,000,000
Buying Equipment	600,000	800,000	800,000

Since the goal is to maximize, and Dua is risk-neutral, she decides to use the *equally likely* decision criterion to make the decision as to which approach to use. According to this criterion, which approach should be used?

·   A.5 The following payoff table provides profits based on various possible decision alternatives and various levels of demand at Adam's software firm:

| | Demand | |
	Low (US$)	High (US$)
Alternative 1	10,000	30,000
Alternative 2	5,000	40,000
Alternative 3	–2,000	50,000

The probability of low demand is 0.4, whereas the probability of high demand is 0.6.
a) What is the highest possible expected monetary value?
b) What is the expected value *with* perfect information (EVwPI)?
c) Calculate the expected value of perfect information for this situation. **Px**

··   A.6 Consider the following decision table, which Tamer has developed for Homs Enterprises:

| | | States of Nature | | |
Decision Alternatives	Probability:	0.40 Low (US$)	0.20 Medium (US$)	0.40 High (US$)
A		40	100	60
B		85	60	70
C		60	70	70
D		65	75	70
E		70	65	80

Which decision alternative maximizes the expected value of the payoff? **Px**

··   A.7 Dab'a Cheese Company is a small manufacturer of several different cheese products. One product is a cheese spread sold to retail outlets. Sameer must decide how many cases of cheese spread to manufacture each month. The probability that demand will be 6 cases is 0.1, for 7 cases it is 0.3, for 8 cases it is 0.5, and for 9 cases it is 0.1. The cost of every case is 45, and the price Sameer gets for each case is 95. Unfortunately, any cases not sold by the end of the month are of no value as a result of spoilage. How many cases should Sameer manufacture each month? **Px**

*Note: **Px** means the problem may be solved with POM for Windows and/or Excel OM.

·· A.8 Noor, president of Jumeeran Industries, is considering whether to build a manufacturing plant in Hama. Her decision is summarized in the following table:

Alternatives	Favorable Market	Unfavorable Market
Build large plant	US$400,000	−US$300,000
Build small plant	US$80,000	−US$10,000
Don't build	US$0	US$0
Market probabilities	0.4	0.6

a) Construct a decision tree.
b) Determine the best strategy using expected monetary value (EMV).
c) What is the expected value of perfect information (EVPI)? **P✗**

·· A.9 Kamal is considering opening a bicycle shop in north Riyadh. Kamal enjoys biking, but this is to be a business endeavor from which he expects to make a living. He can open a small shop, a large shop, or no shop at all. Because there will be a 5-year lease on the building that Kamal is thinking about using, he wants to make sure he makes the correct decision. Kamal is also thinking about hiring his old marketing professor to conduct a marketing research study to see if there is a market for his services. The results of such a study could be either favorable or unfavorable. Develop a decision tree for Kamal. **P✗**

···· A.10 The city of Aleppo is contemplating building a second airport to relieve congestion at the main airport and is considering two potential sites, X and Y. Prem-Quality Hotels would like to purchase land to build a hotel at the new airport. The value of land has been rising in anticipation and is expected to skyrocket once the city decides between sites X and Y. Consequently, Prem-Quality would like to purchase land now. Prem-Quality will sell the land if the city chooses not to locate the airport nearby. Prem-Quality has four choices: (1) buy land at X; (2) buy land at Y; (3) buy land at both X and Y; (4) do nothing. Prem-Quality has collected the following data (which are in millions of US dollars):

	Site X	Site Y
Current purchase price	27	15
Profits if airport and hotel built at this site	45	30
Sale price if airport not built at this site	9	6

Prem-Quality determines there is a 45 percent chance the airport will be built at X (hence, a 55 percent chance it will be built at Y).
a) Set up the decision table.
b) What should Prem-Quality decide to do to maximize total net profit? **P✗**

▶ **Refer to** MyOMLab **for additional homework problems.**

Case Study

▶ Probability Analysis by the National Institute for Liver Diseases

Ahmed Jamil, a robust 50-year-old real estate consultant living in the suburbs of Alexandria, Egypt, has been diagnosed by a specialist at the National Institute for Liver Diseases (Menofya) in Shebeen el Koum as having a decaying liver. Although he is otherwise healthy, Ahmed's liver problem could prove fatal if left untreated.

Firm research data are not yet available to predict the likelihood of survival for a man of Ahmed's age and condition who does not have surgery. However, based on his own experience and recent medical journal articles, the internist tells him that if he elects to avoid surgical treatment of the liver problem, chances of survival will be approximately as follows: only a 60 percent chance of living 1 year, a 20 percent chance of surviving for 2 years, a 10 percent chance for 5 years, and a 10 percent chance of living to age 58. He

places his probability of survival beyond age 58 without a liver transplant to be extremely low.

The transplant operation, however, is a serious surgical procedure. Five percent of patients die during the operation or its recovery stage, with an additional 45 percent dying during the first year. Twenty percent survive for 5 years, 13 percent survive for 10 years, and 8 percent, 5 percent, and 4 percent survive, respectively, for 15, 20, and 25 years.

Discussion Questions

1. Do you think that Ahmed should select the transplant operation?
2. What other factors might be considered?

▶Additional Case Studies: Visit MyOMLab for these additional free case studies:
Arctic, Inc.: A refrigeration company has several major options with regard to capacity and expansion.
Ski Right Corp.: Which of four manufacturers should be selected to manufacture ski helmets?

Main Heading	Review Material	
THE DECISION PROCESS IN OPERATIONS (pp. 552)	To achieve the goals of their organizations, managers must understand how decisions are made and know which decision-making tools to use. Overcoming uncertainty is a manager's mission. Decision tables and decision trees are used in a wide number of OM situations.	
FUNDAMENTALS OF DECISION MAKING (pp. 552–553)	*Alternative*—A course of action or strategy that may be chosen by a decision maker. *State of nature*—An occurrence or a situation over which a decision maker has little or no control. Symbols used in a decision tree: 1. □—A decision node from which one of several alternatives may be selected. 2. ○—A state-of-nature node out of which one state of nature will occur. When constructing a decision tree, we must be sure that all alternatives and states of nature are in their correct and logical places and that we include *all* possible alternatives and states of nature, usually including the 'do nothing' option.	
DECISION TABLES (p. 553)	▪ **Decision table**—A tabular means of analyzing decision alternatives and states of nature. A decision table is sometimes called a payoff table. For any alternative and a particular state of nature, there is a *consequence*, or an *outcome*, which is usually expressed as a monetary value; this is called the *conditional value*.	
TYPES OF DECISION-MAKING ENVIRONMENTS (pp. 554–557)	There are three decision-making environments: (1) decision making under uncertainty; (2) decision making under risk; (3) decision making under certainty. When there is complete *uncertainty* about which state of nature in a decision environment may occur (i.e. when we cannot even assess probabilities for each possible outcome), we rely on three decision methods: (1) maximax; (2) maximin; (3) equally likely. ▪ **Maximax**—A criterion that finds an alternative that maximizes the maximum outcome. ▪ **Maximin**—A criterion that finds an alternative that maximizes the minimum outcome. ▪ **Equally likely**—A criterion that assigns equal probability to each state of nature. Maximax is also called an 'optimistic' decision criterion, while maximin is also called a 'pessimistic' decision criterion. Maximax and maximin present best case/worst case planning scenarios. Decision making under risk relies on probabilities. The states of nature must be mutually exclusive and collectively exhaustive, and their probabilities must sum to 1. ▪ **Expected monetary value (EMV)**—The expected payout or value of a variable that has different possible states of nature, each with an associated probability. The EMV represents the expected value or *mean* return for each alternative *if we could repeat this decision (or similar types of decisions) a large number of times*. The EMV for an alternative is the sum of all possible payoffs from the alternative, each weighted by the probability of that payoff occurring: EMV(Alternative *i*) = (Payoff of 1st state of nature) × (Probability of 1st state of nature) + (Payoff of 2nd state of nature) × (Probability of 2nd state of nature) + ··· + (Payoff of last state of nature) × (Probability of last state of nature) ▪ **Expected value of perfect information (EVPI)**—The difference between the payoff under perfect information and the payoff under risk. ▪ **Expected value with perfect information (EVwPI)**—The expected (average) return if perfect information is available. EVPI represents an upper bound on what you would be willing to spend on state-of-nature information: EVPI = EVwPI – Maximum EMV (EVwPI) = (Best outcome for 1st state of nature) × (Probability of 1st state of nature) + (Best outcome for 2nd state of nature) × (Probability of 2nd state of nature) + ··· + (Best outcome for last state of nature) × (Probability of last state of nature)	Problems: A.1–A.8 Virtual Office Hours for Solved Problems: A.1, A.2

Main Heading	Review Material	MyOMLab
DECISION TREES (pp. 557–561)	When there are two or more sequential decisions, and later decisions are based on the outcome of prior ones, the decision tree (as opposed to decision table) approach becomes appropriate. ■ **Decision tree**—A graphical means of analyzing decision alternatives and states of nature. Analyzing problems with *decision trees* involves five steps: 1. Define the problem. 2. Structure or draw the decision tree. 3. Assign probabilities to the states of nature. 4. Estimate payoffs for each possible combination of decision alternatives and states of nature. 5. Solve the problem by computing the expected monetary values (EMV) for each state-of-nature node. This is done by working *backward*—that is, by starting at the right of the tree and working back to decision nodes on the left: 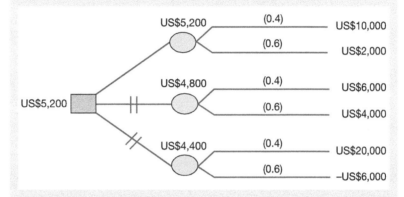 Decision trees force managers to examine all possible outcomes, including unfavorable ones. A manager is also forced to make decisions in a logical, sequential manner. Short parallel lines on a decision tree mean 'prune' that branch, as it is less favorable than another available option and may be dropped.	Problems: A.2, A.8, A.9 Virtual Office Hours for Solved Problem: A.3

Self-Test

■ **Before taking the self-test,** refer to the learning objectives listed at the beginning of the module and the key terms listed at the end of the module.

LO1. On a decision tree, at each state-of-nature node:
   a) the alternative with the greatest EMV is selected
   b) an EMV is calculated
   c) all probabilities are added together
   d) the branch with the highest probability is selected.

LO2. In decision table terminology, a course of action or a strategy that may be chosen by a decision maker is called a(n):
   a) payoff   c) state of nature
   b) alternative   d) all of the above.

LO3. If probabilities are available to the decision maker, then the decision-making environment is called:
   a) certainty   c) risk
   b) uncertainty   d) none of the above.

LO4. What is the EMV for Alternative 1 in the following decision table?

	State of nature	
Alternative	*S1*	*S2*
A1	US$15,000	US$20,000
A2	£10,000	£10,000
Probability	0.30	0.70

   a) US$15,000   d) US$18,500
   b) US$17,000   e) US$20,000.
   c) US$17,500

LO5. The most that a person should pay for perfect information is:
   a) the EVPI
   b) the maximum EMV minus the minimum EMV
   c) the minimum EMV
   d) the maximum EMV.

LO6. On a decision tree, once the tree has been drawn and the payoffs and probabilities have been placed on the tree, the analysis (computing EMVs and selecting the best alternative):
   a) is done by working backward (starting on the right and moving to the left)
   b) is done by working forward (starting on the left and moving to the right)
   c) is done by starting at the top of the tree and moving down
   d) is done by starting at the bottom of the tree and moving up.

LO7. A decision tree is preferable to a decision table when:
   a) a number of sequential decisions are to be made
   b) probabilities are available
   c) the maximax criterion is used
   d) the objective is to maximize regret.

Answers: LO1. b; LO2. b; LO3. c; LO4. d; LO5. a; LO6. a; LO7. a.

QUANTITATIVE MODULE
B
Learning Curves

Medical procedures such as heart surgery follow a learning curve. Research indicates that the death rate from heart transplants drops at a 79 percent learning curve, a learning rate not unlike that in many industrial settings. It appears that as doctors and medical teams improve with experience, so do your odds as a patient. If the death rate is halved every three operations, practice may indeed make perfect.

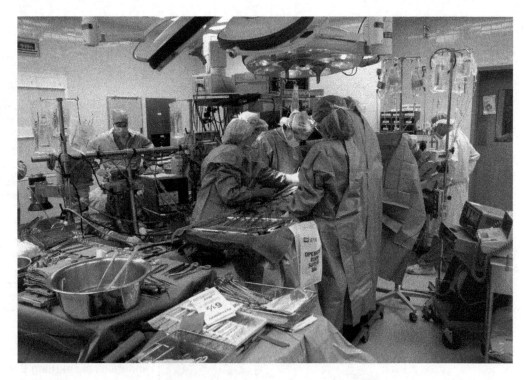

Module B Learning Objectives

WHAT IS A LEARNING CURVE?

Most organizations learn and improve over time. As firms and employees perform a task over and over, they learn how to perform more efficiently. This means that task times and costs decrease.

Learning curves are based on the premise that people and organizations become better at their tasks as the tasks are repeated. A learning-curve graph (illustrated in Figure B.1) displays labor-hours per unit versus the number of units produced. From it we see that the time needed

Learning curves

The premise that people and organizations get better at their tasks as the tasks are repeated; sometimes called experience curves.

► FIGURE B.1

The Learning-Curve Effect States That Time per Repetition Decreases as the Number of Repetitions Increases

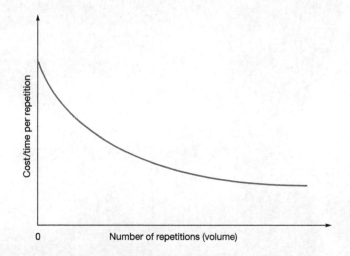

to produce a unit decreases, usually following a negative exponential curve, as the person or company produces more units. In other words, *it takes less time to complete each additional unit a firm produces*. However, we also see in Figure B.1 that the time *savings* in completing each subsequent unit *decreases*. These are the major attributes of the learning curve.

Learning curves were first applied to industry in a report by T. P. Wright of Curtis-Wright Corp. in 1936.[1] Wright described how direct labor costs of making a particular airplane decreased with learning, a theory since confirmed by other aircraft manufacturers. Regardless of the time needed to produce the first plane, learning curves are found to apply to various categories of air frames (e.g. jet fighters versus passenger planes versus bombers). Learning curves have since been applied not only to labor but also to a wide variety of other costs, including material and purchased components. The power of the learning curve is so significant that it plays a major role in many strategic decisions related to employment levels, costs, capacity, and pricing.

LO1: Define learning curve

The learning curve is based on a *doubling* of production: That is, when production doubles, the decrease in time per unit affects the rate of the learning curve. So, if the learning curve is an 80 percent rate, the second unit takes 80 percent of the time of the first unit, the fourth unit takes 80 percent of the time of the second unit, the eighth unit takes 80 percent of the time of the fourth unit, and so forth. This principle is shown as:

$$T \times L^n = \text{Time required for the } n\text{th unit} \qquad \text{(B-1)}$$

where T = unit cost or unit time of the first unit
L = learning curve rate
n = number of times T is doubled

If the first unit of a particular product took 10 labor-hours, and if a 70 percent learning curve is present, the hours the fourth unit will take require doubling twice—from 1 to 2 to 4. Therefore, the formula is:

$$\text{Hours required for unit } 4 = 10 \times (0.7)^2 = 4.9 \text{ hours}$$

LEARNING CURVES IN SERVICES AND MANUFACTURING

AUTHOR COMMENT
Learning is a universal concept, but rates of learning differ widely.

Different organizations—indeed, different products—have different learning curves. The rate of learning varies depending on the quality of management and the potential of the process and product. *Any change in process, product, or personnel disrupts the learning curve.* Therefore, caution should be exercised in assuming that a learning curve is continuing and permanent.

As you can see in Table B.1, industry learning curves vary widely. The lower the number (say 70 percent compared to 90 percent), the steeper the slope and the faster the drop in costs. By tradition, learning curves are defined in terms of the *complements* of their improvement rates.

▼ **TABLE B.1**   **Examples of Learning-Curve Effects**

Example	Improving Parameter	Cumulative Parameter	Learning-Curve Slope (%)
1. Model-T Ford production	Price	Units produced	86
2. Aircraft assembly	Direct labor-hours per unit	Units produced	80
3. Equipment maintenance at GE	Average time to replace a group of parts	Number of replacements	76
4. Steel production	Production worker labor-hours per unit produced	Units produced	79
5. Integrated circuits	Average price per unit	Units produced	72[a]
6. Handheld calculator	Average factory selling price	Units produced	74
7. Disk memory drives	Average price per bit	Number of bits	76
8. Heart transplants	1-year death rates	Transplants completed	79
9. Cesarean section baby deliveries	Average operation time	Number of surgeries	93

[a]Constant dollars.

Sources: W. Y. Fok, L. Y. S. Chan, and T. K. H. Chung. "The Effect of Learning Curves on the Outcome of a Caesarean Section." *BSOG* (November 2006): 1259–1263; James A. Cunningham, "Using the Learning Curve as a Management Tool," *IEEE Spectrum* (June 1980): 45. © 1980 IEEE; and Davis B. Smith and Jan L. Larsson, "The Impact of Learning on Cost: The Case of Heart Transplantation." *Hospital and Health Services Administration* (Spring 1989): 85–97.

[1]T. P. Wright, "Factors Affecting the Cost of Airplanes," *Journal of the Aeronautical Sciences* (February 1936).

For example, a 70 percent learning curve implies a 30 percent decrease in time each time the number of repetitions is doubled. A 90 percent curve means there is a corresponding 10 percent rate of improvement.

Stable, standardized products and processes tend to have costs that decline more steeply than others. Between 1920 and 1955, for instance, the steel industry was able to reduce labor-hours per unit to 79 percent each time cumulative production doubled.

Learning curves have application in services as well as industry. As was noted in the caption for the opening photograph, 1-year death rates of heart transplant patients at Temple University Hospital follow a 79 percent learning curve. The results of that hospital's 3-year study of 62 patients receiving transplants found that every three operations resulted in a halving of the 1-year death rate. As more hospitals face pressure from both insurance companies and the government to enter fixed-price negotiations for their services, their ability to learn from experience becomes increasingly critical. In addition to having applications in both services and industry, learning curves are useful for a variety of purposes. These include:

1. Internal: Labor forecasting, scheduling, establishing costs and budgets.
2. External: Supply-chain negotiations (see the SMT case study at the end of this module).
3. Strategic: Evaluation of company and industry performance, including costs and pricing.

The consequences of learning curves can be far-reaching. For example, there are major problems in scheduling if the learning improvement is not considered: labor and plants may sit idle a portion of the time. Firms may also refuse more work because they ignore their own efficiency improvements.

> **AUTHOR COMMENT**
> Here are the three ways of solving learning curve problems.

APPLYING THE LEARNING CURVE

A mathematical relationship enables us to express the time required to produce a certain unit. This relationship is a function of how many units have been produced before the unit in question and how long it took to produce them. To gain a mastery of this relationship, we will work through learning-curve scenarios using three different approaches: arithmetic analysis, logarithmic analysis, and learning-curve coefficients.

Arithmetic Approach

LO2: Use the arithmetic concept to estimate times

The arithmetic approach is the simplest approach to learning-curve problems. As we noted at the beginning of this module, each time production doubles, labor per unit declines by a constant factor, known as the learning rate. So, if we know that the learning rate is 80 percent and that the first unit produced took 100 hours, the hours required to produce the 2nd, 4th, 8th, and 16th units are as follows:

▶ **TABLE B.2**

Calculation of hours required to produce units at different experience levels

Nth Unit Produced	Hours for Nth Unit
1	100.0
2	$80.0 = (0.8 \times 100)$
4	$64.0 = (0.8 \times 80)$
8	$51.2 = (0.8 \times 64)$
16	$41.0 = (0.8 \times 51.2)$

As long as we wish to find the hours required to produce N units and N is one of the doubled values, then this approach works. Arithmetic analysis does not tell us how many hours will be needed to produce other units. For this flexibility, we must turn to the logarithmic approach.

▼ **TABLE B.3**

Learning-Curve Values of *b*

Learning Rate (%)	*b*
70	−0.515
75	−0.415
80	−0.322
85	−0.234
90	−0.152

Logarithmic Approach

The logarithmic approach allows us to determine labor for *any* unit, T_N, by the formula:

$$T_N = T_1(N^b) \tag{B-2}$$

where T_N = time for the Nth unit
   T_1 = hours to produce the first unit
   b = (log of the learning rate ÷ log 2) = slope of the learning curve

Some of the values for b are presented in Table B.3. Example B1 shows how this formula works.

The learning rate for a typical CPA to conduct a dental practice audit is 80 percent. Ali Zoubi, a new graduate of Durham University, UK, completed his first audit in 100 hours. If the dental offices he audits are about the same, how long should he take to finish his third job?

APPROACH ▶ We will use the logarithmic approach in Equation (B-2).

SOLUTION ▶

$$T_N = T_1(N^b)$$
$$T_3 = (100 \text{ hours}) (3^b)$$
$$= (100)(3^{\log 0.8 + \log 2})$$
$$= (100)(3^{-.322}) = 70.2 \text{ labor-hours}$$

INSIGHT ▶ Ali improved quickly from his first to his third audit. An 80 percent rate means that from just the first to second jobs, his time decreased by 20 percent.

LEARNING EXERCISE ▶ If Ali's learning rate was only 90 percent, how long would the third audit take? [Answer: 84.621 hours.]

RELATED PROBLEMS ▶ B.1, B.2, B.6, B.7, B.8, B.12

EXCEL OM Data File **ModBExB1.xls** can be found at MyOMLab.

The logarithmic approach allows us to determine the hours required for *any* unit produced, but there *is* a simpler method.

Learning-Curve Coefficient Approach

The learning-curve coefficient technique is embodied in Table B.4 and the following equation:

$$T_N = T_1 C \qquad \text{(B-3)}$$

where T_N = number of labor-hours required to produce the Nth unit
   T_1 = number of labor-hours required to produce the first unit
   C = learning-curve coefficient found in Table B.4

The learning-curve coefficient, C, depends on both the learning rate (70 percent, 75 percent, 80 percent, and so on) and the unit number of interest.

Example B2 uses the preceding equation and Table B.4 to calculate learning-curve effects.

It took a Qatari shipyard 125,000 labor-hours to produce the first of several tugboats that you expect to purchase for your shipping company, Arabian Gulf Boats, Inc. Boats 2 and 3 have been produced by the Qataris with a learning factor of 85 percent. At US$40 per hour, what should you, as purchasing agent, expect to pay for the fourth unit?

APPROACH ▶ First, search Table B.4 for the fourth unit and a learning rate of 85 percent. The learning-curve coefficient, C, is 0.723.

SOLUTION ▶ To produce the fourth unit, then, takes:

$$T_N = T_1 C$$
$$T_4 = (125,000 \text{ hours})(0.723)$$
$$= 90,375 \text{ hours}$$

To find the cost, multiply by US$40:

$$90,375 \text{ hours} \times \text{US\$40 per hour} = \text{US\$3,615,000}$$

INSIGHT ▶ The learning-curve coefficient approach is very easy to apply. If we had not factored learning into our cost estimates, the price would have been 125,000 hours × US$40 per hour (same as the first boat) = US$6,000,000.

LEARNING EXERCISE ▶ If the learning factor improved to 80 percent, how would the cost change? [Answer: It would drop to US$3,200,000.]

RELATED PROBLEMS ▶ B.1, B.2, B.3a, B.6, B.7, B.8, B.10, B.12

EXCEL OM Data File **ModBExB2.xls** can be found at MyOMLab.

▼ TABLE B.4   Learning-Curve Coefficients, Where Coefficient, $C = N^{(\text{log of learning rate} \div \text{log } 2)}$

Unit Number (N)	70% Unit Time Co-efficient	70% Total Time Co-efficient	75% Unit Time Co-efficient	75% Total Time Co-efficient	80% Unit Time Co-efficient	80% Total Time Co-efficient	85% Unit Time Co-efficient	85% Total Time Co-efficient	90% Unit Time Co-efficient	90% Total Time Co-efficient
1	1.000	1.000	1.000	1.000	1.000	1.000	1.000	1.000	1.000	1.000
2	0.700	1.700	0.750	1.750	0.800	1.800	0.850	1.850	0.900	1.900
3	0.568	2.268	0.634	2.384	0.702	2.502	0.773	2.623	0.846	2.746
4	0.490	2.758	0.562	2.946	0.640	3.142	0.723	3.345	0.810	3.556
5	0.437	3.195	0.513	3.459	0.596	3.738	0.686	4.031	0.783	4.339
6	0.398	3.593	0.475	3.934	0.562	4.299	0.657	4.688	0.762	5.101
7	0.367	3.960	0.446	4.380	0.534	4.834	0.634	5.322	0.744	5.845
8	0.343	4.303	0.422	4.802	0.512	5.346	0.614	5.936	0.729	6.574
9	0.323	4.626	0.402	5.204	0.493	5.839	0.597	6.533	0.716	7.290
10	0.306	4.932	0.385	5.589	0.477	6.315	0.583	7.116	0.705	7.994
11	0.291	5.223	0.370	5.958	0.462	6.777	0.570	7.686	0.695	8.689
12	0.278	5.501	0.357	6.315	0.449	7.227	0.558	8.244	0.685	9.374
13	0.267	5.769	0.345	6.660	0.438	7.665	0.548	8.792	0.677	10.052
14	0.257	6.026	0.334	6.994	0.428	8.092	0.539	9.331	0.670	10.721
15	0.248	6.274	0.325	7.319	0.418	8.511	0.530	9.861	0.663	11.384
16	0.240	6.514	0.316	7.635	0.410	8.920	0.522	10.383	0.656	12.040
17	0.233	6.747	0.309	7.944	0.402	9.322	0.515	10.898	0.650	12.690
18	0.226	6.973	0.301	8.245	0.394	9.716	0.508	11.405	0.644	13.334
19	0.220	7.192	0.295	8.540	0.388	10.104	0.501	11.907	0.639	13.974
20	0.214	7.407	0.288	8.828	0.381	10.485	0.495	12.402	0.634	14.608
25	0.191	8.404	0.263	10.191	0.355	12.309	0.470	14.801	0.613	17.713
30	0.174	9.305	0.244	11.446	0.335	14.020	0.450	17.091	0.596	20.727
35	0.160	10.133	0.229	12.618	0.318	15.643	0.434	19.294	0.583	23.666
40	0.150	10.902	0.216	13.723	0.305	17.193	0.421	21.425	0.571	26.543
45	0.141	11.625	0.206	14.773	0.294	18.684	0.410	23.500	0.561	29.366
50	0.134	12.307	0.197	15.776	0.284	20.122	0.400	25.513	0.552	32.142

Table B.4 also shows *cumulative values*. These allow us to compute the total number of hours needed to complete a specified number of units. Again, the computation is straightforward. Just multiply the table coefficient value by the time required for the first unit. Example B3 illustrates this concept.

EXAMPLE B3 ▶

Using cumulative coefficients

Example B2 computed the time to complete the fourth tugboat that Arabian Gulf plans to buy. How long will *all four* boats require?

APPROACH ▶ We look at the 'Total Time Coefficient' column in Table B.3 and find that the cumulative coefficient for 4 boats with an 85 percent learning factor is 3.345.

SOLUTION ▶ The time required is:

$$T_N = T_1 C$$
$$T_4 = (125,000)(3.345) = 418,125 \text{ hours in total for all 4 boats}$$

INSIGHT ▶ For an illustration of how Excel OM can be used to solve Examples B2 and B3, see Program B.1 at the end of this module.

LEARNING EXERCISE ▶ What is the value of T_4 if the learning factor is 80 percent instead of 85 percent? [Answer: 392,750 hours.]

RELATED PROBLEMS ▶   B.3b, B.4, B.5, B.11, B.14a

Using Table B.4 requires that we know how long it takes to complete the first unit. Yet, what happens if our most recent or most reliable information available pertains to some other unit? The answer is that we must use these data to find a revised estimate for the first unit and then apply the table coefficient to that number. Example B4 illustrates this concept.

Arabian Gulf Boats, Inc., believes that unusual circumstances in producing the first boat (see Example B2) imply that the time estimate of 125,000 hours is not as valid a base as the time required to produce the third boat. Boat number 3 was completed in 100,000 hours. It wants to solve for the revised estimate for boat number 1.

APPROACH ▶ We return to Table B.4, with a unit value of $N = 3$ and a learning-curve coefficient of $C = 0.773$ in the 85 percent column.

SOLUTION ▶ To find the revised estimate, divide the actual time for boat number 3, 100,000 hours, by $C = 0.773$:

$$\frac{100.000}{0.773} = 129.366 \text{ hours}$$

So, 129.366 hours is the new (revised) estimate for boat 1.

INSIGHT ▶ Any change in product, process, or personnel will change the learning curve. The new estimate for boat 1 suggests that related cost and volume estimates need to be revised.

LEARNING EXERCISE ▶ Boat 4 was just completed in 90,000 hours. Arabian Gulf thinks the 85 percent learning rate is valid but isn't sure about the 125,000 hours for the first boat. Find a revised estimate for boat 1. [Answer: 124,481, suggesting that boat 1's time was fairly accurate after all.]

RELATED PROBLEMS ▶ B.13, B.14b, B.15

EXCEL OM Data File **ModBExB4.xls** can be found at MyOMLab.

STRATEGIC IMPLICATIONS OF LEARNING CURVES

So far, we have shown how operations managers can forecast labor-hour requirements for a product. We have also shown how purchasing agents can determine a supplier's cost, knowledge that can help in price negotiations. Another important application of learning curves concerns strategic planning.

An example of a company cost line and industry price line are so labeled in Figure B.2. These learning curves are straight because both scales are log scales. When the *rate* of change is constant, a log–log graph yields a straight line. If an organization believes its cost line to be the 'company cost' line, and the industry price is indicated by the dashed horizontal line, then the company must have costs at the points below the dashed line (for example, point *a* or *b*) or else operate at a loss (point *c*).

Lower costs are not automatic; they must be managed down. When a firm's strategy is to pursue a curve steeper than the industry average (the company cost line in Figure B.2), it does this by:

1. Following an aggressive pricing policy
2. Focusing on continuing cost reduction and productivity improvement
3. Building on shared experience
4. Keeping capacity growing ahead of demand

Costs may drop as a firm pursues the learning curve, but volume must increase for the learning curve to exist. Moreover, managers must understand competitors before embarking on a learning-curve

LO4: Describe the strategic implications of learning curves

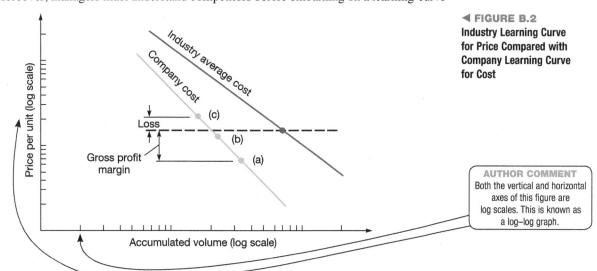

◄ **FIGURE B.2**
Industry Learning Curve for Price Compared with Company Learning Curve for Cost

AUTHOR COMMENT
Both the vertical and horizontal axes of this figure are log scales. This is known as a log–log graph.

strategy. Weak competitors are undercapitalized, stuck with high costs, or do not understand the logic of learning curves. However, strong and dangerous competitors control their costs, have solid financial positions for the large investments needed, and have a track record of using an aggressive learning-curve strategy. Taking on such a competitor in a price war may help only the consumer.

> **AUTHOR COMMENT**
> Determining accurate rates of learning requires careful analysis.

LIMITATIONS OF LEARNING CURVES

Before using learning curves, some cautions are in order:

- Because learning curves differ from company to company, as well as industry to industry, estimates for each organization should be developed rather than applying someone else's.
- Learning curves are often based on the time necessary to complete the early units; therefore, those times must be accurate. As current information becomes available, reevaluation is appropriate.
- Any changes in personnel, design, or procedure can be expected to alter the learning curve, causing the curve to spike up for a short time, even if it is going to drop in the long run.
- While workers and processes may improve, the same learning curves do not always apply to indirect labor and material.
- The culture of the workplace, as well as resource availability and changes in the process, may alter the learning curve. For instance, as a project nears its end, worker interest and effort may drop, curtailing progress down the curve.

MODULE SUMMARY

The learning curve is a powerful tool for the operations manager. This tool can assist operations managers in determining future cost standards for items produced as well as purchased. In addition, the learning curve can provide understanding about company and industry performance. We saw three approaches to learning curves: arithmetic analysis, logarithmic analysis, and learning-curve coefficients found in tables. Software can also help analyze learning curves.

Key Term

Learning curves (p. 570)

Discussion Questions

1. What are some of the limitations of learning curves?
2. Identify three applications of the learning curve.
3. What are the approaches to solving learning-curve problems?
4. Refer to Example B2. What are the implications for Arabian Gulf Boats, Inc. if the engineering department wants to change the engine in the third and subsequent tugboats that the firm purchases?
5. Why isn't the learning-curve concept as applicable in a high-volume assembly line as it is in most other human activities?
6. What are the elements that can disrupt the learning curve?
7. Explain the concept of the 'doubling' effect in learning curves.
8. What techniques can a firm use to move to a steeper learning curve?

Using Software for Learning Curves

Excel, Excel OM, and POM for Windows may all be used in analyzing learning curves. You can use the ideas in the following section on Excel OM to build your own Excel spreadsheet if you wish.

✖ Using Excel OM

Program B.1 shows how Excel OM develops a spreadsheet for learning-curve calculations. The input data come from Example B2 and B3. In cell B7, we enter the unit number for the base unit (which does not have to be 1), and in B8 we enter the time for this unit.

ⓟ Using POM for Windows

The POM for Windows Learning Curve module computes the length of time that future units will take, given the time required for the base unit and the learning rate (expressed as a number between 0 and 1). As an option, if the times required for the first and Nth units are already known, the learning *rate* can be computed. See Appendix IV for further details.

These are used for computations. Do not touch these cells. In cell B11, the time for the first unit is computed, allowing us to use initial units other than unit 1. In cell B12, the power to be raised to is computed, making the formulas in the rest of column B much simpler.

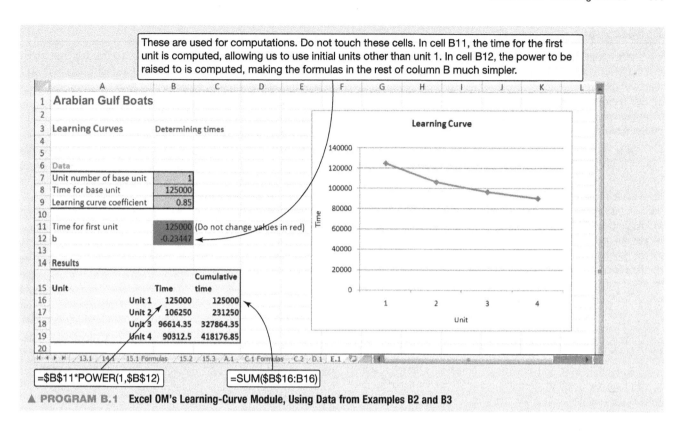

=$B$11*POWER(1,$B$12)

=SUM($B$16:B16)

▲ **PROGRAM B.1** **Excel OM's Learning-Curve Module, Using Data from Examples B2 and B3**

Solved Problems Virtual Office Hours help is available at MyOMLab

▼ SOLVED PROBLEM B.1

Digicomp produces a new telephone system with built-in TV screens. Its learning rate is 80 percent.

a) If the first one took 56 hours, how long will it take Digicomp to make the eleventh system?

b) How long will the first 11 systems take in total?

c) As a purchasing agent, you expect to buy units 12 through 15 of the new phone system. What would be your expected cost for the units if Digicomp charges US$30 for each labor-hour?

▼ SOLUTION

from Table B.4, coefficient for 80 percent unit time

a) $T_N = T_1 C$

$T_{11} = (56 \text{ hours})(0.462) = 25.9 \text{ hours}$

b) Total time for the first 11 units = (56 hours)(6.777) = 379.5 hours

from Table B.4, coefficient for 80 percent total time

c) To find the time for units 12 through 15, we take the total cumulative time for units 1 to 15 and subtract the total time for units 1 to 11, which was computed in part (b). Total time for the first 15 units = (56 hours) (8.511) = 476.6 hours. So, the time for units 12 through 15 is 476.6 – 379.5 = 97.1 hours. (This figure could also be confirmed by computing the times for units 12, 13, 14, and 15 separately using the unit-time coefficient column and then adding them.) Expected cost for units 12 through 15 = (97.1 hours) (US$30 per hour) = US$2,913.

▼ SOLVED PROBLEM B.2

If the first time you performed a job took 60 minutes, how long will the eighth job take if you are on an 80 percent learning curve?

▼ SOLUTION

Three doublings from 1 to 2 to 4 to 8 implies 8^3. Therefore, we have:

$$60 \times (0.8)^3 = 60 \times 0.512 = 30.72 \text{ minutes}$$

or, using Table B.4, we have $C = 0.512$. Therefore:

$$60 \times 0.512 = 30.72 \text{ minutes}$$

Problems*

• **B.1** Amani, an IRS auditor, took 45 minutes to process her first tax return. The IRS uses an 85 percent learning curve. How long will the:
a) 2nd return take?
b) 4th return take?
c) 8th return take? **Px**

• **B.2** Jabal Amman Co. just hired Sally Al-Romani to verify daily invoices and accounts payable. She took 9 hours and 23 minutes to complete her task on the first day. Prior employees in this job have tended to follow a 90 percent learning curve. How long will the task take at the end of:
a) the 2nd day?
b) the 4th day?
c) the 8th day?
d) the 16th day? **Px**

• **B.3** If Professor Mousa takes 15 minutes to grade the first exam and follows an 80 percent learning curve, how long will it take her:
a) to grade the 25th exam?
b) to grade the first 10 exams? **Px**

• **B.4** If it took 563 minutes to complete a hospital's first cornea transplant, and the hospital uses a 90 percent learning rate, what is the cumulative time to complete:
a) the first 3 transplants?
b) the first 6 transplants?
c) the first 8 transplants?
d) the first 16 transplants? **Px**

• **B.5** Muharrag Air has just produced the first unit of a large industrial compressor that incorporated new technology in the control circuits and a new internal venting system. The first unit took 112 hours of labor to manufacture. The company knows from past experience that this labor content will decrease significantly as more units are produced. In reviewing past production data, it appears that the company has experienced a 90 percent learning curve when producing similar designs. The company is interested in estimating the total time to complete the next 7 units. Your job as the production cost estimator is to prepare the estimate. **Px**

• **B.6** Mohammad Ali, a student at the University of Jordan, bought 6 bookcases for his dorm room. Each required unpacking of parts and assembly, which included some nailing and bolting. Mohammad completed the first bookcase in 5 hours and the second in 4 hours.
a) What is his learning rate?
b) Assuming the same rate continues, how long will the 3rd bookcase take?
c) The 4th, 5th, and 6th cases?
d) All 6 cases? **Px**

•• **B.7** Professor Alia Muhanna took 6 hours to prepare the first lecture in a new course. Traditionally, she has experienced a 90 percent learning factor. How much time should it take her to prepare the 15th lecture? **Px**

• **B.8** The first vending machine that Makina, Inc. assembled took 80 labor-hours. Estimate how long the fourth machine will require for each of the following learning rates:
a) 95 percent
b) 87 percent
c) 72 percent. **Px**

• **B.9** Sumaya Systems is installing networks for Baitko Insurance. The first installation took 46 labor-hours to complete. Estimate how long the 4th and the 8th installations will take for each of the following learning rates:
a) 92 percent
b) 84 percent
c) 77 percent. **Px**

•• **B.10** Hussein, the purchasing agent for Qatar Airlines, is interested in determining what she can expect to pay for airplane number 4 if the third plane took 20,000 hours to produce. What would Hussein expect to pay for plane number 5? Number 6? Use an 85 percent learning curve and a US$40-per-hour labor charge. **Px**

•• **B.11** Using the data from Problem B.10, how long will it take to complete the 12th plane? The 15th plane? How long will it take to complete planes 12 through 15 inclusive? At US$40 per hour, what can Hussein, as purchasing agent, expect to pay for all 4 planes? **Px**

•• **B.12** Dynamic Hammam Corp. produces semiconductors and has a learning curve of 0.7. The price per bit is 100 thousandths of a cent when the volume is 0.7×10^{12} bits. a) What is the expected price at 1.4×10^{12} bits? b) What is the expected price at 89.6×10^{12} bits? **Px**

••• **B.13** It takes 28,718 hours to produce the eighth locomotive at a large Egyptian manufacturing firm. If the learning factor is 80 percent, how long does it take to produce the 10th locomotive? **Px**

••• **B.14** As the estimator for Arup Mukherjee Enterprises, your job is to prepare an estimate for a potential customer service contract. The contract is for the service of diesel locomotive cylinder heads. The shop has done some of these in the past on a sporadic basis. The time required to service the first cylinder head in each job has been exactly 4 hours, and similar work has been accomplished at an 85 percent learning curve. The customer wants you to quote the total time in batches of 12 and 20.
a) Prepare the quote.
b) After preparing the quote, you find a labor ticket for this customer for five locomotive cylinder heads. From the notations on the labor ticket, you conclude that the fifth unit took 2.5 hours. What do you conclude about the learning curve and your quote? **Px**

••• **B.15** The service times for a new data entry clerk have been measured and sequentially recorded as shown below:

Report	Time (minutes)
1	66
2	56
3	53
4	48
5	47
6	45
7	44
8	41

Note: **Px** means the problem may be solved with POM for Windows and/or Excel OM.

a) What is the learning curve rate, based on this information?

b) Using an 85 percent learning curve rate and the above times, estimate the length of time the clerk will take to complete the 48th report. **Px**

•• **B.16** If the first unit of a production run takes 1 hour and the firm is on an 80 percent learning curve, how long will unit 100 take? (*Hint:* Apply the coefficient in Table B.4 twice.) **Px**

•••• **B.17** Using the accompanying log-log graph, answer the following questions:

a) What are the implications for management if it has forecast its cost on the optimum line?

b) What could be causing the fluctuations above the optimum line?

c) If management forecast the 10th unit on the optimum line, what was that forecast in hours?

d) If management built the 10th unit as indicated by the actual line, how many hours did it take?

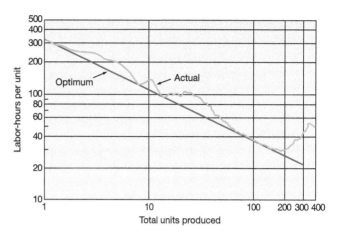

▶ **Refer to** MyOMLab **for additional homework problems.**

Case Study

▶ SMT's Negotiation with IBM

SMT (Simultaneous Multi-Threading) and one other, much larger company were asked by IBM to bid on 80 more units of a particular computer product. The RFQ (request for quote) asked that the overall bid be broken down to show the hourly rate, the parts and materials component in the price, and any charges for subcontracted services. SMT quoted US$1.62 million and supplied the cost breakdown as requested. The second company submitted only one total figure, US$5 million, with no cost breakdown. The decision was made to negotiate with SMT.

The IBM negotiating team included two purchasing managers and two cost engineers. One cost engineer had developed manufacturing cost estimates for every component, working from engineering drawings and cost-data books that he had built up from previous experience and that contained time factors, both setup and run times, for a large variety of operations. He estimated materials costs by working both from data supplied by the IBM corporate purchasing staff and from purchasing journals. He visited SMT facilities to see the tooling available so that he would know what processes were being used. He assumed that there would be perfect conditions and trained operators, and he developed cost estimates for the 158th unit (previous orders were for 25, 15, and 38 units). He added 5 percent for scrap-and-flow loss; 2 percent for the use of temporary tools, jigs, and fixtures; 5 percent for quality control; and 9 percent for purchasing burden. Then, using an 85 percent learning curve, he backed up his costs to get an estimate for the first unit. He next checked the data on hours and materials for the 25, 15, and 38 units already made and found that his estimate for the first unit was within 4 percent of actual cost. His check, however, had indicated a 90 percent learning-curve effect on hours per unit.

In the negotiations, SMT was represented by one of the two owners of the business, two engineers, and one cost estimator. The sessions opened with a discussion of learning curves. The IBM cost estimator demonstrated that SMT had in fact been operating on a 90 percent learning curve. But, he argued, it should be possible to

move to an 85 percent curve, given the longer runs, reduced setup time, and increased continuity of workers on the job that would be possible with an order for 80 units. The owner agreed with this analysis and was willing to reduce his price by 4 percent.

However, as each operation in the manufacturing process was discussed, it became clear that some IBM cost estimates were too low because certain crating and shipping expenses had been overlooked. These oversights were minor, however, and in the following discussions, the two parties arrived at a common understanding of specifications and reached agreements on the costs of each manufacturing operation.

At this point, SMT representatives expressed great concern about the possibility of inflation in material costs. The IBM negotiators volunteered to include a form of price escalation in the contract, as previously agreed among themselves. IBM representatives suggested that if overall material costs changed by more than 10 percent, the price could be adjusted accordingly. However, if one party took the initiative to have the price revised, the other could require an analysis of *all* parts and materials invoices in arriving at the new price.

Another concern of the SMT representatives was that a large amount of overtime and subcontracting would be required to meet IBM's specified delivery schedule. IBM negotiators thought that a relaxation in the delivery schedule might be possible if a price concession could be obtained. In response, the SMT team offered a 5 percent discount, and this was accepted. As a result of these negotiations, the SMT price was reduced almost 20 percent below its original bid price.

In a subsequent meeting called to negotiate the prices of certain pipes to be used in the system, it became apparent to an IBM cost estimator that SMT representatives had seriously underestimated their costs. He pointed out this apparent error because he could not understand why SMT had quoted such a low figure. He wanted to be sure that SMT was using the correct manufacturing process. In any case, if SMT estimators had made a mistake, it should be noted. It was IBM's policy to seek a fair price both for itself and for its suppliers. IBM procurement managers believed that if a vendor was losing money on a job, there would be a tendency to cut corners. In addition, the IBM negotiator felt that by pointing out the error, he generated some goodwill that would help in future sessions.

Discussion Questions

1. What are the advantages and disadvantages to IBM and SMT from this approach?
2. How does SMT's proposed learning rate compare with that of other industries?
3. What are the limitations of the learning curve in this case?

Source: Based on E. Raymond Corey, *Procurement Management: Strategy, Organization, and Decision Making* (New York: Van Nostrand Reinhold).

Main Heading	Review Material	MyOMLab
WHAT IS A LEARNING CURVE? (pp. 570–571)	■ **Learning curves**—The premise that people and organizations get better at their tasks as the tasks are repeated; sometimes called experience curves.	
	Learning usually follows a negative exponential curve.	
	It takes less time to complete each additional unit a firm produces; however, the time *savings* in completing each subsequent unit *decreases.*	
	Learning curves were first applied to industry in a report by T. P. Wright of Curtis-Wright Corp. in 1936. Wright described how direct labor costs of making a particular airplane decreased with learning.	
	Learning curves have been applied not only to labor but also to a wide variety of other costs, including material and purchased components.	
	The power of the learning curve is so significant that it plays a major role in many strategic decisions related to employment levels, costs, capacity, and pricing.	
	The learning curve is based on a *doubling* of production: That is, when production doubles, the decrease in time per unit affects the rate of the learning curve.	
	$$T \times L^n = \text{Time required for the } n\text{th unit} \qquad \text{(B-1)}$$	
	where T = unit cost or unit time of the first unit L = learning curve rate n = number of times T is doubled	
LEARNING CURVES IN SERVICES AND MANUFACTURING (pp. 571–572)	Different organizations—indeed, different products—have different learning curves. The rate of learning varies, depending on the quality of management and the potential of the process and product. *Any change in process, product, or personnel disrupts the learning curve.* Therefore, caution should be exercised in assuming that a learning curve is continuing and permanent.	
	The steeper the slope of the learning curve, the faster the drop in costs.	
	By tradition, learning curves are defined in terms of the *complements* of their improvement rates (i.e. a 75 percent learning rate is better than an 85 percent learning rate).	
	Stable, standardized products and processes tend to have costs that decline more steeply than others.	
	Learning curves are useful for a variety of purposes, including:	
	1. *Internal:* Labor forecasting, scheduling, establishing costs and budgets. 2. *External:* Supply-chain negotiations. 3. *Strategic:* Evaluation of company and industry performance, including costs and pricing.	
APPLYING THE LEARNING CURVE (pp. 572–575)	If learning curve improvement is ignored, potential problems could arise, such as scheduling mismatches, leading to idle labor and productive facilities, refusal to accept new orders because capacity is assumed to be full, or missing an opportunity to negotiate with suppliers for lower purchase prices as a result of large orders.	Problems: B.1–B.16 Virtual Office Hours for Solved Problems: B.1, B.2
	Three ways to approach the mathematics of learning curves are: (1) arithmetic analysis; (2) logarithmic analysis; (3) learning-curve coefficients.	
	The arithmetic approach uses the production doubling Equation (B-1).	
	The logarithmic approach allows us to determine labor for *any* unit, T_N, by the formula:	
	$$T_N = T_1(N^b) \qquad \text{(B-2)}$$	
	where T_N = time for the Nth unit T_1 = hours to produce the first unit b = (log of the learning rate ÷ log 2) = slope of the learning curve	
	The learning-curve coefficient approach makes use of Table B.4 and uses the formula:	
	$$T_N = T_1 C \qquad \text{(B-3)}$$	
	where T_N = number of labor-hours required to produce the Nth unit T_1 = number of labor-hours required to produce the first unit C = learning-curve coefficient found in 'Unit Time Coefficient' columns of Table B.4	
	The learning-curve coefficient, C, depends on both the learning rate and the unit number of interest.	

Main Heading	Review Material
	Formula (B-3) can also use the 'Total Time Coefficient' columns of Table B.4 to provide the total cumulative number of hours needed to complete the specified number of units.
	If the most recent or most reliable information available pertains to some unit other than the first, these data should be used to find a revised estimate for the first unit, and then the applicable formulas should be applied to that revised number.
STRATEGIC IMPLICATIONS OF LEARNING CURVES (pp. 575–576)	When a firm's strategy is to pursue a learning cost curve steeper than the industry average, it can do this by: 1. Following an aggressive pricing policy 2. Focusing on continuing cost reduction and productivity improvement 3. Building on shared experience 4. Keeping capacity growing ahead of demand Managers must understand competitors before embarking on a learning-curve strategy. For example, taking on a strong competitor in a price war may help only the consumer.
LIMITATIONS OF LEARNING CURVES (p. 576)	Before using learning curves, some cautions are in order: ■ Because learning curves differ from company to company, as well as industry to industry, estimates for each organization should be developed rather than applying someone else's. ■ Learning curves are often based on the time necessary to complete the early units; therefore, those times must be accurate. As current information becomes available, reevaluation is appropriate. ■ Any changes in personnel, design, or procedure can be expected to alter the learning curve, causing the curve to spike up for a short time, even if it is going to drop in the long run. ■ While workers and process may improve, the same learning curves do not always apply to indirect labor and material. ■ The culture of the workplace, as well as resource availability and changes in the process, may alter the learning curve. For instance, as a project nears its end, worker interest and effort may drop, curtailing progress down the curve.

Self-Test

■ **Before taking the self-test,** refer to the learning objectives listed at the beginning of the module and the key terms listed at the end of the module.

LO1. A learning curve describes:
  a) the rate at which an organization acquires new data
  b) the amount of production time per unit as the total number of units produced increases
  c) the increase in production time per unit as the total number of units produced increases
  d) the increase in number of units produced per unit time as the total number of units produced increases.

LO2. A surgical procedure with a 90 percent learning curve required 20 hours for the initial patient. The fourth patient should require approximately how many hours?
  a) 18
  b) 16.2
  c) 28
  d) 30
  e) 54.2.

LO3. The first transmission took 50 hours to rebuild at Bilal's Auto Repair, and the learning rate is 80 percent. How long will it take to rebuild the third unit? (Use at least three decimals in the exponent if you use the logarithmic approach.)
  a) under 30 hours
  b) about 32 hours
  c) about 35 hours
  d) about 60 hours
  e) about 45 hours.

LO4. Which one of the following courses of action would *not* be taken by a firm wanting to pursue a learning curve steeper than the industry average?
  a) Following an aggressive pricing policy
  b) Focusing on continuing cost reduction
  c) Keeping capacity equal to demand to control costs
  d) Focusing on productivity improvement
  e) Building on shared experience.

Bibliography

Chapter 1

Broedner, P., S. Kinkel, and G. Lay. "Productivity Effects of Outsourcing." *International Journal of Operations and Production Management* 29, no. 2 (2009): 127.

Hounshell, D. A. *From the American System to Mass Production 1800–1932: The Development of Manufacturing.* Baltimore: Johns Hopkins University Press, 1985.

Lewis, William W. *The Power of Productivity.* Chicago: University of Chicago Press, 2004.

Maroto, A., and L. Rubalcaba. "Services Productivity Revisited." *The Service Industries Journal* 28, no. 3 (April 2008): 337.

Sahay, B. S. "Multi-factor Productivity Measurement Model for Service Organization." *International Journal of Productivity and Performance Management* 54, nos. 1–2 (2005): 7–23.

San, G., T. Huang, and L. Huang. "Does Labor Quality Matter on Productivity Growth?" *Total Quality Management and Business Excellence* 19, no. 10 (October 2008): 1043.

Sprague, Linda G. "Evolution of the Field of Operations Management," *Journal of Operations Management* 25, no. 2 (March 2007): 219–238.

Tangen, S. "Demystifying Productivity and Performance." *International Journal of Productivity and Performance Measurement* 54, no. 1–2 (2005): 34–47.

Taylor, F. W. *The Principles of Scientific Management.* New York: Harper & Brothers, 1911.

van Biema, Michael, and Bruce Greenwald. "Managing Our Way to Higher Service-Sector Productivity." *Harvard Business Review* 75, no. 4 (July–August 1997): 87–95.

Wren, Daniel A. *The Evolution of Management Thought.* New York: Wiley, 1994.

Chapter 2

Beckman, S. L., and D. B. Rosenfield. *Operations Strategy: Competing in the 21st Century.* New York: McGraw-Hill, 2008.

Crotts, J. C., D. R. Dickson, and R. C. Ford. "Aligning Organizational Processes with Mission." *Academy of Management Executive* 19, no. 3 (August 2005): 54–68.

Flynn, B. B., R. G. Schroeder, and E. J. Flynn. "World Class Manufacturing." *Journal of Operations Management* 17, no. 3 (March 1999): 249–269.

Friedman, Thomas. *The World Is Flat: A Brief History of the Twenty-first Century.* New York: Farrar, Straus and Giroux, 2005.

Greenwald, Bruce, and Judd Kahn. "All Strategy Is Local." *Harvard Business Review*, 83, no. 9 (September 2005): 94–104.

Kaplan, Robert S., and David P. Norton. *Strategy Maps.* Boston: Harvard Business School Publishing, 2003.

Kathuria, R., M. P. Joshi, and S. Dellande. "International Growth Strategies of Service and Manufacturing Firms." *International Journal of Operations and Production Management* 28, no. 10 (2008): 968.

Porter, Michael, and Nicolaj Siggelkow. "Contextuality within Activity Systems and Sustainability of Competitive Advantage." *Academy of Management Perspectives* 22, no. 2 (May 2008): 34–36.

Rudberg, Martin, and B. M. West. "Global Operations Strategy." *Omega* 36, no. 1 (February 2008): 91.

Skinner, Wickham. "Manufacturing Strategy: The Story of Its Evolution." *Journal of Operations Management* 25, no. 2 (March 2007): 328–334.

Slack, Nigel, and Mike Lewis. *Operation Strategy*, 2nd ed. Upper Saddle River, NJ: Prentice Hall, 2008.

Wolf, Martin. *Why Globalization Works.* London: Yale University Press, 2004.

Zakaria, Fareed. *The Post American World.* New York: W. W. Norton, 2008.

Chapter 3

Balakrishnan, R., B. Render, and R. M. Stair. *Managerial Decision Modeling with Spreadsheets*, 2nd ed. Upper Saddle River, NJ: Prentice Hall (2007).

Cleland, D. L., and L. R. Ireland. *Project Management*, 5th ed. New York: McGraw-Hill/Irwin (2007).

Gray, C. L., and E. W. Larson. *Project Management with MS Project.* New York: McGraw-Hill/Irwin (2008).

Helgadottir, Hilder. "The Ethical Dimension of Project Management." *International Journal of Project Management* 26, no. 7 (October 2008): 743.

Karlos, A., et al. "Foundations of Project Management." *International Journal of Project Management* 27, no. 1 (January 2009): 1.

Kerzner, H. *Project Management Case Studies*, 3rd ed. New York: Wiley (2009).

Kumar, P. P. "Effective Use of Gantt Chart for Managing Large-Scale Projects." *Cost Engineering* 47, no. 7 (July 2005): 14–21.

Ling, F. Y. Y., et al. "Key Project Management Practices Affecting Singaporean Firms' Project Performance in China." *International Journal of Project Management* 27, no. 1 (January, 2009): 59.

Matta, N. F., and R. N. Ashkenas. "Why Good Projects Fail Anyways." *Harvard Business Review* (September 2003): 109–114.

Maylor, Harvey. *Project Management*, 4th ed. Upper Saddle River, NJ: Prentice Hall (2008).

Meredith, J. R., and S. Mantel. *Project Management*, 7th ed. New York: Wiley (2008).

Oates, David. "Understanding and Solving the Causes of Project Failure." *Knowledge Management Review* 9, no. 5 (May–June 2006): 5.

Render, B., R. M. Stair, and M. Hanna. *Quantitative Analysis for Management*, 10th ed. Upper Saddle River, NJ: Prentice Hall (2009).

Verzuh, Eric. *The Fast Forward MBA in Project Management.* New York: Wiley (2008).

Wysocki, R. K. *Effective Project Management*, 5th ed. New York: Wiley (2009).

Chapter 4

Balakrishnan, R., B. Render, and R. M. Stair. *Managerial Decision Modeling with Spreadsheets*, 2nd ed. Upper Saddle River, NJ: Prentice Hall, 2007.

Berenson, Mark, Tim Krehbiel, and David Levine. *Basic Business Statistics*, 11th ed. Upper Saddle River, NJ: Prentice Hall, 2009.

Campbell, Omar. "Forecasting in Direct Selling Business: Tupperware's Experience." *The Journal of Business Forecasting* 27, no. 2 (Summer 2008): 18–19.

Diebold, F. X. *Elements of Forecasting*, 5th ed. Cincinnati: South-Western College Publishing, 2010.

Fildes, Robert, and Paul Goodwin. "Against Your Better Judgment? How Organizations Can Improve Their Use of

Management Judgment in Forecasting." *Decision Sciences* 37, no. 6 (November–December 2007): 570–576.

Georgoff, D. M., and R. G. Murdick. "Manager's Guide to Forecasting." *Harvard Business Review* 64 (January–February 1986): 110–120.

Gilliland, M., and M. Leonard. "Forecasting Software—The Past and the Future." *The Journal of Business Forecasting* 25, no. 1 (Spring 2006): 33–36.

Hanke, J. E. and D. W. Wichern. *Business Forecasting*, 9th ed. Upper Saddle River, NJ: Prentice Hall, 2009.

Heizer, Jay. "Forecasting with Stagger Charts." *IIE Solutions* 34 (June 2002): 46–49.

Jain, Chaman L. "Benchmarking Forecasting Software and Systems." *The Journal of Business Forecasting* 26, no. 4 (Winter 2007/2008): 30–34.

Onkal, D., M. S. Gonul, and M. Lawrence. "Judgmental Adjustments of Previously Adjusted Forecasts." *Decision Sciences* 39, no. 2 (May 2008): 213–238.

Render, B., R. M. Stair, and M. Hanna. *Quantitative Analysis for Management*, 10th ed. Upper Saddle River, NJ: Prentice Hall, 2009.

Shah, Piyush. "Techniques to Support Better Forecasting." *APICS Magazine* (November/December 2008): 49–50.

Tabatabai, Bijan. "Improving Forecasting." *Financial Management* (October 2008): 48–49.

Urs, Rajiv. "How to Use a Demand Planning System for Best Forecasting and Planning Results." *The Journal of Business Forecasting* 27, no. 2 (Summer 2008): 22–25.

Wilson, J. H., B. Keating, and J. Galt. *Business Forecasting*, 6th ed. New York: McGraw-Hill, 2009.

Yurklewicz, Jack. "Forecasting at Steady State." *Analytics* (Summer 2008): 42–45.

Chapter 5

Ambec, Stefan, and Paul Lanoie. "Does It Pay to Be Green? A Systematic Overview." *Academy of Management Perspectives* 22, no. 4 (November 2008): 13–20.

Brockman, Beverly K., and Robert M. Morgan. "The Role of Existing Knowledge in New Product Innovativeness and Performance." *Decision Sciences* 34, no. 2 (Spring 2003): 385–419.

Camevalli, J. A., and P. A. C. Miguel. "Review, Analysis, and Classification of the Literature on QFD." *International Journal of Production Economics* 114, no. 2 (August 2008): 737.

Ernst, David, and James Bamford. "Your Alliances Are Too Stable." *Harvard Business Review* 83, no. 5 (June 2005): 133–141.

Gerwin, Donald. "Coordinating New Product Development in Strategic Alliances." *The Academy of Management Review* 29, no. 2 (April 2004): 241–257.

Krishnan, V., and Karl T. Ulrich. "Product Development Decisions: A Review of the Literature." *Management Science* 47, no. 1 (January 2001): 1–21.

Loch, C. H., and C. Terwiesch. "Rush and Be Wrong or Wait and Be Late?" *Production and Operations Management* 14, no. 3 (Fall 2005): 331–343.

Miguel, P. A. C., and J. A. Camevalli. "Benchmarking Practices of Quality Function Deployment." *Benchmarking* 15, no. 6 (2008): 657.

Phyper, J. D., and D. MacLean. *Good to Green: Managers Business Risks and Opportunities in an Age of Environmental Awareness*. New York: Wiley, 2009.

Pisano, Gary P., and Roberto Verganti. "Which Kind of Collaboration Is Right for You?" *Harvard Business Review* 86, no. 12 (December 2008): 78–86.

Saaksvuori, A., and A. Immonen. *Product Lifecycle Management*. Berlin: Springer-Verlag, 2004.

Seider, Warren D., et al. *Product and Process Design Principles*. 3rd ed. New York: Wiley, 2008.

Ulrich, K., and S. Eppinger. *Product Design and Development*, 4th ed. New York: McGraw-Hill, 2008.

Chapter 6

Besterfield, Dale H. *Quality Control*, 8th ed. Upper Saddle River, NJ: Prentice Hall, 2009.

Brown, Mark G. *Baldrige Award Winning Quality*, 19th ed. University Park, IL: Productivity Press, 2010.

Crosby, P. B. *Quality Is Still Free*. New York: McGraw-Hill, 1996.

Evans, J. R., and W. M. Lindsay. *Managing for Quality and Performance Excellence*. 7th ed. Mason, OH: Thompson-Southwestern, 2008.

Feigenbaum, A. V. "Raising the Bar." *Quality Progress* 41, no. 7 (July 2008): 22–28.

Gitlow, Howard S. *A Guide to Lean Six Sigma Management Skills*. University Park, IL: Productivity Press, 2009.

Gonzalez-Benito, J., and O. Gonzalez-Benito. "Operations Management Practices Linked to the Adoption of ISO 14001." *International Journal of Production Economics* 113, no. 1 (May 2008): 60.

Gryna, F. M., R. C. H. Chua, and J. A. DeFeo. *Juran's Quality Planning and Analysis for Enterprise Quality*, 5th ed. New York: McGraw-Hill, 2007.

Harrington, D. R., M. Khanna, and G. Deltas. "Striving to Be Green: The Adoption of Total Quality Environmental Management." *Applied Economics* 40, no. 23 (December 2008): 2995.

Mitra, Amit. *Fundamentals of Quality Control and Improvement*. New York: Wiley, 2009.

Pande, P. S., R. P. Neuman, R. R. Cavanagh. *What Is Design for Six Sigma?* New York: McGraw-Hill, 2005.

Schroeder, Roger G., et al. "Six Sigma: Definition and Underlying Theory." *Journal of Operations Management* 26, no. 4 (2008): 536–554.

Soltani, E., P. Lai, and P. Phillips. "A New Look at Factors Influencing Total Quality Management Failure." *New Technology, Work, and Employment* 23, no. 1–2 (March 2008): 125.

Stewart, D. M. "Piecing Together Service Quality: A Framework for Robust Service." *Production and Operations Management* (Summer 2003): 246–265.

Summers, Donna. *Quality Management*, 2nd ed. Upper Saddle River, NJ: Prentice Hall, 2009.

Chapter 7

Davenport, T. H. "The Coming Commoditization of Processes." *Harvard Business Review* 83, no. 6 (June 2005): 101–108.

Debo, L. G., L. B. Toktay, and L. N. Van Wassenhove. "Market Segmentation and Product Technology Selection for Remanufacturable Products." *Management Science* 51, no. 8 (August 2005): 1193–1205.

Duray, R., P. T. Ward, G. W. Milligan, and W. L. Berry. "Approaches to Mass Customization: Configurations and Empirical Validation." *Journal of Operations Management* 18, no. 6 (November 2000): 605–625.

Duray, R. "Mass Customization Origins: Mass or Custom Manufacturing." *International Journal of Operations and Production Management* 22, no. 3 (2002): 314–328.

Gilmore, James H., and Joseph Pine II (eds.). *Markets of One: Creating Customer-Unique Value through Mass Customization*. Boston: Harvard Business Review Book, 2000.

Hall, Joseph M., and M. Eric Johnson. "When Should a Process Be Art, Not Science?" *Harvard Business Review* 87, no. 3 (March 2009): 58–65.

Hegde, V. G., et al. "Customization: Impact on Product and Process Performance." *Production and Operations Management* 14, no. 4 (Winter 2005): 388–399.

Inderfurth, Karl, I. M. Langella. "An Approach for Solving Disassembly-to-order Problems under Stochastic Yields." In *Logistik Management.* Heidelberg: Physica, 2004: 309–331.

Moeeni, F. "From Light Frequency Identification to Radio Frequency Identification in the Supply Chain," *Decision Line* 37, no. 3 (May 2006): 8–13.

Rugtusanatham, M. Johnny, and Fabrizio Salvador. "From Mass Production to Mass Customization." *Production and Operations Management* 17, no. 3 (May–June 2008): 385–396.

Su, J. C. P., Y. Chang, and M. Ferguson. "Evaluation of Postponement Structures to Accommodate Mass Customization." *Journal of Operations Management* 23, nos. 3–4 (April 2005): 305–318.

Swamidass, Paul M. *Innovations in Competitive Manufacturing.* Dordrecht, NL: Kluwer, 2000.

Welborn, Cliff. "Mass Customization." *OR/MS Today* (December 2007): 38–42.

Zipkin, Paul. "The Limits of Mass Customization." *MIT Sloan Management Review* 40, no. 1 (Spring 2001): 81–88.

Chapter 7 Supplement

Anupindi, Ravi, S. Deshmukh, and S. Chopra. *Managing Business Process Flows*, 2nd ed. Upper Saddle River, NJ: Prentice Hall (2007).

Atamturk, A., and D. S. Hochbaum. "Capacity Acquisition, Subcontracting, and Lot-Sizing." *Management Science* 47, no. 8 (August 2001): 1081–1100.

Bowers, John, et al. "Modeling Outpatient Capacity for a Diagnosis and Treatment Center." *Health Care Management Science* 8, no. 3 (August 2005): 205.

Brandl, Dennis. "Capacity and Constraints." *Control Engineering* (February 2008): 24.

Chambers, Chester, Eli M. Snir, and Asad Ata. "The Use of Flexible Manufacturing Capacity in Pharmaceutical Product Introductions." *Decision Sciences* 40, no. 2 (May 2009): 243–268.

Cheng, H. K., K. Dogan, and R. A. Einicki. "Pricing and Capacity Decisions for Non-Profit Internet Service Providers." *Information Technology and Management* 7, no. 2 (April 2006): 91.

Goldratt, Eliyaha. *The Choice.* Great Barrington, MA: North River Press (2009).

Goodale, John C., Rohit Verma, and Madeleine E. Pullman. "A Market Utility-Based Model for Capacity Scheduling in Mass Services." *Production and Operations Management* 12, no. 2 (Summer 2003): 165–185.

Gupta, M. C., and L. H. Boyd. "Theory of Constraints: A Theory for Operations Management." *International Journal of Operations Management* 28, no. 10 (2008): 991.

Jack, Eric P., and Amitabh S. Raturi. "Measuring and Comparing Volume Flexibility in the Capital Goods Industry." *Production and Operations Management* 12, no. 4 (Winter 2003): 480–501.

Jonsson, Patrik, and Stig-Arne Mattsson. "Use and Applicability of Capacity Planning Methods." *Production and Inventory Management Journal* (3rd/4th Quarter 2002): 89–95.

Kekre, Sunder, et al. "Reconfiguring a Remanufacturing Line at Visteon, Mexico." *Interfaces* 33, no. 6 (November–December 2003): 30–43.

Tibben-Lembke, Ronald S. "Theory of Constraints at UniCo." *International Journal of Production Research* 47, no. 7 (January 2009): 1815.

Watson, Kevin J., John H. Blackstone, and Stanley C. Gardiner. "The Evolution of a Management Philosophy: The Theory of Constraints." *Journal of Operations Management* 25, no. 2 (March 2007): 387–402.

Chapter 8

Ballou, Ronald H. *Business Logistics Management*, 5th ed. Upper Saddle River, NJ: Prentice Hall, 2004.

Bartness, A. D. "The Plant Location Puzzle." *Harvard Business Review* 72, no. 2 (March–April 1994).

Denton, B. "Decision Analysis, Location Models, and Scheduling Problems." *Interfaces* 30, no. 3 (May–June 2005): 262–263.

Drezner, Z. *Facility Location: Applications and Theory.* Berlin: Springer-Verlag, 2002.

Florida, R. *The Flight of the Creative Class: The New Global Competition for Talent.* New York: HarperCollins, 2005.

Kennedy, M. *Introducing Geographic Information Systems with ArcGIS.* New York: Wiley, 2006.

Klamroth, K. *Single Facility Location Problems.* Berlin: Springer-Verlag, 2002.

Mentzer, John T. "Seven Keys to Facility Location." *Supply Chain Management Review* 12, no. 5 (May 2008): 25.

Partovi, F. Y. "An Analytic Model for Locating Facilities Strategically." *Omega* 34, no. 1 (January 2006): 41.

Porter, Michael E., and Scott Stern. "Innovation: Location Matters." *MIT Sloan Management Review* (Summer 2001): 28–36.

Render, B., R. M. Stair, and M. Hanna. *Quantitative Analysis for Management*, 10th ed. Upper Saddle River, NJ: Prentice Hall, 2009.

Snyder, L. V. "Facility Location Under Uncertainty." *IIE Transactions* 38, no. 7 (July 2006): 547.

Tallman, Stephen, et al. "Knowledge, Clusters, and Competitive Advantage." *The Academy of Management Review* 29, no. 2 (April 2004): 258–271.

White, G. "Location, Location, Location." *Nation's Restaurant News* 42, no. 27 (July 14, 2008): S10–S11.

Chapter 9

Birchfield, J. C., and J. Birchfield. *Design and Layout of Foodservice Facilities*, 3rd ed. New York, Wiley, 2007.

Francis, R. L., L. F. McGinnis, and J. A. White. *Facility Layout and Location*, 3rd ed. Upper Saddle River, NJ: Prentice Hall, 1998.

Gultekin, H., O. Y. Karasan, and M. S. Akturk. "Pure Cycles in Flexible Robotic Cells." *Computers & Operations Research* 36, no. 2 (February 2009): 329.

Heragu, S. S. *Facilities Design*, 3rd ed. New York: CRC Press, 2008.

Heyer, N., and U. Wemmerlöv. *Reorganizing the Factory: Competing through Cellular Manufacturing.* Portland, OR: Productivity Press, 2002.

Johnson, Alan. "Getting the Right Factory Layout." *Manufacturer's Monthly* (July 2008): 16.

Kator, C. "Crossdocking on the Rise." *Modern Materials Handling* 63, no. 6 (June 2008): 15.

Kee, Micah R. "The Well-Ordered Warehouse." *APICS: The Performance Advantage* (March 2003): 20–24.

Keeps, David A. "Out-of-the-Box Offices." *Fortune* 159, no.1 (January 19, 2009): 45.

Larson, S. "Extreme Makeover—OR Edition." *Nursing Management* (November 2005): 26.

Panchalavarapu, P. R., and V. Chankong. "Design of Cellular Manufacturing System with Assembly Considerations." *Computers & Industrial Engineering* 48, no. 3 (May 2005): 448.

Roodbergen, K. J., and I. F. A. Vis. "A Model for Warehouse Layout." *IIE Transactions* 38, no. 10 (October 2006): 799–811.

Stanowy, A. "Evolutionary Strategy for Manufacturing Cell Design." *Omega* 34, no. 1 (January 2006): 1.

Tompkins, James A. *Facility Planning*, 4th ed. New York: Wiley, 2009.

Upton, David. "What Really Makes Factories Flexible?" *Harvard Business Review* 73, no. 4 (July–August 1995): 74–84.

Zeng, A. Z., M. Mahan, and N. Fleut. "Designing an Efficient Warehouse Layout to Facilitate the Order-Filling Process." *Production and Inventory Management Journal* 43, no. 3–4 (3rd/4th Quarter 2002): 83–88.

Zhao, T., and C. L. Tseng. "Flexible Facility Interior Layout." *The Journal of the Operational Research Society* 58, no. 6 (June 2007): 729–740.

Chapter 10

Aft, Larry, and Neil Schmeidler. "Work Measurement Practices." *Industrial Engineer* 35, no. 11 (November 2003): 44.

Barber, Felix, and Rainer Strack. "The Surprising Economics of a People Business." *Harvard Business Review* 83, no. 6 (June 2005): 81–90.

Barnes, R. M. *Motion and Time Study, Design and Measurement of Work*, 7th ed. New York: Wiley, 1980.

Bridger, R. S. *Introduction to Ergonomics*, 3rd ed. New York: CRC Press, 2008.

De Jong, A., K. De Ruyter, and J. Lemmink. "Service Climate in Self-Managing Teams." *The Journal of Management Studies* 42, no. 8 (December 2005): 1593.

Elnekave, M., and I. Gilad. "Rapid Video-Based Analysis System for Advanced Work Measurement." *International Journal of Production Research* 44, no. 2 (January 2006): 271.

Freivalds, Andris, and B. W. Niebel. *Methods, Standards, and Work Design*, 12th ed. New York: Irwin/McGraw-Hill, 2009.

Huselid, Mark A., Richard W. Beatty, and Brian E. Becker. "'A Players' or 'A Positions'? The Strategic Logic of Workforce Management." *Harvard Business Review* (December 2005): 110–117.

Konz, S., and Steven Johnson. *Work Design: Industrial Ergonomics*, 6th ed. Scottsdale, AZ: Holcomb Hathaway, 2004.

Muthusamy, S. K., J. V. Wheeler, and B. L. Simmons. "Self-Managing Work Teams." *Organization Development Journal* 23, no. 3 (Fall 2005): 53–66.

Pfeffer, Jeffrey. "Producing Sustainable Competitive Advantage Through the Effective Management of People." *Academy of Management Executive* 19, no. 4 (2005): 95.

Sadikoglu, E. "Integration of Work Measurement and Total Quality Management." *Total Quality Management and Business Excellence* 16, no. 5 (July 2005): 597.

Salvendy, G., ed. *Handbook of Human Factors and Ergonomics*, 3rd ed. New York: Wiley, 2006.

Tolo, B. "21st-Century Stopwatch." *Industrial Engineer* 37, no. 7 (July 2005): 34–37.

Walsh, Ellen. "Get Results with Workload Management." *Nursing Management* (October 2003): 16.

Chapter 11

Blackburn, Joseph, and Gary Scudder. "Supply Chain Strategies for Perishable Products." *Production and Operations Management* 18, no. 2 (March–April 2009): 129–137.

Boyer, Kenneth K., and G. Tomas M. Hult. "Extending the Supply Chain: Integrating Operations and Marketing in the Online Grocery Industry." *Journal of Operations Management* 23, no. 6 (September 2005): 642–661.

Chopra, Sunil, and Peter Meindl. *Supply Chain Management*, 4th ed. Upper Saddle River, NJ: Prentice Hall (2010).

Crook, T. Russell, and James G. Combs. "Sources and Consequences of Bargaining Power in Supply Chains." *Journal of Operations Management* 25, no. 2 (March 2007): 546–555.

Hu, J., and C. L. Munson. "Speed versus Reliability Trade-offs in Supplier Selection." *International Journal Procurement Management* 1, no. 1/2 (2007): 238–259.

Kersten, Wolfgang, and Thorsten Blecker (eds.). *Managing Risk in Supply Chains*. Berlin: Erich Schmidt Verlag GmbH & Co. (2006).

Kreipl, Stephan, and Michael Pinedo. "Planning and Scheduling in Supply Chains." *Production and Operations Management* 13, no. 1 (Spring 2004): 77–92.

Linton, J. D., R. Klassen, and V. Jayaraman. "Sustainable Supply Chains: An Introduction." *Journal of Operations Management* 25, no. 6 (November 2007): 1075–1082.

Monczka, R. M., R. B. Handfield, L. C. Gianipero, and J. L. Patterson. *Purchasing and Supply Chain Management*, 4th ed. Mason, OH: Cengage (2009).

Narayanan, Sriram, Ann S. Marucheck, and Robert B. Handfield. "Electronic Data Interchange: Research Review and Future Directions." *Decision Sciences* 40, no. 1 (February 2009): 121–163.

Pisano, Gary P., and Roberto Verganti. "Which Kind of Collaboration Is Right for You?" *Harvard Business Review* 86, no. 12 (December 2008): 78–86.

Sinha, K. K., and E. J. Kohnke. "Health Care Supply Chain Design." *Decision Sciences* 40, no. 2 (May 2009): 197–212.

Stanley, L. L., and V. R. Singhal. "Service Quality Along the Supply Chain." *Journal of Operations Management* 19, no. 3 (May 2001): 287–306.

Wisner, Joel, K. Tan, and G. Keong Leong. *Principles of Supply Chain Management,* 3rd ed., Mason, OH: Cengage (2009).

Chapter 11 Supplement

Aron, R., and J. V. Singh. "Getting Offshoring Right." *Harvard Business Review* (December 2005): 135–143.

Bravard, J., and R. Morgan. *Smarter Outsourcing*. Upper Saddle River, NJ: Pearson (2006).

Champy, James. *Avoiding the Seven Deadly Sins of Outsourcing Relationships*. Plano, TX: Perot Systems (2005).

Friedman, Thomas. *The World Is Flat: A Brief History of the 21st Century*. New York: Farrar, Straus, and Giroux (2005).

Greenwald, Bruce C., and Judd Kahn. *Globalization: The Irrational Fear That Someone in China Will Take Your Job*. New York: Wiley (2009).

Halvey, J. K., and B. M. Melby. *Business Process Outsourcing*, 2nd ed. New York: Wiley (2007).

Hirschheim, R., A. Heinzl, and J. Dibbern. *Information Systems Outsourcing*. Secaucus, NJ: Springer (2009).

Lee, Hau L., and Chung-Yee Lee. *Building Supply Chain Excellence in Emerging Economies*. Secaucus, NJ: Springer (2007).

Messner, W. *Working with India*, Secaucus, NJ: Springer (2009).

Midler, Paul. *Poorly Made in China: An Insider's Account of the Tactics behind China's Production Game*. New York: Wiley (2009).

Thomas, A. R., and T. J. Wilkinson. "The Outsourcing Compulsion." *MIT Sloan Management Review* 48, no. 1 (Fall 2006): 10.

Webb, L., and J. Laborde. "Crafting a Successful Outsourcing Vendor/Client Relationship." *Business Process Management Journal* 11, no. 5 (2005): 437–443.

Whitten, Dwayne, and Dorothy Leidner. "Bringing IT Back: An Analysis of the Decision to Backsource or Switch Vendors." *Decision Sciences* 37, no. 4 (November 2006): 605–621.

Yourdon, Edward. *Outsource: Competing in the Global Productivity Race*. Upper Saddle River, NJ: Prentice Hall (2005).

Chapter 12

Abernathy, Frederick H., et al. "Control Your Inventory in a World of Lean Retailing." *Harvard Business Review* 78, no. 6 (November–December 2000): 169–176.

Arnold, J. R., S. N. Chapman, and L. M. Clive. *Introduction to Materials Management*, 6th ed. Upper Saddle River, NJ: Prentice Hall (2008).

Bradley, James R., and Richard W. Conway. "Managing Cyclic Inventories." *Production and Operations Management* 12, no. 4 (Winter 2003): 464–479.

Burt, D. N., S. Petcavage, and R. Pinkerton. *Supply Management*, 8th ed. Burr Ridge, IL: Irwin/McGraw (2010).

Chapman, Stephen. *Fundamentals of Production Planning and Control*. Upper Saddle River, NJ: Prentice Hall (2006).

Chopra, Sunil, Gilles Reinhardt, and Maqbool Dada. "The Effect of Lead Time Uncertainty on Safety Stocks." *Decision Sciences* 35, no. 1 (Winter 2004): 1–24.

Keren, Baruch. "The Single Period Inventory Model." *Omega* 37, no. 4 (August 2009): 801.

Liu, X., and Z. Lian. "Cost-effective Inventory Control in a Value-added Manufacturing System." *European Journal of Operational Research* 196, no. 2 (July 2009): 534.

McDonald, Stan C. *Materials Management*. New York: Wiley (2009).

Noblitt, James M. "The Economic Order Quantity Model: Panacea or Plague?" *APICS—The Performance Advantage* (February 2001): 53–57.

Render, B., R. M. Stair, and M. Hanna. *Quantitative Analysis for Management*, 11th ed. Upper Saddle River, NJ: Prentice Hall (2011).

Rubin, Paul A., and W. C. Benton. "A Generalized Framework for Quantity Discount Pricing Schedules." *Decision Sciences* 34, no. 1 (Winter 2003): 173–188.

Vollmann, T. E., W. L. Berry, D. C. Whybark, and F. R. Jacobs. *Manufacturing Planning and Control for Supply Chain Management*, 5th ed. Burr Ridge, IL: Irwin/McGraw (2005).

Witt, Clyde E. "Mobile Warehouse Supplies U.S. Marines in Iraq." *Material Handling Management* 60, no. 8 (August 2005): 24–25.

Chapter 13

Chen, Fangruo. "Salesforce Initiative, Market Information, and Production/Inventory Planning." *Management Science* 51, no. 1 (January 2005): 60–75.

Hopp, Wallace J., and Mark L. Spearman. *Factory Physics*, 3rd ed. New York: Irwin/McGraw-Hill (2008).

Kimes, S. E., and G. M. Thompson. "Restaurant Revenue Management at Chevy's." *Decision Sciences* 35, no. 3 (Summer 2004): 371–393.

Metters, R., K. King-Metters, M. Pullman, and S. Walton. *Successful Service Operations Management*. 2nd ed. Mason, OH: Thompson-South-Western (2006).

Metters, Richard, et al. "The 'Killer Application' of Revenue Management: Harrah's Cherokee Casino and Hotel." *Interfaces* 38, no. 3 (May–June 2008): 161–178.

Mukhopadhyay, S., S. Samaddar, and G. Colville. "Improving Revenue Management Decision Making for Airlines." *Decision Science* 38, no. 2 (May 2007): 309–327.

Plambeck, Erica L., and Terry A. Taylor. "Sell the Plant? The Impact of Contract Manufacturing on Innovation, Capacity, and Profitability." *Management Science* 51, no. 1 (January 2005): 133–150.

Silver, E. A., D. F. Pyke, and R. Peterson. *Inventory Management and Production Planning and Scheduling*. New York: Wiley (1998).

Vollmann, T. E., W. L. Berry, D. C. Whybark, and F. R. Jacobs. *Manufacturing Planning and Control for Supply Chain Management*, 5th ed. Burr Ridge, IL: Irwin (2005).

Chapter 14

Barba-Gutierrez, Y., B. Adenso-Diaz, and S. M. Gupta. "Lot Sizing in Reverse MRP for Scheduling Disassembly." *International Journal of Production Economics* 111, no. 2 (February 2008): 741.

Bell, Steve. "Time Fence Secrets." *APICS* 16, no. 4 (April 2006): 44–48.

Bolander, Steven, and Sam G. Taylor. "Scheduling Techniques: A Comparison of Logic." *Production and Inventory Management Journal* 41, no. 1 (1st Quarter 2000): 1–5.

Crandall, Richard E. "The Epic Life of ERP." *APICS* 16, no. 2 (February 2006): 17–19.

Gattiker, Thomas. "Anatomy of an ERP Implementation Gone Awry." *Production and Inventory Management* 43, nos. 3–4 (3rd/4th Quarter 2002): 96–105.

Kanet, J., and V. Sridharan. "The Value of Using Scheduling Information in Planning Material Requirements." *Decision Sciences* 29, no. 2 (Spring 1998): 479–498.

Koh, S. C. L., and S. M. Saad. "Managing Uncertainty in ERP-controlled Manufacturing Environments." *International Journal of Production Economics* 101, no. 1 (May 2006): 109.

Krupp, James A. G. "Integrating Kanban and MRP to Reduce Lead Time." *Production and Inventory Management Journal* 43, no. 3–4 (3rd/4th quarter 2002): 78–82.

Lawrence, Barry F., Daniel F. Jennings, and Brian E. Reynolds. *ERP in Distribution*. Florence, KY: Thomson South-Western (2005).

Moncrief, Stephen. "Push and Pull." *APICS—The Performance Advantage* (June 2003): 46–51.

Norris, G. *E-Business & ERP*. New York: Wiley (2005).

O'Sullivan, Jill, and Gene Caiola. *Enterprise Resource Planning*, 2nd ed. New York: McGraw-Hill (2008).

Segerstedt, A. "Master Production Scheduling and a Comparison of MRP and Cover-Time Planning." *International Journal of Production Research* 44, no. 18–19 (September 2006): 3585.

Summer, M. *Enterprise Resource Planning*. Upper Saddle River, NJ: Prentice Hall (2005).

Wagner, H. M., and T. M. Whitin. "Dynamic Version of the Economic Lot Size Model." *Management Science* 5, no. 1 (1958): 89–96.

Wu, Jen-Hur, et al. "Using Multiple Variables Decision-Making Analysis for ERP Selection." *International Journal of Manufacturing Technology and Management* 18, no. 2 (2009): 228.

Chapter 15

Baker, Kenneth A., and Dan Trietsch. *Principles of Sequencing and Scheduling*. New York: Wiley (2009).

Bard, Jonathan F. "Staff Scheduling in High Volume Service Facilities with Downgrading." *IIE Transactions* 36 (2004): 985–997.

Bolander, Steven, and Sam G. Taylor. "Scheduling Techniques: A Comparison of Logic." *Production and Inventory Management Journal* (1st Quarter 2000): 1–5.

Cayirli, Tugba, and Emre Veral. "Outpatient Scheduling in Health Care: A Review of Literature." *Production and Operations Management* 12, no. 4 (Winter 2003): 519–549.

Chapman, Stephen. *Fundamentals of Production Planning and Control*. Upper Saddle River, NJ: Prentice Hall (2006).

Deng, Honghui, Q. Wang, G. K. Leong, and S. X. Sun. "Usage of Opportunity Cost to Maximize Performance in Revenue Management." *Decision Sciences* 38, no. 4 (November 2008): 737–758.

Dietrich, Brenda, G. A. Paleologo, and L. Wynter. "Revenue Management in Business Services." *Production and Operations Management* 17, no. 4 (July–August 2008): 475–480.

Farmer, Adam, Jeffrey S. Smith, and Luke T. Miller. "Scheduling Umpire Crews for Professional Tennis Tournaments." *Interfaces* 37, no. 2 (March–April 2007): 187–196.

Geraghty, Kevin. "Revenue Management and Digital Marketing." *OR/MS Today* 35, no. 6 (December 2008): 22–28.

Kellogg, Deborah L., and Steven Walczak. "Nurse Scheduling." *Interfaces* 37, no. 4 (July–August 2007): 355–369.

Lopez, P., and F. Roubellat. *Production Scheduling*. New York: Wiley (2008).

Mondschein, S. V., and G. Y. Weintraub. "Appointment Policies in Service Operations." *Production and Operations Management* 12, no. 2 (Summer 2003): 266–286.

Morton, Thomas E., and David W. Pentico. *Heuristic Scheduling Systems*. New York: Wiley (1993).

Pinedo, M. *Scheduling: Theory, Algorithms, and Systems*, 2nd ed. Upper Saddle River, NJ: Prentice Hall (2002).

Plenert, Gerhard, and Bill Kirchmier. *Finite Capacity Scheduling*. New York: Wiley (2000).

Render, B., R. M. Stair, and M. Hanna. *Quantitative Analysis for Management*, 10th ed. Upper Saddle River, NJ: Prentice Hall (2009).

Chapter 16

Burke, Robert, and Gregg Messel. "From Simulation to Implementation: Cardinal Health's Lean Journey." *Target: Innovation at Work* 19, no. 2 (2nd Quarter 2003): 27–32.

Flinchbauh, Jamie. *The Hitchhiker's Guide to Lean*, Dearborn, MI: Society of Manufacturing Engineers (2006).

Graban, Mark. *Lean Hospitals*. New York: CRC Press (2009).

Hall, Robert W. "'Lean' and the Toyota Production System." *Target* 20, no. 3 (3rd Issue 2004): 22–27.

Keyte, Beau, and Drew Locher. *The Complete Lean Enterprise*. University Park, IL: Productivity Press (2004).

Morgan, James M., and Jeffrey K. Liker. *The Toyota Product Development System*. New York: Productivity Press (2007).

Nelson-Peterson, Dana L., and Carol J. Leppa, "Creating an Environment of Caring Using Lean Principles of the Virginia Mason Production System," *Journal of Nursing Administration* 37 (2007): 289.

Parks, Charles M. "The Bare Necessities of Lean." *Industrial Engineer* 35, no. 8 (August 2003): 39.

Schonberger, Richard J. "Lean Extended." *Industrial Engineer* (December 2005): 26–31.

van Veen-Dirks, Paula. "Management Control and the Production Environment." *International Journal of Production Economics* 93 (January 8, 2005): 263.

Womack, James P., and Daniel T. Jones. "Lean Consumption." *Harvard Business Review* 83 (March 2005): 58–68.

Womack, James P., and Daniel T. Jones. *Lean Solutions: How Companies and Customers Can Create Value and Wealth Together*. New York: The Free Press (2005).

Chapter 17

Bauer, Eric, X. Zhang, and D. A. Kimber. *Practical System Reliability*. New York: Wiley (2009).

Blank, Ronald. *The Basics of Reliability*. University Park, IL: Productivity Press (2004).

Cua, K. O., K. E. McKone, and R. G. Schroeder. "Relationships between Implementation of TQM, JIT, and TPM and Manufacturing Performance." *Journal of Operations Management* 19, no. 6 (November 2001): 675–694.

Finigen, Tim, and Jim Humphries. "Maintenance Gets Lean." *IE Industrial Systems* 38, no. 10 (October 2006): 26–31.

Sova, Roger, and Lea A. P. Tonkin. "Total Productive Maintenance at Crown International." *Target: Innovation at Work* 19, no. 1 (1st Quarter 2003): 41–44.

Stephens, M. P. *Productivity and Reliability-Based Maintenance Management*. Upper Saddle River, NJ: Prentice Hall (2004).

Weil, Marty. "Beyond Preventive Maintenance." *APICS* 16, no. 4 (April 2006): 40–43.

Quantitative Modules A

Balakrishnan, R., B. Render, and R. M. Stair Jr. *Managerial Decision Modeling with Spreadsheets*, 2nd ed. Upper Saddle River, NJ: Prentice Hall (2007).

Buchanan, Leigh, and Andrew O'Connell. "A Brief History of Decision Making." *Harvard Business Review* 84, no. 1 (January, 2006): 32–41.

Hammond, J. S., R. L. Kenney, and H. Raiffa. "The Hidden Traps in Decision Making." *Harvard Business Review* 84, no. 1 (January 2006): 118–126.

Keefer, Donald L. "Balancing Drug Safety and Efficacy for a Go/No-Go Decision." *Interfaces* 34, no. 2 (March–April 2004): 113–116.

Miller, C. C., and R. D. Ireland. "Intuition in Strategic Decision Making." *Academy of Management Executive* 19, no. 1 (February 2005): 19.

Parmigiani, G., and L. Inoue. *Decision Theory: Principles and Approaches*. New York: Wiley (2010).

Raiffa, H., and R. Schlaifer. *Applied Statistical Decision Theory*. New York: Wiley (2000).

Render, B., R. M. Stair Jr., and M. Hanna. *Quantitative Analysis for Management*, 10th ed. Upper Saddle River, NJ: Prentice Hall (2009).

Quantitative Modules B

Boh, W. F., S. A. Slaughter, and J. A. Espinosa. "Learning from Experience in Software Development." *Management Science* 53, no. 8 (August 2007): 1315–1332.

Couto, J. P., and J. C. Teixeira. "Using a Linear Model for Learning Curve Effect on Highrise Floor Construction." *Construction Management & Economics* 23 (May 2005): 355.

McDonald, A., and L. Schrattenholzer. "Learning Curves and Technology Assessment." *International Journal of Technology Management* 23 (2002): 718.

Morrison, J. Bradley. "Putting the Learning Curve into Context." *Journal of Business Research* 61, no. 1 (November 2008): 1182.

Ngwenyama, O., A. Guergachi, and T. McLaren. "Using the Learning Curve to Maximize IT Productivity." *International Journal of Production Economics* 105, no. 2 (February 2007): 524.

Smunt, T. L., and C. A. Watts. "Improving Operations Planning with Learning Curves." *Journal of Operations Management* 21 (January 2003): 93.

Weston, M. *Learning Curves*. New York: Crown Publishing (2000).

Appendices

APPENDIX I   NORMAL CURVE AREAS

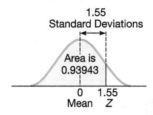

To find the area under the normal curve, you can apply either Table I.1 or Table I.2. In Table I.1, you must know how many standard deviations that point is to the right of the mean. Then, the area under the normal curve can be read directly from the normal table. For example, the total area under the normal curve for a point that is 1.55 standard deviations to the right of the mean is 0.93943.

Table I.1

Z	0.00	0.01	0.02	0.03	0.04	0.05	0.06	0.07	0.08	0.09
0.0	0.50000	0.50399	0.50798	0.51197	0.51595	0.51994	0.52392	0.52790	0.53188	0.53586
0.1	0.53983	0.54380	0.54776	0.55172	0.55567	0.55962	0.56356	0.56749	0.57142	0.57535
0.2	0.57926	0.58317	0.58706	0.59095	0.59483	0.59871	0.60257	0.60642	0.61026	0.61409
0.3	0.61791	0.62172	0.62552	0.62930	0.63307	0.63683	0.64058	0.64431	0.64803	0.65173
0.4	0.65542	0.65910	0.66276	0.66640	0.67003	0.67364	0.67724	0.68082	0.68439	0.68793
0.5	0.69146	0.69497	0.69847	0.70194	0.70540	0.70884	0.71226	0.71566	0.71904	0.72240
0.6	0.72575	0.72907	0.73237	0.73565	0.73891	0.74215	0.74537	0.74857	0.75175	0.75490
0.7	0.75804	0.76115	0.76424	0.76730	0.77035	0.77337	0.77637	0.77935	0.78230	0.78524
0.8	0.78814	0.79103	0.79389	0.79673	0.79955	0.80234	0.80511	0.80785	0.81057	0.81327
0.9	0.81594	0.81859	0.82121	0.82381	0.82639	0.82894	0.83147	0.83398	0.83646	0.83891
1.0	0.84134	0.84375	0.84614	0.84849	0.85083	0.85314	0.85543	0.85769	0.85993	0.86214
1.1	0.86433	0.86650	0.86864	0.87076	0.87286	0.87493	0.87698	0.87900	0.88100	0.88298
1.2	0.88493	0.88686	0.88877	0.89065	0.89251	0.89435	0.89617	0.89796	0.89973	0.90147
1.3	0.90320	0.90490	0.90658	0.90824	0.90988	0.91149	0.91309	0.91466	0.91621	0.91774
1.4	0.91924	0.92073	0.92220	0.92364	0.92507	0.92647	0.92785	0.92922	0.93056	0.93189
1.5	0.93319	0.93448	0.93574	0.93699	0.93822	0.93943	0.94062	0.94179	0.94295	0.94408
1.6	0.94520	0.94630	0.94738	0.94845	0.94950	0.95053	0.95154	0.95254	0.95352	0.95449
1.7	0.95543	0.95637	0.95728	0.95818	0.95907	0.95994	0.96080	0.96164	0.96246	0.96327
1.8	0.96407	0.96485	0.96562	0.96638	0.96712	0.96784	0.96856	0.96926	0.96995	0.97062
1.9	0.97128	0.97193	0.97257	0.97320	0.97381	0.97441	0.97500	0.97558	0.97615	0.97670
2.0	0.97725	0.97784	0.97831	0.97882	0.97932	0.97982	0.98030	0.98077	0.98124	0.98169
2.1	0.98214	0.98257	0.98300	0.98341	0.98382	0.98422	0.98461	0.98500	0.98537	0.98574
2.2	0.98610	0.98645	0.98679	0.98713	0.98745	0.98778	0.98809	0.98840	0.98870	0.98899
2.3	0.98928	0.98956	0.98983	0.99010	0.99036	0.99061	0.99086	0.99111	0.99134	0.99158
2.4	0.99180	0.99202	0.99224	0.99245	0.99266	0.99286	0.99305	0.99324	0.99343	0.99361
2.5	0.99379	0.99396	0.99413	0.99430	0.99446	0.99461	0.99477	0.99492	0.99506	0.99520
2.6	0.99534	0.99547	0.99560	0.99573	0.99585	0.99598	0.99609	0.99621	0.99632	0.99643
2.7	0.99653	0.99664	0.99674	0.99683	0.99693	0.99702	0.99711	0.99720	0.99728	0.99736
2.8	0.99744	0.99752	0.99760	0.99767	0.99774	0.99781	0.99788	0.99795	0.99801	0.99807
2.9	0.99813	0.99819	0.99825	0.99831	0.99836	0.99841	0.99846	0.99851	0.99856	0.99861
3.0	0.99865	0.99869	0.99874	0.99878	0.99882	0.99886	0.99899	0.99893	0.99896	0.99900
3.1	0.99903	0.99906	0.99910	0.99913	0.99916	0.99918	0.99921	0.99924	0.99926	0.99929
3.2	0.99931	0.99934	0.99936	0.99938	0.99940	0.99942	0.99944	0.99946	0.99948	0.99950
3.3	0.99952	0.99953	0.99955	0.99957	0.99958	0.99960	0.99961	0.99962	0.99964	0.99965
3.4	0.99966	0.99968	0.99969	0.99970	0.99971	0.99972	0.99973	0.99974	0.99975	0.99976
3.5	0.99977	0.99978	0.99978	0.99979	0.99980	0.99981	0.99981	0.99982	0.99983	0.99983
3.6	0.99984	0.99985	0.99985	0.99986	0.99986	0.99987	0.99987	0.99988	0.99988	0.99989
3.7	0.99989	0.99990	0.99990	0.99990	0.99991	0.99991	0.99992	0.99992	0.99992	0.99992
3.8	0.99993	0.99993	0.99993	0.99994	0.99994	0.99994	0.99994	0.99995	0.99995	0.99995
3.9	0.99995	0.99995	0.99996	0.99996	0.99996	0.99996	0.99996	0.99996	0.99997	0.99997

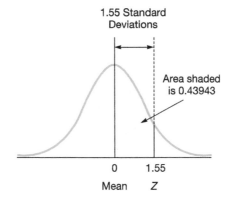

As an alternative to Table I.1, the numbers in Table I.2 represent the proportion of the total area away from the mean, μ, to one side. For example, the area between the mean and a point that is 1.55 standard deviations to its right is 0.43943.

Table I.2

Z	0.00	0.01	0.02	0.03	0.04	0.05	0.06	0.07	0.08	0.09
0.0	0.00000	0.00399	0.00798	0.01197	0.01595	0.01994	0.02392	0.02790	0.03188	0.03586
0.1	0.03983	0.04380	0.04776	0.05172	0.05567	0.05962	0.06356	0.06749	0.07142	0.07535
0.2	0.07926	0.08317	0.08706	0.09095	0.09483	0.09871	0.10257	0.10642	0.11026	0.11409
0.3	0.11791	0.12172	0.12552	0.12930	0.13307	0.13683	0.14058	0.14431	0.14803	0.15173
0.4	0.15542	0.15910	0.16276	0.16640	0.17003	0.17364	0.17724	0.18082	0.18439	0.18793
0.5	0.19146	0.19497	0.19847	0.20194	0.20540	0.20884	0.21226	0.21566	0.21904	0.22240
0.6	0.22575	0.22907	0.23237	0.23565	0.23891	0.24215	0.24537	0.24857	0.25175	0.25490
0.7	0.25804	0.26115	0.26424	0.26730	0.27035	0.27337	0.27637	0.27935	0.28230	0.28524
0.8	0.28814	0.29103	0.29389	0.29673	0.29955	0.30234	0.30511	0.30785	0.31057	0.31327
0.9	0.31594	0.31859	0.32121	0.32381	0.32639	0.32894	0.33147	0.33398	0.33646	0.33891
1.0	0.34134	0.34375	0.34614	0.34850	0.35083	0.35314	0.35543	0.35769	0.35993	0.36214
1.1	0.36433	0.36650	0.36864	0.37076	0.37286	0.37493	0.37698	0.37900	0.38100	0.38298
1.2	0.38493	0.38686	0.38877	0.39065	0.39251	0.39435	0.39617	0.39796	0.39973	0.40147
1.3	0.40320	0.40490	0.40658	0.40824	0.40988	0.41149	0.41309	0.41466	0.41621	0.41174
1.4	0.41924	0.42073	0.42220	0.42364	0.42507	0.42647	0.42786	0.42922	0.43056	0.43189
1.5	0.43319	0.43448	0.43574	0.43699	0.43822	0.43943	0.44062	0.44179	0.44295	0.44408
1.6	0.44520	0.44630	0.44738	0.44845	0.44950	0.45053	0.45154	0.45254	0.45352	0.45449
1.7	0.45543	0.45637	0.45728	0.45818	0.45907	0.45994	0.46080	0.46164	0.46246	0.46327
1.8	0.46407	0.46485	0.46562	0.46638	0.46712	0.46784	0.46856	0.46926	0.46995	0.47062
1.9	0.47128	0.47193	0.47257	0.47320	0.47381	0.47441	0.47500	0.47558	0.47615	0.47670
2.0	0.47725	0.47778	0.47831	0.47882	0.47932	0.47982	0.48030	0.48077	0.48124	0.48169
2.1	0.48214	0.48257	0.48300	0.48341	0.48382	0.48422	0.48461	0.48500	0.48537	0.48574
2.2	0.48610	0.48645	0.48679	0.48713	0.48745	0.48778	0.48809	0.48840	0.48870	0.48899
2.3	0.48928	0.48956	0.48983	0.49010	0.49036	0.49061	0.49086	0.49111	0.49134	0.49158
2.4	0.49180	0.49202	0.49224	0.49245	0.49266	0.49286	0.49305	0.49324	0.49343	0.49361
2.5	0.49379	0.49396	0.49413	0.49430	0.49446	0.49461	0.49477	0.49492	0.49506	0.49520
2.6	0.49534	0.49547	0.49560	0.49573	0.49585	0.49598	0.49609	0.49621	0.49632	0.49643
2.7	0.49653	0.49664	0.49674	0.49683	0.49693	0.49702	0.49711	0.49720	0.49728	0.49736
2.8	0.49744	0.49752	0.49760	0.49767	0.49774	0.49781	0.49788	0.49795	0.49801	0.49807
2.9	0.49813	0.49819	0.49825	0.49831	0.49836	0.49841	0.49846	0.49851	0.49856	0.49861
3.0	0.49865	0.49869	0.49874	0.49878	0.49882	0.49886	0.49889	0.49893	0.49897	0.49900
3.1	0.49903	0.49906	0.49910	0.49913	0.49916	0.49918	0.49921	0.49924	0.49926	0.49929

APPENDIX II VALUES OF $e^{-\lambda}$ FOR USE IN THE POISSON DISTRIBUTION

Values of $e^{-\lambda}$

λ	$e^{-\lambda}$	λ	$e^{-\lambda}$	λ	$e^{-\lambda}$	λ	$e^{-\lambda}$
0.0	10.0000	1.6	0.2019	3.1	0.0450	4.6	0.0101
0.1	0.9048	1.7	0.1827	3.2	0.0408	4.7	0.0091
0.2	0.8187	1.8	0.1653	3.3	0.0369	4.8	0.0082
0.3	0.7408	1.9	0.1496	3.4	0.0334	4.9	0.0074
0.4	0.6703	2.0	0.1353	3.5	0.0302	5.0	0.0067
0.5	0.6065	2.1	0.1225	3.6	0.0273	5.1	0.0061
0.6	0.5488	2.2	0.1108	3.7	0.0247	5.2	0.0055
0.7	0.4966	2.3	0.1003	3.8	0.0224	5.3	0.0050
0.8	0.4493	2.4	0.0907	3.9	0.0202	5.4	0.0045
0.9	0.4066	2.5	0.0821	4.0	0.0183	5.5	0.0041
1.0	0.3679	2.6	0.0743	4.1	0.0166	5.6	0.0037
1.1	0.3329	2.7	0.0672	4.2	0.0150	5.7	0.0033
1.2	0.3012	2.8	0.0608	4.3	0.0136	5.8	0.0030
1.3	0.2725	2.9	0.0550	4.4	0.0123	5.9	0.0027
1.4	0.2466	3.0	0.0498	4.5	0.0111	6.0	0.0025
1.5	0.2231						

APPENDIX III TABLE OF RANDOM NUMBERS

52	06	50	88	53	30	10	47	99	37	66	91	35	32	00	84	57	07
37	63	28	02	74	35	24	03	29	60	74	85	90	73	59	55	17	60
82	57	68	28	05	94	03	11	27	79	90	87	92	41	09	25	36	77
69	02	36	49	71	99	32	10	75	21	95	90	94	38	97	71	72	49
98	94	90	36	06	78	23	67	89	85	29	21	25	73	69	34	85	76
96	52	62	87	49	56	59	23	78	71	72	90	57	01	98	57	31	95
33	69	27	21	11	60	95	89	68	48	17	89	34	09	93	50	44	51
50	33	50	95	13	44	34	62	64	39	55	29	30	64	49	44	30	16
88	32	18	50	62	57	34	56	62	31	15	40	90	34	51	95	26	14
90	30	36	24	69	82	51	74	30	35	36	85	01	55	92	64	09	85
50	48	61	18	85	23	08	54	17	12	80	69	24	84	92	16	49	59
27	88	21	62	69	64	48	31	12	73	02	68	00	16	16	46	13	85
45	14	46	32	13	49	66	62	74	41	86	98	92	98	84	54	33	40
81	02	01	78	82	74	97	37	45	31	94	99	42	49	27	64	89	42
66	83	14	74	27	76	03	33	11	97	59	81	72	00	64	61	13	52
74	05	81	82	93	09	96	33	52	78	13	06	28	30	94	23	37	39
30	34	87	01	74	11	46	82	59	94	25	34	32	23	17	01	58	73
59	55	72	33	62	13	74	68	22	44	42	09	32	46	71	79	45	89
67	09	80	98	99	25	77	50	03	32	36	63	65	75	94	19	95	88
60	77	46	63	71	69	44	22	03	85	14	48	69	13	30	50	33	24
60	08	19	29	36	72	30	27	50	64	85	72	75	29	87	05	75	01
80	45	86	99	02	34	87	08	86	84	49	76	24	08	01	86	29	11
53	84	49	63	26	65	72	84	85	63	26	02	75	26	92	62	40	67
69	84	12	94	51	36	17	02	15	29	16	52	56	43	26	22	08	62
37	77	13	10	02	18	31	19	32	85	31	94	81	43	31	58	33	51

Source: Excerpted from *A Million Random Digits with 100,000 Normal Deviates*, The Free Press (1955): 7, with permission of the RAND Corporation.

APPENDIX IV   USING EXCEL OM AND POM FOR WINDOWS

Two approaches to computer-aided decision making are provided with this text: **Excel OM** and **POM** (Production and Operations Management) **for Windows**. These are the two most user-friendly software packages available to help you learn and understand operations management. Both programs can be used either to solve homework problems identified with a computer logo or to check answers you have developed by hand. Both software packages use the standard Windows interface and run on any IBM-compatible PC operating Windows XP or better.

EXCEL OM

Excel OM has also been designed to help you to better learn and understand both OM and Excel. Even though the software contains 24 modules and more than 50 submodules, the screens for every module are consistent and easy to use. Modules can be accessed through either of two menus that are added to Excel. The Heizer menu lists the modules in *chapter* order as illustrated for Excel 2007 in Program IV.1. The Excel OM menu lists the modules in alphabetical order, as illustrated for earlier versions of Excel in Program IV.2. This software is provided at no cost to purchasers of this textbook at MyOMLab. Excel 2000 or better must be on your PC.

To install Excel OM, after the web page opens, click on the Software option on the left-hand side, click on Excel OM (version 3), and follow the instructions. Default values have been assigned in the setup program, but you may change them if you like. The default folder into which the program will be installed is named **C:\ProgramFiles\ExcelOM3**, and the default name for the program group placed in the START menu is Excel OM 3. Generally speaking, it is simply necessary to click NEXT each time the installation asks a question.

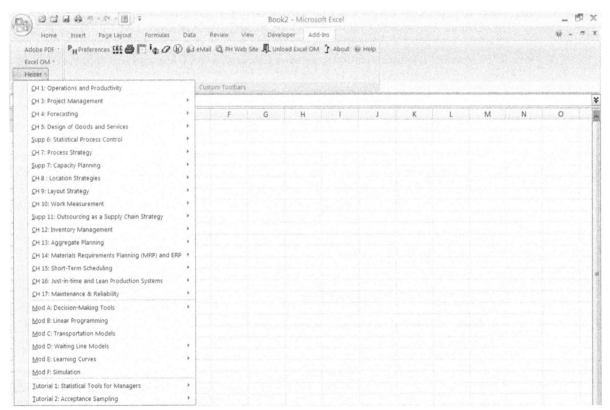

▲ **PROGRAM IV.1**   **Excel OM Modules in Add-Ins Tab in Excel 2007**

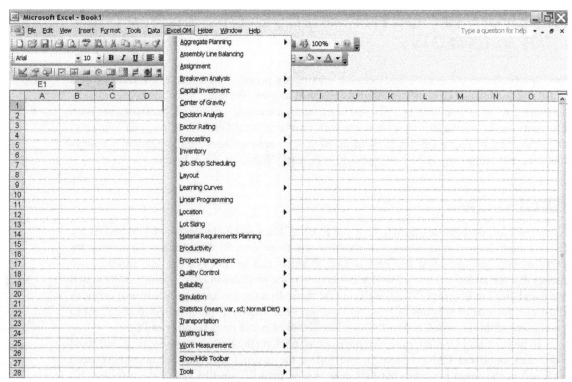

▲ **PROGRAM IV.2**   Excel OM Modules Menu in Main Excel Menu for Versions of Excel Prior to Excel 2007

STARTING THE PROGRAM

To start Excel OM, double-click on the Excel OM 3 shortcut placed on the desktop during installation. Alternatively, you may click on START, PROGRAMS, EXCEL OM 3. In Excel 2007 the Excel OM menu will appear in the Add-Ins tab of the Excel 2007 ribbon as displayed in Program IV.1, while in earlier versions of Excel the Excel OM menu will appear in the main menu of Excel as displayed in Program IV.2.

If you have Excel 2007 and do not see an Add-Ins tab on the ribbon or do not see Excel OM 3 on this tab as displayed in Program IV.1, then your Excel 2007 security settings need to be revised to enable Excel OM 3. Please consult the Excel 2007 instructions at the support site, **www.prenhall.com/weiss**.

Excel OM serves two purposes in the learning process. First, it can simply help you solve homework problems. You enter the appropriate data, and the program provides numerical solutions. POM for Windows operates on the same principle. However, Excel OM allows for a second approach; that is, noting the Excel *formulas* used to develop solutions and modifying them to deal with a wider variety of problems. This 'open' approach enables you to observe, understand, and even change the formulas underlying the Excel calculations, hopefully conveying Excel's power as an OM analysis tool.

POM FOR WINDOWS

POM for Windows is decision support software that is also offered free to students who purchased this text and is available at MyOMLab. Program IV.3 shows a list of 24 OM modules that will be installed on your hard drive. Once you follow the standard setup instructions, a POM for Windows program icon will be added to your start menu and desktop. The program may be accessed by double-clicking on the icon. Updates to POM for Windows are available on the internet through the Pearson download library, found at **www.prenhall.com/weiss**.

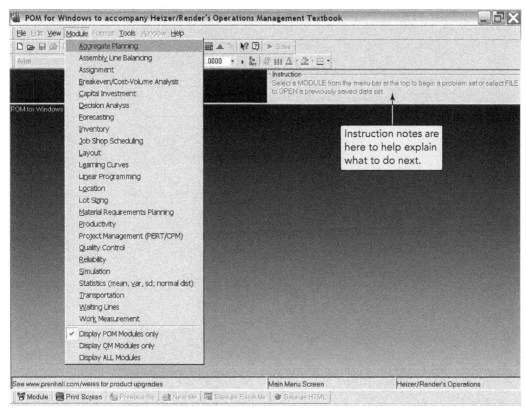

▲ **PROGRAM IV.3   POM for Windows Module List**

APPENDIX V SOLUTIONS TO EVEN-NUMBERED PROBLEMS

Chapter 1

1.2 (a) 2 valves/hr.
   (b) 2.25 valves/hr.
   (c) 12.5%

1.4 Productivity of labor: 9.3%
   Productivity of resin: 11.1%
   Productivity of capital: −10.0%
   Productivity of energy: 6.1%

1.6 (a) 0.0096 rugs/labor-dollar
   (b) 0.00787 rugs/dollar

1.8 Multifactor productivity is:
   375 autos ÷ [(US$20 × 10,000) + (US$1,000 × 500)
   + (US$3 × 100,000)]
   = 375 ÷ (200,000 + 500,000 + 300,000) = 375 ÷ 1,000,000
   = 0.000375 autos per dollar of inputs

1.10 Add one worker.

1.12
$$\text{Old process} = \frac{1,500}{(640 \times 8) + 500 + (1,500 \times 0.35)}$$
$$= \frac{1,500}{6,145} = 0.244$$
$$\text{New process} = \frac{1,875}{(800 \times 8) + 500 + (1,875 \times 0.35)}$$
$$= \frac{1,875}{7,556.25} = 0.248$$
$$\text{Percentage change} = \frac{0.248 - 0.244}{0.244} = 1.6\%$$

Chapter 2

2.2 Cost leadership: Sodexho
   Response: a catering firm
   Differentiation: a fine-dining restaurant

2.4 Some general thoughts to get you going:
   (a) Energy costs change the cost structure of airlines.
   (b) Environmental constraints force changes in process technology (paint manufacturing and application) and product design (autos).

Chapter 3

3.2 Here are some detailed activities for the first two activities for Mr. Aljasser's WBS:
   1.11 Set initial goals for fundraising.
   1.12 Set strategy, including identifying sources and solicitation.
   1.13 Raise the funds.
   1.21 Identify voters' concerns.
   1.22 Analyze competitor's voting record.
   1.23 Establish position on issues.

3.4

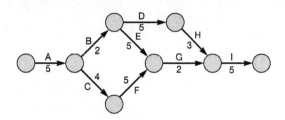

   (a) A–C–F–G–I is critical path.
   (b) 21 days.
   This is an AOA network.

3.6 (a)

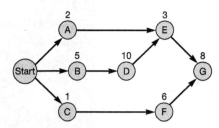

   (b) B–D–E–G
   (c) 26 days.
   (d)

Activity	Slack
A	13
B	0
C	11
D	0
E	0
F	11
G	0

3.8

Activity	Time	ES	EF	LS	LF	Slack	Critical
A	6	0	6	2	8	2	No
B	7	0	7	0	7	0	Yes
C	3	6	9	8	11	2	No
D	2	6	8	12	14	6	No
E	4	7	11	7	11	0	Yes
F	6	7	13	8	14	1	No
G	10	11	21	11	21	0	Yes
H	7	13	20	14	21	1	No

The critical path is given for activities B, E, and G.
Total project completion time is 21 weeks.

3.10

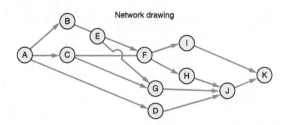

Network drawing

   (a) 12 weeks.
   (b) Variance for C is $\left[\dfrac{(16-8)}{6}\right]^2 = \dfrac{16}{9} = 1.78$
   (c) A–C–F–H–J–K
   (d) = 40.18 weeks (rounded)
   (e) 10.03
   (f) $Z = \dfrac{36 - 40.18}{3.17} = -1.32$, which is about 9.6% chance (0.096 probability) of completing project before week 36.

3.12 (a) A–C–E–H–I–K–M–N; 50 days
   (b) 82.1%
   (c) 58 days

Chapter 4

4.2 (a) None obvious.

    (b) 7, 7.67, 9, 10, 11, 11, 11.33, 11, 9

    (c) 6.4, 7.8, 11, 9.6, 10.9, 12.2, 10.5, 10.6, 8.4

    (d) The 3-yr. moving average.

4.4 (a) 41.6

    (b) 42.3

    (c) Banking industry's seasonality.

4.6 72

4.8 $y = 421 + 33.6x$. When $x = 6$, $y = 622.8$.

4.10 (a)

	Actual	Forecast	|Error|	|% Error|
March	101	120	19	100 (19 ÷ 101) = 18.81%
April	96	114	18	100 (18 ÷ 96) = 18.75%
May	89	110	21	100 (21 ÷ 89) = 23.60%
June	108	108	0	100 (0 ÷ 108) = 0%
			58	61.16%

$$\text{MAD (for management)} = \frac{58}{4} = 14.5$$

$$\text{MAPE (for management)} = \frac{61.16\%}{4} = 15.29\%$$

    (b)

	Actual	Naive	|Error|	|% Error|
March	101	83	18	100 (18 ÷ 101) = 17.82%
April	96	101	5	100 (5 ÷ 96) = 5.21%
May	89	96	7	100 (7 ÷ 89) = 7.87%
June	108	89	19	100 (19 ÷ 108) = 17.59%
			49	48.49%

$$\text{MAD (for naive)} = \frac{49}{4} = 12.25$$

$$\text{MAPE (for naive)} = \frac{48.49\%}{4} = 12.12\%.$$

    Naive outperforms management.

    (c) MAD for the manager's technique is 14.5, while MAD for the naive forecast is only 12.25. MAPEs are 15.29% and 12.12%, respectively. So the naive method is better.

4.12 1,680 boats

4.14 (a) = 13,473 + 37.65(1860) = 83,502

    (b) The predicted selling price is US$83,502, but this is the average price for a house of this size. There are other factors besides square footage that will impact the selling price of a house. If such a house sold for US$95,000, then these other factors could be contributing to the additional value.

    (c) Some other quantitative variables would be age of the house, number of bedrooms, size of the lot, and size of the garage, etc.

    (d) Coefficient of determination = $(0.63)^2$ = 0.397. This means that only about 39.7% of the variability in the sales price of a house is explained by this regression model that only includes square footage as the explanatory variable.

4.16 (a) $y = -0.158 + 0.1308x$

    (b) 2.719

    (c) $r = 0.966$; $r^2 = 0.934$

4.18 Trend adjustment does not appear to give any significant improvement.

Chapter 5

5.2 House of quality for a lunch:

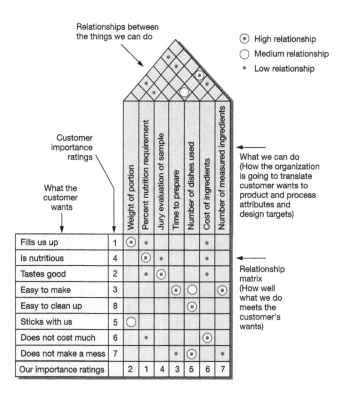

5.4 Individual answer. Build a house of quality similar to the one shown in Problem 5.2, entering the *wants* on the left and entering the *hows* at the top.

5.6 An assembly chart for the eyeglasses is shown below:

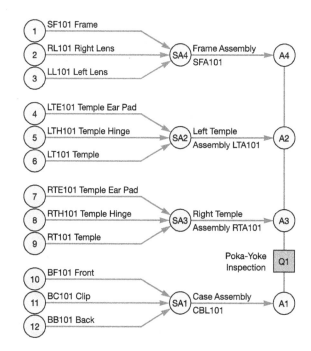

5.8 Assembly chart for a table lamp:

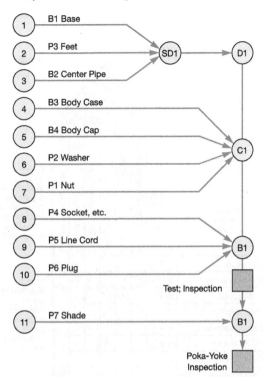

5.10 Possible strategies:

Kindle (growth phase):

Increase capacity and improve balance of production system.

Attempt to make production facilities more efficient.

Netbook (introductory phase):

Increase R&D to better define required product characteristics.

Modify and improve production process.

Develop supplier and distribution systems.

Hand calculator (decline phase):

Concentrate on production and distribution cost reduction.

Chapter 6

6.2 Individual answer, in the style of Figure 6.6(b).

6.4 Individual answer, in the style of Figure 6.6(f).

6.6 Partial flowchart for planning a party:

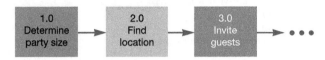

6.8 See figure below.

6.10 Individual answer, in the style of Figure 6.7 in the chapter.

6.12 (a)

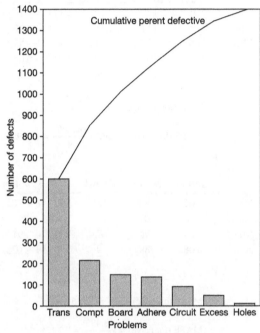

(b) Conclusion: Most of the errors are the result of misplaced transistors.

▼ *Figure for Problem 6.8.*

Fish-Bone Chart for Dissatisfied Airline Customer

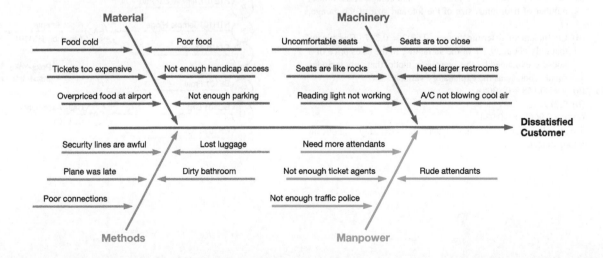

Chapter 7

7.2

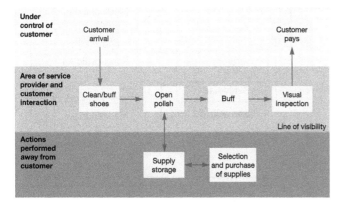

7.4

7.6 GPE is best below 100,000.
FMS is best between 100,000 and 300,000.
DM is best over 300,000.

7.8 Optimal process will change at 100,000 and 300,000.

7.10 (a) Intermittent
(b) US$200,000

Chapter 7 Supplement

S7.2 69.2%

S7.4 88.9%

S7.6 Converting each capacity to a process time, Station 1 = 60 min./hr. ÷ 20 units/hr. = 3 min./unit (for both Machine A and Machine B); Station 2 = 60 min./hr. ÷ 5 units/hr. = 12 min./unit; and Station 3 = 60 min./hr. ÷ 12 units/hr. = 5 min./unit.

(a) Process time for the system (the bottleneck) is Station 2, at 12 min./unit.

(b) Bottleneck operation is Station 2, at 12 min. per unit.

(c) Both paths through the system have the same process cycle time = 3 + 12 + 5 = 20 minutes. (The parallel stations have no effect on process cycle time.)

(d) Weekly capacity = 60 min. × 10 hr. × 5 days ÷ 12 min. at the bottleneck = 3,000 min. ÷ 12 min. for each unit = 250 units per week.

S7.8 (a) US$18,750
(b) 375,000

S7.10 Yes, purchase new equipment and raise price. Profit = US$2,500.

Chapter 8

8.2 India is US$.05 less than elsewhere.

8.4 ICA should locate in Dubai.

8.6 (a) Thailand rates highest (3.1).
(b) Now Thailand's overall score drops to 2.7, just ahead (but not by much) of Taiwan and Singapore.

(c) Now Thailand's score drops to 2.3, leaving the other two countries in a tie for first place.

8.8 (a) Site 1 up to 125, site 2 from 125 to 233, site 3 above 233
(b) Site 2

8.10 (a) The center of gravity is (66.69, 30.22).
(b) The new coordinates become (66.74, 31.18). Coordinate denominators increase (by 2,000 + 2,000) to 72,000. The x-coordinate numerator increases (by 55(2,000) + 80(2,000)) to 4,805,000. The y-coordinate numerator increases (by 45(2,000) + 50(2,000)) to 2,245,000.

Chapter 9

9.2 $(23 \times 10) + (32 \times 5) + (20 \times 8) = 230 + 160 + 160 = 550$
$$\text{Cost} = 550 \times \text{US\$2} = \text{US\$1,100}$$

9.4 B and C should be adjacent, because they have the most trips. Traffic is next heaviest between A and D, so they should be adjacent. Continuing in this fashion, F should be adjacent to D and A should be next to F, but the latter two have already been placed. Finally, E should be placed next to F. Thus, we are left with:

(a) Heuristic solutions:

| B | C | A | D | F | E | = 47,900.

or

| A | D | F | E | B | C | = 44,440.

(*Note:* These are *not* the optimal solution.)

(b) Better layout:

| A | D | F | C | B | E | = 43,880.

9.6 (a)

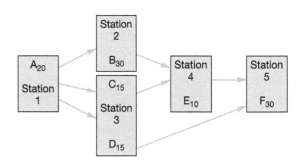

(b) Cycle time = 30 sec./unit

(c) 4 stations = *theoretical* minimum, but 5 are needed

(d) Station 1–Task A; 2–B; 3–C, D; 4–E; 5–F

(e) Total idle = 30 sec.

(f) E = 80% with 5 stations; E = 66.6% with 6 stations

9.8 (a)

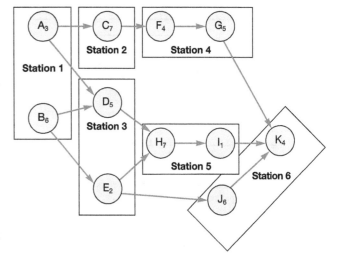

(b) $\left(\dfrac{24\,\text{hr.}}{96\,\text{units}}\right)\left(\dfrac{60\,\text{min.}}{\text{hr.}}\right) = 15\,\text{min.}$

(c) $\left(\dfrac{1\,\text{unit}}{10\,\text{min.}}\right)\left(\dfrac{60\,\text{min.}}{\text{hr.}}\right)\left(\dfrac{24\,\text{hr.}}{\text{day}}\right) = 144\,\text{units per day.}$

(d) $\dfrac{50\,\text{min. per unit}}{10\,\text{min. per cycle}} = 5\,\text{stations}$

(e) Efficiency $= \dfrac{\text{Time needed per unit}}{\text{Time allocated per unit}}$

$= \dfrac{\text{Total task time}}{(\text{Cycle time})\,(\text{Number of stations})}$

$= \dfrac{50}{(10)(6)}$

$= \dfrac{50}{60}$

$= 0.8333,\ \text{or } 83.33\%$

(f) Idle time = Time allocated per unit − Time needed per unit

$= 60 - 50$

$= 10\,\text{min./cycle}$

(g) Best assignment is shown in part (a) with the efficiency shown in part (e) (i.e. 83.33%)

9.10 **(a)** One possible layout is:

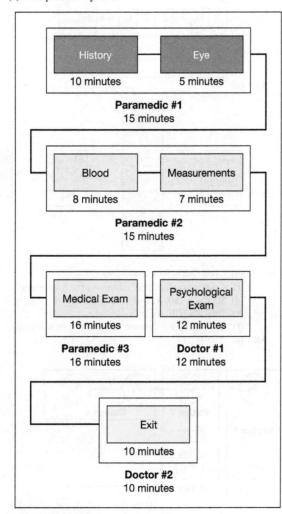

(b) 3.75 patients per hour.

(c) The medical exam station—16 minutes.

(d) Paramedics are idle 2 minutes, and doctors are idle 10 minutes for each patient.

(e) If one more doctor and one more paramedic are added, it is possible to increase the throughput to at least five per hour with this simple layout:

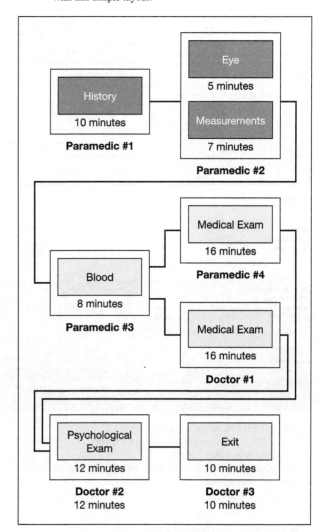

The bottlenecks are now the two stations, psychological exam and eye/measurements, taking 12 minutes.

Chapter 10

10.2

Time	Operator	Time	Machine	Time
1	Prepare Mill	1	Idle	1
2	Load Mill	2		2
3	Idle	3	Mill Operating (Cutting Material)	3
4		4		4
5	Unload Mill	5	Idle	5
6		6		6

10.4

PROCESS CHART _____					**SUMMARY**
CHARTED BY _____				● Operation	14
				➡ Transport	4
				▪ Inspect	1
DATE ____ SHEET 1 OF 1				◗ Delay	
				▽ Store	
PROBLEM Adding A Memory Board				Vert. Dist.	
To Your Computer				Hor. Dist.	68
				Time (min)	24.7

DISTA-NCE (FT)	TIME (MINS)	CHART SYMBOLS	PROCESS DESCRIPTION
	0.2	●➡▪◗▽	Turn computer off
	2.0	●➡▪◗▽	Disconnect all cables
30	1.0	●➡▪◗▽	Move computer to table top
	1.5	●➡▪◗▽	Remove screws from cover
	1.0	●➡▪◗▽	Remove cover
3	0.1	●➡▪◗▽	Set cover on floor
	0.5	●➡▪◗▽	Find board to be replaced
5	0.2	●➡▪◗▽	Bring box with new board to table
	1.0	●➡▪◗▽	Unpack new board
	1.0	●➡▪◗▽	Remove old board
	1.5	●➡▪◗▽	Insert new board
	1.5	●➡▪◗▽	Set jumpers
	1.5	●➡▪◗▽	Set DIP switches
	1.3	●➡▪◗▽	Replace cover
	1.5	●➡▪◗▽	Replace screws in cover
30	0.7	●➡▪◗▽	Move computer to desktop
	2.5	●➡▪◗▽	Install cabling
	0.2	●➡▪◗▽	Turn on computer
	5.5	●➡▪◗▽	Test new memory

10.6 The first portion of the activity chart is shown below.

ACTIVITY CHART

	OPERATOR #1		OPERATOR #2		OPERATIONS: Wash and Dry Dishes
	TIME	%	TIME	%	EQUIPMENT: Sink, Drip Rack, Towels, Soap
WORK	11.75	84	11.75	84	OPERATOR:
IDLE	2.25	16	2.25	16	STUDY NO.: 1 ANALYST: HSM

SUBJECT				DATE	
PRESENT (PROPOSED) DEPT. HOUSECLEANING				SHEET 1 OF 1 CHART BY Hank	
	TIME	Operator #1	TIME	Operator #2	TIME
		Fill sink w/dishes		Idle	
		Fill sink w/soap/water		Idle	
		Wash dishes (2 min.)		Idle	
		Fill sink w/dishes (1 min.)		Rinse (1 min.)	
				Dry dishes (3 min.)	

10.8 $NT = \text{Avg} \times PR = 8.5 \times 1.10 = 9.35$ seconds; worker is faster than normal

10.10   **(a)** $ST = \dfrac{NT}{1 - AF} = \dfrac{9.35}{1 - 0.15} = 11$ seconds

      (b) $ST = \dfrac{NT}{1 - AF} = \dfrac{7.65}{1 - 0.18} = 9.33$ seconds

10.12   **(a)** 12.0 sec.

      (b) 14.12 sec.

10.14   **(a)** Normal time = 3.083 minutes

      (b) Standard time = $\dfrac{\text{Normal time}}{1 - \text{Total allowance}}$

                $= \dfrac{3.083}{1.0 - 0.20} = 3.85$ minutes

10.16   **(a)** 45.36, 13.75, 3.6, 15.09

      (b) 91.53 min.

      (c) 96 samples

10.18   **(a)** $\dfrac{250}{300} = 0.833 = 83.3\%$

      (b) $n = \dfrac{Z^2 p(1 - p)}{h^2}$

          = (at 95% confidence level and 3% acceptable error)

          $n = \dfrac{(1.96)^2 (0.167)(0.833)}{(0.03)^2}$

            $= \dfrac{(3.84)(0.167)(0.833)}{0.0009} = 593.7 \cong 594$

      (c) The sample size was only about half the desired size.

Chapter 11

11.2   Donna, Inc., 8.2; Kay Corp., 9.8

11.4   **(a)** US\$3.13

      (b) US\$7.69

11.6   **(a)** Option a is most economical.

      (b) The customer requirements may demand a faster schedule.

11.8   **(a)** Turnover = $\dfrac{\text{Cost of sales}}{\text{Inventory}} = \dfrac{\text{US\$21,500}}{\text{US\$1,250}} = 17.2$

      (b) Inventory investment = $\dfrac{\text{Inventory}}{\text{Total assets}}$

                       $= \dfrac{\text{US\$1,250}}{\text{US\$16,600}} = 0.0753 \Rightarrow 7.53\%$

      (c) Baker is doing better than the industry. It has a turnover of 17.2 versus 13 for the industry and only 7.5% of its assets invested in inventory versus 8% for the industry.

Chapter 11 Supplement

S11.2   **(a)** Canada, 1.7

       (b) No change

S11.4

Provider	Score
A	$5w + 320 = (60 + 15 + 125 + 15 + 30 + 75)$
B	$4w + 330$
C	$3w + 370$
D	$5w + 255$

Find all w from 1–30 so that:

     $3w + 370 \geq 5w + 320$, or $50 \geq 2w$, or $w \leq 25$

     $3w + 370 \geq 4w + 330$, or $40 \geq w$, or $w \leq 40$

     $3w + 370 \geq 5w + 255$, or $115 \geq 2w$, or $w \leq 57.5$

Company C is recommended for all w such that $1.0 \leq w \leq 25.0$.

Chapter 12

12.2   **(a)** EOQ = $Q = \sqrt{\dfrac{2(19,500)(25)}{4}} = 493.71 = 494$ units

      (b) Annual holdings costs = $[Q \div 2]H = [494 \div 2](4) = $ US\$988

      (c) Annual ordering costs = $[D \div Q]S = [19,500 \div 494](25) = $ US\$987

12.4 (a) 2,100 units
 (b) 4,200 units
 (c) 1,050 units
12.6 (a) 189.74 units
 (b) 94.87
 (c) 31.62
 (d) 7.91
 (e) US$1,897.30
 (f) US$601,897
12.8 (a) 671 units
 (b) 18.63
 (c) 559 = max. inventory
 (d) 16.7%
 (e) US$1,117.90
12.10 (a) 1,217 units
 (b) 1,095 = max. inventory
 (c) 8.22 production runs
 (d) US$657.30
12.12 The solution to any quantity discount model involves determining the total cost of each alternative after quantities have been computed and adjusted for the original problem and every discount. We start the analysis with no discount:

$$\text{EOQ (no discount)} = \sqrt{\frac{2(1,400)(25)}{0.2(400)}} = 29.6 \text{ units}$$

Total cost (no discount)
= Cost of goods + Ordering cost + Carrying cost

$$= \text{US\$400}(1,400) + \frac{1,400(25)}{29.6} + \frac{29.6(\text{US\$400})(0.2)}{2}$$

$$= \text{US\$560,000} + \text{US\$1,183} + \text{US\$1,183} = \text{US\$562,366}$$

The next step is to compute the total cost for the discount:

$$\text{EOQ (with discount)} = \sqrt{\frac{2(1,400)(25)}{0.2(\text{US\$380})}} = 30.3 \text{ units}$$

EOQ (adjusted) = 300 units

Because this last economic order quantity is below the discounted price, we must adjust the order quantity to 300 units. The adjusted EOQ for 300 units is used to compute total cost.

Total cost (with discount)
= Cost of goods + Ordering cost + Carrying cost

$$= \text{US\$380}(1,400) + \frac{1,400(25)}{300} + \frac{300(\text{US\$380})(0.2)}{2}$$

$$= \text{US\$532,000} + \text{US\$117} + \text{US\$11,400} = \text{US\$543,517}$$

The optimal strategy is to order 300 units at a total cost of US$543,517, so the quantity discount should be taken.
12.14 (a) EOQ = 410
 (b) Vendor Suad has slightly lower cost.
 (c) Optimal order quantity = 1,000 @ total cost of US$128,920

12.16 (a) $\mu = 60$; $\sigma = 7$
 Safety stock for 90% service level = σZ(at 0.90)
 $= 7 \times 1.28 = 8.96 \approx 9$
 (b) ROP = $60 + 9 = 69$ BX-5 bandages.
12.18 100 kilos of safety stock
12.20 (a) 2,291 towels
 (b) 291 towels
12.22 (a) ROP = 1,718 cigars
 (b) 1,868 cigars
 (c) A higher service level means a lower probability of stocking out.

Chapter 13

13.2 (a) US$109,120 = total cost
 (b) US$106,640 = total cost
 (c) No, plan 2 is better at US$105,152.
13.4 Extra total cost = US$2,960.
13.6

To / From	Demand Period 1	Demand Period 2	Demand Period 3	Excess	Supply
Initial Inventory	0 / 20	4	8	0	20
Reg. Time Period 1	100 / 20	104 / 10	108	0	30
Overtime Period 1	150	154	158	0 / 10	10
Subcont. Period 2	200	204	208	0 / 5	5
Reg. Time Period 2	∞	100 / 35	104	0	35
Overtime Period 2	∞	150 / 5	154	0 / 7	12
Subcont. Period 3	∞	200	204	0 / 5	5
Reg. Time Period 3	∞	∞	100 / 30	0	30
Overtime Period 3	∞	∞	150 / 10	0	10
Subcont. Period 3	∞	∞	200	0 / 5	5
Demand	40	50	40	32	

Total cost = US$11,790

13.8 **(a)**

Method → Produce to demand (let workforce vary)
Shortages: Lost sales—Shortages not carried from month to month

All months →

| | | Capacities | | | US$1,000 | US$1,300 | US$1,800 | US$200 | US$0 | US$0 | US$0 |
| | | | | | Units | | | | | | |
Month	Demnd	Regtm	Ovrtm	Subcon	Regtm	Ovrtm	Subcon	Holdng	Shortg	Increase	Decrease
Init	0	0	0	0							
Jan	255	235	20	12	235	20	0	0	0	0	0
Feb	294	255	24	16	255	24	15	0	0	20	0
Mar	321	290	26	15	290	26	5	0	0	35	
Apr	301	300	24	17	300	1	0	0	0	10	0
May	330	300	30	17	300	30	0	0	0	0	0
June	320	290	28	19	290	28	2	0	0	0	10
July	345	300	30	19	300	30	15	0	0	10	0
Aug	340	290	30	20	290	30	20	0	0	0	10
Tot	2,506	2,260	212	135	2,260	189	57	0	0	75	20
		Subtotal Costs (US$)			2,260,000	245,700	102,600	0	0	0	0

| Summary Table | | |
Type	Units	Cost (US$)
Regtm	2,260	2,260,000
Ovrtm	189	245,700
Subcon	57	102,600
Holdng	0	0
Shortg	0	0
Increase	75	0
Decrease	20	0
	Total cost =	2,608,300

(b)

Method → Produce to demand (let workforce vary)
Shortages: Lost sales—Shortages not carried from month to month

All pds →

| | | Capacities | | | US$1,000 | US$1,300 | US$1,800 | US$200 | US$0 | US$0 | US$0 |
| | | | | | Units | | | | | | |
Month	Demnd	Regtm	Ovrtm	Subcon	Regtm	Ovrtm	Subcon	Holdng	Shortg	Increase	Decrease
Init	0	0	0	0							
Jan	255	275	20	12	255	0	0	0	0	0	0
Feb	294	275	24	16	275	19	0	0	0	20	0
Mar	321	275	26	15	275	26	15	0	5	0	0
Apr	301	275	24	17	275	24	2	0	0	0	0
May	330	275	30	17	275	30	17	0	8	0	0
June	320	275	28	19	275	28	17	0	0	0	0
July	345	275	30	19	275	30	19	0	21	0	0
Aug	340	275	30	20	275	30	20	0	15	0	0
Tot	2,506	2,200	212	135	2,180	187	90	0	49	20	0
		Subtotal Costs (US$)			2,180,000	243,100	162,000	0	0	0	0

| Summary Table | | |
Type	Units	Cost (US$)
Regtm	2,180	2,180,000
Ovrtm	187	243,100
Subcon	90	162,000
Holdng	0	0
Shortg	49	0
Increase	20	0
Decrease	0	0
Total cost = 2,585,100, or about 50,000 savings		

(c)

Method → Produce to demand (let workforce vary)
Shortages: Lost sales—Shortages not carried from month to month
All months →

			Capacities				Units			
					US$1,000	US$1,400	US$1,800	US$200	US$0	US$0	US$0
Month	**Demnd**	**Regtm**	**Ovrtm**	**Subcon**	**Regtm**	**Ovrtm**	**Subcon**	**Holdng**	**Shortg**	**Increase**	**Decrease**
Init	0	0	0	0							
Jan	255	235	20	12	235	20	0	0	0	0	0
Feb	294	255	24	16	255	24	15	0	0	20	0
Mar	321	290	26	15	290	26	5	0	0	35	0
Apr	301	300	24	17	300	1	0	0	0	10	0
May	330	300	30	17	300	30	0	0	0	0	0
June	320	290	28	19	290	28	2	0	0	0	10
July	345	300	30	19	300	30	15	0	0	10	0
Aug	340	290	30	20	290	30	20	0	0	0	10
Tot	2,506	2,260	212	135	2,260	189	57	0	0	75	20
		Subtotal Costs (US$)			2,260,000	264,600	102,600	0	0	0	0

Summary Table—Overtime Costs: US$1,400

Type	Units	Cost (US$)
Regtm	2,260	2,260,000
Ovrtm	189	264,600
Subcon	57	102,600
Holdng	0	0
Shortg	0	0
Increase	75	0
Decrease	20	0
	Total cost =	2,627,200

There is no change in the solution other than higher cost.

Method → Produce to demand (let workforce vary)
Shortages: Lost sales—Shortages not carried from month to month
All months →

			Capacities				Units			
					US$1,000	US$1,200	US$1,800	US$200	US$0	US$0	US$0
Month	**Demnd**	**Regtm**	**Ovrtm**	**Subcon**	**Regtm**	**Ovrtm**	**Subcon**	**Holdng**	**Shortg**	**Increase**	**Decrease**
Init	0	0	0	0							
Jan	255	235	20	12	235	20	0	0	0	0	0
Feb	294	255	24	16	255	24	15	0	0	20	0
Mar	321	290	26	15	290	26	5	0	0	35	0
Apr	301	300	24	17	300	1	0	0	0	10	0
May	330	300	30	17	300	30	0	0	0	0	0
June	320	290	28	19	290	28	2	0	0	0	10
July	345	300	30	19	300	30	15	0	0	10	0
Aug	340	290	30	20	290	30	20	0	0	0	10
Tot	2,506	2,260	212	135	2,260	189	57	0	0	75	20
		Subtotal Costs (US$)			2,260,000	226,800	102,600	0	0	0	0

Summary Table—Overtime Costs: US$1,200

Type	Units	Cost (US$)
Regtm	2,260	2,260,000
Ovrtm	189	226,800
Subcon	57	102,600
Holdng	0	0
Shortg	0	0
Increase	75	0
Decrease	20	0
	Total cost =	2,589,400

Again there is no change in the solution other than a lower cost.

13.10 **(a)**

Month	Estimated Billable Hours	CPAs	Reg. Time Billable Hours	Reg. Time Cost (US$)	Overtime Hours	Overtime Cost (US$)	Jameel Hours	Jameel Cost (US$)
Jan	660	5	800	25,000	0	0	0	0
Feb	550	5	800	25,000	0	0	0	0
Mar	1,100	5	800	25,000	300	18,750	0	0
Apr	1,320	5	800	25,000	400	25,000	120	15,000
May	715	5	800	25,000	0	0	0	0
June	649	5	800	25,000	0	0	0	0
				150,000	700	43,750	120	15,000

Total cost = US$150,000 + US$43,750 + US$15,000 = US$208,750

(b) With the increase in business, five accountants appear to be necessary. There is still a need for overtime during the tax season, but there is a big saving in Jameel's pay (which is double that of overtime for a regular employee). What Salama needs to do is find additional accounting activities that his staff can work on during the 'off-peak' season.

Chapter 14

14.2 The time-phased plan for the gift bags is:

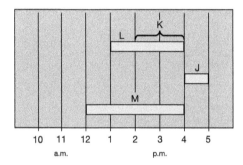

Someone should start on item M by noon.

14.4 Gross material requirements plan:

Item		Week 1	2	3	4	5	6	7	8	Lead Time (wk.)
S	Gross req.							100		
	Order release					100				2
T	Gross req.					100				
	Order release				100					1
U	Gross req.					200				
	Order release			200						2
V	Gross req.				100					
	Order release		100							2
W	Gross req.				200					
	Order release	200								3
X	Gross req.				100					
	Order release			100						1
Y	Gross req.			400						
	Order release	400								2
Z	Gross req.			600						
	Order release		600							1

14.6 Gross material requirements plan, modified to include the 20 units of U required for maintenance purposes:

Item		1	2	3	4	5	6	7	8	Lead Time (wk.)
S	Gross req.							100		
	Order release					100				2
T	Gross req.					100				
	Order release				100					1
U	Gross req.					200	20			
	Order release			200	20					2
V	Gross req.				100					
	Order release		100							2
W	Gross req.				200					
	Order release	200								3
X	Gross req.				100					
	Order release			100						1
Y	Gross req.			400	40					
	Order release	400	40							2
Z	Gross req.			600	60					
	Order release		600	60						1

14.8 (a) Gross material requirements plan for the first three items:

Item		1	2	3	4	5	6	7	8	9	10	11	12
X1	Gross req.								50		20		100
	Order release							50		20		100	
B1	Gross req.							50		20		100	
	Order release					50		20		100			
B2	Gross req.							100		40		200	
	Order release					10		40		200			

Level: 0	Parent:								Quantity:			
Item: X1	**Lead Time:**								**Lot Size: L4L**			

Week No.	1	2	3	4	5	6	7	8	9	10	11	12
Gross Requirement								50		20		100
Scheduled Receipt												
On-hand Inventory								50		0		0
Net Requirement								0		20		100
Planned Order Receipt										20		100
Planned Order Release									20		100	

Level: 1	Parent: X1								Quantity: 1X			
Item: B1	**Lead Time: 2**								**Lot Size: L4L**			

Week No.	1	2	3	4	5	6	7	8	9	10	11	12
									20		100	
Gross Requirement												
Scheduled Receipt												
On-hand Inventory									20		0	
Net Requirement									0		100	
Planned Order Receipt											100	
Planned Order Release									100			

(b) The net materials requirement plan for the first two items:

14.10   Lot-for-Lot Ordering Policy:

	Week											
	1	**2**	**3**	**4**	**5**	**6**	**7**	**8**	**9**	**10**	**11**	**12**
Gross requirement	30		40		30	70	20		10	80		50
Beginning inventory	40	10	10	0	0	0	0	0	0	0	0	0
Ending inventory	10	10	0	0	0	0	0	0	0	0	0	0
Order receipts			30		30	70	20		10	80		50
Order release		30		30	70	20		10	80		50	

C_T = Order cost + holding cost = 7 orders × US$150/order + 20 units × US$2.50/unit/period = US$1,100

14.12   Solution with lead time = 1: Holding cost = US$2.50; Setup cost = US$150. PPB ordering policy:

	Week											
	1	**2**	**3**	**4**	**5**	**6**	**7**	**8**	**9**	**10**	**11**	**12**
Gross requirement	30		40		30	70	20		10	80		50
Beginning inventory	40	10	10	30	30	0	30	10	10	0	50	50
Ending inventory	10	10	30	30	0	30	10	10	0	50	50	0
Order receipts			60			100				130		
Order release		60			100				130			

Calculating EPP:

$$EPP = \frac{\text{Setup cost}}{\text{Holding cost}} = \frac{150}{2.50} = 60$$

Periods Combined	Cumulative Net Req.	Part Periods	Costs Order	Hold
1	0		0 +	25
1, 2	0		0 +	25
1, 2, 3	30		150 +	75
1, 2, 3, 4	30		150 +	75
1, 2, 3, 4, 5*	60	30 × 0 + 30 × 2 = 60	150	
1, 2, 3, 4, 5, 6	130	30 × 0 + 30 × 2 + 70 × 3 = 270	150	

*The part periods for an order encompassing periods 1, 2, 3, 4, and 5 most nearly approximates the EPP of 60.

Note: (1) We have assumed that: (a) a product ordered during a calendar week is available at the beginning of the following week; (b) shipments during a week take place at the beginning of the week. (2) POM for Windows will produce the same answer. Excel OM will produce the same answer when lead time is zero.

Periods Combined	Cumulative Net Req.	Part Periods	Costs Order	Hold
6	70	70 × 0 = 0	150 +	0
6, 7	90	70 × 0 + 20 × 1 = 20		50
6, 7, 8	90	70 × 0 + 20 × 1 = 20		50
6, 7, 8, 9*	100	70 × 0 + 20 × 1 + 10 × 3 = 50		125
6, 7, 8, 9, 10	180	70 × 0 + 20 × 1 + 10 × 3 + 80 × 4 = 370		

*The part periods for an order encompassing periods 6, 7, 8, and 9 most nearly approximates the EPP of 60.

Periods Combined	Cumulative Net Req.	Part Periods	Costs Order	Hold
10	80	80 × 0 = 0	150 +	0
10, 11	80	80 × 0 = 0		0
10, 11, 12*	130	80 × 0 + 50 × 2 = 100		250

*The part periods for an order encompassing periods 10, 11, 12 most nearly approximates the EPP of 60.

Calculate total cost:

C_T = Order cost + Holding cost
   = 3 orders × US$150/order + 230 units × US$2.50/unit/period
   = US$1,025.00

Chapter 15

15.2

Job	Day 1	Day 2	Day 3	Day 4	Day 5	Day 6	Day 7	Day 8	Day 9
D									
E									
F									
G									

Now

15.4 (a) 1–D, 2–A, 3–C, 4–B
   (b) 40
15.6 (a) A, B, C, D, E
   (b) B, A, D, E, C
   (c) E, D, A, B, C
   (d) C, B, A, D, E
   (e) SPT is best.

15.8

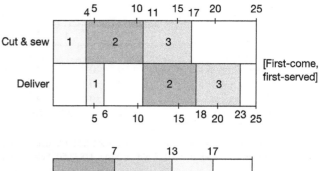

[First-come, first-served]

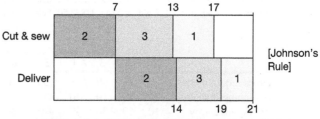

[Johnson's Rule]

Johnson's Rule finishes in 21 days, 2 days faster than the first-come, first-served schedule, which finishes in 23 days.

15.10 Note: Seven employees are needed; six have two consecutive days off. Worker 7 has two consecutive days off but only works 4 days. Days off are circled.

	Monday	Tuesday	Wednesday	Thursday	Friday	Saturday	Sunday
Worker 1	6	5	5	5	6	④	③
Worker 2	5	4	4	4	5	④	③
Worker 3	4	③	③	3	4	4	3
Worker 4	3	3	3	2	3	③	②
Worker 5	2	2	②	①	2	3	2
Worker 6	①	①	2	1	1	2	1
Worker 7	1	1	1	⓪	⓪	1	0

15.12

Period	1	2	3	4	Total
Planned input	80	80	100	100	360
Actual input	85	85	85	85	340
Deviation	+5	+5	−15	−15	−20
Planned output	90	90	90	90	360
Actual output	85	85	80	80	330
Deviation	−5	−5	−10	−10	−30
Backlog: 30	30	30	35	40	

Analysis: The completed input–output report shows that the grinding work center did not process all the jobs that were available during the four periods; therefore, the desired output rate was not achieved. Also, rather than reducing the backlog, the backlog increased to 40 units.

Chapter 16

16.2 3.75, or 4 kanbans
16.4 $D = 2,000$; $H = US\$12$; $S = US\$30$

(a) $EOQ = \sqrt{\dfrac{2(2,000)(30)}{12}} = 100$ lamps

(b) $TC = \dfrac{2,000(30)}{12} + \dfrac{100(12)}{2} = US\$1,200$

(c) No. of orders $= \dfrac{2,000}{100} = 20$ orders/year

16.6 With JIT, purchase/delivery of goods immediately precedes demand. The decrease in EOQ for lamps, from 100 to 10, increases deliveries from 20 to 200. With the new relationship with Specialty Lighting, Jazan-Mart has reduced its inventory costs, a usual pattern for companies using JIT purchasing.

Chapter 17

17.2 From Figure 17.2, about 13% overall reliability.
17.4 Expected daily breakdowns = 2.0
   Expected cost = US\$100 daily
17.6 (a) $FR(\%) = \dfrac{4}{10} = 40\%$

(b) $FR(N) = 4 \div [(10 \times 60,000) - \{(50,000 \times 1) + (35,000 \times 1) + (15,000 \times 2)\}]$
   $= 4 \div [600,000 - 115,000] = 4 \div 485,000$
   $= 0.000008247$ failures per unit hour

(c) $MTBF = 1 \div 0.000008247 = 121,256$ hours

17.8 The overall system has a reliability of 0.9498, or approximately 95%.
17.10 (a) Given the following:

Number of breakdowns	0	1	2	3	4	5
Number of years in which breakdowns occurred	4	3	1	5	5	0

There were a total of $4 \times 0 + 3 \times 1 + 1 \times 2 + 5 \times 3 + 5 \times 4 + 0 \times 5$ = 40 breakdowns over 18 years. Or an expected $40 \div 18 = 2.222$ breakdowns per year.

(b) Cost of current policy = US$2,000/failure × 2.222
expected failures = US$4,444/year
(c) Cost of outsourcing = US$5,000
So the current policy of in-house maintenance is better.
17.12 Reliability is 0.7348. Students will probably argue that reliability should be higher, perhaps over 90 percent. Suggested candidates for backup include fuller inventory, more cashier lanes, and overrides for faulty scanning. Suggested candidates for redesign include bagging and exit.

Quantitative Module A

A.2 (a)

Size of First Station	Good Market (US$)	Fair Market (US$)	Poor Market (US$)	EV Under Equally Likely
Small	50,000	20,000	−10,000	20,000
Medium	80,000	30,000	−20,000	30,000
Large	100,000	30,000	−40,000	30,000
Very large	300,000	25,000	−160,000	55,000

(b) Maximax: Build a very large station.
(c) Maximin: Build a small station.
(d) Equally likely: Build a very large station.
(e)

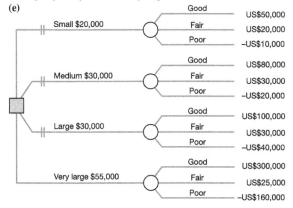

A.4 Buying equipment at US$733,333
A.6 Alternative B; 74
A.8 (a)

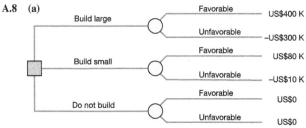

(b) Small plant with EMV = US$26,000
(c) EVPI = US$134,000
A.10 (a)

Decision	At X	At Y	At X	At Y
X	45–27	9–27	18	−18
Y	6–15	30–15	−9	15
X&Y	(45 + 6)–(27 + 15)	(30 + 9)–(27 + 15)	9	−3
Nothing	0	0	0	0
Probability	0.45	0.55	0.45	0.55

(b) EMV (Y) = 4.2, which is best

Quantitative Module B

B.2 (a) 507 min.
(b) 456 min.
(c) 410 min.
(d) 369 min.
B.4 (a) 1,546 min.
(b) 2,872 min.
(c) 3,701 min.
(d) 6,779 min.
B.6 $T_1 = 5$ hr $T_2 = 4$ hr
(a) Learning rate = 4 ÷ 5 = 80%
(b) $T_3 = T_1 \times C = (5)(0.702) = 3.51$
(c) $T_4 = 5(0.640) = 3.2$
$T_5 = 5(0.596) = 2.98$
$T_6 = 5(0.562) = 2.81$
(d) $\sum_{i=1}^{6} T_i = 5(4.299) = 21.5$
B.8 $T_1 = 80$ hours
$T_4 = ?$
Use the doubling effect twice to reach the 4th unit
(a) 95% L.C.
(0.95)(0.95)(80 hours) = 72.2 hours
(b) 87% L.C.
(0.87)(0.87)(80 hours) = 60.552 hours
(c) 72% L.C.
(0.72)(0.72)(80 hours) = 41.472 hours
B.10 US$748,240 for fourth, US$709,960 for fifth, US$679,960 for sixth
B.12 (a) 70 millicents/bit
(b) 8.2 millicents/bit
B.14 (a) 32.98 hr., 49.61 hr.
(b) Initial quote is high.
B.16 0.227 hr.

Online Tutorial 1

T1.2 5.45; 4.06
T1.4 (a) 0.2743;
(b) 0.5
T1.6 0.1587; 0.2347; 0.1587
T1.8 (a) 0.0548;
(b) 0.6554;
(c) 0.6554;
(d) 0.2119

Online Tutorial 2

T2.2 (selected values)

Fraction Defective	Mean of Poisson	$P(x \leq 1)$
0.01	0.05	0.999
0.05	0.25	0.974
0.10	0.50	0.910
0.30	1.50	0.558
0.60	3.00	0.199
1.00	5.00	0.040

T2.4 The plan meets neither the producer's nor the consumer's requirement.

Online Tutorial 3

T3.2 (a) $x_1 + 4x_2 + s_1 = 24$
$x_1 + 2x_2 + s_2 = 16$
(b) See the steps in the tutorial.

(c) Second tableau:

c_j	Mix	x_1	x_2	s_1	s_2	Qty
9	x_2	0.25	1	0.25	0	6
0	s_2	0.50	0	3.50	1	4
	z_j	2.25	9	2.25	0	54
	$c_j - z_j$	0.75	0	32.25	0	

(d) $x_1 = 8$, $x_2 = 4$, Profit = US$60

T3.4 Basis for 1st tableau:
   $A_1 = 80$
   $A_2 = 75$
   Basis for 2nd tableau:
   $A_1 = 55$
   $X_1 = 25$
   Basis for 3rd tableau:
   $X_1 = 14$
   $X_2 = 33$
   Cost = US$221 at optimal solution

T3.6 **(a)** x_1
   (b) A_1

Online Tutorial 4

T4.2 Cost = US$980; 1–A = 20; 1–B = 50; 2–C = 20; 2–Dummy = 30; 3–A = 20; 3–C = 40

T4.4 Total = 3,100 mi.; Morgantown–Coaltown = 35; Youngstown–Coal Valley = 30; Youngstown–Coaltown = 5; Youngstown–Coal Junction = 25; Pittsburgh–Coaltown = 5; Pittsburgh–Coalsburg = 20

T4.6 **(a)** Using VAM, cost = 635; A–Y = 35; A–Z = 20; B–W = 10; B–X = 20; B–Y = 15; C–W = 30.
   (b) Using MODI, cost is also 635 (i.e. initial solution was optimal). An alternative optimal solution is A–X = 20; A–Y = 15; A–Z = 20; B–W = 10; B–Y = 35; C–W = 30.

Online Tutorial 5

T5.2 **(a)** $I_{12} = 12$
   (b) $I_{35} = 7$
   (c) $I_{51} = 4$

T5.4 **(a)** Tour: 1–2–4–5–7–6–8–3–1; 37.9 mi.
   (b) Tour: 4–5–7–1–2–3–6–8–4; 39.1 mi.

T5.6 **(a)** Vehicle 1: Tour
   (b) Vehicle 2: Tour

T5.8 The cost matrix is shown below:

	1	2	3	4	5	6	7	8
1	—	107.26	118.11	113.20	116.50	123.50	111.88	111.88
2		—	113.53	111.88	118.10	125.30	116.50	118.10
3			—	110.56	118.70	120.50	119.90	124.90
4				—	109.90	119.10	111.88	117.90
5					—	111.88	106.60	118.50
6						—	111.88	123.50
7							—	113.20
8								—

Glossary

3D object modeling | نمذجة الهدف ثلاثية الأبعاد
An extension of CAD that builds small prototypes.

5Ss | التوحيدات القياسية الخمسة
A lean production checklist:
Sort
Simplify
Shine
Standardize
Sustain

ABC analysis | التحليل الأبجدي
A method for dividing on-hand inventory into three classifications based on annual dollar volume.

activity chart | الرسم البياني للأنشطة
A way of improving utilization of an operator and a machine or some combination of operators (a crew) and machines.

activity map | خريطة الأنشطة
A graphical link of competitive advantage, KSFs, and supporting activities.

activity-on-arrow (AOA) | النشاط حسب الأسهم
A network diagram in which arrows designate activities.

activity-on-node (AON) | النشاط حسب النقطة
A network diagram in which nodes designate activities.

advanced shipping notice (ASN) | إشعار الشحن المتقدم
A shipping notice delivered directly from vendor to purchaser.

aggregate planning | التخطيط التكاملي
Also known as *aggregate scheduling*; an approach to determine the quantity and timing of production for the intermediate future (usually 3 to 18 months ahead).

alliances | التحالفات
Cooperative agreements that allow firms to remain independent but pursue strategies consistent with their individual missions.

assembly chart | الرسم البياني للتجميع
A graphic means of identifying how components flow into subassemblies and final products.

assembly drawing | رسومات التجميع
An exploded view of the product.

assembly line | خط التجميع
An approach that puts fabricated parts together at a series of workstations; used in repetitive processes.

assembly-line balancing | موازنة خط التجميع
Obtaining output at each workstation on a production line so delay is minimized.

assignment method | أسلوب التخصيص
A special class of linear programming models that involves assigning tasks or jobs to resources.

attribute inspection | التفتيش المميز
An inspection that classifies items as being either good or defective.

automated guided vehicle (AGV) | المركبة الموجهة آلياً
Electronically guided and controlled cart used to move materials.

automated storage and retrieval system (ASRS) | نظام التخزين والاسترداد الآلي
Computer-controlled warehouses that provide for the automatic placement of parts into and from designated places within a warehouse.

automatic identification system (AIS) | نظام التعريف الآلي
A system for transforming data into electronic form, for example bar codes.

autonomous maintenance | الصيانة الذاتية
Operators partner with maintenance personnel to observe, check, adjust, clean, and notify.

average observed time | متوسط الوقت الملاحظ
The arithmetic mean of the times for each element measured, adjusted for unusual influence for each element.

back flush | التدفق الرجعي
A system to reduce inventory balances by deducting everything in the bill of material on completion of the unit.

backsourcing | الرجوع للمصدر
The return of business activity to the original firm.

backward pass | العبور للخلف
An activity that finds all the latest start and latest finish times.

backward scheduling | الجدولة الخلفية
Scheduling that begins with the due date and schedules the final operation first and the other job steps in reverse order.

benchmarking | القياس
Selecting a demonstrated standard of performance that represents the very best performance for a process or an activity.

bias | التنبؤ غير الدقيق
A forecast that is consistently higher or consistently lower than actual values of a time series.

bill of material (BOM) | فاتورة المواد
A list of the components, their description, and the quantity of each required to make one unit of a product.

blanket order | نظام التغطية
A long-term purchase commitment to a supplier for items that are to be delivered against short-term releases to ship.

bottleneck | عنق الزجاجة
The limiting factor or constraint in a system.

breakdown maintenance | صيانة الأعطال
Remedial maintenance that occurs when equipment fails and must be repaired on an emergency or priority basis.

break-even analysis | تحليل نقطة التعادل
A means of finding the point, in monetary terms and units, at which costs equal revenues.

bucketless system | نظام الاسترجاع بالسجلات الزمنية
Time-phased data are referenced using dated records rather than defined time periods, or buckets.

buckets | الوحدات الزمنية
Time units in a material requirements planning system.

build-to-order (BTO) | الإنتاج حسب طلب العميل
Produce to customer order rather than to a forecast.

bullwhip effect | تأثير التأرجح
The increasing fluctuation in orders that often occurs as orders move through the supply chain.

capacity | القدرة الاستيعابية
The 'throughput' or number of units a facility can hold, receive, store, or produce in a period of time.

capacity analysis | تحليل القدرة الاستيعابية
A means of determining throughput capacity of workstations or an entire production system.

cause-and-effect diagram | مخطط السبب والنتيجة
Also known as an *Ishikawa diagram* or a *fish-bone chart*. A schematic technique used to discover possible locations of quality problems.

center-of-gravity method | أسلوب مركز الجاذبية
A mathematical technique used for finding the best location for a single distribution point that services several stores or areas.

channel assembly | تجميع المسارات
Postpones final assembly of a product so the distribution channel can assemble it.

chase strategy | استراتيجية المطاردة
A planning strategy that sets production equal to forecasted demand.

closed-loop MRP system | نظام الحلقة المغلقة لتخطيط الموارد المالية
A system that provides feedback to the capacity plan, master production schedule, and production plan so planning can be kept valid at all times.

clustering | التكتل
The location of competing companies near each other, often because of a critical mass of information, talent, venture capital, or natural resources.

coefficient of correlation | معامل الارتباط
A measure of the strength of the relationship between two variables.

coefficient of determination | معامل التحديد
A measure of the amount of variation in the dependent variable about its mean that is explained by the regression equation.

collaborative planning, forecasting, and replenishment (CPFR) | التخطيط والتوقع والتجديد التعاوني
A joint effort of members of a supply chain to share information in order to reduce supply-chain costs.

competitive advantage | الميزة التنافسية
The creation of a unique advantage over competitors.

computer numerical control (CNC) | التحكم العددي الحاسوبي
Machinery with its own computer and memory.

computer-aided design (CAD) | التصميم بمساعدة الكمبيوتر
Interactive use of a computer to develop and document a product.

computer-aided manufacturing (CAM) | التصنيع بمساعدة الكمبيوتر.
The use of information technology to control machinery.

computer-integrated manufacturing (CIM) | التصنيع التكاملي بمساعدة الكمبيوتر
A manufacturing system in which CAD, FMS, inventory control, warehousing, and shipping are integrated.

concurrent engineering | الهندسة المتزامنة
Use of participating teams in design and engineering activities.

configuration management | إدارة التكوين
A system by which a product's planned and changing components are accurately identified.

consignment inventory | جرد البضاعة
An arrangement in which the supplier maintains title to the inventory until it is used.

consumer market survey | استطلاع السوق الاستهلاكية
A forecasting method that solicits input from customers or potential customers regarding future purchasing plans.

control charts | الرسوم البيانية للمراقبة
Graphic presentations of process data over time, with predetermined control limits.

ConWIP cards | ConWIP بطاقات
Cards that control the amount of work in a work center, aiding input–output control.

core competencies | الكفاءات الأساسية
A set of skills, talents, and activities in which a firm is particularly strong.

cost of quality (COQ) | تكلفة الجودة
The cost of doing things wrong—that is, the price of nonconformance.

crashing | الانهيار
Shortening activity time in a network to reduce time on the critical path so total completion time is reduced.

critical path | المسار الحرج
The computed longest time path(s) through a network.

critical path analysis | تحليل المسار الحرج
A process that helps determine a project schedule.

critical path method (CPM) | أسلوب المسار الحرج
A project management technique that uses only one time factor per activity.

critical ratio (CR) | النسبة الحرجة
A sequencing rule that is an index number computed by dividing the time remaining until due date by the work time remaining.

cross-docking | الالتحام
Avoiding the placement of materials or supplies in storage by processing them as they are received from shipment.

crossover chart | الرسم البياني للنفقات
A chart of costs at the possible volumes for more than one process.

customizing | التخصيص
Using warehousing to add value to a product through component modification, repair, labeling, and packaging through the use of postponement.

cycle counting | حساب الدورات
A continuing reconciliation of inventory with inventory records.

cycle time | زمن الدورة
The time it takes a product to be made.

cycles | الدورات
Patterns in the data that occur every several years.

decision table | جدول القرارات
A tabular means of analyzing decision alternatives and states of nature.

decision tree | شجرة القرارات
A graphical means of analyzing decision alternatives and states of nature.

Delphi method | طريقة دلفي
A forecasting technique using a group process that allows experts to make forecasts.

demand forecasts | توقعات الطلب
Projections of a company's sales for each time period in the planning horizon.

design capacity | القدرة الاستيعابية للتصميم
The theoretical maximum output of a system in a given period under ideal conditions.

design for manufacture and assembly (DFMA) | التصميم من أجل التصنيع والتجميع
Software that allows designers to look at the effect of design on manufacturing of the product.

differentiation | المفاضلة
Distinguishing the offerings of an organization in a way that the customer perceives as adding value.

disaggregation | التفصيل
The process of breaking an aggregate plan into greater detail.

distribution resource planning (DRP) | تخطيط موارد التوزيع
A time-phased stock-replenishment plan for all levels of a distribution network.

division of labor | تقسيم العمالة
Also known as labor specialization or job specialization; the division of labor into unique ('special') tasks.

drop shipping | الشحن المباشر
Shipping directly from the supplier to the end consumer rather than from the seller, saving both time and reshipping costs.

dummy activity | النشاط الوهمي
An activity having no time that is inserted into a network to maintain the logic of the network.

earliest due date (EDD) | أقرب تاريخ استحقاق
Earliest due date jobs are performed first.

economic forecasts | التوقعات الاقتصادية
Planning indicators that are valuable in helping organizations prepare medium- to long-range forecasts.

economic order quantity model | نموذج مقدار الطلب الاقتصادي
An inventory-control technique that minimizes the total of ordering and holding costs.

economic part period (EPP) | فترة المشاركة الاقتصادية
A period of time when the ratio of setup cost to holding cost is equal.

effective capacity | القدرة الاستيعابية الفعالة
The capacity a firm can expect to achieve, given its product mix, methods of scheduling, maintenance, and standards of quality.

efficiency | الكفاءة
Actual output as a percentage of effective capacity.

efficient consumer response (ECR) | الاستجابة الاستهلاكية الفعالة
Supply-chain management systems in the grocery industry that tie sales to buying, to inventory, to logistics, and to production.

electronic data interchange (EDI) | التبادل الالكتروني للبيانات
A standardized data-transmission format for computerized communications between organizations.

employee empowerment | تمكين الموظفين
Enlarging employee jobs so that the added responsibility and authority is moved to the lowest level possible in the organization.

engineering change notice (ECN) | إخطار التغير الهندسي
A correction or modification of an engineering drawing or bill of material.

engineering drawing | الرسم الهندسي
A drawing that shows the dimensions, tolerances, materials, and finishes of a component.

enterprise resource planning (ERP) | تخطيط موارد المؤسسات
An information system for identifying and planning the enterprise-wide resources needed to take, make, ship, and account for customer orders.

E-procurement | الشراء الالكتروني
Purchasing facilitated through the internet.

equally likely | الترجيح المتساوي
A criterion that assigns equal probability to each state of nature.

ergonomics | بيئة العمل
The study of the human interface with the environment and machines.

European Union (EU) | الاتحاد الأوروبي
A European political and trade group that has 27 members.

expected monetary value (EMV) | القيمة النقدية المتوقعة
The expected payout or value of a variable that has different possible states of nature, each with an associated probability.

expected value of perfect information (EVPI) | القيمة المتوقعة للمعلومات الكاملة
The difference between the payoff under perfect information and the payoff under risk.

expected value with perfect information (EVwPI) | القيمة المتوقعة مع المعلومات الكاملة
The expected (average) return if perfect information is available.

experience differentiation | مفاضلة التجارب
Engaging a customer with a product through imaginative use of the five senses, so the customer 'experiences' the product.

exponential smoothing | الصقل الأسي
A weighted-moving-average forecasting technique in which data points are weighted by an exponential function.

fabrication line | خط التصنيع
A machine-paced, product-oriented facility for building components.

factor-rating method | طريقة تصنيف العوامل
A location method that instills objectivity into the process of identifying hard-to-evaluate costs.

finished-goods inventory | قائمة جرد البضائع المنتهية
An end item ready to be sold, but still an asset on the company's books.

finite capacity scheduling | جدولة القدرة المحدودة
Computerized short-term scheduling that overcomes the disadvantage of rule-based systems by providing the user with graphical interactive computing.

first come, first served (FCFS) | ما يأتي أولاً يقدم أولاً
Jobs are completed in the order they arrived.

five forces model | نموذج القوى الخمس
A method of analyzing the five forces in the competitive environment.

fixed-period system | نظام الفترة الثابتة
Also known as a *periodic review*, or *P system*; a system in which inventory orders are made at regular time intervals.

fixed-position layout | تخطيط الوضع الثابت
A system that addresses the layout requirements of stationary projects.

fixed-quantity system | نظام الكمية الثابتة
Also known as a *Q system*; an ordering system with the same order amount each time.

flexibility | المرونة
The ability to respond with little penalty in time, cost, or customer value.

flexible manufacturing system (FMS) | نظام التصنيع المرن
A system that uses an automated work cell controlled by electronic signals from a common centralized computer facility.

flextime | الوقت المرن
A work schedule policy that allows employees, within limits, to determine their own work schedules.

flow diagram | مخطط التدفق
A drawing used to analyze the movement of people or materials.

flowchart | الرسم البياني للتدفق
A drawing used to analyze movement of people or material.

focused factory | المصنع المركز
A facility designed to produce similar products or components.

focused work center | مركز العمل المركز
A permanent or semi-permanent product-oriented arrangement of machines and personnel.

forecasting | التوقع
The art and science of predicting future events.

forward pass | التنبؤ المستقبلي
A process that identifies all the early times.

forward scheduling | الجدولة المستقبلية
Scheduling that begins the schedule as soon as the requirements are known.

Free Trade Zones | مناطق التجارة الحرة
Zones that are free from customs interventions where businesses can manufacture goods from imported products and then export free of duties.

Gantt charts | خرائط جانت
Planning charts used to schedule resources and allocate time.

geographic information system (GIS) | نظام المعلومات الجغرافية
A system that stores and displays information that can be linked to a geographic location.

global strategy | الاستراتيجية العالمية
A strategy in which operating decisions are centralized and headquarters coordinates the standardization and learning between facilities.

graphical techniques | التقنيات التصويرية
Aggregate planning techniques that work with a few variables at a time to allow planners to compare projected demand with existing capacity.

gross material requirements plan | خطة متطلبات المواد الإجمالية
A schedule that shows the total demand for an item (prior to subtraction of on-hand inventory and scheduled receipts) and: (1) when it must be ordered from suppliers; (2) when production must be started to meet its demand by a particular date.

group technology | تكنولوجيا المجموعة
A product and component coding system that specifies the type of processing and the parameters of the processing; it allows similar products to be grouped.

Gulf Cooperation Council (GCC) | مجلس التعاون الخليجي
A political and economic union between Bahrain, Kuwait, Oman, Qatar, Saudi Arabia, and United Arab Emirates.

heuristic | قواعد حل المشاكل
Problem solving using procedures and rules rather than mathematical optimization.

holding cost | تكلفة التحميل
The cost to keep or carry inventory in stock.

house of quality | بيت الجودة
A part of the quality function deployment process that utilizes a planning matrix to relate customer 'wants' to 'how' the firm is going to meet those 'wants.'

infant mortality | معدل وفيات الأطفال
The failure rate early in the life of a product or process.

input–output control | التحكم في المعطيات والنتائج
A system that allows operations personnel to manage facility work flows by tracking work added to a work center and its work completed.

inspection | التفتيش
A means of ensuring that an operation is producing at the quality level expected.

intangible costs | التكاليف غير الملموسة
A category of location costs that cannot be easily quantified, such as quality of life and government.

international business | شركة عالمية
A firm that engages in cross-border transactions.

international strategy | استراتيجية عالمية
A strategy in which global markets are penetrated using exports and licenses.

inventory turnover | دورة الجرد
Cost of goods sold divided by average inventory.

ISO 14000 | 14000 شهادة الأيزو
A series of environmental management standards established by the International Organization for Standardization (ISO).

ISO 9000 | 9000 شهادة الأيزو
A set of quality standards developed by the International Organization for Standardization (ISO).

job design | تصميم المهام
An approach that specifies the tasks that constitute a job for an individual or a group.

job enlargement | توسيع المهام
The grouping of a variety of tasks about the same skill level; horizontal enlargement.

job enrichment | إثراء المهام
A method of giving an employee more responsibility that includes some of the planning and control necessary for job accomplishment; vertical expansion.

job lots | كميات المهام
Groups or batches of parts processed together.

job rotation | دورة المهام
A system in which an employee is moved from one specialized job to another.

Johnson's rule | قاعدة جونسون
An approach that minimizes processing time for sequencing a group of jobs through two work centers while minimizing total idle time in the work centers.

joint ventures | الشركات ذات الملكية المشتركة
Firms establishing joint ownership to pursue new products or markets.

jury of executive opinion | هيئة متخذي القرارات التنفيذية
A forecasting technique that uses the opinion of a small group of high-level managers to form a group estimate of demand.

just-in-time (JIT) | فقط في الوقت المناسب
Continuous and forced problem solving via a focus on throughput and reduced inventory.

just-in-time (JIT) inventory | الجرد فقط في الوقت المناسب
The minimum inventory necessary to keep a perfect system running.

just-in-time (JIT) partnerships | الشراكات فقط في الوقت المناسب
Partnerships of suppliers and purchasers that remove waste and drive down costs for mutual benefits.

kaizen | التركيز على التطوير المستمر
A focus on continuous improvement.

kanban | نظام كانابان
The Japanese word for card, which has come to mean 'signal'; a kanban system moves parts through production via a 'pull' from a signal.

keiretsu | كيرتسو
A Japanese term that describes suppliers who become part of a company coalition.

key success factors (KSFs) | عوامل النجاح الأساسية
Activities or factors that are key to achieving competitive advantage.

knowledge society | مجتمع المعرفة
A society in which much of the labor force has migrated from manual work to work based on knowledge.

labor planning | تخطيط العمالة
A means of determining staffing policies dealing with employment stability, work schedules, and work rules.

labor standards | معايير العمل
The amount of time required to perform a job or part of a job.

lead time | وقت التجهيز
In purchasing systems, the time between placing an order and receiving it; in production systems, the wait, move, queue, setup, and run times for each component produced.

lean operations | العمليات المضغوطة
Eliminates waste through a focus on exactly what the customer wants.

learning curves | منحنيات التعلم
The premise that people and organizations get better at their tasks as the tasks are repeated; sometimes called experience curves.

level material use | الاستخدام القياسي للمواد
The use of frequent, high-quality, small lot sizes that contribute to just-in-time production.

level schedules | الجداول القياسية
Scheduling products so that each day's production meets the demand for that day.

level scheduling | الجدولة القياسية
Maintaining a constant output rate, production rate, or workforce level over the planning horizon.

linear-regression analysis | تحليل الارتداد الخطي
A straight-line mathematical model to describe the functional relationships between independent and dependent variables.

load report | تقرير حجم الأعمال
A report showing the resource requirements in a work center for all work currently assigned there as well as all planned and expected orders.

loading | التعهيد
The assigning of jobs to work or processing centers.

local optimization | التحسين المحلي
When sub-units of a system or members of a group focus on maximizing their immediate interest rather than on the system or the group's overall interest.

locational break-even analysis | التحليل المكاني لنقطة التعادل
A cost–volume analysis to make an economic comparison of location alternatives.

logistics management | إدارة النقل والإمداد
An approach that seeks efficiency of operations through the integration of all material acquisition, movement, and storage activities.

longest processing time (LPT) | أطول وقت تصنيع
Jobs with the longest processing time are completed first.

lot-for-lot | مقدار مقابل مقدار
A lot-sizing technique that generates exactly what is required to meet the plan.

lot-sizing decision | قرار تحديد حجم المقدار
The process of, or techniques used in, determining lot size.

low-cost leadership | القيادة منخفضة التكلفة
Achieving maximum value as perceived by the customer.

low-level coding | ترميز المستوى المنخفض
A number that identifies items at the lowest level at which they occur.

maintenance | الصيانة
The activities involved in keeping a system's equipment in working order.

maintenance/repair/operating (MRO) | الصيانة/التصليح/التشغيل
Maintenance, repair, and operating materials.

make-or-buy decision | قرار التصنيع أو الشراء
A choice between producing a component or service in-house and purchasing it from an outside source.

management coefficients model | نموذج المعاملات الإدارية
A formal planning model built around a manager's experience and performance.

management process | العملية الإدارية
The application of planning, organizing, staffing, leading, and controlling to the achievement of objectives.

manufacturability and value engineering | القدرة على التصنيع وهندسة القيمة
Activities that help improve a product's design, production, maintainability, and use.

manufacturing cycle time | وقت دورة التصنيع
The time between the arrival of raw materials and the shipping of finished products.

mass customization | التخصيص الشامل
Rapid, low-cost production that caters to constantly changing unique customer desires.

master production schedule (MPS) | جدول الإنتاج الرئيسي
A timetable that specifies what is to be made and when.

material requirements planning (MRP) | تخطيط المتطلبات من المواد
A dependent demand technique that uses a bill of material, inventory, expected receipts, and a master production schedule to determine material requirements.

Material requirements planning II (MRP II) | تخطيط المتطلبات من المواد 2
A system that allows, with MRP in place, inventory data to be augmented by other resource variables; in this case, MRP becomes material resource planning.

maximax | وضع الحد الأقصى
A criterion that finds an alternative that maximizes the maximum outcome.

maximin | وضع الحد الأقصى للحد الأدنى للناتج
A criterion that finds an alternative that maximizes the minimum outcome.

mean absolute deviation (MAD) | الانحراف المطلق المتوسط
A measure of the overall forecast error for a model.

mean absolute percent error (MAPE) | نسبة الخطأ المطلق المتوسط
The average of the absolute differences between the forecast and actual values, expressed as a percentage of actual values.

mean squared error (MSE) | الخطأ التربيعي المتوسط
The average of the squared differences between the forecasted and observed values.

mean time between failures (MTBF) | متوسط وقت الأعطال
The expected time between a repair and the next failure of a component, machine, process, or product.

methods analysis | تحليل الأساليب
A system that involves developing work procedures that are safe and produce quality products efficiently.

mission | المهمة
The purpose or rationale for an organization's existence.

mixed strategy | الاستراتيجية المختلطة
A planning strategy that uses two or more controllable variables to set a feasible production plan.

modular bills | الفواتير حسب الوحدة
Bills of material organized by major subassemblies or by product options.

modular design | التصميم حسب الوحدة
A design in which parts or components of a product are subdivided into modules that are easily interchanged or replaced.

modules | الوحدات
Parts or components of a product previously prepared, often in a continuous process.

most likely time | الوقت الأكثر ترجيحاً
The most probable time to complete an activity in a PERT network.

moving average | المتوسط المتحرك
A forecasting method that uses an average of the *n* most recent periods of data to forecast the next period.

multi-domestic strategy | الاستراتيجية المحلية المتعددة
A strategy in which operating decisions are decentralized to each country to enhance local responsiveness.

multi-factor productivity | الإنتاجية متعددة العوامل
Indicates the ratio of the goods and services produced (outputs) to some of the resources (inputs).

multinational corporation (MNC) | التعاون الدولي المتعدد
A firm that has extensive involvement in international business, owning or controlling facilities in more than one country.

multiple regression | الانحسار المتعدد
An associative forecasting method with more than one independent variable.

naive approach | النهج الساذج
A forecasting technique which assumes that demand in the next period is equal to demand in the most recent period.

nearshoring | التجارة القريبة
Choosing an outsource provider in the home country or in a nearby country.

negotiation strategies | استراتيجيات التفاوض
Approaches taken by supply-chain personnel to develop contractual relationships with suppliers.

net material requirements plan | خطة صافي المتطلبات من المواد
The result of adjusting gross requirements for inventory on hand and scheduled receipts.

networked organization | منظمة مترابطة
A group of autonomous units, divisions, or companies that become a single entity, using technology to coordinate and control the process.

normal time | الوقت الطبيعي
The average observed time, adjusted for pace.

North American Free Trade Agreement (NAFTA) | إتفاقية أمريكا الشمالية للتجارة الحرة
A free trade agreement between Canada, Mexico, and the United States.

office layout | تخطيط المكتب
The grouping of workers, their equipment, and spaces/offices to provide for comfort, safety, and movement of information.

offshoring | التجارة الخارجية
Moving a business process to a foreign country but retaining control of it.

operations chart | مخطط العمليات
A chart depicting right- and left-hand motions.

operations decisions | قرارات العمليات
The strategic decisions of OM are goods and service design, quality, process design, location selection, layout design, human resources and job design, supply-chain management, inventory, scheduling, and maintenance.

operations management (OM) | إدارة العمليات
The set of activities that oversees the creation of goods and services.

optimistic time | الوقت التفاؤلي
The 'best' activity completion time that could be obtained in a PERT network.

ordering cost | تكلفة الشراء
The cost of the ordering process.

outsourcing | التعهيد الخارجي
Transferring a firm's activities that have traditionally been internal to external suppliers.

Pareto charts | خرائط باريتو
Graphics that identify the few critical items as opposed to many less important ones.

part period balancing (PPB) | موازنة الفترة الجزئية
An inventory ordering technique that balances setup and holding costs by changing the lot size to reflect requirements of the next lot size in the future.

pass-through facility | مرفق العبور السريع
Expedites shipment by holding merchandise and delivering from shipping hubs.

PDCA | التخطيط والتنفيذ والفحص والتصرف
A continuous improvement model of plan, do, check, act.

pegging | الربط
In material requirements planning systems, tracing upward in the bill of material from the component to the parent item.

perpetual inventory system | نظام الجرد الدائم
A system that keeps track of each withdrawal or addition to inventory continuously, so records are always current.

pessimistic time | الوقت التشاؤمي
The 'worst' activity time that could be expected in a PERT network.

phantom bills of material | فواتير المواد المخيفة
Bills of material for components, usually assemblies, that exist only temporarily; they are never inventoried.

pilferage | الاختلاس
A small amount of theft.

planned order receipt | إيصال أمر الشراء المخطط
The quantity planned to be received at a future date.

planned order release | إصدار أمر الشراء المخطط
The scheduled date for an order to be released.

planning bills | الفواتير المخططة
Also known as *'pseudo' bills, kitted material,* or *kit;* a material grouping created in order to assign an artificial parent to a bill of material.

poka-yoke | بوكا يوكي
Literally translated, 'foolproof'; it has come to mean a device or technique that ensures the production of a good unit every time.

postponement | التأجيل
Delaying any modifications or customization to a product as long as possible in the production process.

predetermined time standards | المعايير الزمنية المحددة سلفاً
A division of manual work into small basic elements that have established and widely accepted times.

preventive maintenance | الصيانة الوقائية
A plan that involves routine inspections, servicing, and keeping facilities in good repair to prevent failure.

priority rules | قواعد الأولوية
Rules used to determine the sequence of jobs in process-oriented facilities.

probabilistic model | النموذج الاحتمالي
A statistical model applicable when product demand or any other variable is not known but can be specified by means of a probability distribution.

process chart | مخطط العملية
A graphic representation that depicts a sequence of steps for a process.

process control | مراقبة العملية
The use of information technology to control a physical process.

process cycle time | زمن دورة العملية
The time it takes for a product to go through the production process with no waiting.

process focus | تركيز العمليات
A production facility organized around processes to facilitate low-volume, high-variety production.

process redesign | إعادة تصميم العمليات
The fundamental rethinking of business processes to bring about dramatic improvements in performance.

process strategy | استراتيجية العمليات
An organization's approach to transforming resources into goods and services.

process time of a station | مدة العمليات لإحدى الوحدات
The time to produce units at a single workstation.

process time of a system | مدة العمليات لإحدى الأنظمة
The time of the longest (slowest) process; the bottleneck.

process-oriented layout | التصميم الموجه بالعملية
A layout that deals with low-volume, high-variety production in which like machines and equipment are grouped together.

product decision | قرار الإنتاج
The selection, definition, and design of products.

product development teams | فرق تطوير المنتجات
Teams charged with moving from market requirements for a product to achieving product success.

product focus | تركيز المنتجات
A facility organized around products; a product-oriented, high-volume, low-variety process.

product life-cycle management (PLM) | إدارة دورة حياة المنتجات
Software programs that tie together many phases of product design and manufacture.

product-by-value analysis | تحليل المنتج حسب القيمة
A list of products, in descending order of their individual monetary contribution to the firm, as well as the total annual monetary contribution of the product.

production | الإنتاج
The creation of goods and services.

production order quantity model | نموذج كمية أوامر شراء المنتجات
An economic order quantity technique applied to production orders.

productivity | الإنتاجية
The ratio of outputs (goods and services) divided by one or more inputs (such as labor, capital, or management).

productivity variables | متغيرات الإنتاجية
The three factors critical to productivity improvement—labor, capital, and the art and science of management.

program evaluation and review technique (PERT) | أسلوب تقييم ومراجعة البرنامج
A project management technique that employs three time estimates for each activity.

project organization | منظمة للمشروعات
An organization formed to ensure that programs (projects) receive the proper management and attention.

pull data | بيانات السحب
Accurate sales data that initiate transactions to 'pull' a product through the supply chain.

pull system | نظام السحب
A concept that results in material being produced only when requested and moved to where it is needed just as it is needed.

Qualifying Industrial Zones (QIZ) | المناطق الصناعية المؤهلة
International factories located in Jordan that receive preferential tariff treatment.

qualitative forecasts | التوقعات الكمية
Forecasts that incorporate such factors as the decision maker's intuition, emotions, personal experiences, and value system.

quality | الجودة
The ability of a product or service to meet customer needs.

quality circle | دورة الجودة
A group of employees meeting regularly with a facilitator to solve work-related problems in their work area.

quality function deployment (QFD) | النشر الجيد للمهام
A process for determining customer wants and translating them into the attributes that each functional area can understand and act on.

quality loss function (QLF) | وظيفة فقدان الجودة
A mathematical function that identifies all costs connected with poor quality and shows how these costs increase as product quality moves from what the customer wants.

quality robust | التمسك بالجودة
Products that are consistently built to meet customer needs in spite of adverse conditions in the production process.

quantitative forecasts | التوقعات النوعية
Forecasts that employ mathematical modeling to forecast demand.

quantity discount | خفض الجودة
A reduced price for items purchased in large quantities.

radio frequency identification (RFID) | نظام تحديد الترددات اللاسلكية
A wireless system in which integrated circuits with antennae send radio waves.

random stocking | التخزين العشوائي
Used in warehousing to locate stock wherever there is an open location.

raw material inventory | قائمة جرد المواد الخام
Materials that are usually purchased but have yet to enter the manufacturing process.

redundancy | الحشو
The use of components in parallel to raise reliability.

reliability | المصداقية
The probability that a machine part or product will function properly for a specified time under stated conditions.

reorder point (ROP) | نقطة إعادة الترتيب
The inventory level (point) at which action is taken to replenish the stocked item.

repetitive process | العملية المتكررة
A product-oriented production process that uses modules.

resources view | استعراض الموارد
A method managers use to evaluate the resources at their disposal and manage or alter them to achieve competitive advantage.

response | الاستجابة
A set of values related to rapid, flexible, and reliable performance.

retail layout | تخطيط التجزئة
An approach that addresses flow, allocates space, and responds to customer behavior.

robot | روبوت (إنسان آلي)
A flexible machine with the ability to hold, move, or grab items. It functions through electronic impulses that activate motors and switches.

robust | قوي
Giving satisfactory answers even with substantial variation in the parameters.

robust design | التصميم القوي
A design that can be produced to requirements even with unfavorable conditions in the production process.

route sheet | خريطة الطريق
A listing of the operations necessary to produce a component with the material specified in the bill of material.

safety stock | المخزون الاحتياطي
Extra stock to allow for uneven demand; a buffer.

sales force composite | مركب قوة البيع
A forecasting technique based on salespersons' estimates of expected sales.

scheduling decisions | قرارات الجدولة
Plans that match production to changes in demand.

seasonal variations | المتغيرات الموسمية
Regular upward or downward movements in a time series that tie to recurring events.

self-directed team | فريق ذاتي التوجيه
A group of empowered individuals working together to reach a common goal.

sequencing | التسلسل
Determining the order in which jobs should be done at each work center.

service blueprinting | خدمة بلو برينتنج
A process analysis technique that lends itself to a focus on the customer and the provider's interaction with the customer.

service level | مستوى الخدمة
The complement of the probability of a stockout.

service recovery | استعادة الخدمة
Training and empowering frontline workers to solve a problem immediately.

service sector | قطاع خدمي
The segment of the economy that includes trade, financial, hospitality, education, legal, medical, and other professional occupations.

services | الخدمات
Economic activities that typically produce an intangible product (such as education, entertainment, hospitality, government, financial, and health services).

servicescape | خدمة سكيب
The physical surroundings in which a service takes place, and how they affect customers and employees.

servitization | التخديم
The inclusion of a service component in each product to better meet the demands of the customers.

setup cost | تكلفة الضبط
The cost to prepare a machine or process for production.

setup time | مدة الضبط
The time required to prepare a machine or process for production.

seven wastes | المخلفات السبعة
Overproduction
Queues
Transportation
Inventory
Motion
Overprocessing
Defective product

shortest processing time (SPT) | أقر وقت للتصنيع
Jobs with the shortest processing times are assigned first.

shrinkage | إنكماش
Retail inventory that is unaccounted for between receipt and sale.

single-factor productivity | إنتاجية العامل الفردي
Indicates the ratio of goods and services produced (outputs) to one resource (input).

single-period inventory model | نموذج قائمة الجرد ذات الفترة ذات الفترة الواحدة
A system for ordering items that have little or no value at the end of a sales period.

single-stage control of replenishment | مرحلة التحكم الفردية في التجديد
Fixing responsibility for monitoring and managing inventory for the retailer.

Six Sigma | القواعد الستة
A program to save time, improve quality, and lower costs.

slack time | زمن الركود
Free time for an activity (Free Float, Free Time, or Free Slack).

slotting fees | رسوم التخزين
Fees manufacturers pay to get shelf space for their products.

smoothing constant | معامل التقريب
The weighting factor used in an exponential smoothing forecast, a number between 0 and 1.

source inspection | التفتيش على المصدر

Controlling or monitoring at the point of production or purchase—at the source.

standard error of the estimate |
الخطأ القياسي للمعيار المقدر لتبادل بيانات المنتجات

A measure of variability around the regression line—its standard deviation.

standard for the exchange of product data (STEP) |
معيار تبادل بيانات المنتجات

A standard that provides a format allowing the electronic transmission of three-dimensional data.

standard time | الزمن القياسي

An adjustment to the total normal time; the adjustment provides allowances for personal needs, unavoidable work delays, and fatigue.

statistical process control (SPC) | مراقبة العملية الإحصائية

A process used to monitor standards, make measurements, and take corrective action as a product or service is being produced.

strategy | إستراتيجية

How an organization expects to achieve its missions and goals.

supermarket | سوبر ماركت

An inventory area that holds common items that are replenished by a kanban system.

supply-chain management | إدارة سلسلة التوريد

Management of activities that procure materials and services, transform them into intermediate goods and final products, and deliver them through a distribution system.

Supply-Chain Operations Reference (SCOR) model |
نموذج إحالة عمليات سلسلة التوريد

A set of processes, metrics, and best practices developed by the Supply-Chain Council (**www.supply-chain.org**).

sustainability | الاستدامة

A production system that supports conservation and renewal of resources.

SWOT analysis |
تحليل نقاط القوة ونقاط الضعف والفرص والتهديدات الخارجية

A method of determining internal strengths and weaknesses and external opportunities and threats.

system nervousness | اضطراب النظام

Frequent changes in an MRP system.

takt time | الوقت المناسب

Pace of production to meet customer demands.

tangible costs | التكاليف الملموسة

Readily identifiable costs that can be measured with some precision.

target-oriented quality | الجودة موجة الأهداف

A philosophy of continuous improvement to bring a product exactly on target.

technological forecasts | التوقعات التكنولوجية

Long-term forecasts concerned with the rates of technological progress.

theory of comparative advantage | نظرية الميزة المقارنة

A theory which states that countries benefit from specializing in (and exporting) products and services in which they have relative advantage, and importing goods in which they have a relative disadvantage.

theory of constraints (TOC) | نظرية القيود

A body of knowledge that deals with anything that limits an organization's ability to achieve its goals.

therbligs | العوامل المادية للحركة

Basic physical elements of motion.

throughput time | مدة الإنتاجية

The time required to move orders through the production process, from receipt to delivery.

time fences | الحدود الزمنية

A means for allowing a segment of the master schedule to be designated as 'not to be rescheduled.'

time measurement units (TMUs) | وحدات قياس الوقت

Units for very basic micromotions in which 1 TMU = 0.0006 minute or 100,000 TMUs = 1 hour.

time series | السلسلة الزمنية

A forecasting technique that uses a series of past data points to make a forecast.

time study | دراسة الوقت

Timing a sample of a worker's performance and using it as a basis for setting a standard time.

time-based competition | المنافسة على أساس الوقت

Competition based on time; rapidly developing products and moving them to market.

time-function mapping | تخطيط الوظائف الزمنية

Also known as *process mapping*; a flowchart with time added on the horizontal axis.

total productive maintenance (TPM) | إجمالي الصيانة الإنتاجية

Combines total quality management with a strategic view of maintenance from process and equipment design to preventive maintenance.

total quality management (TQM) | إدارة الجودة الشاملة

Management of an entire organization so that it excels in all aspects of products and services that are important to the customer.

total slack | الركود الشامل

Time shared among more than one activity.

Toyota Production System (TPS) | نظام الإنتاج الخاص بشركة تويوتا

Focus on continuous improvement, respect for people, and standard work practices.

tracking signal | إشارة التتبع

A measurement of how well a forecast is predicting actual values.

transnational strategy | الاستراتيجية العالمية

A strategy that combines the benefits of global-scale efficiencies with the benefits of local responsiveness.

transportation method of linear programming |
طريقة النقل للبرمجة الخطية

A way of solving for the optimal solution to an aggregate planning problem.

transportation model | نموذج النقل

A technique for solving a class of linear programming problems.

trend projection | عرض الاتجاه

A time-series forecasting method that fits a trend line to a series of historical data points and then projects the line into the future for forecasts.

utilization | الاستفادة

Actual output as a percentage of design capacity.

value analysis | تحليل القيمة

A review of successful products that takes place during the production process.

value-chain analysis | تحليل سلسلة القيمة
A way to identify those elements in the product/service chain that uniquely add value.

value-stream mapping (VSM) | تخطيط اتجاه القيمة
A process that helps managers understand how to add value in the flow of material and information through the entire production process.

variability | التغير
Any deviation from the optimum process that delivers perfect product on time, every time.

variable inspection | التفتيش المتغير
Classifications of inspected items as falling on a continuum scale, such as dimension, or strength.

vendor-managed inventory (VMI) | قائمة الجرد المدارة بواسطة البائع
A system in which a supplier maintains material for the buyer, often delivering directly to the buyer's using department.

vertical integration | التكامل الرأسي
Developing the ability to produce goods or services previously purchased or actually buying a supplier or a distributor.

virtual companies | شركات ظاهرية
Companies that rely on a variety of supplier relationships to provide services on demand. Also known as hollow corporations or network companies.

virtual reality | واقعية ظاهرية
A visual form of communication in which images substitute for reality and typically allow the user to respond interactively.

vision systems | نظم الرؤية
Systems that use video cameras and computer technology in inspection roles.

visual workplace | مكان العمل المرئي
Uses a variety of visual communication techniques to rapidly communicate information to stakeholders.

Wagner–Whitin procedure | إجراء واجنر ويتين
A technique for lot-size computation that assumes a finite time horizon beyond which there are no additional net requirements to arrive at an ordering strategy.

warehouse layout | تخطيط المستودع
A design that attempts to minimize total cost by addressing trade-offs between space and material handling.

work breakdown structure (WBS) | هيكل تعطل العمل
A hierarchical description of a project into more and more detailed components.

work cell | خلية عمل
An arrangement of machines and personnel that focuses on making a single product or family of related products.

work order | أمر عمل
An instruction to make a given quantity of a particular item.

work sampling | أخذ عينة من الأعمال
An estimate, via sampling, of the percentage of the time that a worker spends on various tasks.

work-in-process (WIP) inventory | قائمة الجرد للعمل الجار تنفيذه
Products or components that are no longer raw materials but have yet to become finished products.

World Trade Organization (WTO) | منظمة التجارة العالمية
An international organization that promotes world trade by lowering barriers to the free flow of goods across borders.

yield (or revenue) management | إدارة الناتج (أو الإيرادات)
Capacity decisions that determine the allocation of resources to maximize profit or yield.

Index

Photo Credits